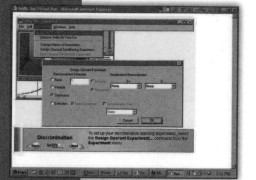

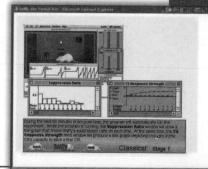

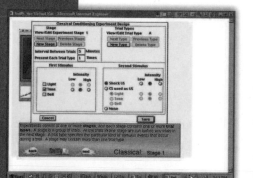

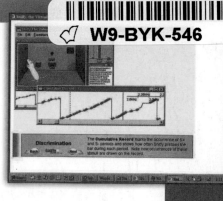

OTHER TITLES OF INTEREST

Biological Psychology

Biological Psychology, 6th edition by James Kalat
Principles of Neuropsychology by Eric Zillmer and Mary Spiers

Behavior Modification

Behavior Modification in Applied Settings, 6th edition by Alan Kazdin
Behavior Modification: Principles and Procedures, 2nd edition by Raymond Miltenberger
First Course in Applied Behavior Analysis by Paul Chance
Principles of Everyday Behavior Analysis, 3rd edition by L. Keith Miller
Self-Directed Behavior: Self Modification for Personal Adjustment, 8th edition by David L. Watson and Roland G. Tharp

Research Methods

Conducting Experiments in Psychology: Measuring the Weight of Smoke, 2nd edition by Brett W. Pelham
Doing Psychology Experiments, 5th edition by David W. Martin
Experimental Psychology, 6th edition by Anne Myers and Christine Hansen
Experimental Psychology: Understanding Psychological Research, 7th edition by Barry H. Kantowitz, Henry L. Roediger, III, and David G. Elmes
Methods Toward a Science of Behavior, 6th edition by William J. Ray
Research Methods, 5th edition by Don McBurney
Research Methods in Psychology, 6th edition by David G. Elmes, Barry H. Kantowitz, and Henry L. Roediger, III
Research Methods Laboratory Manual for Psychology by William Langston

Writing

Writing Papers in Psychology: A Student Guide by Ralph L. Rosnow and Mimi Rosnow
Writing with Style: APA Made Easy, 2nd edition by Lenore Szuchman

THE PRINCIPLES OF LEARNING AND BEHAVIOR

FIFTH EDITION

MICHAEL DOMJAN
University of Texas

with contributions by
J. W. GRAU
Texas A&M University

THOMSON
WADSWORTH

Australia • Canada • Mexico • Singapore • Spain
United Kingdom • United States

THOMSON
WADSWORTH™

Sponsoring Editor: *Marianne Taflinger*
Development Editor: *Jennifer Wilkinson*
Editorial Assistant: *Nicole Root*
Technology Project Manager: *Darin Derstine*
Marketing Manager: *Lori Grebe*
Marketing Assistant: *Laurel Anderson*
Advertising Project Manager: *Brian Chaffee*
Project Manager, Editorial Production: *Mary Noel*
Print/Media Buyer: *Vena Dyer*
Permissions Editor: *Joohee Lee*

Production Service: *Vicki Moran, Publishing Support Services*
Text Designer: *Donna Davis*
Photo Researcher: *Terri Wright*
Copy Editor: *Darlene Bledsoe*
Cover Designer: *Vernon T. Boes*
Cover Image: *Tim Flach/Getty Images*
Cover Printer: *Phoenix Color Corporation, BTP*
Compositor: *TBH Typecast, Inc.*
Printer: *Phoenix Color Corporation, BTP*

Printed in the United States of America
1 2 3 4 5 6 7 06 05 04 03 02

ISBN 0-534-56156-X

THIS BOOK IS PRINTED ON ACID-FREE RECYCLED PAPER

Wadsworth/Thomson Learning
10 Davis Drive
Belmont, CA 94002-3098
USA

Asia
Thomson Learning
5 Shenton Way #01-01
UIC Building
Singapore 068808

Australia
Nelson Thomson Learning
102 Dodds Street
South Melbourne, Victoria 3205
Australia

Canada
Nelson Thomson Learning
1120 Birchmount Road
Toronto, Ontario M1K 5G4
Canada

Europe/Middle East/Africa
Thomson Learning
High Holborn House
50/51 Bedford Row
London WC1R 4LR
United Kingdom

Latin America
Thomson Learning
Seneca, 53
Colonia Polanco
11560 Mexico D.F.
Mexico

Spain
Paraninfo Thomson Learning
Calle/Magallanes, 25
28015 Madrid, Spain

TO ALICE, KATHERINE, AND PAUL

ABOUT THE AUTHOR

Michael Domjan is Professor and Chair of the Psychology Department at the University of Texas at Austin, where he has been teaching undergraduate and graduate courses in learning since 1973. He has served as Editor of the *Journal of Experimental Psychology: Animal Behavior Processes* and Associate Editor of *Learning and Motivation.* He is noted for his research on food-aversion learning and learning mechanisms in sexual behavior. He is recipient of the G. Stanley Hall Award from the American Psychological Association, and his research on sexual conditioning was selected for a MERIT Award by the National Institute of Mental Health. He has served on the Governing Board of the Psychonomic Society and as President of the Division of Behavioral Neuroscience and Comparative Psychology of the American Psychological Association. In addition to *The Principles of Learning and Behavior,* 5th edition, he is author of *Essentials of Conditioning and Learning.*

BRIEF CONTENTS

CONTENTS

4 CLASSICAL CONDITIONING: MECHANISMS 91

5 INSTRUMENTAL CONDITIONING: FOUNDATIONS 124

6 SCHEDULES OF REINFORCEMENT AND CHOICE BEHAVIOR 162

INDEX OF HUMAN EXAMPLES

CHAPTER 1
INTRODUCTION 1

CHAPTER 2
ELICITED BEHAVIOR, HABITUATION, AND SENSITIZATION 28

CHAPTER 3

CLASSICAL CONDITIONING: FOUNDATIONS 59

CHAPTER 4

CLASSICAL CONDITIONING: MECHANISMS 91

CHAPTER 5

INSTRUMENTAL CONDITIONING: FOUNDATIONS 124

CHAPTER 6

SCHEDULES OF REINFORCEMENT AND CHOICE BEHAVIOR 162

CHAPTER 7

INSTRUMENTAL CONDITIONING: MOTIVATIONAL MECHANISMS 191

CHAPTER 8

STIMULUS CONTROL OF BEHAVIOR 217

CHAPTER 9

EXTINCTION OF CONDITIONED BEHAVIOR 251

CHAPTER 10

AVERSIVE CONTROL: AVOIDANCE AND PUNISHMENT 279

CHAPTER 11

ANIMAL COGNITION I: MEMORY MECHANISMS 315

CHAPTER 12

ANIMAL COGNITION II: SPECIAL TOPICS 352

PREFACE

The investigation of learning and behavior has been an integral part of the study of psychology since the late nineteenth century. Studies of learning provide important insights into ways in which long-lasting changes in behavior occur as a result of particular types of experience. Basic associative learning phenomena have contributed significantly to our understanding of the functions of the nervous system. They have provided useful models for various psychological disorders as well as conceptual tools for the construction of intelligent artificial systems and robots. They have also made possible studies of the evolution of cognition and intelligence in various animal species. The methods and analytical models developed to study conditioning and learning have been adopted in studies of infant cognition, behavioral neuroscience, psychopharmacology, behavioral medicine, behavioral toxicology, rehabilitation training, and special education. Thus, the study of learning is at the crossroads of many different aspects of the study of psychology and behavior.

A Bold New Revision

In preparing the fifth edition of *The Principles of Learning and Behavior*, I reviewed all of the research that has appeared in the major journals devoted to this field since 1996, the year I prepared the fourth edition. In particular, I looked at all articles published since 1996 in the *Journal of the Experimental Analysis of Behavior, Animal Learning & Behavior*, the *Journal of Experimental Psychology: Animal Behavior Processes,* the *Quarterly Journal of Experimental Psychology,* and *Learning and Motivation.* I also consulted other sources as needed and reviewed the reprints that were sent to me by numerous investigators in the field. Although I thought I was reasonably well informed before undertaking this review, I was surprised by how much new work has been done in the last five years. I ended up including only about a third of the references that I reviewed, which nevertheless resulted in more than 550 new references being added to the text.

From the early twentieth century to the mid-1960s, the study of learning and behavior provided the foundations of the study of psychology in North America. Prominent investigators of learning, such as Hull, Spence, Mowrer, Tolman, N. E. Miller, and Skinner, were prominent in the field of psychology as a whole rather than major figures in a subspecialty. The thrust of the effort during this period was to develop a general theory of behavior based on extensive laboratory study of a few experimental situations. Much of the research employed laboratory rats and pigeons. Findings derived from this research were assumed to apply to a variety of species and circumstances. The concepts and findings were also used to construct models of abnormal behavior, personality, and the acquisition of special skills, such as language. Students training in psychology were taught the principles of learning and behavior, even if they planned to specialize in some other area.

The field of psychology has changed dramatically during the past 35 years, with the growth of specialties such as cognitive psychology, health psychology, social and developmental psychology, and behavioral neuroscience. The study of learning and behavior no longer has the dominant position in psychology that it once enjoyed, but it remains a vital area that addresses basic aspects of how behavior is governed by environmental events. A remarkably large number of new studies of learning, many with laboratory animals as subjects, continue to appear each year. This trend is evident in two prominent databases, PsycInfo and Medline. PsycInfo lists most of the published literature in psychology, and Medline lists much of the literature in the medical and biological sciences. There is, however, some overlap in the journals covered by the two databases.

Increased Emphasis on Animal Learning

Figure 1 shows the numbers of papers that are found in PsycInfo and Medline for successive 5-year periods since 1970, if one uses the search term "learning" and limits the search to "animal." Notice that Medline shows a steady increase in the numbers of papers that were published on learning in animals from 1970 to 1999. A steady increase is also evident in PsycInfo from 1975 to 1999. The increase in the number of research reports dealing with learning and animals evident in the last quarter of the

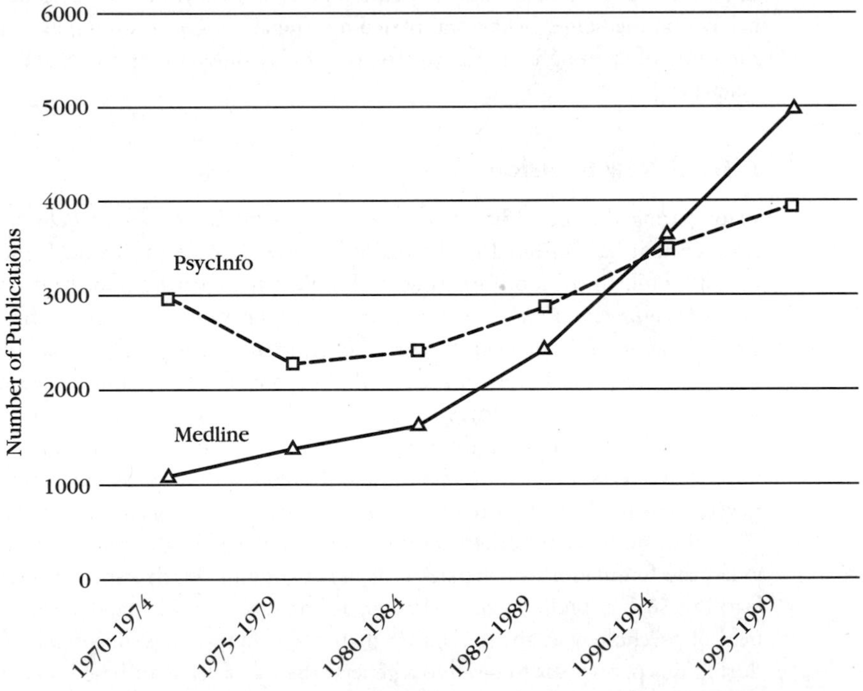

Figure 1 Numbers of papers in Medline and PsycInfo identified by using "learning" as a search term and limiting the search to "animal" in 5-year blocks between 1970 and 1999.

twentieth century resulted in part from an increase in the total number of published papers on learning in general. However, the proportion of all learning publications that involved animal subjects has remained steady since 1975 (see Figure 2). These data indicate that the investigation of learning with animal subjects remains a vital and growing area of scientific inquiry.

Because Medline covers the scientific literature in medicine and biology, the learning papers listed in Medline tend to cover the physiological or biological bases of learning. The dramatic increase in the number of papers on learning in animals during the last 30 years evident in Medline no doubt reflects increased research on the physiological or biological mechanisms of learning. Neuroscientists have focused on learning as one of the key phenomena they are trying to understand at the molecular level. Today, studies of the neural mechanisms of learning probably exceed studies that examine learning at the behavioral level. Notice that for 1995–1999, Medline lists about 5,000 publications dealing with learning in animals, whereas PsycInfo lists only about 4,000 publications. In addition, the numbers of papers dealing with learning in animals shows a much steeper increase from 1975 to 1999 in Medline than in PsycInfo.

Reflects the Biological Bases of Learning

In keeping with increased interest in the biological bases of learning, the 5th edition of the *Principles of Learning and Behavior* includes, for the first time, summaries of some of this research. I am indebted to Professor James W. Grau of Texas A&M

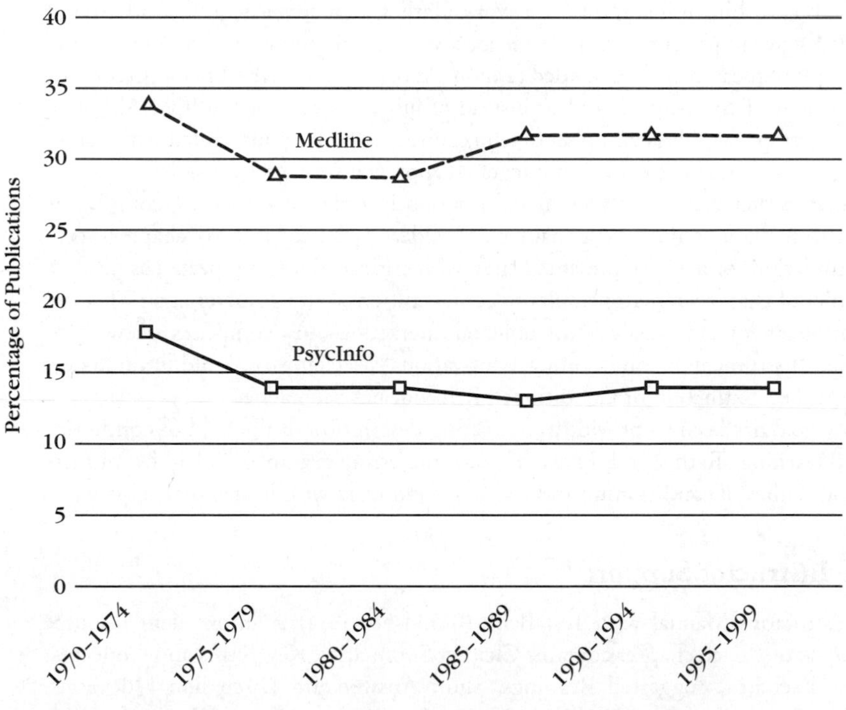

Figure 2 Proportion of papers on learning in Medline and PsycInfo that involves studies with nonhuman animal subjects in 5-year blocks between 1970 and 1999.

University for preparing these summaries, which appear in boxes in Chapters 2, 3, 5, 10, and 11. The emphasis of the book, however, remains on describing learning phenomena at the behavioral level. This emphasis is based on two considerations. First, as the new sections of this text show, scientists are far from having a full understanding of learning at the behavioral level. It therefore remains important to conduct behavioral studies. Second, investigations of the biological bases of learning require first understanding the behavioral characteristics of learning. We cannot study the physiological bases of something without first describing that effect at the behavioral level. Interpretations of the significance and function of various biological processes require relating those processes to well-characterized behavioral end points. The sharp increase in research on the biological bases of learning requires continued attention to the behavioral mechanisms of learning. Without relating the physiology to behavior, we cannot determine the function or significance of a physiological process.

Although the basic paradigms of classical and instrumental conditioning go back about 100 years, our understanding and conceptualization of these types of conditioning continue to evolve in significant ways. Those changes are reflected in numerous revisions I have made to the book. For example, Chapter 7 describes new research on the motivational mechanisms of instrumental behavior, and a new chapter on extinction has been added to the text (Chapter 9).

Balance: Contemporary Findings within a Historic Framework

The fifth edition, like earlier editions, introduces contemporary phenomena and theories about learning and behavior. The emphasis is on presenting recent findings and models, but within an historical framework. Rather than advocate a particular point of view, I strive to present a balanced perspective. I aim to point out the strengths and weaknesses of ideas in an evenhanded fashion. As before, I have tried to emphasize the development of contemporary ideas instead of just listing major findings. Although some contemporary ideas and phenomena cannot yet be fully integrated with earlier findings, I have tried to provide an integrated approach whenever possible.

As in earlier editions, I present information in order of increasing complexity, both within chapters and across chapters. The ideas presented in early chapters serve as a foundation for material presented later, with critical concepts repeated as needed. The order of chapters remains similar to earlier editions, but the material on Theories of Reinforcement and Classical-Instrumental Interactions now comprises a new chapter called Instrumental Conditioning: Motivational Mechanisms. In addition, a new chapter called Extinction of Conditioned Behavior has been added.

My goal has been to provide a captivating description of the field of conditioning and learning. To that end, I have selected interesting examples and added numerous new studies of conditioning and learning conducted with human participants.

More Instructor Support

The Instructor's Manual with Test Bank (0-534-56159-4) is an excellent resource for instructors. Each chapter contains Chapter Summaries, Key Terms and Concepts, In-class Exercises, Suggested Readings, Short Answer and Discussion Questions, Multiple Choice Questions, and material on using Sniffy the Virtual Rat in the classroom. The test items are also available: Examview (0-534-56166-7). The text can also be bundled with a copy of Sniffy, The Virtual Rat, Pro Version (0-534-66694-9)—see endsheets in the front of the book for more information.

Acknowledgments

I am grateful to the friends and colleagues who provided me with material to consider and made useful suggestions for changes. I particularly appreciated Peter Killeen's wisdom and perspective, and Bertram Ploog's persistence. I am also grateful to Marianne Taflinger, who encouraged me to undertake the revision, Vicki Moran who guided me through the production process, and to all of the staff at Wadsworth who helped to make the new edition a reality. I also thank Kevin Holloway for preparing a marvelous instructor's manual and test bank for the book.

I am indebted to all of those who provided thoughtful reviews of an earlier draft of the fifth edition and made numerious helpful suggestions: Kim Dielmann, University of Central Arkansas; Judith Dygdon, Roosevelt University; David Falcone, La Salle University; Edmund Fantino, University of California, San Diego; J. Gregor Fetterman, Indiana University-Purdue University, Indianapolis; Adam Goodie, University of Georgia; Barbara Kucinski, University of Pittsburgh; Sheila Mehta, Auburn University, Montgomery; Thomas Minor, UCLA; Cora Lou Sherburne, Indiana University of Pennsylvania; Lynne Trench, Birmingham-Southern College.

Michael Domjan
Austin, Texas

CHAPTER

1 INTRODUCTION

Historical Antecedents

Historical Developments in the Study of the Mind

Historical Developments in the Study of Reflexes

The Dawn of the Modern Era

Comparative Cognition and the Evolution of Intelligence

Functional Neurology

Animal Models of Human Behavior

Animal Models and Robotics

The Definition of Learning

The Learning-Performance Distinction

Learning and Other Sources of Behavior Change

Different Types of Causal Mechanisms

Methodological Aspects of the Study of Learning

Learning as an Experimental Science

The General-Process Approach to the Study of Learning

Use of Nonhuman Animals in Research on Learning

Rationale for the Use of Nonhuman Animals in Research on Learning

Laboratory Animals and Normal Behavior

Public Debate about Research with Nonhuman Animals

The goal of Chapter 1 is to introduce the reader to the study of learning and behavior. I begin by describing the historical antecedents of key concepts in modern learning theory. This is followed by a discussion of the origins of contemporary experimental research in studies of the evolution of intelligence, functional neurology, and animal models of human behavior, and the implications of contemporary research for the construction of artificial intelligent systems and robots. I then describe the defining characteristics of learning and discuss different causal explanations of learning. Methodological features of studies of learning are described in the next section. Because numerous experiments on learning have been performed with nonhuman animals, I conclude the chapter by discussing the rationale for the use of nonhuman animals in research, with some comments about the public debate about animal research.

People have always been interested in understanding behavior, be it their own or that of others. This interest is more than idle curiosity. Our quality of life is dominated by our actions and the actions of others. Whether you receive a job offer depends on your prior education and record of employment and the decisions of your prospective employer. Whether you get along well with your roommates depends on how they react to the things you do and how you react to the things they do. Whether you get to school on time usually depends on whether you get up early enough and on how crowded the roads are.

Any systematic effort to understand behavior must include consideration of what we learn and how we learn it. Numerous aspects of the behavior of both human and nonhuman animals are the results of learning. We learn to read, to write, and to count. We learn how to walk down stairs without falling, how to open doors, how to ride a bicycle, and how to swim. We also learn when to relax and when to become anxious. We learn what foods we are likely to enjoy and what foods will make us sick. We learn how to tell when someone is unhappy and when that person feels fine. We learn when to carry an umbrella and when to take an extra scarf. Life is filled with activities and experiences that are shaped by what we have learned.

Learning is one of the biological processes that facilitate adaptation to one's environment. The integrity of life depends on successfully accomplishing a number of biological functions such as respiration, digestion, and fighting off disease. Physiological systems have evolved to accomplish these tasks. For many species, however, finely tuned physiological processes do not take care of all adaptive functions required to maintain life. Human and nonhuman animals are faced with climatic changes, changes in food resources, the comings and goings of predators, and other environmental disruptions. Adverse effects of environmental change are often met by behavioral adjustments.

Animals must learn to find new food sources as old ones become used up, they must learn to avoid predators as new ones enter their territory, and they must find new shelter when storms destroy their old one. Accomplishing these tasks obviously requires motor behavior, such as walking and manipulating objects. These tasks also require the ability to predict important events in the environment, such as when and where food will be available. All these things involve learning. Animals learn to go to a new water hole when the old one dries up and to anticipate new sources of danger. These learned adjustments to the environment are as important as physiological processes such as respiration and digestion.

Learning involves acquiring & losing responses/behaviors

We commonly think about learning as involving the acquisition of new behavior. Indeed, learning is required before we can read, ride a bicycle, or play a musical instrument, but learning can just as well consist of the decrease or loss of a previously common response. A child, for example, may learn not to cross the street when the traffic light is red, not to grab food from someone else's plate, and not to yell and scream when someone is trying to take a nap. Learning to withhold responses is just as important as learning to make responses, if not more so.

When considering learning, we are likely to think about forms of learning that require special training—forms of learning that take place in schools and colleges, for example. Solving problems in calculus or making a triple somersault when diving require special instruction. However, we also learn all kinds of things without an expert teacher or coach during the course of routine interactions with our social and physical environment. Children, for example, learn how to open doors and windows, what to do when the phone rings, when to avoid a hot stove, and when to duck so as not to get hit by a flying ball. College students learn how to find their way around campus, how to avoid heartburn from cafeteria food, and how to predict when a roommate will stay out late at night, all without special instruction.

In the coming chapters, I describe research on the basic principles of learning and behavior. This book deals with types of learning and behavior that are fundamental to life but, like breathing, are often ignored. I describe pervasive and basic forms of learning that are normal (and sometimes inevitable) even though they rarely command our attention. I describe the learning of simple relationships between events in the environment, the learning of simple motor movements, and the learning of emotional reactions to stimuli. These forms of learning are investigated in experiments that involve conditioning or "training" procedures of various sorts. However, these forms of learning occur in the lives of human and nonhuman animals without explicit or organized instruction or schooling.

Much of the research that I describe is in the behaviorist tradition of psychology that emphasizes analyzing behavior in terms of its antecedent stimuli and consequences. Conscious reflection and reasoning is deliberately left out of this analysis. I describe automatic procedural learning, which does not require awareness (for example, Lieberman, Sunnucks, & Kirk, 1998), rather than declarative learning, which is more accessible to conscious report. One might argue that this restriction leaves out many interesting aspects of human behavior. However, social psychologists who have been examining these issues empirically have concluded that many important aspects of human behavior occur without awareness. Gosling, John, Craik, and Robins (1998), for example, found that people are relatively inaccurate in reporting about their own behavior. Based on studies of the experience of conscious intent, Wegner and Wheatley (1999) concluded that "the real causal mechanisms underlying behavior are never present in consciousness" (p. 490). Bargh and Chartrand (1999) similarly concluded that "most of a person's everyday life is determined not by their conscious intentions and deliberate choices but by mental processes that are put into motion by features of the environment and that operate outside of conscious awareness and guidance" (p. 462).

HISTORICAL ANTECEDENTS

Theoretical approaches to the study of learning have their roots in the philosophy of René Descartes (see Figure 1.1). Before Descartes, most people thought of human behavior as entirely determined by conscious intent and free will. People's actions were not considered to be controlled by external stimuli or mechanistic natural laws. What a person did was presumed to be the result of his or her will or deliberate intent. Descartes took exception to this view of human nature because he recognized that many things people do are automatic reactions to external stimuli. On the other hand, he was not prepared to abandon entirely the idea of free will and conscious control. He therefore formulated a dualistic view of human behavior known as Cartesian **dualism.**

According to Cartesian dualism, there are two classes of human behavior: involuntary and voluntary. Descartes proposed that involuntary behavior consists of automatic reactions to external stimuli and is mediated by a special mechanism called a **reflex.** Voluntary behavior, by contrast, does not have to be triggered by external stimuli and occurs because of the person's conscious intent to act in that particular manner.

The details of Descartes' dualistic view of human behavior are diagrammed in Figure 1.2. Let us first consider the mechanisms of involuntary, or reflexive, behavior. Stimuli in the environment are detected by the person's sense organs. The sensory information is then relayed to the brain through nerves. From the brain, the impetus for action is sent through nerves to the muscles that create the involuntary response. Thus, sensory input is *reflected* in response output. Hence, Descartes called involuntary behavior *reflexive.*

Bettmann/CORBIS

Figure 1.1
René Decartes
(1596–1650)

Several aspects of this system are noteworthy. Stimuli in the external environment are assumed to be the cause of all involuntary behavior. These stimuli produce involuntary responses by way of a neural circuit that includes the brain. Descartes assumed, however, that only one set of nerves was involved, that the same nerves transmitted information from the sense organs to the brain and from the brain down to the muscles. This circuit, he believed, permitted rapid reactions to external stimuli—for example, quick withdrawal of one's finger from a hot stove.

Descartes assumed that the involuntary mechanism of behavior was the only one available to nonhuman animals. According to this view, all nonhuman animal behavior occurs as reflex responses to external stimuli. Thus, Descartes believed that nonhuman animals lacked free will and were incapable of voluntary, conscious action. He considered free will and voluntary behavior to be uniquely human attributes. This superiority of humans over other animals existed because only human beings were thought to have a mind, or soul.

The mind was assumed to be a nonphysical entity. Descartes believed that the mind was connected to the physical body by way of the pineal gland, near the brain. Because of this connection, the mind could be aware of and keep track of involuntary behavior. Through this mechanism, the mind could also initiate voluntary actions. Because voluntary behavior was initiated in the mind, it could occur independently of external stimulation.

The mind–body dualism introduced by Descartes stimulated two intellectual traditions. One, mentalism, was concerned with the contents and workings of the mind; the other, reflexology, with the mechanisms of reflexive behavior. These two intellectual traditions form the foundations of the modern study of learning.

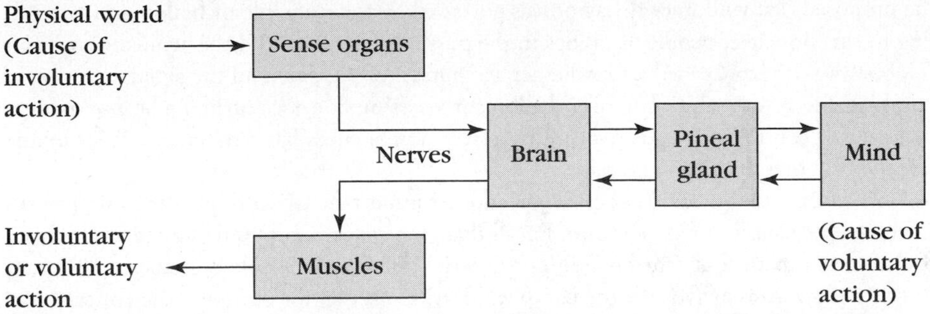

Figure 1.2 Diagram of Cartesian dualism. Events in the physical world are detected by sense organs. From here the information is transmitted to the brain. The brain is connected to the mind by way of the pineal gland. Involuntary action is produced by a reflex arc that involves messages sent first from the sense organs to the brain and then from the brain to the muscles. Voluntary action is initiated by the mind, with messages sent to the brain and then the muscles.

Historical Developments in the Study of the Mind

Philosophers concerned with the mind were interested in what was in the mind and how the mind works. These questions are similar to those that preoccupy present-day cognitive psychologists. Because Descartes thought the mind was connected to the brain by way of the pineal gland, he believed that some of the contents of the mind came from sense experiences. At the same time, he also believed that the mind contained ideas that were innate and existed in all human beings independent of personal experience. He believed, for example, that all humans were born with the concept of God, the concept of self, and certain fundamental axioms of geometry (such as the fact that the shortest distance between two points is a straight line). The philosophical approach that assumes we are born with innate ideas about certain things is called **nativism.**

Some philosophers after Descartes took issue with the nativist position. In particular, the British philosopher John Locke (1632-1704) believed that all the ideas people had were acquired directly or indirectly through experiences after birth. He believed that human beings were born without any preconceptions about the world. According to Locke, the mind started out as a clean slate (*tabula rasa,* in Latin), to be gradually filled with ideas and information as the person had various sense experiences. This philosophical approach to the contents of the mind is called **empiricism.** Empiricism was accepted by a group of British philosophers who lived from the seventeenth to the nineteenth century and who came to be known as the *British empiricists.*

The nativist and empiricist philosophers disagreed not only about what the mind was assumed to contain but also on how the mind was assumed to operate. Descartes believed that the mind did not function in a predictable and orderly manner, according to strict rules or laws that one could identify. One of the first to propose an alternative to this position was the British philosopher Thomas Hobbes (1588–1679). Hobbes accepted the distinction between voluntary and involuntary behavior stated by Descartes and also the notion that voluntary behavior was controlled by the mind. Unlike Descartes, however, Hobbes believed that the mind operated just as predictably and lawfully as a reflex. More specifically,

Hobbes: hedonism - pursue pleasure & avoid pain

he proposed that voluntary behavior was governed by the principle of **hedonism.** According to this principle, people do things in the pursuit of pleasure and the avoidance of pain. Hobbes was not concerned with whether the pursuit of pleasure and the avoidance of pain are laudable or desirable. For him, hedonism was simply a fact of life. The notion that behavior is controlled by positive and negative consequences has remained with us in one form or another to the present day.

According to the British empiricists, another important aspect of how the mind works involved the concept of **association.** Recall that empiricism assumes that all ideas originate from sense experiences. But how do our experiences of various colors, shapes, odors, and sounds allow us to arrive at more complex ideas? Consider, for example, the concept of a car. If someone says the word *car,* you have an idea of what the thing looks like, what it is used for, and how you might feel if you sat in it. Where do all these ideas come from given just the sound of the letters *c, a,* and *r*? The British empiricists proposed that simple sensations were combined into more complex ideas by associations. Because you have heard the word *car* when you saw a car, considered using one to get to work, or sat in one, connections or associations became established between the word *car* and these other attributes of cars. Once the associations are established, the word *car* will activate memories of the other aspects of cars that you have experienced. The British empiricists considered such associations to be the building blocks of mental activity. Therefore, they devoted considerable effort to detailing the rules of associations.

Rules of Associations. The British empiricists accepted two sets of rules for the establishment of associations, one primary and one secondary. The primary rules were originally set forth by the ancient Greek philosopher Aristotle. He proposed three principles for the establishment of associations: contiguity, similarity, and contrast. Of these, the contiguity principle has been the most prominent in studies of associations and continues to play an important role in contemporary work. It states that if two events repeatedly occur together in space or time, they will become associated. For example, if you encounter the smell of tomato sauce with spaghetti often enough, your memory of spaghetti will be activated by the smell of tomato sauce by itself. The similarity and contrast principles state that two things will become associated if they are similar in some respect (both are red, for example) or have some contrasting characteristics (one might be strikingly tall and the other strikingly short, for example). Similarity as a basis for the formation of associations has been confirmed by modern studies of learning (for example, Cusato & Domjan, 2001; Rescorla & Furrow, 1977). However, there is no contemporary evidence that making one stimulus strikingly different from another (contrast) facilitates the formation of an association between the two.

Various secondary laws of associations were set forth by several of the empiricist philosophers—among them, Thomas Brown (1778–1820). Brown proposed that a number of factors influence the formation of associations between two sensations, including the intensity of the sensations and how frequently or recently the sensations occurred together. In addition, the formation of an association between two events was considered to depend on the number of other associations in which each event was already involved, and the similarity of these past associations to the current one being formed.

The British empiricists discussed rules of association as a part of their philosophical discourse. They did not perform experiments to determine whether the rules were valid. Nor did they attempt to determine the circumstances in which one rule was more important than another. Empirical investigation of the mechanisms of associations did not begin until the pioneering work of the nineteenth-century German psychologist Hermann Ebbinghaus (1850–1909).

To study how associations are formed, Ebbinghaus invented **nonsense syllables**—three-letter combinations (*bap,* for example) devoid of any meaning that might influence how someone might react to them. Ebbinghaus used himself as the experimental subject. He studied lists of nonsense syllables and measured his ability to remember them under various experimental conditions. This general method enabled him to answer such questions as how the strength of an association improved with increased training, whether nonsense syllables that appeared close together in a list were associated more strongly with one another than syllables that were farther apart, and whether a syllable became more strongly associated with the next one on the list than with the preceding one. Many of the issues addressed by the British empiricists and Ebbinghaus have their counterparts in modern studies of learning and memory.

Historical Developments in the Study of Reflexes

Descartes made a very significant contribution to the understanding of behavior when he formulated the concept of the reflex. The basic idea that behavior can reflect a triggering stimulus remains an important building block of behavior theory. However, Descartes was mistaken in his beliefs about the details of reflex action. He believed that sensory messages going from sense organs to the brain and motor messages going from the brain to the muscles travel along the same nerves. He thought that nerves are hollow tubes and that neural transmission involves gases called *animal spirits.* The animal spirits, released by the pineal gland, were assumed to flow through the neural tubes and enter the muscles, causing them to swell and create movement. Finally, Descartes considered all reflexive movements to be innate and to be fixed by the anatomy of the nervous system. Over the course of several hundred years after Descartes passed away, all of these ideas about reflexes were proven incorrect.

Charles Bell (1774–1842) in England and François Magendie (1783–1855) in France showed that separate nerves are involved in the transmission of sensory information from sense organs to the central nervous system and of motor information from the central nervous system to muscles. If a sensory nerve is cut, the animal remains capable of muscle movements; if a motor nerve is cut, the animal remains capable of registering sensory information.

The idea that animal spirits are involved in neural transmission was also disproved. In 1669, John Swammerdam (1637–1680) showed that mechanical irritation of a nerve was sufficient to produce a muscle contraction. Thus, infusion of animal spirits from the pineal gland was not necessary. In other studies, Francis Glisson (1597–1677) demonstrated that muscle contractions were not produced by swelling due to the infusion of a gas, as Descartes had postulated.

Descartes and most philosophers after him assumed that reflexes were responsible only for simple reactions to stimuli. The energy in a stimulus was thought to be translated directly into the energy of the elicited response by the neural connections—that is, the more intense the stimulus, the more vigorous the resulting response. This simple view of reflexes is consistent with many casual observations. If you touch a stove, for example, the hotter the stove, the more quickly you withdraw your finger. Some reflexes, however, are much more complicated.

The physiological processes responsible for reflex behavior became better understood in the nineteenth century, and reflexes came to be used as an explanation for a greater range of behaviors. Two Russian physiologists, I. M. Sechenov (1829–1905) (see Figure 1.3) and Ivan Pavlov (1849–1936), were primarily responsible for these developments. Sechenov proposed that stimuli do not elicit reflex responses directly in all cases. Rather, in some

Figure 1.3
I. M. Sechenov
(1829–1905)

cases, a stimulus can release a response from inhibition. Where a stimulus released a response from inhibition, the vigor of the response would not depend on the intensity of the stimulus. This simple idea opened up all sorts of new possibilities.

Since the vigor of an elicited response does not invariably depend on the intensity of its triggering stimulus, it is possible for a very faint stimulus to produce a large response. Small particles of dust in the nose, for example, can cause a vigorous sneeze. Sechenov took advantage of this type of mechanism to provide a reflex analysis of voluntary behavior. He suggested that complex forms of behavior (actions or thoughts) that occurred in the absence of an obvious eliciting stimulus were in fact reflexive responses. In these cases, the eliciting stimuli are so faint as to be unnoticeable. Thus, according to Sechenov, voluntary behavior and thoughts are actually elicited by inconspicuous, faint stimuli.

Sechenov's ideas about voluntary behavior greatly extended the use of reflex mechanisms to explain a variety of aspects of behavior. However, his ideas were philosophical extrapolations from the actual research results he obtained. In addition, Sechenov did not address the question of how reflex mechanisms can account for the fact that the behavior of organisms is not fixed and invariant throughout an organism's lifetime but can be altered by experience. From the time of Descartes, reflex responses were considered to be innate and fixed by the connections of the nervous system. Reflexes were thought to depend on a prewired neural circuit connecting the sense organs to the relevant muscles. According to this view, a given stimulus could be expected to elicit the same response throughout an organism's life. Although this is true in some cases, there are also many examples in which responses to stimuli change as a result of experience. Explanation of such cases by reflex processes had to await the experimental and theoretical work of Ivan Pavlov.

Pavlov showed experimentally that not all reflexes are innate. New reflexes to stimuli can be established through mechanisms of association. Thus, Pavlov's role in the history of the study of reflexes is comparable to the role of Ebbinghaus in the study of the mind. Both were concerned with establishing the laws of associations through empirical research. Pavlov, however, did this in the physiological tradition of reflexology rather than in the mentalistic tradition.

Much of modern behavior theory has been built on the reflex concept of stimulus-response, or S-R units, and the concept associations. S-R units and associations continue to play prominent roles in contemporary behavior theory, but these basic concepts have been elaborated and challenged over the years. As I describe in later chapters, in addition to S-R units or connections, modern studies of learning have also demonstrated the existence of stimulus-stimulus (S-S) connection and modulatory or hierarchical associative structures (Schmajuk & Holland, 1998). Quantitative descriptions of learned behavior that do not employ associations have gained favor in some quarters (for example, Gallistel & Gibbon, 2000, 2001) and have been emphasized by contemporary scientists working in the Skinnerian tradition of behavioral analysis (for example, Mazur, 2001). However, associative analyses continue to have a prominent role in both physiological and behavioral investigations (for example, Dickinson, 2001) even though some have supplemented associative mechanisms with other processes (for example, Denniston, Savastano, & Miller, 2001; Miller & Escobar, 2001).

THE DAWN OF THE MODERN ERA

Experimental studies of basic principles of learning often are conducted with nonhuman animals and in the tradition of reflexology. Research in animal learning came to be pursued with great vigor starting a little more than 100 years ago. Impetus for the research came from three primary sources (see Domjan, 1987). The first of these was interest in comparative cognition and the evolution of the mind. The second was interest in how the nervous system works (functional neurology), and the third was interest in developing animal models to study certain aspects of human behavior. As described in the ensuing chapters, comparative cognition, functional neurology, and animal models of human behavior continue to dominate contemporary research in learning.

Comparative Cognition and the Evolution of Intelligence

Interest in comparative cognition and the evolution of the mind was sparked by the writings of Charles Darwin (see Figure 1.4), who took Descartes' ideas about human nature one step further. Descartes had started chipping away at the age-old notion that human beings have a unique and privileged position in the animal kingdom by proposing that at least some aspects of human behavior (their reflexes) were animal-like. However, Descartes had preserved some privilege for human beings by assuming that humans (and only humans) have a mind.

Darwin attacked this last vestige of privilege. In his second major work, *The Descent of Man and Selection in Relation to Sex,* Darwin argued that "man is descended from some lower form, notwithstanding that connecting-links have not hitherto been discovered" (1897, p. 146). In claiming continuity from nonhuman to human animals, Darwin attempted to characterize not only the evolution of physical traits but also the evolution of psychological or mental abilities. He argued that the human mind is a product of evolution.

Figure 1.4
Charles Darwin
(1809–1882)

In making this claim, Darwin did not deny that human beings had such mental abilities as the capacity for wonder, curiosity, imitation, attention, memory, reasoning, and aesthetic sensibility. Rather, he suggested that nonhuman animals also had these abilities. For example, he maintained that nonhuman animals were capable even of belief in spiritual agencies (p. 95).

Darwin collected anecdotal evidence of various forms of intelligent behavior in animals in an effort to support his claims. Although the evidence was not compelling by modern standards, the research question was. Investigators ever since have been captivated by the possibility of tracing the evolution of intelligence by studying the abilities of various species of animals.

Before investigating the evolution of intelligence in a systematic fashion, a researcher must have a criterion for identifying intelligent behavior in animals. A highly influential proposal for a criterion was offered by George Romanes in his book *Animal Intelligence* (1882). Romanes suggested that intelligence be identified by determining whether an animal learns "to make new adjustments, or to modify old ones, in accordance with the results of its own individual experience" (p. 4). Thus, Romanes defined intelligence in terms of the ability to learn. This definition was widely accepted by comparative psychologists at the end of the nineteenth and the start of the twentieth century and served to make the study of animal learning the key to obtaining information about the evolution of intelligence.

As the upcoming chapters show, little research on mechanisms of animal learning has been concerned with trying to obtain evidence of the evolution of intelligence. Nevertheless, this issue remains of considerable contemporary interest (for example, Papini, 2002; Roitblat & Meyer, 1995; Shettleworth, 1998). I describe some of the fruits of contemporary research on animal cognition in Chapters 11 and 12.

Functional Neurology

The modern era in the study of learning processes was also greatly stimulated by efforts to use studies of learning in nonhuman animals to gain insights into how the nervous system works. This line of research was initiated by the Russian physiologist Ivan Pavlov, quite independently of the work of Darwin, Romanes, and others interested in comparative cognition.

While still a medical student, Pavlov became committed to the principle of **nervism.** According to nervism, all key physiological functions are governed by the nervous system. Armed with this principle, Pavlov devoted his life to documenting how the nervous system controlled various aspects of physiology. Much of his work was devoted to identifying the neural mechanisms of digestion.

Pavlov - nervism: all physio led by NS

For many years, Pavlov's research progressed according to plan. But, in 1902, two British investigators (Bayliss and Starling) published results showing that the pancreas, an important digestive organ, was partially under hormonal rather than neural control. Writing some time later, Pavlov's friend and biographer noted that these novel findings produced a crisis in the laboratory because they "shook the very foundation of the teachings of the exclusive nervous regulation of the secretory activity of the digestive glands" (Babkin, 1949, p. 228).

The evidence of hormonal control of the pancreas presented Pavlov with a dilemma. If he continued his investigations of digestion, he would have to abandon his interest in the nervous system. On the other hand, if he maintained his commitment to nervism, he would have to stop studying digestive physiology. Nervism won out. In an effort to continue studying the nervous system, Pavlov changed from studying digestive physiology to studying the conditioning of reflexes. Thus, Pavlov regarded his studies of conditioning (which is a form of learning) as a way to obtain information about the functions of the nervous system—how the nervous system works. Pavlov's claim that studies of learning reveal how the nervous system functions is well accepted by contemporary neuroscientists. Kandel, for example, has commented that "the central tenet of modern neural science is that all behavior is a reflection of brain function" (Kandel, Schwartz, & Jessell, 1991, p. 3).

The behavioral psychologist is like a driver who tries to find out about an experimental car by taking it out for a test drive instead of first looking under the hood. By driving the car, you can learn a great deal about how it functions. You can discover its acceleration, its top speed, the quality of its ride, its turning radius, and how quickly it comes to a stop. Driving the car will not tell you how these various functions are accomplished, but it will reveal the major functional characteristics of the internal machinery of the car.

Knowledge of the functional characteristics of a car can, in turn, provide clues about its internal machinery. For example, if the car accelerates sluggishly and never reaches high speeds, chances are it is not powered by a rocket engine. If the car only goes forward when facing downhill, it is probably propelled by gravity rather than by an engine. If the car cannot be made to come to a stop quickly, it may not have brakes.

In a similar manner, behavioral studies of learning can provide clues about the machinery of the nervous system. Such studies tell us about the kinds of plasticity the nervous system can exhibit, the conditions under which learning can take place, how long learned responses persist, and the circumstances under which learned information is accessible or inaccessible. By detailing the functions of the nervous system, behavioral studies of learning define the features or functions that have to be explained by neurophysiological investigations.

Animal Models of Human Behavior

The third major impetus for the modern era in the study of animal learning was the belief that research with nonhuman animals can provide information that may help us better understand human behavior. Animal models of human behavior are of more recent origin than comparative cognition or functional neurology. The approach was systematized by Dollard and Miller and their collaborators (Dollard, Miller, Doob, Mowrer, & Sears, 1939; Miller & Dollard, 1941) and developed further by B. F. Skinner (1953).

Drawing inferences about human behavior on the basis of research with other animal species can be hazardous and controversial. The inferences are hazardous if they are unwarranted; they are controversial if the rationale for the model system approach is poorly understood. Model systems have been developed based on research with a variety of species, including several species of primates, pigeons, rats, and mice.

In generalizing from research with rats and pigeons to human behavior, scientists do not make the assumption that rats and pigeons are like people. Animal models are like other types of models. Architects, pharmacologists, medical scientists, and designers of automobiles all rely on models, and the models are often strikingly different from the real thing. Architects, for example, make small-scale models and drawings of buildings they are designing. Obviously, such models and drawings are not the same as a real building. The models are much smaller, made of cardboard and small pieces of wood instead of bricks and mortar, and they support little weight.

As Overmier (1999) pointed out, "Models are basic and powerful tools in science" (p.17). Models are commonly used because they permit investigation of certain aspects of what they represent under conditions that are *simpler, more easily controlled,* and *less expensive.* For example, with the use of a model, an architect can study the design of the exterior of a planned building without the expense of actual construction. The model can be used to determine what the building will look like from various vantage points and how it will appear relative to other nearby buildings. Studying a model in a design studio is much simpler than studying an actual building on a busy street corner. Factors that may get in the way of getting a good view (other buildings, traffic, and power lines, for example) can be controlled and minimized in a model.

In a comparable fashion, a car designer can study the wind resistance of various design features of a new automobile with the use of a model in the form of a computer program. The program can be used to determine how the addition of spoilers or changes in the shape of the car will change its wind resistance. The computer model bears little resemblance to a real car. It has no tires or engine and cannot be driven. However, the model permits testing the wind resistance of a car design under conditions that are much simpler, better controlled, and less expensive than if the actual car were built and driven down the highway under various conditions to measure wind resistance.

Considering all the differences between a model and the real thing, what makes models valid for studying something? For a model to be valid, it must be comparable to the real thing in terms of the feature or function under study—the *relevant feature* or *relevant function.* If the model of a building is used to study the building's exterior appearance, then all the exterior dimensions of the model must be proportional to the corresponding dimensions of the planned building. Other features of the model, such as its structural elements, are irrelevant. In contrast, if the model is used to study how well the building would withstand an earthquake, then its structural elements (beams and how the beams are connected) would be critical.

In a similar manner, the only thing relevant in a computer model of car wind resistance is that the computer program provide calculations for wind resistance that match the results obtained with real cars driven through real air. No other feature is relevant; therefore, the fact that the computer program lacks an engine or rubber tires is of no consequence.

The rationale and strategies associated with using nonhuman animals as models for human behavior are similar to those pertaining to models in other areas of inquiry. Animal models permit investigating problems that are difficult, if not impossible, to study directly with people. A model permits the research to be carried out under circumstances that are simpler, better controlled, and less expensive. Furthermore, the validity of animal models is based on the same criterion as the validity of other types of models. The important thing is similarity between the animal model and human behavior in *relevant features* for the problem at hand. For example, similarities between rats and humans in the way they learn to avoid dangerous foods make a rat model valid for the investigation of human food aversion learning. The fact that rats have long tails and walk on four legs instead of two is entirely irrelevant to food selection.

The critical task in constructing a successful animal model is to identify the relevant similarity between the animal model and the human behavior of interest. The relevant similarity concerns the causal factors that are responsible for particular forms of behavior (Overmier, 1999). We can gain insights into human behavior based on the study of nonhuman animals if the causal relations in the two species are similar. Because animal models are often used to push back the frontiers of knowledge, the correspondence between the animal findings and human behavior always must be carefully verified by empirical data.

The rationale and strategy for the use of animal models of human behavior was stated succinctly by Dollard and Miller (1950):

> In using the results from [research with rats] we are working on the hypothesis that people have all the learning capacities of rats. . . . Even though the facts must be verified at the human level, it is often easier to notice the operation of principles after they have been studied and isolated in simpler situations so that one knows exactly what to look for. Furthermore, in those cases in which it is impossible to use as rigorous experimental controls at the human level, our faith in what evidence can be gathered at that level will be increased if it is in line with the results of more carefully controlled experiments on other mammals. (p. 63)

Dollard and Miller advocated an interplay in which laboratory studies with nonhuman animals are used to isolate and identify phenomena that can then be investigated in people more successfully. The nonhuman animal research is also used to increase confidence in human data obtained with weaker research methods. This interaction between animal and human research continues to make important contributions to our understanding of human behavior (for example, Branch & Hackenberg, 1998; Gosling, 2001) and has also informed our understanding of the behavior of nonhuman animals (for example, Escobar, Matute, & Miller, 2001; Miller & Matute, 1996).

Applications of learning principles got a special boost in the 1960s with the accelerated development of behavior therapy during that period. As O'Donohue commented, "the model of moving from the learning laboratory to the clinic proved to be a extraordinarily rich paradigm. In the 1960s, numerous learning principles were shown to be relevant to clinical practice. Learning research quickly proved to be a productive source of ideas for developing treatments or etiological accounts of many problems" (1998, p. 4). This fervor was tempered during subsequent developments of cognitive behavior therapy. However, recent advances in learning theory have encouraged a return to learning explanations of important human problems such as panic disorder (Bouton, Mineka, & Barlow, 2001).

In the upcoming chapters I describe animal models of love and attachment, drug tolerance and addiction, food aversion learning, learning of fears and phobias, and stress and coping, among others. Animal models have also led to the development of numerous procedures now commonly employed with people, such as biofeedback, programmed instruction, systematic desensitization, token economies, and other techniques of behavior modification. I provide examples of such applications at relevant points in the text. (For additional examples, see Carroll & Overmier, 2001; Haug & Whalen, 1999.)

Animal Models and Robotics

Animal models of learning and behavior are also of considerable relevance to robotics and intelligent artificial systems. Robots are machines that are able to perform specific functions or tasks. The goal in robotics is to make the machines as "smart" as possible. Just as Romanes defined "intelligence" in terms of the ability to learn, contemporary roboticists view the ability to remember and learn from experience an important feature of "smart" artificial systems. Information about the characteristics and mechanisms of such learning may be gleaned from studies of learning in nonhuman animals (for example, McFarland & Bösser, 1993; Meyer, Berthoz, Floreano, Roitblat, & Wilson, 2000; Roitblat & Meyer, 1995; Wilson, 1991). For example, associative mechanisms are frequently used in artificial intelligent systems to enable the response of those systems to be altered by experience.

THE DEFINITION OF LEARNING

Learning is such a common human experience that people rarely reflect on exactly what it means to say that something has been learned. A universally accepted definition of learning does not exist. However, many critical aspects of learning are captured in the following statement (see also Domjan, 2000):

> *Learning is an enduring change in the mechanisms of behavior involving specific stimuli and/or responses that results from prior experience with those or similar stimuli and responses.*

This definition has important implications for the study of learning, as shown in the following sections.

The Learning-Performance Distinction

Whenever we see evidence of learning, we see the emergence of a change in behavior—the performance of a new response or the suppression of a response that occurred previously. A child becomes skilled in snapping the buckles of her sandals or becomes more patient in waiting to eat dinner until everyone has been seated at the table. Such changes in behavior are the only way to tell whether learning has occurred. However, notice that the preceding definition attributes learning to a change in the *mechanisms of behavior,* not to a change in behavior directly.

Why should we define learning in terms of a change in the mechanisms of behavior? The main reason is that behavior is determined by many factors other than learning. Consider, for example, eating. Whether you eat something depends on how hungry you are, how much effort is required to obtain the food, how much you like the food, and whether you know where to find food. Of all these factors, only the last one necessarily involves learning.

Performance refers to an organism's actions at a particular time. Whether you do something or not (your performance) depends on many things. Even the occurrence of a simple response such as jumping into a swimming pool is multiply determined. Whether you jump depends on the availability, depth, and temperature of the water, your physical ability to spring away from the side of the pool, and so forth. Performance is determined by opportunity, motivation, and sensory and motor capabilities, in addition to learning. Therefore, a change in performance cannot be automatically considered to reflect learning.

Learning is defined in terms of a change in the mechanisms of behavior to emphasize the distinction between learning and performance. The behavior of an organism (its performance) is used to provide evidence of learning. However, because performance is determined by many factors in addition to learning, an observer must be very careful in deciding whether a particular aspect of performance does or does not reflect learning. Sometimes evidence of learning cannot be obtained until special test procedures are introduced. Children, for example, learn a great deal about driving a car just by watching others drive, but this learning is not apparent until they are permitted behind the steering wheel. In other cases (next to be discussed), a change in behavior is readily observed but cannot be attributed to learning either because it does not last long enough or because it does not result from experience with specific environmental events.

Learning and Other Sources of Behavior Change

Several mechanisms produce changes in behavior that are too short-lasting to be considered instances of learning. One such process is **fatigue.** Physical exertion may result in a gradual reduction in the vigor of a response because the individual becomes tired or fatigued. This type of change is produced by experience. However, it is not considered an instance of learning, because the decline in responding disappears if the individual is allowed to rest for a while.

Behavior also may be temporarily altered by a *change in stimulus conditions.* If the house lights in a movie theater suddenly come on in the middle of the show, the behavior of the audience is likely to change dramatically. However, this is not an instance of learning, because the audience is likely to return to watching the movie when the house lights are turned off again.

Other short-term changes in behavior that are not considered learning involve *alterations in the physiological or motivational state* of the organism. Hunger and thirst induce responses that are not observed at other times. Changes in the level of sex hormones cause changes in responsiveness to sexual stimuli. Short-lasting behavioral effects may also accompany the administration of psychoactive drugs.

In some cases persistent changes in behavior occur, but without the type of experience with environmental events that satisfies the definition of learning. The most obvious example of this type is **maturation.** A child cannot get something from a high shelf until he grows tall enough. However, the change in behavior in this case is not an instance of learning because it occurs with the mere passage of time. The child does not have to be trained to reach high places as he becomes taller. Maturation can also result in the disappearance of certain responses. For example, shortly after birth, touching an infant's feet results in foot movements that resemble walking, and stroking the bottom of the foot causes the toes to fan out. Both of these reflex reactions disappear as the infant gets older.

*efficient cause:
what is
nec to cause
rxn*

*Material cause:
=neural Δ*

*Formal cause=
behav mech*

Final cause

Generally, the distinction between learning and maturation is based on the importance of special experiences in producing the behavior change of interest. However, the distinction is blurred in cases where environmental stimulation is necessary for maturational development. Experiments with cats, for example, have shown that the visual system will not develop sufficiently to permit perception of horizontal lines unless the subjects have been exposed to such stimuli early in life (for example, Blakemore & Cooper, 1970). The appearance of sexual behavior at puberty also depends on developmental experience. In particular, successful sexual behavior in primates requires interactions with playmates before puberty (for example, Harlow, 1969).

Different Types of Causal Mechanisms

So far I have referred to causal mechanisms but not defined them—and for good reason. Causes can be conceptualized in different terms or at different levels of explanation. In discussing causal mechanisms, it is important to keep in mind what kind of cause you are concerned with. Killeen (2001) has encouraged learning psychologists to think in terms of the four different forms of causality originally described by Aristotle. The first of these, *efficient cause,* is closest to the common definition of cause and refers to the necessary and sufficient conditions for producing a behavioral outcome. In the case of learning, the efficient cause is the training experience with specific stimuli and/or responses that produces the behavior change that is indicative of learning. In contemporary research on learning, efficient causes refer to the procedures that produce the learning. As the upcoming chapters show, there are many different kinds of learning procedures.

The efficient causes of learned behavior are mediated by changes in the nervous system. These neural changes are the *material causes* of learning. Material causes refer to the physical changes in the nervous system that mediate learning. These involve changes in synaptic mechanisms, among other things. Scientists who study the neural mechanisms of learning are studying what Aristotle termed material causes (for example, Greenough & Black, 2000).

Except for the boxes dealing with neural mechanisms prepared by Professor James Grau, this book does not deal with material causes. It deals with what are typically referred to as behavioral mechanisms, explanations of learning at the level of behavior. Behavioral mechanisms are what Aristotle referred to as *formal causes.* Formal causes are theories or models of learning. These theories or models may be expressed in mathematical or computational terms, or they may be stated in terms of theoretical constructs. Associative models of learning are examples of formal causes. This book focuses on such formal causes of learning.

As I noted at the outset of this chapter, learning is a pervasive feature of behavior across the animal kingdom because it is useful, because it enables animals to adjust to changes in their environment. Explanations of learning that emphasize its function or utility involve the fourth type of cause described by Aristotle, namely, *final cause.* In modern biology, the final cause of a behavior or biological process is how that process contributes to the reproductive fitness of the organism. Biological function or final cause is measured in terms of the number of offspring an individual leaves behind. Most scientists would agree that learning mechanisms probably evolved because they increase reproductive fitness. Exactly how the increase in reproductive fitness is achieved has not been identified in many cases, but a few examples of the contributions of learning to reproductive fitness are available (Domjan, Blesbois, & Williams, 1998; Hollis, Pharr, Dumas, Britton, & Field, 1997; see also Domjan & Hollis, 1988).

A common distinction among biologically oriented scientists is between the proximal or immediate causes of behavior and its ultimate causes. Proximate causes correspond to Aristotle's efficient and material causes. Ultimate causes correspond to Aristotle's final causes.

METHODOLOGICAL ASPECTS OF THE STUDY OF LEARNING

There are two prominent methodological features of investigations of learning processes. One of these is a direct consequence of the definition of learning and involves the exclusive use of experimental, as contrasted with observational, research methods. The phenomena of learning cannot be investigated without the use of an experimental methodology. The second methodological feature—reliance on a general-process approach—is more a matter of preference than necessity.

Learning as an Experimental Science

As I described earlier, studies of learning emphasize identifying the causal factors that are responsible for long-term changes in behavior that result from prior experience. Of the four types of causes, learning investigators have focused on efficient, material, and formal causes. Regardless of the type of cause, this emphasis dictates that experimental techniques be used in investigations of learning. Causes cannot be observed directly. They can only be inferred from the results of experimental manipulations.

Consider the following example. Mary opens the door to a dark room. She quickly turns on a switch near the door, and the lights in the room go on. Can you conclude that turning on the switch "caused" the lights to go on? Not from the information provided. Perhaps the lights were on an automatic timer and would have turned on without Mary's actions. Alternatively, the door may have had a built-in switch that turned on the lights after a slight delay. Or, there may have been a motion detector in the room that activated the lights.

How could you determine that manipulation of the wall switch caused the lights to go on? You would have to see what would happen under other circumstances. More specifically, you would have to instruct Mary to enter the room again, but ask her not to turn on the wall switch. If the lights did not go on under these circumstances, certain causal hypotheses could be rejected. You could conclude that the lights were not turned on by a motion detector or by a switch built into the door. To identify a cause, an experiment has to be conducted in which the presumed cause is removed. The results obtained with and without the presumed cause can then be compared. The conclusion that one event causes another requires such comparisons.

In the study of learning, the behavior of living organisms, not lights, is of interest. But observers have to proceed in a similar fashion to identify causes. They have to conduct experiments in which behavior is observed with and without the presumed cause. The most basic question is whether a training procedure produces a particular type of learning effect. To answer this question, the actions of individuals who previously received the training procedure in question have to be compared to the actions of individuals who did not have that training. The only way to prove that the training experience is causing the behavior change of interest is to experimentally vary the presence and absence of that experience. For this reason, *learning can be investigated only with experimental techniques.* Also for this reason, the study of learning is primarily a laboratory science.

The necessity of using experimental techniques to investigate learning is not adequately appreciated by allied scientists. Many aspects of behavior can be studied with observational procedures that do not involve experimental manipulations of the presumed causes of the behavior. For example, observational studies can provide a great deal of information about whether and how animals set up territories, the manner in which they defend those territories, the activities involved in the courtship and sexual behavior of a species, the ways in which animals raise their offspring, and the changes in the activities of the offspring as they mature. Many aspects of animal behavior are accessible to observational study, and much fascinating information has been obtained with observational techniques that involve minimal intrusion into the ongoing activities of the animals.

Unfortunately, learning cannot be observed directly in the same manner as activities such as grooming, aggression, or parental behavior. Researchers can form hypotheses about what animals may be learning by observing their behavior unobtrusively in nature. However, to be sure that the changes in behavior are not due to changes in motivation, sensory development, hormonal fluctuations, or other possible non-learning mechanisms, it is necessary to conduct experiments in which the presumed training experiences are systematically manipulated.

The General-Process Approach to the Study of Learning

The second prominent methodological feature of studies of learning is the use of a general-process approach. This is more a matter of preference than of necessity. However, in adopting a general-process approach, investigators of animal learning are following a longstanding tradition in science.

Elements of the General-Process Approach. The most obvious feature of nature is its diversity. Consider, for example, the splendid variety of minerals that exist in the world. Some are soft, some are hard, some are brilliant in appearance, others are dull, and so on. Plants and animals also are in many different shapes and sizes. Dynamic properties of objects are also diverse. Some things float up, whereas others rapidly drop to the ground; some remain still, and others remain in motion.

In studying nature, one can either focus on differences or try to ignore the differences and search for commonalities. Scientists ranging from physicists to chemists to biologists to psychologists have all elected to search for commonalities. Rather than being overwhelmed by the tremendous diversity in nature, scientists have opted to look for uniformities. They have attempted to formulate *general laws* with which to organize and explain the diversity of events in the universe. Investigators of animal learning have followed this well-established tradition.

Whether or not general laws are discovered often depends on the level of analysis that is pursued. The diversity of the phenomena scientists try to understand and organize makes it difficult to formulate general laws at the level of the observed phenomena. It is difficult, for example, to discover the general laws that govern chemical reactions by simply documenting the nature of the chemicals involved in various reactions. Similarly, it is difficult to explain the diversity of species in the world by cataloging the features of various animals. Major progress in science comes from analyzing phenomena at a more elemental or molecular level. For example, by the nineteenth century, chemists knew many specific facts about what would happen when various chemicals were combined. However, a general account of chemical reactions had to await the development of the periodic table of the elements, which organizes chemical elements in terms of their constituent atomic components.

A fundamental assumption of the general-process approach is that the phenomena of interest are the products of more elemental processes. Furthermore, those elemental processes are assumed to operate in pretty much the same manner no matter where they are found. Thus, generality is assumed to exist at the level of basic or elemental processes.

Investigators of conditioning and learning have been committed to the general-process approach from the inception of this field of psychology. They have focused on the commonalities of various instances of learning and have assumed that learning phenomena are products of elemental processes that operate in much the same way in different learning situations.

The commitment to a general-process approach guided Pavlov's work on functional neurology and conditioning. Commitment to a general-process approach to the study of learning is also evident in the writings of early comparative psychologists. For example, Darwin (1897) emphasized commonalities among species in cognitive functions: "My object . . . is to show that there is no fundamental difference between man and the higher mammals in their mental faculties" (p. 66). Jacques Loeb (1900) pointed out that commonalities occur at the level of elemental processes: "Psychic phenomena . . . appear, invariably, as a function of an elemental process, namely the activity of associative memory" (p. 213). Another prominent comparative psychologist of the time, C. Lloyd Morgan, stated in 1903 that elementary laws of association "are, we believe, universal laws" (p. 219).

The assumption that "universal" elemental laws of association are responsible for learning phenomena does not deny the diversity of stimuli that different animals may learn about, the diversity of responses they may learn to perform, or species differences in rates of learning. The generality is assumed to exist in the rules or processes of learning—not in the content or speed of learning. This idea was clearly expressed nearly a century ago by Edward Thorndike, one of the first prominent American psychologists who studied learning:

> Formally, the crab, fish, turtle, dog, cat, monkey, and baby have very similar intellects and characters. All are systems of connections subject to change by the laws of exercise and effect. The differences are: first, in the concrete particular connections, in what stimulates the animal to response, what responses it makes, which stimulus connects with what response, and second, in the degree of ability to learn. (Thorndike, 1911, p. 280)

What an animal can learn about (the stimuli, responses, and stimulus-response connections it learns about) varies from one species to another. Animals also differ in how fast they learn ("in the degree of ability to learn"). Thorndike assumed that the rules of learning were universal. We no longer share his view that these universal rules of learning are the "laws of exercise and effect." Contemporary scientists do, however, continue to adhere to the idea that universal rules of learning exist. The job of the learning psychologist is to discover those universal laws. (More about the work of Thorndike is found in Chapter 5.)

Methodological Implications of the General-Process Approach. If we assume that universal rules of learning exist, then we should be able to discover those rules in any situation in which learning occurs. Thus, an important methodological implication of the general-process approach is that general rules of learning may be discovered by studying any species or response system that exhibits learning. This implication has encouraged scientists to study learning in a small number of experimental situations. Investigators have converged on a few "standard" or conventional experimental paradigms. Most studies of learning are conducted in one of these paradigms. Figure 1.5, for example, shows an example of a pigeon in a standard Skinner box. I describe other examples of standard experimental paradigms as I introduce various learning phenomena in later chapters.

Conventional experimental paradigms have been fine-tuned over the years to fit well with the behavioral predispositions of the research animals. Because of these improvements, conventional experimental preparations permit laboratory study of reasonably naturalistic responses (Timberlake, 1990).

Robert W. Allan, Lafayette College

Figure 1.5 A pigeon in a standard Skinner box. Three circular disks, arranged at eye level, are available for the bird to peck. Access to food is provided in the hopper below.

Proof of the Generality of Learning Phenomena. The general-process approach has dominated studies of animal learning throughout the twentieth century. As I show in the chapters that follow, the approach has provided an extensive and sophisticated body of knowledge. Given the successes of the general-process approach, it is tempting to conclude that learning processes are indeed universal. However, it is important to keep in mind that the generality of learning processes is not proven by adopting a general-process approach. Assuming the existence of common elemental learning processes is not the same as empirically demonstrating those commonalities.

Direct empirical verification of the existence of common learning processes in a variety of situations remains necessary in efforts to build a truly general account of how learning occurs. A general theory of learning cannot be empirically verified by investigating learning in just a few standard experimental paradigms. The generality of learning processes has to be proven by studying learning in many different species and situations.

The available evidence suggests that elementary principles of learning of the sort that are described in this text have considerable generality (Papini, 2002). Most research on animal learning has been performed with pigeons, rats, and (to a much lesser extent) rabbits. Similar forms of learning have been found with fish, hamsters, cats, dogs, human beings, dolphins, and sea lions. In addition, some of the principles of learning observed with these vertebrate species have been demonstrated in *newts* (Ellins, Cramer, & Martin, 1982); *fruit flies* (Cadieu, Ghadraoui, & Cadieu, 2000; Davis, 1996; Holliday & Hirsch, 1986); *honeybees* (Bitterman, 1988, 1996); *terrestrial mollusks* (Sahley, Rudy, & Gelperin, 1981; Ungless, 1998); *wasps* (Kaiser & De Jong, 1995), and various *marine mollusks* (Carew, Hawkins, & Kandel, 1983; Colwill, Goodrum, & Martin, 1997; Farley & Alkon, 1980; Rogers, Schiller, & Matzel, 1996; Susswein & Schwarz, 1983).

Examples of learning in diverse species provide support for the general-process approach. However, the evidence should be interpreted cautiously. With the exception of the extensive program of research on learning in honeybees conducted by Bitterman and his associates, the various invertebrate species in the studies I cited have been tested on a limited range of learning phenomena. Consequently, we do not know whether their learning was mediated by the same mechanisms that are responsible for analogous instances of learning in vertebrate species.

USE OF NONHUMAN ANIMALS IN RESEARCH ON LEARNING

Many of the experiments discussed in this book have been conducted with nonhuman animal participants. Many types of animals have been used, including rats, mice, rabbits, fish, pigeons, and monkeys. Nonhuman animals are used in the research for both theoretical and methodological reasons.

Rationale for the Use of Nonhuman Animals in Research on Learning

As I have argued, experimental methods are needed to investigate learning phenomena. Experimental methods make it possible to attribute the acquisition of new behaviors to particular previous experiences. Such experimental control of past experience cannot be achieved with the same degree of precision in studies with human participants as in studies with laboratory animals. With laboratory animals, scientists can study how strong emotional reactions are learned and how learning is involved in acquiring food, avoiding pain or distress, or finding potential sexual partners. With people, investigators are limited to trying to modify maladaptive emotional responses after such responses have already been acquired. However, even the development of successful therapeutic procedures for the treatment of maladaptive emotional responses has required knowledge of how such emotional responses are learned in the first place—knowledge that required studies with laboratory animals.

Knowledge of the evolution and biological bases of learning also cannot be obtained without the use of nonhuman animals in research. How cognition and intelligence evolved is one of the fundamental questions about human nature. The answer to this question will shape our view of human nature, just as knowledge of the solar system has shaped our view of the role of Earth in the universe. As I have discussed, investigation of the evolution of cognition and intelligence rests heavily on studies of learning in nonhuman animals.

Knowledge of the biological bases of learning may not change our views of human nature, but it is apt to yield important dividends in the treatment of learning and memory disorders. Such knowledge also rests heavily on research with laboratory animals. The kind of detailed investigations that are necessary to unravel how the nervous system learns and remembers simply cannot be conducted with people. As I pointed out in the Preface, a search for the biological bases of learning first requires documenting the nature of learning processes at the behavioral level. Therefore, behavioral studies of learning in animals are a necessary prerequisite to any animal research on the biological bases of learning. Neuroscience has to be grounded in behavioral science.

Laboratory animals also provide important conceptual advantages over people for studying learning processes. The processes of learning may be simpler in animals reared under controlled laboratory conditions than in people, whose backgrounds are more varied and often poorly documented. The behavior of nonhuman animals is not complicated by linguistic processes that have a prominent role in certain kinds of human behavior. Another important advantage is that demand characteristics are not involved in research with laboratory animals. In research with people, the investigator has to make sure that the actions of the participants are not governed by their efforts to please (or displease) the experimenter. Such factors are not likely to determine what rats and pigeons do in an experiment.

Laboratory Animals and Normal Behavior

Some have suggested that domesticated strains of laboratory animals may not provide useful information because such animals have degenerated as a result of many generations of inbreeding and long periods of captivity (for example, Lockard, 1968). However, this notion is probably mistaken. In an interesting test, Boice (1977) took 5 male and 5 female albino rats of a highly inbred laboratory stock and housed them in an outdoor pen in Missouri without artificial shelter. All 10 rats survived the first winter with temperatures as low as –22°F. The animals reproduced normally and reached a stable population of about 50 members. Only 3 of the rats died before showing signs of old age during the 2-year study period. Given the extreme climatic conditions, this level of survival is remarkable. Furthermore, the behavior of these domesticated rats in the outdoors was very similar to the behavior of wild rats observed in similar circumstances.

Domesticated rats act similarly to wild rats in other tests as well, and there is some indication that they perform better than wild rats in learning experiments (see, for example, Boice, 1973, 1981; Kaufman & Collier, 1983). Therefore, the results I describe in this text should not be discounted simply because many of the experiments were conducted with domesticated animals. In fact, laboratory animals may be preferable in research to their wild counterparts. Human beings in civilized society live in what are largely "artificial" environments. Therefore, research with animals may prove most relevant to human behavior if that research is carried out with domesticated animals that live in artificial laboratory situations. As Boice (1973) commented, "The domesticated rat may be a good model for domestic man" (p. 227).

Public Debate about Research with Nonhuman Animals

There has been much public debate about the pros and cons of research with nonhuman animals. Part of the debate has centered on the humane treatment of animals. Other aspects of the debate have centered on what constitutes ethical treatment of animals, whether human beings have the right to benefit at the expense of animals, and possible alternatives to research with nonhuman animals.

The Humane Treatment of Laboratory Animals. Concern for the welfare of laboratory animals has resulted in the adoption of strict federal standards for animal housing and for the supervision of animal research. Some argue that these rules are needed because without them scientists would disregard the welfare of the animals in their zeal to obtain research data. However, this argument ignores the fact that good science requires good animal care. Scientists, especially those studying behavior, must be concerned about the welfare of their research subjects. Information about normal learning and behavior cannot be obtained from diseased or abused animals. Investigators of animal learning must ensure the welfare of their subjects if they are to obtain useful scientific data.

Laboratory rats cower in a corner if they are sick and anxious. No useful information about their learning and behavior can be obtained under such circumstances. Investigators have to take great pains to make sure their animals are not upset by serving in an experiment.

The animals must be healthy and adapted to handling; the experimental chambers must be suitable for the species; and the animals must be comfortable being in the chamber.

Learning experiments sometimes involve discomfort. However, every effort is made to minimize the degree of discomfort. In studies of food reinforcement, for example, animals are food deprived before each experimental session to ensure their interest in food. However, the hunger imposed is no more severe than the hunger animals are likely to encounter in the wild, and often it is less severe (Poling, Nickel, & Alling, 1990).

The investigation of certain forms of learning and behavior require the administration of aversive stimulation. Important topics, such as punishment or the learning of fear and anxiety, cannot be studied without some discomfort to the participants. However, even in such cases, efforts are made to keep the discomfort to a minimum.

Electric shock is often used in studies of fear and avoidance learning. The term "shock" conjures up images of an electric chair or the pain a child suffers when she accidentally puts her finger in an electrical outlet. However, the shock used in learning experiments is much milder. Unlike other sources of aversive stimulation, electric shock can be precisely regulated, enabling an experimenter to administer shock at controlled low levels. The shock levels employed in studies of animal learning are far lower than the levels experienced from a wall outlet or an electric chair. In addition, in many procedures the animals are permitted to control their exposure by making escape or avoidance responses.

What Constitutes the Ethical Treatment of Animals? Although making sure that animals serving in experiments are comfortable is in the best interests of the animals as well as the research, formulating general ethical principles is difficult. Animal "rights" cannot be identified in the way we identify human rights (Lansdell, 1988), and animals seem to have different "rights" under different circumstances.

Currently, substantial efforts are made to house laboratory animals in conditions that promote their health and comfort. However, a laboratory mouse or rat loses the protection afforded by federal standards when it escapes from the laboratory and takes up residence in the walls of the building (Herzog, 1988). The trapping and extermination of rodents in buildings is a common practice that has not been the subject of either public debate or restrictive federal regulation. Mites, fleas, and ticks are also animals, but we do not tolerate them in our hair or on our pets. Which species have the right to life, and under what circumstances do they have that right? Such questions defy simple answers.

Assuming that a species deserves treatment that meets government-mandated standards, what should those standards be? Appropriate treatment of laboratory animals is sometimes described as being "humane treatment." However, we have to be careful not to take this term literally. "Humane treatment" means treating an individual as we would treat a human being. It is important to keep in mind that rats (and other laboratory animals) are not human beings. Rats prefer to live in dark burrows made of dirt that they never clean. People, in contrast, prefer to live in well-illuminated and frequently cleaned rooms. Well-kept laboratories typically have rats in well-lit rooms that are frequently cleaned. I cannot help but wonder whether the housing standards were dictated more by human considerations than by rat comfort.

Should Human Beings Benefit from the Use of Animals? Part of the public debate about animal rights has been fueled by the argument that people have no right to benefit at the expense of animals, no right to "exploit" animals. This argument goes far beyond issues concerning the use of animals in research. Therefore, I do not discuss the argument in detail here, except to point out that domesticated animals also gain substantial benefits from their relationship to people. In fact, many animals would not exist were it not for their relationship to people. Thus, the relationship is symbiotic rather than just one-sided and exploitative (Hefner, 1999). Furthermore, the use of laboratory animals in research represents but a small proportion of the other human uses of domesticated animals, such as for food.

The U.S. Department of Agriculture is charged with keeping records of the numbers of nonhuman animals (exclusive of rats and mice) that are used in all forms of research in the United States. Since 1973, when these data were first collected, the number of dogs, cats, hamsters, and rabbits used in research has decreased substantially (USDA, 2001). The number of nonhuman primates used in research has remained fairly steady, but only a small proportion of all research animals are nonhuman primates.

Table 1.1 provides estimates of the numbers of animals used in agriculture and all forms of research for 1997, the latest year for which complete data were available from the National Agricultural Statistics Service. More than 8.5 billion animals were used for food in the United States in 1997. Many fewer animals (less than 8.5 million) were used in various forms of research. In fact, all forms of research accounted for less than one tenth of a percent (0.099%) of the total number of animals used between agriculture and research. When the number of animals killed in hunting and in animal shelters is added, the percentage of animals used in research is even smaller. It is difficult to estimate the numbers of animals used in studies of learning, but it is certainly only a tiny proportion of the total number used in research in general.

In addition to the explicit human uses of animals for such things as food, clothing, and hunting, a comprehensive count of human "exploitation" of animals has to include disruptions of habitats that occur whenever we build roads, housing developments, and factories. We should also add the millions of animals that are killed by insecticides and other pest-control efforts in agriculture and elsewhere. In this context, the contributions of animal research to the total "exploitation" of animal life takes on even more trivial dimensions.

In a survey of animal rights advocates, 90% indicated that they would like to eliminate all animal research, and 38% said that this should be the top priority of the animal rights movement (Plous, 1998). Although this percentage is smaller than what had been obtained in an earlier survey (Plous, 1991), the focus of a sizeable proportion of animal rights advocates on curbing animal research efforts is puzzling given the far greater numbers of animals used in other ways. This anti-research focus is also puzzling when we consider that alternatives to the use of animals are much more readily available when it comes to food, clothing, and sports and entertainment.

Alternatives to Research with Animals. Increased awareness of ethical issues involved in the use of nonhuman animals in research has encouraged a search for alternative techniques. Russell and Burch (1959) formulated the "three Rs" for animal research: *replacement* of animals with other testing techniques, *reducing* the number of animals used with statistical techniques, and *refining* the experimental procedures to cause less suffering. Replacement strategies have been successful in the cosmetic industry and in the manufacture of certain vaccines and hormones (Murkerjee, 1997). However, as Gallup and Suarez (1985) pointed out, good research on learning processes cannot be conducted without experiments on live organisms, be they animal or human. Some proposed alternatives are the following:

1. *Observational techniques.* As I discussed earlier, learning processes cannot be investigated with unobtrusive observational techniques. Experimental manipulations of past experience are necessary in studies of learning. Field observations of undisturbed animals cannot yield information about the mechanisms of learning.

2. *Plants.* Learning cannot be investigated in plants because plants lack a nervous system, which is required for learning.

TABLE 1.1 NUMBERS OF ANIMALS USED IN AGRICULTURE AND RESEARCH IN THE UNITED STATES*

AGRICULTURE[1]	
Chickens, Broilers	7,764,200,000
Chickens, Layers	303,604,000
Turkeys	301,251,000
Cattle & Calves	59,801,000
Hogs & Pigs	104,301,000
Sheep & Lambs	6,691,000
Total Agriculture	**8,539,848,000**
RESEARCH[2]	
Dogs	75,429
Cats	26,091
Primates	56,381
Guinea Pigs	217,079
Rabbits	309,322
Farm Animals	159,742
Rats and Mice	7,452,186
Other	150,987
Total Research	**8,452,186**

Percentage of total used in research = 0.099%

*Data for 1997.

[1] Data for chickens (broilers) and turkeys from U.S. Department of Agriculture NASS Bulletin number 958. Data for chickens (layers) from U.S. Department of Agriculture NASS Bulletin number 944. Data for all other agriculture animals from U.S. Department of Agriculture NASS Bulletin number 959a.

[2] Includes all forms of research, not just psychological research. Data for animals, except rats and mice, U.S. Department of Agriculture Animal Welfare Report, Fiscal Year 2000, APHIS 41-35-071. Rats and mice estimated on the assumption suggested by the Institute of Laboratory Animal Research at the National Research Council that 85% of all research vertebrate animals are rats and mice.

3. *Tissue cultures.* Although tissue cultures may reveal the operation of cellular processes, how these cellular processes operate in an intact organism can be discovered only by studying the intact organism. Furthermore, as I pointed out earlier, a search for cellular mechanisms of learning first requires characterizing learning at the behavioral level.

4. *Computer simulations.* Writing a computer program to simulate a natural phenomenon requires a great deal of knowledge about the phenomenon. Before programmers could construct a computer simulation of learning, they would have to have precise and detailed information about the nature of learning phenomena and the mechanisms and factors that determine learning. The absence of such knowledge necessitates experimental research with live organisms. Thus, experimental research with live organisms is a prerequisite for effective computer simulations. For that reason, computer simulations cannot be used in place of experimental research.

Computer simulations can serve many useful functions in science. Simulations are effective in showing us the implications of the experimental observations that have already been obtained. Computer simulations are often used in studies of behavior to show the implications of various theoretical assumptions. They can be used to identify gaps in knowledge and to suggest important future lines of research. However, they cannot be used to generate new, previously unknown facts about behavior. That can be done only by studying live organisms.

Earlier in this chapter, I used the example of a computer simulation to measure the wind resistance of various automobile designs. Why is it possible to construct a computer program to study wind resistance but not possible to construct one to study learning processes? The critical difference is that we know a lot more about wind resistance than we know about learning. Wind resistance is determined by the laws of mechanics—laws that have been thoroughly explored since the days of Sir Isaac Newton. Application of those laws to wind resistance has received special attention in recent years, as the wind resistance of automobiles has become an important factor in increasing gas mileage.

Designing automobiles with low wind resistance is an engineering task. It involves the application of existing knowledge, rather than the discovery of new knowledge and new principles. Research on animal learning involves the discovery of new facts and new principles. It is science, not engineering. As Conn and Parker (1998) pointed out, "scientists depend on computers for processing data that we already possess, but can't use them to explore the unknown in the quest for new information" (p. 1417).

SAMPLE QUESTIONS

1. Describe how historical developments in the study of the mind contributed to the contemporary study of learning.
2. Describe Descartes' conception of the reflex and how the concept of the reflex has changed since his time.
3. Describe the definition of learning and the methodological implications of this definition.
4. Describe Artistotle's four causes and how they may be related to learning.
5. Describe several alternatives to the use of animals in research, and describe their advantages and disadvantages.

KEY TERMS

association A connection between the representations of two events (two stimuli or a stimulus and a response) such that the occurrence of one of the events activates the representation of the other.

dualism The view of behavior according to which actions can be separated into two categories: voluntary behavior controlled by the mind and involuntary behavior controlled by reflex mechanisms.

empiricism A philosophy according to which all ideas in the mind arise from experience.

fatigue A temporary decrease in behavior caused by repeated or excessive use of the muscles involved in the behavior.

hedonism The philosophy proposed by Hobbes according to which the actions of organisms are determined entirely by the pursuit of pleasure and the avoidance of pain.

learning An enduring change in the mechanisms of behavior involving specific stimuli and/or responses that results from prior experience with similar stimuli and responses.

maturation A change in behavior caused by physical or physiological development of the organism in the absence of experience with particular environmental events.

nativism A philosophy according to which human beings are born with innate ideas.

nervism The philosophical position adopted by Pavlov that all behavioral and physiological processes are regulated by the nervous system.

nonsense syllable A three-letter combination (two consonants separated by a vowel) that has no meaning.

performance An organism's activities at a particular time.

reflex A mechanism that enables a specific environmental event to elicit a specific response.

CHAPTER

2

ELICITED BEHAVIOR, HABITUATION, AND SENSITIZATION

Chapter 2 begins the discussion of contemporary principles of learning and behavior with a description of modern research on elicited behavior—behavior that occurs in reaction to specific environmental stimuli. Many of the things we do are elicited by discrete stimuli, and some of the most extensively investigated response systems involve elicited behavior. The chapter begins with a description of the simplest form of elicited behavior, reflexive behavior, and ends with a discussion of complex emotional responses and goal-directed behavior. During this discussion, I describe two of the fundamental and most common forms of behavioral change—habituation and sensitization—which occur in a wide variety of response systems and are potentially involved in all learning procedures.

All animals, whether single-celled paramecia or complex human beings, react to events in their environment. If something moves in the periphery of your vision, you will likely turn your head in that direction. A particle of food in the mouth elicits salivation. Exposure to a bright light causes the pupils of the eyes to constrict. Touching a hot surface elicits a quick withdrawal response. Irritation of the respiratory passages causes sneezing and coughing. These and numerous similar examples illustrate that much of behavior occurs in response to stimuli—that is, it is elicited.

Elicited behavior has been the subject of extensive investigation. Many chapters in this text deal in one way or another with responses to stimuli. I begin the discussion of elicited behavior by describing its simplest form, reflexive behavior.

The Concept of the Reflex

A light puff of air directed at the cornea makes the eye blink. A tap just below the knee causes the leg to kick. A loud noise triggers a startle reaction. These are all examples of reflexes. A reflex involves two closely related events, an *eliciting stimulus* and a *corresponding response,* which are linked. Presentation of the stimulus is followed by the response, and the response rarely occurs in the absence of the stimulus. For example, dust in the nasal passages elicits sneezing, which does not occur in the absence of nasal irritation.

The specificity of the relation between a stimulus and its accompanying reflex response is a consequence of the organization of the nervous system. In vertebrates (including humans), simple reflexes are typically mediated by three neurons, as illustrated in Figure 2.1. The environmental stimulus for a reflex activates a **sensory neuron** (also called **afferent neuron**) that transmits the sensory message to the spinal cord. There, the neural impulses are relayed to the **motor neuron** (also called **efferent neuron**), which activates the muscles involved in the reflex response. However, sensory and motor neurons rarely communicate directly. The impulses from one to the other are relayed through at least one **interneuron.**

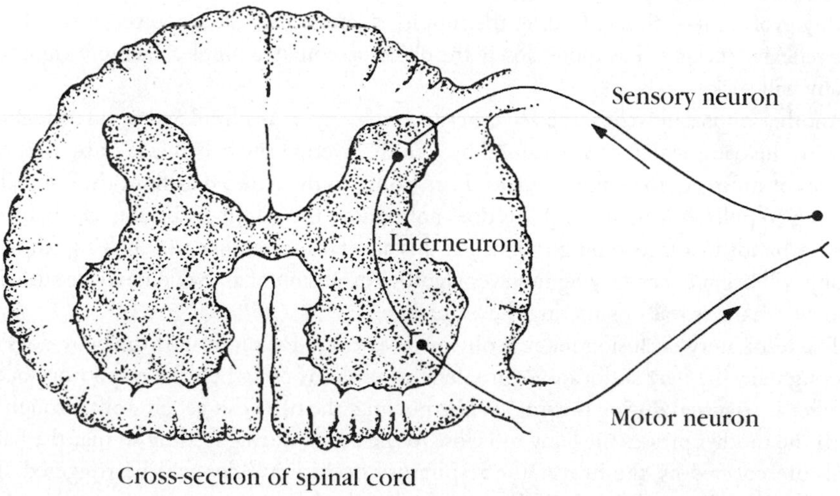

Figure 2.1 Neural organization of simple reflexes. The environmental stimulus for a reflex activates a sensory neuron, which transmits the sensory message to the spinal cord. Here, the neural impulses are relayed to an interneuron, which in turn relays the impulses to the motor neuron. The motor neuron activates muscles involved in movement.

Figure 2.2 Painful stimulation of one limb of a dog causes withdrawal (flexion) of that limb and extension of the opposite limb. (From "Reflexive Behavior," by B. L. Hart in G. Bermant [Ed.], 1973, *Perspectives in Animal Behavior.* Copyright © 1973 by Scott, Foresman. Reprinted by permission.)

The neural circuitry ensures that particular sensory neurons are connected to a corresponding set of motor neurons. Because of this restricted "wiring," a particular reflex response is elicited only by a restricted set of stimuli. The afferent neuron, interneuron, and efferent neuron together constitute the **reflex arc.**

The reflex arc in vertebrates represents the fewest neural connections necessary for reflex action, but additional neural structures may also be involved. For example, the sensory messages may be relayed to the brain, which in turn may modify the reflex reaction in various ways. I discuss such effects later in the chapter. For now, it is sufficient to keep in mind that the occurrence of even simple reflexes can be influenced by higher nervous system activity.

Most reflexes contribute to the well-being of the organism in obvious ways. In many animals, for example, painful stimulation of one limb causes withdrawal, or flexion, of that limb and extension of the opposite limb (Hart, 1973). If a dog stubs a toe while walking, it will automatically withdraw that leg and simultaneously extend the opposite leg (see Figure 2.2). This combination of responses removes the first leg from the source of pain and at the same time allows the animal to maintain balance.

Reflexes constitute much of the behavioral repertoire of newborn infants. If you touch an infant's cheek with your finger, the baby will reflexively turn her head in that direction, with the result that your finger will fall into the baby's mouth. This head-turning reflex probably evolved to facilitate finding the nipple. The sensation of an object in the mouth causes reflexive sucking. The more closely the object resembles a nipple, the more vigorously the baby will suck.

Another important reflex, the *respiratory occlusion reflex,* is stimulated by a reduction of airflow to the baby, which can be caused by a cloth covering the baby's face or by the accumulation of mucus in the nasal passages. In response to the reduced airflow, the baby's first reaction is to pull her head back. If this does not remove the eliciting stimulus, the baby will move her hands in a face-wiping motion. If this also fails to remove the eliciting stimulus, the baby will begin to cry. Crying involves vigorous expulsion of air, which may be sufficient to remove whatever was obstructing the air passages.

The respiratory occlusion reflex is obviously essential for survival. If the baby does not get enough air, she may suffocate. A problem arises, however, when the respiratory occlusion reflex is triggered during nursing. While nursing, the baby can get air only through the nose. If the mother presses the baby too close to the breast during feeding so that the baby's nostrils are covered by the breast, the respiratory occlusion reflex will be triggered. The baby will attempt to pull her head back from the nipple, may move her hands in a face-

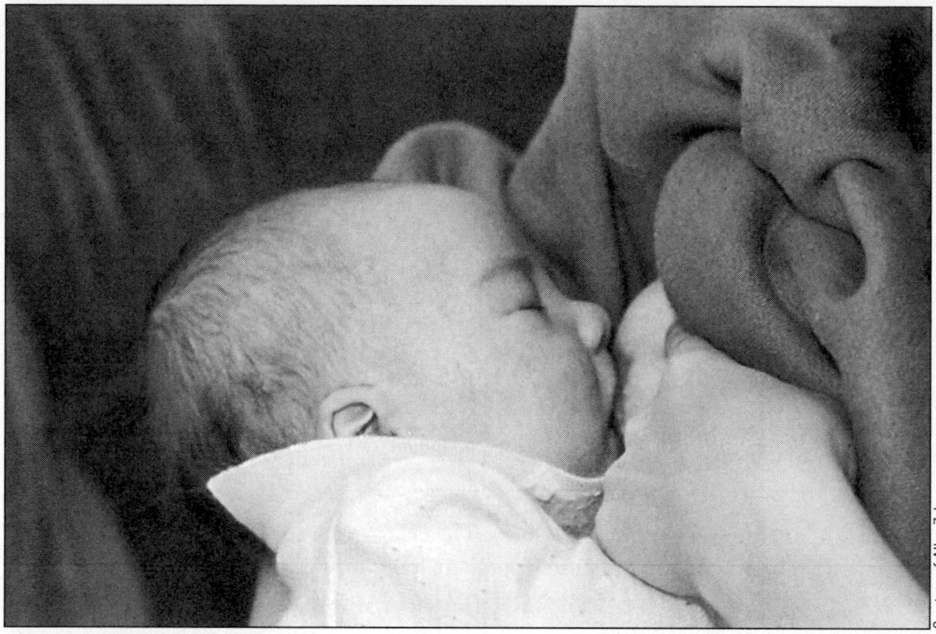

Figure 2.3 Sucking is one of the most prominent reflexes in infants.

wiping motion that pushes away the nipple, and may begin to cry. Successful nursing requires a bit of experience. The mother and child have to adjust their positions so that nursing can progress without stimulation of the respiratory occlusion reflex (Gunther, 1961). (See Figure 2.3.)

Modal Action Patterns

Simple reflex responses, such as pupillary constriction to a bright light and startle reactions to a brief loud noise, are evident in many species. By contrast, other forms of elicited behavior occur in just one species or in a small group of related species. For example, sucking in response to objects placed in the mouth is a characteristic of mammalian infants. Herring-gull chicks are just as dependent on parental feeding as are human infants, but their feeding behavior is very different. When a parent gull returns to the nest from a foraging trip, the chicks peck at the tip of the parent's bill (see Figure 2.4), causing the parent to regurgitate. As the chicks continue to peck, they manage to get some of the parent's regurgitated food, and thus receive nourishment.

Response sequences, such as those involved in infant feeding, that are typical of a particular species are referred to as **modal action patterns** or **MAPs** (Baerends, 1988). Species-typical modal action patterns have been identified in many aspects of animal behavior, including sexual behavior, territorial defense, aggression, and prey capture. Ring doves, for example, begin their sexual behavior with a courtship interaction that culminates in the selection of a nest site and the cooperative construction of the nest by both male and female. By contrast, in the three-spined stickleback, a species of small fish, the male first establishes a territory and constructs a nest. Females that enter the territory after the nest has been built are courted and induced to lay their eggs in the nest. Once a female has deposited her eggs, the male chases her away, leaving him alone to care for and defend the eggs until the offspring hatch.

Figure 2.4 Feeding of herring-gull chicks. The chicks peck a red patch near the tip of the parent's bill, causing the parent to regurgitate food for them.

An important feature of modal action patterns is that the threshold for eliciting such activities varies as a function of circumstances (Camhi, 1984; Baerends, 1988). The same stimulus can have widely different effects, depending on the physiological state of the animal and its recent actions. A male stickleback, for example, will not court a female who is ready to lay eggs until he has completed building his nest. And after the female has deposited her eggs, the male will chase her away rather than court her as he did earlier. Furthermore, these sexual and territorial responses will occur only when environmental cues induce physiological changes that are characteristic of the breeding season in both males and females.

Modal action patterns were initially identified by ethologists, scientists who study the evolution of behavior. Early ethologists, such as Lorenz and Tinbergen, referred to species-specific action patterns as "fixed action patterns" to emphasize that the activities occurred in much the same way in all members of a species. Subsequent detailed observations, however, indicated that action patterns are not performed in exactly the same fashion each time, that they are not strictly "fixed." Because of this variability, we now use the term "modal action pattern" (Baerends, 1988).

Eliciting Stimuli for Modal Action Patterns

The eliciting stimulus is fairly easy to identify in the case of simple reflexes, such as the startle response to a brief loud noise. The stimulus responsible for a modal action pattern can be more difficult to isolate if the response occurs in the course of complex social interactions. For example, consider again the feeding of a herring-gull chick. To get fed, the chick has to peck the parent's beak to stimulate the parent to regurgitate. But what stimulates the chick's pecking response? There are a number of possibilities, but the answer cannot be determined on the basis of casual observation.

The adult herring gull has a long, yellow bill with a striking red patch near the tip. Pecking by the chicks may be elicited by the color, shape, or length of the parent's bill, the noises the parent makes, the head movements of the parent, or some other stimulus. To isolate which one of these stimuli elicits pecking, Tinbergen and Perdeck (1950) tested chicks with various artificial models instead of live adult gulls. Their research showed that a model had to have several characteristics to elicit strong pecking—a long, thin, moving object pointed downward and having a contrasting red patch near the tip. These experiments suggest that the yellow color of the adult's bill, the shape and coloration of its head, and the noises it makes are not required for eliciting pecking in the gull chicks. The specific features required to elicit the pecking behavior are called, collectively, the **sign stimulus** or **releasing stimulus** for this behavior.

A sign or releasing stimulus is sufficient for eliciting a modal action pattern. However, a given action pattern may be controlled by several stimulus features in an additive fashion. In addition, the most effective stimulus for eliciting a modal action pattern may not be one that is likely to occur under natural conditions. These principles are well illustrated by a study of the egg-retrieval behavior of herring gulls (Baerends & Drent, 1982). If a brooding herring gull finds an egg on the rim of its nest, it will pull the egg into the nest. To determine which features of the egg best stimulate this behavior, Baerends and Drent tested gulls with wooden eggs of various sizes, colors, and speckling.

The results indicated that the gulls preferred to retrieve green speckled eggs more than yellow ones, yellow eggs more than brown, and brown eggs more than blue. The preference for green and yellow eggs over brown eggs was remarkable because real gull eggs are brown rather than green or yellow. Increases in the number of speckles and their contrast with the background also increased egg-retrieval behavior, as did increases in the size of the wooden eggs (see Figure 2.5).

G. P. Baerends

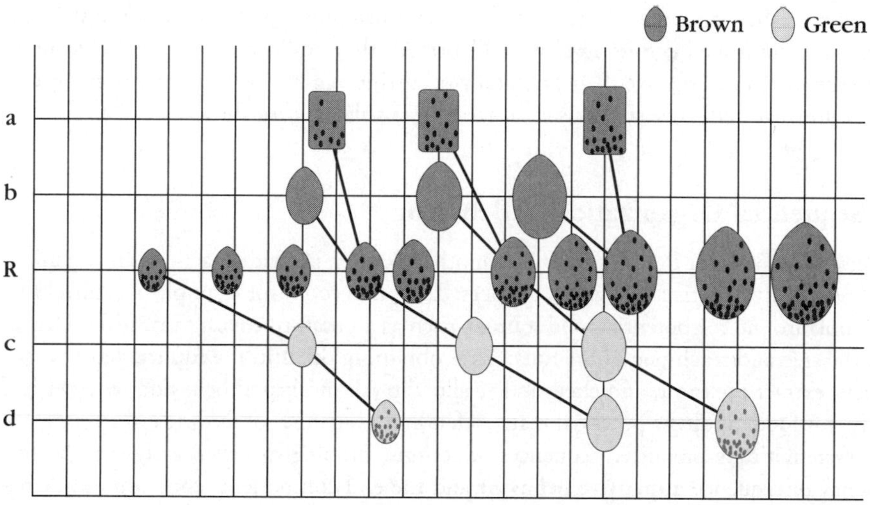

Figure 2.5 Relative effectiveness of various artificial eggs in stimulating egg retrieval behavior in gulls. From left to right, the models increase in effectiveness. Row "R" (for reference series) shows eggs of normal color and speckling. Row "a" shows block-shaped eggs; "b" shows plain brown eggs; "c" shows plain green eggs; and "d" shows speckled green eggs. The oblique lines connect models of the same size. Notice that eggs of a given type can be made more effective by an increase in size. (From "The Herring Gull and Its Egg. Part II: The Responsiveness to Egg Features," by G. P. Baerends and R. H. Drent [Eds.], 1982, *Behaviour, 82,* pp. 1–417. Reprinted by permission.)

BOX 2.1

THE LEARNING OF "INSTINCT"

Because modal action patterns occur in a similar fashion among members of a given species, they include activities that are informally characterized as "instinctive." Instinctive behavior is considered primarily to reflect an individual's genetic history, leading to the impression that modal action patterns are not the product of learning and experience. However, the fact that all members of a species exhibit similar forms of behavior does not necessarily mean that the behavior was not learned through experience. As Tinbergen (1951) recognized many years ago, similar behavior on the part of all members of a species may reflect similar learning experiences. In a more recent expression of this sentiment, Baerends (1988) wrote that "learning processes in many variations are tools, so to speak, that can be used in the building of some segments in the species-specific behavior organization" (p. 801). Thus, learning may be involved in what we commonly refer to as "instinctive" behaviors (Domjan, 1998; Hailman, 1967).

Color, speckling, and size appeared to control the egg-retrieval behavior in an additive fashion. Thus, the attractiveness of an egg could be increased by making it more green, more speckled, or larger. Optimizing all three of these stimulus dimensions resulted in a green, highly speckled, and abnormally large egg. Interestingly, such an egg was more effective in stimulating egg-retrieval behavior than was a real gull egg. Thus, once the stimulus features that controlled egg retrieval were identified, they could be combined to form an object that was more effective than a naturally occurring egg in eliciting the action pattern. Such an unusually effective stimulus is called a **supernormal stimulus.**

The Sequential Organization of Behavior

Responses do not occur in isolation of one another. Rather, individual actions are organized into functionally effective behavior sequences. To obtain food, for example, a squirrel first has to look around for potential food sources, such as a pecan tree with nuts. It then has to climb the tree and reach one of the nuts. After obtaining the nut, the squirrel has to crack the shell, extract the meat, and chew and swallow it. All motivated behavior, whether it is foraging for food, finding a potential mate, defending a territory, or feeding one's young, involves systematically organized sequences of actions. Ethologists called early components of a behavior sequence **appetitive behavior** and the end components **consummatory behavior** (Craig, 1918). The term "consummatory" was meant to convey the idea of *consummation* or *completion.* Thus, consummatory responses are actions that bring a species-typical response sequence to completion. In contrast, appetitive responses occur early in a behavior sequence and serve to bring the organism into contact with the stimuli that will release the consummatory behavior.

Chewing and swallowing are responses that complete activities involved in foraging for food. Hitting and biting are actions that consummate defensive behavior. Copulatory responses serve to complete the sexual behavior sequence. In general, consummatory responses are highly stereotyped, species-typical behaviors that have specific eliciting or releasing stimuli. In contrast, appetitive behaviors are less stereotyped and can take a variety of different forms, depending on the situation (Tinbergen, 1951). In getting to a pecan tree, for example, a squirrel can run up one side or the other or jump from a neighboring tree. These are all possible appetitive responses leading up to actually eating the pecan nut. Once the squirrel is ready to put the pecan meat in its mouth, however, the chewing and swallowing responses that it makes are fairly stereotyped. Consummatory responses tend to be species-typical modal action patterns. In contrast, appetitive behaviors are more variable depending on the environment. As is evident from the varieties of ethnic cuisine, people of different cultures have many different ways of preparing food (appetitive behavior), but they all chew and swallow in much the same way (consummatory behavior). Actions that are considered rude and threatening (appetitive defensive responses) also differ from one culture to another, but people hit and hurt one another (consummatory defensive behavior) in much the same way regardless of culture.

The sequential organization of naturally occurring behavior is very important to scientists interested in understanding how behavior is altered by learning, because learning effects often depend on which component of the behavior sequence is being modified. As I describe in later chapters, the outcomes of Pavlovian and instrumental conditioning depend on how these learning procedures modify the natural sequence of an organism's behavior. Learning theorists are becoming increasingly aware of the importance of considering natural behavior sequences and have expanded on the appetitive and consummatory distinction made by early ethologists (Domjan, 1997; Fanselow, 1997; Timberlake, 1994, 2001).

In considerations of how animals obtain food, for example, it is now common to characterize the foraging response sequence as starting with a **general search mode,** followed by a **focal search mode,** and ending with a **food handling mode.** Thus, in modern learning theory, the appetitive response category has been subdivided into general search and focal search categories (for example, Timberlake, 2001). General search responses occur when the subject does not yet know where to look for food. Before a squirrel has identified a pecan tree, it will move all about looking for potential sources of food. General search responses are not spatially localized. Once the squirrel has found a pecan tree, however, it will switch to the focal search mode and begin to search for pecans only on that tree. Thus, focal search behavior is characterized by considerable spatial specificity. Focal search behavior yields to food handling or consummatory behavior once a pecan nut has been obtained.

EFFECTS OF REPEATED STIMULATION

A common assumption is that an elicited response—in particular, a simple reflex response—will automatically occur the same way every time the eliciting stimulus is presented. This is exactly what Descartes thought. In his view, each occurrence of the eliciting stimulus would produce the same reflex reaction because the energy of the eliciting stimulus is transferred to the motor response through a direct physical connection. If this were true, a baby would suck with the same vigor every time it received a nipple, and you would react with the same pleasure each time you took a sip of your favorite drink. However, if elicited behavior occurred the same way every time, it would be of limited interest, especially for investigators of learning.

Contrary to Descartes' assumptions, elicited behavior is not invariant. One of the most impressive features of elicited behavior is its plasticity. Even simple elicited responses do not

Figure 2.6 Experimental setup for the study of visual attention in infants. The infant is seated in front of a screen that is used to present various visual stimuli. How long the infant looks at the display before diverting his gaze elsewhere is measured on each trial.

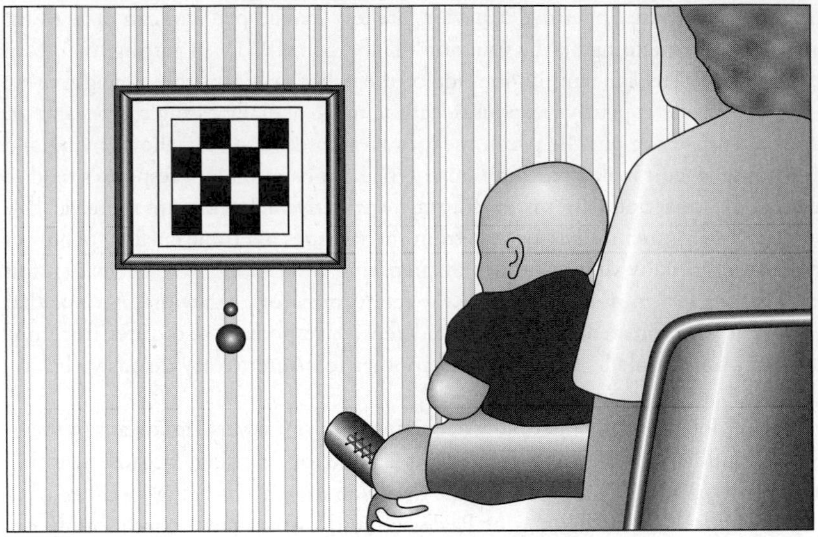

occur the same way each time. As the following examples illustrate, alterations in the nature of elicited behavior often occur simply as a result of repeated presentations of the eliciting stimulus.

Visual Attention in Human Infants

Human infants have a lot to learn about the world, and one way they obtain information is by looking at things in their environment. Visual cues elicit a looking response, which can be measured by how long the infant keeps his eyes on one object before shifting his gaze elsewhere (see Figure 2.6).

In one study of visual attention (Bashinski, Werner, & Rudy, 1985; see also Kaplan, Werner, & Rudy, 1990), 4-month-old infants were assigned to one of two groups, and each group was tested with a different visual stimulus. (The stimuli are shown in the right panel of Figure 2.7.) Both were checkerboard patterns: one had 4 squares on each side (the 4 × 4 stimulus) and the other had 12 (the 12 × 12 stimulus). Each stimulus presentation lasted 10 seconds, and the stimuli were presented eight times at 10-second intervals.

Both stimuli elicited visual attention initially, with the babies spending an average of about 5.5 seconds looking at the stimuli. With repeated presentations of the 4 × 4 stimulus, visual attention progressively decreased. By contrast, the babies increased their gaze at the 12 × 12 stimulus during the second trial as compared to the first. But, after that, visual attention to the 12 × 12 stimulus also decreased.

This relatively simple experiment reveals a great deal about visual attention. The results show that visual attention elicited by a novel stimulus changes as babies gain familiarity with the stimulus. The nature of the change is determined by the nature of the stimulus. With a relatively simple 4 × 4 pattern, visual attention progressively declines. With a more complex 12 × 12 pattern, attention initially increases and then declines. Thus, far from being invariant, the elicited behavior of looking at checkerboard patterns changes in different ways as a result of experience with the stimuli.

Infants cannot tell us in words how they view or think about things. Scientists are therefore forced to use behavioral techniques to study infant perception and cognition. The

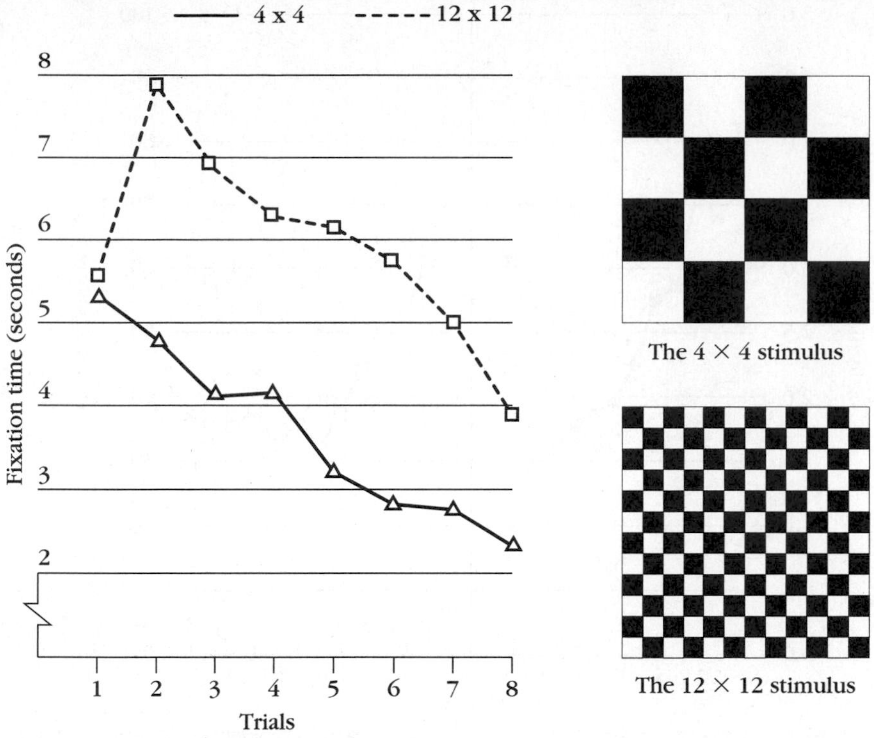

Figure 2.7 Time infants spent looking at a visual stimulus during successive trials. For one group, the stimulus consisted of a 4 × 4 checkerboard pattern. For a second group, the stimulus consisted of a 12 × 12 checkerboard pattern. The stimuli are illustrated to the right of the results. (From "Determinants of Infant Visual Attention: Evidence for a Two-Process Theory," by H. Bashinski, J. Werner, and J. Rudy, *Journal of Experimental Child Psychology, 39,* pp. 580–598. Copyright © 1985 by Academic Press. Reprinted by permission.)

visual attention task can provide information about visual acuity. For example, from the data in Figure 2.7 we may conclude that these infants were able to distinguish the two different checkerboard patterns. The procedure has also been adapted to study a wide range of complicated questions about infant cognition (Fagen & Ohr, 2001).

Salivation and Hedonic Ratings of Taste in People

The taste of food elicits salivation as a reflex response. This can be observed as easily in people as in Pavlov's dogs. In one study, salivation was measured in eight women in response to the taste of either lemon juice or lime juice (Epstein, Rodefer, Wisniewski, & Caggiula, 1992). A tiny amount of one of the flavors (.03 ml) was placed on the subject's tongue on each of 10 trials. On each trial, the subject was asked to rate how much she liked the taste, and her salivation to each taste presentation was also measured. The results are summarized in Figure 2.8. Salivation in response to the taste increased slightly, but from Trial 1 to Trial 2, but response systematically decreased from Trial 2 to Trial 10. A similar decrease was observed in hedonic ratings of the taste. Thus, as the taste stimulus was repeated 10 times, it became less effective in eliciting both salivation and hedonic responses.

On Trial 11, the flavor of the taste was changed (to lime for subjects who had previously been exposed to lemon, and to lemon for subjects who had been exposed to lime). This produced a dramatic recovery in both the salivary reflex and the hedonic rating. Interestingly, this recovery persisted on Trial 12 when the original flavor was presented again.

People often eat because they like the taste of what they are eating. The results presented in Figure 2.8 indicate that people find the taste of a specific food less pleasant the

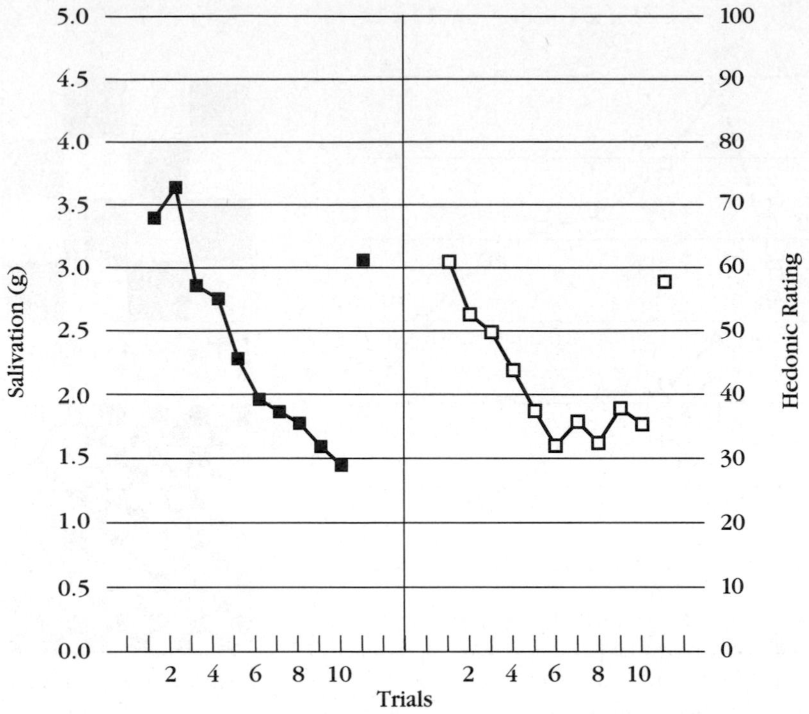

Figure 2.8 Salivation and ratings of pleasantness in response to a taste stimulus (lime or lemon) repeatedly presented to women on Trials 1–10. The alternate taste was presented on Trial 11, causing a substantial recovery in responding. (After Epstein, Rodefer, Wisniewski, & Caggiula, 1992.)

more often they encounter it. The taste of a different food is enough, however, to restore the hedonic rating of a familiar food. These findings suggest that overeating may be discouraged by not varying the foods that are available for consumption.

Startle Response in Rats

The kinds of effects presented in Figures 2.7 and 2.8 have also been extensively examined in laboratory animals. Many of these experiments have involved the startle response. The startle is a defensive response evident in many species, including humans. If someone unexpectedly blows a foghorn behind your back, you are likely to jump. This is the startle response. It consists of a sudden jump and a tensing of the muscles of the upper part of the body, usually involving raising of the shoulders. In rats, the startle reaction can be measured by placing the animal in a *stabilimeter chamber* (see Figure 2.9), which rests on pressure sensors. When startled, the animal jumps and thereby jiggles the chamber. These movements are precisely measured by the pressure sensors under the chamber and are used as indicators of the vigor of the startle reaction.

The startle reaction can be elicited in rats by a variety of stimuli, including brief tones and lights. In one experiment, Davis (1974) investigated the startle reaction of two groups of rats to presentations of a brief (90-millisecond) loud tone (110 decibels [dB], 4,000 cycles per second [cps]). Each group received 100 successive tone presentations separated by 30 seconds. In addition, a noise generator provided background noise that sounded somewhat like water running from a faucet. For one group, the background noise was relatively quiet (60 dB); for the other, it was rather loud (80 dB), but of lower intensity than the brief startle-eliciting tones.

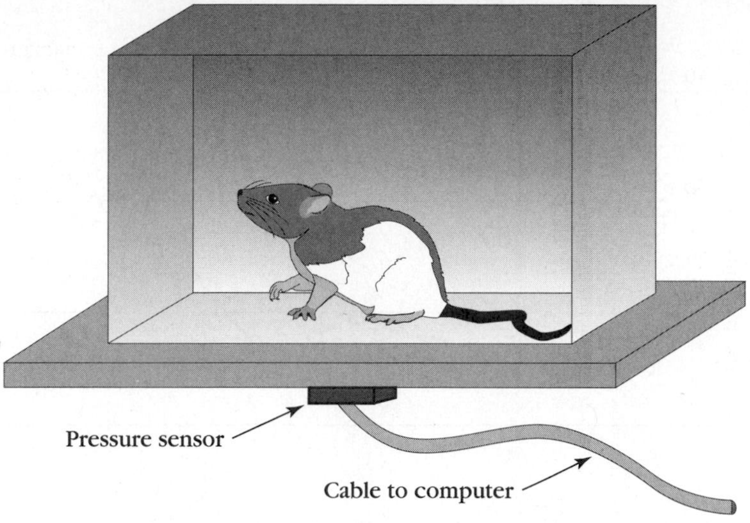

Figure 2.9 Stabilimeter apparatus to measure the startle response of rats. A small chamber rests on pressure sensors. Sudden movements of the rat are detected by the pressure sensors and recorded on a computer. (Adapted from Hoffman and Fleshler, 1964.)

The results of the experiment are shown in Figure 2.10. As in the other examples, repeated presentations of the eliciting stimulus (the 4,000 cps tone) did not always produce the same response. For rats tested in the presence of the soft background noise (60 dB), repetitions of the tone resulted in progressively weaker startle reactions. By contrast, when the background noise was loud (80 dB), repetitions of the tone elicited more vigorous startle reactions.

THE CONCEPTS OF HABITUATION AND SENSITIZATION

The studies described in the previous section show that both decreases and increases in responding can occur with repeated presentation of an eliciting stimulus. Decreases in responsiveness produced by repeated stimulation are technically referred to as **habituation effects.** Increases in responsiveness are called **sensitization effects.** Habituation and sensitization effects are two basic types of behavior change that result from prior experience. They are such fundamental features of how organisms adjust to their environment that they occur in nearly all species and response systems (for recent studies in nematodes and crabs, see Beck & Rankin, 1997). Habituation and sensitization effects can occur in any situation that involves repeated exposures to a stimulus. Therefore, an appreciation of these effects is critical for studies of learning. As I describe in Chapter 3, habituation and sensitization are of primary concern in the design of control procedures for Pavlovian conditioning. They also play a role in operant conditioning (McSweeney, Hinson, & Cannon, 1996; McSweeney & Roll, 1998; see also Bizo, Bogdanov, & Killeen, 1998).

Adaptiveness and Pervasiveness of Habituation and Sensitization

Organisms are constantly bombarded by a host of stimuli. Even a simple situation such as sitting at your desk involves a myriad of sensations. You are exposed to the color, texture, and brightness of the paint on the walls; the sounds of the air-conditioning system; noises

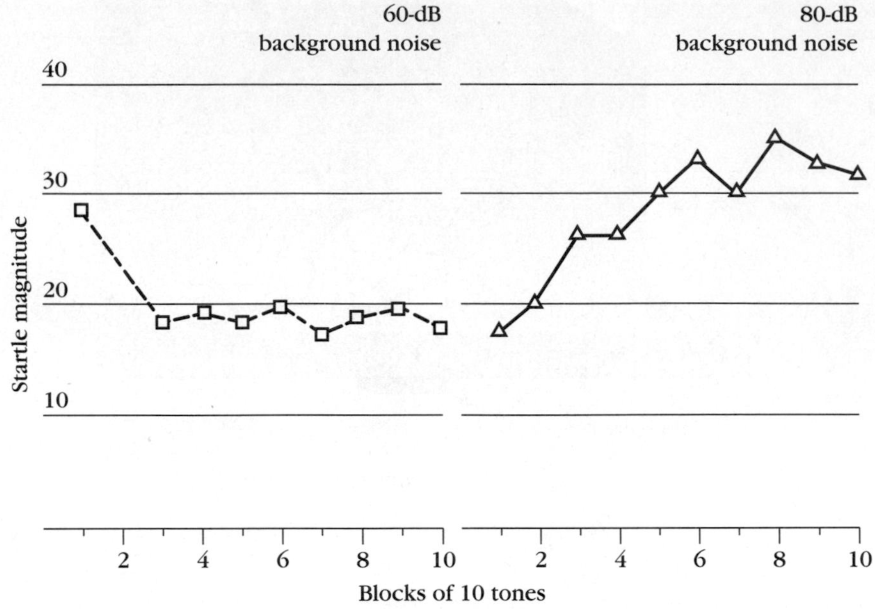

Figure 2.10 Magnitude of the startle response of rats to successive presentations of a tone with background noise of 60 and 80 dB. (From "Sensitization of the Rat Startle Response by Noise," by M. Davis, 1974, *Journal of Comparative and Physiological Psychology,* 87, pp. 571–581. Copyright © 1974 by the American Psychological Association. Reprinted by permission.)

from other rooms; odors in the air; the color and texture of the desk; the tactile sensations of the chair against your legs, seat, and back; and so on. If you were to respond to all of these stimuli, your behavior would be disorganized and chaotic. These effects help sort out what stimuli to ignore and what to respond to. Habituation and sensitization effects are the end products of processes that help organize and focus behavior in the buzzing and booming world of stimuli in which all organisms live.

There are numerous instances of habituation and sensitization in common human experience (Simons, 1996). Consider a grandfather clock, for example. Most people who own such a clock do not notice each time it chimes, because they have completely habituated to the clock's sounds. They are more likely to notice when the clock misses a scheduled chime. In a sense, this is unfortunate, because they may have purchased the clock because they liked its sound. Similarly, people who live on a busy street or near a railroad track may become entirely habituated to the noises that frequently intrude into their homes. Visitors who have not become familiarized with such sounds are much more likely to react and be bothered by them.

Driving a car involves exposure to a large array of complex visual and auditory stimuli. In becoming an experienced driver, a person habituates to the numerous stimuli that are irrelevant to driving, such as details of the color and texture of the road, the kind of telephone poles that line the sides of the highway, tactile sensations of the steering wheel, and routine noises from the engine. Habituation to irrelevant cues is particularly prominent during long driving trips. If you are driving continuously for several hours, you are likely to become oblivious to all kinds of stimuli that are irrelevant to keeping the car on the road. If you then come across an accident or arrive in a new town, you are likely to "wake up" and again pay attention to various things that you had been ignoring. Passing a bad accident or coming to a new town is arousing and sensitizes various orientation responses that were previously habituated.

If you visit a new place or meet a new person, you will likely pay attention to all sorts of stimuli that you ordinarily ignore. In a strange home, for example, you might take notice of the quality of the furniture, the drapes, and some of the knickknacks. You probably ignore such details in familiar places—so much so that you may not be able to either describe the color of the walls in a hallway you pass through every day or recall the type of knob attached to a door you use regularly.

Habituation versus Sensory Adaptation and Response Fatigue

The key characteristic of habituation effects is a decline in the response that was initially elicited by a stimulus. However, habituation is not the only effect that produces a decline in resonse. To understand alternative sources of response decrement, return to the concept of a reflex. A reflex consists of three components. First, a stimulus activates one of the sense organs, such as the eyes or ears. This generates sensory neural impulses that are relayed to the central nervous system (spinal cord and brain). The second component involves relay of the sensory messages through interneurons to motor nerves. Third, the neural impulses in motor nerves in turn activate the muscles that create the observed response.

Given the three components of a reflex, there are several reasons why an elicited response may fail to occur (see Figure 2.11). The response will not be observed if for some reason the sense organs become temporarily insensitive to stimulation. A person may, for example, be temporarily blinded by a bright light or suffer a temporary hearing loss because of repeated exposures to a loud noise. Such decreases in sensitivity are called **sensory adaptation** and are different from habituation. The response also will not occur if the muscles involved become incapacitated by **fatigue.** Sensory adaptation and response fatigue are impediments to responding that are produced outside the nervous system, in sense organs and muscles. Therefore, they are distinguished from habituation.

Habituation and sensitization are assumed to involve neurophysiological changes that hinder or facilitate the transmission of neural impulses from sensory to motor neurons. In habituation, the organism ceases to respond to a stimulus even though it remains fully capable of sensing the stimulus and of making the muscle movements required for the response. The response fails to occur because changes in the nervous system block the relay of sensory neural impulses to the motor neurons.

In studies of habituation, sensory adaptation is ruled out by evidence that *habituation is response-specific.* An organism may stop responding to a stimulus in one aspect of its behavior while continuing to respond to the stimulus in other ways. When a teacher makes an announcement while you are concentrating on taking a test, you may look up from your test at first, but only briefly. You will, however, continue to listen to the announcement until it is over. Thus, your orienting response habituates quickly, but other attentional responses to the stimulus persist.

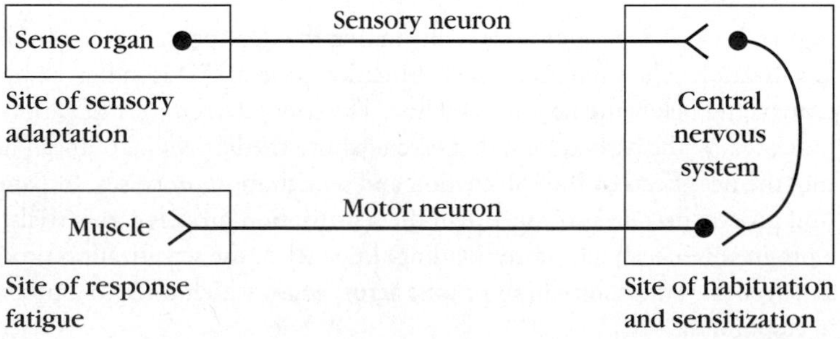

Figure 2.11 Sensory adaptation occurs in the sense organs, and response fatigue occurs in effector muscles. In contrast, habituation and sensitization occur in the nervous system.

Response fatigue as a cause of habituation is ruled out by evidence that *habituation is stimulus-specific.* An habituated response will quickly recover when a new stimulus is introduced. This was illustrated in the taste habituation study summarized in Figure 2.8. After the salivary and hedonic responses had habituated during the first 10 trials, presentation of the alternate taste on Trial 11 resulted in a recovery of both response measures. In an analogous fashion, after your orienting response to a teacher's announcement has habituated, you are likely to look up again if the teacher mentions your name. Thus, a new stimulus will elicit the previously habituated orienting response, indicating that failure of the response was not due to response fatigue.

The Dual-Process Theory of Habituation and Sensitization

Habituation and sensitization effects are changes in behavior or performance. These are outward behavioral manifestations or results of stimulus presentations. What factors are responsible for such changes? To answer this question, we must shift our level of analysis from behavior to presumed underlying process or theory. The dominant theory of habituation and sensitization remains the dual-process theory proposed by Groves and Thompson (1970).

The dual-process theory assumes that different types of underlying neural processes are responsible for increases and decreases in responsiveness to stimulation. One neural process, the **habituation process,** produces decreases in responsiveness. Another, the **sensitization process,** produces increases in responsiveness. These processes are not mutually exclusive. Both may be activated at the same time. The behavioral outcome of these underlying processes depends on which process is stronger. Thus habituation and sensitization processes compete for control of behavior, as illustrated in Figure 2.12.

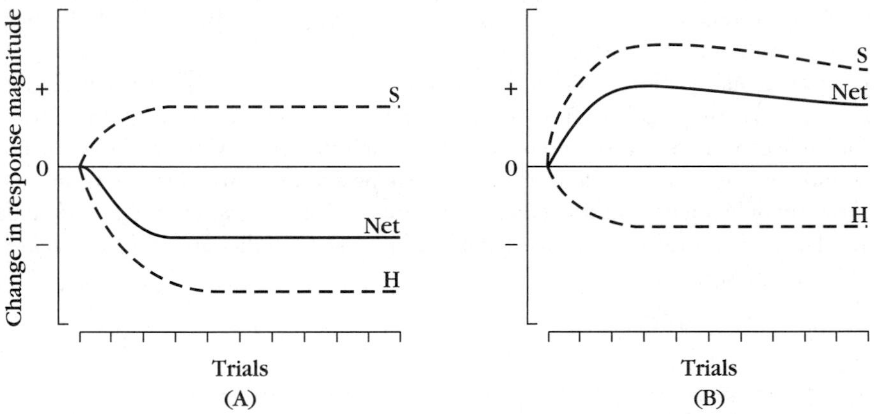

Figure 2.12 Hypothetical data illustrating the dual-process theory of habituation and sensitization. The strength of the habituation process (H) is indicated by the dashed lines that extend below the horizontal 0 line. The strength of the sensitization processes (S) is indicated by the dashed lines that extend above the horizontal 0 line. The solid lines indicate the net effects of the habituation and sensitization processes. In panel A, the habituation process becomes stronger than the sensitization process across trials, which leads to a progressive decrement in responding. In panel B, the sensitization process becomes stronger than the habituation process across trials, which leads to a progressive increase in responding.

The left side of Figure 2.12 illustrates a hypothetical situation in which repetitions of a stimulus intensify the habituation process more than the sensitization process. The net result and behavioral outcome of these changes is a decline in the elicited response across trials (an habituation effect). The right side of Figure 2.12 illustrates the opposite outcome. Here, repetitions of a stimulus strengthen the sensitization process more than the habituation process, and the net result is an increase in the magnitude of the elicited response across trials (a sensitization effect). The change in the elicited response that actually occurs always represents the net effect of the habituation and sensitization processes.

It is unfortunate that the underlying processes that suppress and facilitate responding are called habituation and sensitization. One may be tempted to think that decreased responding or an habituation effect is a direct reflection of the habituation process, and that increased responding or a sensitization effect is a direct reflection of the sensitization process. In fact, as illustrated in Figure 2.12, both habituation and sensitization effects are the sum or net result of both processes. Whether the net result is an increase or a decrease in behavior depends on which underlying process is stronger in a particular situation. The distinction between *effects* and *processes* in habituation and sensitization is analogous to the distinction between *performance* and *learning* discussed in Chapter 1. Effects refer to observable behavior, and processes refer to underlying mechanisms.

On the basis of neurophysiological research, Groves and Thompson (1970) suggested that habituation and sensitization processes occur in different parts of the nervous system (see also Thompson et al., 1973). Habituation processes are assumed to occur in the **S-R system,** which consists of the shortest neural path that connects the sense organs activated by the eliciting stimulus and the muscles involved in making the elicited response. The S-R system may be viewed as the reflex arc. Each presentation of an eliciting stimulus activates the S-R system and causes some buildup of habituation.

Sensitization processes are assumed to occur in the **state system.** This system consists of other parts of the nervous system that determine the organism's general level of responsiveness or readiness to respond. In contrast to the S-R system, which is activated every time an eliciting stimulus is presented, the state system is activated only by arousing events. It is relatively quiescent during sleep, for example. Drugs such as stimulants or depressants may alter the functioning of the state system and thereby change responsiveness. It is also altered by emotional experiences. For example, the heightened reactivity that accompanies fear is caused by activation of the state system.

In summary, the state system determines the organism's general readiness to respond, whereas the S-R system enables the animal to make the specific response that is elicited by the stimulus of interest. Changes in behavior that occur with repetitions of a stimulus reflect the combined actions of the S-R and state systems.

Applications of the Dual-Process Theory. The examples of habituation and sensitization illustrated in the experimental evidence I reviewed earlier can be easily interpreted in terms of the dual-process theory. Repeated exposure to the 4 × 4 checkerboard pattern produced a decrement in visual orientation in infants, presumably because the 4 × 4 stimulus did not create much arousal. In fact, the 4 × 4 stimulus activated primarily the S-R system, and hence activated primarily the habituation process. The more complex 12 × 12 checkerboard pattern produced a greater level of arousal. It presumably activated not only the S-R system but also the state system. Activation of the state system resulted in the increment in visual attention that occurred after the first presentation of the 12 × 12 pattern. However, the arousal or sensitization process was not strong enough to entirely counteract the effects of habituation. As a result, after a few trials, visual attention also declined in response to the 12 × 12 stimulus.

BOX 2.2

TALKING TO A FETUS OR A PRE-VERBAL INFANT

Habituation and sensitization do not require verbal competence. These forms of behavioral plasticity are therefore very useful in studies of the perceptual and cognitive abilities of fetuses and pre-verbal infants (Cohen, 1988; Fagen & Ohr, 2001; Hepper & Shahidullah, 1992; Leinbach & Fagot, 1993; Rose & Orlian, 2001; Smotherman & Robinson, 1992). For example, Kaplan, Goldstein, Huckeby, and Cooper (1995) investigated whether 4-month-old infants could tell the difference between a mother's speech directed toward the infant or toward other adults. To create the speech stimuli, Kaplan et al. recorded a mother saying, "Round and round she goes, and where she stops nobody knows." In one recording, the words were directed toward the mother's infant. In another, the mother was asked to say the words as if talking to another adult. The two kinds of speech were presented while infants were tested for habituation of visual attention to a 4 × 4 checkerboard pattern. Presentation of the infant-directed speech along with the visual stimulus slowed down habituation to the checkerboard pattern. Furthermore, less habituation occurred with infant-directed speech than with adult-directed speech. The babies evidently became more sensitized or aroused by infant-directed speech than by adult-directed speech. This result shows that the babies were able to tell the difference between the two types of speech and found infant-directed speech more stimulating.

A different type of application of the dual-process theory is required for the habituation and sensitization effects I noted in the startle reaction of rats (Figure 2.10). When the rats were tested with a relatively quiet background noise (60 dB), there was little to arouse them. We can therefore assume that the experimental procedures did not produce changes in the state system. Repeated presentations of the startle-eliciting tone merely activated the S-R system, which resulted in habituation of the startle response.

The opposite outcome occurred when the animals were tested in the presence of a loud background noise (80 dB). Stronger startle reactions occurred to successive presentations of the tone. Because the identical tone was used for both groups, the difference in the results cannot be attributed to the tone. One must assume that the loud background noise increased arousal or readiness to respond in the second group. This sensitization of the state system was presumably responsible for increasing the startle reaction to the tone in the second group.

Implications of the Dual-Process Theory. The preceding interpretations of changes in visual attention and startle responding illustrate several important features of the dual-process theory. As discussed earlier, the state and S-R systems are activated differently by repeated presentations of a stimulus. *The S-R system is activated every time a stimulus elicits a response,* because it is the neural circuit that conducts impulses from sensory input to response output. By contrast, *the state system becomes involved only in special circumstances.* Some extraneous event (such as an intense background noise) may increase the individual's alertness and sensitize the state system. Alternatively, the state system may be sensitized by the repeated presentations of the test stimulus itself if that stimulus is sufficiently intense or excitatory (a 12 × 12 checkerboard pattern, as compared with a 4 × 4 pattern). If the arousing stimulus is repeated soon enough so that the second presentation occurs while the organism remains sensitized from the preceding trial, an increase in responding will be observed.

The dual-process theory of habituation and sensitization has been very influential in the study of the plasticity of elicited behavior (for example, Pilz & Schnitzler, 1996), although it has not been successful in explaining all habituation and sensitization effects (for example, Bee, 2001). One of the important contributions of the theory has been the assumption that elicited behavior can be strongly influenced by neurophysiological events that take place outside the reflex arc that is directly involved in a particular elicited response. In the dual-process theory, the state system is assumed to modulate the activity of reflex arcs. The basic idea that certain parts of the nervous system serve to modulate S-R systems that are more directly involved in elicited behavior has also been developed in other recent studies of habituation and sensitization (for example, Borszcz, Cranney, & Leaton, 1989; Davis, Hitchcock, & Rosen, 1987; Falls & Davis, 1994; Frankland & Yeomans, 1995; Lipp, Sheridan, & Siddle, 1994). (For a detailed discussion of other theories of habituation, see Stephenson & Siddle, 1983.)

CHARACTERISTICS OF HABITUATION AND SENSITIZATION

Much research has been performed to determine how various factors influence habituation and sensitization processes. Although the characteristics of habituation and sensitization are not perfectly uniform across all species and response systems, there are many commonalties. In this section, I describe some of the most important ones.

Time Course

Most of the forms of behavior change I describe in later chapters are retained for long periods (weeks or months), a defining characteristic of learning phenomena (see Chapter 1). Instances of habituation and sensitization do not always have this characteristic, and therefore not all instances of habituation and sensitization are properly considered examples of enduring learning.

Time Course of Sensitization. Sensitization processes generally have temporary effects. Although in some instances sensitization persists for more than a week (e.g., Heiligenberg, 1974), the increased responsiveness is generally short-lived. Davis (1974), for example, investigated the sensitizing effect of a 25-minute exposure to a loud noise (80 dB) in rats. As expected, the loud noise sensitized the startle response to a tone, but this increased reactivity lasted only 10–15 minutes after the loud noise was turned off. In other response systems, sensitization dissipates more rapidly. For example, sensitization of the spinal hindlimb-flexion reflex in cats persists for only about 3 seconds (Groves & Thompson, 1970).

In all response systems the duration of sensitization effects is determined by the intensity of the sensitizing stimulus. More intense stimuli produce greater increases in responsiveness, and with more intense stimuli the sensitization effects persist longer.

Time Course of Habituation. Habituation also persists for varying amounts of time. With sensitization, differences in the time course of the effect usually reflect only quantitative differences in the same underlying mechanism. By contrast, there are two qualitatively different types of habituation effects: *Short-term habituation* is similar to most cases of sensitization in that it dissipates relatively quickly—within seconds or minutes. The other type, *long-term habituation* is much longer lasting and may persist for many days.

Short-term and long-term habituation effects are clearly illustrated by Leaton (1976) in an experiment on the startle response of rats. The test stimulus was a high-pitched, loud tone presented for 2 seconds. The animals were first allowed to get used to the experimental chamber without any tone presentations. Each rat then received a single test trial with the tone stimulus once a day for 11 days. Because of the long (24-hour) interval between trials, any decrements in responding produced by the stimulus presentations were assumed to exemplify long-term habituation. The short-term habituation process was illustrated in the next phase of the experiment by giving the rats 300 closely spaced tone presentations (every 3 seconds). Finally, the animals were given a single tone presentation on each of the next 3 days to measure recovery from the short-term habituation effect.

Figure 2.13 shows the results. The most intense startle reaction was observed the first time the tone was presented. Progressively less intense reactions occurred over the next 10 days. Because the animals were tested only once every 24 hours in this phase, the progressive decrements in responding indicate that the habituating effects of the stimulus presentations persisted throughout the 11-day period. It is worth noting, though, that this long-term habituation did not result in complete loss of the startle reflex. Even on the 11th day, the animals reacted a little.

By contrast, startle reactions quickly ceased when the tone presentations occurred every 3 seconds in the second phase of the experiment, but this dramatic loss of responsiveness was only temporary. In the third phase of the experiment, when the animals were tested again just once a day, the startle response recovered to the level of the 11th day of the experiment. This recovery, known as **spontaneous recovery,** occurred simply because the tone had not been presented for a long time (24 hours). *Spontaneous recovery is the identifying characteristic of the short-term habituation effect.*

Repeated presentations of a stimulus do not always result in both long-term and short-term habituation effects. With the spinal leg-flexion reflex in cats, for example, only the

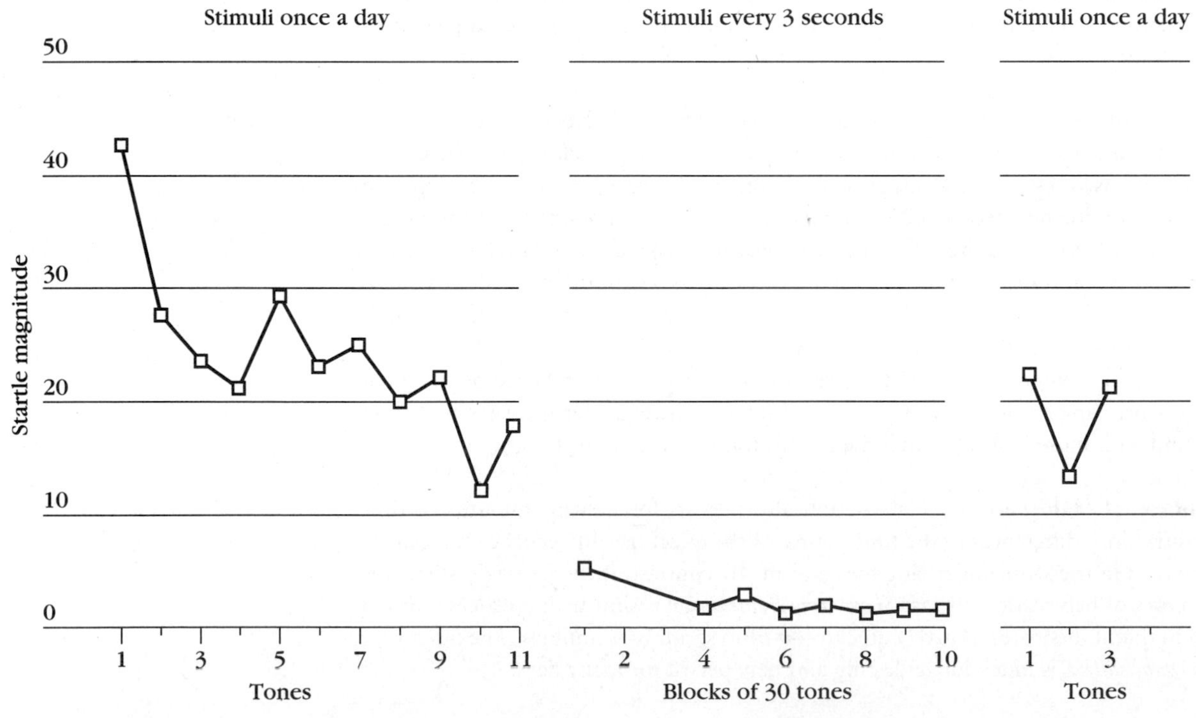

Figure 2.13 Startle response of rats to a tone presented once a day in Phase 1, every 3 seconds in Phase 2, and once a day in Phase 3. (From "Long-Term Retention of the Habituation of Lick Suppression and Startle Response Produced by a Single Auditory Stimulus," by R. N. Leaton, 1976, *Journal of Experimental Psychology: Animal Behavior Processes, 2,* pp. 248–259. Copyright © 1976 by the American Psychological Association. Reprinted by permission.)

short-term habituation effect is observed (Thompson & Spencer, 1966). In such cases, spontaneous recovery completely restores the animal's reaction to the eliciting stimulus if a long enough period of rest is permitted after habituation. By contrast, spontaneous recovery is never complete in situations that also involve long-term habituation effects, as in Leaton's experiment. As Figure 2.13 indicates, the startle response was restored to some extent in the last phase of the experiment, but the animals did not react as vigorously to the tone as they had the first time it was presented.

Short-term habituation typically occurs when the eliciting stimulus is presented frequently, as in the second phase of Leaton's experiment. In contrast, long-term habituation is more likely with more widely spaced stimulus presentations (for example, Beck & Rankin, 1997; Pedreira et al., 1998; Staddon & Higa, 1996).

The dual-process theory of habituation and sensitization was formulated to explain only short-term effects and therefore cannot explain why habituation lasts considerably longer under certain conditions. The most successful explanation of long-term habituation is Wagner's priming theory (for example, Whitlow & Wagner, 1984). I do not discuss this theory here because it involves associative learning mechanisms that are not presented in detail until Chapters 3 and 4. (For recent studies of the associative mechanisms of long-term habituation, see Honey, Good, & Manser, 1998; Jordan, Strasser, & McHale, 2000; Tomsic, Pedreira, Romano, Hermitte, & Maldonado, 1998.)

Stimulus Specificity

Stimulus Specificity of Habituation. Habituation is specific to the stimulus that is repeatedly presented (Thompson & Spencer, 1966). A response that has been habituated to one stimulus can be evoked in full strength by altering a critical feature of the stimulus. This outcome was shown in the experiment on habituation of salivation and hedonic ratings in response to a taste (see Figure 2.8). After the salivary and emotional responses to one taste stimulus (for example, lime) had substantially habituated (Trials 1-10), the responses showed total recovery when a different taste (lemon) was presented (Trial 11). Similar effects occur in common experience. For example, after you have become habituated to the chimes of a grandfather clock, your attention to the clock is likely to be entirely restored if the clock malfunctions and makes a new sound. After complete habituation of the orienting response to one stimulus, the response will occur in its normal strength if a sufficiently novel stimulus is presented. Stimulus specificity has been considered one of the defining characteristics of habituation (Thompson & Spencer, 1966).

Although habituation effects are always stimulus-specific, some generalization of the effects may occur. If you have become habituated to a particular clock chime, you may also not respond to another clock chime that is similar to the original one. This phenomenon is called *stimulus generalization of habituation.* However, even in cases of stimulus generalization, as test stimuli are made increasingly different from the habituated stimulus, the organism will show progressively less habituation or suppression of responding to the test stimuli.

Stimulus Specificity of Sensitization. Unlike habituation, sensitization is not highly stimulus-specific. If an animal becomes aroused or sensitized for some reason, its reactivity will increase to a range of cues. For example, pain induced by footshock increases the reactivity of laboratory rats to both auditory and visual cues. Similarly, feelings of sickness or malaise increase the reactivity of rats to a wide range of novel tastes. However, shock-induced sensitization appears to be limited to exteroceptive cues, and illness-induced sensitization is limited to gustatory stimuli (Miller & Domjan, 1981). Cutaneous pain and internal malaise seem to activate separate sensitization systems.

Effects of a Strong Extraneous Stimulus

As I have noted, changing the nature of the eliciting stimulus can produce recovery of an habituated response. However, this is not the only way to quickly restore responding after habituation. The habituated response can also be restored by sensitizing the organism with exposure to an extraneous stimulus. This phenomenon is called **dishabituation.**

Figure 2.14 illustrates the results of a study involving dishabituation of the visual-attention response of human infants (Kaplan, Werner, & Rudy, 1990). The infants were shown a 4 × 4 checkerboard pattern during each of the first eight trials of the experiment and displayed a familiar habituation effect. During Trial 9, a 75 dB, 1,000 cps tone was sounded along with the visual stimulus for one group of infants, while the other group continued to receive the visual stimulus but without the tone. The presence of the tone greatly elevated responding. Furthermore, responding continued to be elevated in Trials 10, 11, and 12, during which the tone was again omitted and only the 4 × 4 visual stimulus was available.

It is important to keep in mind that dishabituation refers to recovery in the response to the previously habituated stimulus—the 4 × 4 pattern in the above example. Responding directly to the sensitizing or dishabituating tone was not of interest. In fact, the increased visual fixation that was observed when the tone was presented on Trial 9 could not be explained as a response to the tone because the tone was presented through a speaker located above and behind the infant. If the infant had oriented toward the source of the tone, he or she would have ended up looking away from the visual stimulus.

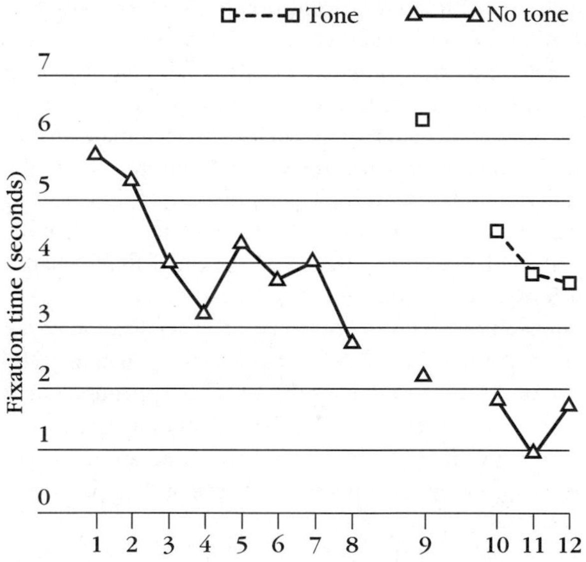

Figure 2.14 Fixation time of human infants plotted as a function of presentations of a 4 × 4 checkerboard pattern. On the 9th trial, some of the infants were exposed to a 10-second, 1,000 Hz, 75 dB tone. This caused an increase in responding to the checkerboard pattern. (From "Habituation, Sensitization, and Infant Visual Attention," by P. S. Kaplan, J. S. Werner, and J. W. Rudy, 1990, in *Advances in Infancy Research,* Vol. 6, pp. 61–109, C. Rovee-Collier and L. P. Lipsitt [Eds.]. Copyright © 1990 by Ablex Publishing Company. Reprinted by permission.)

BOX 2.3

LEARNING IN AN INVERTEBRATE

How does the brain acquire, store, and retrieve information? To answer this question, we need to know how neurons operate and how neural circuits are modified by experience. Studying these issues requires that we delve into the neural machinery, to record and manipulate its operations. Naturally, people are not keen on volunteering for such experiments. Therefore, such research has to be conducted on other species.

Much can be learned from the vertebrates (rats, rabbits) that are typically used in behavioral studies of learning. Yet, at a neural level, even a rat poses technical challenge for a neurobiologist. Therefore, neurobiologists have focused on creatures with simpler nervous systems. Invertebrates are attractive because some of their neurons are very large (for example, the motor neuron that drives escape in a squid), and they have far simpler nervous systems. Using this approach, Eric Kandel and his colleagues have uncovered the mechanisms that mediate some basic learning processes in the marine snail *Aplysia.* Here I provide an overview of the mechanisms that underlie habituation and sensitization. For more information on this topic and others related to the neurobiology of learning, see Dudai (1989) and Kandel, Schwartz, and Jessell (2000).

The *Aplysia* has two winglike flaps (the parapodium) on its back or dorsal surface. These flaps cover the gill and other components of the respiratory apparatus (see Figure 2.15). The gill lies under a mantle shelf and a siphon helps to circulate water across the gill. In the relaxed state, the gill is extended (left side of Figure 2.15), maximizing chemical exchange across its surface. The gill is a fragile organ that must be protected, and thus nature has given *Aplysia* a protective gill withdrawal reflex. This reflex can be elicited by a light touch applied to the siphon or mantle. In the laboratory, the reflex is often elicited by a water jet produced from a Water Pik. While the mechanisms that underlie this reflex can be studied in the intact organism, it is often easier to study the underlying system after the essential components have been removed and placed in a nutrient bath that sustains the tissue.

With this simple preparation, it is an easy matter to demonstrate both habituation and sensitization (see Figure 2.15). Habituation can be produced by repeatedly applying the tactile stimulus to the siphon. With continued exposure, the magnitude of the gill withdrawal reflex becomes smaller (habituates). Interestingly, this experience has no effect on the magnitude of the gill withdrawal elicited by touching the mantle shelf. Conversely, if we repeatedly touch the mantle, the withdrawal response observed habituates without affecting the response elicited by touching the siphon. A modification in one stimulus-response (S-R) pathway has no effect on the response vigor in the other.

In vertebrates, a painful shock engages a mechanism that generally sensitizes behavior, augmenting a variety of response systems including those that generate a startle response (Davis, 1989). A similar effect can be demonstrated in *Aplysia.* If a shock stimulus is applied to the tail, it sensitizes the gill withdrawal response elicited by touching the mantle or siphon (Walters, 1994). Notice that this is a general effect that augments behavioral reactivity in both the mantle and the siphon circuits.

The essential neural components that underlie gill withdrawal in response to a siphon touch are illustrated in Figure 2.15. A similar diagram could be drawn for the neurons that underlie the gill withdrawal elicited by touching the mantle.

Touching the siphon skin engages a mechanical receptor that is coupled to a sensory neuron (SN). Just one receptor is illustrated here, but additional receptors and neurons innervate adjoining regions of the siphon skin. The degree to which a particular receptor is engaged will depend on its proximity to the locus of stimulation, being greatest at the center of stimulation and weakening as distance increases. This yields the neural equivalent to a generalization gradient, with the maximum activity being produced by the neuron that provides the primary innervation for the receptive field stimulated.

The mechanical receptors that detect a touch engage a response within the dendrites of the sensory neuron (SN).

(continued)

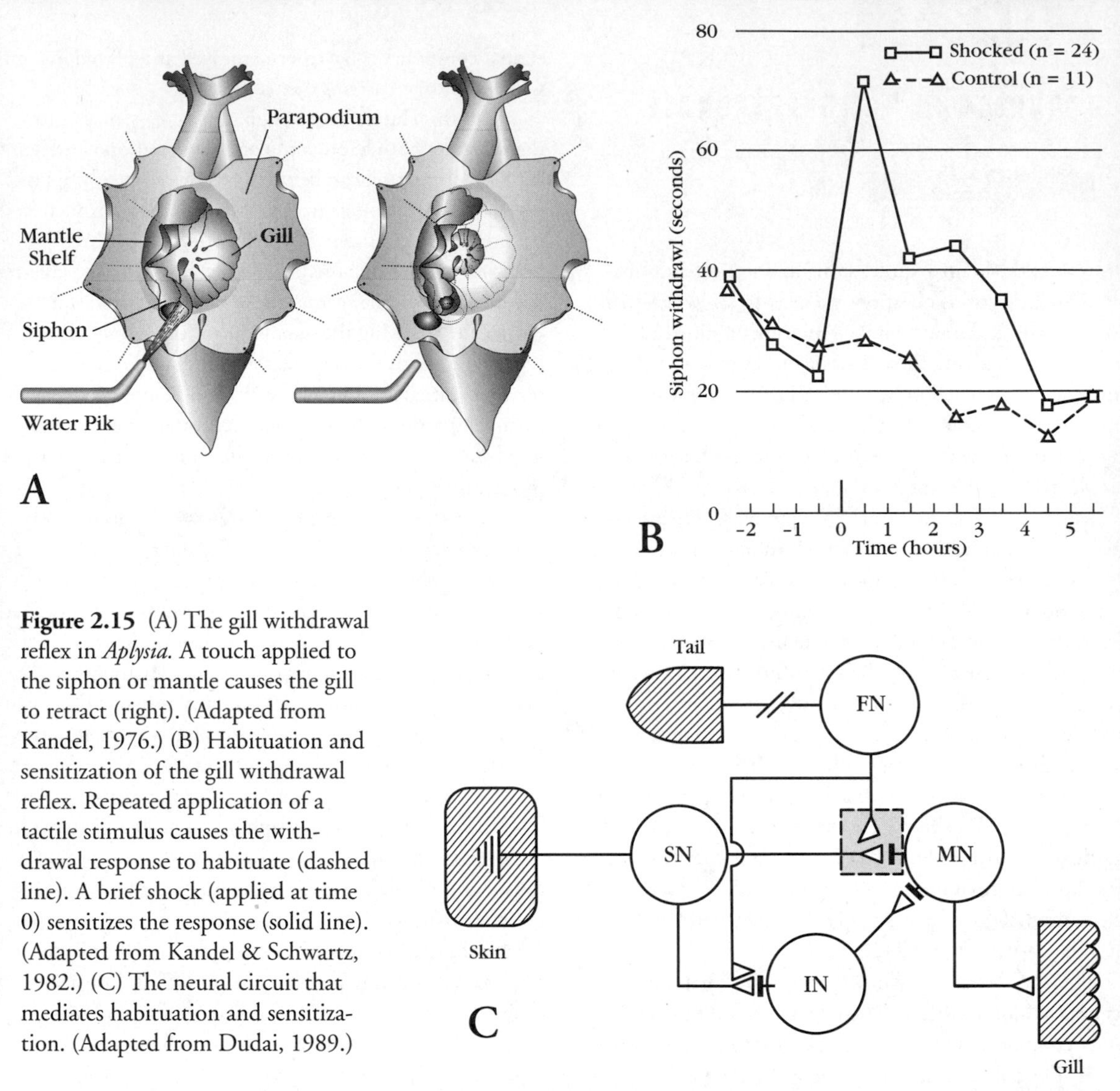

Figure 2.15 (A) The gill withdrawal reflex in *Aplysia.* A touch applied to the siphon or mantle causes the gill to retract (right). (Adapted from Kandel, 1976.) (B) Habituation and sensitization of the gill withdrawal reflex. Repeated application of a tactile stimulus causes the withdrawal response to habituate (dashed line). A brief shock (applied at time 0) sensitizes the response (solid line). (Adapted from Kandel & Schwartz, 1982.) (C) The neural circuit that mediates habituation and sensitization. (Adapted from Dudai, 1989.)

This neural response is conveyed to the cell body (soma) and down a neural projection, the axon, to the motor neuron (MN). The sensory neuron is the presynaptic cell. The motor neuron is the postsynaptic cell. The motor neuron is engaged by the release of a chemical (neurotransmitter) from the sensory neuron. The motor neuron, in turn, carries the signal to the muscles that produce the gill withdrawal response. Here, the release of neurotransmitter activates muscle fibers that cause the gill to retract.

The sensory neuron also engages other cells, interneurons that contribute to the performance of the gill withdrawal response. However, because an understanding of the basic mechanisms that underlie learning does not hinge on their function, we will pay little attention to the interneurons engaged by the sensory neuron. We cannot, however, ignore another class of interneurons, those engaged by applying a shock to a tail. A tailshock engages neurons that activate an interneuron called the facilitory interneuron (FN). As shown in the figure, the facilitory interneuron impinges upon the end of the presynaptic, sensory, neuron. In more technical terms, the facilitory interneuron presynaptically innervates the sensory neuron. Because of this, the facilitory interneuron can alter the operation of the sensory neuron.

The magnitude of the gill withdrawal response depends on the amount of neurotransmitter released from the motor neurons. The more that is released, the stronger is the response. Similarly, the probability that a response will be engaged in the motor neuron, and the number of motor neurons that are engaged, depend on the amount of neurotransmitter released from the sensory neuron. Increasing the amount released will, on average, enhance the motor neuron response and gill withdrawal response.

Research has shown that repeated stimulations of the sensory neuron cause no change in the action potential generated within the sensory neuron, but result in less transmitter being released, thereby producing the behavioral phenomenon of habituation.

Sensitization, in contrast, engages the facilitory interneuron, which produces a change within the sensory neuron that causes it to release more neurotransmitter. Because more transmitter is released, the motor neurons are engaged to a greater extent, and the gill withdrawal response is more vigorous. Thus, behavioral sensitization occurs because tailshock augments the release of neurotransmitter from the sensory neuron.

—J. W. Grau

EXTENSIONS TO EMOTIONS AND MOTIVATED BEHAVIOR

My discussion of changes produced by repetitions of an eliciting stimulus has so far been limited to relatively simple responses. Stimuli may also evoke complex emotions, such as love, fear, euphoria, terror, or satisfaction. I have already described habituation of an emotional response to repeated presentations of a taste (Figure 2.8), but the concepts of habituation and sensitization also have been extended to changes in more complex emotions (Hoffman & Solomon, 1974; Solomon & Corbit, 1974) and various forms of motivated behavior such as feeding, drinking, exploration, aggression, courtship and sexual behavior (McSweeney & Swindell, 1999), and drug addiction (for example, Koob, Caine, Parsons, Markou, & Weiss, 1997; Solomon, 1977; Solomon & Corbit, 1973).

Courtesy Donald A. Dewsbury

R. L. Solomon

Emotional Reactions and Their Aftereffects

In their review of examples of emotional responses to various stimuli, including drugs, Solomon and Corbit (1974) noticed a couple of striking features. First, intense emotional reactions are often biphasic. One emotion occurs during the eliciting stimulus, and the opposite emotion is observed when the stimulus is terminated. Consider, for example, the psychoactive effects of alcohol. A person who has a beer or a glass of wine becomes mellow and relaxed, feelings that are generally pleasant. These reactions reflect the primary sedative effects of alcohol. In contrast, something quite different occurs after a serious bout of drinking. Once the sedative effects of alcohol have dissipated, the person is likely to become irritable and may experience headaches and nausea. The pleasant sedative effects of alcohol give way to the unpleasant sensations of a hangover. Furthermore, both the primary reaction and the aftereffect depend on the drug dosage. The more you drink, the more sedated or drunk you become and the more intense is the hangover afterward. Similar biphasic responses are observed with other drugs. Amphetamine, for example, creates feelings of euphoria, a sense of well-being, self-confidence, wakefulness, and a sense of control. After the drug has worn off, you are likely to feel tired, depressed, and drowsy.

Another common characteristic of emotional reactions is that they change with experience. The primary reaction becomes weaker, and the after-reaction becomes stronger. An habitual drinker is not as debilitated by a few beers as is someone drinking for the first time. However, an habitual drinker experiences more severe withdrawal symptoms after a bout of drinking.

Habituation of the primary drug reactions is called **drug tolerance,** which refers to a decline in the effectiveness of a drug with repeated exposures. Habitual users of alcohol, nicotine, heroin, caffeine, and other drugs are not as greatly affected by the presence of the drug as are first-time users. An amount of alcohol that would make a casual drinker a bit tipsy is not likely to have any effect on a frequent drinker. (I revisit the role of opponent processes in drug tolerance in Chapter 4.)

Because of the development of tolerance, habitual drug users sometimes do not enjoy taking the drug as much as naive users. People who smoke frequently, for example, do not always derive much enjoyment from doing so. Accompanying this decline in the primary drug reaction is a growth in the opponent after-reaction. Accordingly, habitual drug users experience much more severe "hangovers" on termination of the drug than do naive users. Most people who stop smoking cigarettes, for example, experience headaches, irritability, anxiety, tension, and general dissatisfaction. A heavy drinker who stops taking alcohol is likely to experience hallucinations, memory loss, psychomotor agitation, delirium tremens, and other physiological disturbances. For an habitual user of amphetamine, the fatigue and depression that characterize the opponent aftereffect may be severe enough to cause suicide.

Solomon and Corbit (1974) noted that similar patterns of emotional reaction occur with other emotion-arousing stimuli. Consider, for example, love and attachment. Newlyweds are usually very excited about each other and are very affectionate whenever they are together, but this primary emotional reaction habituates as the years go by. The couple gradually settles into a comfortable mode of interaction that lacks the excitement of the honeymoon. Furthermore, habituation of the primary emotional reaction is accompanied by a strengthening of the affective after-reaction. Couples who have been together for many years become more intensely unhappy if they are separated by death or disease than do most newlyweds. After partners have been together for several decades, the death of one partner may cause an intense grief reaction in the survivor. This strong affective after-reaction is remarkable, considering that by this stage in their relationship the couple may have entirely ceased to show any overt signs of affection.

The Opponent-Process Theory of Motivation

The above examples illustrate three common characteristics of emotional reactions: (1) Emotional reactions are biphasic; a primary reaction is followed by an opposite after-reaction. (2) The primary reaction becomes weaker with repeated stimulations. (3) The weakening of the primary reaction with experience is accompanied by a strengthening of the after-reaction. The *opponent-process theory of motivation* (Solomon & Corbit, 1973, 1974) was designed to explain these three prominent features of emotions.

The opponent-process theory assumes that neurophysiological mechanisms involved in emotional behavior serve to maintain emotional stability. Thus, the opponent-process theory is a *homeostatic* theory. It is built on the premise that an important function of mechanisms that control emotional behavior is to minimize deviations from emotional neutrality or stability. (The concept of homeostasis has been very important in the analysis of behavior. I discuss other types of homeostatic theories in later chapters.)

How might physiological mechanisms maintain emotional stability or neutrality? Maintaining any system in a neutral or stable state requires that a disturbance that moves the system in one direction be met by an opposing force that counteracts the disturbance. Consider, for example, trying to keep a seesaw level. If something pushes one end of the seesaw down, the other end will go up. To keep the seesaw level, a force pushing one end down has to be met by an opposing and equal force on the other side.

The concept of opponent forces or processes serving to maintain a stable state is central to the opponent-process theory of motivation. The theory assumes that an emotion-arousing stimulus pushes a person's emotional state away from neutrality. This shift away from emotional neutrality is assumed to trigger an opponent process that counteracts the shift. The patterns of emotional behavior observed both initially and after extensive experience with a stimulus are the net results of the opponent process and changes in the opponent process with experience.

The opponent-process theory assumes that the presentation of an emotion-arousing stimulus initially elicits what is called the **primary process,** or ***a* process,** which is responsible for the quality of the emotional state (happiness, for example) that occurs in the presence of the stimulus. The primary, or *a,* process is assumed to elicit, in turn, an **opponent process,** or ***b* process,** that generates the opposite emotional reaction (unhappiness, for example). The emotional changes observed when a stimulus is presented and then removed are assumed to reflect the net result of the primary and opponent processes. The strength of the opponent process subtracts from the strength of the primary process to provide the emotions that actually occur. Thus, the primary and opponent processes are internal mechanisms whose net effects are the emotional changes that are observed. (The idea is similar to the proposal, illustrated in Figure 2.12, that habituation and sensitization processes are internal mechanisms whose net effects are observed in the magnitude of the startle reflex.)

An additional assumption that is basic to the opponent-process theory is that the opponent process is a bit inefficient. It lags behind the primary emotional disturbance at first and therefore is not strong enough to entirely counteract the primary emotion initially. However, the opponent process becomes quicker and more powerful with practice or repeated experience with the emotion-arousing stimulus. In a sense, the opponent process becomes sensitized as a result of repeated activation. It eventually becomes strong enough to block most of the primary emotional reaction, at which point it also produces a very strong after-reaction when the emotion-arousing stimulus is terminated.

Opponent Mechanisms during Initial Stimulus Exposure. Figure 2.16 shows how the primary and opponent processes determine the initial responses of an organism to an emotion-arousing stimulus. The underlying primary and opponent processes are represented at the bottom of the figure. The net effects of these processes (the observed emotional reactions) are represented in the top panel. When the stimulus is first presented, the *a* process occurs unopposed by the *b* process. This permits the primary emotional reaction to reach its peak quickly. The *b* process then becomes activated and begins to oppose the *a* process. On the first presentation of the stimulus, however, the *b* process is not strong enough to entirely counteract the primary emotional response, which therefore persists during the eliciting stimulus. When the stimulus is withdrawn, the *a* process quickly stops, but the *b* process lingers for awhile. At this point, the *b* process has nothing to oppose, and emotional responses characteristic of the opponent process become evident for the first time. These emotions are typically opposite to those observed during the presence of the stimulus.

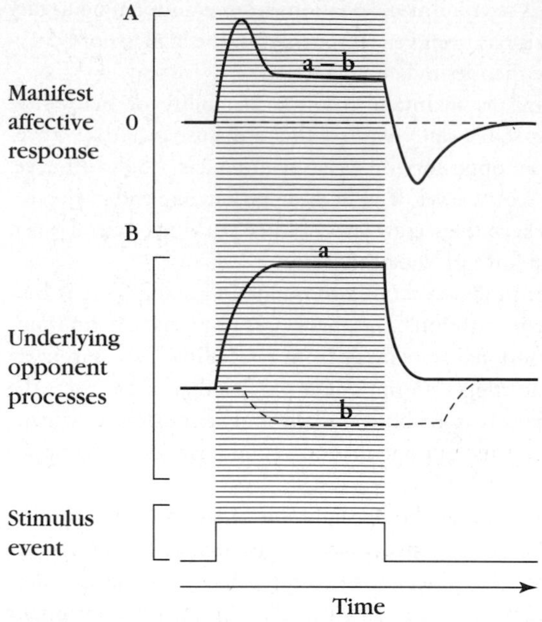

Figure 2.16 Opponent-process mechanism during the initial presentation of an emotion-arousing stimulus. The observed emotional reactions are represented in the top panel. The underlying opponent processes are represented in the bottom panel. Notice that the *b* process starts a bit after the onset of the *a* process. In addition, the *b* process ends much later than the *a* process. This last feature allows the opponent emotions to dominate after the end of the stimulus. (From "An Opponent-Process Theory of Motivation: I. The Temporal Dynamics of Affect," by R. L. Solomon and J. D. Corbit, 1974, *Psychological Review, 81,* pp. 119–145. Copyright © 1974 by the American Psychological Association. Reprinted by permission.)

Opponent Mechanisms after Extensive Stimulus Exposure. Figure 2.17 shows how the primary and opponent processes operate after extensive exposure to a stimulus. As I noted earlier, a highly familiar stimulus does not elicit strong emotional reactions, but the affective after-reaction tends to be much stronger when a highly familiar stimulus is terminated. The opponent-process theory explains this outcome by assuming that the *b* process becomes strengthened by repeated exposures to the stimulus. The strengthening of the *b* process is reflected in several of its characteristics: It becomes activated sooner after the onset of the stimulus, its maximum intensity becomes greater, and it becomes slower to decay when the stimulus ceases. In contrast, the *a* process is assumed to remain unchanged. Thus, after repeated presentations of a stimulus, the primary emotional responses are more effectively counteracted by the opponent process. This growth in the opponent process reduces the intensity of the observed primary emotional responses during presentation of the emotion-arousing stimulus. It also leads to the excessive affective after-reaction when the stimulus is withdrawn (see Figure 2.17).

Opponent Aftereffects and Motivation. If the primary pleasurable effects of a psychoactive drug are gone for habitual users, why do they continue taking the drug? Why are they addicted? The opponent-process theory suggests that drug addiction is mainly an attempt

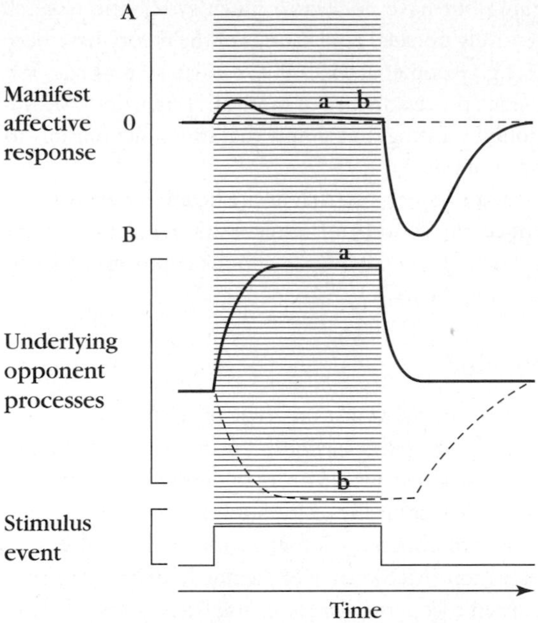

Figure 2.17 Opponent-process mechanism that produces the affective changes to an habituated stimulus. The observed emotional reactions are represented in the top panel. The underlying opponent processes are represented in the bottom panel. Notice that the *b* process starts promptly after the onset of the *a* process and is much stronger than in Figure 2.16. In addition, the *b* process ends much later than the *a* process. Because of these changes in the *b* process, the primary emotional response is nearly invisible during the stimulus, but the affective after-reaction is very strong. (From "An Opponent-Process Theory of Motivation: I. The Temporal Dynamics of Affect," by R. L. Solomon and J. D. Corbit, 1974, *Psychological Review, 81,* pp. 119–145. Copyright © 1974 by the American Psychological Association. Reprinted by permission.)

to reduce the aversiveness of the affective after-reaction to the drugs—the bad hangovers, the amphetamine "crashes," and the irritability that comes from not having the usual cigarette. There are two ways to reduce the aversive opponent after-reactions of drugs. One is simply to wait long enough for them to dissipate—an act known as "cold turkey." For heavy drug users, cold turkey may take a long time and may be very painful. The opponent after-reaction can be reduced much more quickly by taking the drug again. This will reactivate the primary process and stave off the agonies of withdrawal. According to the theory, addicts are "trapped" not by the direct pleasure they derive from their drug, but by their need to take the drug to reduce withdrawal pains.

Overall Assessment of the Opponent-Process Theory. The opponent-process theory was very attractive when it was first introduced because it encompassed a wide range of situations and provided a provocative account of drug tolerance, dependence, and drug addiction. The theory has been extended to research on social attachment in monkeys (Mineka, Suomi, & DeLizio, 1981; Suomi, Mineka, & Harlow, 1983) and ducklings (Hoffman & Solomon, 1974; Starr, 1978). It has also been supported by research on human breast-feeding (Myers & Siegel, 1985). Applications of the theory to other aspects of human experience, such as love and attachment, have been intriguing but have not led to much systematic research (Tzeng & Gomez, 1992). The most extensively pursued applications of the theory have been to the understanding of drug addiction (e.g., Koob et al., 1997). On balance, however, it is fair to say that the promises of the opponent-process theory of motivation remain to be fulfilled. It is not that the theory has been found wanting, but simply that its predictions in various situations have not been put to empirical test.

Although the theory has not stimulated as much research as predicted, it has made an important contribution in that it extended the concept of homeostatic regulation to the analysis of emotions and motivation. As I describe in Chapter 4, opponent-process concepts continue to have a prominent role in learning theory.

Variations in Goal-Directed Behavior

Responding to escape the discomfort of withdrawal is just one type of motivated or goal-directed behavior. I say a lot more about goal-directed behavior in Chapters 5, 6, and 7, focusing on situations in which individuals make a response in order to produce a desirable or rewarding stimulus. A rewarding goal object is technically called a **reinforcer.** Situations in which organisms repeatedly make a response to obtain a reinforcer show many of the common properties of habituation and sensitization (McSweeney & Swindell, 1999). Consider, for example, turning on a CD player to listen to a particular song. You become less likely to turn on the CD player if the outcome is the same song over and over again (habituation), but this loss of interest is specific to the repeated song (stimulus specificity). Furthermore, you will regain your interest in the original song if you don't hear it for a few days (spontaneous recovery). Your interest in the familiar song can also be restored by exposure to novel stimuli, such as the excitement of meeting a friend (sensitization).

Habituation and sensitization effects are common with sensory reinforcers such as pieces of music. Phenomena similar to habituation and sensitization also occur with consumable goal objects such as food and water. For example, repeated exposures to food will produce a decline in food-directed behavior. Decreases in food-directed behavior are often attributable to a reduction of hunger or satiation (Bizo, Bogdanov, & Killeen, 1998), but more general habituation mechanisms may also be involved (McSweeney & Roll, 1998).

CONCLUDING COMMENTS

The quality of life and survival itself depend on an intricate coordination of behavior with the complexities of the environment. Elicited behavior represents one of the fundamental ways in which the behavior of all animals—from single-celled organisms to people—is adjusted to environmental events.

Elicited behavior takes many forms, ranging from simple reflexes mediated by just three neurons to complex emotional reactions. Although elicited behavior occurs as a reaction to a stimulus, it is not rigid and invariant. In fact, one of its remarkable features is that elicited behavior is altered by experience. If an eliciting stimulus does not arouse the organism, repeated presentations of the stimulus will evoke progressively weaker responses (an habituation effect). If the eliciting stimulus is particularly intense or of significance to the individual, repeated presentations will lead to progressively stronger reactions (a sensitization effect).

Environmental events activate habituation and sensitization processes to varying degrees. The resultant level of responding reflects the net effect of the habituation and sensitization processes. Therefore, if one does not know the past experiences of the organism, it is impossible to predict how strong a reaction will be elicited by a particular stimulus presentation.

Repeated presentations of an eliciting stimulus produce changes in simple responses as well as in more complex emotional reactions. Organisms tend to minimize changes in emotional state caused by external stimuli. According to the opponent-process theory of motivation, emotional responses stimulated by an environmental event are counteracted by an opposing process in the organism. This compensatory, or opponent, process is assumed to become stronger each time it is activated, and this leads to a reduction of the primary emotional responses. The strengthened opponent emotional state is evident as an after-reaction when the stimulus is removed.

Habituation, sensitization, and changes in the strength of opponent processes are the simplest mechanisms whereby organisms adjust their reactions to environmental events on the basis of past experience.

SAMPLE QUESTIONS

1. Compare and contrast appetitive and consummatory behavior, and describe how these are related to general search, focal search, and food handling.
2. Describe the distinction between habituation, sensory adaptation, and fatigue.
3. Describe the difference between habituation and sensitization effects and habituation and sensitization processes.
4. Describe the two processes of the dual-process theory of habituation and sensitization and the differences between these processes.
5. Describe the opponent-process theory of motivation and how it explains habituation and sensitization effects.
6. Describe how habituation and sensitization are relevant to goal-directed behavior.

KEY TERMS

***a* process** Same as *primary process* in the opponent process theory of motivation.

afferent neuron A neuron that transmits messages from sense organs to the central nervous system. Also called *sensory neuron.*

appetitive behavior Behavior that occurs early in a natural behavior sequence and serves to bring the organism into contact with a releasing stimulus. (See also *general search mode* and *focal search mode.*)

***b* process** Same as *opponent process* in the opponent-process theory of motivation.

consummatory behavior Behavior that serves to bring a natural sequence of behavior to consummation or completion. Consummatory responses are usually species-typical modal action patterns. (See also *food handling mode.*)

dishabituation Recovery of an habituated response as a result of a strong extraneous stimulus.

drug tolerance Reduction in the effectiveness of a drug as a result of repeated use of the drug.

efferent neuron A neuron that transmits impulses to muscles. Also called a *motor neuron.*

fatigue A temporary decrease in behavior caused by repeated or excessive use of the muscles involved in the behavior.

focal search mode The second component of the feeding behavior sequence, following general search, in which the organism engages in behavior focused on a particular location or stimulus that is indicative of the presence of food. Focal search is a form of appetitive behavior that is more closely related to food than is general search.

food handling mode The last component of the feeding behavior sequence, in which the organism handles and consumes the food. This is similar to what ethologists referred to as consummatory behavior.

general search mode The earliest component of the feeding behavior sequence, in which the organism engages in nondirected locomotor behavior. General search is a form of appetitive behavior.

habituation effect A progressive decrease in the vigor of elicited behavior that may occur with repeated presentations of the eliciting stimulus.

habituation process A neural mechanism activated by repetitions of a stimulus that reduces the magnitude of responses elicited by that stimulus.

interneuron A neuron in the spinal cord between the afferent (or sensory) neuron and the efferent (or motor) neuron in the reflex arc.

MAP Abbreviation for *modal action pattern.*

modal action pattern A response pattern exhibited in much the same way by most, if not all, members of a species. Modal action patterns are used as basic units of behavior in ethological investigations of behavior. Abbreviated *MAP.*

motor neuron Same as *efferent neuron*

opponent process A compensatory mechanism that occurs in response to the primary process elicited by biologically significant events. The opponent process causes physiological and behavioral changes that are the opposite of those caused by the primary process. Sometimes referred to as the *b process.*

primary process The first process elicited by a biologically significant stimulus. Sometimes referred to as the *a process.*

reflex arc Neural structures, consisting of the efferent (sensory) neuron, interneuron, and afferent (motor) neuron, that enable a stimulus to elicit a reflex response.

reinforcer A stimulus whose delivery shortly following a response increases the future probability of that response.

releasing stimulus Same as *sign stimulus.*

sensitization effect An increase in the vigor of elicited behavior that may result from repeated presentations of the eliciting stimulus or from exposure to a strong extraneous stimulus.

sensitization process A neural mechanism that increases the magnitude of responses elicited by a stimulus.

sensory adaptation A temporary reduction in the sensitivity of sense organs caused by repeated or excessive stimulation.

sensory neuron Same as *afferent neuron.*

sign stimulus A specific feature of an object or animal that elicits a modal action pattern in another organism. Also called *releasing stimulus.*

spontaneous recovery Recovery of a response produced by a period of rest after habituation or extinction. (Extinction is discussed in Chapters 3 and 9.)

S-R system The shortest neural pathway that connects the sense organs stimulated by an eliciting stimulus and the muscles involved in making the elicited response.

state system Neural structures that determine the general level of responsiveness, or readiness to respond, of the organism.

supernormal stimulus An artificially enlarged or exaggerated sign stimulus that elicits an unusually vigorous response.

CHAPTER

3

CLASSICAL CONDITIONING: FOUNDATIONS

Chapter 3 provides an introduction to another basic form of learning, classical conditioning. Investigations of classical conditioning began with the work of Pavlov, who studied how dogs learn to anticipate feeding episodes. Since then, the research has been extended to a variety of other organisms and response systems. Some classical conditioning procedures establish an excitatory association between two stimuli. Others serve to inhibit the operation of excitatory associations. I describe both excitatory and inhibitory conditioning procedures and discuss how these are involved in a variety of important life experiences.

Chapter 2 described how environmental events can elicit behavior and how such elicited behavior can be modified by sensitization and habituation. These relatively simple processes help to bring the behavior of organisms in tune with their environment. However, if human and nonhuman animals only had the behavioral mechanisms described in Chapter 2, they would remain rather limited in the kinds of things they could do. For one thing, habituation and sensitization involve changes only in responses that are already in the organism's repertoire. They do not involve the learning of new responses or responses to new stimuli. And for the most part, habituation and sensitization involve learning about just one stimulus. Events in the world, however, do not occur in isolation, independent of one another. They occur in predictable and consistent combinations.

Cause-and-effect relationships ensure that certain things occur in combination with others. A car's engine does not run unless the ignition has been turned on; you cannot walk through a doorway unless the door is first opened; it does not rain unless there are clouds in the sky. Social institutions and customs also ensure that events occur in a predictable order. Classes are scheduled at predictable times; people are better dressed at church than at a picnic; you can predict whether someone will talk to you by the way the person looks at you. Learning to predict events in the environment and learning what stimuli tend to occur together are important for bringing behavior in line with the environment. Imagine how much trouble you would have if you could not predict how long it takes to make coffee, when stores are likely to be open, or whether your key works to unlock your apartment.

Classical conditioning is the simplest mechanism whereby organisms learn about relations between stimuli and come to alter their behavior accordingly. It enables human and nonhuman animals to take advantage of the orderly sequence of events in their environment and learn which stimuli tend to go with which events. On the basis of this learning, organisms come to make new responses to stimuli. For example, classical conditioning is the process whereby we learn to predict when and what we might eat, when we are likely to face danger, and when we are likely to be safe. It is also integrally involved in the learning of new emotional reactions such as fear and pleasure to stimuli that initially do not elicit these emotions.

THE EARLY YEARS OF CLASSICAL CONDITIONING

Systematic studies of classical conditioning began with the work of the great Russian physiologist Ivan P. Pavlov (see Box 3.1). Classical conditioning was also independently discovered by Edwin B. Twitmyer. In a Ph.D. dissertation submitted to the University of Pennsylvania in 1902 (see Twitmyer, 1974), Twitmyer repeatedly tested the knee-jerk reflex of college students by sounding a bell 0.5 seconds before hitting the patellar tendon just below the kneecap. After several of these trials, the bell was sufficient to elicit the knee-jerk reflex in some of the students. But Twitmyer did not develop the implications of his discoveries, and his findings did not attract much attention.

Pavlov's studies of classical conditioning were an extension of his research on the processes of digestion. He made major advances in the study of digestion by developing surgical techniques that enabled dogs to survive for many years with artificial tubes or fistulae that permitted the collection of various digestive juices. With the use of a stomach fistula, for example, Pavlov was able to collect stomach secretions in dogs that otherwise lived normally. Technicians in the laboratory soon discovered that the dogs would secrete stomach juices in response to the sight of food, or even just upon seeing the person who usually fed

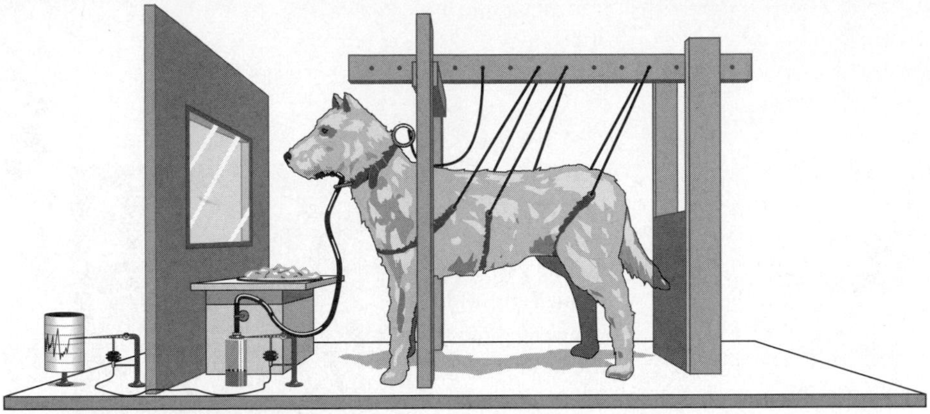

Figure 3.1 Diagram of the Pavlovian salivary conditioning preparation. A cannula attached to the animal's salivary duct conducts drops of saliva to a data-recording device. (From "The Method of Pavlov in Animal Psychology," by R. M. Yerkes and S. Morgulis, 1909, *Psychological Bulletin, 6,* pp. 257–273.)

them. The laboratory produced considerable quantities of stomach juice in this manner and sold the excess to the general public. The popularity of this juice as a remedy for various stomach ailments supplemented the income of the laboratory for several years.

Assistants in the laboratory referred to stomach secretions elicited by food-related stimuli as "psychic secretions" because they seemed to be a response to the expectation or thought of food. For many years, however, the phenomenon of psychic secretions generated little scientific interest.

The Discoveries of Vul'fson and Snarskii

The first systematic studies of classical conditioning were performed by S. G. Vul'fson and A. T. Snarskii in Pavlov's laboratory (Boakes, 1984; Todes, 1997). Both students focused on the salivary glands, which are the first digestive glands involved in the breakdown of food. Some of the salivary glands are rather large and have ducts that are accessible and can be easily externalized with a fistula (see Figure 3.1). Vul'fson studied salivary responses to various substances placed in the mouth, such as dry food, wet food, sour water, and sand. After the dogs had experienced these substances placed in the mouth, the mere sight of the substances was enough to make them salivate.

Whereas Vul'fson used naturally occurring substances in his studies, Snarskii extended these observations to artificial substances. In one experiment, for example, Snarskii first gave his dogs sour water (such as strong lemon juice) that was artificially colored black. After several encounters with the black sour water, the dogs also salivated to plain black water or to the sight of a bottle containing a black liquid.

The substances tested by Vul'fson and Snarskii could be identified at a distance by sight. The substances also produced distinctive texture and taste sensations in the mouth. Such sensations are called *orosensory stimuli.* The first time that sand was placed in a dog's mouth, only the feel of the sand in the mouth elicited salivation. After sand had been placed in the mouth several times, the sight of sand (its visual features) also came to elicit salivation. Presumably, the dog learned to associate the visual features of the sand with its

BOX 3.1

IVAN P. PAVLOV: BIOGRAPHICAL SKETCH

Bettmann Archive

Born in 1849 into the family of a priest in Russia, Pavlov dedicated his life to scholarship and discovery. He received his early education in a local theological seminary and planned a career of religious service. His interests soon changed, and when he was 21, he entered the university in St. Petersburg, where his studies focused on chemistry and animal physiology. After obtaining the equivalent of a bachelor's degree, he went to the Imperial Medico-Surgical Academy in 1875 to further his education in physiology. Eight years later, he received a doctoral degree for his research on the efferent nerves of the heart. He then began investigating various aspects of digestive physiology. In 1888, Pavlov discovered the nerves that stimulate the digestive secretions of the pancreas—a finding that initiated a series of experiments for which he was awarded the Nobel Prize in Physiology in 1904.

Pavlov did a great deal of original research while a graduate student, as well as after obtaining his doctoral degree. Interestingly, he did not have a faculty position or his own laboratory until 1890, when he was appointed professor of pharmacology at the St. Petersburg Military Medical Academy. In 1895 he became professor of physiology at the same institution. Pavlov remained active in the laboratory until close to his death in 1936. Much of the research for which he is famous today was performed after he received the Nobel Prize.

object learning
assoc visual features w/ orosensory features

orosensory features. Such learning is referred to as **object learning** because it involves associating different features of the same object.

To study the mechanisms of associative learning, the stimuli to be associated have to be manipulated independently of one another. This is difficult to do when the two stimuli are properties of the same object. Therefore, in later studies of conditioning, Pavlov used procedures in which the stimuli to be associated came from different sources. This led to the experimental methods that continue to dominate studies of classical conditioning to the present day.

CS = tone/light
response depends on pairing trials

US = food/taste
response is not dependent on pairing

The Classical Conditioning Paradigm

Pavlov's basic procedure for the study of conditioned salivation is now familiar to college students. The procedure involves two stimuli: (1) a tone or a light that does not elicit salivation at the outset of the experiment, and (2) food or the taste of a sour solution placed in the mouth. In contrast to the first stimulus, the second one elicits vigorous salivation the first time it is presented.

Pavlov referred to the tone or light as the **conditional stimulus** because the effectiveness of this stimulus in eliciting salivation depended on (or was conditional on) pairing it several times with the presentation of food. By contrast, the food or sour-taste stimulus was called the **unconditional stimulus** because its effectiveness in eliciting salivation was not dependent on any prior training. The salivation that was eventually elicited by the tone or light was called the **conditional response,** and the salivation that was always

CR vs UR - depends on whether the response was elicited by CS or US elicited by the food or sour taste was called the **unconditional response.** In other words, stimuli and responses whose properties did not depend on prior training were called "unconditional," and stimuli and responses whose properties emerged only after training were called "conditional."

In the first English translation of Pavlov's writings, the term unconditional was erroneously translated as unconditioned, and the term conditional was translated as conditioned. The -ed suffix was used exclusively in English writings for many years. However, the term conditioned does not capture Pavlov's original meaning of "dependent on" as well as the term conditional (Gantt, 1966). The words conditional and unconditional are more common in modern writings on classical conditioning and are now used interchangeably with conditioned and unconditioned.

Because the terms "conditioned (unconditioned) stimulus" and "conditioned (unconditioned) response" are used frequently in discussions of classical conditioning, they are often abbreviated. Conditioned stimulus and conditioned response are abbreviated **CS** and **CR,** respectively. Unconditioned stimulus and unconditioned response are abbreviated **US** and **UR,** respectively.

"conditional" assumes conditioning took place.

EXPERIMENTAL SITUATIONS

Classical conditioning has been investigated in a variety of situations and species (Hollis, 1997; Turkkan, 1989). Pavlov did most of his experiments with dogs using the salivary-fistula technique. Most contemporary experiments on Pavlovian conditioning are carried out with domesticated rats, rabbits, and pigeons using procedures developed by North American scientists during the second half of the twentieth century.

~~Pavlov used~~ rats, rabbits & pigeons used now to study cond.

Fear Conditioning

Following the early work of Watson and Rayner (1920), a major focus of investigators of Pavlovian conditioning has been the conditioning of emotional reactions. Watson and Rayner believed that infants are at first limited in their emotional reactivity. Given this belief, they assumed that "there must be some simple method by means of which the range of stimuli which can call out these emotions and their compounds is greatly increased" (p. 1). That simple method was Pavlovian conditioning. In a famous demonstration, Watson and Rayner conditioned a fear response in a 9-month- old infant, Albert, to the presence of a docile white laboratory rat.

There was hardly anything that Albert was afraid of. After testing a variety of stimuli, Watson and Rayner found that little Albert reacted with alarm when he heard the loud noise of a steel bar being hit by a hammer behind his head. Watson and Rayner then used this unconditioned alarm response to condition fear to a white rat. Each conditioning trial consisted of presenting the rat to Albert and then striking the steel bar. At first, Albert reached out to the rat when it was presented to him. But after just two conditioning trials, he became reluctant to touch the rat. After five additional conditioning trials, Albert showed strong fear responses to the rat. He whimpered or cried, leaned as far away from the rat as he could, and sometimes fell over and moved away on all fours. Significantly, these fear responses were not evident when Albert was presented with his toy blocks. However, the conditioned fear generalized to other furry things (a rabbit, a fur coat, cotton wool, a dog, and a Santa Claus mask).

Fear and anxiety are the source of considerable human discomfort, and if sufficiently severe they can lead to serious psychological and behavioral problems. There is considerable

US – noise
CS – rat
UR/CR – fear

generalized to furry things

interest in how fear and anxiety are acquired, what the neural mechanisms of fear are, and how fear may be attenuated with pharmacological and behavioral treatments. Many of these kinds of questions are difficult to address experimentally using human subjects. Therefore, since Watson and Rayner's study with little Albert, investigators have examined fear conditioning using primarily laboratory rats. The aversive unconditioned stimulus in these studies is a brief electrical current delivered to the feet through a metal grid floor. Shock is used because it can be regulated with greater precision than striking a steel bar with a hammer. The shock US is of such low intensity and brief duration that no tissue damage occurs. The shock is aversive primarily because it is startling—unlike anything the animal has encountered before. The conditioned stimulus may be a tone or a light. Thus, the basic procedure involves presenting a tone or a light shortly before the presentation of a brief shock US. Unlike little Albert who showed fear by whimpering and crying, rats show their fear by freezing. Freezing is a species-typical defense response that occurs in a variety of animals in response to the anticipation of aversive stimulation (see Chapter 10).

Although the primary fear response of rats is to become motionless, investigators of fear conditioning often do not measure freezing directly. Instead, they measure conditioned fear indirectly by recording how the conditioned stimulus disrupts the animal's ongoing activity. A popular technique for the indirect measurement of conditioned fear is the **conditioned emotional response,** or **conditioned suppression,** procedure (abbreviated **CER**). The CER procedure was devised by Estes and Skinner (1941) and has since been used extensively in the study of Pavlovian conditioning (Kamin, 1965). Rats are first trained to press a response lever for food reward in a small experimental chamber (see Figure 3.2A). Food is provided for every few lever presses. After sufficient training, the rats press the lever at a steady rate. The classical conditioning phase of the experiment is then introduced. During each conditioning trial, the CS is presented for 1 or 2 minutes, followed immediately by brief exposure to the shock US. Trials are scheduled 15–30 minutes apart.

Rats cannot press the lever when they freeze because of fear. This makes the CER procedure useful for measuring response suppression induced by fear (Bouton & Bolles, 1980; Mast, Blanchard, & Blanchard, 1982; for additional factors involved in conditioned suppression, see Bevins & Ayres, 1994). The acquisition of fear to the CS results in disruption of the food-rewarded lever-press response. After several pairings of the CS with shock, the animals suppress their lever pressing when the CS appears. Within three to five conditioning trials, the conditioned suppression may be complete (Kamin & Brimer, 1963), with the rats not pressing the lever at all during the CS. However, the suppression is specific to the CS. Soon after the CS is turned off, the animals resume their food-rewarded behavior.

To measure the conditioned suppression quantitatively, a suppression ratio is calculated. The ratio compares the number of lever presses that occur during the CS with the number that occur during a comparable baseline period before the CS is presented (the pre-CS period). The specific formula is as follows:

$$\text{Suppression Ratio} = \text{CS responding} \div (\text{CS responding} + \text{pre-CS responding})$$

Notice that the *suppression ratio* has a value of 0 if the rat suppresses lever pressing completely during the CS, because in this case the numerator of the formula is 0. At the other extreme, if the rat does not alter its rate of lever pressing at all when the CS is presented, the ratio has a value of .5. For example, assume that the CS is presented for 2 minutes and that in a typical 2-minute period the rat makes 30 responses. If the CS does not disrupt lever pressing, the animal will make 30 responses during the CS, so that the numerator of the ratio will be 30. The denominator will be 30 (CS responses) + 30 (pre-CS responses), or 60. Therefore, the ratio will be 30 ÷ 60 or 0.5. Decreasing values of the ratio from 0.5 to 0 indicate greater degrees of response suppression, or conditioned fear. Thus, the scale is in-

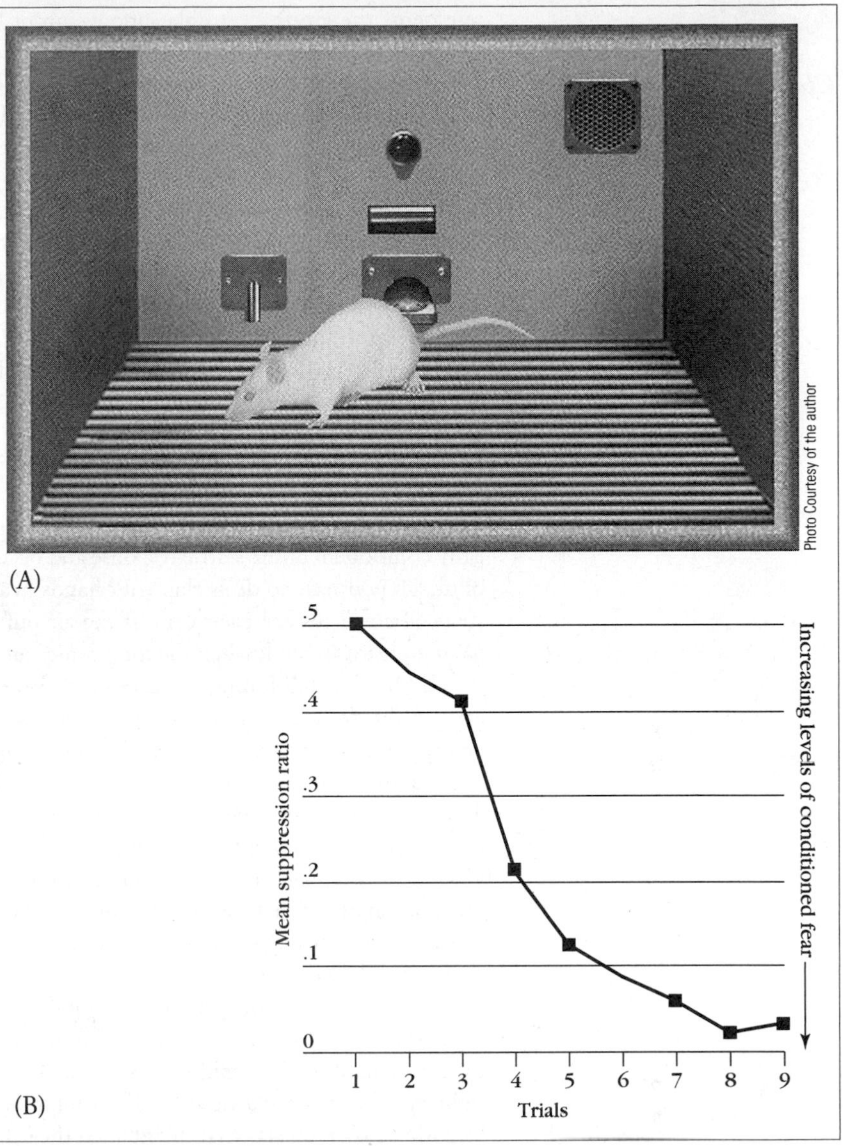

Figure 3.2 (A) Representation of a rat in a Skinner box. The floor is made of metal rods. The response lever is located in the center of the wall above the food cup. (From *Sniffy, The Virtual Rat,* Wadsworth/Thomson Learning.) (B) Sample results of a conditioned suppression experiment with rats (from Domjan, unpublished). Three conditioning trials were conducted on each of 3 days of training. The CS was an audiovisual stimulus and the US was a brief shock through the grid floor. A suppression ratio of .5 indicates that the participants did not suppress their lever pressing during the CS. A suppression ratio of 0 indicates complete suppression of responding during the CS.

verse. Greater disruptions of lever pressing are represented by lower values of the suppression ratio.

Figure 3.2B shows sample results of a conditioned suppression experiment with rats. Three conditioning trials were conducted on each of 3 days of training. Very little suppression occurred the first time the CS was presented, and not much acquisition of suppression was evident during the first day of training. A substantial increase in suppression occurred from the last trial on Day 1 (Trial 3) to the first trial on Day 2 (Trial 4). With continued training, responding gradually became more and more suppressed, until the animals hardly ever pressed the response lever when the CS was presented.

Interpreting conditioned suppression data can be confusing because the scale is inverse. Keep in mind that a suppression ratio of 0 indicates zero responding during the CS, which represents the greatest possible suppression of lever pressing. The smaller the suppression ratio, the more motionless is the animal, because the CS elicits more conditioned fear.

In the conditioned suppression procedure, the baseline level of responding is provided by lever pressing for food reinforcement. In a related procedure, thirsty rats are permitted to lick a waterspout. The presentation of a conditioned fear stimulus causes a suppression in this licking behavior. Hence, this is called the **conditioned lick suppression** procedure. Some investigators favor the lick suppression procedure because getting rats to lick a waterspout requires less training than getting them to press a response lever for food. In the lick suppression procedure, how long it takes subjects to complete a total of 5 seconds of drinking is recorded as a measure of response suppression. The more fearful the rats are, the longer they will take to accumulate the criterion 5 seconds of drinking (for example, Figures 3.12 and 3.13). (For an adaptation of the conditioned suppression in the form of a video game for testing human subjects, see Arcediano, Ortega, & Matute, 1996.)

Eyeblink Conditioning

The eyeblink reflex is a discrete reflex, much like the patellar knee-jerk response. It is an early component of the startle response and occurs in a variety of species. To get someone to blink, all you have to do is clap your hands near their eyes or blow a puff of air through a straw directed toward their eyes. If the air puff is preceded by a brief tone, the person is likely to learn to blink when the tone comes on, in anticipation of the puff.

Eyeblink conditioning was extensively investigated in studies with human participants early in the development of learning theory (see Hilgard & Marquis, 1940; Kimble, 1961) and is the topic of renewed interest in contemporary research (for example, Clark & Squire, 1999; Durkin, Prescott, Furchtgott, & Cantor,1993; Green, Ivry, & Woodruff-Pak, 1999; Tracy, Ghose, Stecher, McFall, & Steinmetz, 1999) because of advances in our understanding of the neurobiological substrates of this type of learning (see Box 3.2). Steinmetz (1999), for example, noted, "Eyeblink conditioning provides an excellent means for direct observation of simple behavior . . . [and] can be used to assess basic biological-psychological processes in humans, such as basic learning and memory, development, awareness, attention, arousal, and normal aging" (p. 24).

In a recent study of eyeblink conditioning, 2 groups of 5-month-old infants were compared (Ivkovich, Collins, Eckerman, Krasnegor, & Stanton, 1999). The CS was a 1,000 cps tone presented for 750 milliseconds, and the US was a gentle puff of air delivered to the right eye through a plastic tube. Each infant sat on a parent's lap facing a platform with brightly colored objects that maintained the infant's attention during the experimental sessions. Eyeblinks were recorded by video cameras. For Group 1, the CS always ended with the puff of air, and these conditioning trials occurred an average of 12 seconds apart. Group 2 received the same number and distribution of CS and US presentations, but for them the CSs and USs were spaced 4–8 seconds apart in an explicitly unpaired fashion. Thus, Group 2 served as a control. Each subject received 2 training sessions, 1 week apart.

The results of the experiment are presented in Figure 3.3 in terms of the percentage of trials on which the subjects blinked during the CS. The rate of eyeblinks for the 2 groups of subjects did not differ statistically during the first experimental session. However, the paired group responded to the CS at a significantly higher rate during Session 2 than the unpaired control group. Furthermore, additional research indicated that the high level of performance in the paired group during Session 2 was due in part to the CS-US association they started to learn during Session 1.

This experiment illustrates a number of important points about learning. First, it shows that classical conditioning requires the pairing of a CS and a US. Responding to the

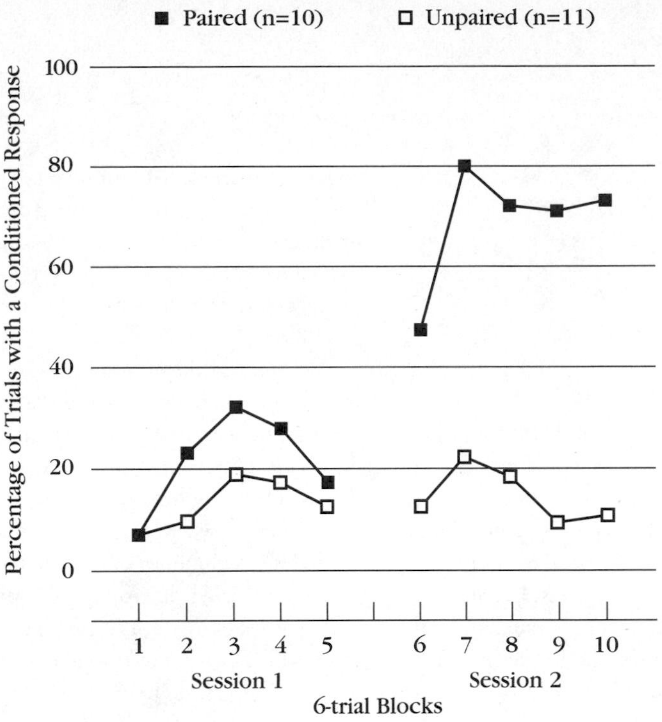

Figure 3.3 Eyeblink conditioning in 5-month-old infants. For the infants in the paired group, a tone CS ended in a gentle puff of air to the eye. For the infants in the unpaired group, the tone and air puff never occurred together. (After Ivkovich, Collins, Eckerman, Krasnegor, & Stanton, 1999.)

CS did not develop in the unpaired control group. Second, initial learning may not be directly observable. Although the infants in the paired group did not respond much in Session 1, they were starting to learn that the CS was related to the US. This learning was evident when the subjects were returned to the experimental situation for Session 2.

As I noted earlier, recent interest in eyeblink conditioning in humans stems from the fact that substantial progress has been made in understanding the neurobiological substrates of this type of learning. Neurobiological investigations of eyeblink conditioning have been conducted primarily in studies with domesticated rabbits. The rabbit eyeblink preparation was developed by Gormezano (see Gormezano, 1966; Gormezano, Kehoe, & Marshall, 1983). Domesticated rabbits are ideal for this type of research because they are readily available, they are sedentary and tolerate mild restraint well, and they rarely blink in the absence of an air puff or other irritation of the eye. In an eyeblink conditioning experiment, the rabbit is placed in a small enclosure and attached to equipment that enables measurement of the blink response. The unconditioned stimulus to elicit blinking is provided by a small puff of air or mild irritation of the skin below the eye with a brief (0.1-second) electrical current. The conditioned stimulus may be a light, a tone, or a mild vibration of the animal's abdomen.

I. Gormezano

In the typical conditioning experiment, the CS is presented for half a second and is followed immediately by delivery of the unconditioned stimulus. The US elicits a rapid and vigorous eyelid closure. As the CS is repeatedly paired with the US, the eyeblink response also comes to be made to the CS. Investigators record the percentage of trials in which a conditioned blink response is observed. Rabbit eyeblink conditioning is relatively slow, requiring several hundred trials for substantial levels of conditioned responding.

BOX 3.2

EYEBLINK CONDITIONING AND THE SEARCH FOR THE ENGRAM

When an organism learns something, the results of this learning must be stored within the brain. Somehow, the network of neurons that makes up the central nervous system is able to encode the relationship between biologically significant events and use this information to guide the selection of ongoing behavior. This biological memory is known as an *engram.* The traditional view is that the engram for a discrete conditioned response is stored in localized regions of the brain. This raises a basic question in neurobiology: Where is the engram located?

This question has been pursued for nearly four decades by Richard Thompson and his collaborators (for recent reviews, see Steinmetz, Gluck, & Solomon, 2001). Thompson recognized that locating the engram would require a well-defined behavioral system in which both the conditions for learning and the motor output were precisely specified. These considerations led him to study the mechanisms that underlie eyeblink conditioning. In the eyeblink conditioning situation, a CS (for example, a tone) is repeatedly paired with an air puff to the eye (the US) and acquires the ability to elicit a defensive eyeblink response. To pursue his neurobiological investigations, Thompson studied eyeblink conditioning in rabbits.

The search for the engram began with the hippocampus. Studies of humans with damage to this region revealed that the ability to consciously remember a recent event requires that the hippocampus remain intact. In animal subjects, small electrodes were lowered into the hippocampus and neural activity was recorded during eyeblink conditioning. These studies revealed that cells in this region reflect the learning of a CS-US association. To the surprise of many investigators, however, removing the hippocampus did not eliminate the animal's ability to acquire and retain a conditioned eyeblink response. In fact, removing all of the brain structures above the midbrain (see Figure 3.4) had little effect on eyeblink conditioning with a delayed conditioning procedure. This suggests that the essential circuitry for eyeblink conditioning lies within the lower neural structures of the brainstem and cerebellum. Subsequent experiments clearly showed that the acquisition of a well-timed conditioned eyeblink response depends on a neural circuit that lies within the cerebellum (Steinmetz et al., 2001).

The unconditioned response elicited by an airpuff to the eye is mediated by neurons that project to a region of the brainstem known as the trigeminal nucleus (see Figure 3.4B). From there, neurons travel along two routes, either directly or through the reticular formation, to the cranial motor nucleus where the behavioral output is organized. Three basic techniques were used to define this pathway. The first involved electrophysiological recordings to verify that neurons in this neural circuit are engaged in response to the US. The second technique involved inactivating the neural circuit, either permanently (by killing the cells) or temporarily (by means of a drug or cooling), to show that the circuit plays an essential role in the unconditioned response. If the circuit is necessary, disrupting its function should eliminate the behavioral output. Finally, the circuit was artificially stimulated to show that activity in this circuit is sufficient to produce the behavioral response.

The same techniques (electrical recording, inactivation, and stimulation) have been used to define the neural pathway that mediates the acquisition and performance of the conditioned response. As illustrated in Figure 3.4B, the CS input travels to a region of the brainstem known as the pontine nucleus. From there, it is carried by mossy fibers that convey the signal to the cerebellum. The US signal is carried into the cerebellum through the climbing fibers. These two signals meet in the cerebellar cortex where coincident activity brings about a synaptic modification that alters the neural output from the cerebellum. In essence, the climbing fibers act as teachers, selecting a subset of connections to be modified. This change defines the stimulus properties (the characteristics of the CS) that engage a discrete motor output. This output is mediated by neurons that project from the interpositus nucleus to the red nucleus, and finally, to the cranial motor nucleus.

As a conditioned response is acquired, conditioned activity develops within the interpositus nucleus. Neurons from the interpositus nucleus project back to the US pathway and inhibit the US signal within the inferior olive.

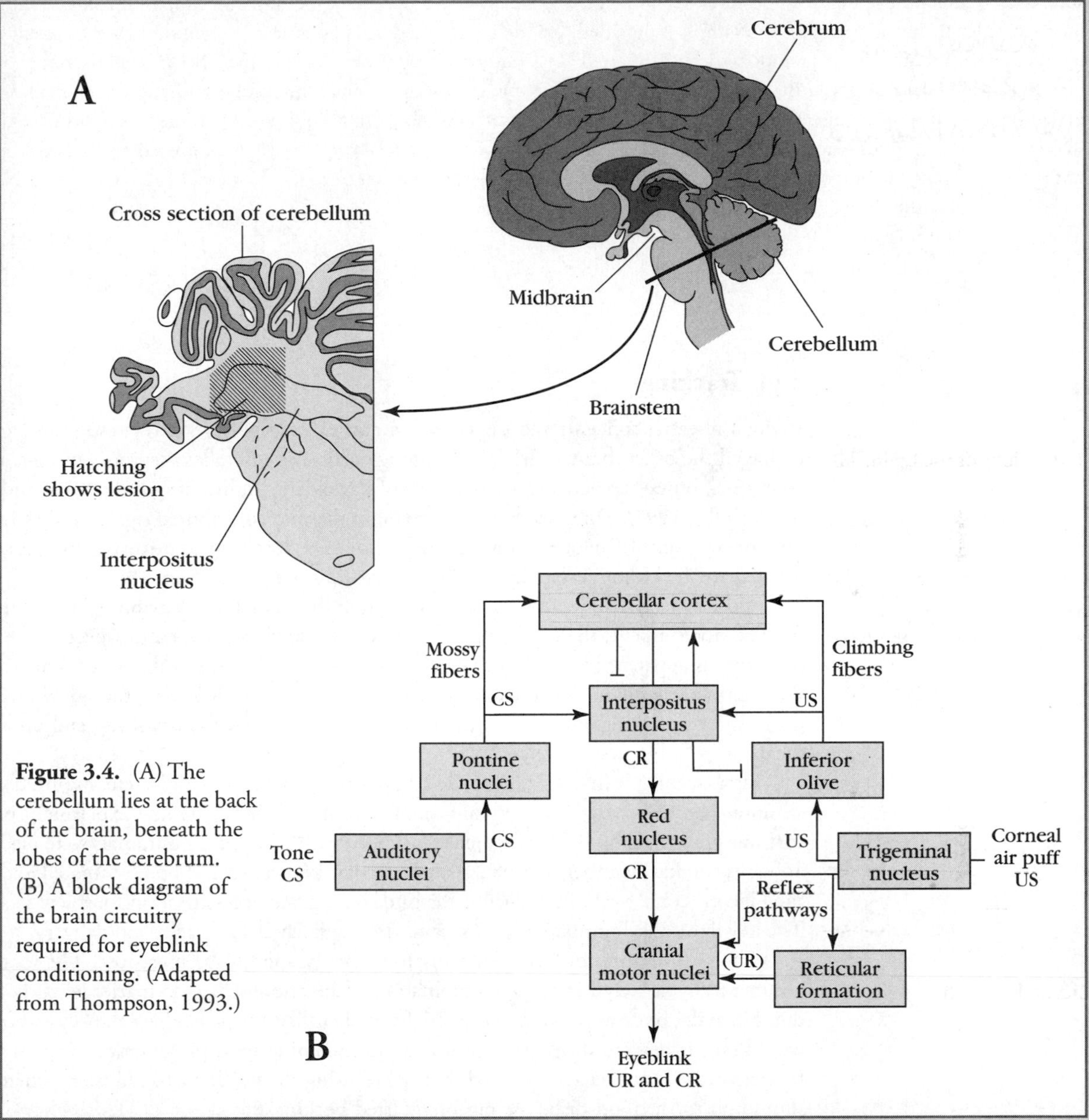

Figure 3.4. (A) The cerebellum lies at the back of the brain, beneath the lobes of the cerebrum. (B) A block diagram of the brain circuitry required for eyeblink conditioning. (Adapted from Thompson, 1993.)

This provides a form of negative feedback that decreases the effectiveness of the US. Many researchers believe that phenomena such as blocking and overshadowing occur because a predicted CS is less effective (see Chapter 4). Within an eyeblink paradigm, this might occur because the US input is inhibited within the inferior olive. Supporting this, Kim et al. (1998) showed that eliminating this source of inhibition eliminated the blocking effect.

(continued)

Box 3.2 (continued)

Earlier I noted that the hippocampus is not needed for simple delayed conditioning. It is, however, required for more complex forms of learning. An example is provided by trace conditioning, where a temporal delay is inserted between the end of the CS and the start of the US. A normal animal can readily acquire a conditioned eyeblink to a CS that ends 0.5 seconds before the US. However, it cannot span this gap if the hippocampus is removed. A similar pattern of results is observed in amnesic patients who have damage to the hippocampus (Clark & Squire, 1998). These patients cannot consciously remember the CS-US relation. In the absence of this explicit memory, they fail to learn with a trace conditioning procedure. Learning in the delayed procedure is not affected, even though the patient cannot consciously remember the CS-US relation from one session to the next. Interestingly, disrupting conscious awareness in a normal subject undermines the appreciation of the CS-US relation with the trace procedure. Again, subjects who cannot explicitly report the relation, fail to learn.

—J. W. Grau

Sign Tracking

Pavlov's research concentrated on salivation and other highly reflexive responses and encouraged the belief that classical conditioning occurs only in reflex response systems. In recent years, however, such a restrictive view of Pavlovian conditioning has been abandoned (e.g., Hollis, 1997). One experimental paradigm that has contributed significantly to modern conceptions of Pavlovian conditioning is the **sign tracking** or **autoshaping** paradigm (Hearst, 1975; Hearst & Jenkins, 1974; Locurto, Terrace, & Gibbon, 1981).

Animals tend to approach and contact stimuli that signal the availability of food. In the natural environment, the availability of food can be predicted by some aspect of the food itself that is apparent at a distance (such as the visual appearance of the food). For a hawk, for example, the sight and movements of a mouse are cues indicating the possibility of a meal. By approaching and contacting these distant food cues, the hawk can end up with a meal.

Sign tracking is investigated in the laboratory by presenting a discrete, localized visual stimulus just before each delivery of a small amount of food. The first experiment of this sort was performed by Brown and Jenkins (1968) with pigeons. The animals were placed in an experimental chamber that had a small circular key that could be illuminated and that the pigeons could peck. Periodically, the birds were given access to food for a few seconds. The key light was illuminated for 8 seconds immediately before each food delivery.

The pigeons did not have to do anything for the food to be presented. The food was automatically delivered after each illumination of the response key no matter what the birds did. Since the birds were hungry, one might predict that when they saw the key light, they would go to the food dish and wait for the forthcoming food presentation. Interestingly, however, that is not what happened. Instead of using the key light to tell them when they should go to the food dish, the pigeons started pecking the key itself. This behavior was remarkable because it was not required to gain access to the food.

Since its discovery, many experiments have been done on sign tracking in a variety of species, including chicks, quail, goldfish, lizards, rats, rhesus monkeys, squirrel monkeys, and human adults and children (see Tomie, Brooks, & Zito, 1989.) These experiments have shown that sign tracking is a useful technique for the investigation of associative learning. In pigeon sign-tracking experiments, the *conditioned stimulus* is illumination of the response key and the *unconditioned stimulus* is presentation of food. Learning proceeds most rapidly

Figure 3.5 The "long box" used in the sign-tracking experiment with pigeons by Jenkins. The conditioned stimulus was illumination of the key light at one end of the experimental chamber. Food was delivered in the middle of the chamber. (Based on Jenkins, personal communication, 1980.)

when the CS is presented just before the US. Pigeons do not approach and peck the CS if the CS and US are presented at random times in relation to each other (Gamzu & Williams, 1971, 1973).

The tracking of signals for food is dramatically illustrated by instances in which the signal is located far away from the food cup. In one such experiment (see Hearst & Jenkins, 1974), pigeons were placed in a 6-foot (182 cm) alley that had a food dish in the middle (see Figure 3.5). Each end of the alley had a circular disk or response key. Presentation of food was always preceded by illumination of the key at one end of the alley. The key light at the opposite end was uncorrelated with food. One other aspect of the experiment is important to point out: the food was available for only 4 seconds each time. Therefore, if the bird did not reach the food cup within 4 seconds, it did not get any food on that trial.

As conditioning progressed, the pigeons started behaving in a most remarkable manner. As soon as the key light came on, they ran to that end of the alley, pecked the key, and then ran to the center of the alley to get the food. Because the alley was very long, the pigeons did not always get to the food dish before the brief food presentation ended. The sign-tracking behavior was amazing because it was entirely unnecessary. The birds did not have to peck the key light to get the food US. They could have just stayed in the middle of the alley and waited by the food dish. The fact that they approached the key light is evidence of the compelling attraction of classically conditioned signals for food. The pigeons did not consistently approach the light at the other end of the chamber, which was uncorrelated with food presentations. (For similar experiments with domesticated quail, see Burns & Domjan, 2000.)

Sign tracking is possible only in situations where the conditioned stimulus is localized and therefore can be approached and "tracked." In one study, diffuse spatial and contextual cues of the chamber in which pigeons were given food periodically served as the conditioned stimulus. This time the learning of an association was evident in an increase in activity, rather than in a specific approach response (Rescorla, Durlach, & Grau, 1985). In another experiment (conducted with laboratory rats), a localized light and a sound were compared as conditioned stimuli for food (Cleland & Davey, 1983). Only the light stimulated conditioned approach or sign-tracking behavior. The auditory CS elicited approach to the food cup rather than approach to the sound source. These experiments illustrate that for sign tracking to occur, the conditioned stimulus has to be of the proper modality and configuration. Another important factor is how much time the subjects spend in the experimental context relative to the duration of each CS presentation. Greater levels of sign tracking occur with longer exposures to the experimental context relative to the duration of the CS (Burns & Domjan, 2001). I say more about this variable in Chapter 4.

Taste-Aversion Learning

The normal course of eating provides numerous opportunities for the learning of associations. Rozin and Zellner (1985) concluded a review of the role of Pavlovian conditioning in the foods people will like or dislike with the note that "Pavlovian conditioning is alive and well, in the flavor-flavor associations of the billions of meals eaten each day, . . . in the associations of foods and offensive objects, and in the associations of foods with some of their consequences" (p. 199).

Taste aversions can be learned if ingestion of a novel flavor is followed by illness or other aversive consequences. In contrast, a taste preference may be learned if a flavor is paired with nutritional repletion or other positive consequences (for example, Capaldi, Hunter, & Lyn, 1997; Ramirez, 1997). Taste-aversion and taste-preference learning as examples of Pavlovian conditioning have been investigated extensively in various animal species (see Riley & Tuck, 1985; Pérez, Fanizza, & Sclafani, 1999; Sclafani, 1997). A growing body of evidence indicates that many human taste aversions are also the result of Pavlovian conditioning. Much of this evidence has been provided by questionnaire studies (Batsell & Brown, 1998; Garb & Stunkard, 1974; Logue, Ophir, & Strauss, 1981; Logue, 1985, 1988a). People report having acquired at least one food aversion during their lives. The typical aversion learning experience involves eating a distinctively flavored food and then getting sick. Such a flavor–illness pairing can produce a conditioned food aversion in just one trial, and the learning can occur even if the illness is delayed several hours after ingestion of the food. Another interesting finding is that in about 20% of the cases, the individuals were certain that their illness was not caused by the food they ate. Nevertheless, they learned an aversion to the food. This indicates that food aversion learning can be independent of rational thought processes and can go against a person's conclusions about the causes of the illness.

Questionnaire studies offer provocative data, but systematic experimental research is required to isolate the mechanism of learning. Experimental studies of taste aversion learning have been conducted with people in situations where they encounter illness during the course of medical treatment. Chemotherapy for cancer is one such situation. Chemotherapy often causes nausea as a side effect. Both child and adult cancer patients have been shown to acquire aversions to foods eaten before a chemotherapy session (Bernstein, 1978, 1991; Bernstein & Webster, 1980; Carrell, Cannon, Best, & Stone, 1986). Such conditioned aversions may contribute to the lack of appetite commonly found among chemotherapy patients. (For laboratory studies on the role of nausea in the conditioning of taste aversions, see Limebeer & Parker, 1999, 2000.)

Conditioned food aversions also may contribute to the suppression of food intake or anorexia observed in other clinical situations (see Bernstein & Borson, 1986, for a review.) The anorexia that accompanies the growth of some tumors may result from food aversion learning. Animal research indicates that the growth of tumors can result in the conditioning of aversions to food ingested during the disease. Food aversion learning may also contribute to anorexia nervosa, a disorder characterized by severe and chronic weight loss. Suggestive evidence indicates that people suffering from anorexia nervosa experience digestive disorders that may increase their likelihood of learning food aversions. Increased susceptibility to food aversion learning may also contribute to loss of appetite evident in people suffering from severe depression.

Many of our ideas about food aversion learning in people have their roots in research with laboratory animals. In the typical procedure, the subjects receive a distinctively flavored food or drink and are then made to feel sick by the injection of a drug or exposure to radiation. As a result of the taste-illness pairing, the animals acquire an aversion to the taste. Their ingestion of the taste solution is suppressed by the conditioning procedure (see Barker, Best, & Domjan, 1977; Braveman & Bronstein, 1985).

Taste aversion learning is a result of the pairing of a CS (in this case, a taste) and a US (drug injection or radiation exposure) in much the same manner as in other examples of classical conditioning and follows standard rules of learning in many respects (for example, Domjan, 1980, 1983). It also has some special features. First, laboratory studies have clearly demonstrated that strong taste aversions can be learned with just one pairing of the flavor and illness. Although one-trial learning also occurs in fear conditioning, such rapid learning is rarely, if ever, observed in eyeblink conditioning, salivary conditioning, or sign tracking.

J. Garcia

The second unique feature of taste aversion learning is that it occurs even if the animals do not get sick until several hours after exposure to the novel taste (Garcia, Ervin, & Koelling, 1966; Revusky & Garcia, 1970). Dangerous substances in food often do not have their poisonous effects until the food has been digested, absorbed into the bloodstream, and distributed to various body tissues. This process takes time. *Long-delay learning* of taste aversions probably evolved to enable human and nonhuman animals to avoid poisonous foods that have delayed ill effects.

A dramatic example of long-delay taste aversion learning was provided by an experiment by Smith and Roll (1967). Laboratory rats were first adapted to a water deprivation schedule so that they would readily drink when a water bottle was placed on their cage. On the conditioning day, the rats were given a novel 0.1% saccharin solution to drink for 20 minutes. At various times after the saccharin presentation, ranging from 0 to 24 hours, different groups of rats were exposed to radiation from an X-ray machine. Control groups of rats were also taken to the X-ray machine but were not irradiated. They were called the sham irradiated groups. Starting a day after the radiation or sham treatment, each rat was given a choice of saccharin solution or plain water to drink for 2 days.

The preference of each group of animals for the saccharin solution is shown in Figure 3.6. Animals exposed to radiation within 6 hours after tasting the saccharin solution showed a profound aversion to the saccharin flavor in the postconditioning test. They drank less

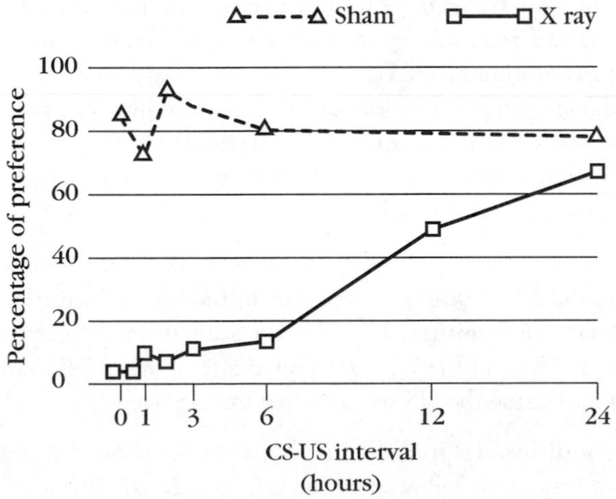

Figure 3.6 Mean percent preference for the CS flavor during a test session conducted after the CS flavor was paired with X irradiation (the US) or sham exposure. Percent preference is the percentage of a participant's total fluid intake (saccharin solution plus water) that consisted of the saccharin solution. During conditioning, the interval between exposure to the CS and the US ranged from 0 to 24 hours for different groups of rats. (From "Trace Conditioning with X-rays as an Aversive Stimulus," by J. C. Smith and D. L. Roll, *Psychonomic Science,* 1967, *9,* pp. 11–12. Copyright © 1967 by Psychonomic Society. Reprinted by permission.)

than 20% of their total fluid intake from the saccharin drinking tube. Much less aversion was evident in animals irradiated 12 hours after the saccharin exposure, and hardly any aversion was observed in rats irradiated 24 hours after the taste exposure. In contrast to this gradient of saccharin avoidance observed in the irradiated rats, all the sham irradiated groups strongly preferred the saccharin solution. They drank more than 70% of their total fluid intake from the saccharin drinking tube.

EXCITATORY PAVLOVIAN CONDITIONING PROCEDURES

What I have been discussing so far are instances of excitatory Pavlovian conditioning. In excitatory conditioning, organisms learn an association between the conditioned and the unconditioned stimuli. As a result of this association, presentation of the CS activates behavioral and neural activity related to the US—in the absence of the actual presentation of the unconditioned stimulus. These US-related processes are responsible for the conditioned responses that are observed. Thus, dogs come to salivate in response to the sight of sand or black water, pigeons learn to approach and peck a key light that is followed by food, rats learn to freeze to a sound that precedes foot shock, rabbits learn to blink in response to a tone that precedes a puff of air, and rats learn to avoid drinking saccharin that is followed by illness. In all these cases, the conditioned stimulus comes to activate behavior related to the associated US.

Common Pavlovian Conditioning Procedures

One of the critical factors that determines the course of classical conditioning is the relative timing of the conditioned stimulus and the unconditioned stimulus. In most conditioning situations, seemingly small and trivial variations in how a CS is paired with a US can have profound effects on how vigorous the conditioned response becomes.

Five common classical conditioning procedures are illustrated in Figure 3.7. The horizontal distance in each diagram represents the passage of time; vertical displacements represent when a stimulus begins and ends. Each configuration of CS and US represents a single **conditioning trial.**

In a typical classical conditioning experiment, CS-US episodes are repeated a number of times during a *training session.* The time from the end of one conditioning trial to the start of the next trial is called the **intertrial interval.** By contrast, the time from the start of the CS to the start of the US within a conditioning trial is called the **interstimulus interval** or **CS-US interval.** For conditioned responding to develop, the interstimulus interval has to be much shorter than the intertrial interval. In many experiments the interstimulus interval is less than 1 minute, whereas the intertrial interval may be 5 minutes or more. (A more detailed discussion of these parameters is provided in Chapter 4.)

1. *Short-delayed conditioning.* The most frequently used procedure for Pavlovian conditioning involves delaying the start of the US slightly after the start of the CS on each trial. This procedure is called **short-delayed conditioning.** The critical feature of short-delayed conditioning is that the CS starts each trial and the US is presented after a brief (less than 1 minute) delay. The CS may continue during the US or end when the US begins.

2. *Trace conditioning.* The **trace conditioning** procedure is similar to the short-delayed procedure in that the CS is presented first and is followed by the US. In trace conditioning,

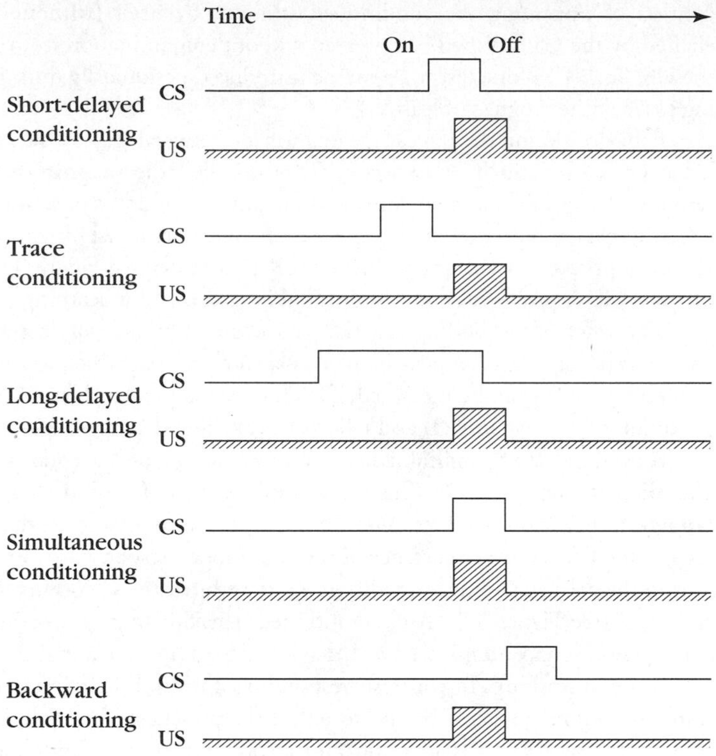

Figure 3.7 Five common classical conditioning procedures.

however, the US is not presented until some time after the CS has ended. This leaves a gap between the CS and the US. The gap is called the **trace interval.**

3. *Long-delayed conditioning.* The long-delayed conditioning procedure is also similar to the short-delayed conditioning in that the CS starts before the US. In this case, however, the US is delayed much longer (5–10 minutes) than in the short-delay procedure. Most important, the long-delayed procedure does not include a trace interval. The CS lasts until the US begins.

4. *Simultaneous conditioning.* Perhaps the most obvious way to expose subjects to a CS in conjunction with a US is to present the two stimuli at the same time. This procedure is called **simultaneous conditioning** because the conditioned and unconditioned stimuli are presented concurrently.

5. *Backward conditioning.* The last procedure depicted in Figure 3.7 differs from the others in that the US occurs shortly *before,* rather than after, the CS. This technique is called **backward conditioning** because the CS and US are presented in a "backward" order compared to the other procedures.

Measurement of Conditioned Responses

Pavlov and others after him have conducted systematic investigations of procedures like those depicted in Figure 3.7 to find out how the conditioning of a CS depends on the temporal relation between CS and US presentations. To make comparisons among the various procedures, the investigator must use a method for measuring conditioning that is equally applicable to all the procedures. This is typically done with the use of a **test trial.** A test trial consists of presenting the conditioned stimulus by itself (without the US). Responses elicited by the CS can then be observed without contamination from responses elicited by the US. Such CS-alone test trials can be introduced periodically during the course of training to track the progress of learning.

Behavior during the CS can be quantified in several ways. One aspect of conditioned behavior is how much of it occurs. This is called the **magnitude** of the conditioned response. Pavlov, for example, measured the number of drops of saliva that were elicited by a CS. Other examples of the magnitude of conditioned responses are the amount of response suppression that occurs in the CER procedure (see Figure 3.2) and the degree of depressed flavor preference that is observed in taste aversion learning (see Figure 3.6).

The vigor of responding can also be measured by how often the CS elicits a conditioned response. For example, the percentage of trials on which a conditioned response is elicited by the CS can be measured. This measure is frequently used in studies of eyeblink conditioning (see Figure 3.3) and reflects the likelihood or **probability** of responding.

A third aspect of conditioned responding is how soon the conditioned response occurs after presentation of the CS. This measure of the vigor of conditioned behavior is called the **latency** of the conditioned response. Latency is the amount of time that elapses between the start of the CS and the occurrence of the conditioned response.

In the delayed and trace conditioning procedures, the CS occurs by itself at the start of each trial (see Figure 3.7). Any conditioned behavior that occurs during this initial CS-alone period is uncontaminated by behavior elicited by the US and therefore can be used as a measure of learning. In contrast, responding during the CS in simultaneous and backward conditioning trials is bound to reflect the presence of the US or its recent presentation. Therefore, test trials are critical for assessing learning in simultaneous and backward conditioning.

Control Procedures for Classical Conditioning

Devising an effective test trial is not enough to obtain conclusive evidence of classical conditioning. As I noted in Chapter 1, learning is an inference about the causes of behavior based on a comparison of at least two conditions. To be certain that a conditioning procedure is responsible for certain changes in behavior, those changes must be compared to the effects of a control procedure. What should the control procedure be? In studies of habituation and sensitization, only the effects of prior exposure to a stimulus were of interest. Therefore, the comparison or control procedure was rather simple: it consisted of no prior stimulus exposure. In studies of classical conditioning, our interest is in how conditioned and unconditioned stimuli become associated. Because this is a more complicated issue, it requires more complicated control procedures.

An association between a CS and a US implies that the two events have become connected in some way. After an association has been established, the CS is able to activate processes related to the US. An association requires more than just familiarity with the CS and US. It presumably depends on having the two stimuli experienced in connection with each other. Therefore, to conclude that an association has been established, one has to make sure that the observed change in behavior could not have been produced by prior separate presentations of the CS or the US.

As described in Chapter 2, increased responding could occur as a result of sensitization, which is not an associative process. Presentations of an arousing stimulus, such as food to a hungry animal, can increase the behavior elicited by a more innocuous stimulus, such as a tone, without an association having been established between the two stimuli. (Recall, for example, the phenomenon of dishabituation, discussed under "Characteristics of Habituation and Sensitization" in Chapter 2.) Therefore, increases in responding observed with repeated CS-US pairings can sometimes result from exposure to just the US. Instances in which exposure to just the US produces responses like the conditioned response are called **pseudoconditioning.** Control procedures are required to determine whether responses that develop to the CS represent an association between the CS and US rather than sensitization effects of exposure to the conditioned and unconditioned stimuli.

Investigators have debated at length about the proper controls for classical conditioning. Ideally, a control procedure for the learning of an association would involve the same number and distribution of CS and US presentations as the experimental procedure, but with the CSs and USs arranged so that they would not become associated. One possibility is to present the CS and US at random during the course of an experimental session (Rescorla, 1967b). This is called the **random control** procedure. Unfortunately, evidence from a variety of sources indicates that the random control procedure can produce associative learning (see Papini & Bitterman, 1990; Rescorla, 2000)

A more successful control procedure involves presenting the conditioned and unconditioned stimuli on separate trials. Such a procedure is called the **explicitly unpaired control.** In the explicitly unpaired control, the CS and US are presented far enough apart to prevent their association. How much time has to elapse between them depends on the response system. In taste-aversion learning, much longer separation is necessary between the CS and US than in other forms of conditioning. In one variation of the explicitly unpaired control, only CSs are presented during one session and only USs are presented during a second session. (For a further discussion of control methodology, see Gormezano et al., 1983.)

Effectiveness of Common Conditioning Procedures

There has been considerable interest in determining which of the procedures depicted in Figure 3.7 produces the strongest evidence of learning. Traditionally, investigators followed Pavlov's lead in focusing on a single direct measure of learning. Learning laboratories were set up to conduct experiments using just one of the common conditioning preparations (fear conditioning, eyeblink conditioning, sign tracking, or taste aversion learning), and equipment was specially adapted to record only the particular response of interest for that laboratory. Fear conditioning laboratories, for example, measured only conditioned suppression or freezing; and eyeblink laboratories measured only the conditioned blink responses. After settling on a specific measure of learning, the investigator was ready to examine learning in delayed, simultaneous, trace, and backward conditioning procedures. The assumption was that Pavlovian conditioning would produce a CS-US association whose strength would be directly reflected in the vigor of the conditioned response.

The outcome of many early studies of the five conditioning procedures depicted in Figure 3.7 can be summarized by focusing on the interval between the start of the CS and the start of the US—the *interstimulus interval* or *CS-US interval.* In general, little conditioned responding was observed in simultaneous conditioning procedures, where the CS-US interval is zero (for example, Bitterman, 1964; Smith, Coleman, & Gormezano, 1969). Delaying the presentation of the US slightly after the CS often facilitated conditioned responding. However, this facilitation was fairly limited (Ost & Lauer, 1965; Schneiderman & Gormezano, 1964). If the CS-US interval was increased further, conditioned responding declined, as illustrated in Figure 3.8. Even in the taste-aversion conditioning procedure, where learning is possible with CS-US intervals of 1 or 2 hours, conditioned responding declines as the CS-US interval is increased (see Figure 3.6).

Trace conditioning procedures are interesting because they can have the same CS-US interval as delayed conditioning procedures. However, in trace procedures the CS is turned

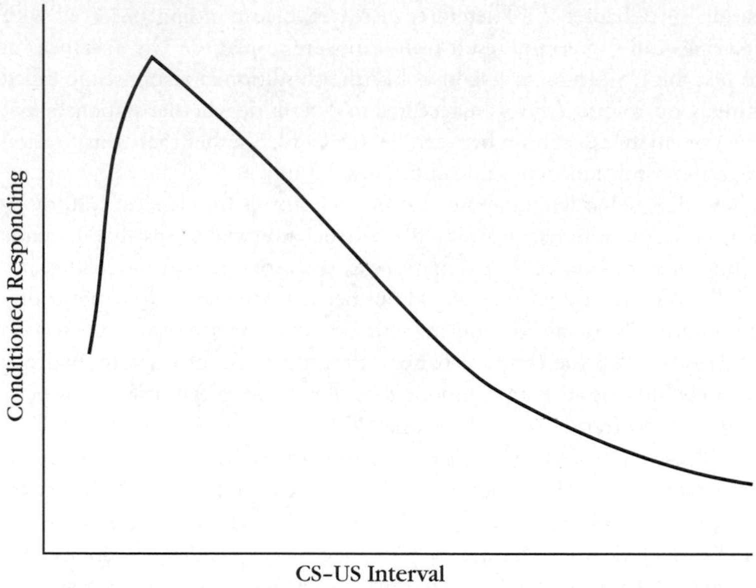

Figure 3.8 Traditional effects of the CS-US interval on the vigor of Pavlovian conditioned responding. (Idealized data.)

off a short time before the US occurs, resulting in a *trace interval.* Trace conditioning has traditionally been considered to be less effective than delayed conditioning (Ellison, 1964; Kamin, 1965) because of the trace interval (Kaplan & Hearst, 1982; Rescorla, 1982a). As with delayed conditioning, however, less conditioned responding is evident with a trace procedure if the interval between the CS and the US is increased (Kehoe, Cool, & Gormezano, 1991).

The above findings encouraged the conclusion that conditioning is most effective when the CS is a good signal that the US will soon occur. The signal value of the CS is best in the short-delayed procedure, where the US occurs shortly after the onset of the CS. The signal value of the CS decreases as the CS–US interval is increased. The CS is also a poor predictor of the US in simultaneous and trace procedures. In simultaneous conditioning, the US occurs at the same time as the CS and is therefore not signaled by the CS. In trace conditioning, the CS is followed by the trace interval rather than the US.

The one procedure whose results were difficult to interpret in terms of the CS-US interval and CS signal value is backward conditioning. Backward conditioning produced mixed results. Some investigators observed excitatory responding produced by backward pairings of a CS and a US (for example, Ayres, Haddad, & Albert, 1987; Hearst, 1989; Shurtleff & Ayres, 1981; Spetch, Wilkie, & Pinel, 1981). Others reported primarily inhibition of conditioned responding as a result of backward conditioning (for example, Maier, Rapaport, & Wheatley, 1976; Siegel & Domjan, 1971). To make matters even more confusing, in a rather remarkable experiment, Tait and Saladin (1986) found both excitatory and inhibitory conditioning effects resulting from the same backward conditioning procedure (see also McNish, Betts, Brandon, & Wagner, 1997).

The simple assumption that CS signal value determines whether a procedure will produce conditioned responding clearly cannot explain the complexity of findings that have been obtained in backward conditioning. The idea that there is a unitary hypothetical construct such as signal value or associative strength that varies as a function of the CS–US interval has also been challenged by the results of recent experiments that have employed sophisticated and multiple measures of learning. These studies have documented that delayed, simultaneous, trace, and backward conditioning can all produce strong learning and vigorous conditioned responding (for example, Albert & Ayres, 1997; Akins & Domjan, 1996; Marchand & Kamper, 2000; Romaniuk & Williams, 2000; Schreurs, 1998; Williams & Hurlburt, 2000). The challenge is to formulate new theoretical ideas to explain these diverse findings.

An entirely new conceptualization of the relative effectiveness of various Pavlovian conditioning procedures is beginning to emerge. According to contemporary views, delayed, simultaneous, trace, and backward conditioning all produce robust learning, but these procedures differ in what the subject learns. Instead of learning just a CS-US association, the subject is assumed to also learn when the US occurs in relation to the CS. Depending on the specific conditioning procedure, the subject can learn that the US occurs at the same time as the CS, before the CS, or with a short or a long delay after the CS. Thus, the subject learns not only that the CS is associated with the US but exactly when the US occurs in relation to the CS. This view is called the **temporal coding hypothesis** (Barnet, Cole, & Miller, 1997; Brown, Hemmes, & de Vaca, 1997; Cole, Barnet, & Miller, 1995b; Savastano & Miller, 1998). In Chapter 4, I describe in greater detail how the temporal information the CS provides about the US is manifest in conditioned behavior. In brief, the idea is that different types of conditioned responses occur depending on the temporal information the CS provides about the US (for example, Akins, 2000; Silva & Timberlake, 2000; Silva, Timberlake, & Cevik, 1998).

INHIBITORY PAVLOVIAN CONDITIONING

So far I have discussed Pavlovian conditioning in terms of learning to predict when a significant event or unconditioned stimulus will occur. But there is another type of Pavlovian conditioning—one in which participants learn to predict the absence of the unconditioned stimulus. Why would they want to predict the absence of something?

Consider being in an environment where bad things happen to you without warning. A child in an abusive home experiences something like that. His parents may yell at him and hit him unpredictably for no particular reason. Bad things can also happen with little warning if you are driving in heavy traffic. Getting pushed and shoved in a crowd also involves danger that arises without much warning and pretty much independent of what you might be doing. Research with laboratory animals has shown that exposure to unpredictable aversive stimulation is highly aversive and results in stomach ulcers and other physiological symptoms of stress. Stressful work environments are similar in involving unpredictable aversive events.

Another source of stress is a panic attack. A panic attack is a sudden sense of fear or discomfort, accompanied by physical symptoms (for example, heart palpitations) and a sense of impending doom. If such attacks are fairly frequent and become the source of considerable anxiety, the individual is said to suffer from panic disorder. At some point in their lives, 3.5% of the population experience panic disorder (Kessler et al., 1994). Individuals with panic disorder can sometimes predict the onset of a panic attack; at other times, they may experience an attack without warning. In a study of individuals who experienced both predictable and unpredictable panic attacks, Craske, Glover, and DeCola (1995) measured the general anxiety of the subjects before and after each type of attack. The results are summarized in Figure 3.9. Before the attack, anxiety ratings were similar whether the attack was predictable or not. Interestingly, however, anxiety significantly increased after an

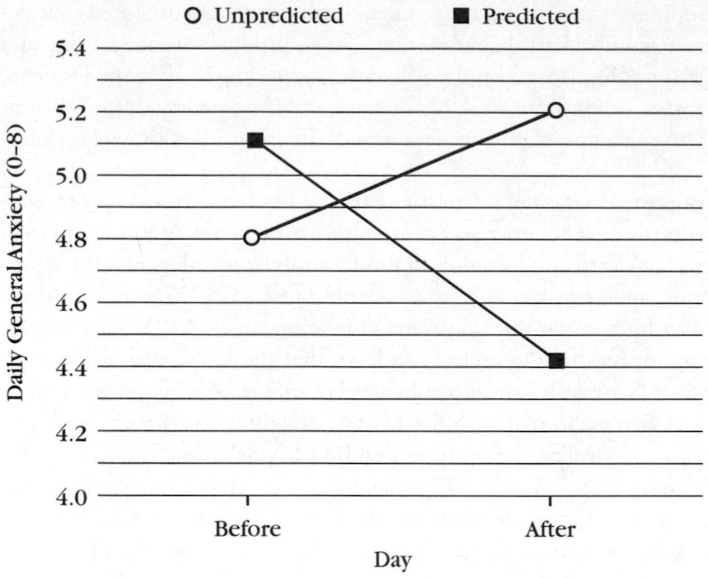

Figure 3.9 Ratings of general anxiety in individuals with panic disorder before and after predicted and unpredicted panic attacks. (From Craske, Glover, & DeCola, 1995.)

unpredicted panic attack and decreased after a predicted attack. Such results indicate that the anxiety generated by the experience of panic attacks occurs primarily because of the unpredictability of the attacks. Consistent with such findings, laboratory research with human and nonhuman subjects has shown that if one has to be exposed to aversive stimulation, predictable or signaled aversive stimuli are preferable to unpredictable aversive stimulation (Mineka & Henderson, 1985).

Why might predictable aversive stimuli be preferable to unpredicted events? A good possibility is that the ability to predict when an aversive event will occur also enables you to predict the absence of aversive stimulation. Being able to predict that absence may be the critical factor. Consistent with this reasoning, many effective stress-reduction techniques (such as relaxation training or meditation) involve creating a predictable period of safety or a time when you can be certain that aversive events will not occur. Stress management consultants recognize that it is often impossible to eliminate aversive events from one's life. for example, a teacher supervising a playground with 25 small children is bound to encounter unexpected and unpleasant events. One cannot entirely prevent accidents or avoid having one child hurt another. Eliminating aversive stimulation is often not a feasible stress management procedure. However, introducing even short periods of predictable safety (by allowing the teacher to take a break, for example) can substantially reduce stress.

Signals that predict the absence of an aversive stimulus are conditioned inhibitory stimuli. Although one can learn to predict the absence of a positive US just as well as a negative or aversive US, much of the research on conditioned inhibition has employed aversive stimulation.

Although Pavlov discovered inhibitory conditioning early in the twentieth century, this type of learning did not command the serious attention of psychologists until decades later (Boakes & Halliday, 1972; Rescorla, 1969b). The concept of conditioned inhibition was ignored because investigators thought evidence for inhibitory processes could be explained in other ways (for a historical discussion, see Williams, Overmier, & LoLordo, 1992). In contrast to excitatory conditioning, conditioned inhibition remains a controversial topic (for example, Miller & Matzel, 1988; Papini & Bitterman, 1993). Nevertheless, a considerable body of research has addressed problems related to conditioned inhibition (for reviews, see Fowler, Lysle, & DeVito, 1991; Miller & Spear, 1985; Savastano, Cole, Barnet, & Miller, 1999). The following section describes the major procedures used to produce conditioned inhibition as well as the special tests used to detect and measure conditioned inhibition.

Procedures for Inhibitory Conditioning

Unlike excitatory conditioning, which can proceed without special preconditions, conditioned inhibition has an important prerequisite. For the absence of a US to be a significant event, the US has to occur periodically in the situation. There are many signals for the absence of events in our daily lives. Signs such as "Closed," "Out of Order," and "No Entry" are all of this type, but they provide meaningful information and influence what we do only if they indicate the absence of something we otherwise expect to see. For example, if we encounter the sign "Out of Gas" at a service station, we may become frustrated and disappointed; the sign provides important information because service stations are expected to have gasoline. The same sign does not tell us anything of interest if it is in the window of a lumber yard, and it is not likely to discourage us from going to buy lumber.

The example I just gave illustrates the general rule that inhibitory conditioning and inhibitory control of behavior occur only if there is an excitatory context for the US in question (for example, Baker & Baker, 1985; Fowler, Kleiman, & Lysle, 1985; LoLordo & Fairless, 1985). This principle makes inhibitory conditioning very different from excitatory conditioning. Excitatory conditioning is not dependent on a special context in the same fashion.

Standard Procedure for Conditioned Inhibition. Pavlov recognized the importance of an excitatory context for the conditioning of inhibition and was careful to provide such a context in his standard inhibitory training procedure (Pavlov, 1927). The procedure he used, diagrammed in Figure 3.10, involves two conditioned stimuli and two kinds of conditioning trials, one for excitatory conditioning and the other for inhibitory conditioning. The US is presented on excitatory conditioning trials (trial Type A in Figure 3.10), and whenever the US occurs, it is announced by the conditioned stimulus labeled CS+ (a tone, for example). Because of its pairings with the US, the CS+ becomes a signal for the US and can then provide the excitatory context for the development of conditioned inhibition.

During inhibitory conditioning trials (trial Type B in Figure 3.10), the CS+ is presented together with the second conditioned stimulus, the CS– (a light, for example), and the US does not occur. Thus, the CS– is presented in the excitatory context provided by the CS+, but the CS– is not paired with the US. This makes the CS– a conditioned inhibitor. During the course of training, A type and B type trials are alternated randomly. As the animal receives repeated trials of CS+ followed by the US and CS+/CS– followed by no US, the CS– gradually acquires inhibitory properties (Marchant, Mis, & Moore, 1972).

The standard conditioned inhibition procedure is analogous to a situation in which something is introduced that prevents an outcome that would occur otherwise. A red traffic light at a busy intersection is a signal (CS+) of potential danger (the US). However, if a police officer indicates that you should cross the intersection despite the red light (perhaps because the traffic lights are malfunctioning), you will probably not have an accident. The red light (CS+) together with the gestures of the officer (CS–) are not likely to be followed by danger. The gestures act like a CS– to inhibit, or block, your hesitation to cross the intersection because of the red light.

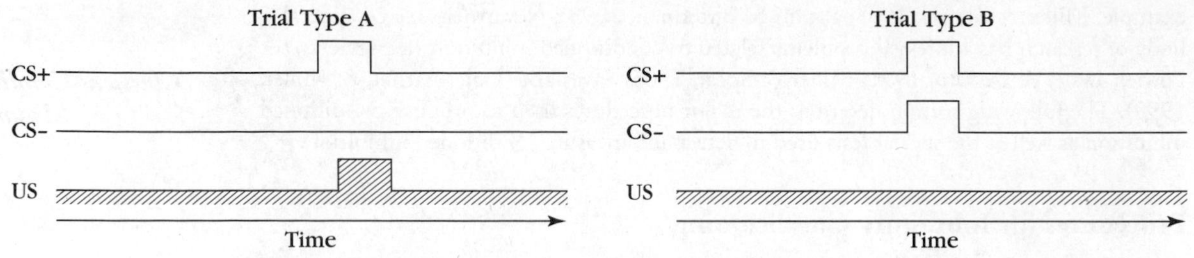

Figure 3.10 Standard procedure for conditioned inhibition. On some trials (Type A), the CS+ is paired with the US. On other trials (Type B), the CS+ is presented with the CS– and the US is omitted. The procedure is effective in conditioning inhibitory properties to the CS–.

Negative CS-US Contingency or Correlation Another common procedure for producing conditioned inhibition does not involve an explicit excitatory stimulus or CS+; rather, it involves only a CS– that is negatively correlated with the US. A negative correlation or contingency means that the US is less likely to occur after the CS than at other times. Thus, the CS signals a reduction in the probability that the US will occur. A sample arrangement that meets this requirement is diagrammed in Figure 3.11. The US is periodically presented by itself. However, each occurrence of the CS is followed by the predictable absence of the US for a while.

R. A. Rescorla

Consider a child who periodically gets picked on by her classmates when the teacher is out of the room. This is like periodically getting an aversive stimulus or US. When the teacher returns, the child can be sure she will not be bothered. Thus, the teacher serves as a CS– that signals a period free from harassment, or the absence of the US.

Conditioned inhibition is reliably observed in procedures in which the only explicit conditioned stimulus is negatively correlated with the US (Rescorla, 1969a). What provides the excitatory context for this inhibition? In this case, the environmental cues of the experimental chamber provide the excitatory context (Dweck & Wagner, 1970). Because the US occurs periodically in the experimental situation, the contextual cues of the experimental chamber acquire excitatory properties. This in turn permits the acquisition of inhibitory properties by the CS.

In a negative CS-US contingency procedure, the aversive US may occasionally occur shortly after the CS but this is unlikely. The aversive US is much more likely to occur in the absence of the CS, leading to the negative CS/US contingency. Even in the absence of the CS, however, the exact timing of the US cannot be predicted exactly. The US occurs probabilistically, in contrast to the standard procedure for conditioned inhibition. In the standard procedure, the US always occurs at the end of the CS+ and does not occur when the CS– is presented together with the CS+. Since the standard procedure permits predicting the exact timing of the US, it also permits predicting exactly when the US will *not* occur. (The US will not occur at the end of CS+ if the CS+ is presented with the CS–.) Thus, the standard procedure for conditioned inhibition permits temporal coding of the absence of the US (Denniston, Cole, & Miller, 1998; Denniston, Blaisdell, & Miller, 1998).

Measuring Conditioned Inhibition

How are conditioned inhibitory processes manifest in behavior? For conditioned excitation, the answer is straightforward. Conditioned excitatory stimuli come to elicit responses that

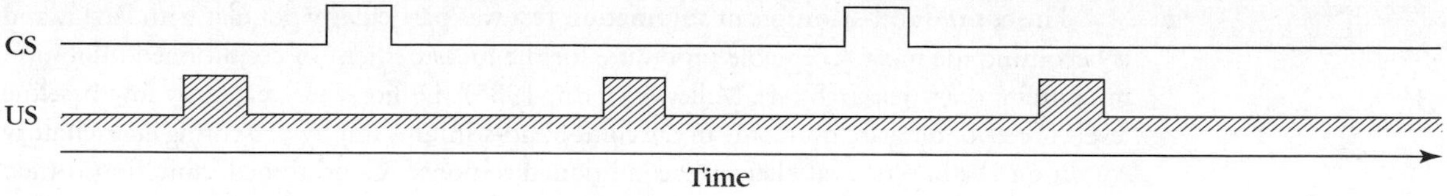

Figure 3.11 A negative CS-US contingency procedure for conditioning inhibitory properties to the CS. Notice that the CS is always followed by a period without the US.

were not evident before. Conditioned excitatory stimuli come to elicit new responses such as salivation, approach, or eyeblinking, depending on what was the unconditioned stimulus. One might expect that conditioned inhibitory stimuli would elicit the opposites of these reactions—namely, suppression of salivation, approach, or eyeblinking. But how can these response opposites be measured?

Bidirectional Response Systems. Identification of opposing response tendencies is easy with response systems that can change in opposite directions from baseline or normal performance. This is characteristic of many physiological responses. Heart rate, respiration, and temperature, for example, can either increase or decrease from a baseline level. Certain behavioral responses are also bidirectional. For example, animals can either approach or withdraw from a stimulus, and their rate of lever pressing for a food reward can either increase or decrease. In these cases, conditioned excitation results in a change in behavior in one direction, and conditioned inhibition results in a change in behavior in the opposite direction.

The sign-tracking procedure, for example, has been used to provide evidence of inhibitory conditioning through bidirectional responses. As noted earlier, a pigeon will approach a key light associated with the forthcoming presentation of food. By contrast, if an inhibitory conditioning procedure is used, the pigeon will withdraw from the CS (Hearst & Franklin, 1977; Wasserman, Franklin, & Hearst, 1974; Janssen, Farley, & Hearst, 1995; see also Palya, 1993). Although bidirectional responses can provide evidence of conditioned inhibition, the technique is limited and has not come to be widely used. One limitation, of course, is that this approach works only with responses that can go in opposite directions. Another, less obvious, limitation is that this technique can show only the net effects of excitation and inhibition. The subject will approach the CS if the excitatory properties of the CS are greater than its inhibitory properties, and it will withdraw from the CS if the inhibitory properties exceed the excitatory properties. The pigeon cannot both approach and withdraw at the same time. This makes the procedure of little use in instances where a CS acquires both excitatory and inhibitory properties. (For further discussion of this point, see Savastano et al., 1999.)

The Compound-Stimulus, or Summation, Test. How could researchers measure inhibition if the target behavior is not bidirectional? Consider, for example, the eyeblink response, which is frequently studied with rabbits. In the absence of an eliciting stimulus, rabbits rarely blink. If a stimulus had been conditioned to inhibit the eyeblink response, researchers would also not observe eyeblinks when this stimulus was presented. How could they tell whether the lack of responding reflected an active suppression of blinking or merely the low baseline level of this behavior? To conclude that a stimulus actively inhibits blinking, researchers have to use more sophisticated test procedures. One of these is the *compound-stimulus test.*

The **compound-stimulus** or **summation test** was particularly popular with Pavlov and is becoming the most acceptable procedure for the measurement of conditioned inhibition in contemporary research (see Miller & Spear, 1985). Difficulties created by low baseline levels of responding are overcome in the compound-stimulus test by presenting an excitatory conditioned stimulus that elicits the conditioned response. Conditioned inhibition is then measured in terms of the reduction or inhibition of this conditioned responding. Thus, the test involves observing the effects of an inhibitory CS in compound with an excitatory CS+. The procedure may also be conceptualized as one that involves observing the summation of the effects of the inhibitory stimulus (CS–) and an excitatory stimulus (CS+).

A particularly well-controlled demonstration of conditioned inhibition using the compound-stimulus or summation test was reported by Cole, Barnet, and Miller (1997). The experiment was conducted using the lick suppression procedure with laboratory rats. The subjects received inhibitory conditioning in which the presentation of a flashing light by itself always ended in a brief shock (A+), and the presentation of an auditory cue (X) together with the light ended without shock (AX–). Thus, the standard procedure for conditioned inhibition was used. Inhibitory conditioning was conducted over 7 sessions in which the subjects received a total of 28 A+ trials and 56 AX– trials. The subjects also received training with another auditory stimulus (B) in a different experimental chamber, and this stimulus always ended in the brief shock (B+). The intent of these procedures was to establish conditioned excitation to two different stimuli, A and B, and conditioned inhibition to X.

Cole et al. then asked whether the presumed inhibitor X would suppress responding to the excitatory stimuli A and B. The results of those tests are summarized in Figure 3.12. How long the subjects took to accumulate 5 seconds of uninterrupted drinking was measured. Notice that when the excitatory stimuli A and B were presented by themselves, the rats required substantial amounts of time to complete the 5-second drinking criterion. In contrast, when the excitatory stimuli were presented together with the conditioned inhibitor (AX and BX tests), the drinking requirement was completed much faster. Thus, presenting stimulus X with A and B reduced the drinking suppression that occurred when A and B were presented by themselves. Figure 3.12 includes yet another test condition, stimulus B tested with another auditory cue Y. Stimulus Y was not previously conditioned as an inhibitor and was presented in order to be sure that introducing a new stimulus with stimulus B would not cause disruption of the conditioned fear response. As Figure 3.12 illustrates, no such disruption occurred with stimulus Y. Thus, the inhibition of conditioned fear was limited to the stimulus (X) that had participated in the conditioned inhibition training. Another important aspect of these results is that X was able to inhibit conditioned fear not only to the exciter with which it was trained (A) but also to another exciter (B) that had never been presented with X during training.

The compound-stimulus test procedure for conditioned inhibition suggests that the presentation of a conditioned inhibitor or safety signal can reduce the stressful effects of an aversive experience. This prediction was tested with patients who were prone to experience panic attacks (Carter, Hollon, Carson, & Shelton, 1995). Panic attack patients were invited to the laboratory, accompanied by someone with whom they felt safe. Panic was experimentally induced in the participants by having them inhale a mixture of gas containing elevated levels of carbon dioxide. The participants were then asked to report on their perceived levels of anxiety and catastrophic ideation triggered by the carbon dioxide exposure. The experimental manipulation was the presence of another person with whom the participants felt safe. Half the participants were allowed to have their trusted acquaintance in the room with them during the experiment, whereas the remaining participants took part in the

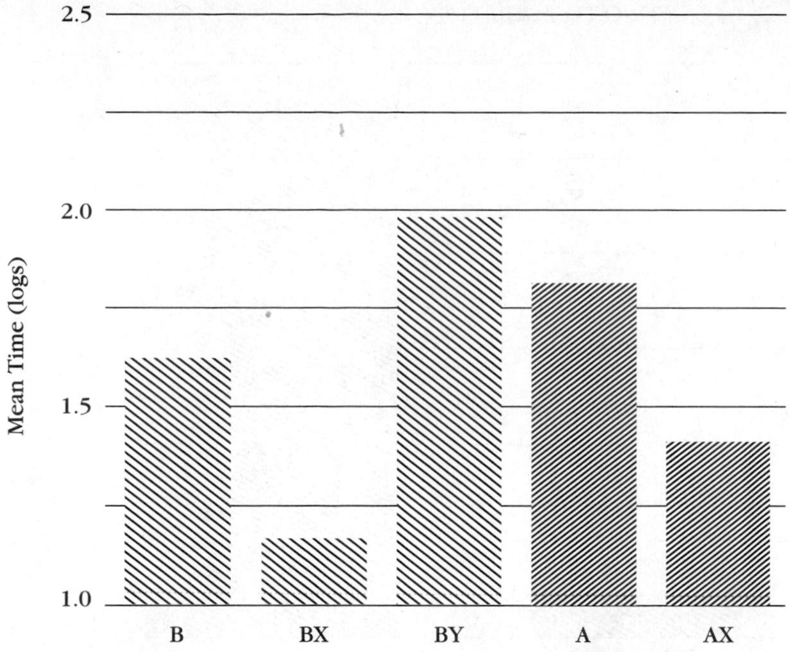

Figure 3.12 Compound-stimulus test of inhibition in a lick suppression experiment. Stimuli A and B were conditioned as excitatory stimuli by being presented alone with shock (A+ and B+). Stimulus X was conditioned as an inhibitor by being presented with stimulus A without shock (AX–). Stimulus Y was a control stimulus that had not participated in either excitatory or inhibitory conditioning. A was a flashing light. B, X, and Y were auditory cues (a clicker, white noise, and a buzzer, counterbalanced across subjects). A, and AX were tested in the original training context. B, BX, and BY were tested in a different context. (For additional details, see Cole, Barnet, & Miller, 1997, Experiment 1.)

experiment alone. The results indicated that the presence of a safe acquaintance reduced the anxiety and catastrophic ideation associated with the panic attack.

The Retardation-of-Acquisition Test. Another frequently used indirect test of conditioned inhibition is the **retardation-of-acquisition test** (for example, Hammond, 1968; Rescorla, 1969a). The rationale for this test is also rather straightforward. If a stimulus actively inhibits a particular response, then it should be especially difficult to condition that stimulus to elicit the behavior. In other words, the rate of acquisition of an excitatory conditioned response should be retarded if the CS is a conditioned inhibitor. This prediction was tested by Cole et al. (1997) in an experiment very similar to their summation test study described earlier.

After the same kind of inhibitory conditioning that produced the results summarized in Figure 3.12, Cole et al. took stimulus X (which had been conditioned as an inhibitor) and stimulus Y (which had not been used in a conditioning procedure before) and conducted a retardation-of-acquisition test by pairing each stimulus with shock on three occasions. (This retardation-of-acquisition test was conducted in an experimental chamber different from the chamber in which the subjects previously received inhibitory training.)

TWO-TEST STRATEGY

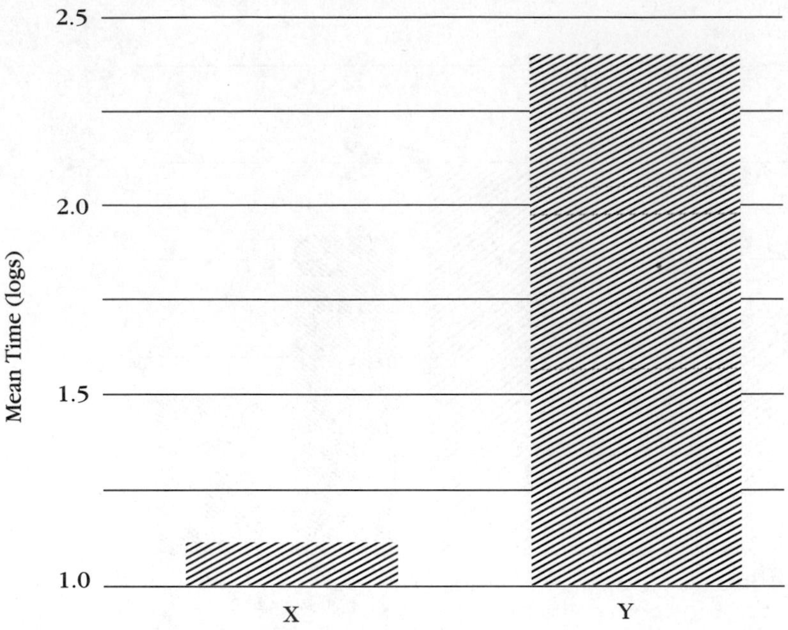

Figure 3.13 Effects of a retardation-of-acquisition test of inhibition in a lick suppression experiment after the same kind of inhibitory conditioning as was conducted to produce the results presented in Figure 3.12. Stimulus X was previously conditioned as an inhibitory stimulus, and stimulus Y previously received no training. (For additional details, see Cole, Barnet, & Miller, 1997, Experiment 2.)

After the three acquisition trials, each stimulus was tested to see which would cause a greater suppression of drinking. The results are presented in Figure 3.13. The time to complete a cumulative of 5 seconds drinking took much longer in the presence of the control stimulus Y than in the presence of stimulus X, which had previously been trained as a conditioned inhibitor. Thus, the initial inhibitory training of X retarded its acquisition of excitatory conditioned fear properties.

Conditioned inhibition can be difficult to distinguish from other behavioral processes. Therefore, the best strategy is to use more than one test and be sure that the different tests all point to the same conclusion. Rescorla (1969b) advocated using both the compound stimulus test and the retardation-of-acquisition test. This dual test strategy has remained popular ever since (Savastano et al., 1999; Williams et al., 1992).

PREVALENCE OF CLASSICAL CONDITIONING

Classical conditioning is typically investigated in laboratory situations. However, we do not have to know much about classical conditioning to realize that it also occurs in a wide range of situations outside the laboratory. Classical conditioning is most likely to develop when one event reliably precedes another in a short-delayed CS-US pairing. This occurs in many aspects of life. As I mentioned at the beginning of the chapter, stimuli in the environment occur in an orderly temporal sequence, largely because of the physical constraints of causation. Some events simply cannot happen before other things have occurred. Social institutions and customs also ensure that things happen in a predictable order. Whenever one stimulus reliably precedes another, classical conditioning may take place.

One area of research that has been of particular interest is how people come to judge one event as the cause of another. In studies of human causal judgment, participants are exposed to repeated occurrences of two events (pictures of a blooming flower and a water can briefly presented on a computer screen) in various temporal arrangements. In one condition, for example, the water can may always occur before the flower; in another, it may occur at random times relative to the flower. After observing numerous appearances of both objects, the subjects are asked to indicate their judgment about the strength of causal relation between them. Studies of human causal judgment are analogous to studies of Pavlovian conditioning in that both involve repeated experiences with two events and responses based on the extent to which those two events are related to one another. Given this correspondence, one might suspect that there is considerable commonality in the outcomes of causal judgment and Pavlovian conditioning experiments. That prediction has been borne out in numerous studies (Miller & Matute, 1996; Shanks & Dickinson, 1987; Wasserman, 1990), suggesting that Pavlovian associative mechanisms are not limited to Pavlov's dogs but may play a role in the numerous informal judgments of causality we all make during the course of our daily lives.

Courtesy of Donald A. Dewsbury

M. E. Bouton

As I described earlier in the chapter, Pavlovian conditioning can result in the conditioning of food preferences and aversions. It can also result in the acquisition of fear. Conditioned fear responses have been of special interest because they may contribute significantly to anxiety disorders, phobias, and panic disorder (Bouton, 2001; Bouton, Mineka, & Barlow, 2001). As I discuss further in Chapter 4, Pavlovian conditioning is also involved in drug tolerance and addiction. Cues that reliably accompany drug administration can come to elicit drug-related responses through conditioning. In discussing this type of learning among crack addicts, Dr. Scott Lukas of McLean Hospital in Massachusetts described the effects of drug-conditioned stimuli by saying, "These cues turn on crack-related memories, and addicts respond like Pavlov's dogs" (*Newsweek,* February 12, 2001, p. 40).

Pavlovian conditioning is also involved in infant and maternal responses in nursing. Suckling involves mutual stimulation for the infant and the mother. To successfully nurse, the mother has to hold the baby in a particular position, which provides special tactile stimuli for both the infant and the mother. The tactile stimuli experienced by the infant may become conditioned to elicit orientation and suckling responses on the part of the baby (Blass, Ganchrow, & Steiner, 1984). The tactile stimuli experienced by the mother may also become conditioned, in this case to elicit the milk let-down response of the mother in anticipation of having the infant suckle. Mothers who nurse their babies frequently may experience the milk let-down reflex when the baby cries or when the usual time for breast-feeding arrives. All these stimuli (special tactile cues, the baby's crying, and the time of normal feedings) reliably precede suckling by the infant. Therefore, they may become conditioned by the suckling stimulation and come to elicit milk secretion as a conditioned response. The anticipatory conditioned orientation and suckling responses and the anticipatory conditioned milk let-down response make the nursing experience more successful for both the baby and the mother.

Pavlovian conditioning is also important in learning about sexual situations. Although clinical observations indicate that human sexual behavior can be shaped by learning experiences, the best experimental evidence of sexual conditioning has been obtained in studies

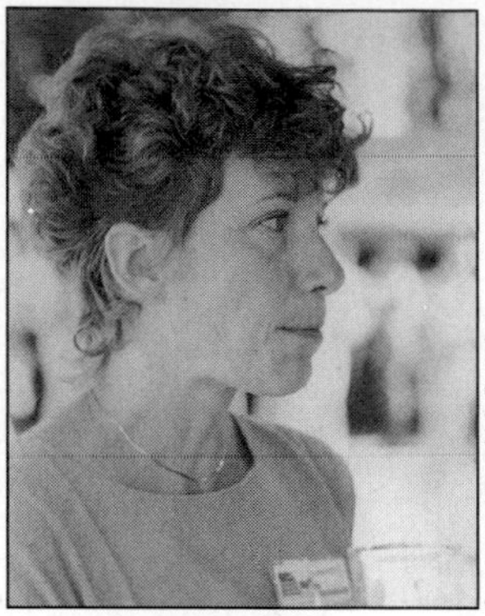

Courtesy of Donald A. Dewsbury

K. L. Hollis

with laboratory animals (Domjan & Holloway, 1998). In these studies, males typically serve as participants, and the unconditioned stimulus is provided either by the sight of a sexually receptive female or by physical access to a female (Domjan, 1998). Subjects come to approach stimuli that signal the availability of a sexual partner (Burns & Domjan, 1996; Hollis, Cadieux, & Colbert, 1989). The presentation of a sexually conditioned stimulus also facilitates various aspects of reproductive behavior. Studies with rats, quail, and a fish species have shown that after exposure to a sexual CS, males are quicker to perform copulatory responses (Zamble, Hadad, Mitchell, & Cutmore, 1985), compete more successfully with other males for access to a female (Gutiérrez & Domjan, 1996), show more courtship behavior (Hollis et al., 1989), release greater quantities of sperm (Domjan, Blesbois, & Williams, 1998), and show increased levels of testosterone and leuteinizing hormone (Graham & Desjardins, 1980). Although these various manifestations of sexual conditioning are noteworthy, the ultimate payoff for sexual behavior is the numbers of offspring that are produced. In an important study with a fish species, Hollis, Pharr, Dumas, Britton, and Field (1997) found that the presentation of a Pavlovian CS+ before a sexual encounter greatly increased the numbers of offspring that resulted from the reproductive behavior. Similar findings are emerging in studies with domesticated quail (Domjan & Mahometa, 2001).

CONCLUDING COMMENTS

Chapter 3 continued the discussion of elicited behavior by turning attention from habituation and sensitization to classical conditioning. Classical conditioning is a bit more complex than habituation and sensitization in that it involves associatively mediated elicited behavior. Classical conditioning is one of the major techniques for investigating how associations are learned. As we have seen, classical conditioning may be involved in many different important aspects of behavior. Depending on the procedure used, the learning may occur quickly or slowly. With some procedures, excitatory response tendencies are learned; with other procedures, the organism learns to inhibit a particular response in the presence of the conditioned stimulus. Excitatory and inhibitory conditioning occur in many aspects of common experience and serve to increase how effectively we cope with significant biological events.

SAMPLE QUESTIONS

1. Describe similarities and differences between habituation, sensitization, and classical conditioning.
2. What is object learning, and how is it similar or different from conventional classical conditioning?
3. What is the most effective procedure for excitatory conditioning and how is it different from other possibilities?
4. What is a control procedure for excitatory conditioning, and what processes are the control procedure intended to rule out?
5. Are conditioned excitation and conditioned inhibition related, and if so how?
6. Describe procedures for conditioning and measuring conditioned inhibition.

KEY TERMS

autoshaping Same as *sign tracking.*

backward conditioning A procedure in which the conditioned stimulus is presented after the unconditioned stimulus on each trial.

CER Abreviation for *conditioned emotional response.*

compound-stimulus test A test procedure that identifies a stimulus as a conditioned inhibitor if that stimulus reduces the responding elicited by a conditioned excitatory stimulus. Also called *summation test.*

conditional or conditioned response The response that comes to be made to the conditioned stimulus as a result of classical conditioning. Abbreviated *CR.*

conditional or conditioned stimulus A stimulus that does not elicit a particular response initially, but comes to do so as a result of becoming associated with an unconditioned stimulus. Abbreviated *CS.*

conditioned emotional response Suppression of positively reinforced instrumental behavior (for example, lever pressing for food pellets) caused by the presentation of a stimulus that has become associated with an aversive stimulus. Abbreviation *CER.* Also called *conditioned suppression.*

conditioned suppression Same as *conditioned emotional response.*

conditioned lick suppression Similar to the conditioned emotional response (CER) or conditioned suppression procedure. However, instead of lever pressing for food serving as the behavior that is suppressed by conditioned fear, the baseline is licking a waterspout by thirsty rats. The presentation of a fear-conditioned CS slows down the rate of licking.

conditioning trial A training episode involving presentation of a conditioned stimulus with (or without) an unconditioned stimulus.

CR Abbreviation for *conditioned response.*

CS Abbreviation for *conditioned stimulus.*

CS-US interval Same as *interstimulus interval.*

explicitly unpaired control A procedure in which both conditioned and unconditioned stimuli are presented, but with sufficient time between them so that they do not become associated with each other.

interstimulus interval The amount of time that elapses between presentations of the conditioned stimulus (CS) and the unconditioned stimulus (US) during a classical conditioning trial. Also called the *CS-US interval.*

intertrial interval The amount of time that elapses between two successive trials.

latency The time elapsed between a stimulus (or the start of a trial) and the response that is made to the stimulus.

magnitude of a response A measure of the size, vigor, or extent of a response.

object learning Learning associations between different stimulus elements of an object.

probability of a response The likelihood of making the response, usually represented in terms of the percentage of trials on which the response occurs.

pseudoconditioning Increased responding that may occur to a stimulus whose presentations are intermixed with presentations of an unconditioned stimulus (US) in the absence of the establishment of an association between the stimulus and the US.

random control A procedure in which the conditioned and unconditioned stimuli are presented at random times with respect to each other.

retardation-of-acquisition test A test procedure that identifies a stimulus as a conditioned inhibitor if that stimulus is slower to acquire excitatory properties than a comparison stimulus.

short-delayed conditioning A classical conditioning procedure in which the conditioned stimulus is initiated shortly before the unconditioned stimulus on each conditioning trial.

sign tracking Movement toward and possibly contact with a stimulus that signals the availability of a positive reinforcer, such as food. Also called *autoshaping.*

simultaneous conditioning A classical conditioning procedure in which the conditioned stimulus and the unconditioned stimulus are presented simultaneously on each conditioning trial.

summation test Same as *compound-stimulus test.*

temporal coding hypothesis The idea that Pavlovian conditioning procedures lead not only to learning that the US happens but exactly when the US occurs in relation to the CS. The CS comes to represent (or code) the timing of the US.

test trial A trial in which the conditioned stimulus is presented without the unconditioned stimulus. This allows measurement of the conditioned response in the absence of the unconditioned response.

trace conditioning A classical conditioning procedure in which the unconditioned stimulus is presented after the conditioned stimulus has been terminated for a short period.

trace interval The interval between the end of the conditioned stimulus and the start of the unconditioned stimulus in trace-conditioning trials.

unconditional or unconditioned response A response that occurs to a stimulus without the necessity of prior training.

unconditional or unconditioned stimulus A stimulus that elicits a particular response without the necessity of prior training.

UR Abbreviation for *unconditioned response.*

US Abbreviation for *unconditioned stimulus.*

CHAPTER

4 CLASSICAL CONDITIONING: MECHANISMS

Chapter 4 continues the discussion of classical conditioning, focusing on the mechanisms and outcomes of this type of learning. The discussion is organized around three key issues: (1) features of conditioned and unconditioned stimuli that influence their effectiveness in classical conditioning procedures, (2) factors that determine the types of responses that come to be made to conditioned stimuli, and (3) mechanisms involved in the formation of associations between conditioned and unconditioned stimuli and the mechanisms involved in the acquisition of conditioned behavior.

WHAT MAKES EFFECTIVE CONDITIONED AND UNCONDITIONED STIMULI?

This is perhaps the most basic question about classical conditioning. It was originally addressed by Pavlov and is also increasingly attracting the attention of contemporary researchers.

Initial Responses to the Stimuli

Pavlov addressed the effectiveness criteria for conditioned and unconditioned stimuli in his definitions of the terms *conditioned* and *unconditioned.* According to these definitions, the conditioned stimulus (CS) does not elicit the conditioned response initially, but comes to do so as a result of becoming associated with the unconditioned stimulus (US). By contrast, the US is effective in eliciting the target response from the outset without any special training.

Pavlov's definitions were stated in terms of the elicitation of a particular response—the one to be conditioned. Because of this, identifying potential CSs and USs requires comparing the responses elicited by each stimulus before conditioning. Such a comparison makes the identification of CSs and USs *relative.* A particular event may serve as a CS relative to one stimulus and as a US relative to another.

Consider, for example, a palatable saccharin solution for thirsty rats. The taste may serve as a CS in a taste-aversion experiment, with illness serving as the US. In this case, conditioning trials would consist of exposure to the saccharin flavor followed by injection of a drug that induces malaise, and the animals would learn to stop drinking the saccharin solution.

The same saccharin solution may also serve as a US—in a sign-tracking experiment, for example. The conditioning trials in this case would involve the illumination of a light just before each presentation of a small amount of saccharin. After a number of these trials, the animals would begin to approach the light CS. Thus, whether the saccharin solution is considered a US or a CS depends on its relation to other stimuli in the situation.

The Novelty of Conditioned and Unconditioned Stimuli

As studies of habituation show, the behavioral impact of a stimulus depends on its novelty. Highly familiar stimuli do not elicit as vigorous reactions as do novel stimuli. Novelty is also important in classical conditioning. If either the conditioned or the unconditioned stimulus is highly familiar, learning proceeds more slowly than if the CS and US are novel.

Investigations of the role of novelty in classical conditioning are usually conducted in two phases. Subjects are first given repeated presentations of the stimulus that is later to be used as the CS. During this initial phase of the experiment, the CS-to-be is always presented by itself. After the preexposure phase, the CS is paired with an unconditioned stimulus using conventional classical conditioning procedures. Initial familiarization with a stimulus presented by itself usually retards the subsequent conditioning of that stimulus. This phenomenon is called the **CS-preexposure effect** or the **latent-inhibition effect** (Hall, 1991; Lubow, 1989; Lubow & Gewirtz, 1995; for implications for psychopathology, see Lubow, 1998; Oberling, Gosselin, & Miller, 1997).

The function of the CS-preexposure effect is similar to the function of habituation. Both phenomena serve to limit processing and attention to stimuli that have proven to be inconsequential. Habituation serves to bias elicited behavior in favor of novel stimuli;

latent inhibition serves to bias learning in favor of novel stimuli. As Lubow and Gewirtz (1995) noted, latent inhibition "promotes the stimulus selectivity required for rapid learning" (p. 87).

Experiments on the importance of US novelty are similar in design to CS-preexposure experiments. Subjects are first given repeated exposures to the US presented by itself. The US is then paired with a CS, and the progress of learning is monitored. Subjects familiarized with a US before its pairings with a CS are slower to develop conditioned responding to the CS than participants for whom the US is novel during the CS-US pairings. This result is called the **US-preexposure effect** (Randich, 1981; Randich & LoLordo, 1979; Riley & Simpson, 2001; Saladin, ten Have, Saper, Labinsky, & Tait, 1989).

The mechanisms of CS- and US-preexposure effects have been the subject of extensive research and debate. No one theory has been successful in explaining all of the data. A reasonable conclusion at this time is that several mechanisms are involved (see Hall, 1991, for a discussion of this in relation to the CS-preexposure effect). One mechanism involves *associative interference.* According to the associative interference account, preconditioning exposures to the CS or US make these stimuli less able to enter into new associations (Lubow, Weiner, & Schnur, 1981; McPhee, Rauhut, & Ayres, 2001; Riley & Simpson, 2001).

The second explanation of CS- and US-preexposure effects is *memory interference.* According to the memory interference account, conditioned responding is disrupted because participants remember what happened in both phases of the experiment. They remember having received the CS (or US) by itself repeatedly during the preexposure phase and having received the CS paired with the US in the conditioning phase. The memory of the preexposure phase disrupts responding because the CS- and US-preexposure procedures do not stimulate the conditioned response. Consistent with this mechanism, procedures that reduce the memory of preexposure at the time of testing result in enhanced conditioned responding (for example, Graham, Barnet, Gunther, & Miller, 1994; Rosas & Bouton, 1997; Westbrook, Jones, Bailey, & Harris, 2000).

CS and US Intensity and Salience

Another important stimulus variable for classical conditioning is the intensity of the conditioned and unconditioned stimuli. Most biological and physiological effects of stimulation are related to the intensity of the stimulus input. This is also true of Pavlovian conditioning. More vigorous conditioned responding occurs when more intense conditioned and unconditioned stimuli are used (for example, Bevins, McPhee, Rauhut, & Ayres, 1997; Kamin & Brimer, 1963; Ploog & Zeigler, 1996; Scavio & Gormezano, 1974).

Stimulus intensity is one factor that contributes to what is more generally called **stimulus salience.** The term *salience* is not well defined, but it roughly corresponds to significance or noticeability. Theories of learning typically assume that learning will occur more rapidly with more salient stimuli (for example, McLaren & Mackintosh, 2000; Pearce & Hall, 1980). A stimulus can be made more salient, or significant, by making it more intense and hence more attention getting. Investigators can also make a stimulus more salient by making it more relevant to the biological needs of the organism. For example, animals become more attentive to the taste of salt if they suffer a nutritional salt deficiency (Kriekhaus, & Wolf, 1968). Consistent with this outcome, Sawa, Nakajima, and Imada (1999) found that sodium-deficient rats learn stronger aversions to the taste of salt than do nondeficient control subjects.

Another way to increase the salience of a CS is to make the laboratory CS more similar to the kinds of stimuli an animal is likely to encounter in its natural environment. Studies of sexual conditioning with domesticated quail provide an example. In the typical

[handwritten margin notes:]
taste predicts sickness

sound predicts shock

but

taste wx predict shock

sound wx predict sickness

experiment, access to a female quail serves as the US for a male, and this sexual opportunity is signaled by the presentation of a CS. The CS can be an "arbitrary" cue such as a light or a terrycloth object. Alternatively, the CS can be made more natural or salient by adding partial cues of a female (see Figure 4.1). Studies have shown that more vigorous sexually conditioned responding occurs to a CS object that includes some of the stimulus features of a female quail (Cusato & Domjan, 1998, 2000; Domjan, 1998).

CS-US Relevance, or Belongingness

Another variable that governs the rate of classical conditioning is the extent to which the CS is relevant to, or belongs with, the US. The importance of stimulus relevance was first clearly demonstrated in a classic experiment by Garcia and Koelling (1966). The investigators compared learning about peripheral pain (induced by footshock) and learning about illness (induced by irradiation or a drug injection) in a study conducted with laboratory rats.

In their natural environment, rats are likely to get sick after eating a poisonous food. In contrast, they are likely to encounter peripheral pain after being chased and bitten by a predator that they can hear and see. To represent food-related cues, Garcia and Koelling used a flavored solution of water as the CS; to represent predator-related cues, they used an audiovisual CS.

The experiment, diagrammed in Figure 4.2, involved having the rats drink from a drinking tube before administration of one of the unconditioned stimuli. The drinking tube was filled with water flavored either salty or sweet. In addition, each lick on the tube activated a brief audiovisual stimulus (the click of a relay and a flash of light). Thus, the rats encountered the taste and audiovisual stimuli at the same time. After exposure to these conditioned stimuli, the animals either received a brief shock through the grid floor or were made sick.

Because the unconditioned stimuli used were aversive, the rats were expected to learn an aversion of some kind. The investigators measured the response of the animals to the taste and audiovisual CSs presented individually after conditioning. During tests of the taste CS, the water was flavored as before, but now licks did not activate the audiovisual cue. During tests of the audiovisual CS, the water was unflavored, but the audiovisual cue was briefly turned on each time the animal licked the spout. The degree of conditioned aversion to the taste or audiovisual CS was inferred from the suppression of drinking.

Figure 4.1 CS objects used as signals for copulatory opportunity in studies of sexual conditioning with male quail. The object on the left is "arbitrary" and made entirely of terrycloth. The object on the right includes limited female cues provided by the head and some neck feathers from a taxidermically prepared female bird. (From Cusato & Domjan, 1998.)

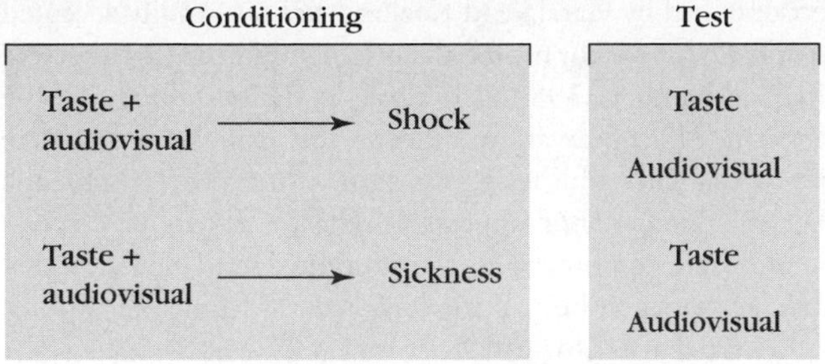

Figure 4.2 Diagram of Garcia and Koelling's (1966) experiment. A compound taste-audiovisual stimulus was first paired with either shock or sickness for separate groups of laboratory rats. The subjects were then tested with the taste and audiovisual stimuli separately.

The results of the experiment are summarized in Figure 4.3. Animals conditioned with shock subsequently suppressed their drinking much more when tested with the audiovisual stimulus than when tested with the taste CS. The opposite result occurred for animals that had been conditioned with sickness—these rats suppressed their drinking much more when the taste CS was presented than when drinking produced the audiovisual stimulus.

Garcia and Koelling's experiment demonstrates the principle of CS-US relevance, or belongingness. Learning depended on the relevance or appropriateness of the CS to the US that was administered. Taste became readily associated with illness, and audiovisual cues became readily associated with peripheral pain. Rapid learning occurred only if the CS was combined with the appropriate US. The audiovisual CS was not generally more effective than the taste CS. Rather, the audiovisual CS was more effective only when shock served as the US. Correspondingly, the shock US was not generally more effective than the sickness US. Rather, shock conditioned stronger aversions than sickness only when the audiovisual cue served as the CS.

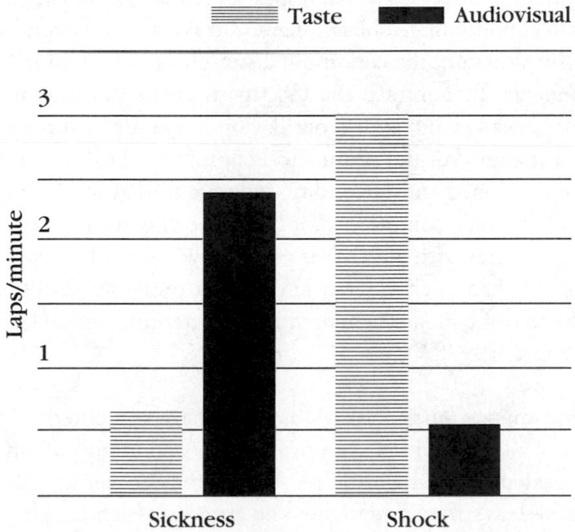

Figure 4.3 Results of Garcia and Koelling's (1966) experiment. Rats conditioned with sickness learned a stronger aversion to taste than to audiovisual cues. By contrast, rats conditioned with shock learned a stronger aversion to audiovisual than to taste cues. (Adapted from Garcia and Koelling, 1966.)

The CS-US relevance effect obtained by Garcia and Koelling was not readily accepted at first, but numerous subsequent studies have confirmed the original findings (for a review, see Domjan, 1983). Gemberling and Domjan (1982), for example, demonstrated that the effect occurs in rats 1 day after birth. This observation indicates that extensive experience with tastes and sickness (or audiovisual cues and peripheral pain) is not necessary for the stimulus relevance effect. Rather, the phenomenon appears to reflect a genetic predisposition for the selective association of certain combinations of conditioned and unconditioned stimuli. (For evidence of stimulus relevance in human food aversion learning, see Garb & Stunkard, 1974; Logue et al., 1981; Pelchat & Rozin, 1982).

Stimulus relevance effects have also been documented in other situations. For example, LoLordo and his associates investigated how pigeons learn about food as compared with peripheral pain. They found that pigeons associate visual cues with food much more easily than they associate auditory cues with food. By contrast, if the conditioning situation involves shock, auditory cues are more effective as the CS than are visual cues. These results suggest that, for pigeons, visual cues are relevant to feeding and auditory cues are relevant to defensive behavior (see LoLordo, Jacobs, & Foree, 1982; Kelly, 1986; Shapiro, Jacobs, & LoLordo, 1980; Shapiro & LoLordo, 1982).

Stimulus relevance effects are also evident in the acquisition of fear. Rhesus monkeys can become fearful of a live snake or a toy snake as a result of observing another monkey react with fear to the snakes. Cook and Mineka (1990) found that observational learning of fear was more likely if the demonstrator showed fear of a toy snake than if the demonstrator acted fearfully in the presence of artificial flowers. However, the artificial flower CS was just as effective as the toy snake in a learning task involving food. Thus, monkeys seem to be predisposed to learn to fear snakes.

People also exhibit stimulus selectivity in their learning of fear. They are more likely to report being afraid of snakes and spiders than of electric outlets or hammers that can also inflict severe pain (Seligman, 1971). Laboratory studies have shown that human participants associate pictures of snakes and spiders with shock more readily than pictures of flowers and houses (Öhman, Dimberg, & Öst, 1985). The mechanisms of these selective learning effects remain the subject of lively debate (Davey, 1995).

The Concept of Biological Strength

In all the examples of classical conditioning discussed so far, responses to the CS were not as strong as responses to the US prior to conditioning. The familiar example of salivary conditioning is a good case in point. In this situation, the conditioned stimulus (a tone) initially elicits only weak orientation movements. By contrast, the US (food) elicits vigorous approach, ingestion, salivation, chewing, swallowing, and so on. Pavlov was aware of this significant difference in the "biological strength" of the stimuli and considered the difference necessary for their effectiveness as conditioned and unconditioned stimuli (Pavlov, 1927). Pavlov suggested that for a stimulus to become conditioned, it had to be of weaker biological strength than the unconditioned stimulus with which it is paired. By "weaker biological strength," he meant that the CS initially had to elicit fewer and weaker responses than the US. (For a recent examination of the role of biological strength in the determination of CSs and USs, see Gunther, Miller, & Matute, 1997.)

Higher-Order Conditioning. One implication of Pavlov's biological strength criterion is that a stimulus may serve in the role of a US after it has become strongly conditioned. Consider, for example, a tone that is repeatedly paired with food. After sufficient pairings, the tone will come to elicit salivation, as well as strong orientation and approach (sign tracking)

BOX 4.1

BEHAVIORAL APPROACHES TO THE CONTROL OF SMOKING

A variety of aversion conditioning procedures have been developed to discourage cigarette smoking (Hall, Hall, & Ginsberg, 1990). Early efforts involved aversion therapy in which smoking was paired with pain induced by electric shock. More recent techniques have been based on findings indicating that the aversion conditioning is more effective if the aversive stimulus is "relevant" to the situation. In these procedures, cigarette smoking itself is used to provide the aversive stimulus. A frequently employed procedure is *rapid smoking* (USDHHS, 1996), which requires the subject to inhale every 6 seconds either for a fixed period or until nausea or dizziness develops. Such rapid smoking is aversive and serves to condition an aversion to smoking.

Aversion conditioning procedures are most effective in discouraging smoking when they are combined with other behavior modification techniques. Rapid smoking, for example, may be effectively combined with training in self-monitoring and self-management procedures. Individuals are first required to maintain an accurate record of the number of cigarettes they smoke, and the time, place, and circumstances of the smoking. Once the frequency and circumstances of a person's usual smoking behavior are known, two objectives are introduced with the goal of gradually reducing smoking: to reduce the total number of cigarettes smoked each day, and to reduce the number of situations in which the person is allowed to smoke. These objectives serve in combination to restrict smoking behavior. Compliance can be encouraged by setting up a contract system. For example, the person may deposit a sizable sum of money at the start of treatment and receive portions of this deposit back each time a specified objective is met.

responses. According to the concept of biological strength, at this point the tone should be effective in conditioning salivation to a novel light stimulus that does not initially elicit strong responses. Pairings of the previously conditioned tone with the novel light should gradually result in the conditioning of salivation to the light. Indeed, this effect is often observed and is called **higher-order conditioning**. Figure 4.4 summarizes the sequence of events that brings about higher-order conditioning.

As the term *higher order* implies, conditioning may be considered to operate at different levels. In the preceding example, pairings of the tone with food is considered *first-order conditioning.* Pairings of the light with the previously conditioned tone is considered *second-order conditioning.* If after becoming conditioned, the light were used to condition yet another stimulus—say, an odor—that would be *third-order conditioning.*

The procedure for second-order conditioning shown in Figure 4.4 is similar to the standard procedure for inhibitory conditioning described in Chapter 3 (see Figure 3.10). In both cases, one conditioned stimulus (CS_1 or the CS^+) is paired with the US ($CS_1 \rightarrow$ US or $CS^+ \rightarrow$ US), and a second CS (CS_2 or CS^-) is paired with the first one without the unconditioned stimulus ($CS_1/CS_2 \rightarrow$ noUS or $CS^+/CS^- \rightarrow$ noUS). Why does such a procedure produce conditioned inhibition in some cases and excitatory second-order conditioning under other circumstances? The critical factor appears to be the number of noUS trials. With a few nonreinforced trials, second-order excitatory conditioning occurs. With extensive training, conditioned inhibition develops (Yin, Barnet, & Miller, 1994).

Although second-order conditioning is a well-known robust phenomenon (Rescorla, 1980a), little research has been done to evaluate the mechanisms of third- and higher orders

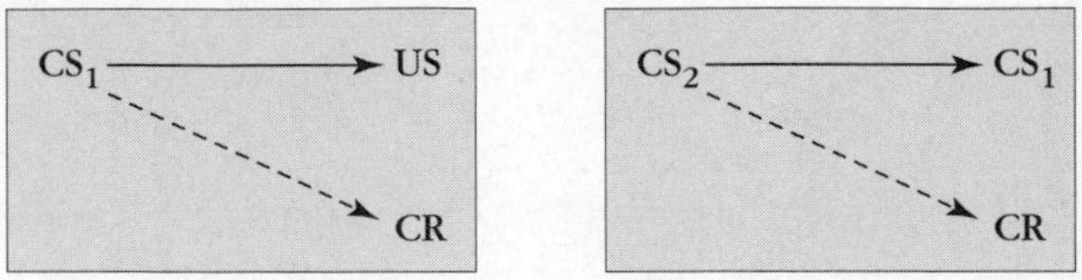

Figure 4.4 Procedure for higher-order conditioning. CS_1 is first paired with the US and comes to elicit the conditioned response. A new stimulus (CS_2) is then paired with CS_1 and also comes to elicit the conditioned response.

of conditioning. However, even the existence of second-order conditioning is of considerable significance because it greatly increases the range of situations in which classical conditioning can take place. With higher-order conditioning, classical conditioning can occur without a primary unconditioned stimulus. The only requirement is that a previously conditioned stimulus be available.

Many instances of conditioning in human experience involve higher-order conditioning. For example, money is a powerful conditioned stimulus for human behavior because of its association with candy, toys, movies, and other things it can buy. A child may become fond of his uncle if the uncle gives him some money on each visit. The positive conditioned emotional response to the uncle develops because the child comes to associate the uncle with money, in a case of second-order conditioning.

Second-order conditioning is also of interest as a technique for confirming the occurrence of first-order conditioning. Sometimes, first-order conditioning is not evident in a clear conditioned response even though the first-order CS can support second-order conditioning (Barnet, Arnold, & Miller, 1991; Bevins, Delzer, & Bardo, 1996; Cole & Miller, 1999).

Counterconditioning. Many instances of association learning, including higher-order conditioning, satisfy the criterion of differential biological strength. However, this criterion is not met in all situations that permit the learning of associations between stimuli. In **counterconditioning,** two stimuli can become associated with each other even though both elicit strong responses initially. The response an animal makes to a CS is reversed, or "countered," by pairing this stimulus with a US that promotes the opposite type of reaction.

In one study of counterconditioning (Pearce & Dickinson, 1975), the aversive properties of brief shock were reduced or reversed by pairing the shock with food. In the first phase of the experiment, rats in the counterconditioned group received shock periodically, but each shock delivery ended in a food pellet. Animals in control groups received the shocks and food pellets unpaired, or they received only one or the other of the USs. How these treatments changed the aversiveness of shock was then measured by using the shock in a conditioned-suppression procedure. As expected, the animals that previously had shock paired with food showed less conditioned suppression than the control groups. This result indicates that the counterconditioning procedure had reduced the aversive properties of the shock. (For other examples of counterconditioning, see Dickinson & Dearing, 1979.)

Sensory Preconditioning. Associations can also be learned between two stimuli, each of which elicits only a mild orienting response before conditioning. Consider, for example, the flavors vanilla and cinnamon that you often encounter together in pastry without ill effects. Because of these pairings, the vanilla and cinnamon flavors may become associated with one another. What would happen if you then acquired an aversion to cinnamon through food

BOX 4.2

HIGHER-ORDER CONDITIONING OF FEAR

Irrational fears sometimes develop through higher-order conditioning. For example, Wolpe (1990) describes the case of a woman who initially developed a fear of crowds. How this fear had been originally conditioned is unknown, but crowds had become fear-eliciting stimuli. To avoid arousing her fear, the woman would go to the movies only in the daytime when few people were present. On one such visit, the theater suddenly became crowded with students. The woman became extremely upset by this, and came to associate movie houses with crowds. Thus, one fear-conditioned stimulus (crowds) had conditioned fear to other stimuli (movie houses) that previously were innocuous, as in higher-order conditioning. The remarkable aspect of this experience was that an aversion became conditioned to movie-house stimuli even though those cues had not been directly paired with an aversive unconditioned stimulus.

After her frightening experience in the movie house, the woman avoided going to the movies even when she was unlikely to encounter many other people there. Furthermore, her newly acquired fear of movie houses generalized to other public places, such as restaurants, churches, and public buildings. She also avoided these, even if they were empty.

poisoning or illness? Chances are your acquired aversion to cinnamon would also lead you to now reject foods with the taste of vanilla because of the prior association of vanilla with cinnamon. This is an example of **sensory preconditioning.**

The basic procedure for sensory preconditioning is diagrammed in Figure 4.5. In a sensory preconditioning experiment, subjects first receive repeated pairings of two biologically weak stimuli or CSs. The stimuli may be two visual cues—a triangle △ and a square □, for example. No response conditioning is evident in this phase of training. Neither the triangle △ nor the square □ comes to elicit a conditioned response. Conditioned behavior is acquired in the second phase of the experiment, in which the triangle △ is now paired with an unconditioned stimulus, such as shock. With shock as the US, a conditioned fear response comes to be elicited by the triangle △.

Once the triangle △ has come to elicit conditioned fear, an interesting thing happens: the square □ now also elicits this response because of its prior association with the triangle △. Thus, the square □ comes to elicit conditioned fear not because of its own pairings with shock but because its associated stimulus (the triangle △) became paired with shock. The

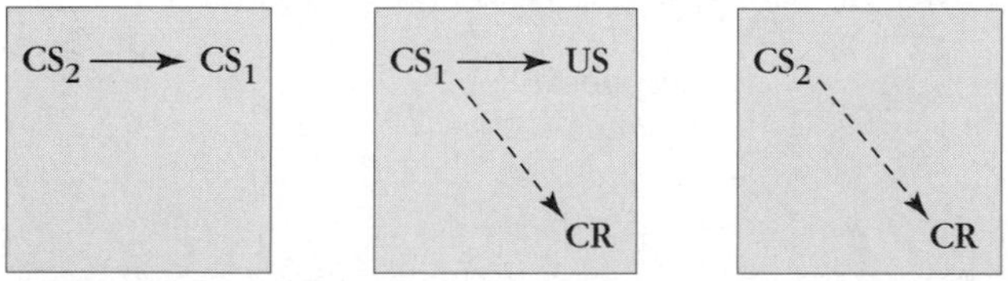

Figure 4.5 Procedure for sensory preconditioning. First, CS_2 is paired with CS_1 without a US in the situation. Then, CS_1 is paired with a US and comes to elicit a conditioned response (CR). In a later test session, CS_2 is also found to elicit the CR, even though CS_2 was never paired with the US.

association of the two innocuous visual cues with each other becomes evident when one of the stimuli is later conditioned to elicit a vigorous response. (For additional examples of sensory preconditioning, see Berridge & Schulkin, 1989; Lavin, 1976; Rescorla & Durlach, 1981; Ward-Robinson & Hall, 1996, 1998.)

WHAT DETERMINES THE NATURE OF THE CONDITIONED RESPONSE?

In this chapter and in Chapter 3, I describe numerous examples of classical conditioning. In each of these examples, conditioning is identified by the development of new responses to the conditioned stimulus. I describe a variety of responses that can become conditioned, including salivation, eyeblinking, fear, locomotor approach and withdrawal, and aversion responses. I now address why one set of responses becomes conditioned in one situation and other responses are learned in other circumstances.

The Stimulus Substitution Model

The first and most enduring explanation for the nature of the conditioned response (CR) is Pavlov's **stimulus substitution** model. According to this model, the association of the CS with the US turns the CS into a surrogate US. The CS comes to function much like the US did previously. Thus, the CS is assumed to activate neural circuits previously activated only by the US and to elicit responses similar to the US.

Pavlov suggested that conditioning results in the establishment of new functional neural pathways (see Figure 4.6). During the course of repeated pairings of the conditioned and unconditioned stimuli, a new connection develops between the neural circuits previously activated by the CS and the circuits previously activated only by the US. Once this new connection has been established, presentation of the CS results in activation of the US circuits, which in turn generate the unconditioned response. Therefore, according to Pavlov's model, conditioning enables the CS to elicit the unconditioned response. The CS becomes a *substitute* for the US.

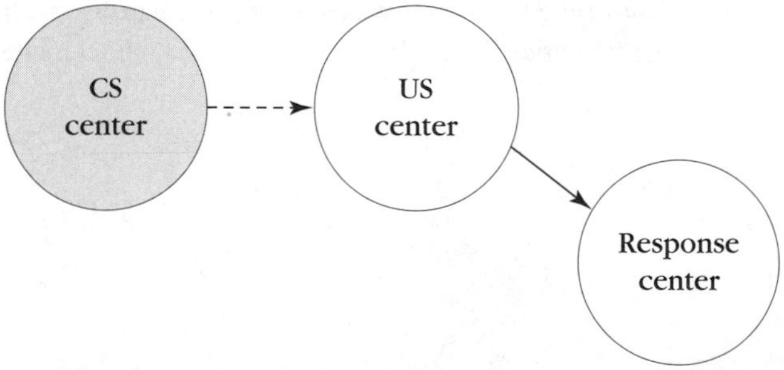

Figure 4.6 Diagram of Pavlov's stimulus substitution model. The solid arrow indicates preexisting neural connection. The dashed arrow indicates a learned neural connection. The CS comes to elicit a response by activating neural structures previously activated only by the US. Because of this, as conditioning progresses, the CS comes to elicit a response similar to the response to the US.

The US as a Determining Factor for the CR. Different unconditioned stimuli elicit different unconditioned responses. Food elicits salivation and approach; shock elicits aversion and withdrawal. If conditioning turns a CS into a surrogate US, CSs conditioned with different USs should elicit different types of conditioned responses. This is obviously true. Animals learn to salivate when conditioned with food and to blink when conditioned with a puff of air to the eye. Salivation is not conditioned in eyeblink conditioning experiments, and eyeblink responses are not conditioned in salivary conditioning experiments.

Evidence that the nature of the conditioned response depends on the US is also available from more subtle comparisons. In one famous experiment, Jenkins and Moore (1973) compared Pavlovian conditioning in pigeons with food versus water as the US. A pigeon eating grain makes rapid, hard pecking movements directed at the grain with its beak open just before contact with the piece of grain. (The beak opening is related to the size of the grain about to be pecked.) By contrast, a pigeon drinks by lowering its beak into the water with the beak mostly closed. Once its beak is underwater, the bird opens it periodically to suck up the water (Klein, LaMon, & Zeigler, 1983). Thus, the unconditioned responses of eating and drinking differ in both speed and form. Jenkins and Moore (1973) were interested in whether responses conditioned with food and water would differ in a corresponding fashion.

The CS was illumination of a pecking key for 8 seconds. The CS was paired with either the presentation of grain or the access to water. Conditioning resulted in pecking of the key light in both cases. However, the form of the conditioned response differed depending on the US. When food was the US, the pigeons pecked the response key as if eating: the pecks were rapid, with the beak open at the moment of contact. With water as the US, the pecking movements were slower, made with the beak closed, and were often accompanied by swallowing. Thus, the form of the conditioned response resembled the form of the unconditioned response. Eating-like pecks occurred to the food-conditioned CS, and drinking-like responses occurred to the water-conditioned CS (see also Allan & Zeigler, 1994; Ploog & Zeigler, 1996; Ploog, 2001; Spetch, Wilkie, & Skelton, 1981; Stanhope, 1992). Similar findings have been obtained with food pellets and milk as unconditioned stimuli with laboratory rats (Davey & Cleland, 1982; Davey, Phillips, & Cleland, 1981).

Learning and Homeostasis: A Special Case of Stimulus Substitution

Proper functioning of the body requires that certain physiological parameters such as blood sugar, blood oxygen, and temperature be maintained within acceptable limits. For example, having a body temperature of 98.6 °F is so critical that substantial deviations from that value are considered symptoms of illness. The concept of **homeostasis** was introduced by Water Cannon to refer to physiological mechanisms that serve to maintain critical aspects of the body within acceptable limits.

How is a desired or homeostatic level achieved and defended against challenges? I described the concept of homeostasis in discussions of the opponent-process theory of motivation in Chapter 2. As I noted, maintaining any system within a desirable range requires that a disturbance that moves the system in one direction be met by opponent processes that counteract the disturbance. Thus, achieving homeostasis requires that a challenge to the homeostatic level trigger a compensatory reaction that will neutralize the disturbance. Consider, for example, homeostatic mechanisms of temperature regulation. In warm-blooded animals, any lowering of body temperature caused by exposure to cold reflexively triggers compensatory reactions that help to conserve and increase temperature. These compensatory reactions include peripheral vasoconstriction and shivering. The system operates through a *negative feedback loop*. A drop in body temperature is detected and this serves as a stimulus to activate compensatory responses.

Water Cannon lived from 1871 to 1945 and met Pavlov in 1923 when Pavlov visited the United States. They had considerable respect for each other's work, but it wasn't until more than half a century after both of them had died that Cannon's concept of homeostasis became integrated with studies of Pavlovian conditioning (Dworkin, 1993). Homeostatic mechanisms, as conceived by Cannon, operated by negative feedback processes that served to counteract a challenge after the disturbance had already caused a deviation from the homeostatic level. This can be rather inefficient, particularly if the corrective or compensatory process is slow to become activated. Dworkin (1993) pointed out that challenges to homeostasis can be met more effectively if those challenges are anticipated. Pavlovian conditioning provides the means for such feed-forward anticipation.

Consider, for example, exposure to cold. Feedback processes require that a drop in body temperature occur before compensatory shivering and vasoconstriction will occur to counteract the cold. However, if subjects can learn the cues that signal when they will get cold, they can make feed-forward compensatory adjustments in anticipation of the cold and thereby avoid suffering a drop in body temperature (Riccio, MacArdy, & Kissinger, 1991). According to this view, the conditioned response to a physiological challenge is the same as the reflexive compensatory response to the challenge. Thus, the conditioned response is the same as the unconditioned response, but the unconditioned response is considered to be the compensatory reaction to the physiological disturbance.

Conditioned homeostatic responses have been examined most extensively in studies of how organisms respond to the administration of a psychoactive drug (Poulos & Cappell, 1991; Ramsey & Woods, 1997; Siegel & Allan, 1998). (For studies of conditioned homeostatic mechanisms in color perception, see Siegel and Allan, 1998; for studies of Pavlovian feed-forward mechanisms in the control of social behavior, see Domjan, Cusato, & Villarreal, 2000.) Drugs often cause physiological challenges to homeostasis that trigger unconditioned compensatory reactions. Cues that become associated with the drug-induced physiological challenge can come to elicit these compensatory reactions as anticipatory or feed-forward conditioned responses. Drug craving in habitual drug users, for example, is a manifestation of these drug anticipatory conditioned responses.

Courtesy of Donald A. Dewsbury

S. Seigel

It has been recognized for a long time that the administration of a drug constitutes a conditioning trial in which cues related to drug administration are paired with the pharmacological effects of the drug. Caffeine, for example, is a commonly used drug, whose pharmacological effects are typically preceded by the smell and taste of coffee. Thus, the taste and smell of coffee can serve as a conditioned stimulus that is predictive of the physiological effects of caffeine (for example, Flaten & Blumenthal, 1999). Studies of drug conditioning have been conducted with a wide range of pharmacological agents, including alcohol, heroin, morphine, and cocaine, and there has been considerable interest in how Pavlovian conditioning may contribute to drug tolerance, drug craving, and drug addiction (Baker & Tiffany, 1985; Cunningham, 1998; Siegel, 1983, 1989, 1999; Siegel, Baptista, Kim, McDonald, & Weise-Kelly, 2000).

Studies of drug conditioning have been conducted with both human and nonhuman animals and in laboratory and field settings. For example, in a study of naturally acquired drug-conditioned responses, Ehrman, Robbins, Childress, and O'Brien (1992) tested men with a history of freebasing and smoking cocaine (but no history of heroin use). A control group that had never used cocaine or heroin also provided data. The participants were observed under three test conditions. In one test, cues related to cocaine use were presented. The participants listened to an audiotape of people talking about their experiences freebasing and smoking cocaine, watched a videotape of people buying and using cocaine, and were asked to go through the motions of freebasing and smoking. In another test, cues related to heroin use were presented in the same manner as the cocaine stimuli. In the third test, control stimuli unrelated to drug use were presented. During each test, both physiological responses and self-reports of feelings were recorded.

Both the physiological measures and the self-reports of mood provided evidence that cocaine-related stimuli elicited conditioned responses. Figure 4.7 shows the results of measures of heart rate. Cocaine users exposed to cocaine-related stimuli experienced a significant increase in heart rate during the test. Furthermore, this increased heart rate response was specific to the cocaine-related stimuli. The heart rate of cocaine users did not change in response to heroin-related stimuli or nondrug stimuli. The increased heart rate response was also specific to the cocaine users. Participants in the control group did not show elevations in heart rate in any of the tests.

Participants with a history of cocaine use also reported feelings of cocaine craving and withdrawal elicited by the cocaine-related stimuli. They did not report these emotions in response to either the heroin-related or the nondrug stimuli. Feelings of cocaine craving and withdrawal were also not reported by participants in the control group. Thus, the results suggest that cocaine users acquired both physiological and emotional conditioned responses to cocaine-related stimuli during the course of their drug use.

The Conditioning Model of Drug Tolerance. The role of Pavlovian conditioning has been examined perhaps most extensively in relation to the development of **drug tolerance.** Tolerance to a drug is said to develop when repeated administrations of the drug have progressively less effect. Increasing doses are then required to produce the same drug effect. Drug tolerance has traditionally been considered to result from pharmacological processes. In contrast to this traditional approach, Shepard Siegel has proposed a model of drug tolerance based on classical conditioning.

The conditioning model takes advantage of the concepts of learned homeostasis. According to these concepts, the administration of a psychoactive drug causes physiological changes that disrupt homeostasis. Those physiological changes constitute the unconditioned stimulus that in turn triggers unconditioned compensatory adjustments to counteract the disturbance. These reflexive compensatory adjustments are the unconditioned

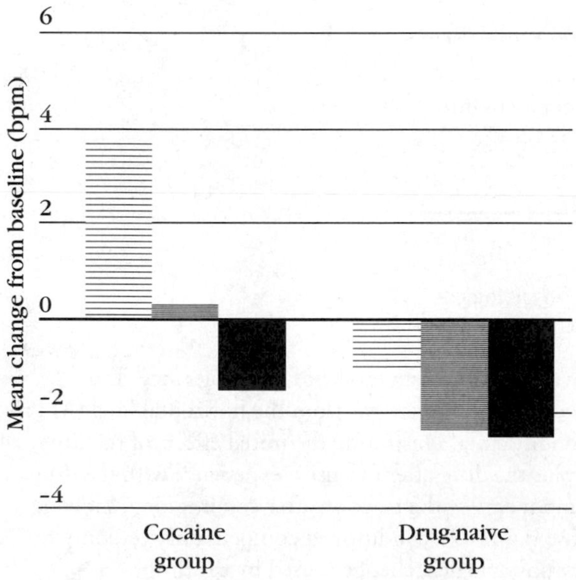

Figure 4.7 Mean change in heart rate from baseline levels for men with a history of cocaine use and a drug-naive control group during tests involving exposure to cocaine-related stimuli (light bars), heroin-related stimuli (medium bars), or nondrug stimuli (dark bars). (From "Conditioned Responses to Cocaine-Related Stimuli in Cocaine Abuse Patients," by R. N. Ehrman, S. J. Robbins, A. R. Childress, and C. P. O'Brien, 1992, *Psychopharmacology, 107,* pp. 523–529. Copyright © 1992 by Springer-Verlag. Reprinted by permission.)

response to the drug US. Through Pavlovian conditioning, stimuli that accompany the drug administration become associated with the drug US. These conditioned stimuli might be the time of day, the sensations involved in preparing a syringe, or the distinctiveness of the place where the drug is usually taken. As a result of association with the drug US, the drug administration cues come to elicit the drug compensatory responses that were previously triggered as unconditioned responses to the homeostatic challenge, and thereby come to attenuate the drug effects that were observed initially. Because the conditioned responses counteract the drug effects, the reaction otherwise elicited by the drug is reduced, resulting in drug tolerance (see Figure 4.8).

The conditioning model of drug tolerance attributes tolerance to compensatory responses conditioned to environmental stimuli paired with drug administration. A key prediction of the model is that drug tolerance will be attenuated if subjects receive the drug under novel circumstances or in the absence of the usual drug-predictive cues. The model also predicts that various factors (such as CS preexposure) that attenuate the development of conditioned responding should also attenuate the development of drug tolerance. These and other predictions of the conditioning model have been confirmed by Siegel and his colleagues, as well as by numerous other investigative teams in laboratory studies with opiates (morphine and heroin), alcohol, scopolamine, benzodiazepines, and amphetamine (see reviews by Siegel, 1989, 1999; Siegel & Allan, 1998; Stewart & Eikelboom, 1987).

When the conditioning model of drug tolerance was originally formulated, the assumption was that all drug-conditioned responses would be opposite the direct effects of the drug. However, as Siegel (1999) himself has acknowledged, this was an oversimplification. In the recently revised model (for example, Ramsey & Woods, 1997; Siegel, 1999), the initial effect of the drug is viewed as an unconditioned stimulus that triggers homeostatic compensatory reactions. The CS comes to elicit these compensatory URs. An important

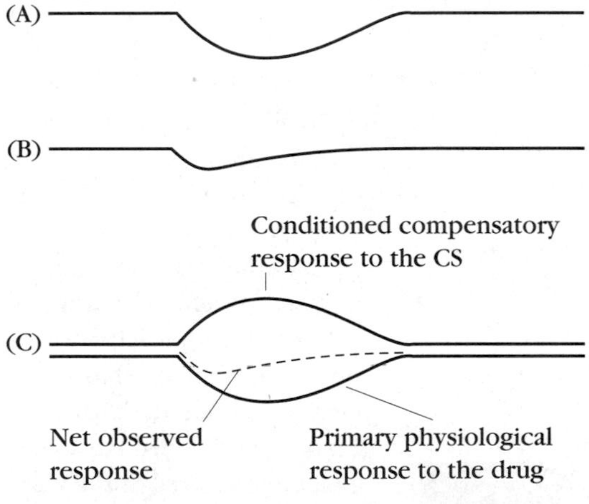

Figure 4.8 Diagram of the Pavlovian conditioning model of drug tolerance. The strength of the drug reaction is represented by deviations from the horizontal line. (A) Primary reaction to the drug before conditioning, illustrating the initial effects of the drug. (B) Attenuated reaction to the CS plus the drug after extensive experience with the drug, illustrating drug tolerance. (C) Components of the reaction after conditioning, showing that the net attenuated drug response is due to a conditioned compensatory response to the CS that counteracts the primary physiological change caused by the drug.

prediction of this view is that conditioned compensatory responses will develop only for physiological systems that are homeostatically controlled. Compensatory conditioned responses are not predicted in situations that lack homeostatic unconditioned responses.

The CS as a Determinant of the Form of the CR

The discussion thus far has considered how the form of the conditioned response is determined by the unconditioned stimulus. However, the US is not the only important factor. The form of the CR is also influenced by the nature of the CS. This was first illustrated by a rather unusual experiment by Timberlake and Grant (1975).

Timberlake and Grant investigated classical conditioning in rats with food as the US. Instead of a conventional light or tone, the CS was the presentation of another rat just before food delivery. One side of the experimental chamber was equipped with a sliding platform that could be moved in and out of the chamber through a flap door (see Figure 4.9). A live rat was gently restrained on the platform. Ten seconds before each delivery of food, the platform was moved into the experimental chamber, thereby transporting the stimulus rat through the flap door.

The stimulus-substitution model predicts that CS-US pairings will generate responses to the CS that are similar to responses elicited by the food US. Since the food US elicited gnawing and biting, these responses were also expected to be elicited by the CS. Contrary to prediction, the CS did not elicit gnawing and biting. Instead, as the CS rat was repeatedly paired with food, it came to elicit orientation, approach, and sniffing movements, as well as social contacts. Such responses did not develop if the CS rat was not paired with food or was presented at times unrelated to food.

The outcome of this experiment does not support any model that explains the form of the conditioned response solely in terms of the unconditioned stimulus that is used. The pattern of conditioned responses, particularly the social behavior elicited by the CS rat, was no doubt determined by the nature of the CS (see also Timberlake, 1983a). Other kinds of food-conditioned stimuli elicit different conditioned responses. For example, Peterson, Ackil, Frommer, and Hearst (1972) inserted an illuminated response lever into the experimental chamber immediately before presenting food to rats. With the protruding metal lever as the CS, the conditioned responses were "almost exclusively oral and consisted

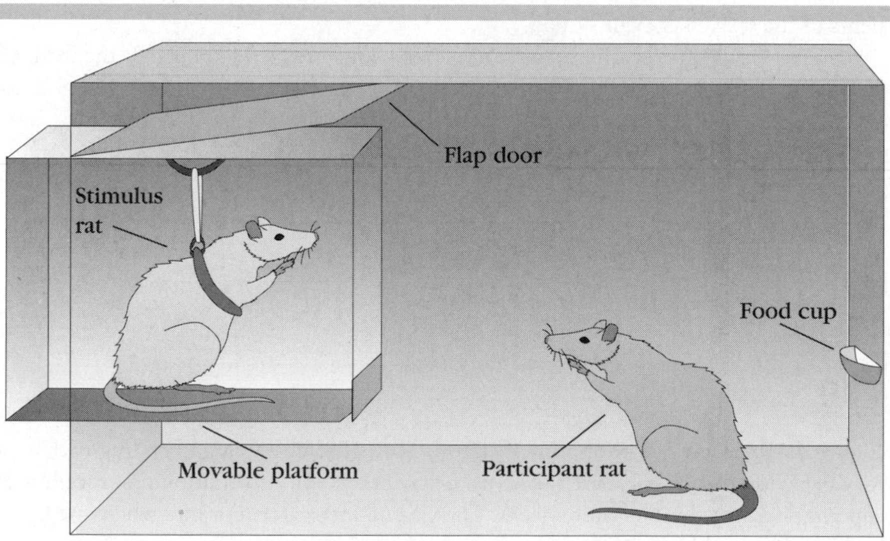

Figure 4.9 Diagram of the experiment by Timberlake and Grant (1975). The CS for food is presentation of a stimulus rat on a movable platform through a flap door on one side of the experimental chamber.

mainly of licking . . . and gnawing" (p. 1010). (For other investigations of how the CS determines the nature of the conditioned response, see Akins, 2000; Cusato & Domjan, 1998, 2000; Holland, 1977, 1980, 1984; Kim, Rivers, Bevins, & Ayres, 1996; Sigmundi & Bolles, 1983).

Conditioned Behavior and Behavior Systems

The approaches to the form of the conditioned response I have discussed so far have their intellectual roots in Pavlov's physiological model systems method for the study of learning. In this method, one or two responses are isolated for investigation and are used as indices of associative learning. This method continues to provide rich dividends in new knowledge, but it is becoming evident that complete understanding of the nature of conditioned behavior will require a broader perspective. Holland (1984), for example, has commented that the understanding of conditioned behavior will ultimately require "knowledge of the normal functions of behavior systems engaged by the various CSs, the natural, unlearned organization within those systems, and the ontogeny of those systems" (p. 164).

Different systems of behavior have evolved to enable animals to accomplish various critical tasks such as procuring and eating food, defending a territory, avoiding predation, producing and raising offspring, and so on. As I discussed in Chapter 2, each behavior system consists of a series of response modes, each with its own controlling stimuli and responses, arranged spatially and/or temporally. Consider, for example, the sexual behavior of male quail. When sexually motivated, the male will engage in a general search response to bring him into the vicinity of a female. Once there, he will engage in a more focal search response to actually locate her. Having found her, the male will then engage in courtship and copulatory responses. This sequence is illustrated in Figure 4.10.

Behavior systems theory assumes that the presentation of a US in a Pavlovian conditioning procedure activates the behavior system relevant to that US. Food unconditioned stimuli activate the foraging and feeding system. A sexual US, by contrast, will activate the sexual behavior system. Classical conditioning procedures involve superimposing a CS-US relationship on the behavioral system activated by the US. As a conditioned stimulus becomes associated with the US, it becomes integrated into the behavior system and comes to elicit component responses of that system. Thus, food-conditioned stimuli come to elicit components of the feeding system, and sexual conditioned stimuli come to elicit components of the sexual behavior system.

An especially provocative prediction of behavior systems theory is that the form of the CR will depend on the CS-US interval that is used. The CS-US interval is assumed to

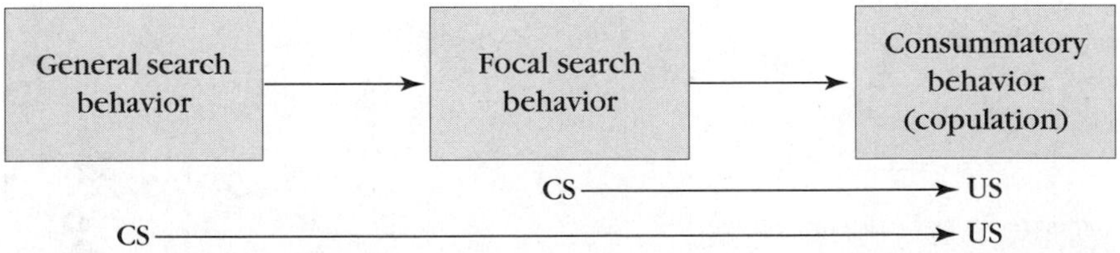

Figure 4.10 Sequence of responses, starting with general search and ending with copulatory behavior, that characterize the sexual behavior system. A conditioning procedure is superimposed on this behavior system. The CS-US interval determines where the CS becomes incorporated into the behavioral sequence.

determine where the CS becomes incorporated into the sequence of responses that makes up the behavior system.

Consider what might happen if a Pavlovian conditioning procedure were superimposed on the sexual behavior system. In the sexual conditioning of male quail, access to a female is the US. Access to the female activates the courtship and copulatory responses that characterize the end of the sexual behavior sequence. With a short CS-US interval, the CS occurs shortly before access to the female. If the CS becomes incorporated into the behavior system at this point, the CS should elicit focal search behavior: the male should approach and remain near the CS. The CR should be different if a long CS-US interval is used. In this case (see Figure 4.10), the CS should become incorporated into an earlier portion of the behavior system and elicit general search rather than focal search behavior. General search behavior should be manifest in increased nondirected locomotor behavior.

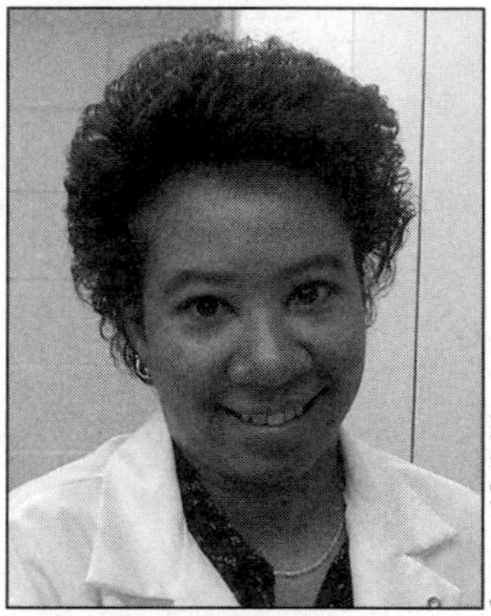

C. K. Akins

These predictions were recently tested in an experiment conducted with domesticated quail (Akins, 2000). Akins used a large rectangular experimental chamber. During each conditioning trial, a small visual CS was presented at one end either 1 minute before the male birds received access to a female or 20 minutes before the release of the female. Control groups were exposed to the CS and US in an unpaired fashion. To detect focal search behavior, Akins measured how much time the males spent close to the conditioned stimulus. To detect general search behavior, she measured pacing between one half of the experimental chamber and the other.

The results of the focal search and general search CR measures are presented in Figure 4.11. With a 1-minute CS-US interval, the conditioning procedure produced significant focal search but not general search behavior. In contrast, with the 20-minute CS-US interval, conditioning produced significant general search but not focal search responding. These results are precisely what is predicted by behavior systems theory. According to the theory,

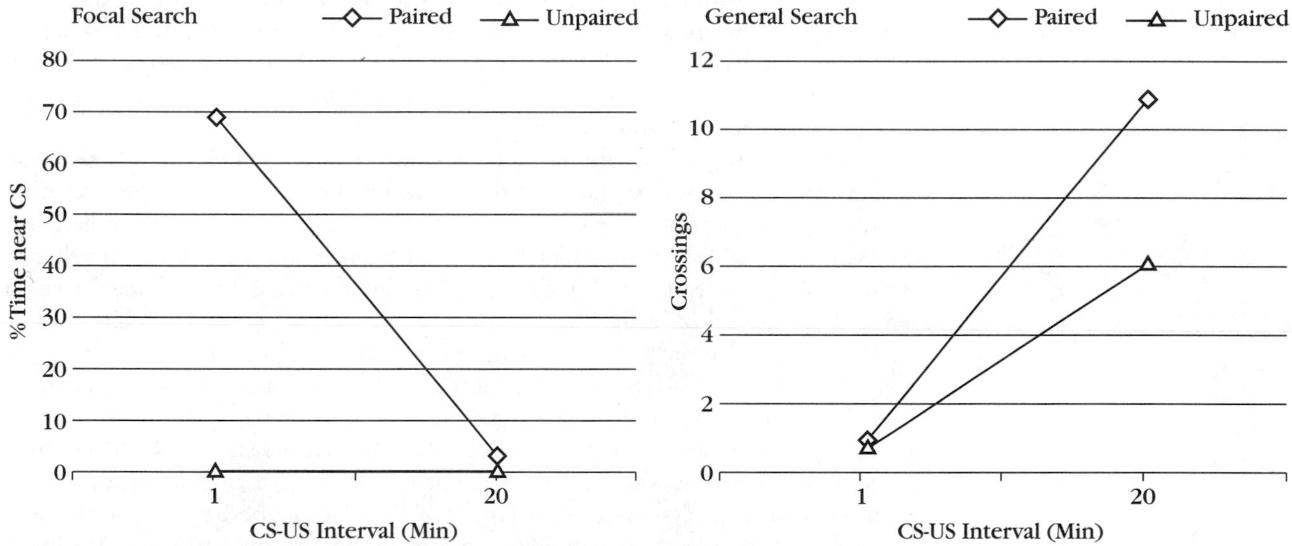

Figure 4.11 Effects of the CS-US interval on the conditioning of focal search and general search responses in male domesticated quail. When the CS-US interval was 1 minute, conditioning resulted in increased focal search behavior. When the CS-US interval was 20 minutes, conditioning resulted in increased general search behavior. (Adapted from Akins, 2000.)

the CS does not come to either substitute for or compensate for the US. Rather, the CS comes to substitute for a stimulus in the behavior system at a point that is determined by the CS-US interval. (For related studies, see Akins, Domjan, & Gutiérrez, 1994; Silva & Timberlake, 1997).

Behavior systems theory has been developed most extensively by William Timberlake (Timberlake, 1983a, 1983b, 2001; Timberlake & Lucas, 1989) and is consistent with much of what is known about the nature of classically conditioned behavioral responses. The theory is clearly consistent with the fact that the form of conditioned responses is determined by (1) the nature of the US, since different unconditioned stimuli activate different behavior systems; and (2) the nature of the conditioned stimulus. Certain types of stimuli are more effective than others in eliciting particular component responses of a behavior system. Therefore, the nature of the CS is expected to determine how the CS becomes incorporated into the behavior system (for example, Cusato & Domjan, 1998). Finally, behavior systems theory makes unique predictions about differences in conditioned behavior as a function of the CS-US interval.

S-R versus S-S Learning

I turn now to how a CS produces responding. Historically, conditioned behavior was viewed as a response elicited directly by the CS. According to **S-R learning,** conditioning establishes a new *stimulus-response* or S-R connection between the CS and the CR. A more contemporary alternative view is that subjects learn a new *stimulus-stimulus* or S-S connection between the CS and the US. According to the **S-S learning** view, subjects respond to the CS not because it elicits a CR directly but because the CS activates a representation of the US. In a sense, presentation of the CS makes the subject "think about" the US—these thoughts cause the conditioned behavior. Conditioned behavior is assumed to reflect the status of the US representation activated by the CS.

How might investigators decide between these two interpretations? One important research method used to decide between S-R and S-S learning involves the technique of **US devaluation,** which has been applied to a variety of issues in behavior theory. (I will describe applications of it in instrumental conditioning in Chapter 7.) Therefore, it is important to understand its rationale.

The basic strategy of a US devaluation experiment is illustrated in Figure 4.12. Holland and Rescorla (1975a), for example, first conditioned two groups of mildly food-deprived rats by repeatedly pairing a tone with pellets of food. This initial phase of the experiment was assumed to establish an association between the tone CS and the food US, as well as to get the rats to form a representation of the food US. Conditioned responding was evident in increased activity elicited by the tone.

In the next phase of the experiment, the experimental group received a treatment designed to make the US less valuable to them. This US devaluation was accomplished by giving the subjects sufficient free food to satisfy their hunger completely. Food satiation presumably reduces the value of food and thus devalues the US representation. The deprivation state of the control group was not changed in Phase 2; therefore, the US representation was assumed to remain intact for the control group (see Figure 4.12). Both groups then received a series of test trials with the tone-conditioned stimulus. During these tests, the experimental group showed significantly less conditioned responding than the control group. These results are indicative of S-S learning rather than S-R learning.

If conditioning had established a new reflex connection between the CS and the CR (an S-R connection), the CR would have been elicited whenever the CS occurred. That did

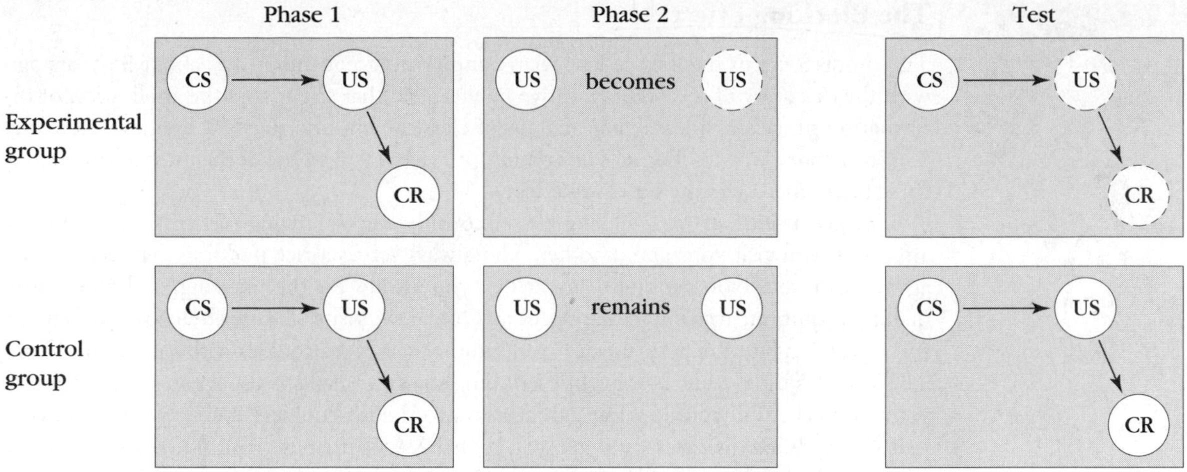

Figure 4.12 Basic strategy and rationale involved in US-devaluation experiments. In Phase 1 the experimental and control groups receive conventional conditioning to establish an association between the CS and the US and to lead the participants to form a representation of the US. In Phase 2 the US representation is devalued for the experimental group but remains unchanged for the control group. If the CR is elicited by way of the US representation, devaluation of the US representation should reduce responding to the CS.

not happen. Instead, conditioning resulted in an association between the CS and a representation of the US (S-S learning). Presentation of the CS activated the US representation, and the CR depended on the status of that US representation.

Evidence of S-S learning is available from a variety of classical conditioning situations (for example, Cleland & Davey, 1982; Colwill & Motzkin, 1994; Holland & Straub, 1979; Holloway & Domjan, 1993; Kraemer, Hoffmann, Randall, & Spear, 1992; Rescorla, 1973; Hilliard, Domjan, Nguyen, & Cusato, 1998). However, not all instances of classical conditioning involve S-S learning. Participants in some cases appear to learn a direct association between the CS and the CR. Evidence for S-R learning comes from studies of second-order conditioning (for example, Holland & Rescorla, 1975a, 1975b). However, some instances of second-order conditioning involve S-S learning (Rashotte, Griffin, & Sisk, 1977; Rescorla, 1982b).

HOW DO CONDITIONED AND UNCONDITIONED STIMULI BECOME ASSOCIATED?

The issue of how conditioned and unconditioned stimuli become associated is a critical one. What are the mechanisms of association learning—the underlying processes that are activated by conditioning procedures to produce learning? This question has been the subject of intense scholarly work. The evolution of theories of classical conditioning continues today, as investigators strive to formulate comprehensive accounts of the mechanisms of association learning that can embrace all the diverse research results. (For recent reviews, see Pearce & Bouton, 2001; Hall, 1994; Mowrer & Klein, 2001; Wasserman & Miller, 1997).

The Blocking Effect

The modern era in theories of Pavlovian conditioning got under way about 35 years ago with the discovery of several provocative phenomena that stimulated the application of information processing ideas to the analysis of classical conditioning (for example, Rescorla, 1967b, 1968b; Wagner, Logan, Haberlandt, & Price, 1968). One of the most prominent of these phenomena was the **blocking effect.**

A+ AX+ X → cr
prior learning of A w/US prevents learning of X w/US

To get a sense of the blocking effect, consider the following scenario: Each Sunday afternoon you visit your grandmother, who always serves a rice pudding that slightly disagrees with you. Not wanting to upset her, you always eat the pudding, and you consequently acquire an aversion to rice pudding. One of the visits falls on a holiday, and to make the occasion a bit more festive, your grandmother serves tea cookies with the rice pudding. This time, as usual, you eat some of everything she serves, and as usual you get a bit sick to your stomach. Will you now learn an aversion to the tea cookies? Probably not. Knowing that rice pudding disagrees with you, you probably will attribute your illness to the proven culprit and not learn to dislike the tea cookies.

The blocking effect involves a similar sequence of events. First, an association is established between one conditioned stimulus (stimulus A) and the US. Once CS_A is well conditioned, a second stimulus (stimulus B) is added to stimulus A during the conditioning trials. The basic finding is that prior conditioning of stimulus A interferes with or blocks the development of conditioned responding to the added stimulus B.

Courtesy of L. J. Kamin

L. J. Kamin

The blocking effect was initially investigated using the conditioned suppression technique with rats (Kamin, 1968, 1969). Subsequently, the phenomenon has been demonstrated in various other conditioning preparations with both human and nonhuman animals (for example, Giftakis & Tait, 1998; Goddard, 1996; Khallad & Moore, 1996; Oades, Roepcke, & Schepker, 1996; Roberts & Pearce, 1999; Symonds & Hall, 1997). The basic procedure involves three phases and employs two conditioned stimuli, such as a tone and a light. In Phase 1 (see Figure 4.13), the experimental group receives repeated pairings of one of the stimuli (A) with the US. This phase of training is continued until a strong conditioned response develops to stimulus A. In Phase 2, stimulus B is presented together with stimulus A and paired with the US. After several such conditioning trials, stimulus B is presented alone in a test trial to see if it also elicits the conditioned response. Interestingly, very little responding occurs to stimulus B even though B was repeatedly paired with the US during Phase 2.

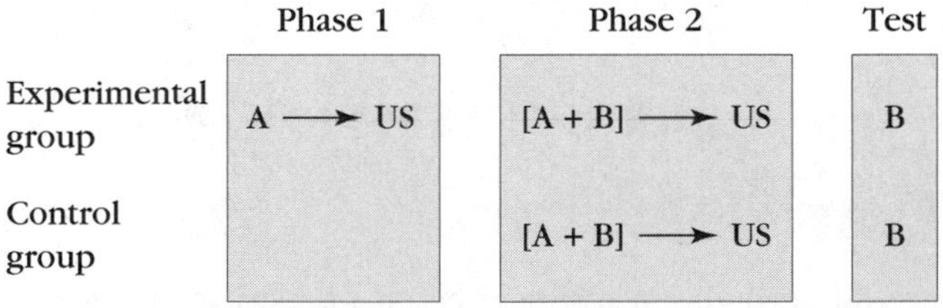

Figure 4.13 Diagram of the blocking procedure. During Phase 1, stimulus A is conditioned with the US in the experimental group, while the control group receives stimulus A presented unpaired with the US. During Phase 2, both experimental and control groups receive conditioning trials in which stimulus A is presented simultaneously with stimulus B and paired with the US. A later test of stimulus B alone shows that less conditioned responding occurs to stimulus B in the experimental group than in the control group.

BOX 4.3

THE PICTURE-WORD PROBLEM IN TEACHING READING: A FORM OF BLOCKING

Early instruction in reading often involves showing children a written word, along with a picture of what that word represents. Thus, two stimuli are presented. The children have already learned what the picture is called (a "horse," for example). Therefore, the two stimuli in the picture-word compound include one that is already known (the picture) and one that is not (the word). This makes the picture-word compound much like the compound stimulus in a blocking experiment: a known stimulus is presented along with a new stimulus the child does not know. Research on the blocking effect predicts that the presence of the previously learned picture should disrupt learning about the word. Singh and Solman (1990) found that this occurs when using picture-word compounds in teaching reading to mentally retarded students.

The children were taught to read words such as knife, lemon, radio, stamp, and chalk. Some of the words were taught using a variation of the blocking design in which the picture of the object was presented first and the student was asked to name it. The picture was then presented, together with its written word, and the student was asked, "What is that word?" In other conditions, the words were presented without corresponding pictures. All 8 students showed the slowest learning for the words that were taught in the blocking procedure. By contrast, 6 of the 8 students showed the fastest learning of the words that were taught without corresponding pictures. (The remaining 2 students learned most rapidly with a modified procedure.) These results suggest that processes akin to blocking may occur in learning to read. They also suggest that pictorial prompts should be used with caution in reading instruction because they may disrupt rather than facilitate learning. (See also Didden, Prinsen, & Sigafoos, 2000.)

The control group in the blocking design receives the same kind of conditioning trials with stimulus B as the experimental group (Phase 2 of Figure 4.13); that is, stimulus B is presented simultaneously with stimulus A. For the control group, however, stimulus A is not conditioned prior to these compound-stimulus trials. Rather, during Phase 1, the control group receives presentations of stimulus A and the US in an unpaired fashion. In many replications of this design, stimulus B invariably produced less conditioned responding in the experimental group than in the control group.

A recent study examined the blocking effect in a conditioned suppression procedure with college students in Spain (Acediano, Matute, & Miller, 1997). In the typical conditioned suppression procedure with laboratory rats, the subjects are periodically reinforced with food for pressing a response lever. In the study with college students, the task was a variation on a video game that required the students to repeatedly fire a "laser gun" to prevent invading Martians from landing. (The laser gun was the space bar.) To create suppression of this behavior, periodically an anti-laser shield was activated during which lots of Martians would land in large numbers if the subject continued to shoot. The presence of the anti-laser shield was indicated by a flashing light and constituted the unconditioned stimulus or US.

In Phase 1, presentations of the US were signaled by a visual CS that consisted of a change in the color of the background of the computer screen. In Phase 2, this visual CS was presented together with an auditory CS (a complex tone), and this stimulus compound ended with the US. For subjects in the experimental group, compound conditioning (in

Phase 2) was preceded by conditioning of the light alone (in Phase 1). In contrast, subjects in the control group received the light CS unpaired with the US in Phase 1. Subsequent tests of conditioned suppression to the tone CS after Phase 2 indicated that the experimental group showed significantly less conditioned suppression than the control group. The mean suppression ratio for the experimental group was 0.39 (standard error = .02). In contrast, the mean suppression ratio for the control group was 0.27 (standard error = .04). (Keep in mind that lower values of the suppression ratio indicate greater levels of conditioned suppression.)

Since the time of Aristotle, temporal contiguity has been considered the primary means by which stimuli become associated. The blocking effect has become a landmark phenomenon in classical conditioning because it called into question the assumption that temporal contiguity is sufficient for learning. The blocking effect clearly shows that pairings of a CS with a US are not enough for conditioned responding to develop. During Phase 2 of the blocking experiment, CS_B is paired with the US in an identical fashion for the experimental and the control groups. Nevertheless, CS_B comes to elicit vigorous conditioned responding only in the control group.

Why does the presence of the previously conditioned stimulus A block the acquisition of responding to the added cue B? Kamin, the originator of the blocking effect, explained the phenomenon by proposing that a US has to be surprising to be effective in producing learning. If the US is signaled by a previously conditioned stimulus (A), it will not be surprising and therefore will not function well in conditioning the added stimulus (B). Kamin reasoned that if the US is not surprising, it will not startle the animal and stimulate the "mental effort" needed for the formation of an association. Unexpected events are events to which the organism has not adjusted yet. Therefore, unexpected events activate processes leading to new learning. To be effective, the US has to be unexpected or surprising.

A. R. Wagner

The Rescorla–Wagner Model

The idea that the effectiveness of an unconditioned stimulus is determined by how surprising it is forms the basis of a formal mathematical model of conditioning by Robert Rescorla and Allan Wagner (Rescorla & Wagner, 1972; Wagner & Rescorla, 1972). With the use of this model, the implications of the concept of US surprisingness were extended to a wide variety of conditioning phenomena. The Rescorla–Wagner model dominated research on classical conditioning for about 10 years after its formulation and continues to be used in a variety of areas of psychology (Siegel & Allan, 1996).

What does it mean to say that something is surprising? How might observers measure the surprisingness of an unconditioned stimulus? By definition, *an event is surprising if it is different from what is expected.* If you expect a small gift for your birthday and get a car, you will be very surprised. This is analogous to an unexpectedly large US. Correspondingly, if you expect a car and receive a box of candy, you will also be surprised. This is analogous to an unexpectedly small US. According to the Rescorla–Wagner model, an unexpectedly large US is the basis for excitatory conditioning or increases in associative value, and an unexpectedly small US is the basis for inhibitory conditioning or decreases in associative value.

Rescorla and Wagner assumed that the surprisingness, and hence the effectiveness, of a US depends on how different the US is from what the individual expects. They also assumed that expectation of the US is related to the conditioned or associative properties of the stimuli that precede the US. Strong conditioned responding indicates strong expectation that the US will occur; weak conditioned responding indicates a low expectation of the US.

These ideas can be expressed mathematically by using λ to represent the asymptote of learning possible with the US being used, and V to represent the associative value of the stimuli that precede the US. The surprisingness of the US will then be $(\lambda - V)$. The amount of learning on a given trial is assumed to be proportional to $(\lambda - V)$ or US surprisingness. The value of $(\lambda - V)$ is large at the start of learning (because V, the associative value of the stimuli preceding the US, is close to zero at this point). Hence, substantial increments in associative strength occur during early conditioning trials. Once the associative value of the cues that precede the US has increased, $(\lambda - V)$ will be small, and little additional learning will occur.

Learning on a given conditioning trial is the change in the associative value of a stimulus. That change can be represented as ΔV. Using these symbols, the idea that learning depends on the surprisingness of the US can be expressed as follows:

$$\Delta V = k(\lambda - V),$$

where "k" is a constant related to the salience of the CS and US. This is the fundamental equation of the Rescorla–Wagner model.

Blocking

$V_{surprise} = \lambda$

Application to the Blocking Effect. The basic ideas of the Rescorla–Wagner model clearly predict the blocking effect. In applying the model, it is important to keep in mind that expectations of the US are based on all of the cues available to the organism during the conditioning trial. As presented in Figure 4.13, the experimental group in the blocking design first receives extensive conditioning of stimulus A so that it acquires a perfect expectation that the US will occur whenever it encounters stimulus A. Therefore, V_A equals the asymptote of learning or λ ($V_A = \lambda$). In Phase 2, stimulus B is presented together with stimulus A, and the two CSs are followed by the US. According to the Rescorla–Wagner model, no conditioning of stimulus B will occur in Phase 2 because the US is now perfectly predicted by the presence of stimulus A: $(\lambda - V_{A+B}) = 0$.

The control group receives the identical training in Phase 2, but for them the presence of stimulus A does not lead to an expectation of the US. Therefore, the US in Phase 2 is surprising for the control group and produces new learning.

Loss of Associative Value Despite Pairings with the US. The Rescorla–Wagner model is consistent with fundamental facts of classical conditioning such as acquisition and the blocking effect. Much of the importance of the model, however, has come from its unusual predictions. One such prediction is that under certain circumstances the conditioned properties of stimuli will decline despite continued pairings with the US. How might this happen? Stimuli are predicted to lose associative value if they are presented together on a conditioning trial after having been trained separately. Such an experiment is outlined in Figure 4.14.

Figure 4.14 shows a 2-phase experiment. In Phase 1, stimuli A and B are paired with the same US (one pellet of food, for example) on separate trials. This continues until both A and B have been conditioned completely—until both stimuli predict perfectly the one-food-pellet US, or $V_A = V_B = \lambda$. Phase 2 is then initiated. In Phase 2, stimuli A and B are presented simultaneously for the first time, and this stimulus compound is followed by the same US—one food pellet. The question is, What happens to the conditioned properties of stimuli A and B as a result of the Phase 2 training?

Note that the same US that was used in Phase 1 continues to be presented in Phase 2. Given that there is no change in the US, informal reflection suggests that the conditioned properties of stimuli A and B should also remain unchanged during Phase 2. In contrast to this commonsense prediction, the Rescorla–Wagner model predicts that the conditioned properties of the individual stimuli A and B will decrease in Phase 2.

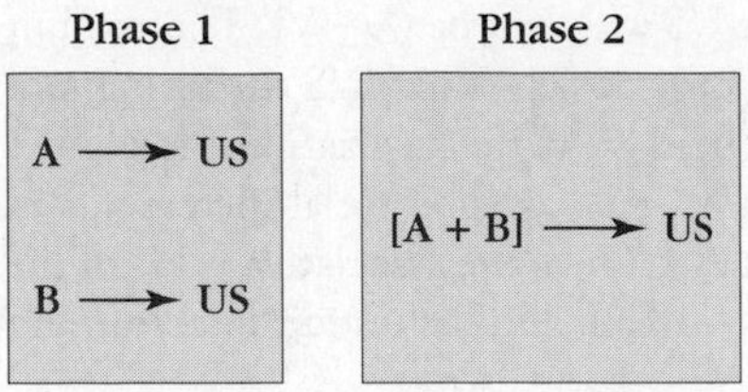

Figure 4.14 Loss of associative value despite continued presentations of the US. Stimuli A and B are conditioned separately to asymptote in Phase 1 so that each CS perfectly predicts the US. In Phase 2, stimuli A and B are presented simultaneously and paired with the same US that was used in Phase 1. This produces an overexpectation of the US. Because the delivered US is surprisingly small at the start of Phase 2, the conditioned properties of stimuli A and B decrease until the simultaneous presentation of the two CSs no longer produces the overexpectation.

As a result of training in Phase 1, stimuli A and B both come to predict the one-food-pellet US ($V_A = \lambda$; $V_B = \lambda$). When stimuli A and B are presented simultaneously for the first time, in Phase 2, the expectations based on the individual stimuli are assumed to add together, with the result that two food pellets are predicted as the US ($V_{A+B} = V_A + V_B = 2\lambda$). This is an overexpectation because the US remains only one food pellet. Thus, a discrepancy exists between what is expected (two pellets) and what occurs (one pellet). At the start of Phase 2, the participants find the US surprisingly small. To bring their expectations of the US in line with what actually occurs in Phase 2, the participants have to decrease their expectancy of the US based on stimuli A and B. Thus, stimuli A and B are predicted to lose associative value despite continued presentations of the same US. The loss in associative value is predicted to continue until the sum of the expectancies based on A and B equals one food pellet. The predicted loss of conditioned response to the individual stimuli A and B in this type of procedure is highly counterintuitive but has been verified experimentally (see Kremer, 1978; Khallad & Moore, 1996; Lattal & Nakajima, 1998; Rescorla, 1999b).

Conditioned Inhibition. How does the Rescorla–Wagner model explain the development of conditioned inhibition? Consider, for example, the standard inhibitory conditioning procedure (see Figure 3.10). This procedure involves two kinds of trials—trials on which the US is presented (reinforced trials), and trials on which the US is omitted (nonreinforced trials). On reinforced trials, a conditioned excitatory stimulus (CS+) is presented. On nonreinforced trials, the CS+ is presented together with the conditioned inhibitory stimulus, CS–.

Application of the Rescorla–Wagner model to such a procedure requires considering reinforced and nonreinforced trials separately. To accurately anticipate the US on reinforced trials, the CS+ has to gain excitatory properties. The development of such conditioned excitation is illustrated in the left-hand panel of Figure 4.15. Excitatory conditioning involves the acquisition of positive associative value and ceases once the organism predicts the US perfectly on each reinforced trial.

What happens on nonreinforced trials? Both the CS+ and the CS– occur. Once the CS+ has acquired some degree of conditioned excitation (because of its presentation on reinforced trials), the organism will expect the US whenever the CS+ occurs, including on nonreinforced trials. However, the US does not happen on nonreinforced trials. Therefore, this is a case of overexpectation, similar to the example illustrated in Figure 4.14. To accurately predict the absence of the US on nonreinforced trials, the associative value of the CS+ and the value of the CS– have to sum to zero (the value represented by no US). How can this be achieved? Given the positive associative value of the CS+, the only way to achieve a net zero expectation of the US on nonreinforced trials is to make the associative value of the CS– negative. Hence, the Rescorla–Wagner model explains conditioned inhibition by assuming that the CS– acquires negative associative value (see the left-hand panel of Figure 4.15).

Extinction of Excitation and Inhibition. In an extinction procedure, the conditioned stimulus is presented repeatedly without the US. (I say more about extinction in Chapter 10.) Consider predictions of the Rescorla–Wagner model for extinction, illustrated in the right-hand panel of Figure 4.15. If a CS has acquired excitatory properties (see CS+ in Figure 4.15), there will be an overexpectation of the US the first time the CS is presented by itself in extinction. With continued CS-alone trials, the expectation elicited by the CS will be brought in line with the absence of the US by gradual reduction of the associative value of the CS+ to zero.

The Rescorla–Wagner model predicts an analogous scenario for extinction of conditioned inhibition. At the start of extinction, the CS– has negative associative value. This may be thought of as creating an underprediction of the US; the organism predicts less than the zero US that occurs on extinction trials. To bring expectations in line with the absence of the US, the negative associative value of the CS– is gradually lost and the CS– ends up with zero associative strength.

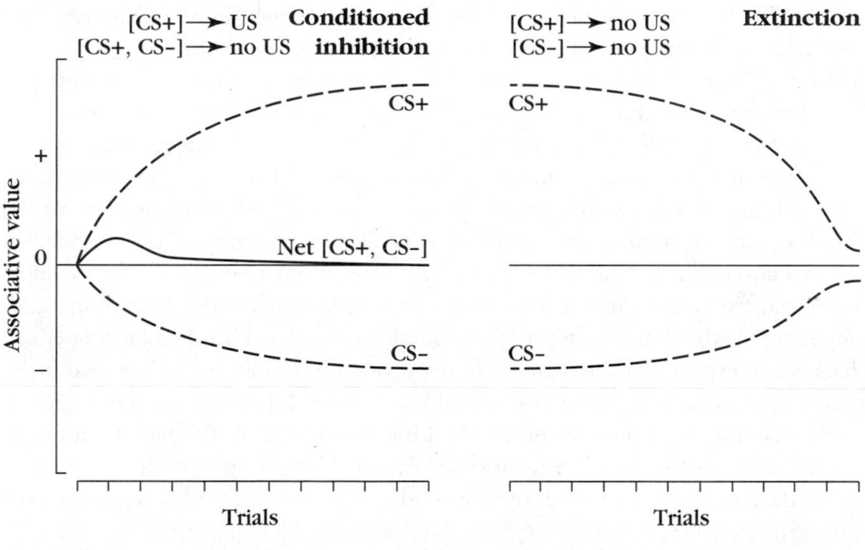

Figure 4.15 Predicted associative values of CS+ and CS– during the course of conditioned inhibition training (left) and extinction (right). During conditioned inhibition training, when the CS+ is presented alone, it is followed by the US; by contrast, when the CS+ is presented with the CS–, the US is omitted. The net associative value of CS+ and CS– is the sum of the associative values of the individual stimuli. During extinction, the conditioned stimuli are presented alone, and the US never occurs.

Problems with the Rescorla–Wagner Model. The Rescorla–Wagner model stimulated a great deal of research and led to the discovery of many new and important phenomena in classical conditioning (Siegel & Allan, 1996). Not unexpectedly, however, the model has also encountered some difficulties since it was proposed about 30 years ago (see Miller, Barnet, & Grahame, 1995).

One of the difficulties with the model that became evident early on is that its analysis of the extinction of conditioned inhibition is incorrect. The model (see Figure 4.15) predicts that repeated presentations of a conditioned inhibitor (CS–) by itself will lead to loss of conditioned inhibition, but this does not occur (Zimmer-Hart & Rescorla, 1974; Witcher & Ayres, 1984). On the contrary, some investigators have found that repeated nonreinforcement of a CS– can enhance its conditioned inhibitory properties (for example, DeVito & Fowler, 1987; Hallam, Grahame, Harris, & Miller, 1992). Curiously, an effective procedure for reducing the conditioned inhibitory properties of a CS– does not involve presenting the CS– at all. Rather, it involves extinguishing the excitatory properties of the CS+ with which the CS– was presented during inhibitory training (Best, Dunn, Batson, Meachum, & Nash, 1985; Lysle & Fowler, 1985). (For a more complete discussion of procedures for extinguishing conditioned inhibition, see Fowler et al., 1991.)

Another difficulty is that the Rescorla–Wagner model views extinction as the reverse of acquisition, or the return of the associative value of a CS to zero. A growing body of evidence indicates that extinction should not be viewed as simply the reverse of acquisition (see Chapter 10). Extinction appears to involve the learning of a new relationship between the CS and the US (namely, that the US no longer follows the CS).

Another puzzling finding that has been difficult to incorporate into the Rescorla–Wagner model is that under certain conditions, the same CS may have both excitatory and inhibitory properties (Barnet & Miller, 1996; Matzel, Gladstein, & Miller, 1988; McNish, Betts, Brandon, & Wagner, 1997; Robbins, 1990; Tait & Saladin, 1986; Williams & Overmier, 1988b). The Rescorla–Wagner model allows for conditioned stimuli to have only one associative value. That value can be excitatory or inhibitory, but not both.

Finally, the Rescorla–Wagner model has difficulty explaining recent findings obtained in taste- and odor-aversion learning. These experiments employed a 2-phase procedure very similar to the blocking design (Figure 4.13). In Phase 1, laboratory rats received one CS (taste or odor) paired with lithium-induced malaise to condition an aversion to that stimulus. In Phase 2, this previously conditioned stimulus was presented simultaneously with a new stimulus, and the compound was paired with lithium toxicosis. The CS added in Phase 2 was a novel odor for the taste-conditioned subjects and a novel taste for the odor-conditioned subjects. Thus, Phase 2 involved the presentation of an odor-taste compound, one component of which had been previously conditioned. Based on the blocking effect, researchers would expect that the presence of the previously conditioned CS would interfere with the conditioning of the CS that was added in Phase 2. Just the opposite result has been found—an **augmentation** or **contra-blocking effect** (Batsell, Paschall, Gleason, & Batson, 2001; Batsell & Batson, 1999; Batson & Batsell, 2000). Instead of disrupting conditioning of the added CS in Phase 2, the previously conditioned stimulus augmented the conditioning of the added CS. The augmentation, or contra-blocking effect, is a relatively new discovery and not much is known about its boundary conditions. However, it presents a serious challenge to the Rescorla–Wagner model, which was built on the opposite outcome, a blocking rather than a contra-blocking effect.

Other Models of Classical Conditioning

Devising a comprehensive theory of classical conditioning is a formidable challenge. Given the nearly 100 years of research on classical conditioning, a comprehensive theory must account for many diverse findings. No theory available today has been entirely successful in accomplishing that goal. Nevertheless, interesting new ideas about classical conditioning continue to be proposed and examined. Some of these proposals supplement the Rescorla–Wagner model; others are incompatible with it and move the theoretical debate in some startling new directions.

Courtesy of Donald A. Dewsbury

N. J. Mackintosh

Attentional Models of Conditioning. In the Rescorla–Wagner model, how much is learned on a conditioning trial depends on the effectiveness of the unconditioned stimulus. Psychologists in North America have favored theories of learning that focus on changes in US effectiveness. In contrast, those in Great Britain have approached phenomena such as the blocking effect by postulating changes in how well the CS commands the subject's attention. The general assumption is that for conditioning to occur subjects have to pay attention to the CS. Procedures that disrupt attention to the CS are expected to also disrupt learning (Mackintosh, 1975; McLaren & Mackintosh, 2000; Pearce & Hall, 1980).

Attentional theories differ in their assumptions about what determines the salience, or noticeability, of the CS on a given trial. Pearce and Hall (1980), for example, assumed that how much attention an animal devotes to the CS on a given trial is determined by how surprising the US was on the preceding trial (see also Hall, Kaye, & Pearce, 1985; McLaren & Mackintosh, 2000). Animals to whom the US was surprising on the preceding trial have a lot to learn and will therefore pay closer attention to that CS on the next trial. In contrast, if a CS was followed by an expected US, the subject will pay less attention to that CS on the next trial. An expected US is assumed to decrease the salience or attention commanded by the CS.

An important feature of attentional theories is that they assume that the surprisingness of the US on a given trial alters the degree of attention commanded by the CS on future trials. For example, if Trial 10 ends in a surprising US, that will increase the salience of the CS on Trial 11. Thus, US surprisingness is assumed to have only a *prospective* or *proactive* influence on attention and conditioning. This is an important contrast to US-reduction models such as the Rescorla–Wagner model, in which the surprisingness of the US on a given trial determines what is learned on that same trial.

The assumption that the US on a given trial influences only what is learned on the next trial has permitted attentional models to explain certain findings (for example, Mackintosh, Bygrave, & Picton, 1977). That assumption has made it difficult for the models to explain other results. In particular, the models cannot explain blocking that occurs on the first trial of Phase 2 of the blocking experiment (for example, Azorlosa & Cicala, 1986; Balaz, Kasprow, & Miller, 1982; Dickinson, Nicholas, & Mackintosh, 1983; Gillan & Domjan, 1977). According to attentional models, blocking occurs because in Phase 2 of the blocking experiment the lack of surprisingness of the US reduces attention to the added CS. Because that reduction in salience can occur only after the first Phase 2 trial, attentional models cannot explain the blocking that occurs on the first trial of Phase 2 of the blocking experiment.

Temporal Factors and Conditioned Responding. Neither the Rescorla–Wagner model nor CS modification models were designed to explain the effects of time in conditioning, although time is obviously a critical factor. One important temporal variable is the CS-US interval. As noted in Chapter 3, conditioned responding is inversely related to the CS-US interval or CS duration. Beyond an optimal point, procedures with longer CS-US intervals produce less responding (see Figure 3.8). This relation appears to be a characteristic primarily of responses closely related to the US (such as focal search). If behaviors that are ordinarily farther removed from the US are measured (such as general search), responding is greater with procedures that involve longer CS-US intervals (see Figure 4.11). Both types of

Courtesy of J. Gibbon

J. Gibbon

findings illustrate that the duration of the CS is an important factor in conditioning. (For other research on the importance of the CS-US interval in conditioning, see studies of the *temporal coding hypothesis,* Barnet, Cole, & Miller, 1997; Brown, Hemmes, & de Vaca, 1997; Cole, Barnet, & Miller, 1995; Savastano & Miller, 1998.)

Another important temporal variable is the interval between successive trials. In general, more conditioned responding is observed with procedures in which trials are spaced farther apart. Of greater interest, however, is the fact that the intertrial interval and the CS duration act in combination to determine responding. Numerous studies have shown that the critical factor is the relative duration of these two temporal variables rather than the absolute value of either one by itself (Gibbon & Balsam, 1981; Gallistel & Gibbon, 2000). A particularly clear example of this relationship was recently reported by Holland (2000).

Holland's experiment was conducted with laboratory rats. Food was presented periodically in a cup as the US, and presentations of the food were signaled by a CS that was white noise. Initially, the rats went to the food cup only when the food was delivered. As conditioning proceeded, they started going to the food cup as soon as they heard the noise CS. Thus, nosing of the food cup served as the anticipatory conditioned response. Each group was conditioned with one of two CS durations, either 10 seconds or 20 seconds, and one of six intertrial intervals (ranging from 15 seconds to 960 seconds). Each procedure could be characterized in terms of the ratio of the intertrial interval (I) and the CS duration, which Holland called the trial duration (T). The results of the experiment are summarized in Figure 4.16. Time spent nosing the food cup during the CS is shown as a function of the relative value of the intertrial interval (I) and the trial duration (T) for each group of subjects. Notice that conditioned responding was directly related to the I/T ratio. At each I/T ratio, the groups that received the 10-second CS responded similarly to those that received the 20-second CS. (For other recent studies of the role of the I/T ratio in conditioning, see Burns & Domjan, 2001; Kirkpatrick & Church, 2000; Lattal, 1999.)

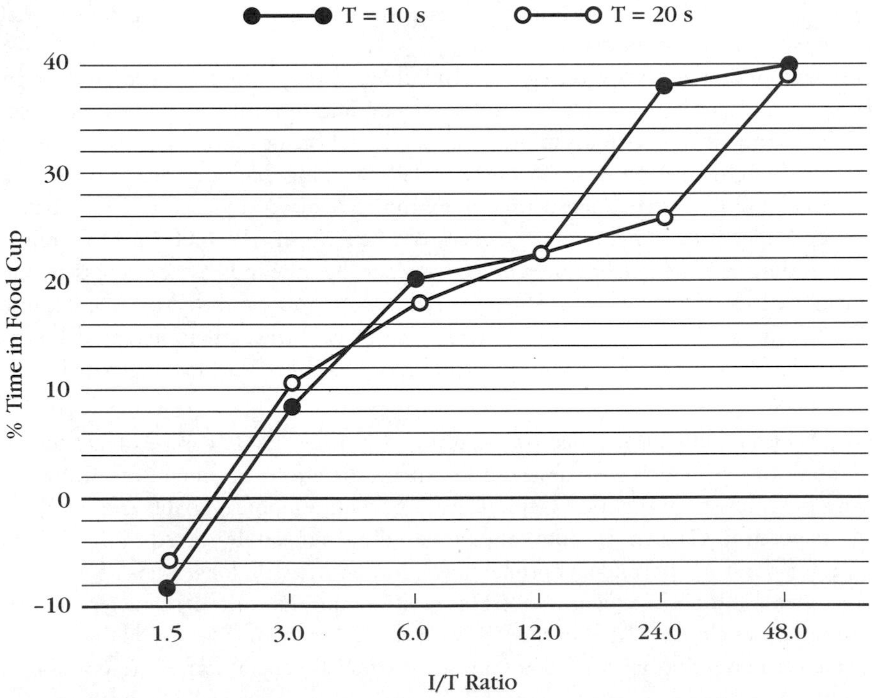

Figure 4.16 Percent time rats spent nosing the food cup during an auditory CS in conditioning with either a 10-second or a 20-second trial duration (T) and various intertrial intervals (I) that created I/T ratios ranging from 1.5 to 48.0. Data are shown in relation to responding during baseline periods when the CS was absent. (From Figure 2, p. 125, P. C. Holland, in *Animal Learning & Behavior,* Vol. 28, Copyright 2000 Psychonomic Society, Inc. Reprinted with permission.)

Various interpretations have been offered for why conditioned responding is so strongly determined by the I/T ratio. An early explanation was the **relative waiting time hypothesis** (Jenkins, Barnes, & Barrera, 1981; see also scalar expectancy theory, Gibbon & Balsam 1981). This hypothesis was built on the assumption that a CS is informative about the occurrence of the US only if the subject has to spend less time waiting for the US when the CS is present than in the experimental situation irrespective of the CS. With a low I/T ratio, the CS waiting time is similar to the context waiting time. In this case, the CS provides little new information about when the US will occur, and not much conditioned responding will develop. In contrast, with a high I/T ratio, the CS waiting time is much shorter than the context waiting time. This makes the CS highly informative about when the US will occur, and conditioned responding will be more vigorous.

More recently, these ideas have been elaborated within the context of a comprehensive theory of temporal factors and conditioning in what is called *rate expectancy theory* (Gallistel & Gibbon, 2000). I discuss timing further in Chapter 12. It is now well accepted that organisms perceive and remember temporal aspects of a conditioning procedure (such as the intertrial interval and the CS duration) and that conditioned responding depends on decision processes that involve comparing these temporal variables. Originally, these temporal variables were considered to be performance factors that just influenced the behavioral manifestations of learning. It is now clear that they are directly involved in the basic learning processes themselves (Holland, 2000; Lattal, 1999).

Courtesy of M. Burns

M. Burns

The Comparator Hypothesis. The relative waiting time hypothesis and related theories were developed to explain certain temporal features of excitatory conditioning and manipulations of CS-US contingency. One of their important contributions was to emphasize that conditioned responding depends not only on what happens during the CS but also on what happens in the experimental situation in general. The idea that both of these factors influence many learning phenomena has been developed in greater detail by R. Miller and his collaborators in the **comparator hypothesis** (Denniston, Savastano, & Miller, 2001; Miller & Matzel, 1988, 1989).

Courtesy of Donald A. Dewsbury

P. D. Balsam

The comparator hypothesis is similar to the relative waiting time hypothesis in assuming that conditioned responding depends not only on associations between a target CS and the US but also on possible associations that may be learned between contextual cues and the US. The associative strength of other cues present during training with the target CS is especially important. Another restriction of the comparator hypothesis is that it only allows for the formation of excitatory associations with the US. Whether conditioned responding reflects excitation or inhibition is assumed to be determined by the relative strengths of excitation conditioned to the target CS as compared to the excitatory value of the contextual cues that were present with the target CS during training.

The comparator process is represented by the balance in Figure 4.17. As Figure 4.17 illustrates, a comparison is made between the excitatory value of the target CS and the excitatory value of the other cues that are present during the training of the CS. If CS excitation exceeds the excitatory value of the contextual cues, the balance of the comparison will be tipped in favor of excitatory responding to the target CS. As the excitatory value of the other cues becomes stronger, the balance of the comparison will become less favorable for excitatory responding. If the excitatory value of the contextual cues becomes sufficiently strong, the balance may become tipped in favor of inhibitory responding to the target CS.

Unlike the relative waiting time hypothesis, the comparator hypothesis emphasizes associations rather than time. It assumes that organisms learn three associations during the course of conditioning (see Figure 4.18). The first association (Link 1 in Figure 4.18) is between the target CS (X) and the US. The second association (Link 2) is between the

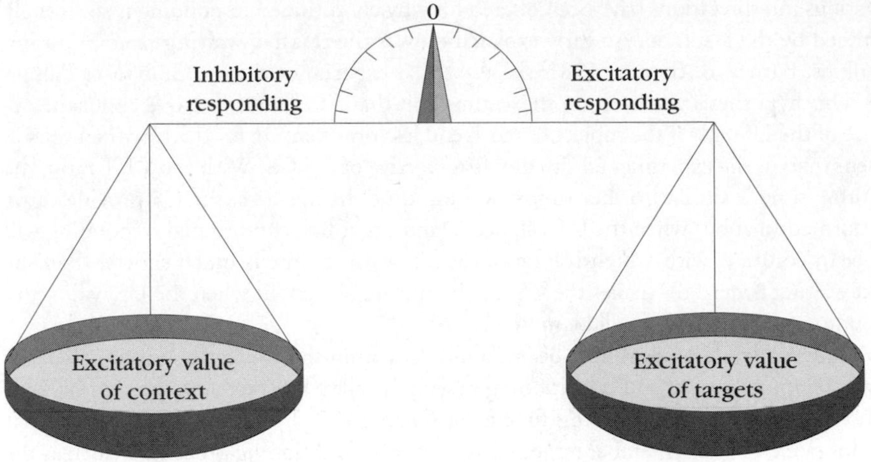

Figure 4.17 Illustration of the comparator hypothesis. Responding to the target CS is represented by the reading on the balance. If the excitatory value of the target CS exceeds the excitatory value of the other cues present during training of the target CS, the balance tips in favor of excitatory responding to the CS. As the associative value of the contextual cues increases, the comparison becomes less favorable for excitatory responding and may tip in favor of inhibitory responding.

target CS (X) and the comparator contextual cues. Finally, there is an association between the comparator stimuli and the US (Link 3). With all three links in place, once the CS is presented, it activates the US representation directly (through Link 1) and indirectly (through Links 2 and 3). A comparison of the direct and indirect activations determines the degree of excitatory or inhibitory responding that occurs.

Courtesy of R. R. Miller

R. R. Miller

It is important to note that the comparator hypothesis makes no assumptions about how associations become established. Rather, it describes how CS-US and context-US associations determine responding to the target CS. Thus, unlike US-modification and attentional models, the comparator hypothesis is a theory of *performance,* not a theory of learning.

An important corollary to the comparator hypothesis is that the comparison of CS-US and context-US associations is made at the time of testing for conditioned responding. Because of this assumption, the comparator hypothesis makes the unusual prediction that extinction of context-US associations following training of a target CS will enhance responding to that target CS. This prediction has been repeatedly confirmed (for example, Blaisdell, Gunther, & Miller, 1999; Cole, Oberling, & Miller, 1999; Miller, Barnet, & Grahame, 1992). US-modification and attentional theories of learning cannot explain such results.

The comparator hypothesis has also been tested in studies of conditioned inhibition (see Friedman, Blaisdell, Escobar, & Miller, 1998; Kasprow, Schachtman, & Miller, 1987; Schachtman, Brown, Gordon, Catterson, & Miller, 1987). The hypothesis attributes inhibitory responding to situations in which the association of the target CS with the US is weaker than the association of contextual cues with the US. The contextual cues in this case are the stimuli that provide the excitatory context for inhibitory conditioning. Interestingly, the hypothesis predicts that extinction of these conditioned excitatory stimuli following inhibitory conditioning will reduce inhibitory responding. Thus, the comparator hypothe-

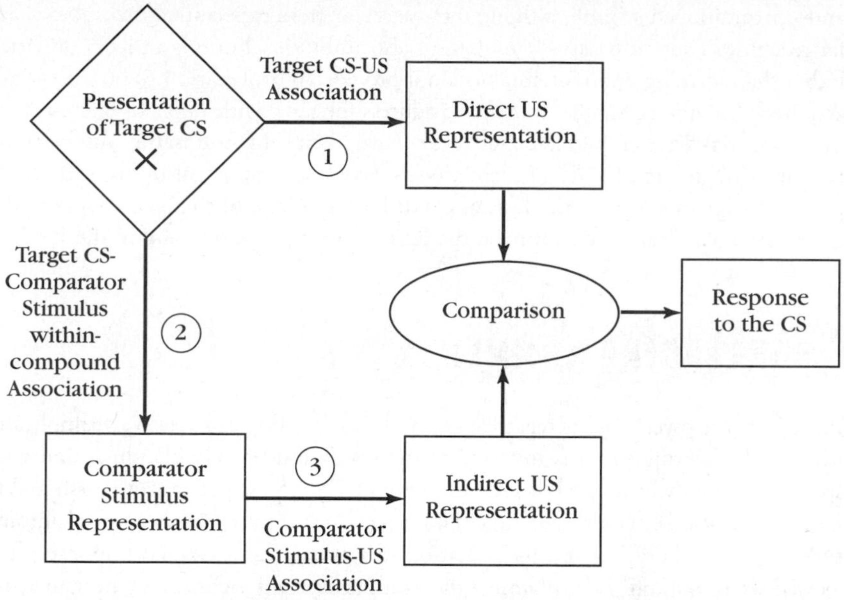

Figure 4.18 The associative structure of the comparator hypothesis. The target CS is represented as X. Excitatory associations result in activation of the US representation, either directly by the target (Link 1) or indirectly (through Links 2 and 3). (From Friedman et al., 1998.)

sis is unique in predicting that extinction of conditioned inhibition is best accomplished not by presenting the CS– alone but by extinguishing the CS+ cues that provided the excitatory context for inhibitory conditioning. As I noted earlier in the discussion of the extinction of conditioned inhibition, this unusual prediction has been confirmed (Best et al., 1985; Lysle & Fowler, 1985).

Although the comparator hypothesis has accurately predicted the results of studies involving extinction of contextual and other comparator cues after training, efforts to obtain the opposite effect have been less successful. The model predicts that increasing the excitatory value of contextual cues after training (Link 3 in Figure 4.18) will reduce conditioned responding to the target CS. A number of experiments have failed to find this outcome (Miller, Hallam, & Grahame, 1990; Robbins, 1988), but this failure is not universal. Furthermore, the negative findings are not entirely unexpected since increasing the excitatory value of the contextual cues may weaken the association between the target stimulus and the comparator (Link 2 in Figure 4.18) (see Denniston et al., 2001).

On balance, the comparator hypothesis has identified some important contextual constraints on conditioned responding. One of its major contributions has been to emphasize that differences in conditioned responding may reflect differences in performance rather than learning. In fact, it views even a robust phenomenon such as the blocking effect as a failure of performance rather than learning. It predicts, for example, that postconditioning extinction of a blocking stimulus will elevate conditioned responding to the blocked CS. Recent studies have verified this unusual prediction (Blaisdell et al., 1999). Given these successes, other theories of learning will have to address such postconditioning modulations of responding more successfully to be viable. Rate estimation theory (Gallistel & Gibbon, 2001) has risen to this challenge.

Overview of Theoretical Alternatives. Each of the new models I have described emphasizes a different aspect of classical conditioning. The relative waiting time hypothesis addresses a fairly small range of phenomena involving the temporal distribution of conditioned and unconditioned stimuli, although its successor (rate expectancy theory) is much more far-reaching. The comparator hypothesis is also ambitious, but it is a theory of performance rather than learning and therefore does not provide an explanation of how associations are acquired. Attentional models attempt to address the same wide range of phenomena as does the Rescorla–Wagner model, but they have some of the same difficulties as the Rescorla–Wagner model. All of these models have been important in directing attention to previously ignored aspects of classical conditioning. None of them has come to dominate the study of classical conditioning as the Rescorla–Wagner model did in the 1970s.

CONCLUDING COMMENTS

Initially, some psychologists regarded classical conditioning as a relatively simple and primitive type of learning that is involved in the regulation of only glandular and visceral responses, such as salivation. The establishment of CS-US associations was assumed to occur fairly automatically with the pairing of a CS and a US. Given the simple and automatic nature of the conditioning and its limitation to glandular and visceral responses, it was not viewed as important in explaining the complexity and richness of human experience. Clearly, this view of classical conditioning is no longer tenable.

The research reviewed in Chapters 3 and 4 has shown that classical conditioning involves numerous complex processes and is involved in the control of a wide variety of responses, including emotional behavior and approach-and-withdrawal responses. The learning does not occur automatically with the pairing of a CS with a US. It depends on the organism's prior experience with each of these stimuli, the presence of other stimuli during the conditioning trial, and the extent to which the CS and the US are relevant to each other. Furthermore, the processes of classical conditioning are not limited to CS-US pairings. Learned associations can occur between two biologically weak stimuli (sensory preconditioning), in the absence of an unconditioned stimulus (higher-order conditioning), or in the absence of conventional conditioned stimuli (counterconditioning).

Given these and other complexities of classical conditioning processes, it is a mistake to disregard classical conditioning in attempts to explain complex forms of behavior. The richness of classical conditioning mechanisms makes them relevant to the richness and complexity of human experience.

SAMPLE QUESTIONS

1. What, if any, limits are there on the kinds of stimuli that can serve as conditioned and unconditioned stimuli in Pavlovian conditioning?
2. How can Pavlovian conditioning mechanisms explain drug tolerance, and what are some of the implications of these mechanisms?
3. How can you distinguish between S-R and S-S learning experimentally?
4. Describe the basic idea of the Rescorla–Wagner model. What aspect of the model allows it to explain the blocking effect and make some unusual predictions?
5. In what respects are attentional theories of learning different from other theories?
6. How would the comparator hypothesis explain the blocking effect?

KEY TERMS

augmentation Facilitation of the conditioning of a novel stimulus because of the presence of a previously conditioned stimulus. Also called the *contra-blocking effect.*

blocking effect Interference with the conditioning of a novel stimulus because of the presence of a previously conditioned stimulus.

comparator hypothesis The idea that conditioned responding depends on a comparison between the associative strength of the conditioned stimulus (CS) and the associative strength of other cues present during training of the target CS.

conditioned homeostatic-response A conditioned response that is similar to the unconditioned homeostatic reactions that are elicited by some unconditioned stimuli.

contra-blocking effect Same as *augmentation.*

counterconditioning A conditioning procedure that reverses the organism's previous response to a stimulus. For example, an animal may be conditioned to approach a stimulus that initially elicited withdrawal reactions.

CS-preexposure effect Interference with conditioning produced by repeated exposures to the conditioned stimulus before the conditioning trials. Also called *latent-inhibition effect.*

drug tolerance Reduction in the effectiveness of a drug as a result of repeated use of the drug.

higher-order conditioning A procedure in which a previously conditioned stimulus (CS_1) is used to condition a new stimulus (CS_2).

homeostasis A concept introduced by Water Cannon to refer to physiological mechanisms that serve to maintain critical aspects of the body (such as blood sugar level and temperature) within acceptable limits. The homeostatic level is typically achieved by the operation of negative feedback mechanisms that serve to counteract the effects of challenges to the homeostatic level.

latent-inhibition effect Same as *CS-preexposure effect.*

relative waiting time hypothesis The idea that conditioned responding depends on how long the organism has to wait for the unconditioned stimulus (US) in the presence of the conditioned stimulus (CS), as compared to how long the organism has to wait for the US in the experimental situation irrespective of the CS.

S-R learning The learning of an association between a stimulus and a response, with the result that the stimulus comes to elicit the response. Same as *stimulus-response learning.*

S-S learning The learning of an association between two stimuli, with the result that exposure to one of the stimuli comes to activate a representation, or "mental image," of the other stimulus. Same as *stimulus-stimulus learning.*

sensory preconditioning A procedure in which one biologically weak stimulus (CS_2) is repeatedly paired with another biologically weak stimulus (CS_1). Then, CS_1 is conditioned with an unconditioned stimulus. In a later test trial, CS_2 also will elicit the conditioned response, even though CS_2 was never directly paired with the unconditioned stimulus.

stimulus-response learning Same as *S-R learning.*

stimulus-stimulus learning Same as *S-S learning.*

stimulus salience The significance or noticeability of a stimulus to the organism. In general, conditioning proceeds more rapidly with more salient conditioned and unconditioned stimuli.

stimulus substitution The theoretical idea that the outcome of classical conditioning is that organisms come to respond to the conditioned stimulus in much the same way that they respond to the unconditioned stimulus.

US-preexposure effect Interference with conditioning produced by repeated exposures to the unconditioned stimulus before the conditioning trials.

US devaluation Reduction in the attractiveness of an unconditioned stimulus, usually achieved by aversion conditioning or satiation.

CHAPTER

5

INSTRUMENTAL CONDITIONING: FOUNDATIONS

Chapter 5 begins a discussion of instrumental conditioning and goal-directed behavior. In this type of conditioning, presentations of stimuli depend on the prior occurrence of designated responses. First, I describe the origins of research on instrumental conditioning and the investigative methods used in contemporary research. This discussion lays the groundwork for the section following, in which the four basic types of instrumental conditioning procedures are described. I conclude the chapter with a discussion of three fundamental elements of the instrumental conditioning paradigm: the instrumental response, the goal event, and the relation between the instrumental response and the goal event.

In the preceding chapters I described various aspects of how responses are elicited by discrete stimuli. Studies of habituation, sensitization, and classical conditioning are all concerned with analyses of the mechanisms of elicited behavior. Because of this emphasis, experiments on habituation, sensitization, and classical conditioning use procedures in which the organism has no control over the stimuli to which it is exposed. In this chapter, I turn to the analysis of learning situations in which the stimuli an organism encounters are a direct result of its behavior. Such behavior is commonly referred to as "goal-directed."

By studying hard, a student can earn a better grade in a class; by turning the car key in the ignition, a driver can start the engine; by putting a coin in a vending machine, a child can obtain a piece of candy. In all these instances, some aspect of the person's behavior is instrumental in producing a significant stimulus or outcome. Furthermore, the behavior occurs because similar actions produced the same type of outcome in the past. Students would not study if studying did not yield better grades; drivers would not turn the ignition key if this did not start the engine; and children would not put coins in a candy machine if they did not get candy in return. Behavior that occurs because it was previously instrumental in producing certain consequences is called **instrumental behavior.**

The fact that the consequences of an action can determine future occurrences of that action is obvious to everyone. If you happen to find a dollar bill when you glance down, you will keep looking at the ground as you walk. How such consequences influence future behavior is not so readily apparent. Much of the remainder of this text is devoted to a discussion of the mechanisms responsible for the control of behavior by its consequences. In this chapter, I describe some of the history, basic techniques, procedures, and issues in the experimental analysis of instrumental, or goal-directed, behavior.

How might instrumental behavior be investigated? One way would be to look for examples of goal-directed behavior in the natural environment. This approach, however, is not likely to lead to definitive results because factors responsible for goal-directed behavior are difficult to isolate without experimental manipulation.

Consider, for example, a dog sitting comfortably in its yard. When an intruder approaches, the dog starts to bark vigorously, with the result that the intruder goes away. Because the dog's barking has a clear consequence (departure of the intruder), it is tempting to conclude that the dog barked in order to produce this consequence—that barking was goal-directed. An equally likely possibility is that barking was elicited by the novelty of the intruder and persisted as long as the eliciting stimulus was present. The response consequence—departure of the intruder—may have been incidental to the dog's barking. Deciding between such alternatives is difficult without experimental manipulations of the relation between barking and its consequences. (For an experimental analysis of a similar situation in a fish species, see Losey & Sevenster, 1995).

The type of research I discuss in this chapter brings instrumental behavior into the laboratory. The idea, as with elicited behaviors, is to study representative instrumental responses in the hope of discovering general principles.

EARLY INVESTIGATIONS OF INSTRUMENTAL CONDITIONING

Laboratory and theoretical analyses of instrumental conditioning began in earnest with the work of E. L. Thorndike. Thorndike's original intent was to study animal intelligence (Thorndike, 1898, 1911; for recent commentaries, see Catania, 1999; Dewsbury, 1998;

Lattal, 1998). As I noted in Chapter 1, the publication of Darwin's theory of evolution stimulated people to speculate about the extent to which human intellectual capacities were present in animals. Thorndike pursued this question through empirical research. He devised a series of puzzle boxes for his experiments. His training procedure consisted of placing a hungry cat (or dog or chicken) in the puzzle box with some food left outside in plain view of the animal. The task for the cat was to learn how to get out of the box and obtain the food.

Different puzzle boxes required different responses to get out, and some were easier than others. Figure 5.1 illustrates two of the easier puzzle boxes. In Box A, the required response was to pull a ring to release a latch that blocked the door on the outside. In Box I, the required response was to press down on a lever, which released a latch. Initially, the subjects were slow to make the correct response, but with continued practice on the task, their latencies became shorter and shorter. Figure 5.2 shows the latencies of a cat to get out of Box A on successive trials. The cat took 160 seconds to get out of Box A on the first trial. Its shortest latency later on was 6 seconds (Chance, 1999).

Thorndike's careful empirical approach was a significant advance in the study of "animal intelligence." Another important contribution was his strict avoidance of anthropomorphic interpretations of the behavior he observed. Although Thorndike titled his treatise "Animal Intelligence," he thought many aspects of his subjects' behavior seemed rather unintelligent. He did not think that the subjects got faster in escaping from a puzzle box because they gained insight into the task or figured out how the release mechanism was designed. Rather, Thorndike interpreted the results of his studies as reflecting the learning of an S-R association. When a cat was initially placed in a box, it displayed a variety of responses typical of a confined animal. Some of these responses eventually resulted in opening the door. Thorndike believed that such successful escapes led to the learning of an association between the stimuli inside the puzzle box and the escape response. As the association, or connection, between the box cues and the successful response became stronger,

Figure 5.1 Two of Thorndike's puzzle boxes, A and I. In Box A, the subject had to pull a loop to release the door. In Box I, pressing down on a lever released a latch on the other side. *Left:* Chance (1999). *Journal of Experimental Analysis of Behavior, 72,* 433–440. Copyright 1999 by the Society for the Experimental Analysis of Behavior, Inc. *Right:* Thorndike (1898). *Animal Intelligence: Experimental Studies.*

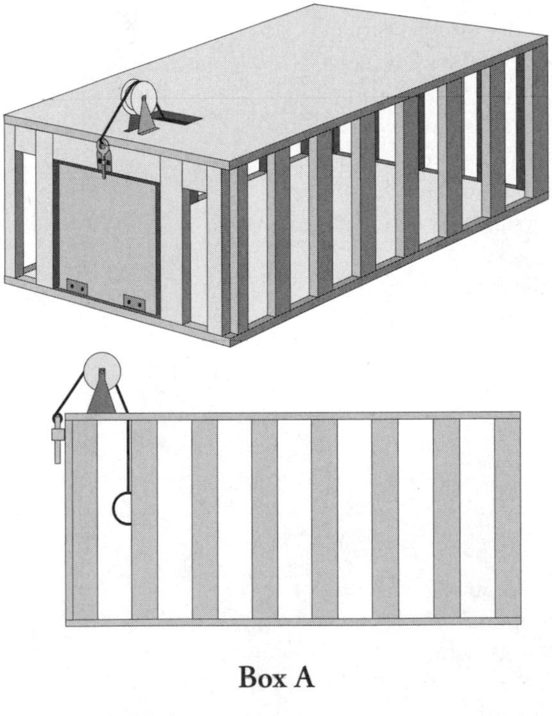

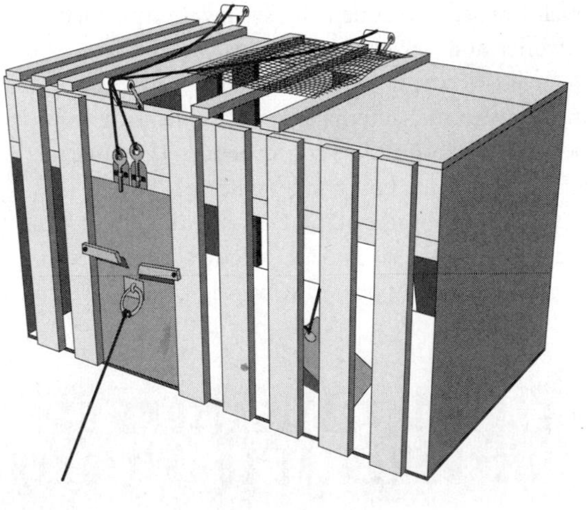

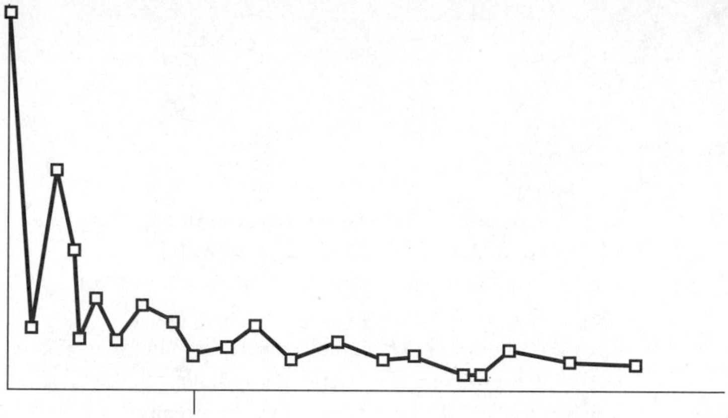

Figure 5.2 Latencies to escape from Box A during successive trials. The longest latency was 160 seconds; the shortest was 6 seconds. (Notice that the axes are not labeled, as in Thorndike's original report.)

the cat came to make that response more quickly. The consequence of the successful response—escaping the box—strengthened the association between the box stimuli and that response.

On the basis of his research, Thorndike formulated the **law of effect.** This law states that if a response in the presence of a stimulus is followed by a *satisfying event,* the association between the stimulus (S) and the response (R) is strengthened. If the response is followed by an *annoying event,* the S-R association is weakened. It is important to stress that according to the law of effect, animals learn an association between the response and the stimuli present at the time of the response. Notice that the consequence of the response is not one of the elements in the association. The satisfying or annoying consequence simply serves to strengthen or weaken the association, or bond, between the response and the stimulus situation. Thus, Thorndike's law of effect involves *S-R learning.*

MODERN APPROACHES TO THE STUDY OF INSTRUMENTAL CONDITIONING

Thorndike used 15 different puzzle boxes in his investigations. Each box required different manipulations for the cat to get out. As more scientists became involved in studying instrumental learning, the range of tasks they used became much smaller. A few of these became "standard" and have been used repeatedly to facilitate comparison of results obtained in different laboratories.

Discrete-Trial Procedures

Discrete-trial procedures are similar to the method Thorndike used in that each training trial ends with removal of the animal from the apparatus, and the instrumental response is performed only once during each trial. Discrete-trial investigations of instrumental behavior are often conducted in some type of maze. The use of mazes in investigations of learning was introduced at the turn of the twentieth century by the American psychologist W. S.

BOX 5.1

E. L. THORNDIKE: BIOGRAPHICAL SKETCH

As an undergraduate at Wesleyan University, Edward Lee Thorndike (1874–1949) became interested in the work of William James, then at Harvard. Thorndike himself entered Harvard as a graduate student in 1895, where he began his research on instrumental behavior, at first using chicks. Having no laboratory space at Harvard, he set up his project in William James's cellar. He was soon offered a fellowship at Columbia University, where he located his laboratory in the attic of psychologist James Cattell.

Thorndike received his Ph.D. from Columbia in 1898, for his work entitled "Animal Intelligence: An Experimental Analysis of Associative Processes in Animals." This included the famous puzzle-box experiments. After a short stint at Western Reserve University in Cleveland, Thorndike returned to Columbia, where for many years he served as professor of educational psychology in the Teachers College. Among other things, he attempted to apply to children the principles of trial-and-error learning he had uncovered with animals. He also became interested in psychological testing and became a leader in this newly formed field. By the time of his retirement, he had written 507 scholarly works, about 50 of them books (Cumming, 1999). Several years before his death, Thorndike returned to Harvard as the William James Lecturer—a fitting honor considering the origins of his interests in psychology.

Small (1899, 1900). Small was interested in studying rats and decided to use a maze after reading an article in *Scientific American* that described the complex system of underground burrows that kangaroo rats build in their natural habitat. He reasoned that a maze would take advantage of the rats' "propensity for small winding passages."

Figure 5.3 shows two mazes frequently used in contemporary research. The runway or straight-alley maze contains a start box at one end and a goal box at the other. The rat is placed in the start box at the beginning of each trial. The movable barrier separating the start box from the main section of the runway is then lifted. The rat is allowed to make its way down the runway until it reaches the goal box, which usually contains a reinforcer, such as food or water.

Another frequently used maze is the T-maze, shown on the right in Figure 5.3. The T-maze consists of a start box and alleys arranged in the shape of a T. A goal box is located at the end of each arm of the T. Because it has two goal boxes, the T maze is well suited to studying choice behavior. For example, one goal box may be baited with plain food and the other with food flavored with artificial sweetener. By seeing which arm the rat chooses over a series of trials, the experimenter can measure preference for one food over the other.

Behavior in a maze can be quantified by measuring the **running speed**—how fast the animal gets from the start box to the goal box. The running speed typically increases with repeated training trials. Another common measure of behavior in runways is the **latency**—the time it takes the animal to leave the start box and begin moving down the alley. Typically, latencies become shorter as training progresses.

Free-Operant Procedures

In a runway or a T-maze, after reaching the goal box, the animal is removed from the apparatus for a while before being returned to the start box for its next trial. The animal conse-

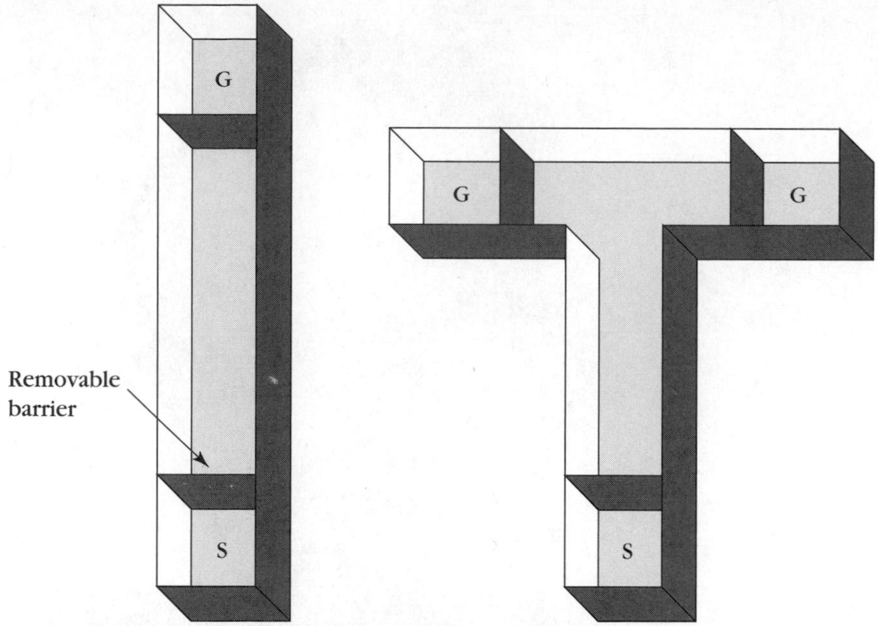

Figure 5.3 Top view of a runway and a T-maze. S is the start box; G is the goal box.

quently has limited opportunities to respond, and those opportunities are scheduled by the experimenter. By contrast, **free-operant** procedures allow the animal to repeat the instrumental response over and over again without constraint. The free-operant method was devised by B. F. Skinner (1938) to study behavior in a more continuous manner than is possible with mazes.

Skinner (Figure 5.4) was interested in analyzing in the laboratory a form of behavior that would be representative of all naturally occurring ongoing activity. He recognized, however, that before behavior can be experimentally analyzed, a measurable unit of behavior must be defined. Casual observation suggests that ongoing behavior is continuous; one activity leads to another. Behavior does not fall neatly into units as do molecules of a chemical solution. Skinner proposed the concept of the operant as a way of dividing behavior into meaningful measurable units.

Figure 5.5 shows a typical Skinner box used to study free-operant behavior in rats. (A Skinner box used to study pecking in pigeons is presented in Figure 1.5.) The box is a small chamber that contains a lever that the rat can push down repeatedly. The chamber also has a mechanism that can deliver a reinforcer, such as food or water. In the simplest experiment, a hungry rat is placed in the chamber. The lever is electronically connected to the food-delivery system. When the rat depresses the lever, a pellet of food automatically falls into the food cup.

An **operant response,** such as the lever press, is defined in terms of the effect that it has on the environment. Activities that have the same environmental effect are considered to be instances of the same operant response. The critical thing is not the muscles involved in the behavior but the way in which the behavior "operates" on the environment. For example, the lever-press operant in rats is typically defined as sufficient depression of the lever to cause the closure of a microswitch. The rat may press the lever with its right paw, its left paw, or its tail. These different muscle responses constitute the same operant if they all

Figure 5.4 B. F. Skinner (1904–1990)

depress the lever the required amount. Various ways of pressing the lever are assumed to be functionally equivalent because they all have the same effect on the environment—namely, closing the microswitch.

Magazine Training and Shaping. Most rats, when placed in a Skinner box, do not press the lever frequently. There are some preliminary steps for establishing the lever-press behavior. First, the animals have to learn when food is available in the food cup. This involves classical conditioning: the sound of the food-delivery device is repeatedly paired with the delivery of a food pellet into the cup. The food-delivery device is called the *food magazine.* After enough pairings of the sound of the food magazine with the food delivery, the sound comes to elicit a sign tracking response: the animal goes to the food cup and picks up the food pellet. This preliminary phase of conditioning is called **magazine training.**

After magazine training, the organism is ready to learn the required instrumental response. If the response is not something the animal already does occasionally, it may never happen on the response that produces the reinforcer on its own. To facilitate the acquisition of a new operant response, experimenters employ a strategy that has been used by animal trainers for centuries. At first, food is given if the animal does anything remotely related to the desired response. For example, at first a rat may be given a food pellet each time it gets up on its hind legs anywhere in the experimental chamber. Once the rearing response has been established, the food pellet may be given only if the rat makes the rearing response over the response lever. Rearing in other parts of the chamber would no longer be reinforced. Once rearing over the lever has been established, the food pellet may be given only after the rat actually depresses the lever. Such a sequence of training steps is called **shaping.** Shaping

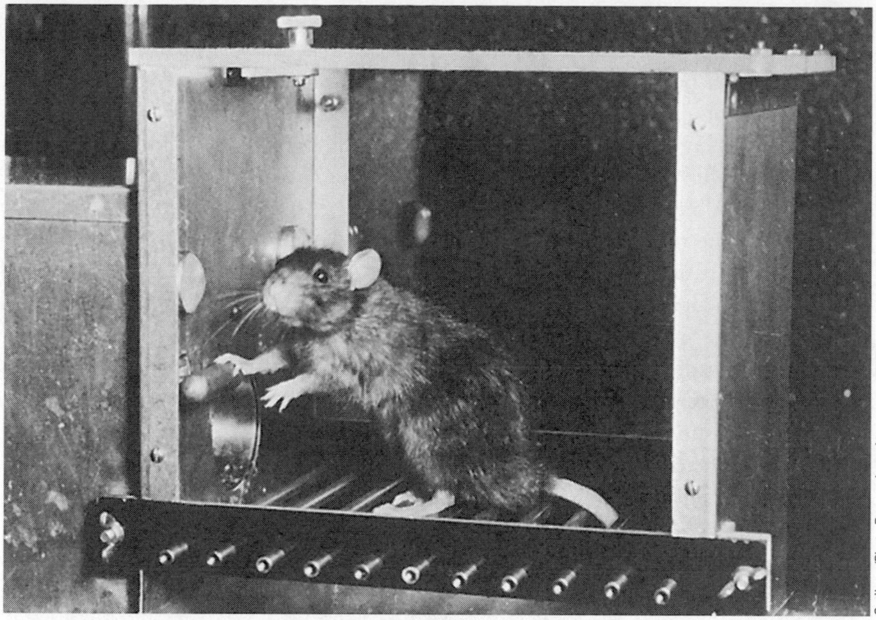

Figure 5.5 A Skinner box equipped with a response lever and a food-delivery device. Electronic equipment is used to program procedures and record responses automatically.

involves two complementary tactics: *reinforcement of successive approximations* to the required response and *nonreinforcement of earlier response forms.*

As illustrated in the preceding example, the shaping of a new operant requires training response components or approximations to the final behavior. Once an operant response such as lever pressing has become established, the manner in which the organism accomplishes the required operation on the environment does not matter. Nevertheless, the steps used in shaping the behavior continue to influence how the response is made. For example, if rearing was one of the reinforced approximations during shaping, the rat is likely to continue to rear as it presses the lever (Stokes & Balsam, 1991). With extensive training, responding becomes more efficient and comes to involve less energy expenditure (Brener & Mitchell, 1989; Mitchell & Brener, 1991).

Shaping and New Behavior. Shaping procedures are often used to generate new behavior, but exactly how new are those responses? Consider, for example, a rat's lever-press response. To press the bar, the rat has to approach the bar, stop in front of it, raise its front paws, and then bring the paws down on the bar with sufficient force to push it down. All of these response components are things the rat is likely to have done at one time or another in other situations (while exploring its cage, interacting with another rat, or handling pieces of food). In teaching the rat to press the bar, the investigator is not teaching new response components. He or she is teaching the rat how to combine familiar responses into a new activity. Instrumental conditioning often involves the construction or synthesis of a new behavioral unit from preexisting response components that already occur in the subject's repertoire (Balsam, Deich, Ohyama, & Stokes, 1998; Reid, Chadwick, Dunham, & Miller, 2001; Schwartz, 1981).

Instrumental conditioning can also be used to produce responses unlike anything the individual is likely to do without training. Consider, for example, throwing a football 60 yards down the field. It takes more than putting familiar behavioral components together to achieve such a feat. The force, speed, and coordination involved in throwing a football 60 yards is unlike anything an untrained individual might do. It is an entirely new response. Expert performance in sports, in playing a musical instrument, or in ballet involves novel response forms. Such novel responses are also created by shaping.

In a laboratory study, for example, Deich, Allan, and Zeigler (1988) shaped the gape response of pigeons pecking for food reinforcement. As I pointed out in Chapter 4, pigeons peck for food with their beaks opened a bit. Deich et al. used a special transducer to measure how far the birds opened their beaks as they pecked a response key. In a baseline phase, the pigeons were reinforced for pecking irrespective of the size of their gape. In another phase of the experiment, food was provided only if their beaks were opened wider than a criterion value. The criterion was chosen based on the previous day's performance so that at least 20% of the birds' pecks would be reinforced. As the birds met each new criterion, the criterion was made more stringent, thereby shaping the birds to peck with increasingly wider gapes. In a comparable manner, decreases in the gape response were shaped in another phase of the experiment.

Figure 5.6 shows the results for one pigeon. During the baseline phase, when reinforcement was independent of the bird's gape, the pigeon made intermediate gape responses. After the shaping procedure in which the criterion for reinforcement required progressively wider gapes, the pigeon learned to peck with its beak opened wider. By contrast, after shaping in which the criterion for reinforcement involved progressively smaller gapes, the pigeon learned to peck with its beak more tightly closed. These changes occurred fairly rapidly. The data in the middle panel of Figure 5.6 were obtained during the 5th

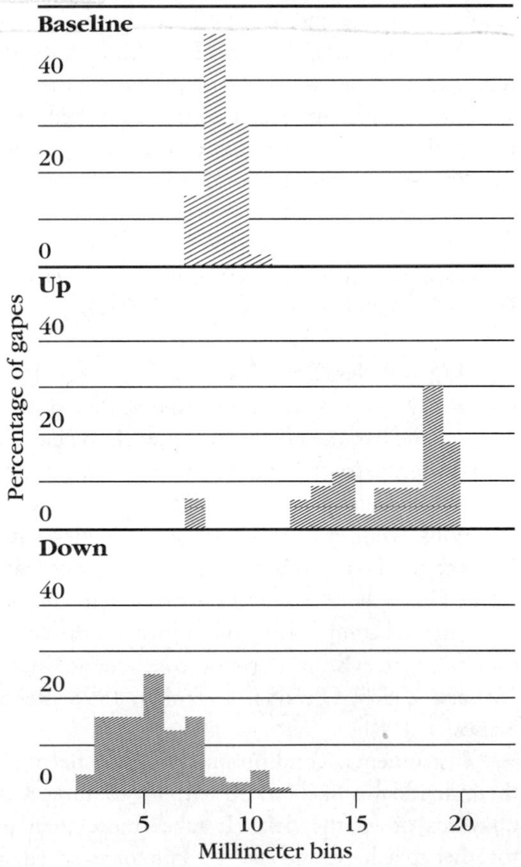

Figure 5.6 Illustration of the shaping of gape size in pigeons. Each panel shows the relative frequency of gapes of various sizes observed in the pecking behavior of a pigeon. During the baseline phase (top panel), pecking was reinforced with food irrespective of the size of the gape. In the other phases, pecking was reinforced only if it occurred with gapes that either exceeded a progressively increasing criterion (middle panel) or were less than a progressively decreasing criterion (bottom panel). (From "Conjunctive Differentiation of Gape During Food-Reinforced Keypecking in the Pigeon," by J. D. Deich, R. W. Allan, and H. P. Zeigler, 1988, *Animal Learning & Behavior, 16,* pp. 268–276. Copyright © 1988 by the Psychonomic Society. Reprinted by permission.)

training session, and the data in the bottom panel came from the 7th session of that condition. (Each session had 32 trials.)

The results presented in Figure 5.6 illustrate several important aspects of the process of shaping. Most responses are like the gape response in that they occur with some variability. The gape response was most uniform during the baseline phase. However, even then, the pigeon pecked with gapes of 7 to 10 mm. This variability in responding helps to ensure that at least a few responses occur that are in the direction you may want to shape the behavior. Thus, *shaping takes advantage of the inherent variability of behavior.* Without such variability, shaping procedures could not succeed. (For a recent study of response variability and shaping, see Stokes, Mechner, & Balsam, 1999.)

When a gape-size criterion was introduced, the distribution of gape sizes shifted in the direction of the reinforcement criterion. Presenting food only if the gape exceeded a certain size, for example, served to shift the distribution of gape sizes to higher values. It was important to set each new criterion so that at least some of the pigeon's existing responses could be reinforced. For example, the first shaping criterion could not have been set at 15 mm because during the baseline phase the pigeon never made a peck with its beak more than 10 mm apart.

As the criterion for reinforcement was gradually shifted during shaping, the pigeon's responses shifted correspondingly. Eventually, the pigeon started making responses that it had never displayed prior to training. For example, after the pigeon was trained to peck with progressively larger gapes, it pecked with its beak opened 20 mm some of the time. By contrast, during the baseline phase, gapes had never exceeded 10 mm. In an analogous fashion, shaping of small gapes produced pecks with gapes as small as 4 mm, which had never been observed during the baseline phase. These aspects of the results illustrate that *shaping can produce new response forms,* forms never before performed by the organism. (For additional discussions of shaping, see Galbicka, 1988; Midgley, Lea, & Kirby, 1989; Pear & Legris, 1987; Platt, 1973.)

Response Rate as a Measure of Operant Behavior. In contrast to discrete-trial techniques for studying instrumental behavior, free-operant methods permit continuous observation of behavior over long periods. With continuous opportunity to respond, the organism rather than the experimenter determines the frequency of its instrumental response. Hence, free-operant techniques provide a special opportunity to observe changes in the likelihood of behavior over time.

How might a researcher take advantage of this opportunity and measure the probability of an operant response? Measures of response latency and speed that are commonly used in discrete-trial procedures do not characterize the likelihood of repetitions of a response. Skinner proposed that the *rate of occurrence* of operant behavior (frequency of the response per minute, for example) be used as a measure of response probability. Highly likely responses occur frequently and have a high rate. In contrast, unlikely responses occur seldom and have a low rate.

INSTRUMENTAL CONDITIONING PROCEDURES

In all instrumental conditioning situations, the subject makes a response and thereby produces an outcome. Paying the boy next door for mowing the lawn, yelling at a cat for getting on the kitchen counter, closing a window to prevent the rain from coming in, and canceling a teenager's driving privileges for staying out late are all forms of instrumental

TABLE 5.1 TYPES OF INSTRUMENTAL CONDITIONING PROCEDURES

NAME OF PROCEDURE	RESPONSE-OUTCOME CONTINGENCY	RESULT
Positive reinforcement	*Positive:* Response produces an appetitive stimulus	*Reinforcement* or increase in response rate
Punishment (positive punishment)	*Positive:* Response produces an aversive stimulus	*Supression* or decrease in response rate
Negative reinforcement (escape or avoidance)	*Negative:* Response eliminates or prevents the occurrence of an aversive stimulus	*Reinforcement* or increase in response rate
Omission training (DRO)	*Negative:* Response eliminates or prevents the occurrence of an appetitive stimulus	*Supression* or decrease in response rate

conditioning. Two of these examples involve pleasant events (getting paid, driving a car) whereas the other two involve unpleasant stimuli (the sound of yelling, and rain coming in the window). A pleasant outcome is technically called an **appetitive stimulus.** An unpleasant outcome is technically called an **aversive stimulus.** The instrumental response may turn on the stimulus, as when the boy next door gets paid for mowing the lawn. In this case a *positive contingency* is said to be in effect between the response and its stimulus outcome. Alternatively, the instrumental response may turn off or eliminate a stimulus, as in closing a window to stop the incoming rain. In that case a *negative contingency* is said to be in effect between the response and its outcome. Whether the result of a conditioning procedure is an increase or a decrease in the rate of responding depends both on response-outcome contingency and on the nature of the outcome.

Table 5.1 describes four common instrumental conditioning procedures. The procedures differ in what type of stimulus (appetitive or aversive) is controlled by the instrumental response and whether the response produces or eliminates the stimulus.

Positive Reinforcement. A father gives his daughter a cookie when she puts her toys away; a teacher praises a student when the student hands in a good report; an employee receives a bonus check when he performs well on the job. These are all examples of **positive reinforcement.** Positive reinforcement is a procedure in which the instrumental response turns on or produces an appetitive stimulus. If the response occurs, the appetitive stimulus is presented; if the response does not occur, the appetitive stimulus is not presented. Thus, a positive contingency exists between the instrumental response and the appetitive stimulus. Positive reinforcement produces an increase in the rate of responding. Giving a hungry rat a food pellet whenever it presses a response lever but not when it does not press the lever is a common laboratory example of positive reinforcement.

Punishment. A mother reprimands her child for running into the street; your boss criticizes you for being late to a meeting; your teacher gives you a failing grade for answering too many test questions incorrectly. These are examples of **punishment.** In a *punishment* procedure, the instrumental response produces or turns on an unpleasant, or aversive, stimulus.

There is a positive contingency between the instrumental response and the stimulus outcome, but the outcome is an aversive stimulus. Effective punishment procedures produce a decline in the instrumental response.

Negative Reinforcement. Both positive reinforcement and punishment involve a positive contingency between the instrumental response and the stimulus outcome. I now turn to procedures that involve a *negative contingency* between the instrumental response and an environmental event. In a negative contingency, the response turns off or prevents the presentation of the environmental event. A procedure in which the instrumental response terminates or prevents the delivery of an *aversive* stimulus is called **negative reinforcement.**

There are two types of negative reinforcement procedures: escape and avoidance. In **escape,** the aversive stimulus is present but can be terminated by the instrumental response. You may escape the unpleasant static of a radio by turning it off. People may leave a movie theater to escape the experience of a bad movie. In the laboratory, a rat may be exposed to a continuous loud noise at the beginning of a trial. By jumping over a barrier or pressing a lever, the rat can escape the noise. In all these cases, the presence of the aversive stimulus sets the occasion for the instrumental response. The instrumental response is then reinforced by termination of the aversive stimulus.

Avoidance involves an aversive stimulus that is scheduled to be presented sometime in the future. In this case the instrumental response prevents delivery of the aversive stimulus. People do many things to prevent the occurrence of something bad. Students study before an examination to avoid receiving a bad grade; factory workers may avoid injury by responding to a fire alarm; people get their cars tuned up regularly to avoid unexpected breakdowns. In the laboratory, a rat may be scheduled to receive shock at the end of a warning stimulus. However, if the rat makes the instrumental response during the warning stimulus, the shock will not be delivered. I have more to say about avoidance behavior in Chapter 10.

Omission Training. Another type of procedure that involves a negative contingency between the instrumental response and an environmental event is called **omission training.** In this case, the instrumental response prevents the delivery of a pleasant or an appetitive stimulus. Omission training is often a preferred method of discouraging human behavior because, unlike punishment, it does not involve delivering an aversive stimulus. Omission training is being used when a child is told to go to his room after doing something bad. The child does not receive an aversive stimulus when he is told to go to his room. There is nothing aversive about the child's room. Rather, by sending the child to the room, the parent is withdrawing sources of positive reinforcement, such as playing with friends or watching television. Suspending a person's driver's license for drunken driving also constitutes omission training (withdrawal of the pleasure and convenience of driving).

Omission training procedures are sometimes called **differential reinforcement of other behavior,** or **DRO.** This term highlights the fact that the individual periodically receives the appetitive stimulus provided he is engaged in behavior other than the response specified by the procedure. Making the target response results in omission of the reward that would have been delivered had the individual performed some "other" behavior. Thus, omission training involves the reinforcement of "other" behavior.

The terms used to describe instrumental conditioning procedures are a bit confusing. For example, people tend to confuse negative reinforcement and punishment. Although an aversive stimulus is used in both procedures, the relation of the instrumental response to the aversive stimulus in each is drastically different. In what is commonly called punishment, a positive contingency exists between the instrumental response and the aversive stimulus.

BOX 5.2

Omission Training as a Therapeutic Procedure

Omission training, or differential reinforcement of other behavior (DRO), involves the delivery of an appetitive stimulus when the individual fails to perform the target response. Therefore, such procedures can be used to discourage undesired responses. In one study (Barton, Brulle, & Repp, 1986), omission training was used with mentally retarded students of elementary school age. The reinforcers were things like apples, raisins, grapes, and juice. One student engaged in recurrent handflapping (moving the hand up and down or back and forth). The rate of this behavior was first observed under baseline conditions (in the absence of special intervention) for 12 days. Then, an omission training (DRO) procedure was introduced for the next 29 days. Omission training consisted of providing a reinforcer whenever a 1-minute period elapsed without any handflapping. The omission training phase was then followed by return to the baseline condition, followed by reintroduction of omission training.

The results of the study are summarized in Figure 5.7. During the first baseline phase, the student engaged in handflapping about once a minute. This rate of responding declined to near zero during the first omission training (DRO) phase. Removal of the omission procedure resulted in recovery of the handflapping response. Reintroduction of omission training at the end of the study produced another decline in responding. Interestingly, responding dropped to close to zero faster the second time the omission contingency (DRO) was introduced. These results indicate that omission training is an effective procedure for suppressing responding. Omission training or DRO procedures have also been used successfully to suppress self-injurious behavior and aggression in individuals diagnosed with mental retardation (Lindberg et al., 1999; Progar et al., 2001).

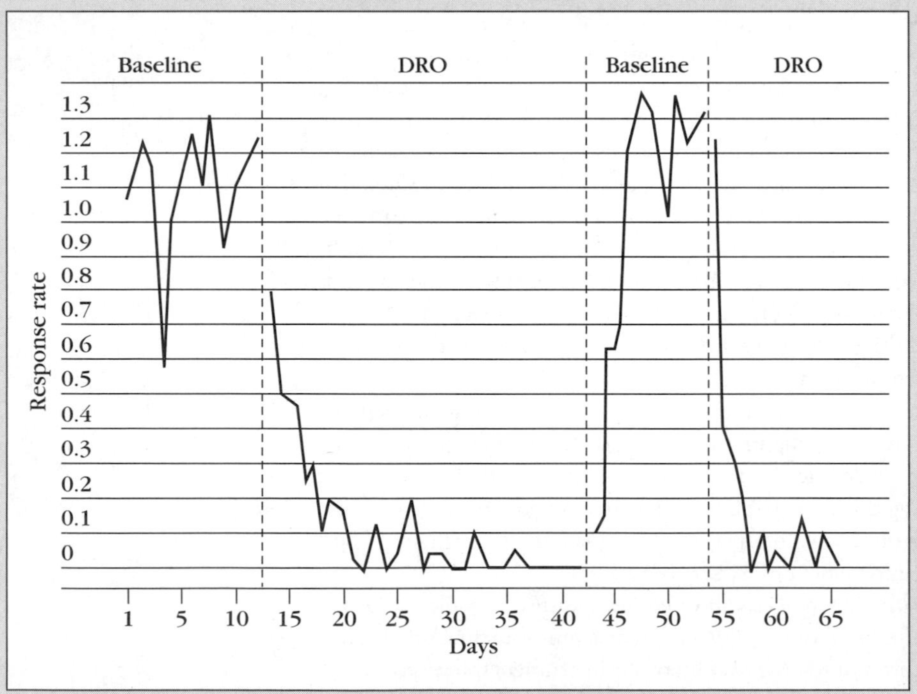

Figure 5.7 Rate of handflapping (responses per minute) by a mentally retarded student during baseline conditions, when reinforcement was not provided, and during omission training phases (DRO), when reinforcement was provided for 1-minute periods without handflapping. (From "Maintenance of Therapeutic Change by Momentary DRO," by L. E. Barton, A. R. Brulle, and A. C. Repp, 1986, *Journal of Applied Behavior Analysis, 19,* 277–282. Copyright © 1986 by the *Journal of Applied Behavior Analysis.* Reprinted by permission.)

(The response results in delivery of the aversive stimulus.) By contrast, in negative reinforcement, there is a negative response-outcome contingency. (The response either terminates or prevents the delivery of the aversive stimulus.) This difference in the contingencies produces very different outcomes. The instrumental response is decreased by punishment and increased by negative reinforcement.

FUNDAMENTAL ELEMENTS OF INSTRUMENTAL CONDITIONING

As I show in the coming chapters, analysis of instrumental conditioning involves numerous factors and variables. However, the essence of instrumental behavior is that it is controlled by its consequences. Instrumental conditioning involves three key elements: a response, an outcome (the reinforcer), and a relation, or contingency, between the response and the outcome. In the remainder of this chapter, I describe how each of these elements influences the course of instrumental conditioning.

The Instrumental Response

The outcome of instrumental conditioning procedures depends in part on the nature of the response being conditioned. Some responses are more easily modified than others. In Chapter 10, I describe how the nature of the response influences the outcome of negative reinforcement (avoidance) and punishment procedures. The following section describes how the nature of the response determines the results of positive reinforcement procedures.

Behavioral Variability versus Stereotypy. Thorndike described instrumental behavior as involving the "stamping in" of an S-R association. Skinner wrote about behavior being "reinforced" or strengthened. Both pioneers emphasized that reinforcement increases the likelihood that the instrumental response will be repeated in the future. This emphasis encouraged the belief that instrumental conditioning produces repetitions of the same response—that it produces uniformity or stereotypy in behavior. Increasingly stereotyped responding does develop if that is allowed or required by the instrumental conditioning procedure (for example, Pisacreta, 1982; Schwartz, 1980, 1985, 1988.) However, that does not mean that instrumental conditioning cannot also be involved in producing creative or variable responses.

We are accustomed to thinking about the requirement for reinforcement being an observable action, such as movement of an individual's leg, torso, or hand. Interestingly, however, the criteria for reinforcement can also be defined in terms of more abstract dimensions of behavior, such as its variability. For example, organisms can learn to obtain reinforcement in a situation where they are required to do something new, something unlike what they did on the preceding four or five trials. *Response variability* can be the basis for instrumental reinforcement.

In one study of the instrumental conditioning of response variability (Page & Neuringer, 1985), pigeons had to peck two response keys eight times to obtain food. The eight pecks could be distributed between the two keys in any manner. All the pecks could be on the left or the right key, or the pigeons could alternate between the keys in various ways (two pecks on the left, followed by one on the right, one on the left, three on the right, and one on the left, for example). However, to obtain food on a given trial, the

A. Neuringer

sequence of left-right pecks had to be different from the pattern of left-right pecks the bird made on the preceding 50 trials. Thus, the pigeons had to generate novel patterns of left-right pecks and not repeat any pattern for 50 trials. In a control condition, food was provided at the same frequency for eight pecks distributed between the two keys, but now the sequence of right and left pecks did not matter. The pigeons did not have to generate novel response sequences in the control condition.

Sample results of the experiment are presented in Figure 5.8 in terms of the percentage of response sequences performed during each session that were different from each other. Results for the first and last 5 days on each procedure are presented separately. About 50% of the response sequences performed were different from each other during the first five sessions of each procedure. When the instrumental conditioning procedure required response variability, variability in responding increased to about 75%. By contrast, in the control condition, when the pigeons were reinforced regardless of the sequence of left-right pecks they made, variability in performed sequences dropped to less than 20%.

This study illustrates two interesting facts about instrumental conditioning. First, it shows that variability in responding can be maintained and increased by reinforcement. Thus, response variability can be established as an operant (see also Machado, 1989, 1992; Morgan & Neuringer, 1990; Morris, 1987; Neuringer, 1991, 1992, 1993; Neuringer, Deiss, & Olson, 2000). The results also show that in the absence of explicit reinforcement

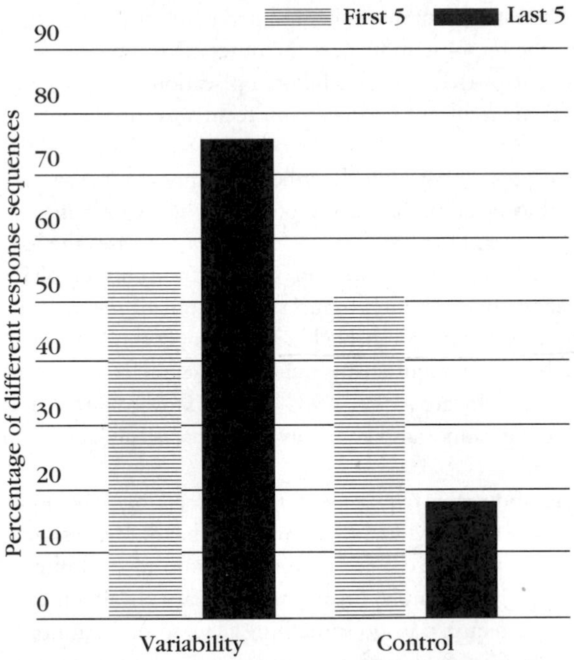

Figure 5.8 Percentage of novel left-right response sequences pigeons performed when variability in response sequences was required for food reinforcement (left) and when food reinforcement was provided regardless of the response sequence performed (right). Data are presented separately for the first five and last five sessions of each procedure. (After "Variability as an Operant," by S. Page and A. Neuringer, 1985, *Journal of Experimental Psychology: Animal Behavior Process, 11,* 429–452. Copyright © 1985 by the American Psychological Association).

BOX 5.3

DETRIMENTAL EFFECTS OF REWARD: MORE MYTH THAN REALITY

Reinforcement procedures have become commonplace in educational settings as a way to encourage students to read and do their assignments. However, some have been concerned that reinforcement may actually undermine a child's intrinsic interest and willingness to perform a task once the reinforcement procedure is removed (for example, Lepper, Greene, & Nisbett, 1973). Similar concerns have been expressed about possible detrimental effects of reinforcement on creativity or originality. Extensive research on these questions has produced inconsistent results. However, a meta-analysis of nearly 100 studies indicated that overall there is little evidence to support the claim that reinforcement undermines intrinsic motivation or performance (Cameron & Pierce, 1994). The only circumstance in which reinforcement consistently undermined performance was if the reward was given irrespective of behavior. Research with children also indicated that reinforcement makes children respond with less originality only under special circumstances (see Eisenberger & Cameron, 1996). Reinforcement can increase or decrease originality, depending on the criterion for reinforcement. If highly original responding is required to obtain reinforcement, originality increases, provided that the reinforcer is not so salient as to distract the participant from the task. (For a discussion of how such contingencies and other task constraints promote creativity in gifted children and artists, see Stokes, 2001.)

of variability, responding becomes more stereotyped with continued instrumental conditioning. Pigeons in the control condition decreased the range of different response sequences they performed as training progressed. Thus, the typical consequence of instrumental reinforcement is a decrease in response variability. (For other conditions that decrease response variability, see Cherot, Jones, & Neuringer, 1996.)

Relevance or Belongingness in Instrumental Conditioning. As the preceding section showed, instrumental conditioning can act on overt response components or on abstract dimensions of behavior (such as variability). How far do these principles extend? Are there any limits on the types of new behavioral units or response dimensions that may be modified by instrumental conditioning? A growing body of evidence indicates that there are important limitations.

In Chapter 4, I described how classical conditioning occurs at different rates depending on the combination of CS and US that is used. Rats readily learn to associate tastes with sickness, for example, whereas associations between tastes and shock are not so easily learned. For conditioning to occur rapidly, the CS has to "belong" with the US, or be "relevant" to the US. Analogous belongingness, or relevance, relations occur in instrumental conditioning.

Thorndike was the first to observe differences in the ease of conditioning of various responses. In many of the puzzle-box experiments, the cat had to manipulate a latch or a string to escape from the box. Thorndike also tried to condition scratching and yawning as instrumental responses. The cats could learn to make these responses, but, interestingly, the form of the responses changed as training proceeded. At first, the cat would scratch itself vigorously to be let out of the box. On later trials, it would only make "aborted" scratching movements. It might put its leg to its body but would not make a true scratch response.

Similar results were obtained in attempts to condition yawning. As training progressed, the animal would open its mouth to be let out of the box, but it would not give a bona fide yawn.

Thorndike proposed the concept of **belongingness** to explain the failures to train scratching and yawning. According to this concept, certain responses naturally "belong with" the reinforcer because of the animal's evolutionary history. Operating a latch and pulling a string are manipulatory responses that are naturally related to release from confinement. By contrast, scratching and yawning characteristically do not help animals escape from confinement and therefore do not "belong with" release from a puzzle box. Presumably, this is why scratching and yawning do not persist as vigorous bona fide instrumental responses when reinforced by release from the box.

The concept of belongingness in instrumental conditioning is well illustrated by a more recent study involving a small fish species, the three-spined stickleback (*Gasterosteus aculeatus*). During the mating season each spring, male sticklebacks establish territories from which they court females but chase away and fight other males. Sevenster (1973) used the presentation of another male or a female as a reinforcer in instrumental conditioning of male sticklebacks. One group of fish was required to bite a rod to obtain access to the reinforcer. Biting is a component of the aggressive behavior that occurs when a resident male encounters an intruder male. When the reinforcer was another male, biting behavior increased; access to another male was an effective reinforcer for the biting response. By contrast, biting did not increase when it was reinforced with courtship opportunity. However, courtship opportunity was an effective reinforcer for other responses, such as swimming through a ring. A belongingness relation evidently exists between biting and the consequent presentation of another male, but biting does not "belong with" presentation of a female, which typically elicits courtship rather than aggression.

Various limitations on instrumental conditioning were also observed by Breland and Breland (1961) in attempts to condition instrumental responses with food reinforcement in several species. Their goal was to train animals to perform entertaining response chains for displays to be used in amusement parks and zoos. During the course of this work, they observed dramatic behavior changes that were not consistent with the reinforcement procedures they were using. For example, they describe a raccoon that was reinforced for picking up a coin and depositing it in a coin bank.

Courtesy of Donald A. Dewsbury

M. Breland-Bailey

> We started out by reinforcing him for picking up a single coin. Then the metal container was introduced, with the requirement that he drop the coin into the container. Here we ran into the first bit of difficulty: he seemed to have a great deal of trouble letting go of the coin. He would rub it up against the inside of the container, pull it back out, and clutch it firmly for several seconds. However, he would finally turn it loose and receive his food reinforcement. Then the final contingency: we [required] that he pick up [two] coins and put them in the container.
>
> Now the raccoon really had problems (and so did we). Not only could he not let go of the coins, but he spent seconds, even minutes, rubbing them together (in a most miserly fashion), and dipping them into the container. He carried on this behavior to such an extent that the practical application we had in mind—a display featuring a raccoon putting money in a piggy bank—simply was not feasible. The rubbing behavior became worse and worse as time went on, in spite of nonreinforcement. (p. 682)

From "The Misbehavior of Organisms," by K. Breland and M. Breland, 1961. In *American Psychologist, 16,* 682.

The Brelands had similar difficulties with other species. Pigs, for example, also could not learn to put coins in a piggy bank. After initial training, they began rooting the coins

Animal Behavior Enterprises

Raccoons are adept at doing some things, like tearing up a package, but it is difficult to condition them to drop coins into a container for food reinforcement.

along the ground. The Brelands called the development of such responses as rooting in the pigs and rubbing coins together in the raccoons **instinctive drift.** As the term implies, the extra responses that developed in these food reinforcement situations were activities the animals instinctively perform when obtaining food. Pigs root along the ground in connection with feeding, and raccoons rub and dunk food-related objects. These natural food-related responses were apparently very strong and competed with the responses required by the experimenter. The Brelands emphasized that such instinctive response tendencies have to be taken into account in the analysis of behavior.

Behavior Systems and Constraints on Instrumental Conditioning. The response limitations on instrumental conditioning I have described are consistent with behavior systems theory, which I described in Chapter 4, in discussions of the nature of the conditioned response (see Timberlake, 1983a, 2001; Timberlake & Lucas, 1989). According to behavior systems theory, when an animal is food-deprived and is in a situation where it might encounter food, its feeding system becomes activated, and it begins to engage in foraging and other food-related activities. An instrumental conditioning procedure is superimposed on this behavior system. The effectiveness of the procedure in increasing an instrumental response will depend on the compatibility of that response with the preexisting organization of the feeding system. Furthermore, the nature of other responses that emerge during the course of training (or instinctive drift) will depend on the behavioral components of the feeding system that become activated by the instrumental conditioning procedure.

According to the behavior systems approach, we should be able to predict which responses will increase with food reinforcement by studying what animals do when their feeding system is activated in the absence of instrumental conditioning. This prediction has been confirmed. In a study of hamsters, Shettleworth (1975) found that food deprivation decreases the probability of self-care responses, such as face washing and scratching, but increases the probability of environment-directed activities, such as digging, scratching at a wall (scrabbling), and rearing on the hind legs. These results suggest that self-care responses (face washing and scratching) are not part of the feeding system activated by hunger,

Courtesy of Donald A. Dewsbury

S. J. Shettleworth

whereas environment-directed activities (digging, scrabbling, and rearing) are part of the feeding system. Given these findings, behavior systems theory predicts that food reinforcement should produce increases in digging, scrabbling, and rearing but not increases in face washing and scratching. This pattern of results is precisely what has been observed in studies of instrumental conditioning (Shettleworth, 1975). Thus, the susceptibility of various responses to food reinforcement can be predicted from how those responses are altered by food deprivation, which presumably reflects their compatibility with the feeding system.

As discussed in Chapter 4, another way to diagnose whether a response is a part of a behavior system is to perform a classical conditioning experiment. Through classical conditioning, a CS comes to elicit components of the behavior system activated by the US. If instinctive drift reflects responses of the behavior system, responses akin to instinctive drift should be evident in a classical conditioning experiment. Timberlake and his associates (see Timberlake, 1983b; Timberlake, Wahl, & King, 1982) tested this prediction with rats in a modification of the coin-handling studies conducted by Breland and Breland.

The apparatus used by Timberlake et al. (1982) delivered a ball bearing into the experimental chamber at the start of each trial. The floor of the chamber was tilted so that the ball bearing would roll from one end of the chamber to the other and exit through a hole. In one experimental condition, the rats were required to make contact with the ball bearing to obtain food reinforcement. Other conditions employed a classical conditioning procedure: food was provided after the ball bearing rolled across the chamber whether or not the rat touched the ball bearing. Consistent with the behavior systems view, in both procedures the rats came to touch and extensively handle the ball bearings instead of letting them roll into the hole. (Some animals picked up the bearing, put it in their mouth, carried it to the other end of the chamber, and sat and chewed it.) Such instinctive drift developed with both instrumental and classical conditioning procedures. These results indicate that touching and handling the ball bearing are manifestations of the feeding behavior system in rats. Thus, instinctive drift represents the intrusion of responses appropriate to the behavior system activated during the course of instrumental conditioning. (For additional research on the implications of behavior systems for instrumental conditioning, see Timberlake, 1983b; Timberlake & Washburne, 1989).

The Instrumental Reinforcer

Several aspects of a reinforcer determine its effects on the learning and performance of instrumental behavior. I first discuss the direct effects of the quantity and quality of a reinforcer on instrumental behavior. I then describe how responding to a particular reward amount and type depends on the organism's past experience with other reinforcers.

Quantity and Quality of the Reinforcer. Although the quantity and quality of the reinforcer are logically different characteristics, sometimes it is difficult to separate them experimentally. A change in the quantity of the reinforcer may also make the reinforcer qualitatively different. In a systematic study, Hutt (1954) tried to isolate the effects of the quantity and quality of a liquid food reinforcer by systematically varying both features. Independent groups of rats were trained to press a response lever to receive either small, medium, or large amounts of a fluid mixture of water, milk, and flour. Some of the rats were tested with the basic mixture; others were given a mixture that had been improved by adding saccharin. For yet other groups of rats, the quality of the fluid was reduced by adding a small amount of citric acid. Figure 5.9 shows the average rate of bar pressing for each group. Increases in either the quality or the quantity of the reinforcer produced higher rates of responding.

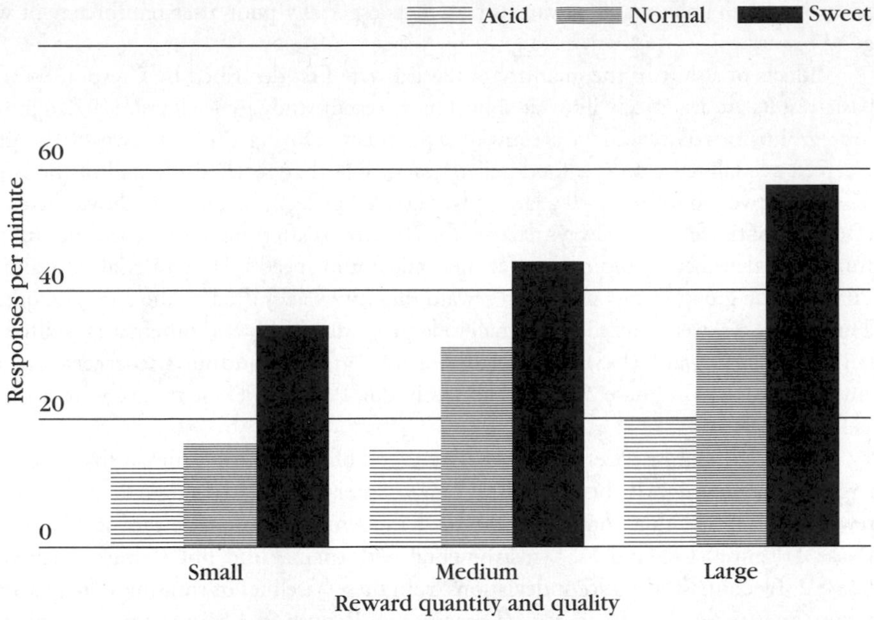

Figure 5.9 Average rates of responding in groups of rats for which responding was reinforced with reinforcers varying in quantity and quality. (From "Rate of Bar Pressing as a Function of Quality and Quantity of Food Reward," by P. J. Hutt, 1954, *Journal of Comparative and Physiological Psychology, 47,* pp. 235–239.)

Results similar to the findings of Hutt are typically obtained in runway experiments (see Mackintosh, 1974, for a review). Rats, for example, run faster for larger and more palatable reinforcers. In free-operant situations, however, the effects of reinforcer magnitude are more complex and depend on the schedule of reinforcement used and other factors (for example, Bizo, Kettle, & Killeen, 2001; Collier, Johnson, & Morgan, 1992; Leslie, Boyle, & Shaw, 2000; Reed, 1991; Reed & Wright, 1989). (I discuss schedules of reinforcement in Chapter 6.)

Shifts in Reinforcer Quality or Quantity. In the study by Hutt (1954), a given group of rats received only one particular quantity and quality of liquid food throughout the experiment. What would happen if the quantity or quality of the reinforcer were shifted from one value to another for the same individual? This is an interesting question because it raises the possibility that the effectiveness of a reinforcer depends not only on its own properties but also on how that reinforcer compares with others the individual has experienced.

I noted in Chapter 4 that the effectiveness of an unconditioned stimulus in classical conditioning depends on how the US compares with the individual's expectations based on prior experience. This idea serves as the foundation of the Rescorla–Wagner model. If the US is larger (or more intense) than expected, it will support excitatory conditioning. By contrast, if the US is smaller (or weaker) than expected, it will support inhibitory conditioning. Are there analogous effects in instrumental conditioning? Common experience suggests definitely yes. If you have been working for $9.50 per hour for the past 6 months, getting that rate of pay will not be too exciting. However, if you have been working for $7.50/hr, an increase to $9.50/hr will be especially attractive. Experimental evidence confirms these impressions. Numerous studies have shown that the effects of a particular amount and type of reinforcer depend on the quantity and quality of the reinforcers the individual experienced previously. (For reviews, see Flaherty, 1982, 1991, 1996.) Speaking loosely, a favorable reward is treated as especially good after reinforcement with a poor reward, and an unfavorable reward is treated as especially poor after reinforcement with a good reward.

Effects of a shift in the quantity of reward were first described by Crespi (1942). The basic results are also nicely illustrated by a more recent study by Mellgren (1972), in which four groups of rats served in a runway experiment. During Phase 1, two of the groups received a small reward (S: 2 food pellets) each time they reached the end of the runway. The other two groups received a large reward (L: 22 pellets) for each trip down the runway. (Delivery of the food was always delayed for 20 seconds after the rats reached the end of the runway so that they would not run at their maximum speed.) After 11 trials of training in Phase 1, one group of rats with each reward quantity was shifted to the alternate quantity. Thus, some rats were shifted from small to large reward (S-L), and others were shifted from large to small reward (L-S). The remaining two groups continued to receive the same amount of reward in Phase 2 as they had received in Phase 1. (These groups were designated as L-L and S-S.)

R. L. Mellgren

Figure 5.10 summarizes the results. At the end of Phase 1, the animals that received the large reward ran slightly, but not significantly, faster than the rats that received the small reward. For groups that continued to receive the same amount of reward in Phase 2 as in Phase 1 (groups L-L and S-S), instrumental performance did not change much during Phase 2. By contrast, significant deviations from these baselines of running were observed in groups that received shifts in reward magnitude. Rats shifted from large to small reward (group L-S) rapidly decreased their running speeds, and rats shifted from small to large reward (group S-L) soon increased their running speeds.

The most significant finding was that following a shift in reward magnitude, running speed was not entirely determined by the new reward magnitude. Rather, the effects of the

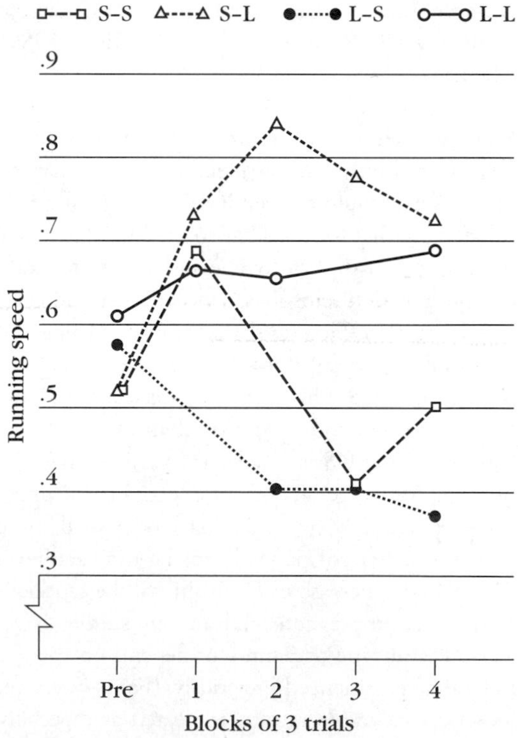

Figure 5.10 Running speeds of four groups of rats in blocks of 3 trials. Block "Pre" represents running speeds at the end of Phase 1. Blocks 1–4 represent running speeds in Phase 2. At the start of Phase 2, groups S-L and L-S experienced a shift in amount of reward from small to large and large to small, respectively. Groups S-S and L-L received small and large rewards, respectively, throughout the experiment. (From "Positive and Negative Contrast Effects Using Delayed Reinforcement," by R. L. Mellgren, 1972, *Learning and Motivation, 3,* pp. 185–193. Copyright © 1972 by Academic Press. Reprinted by permission.)

new reward were enhanced by previous experience with a contrasting reward magnitude. Rats shifted from a small to a large reward (group S-L) ran faster for the large reward than rats that always received the large reward (group L-L). Correspondingly, animals shifted from a large to a small reward (group L-S) ran more slowly for the small reward than animals that always received the small reward (group S-S).

The results Mellgren obtained illustrate the phenomena of successive positive and negative contrast. **Positive contrast** refers to elevated responding for a favorable reward resulting from prior experience with a less attractive outcome. More informally, the favorable reward looks especially good to individuals who experienced a worse outcome previously. **Negative contrast** refers to depressed responding for an unfavorable reward because of prior experience with a better outcome. In this case, the unfavorable reward looks especially bad to individuals who experienced a better reward previously.

In Mellgren's study, the two reward conditions were presented in different phases of the experiment, and only one shift in reward magnitude occurred for the shifted groups. Because of this, the results are called *successive* positive and negative contrast. Contrast effects also occur if reward conditions are shifted back and forth frequently, with a different cue signaling each reward condition (for example, McSweeney & Melville, 1993; Williams, 1983, 1990, 1992b, 1997b). These effects are examples of **simultaneous behavioral contrast.**

Courtesy of Donald A. Dewsbury

C. F. Flaherty

Different contrast effects are mediated by different mechanisms (see Flaherty, 1996; Williams, 1997b). However, all contrast effects illustrate that the effectiveness of a reinforcer in one situation is determined in part by the organism's experiences with reinforcers in other situations. For reasons that are not entirely clear, negative contrast has been obtained more readily than positive contrast. Negative contrast has traditionally been attributed to the aversive or frustrative effects of getting an unexpectedly small reward (Amsel, 1992). Studies with anti-anxiety drugs, however, suggest that the emotional effects of a downshift in reward value do not occur immediately (Flaherty, Grigson, & Lind, 1990). Current thinking is that a downshift in reward magnitude activates a series of cognitive and behavioral changes (Flaherty, 1996). The initial encounter with the unexpectedly small reward activates exploratory and search responses that might result in finding a better source of food (Flaherty, Greenwood, Martin, & Leszczuk, 1998; Pecoraro, Timberlake, & Tinsley, 1999). Emotional disappointment sets in when the search responses are unsuccessful and the subject has to contend with the small reward. This is then followed by an accommodation to the continued availability of only the small reward.

The Response-Reinforcer Relation

As I have said, instrumental behavior produces and is controlled by its consequences. In some cases, there is a strong relation between what a person does and the consequence that follows. If you put 75¢ into a soda machine, you will get a can of soda. As long as the machine is working, you will get a can of soda every time you put in the required 75¢. In other cases, there is no relation between behavior and an outcome. You may wear a red shirt to an examination and receive a good grade, but the grade would not be related to your having worn the red shirt. The relation between behavior and its consequences can also be probabilistic. For example, you might have to make several phone calls before finding someone who is willing to help you with a problem.

Human and nonhuman animals perform a continual stream of responses and experience all kinds of environmental events. You are always doing something, even if it is just sitting around, and things are continually happening in your environment. An organism must organize its behavior to meet various challenges, and it must do so in a way that makes the best use of its time and energy. There is no point in working hard to make the sun rise each morning, because that will happen anyway. It makes more sense to devote energy to fixing breakfast or working for a paycheck—things that do not become available without your effort. To be efficient, you have to know when you have to do something to obtain a reinforcer and when the reinforcer is likely to be delivered independent of your actions. Efficient instrumental behavior requires sensitivity to the response-reinforcer relation.

Two types of relationships exist between a response and a reinforcer. One is the *temporal relation,* which refers to the time between the response and the reinforcer. A special type of the temporal relation is the **temporal contiguity,** which refers to the delivery of the reinforcer immediately after the response. The second type of relation between a response and the reinforcer is the *causal relation* or **response-reinforcer contingency.** The response-reinforcer contingency refers to the extent to which the instrumental response is necessary and sufficient for the occurrence of the reinforcer.

Temporal and causal factors are independent of each other. A strong temporal relation does not require a strong causal relation, and vice versa. For example, there is strong causal relation between submitting an application for admission to college and getting accepted. (If you don't apply, you are guaranteed not to be accepted.) However, the temporal relation between applying and getting admitted is weak. You may not hear about the acceptance for several weeks (or months) after submitting your application.

Effects of Temporal Contiguity. Both conventional wisdom and experimental evidence tell us that immediate reinforcement is preferable to delayed reinforcement (McDevitt & Williams, 2001). In addition, since the early work of Grice (1948), learning psychologists have emphasized that instrumental conditioning requires providing the reinforcer immediately after the occurrence of the instrumental response. Grice reported that instrumental learning can be disrupted by delays as short as 0.5 seconds. More recent research has indicated that instrumental conditioning is possible with delays as long as 30 seconds (Critchfield & Lattal, 1993; Lattal & Gleeson, 1990; Lattal & Metzger, 1994; Sutphin, Byrne, & Poling, 1998; Williams & Lattal, 1999). The fact remains that instrumental learning is disrupted by delaying the delivery of the reinforcer after the occurrence of the instrumental response.

The effects of delayed reinforcement on learning to press a response lever is shown in Figure 5.11 (Dickinson, Watt, & Griffiths, 1992). Each time a rat pressed the lever, a food pellet was delivered after a fixed delay. For some subjects, the delay was short (2–4 seconds); for others, the delay was considerable (64 seconds). In this study, if the subject pressed the lever again during the delay interval, the new response resulted in another food pellet after the specified delay. (In other studies, such "extra" responses are programmed to reset the delay interval.) In Figure 5.11, response rates are shown as a function of the mean delay of reinforcement experienced by each group. The results indicate that responding dropped off fairly rapidly with increases in the delay of reinforcement. No learning was evident with a 64-second delay of reinforcement in this experiment.

Why is instrumental conditioning so sensitive to a delay of reinforcement? There are several contributing factors. One stems from the fact that a delay makes it difficult to figure out which response deserves the credit for the reinforcer that is delivered. As I pointed out earlier, behavior consists of an ongoing, continual stream of activities. When reinforcement is delayed after performance of a specified response, R1, the organism does not stop doing things. After performing R1, the organism may perform R2, R3, R4, and so on. If the reinforcer is set up by R1 but not delivered until some time later, the reinforcer may occur immediately after some other response, say, R6. To associate R1 with the reinforcer, the organism has to have some way to distinguish R1 from the other responses it performs during the delay interval.

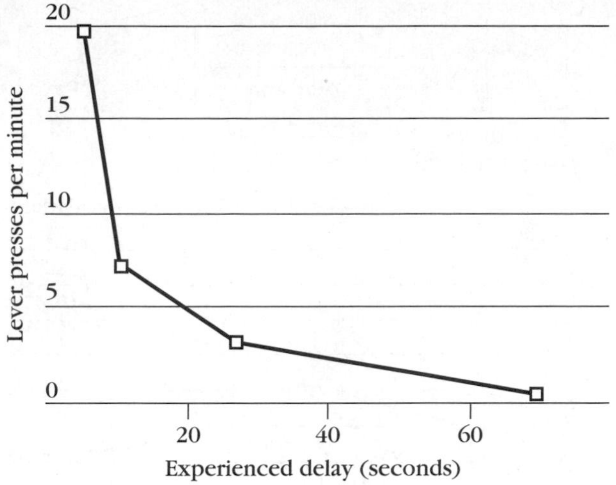

Figure 5.11 Effects of delay of reinforcement on acquisition of lever pressing in rats. (From "Free-Operant Acquisition with Delayed Reinforcement," by A. Dickinson, A. Watt, and W. J. H. Griffiths, 1992, *The Quarterly Journal of Experimental Psychology, 45B,* pp. 241–258. Copyright © 1992 by The Experimental Psychology Society. Reprinted by permission.)

There are a couple of ways to overcome this problem. The first technique, used by animal trainers and coaches for centuries, is to provide a secondary or conditioned reinforcer immediately after the instrumental response, even if the primary reinforcer cannot occur until some time later. A **secondary** or **conditioned reinforcer** is a conditioned stimulus that was previously associated with the reinforcer. Verbal prompts in coaching, such as "good" and "that's the way," are conditioned reinforcers that can provide immediate reinforcement for appropriate behavior. Good coaches are constantly providing such immediate verbal feedback or conditioned reinforcement. Conditioned reinforcers can serve to "bridge" a delay between the instrumental response and the delivery of the primary reinforcer (Cronin, 1980; Winter & Perkins, 1982; Williams, 1991, 1993; for an analogous outcome in human judgments of causality, see Reed, 1999).

Another technique that facilitates learning with delayed reinforcement is to *mark* the target instrumental response in some way to make it distinguishable from the other activities of the organism. The effectiveness of a **marking procedure** was first demonstrated by Lieberman, McIntosh, and Thomas (1979). Rats served in the experiment, and the apparatus was a special maze, shown at the top in Figure 5.12. After release from the start box, the rats had a choice between entering a white or a black side arm. Entering the white arm was designated as the correct instrumental response and was reinforced with access to food in the goal box after a delay of 60 seconds.

D. A. Lieberman

Two groups of animals were tested, and they were differentiated by what happened to them immediately after making the correct choice. Rats in the "marked" group were picked up by the experimenter and placed in the delay box. By contrast, the animals in the "unmarked" group were undisturbed. After they made the correct response, the door at the end of the choice alley was opened for them, and they were allowed to walk into the delay box without being handled. Sixty seconds after the instrumental response, both groups were placed in the goal box to obtain the reinforcer. The same sequence of events occurred when the rats made an incorrect response, except that in this case they were not reinforced at the end of the delay interval. Because the same marking stimulus (handling) occurred on both reinforced and nonreinforced trials, the marking stimulus was not specifically correlated with reinforcement.

Results of the experiment are shown in the graph in Figure 5.12. Rats in the marked group learned the instrumental response with the 60-second delay of reinforcement much

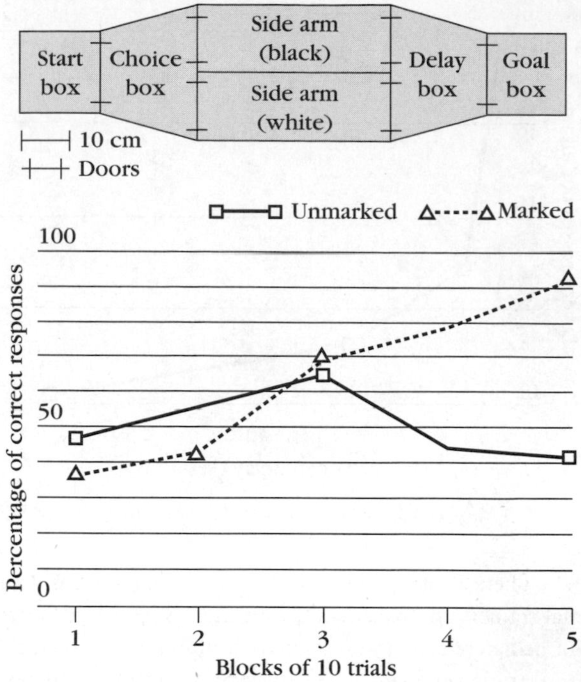

Figure 5.12 Top view of apparatus and results of an experiment to test the effects of marking an instrumental response on instrumental conditioning with reinforcement delayed 60 seconds. Choosing the white side arm was designated as the correct response. Rats spent the delay interval in the delay box. Those in the "Marked" group were placed in the delay box after each choice response. Those in the "Unmarked" group were allowed to walk into the delay box undisturbed. (From "Learning When Reward Is Delayed: A Marking Hypothesis," by D. A. Lieberman, D. C. McIntosh, and G. V. Thomas, 1979, *Journal of Experimental Psychology: Animal Behavior Processes, 5,* pp. 224–242. Copyright © 1979 by the American Psychological Association. Reprinted by permission.)

better than animals in the unmarked group. At the end of 50 training trials, the marking procedure resulted in the correct choice 90% of the time. By contrast, without the marking procedure, the correct choice occurred about 50% of the time, which is chance performance.

In another experiment, Lieberman and his colleagues demonstrated successful learning with delayed reinforcement when the instrumental response was marked by a brief, intense light or noise (Lieberman et al., 1979). These effects of marking cannot be explained in terms of secondary or conditioned reinforcement, because the marking stimulus was presented after both correct and incorrect choices. Any conditioned reinforcement effects would have increased both correct and incorrect choices and thus cannot be responsible for the preponderance of correct responses that was observed (see also Lieberman, Davidson, & Thomas, 1985; Lieberman & Thomas, 1986; Ploog, 2001; Thomas & Lieberman, 1990; Urcuioli & Kasprow, 1988).

Secondary reinforcement and marking procedures both focus on better connecting the target instrumental response to the delayed reinforcer. Another way to think about this issue is that when reinforcement is delayed, it is treated as if the reinforcer occurred independent of behavior. What are the consequences of response-independent reinforcement that could contribute to the deleterious effects of delayed reinforcement? When a reinforcer is presented independent of behavior, the subject cannot easily tell when it will get reinforced. Not being able to predict when it will get fed, the subject may look into the food hopper more frequently, and these hopper-observing responses will interfere with the target instrumental response. Experiments with pigeons have provided data in support of this interpretation (Schaal, Shahan, Kovera, & Reilly, 1998; see also Lattal & Abreu-Rodrigues, 1997).

Another consequence of response-independent reinforcement is the conditioning of contextual cues. If there is a delay between the target response and the delivery of the reinforcer, the reinforcer will occur in the experimental context without being signaled by the response. This will permit conditioning of the contextual cues. By becoming associated with the reinforcer, these contextual cues can then block the formation of an association between the target response and the reinforcer. Consistent with this interpretation, Dickinson, Watt, and Varga (1996) found that procedures that disrupt the conditioning of contextual cues help to overcome the deleterious effects of delayed reinforcement on instrumental conditioning.

The Response-Reinforcer Contingency. As I noted earlier, the response-reinforcer contingency refers to the extent to which the delivery of the reinforcer is dependent on the prior occurrence of the instrumental response. In studies of delay of reinforcement, there is a perfect causal relation between the response and the reinforcer. Although the reinforcer is delayed, it is only provided if the organism makes the instrumental response. Studies of delay of reinforcement show that a perfect causal relation between the response and the reinforcer is not sufficient to produce vigorous instrumental responding. Even with a perfect causal relation, conditioning does not occur if reinforcement is delayed too long. Such data encouraged early investigators to conclude that response-reinforcer contiguity rather than contingency was the critical factor producing instrumental learning. However, this view has turned out to be unjustified by subsequent research. The response-reinforcer contingency is also important.

Skinner's Superstition Experiment. A landmark experiment in the debate about the role of contiguity versus contingency in instrumental learning was Skinner's superstition experiment (Skinner, 1948). Skinner placed pigeons in separate experimental chambers and set the equipment to deliver a bit of food every 15 seconds irrespective of what the pigeons were doing. The birds were not required to peck a key or perform any other specified response to get the food. After some time, Skinner returned to see what his birds were doing. He described some of what he saw as follows:

> In six out of eight cases the resulting responses were so clearly defined that two observers could agree perfectly in counting instances. One bird was conditioned to turn counterclockwise about the cage, making two or three turns between reinforcements. Another repeatedly thrust its head into one of the upper corners of the cage. A third developed a "tossing" response, as if placing its head beneath an invisible bar and lifting it repeatedly. (p. 168)

The pigeons appeared to be responding as if their behavior controlled the delivery of the reinforcer, when, in fact, food was provided independently of behavior. Accordingly, Skinner called this **superstitious behavior.**

Skinner's explanation of superstitious behavior rests on the idea of **accidental,** or **adventitious, reinforcement.** Adventitious reinforcement refers to the accidental pairing of a response with delivery of the reinforcer. Animals are always doing something, even if no particular responses are required to obtain food. Skinner suggested that whatever response a subject happened to make just before it got free food became strengthened and subsequently increased in frequency because of adventitious reinforcement. One accidental pairing of a response with food increases the chance that the same response will occur just before the next delivery of the food. A second accidental response-reinforcer pairing further increases the probability of the response. In this way, each accidental pairing helps to "stamp in" a particular response. After a while, the response will occur frequently enough to be identified as superstitious behavior.

Skinner's interpretation of his experiment was appealing and consistent with views of reinforcement that were widely held at the time. Impressed by studies of delay of reinforcement, theoreticians thought that temporal contiguity was the main factor responsible for

J. E. R. Staddon

learning. Skinner's experiment appeared to support this view and suggested that a positive response-reinforcer contingency is not necessary for instrumental conditioning.

1. *Reinterpretation of the Superstition Experiment.* Skinner's bold claim that response-reinforcer contiguity rather than contingency is most important for instrumental conditioning has been challenged by subsequent empirical evidence. In a landmark study, Staddon and Simmelhag (1971) attempted to replicate Skinner's experiment. However, Staddon and Simmelhag made much more extensive and systematic observations. They defined and measured the occurrence of many responses, such as orienting to the food hopper, pecking the response key, wing flapping, turning in quarter circles, and preening. They then recorded the frequency of each response according to when it occurred during the interval between successive free deliveries of food.

Figure 5.13 shows the data obtained by Staddon and Simmelhag for several responses for one pigeon. Clearly, some of the responses occurred predominantly toward the end of the interval between successive reinforcers. For example, R1 and R7 (orienting to the food magazine and pecking at something on the magazine wall) were much more likely to occur at the end of the food-food interval than at other times. Staddon and Simmelhag called these **terminal responses.** Other activities increased in frequency after the delivery of food and then decreased as the time for the next food delivery drew closer. The pigeons were most likely to engage in R8 and R4 (moving along the magazine wall and making a quarter turn) somewhere near the middle of the interval between food deliveries. These activities were called **interim responses.**

Which actions were terminal responses and which were interim responses did not vary much from one pigeon to another. Furthermore, Staddon and Simmelhag failed to find evi-

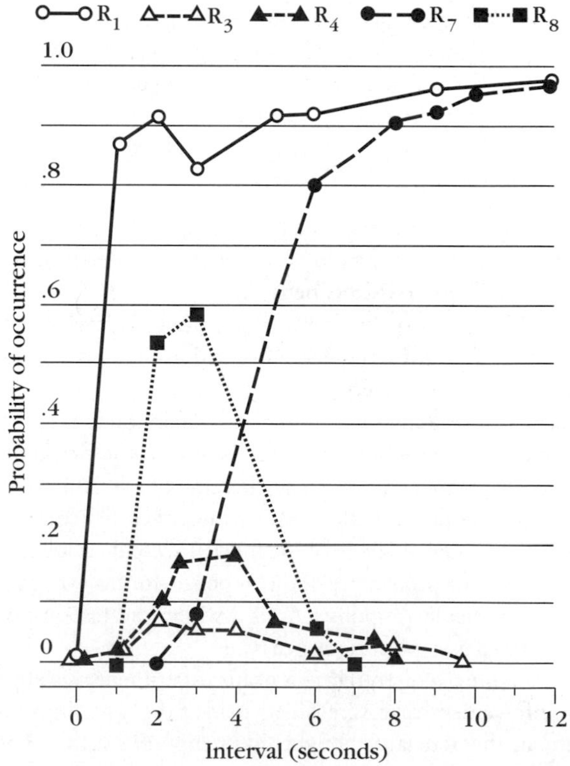

Figure 5.13 Probability of several responses as a function of time between successive deliveries of a food reinforcer. R1 (orienting toward the food magazine wall) and R7 (pecking at something on the magazine wall) are terminal responses, having their highest probabilities at the end of the interval between food deliveries. R3 (pecking at something on the floor), R4 (a quarter turn), and R8 (moving along the magazine wall) are interim responses, having their highest probabilities somewhere near the middle of the interval between food deliveries. (From "The 'Superstition' Experiment: A Reexamination of Its Implications for the Principles of Adaptive Behavior," by J. E. R. Staddon and V. L. Simmelhag, 1971, *Psychological Review, 78,* pp. 3–43. Copyright © 1971 by the American Psychological Association. Reprinted by permission.)

dence for accidental reinforcement effects. Responses did not always increase in frequency merely because they occurred coincidentally with food delivery. Food delivery appeared to influence only the strength of terminal responses, even in the initial phases of training.

Subsequent research has provided much additional evidence that periodic presentations of a reinforcer produce behavioral regularities, with certain responses predominating late in the interval between successive food presentations, and other responses predominating earlier in the food-food interval (Anderson & Shettleworth, 1977; Innis, Simmelhag-Grant, & Staddon, 1983; Silva & Timberlake, 1998). It is not clear why Skinner failed to observe such regularities in his experiment. One possibility is that he focused on different aspects of the behavior of different birds in an effort to document that each bird responded in a unique fashion. For example, he may have focused on the terminal response of one bird and interim responses in other birds. Subsequent investigators have also noted some variations in behavior between individuals but have emphasized what are even more striking similarities among animals that are given food periodically, independent of their behavior.

2. *Explanation of the Periodicity of Interim and Terminal Responses.* What is responsible for the development of similar terminal and interim responses in animals exposed to the same schedule of response-independent food presentations? Staddon and Simmelhag (1971) suggested that terminal responses are species-typical responses that reflect the anticipation of food as time draws nearer to the next food presentation. By contrast, they viewed interim responses as reflecting other sources of motivation that become prominent early in the interfood interval, when food presentation is unlikely. In contrast, subsequent investigators have favored approaches in which terminal and interim responses are considered to be different manifestations of the same motivational system (for example, Innis, Reberg, Mann, Jacobson, & Turton, 1983; Matthews, Bordi, & Depollo, 1990; but see Lawler & Cohen, 1992). The best developed of these alternative formulations is behavior systems theory (Lucas, Timberlake, & Gawley, 1988; Timberlake & Lucas, 1985, 1991; Silva & Timberlake, 1998).

According to behavior systems theory, the feeding system (and its accompanying foraging responses) is activated in food-deprived animals that are periodically given small portions of food. Behavior under these circumstances is assumed to be a reflection of preorganized species-typical foraging and feeding behavior. Different behaviors occur depending on when food was last delivered and when food is going to occur again. Just after the delivery of food, the organism is assumed to display *post-food focal search* responses that involve activities near the food cup. In the middle of the interval between food deliveries (when the subjects are least likely to get food), *general search* responses are evident that take the subject away from the food cup. As time for the next food delivery approaches, subjects exhibit *focal search* responses that are again concentrated near the food cup. In Figure 5.13, the terminal responses, R1 and R7 were distributed in time in the manner expected of focal search behavior, and R4 and R8 were distributed in the manner expected of general search responses. (For studies examining these issues in greater detail, see Timberlake & Lucas, 1985; Matthews et al., 1990; Silva & Timberlake, 1998.)

Consistent with behavior systems theory, the distribution of activities that develops with periodic deliveries of a reinforcer depend on the nature of that reinforcer. For example, different patterns of behavior develop with food versus water presentations (Innis et al., 1983; Papadouka & Matthews, 1995; Reberg, Innis, Mann, & Eizenga, 1978; Timberlake & Lucas, 1991), presumably because food and water activate different foraging patterns.

Effects of the Controllability of Reinforcers. A strong contingency between an instrumental response and a reinforcer essentially means that the response controls the reinforcer. With a strong contingency, whether the reinforcer occurs depends on whether the instrumental response has occurred. Studies of the effects of control over reinforcers have provided the most extensive body of evidence on the sensitivity of behavior to response-reinforcer contingencies. Although some of these studies have involved positive reinforcement (for example, Caspy & Lubow, 1981; Ferguson & Job, 1997; Job, 1987, 1989), most of the research has focused on the effects of control over aversive stimulation (see reviews by LoLordo & Taylor, 2001; Overmier & LoLordo, 1998; Maier & Jackson, 1979; Peterson, Maier, & Seligman, 1993).

Contemporary research on the effects of the controllability of aversive stimulation on learning originated with the pioneering studies of Seligman, Overmier, and Maier (Overmier & Seligman, 1967; Seligman & Maier, 1967), who investigated the effects of exposure to uncontrollable shock on subsequent escape-avoidance learning in dogs. The major finding was that exposure to uncontrollable shock disrupted subsequent learning. This phenomenon has come to be called the **learned-helplessness effect.**

The learned-helplessness effect continues to be the focus of a great deal of research, but dogs are no longer used in the experiments. Instead, most of the research is now done with laboratory rats and human participants. The results of the research with humans has turned out to be more relevant to issues in social and clinical psychology than behavior theory (see Mikulincer, 1994, for a review); consequently, I mention that work only briefly.

1. *The Triadic Design.* Learned-helplessness experiments are usually conducted using the *triadic design* presented in Table 5.2. The design involves two phases: exposure and conditioning. During the exposure phase, one group of rats (E, for *e*scape) is exposed to periodic shocks that can be terminated by performing an escape response (rotating a small wheel or tumbler, for example). Each subject in the second group (Y, for *y*oked) is yoked to an animal in Group E and receives the same shocks as its Group E partner. However, animals in Group Y cannot do anything to turn off the shocks. The third group (R, for *r*estricted) receives no shocks during the exposure phase but is restricted to the apparatus for as long as the other groups. During the conditioning phase, all three groups receive escape-avoidance training. This is usually conducted in a shuttle apparatus that has two adjacent compartments (see Figure 10.4). The animals have to go back and forth between the two compartments to avoid shock (or escape any shocks that they did not avoid).

The remarkable finding in experiments on the learned-helplessness effect is that the effects of aversive stimulation during the exposure phase depend on whether or not shock is escapable. Exposure to uncontrollable shock (Group Y) produces a severe disruption in subsequent escape-avoidance learning. In the conditioning phase of the experiment, Group Y typically shows much poorer escape-avoidance performance than both Group E and Group R. By contrast, little or no deleterious effects are observed after exposure to escapable shock. In fact, Group E often learns the subsequent escape-avoidance task as rapidly as Group R, which received no shock during the exposure phase. Similar detrimental effects of exposure to yoked inescapable shock have been reported on subsequent responding for food reinforcement (for example, Rosellini & DeCola, 1981; Rosellini, DeCola, & Shapiro, 1982; see also DeCola & Rosellini, 1990).

The fact that Group Y shows a deficit in subsequent learning in comparison to Group E indicates that the animals are sensitive to the procedural differences between escapable and yoked inescapable shock. The primary procedural difference between Groups E and Y is the presence of a response-reinforcer contingency for Group E but not for Group Y. Therefore, the difference in the rate of learning between these two groups shows that the animals are sensitive to the response-reinforcer contingency.

2. *The Learned-Helplessness Hypothesis.* The first major explanation of studies employing the triadic design—the **learned-helplessness hypothesis**—was based on the conclusion that

TABLE 5.2 THE TRIADIC DESIGN USED IN STUDIES OF THE LEARNED-HELPLESSNESS EFFECT

GROUP	EXPOSURE PHASE	CONDITIONING PHASE	RESULT
Group E	Escapable shock	Escape-avoidance	Rapid avoidance learning
Group Y	Yoked inescapable shock	Escape-avoidance	Slow avoidance learning
Group R	Restricted to apparatus	Escape-avoidance	Rapid avoidance learning

animals can perceive the contingency between their behavior and the delivery of a reinforcer (Maier & Seligman, 1976; Maier, Seligman, & Solomon, 1969). The learned-helplessness hypothesis assumes that during exposure to uncontrollable shocks, animals learn that the shocks are independent of their behavior—that they can do nothing to control the shocks. Furthermore, they come to expect that reinforcers will continue to be independent of their behavior in the future. This expectation of future lack of control undermines their ability to learn a new instrumental response. The learning deficit occurs for two reasons. First, the expectation of lack of control reduces the motivation of the subjects to perform an instrumental response. Second, even if they make the response and get reinforced in the conditioning phase, the previously learned expectation of lack of control makes it more difficult for the subjects to learn that their behavior is now effective in producing reinforcement.

Courtesy of Donald A. Dewsbury

S. F. Maier

It is important to distinguish the learned-helplessness *hypothesis* from the learned-helplessness *effect.* The learned-helplessness effect is the pattern of results obtained with the triadic design (poorer learning in Group Y than in Groups E and R). The learned-helplessness effect has been replicated in numerous studies and is a well-established finding. By contrast, the learned-helplessness hypothesis has been a provocative and controversial explanation of the learned-helplessness effect since its introduction (see Black, 1977; Levis, 1976; LoLordo & Taylor, 2001; Overmier & LoLordo, 1998).

Courtesy of M. E. P. Seligman

M. E. P. Seligman

3. *Activity Deficits.* Early in the history of research on the learned-helplessness effect, investigators became concerned that the learning deficit observed in Group Y was a result of these animals learning to be inactive in response to shock during the exposure phase. Consistent with this hypothesis, in some situations, inescapable shock produces a decrease in motor movement, or response perseveration, and this is responsible for subsequent performance deficits (Anderson, Crowell, Cunningham, & Lupo, 1979; Anisman, de Catanzaro, & Remington, 1978; Anisman, Hamilton, & Zacharko, 1984; Irwin, Suissa, & Anisman, 1980). There are also situations in which effects on learning are not likely to be due to the suppression of movement caused by inescapable shock (for example, Jackson, Alexander, & Maier, 1980; Rosellini, DeCola, Plonsky, Warren, & Stilman, 1984). Therefore, a learned inactivity hypothesis cannot explain all instances of learned-helplessness effects (Maier & Jackson, 1979).

4. *Attentional Deficits.* Why might lack of control over reinforcers produce a deficit in learning if the effect is not due to a deficit in activity? One interesting possibility is that inescapable shock causes animals to pay less attention to their actions. If an animal fails to pay attention to its behavior, it will have difficulty associating its actions with reinforcers in escape-avoidance or other forms of instrumental conditioning.

BOX 5.4

HUMAN EXTENSIONS OF ANIMAL RESEARCH ON THE CONTROLLABILITY OF REINFORCERS

The fact that a history of lack of control over reinforcers can severely disrupt subsequent instrumental performance has important implications for human behavior. The concept of helplessness has been extended and elaborated to many areas of human concern, including aging, athletic performance, chronic pain, academic achievement, susceptibility to heart attacks, and victimization and bereavement (see Garber & Seligman, 1980; Peterson, Maier, & Seligman, 1993). Perhaps the most prominent area to which the concept of helplessness has been applied is depression (Seligman, 1975; see also Abramson, Metalsky, & Alloy, 1989; Peterson & Seligman, 1984).

Animal research on uncontrollability and unpredictability has also been used to gain insights into human posttraumatic stress disorder (Foa, Zinbarg, & Rothbaum, 1992). Victims of rape, assault, or combat stress have symptoms that correspond to the effects of chronic uncontrollable and unpredictable shock in animals. Recognition of these similarities promises to provide new insights into the origin and treatment of posttraumatic stress disorder.

In a fascinating experiment, Maier, Jackson, and Tomie (1987) tested this attention-deficit hypothesis with rats. They reasoned that an animal that fails to pay attention to its behavior because of exposure to inescapable shock is faced with the same problem as an animal that receives delayed reinforcement. In both cases, the animals have difficulty figuring out which of their actions causes the delivery of the reinforcer. This analogy suggested to Maier and his colleagues that manipulations that facilitate learning with delayed reinforcement might also help animals exposed to inescapable shock.

As I described earlier in this chapter, the problem of identifying which response is responsible for delayed reinforcement can be solved by marking the target response with an immediate external feedback stimulus of some sort. Maier and his colleagues reasoned that reduced attention to instrumental behavior also may be alleviated by introducing an external response feedback cue or marking stimulus. Thus, they predicted that rats given inescapable shock will not be disrupted in their subsequent escape learning if each instrumental response is marked by an external stimulus.

The relevant results of their experiment are presented in Figure 5.14. The figure shows the latency of escape responses performed by various groups during conditioning—the second phase of the experiment. Higher values indicate slower escape responses, and hence poorer escape learning. Groups E, Y, and R were the standard groups of the triadic design and yielded the usual learned-helplessness effect. Group E, which received escapable shocks during the exposure phase, performed with as short latencies as Group R, which was not given shock during the exposure phase. By contrast, Group Y, which received inescapable shocks at first, had significantly longer escape latencies.

The fourth group, Group Y-M (yoked-marker) received the same type of shocks as Group Y during the exposure phase. During the conditioning phase, Group Y-M received a marking stimulus after each escape response. The marker consisted of turning off the house lights for 0.75 second and having the floor tilt slightly as the rat crossed from one side of the shuttle box to the other. The presence of this marker completely eliminated the deficit in learning that was otherwise produced by prior exposure to inescapable shock. Group Y-M performed much better than Group Y and as well as Groups R and E. (Other aspects of the experiment ruled out nonspecific effects of the marking stimulus.) Thus, as predicted, mark-

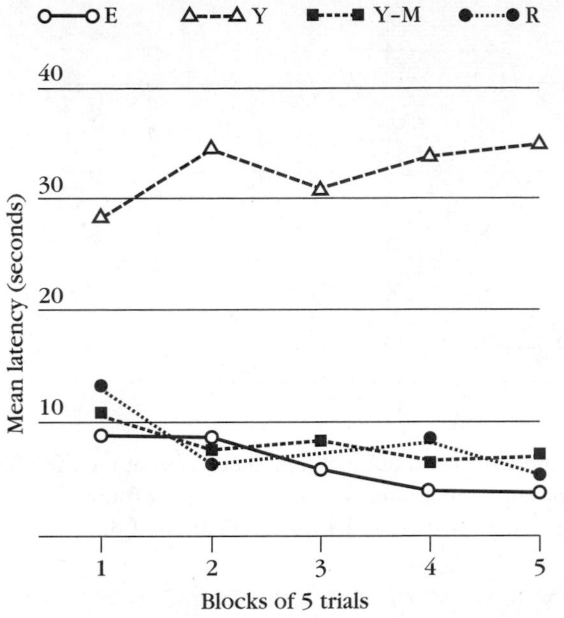

Figure 5.14 Mean escape latency during the conditioning phase for four groups of rats in a learned-helplessness experiment. During the exposure phase, Group E received escapable shocks, Groups Y and Y-M received yoked inescapable shocks, and Group R received no shock. During the conditioning phase, a brief marking stimulus was presented after each escape response for subjects in Group Y-M. (From "Potentiation, Overshadowing, and Prior Exposure to Inescapable Shock," by S. F. Maier, R. L. Jackson, and A. Tomie, 1987, *Journal of Experimental Psychology: Animal Behavior Processes, 13,* pp. 260–270. Copyright © 1987 by the American Psychological Association. Reprinted by permission.)

ing the instrumental response overcame the learned-helplessness deficit. This outcome suggests that one of the sources of the learning deficit is a reduction in attention to the responses the animal performs (see also Lee & Maier, 1988; Rodd, Rosellini, Stock, & Gallup, 1997).

5. *Stimulus Relations in Escape Conditioning.* The interpretations of the learned-helplessness effect I have described so far have focused on the deleterious effects of exposure to inescapable shock. An equally important question is why exposure to shock is not as harmful if the animal can perform a response to escape the shock (Minor, Dess, & Overmier, 1991). This question has stimulated a closer look at what happens when animals are permitted to escape shock in the exposure phase of the triadic design. It is apparent that escape training is more complex than was previously thought.

N. K. Dess

The defining feature of escape behavior is that the instrumental response results in the termination of an aversive stimulus. However, there are also special stimulus relations in an escape procedure that are potentially very important. These are illustrated in Figure 5.15. Making the escape response results in internal response feedback cues. Some of these response-produced stimuli are experienced at the start of the escape response, just before the shock is turned off, and are called *shock-cessation feedback cues.* Other response-produced stimuli are experienced as the animal completes the response, just after the shock has been turned off at the start of the intertrial interval. These are called *safety-signal feedback cues.*

At first, investigations of stimulus factors involved with escapable shock centered on the possible significance of safety-signal feedback cues. Safety-signal feedback cues are reliably followed by the intertrial interval, and hence by the absence of shock. Therefore, such feedback cues can become conditioned inhibitors of fear and limit or inhibit fear elicited by contextual cues of the experimental chamber. No such safety signals exist for animals given yoked inescapable shock because, for them, shocks and shock-free periods are not predictable. Therefore, contextual cues of the chamber in which shocks are delivered are more likely to become conditioned to elicit fear with inescapable shock. These considerations have encouraged analyzing the triadic design in terms of group differences in signals for safety rather than in terms of differences in response-reinforcer contingencies.

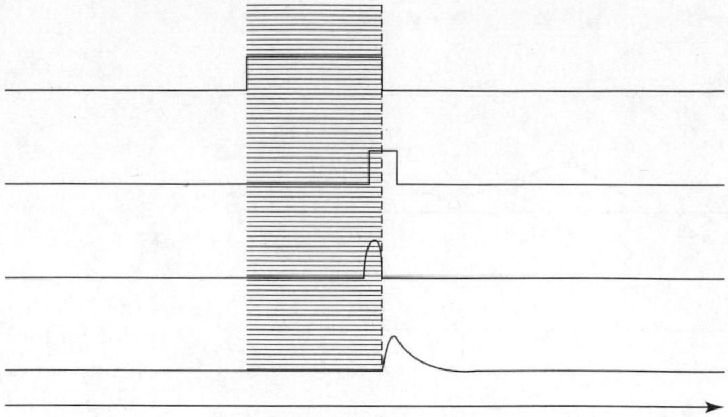

Figure 5.15 Stimulus relations in an escape conditioning trial. Shock-cessation feedback cues are experienced at the start of the escape response, just before the termination of shock. Safety-signal feedback cues are experienced just after the termination of shock, at the start of the intertrial interval.

T. R. Minor

Although some studies have indicated that group differences in signals for safety can account for the learned-helplessness effect (Jackson & Minor, 1988), findings from other experiments have not supported this conclusion (DeCola, Rosellini, & Warren, 1988; Maier, 1990; Maier & Warren, 1988; Rosellini, Warren, & DeCola, 1987). These considerations have encouraged focusing on other aspects of escape responding that may protect animals from the deleterious effects of exposure to shock. One study suggests, for example, that the critical aspect of an escape response may be that it indicates that the shock is being terminated (Minor, Trauner, Lee, & Dess, 1990). Thus, cessation signals may mimic critical features of an escape response more effectively than safety signals.

Focusing on stimulus factors in escape conditioning rather than on response-reinforcer contingencies has not yet yielded a comprehensive account of the results of all experiments with the triadic design. However, the available evidence indicates that significant differences in how animals cope with aversive stimulation can result from differences in signal relations. The more restricted focus of the learned-helplessness hypothesis cannot explain such findings. On balance, the triadic design has been invaluable in focusing attention on the possible importance of response-reinforcer contingencies. Recent research, however, has uncovered important factors other than the response-reinforcer contingency that also determine the effects of exposure to uncontrollable aversive stimulation (for reviews, see LoLordo & Taylor, 2001; Overmier & LoLordo, 1998).

CONTIGUITY AND CONTINGENCY: CONCLUDING COMMENTS

As I have described, organisms are sensitive to the contiguity as well as the contingency between an instrumental response and a reinforcer. Typically, these two aspects of the relation between response and reinforcer act jointly to produce learning (Davis & Platt, 1983). Both

BOX 5.5

HELPLESSNESS WITHIN THE SPINAL CORD

If someone asks you where learning occurs, you would likely give a quick response accompanied by an expression of disbelief. Everyone knows that learning occurs within the brain. But what about the neural tissue that lies below the brain, the cylinder of axons and gray matter that is protected by the bones of the vertebrate column? Can it learn? Recent work suggests that neurons within this region are sensitive to environmental relations and can exhibit some simple forms of learning (for a review, see Patterson & Grau, 2001).

The spinal cord is composed of two regions (see Figure 5.16A). The inner region (the central gray) is composed of neurons that form a network that can modulate signals and organize some simple behaviors. The central gray is surrounded by a band of axons (the white matter) that carry neural signals up and down the spinal cord, relaying information between the periphery and the brain. When an individual has an accident that causes paralysis below the waist (paraplegia), the loss of sensory and motor function is due to disruption in the relay cable formed by the axons of the white matter.

Spinal injury does not eliminate neural control of reflex responses. Below the point of injury, the neurons of the central gray retain the capacity to organize some simple behaviors. These spinal reflexes can be studied in nonhuman subjects such as rats by surgically cutting the spinal cord, disconnecting the lower region of the spinal cord (the lumbar-sacral region) from the brain. After the spinal injury, pressure applied to the rear paw will still elicit an upward movement of the paw (a flexion response). This protective reflex is designed to move the limb away from noxious stimuli that might cause damage to the skin. The reflex is mediated by neurons within the lumbosacral region of the spinal cord. The flexion response does not require the brain.

Groves and Thompson (1990) have shown that the vigor of a spinal reflex can change with experience. Repeated stimulation produces habituation while an intense stimulus can induce sensitization. These observations formed the cornerstone of the dual-process theory of nonassociative learning that was described in Chapter 2 (Groves & Thompson, 1970).

More recently, Grau and his colleagues have shown that neurons within the spinal cord can also support a simple form of instrumental learning (reviewed in Grau & Joynes, 2001). In these studies, the spinal cord was cut and subjects were trained using a shock that elicited a hindlimb flexion response. One group (the master rats) received legshock whenever the leg was extended. Subjects in a yoked group were experimentally coupled to the master subjects. Each time a master rat received shock, its yoked partner did, too. Master rats quickly learned to hold the leg up, effectively minimizing net shock exposure (Figure 5.16B). In contrast, the yoked rats, which received shock independent of leg position, failed to learn. This difference between master and yoked rats indicates that neurons within the spinal cord are sensitive to an instrumental (response-reinforcer) relation (for additional evidence, see Grau & Joynes, 2001).

Master and yoked rats were then tested under common conditions with controllable shock. As you would expect, master rats learned faster than control subjects that previously had not received shock. In contrast, the yoked rats failed to learn. Their behavioral deficit resembles the phenomenon of learned helplessness (Maier & Seligman, 1976). Crown and Grau (2001) have gone on to show that prior exposure to controllable shock has an immunizing effect that can protect the spinal cord from becoming helpless. Other experiments demonstrated that a combination of behavioral and drug treatments can restore the spinal cord's capacity for learning.

Across a range of behavioral manipulations, the spinal cord has yielded a pattern of results remarkably similar to those derived from brain-mediated behaviors. These results indicate that learning theorists have identified some very

(continued)

Figure 5.16 (A) A cross section of the spinal cord. The inner region (central gray) is composed of cell bodies, interneurons, and glia. It is surrounded by a band of axons (the white matter) that relay signals to and from the brain, segments of the cord, and the periphery. (B) *Training with response-contingent shock.* Master rats receive shock whenever one leg is extended. Even though the spinal cord has been surgically disconnected from the brain, they learn to hold the leg up (an increase in flexion duration) to minimize net shock exposure. Yoked rats, which receive the same amount of shock independent of leg position, fail to learn. *Testing learned helplessness after noncontingent shock.* When subjects are subsequently tested with response-contingent shock, master rats quickly re-learn the required response. Yoked rats, which had previously received shock independent of leg position, fail to learn. (Adapted from Grau & Joynes, 2001.)

A

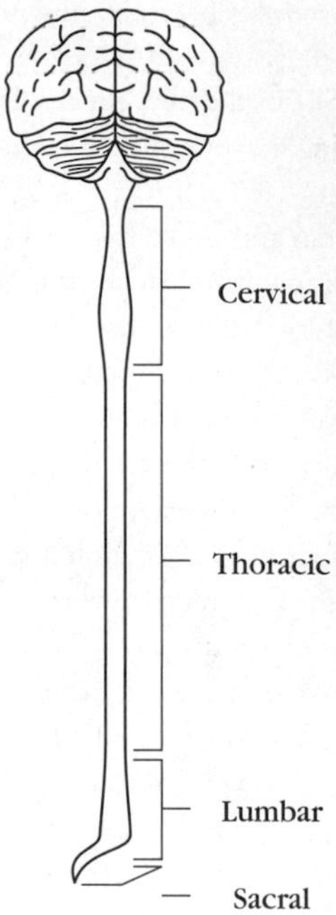

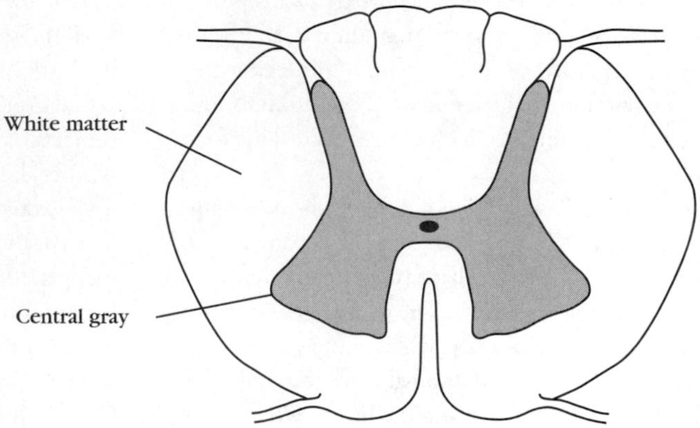

B

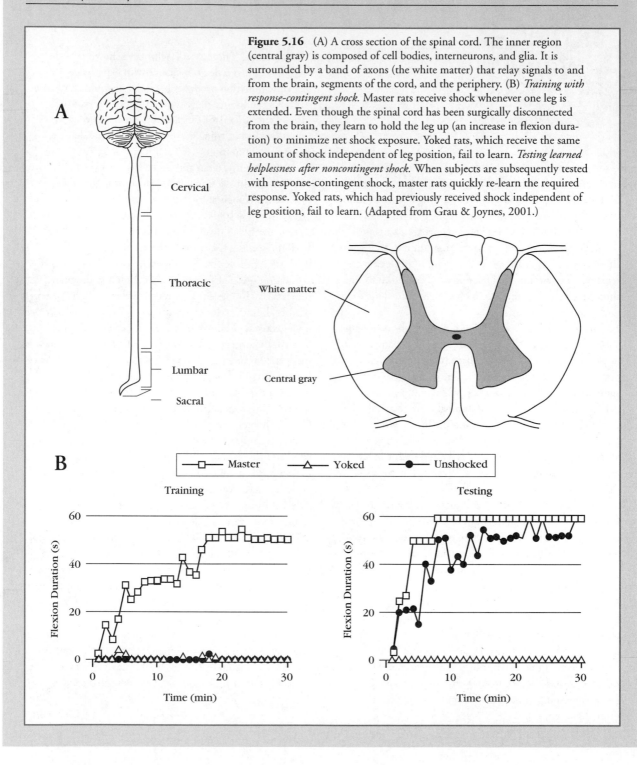

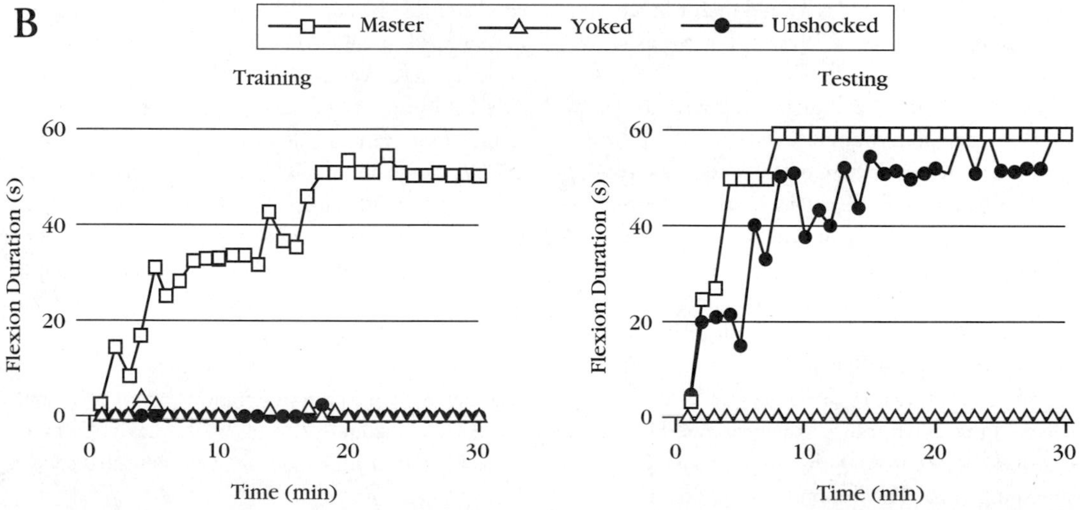

general principles of learning, principles that apply across a range of species (from *Aplysia* to humans) and across different levels of the neural axis (from spinal cord to forebrain). Of course, higher neural systems enable more complex functional capacity. However, there appear to be some core principles of neural plasticity that are evident in all learning situations.

Other researchers have shown that spinal cord neurons can also support stepping behavior (Edgerton, Roy, & de Leon, 2001). In these studies, the spinal cord was cut and the animal's hindlegs were suspended over a treadmill. The movement of the treadmill against the paws engaged a neural circuit that organizes stepping behavior. With experience, and some shaping of the response, an animal can recover the capacity to step over a range of treadmill speeds. Moreover, this system can be modified by experience. If an obstacle is placed in the path of the paw so that the paw hits it while the leg swings forward, the spinal cord will learn to lift the paw higher to minimize contact with the obstacle.

On the basis of these observations, Anton Wernig (Wernig, Muller, Nanassy, & Cagol, 1995) attempted to shape locomotive behavior in humans who were paraplegic. The participants were suspended over a treadmill and step training was conducted over a period of 12 weeks. Over the course of this experience, the spinal cord appeared to regain the capacity to organize stepping. The participants regained additional leg support and learned to engage the stepping circuit, allowing them to walk forward using a wheeled walker (rollator). The results were remarkable. At the start of training, 86% of the participants were confined to a wheelchair. By the end, 86% were able to move about using a walker or rollator. Very few (7%) of the subjects in a comparison group that received conventional therapy exhibited any improvement. These studies were conducted in the mid-1990s. Today, step training is a common behavioral treatment available across the country. For other examples of how animal research has benefited society, see Carroll & Overmier (2001).

—J. W. Grau

factors serve to focus the effects of reinforcement on the instrumental response. The causal relation, or contingency, ensures that the reinforcer is delivered only after occurrence of the specified instrumental response. The contiguity relation ensures that other activities do not intrude between the specified response and the reinforcer to interfere with conditioning of the target response.

SAMPLE QUESTIONS

1. Compare and contrast free-operant and discrete-trial methods for the study of instrumental behavior.
2. What are the similarities and differences between positive and negative reinforcement?
3. What is the current thinking about instrumental reinforcement and creativity, and what is the relevant experimental evidence?
4. What are the effects of a delay of reinforcement on instrumental learning, and what causes these effects?
5. What was the purpose of Skinner's superstition experiment? What were the results, and how have those results been reinterpreted?
6. Describe alternative explanations of the learned-helplessness effect.

KEY TERMS

accidental reinforcement An instance in which the delivery of a reinforcer happens to coincide with a particular response even though that response was not responsible for the reinforcer presentation. Also called *adventitious reinforcement.*

adventitious reinforcement Same as *accidental reinforcement.*

appetitive stimulus A pleasant or satisfying stimulus that can be used to positively reinforce an instrumental response.

aversive stimulus An unpleasant or annoying stimulus than can be used to punish an instrumental response.

avoidance An instrumental conditioning procedure in which the instrumental response prevents the delivery of an aversive stimulus.

belongingness The theoretical idea, originally proposed by Thorndike, that an organism's evolutionary history makes certain responses fit or belong with certain reinforcers. Belongingness facilitates learning.

conditioned reinforcer A stimulus that becomes an effective reinforcer because of its association with a primary or an unconditioned reinforcer. Also called *secondary reinforcer.*

contiguity The simultaneous (or almost simultaneous) occurrence of two events, such as a response and a reinforcer. Also called *temporal contiguity.*

differential reinforcement of other behavior An instrumental conditioning procedure in which a positive reinforcer is periodically delivered only if the participant fails to perform a particular response. Abbreviated *DRO.*

discrete-trial method A method of instrumental conditioning in which the participant can perform the instrumental response only during specified periods usually determined either by placement of the participant in an experimental chamber or by the presentation of a stimulus.

DRO Abbreviation for *differential reinforcement of other behavior.*

escape An instrumental conditioning procedure in which the instrumental response terminates an aversive stimulus. (See also *negative reinforcement.*)

free-operant method A method of instrumental conditioning that permits repeated performance of the instrumental response without the participant being removed from the experimental chamber. (Compare with *discrete-trial method.*)

instinctive drift A gradual drift of instrumental behavior away from the responses required for reinforcement to species-typical or "instinctive" responses related to the reinforcer and to other stimuli in the experimental situation.

instrumental behavior An activity that occurs because it is effective in producing a particular consequence or reinforcer.

interim response A response that increases in frequency after the delivery of a periodic reinforcer and then declines as time for the the next reinforcer approaches.

latency The time between the start of a trial (or the start of a stimulus) and the instrumental response.

law of effect A rule for instrumental behavior, proposed by Thorndike, which states that if a response in the presence of a stimulus is followed by a satisfying event, the association between the stimulus and the response will be strengthened; if the response is followed by an annoying event, the association will be weakened.

learned-helplessness effect Interference with the learning of new instrumental responses as a result of exposure to inescapable and unavoidable aversive stimulation.

learned-helplessness hypothesis A theoretical idea that assumes that during exposure to inescapable and unavoidable aversive stimulation, participants learn that their behavior does not control environmental events.

magazine training A preliminary stage of instrumental conditioning in which a stimulus is repeatedly paired with the reinforcer to enable the participant to learn to go and get the reinforcer when it is presented. The sound of the food-delivery device, for example, may be repeatedly paired with food so that the animal will learn to go to the food cup when food is delivered.

marking procedure A procedure in which the instrumental response is immediately followed by a distinctive event (the participant is picked up or a flash of light is presented) that makes the instrumental response more memorable and helps overcome the deleterious effects of delayed reinforcement.

negative contrast Less responding for an unfavorable reinforcer following previous experience with a more desired reinforcer than in the absence of such prior experience.

negative reinforcement An instrumental conditioning procedure in which there is a negative contingency between the instrumental response and an aversive stimulus. If the instrumental response is performed, the aversive stimulus is terminated or prevented from occurring; if the instrumental response is not performed, the aversive stimulus is presented.

omission training An instrumental conditioning procedure in which the instrumental response prevents the delivery of a reinforcing stimulus. (See also *differential reinforcement of other behavior.*)

operant response A response that is defined by the effect it produces in the environment. Examples include pressing a lever and opening a door. Any sequence of movements that depresses the lever or opens the door constitutes an instance of that particular operant.

positive contrast Greater responding for a favorable reinforcer following previous experience with a less desired reinforcer than in the absence of such prior experience.

positive reinforcement An instrumental conditioning procedure in which there is a positive contingency between the instrumental response and a reinforcing stimulus. If the participant performs the response, it receives the reinforcing stimulus; if the participant does not perform the response, it does not receive the reinforcing stimulus.

punishment An instrumental conditioning procedure in which there is a positive contingency between the instrumental response and an aversive stimulus. If the participant performs the instrumental response, it receives the aversive stimulus; if the participant does not perform the instrumental response, it does not receive the aversive stimulus.

response-reinforcer contingency The causal relation between a response and a reinforcer, measured in terms of the probability of getting reinforced for making the response as compared to the probability of getting reinforced in the absence of the response.

running speed How fast (in feet per second, for example) an animal moves in a runway.

secondary reinforcer Same as *conditioned reinforcer.*

shaping Reinforcement of successive approximations to a desired instrumental response.

simultaneous behavioral contrast Behavioral contrast effects (positive and negative contrast) that are produced by frequent shifts between a favorable and an unfavorable reward condition, with each reward condition associated with its own distinctive stimulus.

superstitious behavior Behavior that increases in frequency because of accidental pairings of the delivery of a reinforcer with occurrences of the behavior.

temporal contiguity Same as *contiguity.*

terminal response A response that is most likely at the end of the interval between successive reinforcements that are presented at fixed intervals.

CHAPTER

6 SCHEDULES OF REINFORCEMENT AND CHOICE BEHAVIOR

Chapter 6 continues the discussion of the importance of the response-reinforcer relation in instrumental behavior by describing the effects of various schedules of reinforcement. A schedule of reinforcement is a program or rule that determines how presentations of the reinforcer are related to occurrences of the instrumental response. Schedules of reinforcement are important because they determine the rate and pattern of instrumental responses. I first describe simple fixed and variable ratio and fixed and variable interval schedules, and the patterns of instrumental responding produced by these schedules. I then describe response-rate schedules of reinforcement, before moving on to discuss choice behavior. A great deal of research has dealt with how schedules of reinforcement determine choice between different response alternatives. Concurrent and concurrent-chain schedules of reinforcement are techniques used in the empirical and theoretical analyses of choice. A particularly interesting form of choice is between modest short-term gains versus larger long-term gains, because these alternatives represent the dilemma of self-control.

Schedules of Reinforcement and Choice Behavior

In describing various instrumental conditioning procedures in Chapter 5, I may have given the impression that every occurrence of the instrumental response invariably results in delivery of the reinforcer in these procedures. Casual reflection suggests that such a perfect contingency between response and reinforcement is rare in the real world. You do not get a high grade on a test every time you spend many hours studying. You cannot get on a bus every time you go to the bus stop. Inviting someone over for dinner does not always result in a pleasant evening. In fact, in most cases the relation between instrumental responses and consequent reinforcement is rather complex. Attempts to study how these complex relations control the occurrence of instrumental responses have led to laboratory investigations of schedules of reinforcement.

A **schedule of reinforcement** is a program, or rule, that determines how and when the occurrence of a response will be followed by a reinforcer. Such a program could be set up in an infinite number of ways. The delivery of a reinforcer could depend on the occurrence of a certain number of responses, the passage of time, the presence of certain stimuli, the occurrence of other responses of the animal, or any number of other things. Cataloging the behavioral effects produced by the various possible schedules of reinforcement might seem to be a difficult task, but research has shown that the job is quite manageable. Reinforcement schedules that involve similar relations among stimuli, responses, and reinforcers usually produce similar patterns of behavior. The exact rate of responding may differ from one situation to another, but the pattern of results is highly predictable. This regularity has made the study of reinforcement schedules both interesting and fruitful.

Schedules of reinforcement influence both how an instrumental response is learned and how it is then maintained by reinforcement. Traditionally, however, investigators of schedule effects have been concerned primarily with the maintenance of behavior. Reinforcement schedules are typically investigated in Skinner boxes that permit continuous observation of behavior so that changes in the rate of responding can be readily observed and analyzed (Ferster & Skinner, 1957). The manner in which the operant response is initially shaped and conditioned is rarely of interest. Thus, investigations of reinforcement schedules have provided a great deal of information about the factors that control the maintenance and repetitive performance of instrumental behavior rather than its original acquisition.

Schedules of reinforcement are important for managers who have to make sure their employees continue to perform a job after having learned it. Even teachers are often concerned with encouraging the occurrence of already learned responses rather than teaching new ones. Many students who do poorly in school know how to do their homework and how to study, but simply choose not to. Schedules of reinforcement can be used to motivate more frequent studying behavior.

The study of schedules of reinforcement is critical to the understanding of instrumental behavior because of what such studies tell us about the reinforcement process and because "they serve as useful baselines for the study of other behavioral processes" (Lattal & Neef, 1996, p. 214). The influence of drugs, changes in motivation, and other manipulations often depend on the schedule of reinforcement that is in effect at the time. This makes the understanding of schedule performance critical to the study of a variety of other issues in behavior theory and behavioral neuroscience. Because of their pervasive importance, Zeiler (1984) called reinforcement schedules the "sleeping giant" in the analysis of behavior.

SIMPLE SCHEDULES OF INTERMITTENT REINFORCEMENT

Processes that organize and direct instrumental performance are activated in different ways by different schedules of reinforcement. In "simple" schedules, a single factor determines which occurrence of the instrumental response is reinforced.

Ratio Schedules

The defining characteristic of a **ratio schedule** is that reinforcement depends only on the number of responses the organism has performed. A ratio schedule requires merely counting the number of responses that have occurred and delivering the reinforcer each time the required number is reached. If the required number is one, every occurrence of the instrumental response results in delivery of the reinforcer. Such a schedule is technically called **continuous reinforcement** (abbreviated CRF).

Continuous reinforcement rarely occurs outside the laboratory because the world is not perfect. Pushing an elevator button usually brings the elevator, but all elevators occasionally malfunction so that nothing may happen when you push the button. Other forms of instrumental behavior also may result in reinforcement only some of the time. Situations in which responding is reinforced only some of the time are said to involve **partial** or **intermittent reinforcement.**

Fixed Ratio. Consider, for example, delivering the reinforcer after every 10th lever-press response in a study with laboratory rats. In such a schedule, there would be a fixed ratio between the number of responses the rat made and the number of reinforcers it got. (There would always be 10 responses per reinforcer.) This makes the procedure a **fixed ratio schedule.** More specifically, the procedure would be called a *fixed ratio 10* schedule of reinforcement (abbreviated FR 10).

Fixed ratio schedules are found in daily life wherever a fixed number of responses are always required for reinforcement. The delivery person who always has to visit the same number of houses to complete his route is working on a fixed ratio schedule. Checking class attendance by reading the roll involves a fixed ratio schedule, set by the number of students on the class roster. Piecework in factories is usually set up on a fixed ratio schedule: workers get paid for every so many "widgets" they put together. Making a phone call involves a fixed ratio schedule: you have to dial a fixed number of digits to complete each call.

A continuous reinforcement schedule is also a fixed ratio schedule. Continuous reinforcement involves a fixed ratio of one response per reinforcer. On a continuous reinforcement schedule, organisms typically respond at a steady but moderate rate. Only brief and unpredictable pauses occur. On a CRF schedule, a pigeon, for example, will peck a key for food steadily at first and will then slow down as it satisfies its hunger.

A very different pattern of responding occurs when an intermittent fixed ratio schedule of reinforcement is in effect. You are not likely to pause in the middle of dialing a phone number, but you may take a while before starting to make the call. This is the typical pattern for fixed ratio schedules. A steady and high rate of responding exists once the behavior gets under way, but there may be a pause before the start of the required number of responses. These features of responding are clearly evident in a **cumulative record** of the behavior.

A cumulative record is a special way of representing how a response is repeated over time. It shows the total (or cumulative) number of responses that have occurred up to a particular point in time. Before computers became common, cumulative records were obtained

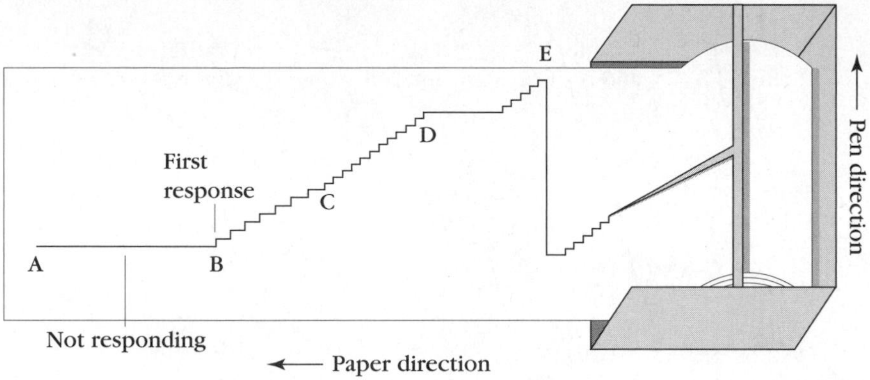

Figure 6.1 The construction of a cumulative record by a cumulative recorder for the continuous recording of behavior. The paper moves out of the machine toward the left at a constant speed. Each response causes the pen to move up the paper one step. No responses occurred between points A and B. A moderate rate of responding occurred between points B and C, and a rapid rate occurred between points C and D. At point E, the pen reset to the bottom of the page.

with the use of a chart recorder (see Figure 6.1). The recorder consisted of a rotating drum that pulled paper out of the recorder at a constant speed. A pen rested on the surface of the paper. If no responses occurred, the pen remained stationary and made a horizontal line as the paper came out of the machine. If the subject performed a lever-press response, the pen moved one step vertically on the paper. Since each lever-press response caused the pen to move one step up the paper, the total vertical distance traveled by the pen represented the cumulative (or total) number of responses the subject made. Because the paper came out of the recorder at a constant speed, the horizontal distance on the cumulative record provided a measure of how much time had elapsed in the session. The slope of the line made by the cumulative recorder represents the subject's *rate of responding.*

The cumulative record provides a complete visual representation of when and how frequently the subject responds during a session. In the record of Figure 6.1, for example, the subject did not perform the response between points A and B, and a slow rate of responding occurred between points B and C. Responses occurred more frequently between points C and D, but the subject paused at D. After responding resumed, the pen reached the top of the page (at point E) and reset to the bottom for additional responses.

Figure 6.2 shows the cumulative record of a pigeon whose responding had stabilized on a reinforcement schedule that required 120 pecks for each delivery of the reinforcer (an FR 120 schedule). Each food delivery is indicated by the small downward deflections of the recorder pen. The bird stopped responding after each food delivery; when it resumed pecking, it responded at a high and steady rate. The zero rate of responding that occurs just after reinforcement is called the **postreinforcement pause.** The high and steady rate of responding that completes each ratio requirement is called the **ratio run.**

If the ratio requirement is increased a little (from FR 120 to FR 150, for example), the rate of responding during the ratio run may remain the same. With higher ratio requirements, longer postreinforcement pauses tend to occur (for example, Baron & Herpolsheimer, 1999; Felton & Lyon, 1966). If the ratio requirement undergoes a sudden and significant increase (from FR 120 to FR 500, for example), the animal is likely to pause periodically before the completion of the ratio requirement (for example, Stafford & Branch,

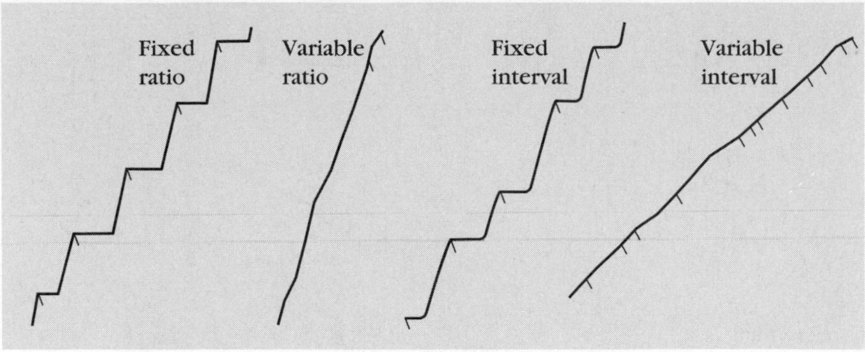

Figure 6.2 Sample cumulative records of different pigeons pecking a response key on four simple schedules of food reinforcement: fixed ratio 120, variable ratio 360, fixed interval 4 minute, and variable interval 2 minute. (From *Schedules of Reinforcement,* by C. B. Ferster and B. F. Skinner, 1957, Appleton-Century-Crofts.)

1998). This effect is called **ratio strain.** In extreme cases, ratio strain may be so great that the animal stops responding altogether. In using ratio schedules, an investigator must be careful not to raise the ratio requirement (or, more generally, the difficulty of a task) too quickly, because ratio strain may occur and the organism may give up altogether.

Although the pause that occurs before a ratio run in fixed ratio schedules is historically called the *postreinforcement pause,* research has shown that the length of the pause is controlled by the upcoming ratio requirement (for example, Baron & Herpolsheimer, 1999). If you procrastinate before starting a ratio task such as washing your car, it is because you are not quite ready to tackle the job, not because you are "resting" from the previous time you did the work. Thus, the postreinforcement pause would be more correctly labeled the *preratio pause.*

Variable Ratio. In a fixed ratio schedule, a predictable number of responses is required for each reinforcer. This predictability can be disrupted by varying the number of responses required for reinforcement from one occasion to the next. Such a procedure is still a ratio schedule because reinforcement still depends on how many responses the organism makes. A procedure in which a different number of responses is required for the delivery of each reward is called a **variable ratio schedule** (abbreviated VR). Investigators may, for example, require a pigeon to make 10 responses to earn the first reward, 13 to earn the second reward, 7 for the next one, and so on. The numerical value of a variable ratio schedule indicates the average number of responses required per reinforcer. Thus, the procedure in this case would be a variable ratio 10 schedule (abbreviated VR 10).

Variable ratio schedules are found in daily life whenever an unpredictable amount of effort is required to obtain a reinforcer. For example, each time a custodian goes into a room on his rounds, he knows that some amount of cleaning will be necessary, but he does not know exactly how dirty the room will be. Gamblers playing a slot machine are responding on a VR schedule. They have to play the machine to win, but they never know how many plays will produce the winning combination. Variable ratio schedules are also common in sports. A certain number of strokes are always required to finish a hole in golf, but players cannot be sure how many strokes they will need when they start.

Because the number of responses required for reinforcement is not predictable, predictable pauses in the rate of responding are less likely with VR schedules than with FR

BOX 6.1

THE POSTREINFORCEMENT PAUSE AND PROCRASTINATION

The postreinforcement pause that occurs in fixed ratio schedules in the laboratory is also evident in common human experience. In FR schedules, the pause occurs because a predictably large number of responses are always required to produce the next reward. Such procrastination is legendary in human behavior. Consider, for example, a semester in which you have several term papers to write. You are likely to work on one term paper at a time. When you have completed one, however, you probably will not start working on the next one right away. There will be a postreinforcement pause. After completing a large project, people tend to take some time off before starting the next one. Procrastination between tasks or before the start of a new job is the rule rather than the exception.

Laboratory results provide a suggestion for overcoming procrastination. Fixed ratio schedule performance in the laboratory indicates that once animals begin to respond on a ratio run, they respond at a high and steady rate until they complete the ratio requirement. This suggests that if somehow you got yourself to start on a job, chances are you would not find it difficult to keep going. Only the beginning is hard. One technique that works pretty well in getting started is to tell yourself that you will start by just doing a little bit of the job. If you are trying to write a paper, tell yourself that you will write only one paragraph to start with. Once you have completed the first paragraph, you may find it easier to write the second one, then the one after that, and so on. If you are procrastinating about spring cleaning, try not to think about doing the entire job. Start with a small part of it, such as washing the kitchen floor. The rest will then come more easily.

schedules. Rather, organisms respond at a fairly steady rate on VR schedules. Figure 6.2 shows a cumulative record for a pigeon whose pecking behavior was maintained on a VR 360 schedule of reinforcement. Notice that even though the VR 360 schedule required, on average, many more pecks for each reinforcer than the FR 120 schedule, the VR 360 schedule maintained a much steadier pattern of responding.

Although postreinforcement pauses can occur on variable ratio schedules (see Blakely & Schlinger, 1988; Schlinger, Blakely, & Kaczor, 1990), such pauses are longer and more prominent with fixed ratio schedules. The overall response rate on FR and VR schedules is similar provided that, on average, similar numbers of responses are required. However, the overall response rate tends to be distributed in a pause-run pattern with FR schedules, whereas a steadier pattern of responding is observed with VR schedules (for example, Crossman, Bonem, & Phelps, 1987). (For additional analyses of ratio schedules, see Bizo & Killeen, 1997.)

Interval Schedules

In ratio schedules, reinforcement depends only on the number of responses the organism has performed. In **interval schedules,** responses are reinforced only if the responses occur after a certain amount of time has passed.

Fixed Interval. In a simple interval schedule, a response is reinforced only if it occurs more than a set amount of time after the last delivery of the reinforcer. In a **fixed interval schedule** (abbreviated FI), the set time is constant from one occasion to the next. Fixed interval schedules are found in situations where a fixed amount of time is required to prepare or set up the reinforcer. For example, washing clothes in a washing machine requires a certain amount of time to complete the wash cycle. No matter how many times you open the washing machine before the required amount of time has passed, you will not be reinforced with clean clothes. Once the cycle is finished, the reinforcer becomes available, and you can take out your clean clothes any time after that.

Similar contingencies can be set up in the laboratory. Consider, for example, a fixed interval 4-minute schedule (FI 4 min) for pecking in pigeons. A bird on this schedule would get reinforced for the first peck it made after 4 minutes have passed since the last food delivery (or the beginning of the schedule cycle). Because pecks made less than 4 minutes after each food delivery are never reinforced, the subjects learn to wait to respond until the end of the FI (see Figure 6.2). As the time for the availability of the next reinforcer draws closer, the response rate increases. This increase in response rate is evident as an acceleration in the cumulative record toward the end of the FI. The pattern of responding that develops with FI reinforcement schedules is accordingly called the **fixed interval scallop.**

Performance on an FI schedule reflects the subject's accuracy in telling time. If the subject were entirely incapable of telling time, it would respond equally throughout the FI cycle. The postreinforcement pause and the subsequent acceleration toward the end of the interval reflect a rudimentary ability to tell time. How could this ability be improved? Common experience suggests that having a clock of some sort makes it much easier to judge time intervals. The same thing happens with pigeons on an FI schedule. In one study, the clock consisted of a spot of light that grew into a slit as time passed during the FI cycle. Introduction of this clock stimulus increased the duration of the postreinforcement pause and caused responding to shift closer to the end of the FI cycle (Ferster & Skinner, 1957). As expected, the clock stimulus increased the efficiency of performance on the FI schedule.

It is important to realize that an FI schedule does not guarantee that the reinforcer will be provided at a certain point in time. Pigeons on an FI 4-min schedule do not automatically receive access to grain every 4 minutes. Instrumental responses are required for the reinforcer in interval schedules, just as in ratio schedules. The interval determines only when the reinforcer *becomes available,* not when it is delivered. In order to receive the reinforcer after it has become available, the subject still has to make the instrumental response. (For recent analyses of FI schedule performance, see Baron & Leinenweber, 1994; Hoyert, 1992; Lejeune & Wearden, 1991; Machado, 1997b; Wynne, Staddon, & Delius, 1996).

The scheduling of tests in college courses has important similarities to the basic FI schedule. Usually, each course has only two or three tests, and they are evenly distributed during the term. There may be only a midterm and a final exam. Such a schedule encourages a pattern of studying that is very similar to what is observed with an FI schedule in the laboratory. Students spend little effort studying at the beginning of the semester or just after the midterm exam. Instead, they begin to study a week or so before each exam, and the rate of studying rapidly increases as the day of the exam approaches.

Variable Interval. In fixed interval schedules, responses are reinforced if they occur after a fixed amount of time has passed since the delivery of the previous reinforcer (or the beginning of the schedule cycle). Interval schedules also can be unpredictable. With a **variable interval schedule** (abbreviated VI), responses are reinforced if they occur after a variable interval since the delivery of the previous reinforcer (or the beginning of the schedule cycle).

Variable interval schedules are found in situations where an unpredictable amount of time is required to prepare or set up the reinforcer. A mechanic who cannot tell you how long it will take to fix your car has imposed a VI schedule on you. The car will not be ready for some time, during which attempts to get it will not be reinforced. How much time has to pass before the car will be ready is unpredictable. A sales clerk at a bakery is also on a VI schedule of reinforcement. Some time has to pass after waiting on a customer before another will enter the store to buy something. The interval between customers is unpredictable.

In a laboratory study, a VI schedule could be set up in which the first reinforcer became available when at least 1 minute has passed since the beginning of the session, the second reinforcer became available when at least 3 minutes have passed since the first reward, and the third reinforcer became available when at least 2 minutes have passed since the second reward. In this procedure, the average interval that has to pass before successive rewards become available is 2 minutes. Therefore, the procedure would be called a variable interval 2-minute schedule, or VI 2 min.

As in fixed interval schedules, the subject in VI schedules has to perform the instrumental response to obtain the reinforcer. Reinforcers are not given "free"; they are given only if the organism responds after the variable interval. Like variable ratio schedules, VI schedules maintain steady and stable rates of responding without regular pauses (see Figure 6.2).

Interval Schedules and Limited Hold. In simple interval schedules, once the reinforcer becomes available, it remains available until the required response is made, no matter how long that may take. On an FI 2-min schedule, for example, the reinforcer becomes available 2 minutes after the start of the schedule cycle. If the animal responds at exactly this time, it will be reinforced. If it waits and responds 90 minutes later, it will still get reinforced. Once the reinforcer has been set up, it remains available until the response occurs.

With interval schedules outside the laboratory, it is more common for reinforcers to become available only for limited periods. Consider, for example, a dormitory cafeteria. Meals are served only at fixed intervals; therefore, going to the cafeteria is reinforced only after a certain amount of time has passed since the last meal. Once a meal becomes available, however, you have a limited amount of time in which to get it. This kind of restriction on how long the reinforcer remains available is called a **limited hold.** Limited hold restrictions can be added to both fixed interval and variable interval schedules.

Comparison of Ratio and Interval Schedules

There are striking similarities between the patterns of responding maintained by simple ratio and interval schedules. As I have described, both fixed ratio and fixed interval schedules have a postreinforcement pause after each delivery of the reinforcer. In addition, both FR and FI schedules produce high rates of responding just before the delivery of the next reinforcer. By contrast, variable ratio and variable interval schedules maintain steady rates of responding, without predictable pauses. Does this mean that interval and ratio schedules motivate behavior in the same way? Hardly! The surface similarities hide fundamental differences in underlying mechanisms between interval and ratio schedules.

Ratio and interval schedules activate different neurochemical changes in the brain (Barrett & Hoffmann, 1991). As might be expected, behavior maintained by interval schedules is mediated by the organism's sense of time, whereas timing mechanisms are not involved with ratio performance (Staddon, Wynne, & Higa, 1991). (I discuss mechanisms of timing in greater detail in Chapter 12.)

Early evidence of fundamental differences between ratio and interval schedules was provided by an important experiment by Reynolds (1975). Reynolds compared the rate of key pecking in pigeons reinforced on variable ratio and variable interval schedules. Two pigeons were trained to peck the response key for food reinforcement. One bird was reinforced on a VR schedule—the frequency of reinforcement was entirely determined by the bird's rate of responding. The other bird was reinforced on a VI schedule. To make sure that the opportunities for reinforcement would be identical for the two birds, the VI schedule was controlled by the behavior of the bird reinforced on the VR schedule. Each time the VR pigeon was just one response short of the requirement for reinforcement on that trial, the experimenter set up the reinforcer for the VI bird. With this arrangement, the next response made by each bird was reinforced. Thus, the frequency of reinforcement was virtually identical for the two animals.

Figure 6.3 shows the cumulative record of pecking exhibited by each bird. Even though the two pigeons received the same frequency and distribution of reinforcers, they behaved very differently. The pigeon reinforced on the VR schedule responded at a much higher rate than the pigeon reinforced on the VI schedule. The VR schedule motivated much more vigorous instrumental behavior (see also Baum, 1993; Cole, 1994).

Similar results have been found in a study of schedule effects with undergraduate students (Raia, Shillingford, Miller, & Baier, 2000). The task was akin to a video game. A target appeared on a computer screen, and the students had to maneuver a spaceship and "fire" at the target with a joystick as the instrumental response. Following a direct hit of the target, the subjects received 5 cents. However, not every "hit" was reinforced. Which occurrence of the instrumental response was reinforced depended on the schedule of reinforcement programmed into the software. The students were assigned to pairs, but each worked in a separate cubicle and didn't know that he or she had a partner. One member of each pair received reinforcement on a variable ratio schedule. The other member of the pair was reinforced on a variable interval schedule that was yoked to the VR schedule. Thus, as in the pigeon experiment, reinforcers became available to both subjects at the same time, but one controlled access to the reinforcer through a VR schedule and the other did not.

Raia et al. (2000) studied the effects of response shaping, instructions, and the presence of a consummatory response on performance on the VR-VI yoking procedure. (The consummatory response was being required to pick up the 5-cent reinforcer each time it was delivered and put it into a piggy bank.) One set of conditions was quite similar to the pigeon studies: the students were shaped to make the instrumental response, they received

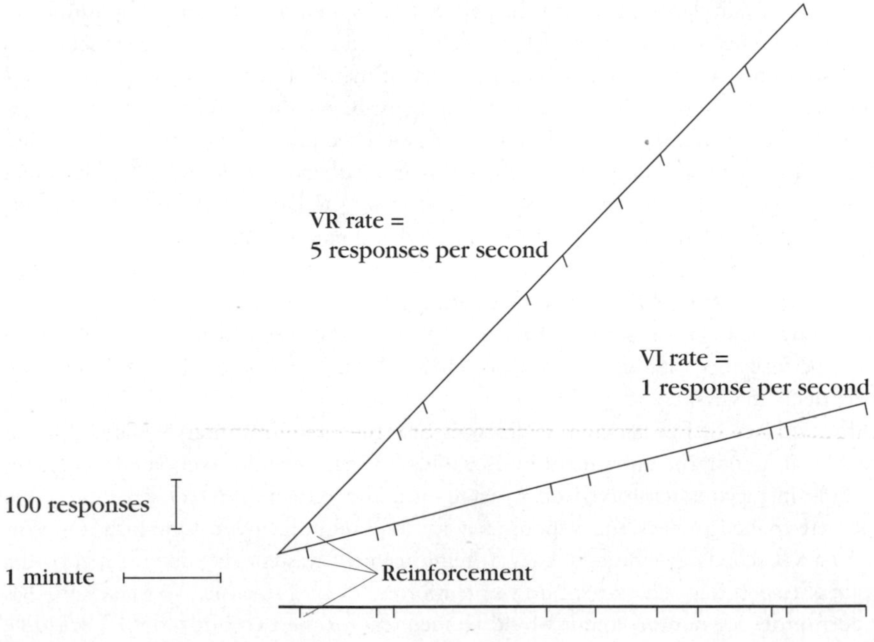

Figure 6.3 Cumulative records for two pigeons, one reinforced on a variable ratio (VR) schedule and the other yoked to it on a variable interval (VI) schedule. Although the two pigeons received the same rate of reinforcement, the VR bird responded five times as fast as the VI bird. (From *A Primer of Operant Conditioning,* 2nd ed., by G. S. Reynolds. Copyright © 1975 by Scott, Foresman. Reprinted by permission.)

minimal instructions, and they were required to make the consummatory response. Interestingly, under these conditions, the college students performed just like the pigeons. Higher rates of responding occurred for the individual of each pair who was reinforced on the variable ratio schedule.

Differential Reinforcement of Interresponse Times. Why might ratio schedules produce higher rates of responding than interval schedules? The answer has not been easy to find, but research is converging on the idea that what is critical is the spacing between responses just before reinforcement. The interval between one response and the next is called the **interresponse time** or **IRT.** I noted in Chapter 5 that a variety of different features of behavior can be increased in probability by reinforcement. The interval between successive responses is also a behavioral parameter than can be shaped by reinforcement. If short IRTs are reinforced, the subject becomes more likely to make short IRTs. If long IRTs are reinforced, the subject becomes more likely to make long IRTs. A subject that shows mostly short interresponse times will be responding at a high rate. By contrast, a subject that shows mostly long interresponse times will be responding at a low rate.

How do ratio and interval schedules determine the reinforcement of interresponse times? With a ratio schedule, there are no constraints on when responses count toward obtaining the reinforcer. In fact, the faster the subject completes the ratio requirement, the faster it will receive the reinforcer. Thus, a ratio schedule favors not waiting long between responses. It favors short interresponse times.

In contrast, interval schedules provide little advantage for short interresponse times; they favor the performance of long IRTs. Consider, for example, an FI 2-min schedule of food reinforcement. Each food pellet becomes available 2 minutes after the last one was delivered. If the subject responds frequently before the food pellet is set up, those responses and short IRTs will not be reinforced. On the other hand, if the subject waits a long time between responses (emitting long IRTs), its response is more likely to occur after the reinforcer has been set up, and it is more likely to be reinforced. Thus, interval schedules differentially reinforce long IRTs, and this results in lower rates of responding than what is observed with ratio schedules (Cole, 1999; Reed, Soh, Hildebrandt, DeJongh, & Shek, 2000; see also Baum, 1993; Cole, 1994; Dawson & Dickinson, 1990; McDowell & Wixted, 1988; Wearden & Clark, 1988; see also Lattal, Reilly, & Kohn, 1998).

Response-Rate Schedules of Reinforcement

Although ratio schedules produce higher rates of responding than comparable interval schedules, neither type of schedule requires a specific rate of responding for reinforcement. By contrast, **response-rate schedules** specifically require that the organism respond at a particular rate to get reinforced.

In response-rate schedules, whether a response is reinforced depends on how soon it occurs after the preceding response. A reinforcement schedule can be set up, for example, in which a response is reinforced only if it occurs within 5 seconds following the preceding response. If the animal makes a response every 5 seconds, its rate of response will be 12 per minute. Thus, the schedule provides reinforcement if the rate of response is 12 per minute or greater. The organism will not be reinforced if its rate of response falls below 12 per minute. As you might suspect, this procedure encourages responding at high rates. It is called **differential reinforcement of high rates,** or DRH.

In DRH schedules, a response is reinforced only if it occurs *before* a certain amount of time has elapsed following the preceding response. The opposite result is achieved if a response is reinforced only if it occurs *after* a certain amount of time has elapsed following

BOX 6.2

Wage Scales and Schedules of Reinforcement

The basis for determining the wages paid for work performed in a company constitutes a schedule of reinforcement. Laboratory research indicates that different schedules of reinforcement maintain different patterns and rates of responding. We may expect different wage systems to produce different rates of responding in work situations as well. A study of productivity among servers at three family restaurants illustrates such effects (George & Hopkins, 1989).

As is customary, the servers were paid an hourly wage. Most earned $1.90 plus tips, and a few earned more based on seniority. The employees complained that they were underpaid. The owners decided that they could not increase wages without an increase in productivity because the restaurants were already losing money. The servers claimed that because of their low wages, they had no incentive to increase productivity. The two sides thus found themselves stuck in a common labor–management dispute.

Following the advice of behavioral consultants, the owners adopted a performance-contingent pay scale. Such a system is a variant of a fixed ratio schedule in which rate of reinforcement is directly related to rate of responding. In a performance-contingent pay scale, each server is paid a fixed proportion of his or her gross sales. The proportion was set at 7%. Servers could easily make at least $1.90 per hour at 7% of gross sales, and 7% seemed to be the break-even point for profitability of the restaurant.

Introduction of the performance-contingent pay scale increased the hourly earning of the servers 24–30% in the three restaurants. The new schedule of reinforcement also increased productivity. Gross sales per labor hour increased 18–36%. This increase occurred primarily because of increases of 18–26% in the number of customers served per labor hour, rather than because of how much was purchased by each customer.

the previous response. This type of procedure is called **differential reinforcement of low rates,** abbreviated DRL. As you might suspect, DRL schedules encourage subjects to respond slowly.

Response-rate schedules are found outside the laboratory in situations that require particular rates of responding. DRH schedules are in effect in sports where speed is of the essence. For example, running from home plate to first base in a baseball game is reinforced only if it occurs faster than the time it takes to throw the ball to first base. In other circumstances, responding is reinforced only if it occurs at a specified rate. This is typically the case in dancing and music. Response-rate schedules are also in effect on an assembly line, where the speed of movement of the line dictates the rate of response for the workers. If an employee responds more slowly than the specified rate, he or she will not be reinforced and may, in fact, get fired. However, workers must be careful not to work too fast. Those who work faster than the accepted norm may be disliked by their peers.

CHOICE BEHAVIOR: CONCURRENT SCHEDULES

The reinforcement schedules I have described thus far involve a single response and reinforcement of that response. However, experiments in which only one response is being measured are not likely to provide a complete account of behavior. Behavior involves more than the repetition of individual responses. Even in a simple situation such as a Skinner box, organisms engage in a variety of activities and are continually choosing among possible alternatives. People are also constantly having to make choices about what to do. Should you go to the movies or stay at home and study? Should you go shopping tonight or watch television and go shopping tomorrow? Understanding the mechanisms of choice is fundamental to the understanding of behavior because the choices organisms make determine the occurrence of individual responses.

Choice situations can be rather complicated. For example, a person may have a choice of 12 different activities (reading the newspaper, watching television, going for a walk, playing with the dog, and the like), each of which produces a different type of reinforcer according to a different reinforcement schedule. Analyzing all the factors that control the individual's behavior in such a situation is a formidable task, if not an impossible one. Therefore, psychologists have begun experimental investigations of the mechanisms of choice by studying simpler situations. The simplest choice situation has two response alternatives, with each response followed by a reinforcer according to its own schedule of reinforcement.

Historically, research on choice behavior was conducted using mazes, particularly the T maze (see Woodworth & Schlosberg, 1954). Recent approaches to the study of choice use Skinner boxes equipped with two manipulanda, such as two pecking keys. In the typical experiment, responding on each key is reinforced on some schedule of reinforcement. The two schedules are in effect at the same time (or concurrently), and the subject is free to switch from one response key to the other. This type of procedure is called a **concurrent schedule.** It allows for continuous measurement of choice because the organism is free to change back and forth between the response alternatives at any time.

Figure 6.4 shows an example of a concurrent schedule. If the pigeon pecks the left key, it receives food according to a VI 60-sec schedule. Pecks on the right-hand key produce food according to an FR 10 schedule. The subject is free to peck on either key at any time. The point of the experiment is to see how the pigeon distributes its pecks on the two keys and how the schedule of reinforcement on each key influences its choices.

Measures of Choice Behavior

The individual's choice in a concurrent schedule is reflected in the distribution of its behavior between the two response alternatives. This can be measured in several ways. One common technique is to calculate the *relative rate of responding* on each alternative. The relative

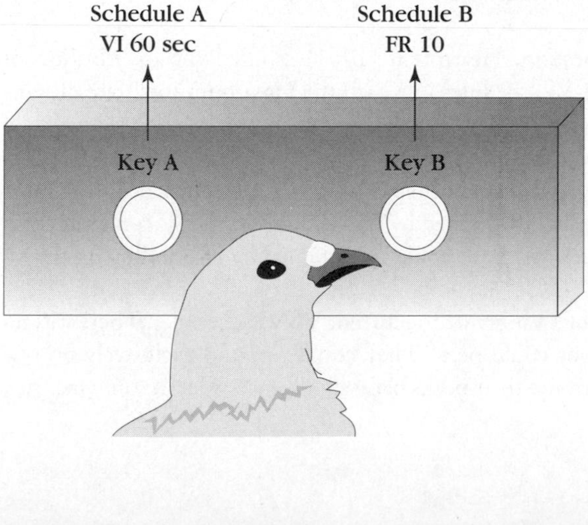

Figure 6.4 Diagram of a concurrent schedule. Pecks on key A are reinforced according to a VI 60-sec schedule of reinforcement. Pecks on key B are reinforced according to an FR 10 schedule of reinforcement.

rate of responding on key A, for example, is calculated by dividing the response rate on key A by the total rate of responding (rate on key A plus rate on key B):

$$R_A/(R_A + R_B) \tag{6.1}$$

where R_A is the rate of responding on key A and R_B is the rate on key B. If the pigeon pecks equally often on the two response keys, this ratio will be 0.5. If the rate of responding on key A is greater than on key B, the ratio will be greater than 0.5. On the other hand, if the rate of responding on key A is less than on key B, the ratio will be less than 0.5. The relative rate of responding on key B can be calculated in a comparable manner.

As you might suspect, how an organism distributes its behavior between the two response alternatives is greatly influenced by the reinforcement schedule in effect for each response. For example, if the same variable interval reinforcement schedule is available for each response alternative, as in a concurrent VI 60-sec VI 60-sec procedure, the pigeon will peck the two keys equally often. The relative rate of responding for pecks on each side will be 0.5. This result is intuitively reasonable. If the pigeon spent all its time pecking on one side, it would receive only the reinforcers programmed for that side. The bird can get more reinforcers by pecking on both sides. Since the VI schedule available on each side is the same, there is no advantage in responding more on one side than on the other.

By responding equally often on each side of a concurrent VI 60-sec VI 60-sec schedule, the pigeon will also earn reinforcers equally often on each side. The relative rate of reinforcement earned for each response alternative can be calculated in a manner comparable to the relative rate of response. For example, the relative rate of reinforcement for alternative A is the rate of reinforcement of response A divided by the total rate of reinforcement (the sum of the rate of reward earned on side A plus the rate of reward earned on side B). This is expressed in the formula

$$r_A/(r_A + r_B) \tag{6.2}$$

where r_A and r_B represent the rates of reinforcement earned on each response alternative. On a concurrent VI 60-sec VI 60-sec schedule, the relative rate of reinforcement for each response alternative will be 0.5 because the subject earns rewards equally often on each side.

The Matching Law

As I have described, with a concurrent VI 60-sec VI 60-sec schedule, both the relative rate of responding and the relative rate of reinforcement for each response alternative are 0.5. Thus, the relative rate of responding is equal to the relative rate of reinforcement. Will this equality also occur if the two response alternatives are not reinforced according to the same schedule?

Courtesy of Donald A. Dewsbury

R. J. Herrnstein

To answer this important question, Herrnstein (1961) studied the distribution of responses on various concurrent VI-VI schedules in which the maximum total rate of reinforcement the pigeons could earn was fixed at 40 per hour. Depending on the exact value of each VI schedule, different proportions of the 40 reinforcers could be obtained by pecking the left and right keys. For example, with a concurrent VI 6-min VI 2-min schedule, a maximum of 10 reinforcers per hour could be obtained by responding on the VI 6-min alternative, and a maximum of 30 reinforcers per hour could be obtained by responding on the VI 2-min alternative.

Herrnstein studied the effects of a variety of concurrent VI-VI schedules. There was no constraint on which side the pigeons could peck. They could respond exclusively on one side or the other, or they could distribute their pecks between the two sides in some manner.

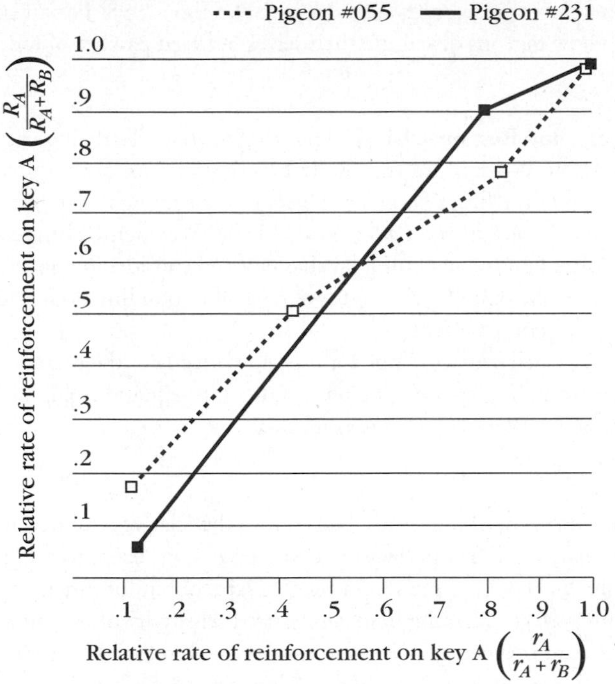

Figure 6.5 Various combinations of VI schedules were tested whose combined reinforcement rate was 40 reinforcements per hour. Note that throughout the range of schedules, the relative rate of responding nearly equals (matches) the relative rate of reinforcement. (From "Relative and Absolute Strength of Response as a Function of Frequency of Reinforcement," by R. J. Herrnstein, 1961, *Journal of the Experimental Analysis of Behavior, 4*, pp. 267–272. Copyright © 1961 by the Society for the Experimental Analysis of Behavior, Inc. Reprinted by permission.)

As it turned out, the pigeons distributed their responses in a highly predictable fashion. The results, summarized in Figure 6.5, indicate that the relative rate of responding on a given alternative was always very nearly equal to the relative rate of reinforcement earned on that alternative. If the pigeons earned a greater proportion of their reinforcers on alternative A, they made a correspondingly greater proportion of their responses on alternative A. Thus, the relative rate of responding on an alternative *matched* the relative rate of reinforcement on that alternative. Similar findings have been obtained in a variety of situations, which encouraged Herrnstein to state the relation as a law of behavior, the **matching law.** (For an anthology of Herrnstein's papers on this topic, see Herrnstein, 1997.)

There are two common mathematical expressions of the matching law. In one formulation, rates of responding and reinforcement on one alternative are expressed as a proportion of total response and reinforcement rates, as follows:

$$R_A/(R_A + R_B) = r_A/(r_A + r_B) \quad (6.3)$$

As before, R_A and R_B in this equation represent the rates of responding on keys A and B, and r_A and r_B represent the rates of reinforcement earned on each response alternative.

The second formulation of the matching law is simpler but mathematically equivalent to equation 6.3. In the second version, the rates of responding and reinforcement on one alternative are expressed as a proportion of the rates of responding and reinforcement on the other alternative, as follows:

$$R_A/R_B = r_A/r_B \quad (6.4)$$

Both mathematical expressions of the matching law represent the same basic principle, namely, that *relative rates of responding match relative rates of reinforcement.* (For an example

W. M. Baum

of matching involving a drug reinforcer in monkeys, see Meisch & Spiga, 1998. For an extension of the matching law to how pigeons distribute themselves between patches of food, see Baum & Kraft, 1998.)

Undermatching, Overmatching, and Response Bias. The matching law clearly indicates that choices are not made capriciously—they are an orderly function of rates of reinforcement. The precise characterization of the function is the subject of continuing research (see reviews by Baum, 1979; Davison & McCarthy, 1988; Nevin, 1998; Wearden & Burgess, 1982; Williams, 1988, 1994). Although the matching law has enjoyed considerable success and has guided much research over the past 30 years, relative rates of responding do not always exactly match relative rates of reinforcement.

Most instances in which choice behavior does not correspond perfectly to the matching relation can be accommodated by adding two parameters, *b* and *s*, to equation 6.4. This generalized form of the matching law (Baum, 1974) is as follows:

$$R_A/R_B = b(r_A/r_B)^s \qquad (6.5)$$

The parameter *s* represents *sensitivity* of the choice behavior to the relative rates of reinforcement for the response alternatives. When perfect matching occurs, *s* is equal to 1.0, in which case relative response rates are a direct function of relative rates of reinforcement.

One type of deviation from perfect matching involves reduced sensitivity of the choice behavior to the relative rates of reinforcement. Such results are referred to as **undermatching** and can be accommodated by equation 6.5 by making the exponent *s* less than 1.0. Notice that if the exponent *s* is less than 1.0, the value of the term representing relative reinforcer rates—$(r_A/r_B)^s$—becomes smaller, indicating the reduced sensitivity to the relative rate of reinforcement.

In other instances, the relative rate of responding is more sensitive to the relative rate of reinforcement than what is predicted by perfect matching. Such outcomes are called **overmatching** and can be accommodated by equation 6.5 by making the exponent greater than 1.0. In this case, the value of the term representing the relative rate of reinforcement—$r_A/r_B)^s$—is increased, indicating the increased sensitivity to this factor.

Choices are more likely to exhibit reduced sensitivity to relative reinforcement rates than they are to exhibit enhanced sensitivity to reinforcement rates. Consequently, undermatching is found more often than overmatching. The sensitivity parameter can be influenced by numerous variables, including the species tested, the effort or difficulty involved in switching from one alternative to the other, and the details of how the schedule alternatives are constructed (for example, see Aparicio, 2001; Davison, 1991a; Davison & Jones, 1995; Dreyfus, DePorto-Callan, & Pesillo, 1993; Elliffe & Alslop, 1996; Foster, Temple, Robertson, Nair, & Poling, 1996). In general, making it more difficult to switch from one response alternative to the other increases the sensitivity parameter; when switching is more difficult, organisms are more sensitive to the relative rates of reinforcement for the response alternatives.

The parameter *b* in equation 6.5 represents response *bias.* In Herrnstein's original experiment (and in most others that have followed), animals chose between two responses of the same type (pecking a response key), and each response was reinforced by the same type of reinforcer (a short period of access to food). Response bias influences choice when the response alternatives are different (for example, pecking a key and stepping on a treadle). Parameter *b* is also important when the reinforcer provided for the two responses is different. In the case of pigeons, one reinforcer may be buckwheat and the other hemp seed. A preference (or bias) for one response or one reinforcer over the other influences the bias parameter *b* (see Hanson & Green, 1986; Miller, 1976; Sumpter, Temple, & Foster, 1998).

In the absence of bias, *b* is equal to 1.0. Depending on the nature of the bias or preference, *b* will be greater or less than 1.0.

The Matching Law and Reinforcer Value. The matching relation has been extended to aspects of reinforcers other than their rate of occurrence. For example, the relative rate of responding has been found to be a function of the relative amount of each reinforcer, as well as the relative delay of reinforcement (for example, Gibbon & Fairhurst, 1994; Grace, 1995; see also Ho, Wogar, Bradshaw, & Szabadi, 1997). Relative rates of responding have also been found to be determined by the palatability of the reinforcers (Shah, Bradshaw, & Szabadi, 1991). Features of a reinforcer such as its amount, palatability, and delay can be considered to be aspects of its general value. Larger, more palatable, and more immediate reinforcers presumably are of greater value. However, it is not yet clear exactly how various features of a reinforcer combine to determine reinforcer value. (For further discussion of this issue, see McLean & Blampied, 2001; Nevin, 1998; Williams, 1994b.)

The Matching Law and Simple Reinforcement Schedules. If the matching law represents a fundamental fact about behavior, then it should also characterize responding on simple schedules of reinforcement. But simple schedules have only one response manipulandum. How can a law that describes the distribution of responses among several alternatives be applied to single response?

As Herrnstein (1970) pointed out, even single-response situations can involve a choice. The choice is between making the specified response (bar pressing or pecking a key, for example) and engaging in other possible activities (grooming, walking around, pecking the floor, sniffing holes in the experimental chamber). On a simple schedule, the subject receives not only explicit reinforcement for making a specific operant response but also intrinsic rewards for the other activities in which it may engage. Hence, the total reinforcement includes the programmed extrinsic rewards as well as the unprogrammed sources of reinforcement. This type of analysis permits application of the matching law to single-response reinforcement schedules.

Assume that R_A represents the rate of the specified operant response in the schedule, R_O represents the rate of the animal's other activities, r_A is the rate of the explicit programmed reinforcement, and r_O is the rate of the intrinsic reinforcement for the other activities. With these values substituted into equation 6.3, the matching law for single-response situations can be stated as follows:

$$R_A/(R_A + R_O) = r_A/(r_A + r_O) \qquad (6.6)$$

Solving this equation for R_A provides the following:

$$R_A = (R_A + R_O)r_A/(r_A + r_O) \qquad (6.7)$$

This equation can be solved if the investigator assumes that $(R_A + R_O)$ is equal to a constant irrespective of the reinforcer that is employed. If this constant is labeled *k,* equation 6.7 can be rewritten as

$$R_A = kr_A/(r_A + r_O)$$

This equation predicts that the rate of responding (R_A) will be directly related to the rate of reinforcement for that response in a negatively accelerating fashion. Another implication of the equation, of particular clinical interest, is that the rate of responding will decline as the rate of alternative sources of reinforcement (r_O) is increased. Thus, equation 6.8 provides two ways of changing the rate of a response (by changing its rate of reinforcement or by changing the rate of other sources of reinforcement).

BOX 6.3

THE MATCHING LAW, HUMAN BEHAVIOR, AND BEHAVIOR THERAPY

The matching law and its implications have been found to apply to a wide range of human behavior (see, for example, Baum, 1975; Conger & Killeen, 1974; Martens, Lochner, & Kelly, 1992; McDowell, 1982). In an interesting study, Vollmer and Bourret (2000) examined the choices that college basketball players made during the course of intercollegiate games. A basketball player can elect to shoot at the basket from an area close to the basket and thereby get 2 points, or from farther away and get 3 points. Teams compile statistics on the number of 2- and 3-point shots attempted and made by individual players. These data provide information about the relative rates of selecting each response alternative. The team data also include information about the success of each attempt and can be used to calculate the rate of reinforcement for each response alternative. Vollmer and Bourret examined the data for 13 players on the men's team and 13 players on the women's team of a large university and found that the relative choice of the different types of shots was proportional to the relative rates of reinforcement for those shots. Thus, the choice behavior of these athletes during regular games followed the matching law.

The matching law has important implications for behavior therapy (McDowell, 1982; Noll, 1995). According to this law, the tendency to make a particular response depends not only on the rate of reinforcement for that response but also on the rates of reinforcement available for alternative activities. This implies that analysis of a problematic behavior (truancy from school, for example) has to include not only consideration of the rewards available for that particular behavior but also the rewards the person can obtain in other ways. Thus, the matching law suggests that accurate assessment of a behavior problem requires consideration of the individual's full range of activities and sources of reinforcement.

The matching law also suggests novel techniques for decreasing undesired responses and increasing desired responses. According to the matching law, an undesired response can be decreased by providing more reinforcement for other activities or by simply providing more "free" reinforcers. Conversely, a desired response can be increased by withdrawing reinforcement for other activities.

The extension of the matching law to single-response situations has enjoyed considerable success (for example, Belke & Heyman, 1994a, 1994b; Heyman & Monaghan, 1994; Petry & Heyman, 1994). It is now well established that responding in single-response situations is a negatively accelerating function of the rate of reinforcement for that response. However, recent studies varying the reinforcer but not the instrumental response have called into question the assumption that $(R_A + R_O)$ is constant for a particular instrumental situation. Because of that, the usefulness of matching as a theory of behavior in single-operant situations is currently in doubt (Belke, 1998; Dallery, McDowell, & Lancaster, 2000; McDowell & Dallery, 1999).

Mechanisms of the Matching Law

The matching law describes how organisms distribute their responses in a choice situation but does not explain what mechanisms are responsible for this response distribution. It is a descriptive law of nature rather than a mechanistic law. Factors that may be responsible for matching in choice situations have been the subject of continuing experimentation and theoretical debate (see Commons, Herrnstein, & Rachlin, 1982; Davison & McCarthy, 1988; Herrnstein, 1997; Williams, 1988, 1994b).

The matching law is stated in terms of rates of responding and reinforcement averaged over the entire duration of experimental sessions. It ignores when individual responses are made. Similarly, *molar theories* of matching ignore what might occur at the level of individual responses. Molar theories explain aggregates of responses and deal with the overall distribution of responses and reinforcers in choice situations.

In contrast to molar theories, *molecular theories* focus on what happens at the level of individual responses and view the matching relation as the net result of these individual choices. Yet other theories provide characterizations of behavior that are neither molar nor molecular but somewhere in between; one such theory is *melioration.* The following is a discussion of molecular, molar, and melioration theories of choice. (For a theoretical treatment that takes both long-term and short-term factors into account, see Dragoi & Staddon, 1999.)

B. A. Williams

Matching and Maximizing Rates of Reinforcement. The most extensively investigated explanations of choice behavior are based on the intuitively reasonable idea that organisms distribute their actions among response alternatives in order to receive the maximum amount of reinforcement possible in the situation (for a good overview, see Baum & Aparicio, 1999). According to this idea, animals switch back and forth between response alternatives so as to receive as many reinforcers as they possibly can. The idea that organisms maximize reinforcement has been used to explain choice behavior at both molecular and molar levels of analysis.

1. *Molecular Maximizing.* According to molecular theories of maximizing, organisms always choose whichever response alternative is most likely to be reinforced at the time (Hinson & Staddon, 1983a, 1983b). Shimp (1966, 1969) proposed an early version of molecular matching. He suggested that when two schedules (A and B) are in effect simultaneously, the subject switches from schedule A to schedule B as the probability of reinforcement for schedule B increases. Consider, for example, a pigeon working on a concurrent VI-VI schedule. As the pigeon pecks key A, the timer controlling reinforcement for key B is still operating. The longer the pigeon stays on key A, the greater the probability that the requisite interval for key B will elapse and reinforcement will become available for pecking key B. By switching, the pigeon can pick up the reinforcer on key B. Now, the longer it continues to peck key B, the more likely key A will become set for reinforcement. Shimp proposed that the matching relation is a by-product of prudent switching when the probability of reinforcement on the alternative response key becomes greater than the probability of reinforcement on the current response key.

Detailed studies of the patterns of switching from one to another response alternative have not always supported the molecular maximizing theory proposed by Shimp. In fact, some studies have shown that matching is possible in the absence of momentary maximizing (for example, Nevin, 1969, 1979; see also Machado, 1994; Williams, 1991, 1992a). However, recent approaches to molecular analyses of choice behavior have met with more success.

One approach has emphasized analyzing a two-alternative choice in terms of reinforcement for staying with a particular alternative and reinforcement for switching to the other option. For example, a situation in which a laboratory rat has two response levers available can be analyzed as involving four different options: staying on the right lever, switching from the right lever to the left one, staying on the left lever, and switching from the left lever to the right one. Each of these four options has its own reinforcement contingency by virtue of the schedule of reinforcement that is programmed on each lever. The relative distribution of right and left responses is presumed to depend on the relative rate of reinforcement for staying on each lever versus switching to the other lever (MacDonall, 1998, 1999, 2000). The success of these analyses suggests that such molecular mechanisms can contribute to the performance that is observed on concurrent schedules, but the extent to which such molecular processes are responsible for (or necessary for) matching remains in dispute (Machado & Keen, 1999). (For other recent molecular accounts of choice in concurrent schedules, see Cleaveland, 1999; Gallistel & Gibbon, 2000.)

2. *Molar Maximizing.* Molar theories of maximizing assume that organisms distribute their responses among various alternatives in order to maximize the amount of reinforcement they earn over the long run (for example, Rachlin, Battalio, Kagel, & Green, 1981; Rachlin, Green, Kagel, & Battalio, 1976). What is long enough to be considered a "long run" is not clearly specified. In contrast to molecular theories, however, molar theories focus on aggregates of behavior over some period of time rather than on individual choice responses.

Molar maximizing theory was originally formulated to explain choice on concurrent schedules made up of ratio components. In concurrent ratio schedules, animals rarely switch back and forth between response alternatives; instead, they respond exclusively on the ratio component that requires the fewest responses. On a concurrent FR 20–FR 10 schedule, for example, the organism is likely to respond only on the FR 10 alternative. In this way it maximizes its rate of reinforcement with the least effort.

In many situations, molar maximizing accurately predicts the results of choice procedures, but certain findings present difficulties. One difficulty arises from the results of concurrent VI-VI schedules of reinforcement in which organisms can earn close to all of the available rewards on both schedules, provided they occasionally sample each alternative. The total amount of reinforcement obtained on a concurrent VI-VI schedule can therefore be close to the same despite wide variations in how responding is distributed between the two alternatives. The matching relation is only one of many different possibilities that yield close to maximal rates of reinforcement. Because other response distributions can yield similar amounts of total reward, molar maximizing cannot explain why choice behavior is distributed so close to the matching relation on concurrent VI-VI schedules and not in other equally effective ways (Heyman, 1983).

Another challenge for molar matching is provided by results of studies in which there is a choice between a variable ratio and a variable interval schedule. On a variable ratio schedule, the organism can obtain reinforcement at any time by making the required number of responses. By contrast, on a variable interval schedule, the subject has to respond only occasionally to obtain close to the maximum number of rewards possible. Given these differences, for maximum return on a concurrent VR-VI schedule, subjects should concentrate their responses on the variable ratio alternative and respond only occasionally on the variable interval component. Evidence shows that animals do favor the VR component but not as strongly as molar maximizing predicts (Baum, 1981; DeCarlo, 1985; Herrnstein & Heyman, 1979; Heyman & Herrnstein, 1986; see also Vyse & Belke, 1992; but see Baum & Aparicio, 1999). Human participants also respond much more on the VI alternative than is prudent if they are trying to maximize their rate of reinforcement (Savastano & Fantino, 1994).

3. *Melioration.* The third major mechanism of choice, melioration, is neither a molecular nor a molar mechanism. Melioration mechanisms operate on a timescale that is between the timescale of molar and molecular theories.

Many aspects of behavior are not optimal in the long run. People make choices that result in their being overweight, being addicted to cigarettes or other drugs, or being without close friends. No one chooses these end points. As Herrnstein (1997) has pointed out,

"A person does not normally make a once-and-for-all decision to become an exercise junkie, a miser, a glutton, a profligate, or a gambler; rather he slips into the pattern through a myriad of innocent, or almost innocent choices, each of which carries little weight" (p. 285). It is these "innocent choices" that meliation is intended to characterize.

The term *melioration* refers to making something better. Notice that melioration does not refer to selecting the best alternative at the moment (molecular maximizing) or making something as good as it can be in the long run (molar maximizing). Melioration refers to the more modest (or "innocent") goal of just making the situation better. Better than what? Better than how that situation has been in the recent past. The benefits are assessed specific to a limited situation—not overall or in the long run.

An important term in translating these ideas to testable experimental predictions is the *local rate* of responding and reinforcement. Molar theories focus on overall rates of responding and reinforcement, which are calculated over the entire duration of an experimental session. In contrast, local rates are calculated only over the time period that a subject devotes to a particular choice alternative. For example, if the situation involves two options (A and B), the local rate of responding on A is calculated by dividing the frequency of responses on A by the time the subject devoted to responding on A.

The local rate of a response is always higher than its overall rate. If the subject responds 75 times in an hour on alternative A, the overall rate for response A will be 75/hour. However, those 75 responses might be made during just 20 minutes of the session, with the subject working on response B the rest of the time. Therefore, the local rate of response A will be 75/20 minutes, or 225/hour.

Melioration theory assumes that organisms change from one response alternative to another to improve on the local rate of reinforcement they are receiving (Herrnstein, 1997; Herrnstein & Vaughan, 1980; Vaughan, 1981, 1985). Adjustments in the distribution of behavior between alternatives are assumed to continue until the organism is obtaining the same local rate of reward on all alternatives. It can be shown mathematically that when subjects distribute their responses to obtain the same local rate of reinforcement on each response alternative, they are behaving in accordance with the matching law. Therefore, the mechanism of melioration results in matching.

To see how melioration works, consider a concurrent VI 1-min VI 3-min schedule. During the first hour of exposure to this schedule, a pigeon will switch back and forth between the two alternatives and may end up accumulating a total of 30 minutes responding on each component, earning all of the available reinforcers. On a VI 1-min schedule, at most 60 reinforcers are available in 1 hour. The pigeon could get all of these during the course of spending 30 minutes on the VI 1-min schedule, provided it distributed its responses appropriately. If the pigeon received all 60 reinforcers during the course of accumulating 30 minutes on the VI 1-min schedule, its local rate of reinforcement will be 60 reinforcers in 30 minutes, or *120 per hour.* On a VI 3-min schedule, at most 20 reinforcers are available in 1 hour. If the pigeon got all of these during the course of accumulating a total of 30 minutes on the VI 3-min schedule, its local rate of reinforcement on the VI 3-min component will be 20 reinforcers in 30 minutes, or *40 per hour.*

According to melioration theory, the pigeon will shift its preference in favor of the response alternative that yields the higher local rate of reinforcement. Since the local rate of reinforcement on the VI 1-min schedule (120/hr) was much higher than on the VI 3-min schedule (40/hr), the pigeon will shift its behavior in favor of the VI 1-min alternative. However, if it begins to spend too much time on the VI 1-min schedule and samples the VI 3-min schedule only rarely, it may be reinforced every time it pecks the VI 3-min key. This will make the local rate of reinforcement on the VI 3-min key higher than the local rate of reinforcement on the VI 1-min alternative. That in turn would produce a shift in favor of the VI 3-min schedule. According to melioration theory, such shifts back and forth will continue until the local rates of reinforcement earned on the two alternatives are equal.

Although tests of the melioration hypothesis have yielded confirmatory evidence (for example, McSweeney, Melville, Buck, & Whipple, 1983), the hypothesis has also encountered some difficulties (for example, Belke, 1992; Williams, 1993). Given the complexity of choice behavior, it is not surprising that investigators are continuing their exploration of alternative approaches to explaining how organisms choose between different sources of reinforcement (for example, Davis, Staddon, Machado, & Palmer, 1993; Dragoi & Staddon, 1999; Gallistel & Gibbon, 2000; Grace, 1994; Mazur, 2001).

CHOICE WITH COMMITMENT

In a standard concurrent schedule of reinforcement, two (or more) response alternatives are available at the same time, and switching from one to the other can occur at any time. Many choice situations outside the laboratory are of this type. If you have a plate of roast beef, vegetables, and mashed potatoes, you can switch from one food to another at any time during the meal. You can similarly switch back and forth among television channels or parts of a newspaper. In some cases, however, choosing one alternative makes other alternatives unavailable, and the choice may involve assessing complex, long-range goals.

Should you go to college and get a degree in engineering or start in a full-time job without a college degree? You cannot switch back and forth between such alternatives. Furthermore, to make the decision, you need to consider long-range goals. A degree in engineering may enable you to get a higher paying job eventually, but it may require significant economic sacrifices initially. Getting a job without a college degree would enable you to make money sooner, but in the long run you would not earn as much.

Important choices in life often involve a short-term small benefit versus a more delayed but larger benefit. This is fundamentally the problem of self-control. People are said to lack self-control if they choose a small short-term reward instead of waiting for a larger but more delayed benefit. The student who talks with a friend instead of studying is selecting a small short-term reward over the more delayed but larger reward of successfully completing college. The heroin addict who uses a friend's needle instead of getting a clean one is similarly selecting the smaller, quicker reward, as is the drunk who elects to drive home now instead of waiting to sober up.

Concurrent-Chain Schedules

Obviously, investigators cannot conduct experiments that directly involve choosing between college and a job after high school, or driving while intoxicated versus waiting to sober up. However, simplified analogous questions may be posed in laboratory experiments. Many such studies have been done with pigeons, rats, and monkeys, and these experiments have stimulated analogous studies with human subjects (see, for example, studies by Forzano & Corry, 1998; Ito & Nakamura, 1998; Logue, Forzano, & Ackerman, 1996). The basic technique in this area of research is the **concurrent-chain schedule** of reinforcement.

We have all heard that variety is the spice of life. How could investigators determine whether this is true? One implication may be that subjects will prefer a variable ratio schedule of reinforcement (which provides variety in the number of responses required for successive reinforcers) over a fixed ratio schedule (which requires the same number of responses per reinforcer). A concurrent-chain schedule is ideal for answering such questions.

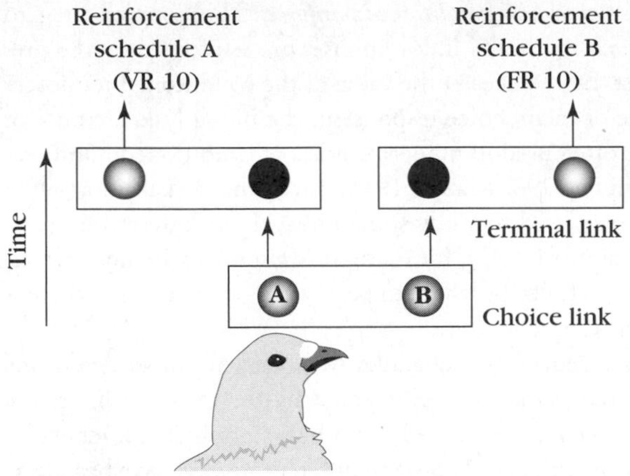

Figure 6.6 Diagram of a concurrent-chain schedule. Pecking the left key in the choice link puts into effect reinforcement schedule A in the terminal link. Pecking the right key in the choice link puts into effect reinforcement schedule B in the terminal link.

A concurrent-chain schedule of reinforcement involves at least two stages or links (see Figure 6.6). During the first stage, the *choice link,* the participant is allowed to choose between two schedule alternatives by making one of two responses. In the example diagrammed in Figure 6.6, the pigeon makes its choice by pecking either the left or the right response key. Pecking the left key produces alternative A, the opportunity to peck the left key for 10 minutes on a VR 10 schedule of reinforcement. If the pigeon pecks the right key in the choice link, it produces alternative B, which is the opportunity to peck the right key for 10 minutes on an FR 10 schedule. Responding on either key during the choice link does not yield food. The opportunity for reinforcement occurs only after the initial choice has been made and the pigeon has entered the *terminal link.* Another important feature of the concurrent-chain schedule is that once the participant has made a choice, it is stuck with that choice until the end of the terminal link of the schedule (10 minutes in the hypothetical example). Thus, concurrent-chain schedules involve *choice with commitment.*

The pattern of responding that occurs in the terminal component of a concurrent-chain schedule is characteristic of whatever schedule of reinforcement is in effect during that component. In the example, if the pigeon selects alternative A, its pattern of pecking during the terminal component will be similar to the usual response pattern for a VR 10 schedule. If the pigeon selects alternative B, its pattern of pecking during the terminal component will be characteristic of an FR 10 schedule.

Studies of this sort have shown that subjects do prefer the variable ratio alternative. In fact, pigeons favor the VR alternative even if it requires, on average, more responses per reinforcer than the FR alternative. To this extent, variety does seem to be the spice of life. The preference for the VR schedule is driven by the fact that occasionally a VR schedule provides reinforcement for relatively few responses (Field, Tonneau, Ahearn, & Hineline, 1996). (For other studies of preference for a schedule in which reinforcers are unpredictable over one that provides reinforcement in a predictable fashion, see Belke & Spetch, 1994; Bruner, Gibbon, & Fairhurst, 1994; Mazur, 1991; Mazur & Romano, 1992; Spetch, Mondloch, Belke, & Dunn, 1994).

As I noted, the consequence of responding during the initial (choice) link of a concurrent schedule is not the primary reinforcer (food). It is entry into one of the terminal links, each of which is typically designated by a particular color on the pecking key. Thus, the immediate consequence of an initial link response is a stimulus that is associated with the terminal link that was chosen. Since that stimulus is present when the primary reinforcer is provided, the terminal link stimulus becomes a *conditioned reinforcer.* Thus, one may regard a concurrent schedule as one in which the initial link responses are reinforced by the presentation of a conditioned reinforcer. Differences in the value of the conditioned reinforcer will then determine the relative rate of each choice response in the initial link. Because of this, concurrent-chain schedules are often used in modern studies of conditioned reinforcement (Goldshmidt, Lattal, & Fantino, 1998; Mazur, 1998; Savastano & Fantino, 1996; Williams, 1997a). They have been also used to study some unusual and interesting questions about behavior. Cerutti and Catania (1997), for example, examined whether pigeons prefer a situation in which they have a choice of where to peck versus one in which there is only one place where pecking will yield food.

Courtesy of Donald A. Dewsbury

E. Fantino

Although many studies of concurrent-chain schedules were carried out to determine how organisms select between different situations represented by the terminal links, the consensus of opinion is that choice behavior is governed by both the terminal link schedules and whatever schedule is in effect in the initial link. Several different models have been proposed to explain how variables related to the initial and terminal links act in concert to determine concurrent choice performance (for an excellent review, see Mazur, 2000, 2001).

Studies of "Self-Control"

Self-control is often a matter of choosing a large delayed reward over an immediate small reward. For example, self-control in eating involves selecting the large delayed reward of being thin over the immediate small reward of eating a piece of cake. When a piece of cake is in plain view, it is very difficult to choose the delayed reward; it is difficult to pass up the piece of cake in favor of being thin. Self-control is easier if the tempting alternative is not as readily available. It is easier to pass up a piece of cake if you are deciding on what to eat at the next meal. Rachlin and Green (1972) set up a laboratory analog of self-control with pigeons based on these ideas.

The basic concurrent-chain schedule used by Rachlin and Green is shown in Figure 6.7. In the terminal components of the schedule, responding was rewarded by either immediate access to a small amount of grain (alternative A) or access to a large amount of grain that was delayed by 4 seconds (alternative B). The pigeons could choose between these two alternatives by pecking either key A or key B during the initial component of the schedule.

Rachlin and Green tested the choice behavior of the pigeons under two different conditions. In one case ("direct-choice procedure" in Figure 6.7), the small immediate reward and the delayed large reward were available as soon as the pigeons pecked the corresponding choice key once. Under these conditions, the pigeons lacked self-control. They predominantly selected the small immediate reward. In the second case ("concurrent-chain procedure" in Figure 6.7), the terminal components of the concurrent-chain schedule were delayed after the pigeons made their initial choice. If a sufficient delay was imposed before the terminal components, the pigeons showed self-control; they primarily selected the large delayed reward.

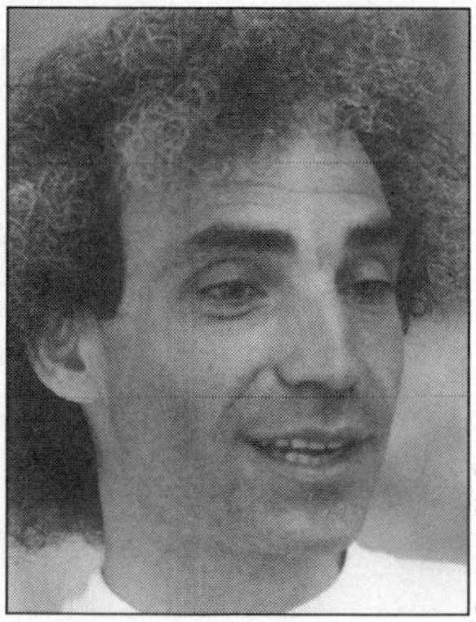

Courtesy of L. Green

L. Green

The phenomenon of self-control as illustrated by the Rachlin and Green experiment has stimulated much research and theorizing. Many investigators have found, in agreement with Rachlin and Green, that preferences shift in favor of the delayed large reward as participants are required to wait longer to receive either reward after making their choice. If rewards are delivered shortly after a choice response, subjects generally favor an immediate small reward over a delayed large reward. However, if a constant delay is added to the delivery of both rewards, individuals are more likely to show self-control and favor the delayed large reward. This crossover in preference has been obtained in laboratory experiments with both human and nonhuman animals and thus represents a general property of choice

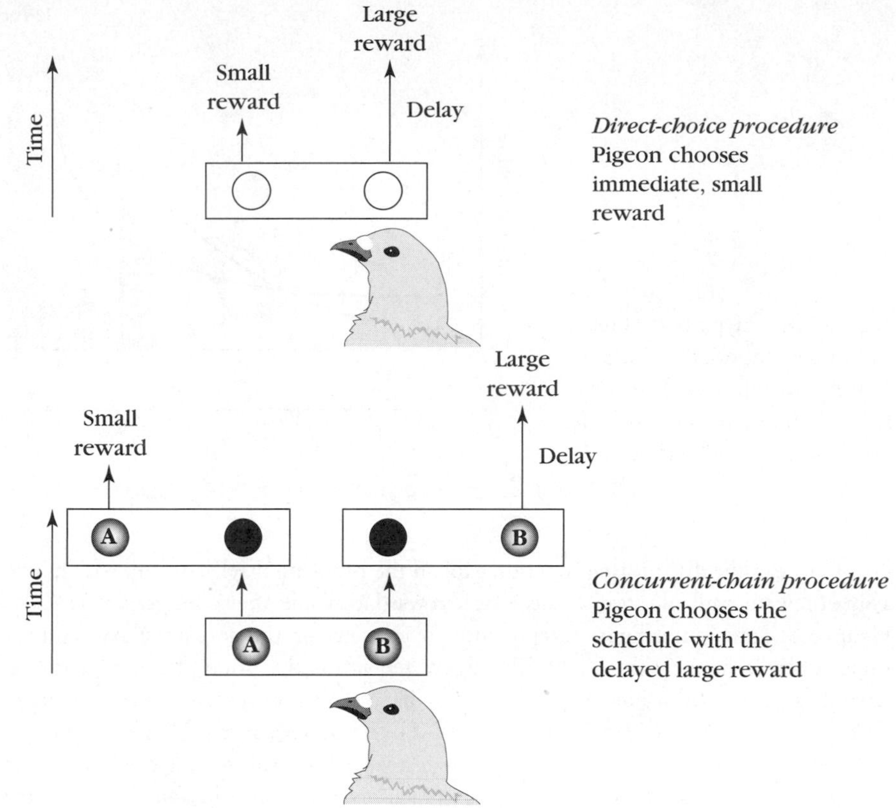

Figure 6.7 Diagram of the experiment by Rachlin and Green (1972) on self-control. The direct-choice procedure is shown at the top; the concurrent-chain procedure, at the bottom.

behavior. (For applications of these concepts to university administration, see Logue, 1998a; For more comprehensive reviews of self-control, see Logue, 1988b, 1995, 1998b.)

Courtesy of A. W. Logue

A. W. Logue

Explanations of Self-Control. Which would you prefer, $1,000 today or $1,000 next year? For most people, the answer is obvious: $1,000 today would be of much greater value. How about $1,000 next week, or next month? Most people would agree that the longer one has to wait for the $1,000, the less exciting is the prospect of getting the money. This illustrates a general principle that is the key to behavioral explanations of self-control, namely, that the value of a reinforcer is reduced by how long you have to wait to get it. The mathematical function describing this decrease in value is called the **value discounting function**. The exact mathematical form of the value discounting function has taken a bit of empirical effort to pin down. But the current consensus is that the value of a reinforcer (V) is directly related to reward magnitude (M) and inversely related to reward delay (D), according to the formula,

$$V = M/(1 + KD) \qquad (6.9)$$

where K is the discounting rate parameter (Mazur, 1987). Equation 6.9 is called the *hyperbolic decay function.* (For a generalized version of the hyperbolic decay function, see Grace, 1999.) According to this equation, if the reinforcer is delivered with no delay (D=0), the value of the reinforcer is directly related to its magnitude (larger reinforcers have larger values). The longer the reinforcer is delayed, the smaller its value.

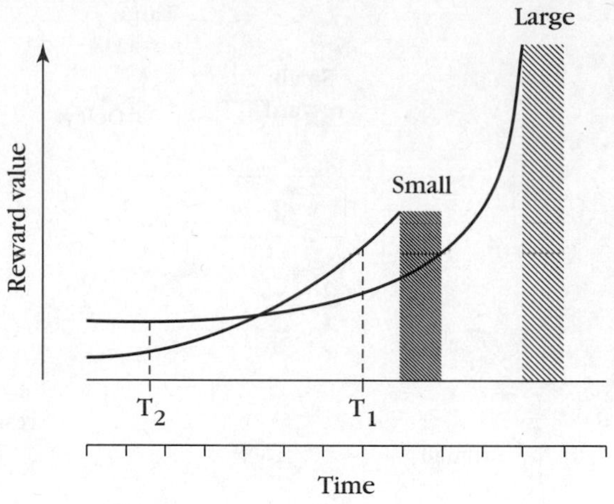

Figure 6.8 Hypothetical relations between reward value and waiting time to reward delivery for a small reward and a large reward presented some time later.

How can the discounting function explain the problem of self-control, which involves a small reward available soon versus a large reward available after a longer delay? Consider Figure 6.8. Time in this figure is represented by distance on the horizontal axis, and reward value is represented by the *y* axis. The figure represents the value of a large and a small reward as a function of how long participants have to wait to receive the reward. Two different points in time are identified, T_1 and T_2. The usual self-control dilemma involves considering the reward values at T_1, where there is a very short wait for the small reward and a longer wait for the large reward. Waiting for each reward reduces its value. Because reward value decreases rapidly at first, given the delays involved at T_1 the value of the large reward is smaller than the value of the small reward. Hence, the model predicts that if the choice occurs at T_1, participants will select the small reward (the impulsive option). However, the discounting functions cross over with further delays. The value of both rewards is less at T_2 than at T_1 because T_2 involves longer delays. Notice, however, that at T_2 the value of the large reward is now greater than that of the small reward. Therefore, a choice at T_2 would have participants select the large reward (the self-control option).

The value discounting functions illustrated in Figure 6.8 predict the results of Rachlin and Green (1972) described earlier, as well as numerous other studies of self-control. Increasing the delay to both small and large rewards makes it easier to exhibit self-control by selecting the larger but more delayed reinforcer.

Discounting Functions and the Problems of Self-Control in Drug Addiction. As I have noted, the parameter K in equation 6.8 indicates how rapidly reward value declines as a function of delay. The steeper a person's delay discounting function, the more difficulty he or she will have in exhibiting self-control (electing the larger delayed reward) rather than impulsivity (electing the smaller, quicker reward). A team of investigators at the University of Vermont led by Warren Bickel and Gregory Madden has been using the delay discounting function to study how problems of self-control are involved in drug addiction.

Madden, Petry, Badger, and Bickel (1997) noted that "substance abuse frequently reflects a series of impulsive choices" (p. 256). Addicts will choose the relatively quick small reward of drug intoxication at the risk of more delayed negative consequences of interpersonal problems, and loss of social support, steady employment, and good health. Such choices suggest discounting the value (or threat) of long-term consequences. If this is true,

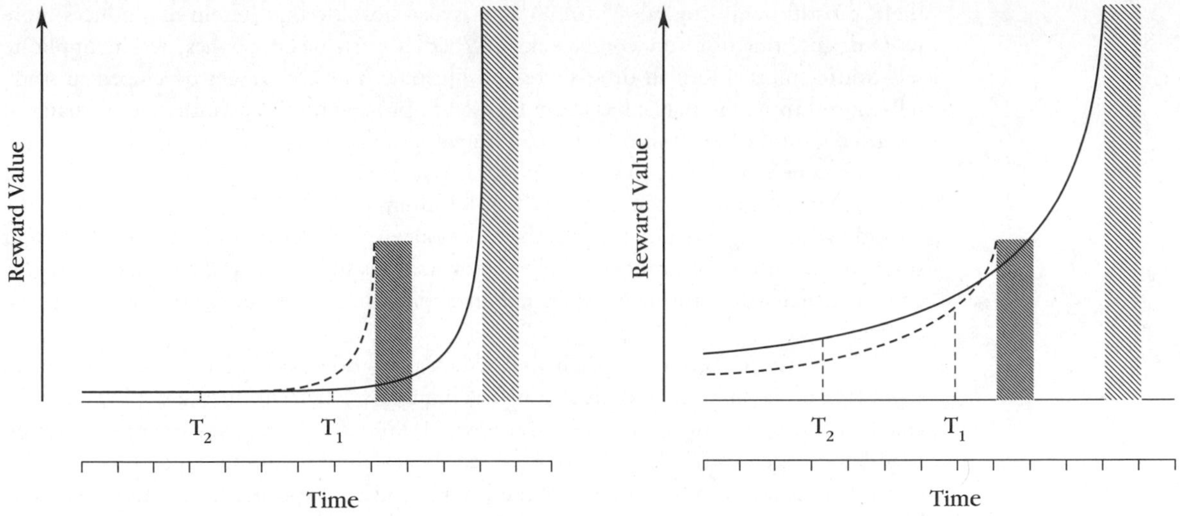

Figure 6.9 Reward discount functions for a large and smaller monetary reward. The left panel shows the discount functions obtained with a group of heroin-dependent subjects. The right panel shows data from a control group. (From "Impulsive and Self-Control Choices in Opioid-Dependent Patients and Non-Drug-Using Control Participants: Drug and Monetary Rewards," by G. J. Madden, N. M. Petry, G. J. Badger, and W. K. Bickel, 1997, *Experimental and Clinical Psychopharmacology, 5,* pp. 256–262. Reprinted by permission.)

then drug addicts should show steeper reward discount functions than other individuals. Madden et al. (1997) tested this prediction with a group of heroin-dependent patients enrolled in a substance abuse program and a group of nondependent individuals matched for age, gender, education, and IQ.

The procedure was a variant of the adjusting-delay procedure developed by Mazur (1987) in studies with pigeons. On each trial, the subjects were asked to choose between two hypothetical scenarios: getting $1,000 sometime in the future or a smaller amount of money right away. In different repetitions of the task, the $1,000 was to be received at one of seven future times ranging from 1 week to 25 years. For each delay period, the magnitude of the smaller immediate alternative was varied across trials until the investigators determined how much money obtained immediately was as attractive as the $1,000 sometime in the future. Using these data, Madden et al. (1997) were able to construct reward discount functions for both heroin-dependent and control subjects.

The results are summarized in Figure 6.9. Keep in mind that these are reward discount functions for hypothetical choices between different amounts of money to be received soon (T_1) or after a substantial delay (T_2). The data for the heroin addicts are presented in the left panel, and the data for the control subjects appear in the right panel. One striking finding was that the reward discount functions were much steeper for the heroin addicts; that is, for heroin-dependent subjects the value of money dropped very quickly if receipt of the money was to be delayed. This steep reward discounting function is indicative of lack of control and impulsivity. Madden et al. (1997) speculated that because drug-dependent subjects showed more rapid discounting of reward value, "heroin-addicted individuals may be more likely to engage in criminal and dangerous activities to obtain immediate rewards (e.g., theft, prostitution, drug sales)" (p. 261). It is also possible that heroin use induces more rapid discounting of future consequences. Whether cause or effect, these results implicate self-control mechanisms in drug abuse and illustrate how techniques developed to study self-control in nonhuman subjects can be used to provide precise quantitative estimates of reward discounting relevant to important human problems.

Subsequent work extended this type of analysis to cigarette smokers and the problem of needle sharing among heroin addicts. Bickel, Odum, and Madden (1999) found that the reward discounting function for hypothetical monetary choices is much steeper for current smokers than it is for nonsmokers and ex-smokers. This suggests that the same kind of self-control deficits that are involved in heroin addiction are also evident among cigarette addicts.

The sharing of needles among heroin addicts may also reflect lack of self-control due to rapid reward discounting. Needle sharing is a highly risky behavior because it increases the chance of getting various infectious diseases (AIDS and hepatitis, for example). Odum, Madden, Badger, and Bickel (2000) measured the reward discounting functions of heroin-dependent patients in a substance abuse program using hypothetical monetary choices. They then asked the subjects to select between two hypothetical scenarios: using a friend's needle right away or waiting a week to obtain a new sterile needle. Interestingly, the subjects who expressed a willingness to share a needle had much steeper reward discount functions than subjects who preferred to wait for a new needle. This difference, however, was observed only when the task involved hypothetical monetary amounts. When the subjects were asked to judge the relative value of a small amount of heroin now or a larger amount later, the two groups of patients showed similarly rapid discount functions. (For related work, see Kirby, Petry, & Bickel, 1999; Madden, Bickel, & Jacobs, 1999.)

Can Self-Control Be Trained? A person who cannot tolerate the waiting time required for large rewards has to forgo obtaining those reinforcers. Self-control, or the preference for a large delayed reward over a small immediate reward, is often a sensible strategy. In fact, some have suggested that self-control is a critical component of socialization and emotional adjustment. This raises an interesting question: Can self-control be trained? Fortunately for society, the answer is yes.

Training people with delayed reward appears to have generalized effects in increasing their tolerance for delayed reward. In one study (Eisenberger & Adornetto, 1986), second- and third-grade students in a public elementary school were first tested for self-control by being asked whether they wanted to get 2¢ immediately or 3¢ at the end of the day. Children who elected the immediate reward were given 2¢; for those who elected the delayed reward, 3¢ was placed in a cup to be given to the child later. The procedure was repeated eight times to complete the pretest. The children then received three sessions of training with either immediate or delayed reward.

During each training session, various problems were presented: one involved counting objects on a card, another was a picture–memory task, and the third was a shape-matching task. For half the students, correct responding was reinforced immediately with 2¢. For the remaining students, correct responses resulted in 3¢ being placed in a cup that was given to the child at the end of the day. After the third training session, preference for small immediate reward versus larger delayed reward was measured as in the pretest. Provided that the training tasks involved low effort, training with delayed reward increased preference for the larger delayed reward during the posttest. Thus, training with delayed reinforcement produced generalized self-control. (For other approaches to increasing self-control, see Logue, 1998b; Schweitzer & Sulzer-Azaroff, 1988).

CONCLUDING COMMENTS

The basic principle of instrumental conditioning is very simple: reinforcement increases (and punishment decreases) the future probability of an instrumental response. However, as I have described, the experimental analysis of instrumental behavior can be rather intricate. Many important aspects of instrumental behavior are determined by the schedule of reinforcement. There are numerous schedules by which responses can be reinforced. Reinforcement can depend on how many responses have occurred, the passage of time, or the rate of responding. Furthermore, more than one reinforcement schedule may be available to the organism at the same time. The pattern of instrumental behavior, as well as choices between various response alternatives, is strongly determined by the schedule of reinforcement that is in effect. These various findings have revealed a great deal about how reinforcement controls behavior in a variety of circumstances and have encouraged many powerful applications of reinforcement principles to human behavior.

SAMPLE QUESTIONS

1. Compare and contrast ratio and interval schedules in terms of how the contingencies of reinforcement are set up and the effects they have on the instrumental response.
2. Describe how response rate schedules are designed and what their effects are.
3. Describe the generalized matching law equation, and explain each of its parameters.
4. Describe various theoretical explanations of the matching law.
5. How are concurrent-chain schedules different from concurrent schedules, and what kinds of research questions require the use of concurrent-chain schedules?
6. What is a reward discounting function, and how is it related to the problem of self-control?

KEY TERMS

concurrent-chain schedule A complex reinforcement procedure in which the participant is permitted to choose which of several simple reinforcement schedules will be in effect. Once a choice has been made, the rejected alternatives become unavailable for some time.

concurrent schedule A complex reinforcement procedure in which the participant can choose any one of two or more simple reinforcement schedules that are available simultaneously. Concurrent schedules allow for the measurement of choice between simple schedule alternatives.

continuous reinforcement A schedule of reinforcement in which every occurrence of the instrumental response produces the reinforcer. Abbreviated CRF.

cumulative record A graphical representation of how a response is repeated over time, with the passage of time represented by the horizontal distance (or *x* axis), and the total or cumulative number of responses that have occurred up to a particular point in time represented by the vertical distance (or *y* axis).

differential reinforcement of high rate A reinforcement schedule in which a response is reinforced only if it occurs *before* a specified amount of time has elapsed following the preceding response. Abbreviated DRH.

differential reinforcement of low rate A reinforcement schedule in which a response is reinforced only if it occurs *after* a specified amount of time has elapsed following the preceding response. Abbreviated DRL.

fixed interval scallop The gradually increasing rate of responding that occurs between successive reinforcements on a fixed interval schedule.

fixed interval schedule A reinforcement schedule in which the reinforcer is delivered for the first response that occurs after a fixed amount of time following the last reinforcer. Abbreviated FI.

fixed ratio schedule A reinforcement schedule in which a fixed number of responses must occur in order for the next response to be reinforced. Abbreviated FR.

intermittent reinforcement A schedule of reinforcement in which only some of the occurrences of the instrumental response are reinforced. The instrumental response is reinforced occasionally, or intermittently. Also called *partial reinforcement.*

interresponse time or **IRT** The interval between one response and the next. IRTs can be differentially reinforced in the same fashion as other aspects of behavior, such as response force or variability.

interval schedule A reinforcement schedule in which a response is reinforced only if it occurs after a set amount of time following the last reinforcement.

limited hold A restriction on how long reinforcement remains available. In order for a response to be reinforced, it must occur during the limited-hold period.

matching law A rule for instrumental behavior, proposed by R. J. Herrnstein, which states that the relative rate of responding on a particular response alternative equals the relative rate of reinforcement for that response alternative.

melioration A mechanism for achieving matching by responding so as to improve the local rates of reinforcement for response alternatives.

overmatching Greater sensitivity to the relative rate of reinforcement than predicted by perfect matching.

partial reinforcement Same as *intermittent reinforcement.*

postreinforcement pause A pause in responding that typically occurs after the delivery of the reinforcer on fixed ratio and fixed interval schedules of reinforcement.

ratio run The high and invariant rate of responding observed after the postreinforcement pause on fixed ratio reinforcement schedules. The ratio run ends when the necessary number of responses have been performed, and the participant is reinforced.

ratio schedule A reinforcement schedule in which reinforcement depends only on the number of responses the participant performs, irrespective of when those responses occur.

ratio strain Disruption of responding that occurs when a fixed ratio response requirement is increased too rapidly.

response-rate schedule A reinforcement schedule in which a response is reinforced depending on how soon that response is made after the previous occurrence of the behavior.

schedule of reinforcement A program, or rule, that determines how and when the occurrence of a response will be followed by the delivery of the reinforcer.

undermatching Less sensitivity to the relative rate of reinforcement than predicted by perfect matching.

value discounting function The mathematical function that describes how reinforcer value decreases as a function of how long a participant has to wait for delivery of the reinforcer.

variable interval schedule A reinforcement schedule in which reinforcement is provided for the first response that occurs after a variable amount of time from the last reinforcement. Abbreviated VI.

variable ratio schedule A reinforcement schedule in which the number of responses necessary to produce reinforcement varies from trial to trial. The value of the schedule refers to the average number of responses needed for reinforcement. Abbreviated VR.

CHAPTER 7

INSTRUMENTAL CONDITIONING: MOTIVATIONAL MECHANISMS

Chapter 7 is devoted to a discussion of processes that motivate and direct instrumental behavior. Two distinctively different approaches have been pursued in an effort to understand why instrumental behavior occurs. One of these originated in the work of Thorndike and Pavlov and focuses on identifying the associative structure of instrumental conditioning. The other approach originated in the work of Skinner and focuses on how behavior is regulated in the face of limitations or restrictions created by an instrumental conditioning procedure. Behavior regulation theories describe reinforcement effects within the broader context of an organism's behavioral repertoire, using concepts from several areas of inquiry, including behavioral economics and behavioral ecology. The associationist approach considers molecular mechanisms and is not concerned with the long-range goal or function of instrumental behavior. In contrast, the behavioral regulation approach considers molar aspects of behavior and regards instrumental conditioning effects as manifestations of maximization or optimization processes. These two approaches provide an exciting illustration of the sometimes turbulent course of scientific inquiry. Investigators studying the motivational substrates of instrumental behavior have moved boldly to explore radically new conceptions when older ideas did not meet the challenges posed by new empirical findings.

In Chapters 5 and 6 I defined instrumental behavior, pointed out how it is investigated, and described how such behavior is influenced by various experimental manipulations, including schedules of reinforcement. I did not say much about what motivates instrumental responding, perhaps because the answer seemed obvious. Informal reflection suggests that instrumental behavior occurs because the subject is motivated to obtain the reinforcer and can do so only by performing the instrumental response. But what does it mean to be "motivated" to obtain the reinforcer? And what is the full impact of setting up a situation so that the reinforcer is accessible only by making the required instrumental response? Answers to these questions have occupied scientists for more than a century and have encompassed some of the most important and interesting research in the analysis of behavior.

The motivation of instrumental behavior has been considered from two radically different perspectives. The first originated with Thorndike and involves analysis of the *associative structure of instrumental conditioning.* As the label implies, this approach relies heavily on the concept of associations and hence is compatible with the theoretical tradition of Pavlovian conditioning. In fact, much of the research relevant to the associative structure of instrumental conditioning was stimulated by efforts to identify the role of Pavlovian mechanisms in instrumental learning. In addition, some of the investigative tactics that were developed to study Pavlovian conditioning were imported to the problem of instrumental learning.

The associative approach takes a molecular perspective. It focuses on individual responses and their specific stimulus antecedents and outcomes. To achieve this level of detail, the associative approach examines instrumental learning in isolated behavioral preparations, not unlike studying something in a test tube or a petri dish. Because associations can be substantiated in the nervous system, the associative approach provides a convenient framework for studying the neural mechanisms of instrumental conditioning.

The alternative approach to motivational processes in instrumental learning is *behavioral regulation.* This approach developed within the Skinnerian tradition and involves considering instrumental conditioning within the broader context of the numerous things organisms are constantly doing. In particular, the behavioral regulation approach is concerned with how an instrumental conditioning procedure sets limits on the organism's free flow of activities and the behavioral consequences of such constraints. Unlike the associative approach, behavioral regulation considers the motivation of instrumental behavior from a more molar perspective. It considers "goals" and how organisms take advantage of the complexities of their environment and their multiple behavioral options in achieving their goals. Thus, the behavioral regulation theory views instrumental behavior from a more functional perspective. Because it takes a molar approach, behavioral regulation does not provide a convenient framework for studying the neural mechanisms of instrumental learning.

The associative and behavioral regulation approaches have thus far proceeded nearly independently of each other. Each approach has identified important issues, but neither can stand alone. The hope is that at some point the molecular analyses of the associative approach will make sufficient contact with the more molar functional analyses of behavioral regulation to provide a comprehensive integrated account of the motivation of instrumental behavior.

THE ASSOCIATIVE STRUCTURE OF INSTRUMENTAL CONDITIONING

Edward Thorndike was the first to recognize that instrumental conditioning involves more than just a response and a reinforcer. The instrumental response occurs in the presence of particular stimuli. Three events must be considered in an analysis of instrumental

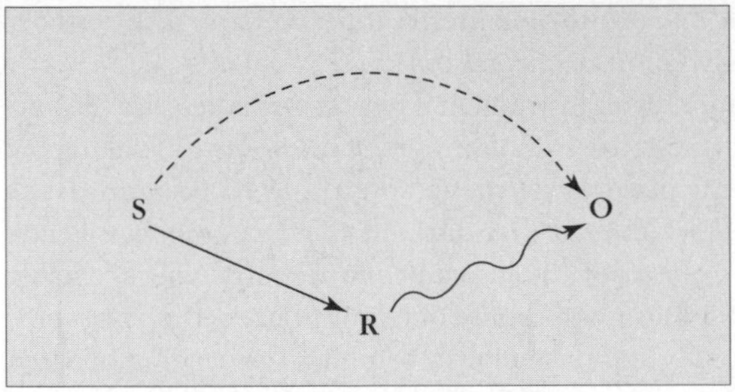

Figure 7.1 Diagram of instrumental conditioning. The instrumental response (R) occurs in the presence of distinctive stimuli (S) and results in delivery of the reinforcer outcome (O). This allows for the establishment of several different types of associations.

conditioning: the stimulus context (S), the instrumental response (R), and the response outcome (O), or reinforcer. Skinner also subscribed to the three-event notion and described instrumental conditioning in terms of a *three-term contingency* involving S, R, and O. (For a contemporary treatment, see Davison & Nevin, 1999.) The traditional conception of how these three terms are related is presented in Figure 7.1.

The S-R Association and the Law of Effect

The basic structure of an instrumental conditioning procedure permits the development of several different types of associations. The first of these is an association between the contextual stimuli S and the instrumental response R, the *S-R association.* The S-R association was postulated by Thorndike to be the key to instrumental learning in his *Law of Effect.* According to the Law of Effect, the role of the reinforcer or response outcome is to establish or "stamp in" an association between the contextual cues S and the instrumental response R. Thorndike thought that once established, this S-R association was solely responsible for the occurrence of the instrumental response. Thus, the basic impetus or motivation for the instrumental response was the activation of the S-R association by exposing the subject to the stimuli in the presence of which the instrumental response was previously reinforced. (For a discussion of the role of S-R associations in contemporary theorizing, see Donahoe, Palmer, & Burgos, 1997, and following commentary.)

An important implication of the Law of Effect is that instrumental conditioning does not involve learning about the reinforcer (O) or the relation between the response and the reinforcing outcome (the R-O association). The Law of Effect assumes that the only role of the reinforcer is to create the S-R association, that the reinforcer itself is not a party or participant in this association. This is a rather counterintuitive assumption, and perhaps because of that, it is not always appreciated. It is tempting to think that instrumental conditioning involves learning to expect the reinforcer or learning to expect that the response will produce the reinforcer. Rigorous formulations or tests of these ideas were unavailable at the turn of the twentieth century, and therefore Thorndike and Skinner shied away from the cognitive notion of an expectancy. The idea that reward expectancy may motivate instrumental behavior had to await modern developments in Pavlovian conditioning, and the integration of those developments into a consideration of instrumental behavior.

Expectancy of Reward and the S-O Association

How might we capture the notion that subjects learn to expect the reinforcer during the course of instrumental conditioning? Both human and nonhuman animals come to expect that something important will happen when they encounter a stimulus that signals a significant event or allows them to predict that the event will occur. Pavlovian conditioning is the basic process of signal learning. Hence, one way to look for reward expectancy is to consider how Pavlovian processes may be involved in instrumental learning.

As Figure 7.1 illustrates, specification of an instrumental response ensures that the participant will always experience certain distinctive stimuli (S) in connection with making the response. These stimuli may involve the place where the response is to be performed, the texture of the object the participant is to manipulate, or distinctive olfactory or visual cues. Whatever the stimuli may be, reinforcement of the instrumental response will inevitably result in a pairing between S and the reinforcer or response outcome (O). Such pairings provide the potential for classical conditioning and the establishment of an association between S and O. This S-O association is represented by the dashed line in Figure 7.1 and is the basis for reward expectancy in instrumental conditioning.

One of the earliest and most influential accounts of the role of classical conditioning in instrumental behavior was proposed by Clark Hull (1930, 1931) and later elaborated by Kenneth Spence (1956). Their basic assumption was that during the course of instrumental conditioning, the instrumental response comes to be instigated or motivated by two factors. First, the presence of S comes to evoke the instrumental response directly by association with R, through the Thorndikian S-R association. Second, the instrumental activity also comes to be made in response to the expectancy of reward because of the establishment of an S-O association. Exactly how the S-O association comes to motivate instrumental behavior has been the subject of considerable debate and experimental investigation (see review by Black, 1971). A particularly influential formulation was *modern two-process theory* (Rescorla & Solomon, 1967).

Modern Two-Process Theory. Modern two-process theory assumes that there are two distinct types of learning, Pavlovian and instrumental conditioning. (Nothing too radical there.) The theory further assumes that these two learning processes are related in a special way. In particular, during the course of instrumental conditioning, the stimuli (S)—in the presence of which the instrumental response is reinforced—are presumed to become associated with the response outcome (O) through Pavlovian conditioning to establish an S-O association. Through the S-O association, stimulus S comes to motivate the instrumental behavior by activating a *central emotional state.* The nature of that emotional state or motivation will depend on the nature of the reinforcer. For example, in an instrumental conditioning procedure in which the response is reinforced by the presentation of food (or other appetitive reinforcers), the S-O association activates the expectancy of food, or what Mowrer (1960) more generally called "hope." (For a contemporary discussion of these ideas, see Berridge, 2001.)

How could investigators test the notion that "hope" or some other Pavlovian expectancy motivates instrumental behavior? Rescorla and Solomon (1967) pointed out that if a Pavlovian expectancy motivates instrumental behavior, then the presentation of a Pavlovian conditioned stimulus should alter the course of instrumentally reinforced responding. Thus, the basic implication of modern two-process theory is that *the rate of an instrumental response will be modified by the presentation of a classically conditioned stimulus.* This prediction is based on the following considerations. During instrumental conditioning, a conditioned central emotional state is assumed to develop to motivate the instrumental response. Reinforcing a lever-press response with food, for example, creates the expectancy of food and the emotion of "hope." Classically conditioned stimuli also are assumed to elicit central emotional states. A CS+ for food will also elicit "hope" of getting food. Therefore, presentation of a classically conditioned CS+ for food during performance of a food-reinforced response should enhance the "hope" that was created by the instrumental contingency and increase responding.

Results Consistent with Modern Two-Process Theory. Studies that evaluate modern two-process theory typically employ an experimental design called the **transfer-of-control experiment.** Such experiments basically consist of three phases. Phase 1 involves instrumental conditioning of an operant response using some schedule of positive or negative reinforcement. In Phase 2 the participants are given classical conditioning in which an explicit CS is associated with either the presence or the absence of an unconditioned stimulus. The instrumental conditioning procedure need not be in effect during the Pavlovian conditioning phase. Phase 3 is the critical *transfer phase.* Here the participants are allowed to engage in the instrumental response, and the CS from Phase 2 is periodically presented to observe its effect on the rate of the instrumental behavior.

Modern two-process theory has stimulated a great deal of research using the transfer-of-control design. We have already seen an example of this in the conditioned emotional response (CER) procedure described in Chapter 3. In that procedure, animals are first trained to press a response lever for food reinforcement; then a discrete stimulus, such as a light or a tone, is repeatedly paired with shock. This classically conditioned fear stimulus is then presented while the subjects are lever pressing for food. Presentation of the CS+ for shock produces a decrease in the rate of the lever-press response (Blackman, 1977; Davis, 1968; Lyon, 1968). This occurs because the Pavlovian CS elicits an emotional state (fear) that is contrary to the emotion or expectancy (hope) that is established in instrumental conditioning with food.

How would these same subjects respond if they were presented with a Pavlovian CS that had been paired with food (and presumably elicited "hope")? The emotion elicited by the Pavlovian CS would be compatible with the emotion established during instrumental conditioning, and an increase in responding should occur during the Pavlovian signal. Evidence consistent with this prediction has been obtained (for example, Estes, 1943, 1948; LoLordo, 1971; Lovibond, 1983). (For a more detailed discussion of other predictions of modern two-process theory, see Domjan, 1993.)

Response Interactions in Transfer-of-Control Experiments. Classically conditioned stimuli elicit not only emotional states but also overt responses. Consequently, a classically conditioned stimulus may influence instrumental behavior through the overt responses it elicits. Consider a hypothetical situation in which the classically conditioned stimulus makes the animal remain still, and the instrumental response is shuttling back and forth in a shuttle box. In this example, presentation of the CS will decrease the instrumental response simply because the tendency to stop moving elicited by the CS will interfere with the shuttle behavior. An appeal to central emotional states is not necessary to understand such an outcome. An appeal to central emotional states is also unnecessary if a classically conditioned stimulus elicited overt responses that were similar to the instrumental behavior. In this case, presentation of the CS would increase responding because responses elicited by the CS would be added to the responses being performed by the animal to receive instrumental reinforcement.

Investigators have been very concerned with the possibility that the results of transfer-of-control experiments are due to Pavlovian CSs eliciting overt responses that either interfere with or facilitate the behavior required for instrumental reinforcement. A number of experimental strategies have been designed to rule out such response interactions (for a review, see Overmier & Lawry, 1979). These strategies have generally been successful in showing that many transfer-of-control effects are not produced by interactions between overt responses. However, overt classically conditioned responses have been important in some transfer-of-control experiments (for example, Karpicke, 1978; LoLordo, McMillan, & Riley, 1974; Schwartz, 1976).

Conditioned Central Emotional States or Reward-Specific Expectancies? Modern two-process theory assumes that classical conditioning mediates instrumental behavior through the conditioning of central emotional states such as hope (in the case of positive reinforcement) or fear (in the case of negative reinforcement). However, animals also acquire specific reward expectancies instead of more general central emotional states during instrumental and classical conditioning (Peterson & Trapold, 1980).

In one study, for example, solid food pellets and a sugar solution were used as USs in the classical and instrumental conditioning of rats (Kruse, Overmier, Konz, & Rokke, 1983). A CS+ for food facilitated instrumental responding reinforced with food much more than instrumental behavior reinforced with the sugar solution. Correspondingly, a CS+ for sugar increased instrumental behavior reinforced with sugar more than instrumental behavior reinforced with food pellets. Thus, expectancies for specific rewards rather than a general central emotional state of hope determined the results.

This study as well as similar experiments clearly indicate that under some circumstances, animals acquire reinforcer-specific expectancies rather than the more general emotional state of "hope" during instrumental and classical conditioning. (For additional evidence of reinforcer-specific expectancies, see Baxter & Zamble, 1982; DeMarse & Urcuioli, 1993; Henderson, Patterson, & Jackson, 1980; Urcuioli & DeMarse, 1996; Sherburne & Zentall, 1998.) Reinforcer-specific expectancy learning is a challenging alternative to modern two-process theory in explaining certain types of results. This alternative is, however, based on the assumption that instrumental conditioning involves the learning of an S-O association.

S-O associations appear to be fundamental to the motivation of instrumental behavior. In a recent analysis, Berridge (2001) pointed out that the S-O association is the basis for the core process of "wanting" the reinforcer. Through the S-O association, S becomes an incentive stimulus; S itself becomes attractive. This acquired incentive motivation contributes significantly to the motivation of the instrumental response.

R-O and S(R-O) Relations in Instrumental Conditioning

So far I have explained two different associations that can motivate instrumental behavior, Thorndike's S-R association and the S-O association, which activates a reward-specific expectancy or emotional state. For a couple of reasons, it would be odd to explain all of the motivation of instrumental behavior in terms of these two associations (see Colwill & Rescorla, 1986). First, notice that neither the S-R nor the S-O association involves a direct link between the response R and the reinforcer, or response outcome, O. The response outcome O is not directly represented in the S-R association, or otherwise associated with the response. This is counterintuitive. If you ask someone why she is performing an instrumental response, her reply would be that she expected the response (R) to result in the reinforcer (O). Intuition suggests that instrumental behavior involves R-O associations. You comb your hair because you expect that doing so will improve your appearance; you go to see a movie because you expect that watching the movie will be entertaining; and you open the refrigerator because you anticipate that doing so will enable you to get something to eat. Although informal explanations of instrumental behavior emphasize R-O associations, such associations do not exist in two-process models.

Another peculiarity of the associative structure of instrumental conditioning assumed by two-process theories is that S is assumed to become associated directly with O on the assumption that the pairing of S with O is sufficient for the occurrence of classical conditioning. However, as I explained in Chapter 4, CS-US pairings are not sufficient for the development of Pavlovian associations. The CS must also provide information about the US, or in some way be related to the US. In an instrumental conditioning situation, the reinforcer O cannot be predicted from S alone. Rather, O occurs if the participant makes response R in the presence of S. Thus, instrumental conditioning involves a conditional relation in which S is followed by O only if R occurs. This conditionality in the relation of S to O is ignored in two-process theories.

Evidence of R-O Associations. A number of investigators have suggested that instrumental conditioning leads to the learning of response-outcome associations (for example, Bolles, 1972b; Mackintosh & Dickinson, 1979), and several different types of evidence have been obtained in support of this possibility. A common technique involves devaluing the reinforcer after conditioning to see if this decreases the instrumental response. (For reviews, see Dickinson & Balleine, 1994; Colwill, 1994; Colwill & Rescorla, 1986; Rescorla, 1991.) This strategy is analogous to the strategy of US devaluation in studies of Pavlovian conditioning (see Chapter 4). In Pavlovian conditioning, US devaluation is used to determine whether the conditioned response is mediated by a CS-US association. If US devaluation after conditioning disrupts the CR, investigators may conclude that the CR was mediated by the CS-US association. In a corresponding fashion, reinforcer devaluation has been used to determine if an instrumental response is mediated by an association between the response and its reinforcer outcome.

In one definitive demonstration, Colwill and Rescorla (1986) first reinforced rats for pushing a vertical rod to either the right or the left. Responding in either direction was reinforced on a variable interval 1-minute schedule of reinforcement. Both response alternatives were always available during training sessions. The only difference was that responses in one direction were reinforced with food pellets, and responses in the opposite direction were always reinforced with a bit of sugar solution (sucrose).

After both responses had become well established, the rod was removed and the reinforcer devaluation procedure was introduced. One of the reinforcers (either food pellets or sugar solution) was periodically presented in the experimental chamber, followed by an injection of lithium chloride to condition an aversion to that reinforcer. After an aversion to the selected reinforcer had been conditioned, the vertical rod was returned, and the rats received a test during which they were free to push the rod either to the left or to the right but neither food nor sucrose was provided.

The results of the test are presented in Figure 7.2. The important finding was that the rats were less likely to make the response whose reinforcer had been made aversive by pairings with lithium chloride. For example, if sucrose was used to reinforce responses to the left and an aversion was then conditioned to sucrose, the rats were less likely to push the rod to the left than to the right.

The selective response suppression that was obtained is difficult to explain in terms of the S-O or S-R associations that are assumed to be learned according to two-process theory. S-R associations cannot produce the results because the reinforcer is not included in an S-R association. Therefore, changes in the value of the reinforcer cannot alter behavior mediated by an S-R association. The results cannot be explained in terms of S-O associations because the two responses, pushing the vertical rod left or right, were made in the same place, with the same manipulandum, and therefore in the presence of the same external S stimuli. If devaluation of one of the reinforcers had altered the properties of S, that should have changed the two responses equally. Instead, devaluation of a reinforcer selectively depressed the particular response that had been trained with that reinforcer. This finding indicates that each response was associated separately with its own reinforcer. The participants evidently

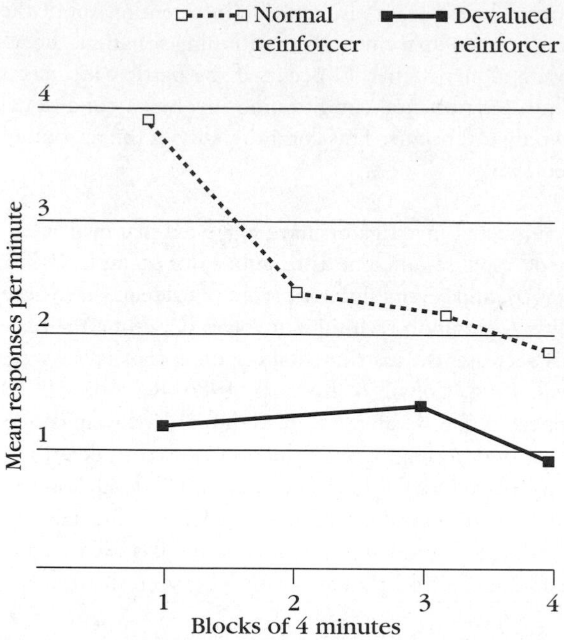

Figure 7.2 Effects of reinforcer devaluation on instrumental behavior. Devaluation of a reinforcer selectively reduces the response that was previously reinforced with that reinforcer. (From "Associative Structures in Instrumental Learning," by R. M. Colwill and R. A. Rescorla, in G. H. Bower [Ed.], 1986, *The Psychology of Learning and Motivation,* Vol. 20, pp. 55–104. Copyright © 1986 Academic Press. Reprinted by permission.)

learned separate R-O associations. (For further consideration of the role of R-O associations and the motivation of instrumental behavior, see Balleine, 2001; Dickinson & Balleine, 1994. For an alternative perspective on the effects of reinforcer devaluation, see Donahoe & Burgos, 2000.)

Evidence of the Learning of a Hierarchical S-(R-O) Relation. The evidence cited earlier clearly shows that organisms learn to associate an instrumental response with its outcome. However, R-O associations cannot act alone to produce instrumental behavior. As Mackintosh and Dickinson (1979) point out, the fact that the instrumental response activates an expectancy of the reinforcer is not sufficient to tell us what causes the response. An additional factor is required to activate the R-O association. One possibility is that the R-O association is activated by the stimuli S that are present when the response is reinforced. According to this view, S does not activate R directly, but rather it activates the R-O association. The subject comes to think of the R-O association when it encounters S, and that motivates it to make the instrumental response.

Skinner (1938) suggested many years ago that S, R, and O in instrumental conditioning are connected through a conditional S-(R-O) relation. This suggestion has been vigorously pursued in recent years. A variety of direct and indirect lines of evidence have been developed that point to the learning of S-(R-O) relations in instrumental conditioning (Colwill & Rescorla, 1990; Davidson, Aparicio, & Rescorla, 1988; Holman & Mackintosh, 1981; Goodall & Mackintosh, 1987; Rescorla, 1990a, 1990b). Most of these studies have involved rather complicated discrimination training procedures that are beyond the scope of this book. (For an especially good example, see Colwill & Delameter, 1995, Experiment 2.)

BEHAVIORAL REGULATION

Although contemporary associative analyses of instrumental motivation go far beyond Thorndike's S-R mechanisms, they are a part of the Thorndikian and Pavlovian tradition that views the world of behavior in terms of stimuli, responses, and associations. Behavioral regulation analyses are based on a radically different worldview. Instead of considering instrumental conditioning in terms of the reinforcement of a response in the presence of certain stimuli, behavioral regulation analyses focus on how instrumental contingencies put limitation on an organism's activities.

Antecedents of Behavioral Regulation

Reinforcers were initially considered to be special kinds of stimuli. Thorndike, for example, characterized a reinforcer as a stimulus that produces a "satisfying state of affairs." Various proposals were made about the special characteristics a stimulus must have for it to serve as a reinforcer. Although there were differences of opinion, for about a half century after Thorndike's Law of Effect, theoreticians agreed that reinforcers were special stimuli that "strengthened" instrumental behavior.

Consummatory Response Theory. The first challenge to the idea that reinforcers are stimuli came from Fred Sheffield and his colleagues, who formulated the **consummatory response theory.** Many reinforcers, such as food and water, elicit species-typical unconditioned responses, such as chewing, licking, and swallowing. The consummatory response theory attributes reinforcement to these species-typical behaviors. It asserts that species-typical consummatory responses—eating, drinking, and the like—are themselves the critical feature of reinforcers. In support of this idea, Sheffield, Roby, and Campbell (1954) showed that saccharin, an artificial sweetener, can serve as an effective reinforcer, even though it has no nutritive value and hence cannot satisfy a biological need. The reinforcing properties of artificial sweeteners now provide the foundations of a flourishing diet drink industry. Apart from their commercial value, however, artificial sweeteners were important in advancing scientific thinking about instrumental motivation.

The consummatory response theory was a radical innovation because it moved the search for reinforcers from special kinds of stimuli to special types of responses. Reinforcer responses were assumed to be special because they involved the consummation or completion of an instinctive behavior sequence. (See discussion of consummatory behavior in Chapter 2.) The theory assumed that consummatory responses (chewing and swallowing, for example) are fundamentally different from various potential instrumental responses, such as running, jumping, or pressing a lever. David Premack took issue with this theory and suggested that reinforcer responses are special only because they are more likely to occur than the instrumental responses they follow.

The Premack Principle. Premack pointed out that responses involved with commonly used reinforcers are activities that animals are highly likely to perform. For example, animals in a food reinforcement experiment are typically food deprived and therefore are highly likely to engage in eating behavior. By contrast, instrumental responses are typically low-probability activities. An experimentally naive rat, for example, is much less likely to press a response lever than it is to eat. Premack (1965) proposed that this difference in response probabilities is critical for reinforcement. Formally, the **Premack principle** can be stated as follows:

> Given two responses of the different likelihood, H and L, the opportunity to perform the higher probability response H after the lower probability response L will result in reinforcement of response L. (L→H reinforces L.) The opportunity to perform the lower probability response L after the higher probability response H will not result in reinforcement of response H. (H→L does not reinforce H.)

The Premack principle focuses on the difference in the likelihood of the instrumental and reinforcer responses; therefore, it is also called the **differential probability principle.**

Eating will reinforce bar pressing because eating is typically more likely than bar pressing. Under ordinary circumstances, bar pressing cannot reinforce eating. Premack's theory suggests, however, that if for some reason bar pressing became more probable than eating, it would reinforce eating. Premack's theory denies that a fundamental distinction exists between reinforcers and instrumental responses. There is nothing inherently unique about reinforcers; rather, the effectiveness of a reinforcer is a relative matter. The reinforcing response is simply more likely to occur at the outset than the instrumental response. This relative property of reinforcers makes it possible to use a wide variety of responses as reinforcers.

Premack and his colleagues conducted many experiments to test his theory (see Premack, 1965, 1971a). One of the early studies was conducted with young children. Premack first gave the children two response alternatives (eating candy and playing a pinball machine) and measured which response was more probable for each child. Some of the children preferred eating candy over playing pinball; others preferred the pinball machine. In the second phase of the experiment (see Figure 7.3), the children were tested with one of two procedures. In one procedure, eating was specified as the reinforcing response, and playing pinball was the instrumental response—that is, the children had to play the pinball machine in order to get access to candy. The question was whether all the children would increase their pinball playing. Consistent with Premack's theory, only those

Figure 7.3 Diagram of Premack's (1965) study.

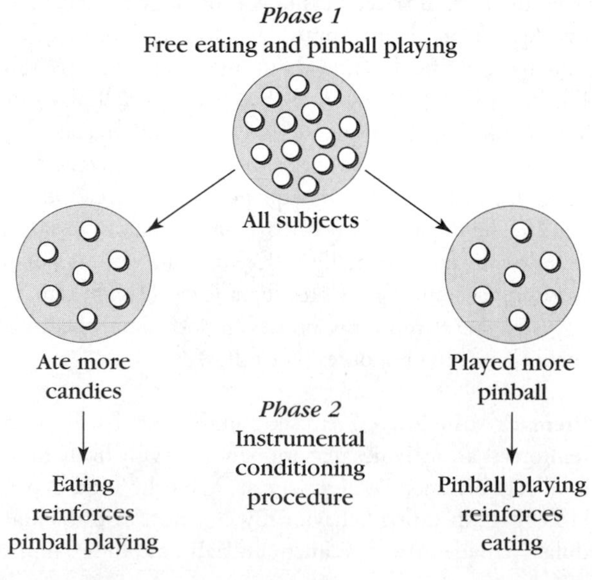

children who preferred eating to playing pinball showed a reinforcement effect under these circumstances.

In another test, the roles of the two responses were reversed: eating was the instrumental response, and playing pinball was the reinforcing response. The children had to eat candy to get access to the pinball machine. In this situation, only those children who preferred playing pinball to eating showed a reinforcement effect.

Premack (1962) also tested his theory in studies of drinking and wheel running in laboratory rats (see Figure 7.4). Premack altered the probabilities of the drinking and wheel running by changing deprivation conditions. In one procedure, the rats were deprived of water but not of the opportunity to run in the wheel. Under these circumstances drinking was more probable than running, and the opportunity to drink was effective in reinforcing running. In the second procedure, the rats were not deprived of water. Under these circumstances, they were more likely to run in the wheel than to drink. Now the opportunity to run in the wheel could reinforce drinking, but drinking could no longer be used to reinforce running. This study shows that running and drinking could be used interchangeably as instrumental and reinforcing responses, depending on the animal's state of water deprivation. Nothing inherent to one response or the other made it a reinforcer.

The Premack principle advanced scientific thinking about reinforcement in significant ways. It encouraged thinking about reinforcers as responses rather than as stimuli, and it

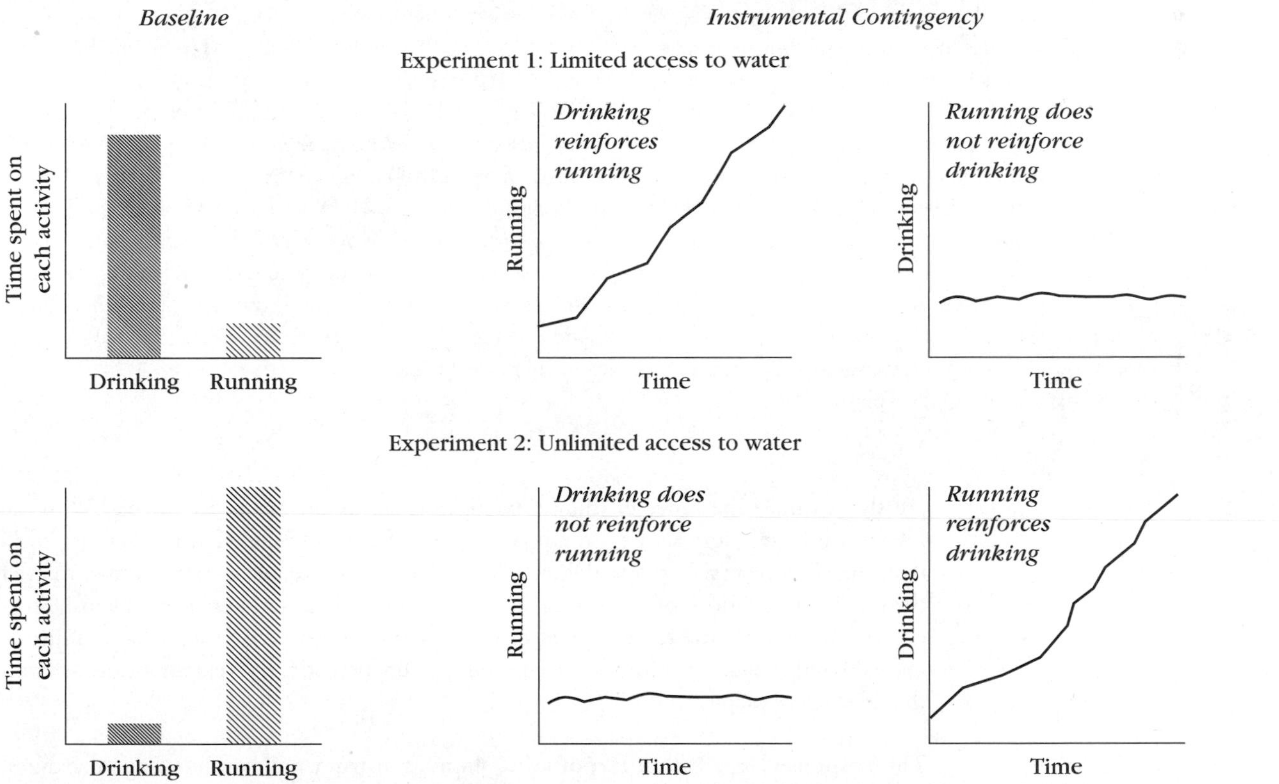

Figure 7.4 When a rat is water-deprived (Experiment 1), it drinks more than it runs. Therefore, drinking reinforces running, but running does not reinforce drinking. When a rat is not water-deprived (Experiment 2), it runs more than it drinks. This time running reinforces drinking, but drinking does not reinforce running.

BOX 7.1

APPLICATIONS OF THE PREMACK PRINCIPLE

Using reinforcement procedures to encourage appropriate behavior in children requires identifying an effective reinforcer. Food is often a good choice, but practical and ethical considerations have encouraged investigators to identify other forms of reinforcement. The Premack principle has been a great help in this regard because it suggests that any activity that is more likely than the response to be reinforced can serve as an effective reinforcer.

Children, like adults, vary in their preferred activities. Some prefer playing ball after school; others prefer talking to friends on the phone. By measuring the relative probability of different activities for each child, reinforcement procedures can be personalized to take advantage of each individual's unique response preferences. This may result in some rather unusual responses serving as reinforcers.

Children with autism often engage in repetitive aberrant behaviors. One such behavior, called *delayed echolalia,* involves repeating words. For example, one autistic child was heard to say over and over again, "Ding! ding! ding! You win again," and "Match Game 83." Another form of aberrant behavior, *perseverative behavior,* involves persistent manipulation of an object. For example, the child may repeatedly handle only certain plastic toys.

The high probability of echolalia and perseverative behavior in children with autism suggests that these responses may be effectively used as reinforcers in treatment procedures. This possibility has been explored by several investigators. In a study by Charlop, Kurtz, and Casey (1990), the effectiveness of different forms of reinforcement was compared in training various academic-related skills in autistic children. The tasks included identifying which of several objects was the same or different from the one held up by the teacher, adding up coins, and correctly responding to sentences designed to teach receptive pronouns or prepositions. In one experimental condition, a preferred food (such as a small piece of chocolate, cereal, or a cookie) served as the reinforcer, in the absence of programmed food deprivation. In another condition, the opportunity to perform an aberrant response for 3 to 5 seconds served as the reinforcer.

Some results of the study are illustrated in Figure 7.5. Each panel represents the data for a different student. Notice that in each case, the opportunity to engage in a prevalent aberrant response resulted in better performance on the training tasks than food reinforcement. Both delayed echolalia and perseverative behavior served to increase task performance above what was observed with food reinforcement. These results indicate that high-probability responses can serve to reinforce lower-probability responses, even if the reinforcer responses are not characteristic of normal behavior.

greatly expanded the range of things investigators started to use as reinforcers. With the Premack principle, any activity could serve as a reinforcer provided that it was more likely than the instrumental response. Differential probability as the key to reinforcement paved the way for applications of reinforcement procedures to all sorts of human problems. However, problems with the measurement of response probability, and a closer look at instrumental conditioning procedures, moved subsequent theoretical developments away from the Premack principle.

The Response Deprivation Hypothesis. In most instrumental conditioning procedures, the momentary probability of the reinforcer response is kept at a high level by restricting access to the reinforcing response. A rat lever pressing for food, for example, typically comes into the experimental situation not having eaten much and does not receive a whole meal for each lever-press response. These limitations on the reinforcing response are very impor-

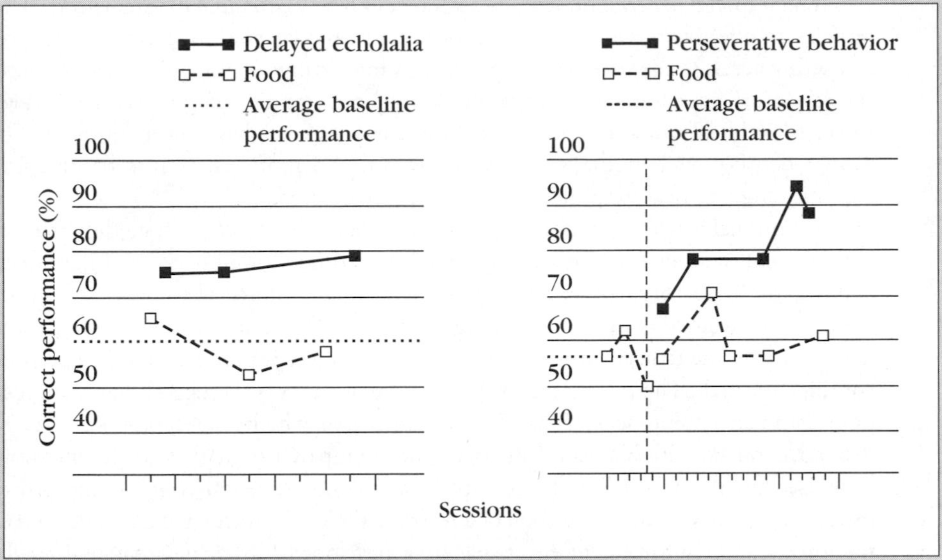

Figure 7.5 Task performance data for two children with autism. One student's behavior was reinforced with food or the opportunity to engage in delayed echolalia. Another student's behavior was reinforced with food or the opportunity to engage in perseverative responding. (Responding during baseline periods was also reinforced with food.) (From "Using Aberrant Behaviors as Reinforcers for Autistic Children," by M. H. Charlop, P. F. Kurtz, & F. G. Casey, *Journal of Applied Behavior Analysis, 23,* pp. 163–181. Copyright © 1990 by the Society for the Experimental Analysis of Behavior, Inc. Reprinted by permission.)

tant. If an investigator were to give the rat a full meal for pressing the lever once, chances are it would not increase its rate of responding very much. Restrictions on the opportunity to engage in the reinforcing response serve to increase its effectiveness as a reinforcer.

Premack (1965) recognized the importance of restricting access to the reinforcer response for instrumental conditioning. He regarded response deprivation as not only a necessary condition for reinforcement but also an adjunct to the differential probability principle. In his view, the reinforcer response still had to be a more likely behavior than the instrumental response. By contrast, Timberlake and Allison (1974; see also Allison, 1993) abandoned the differential probability principle altogether and argued that restriction of the reinforcer response was the critical factor for instrumental reinforcement. This proposal is called the **response deprivation hypothesis.**

In particularly decisive tests of the response deprivation hypothesis, several investigators found that even access to a low-probability response can serve as a reinforcer, provided that

W. Timberlake

J. Allison

subjects are restricted from making this response (Timberlake & Allison, 1974; Eisenberger, Karpman, & Trattner, 1967). Thus, with response deprivation, even a low-probability response can be used to reinforce a higher-probability response. This set of conditions seriously violates the Premack principle and shows that response deprivation is more basic to the motivation of instrumental behavior than differential response probability.

The response deprivation hypothesis provides a new principle for predicting what will serve as an effective reinforcer. It also provides a new procedure for creating reinforcers—restricting access to the reinforcer response. It is interesting to note that restricting access to the reinforcer response is inherent in all instrumental conditioning procedures—the reinforcer is withheld until the specified instrumental response has been performed. The response deprivation hypothesis points out that this definitional feature of instrumental conditioning is critical for producing a reinforcement effect.

Traditional views of reinforcement assume that a reinforcer is something that exists independent of an instrumental conditioning procedure. Stimulus views of reinforcement and the consummatory response theory all assume that reinforcers exist whether or not they are used in an instrumental conditioning procedure. The response deprivation hypothesis makes explicit the radically different idea that a reinforcer is produced by the instrumental contingency itself. The Premack principle was the first theory to suggest that reinforcers do not exist in an absolute sense. In the Premack principle, whether a response was a reinforcer depended on how its likelihood of occurrence compared with that of the instrumental response, but the principle did not imply that the instrumental conditioning procedure itself was responsible for the creation of a reinforcer. How instrumental contingencies create reinforcers and reinforcement effects has been developed further in behavioral regulation theories.

Behavioral Regulation and the Behavioral Bliss Point

Regulation is a recurrent theme in learning theory. I discussed regulatory processes in Chapter 2 in connection with the opponent-process theory of motivation, and in Chapter 4 in connection with the role of learning in physiological homeostasis. Physiological homeostasis refers to mechanisms that serve to maintain critical aspects of the body (such as blood sugar level and temperature) within acceptable limits. A shift away from the physiologically optimal or homeostatic level triggers changes that serve to return the system to the homeostatic level.

Behavioral regulation theories assume that analogous homeostatic mechanisms exist with respect to behavior. Within the framework of behavioral regulation, organisms are presumed to have a preferred or an optimal distribution of activities that they work to maintain in the face of challenges or disruptions. Behavioral regulation theories focus on the extent to which an instrumental response-reinforcer contingency disrupts behavioral stability and forces the individual away from its preferred or optimal distribution of activities (see Allison, 1983, 1989; Hanson & Timberlake, 1983; Tierney, 1995; Timberlake, 1980, 1984, 1995).

An individual has to eat, breathe, drink, keep warm, exercise, entertain itself, and so on. All these activities have to occur in particular proportions—an individual should not eat too much or too little, or exercise too much or too little. If the preferred or optimal balance of activities is upset, behavior is assumed to change so as to correct the deviation from the homeostatic level. This basic assumption of behavioral regulation is fairly simple. However, numerous factors (some of which are a bit complicated) can influence how organisms meet challenges to their preferred or optimal distribution of responses.

The Behavioral Bliss Point. Every situation provides various response opportunities. In an experimental chamber, for example, an animal may run in a wheel, drink, eat, scratch itself, sniff holes, or manipulate a response lever. Behavioral regulation theory assumes that if organisms are free to distribute their responses among the available alternatives, they will do so in a way that is most comfortable or in some sense "optimal" for them. This response distribution defines the **behavioral bliss point.**

The particular distribution of activities that constitutes the bliss point will vary from one situation to another. For example, if the running wheel is made very difficult to turn or the participant is severely deprived of water, the relative likelihood of running and drinking will change. However, for a given circumstance, the behavioral bliss point, as revealed in unconstrained choices among response alternatives, is assumed to be stable across time.

The behavioral bliss point can be identified by the relative frequency of occurrence of all the responses of an organism in an unconstrained situation. To simplify analysis, I focus on just two responses. Consider how a high school student may distribute his activities between studying and watching TV. Figure 7.6 represents time spent watching TV on the vertical axis and time spent studying on the horizontal axis. If no restrictions are placed on the student's behavior, he will probably spend a lot more time watching TV than studying. This is represented by the open circle in Figure 7.6 and is the *behavioral bliss point* in this situation. At the bliss point, the student watches TV for 60 minutes for every 15 minutes that he spends studying.

Imposing an Instrumental Contingency. How would the introduction of an instrumental contingency between studying and watching TV disrupt the student's behavioral bliss? That depends on the nature of the contingency. Figure 7.6 shows a schedule line starting at

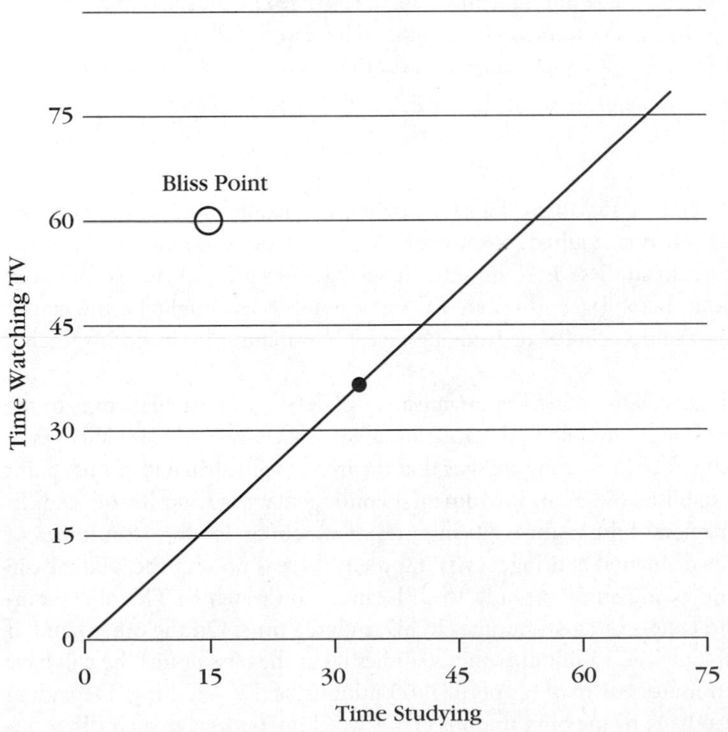

Figure 7.6 Allocation of behavior between watching TV and studying. The open circle shows the optimal allocation, or behavioral bliss point, obtained when there are no constraints on either activity. The schedule line represents a schedule of reinforcement in which the student is required to study for the same amount of time that he or she gets to watch TV. Notice that once this schedule of reinforcement is imposed, it is no longer possible for the student to achieve the behavioral bliss point. The schedule deprives the student of access to the TV and forces or motivates an increase in studying.

BOX 7.2

THE BLISS POINT APPROACH AND BEHAVIOR THERAPY

Behavior regulation theories of reinforcement not only provide new insights into age-old theoretical issues concerning reinforcement but also suggest new approaches to behavior therapy (Timberlake & Farmer-Dougan, 1991). The bliss point approach, for example, forces investigators to consider the behavioral context in which an instrumental contingency is introduced. Depending on that behavioral context, a reinforcement procedure may increase or decrease the target response. The bliss point approach can therefore provide insights into situations in which a reinforcement procedure produces an unexpected decrease in the instrumental response.

One area of behavior therapy in which reinforcement procedures are surprisingly ineffective is the use of parental social reinforcement to increase a child's prosocial behavior. A parent whose child frequently misbehaves is encouraged to provide more social reinforcement for positive behavior on the assumption that low rates of parental reinforcement are responsible for the child's misbehavior. Viken and McFall (1994) have pointed out that the common failure of such reinforcement procedures is predictable when the behavioral bliss point of the child is considered.

Figure 7.7 shows the behavioral space for parental social reinforcement and positive child behavior. The open circle represents the child's presumed bliss point. Left to her own devices, the child prefers a lot of social reinforcement while emitting few positive behaviors. The dashed line represents the low rate of parental reinforcement in effect before a therapeutic intervention. According to this schedule line, the child has to perform two positive responses to receive each social reinforcer from her parent. The filled circle on the line indicates the equilibrium point, where positive responses by the child and social reinforcers earned are equally far from their respective bliss point values.

The therapeutic procedure involves increasing the rate of social reinforcement, say, to a ratio of 1:1. This is illustrated by the solid line in Figure 7.7. Now the child receives one social reinforcer for each positive behavior. The equilibrium point is again illustrated by the filled data point. Notice that with the increased social reinforcement, the child can get more of the social reinforcers she wants without having to make more positive responses. In fact,

the origin and increasing at a 45° angle. This line defines a schedule of reinforcement, according to which the student is required to study for the same amount of time that he wants to watch TV. If the student studies for 10 minutes, he will get to watch TV for 10 minutes; if he studies for 1 hour, he will get to watch TV for 1 hour. What might be the consequences of disrupting the free choice of studying and TV watching by imposing such a schedule constraint?

Behavioral regulation theory states that organisms will defend against challenges to the behavioral bliss point, just as physiological regulation involves defense against challenges to a physiological set point. The interesting thing is that the free-baseline behavioral bliss point cannot always be reestablished after an instrumental contingency has been introduced. In my example, the behavioral bliss point is 60 minutes of watching TV for 15 minutes of studying. Once the instrumental contingency is imposed, there is no way the student can watch TV for 60 minutes and study for only 15. If he insists on watching TV for 60 minutes, he will have to tolerate adding 45 minutes to his studying time. On the other hand, if he insists on spending only the 15 minutes on his studies (as at the bliss point), he will have to make do with 45 minutes less than his optimal 60 minutes of TV watching. Defending the bliss amount of studying or the bliss amount of TV watching both have their disadvan-

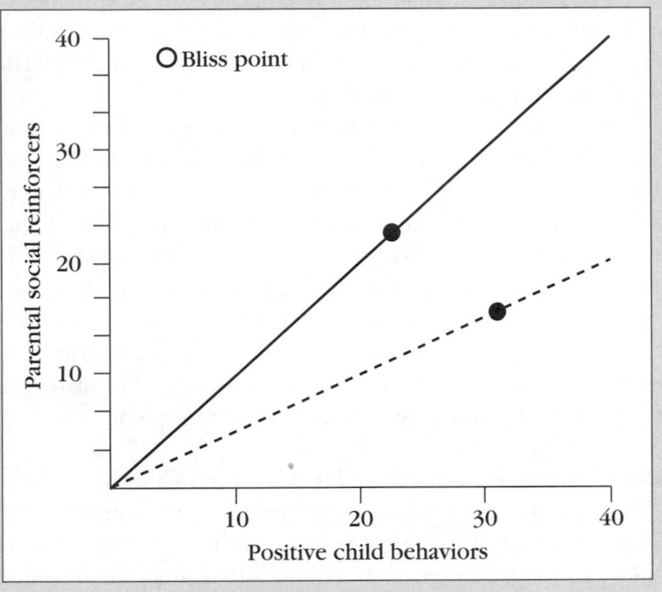

Figure 7.7 Hypothetical data on parental social reinforcement and positive child behavior. The behavioral bliss point for the child is indicated by the open circle. The dashed line represents the rate of social reinforcement for positive behavior in effect prior to introduction of a treatment procedure. The solid line represents the rate of social reinforcement for positive behavior set up by the behavior therapy procedure. The solid point on each line represents the equilibrium point for each schedule.

she can increase her rate of social reinforcement while performing fewer positive responses. No wonder, then, that the therapeutic reinforcement procedure does not increase the rate of positive responses. The unexpected results of increased social reinforcement illustrated in Figure 7.7 suggest that solutions to behavior problems require considering the complex context in which reinforcement procedures are introduced.

tages. That is often the dilemma posed by an instrumental contingency. It does not permit getting back to the bliss point.

Although the instrumental contingency shown in Figure 7.6 makes it impossible to return to the behavioral bliss point, this does not mean that the bliss point becomes irrelevant. To the contrary. The bliss point still provides the motivation for instrumental behavior. Behavioral regulation theory assumes that returning to the behavioral set point remains a goal of response allocation. When this goal cannot be reached, the redistribution of responses between the instrumental and contingent behaviors becomes a matter of compromise. The rate of one response is brought as close as possible to its preferred level without moving the other response too far away from its preferred level.

Staddon, for example, proposed a **minimum deviation model** of behavioral regulation to solve the dilemma of schedule constraints (Staddon, 1979; see also Staddon, 1983). According to this model, introduction of a response-reinforcer contingency causes organisms to redistribute their behavior between the instrumental and contingent responses in a way that minimizes the total deviation of the two responses from the optimal or bliss point. The minimum deviation point is shown by the filled circle on the schedule line in Figure 7.6. For situations in which the free-baseline behavioral bliss point cannot be achieved, the minimum deviation model provides one view of how organisms settle for the next best thing.

Explanation of Reinforcement Effects. How are reinforcement effects produced by behavioral regulation? Behavioral regulation involves the defense of a behavioral bliss point in the face of restrictions on responding imposed by a response-reinforcer contingency. As noted earlier, this defense may require settling for something close to but not exactly at the free-baseline bliss point. How do these mechanisms lead to increases in instrumental behavior in typical instrumental conditioning procedures?

A reinforcement effect is identified by an increase in the occurrence of an instrumental response above the level of that behavior in the absence of the response-reinforcer contingency. The schedule line shown in Figure 7.6 involves restricting access to TV watching below the level specified by the bliss point. To move toward the behavioral bliss point, the student has to increase his studying in order to gain more opportunity to watch TV. This is precisely what occurs in typical instrumental conditioning procedures. Access to the reinforcer is restricted; to gain more opportunity to engage in the reinforcer response, the individual has to perform more of the instrumental response. Thus, increased performance of the instrumental response (a reinforcement effect) results from behavioral regulatory mechanisms that function to minimize deviations from the behavioral bliss point.

Viewing Reinforcement Contingencies in a Broader Behavioral Context. The earlier explanation of how schedule constraints produce reinforcement effects considers only the instrumental and reinforcer responses (studying and watching TV). A student's environment most likely provides a much greater range of options. Instrumental contingencies do not occur in a behavioral vacuum or test tube. They occur in the context of a variety of responses and reinforcers the subject may obtain. Furthermore, that broader behavioral context can significantly influence how the subject adjusts to a schedule constraint. For example, if the student enjoys listening to the radio as much as watching TV, restrictions on access to the TV may not increase studying behavior. The student may switch to listening to the radio, or he may switch to reading comic books or going to the movies. Any of these options will undermine the instrumental contingency. If the student opts for listening to the radio or going to the movies in place of watching TV, he will not increase his studying behavior to obtain his preferred amount of TV time.

This example illustrates that accurate prediction of the effects of an instrumental conditioning procedure requires considering the broader context of the organism's response options. Focusing on just the instrumental response and its antecedent and consequent stimuli (that is, the associative structure of instrumental behavior) ignores the broader behavioral context in which instrumental contingencies operate. It is important to consider that broader behavioral context because it can significantly influence the outcome of particular instrumental conditioning procedures. The effect of a particular instrumental conditioning procedure may depend on what alternative sources of reinforcement are available to the organism, how those other reinforcers are related to the particular reinforcer involved in the instrumental contingency, and the costs of obtaining those alternative reinforcers. These issues have been systematically considered with the application of economic concepts to the problem of response allocation.

Economic Concepts and Response Allocation

The bliss point approach redefined the fundamental issue in the analysis of instrumental motivation. It shifted attention away from the notion that reinforcers are special stimuli that enter into special associative relations with the instrumental response and its antecedents.

With the bliss point approach, the fundamental question in instrumental motivation became, "How do the constraints of an instrumental conditioning procedure produce changes in behavior?"

Students who have studied economics may recognize a similarity here to problems addressed by economists. Economists, like psychologists, strive to understand changes in behavior in terms of preexisting preferences and restrictions on fulfilling those preferences. As Bickel, Green, and Vuchinich (1995) noted, "economics is the study of the allocation of behavior within a system of constraint" (p. 258). In the economic arena, the restrictions on behavior are imposed by an individual's income and the price of the goods that he or she wants to purchase. In instrumental conditioning situations, the restrictions are provided by the number of responses an organism is able to make and the number of responses required to obtain each reinforcer.

Psychologists have become interested in the similarities between economic restrictions in the marketplace and schedule constraints in instrumental conditioning. In the following section, I discuss how economic ideas have influenced behavior regulation theories of reinforcement. For the sake of simplicity, I concentrate on the basic ideas that have had the most impact on understanding reinforcement. (For further details, see Allison, 1983, 1993; Green & Freed, 1998; Hursh, 1984; Lea, 1978; Rachlin, 1989; Rachlin et al., 1976.)

Consumer Demand. Fundamental to the application of economic concepts to the problem of reinforcement is the relation between the price of a commodity and how much of it is purchased. This relation is called the **demand curve.** Figure 7.8 shows three examples of demand curves. Curve A illustrates a situation in which the consumption of a commodity is very easily influenced by its price, such as is the case with candy. If the price of candy increases substantially, the amount purchased quickly drops. Other commodities are less responsive to price changes (Curve C in Figure 7.8). The purchase of gasoline, for example, is not as easily discouraged by increases in price. People continue to purchase gas for their cars even if the price increases substantially.

The degree to which price influences consumption is called **elasticity of demand.** Demand for candy is highly elastic. The more candy costs, the less people will buy. In contrast, demand for gasoline is much less elastic. People continue to purchase gas even if the price increases a great deal.

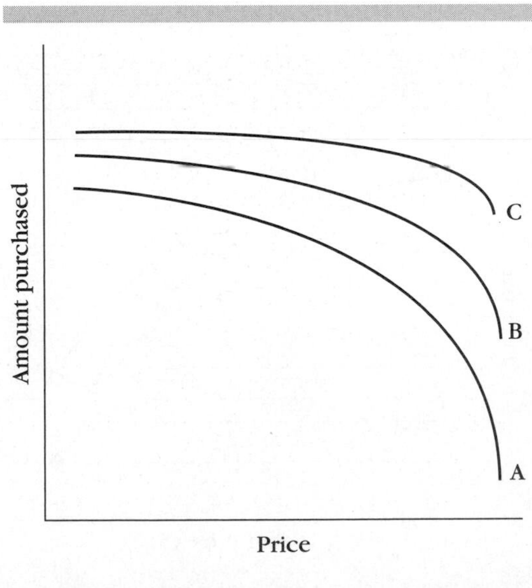

Figure 7.8 Hypothetical consumer demand curves illustrating high sensitivity to price (Curve A), intermediate sensitivity (Curve B), and low sensitivity (Curve C).

The concept of consumer demand can be used to analyze instrumental reinforcement by considering the number of responses performed (or time spent responding) to be analogous to money. The "price" of a reinforcer is the time or number of responses required to obtain the reinforcer. Thus, the "price" of the reinforcer is determined by the schedule of reinforcement. The goal is to understand how instrumental behavior ("spending") is controlled by instrumental contingencies ("prices").

Madden and Bickel (1999) investigated the elasticity of demand for cigarettes in smokers who were not trying to quit. Subjects used a special apparatus that had two plungers they could pull. One of the plungers was designated as the instrumental response, and pulling this plunger was reinforced with 10¢ each time a subject completed 100 responses (an FR 100). After a subject had accumulated enough money, he or she could pull the second plunger and obtain two puffs on a lit cigarette. The price for the two puffs varied from one session to the next in random order, ranging from 2¢ to 120¢. The subjects went through the test series twice. In the abstinence condition, they were required to go without cigarettes for 5–6 hours before coming to the laboratory. In the nonabstinence condition, they were allowed to smoke normally before coming to the laboratory. The goal of the experiment was to see if working for access to a cigarette would be a function of price (elasticity of demand), and if the demand curve would be influenced by abstinence.

The results of the experiment are summarized in Figure 7.9. As might be expected, subjects who were abstinent when they started each session worked to obtain more puffs on the cigarette than did subjects who had been allowed to smoke as usual before the session. However, regardless of whether the participants abstained before coming to the lab, they showed considerable sensitivity to price (elasticity of demand). Smoking significantly decreased with increases in price. (For additional studies of the behavioral economics of smoking, see Bickel, DeGrandpre, Hughes, & Higgins, 1991; Bickel, Madden, & DeGrandpre, 1997; Madden, Bickel, & Jacobs, 2000. For recent studies of price effects in research with nonhuman animals, see Collier & Johnson, 1997, 2000; Sumpter, Temple, & Foster, 1999.)

Determinants of the Elasticity of Demand. The application of economic concepts to the analysis of instrumental conditioning would be of little value if the application did not provide new insights into the mechanisms of reinforcement. As it turns out, economic concepts have helped to identify three major factors that influence how schedule constraints shape

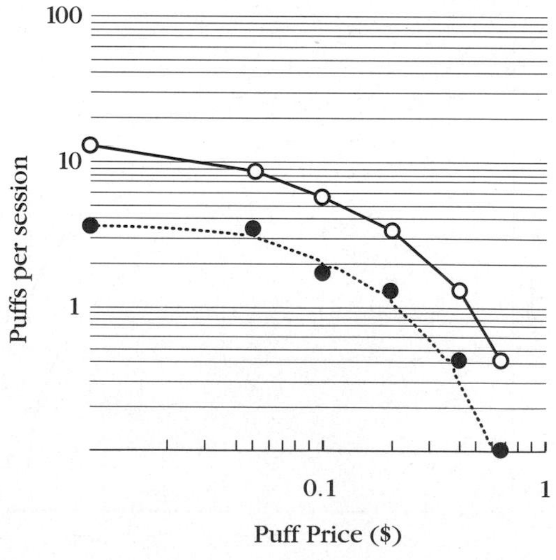

Figure 7.9 Number of cigarette puffs obtained as a function of price for cigarette smokers who were not planning to quit. Data for subjects who abstained from smoking for 5–6 hours before the session are shown by the open circles. Data for subjects who did not abstain from smoking before the session are shown by the filled circles. (After Madden & Bickel, 1999. Only data from the first half of each session are presented.)

the reallocation of behavior. Each of these factors determines the degree of elasticity of demand, or the extent to which increases in price cause a decrease in consumption.

1. *Availability of Substitutes.* Perhaps the most important factor that influences the elasticity of demand is the availability of substitutes. Whether increases in the price of one item cause a decline in consumption depends on the availability (and price) of other goods that can be used in place of the original item. The availability of substitutes increases the sensitivity of the original item to higher prices.

Coffee and tea are good examples of substitutes. Both are common sources of caffeine. Furthermore, many people find tea a good substitute for coffee. Therefore, if the price of coffee increases substantially, they will switch to tea. The elasticity of the demand for coffee is influenced by the availability of tea as a substitute for coffee. In contrast to coffee, how much gasoline people buy is not highly influenced by price, because there are no readily available substitutes for gasoline to fuel a car.

The availability of drug substitutes on elasticity of demand for food was recently examined by Foltin (1999) in an experiment conducted with baboons. The subjects had to press a response lever to obtain food pellets. The "price" of the pellets was varied by requiring different numbers of lever presses for each pellet (using fixed ratio schedules). Foltin was interested in whether food intake would decrease as the price of food was increased, and whether the availability of alternative reinforcers would influence this function. In different experimental conditions, responses on a second lever produced either nothing, a sugar solution, or solutions with different concentrations of cocaine. The availability of these alternative reinforcers always required two presses (FR 2) on the alternate lever. In general, increases in the "price" of food resulted in fewer pellets being obtained. More interesting, the availability of cocaine on the alternate response lever increased the elasticity of demand for food. This effect was particularly striking in baboon #3.

The results for baboon #3 are shown in Figure 7.10. Notice that for this subject increasing the price of food had little effect if the alternate response lever produced either nothing or dextrose (a sugar solution). However, when the alternate response lever yielded cocaine, increases in the price of food resulted in a precipitous decline in food-reinforced responding. The largest effect was obtained with the intermediate cocaine concentration. With this concentration, availability of cocaine on the alternate lever dramatically increased the elasticity of demand for food. This study illustrates a powerful example of substitutability on the elasticity of demand. In addition, it shows how the methodology provided by behavioral economic concepts can be used to identify substitutable reinforcers. For baboon #3 an intermediate concentration of cocaine was an excellent substitute for food.

One source of substitutable reinforcers is the availability of the reinforcer outside the experimental session. When food is used as the reinforcer in experiments with laboratory animals, the subjects are typically given a certain amount of food each day. Any part of this ration that they fail to earn during an experimental session is given to them later as "free" food in the home cage. Such a situation is called an *open economy.* This is contrasted with a *closed economy,* in which subjects do not receive supplemental feedings. In a closed economy, if the subjects fail to obtain their daily food ration during the experimental session, they have to wait until the next session to make up the deficit. In general, elasticity of demand is greater in open economy situations than in closed economies (Hursh, 1991; see also Foster, Blackman, & Temple, 1997). (For additional studies of substitutability with laboratory animals, see Collier & Johnson, 2000; Foltin, 1997; Green & Freed, 1993; Schultz, Collier, & Johnson, 1999. For a recent study of substitutability among heroin addicts who also use other drugs, see Petry & Bickel, 1998.)

2. *Price Range.* Another important determinant of the elasticity of demand is the price range of the commodity. Generally, an increase in price has less effect at low prices than at

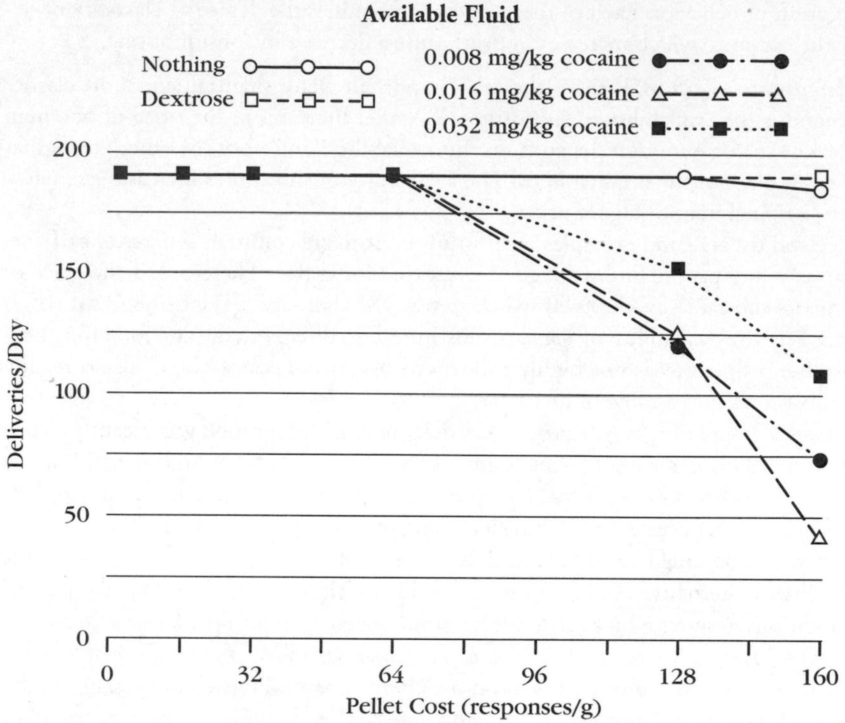

Figure 7.10 Number of food pellets obtained as a function of increases in the response requirement for food for a baboon that could also press an alternate response lever that produced either nothing, a solution of dextrose (a type of sugar), or different concentrations of cocaine. Notice that the elasticity of demand for food dramatically changed with the availability of cocaine. (After Foltin, 1999.)

high prices. Consider, for example, the cost of candy. A 10% increase in the price from 50¢ to 55¢ is not likely to discourage consumption. But if the candy costs $5.00, a 10% increase to $6.00 might well discourage purchases.

Price effects on elasticity of demand are evident in Figures 7.9 and 7.10. Notice that at low prices, there is little change in the number of reinforcers obtained as the price increases a bit. However, dramatic declines occur in the number of reinforcers obtained in the high range of prices. Price effects on the elasticity of demand for food have also been documented in studies with laboratory rats and baboons (Hursh, Raslear, Shurtleff, Bauman, & Simmons, 1988; Foltin, 1991, 1994). In these experiments, the price of food was increased by increasing the number of responses required for reinforcement, using fixed ratio schedules. As the price of food increased, the animals at first increased their responding correspondingly to obtain the same amount of food as before. Thus, over a range of low prices, demand for food was inelastic. Responding failed, however, to keep up with further increases in price, and at the high FR schedules, food consumption declined.

3. *Income Level.* A third factor that determines elasticity of demand is the level of income. In general, the higher the income, the less deterred a consumer will be by increases in price. This is also true for reinforcers obtained on schedules of reinforcement. In studies of instrumental conditioning, the number of responses or amount of time available for responding corresponds to income. These are resources an organism can use to respond to a schedule

BOX 7.3

Concepts of Consumer Demand in the Analysis of Drug Abuse

The use of illicit drugs such as heroin and cocaine is instrumental behavior. Going to obtain an illicit drug and paying for it provides the opportunity to use it. Government efforts to reduce the use of illicit drugs have involved manipulating various aspects of its cost or "price." Confiscating shipments limits the availability of a drug and increases its monetary cost, as shortages drive up the price. Severe penalties for drug possession also impose a "cost," but only after the drug has been obtained.

Laboratory studies of rats, monkeys, and people self-administering drugs under various schedules of reinforcement have shown that the concepts of consumer demand are useful in the analysis of instrumental drug-seeking behavior (for example, Bickel et al., 1991; Carroll, Carmona, & May, 1991; English, Rowlett, & Woolverton, 1995; Petry & Heyman, 1995). The results of experimental studies of consumer demand have also been extended to analyses of drug abuse policy (Hursh, 1991).

The effectiveness of policies intended to curb drug use depend on the drug's elasticity of demand. As I have described, increasing the cost of a commodity fails to reduce its consumption if the price remains relatively low, if there are no substitutes for the item, or if the consumer has a high income level. These considerations suggest that to discourage drug use, more than the cost of the drug needs to be considered. A highly effective technique for increasing the elasticity of demand for an item involves making available an effective substitute. Interestingly, under certain circumstances, nondrug reinforcers can serve as effective substitutes for a drug reinforcer (for example, Carroll et al., 1991).

constraint. The more responses or time animals have available, the less their behavior is influenced by increases in the cost of the reinforcer (Hastjarjo, Silberberg, & Hursh, 1990; Silberberg, Warren-Bouton, & Asano, 1987; see also Hastjarjo & Silberberg, 1992; DeGrandpre, Bickel, Rizvi, & Hughes, 1993).

Problems with Behavioral Regulation Approaches

Behavioral regulation theories have done much to change the way we think about reinforcement and instrumental conditioning, but several major shortcomings have emerged.

Behavioral regulation approaches are based on the assumption that individuals seek to defend an "optimal" or preferred combination of activities, or bliss point. This bliss point is defended by reallocating behavior between insrumental and reinforcer responses or by opting for substitute reinforcers. The bliss point is a molar characteristic of behavior. It is based on a measure of each response totaled over a large block of time (such as an entire free-baseline session). A given molar bliss point can be achieved in a variety of ways. In the hypothetical example in Figure 7.6, the student was allowed to choose between watching TV and studying during the free-baseline period and ended up watching TV for 60 minutes and studying for 15. This could have been achieved by doing all the TV watching before any studying or by switching back and forth between the two activities. According to the behavioral bliss point approach, such differences in response patterns should not matter. But experimental evidence indicates that how the molar bliss point is achieved is important (for example, Gawley, Timberlake, & Lucas, 1987; Tierney, Smith, & Gannon, 1987). Therefore, an adequate characterization of "behavioral bliss" requires information about molecular choice patterns.

Another, and perhaps more serious, difficulty is that responses during a free-operant baseline period do not always have the same "value" as responses that occur as a part of an arranged instrumental contingency. In behavioral regulation approaches, the outcome of instrumental contingencies is predicted from the free-baseline distribution of responses. For such predictions to work, an investigator has to assume that responses performed in the absence of experimenter-imposed constraints are basically the same as the responses that occur when an instrumental contingency is imposed. For example, studying in the absence of an externally imposed response constraint has to be of the same "value" as studying in order to gain access to the TV. This assumption has been found to be incorrect in several experiments (Allison, Buxton, & Moore, 1987; Gawley et al., 1987; Tierney et al., 1987). Doing something when there are no externally imposed requirements (jogging for pleasure, for example) appears to be different from doing the same thing when it is required by an imposed instrumental contingency (jogging in a physical education class, for example).

Finally, because behavioral regulation and economic approaches to instrumental behavior do not deal with molecular behavioral processes, they say nothing about how organisms manage to defend a preferred combination of goods or activities. As Killeen (1995) pointed out, economics "provides an approach to understanding the trade-offs animals make between alternate packages of goods" (p. 426), but it does not tell us the processes that are involved in making those trade-offs.

Contributions of Behavioral Regulation

The behavioral regulation approach emerged from the theoretical developments that originated with Premack and his differential probability principle. Although this line of theorizing encountered some serious difficulties, it has also made major contributions to how we think about the motivation of instrumental behavior (see Tierney, 1995). It is instructive to review some of these contributions.

1. Behavioral regulation and the Premack principle moved us away from thinking about reinforcers as special kinds of stimuli or as special kinds of responses. We are now encouraged to look for the causes of reinforcement in how instrumental contingencies constrain the free flow of behavior. Reinforcement effects are seen as produced by schedule constraints on an organism's ongoing activities.

2. Instrumental conditioning procedures are no longer considered to "stamp in" or to "strengthen" instrumental behavior. Rather, instrumental conditioning is seen as creating a new distribution, or allocation, of responses. Typically, the reallocation of behavior involves an increase in the instrumental response and a decrease in the reinforcer response. These two changes are viewed as equally important features of the redistribution of behavior.

3. There is no fundamental distinction between instrumental and reinforcer responses. Reinforcer responses are not assumed to be more likely than instrumental responses. They are not assumed to provide any special physiological benefits or to have any inherent characteristics that make them different from instrumental responses. Rather, instrumental and reinforcer responses are distinguished only by the roles assigned to them by an instrumental conditioning procedure.

4. Behavioral regulation and behavioral economics embrace the assumption that organisms respond in order to maximize benefits. The idea of optimization or maximization is not original with behavioral regulation. I introduced the idea (maximizing rates of reinforcement) earlier in discussions of concurrent schedules. The bliss point approach suggests

that the optimal distribution of activities is determined not only by physiological needs but also by the organism's ecological niche and natural or phylogenetically determined response tendencies. It is not always clear what is being maximized. In fact, studies of behavior can be used to identify what organisms value and work to conserve (Rachlin, 1995).

5. Behavioral regulation and behavioral economics have provided new and precise ways of describing constraints that various instrumental conditioning procedures impose on an organism's repertoire of behavior. More important, they have emphasized that instrumental behavior cannot be studied in a vacuum or behavioral test tube. All of the organism's response options at a given time must be considered as a system. Changes in one part of the system influence changes in other parts. Constraints imposed by instrumental procedures are more or less effective depending on the nature of the constraint, the availability of substitutes, and the organism's level of "income."

CONCLUDING COMMENTS

Motivational processes in instrumental behavior have been addressed from two radically different perspectives and intellectual traditions: the associationist perspective rooted in Thorndike's Law of Effect and Pavovian conditioning, and the behavioral regulation perspective rooted in Skinnerian behavioral analysis. These two approaches differ in more ways than they are similar, making it difficult to imagine how they might be integrated. For example, the fundamental concept in the associationist approach (the concept of an association) is entirely ignored in behavioral regulation. Correspondingly, the critical concepts of behavioral regulation (bliss points and schedule constraints) have no correspondence in the associationist approach. The associationist approach readily lends itself to explorations of the neural circuitry of instrumental conditioning. On the other hand, it is difficult to see how the behavioral regulation approach could be used to guide neurophysiological research.

The two approaches appear to be focused on entirely different things, but both have contributed significantly to our understanding of the motivation of instrumental behavior. It is obvious that one approach cannot be ignored in favor of the other, but how does each approach contribute to our complete understanding of instrumental motivation?

One way to think about the two approaches is that they involve different levels of analysis. The associationist approach involves the molecular level where the focus is on specific stimuli, responses, and their connections. In contrast, as I have described, behavioral regulation operates at a molar level of aggregates of behavior and the broader behavioral context in which instrumental contingencies operate. Thus, the behavioral regulation approach makes better contact with the complexities of an organism's ecology.

Another way to think about the relation between the two approaches is that one is concerned with processes and the other is more concerned with functions or long-range goals. The associationist approach describes specific processes [S-R, S-O, R-O, and S-(R-O) associations] that serve to generate and direct instrumental behavior, but it ignores the long-range "purpose" or function of instrumental learning. That is the purview of behavioral regulation and behavioral economics, which assumes that organisms work to defend an optimal distribution of activities. The defense of the behavioral bliss point is achieved through the molecular mechanisms of associations. (For a formal discussion of the relations between processes, ecology, and function, see Killeen, 1995.)

The conceptual developments in the study of the motivation of instrumental behavior provide an exciting illustration of the course of scientific inquiry. This inquiry has spanned intellectual developments from simple stimulus-response formulations to comprehensive considerations of how the organism's repertoire is constrained by instrumental contingencies and how organisms solve complex ecological problems. In this aspect of the study of conditioning and learning, perhaps more than in any other, investigators have moved boldly to explore radically new conceptions when older ideas did not meet the challenges posed by new empirical findings.

SAMPLE QUESTIONS

1. What is an S-O association, and what research tactic provides the best evidence for it?
2. What investigative techniques are used to provide evidence of R-O associations? Why is it not possible to explain instrumental behavior by assuming only R-O association learning?
3. Describe similarities and differences between the Premack principle and subsequent behavioral regulation theory.
4. What are the primary contributions of economic concepts to the understanding of the motivational bases of instrumental behavior?
5. What are the shortcomings of behavioral regulation theory?
6. Describe implications of modern concepts of reinforcement for behavior therapy.

KEY TERMS

behavioral bliss point The preferred distribution of an organism's activities before an instrumental conditioning procedure is introduced that sets constraints and limitations on response allocation.

consummatory response theory A theory that assumes that species-typical consummatory responses (eating, drinking, and the like) are the critical features of reinforcers.

demand curve The relation between how much of a commodity is purchased and the price of the commodity.

differential probability principle A principle that assumes that reinforcement depends on how much more likely the organism is to perform the reinforcer response than the instrumental response before an instrumental conditioning procedure is introduced. The greater the differential probability of the reinforcer and instrumental responses during baseline conditions, the greater will be the reinforcement effect of providing opportunity to engage in the reinforcer response after performance of the instrumental response. Also known as the *Premack principle.*

elasticity of demand The degree to which price influences the consumption or purchase of a commodity. If price has a large effect on consumption, elasticity of demand is high. If price has a small effect on consumption, elasticity of demand is low.

minimum deviation model A model of instrumental behavior, according to which participants respond to a response-reinforcer contingency in a manner that gets them as close as possible to their behavioral bliss point.

Premack principle Same as *differential probability principle.*

response deprivation hypothesis An explanation of reinforcement according to which restricting access to a response below its baseline rate of occurrence (response deprivation) is sufficient to make the opportunity to perform that response an effective positive reinforcer.

transfer-of-control experiment An experiment that assesses the effects of a classically conditioned stimulus (CS) on the performance of instrumental behavior. The CS and the instrumental response are first conditioned in independent phases of the experiment. The effects of the CS on instrumental reponding are then determined in the transfer phase.

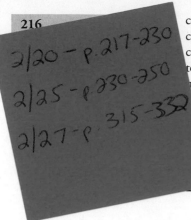

CHAPTER

8 STIMULUS CONTROL OF BEHAVIOR

Chapter 8 is organized around the principles of stimulus control. Although most of the chapter deals with the ways in which instrumental behavior comes under the control of particular stimuli that are present when the response is reinforced, the concepts are equally applicable to classical conditioning. The chapter begins with a definition of stimulus control and the basic concepts of stimulus discrimination and generalization. I then discuss factors that determine the extent to which behavior comes to be restricted to particular stimulus values. Along the way, I describe special forms of stimulus control (intradimensional discrimination) and control by special categories of stimuli (compound stimuli and contextual cues). The chapter concludes with a discussion of the learning of conditional relations in both instrumental and classical conditioning.

As I pointed out in earlier chapters, both Thorndike and Skinner recognized that instrumental responses and reinforcers occur not in a vacuum, but in the presence of particular stimuli. As I described in Chapter 7, research on the associative structure of instrumental conditioning emphasized that these stimuli can come to determine whether the instrumental response is performed. The importance of antecedent stimuli has been examined further in studies of the stimulus control of instrumental behavior, which is the topic of this chapter.

The stimulus control of instrumental behavior is evident in many aspects of life. Studying, for example, is under the strong control of school-related stimuli. College students who have fallen behind in their work may resolve to study a lot when they return home for the holidays, but they rarely carry out such good intentions. Holiday stimuli are very different from the stimuli students experience when classes are in session and consequently do not engender effective studying behavior.

The proper fit between an instrumental response and the stimulus context in which the response is performed is so important that the failure of appropriate stimulus control is often considered abnormal. Getting undressed, for example, is acceptable instrumental behavior in the privacy of your bedroom, but doing so on a public street will get you arrested. Staring at a television set is considered appropriate if the TV is turned on, whereas staring at a blank television screen may be a symptom of behavior pathology. If you respond in a loving manner in the presence of your spouse or other family members, your behavior is welcomed. Directing the same behavior toward strangers is likely to be greeted with far less acceptance.

The stimulus control of behavior is an important aspect of how organisms adjust to their environment. The survival of both human and nonhuman animals depends on their ability to perform responses that are appropriate to the situation. With seasonal changes in food supply, for example, animals have to change how they forage for food. Within the same season, they have to respond one way in the presence of predators or intruders and in other ways in the absence of nearby danger. In cold weather, animals may seek comfort by going to uncovered areas warmed by the sun; on rainy days, they may seek covered areas sheltered from the rain. To effectively obtain comfort and avoid pain, animals have to behave in ways that are appropriate to their changing circumstances.

IDENTIFICATION AND MEASUREMENT OF STIMULUS CONTROL

To investigate the stimulus control of behavior, a researcher first has to figure out how to identify and measure it. How can he or she tell that an instrumental response has come under the control of certain stimuli?

Differential Responding and Stimulus Discrimination

Consider, for example, an experiment by Reynolds (1961). Two pigeons were reinforced on a variable interval schedule for pecking a circular response key. Reinforcement for pecking was available whenever the response key was illuminated by a visual pattern consisting of a white triangle on a red background (see Figure 8.1). Thus the stimulus on the key had two components—the white triangle and the red color of the background. Reynolds was interested in which of these stimulus components gained control over the pecking behavior.

After the pigeons learned to peck steadily at the triangle on the red background, Reynolds measured the amount of pecking that occurred when only one of the stimuli was presented. On some of the test trials, the white triangle was projected on the response key without the red color; on others, the red background color was projected on the response key without the white triangle.

The results are summarized in Figure 8.1. One of the pigeons pecked a great deal more when the response key was illuminated with the red light than when it was illuminated with the white triangle. This outcome shows that the bird's pecking behavior was much more strongly controlled by the red color than by the white triangle. By contrast, the other pigeon pecked a great deal more when the white triangle was projected on the response key than when the key was illuminated by the red light. Thus, for the second bird, the pecking behavior was more strongly controlled by the triangle. (For a more recent similar study, see Cheng & Spetch, 1995.)

This experiment illustrates several important ideas. First, it shows researchers how to determine whether instrumental behavior has come under the control of a particular stimulus. *The stimulus control of instrumental behavior is demonstrated by variations in responding (differential responding) related to variations in stimuli.* If an organism responds one way in the presence of one stimulus, and a different way in the presence of another stimulus, its behavior has come under the control of those stimuli. Such differential responding was evident in the behavior of both pigeons Reynolds tested.

Differential responding to two stimuli also indicates that the pigeons were treating each stimulus as different from the other. This is called **stimulus discrimination.** *An organism is said to exhibit stimulus discrimination if it responds differently to two or more stimuli.* Stimulus discrimination and stimulus control are two ways to consider the same phenomenon: one does not exist without the other. If an organism does not discriminate between two stimuli, its behavior is not under the control of those cues.

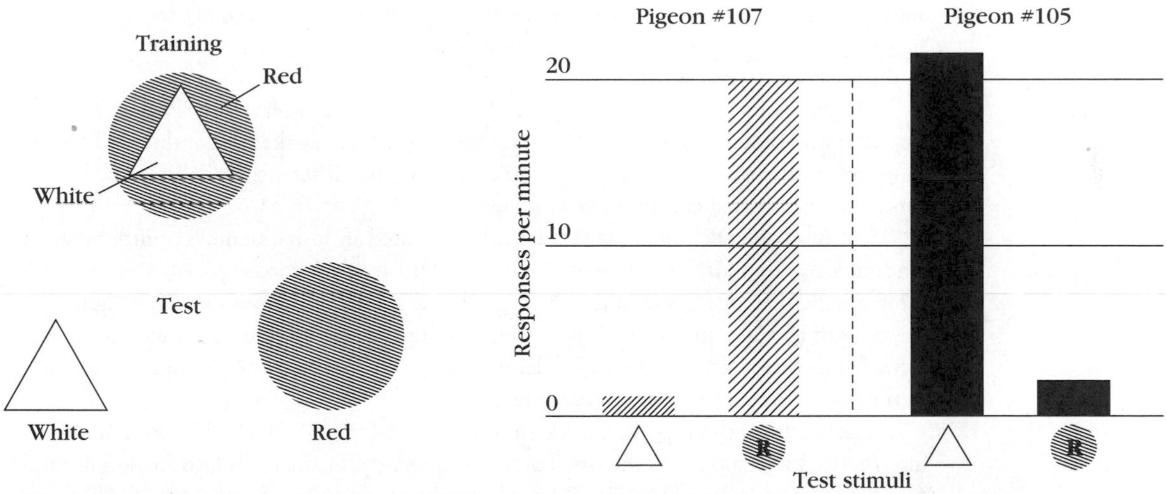

Figure 8.1 Summary of procedure and results of an experiment by Reynolds (1961). Two pigeons were first reinforced for pecking whenever a compound stimulus consisting of a white triangle on a red background was projected on the response key. The rate of pecking was then observed with each pigeon when the white triangle and the red background stimuli were presented separately.

Another interesting aspect of the results of Reynolds's experiment was that the pecking behavior of each bird came under the control of a different stimulus. The behavior of bird 107 came under the control of the red color, whereas the behavior of bird 105 came under the control of the triangle. The procedure used by Reynolds did not direct attention to one of the stimuli at the expense of the other. Therefore, it is not surprising that each bird came to respond to a different aspect of the situation. The experiment was comparable to showing a group of children a picture of a cowboy grooming a horse. Some of the children may focus on the cowboy; others may find the horse more interesting. In the absence of special procedures (that I describe later in the chapter), investigators cannot always predict which of the various stimuli an organism experiences will gain control over its instrumental behavior.

Stimulus Generalization

Identifying and differentiating various stimuli is not a simple matter (Fetterman, 1996). Stimuli may be defined in all kinds of ways. Sometimes widely different objects or events are considered instances of the same stimulus because they all share the same function. A wheel, for example, may be small or large, spoked or not spoked, and made of wood, rubber, or metal, but it is still a wheel. By contrast, stimuli in other cases are identified and distinguished in terms of precise physical features, such as the wavelength of light or the frequency of radio waves. For example, to listen to a particular FM radio station, you have to tune your radio within a very small range of the FM band. Small variations in tuning will significantly change the quality of the reception.

Psychologists and physiologists have long been concerned with how organisms identify and distinguish different stimuli. Some have suggested that this is the single most important question in psychology (Stevens, 1951). The problem is central to the analysis of stimulus control. As this chapter shows, numerous factors are involved in the identification and differentiation of stimuli. Experimental analyses of the problem have depended mainly on the phenomenon of **stimulus generalization,** which in a sense is the opposite of differential responding, or stimulus discrimination. *An organism is said to show stimulus generalization if it responds in a similar fashion to two or more stimuli*—if the same level of behavior is observed in the presence of different stimuli.

The phenomenon of stimulus generalization was first observed by Pavlov. He found that after one stimulus was used as a CS, his dogs would also make the conditioned response to other, similar stimuli. That is, they failed to respond differentially to stimuli that were similar to the original conditioned stimulus.

Stimulus generalization has also been investigated in instrumental conditioning. In a landmark experiment, Guttman and Kalish (1956) first reinforced pigeons on a variable interval schedule for pecking a response key illuminated by a yellowish-orange light with a wavelength of 580 nanometers (nm). After training, the birds were tested with a variety of other colors presented in a random order without reinforcement, and the rate of responding in the presence of each color was recorded.

The results of the experiment are summarized in Figure 8.2. The highest rate of pecking occurred in response to the original 580-nm color. But the birds also made substantial numbers of pecks when lights of 570-nm and 590-nm wavelength were tested, which indicates that responding generalized to the 570-nm and 590-nm stimuli. However, as the color of the test stimuli became increasingly different from the color of the original training stimulus, progressively fewer responses occurred. The results showed a gradient of responding as a function of how similar each test stimulus was to the original training stimulus. This is an example of a **stimulus generalization gradient.**

Stimulus Generalization Gradients as Measures of Stimulus Control

Stimulus generalization gradients are often used to measure stimulus control because they provide information about how sensitive the organism's behavior is to variations in a particular aspect of the environment (for a review of this technology, see Honig & Urcuioli, 1981). With the use of stimulus generalization gradients, investigators can determine exactly how much a stimulus has to be altered to produce a change in behavior.

Consider, for example, the gradient in Figure 8.2. The pigeons responded much more when the original 580-nm training stimulus was presented than when the response key was illuminated by lights whose wavelengths were 520, 540, 620, and 640 nm. Differences in color controlled different levels of responding, but this control was not very precise. Responding to the 580-nm color generalized to the 570-nm and 590-nm stimuli. The wavelength of the 580-nm training stimulus had to be changed by more than 10 nm before a decrement in performance was observed. This aspect of the stimulus generalization gradient provides precise information about how much the stimulus has to be changed for the pigeons to respond to the change.

How do you suppose color-blind pigeons would have responded? They could not have distinguished lights on the basis of color or wavelength and therefore would have responded in much the same way regardless of what color was projected on the response key. Figure 8.3 presents hypothetical results of an experiment of this sort. If the pigeons did not respond on the basis of the color of the key light, similar high rates of responding would have occurred as different colors were projected on the key. Thus, the stimulus generalization gradient would have been flat.

A comparison of the results obtained by Guttman and Kalish (1956) and the hypothetical experiment with color-blind pigeons indicates that *the steepness of a stimulus generalization gradient provides a precise measure of the degree of stimulus control.* A flat generalization gradient (Figure 8.3) is obtained if the organism responds in a similar fashion to all the test stimuli. Such lack of differential responding shows that the stimulus feature that is varied in the generalization test does not control the instrumental behavior. By contrast, a steep generalization gradient (Figure 8.2) is obtained if the organism responds more to some of the test stimuli than to others. Such differential responding is evidence that the instrumental behavior is under the control of the stimulus feature that is varied among the test stimuli.

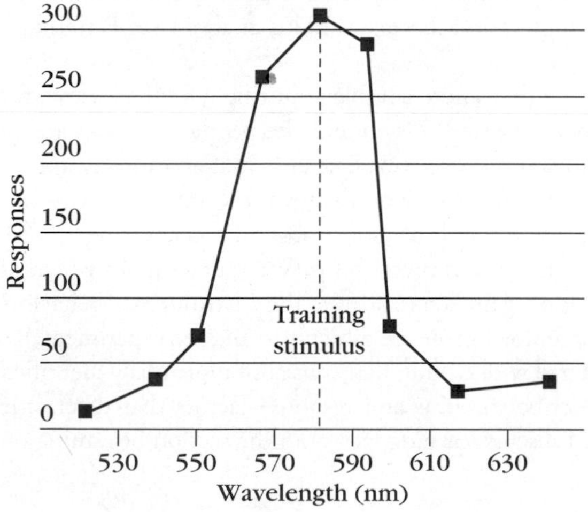

Figure 8.2 Stimulus generalization gradient for pigeons that were trained to peck in the presence of a colored light of 580-nm wavelength and were then tested in the presence of other colors. (From "Discriminability and Stimulus Generalization," by N. Guttman and H. I. Kalish, 1956, *Journal of Experimental Psychology, 51,* pp. 79–88.)

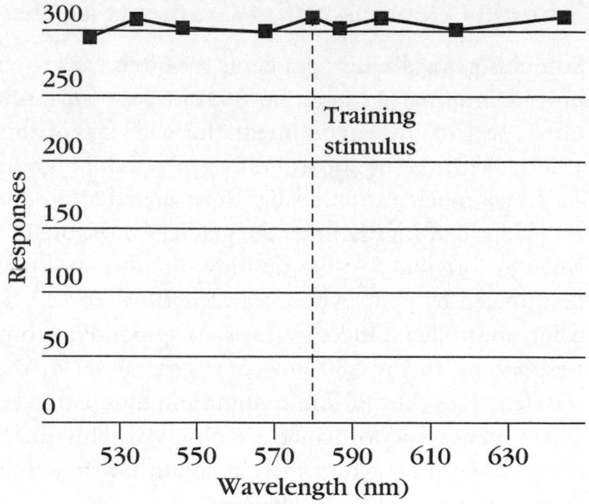

Figure 8.3 Hypothetical stimulus generalization gradient for color-blind pigeons trained to peck in the presence of a colored light of 580-nm wavelength and then tested in the presence of other colors.

Generalization and differential responding are opposites. If a great deal of generalization occurs, there is little differential responding. If responding is highly differential to stimuli, little generalization is obtained.

STIMULUS AND RESPONSE FACTORS IN STIMULUS CONTROL

In the experiment by Reynolds (1961) described at the outset of this chapter, pigeons pecked a response key that had a white triangle on a red background. Such a stimulus obviously has two features: the color of the background and the shape of the triangle. Perhaps less obvious is the fact that all stimulus situations can be analyzed in terms of multiple features. Even if the response key had only the red background, it could be characterized in terms of its brightness, shape, or location in the experimental chamber, in addition to its color. (For a more complete discussion of approaches to stimulus analysis, see Fetterman, 1996.)

Situations outside the laboratory are even more complex. During a football game, for example, cheering is reinforced by social approval if you and the people near you are all rooting for the same team, and if that team is doing well. The cues that accompany appropriate cheering include your team making a good play on the field, the announcer describing the play, cheerleaders dancing exuberantly, and the people around you cheering.

The central issue in the analysis of the stimulus control is, What determines which of the many features of a stimulus situation gains control over the instrumental behavior? Stimuli as complex as those found at a football game are difficult to analyze experimentally. Laboratory studies are typically conducted with stimuli that consist of more easily identified features. In the present section, I describe stimulus and response factors that determine which cues come to control behavior. I discuss learning factors in the section beginning on page 230.

BOX 8.1

GENERALIZATION OF TREATMENT OUTCOMES

Stimulus generalization is critical to the success of behavior therapy. Behavior therapy, like other forms of therapy, is typically conducted under specific circumstances (in a therapist's office, for example). For the treatment to be maximally useful, what is learned during treatment should generalize outside the training situation. An autistic child, for example, who is taught certain communicative responses in interactions with a particular therapist should also exhibit those responses in interactions with other people. The following, sometimes contradictory, techniques have been proposed to facilitate generalization of treatment outcomes (for example, Schreibman, Koegel, Charlop, & Egel, 1990; Stokes & Baer, 1977):

1. The treatment situation should be made as similar as possible to the natural environment of the client. For example, if the natural environment provides reinforcement only intermittently, it is a good idea to reduce the frequency of reinforcement during treatment sessions as well. It is also best to use the same reinforcers the client is likely to encounter in the natural environment.
2. Conduct the treatment procedure in new settings. This strategy is called *sequential modification.* After a behavior has been conditioned in one situation (a classroom), training is conducted in a new situation (the playground). If that does not result in sufficient generalization, training can be extended to a third environment (the school cafeteria, for example).
3. Use numerous exemplars during training. In trying to extinguish fear of elevators, for example, conduct training with various types of elevators.
4. Condition the new responses to stimuli that are common to various situations. Language provides effective mediating stimuli. Responses conditioned to verbal or instructional cues are likely to generalize to new situations in which those instructional stimuli are encountered.
5. Make the training procedure indiscriminable or incidental to other activities. In one study (McGee, Krantz, & McClannahan, 1986), for example, the investigators took advantage of the interest that autistic children showed in specific toys during a play session to teach the children how to read the names of the toys.
6. Generalization outside a training situation is achieved if the training helps bring the individual into contact with contingencies of reinforcement available in the natural environment (Baer & Wolf, 1970). Once a response is acquired through special training, the behavior often can be maintained by naturally available reinforcers. Reading, calculating simple arithmetic problems, and riding a bicycle are all responses that are maintained by natural reinforcers once the responses have been acquired through special training.

Sensory Capacity and Orientation

The most obvious factor that determines whether a particular stimulus feature comes to control responding is the organism's sensory capacity and orientation. The range of stimuli that potentially can control behavior is determined by the organism's sensory world—the world of sensations experienced by a particular individual. Sensory capacity and orientation determine which stimuli are included in an organism's sensory world. Presentation of stimuli with certain features of interest to one organism does not guarantee that another organism will respond to the same features. The individual's own (and possibly unique) point of view or sensory world must always be considered.

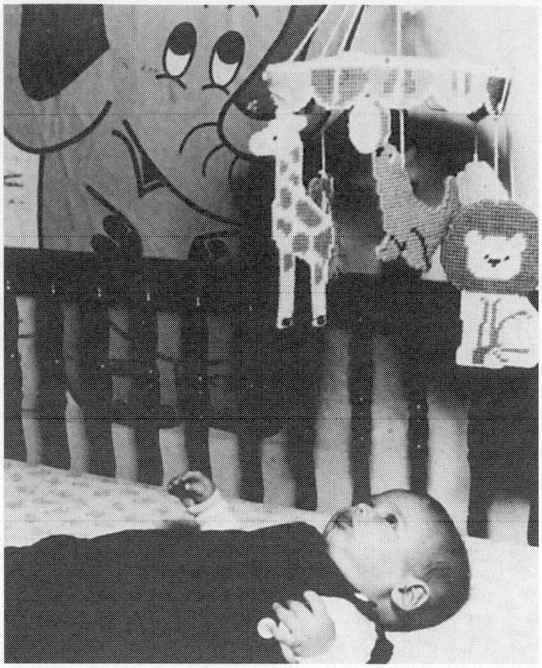

Figure 8.4 An infant looking up at a mobile.

Events outside the range of what an organism can detect with its sense organs simply do not exist for that individual unless the stimuli are amplified or transduced into something the individual can detect. People, for example, cannot hear sounds above about 20,000 cps. Such stimuli are called "ultrasounds" because they are outside the range of human hearing. Because ultrasounds are inaudible to people, such sounds cannot come to control human behavior. Other species, however, are able to hear ultrasounds. Dogs, for example, can hear whistles outside the range of human hearing and therefore can be trained to respond to such sounds.

Limitations on the stimuli that can come to control behavior are also set by whether the individual comes into contact with the stimulus. Consider, for example, a child's crib. Parents often place mobiles and other decorations on and around the crib to provide interesting stimuli for the child to look at; for example, the mobile shown in Figure 8.4 consists of several animal figures (a giraffe, a seal, and a lion) made of thin needlework.

Which aspects of the mobile in the crib in Figure 8.4 can potentially control the child's behavior? To answer this question, first consider what the child sees about the mobile rather than what the mobile looks like to adults. From the child's vantage point under the mobile, only the bottom edges of the animal figures are visible. The shapes of the animals and their surface decorations cannot be seen from below and thus are not likely to gain control of the child's looking behavior. (For findings illustrating the importance of orientation for the acquisition of stimulus control in laboratory animals, see, for example, Gillette, Martin, & Bellingham, 1980.)

Relative Ease of Conditioning Various Stimuli

Having the necessary sense organs and the appropriate sensory orientation does not guarantee that the organism's behavior will come under the control of a particular stimulus. Whether a stimulus comes to control behavior also depends on the presence of other cues in the situation. In particular, how strongly organisms learn about one stimulus depends on how easily other cues in the situations can become conditioned. This phenomenon is called **overshadowing,** which illustrates competition among stimuli for access to the processes of learning.

Consider, for example, trying to teach a child to read by having her follow along as you read a children's book that has a big picture and a short sentence on each page. Learning about pictures is easier than learning words; therefore, the pictures may well overshadow the words. The child will quickly memorize the story based on the pictures rather than the words and will soon appear to be "reading" without error.

Pavlov (1927) was the first to observe that if two stimuli are presented at the same time, the presence of the more easily trained stimulus may hinder learning about the other one. In many of his experiments, the two stimuli differed in intensity. In general, the more intense stimulus became conditioned more rapidly and overshadowed learning about the weaker stimulus. Pavlov found that the weak stimulus could become conditioned (somewhat slowly) if it was presented by itself. Less conditioning occurred if the weak stimulus was presented simultaneously with a more intense stimulus. (For more recent studies of overshadowing, see March, Chamizo, & Mackintosh, 1992; Schachtman, Kasprow, Meyer, Bourne, & Hart, 1992; Spetch, 1995)

Type of Reinforcement

Courtesy of Donald A. Dewsbury

V. M. LoLordo

The development of stimulus control also depends on the type of reinforcement that is used. Certain types of stimuli are more likely to gain control over the instrumental behavior with positive reinforcement than with negative reinforcement. This relation has been extensively investigated in experiments with pigeons (see LoLordo, 1979).

In one study (Foree & LoLordo, 1973), two groups of pigeons were trained to press a foot treadle in the presence of a compound stimulus consisting of a red light and a tone whose pitch was 440 cps. When the light/tone compound was absent, responses were not reinforced. For one group of pigeons, reinforcement for treadle pressing was provided by food. For the other group, treadle pressing was reinforced by the avoidance of shock. If the avoidance group pressed the treadle in the presence of the light/tone stimulus, no shock was delivered on that trial; if they failed to respond during the light/tone stimulus, a brief shock was periodically applied until a response occurred.

Both groups of pigeons learned to respond during the light/tone compound. Foree and LoLordo then sought to determine which of the two elements of the compound stimulus was primarily responsible for the treadle-press behavior. Test trials were conducted during which the light and tone stimuli were presented one at a time. The results are summarized in Figure 8.5.

Pigeons that were trained with food reinforcement responded much more when tested with the light stimulus alone than when tested with the tone alone. In fact, their rate of treadle pressing in response to the isolated presentation of the red light was nearly as high as when the light was presented simultaneously with the tone. Therefore, the investigators concluded that the behavior of these birds was nearly exclusively controlled by the red light.

A contrasting pattern of results occurred with the pigeons trained with shock-avoidance reinforcement. These birds responded much more when tested with the tone alone than when tested with the light alone. Thus, with shock-avoidance reinforcement the tone acquired more control over the treadle response than did the red light.

Similar results have been obtained in a variety of other experiments conducted with both pigeons and rats (for example, Kelly, 1986; Kraemer & Roberts, 1985; Schindler & Weiss, 1982; Shapiro et al., 1980; Shapiro & LoLordo, 1982; Weiss & Panlilio, 1999).

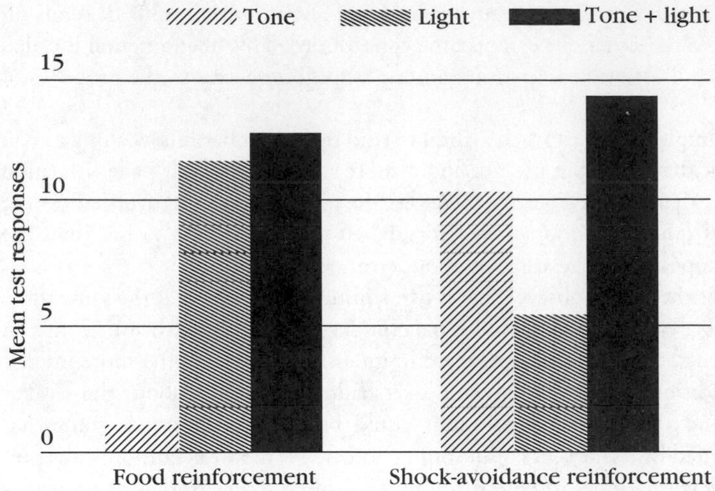

Figure 8.5 Effects of type of reinforcement on stimulus control. A treadle-press response in pigeons was reinforced in the presence of a compound stimulus consisting of a tone and a red light. With food reinforcement, the light gained much more control over the behavior than the tone. With shock-avoidance reinforcement, the tone gained more control over behavior than the light. (Adapted from Foree & LoLordo, 1973.)

These findings indicate that stimulus control of instrumental behavior is determined in part by the type of reinforcement used. Although the mechanisms responsible for this effect are still being worked out (Weiss, Panlilio, & Schindler, 1993a, 1993b), the results are clear. Visual stimuli are more likely to gain control over behavior in appetitive situations than are auditory cues, whereas auditory cues are more likely to gain control in aversive situations.

The dominance of visual control in appetitive situations and auditory control in aversive situations is probably related to the behavior systems that are activated in the two cases. Food-reinforcement procedures activate the feeding system. Food eaten by pigeons and rats is more likely to be identified by visual cues than by auditory cues. Therefore, activation of the feeding system may involve increased sensitivity to visual stimuli. In contrast, shock-avoidance procedures activate the defensive behavior system. Responding to auditory cues may be particularly adaptive in avoiding danger.

Unfortunately, we do not know enough about the evolutionary history of pigeons or rats to be able to calculate the adaptive value of different types of stimulus control in feeding versus defensive behavior. We also do not know much about how stimulus control varies as a function of the type of reinforcement in other species. This issue remains a fertile area for future research.

Type of Instrumental Response

Another factor that can determine which of several features of a compound stimulus gains control over behavior is the nature of the response required for reinforcement. The importance of the instrumental response for stimulus control is illustrated by an experiment by Dobrzecka, Szwejkowska, and Konorski (1966). These investigators studied the control of instrumental behavior by auditory stimuli in dogs. The dogs were gently restrained in a harness, with a metronome placed in front of them and a buzzer placed behind them. The metronome and buzzer provided qualitatively different types of sounds, a periodic beat versus a continuous rattle. The two stimuli also differed in spatial location, one in front of the animal and the other behind it. The investigators were interested in which of these two stimulus characteristics (sound quality or location) would come to control behavior.

Two groups of dogs served in the experiment (see Figure 8.6). Each group differed in what responses were required for reinforcement in the presence of the buzzer and the met-

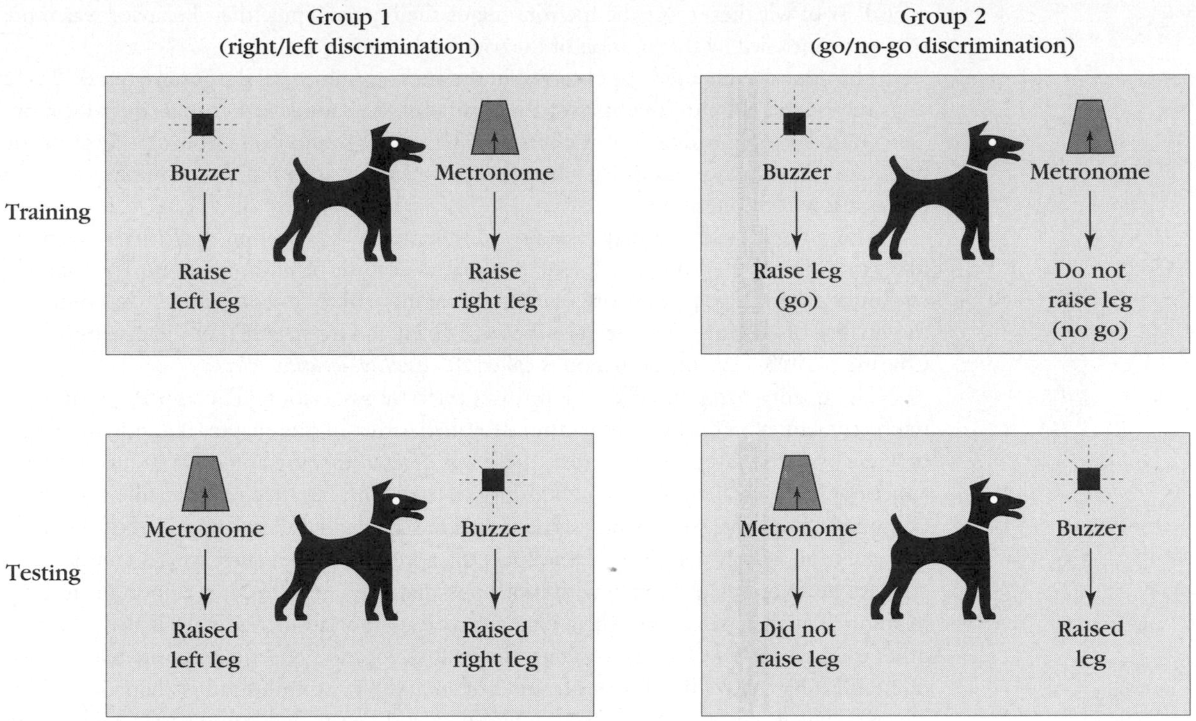

Figure 8.6 Diagram of the experiment by Dobrzecka, Szwejkowska, and Konorski (1966). Dogs were trained on a left/right or go/no-go task (Groups 1 and 2, respectively) with auditory stimuli that differed both in location (in front or in back of the animals) and in quality (the sound of a buzzer or a metronome). During testing, the location of the two sounds was reversed. The results showed that the left/right differential response was controlled mainly by the location of the sounds, whereas the go/no-go differential response was controlled mainly by the quality of the sounds.

ronome stimuli. Group 1 received training in a right/left task. When the metronome was sounded, dogs in this group were reinforced for raising the right leg; when the buzzer was sounded, they were reinforced for raising the left leg. Thus, the location of the response (right/left) was important for reinforcement in this group.

Group 2 received training on a go/no-go task. In this case, the dogs had to raise the right leg when the buzzer sounded and not raise the leg when the metronome sounded. Thus, the quality of the response (go/no-go) rather than its location was important for reinforcement for this group.

What aspect of the auditory cues—quality or location—gained control over the instrumental behavior in the two groups? To answer this question, investigators reversed the positions of the metronome and the buzzer—the buzzer was placed in front of the dogs and the metronome behind them (see Figure 8.6). This manipulation produced different test results in the two groups.

Dogs trained on the right/left task responded mainly on the basis of the location of the auditory cues rather than their quality. The participants in Group 1 raised the right leg in response to sound from the front, regardless of whether the sound was made by the metronome or the buzzer. When the sound came from the back, they raised the left leg, again regardless of whether it was the metronome or the buzzer. Thus, their behavior was more strongly controlled by the location of the sounds than their quality.

The opposite outcome was observed in the animals trained on the go/no-go task. These dogs responded more on the basis of the quality of the sounds rather than their location. They raised a leg in response to the buzzer whether the sound came from the front or the back, and they did not raise a leg when the metronome was sounded, again irrespective of the location of the metronome.

These results indicate that responses differentiated by location (right/left) are more likely to come under the control of the spatial feature of auditory cues. By contrast, responses differentiated by quality (go/no-go) are more likely to come under the control of the quality of auditory cues (see also Bowe, Miller, & Green, 1987; Williams, Butler, & Overmier, 1990). The phenomenon is called the *quality–location effect.*

The quality–location effect is a form of selective association. The appetitive–aversive reinforcement effect on stimulus control described earlier in this chapter is another example of a selective association. In that case, there was greater learning about visual features with appetitive reinforcement and about auditory features with negative reinforcement. Another example of a selective association was described in Chapter 4, where I pointed out that taste cues are more readily associated with illness than are audiovisual cues, whereas audiovisual cues are more readily associated with footshock than are taste cues. It is important to keep in mind that these selective associations are typically not all or none. As is the case with other examples of selective associations, the quality–location effect reflects the relative ease of establishing control by different features of an auditory stimulus rather than all-or-none effects. That is, the quality–location effect does not mean that subjects can never learn about the quality of sounds when spatially differentiated responses are involved or that they can never learn about the location of sounds in a go/no-go task. With judicious placement of the sound sources (one much closer to the response than the other), subjects can come to respond to location features of sounds in a go/no-go task (Neill & Harrison, 1987).

Stimulus Elements versus Configural Cues in Compound Stimuli

In the discussion so far of control of behavior by various stimulus elements, I have assumed that organisms treat these stimulus elements as distinct and separate features of the environment. This is called the **stimulus-element approach.** Thus, in the quality–location effect, the quality and location of an auditory stimulus were considered to be separate features of the auditory cues. The assumption was that a particular stimulus feature (sound quality) was perceived the same way regardless of the status of the other feature (sound location). An important alternative theoretical approach assumes that organisms treat a complex stimulus as an integral whole that is not divided into parts or elements. This is called the **configural-cue approach.**

According to the configural-cue approach, individuals respond to a compound stimulus in terms of the unique configuration of its elements. It is assumed that the elements are not treated as separate entities. In fact, they may not even be identifiable when the stimulus compound is presented. In the configural-cue approach, stimulus elements are important not because of their individuality but because of the way they contribute to the entire configuration of stimulation provided by the compound.

The concept of a configural cue may be illustrated by considering the sound made by a symphony orchestra. The orchestral sound originates from the sounds of the individual instruments. The sound of the entire orchestra, however, is very different from the sound of any of the individual instruments, some of which are difficult to identify when the entire orchestra is playing. We primarily hear the configuration of the sounds made by the individual instruments.

TABLE 8.1 CONFIGURAL EXPLANATION OF OVERSHADOWING

GROUP	TRAINING STIMULI	TEST STIMULUS	GENERALIZATION FROM TRAINING TO TEST
Overshadowing group	aB	a	Decrement
Control group	a	a	No decrement

The configural-cue approach has been encouraged by the theoretical work of John Pearce (1987, 1994), who showed that many learning phenomena are consistent with this framework. Consider, for example, the overshadowing effect (see Table 8.1). An overshadowing experiment involves two groups of subjects and two stimulus elements, one of low intensity (*a*) and the other of high intensity (*B*). For the overshadowing group, the two stimuli are presented together (*aB*) as a compound cue and paired with reinforcement during conditioning. For the control group, only the low-intensity stimulus (*a*) is presented during conditioning. Tests are then conducted for each group with the weaker stimulus element (*a*) presented alone. These tests show less responding to *a* in the overshadowing group than in the control group. Thus, the presence of *B* during conditioning disrupts control of behavior by the weaker stimulus *a.*

According to the configural-cue approach, overshadowing reflects different degrees of generalization decrement from training to testing for the overshadowing and the control groups (Pearce, 1987). There is no generalization decrement for the control group when it is tested with the weak stimulus *a* because that is the same as the stimulus it received during conditioning. In contrast, considerable generalization decrement occurs when the overshadowing group is tested with stimulus *a* after conditioning with the compound *aB.* For the overshadowing group, responding becomes conditioned to the *aB* compound, which is very different from *a* presented alone during testing. Therefore, responding conditioned to *aB* suffers considerable generalization decrement. According to the configural-cue approach, this greater generalization decrement is responsible for the overshadowing effect.

Courtesy of Donald A. Dewsbury

J. M. Pearce

The configural-cue approach has enjoyed considerable success (see Pearce & Bouton, 2001, for a review). Under certain conditions, organisms clearly respond to compound stimuli primarily in terms of the configuration of the elements that make up the compound (for recent examples, see Nakajima, 1997, 1998; Nakajima & Urushihara, 1999; Pearce, Aydin, & Redhead, 1997). However, some experimental results favor analyses of stimulus control in terms of stimulus elements (for example, Myers, Vogel, Shin, & Wagner, 2001; Rescorla, 1997e, 1999a). In addition, the configural-cue approach is incompatible with the various examples of selective associations that I described earlier. For example, the configural-cue approach does not explain why stimulus control is a function of the type of reinforcement used or the type of response that is required. The most prudent conclusion at this point is that organisms respond to stimulus compounds both in terms of the stimulus elements that make up the compound and in terms of unique stimulus configurations created by the stimulus elements. Under certain circumstances elemental control predominates, whereas under other conditions control by configural features of stimulus compounds predominates. What is required is a comprehensive theory that deals successfully with both types of phenomena.

The structure of such a unified theory was recently described by Wagner and Brandon (2001). According to the Wagner–Brandon theory, stimuli such as the sound of a tone consist of distinctive features (pitch, loudness, and location). When one stimulus is combined with another (a tone combined with a clicker, for example), new configural stimulus elements that are unique to this new stimulus combination are created. In addition, some of the individual features of the original stimuli are lost in the combination. This biases stimulus control in favor of the configural elements and produces results consistent with the configural-cue approach.

LEARNING FACTORS IN STIMULUS CONTROL

The stimulus and response factors described in the preceding section set the preconditions for how human and nonhuman animals learn about the environmental stimuli they encounter. Stimulus and response factors are the starting points for stimulus control. The fact that certain stimuli can be perceived does not ensure that those stimuli will come to control behavior. A child, for example, may see Ford and Chevy pickups but may not be able to distinguish between them. A novice chess player may be able to look at two different patterns on a chess board without being able to identify which represents the more favorable configuration. Whether certain stimuli come to control behavior often depends on what the organism has learned about those stimuli—not just whether the stimuli can be detected.

The suggestion that experience with stimuli may determine the extent to which those stimuli come to control behavior originated in efforts to explain the phenomenon of stimulus generalization. As I noted earlier, stimulus generalization refers to the fact that a response conditioned to one stimulus will also occur when other stimuli similar to the original cue are presented. Pavlov suggested that stimulus generalization occurs because learning about a CS becomes transferred to other stimuli on the basis of the physical similarity of those test stimuli to the original CS.

In a spirited attack, Lashley and Wade (1946) took exception to Pavlov's proposal. They rejected the idea that stimulus generalization reflects the transfer of learning and argued that it reflects the *absence* of learning. In particular, they proposed that stimulus generalization occurs if organisms have not learned to distinguish differences among the stimuli. Lashley and Wade proposed that animals have to learn to treat stimuli as different from one another. Thus, in contrast to Pavlov, Lashley and Wade considered the shape of a stimulus generalization gradient to be determined primarily by the organism's previous learning experiences rather than by the physical properties of the stimuli tested.

Stimulus Discrimination Training

Lashley and Wade were closer to the truth than Pavlov. Numerous studies have shown that stimulus control can be dramatically altered by learning experiences. Perhaps the most powerful procedure for bringing behavior under the control of a stimulus is stimulus discrimination training. In a **stimulus discrimination procedure,** the participants are exposed to at least two different stimuli—a red and a green light, for example—but reinforcement for performing the instrumental response is available only in the presence of one of the colors. The participants could be reinforced for responding when the red light is on but not when the green light is on. In this procedure, diagrammed in Figure 8.7, the red light signals the availability of reinforcement for responding. The green light signals that responding will not be reinforced. The stimulus that signals the availability of reinforcement is called the S+ or

S^D (pronounced "ess dee"). By contrast, the stimulus that signals the lack of reinforcement is called the S– or S^Δ (pronounced "ess delta").

With sufficient exposure to a discrimination procedure, participants will come to respond during S+ and withhold responding during S–. The acquisition of this pattern of responding is illustrated in the cumulative record in Figure 8.7. Initially, organisms respond similarly in the presence of the S+ and the S–. As training progresses, responding in the presence of the S+ persists, and responding in the presence of the S– declines. The emergence of greater responding to the S+ than to the S– indicates differential responding to these stimuli. Thus, *stimulus discrimination procedures establish control by the stimuli that signal when reinforcement is and is not available.* Once the S+ and S– have gained control over the organism's behavior, they are called **discriminative stimuli.** The S+ is a discriminative stimulus for performing the instrumental response, and the S– is a discriminative stimulus for not performing the response.

The procedure diagrammed in Figure 8.7 is the standard procedure for stimulus discrimination training in instrumental conditioning. Stimulus discriminations can also be established with the use of classical conditioning procedures: one stimulus (the CS+) is paired with the unconditioned stimulus and another (the CS–) is presented in the absence of the US. With repeated pairings of the CS+ with the US, and presentations of the CS– by itself, conditioned responding comes to be elicited by the CS+ but not by the CS–. (In fact, the CS– might become a conditioned inhibitor.)

Instrumental stimulus discrimination procedures are different from classical conditioning procedures only in that the reinforcer is presented contingent on responding during the S+. Responding is not required for pairings of the CS+ with the US in classical conditioning. Unlike a CS+, an S+ does not signal that the reinforcer will inevitably occur. Rather, the S+ indicates that the instrumental response will be reinforced.

The stimulus discrimination procedure shown in Figure 8.7 is a special case of a **multiple schedule of reinforcement.** In a multiple schedule, different schedules of reinforcement

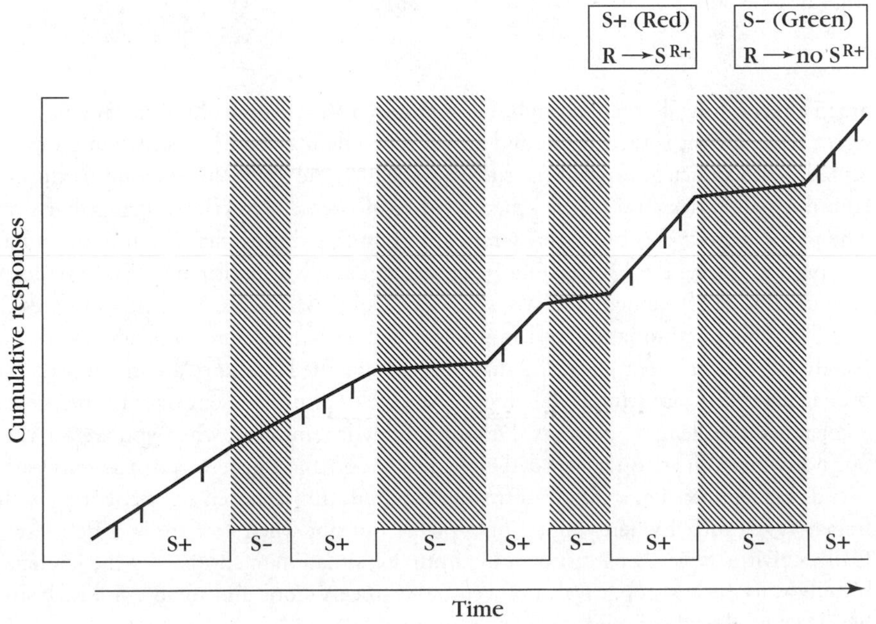

Figure 8.7 Procedure and hypothetical results (presented as a cumulative record) of stimulus discrimination training. Responding is reinforced on a variable interval schedule in the presence of the S+ (a red light) and is not reinforced in the presence of the S– (a green light). Differential responding gradually develops to the two stimuli. (Hatch marks on the cumulative record indicate reinforcements.)

BOX 8.2

STIMULUS CONTROL OF SLEEPING IN CHILDREN

Getting young children to go to sleep in the evening and remain asleep during the night can be difficult. Night wakings by young children can be stressful for parents and have been linked to increased maternal malaise, marital discord, and child abuse. Behavioral approaches to the treatment of night waking have stressed the concepts of stimulus control and extinction.

In the absence of special intervention, a child may wake up at night and cry or call a parent. The parent visits with the child and tries to put him back to sleep either in the child's own bed or in the parent's bed, where the child eventually falls asleep. This scenario may serve to maintain the sleep disturbance in two ways. First, parental attention upon waking may serve to reinforce the child for waking up. Second, special efforts the parent makes to encourage the child to go back to sleep (taking the child into the parent's bed, for example) may introduce special discriminative stimuli for getting back to sleep. In the absence of those cues, getting back to sleep may be especially difficult.

In a study of behavioral treatment of night waking in infants from 8 to 20 months old, France and Hudson (1990) gave parents the following instructions:

> At bedtime, carry out the usual bed-time routine (story, song, etc.). Then place (*child's name*) in bed. Bid him or her "Good night" and immediately leave the room. Do not return unless absolutely necessary. If absolutely necessary, check your child (when illness or danger is suspected), but do so in silence and with a minimum of light." (p. 93)

This procedure was intended to minimize reinforcement of the child for waking up. The procedure was also intended to make the child's own bed in the absence of parental interaction a discriminative stimulus for getting back to sleep should the child wake up at night. With the introduction of these procedures, all seven infants in the study were reported to decrease the number of times they woke up and cried or called for their parents during the night. Before introduction of the procedure, the mean number of nightly awakenings was 3.3. After the treatment procedure, this declined to 0.8. These gains were maintained during follow-up tests conducted 3 months and 2 years later.

are in effect during different stimuli. For example, a VI schedule of reinforcement may be in effect when a light is turned on, and an FR schedule may be in effect when a tone is presented. With sufficient exposure to such a procedure, the pattern of responding during each stimulus will correspond to the schedule of reinforcement in effect during that stimulus. The participants will show a steady rate of responding during the VI stimulus and a stop-run pattern during the FR stimulus. (For a recent study of multiple schedule performance with cocaine reinforcement, see Weiss, Kearns, Cohn, Schindler, & Panlilio, in press.)

Stimulus discrimination and multiple schedules are common outside the laboratory. Nearly all reinforcement schedules that exist outside the laboratory are in effect only in the presence of particular stimuli. Playing a game yields reinforcement only in the presence of enjoyable or challenging partners. Driving rapidly is reinforced when you are on a freeway but not when you are on a crowded city street. Loud and boisterous discussions with your friends are reinforced at a party but frowned upon during a church service. Eating with your fingers is reinforced when you are on a picnic but not when you are in a fine restaurant. Daily activities typically consist of going from one situation to another (to the kitchen to get breakfast, to the bus stop, to your office, to the grocery store, and so on), and each situation has its own schedule of reinforcement.

Effects of Discrimination Training on Stimulus Control

Discrimination training brings the instrumental response under the control of the S+ and S−. How precise is the control that S+ acquires over the instrumental behavior, and what factors determine the precision of the stimulus control that is achieved? To answer these questions, it is not enough to observe differential responding to S+ versus S−. Investigators must also find out how steep the generalization gradient is when the participants are tested with stimuli that systematically vary from the S+. Furthermore, it must be determined which aspect of the discrimination training procedure is responsible for the type of stimulus generalization gradient that is obtained. These issues were first addressed in classic experiments by Jenkins and Harrison (1960, 1962).

Jenkins and Harrison examined how auditory stimuli that differed in pitch came to control the pecking behavior of pigeons reinforced with food. They measured how pigeons responded to tones of various frequencies after three types of training procedures. One group of birds was reinforced for pecking in the presence of a 1,000-cps tone and received no reinforcement when the tone was off. The 1,000-cps tone served as the S+ and the absence of tones served as the S−.

For the second group, the 1,000-cps tone again served as the S+, but the S− was a 950-cps tone. The third group of pigeons served as a control and did not receive discrimination training. The 1,000-cps tone was continuously turned on for these animals, and they could always receive reinforcement for pecking in the experimental chamber.

Upon completion of the three different training procedures, each group was tested for pecking in the presence of tones of various frequencies to see how precisely pecking was controlled by pitch. Figure 8.8 shows the generalization gradients that were obtained. The control group, which had not received discrimination training, responded nearly equally in the presence of all the test stimuli: the pitch of the tones did not control their behavior. Each of the other two training procedures produced more stimulus control by pitch. The steepest generalization gradient, and hence the strongest stimulus control, was observed in birds that had been trained with the 1,000-cps tone as S+ and the 950-cps tone as S−. Pigeons that previously received discrimination training between the 1,000-cps tone (S+) and the absence of tones (S−) showed an intermediate degree of stimulus control by tonal frequency.

The Jenkins and Harrison experiment provided two important principles: (1) discrimination training increases the stimulus control of instrumental behavior, and (2) a particular stimulus dimension (such as tonal frequency) is most likely to gain control over responding if the S+ and S− differ along that stimulus dimension. The most precise control by tonal frequency was observed after discrimination training in which the S+ was a tone of one frequency (1,000 cps) and the S− was a tone of another frequency (950 cps). Discrimination training did not produce as strong control by pitch if the S+ was a 1,000-cps tone and the S− was the absence of tones. The discrimination between the presence and absence of the 1,000-cps tone could have been based on the loudness or timbre of the tone in addition to its frequency. Hence, tonal frequency did not gain as much control in this case. (For further discussion of these and related issues, see Balsam, 1988; Dinsmoor, 1995; Hinson & Cannon, 1999; Hinson, Cannon, & Tennison, 1999.)

Range of Possible Discriminative Stimuli

Discrimination procedures can be used to bring an organism's instrumental behavior under the control of a wide variety of stimuli. D'Amato and Salmon (1982), for example, used two different tunes as discriminative stimuli for rats and monkeys. Porter and Neuringer

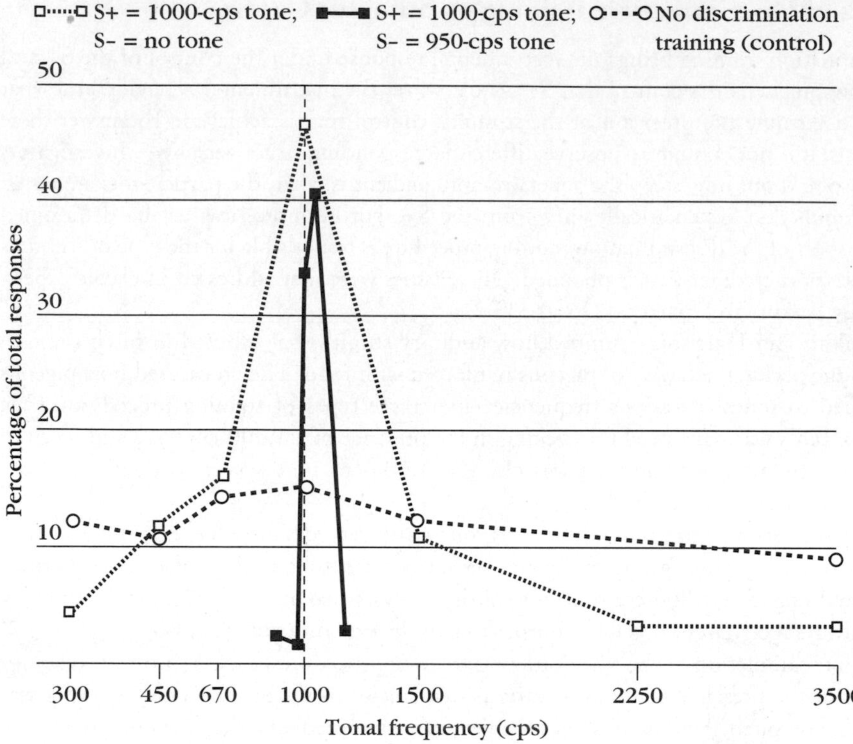

Figure 8.8 Generalization gradients of response to tones of different frequencies after various types of training. One group received discrimination training in which a 1,000-cps tone served as the S+ and the absence of tones served as the S−. Another group received training in which a 1,000-cps tone served as the S+ and a 950-cps tone served as the S−. The control group did not receive discrimination training before the generalization test. (From "Effects of Discrimination Training on Auditory Generalization," by H. M. Jenkins and R. H. Harrison, 1960, *Journal of Experimental Psychology, 59,* pp. 246–253; also from "Generalization Gradients of Inhibition Following Auditory Discrimination Learning," by H. M. Jenkins and R. H. Harrison, 1962, *Journal of Experimental Analysis of Behavior, 5,* pp. 435–441.

(1984) showed that pigeons are able to discriminate music by Bach from music by Stravinsky and generalize this discrimination to music of other composers from the same periods in musical history. In another study, pigeons learned to distinguish color slides of paintings by Monet from paintings of Picasso (Watanabe, Sakamoto, & Wakita, 1995). Discrimination procedures used with laboratory rats and pigeons have also been based on internal cues related to level of hunger (Davidson, Flynn, & Jarrard, 1992), number of stimuli in a visual array (Emmerton, 1998), the relative frequency of events (Keen & Machado, 1999; Machado & Cevik, 1997), time of day (morning versus afternoon; Budzynski & Bingman, 1999), or video images of different pigeons or their actions (Jitsumori, Natori, & Okuyama, 1999).

Discrimination training procedures are often used to evaluate the sensory capacity of animals. Schusterman and his colleagues, for example, have used discrimination training to determine the visual and hearing thresholds of several species of pinniped (sea lions, harbor seals, and elephant seals) (Levenson & Schusterman, 1999; Kastak & Schusterman, 1998). The pinnipeds in these studies were first reinforced (with a piece of fish) for resting the chin on a piece of PVC pipe. This was done so that the head of the subject would be in a standard position at the start of each trial. Trials then consisted of the presentation of a visual or an auditory cue (the S+) or no stimulus (the S–). In the presence of the S+, the subject had to move the head to one side to press on a paddle or ball to obtain a piece of fish. Responses during the S– were not reinforced. After the discrimination was well learned, the intensity of the visual or auditory S+ was systematically varied to obtain estimates of the visual and auditory thresholds of the subject (see also Kastak, Schusterman, Southall, & Reichmuth, 1999).

Investigators have also been interested in studying whether animals can detect the internal sensations created by a drug state. Can a pigeon, for example, tell when it is under the influence of pentobarbital (a sedative), and do other drugs (chlordiazepoxide, alcohol, and methamphetamine, for example) produce sensations similar those of pentobarbital? Discrimination training with drug stimuli and tests of stimulus generalization can provide answers to such questions (for recent examples, see McMillan & Li, 1999, 2000; McMillan, Li, & Hardwick, 1997; Snodgrass & McMillan, 1996; Zarcone & Ator, 2000).

This research has shown that the mechanisms of stimulus control by drug stimuli are remarkably similar to the mechanisms identified by Jenkins and Harrison (1960, 1962) for the control of key pecking by visual cues in pigeons.

Schaal and his colleagues, for example, compared the extent of stimulus control by drug stimuli before and after discrimination training (Schaal, McDonald, Miller, & Reilly, 1996). Pigeons were reinforced for pecking a response key on a variable interval 2-minute schedule of reinforcement. In the first phase of the experiment (no discrimination training), the birds were injected with 3.0 mg/kg cocaine before each session. After responding stabilized, generalization tests were periodically interspersed between training sessions. During these tests, the subjects received no drug (saline) or various doses of cocaine ranging from 0.3 to 5.6 mg/kg. (Responding was not reinforced during the test sessions.) The results obtained with one of the birds (P1) are presented in the left panel of Figure 8.9. Notice that the generalization gradient as a function of drug dose is fairly flat, indicative of weak stimulus control.

Figure 8.9 Responding as a function of cocaine dose for a pigeon before (left panel) and after (right panel) discrimination training in which 3.0 mg/kg of cocaine was present during S+ sessions and a saline injection (no drug) was given prior to S– sessions. (After Schaal et al., 1996.)

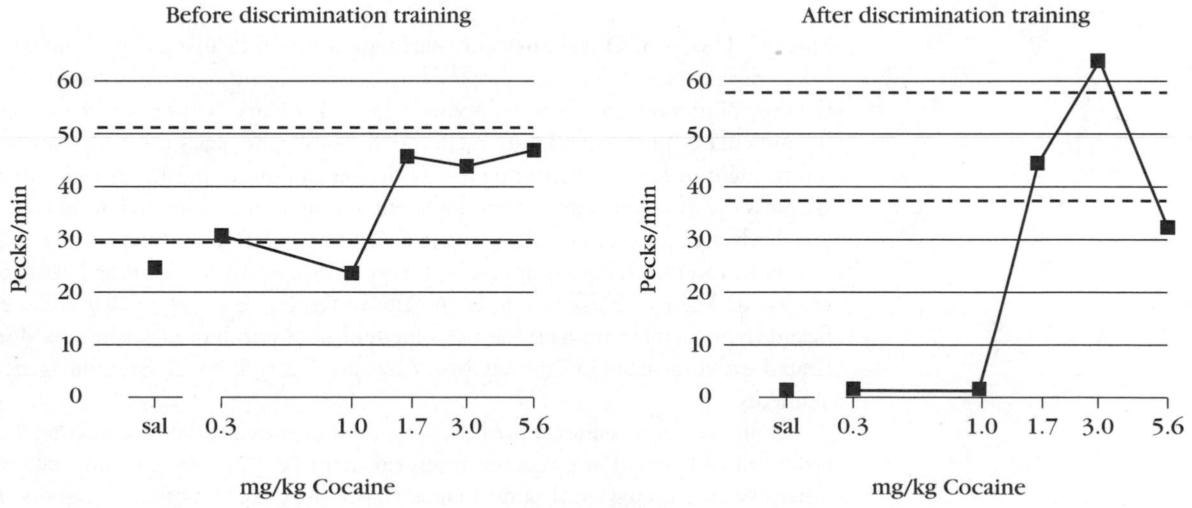

During the next phase of the experiment, a discrimination procedure was introduced. During this phase, some sessions were preceded with an injection of cocaine as before, and pecking was reinforced. In addition, the subjects received sessions without the drug during which pecking was not reinforced. Thus, cocaine in the bird's system served as the S+. The subjects learned the discrimination, responding strongly during S+ sessions and much less during S- sessions. Once the discrimination was established, generalization tests were conducted as before. The results of those tests are shown in the right panel of Figure 8.9. Notice that now the generalization gradient was much steeper, indicating much stronger control by the drug stimuli. The greatest level of responding occurred when the pigeon was tested with the 3.0 mg/kg of cocaine that had been used during reinforced sessions. Virtually no responding occurred during sessions with no drug or with just 0.3 or 1.0 mg/kg of cocaine. Interestingly, responding also declined a bit when the test dose was 5.6 mg/kg, which exceeded the training dose. Thus, as was the case with stimulus control of behavior by tonal frequency (Figure 8.8), discrimination training increased stimulus control by the internal sensations created by cocaine.

The fact that stimulus discrimination procedures can be used to bring behavior under the control of a wide variety of stimuli makes these procedures powerful tools for the investigation of how animals process information. Some impressive results of this research are presented in discussions of animal cognition in Chapters 11 and 12.

What Is Learned in Discrimination Training?

Investigators have been interested in what is learned during discrimination training because of the profound effect it has on stimulus control. Consider the following relatively simple situation: Responses are reinforced whenever a red light is turned on (S+) and not reinforced whenever a loud tone is presented (S–). What strategies could a subject use to make sure that most of its responses were reinforced in this situation? One possibility is to learn to respond whenever the S+ is present and not learn anything about the S–. If an organism adopted this strategy, it would end up responding much more to S+ than to S– and could obtain all of the available reinforcers. Another possibility is to learn to suppress responding during S– but not learn anything about S+. This would constitute following the rule, "Suppress responding only when S– is present." This strategy would also lead to more responding during S+ than during S–. A third possibility is to learn the significance of both S+ and S–, to learn both to respond to S+ and to suppress responding to S–.

Spence's Theory of Discrimination Learning. One of the first and most influential theories of discrimination learning, proposed by Kenneth Spence (1936), is based on the last of the possibilities described above. According to this theory, reinforcement of a response in the presence of the S+ conditions excitatory response tendencies to S+. By contrast, nonreinforcement of responding during S– conditions inhibitory properties to S– that serve to suppress the instrumental behavior. Differential responding to S+ and S– is assumed to reflect both the excitation of responding to S+ and the inhibition of responding to S–.

How can the excitation-inhibition theory of discrimination learning be experimentally evaluated? The mere observation that organisms respond more to S+ than to S– is not sufficient to prove that they have learned something about both of these stimuli. More sophisticated experimental tests are required. One possibility is to use stimulus generalization gradients.

If an excitatory tendency has become conditioned to S+, then stimuli that increasingly differ from S+ should be progressively less effective in evoking the instrumental response. In other words, a steep generalization gradient, with the greatest amount of responding occurring to S+ should be observed. Such an outcome is called an **excitatory stimulus generalization gradient.** Conversely, if an inhibitory tendency has become conditioned to S–, then stimuli that increasingly differ from S– should be progressively less effective in inhibiting the instrumental response. Such an outcome is called an **inhibitory stimulus generalization gradient.**

When Spence proposed his theory, behavioral techniques were not sufficiently sophisticated to allow direct observation of the excitatory and inhibitory generalization gradients assumed in his theory. Experimental tests conducted decades later, however, proved that his ideas were substantially correct. In a landmark experiment, two groups of pigeons received discrimination training with visual stimuli before tests of stimulus generalization (Honig, Boneau, Burstein, & Pennypacker, 1963). One group was reinforced for pecking when the response key was illuminated by a white light that had a black vertical bar superimposed on it (S+) and was not reinforced when the white light was presented without the vertical bar (S–). The second group of animals received the same type of discrimination training, but with the S+ and S– stimuli reversed—the black vertical bar served as the S–, and the white key without the bar served as the S+. After both groups had learned to respond much more to S+ than to S–, tests of stimulus generalization were conducted to see how much control the vertical bar had gained over the instrumental behavior in the two groups. The test stimuli consisted of the black bar on a white background, with the bar tilted at various angles away from the vertical position during the test trials.

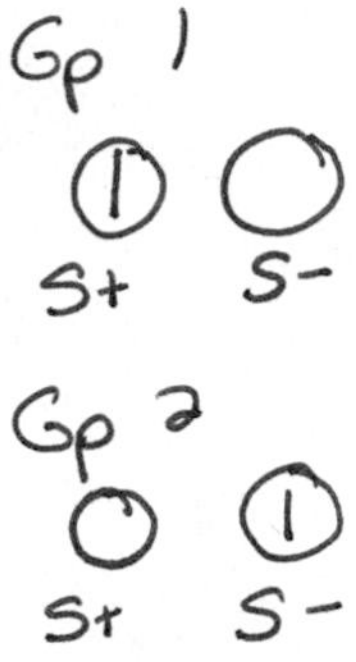

The results of the experiment are summarized in Figure 8.10. First, consider the outcome for Group 1, which received the vertical bar as the S+ during discrimination training. These birds came to respond in the presence of the vertical bar. During the generalization test, the highest rate of responding occurred when the bar was presented in the original

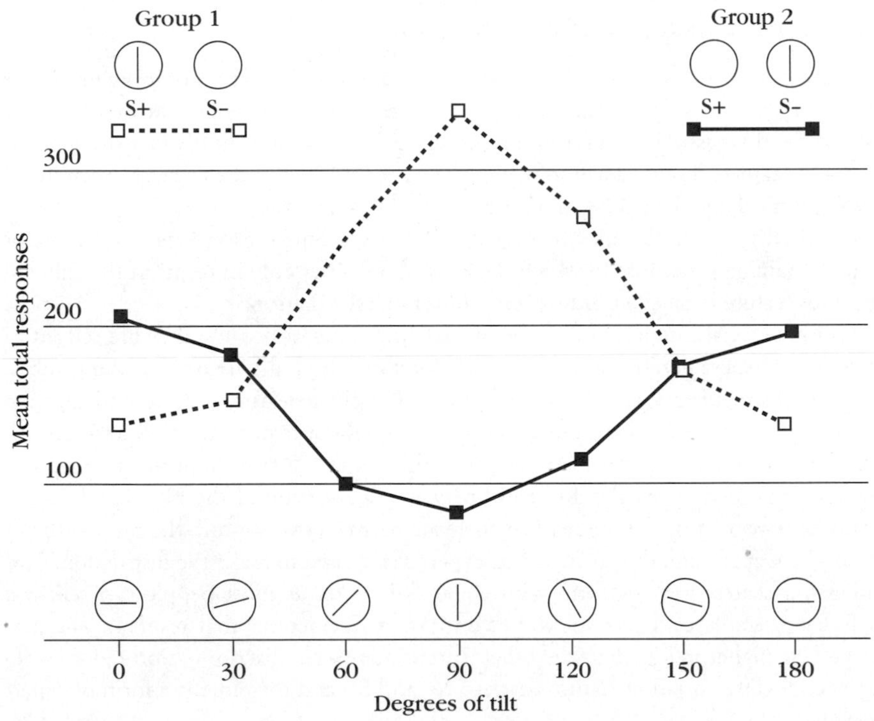

Figure 8.10 Stimulus generalization gradients for line-tilt stimuli in two groups of pigeons after discrimination training. For Group1, a vertical black bar on a white background served as the S+, and the white light without the bar served as the S–. For Group 2, the functions of the stimuli were reversed. (From "Positive and Negative Generalization Gradients Obtained Under Equivalent Training Conditions," by W. K. Honig, C. A. Boneau, K. R. Burstein, and H. S. Pennypacker, 1963, *Journal of Comparative and Physiological Psychology,* 56, p. 111–116.)

vertical position, and progressively less responding was observed when the bar was tilted more and more away from the vertical. These results illustrate an excitatory stimulus generalization gradient around S+.

Group 2, which received the vertical bar as the S– during discrimination training, did not peck when the vertical bar was projected on the response key. Results of the generalization test indicated that this failure to respond to the vertical bar was due to active inhibition of the pecking behavior in response to the position of the vertical bar. As the bar was tilted away from the original vertical position, progressively more pecking occurred. Stimuli that were increasingly different from the original S– produced progressively less inhibition of the pecking behavior, illustrating an inhibitory stimulus generalization gradient.

This experiment shows that discrimination training can produce both excitatory conditioning to S+ and inhibitory conditioning to S–. The excitatory gradient had an inverted-U shape, with greatest responding occurring to the original S+. The inhibitory gradient had the opposite shape, with the least responding occurring to the original S–. The fact that gradients of excitation and inhibition can occur around S+ and S– provides strong support for Spence's theory of discrimination learning.

The choice of the stimuli that served as S+ and S– was very important for the success of this experiment. Consider, for example, Group 2, which received the vertical bar on a white background as the S– and the white background without a bar as the S+. Responding in the inhibitory generalization gradient increased as the bar was tilted away from vertical. This outcome cannot be explained by claiming that tilting the black bar made the test stimuli more similar to the S+. Changing the orientation of the black bar does not make a bar more or less similar to the white background that served as the S+. The bar stimuli are qualitatively different from the background alone. As I point out in the following section, different results occur if the S+ and S– stimuli differ quantitatively in one feature rather than qualitatively (involving many features).

Interactions between S+ and S–: Peak Shift

So far I have described general characteristics of stimulus discrimination training under the assumption that what subjects learn about S+ is pretty much independent of what they learn about S–. This assumption is too simplistic. Learning is not so neatly compartmentalized. What is learned about S+ can influence the response to S– and vice versa. Such interactions are particularly likely if S+ and S– are related in some way.

One way that S+ and S– may be related is if they are similar except for one feature or attribute. A training procedure in which the S+ and S– differ only in terms of the value of one stimulus feature is called an **intradimensional discrimination.**

Intradimensional discriminations are of particular interest because they are related to the problem of expert performance. Expert performance typically involves making subtle distinctions. Distinguishing stimuli that differ only in a single feature is more difficult than distinguishing stimuli that differ in many respects. It does not require much expertise to tell the difference between a compact car and a bus. In contrast, a fairly sophisticated knowledge of cars is needed to tell the difference between one version of the Honda Civic and another. The fewer distinguishing features there are between two stimuli, the more difficult it is to tell them apart, and the greater is the expertise required to make the distinction. Two championship skaters may perform with equal skill as far as most people can tell, but expert judges are able to detect subtle but important distinctions that result in one performer getting higher marks than the other. Intradimensional discrimination requires detecting a single differentiating feature between S+ and S– and therefore is a form of expert performance.

An important characteristic of intradimensional discriminations is that sometimes they result in an interesting interaction between S+ and S– performance. This was illustrated by Hanson (1959) in a landmark experiment that examined the effects of intradimensional discrimination training on the extent to which various colors controlled the pecking behavior of pigeons. All the participants in the experiment were reinforced for pecking in the presence of a light whose wavelength was 550 nm. Thus, the S+ was the same for all of the subjects. The groups differed in how similar the S– was to the S+ (how expert the pigeons had to become in telling the colors apart). One group received discrimination training in which the S– was a color of 590-nm wavelength, 40 nm away from the S+. For another group, the wavelength of the S– was 555 nm, only 5 nm away from the S+. The performance of these pigeons was compared with the behavior of a control group that did not receive discrimination training but was also reinforced for pecking in the presence of the 550-nm stimulus.

After their different training experiences, all of the birds were tested for their rate of pecking in the presence of stimuli of various colors. The results are shown in Figure 8.11. The control group showed the highest rates of response to the S+ stimulus, and progressively lower rates of responding occurred as the pigeons were tested with stimuli increasingly different from the S+. Thus, the control group showed the usual excitatory stimulus generalization gradient centered around the S+.

Different results were obtained after discrimination training with the 590-nm color as S–. These pigeons also responded at high rates to the 550-nm color that had served as the S+, but they showed much more generalization of the pecking response to the 540-nm color. Their rate of response was slightly higher to the 540-nm color than to the original 550-nm S+. This shift of the peak responding away from the original S+ was even more dramatic after discrimination training with the 555-nm color as S–. These birds showed much lower rates of responding to the original S+ (550 nm) than either of the other two groups. Furthermore, their highest response rates occurred to colors of 540- and 530-nm wavelength. This shift of the peak of the generalization gradient away from the original S+ is remarkable because in the earlier phase of discrimination training, responding was never reinforced in the presence of the 540-nm or the 530-nm stimuli. Thus, the highest rates of pecking occurred to stimuli that had never been presented during original training.

The shift of the peak of the generalization gradient away from the original S+ is called the **peak-shift** phenomenon. The peak-shift effect is a result of intradimensional discrimination training. A peak shift did not occur in the control group, which had not received discrimination training. The peak-shift effect was a function of the similarity of the S– to the S+ used in discrimination training. The biggest peak shift occurred after training in which the S– was very similar to the S+ (555 nm and 550 nm, respectively). Less peak shift occurred after discrimination training with more widely different colors (590 nm compared with 550 nm). It is interesting to note that a small peak-shift effect is also evident in Figure 8.8 for pigeons that received discrimination training with the 1,000-cps tone as S+ and the 950-cps tone as S–.

The peak-shift effect can result from any intradimensional discrimination, not just pitch and color. The S+ and S– may be lines of different orientations, tones of different loudness, squares of different size, or different positions on a computer screen (see Cheng, Spetch, & Johnson, 1997; Dougherty & Lewis, 1991; Moye & Thomas, 1982; Weiss & Schindler, 1981; Weiss & Weissman, 1992; Wills & Mackintosh, 1998).

Spence's Explanation of Peak Shift. The peak-shift effect is remarkable because it shows that the only stimulus in whose presence responding is reinforced (the S+) is not necessarily the stimulus that evokes the highest response rate. How can this be? Excitatory stimulus generalization gradients are supposed to peak at the S+. Can the peak shift effect be explained in terms of standard excitatory and inhibitory gradients such as those shown in Figure 8.10? In an ingenious analysis, Spence (1937) suggested that excitatory and inhibitory gradients may produce the peak-shift phenomenon. His analysis is particularly remarkable because it was proposed more than 20 years before the peak-shift effect and gradients of excitation and inhibition were experimentally demonstrated.

Spence assumed that intradimensional discrimination training produces excitatory and inhibitory stimulus generalization gradients centered at S+ and S−, respectively, in the usual fashion. However, because the S+ and S− are similar in intradimensional discrimination tasks (both being colors, for example), the generalization gradients of excitation and inhibition will overlap. Furthermore, the degree of overlap will depend on the degree of similarity between S+ and S−. Because of this overlap, generalized inhibition from S− will suppress responding to S+, resulting in a peak-shift effect. More inhibition from S− to S+ will occur if S− is closer to S+, and this will result in a greater peak-shift effect, just as Hanson (1959) found (see Figure 8.11). (For other evidence in support of Spence's theory, see Hearst, 1968, 1969; Klein & Rilling, 1974; Marsh, 1972).

Courtesy of Donald A. Dewsbury

M. E. Rilling

Alternative Accounts of Peak Shift. As I noted earlier, studies of stimulus control can reveal a great deal about how human and nonhuman animals view the world. An important question that has been a source of debate for decades is whether we view stimuli in terms of their individual and absolute properties or in terms of their relation to other stimuli that we experience (for example, Köhler, 1939). Evidence consistent with each of these approaches to the analysis of stimulus control is available, suggesting that both types of mechanisms are involved in how organisms respond (for example, Hulse, Page, & Braaten, 1990).

Spence's model of discrimination learning is an absolute stimulus learning model. It predicts behavior based on the net excitatory properties of individual stimuli. An alternative approach assumes that organisms learn to respond to a stimulus based on the relation of that stimulus to other cues in the situation. An interesting prediction of this approach is

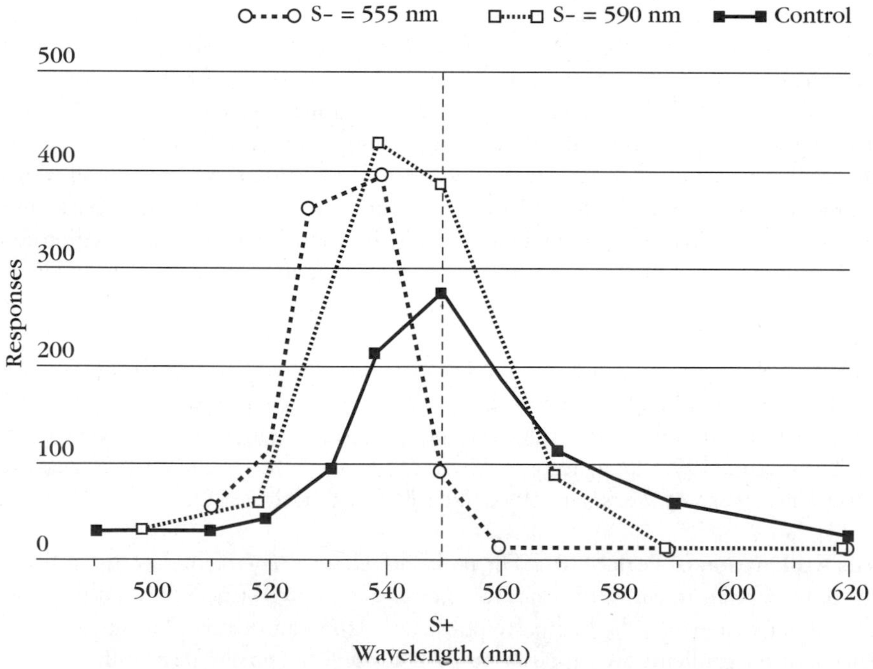

Figure 8.11 Effects of intradimensional discrimination training on stimulus control. All three groups of pigeons were reinforced for pecking in the presence of a 550-nm light (S+). One group received discrimination training in which the S– was a 590-nm light. For another group, the S– was a 555-nm light. The third group served as a control and did not receive discrimination training before the test for stimulus generalization. (From "Effects of Discrimination Training on Stimulus Generalization," by H. M. Hanson, 1959, *Journal of Experimental Psychology, 58,* pp. 321–333.)

that the shape of a generalization gradient will change as a function of the range of test stimuli that are presented during the generalization test session. These and other predictions of the relational approach have been confirmed in studies with human participants (see Thomas, 1993).

Stimulus Equivalence Training

The peak-shift effect is a curious and counterintuitive outcome of intradimensional discrimination training. However, as the studies of Jenkins and Harrison showed (see Figure 8.8), even with this effect, discrimination training dramatically increases the stimulus control of behavior. It limits the generalization of behavior from S+ to other cues and increases the steepness of generalization gradients. This raises questions: Are there learning procedures that have the opposite effect? Are there learning procedures that increase stimulus generalization? How might we construct such procedures?

In a discrimination procedure, stimuli are treated differently—they have different consequences. One stimulus is associated with reinforcement, whereas the other is not. The differential treatment or significance of the stimuli leads organisms to respond to them as distinct from each other. What would happen if two stimuli were treated in the same or equivalent fashion? Would such a procedure lead organisms to respond to the stimuli as similar or equivalent? The answer seems to be yes. Just as discrimination training encourages differential responding, equivalence training encourages generalized responding or **stimulus equivalence.**

Several approaches are available to promote generalization rather than discrimination among stimuli. In Chapter 12, I describe research on perceptual concept learning that involves learning to treat various physically different instances of a perceptual concept in the same manner. For example, pigeons can be trained to respond in a similar fashion to different photographs, all of which include water in some form (ocean, lake, puddle, stream) (Herrnstein, Loveland, & Cable, 1976). The basic training strategy is to reinforce the same response (pecking a response key) in the presence of various pictures containing water, and to not reinforce that response when photographs without water appear. Herrnstein et al. trained such a discrimination using 500–700 photographs of various scenes in New England. Once the pigeons learned the water/no-water discrimination, their behavior generalized to novel photographs that had not been presented during training. (For additional discussion of perceptual concept learning, see Chapter 12.)

Investigators have also explored the possibility that functional equivalence between two different stimuli might be established by linking each of the distinct cues with a common third stimulus (Saunders & Green, 1999; Zentall, 1998; Zentall & Smeets, 1996). In an experiment by Honey and Hall (1989), for example, rats first received presentations of two different auditory cues, a noise and a clicker. For one group of animals, both the noise and the clicker were paired with food. The common food outcome was expected to create functional equivalence between the noise and the clicker stimuli. The control group also received presentations of the noise and the clicker, but for that group only the clicker was paired with food. Both groups then had the noise paired with mild footshock, resulting in the conditioning of fear to the noise. The investigators were interested in the extent to which this conditioned fear of the noise would generalize to the clicker. Significantly more generalization occurred in the equivalence-trained animals than in the control group. The equivalence-trained animals were more apt to treat the clicker and the noise similarly than was the control group. (For additional research along these lines, see Bonardi, Rey, Richmond, & Hall, 1993; Hall, 1991; Hall, Ray, & Bonardi, 1993; Honey & Hall, 1991; Honey & Watt, 1998, 1999; Ward-Robinson & Hall, 1999.)

Pairing different stimuli with the same outcome creates *functional equivalence* among those stimuli, with the consequence that a response conditioned to one of the stimuli generalizes to the others. A more formal definition of *equivalence class* has been proposed by Sidman and his colleagues (Sidman, 1990, 1994, 2000; Sidman & Tailby, 1982; see also Tierney & Bracken, 1998). An equivalence class is said to exist if its members possess three mathematical properties: (1) reflexivity or sameness, (2) symmetry, and (3) transitivity. Consider, for example, an equivalence class consisting of the three stimuli A, B, and C. *Reflexivity* or sameness refers to the relation A=A, B=B, and C=C. *Symmetry* is said to exist if a relationship is bidirectional. For example, if A leads to B (A→B), then symmetry requires that B leads to A (B→A). Finally, *transitivity* refers to the integration of two relationships into a third one. For example, given the relations A→B and B→C, transitivity requires that A→C.

The concept of equivalence class has been particularly important in analyses of language. The word *apple,* for example, derives its meaning from the fact that the word is in an equivalence class that includes other items that we call "apple," such as an actual apple and a photograph or drawing of an apple. These physically different objects have the property of reflexivity (apple = apple). They also have the property of symmetry. If you learned to say the word apple when you saw a picture of one, you will be able to pick out the picture if asked to identify what the word apple signifies. Finally, these items exhibit transitivity. If you learned that the word refers to the picture (A→B), and the picture refers to the physical apple object (B→C), you will be able to identify the object when given the word (A→C).

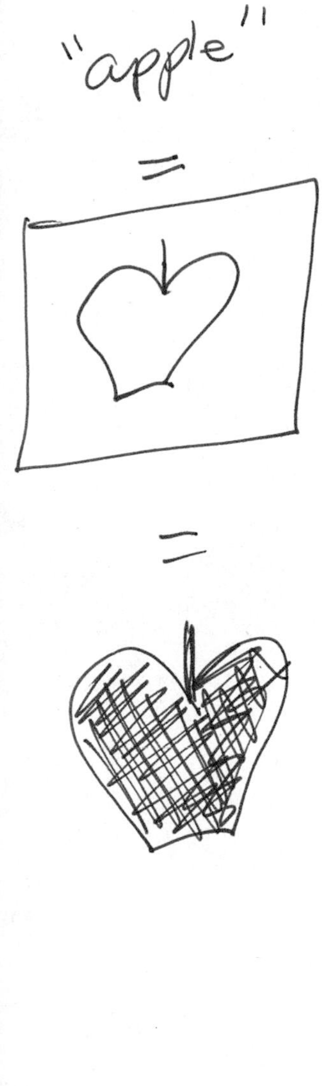

In general, individuals with good verbal skills learn equivalence classes more easily than those with poor verbal skills. This has encouraged some investigators to suggest that verbal skill and the formation of equivalence classes are integrally related (see Horne & Lowe, 1996, 1997, and related commentary). Consistent with this view, Zentall (1998) concluded that the "evidence for the emergence of the component relations presumed to underlie stimulus equivalence in [nonhuman] animals has not been overwhelming. Nor has there been extensive evidence for equivalence (as defined by Sidman, 1990) in animals" (p. 373). (See also Dugdale & Lowe, 2000.) The ability to use verbal labels facilitates equivalence class formation (for example, Randell & Remington, 1999). However, the ability to name stimuli and objects may not be essential for the acquisition of stimulus equivalence (Carr & Blackman, 2001; Carr, Wilkinson, Blackman, & McIlvane, 2000). Given the potential of equivalence classes to produce emergent stimulus relations that need not be specifically trained (such as symmetry and transitivity), this promises to be an exciting area for continued research.

CONTEXTUAL CUES AND CONDITIONAL RELATIONS

So far I have been discussing the control of behavior by discrete stimuli, such as a tone or a light, presented individually or in combination with one another. A stimulus is said to be *discrete* if it is presented for a brief period and has a clear beginning and end. Although studies with discrete stimuli have provided much information about the stimulus control of instrumental behavior, such studies do not tell the whole story. A more comprehensive analysis of the stimuli organisms experience during the course of instrumental conditioning indicates that discrete discriminative stimuli occur in the presence of background contextual cues. The contextual cues may be visual, auditory, or olfactory cues of the room or place where the discrete discriminative stimuli are presented. Recent research indicates that contextual cues can provide an important additional source of control of learned behavior.

Control by Contextual Cues

Several examples of stimulus control described at the beginning of this chapter involved the control of behavior by contextual cues. It is easier to concentrate on studying in the school library than at home during holidays because of contextual control of studying behavior by stimuli experienced in the library. Cheering at a football game but not during a church sermon also illustrates the power of contextual cues.

Contextual cues can come to control behavior in a variety of ways (see Balsam, 1985; Balsam & Tomie, 1985). In a study of sexual conditioning, for example, Akins (1998, Experiment 1) used contextual cues as a signal for sexual reinforcement, in much the same way that discrete stimuli might be used. Male domesticated quail served as subjects, and the apparatus consisted of two large compartments that were distinctively different. One compartment had sand on the floor, and the walls and ceiling were colored orange. The other compartment had a wire-mesh floor and green walls and ceiling. Before the start of the conditioning trials, the subjects were allowed to move back and forth between the two compartments during a 10-minute preference test to determine their baseline preference. The nonpreferred compartment was then designated as the CS. Conditioning trials consisted of placing the male subject in its CS context for 5 minutes, at which point a sexually receptive female was placed with them for another 5 minutes. Thus, these subjects received exposure to the CS context paired with the sexual US. Subjects in a control group received access to a female in their home cages 2 hours before being exposed to the CS context. Thus, the CS and US were unpaired for the control subjects.

In addition to the preference test conducted before the start of conditioning, tests were conducted after the 5th and 10th conditioning trials. The results of these tests are presented in Figure 8.12. Notice that the Paired and Unpaired groups showed similar low preferences for the CS compartment at the outset of the experiment. This low preference persisted in the control group. In contrast, subjects that received the CS context paired with sexual reinforcement came to prefer that context. Thus, the association of contextual cues with sexual reinforcement increased preference for those cues.

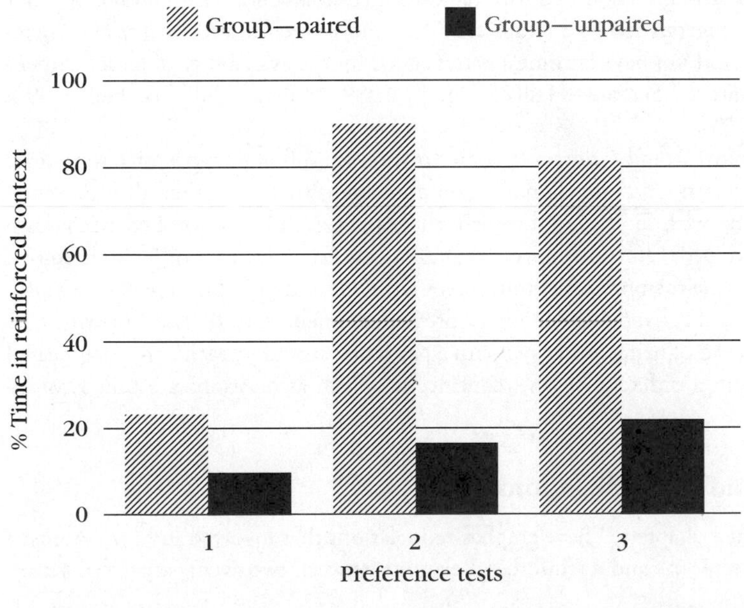

Figure 8.12 Development of a preference for a distinctive context paired (or unpaired) with sexual reinforcement in male domesticated quail. Five conditioning trials were conducted between successive tests for the subjects in the Paired group. (From Figure 1, p. 419, C. K. Akins in *Animal Learning & Behavior,* Vol. 26. Copyright 1998 Psychonomic Society, Inc. Reprinted with permission.)

Experiments like the one by Akins illustrate that contextual cues can come to control behavior if they serve as a signal for a US or a reinforcer. Do contextual cues come to control behavior when they do not signal reinforcement—when they are truly "background" stimuli that the organism is not specifically required to pay attention to? This is a major issue in the stimulus control of instrumental behavior. Much work has been devoted to it, and the answer is clearly yes.

In one experiment, for example, Thomas, McKelvie, and Mah (1985) first trained pigeons on a line-orientation discrimination in which a vertical line (90°) served as the S+ and a horizontal line (0°) served as the S–. The pigeons were periodically reinforced with food for pecking on S+ trials and were not reinforced on S– trials. The training took place in a standard Skinner box (Context 1), but the availability of reinforcement was signaled by the line-orientation S+ and S– stimuli rather than by contextual cues.

After the discrimination was well learned, the contextual cues of the experimental chamber were changed by altering both the lighting and the type of noise in the chamber. In the presence of these new contextual cues (Context 2), the discrimination training contingencies were reversed. Now, the horizontal line (0°) served as the S+ and the vertical line (90°) served as the S–. Notice that the pigeons were not specifically required to pay attention to the contextual cues. They were only required to learn a new discrimination problem. (They could have learned this new problem had the contextual cues not been changed.)

After mastery of the reversal problem, the birds received generalization tests in which lines of various orientations between 0° and 90° were presented. One such generalization test was conducted in Context 1, and another was conducted in Context 2. The results of these tests are presented in Figure 8.13. Remarkably, the shape of the generalization gradient in each context was appropriate to the discrimination problem that was in effect in that context. Thus, in Context 1, the birds responded most to the 90° stimulus, which had served as the S+ in that context, and least to the 0° stimulus, which had served as the S–. The opposite pattern of results occurred in Context 2. Here, the pigeons responded most to the 0° stimulus and least to the 90° stimulus, appropriate to the reverse discrimination contingencies that had been in effect in Context 2.

These results clearly illustrate that contextual cues can come to control instrumental behavior. The results also illustrate that contextual stimulus control can occur without one context being more strongly associated with reinforcement than another. In both Context 1 and Context 2, the pigeons received reinforced (S+) and nonreinforced (S–) trials. Therefore, one context could not have become a better signal for the availability of reinforcement than the other context. (See also Hall & Honey, 1989; Honey, Willis, & Hall, 1990; Swartzentruber, 1993.)

How did Context 1 and Context 2 come to produce different types of responding? Since one context was not a better signal for reinforcement than the other, direct associations of each context with food cannot explain the results. A different kind of mechanism must have been involved. One possibility is that each context activated a different memory. Context 1 activated the memory of reinforcement with 90° and nonreinforcement with 0°. In contrast, Context 2 activated the memory of reinforcement with 0° and nonreinforcement with 90°. Instead of being associated with a particular stimulus, each context appeared to be associated with a different S+ /S– contingency. Such associations are called conditional relations.

Control by Conditional Relations

In many of the earlier chapters, I have emphasized relations that involved just two events: a CS and a US, or a response and a reinforcer. Relations between two events are called *binary*

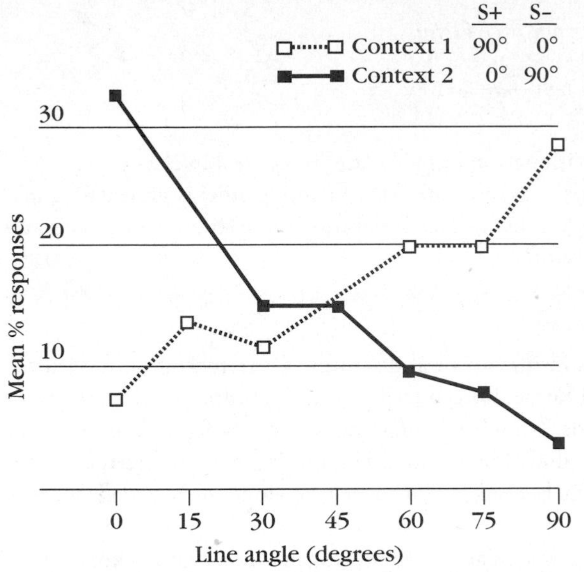

Figure 8.13 Generalization gradients obtained with various line-angle stimuli following training in two different contexts. In Context 1, the 90° stimulus served as the S+ and the 0° stimulus served as the S–. In Context 2, the 0° stimulus served as the S+ and the 90° stimulus served as the S–. (From "Context as a Conditional Cue in Operant Discrimination Reversal Learning," by D. R. Thomas, A. R. McKelvie, & W. L. Mah, 1985, *Journal of Experimental Psychology: Animal Behavior Processes, 11,* pp. 317–330. Copyright © 1985 by the American Psychological Association. Reprinted by permission.)

relations. Under certain circumstances, the nature of a binary relation is determined by a third event, called a **modulator.** In the experiment by Thomas et al. (1985), each context was a modulator. Whether a particular line-angle stimulus was associated with reinforcement depended on which contextual cues were present. The relation of a modulator to the binary relation that it signals is called a **conditional relation.** Numerous experiments have indicated that animals can learn to use modulators to tell when a particular binary relation is in effect (see reviews by Holland, 1984, 1992; Schmajuk & Holland, 1998; Swartzentruber, 1995).

I have already described some conditional relations without having identified them as such. One example is instrumental stimulus discrimination training, a procedure in which the organism is reinforced for responding during S+ but is not reinforced during S–. The discriminative stimuli S+ and S– are modulators that signal the relation between the response and the reinforcer. One response-reinforcer relation exists during S+ (positive reinforcement), and a different relation exists during S– (nonreinforcement). Thus, instrumental discrimination procedures involve conditional control of the relation between the response and the reinforcer (Davidson, Aparicio, & Rescorla, 1988; Goodall & Mackintosh, 1987; Holman & Mackintosh, 1981; Jenkins, 1977; Skinner, 1938).

Conditional Control in Pavlovian Conditioning. Conditional relations have been extensively investigated using Pavlovian conditioning procedures. The fundamental concept of conditional control is that one event signals the relation between two other events. Classical conditioning is typically conceived as involving a binary relation between a conditioned and an unconditioned stimulus. The CS may be brief illumination of a localized response key with an orange light, and the US may be food. A strong relation exists between the CS and the US if food is presented immediately after each occurrence of the CS but not at other times. How could conditional control be established over such a CS-US relation?

Establishing a conditional relation requires introducing a third event (the modulator) that indicates when presentation of the key light will end in food. For example, a noise stimulus could be introduced, in the presence of which the key light would be followed by food. In the absence of the noise stimulus, the key light would not end with food. This procedure

Reinforced trials	*Nonreinforced trials*
Noise	No noise
Key light → food	Key light → no food

Figure 8.14 Procedure for establishing conditional stimulus control in classical conditioning. On reinforced trials, a noise stimulus (the modulator) is presented, and a key-light CS is paired with food. On nonreinforced trials, the noise stimulus is absent, and the key-light CS is presented without food.

is diagrammed in Figure 8.14. As in instrumental discrimination procedures, the participants receive both reinforced and nonreinforced trials. During reinforced trials, the noise stimulus is turned on for 15 seconds. Ten seconds later, the orange key-light CS is turned on for 5 seconds and is immediately followed by the food US. During nonreinforced trials, the noise stimulus is not presented. The key-light CS is turned on alone for 5 seconds without the food US.

The procedure I just described is similar to one investigated in a sign tracking experiment with pigeons by Rescorla, Durlach, and Grau (1985). A noise stimulus was used as the modulator on reinforced trials for half the pigeons. For the rest of the birds, a diffuse flashing light was used in place of the noise. The measured conditioned response was pecking the response key when it was illuminated with the orange key-light CS. Since pecking is not elicited by diffuse auditory or visual stimuli, the key-peck behavior could be interpreted as a response only to the orange key-light CS.

The results of the experiment are illustrated in Figure 8.15. The birds pecked the orange key much more when it was presented after presentation of the modulator than when it was presented as an isolated element. Thus, the presence of the modulator facilitated responding to the key-light CS. It is important to keep in mind that the modulator itself did not elicit pecking, because pigeons do not peck in response to diffuse auditory and visual stimuli. Rather, the modulator increased the ability of the orange key-light CS to elicit pecking. The diffuse modulator gained conditional control over the effectiveness of the key-light CS in eliciting the conditioned response. Just as a discriminative stimulus facilitates instrumental behavior, the modulator facilitated CS-elicited responding in the present study. (See also Boakes, Westbrook, Elliott, & Swinbourne, 1997; Parker, Serdikoff, Kaminski, & Critchfield, 1991.)

In instrumental discrimination procedures, modulators (S+ and S–) are called "discriminative stimuli." In Pavlovian conditioning, some investigators have called conditional control of responding **facilitation** because the modulator facilitates responding to the CS (Rescorla, 1985; Rescorla et al., 1985). In this terminology, the modulator is called a *facilitator.* More commonly, conditional control in classical conditioning is called **occasion setting** because the modulator sets the occasion for pairings of the CS with the US (Holland, 1985; Ross, 1983; Ross & Holland, 1981). In this terminology, the modulator is called an *occasion setter.*

Note that the procedure outlined in Figure 8.14 is the converse of the standard procedure for inhibitory conditioning (see Figure 3.10). To turn the procedure outlined in Figure 8.14 into one that will result in the conditioning of inhibitory properties to the noise, all the investigator has to do is to reverse the type of trial on which the noise is presented. Instead of being presented on reinforced trials, the noise would be presented on nonreinforced trials.

As I noted in Chapter 3, conditioned inhibition develops if a stimulus signals the absence of the US that is otherwise expected to occur. Presenting the noise stimulus on non-

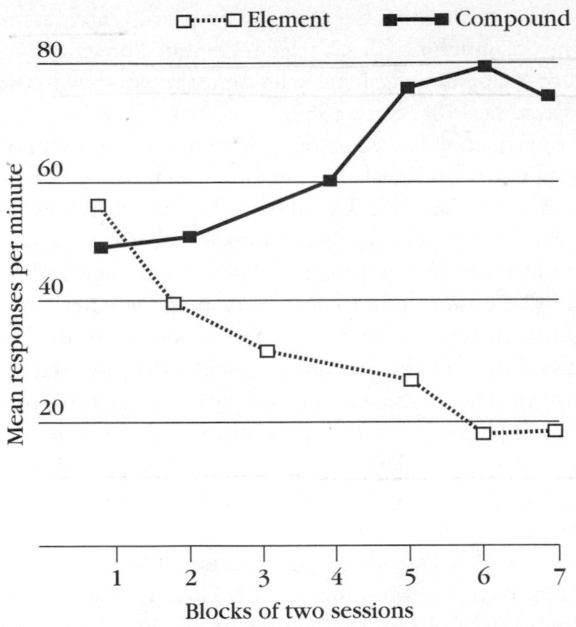

Figure 8.15 Acquisition of pecking to an orange key light in a study of conditional stimulus control of Pavlovian conditioned key pecking in pigeons. An orange key-light CS was paired with food in the presence of a modulator (compound trials) and was presented without food in the absence of the modulator (element trials). (From "Contextual Learning in Pavlovian Conditioning" by R. A. Rescorla, P. J. Durlach, & J. W. Grau. In P. Balsam & A. Tomie [Eds.], *Context and Learning.* Copyright © 1985, Lawrence Erlbaum and Associates. Reprinted by permission.)

reinforced trials would make the noise a signal for nonreinforcement of the key light, and would make the noise a conditioned inhibitor. This illustrates that the procedure for inhibitory Pavlovian conditioning involves a conditional relation, just as positive occasion setting and facilitation procedures do. This argument also suggests that conditioned inhibition may be the conceptual opposite of facilitation or occasion setting rather than the opposite of conditioned excitation. In certain circumstances, this indeed appears to be the case (Rescorla, 1987, 1988a).

Distinction between Excitation and Modulation. Occasion setting is an important aspect of classical conditioning not only because it illustrates that classical conditioning is subject to conditional control, but also because it appears to involve different mechanisms of learning from those considered previously. As discussed in Chapter 4, pairings of a CS with a US result in an association between the two events such that presentation of the CS comes to activate a representation of the US. I have referred to this kind of learning as the conditioning of excitation to the CS. Modulatory properties of stimuli are different from conditioned excitation.

In several studies, attempts to obtain evidence of conditioned excitatory properties of modulators failed to reveal such evidence (for example, Bouton & Swartzentruber, 1986; Puente, Cannon, Best, & Carrell, 1988). These experiments indicate that a stimulus can set the occasion for conditioned responding elicited by another cue without itself eliciting visible conditioned responding. Other studies have shown that conditioning simple excitatory properties to a stimulus does not make that stimulus function as a modulator (see Holland, 1985; Rescorla, 1985; but see Gewirtz, Brandon, & Wagner, 1998; Swartzentruber, 1997).

Additional evidence for a distinction between modulation and conditioned excitation is based on the effects of extinction procedures. *Extinction* refers to a procedure in which a previously conditioned stimulus is presented repeatedly but now without the US. I describe extinction in greater detail in Chapter 9. The typical outcome of extinction is that conditioned responding declines. Interestingly, the same procedure (repeated nonreinforced stimulus presentations) carried out with an occasion setter often has no effect. Once a stimulus has become established to set the occasion for a CS-US relation, repeated presentations of the stimulus by itself do not reduce its ability to facilitate conditioned responding to the CS (for example, Holland, 1989a; Rescorla, 1985; Ross, 1983).

The difference in the effects of an extinction procedure on conditioned excitatory stimuli and occasion setters may be related to what is signaled. A conditioned excitatory stimulus signals the forthcoming presentation of the US. The absence of the US following presentation of the CS during extinction is a violation of that expectancy. Hence, the signal value of the CS has to be readjusted in extinction to bring it in line with the new reality. Such a readjustment is not required by an extinction procedure for an occasion setter.

An occasion setter signals a relation between a CS and a US. The absence of the US when the occasion setter is presented alone in extinction does not mean that the relation between the CS and the US has changed. The information signaled by an occasion setter is not proved incorrect by presenting the modulator by itself during extinction. Therefore, the ability of the modulator to promote responding elicited by the CS remains intact during extinction. However, a modulator's effectiveness is reduced if the CS-US relation signaled by the modulator is altered (Rescorla, 1986).

Another line of evidence that supports the conclusion that occasion setting is distinct from conventional excitation has been obtained from transfer tests. These tests were conducted to determine whether a stimulus that has been conditioned to set the occasion for responding to a particular target CS will also increase responding to other CSs. Evidence of successful transfer of the effects of a modulator to new target CSs has been obtained. Of particular interest is the type of properties the targets must have in order to be subject to the influence of a modulator. Transfer effects are most likely to be obtained if the new target stimuli had previously served as targets of other modulator stimuli (Holland, 1992; Swartzentruber, 1995). Little transfer is obtained if the new target previously served as a conditioned excitatory stimulus, or if it had a history of reinforcement and nonreinforcement but was not a part of a conditional relation. Such limitations on transfer effects would not occur if a modulator increased responding to a target stimulus because the excitatory properties of the modulator summated with the excitatory properties of the target. Therefore, limitations on transfer provide additional evidence that modulators have their effects by some mechanism other than conventional excitation. (For further evidence of limitations on transfer of occasion setting, see Bonardi, 1996; Goddard & Holland, 1996; Nakajima, 1997; Skinner, 2000.)

Modulation versus Configural Conditioning. Not all conditional discrimination procedures of the type illustrated in Figure 8.14 result in the learning of a conditional relation between the stimuli involved. On reinforced trials in this procedure, a compound stimulus consisting of the noise and the key light was presented. As I noted earlier, organisms can respond to a compound stimulus either in terms of the elements that make up the compound, or in terms of the unique stimulus configuration produced by the elements. For the noise to serve as a signal that the key light will be paired with food, the noise and key light have to be treated as independent events rather than as a combined configural cue. Thus, modulatory effects require responding to the stimulus compound as consisting of independent stimulus elements (Holland, 1992).

To encourage organisms to treat stimulus compounds as consisting of independent elements, investigators have presented the elements one after the other, rather than simultaneously, in what is called a *serial compound.* On reinforced trials, the occasion setter is usually presented first, followed by the target CS and reinforcement. For example, in many of his experiments on occasion setting, Holland has even inserted a 5-second gap between the modulator and the target CS. Such procedures discourage the perception of a stimulus configuration based on the occasion setter and the target CS. In numerous studies, Holland and his associates have found that organisms respond to conditional discriminations involving serial compounds in terms of conditional relations. By contrast, the use of simultaneous compounds in conditional discriminations often does not result in modulatory effects (for example, Holland, 1986, 1989a, 1989c, 1991; Ross & Holland, 1981; see also Holland, 1989b; Thomas, Cook, & Terrones, 1990; Thomas, Curran, & Russell, 1988).

CONCLUDING COMMENTS

Stimulus control refers to how precisely tuned an organism's behavior is to specific features of the environment. Therefore, issues concerning the stimulus control of behavior are critical for understanding how an organism interacts with its environment. Stimulus control is measured in terms of the steepness of generalization gradients. A steep generalization gradient indicates that small variations in a stimulus produce large differences in responding. Weaker stimulus control is indicated by flatter generalization gradients.

The degree of stimulus control is determined by numerous factors, including the sensory capacity and sensory orientation of the organism, the relative salience of other cues in the situations, the type of reinforcement used, and the type of response required for reinforcement. Stimulus control is also a function of learning. Discrimination training increases the stimulus control of behavior whether that training involves stimuli that differ in several respects or stimuli that differ in only one respect. Discrimination training with stimuli that differ in only one dimension produces more precise stimulus control and may lead to the counterintuitive outcome that the peak level of responding is shifted away from the reinforced stimulus. The converse of discrimination training is equivalence training, which increases the generalization of behavior.

Not only discrete stimuli but also background contextual cues can come to control behavior. Stimulus control by contextual cues can develop even if attention to contextual cues is not required to optimize reinforcement. Contextual cues can become associated with a US directly or can serve to modulate the relation between a discrete CS and a US.

SAMPLE QUESTIONS

1. Describe the relationship between stimulus discrimination and stimulus generalization.
2. Describe the phenomenon of overshadowing, and describe how it may be explained by elemental and configural approaches to stimulus control.
3. Describe how the steepness of a generalization gradient may be altered by experience and learning.
4. Describe the difference between intradimensional and interdimensional discrimination training.
5. Describe the peak-shift effect and its determinants.
6. Compare and contrast conditioned excitation and occasion setting or facilitation.

KEY TERMS

conditional relation A relation in which the significance of one stimulus or event depends on the status of another stimulus.

configural-cue approach An approach to the analysis of control by compound stimuli that assumes that organisms respond to a compound stimulus as an integral whole rather than a collection of separate and independent stimulus elements. (Compare with *stimulus element approach.*)

discriminative stimulus A stimulus that controls the performance of instrumental behavior because it signals the availability (or nonavailability) of reinforcement.

excitatory stimulus generalization gradient A gradient of responding that is observed when organisms are tested with the S+ from a discrimination procedure and with stimuli that increasingly differ from the S+. The highest level of responding occurs to stimuli similar to the S+; progressively less responding occurs to stimuli that increasingly differ from the S+ . Thus, the gradient has an inverted-U shape.

facilitation A procedure in which one cue designates when another cue will be reinforced. Also called *occasion setting.*

inhibitory stimulus generalization gradient A gradient of responding observed when organisms are tested with the S− from a discrimination procedure and with stimuli that increasingly differ from the S−. The lowest level of responding occurs to stimuli similar to the S−; progressively more responding occurs to stimuli that increasingly differ from S−. Thus, the gradient has a U shape.

intradimensional discrimination A discrimination between stimuli that differ only in terms of the value of one stimulus feature, such as color, brightness, or pitch.

modulator A stimulus that signals the relation between two other events. The nature of a binary relation is determined by the modulator.

multiple schedule of reinforcement A procedure in which different reinforcement schedules are in effect in the presence of different stimuli presented in succession. Generally, each stimulus comes to evoke a pattern of responding that corresponds to whatever reinforcement schedule is in effect during that stimulus.

occasion setting Same as *facilitation.*

overshadowing Interference with the conditioning of a stimulus because of the simultaneous presence of another stimulus that is easier to condition.

peak shift A displacement of the highest rate of responding in a stimulus generalization gradient away from the S+ in a direction opposite the S− after intradimensional discrimination training.

stimulus discrimination Differential responding in the presence of two or more stimuli.

stimulus discrimination procedure (in classical conditioning) A classical conditioning procedure in which one stimulus (the CS+) is paired with the unconditioned stimulus on some trials and another stimulus (the CS−) is presented without the unconditioned stimulus on other trials. As a result of this procedure, the CS+ comes to elicit a conditioned response, and the CS− comes to inhibit this response. (Also called *differential inhibition.*)

stimulus discrimination procedure (in instrumental conditioning) A procedure in which reinforcement for responding is available whenever one stimulus (the S+, or S^D) is present and not available whenever another stimulus (the S−, or S^Δ) is present.

stimulus-element approach An approach to the analysis of control by compound stimuli that assumes that participants respond to a compound stimulus in terms of the stimulus elements that make up the compound. (Compare with *configural-cue approach.*)

stimulus equivalence Responding to physically distinct stimuli as if they were the same because of common prior experiences with the stimuli.

stimulus generalization The occurrence of behavior learned through habituation or conditioning in the presence of stimuli that are different from the stimuli used during training.

stimulus generalization gradient A gradient of responding that is observed if participants are tested with stimuli that increasingly differ from the stimulus that was present during training. (See also *excitatory stimulus generalization gradient* and *inhibitory stimulus generalization gradient.*)

CHAPTER 9

EXTINCTION OF CONDITIONED BEHAVIOR

Chapter 9 represents a departure from previous chapters in that it focuses on extinction, a procedure that produces a decline in responding. Extinction can be conducted only after a response or association has been established using Pavlovian or instrumental conditioning. Often the goal is to reverse the effects of acquisition, but a true reversal is rarely achieved and may not be possible. Phenomena such as spontaneous recovery, renewal, and reinstatement all show that extinction does not erase what was learned originally. Studies of reinforcer devaluation suggest that extinction has virtually no measurable impact on S-O and R-O associations. Rather, extinction seems to involve the new learning of an inhibitory S-R association that is superimposed on what was learned earlier. The inhibition arises from the frustrative effects of the unexpected absence of reward. The frustration produced by nonreward is responsible for a number of "paradoxical" reward effects, including the partial reinforcement extinction effect. Intermittent or partial reinforcement permits organisms to learn about nonreward in ways that serve to immunize them against the effects of extinction. This kind of resistance to change is also the subject of studies of behavioral momentum that are described at the end of the chapter.

So far, my descriptions of classical and instrumental conditioning have centered on various aspects of the acquisition and maintenance of new associations and new responses. Learning mechanisms are important because they provide needed flexibility in how individuals interact with their environment. Learning mechanisms are more useful than unconditioned response processes because the behavioral plasticity that they enable promotes adjustments to a changing environment. But if learned behavior is an adaptation to a changing environment, then the loss of conditioned behavior should be just as prevalent as its acquisition. Not many reinforcement schedules remain in effect throughout an organism's lifetime. Responses that are successful at one stage may cease to be effective as circumstances change. Children, for example, are praised for drawing crude representations of people and objects in nursery school, but the same type of drawing is not considered good if made in sixth grade. Dating someone may be extremely pleasant and rewarding at first, but stops being reinforcing when that person falls in love with someone else.

Acquisition of conditioned behavior involves procedures in which a reinforcing outcome is presented. In Pavlovian conditioning, the reinforcing outcome or unconditioned stimulus is presented as a consequence of a conditioned stimulus. In instrumental conditioning, the reinforcing outcome is presented as a consequence of the instrumental response. **Extinction** involves omitting the US or reinforcer. Thus, extinction in classical conditioning involves repeated presentations of the conditioned stimulus by itself. Extinction in instrumental conditioning involves no longer presenting the reinforcer as a consequence of the instrumental response. The typical result is that conditioned responding, be it classical or instrumental, declines. Thus, the behavioral change that occurs in extinction is the reverse of what was observed in acquisition. Because this reverse behavioral change is produced by omitting the reinforcer or US that motivated the original learning, extinction appears to be the opposite of acquisition. Indeed, that is how extinction has been characterized in traditional theories of learning, such as the Rescorla–Wagner model (see Chapter 4). However, as the evidence described in the present chapter shows, this view of extinction is incorrect.

It is important to point out that the loss of the conditioned response that occurs as a result of extinction is not the same as the loss of behavior that may occur because of **forgetting.** Extinction is produced by omitting the US following presentations of the CS or omitting the reinforcer following occurrences of the instrumental response. Forgetting, by contrast, is a decline in conditioned responding that may occur simply because of the passage of time. Extinction occurs as a consequence of repeated presentations of the CS by itself or repeated instances of the instrumental response by itself. Forgetting occurs with prolonged absence of experience with the conditioned stimulus or the instrumental response.

Understanding extinction is important for both behavior theory and behavior therapy (Bouton & Nelson, 1998; Falls, 1998). Individuals seek therapy when some aspect of their behavior is creating a problem for them. One approach to alleviating the difficulty is to extinguish the problematic response. Presumably, if a problematic behavior developed because of Pavlovian or instrumental conditioning, the behavior should be susceptible to extinction. However, extinction does not always work in behavior therapy. An observer may be tempted to conclude that in these cases the original behavioral problem was not acquired through conditioning. However, recent advances in the understanding of extinction suggest that failures of extinction reflect the normal limitations of extinction. Extinction does not reverse the effects of acquisition. Rather, it involves learning something new that is superimposed on what was learned earlier (without the loss of that earlier learning).

EFFECTS OF EXTINCTION PROCEDURES

What would you do if you unexpectedly did not succeed in opening the door to your apartment with your key? Chances are you would not give up after the first attempt but would try several more times, perhaps jiggling the key in different ways each time. But, if none of those response variations worked, you would eventually quit trying. This illustrates two basic behavioral effects of extinction. The most obvious behavioral effect is that responding decreases when the response no longer results in reinforcement. This is the primary behavioral effect of extinction, the one that scientists have given the most attention. Investigations of extinction have focused on the rate or probability of the instrumental response during the course of extinction and have been concerned with how rapidly responding decreases. If the key to your apartment no longer opens the door, you will give up trying. Notice, however, that before you give up entirely, you are likely to jiggle the key in various ways in an effort to make it work. This illustrates the second basic behavioral effect of extinction, namely, that it increases response variability.

The two basic behavioral effects of extinction are illustrated in a recent study by Neuringer, Kornell, and Olufs (2001). Two groups of rats served in the experiment. During the first phase, both groups were reinforced for making instrumental responses, but only one group was required to vary its instrumental behavior. The two groups were then observed in extinction, to see how the rate and variability of their responses would be altered by nonreinforcement. As I described in Chapter 5, reinforcement can increase the probability of response variability if variation in responding is required for reinforcement. The study by Neuringer et al. was designed to examine the effects of extinction on this phenomenon.

The experimental chamber had two response levers on one wall and a round response key on the opposite wall. During the reinforcement phase, the rats had to make three responses in a row to obtain a food pellet. For example, they could press the left lever three times (LLL), press each lever and the response key once (RLK), or press the left lever twice and the key once (LLK). For the subjects in Group 1, a sequence of three responses was reinforced only if this sequence was different from 95% of the previous response sequences the subjects performed (adjusted for recency). Thus, Group 1 had to vary their response sequences to obtain reinforcement. Each subject in the Group 2 was yoked to a subject in the variability group (Group 1) and received reinforcement on a particular trial only if its yoked partner got reinforced. Subjects in the yoked group also had to make three responses to get reinforced, but whether they got a food pellet did not depend on the variability of their response sequences. After behavior was well established by the reinforcement contingencies, both groups were shifted to a phase of extinction.

Figure 9.1 shows the results of the experiment for the last four sessions of the reinforcement phase and the first four sessions of the extinction phase. The left panel represents the variability in the response sequences each group performed; the right panel represents their rates of responding. Notice that reinforcement produced the expected difference between the two groups in terms of the variability of their response sequences. Subjects reinforced for varying their responses (Group 1) showed much more variability than the yoked subjects (Group 2), which did not have to vary their behavior. Interestingly, the yoked subjects responded somewhat faster, perhaps because they did not have to move as frequently from one response lever to the other.

As expected, extinction produced a decline in the rate of responding in both groups (see right panel of Figure 9.1). Interestingly, this decline in responding occurred in the face

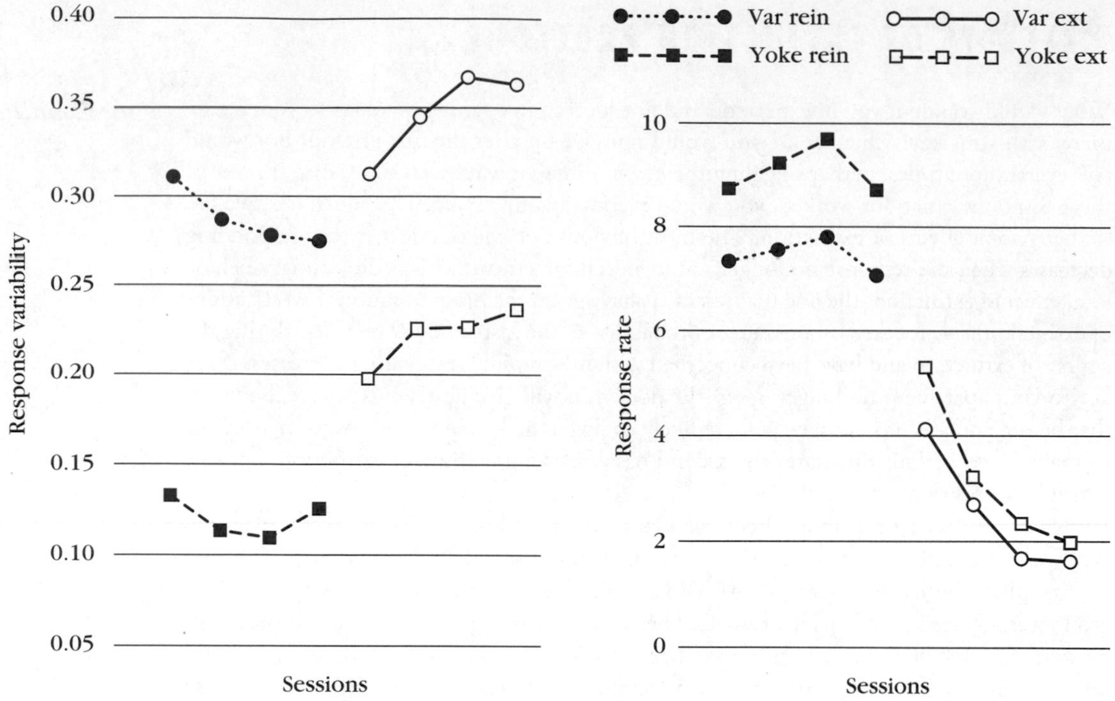

Figure 9.1 Effects of extinction on response variability (left panel) and response rate (right panel) for a group of rats that was required to perform variable response sequences for reinforcement (Var) or received reinforcement regardless of their response sequences (Yoke). The filled symbols represent the last four sessions of the reinforcement phase. The open symbols represent the first four sessions of the extinction phase. (Response variability was measured in terms of the probability of meeting the variability criterion. Response rate was measured in terms of the number of three-response sequences that were completed per minute.) (After Neuringer, Kornell, & Olufs, 2001.)

of an increase in the variability of the response sequences the subjects performed (see left panel of Figure 9.1). Both groups showed a significant increase in the variability of the response sequences they performed during extinction. The increase in response variability was evident during the first extinction session and increased during subsequent sessions. Thus, extinction produced a decline in the number of response sequences the subjects performed, but it increased the variability of those sequences. (For another example of increased response variability due to nonreinforcement, see Gharib, Derby, & Roberts, 2001.)

Another interesting finding in the study by Neuringer et al. (2001) was that the increase in response variability that occurred during extinction did not come at the expense of the subjects repeating response sequences that they had performed during the reinforcement phase. Response sequences that were highly likely to occur during the reinforcement phase continued to occur during extinction but were supplemented by sequences that the subjects had rarely tried previously. This last outcome confirms previous conclusions that the basic structure of instrumental behavior is altered very little by the introduction of extinction (Machado & Cevik, 1998; Schwartz, 1981; for similar evidence in Pavlovian conditioning, see Ohyama, Gibbon, Deich, & Balsam, 1999). Extinction decreases the rate of responding and increases response variability, but otherwise does not alter the structure of behavior.

In addition to the behavioral effects illustrated in Figure 9.1, extinction procedures may produce strong emotional effects (see Papini & Dudley, 1997, for a recent review). If an organism has become accustomed to receiving reinforcement for a particular response, it may become upset when reinforcers are no longer delivered. The emotional reaction induced by withdrawal of an expected reinforcer is called **frustration.** Frustrative nonreward energizes behavior (for carefully controlled studies, see Dudley & Papini, 1995, 1997; Thomas & Papini, 2001). Under certain conditions, frustration may be sufficiently severe to include aggressive reactions. When a vending machine breaks down and no longer delivers a soft drink or candy after you put in your money, you may become abusive and pound and kick the machine. If your spouse has coffee ready for you every morning, you are likely to get angry the first time the coffee is not ready when you get up. If your partner takes you on a date every Saturday evening, you will surely be very upset if your partner unexpectedly calls one Saturday afternoon to cancel the date.

Frustrative aggression induced by extinction is dramatically demonstrated by experiments in which two animals—pigeons, for example—are placed in the same Skinner box (Azrin, Hutchinson, & Hake, 1966). One pigeon is initially reinforced for pecking a response key, while the other animal is restrained in a corner of the experimental chamber. The key-pecking bird largely ignores the other one as long as reinforcers are provided. However, when extinction is introduced and reinforcement ceases, the previously rewarded bird is likely to attack its innocent partner. Similar aggression occurs if a stuffed model instead of a real animal is placed in the Skinner box. Extinction-induced aggression has also been investigated in studies with rats and with people (for example, Lewis, Alessandri, & Sullivan, 1990; Nation & Cooney, 1982; Tomie, Carelli, & Wagner, 1993) and can be a problem when extinction is used as a therapeutic procedure (Lerman, Iwata, & Wallace, 1999).

EXTINCTION AND ORIGINAL LEARNING

Although extinction produces important behavioral and emotional effects, it does not reverse the effects of acquisition. Evidence that extinction does not erase what was originally learned has been obtained through studies of spontaneous recovery, renewal, reinstatement, and reinforcer devaluation effects.

Spontaneous Recovery

Spontaneous Recovery following Pavlovian Conditioning. One of the hallmark features of extinction is that it dissipates with time. The consequence of this loss of the extinction effect over time is that the originally conditioned response returns if the subject is tested after a delay following the extinction procedure. In a recent study with laboratory rats as subjects, for example, Rescorla (1997b) used two appetitive unconditioned stimuli, sucrose and a solid food pellet, delivered into cups recessed in one wall of the experimental chamber. Infrared detectors identified each time the rat poked its head into the food cups. This magazine entry behavior is a form of goal tracking (see Chapter 3). The experimental chamber was usually dark. During the initial acquisition phase, one of the unconditioned stimuli was signaled by a noise CS and the other was signaled by a light CS. As conditioning progressed, each CS quickly came to elicit the goal tracking conditioned response, with the two CSs eliciting similar levels of responding. The mean number of magazine entries per minute at the end of acquisition was 15.6 during the CSs (and 4.6 during the intertrial intervals).

Two extinction sessions (of 16 trials each) were then conducted with each CS, followed by a series of 4 test trials. The experimental manipulation of primary interest was that for one of the CSs (CS-No rest), the extinction trials immediately preceded the test trials. In contrast, an 8-day rest period separated extinction and testing for the other CS (CS-Rest). Responses to both of the stimuli during the test trials are shown in Figure 9.2. Both CSs elicited very little responding at the end of the extinction phase. (Mean response rates were below 2 per minute.) This low level of responding persisted during the test session for the stimulus (CS-No rest) that was tested immediately after extinction. In contrast, for the stimulus that was tested 8 days after extinction (CS-Rest), responding was substantially higher, especially during the first trial. This represents *spontaneous recovery.* Notice, however, that the recovery was not complete. At the end of the acquisition phase, the rate of magazine entries had been 15.6 responses/min. During the first trial after the rest period, the mean response rate was about 6.2 responses/min. (For other studies of spontaneous recovery of Pavlovian conditioned responding after extinction, see Brooks & Bouton, 1993; Robbins, 1990; Rosas & Bouton, 1996.)

Spontaneous Recovery after Instrumental Conditioning. Spontaneous recovery is also a prominent phenomenon in extinction after instrumental conditioning. A particularly clear demonstration of the phenomenon was provided by a study with laboratory rats (Rescorla, 1996c). The rats were first trained to make two different instrumental responses for food reinforcement (pressing a response lever and poking their nose into a small opening). Separate training sessions were conducted with each response, and reinforcement was provided on a variable interval 1-min schedule. This instrumental conditioning resulted in mean response rates of about 17 per minute for each response.

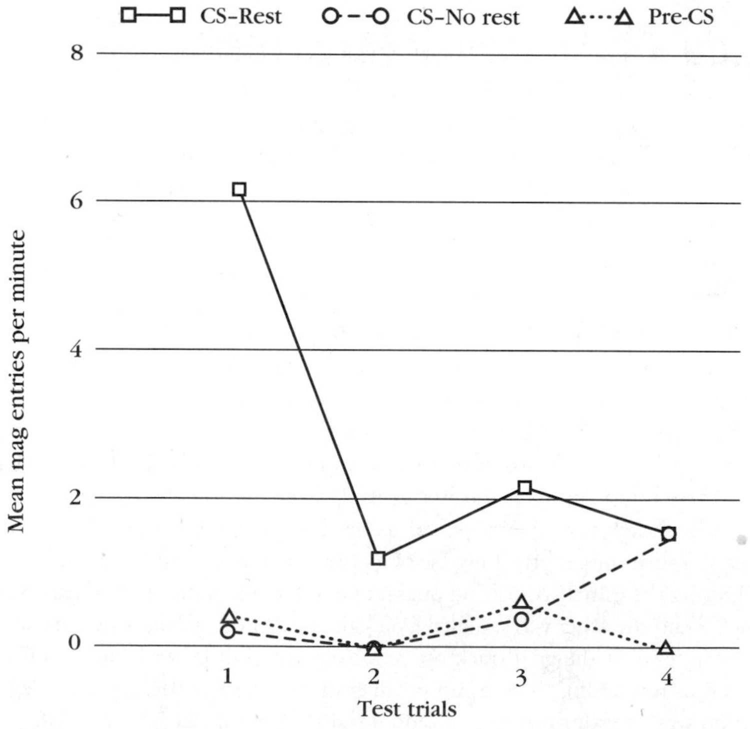

Figure 9.2 Rate of goal tracking for two different CSs during a test session for spontaneous recovery. Both CSs were initially conditioned by pairing them with food reinforcement. Each CS was then extinguished. For CS-Rest, the test session occurred 8 days after the extinction phase. For CS-No Rest, the test session occurred immediately after the extinction phase. Notice that the 8-day rest period caused a substantial recovery in the rate of responding. (From "Spontaneous recovery after Pavlovian conditioning with multiple outcomes" by R. A. Rescorla, in *Animal Learning & Behavior,* Vol. 25, p. 101. Copyright 1997 Psychonomic Society, Inc. Reprinted with permission.)

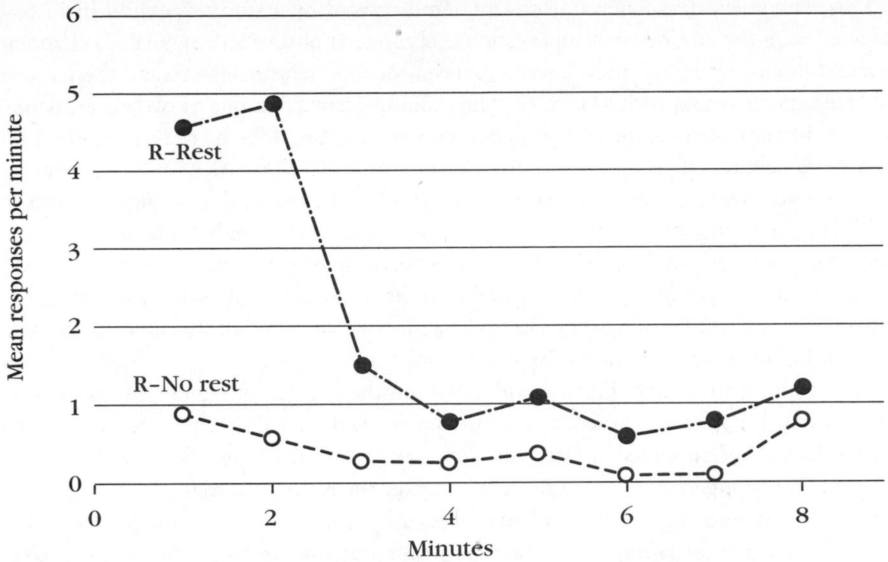

Figure 9.3 Instrumental responding during a recovery test to demonstrate spontaneous recovery. At first, laboratory rats were trained to make two different instrumental responses for food reinforcement (a lever press and a nose-poke response). One response was then extinguished shortly before the recovery test (R-No rest), and the other was extinguished 7 days before the test (R-Rest). Notice that much more responding occurred during the recovery test if extinction was followed by the 7-day rest period. (From Figure 2, p. 13, in R. A. Rescorla, in *Animal Learning & Behavior*, Copyright 1996 Psychonomic Society, Inc. Reprinted with permission.)

After the acquisition phase, two 20-minute extinction sessions were conducted with each response. For one of the responses (counterbalanced across subjects), the extinction phase occurred shortly before a recovery test. For the other response, the extinction phase occurred 7 days before the recovery test. By the end of the extinction phase, mean response rates did not exceed 2 per minute for either response. The results of the test sessions conducted with each response are displayed in Figure 9.3. Notice that the response whose recovery was tested after a rest period after extinction (R-Rest) occurred at a much higher rate than the response whose recovery was tested without a rest period after extinction (R-No rest). Introducing a period of rest after extinction produced a substantial recovery in responding, illustrating the phenomenon of spontaneous recovery. (For other examples of spontaneous recovery of instrumental and more complex forms of behavior, see Devenport, 1998; Rescorla, 1997c.)

Renewal of Original Excitatory Conditioning

Another strong piece of evidence that extinction does not result in unlearning is the phenomenon of **renewal** identified by Mark Bouton and his colleagues. Renewal refers to a recovery of acquisition performance when the contextual cues that were present during extinction are changed. The change can be a return to the context of original acquisition or a shift to a "neutral" context. Renewal is particularly troublesome for behavior therapy because it means that irrational fears that are extinguished in the context of a therapist's office can easily return when the subject moves to a different context.

The phenomenon of renewal is clearly demonstrated by a study of conditioned fear conducted with the conditioned suppression technique (Bouton & King, 1983). Laboratory rats were first trained to press a response lever for food reinforcement, and then a tone CS was repeatedly paired with footshock. The training occurred in one of two experimental chambers that provided distinctively different contextual cues. Which context was used for training was counterbalanced across subjects and labeled Context A. As usual, excitatory conditioning resulted in a conditioned suppression of lever pressing during presentations of the CS. For the next phase of the experiment, the subjects were divided into three groups. Two of the groups received 20 extinction trials consisting of presentations of the tone CS without shock. For Group A, these extinction trials occurred in the same context (A) as original excitatory conditioning. For Group B, extinction occurred in the alternate context (B). A third group (NE) did not receive extinction.

The results of the extinction trials are shown on the left side of Figure 9.4. Recall that in a conditioned suppression procedure, greater levels of conditioned fear are represented by smaller values of the suppression ratio (see Chapter 3). Groups A and B showed similarly strong levels of suppression to the tone at the start of the extinction trials. This shows that the fear that had been conditioned in Context A easily generalized when the tone was presented in Context B for Group B. As the tone was repeatedly presented during the extinction phase, conditioned suppression gradually dissipated, and did so in a similar fashion for subjects extinguished in Context A or Context B.

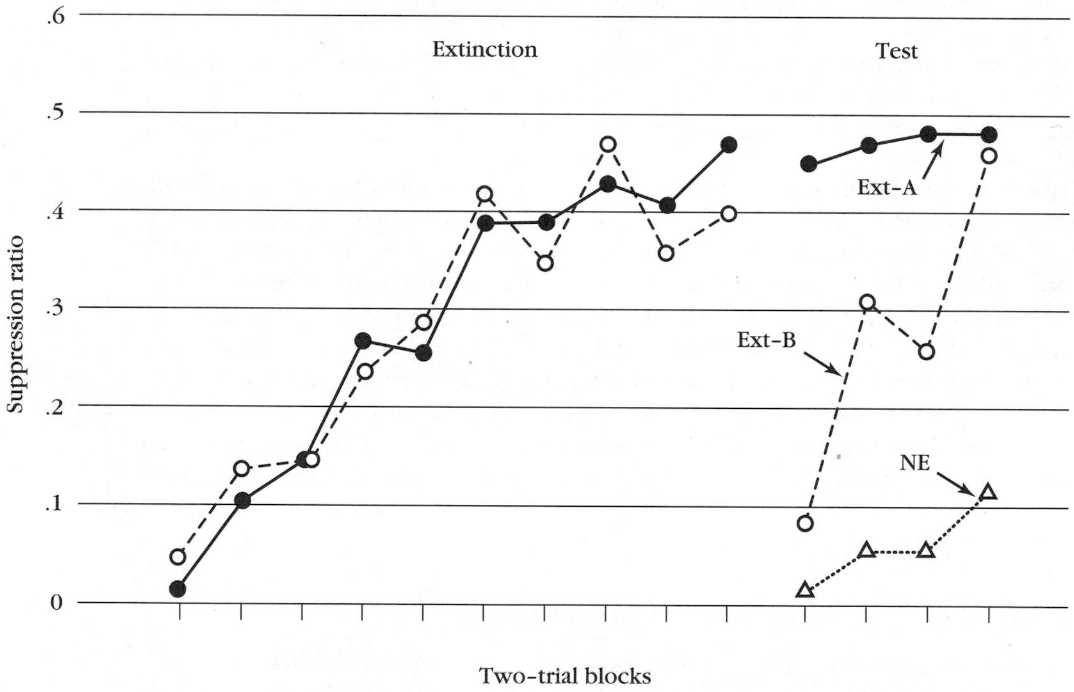

Figure 9.4 Demonstration of the renewal effect in conditioned suppression. All of the subjects first received pairings of a tone with footshock in Context A (data not shown). Groups A and B then received extinction trials either in Context A or Context B. Group NE did not receive extinction. Test sessions were then conducted in Context A for all subjects. (From Bouton & King, 1983.)

Following extinction in either Context A or Context B, all subjects received a series of test trials in Context A, where they had been trained originally. The results of these test trials are presented on the right side of Figure 9.4. Group NE, which did not receive extinction, showed the strongest degree of suppression to the tone during the test trials. The least suppression was evident in Group A, which received extinction in the same context as the context of testing. Group B, which also received extinction but in Context B, showed substantial levels of suppression when first returned to Context A. Group B's conditioned fear during the first three test trials was substantially greater than it had been at the end of the extinction phase. Thus, conditioned fear was *renewed* when Group B was removed from the extinction context and returned to the context of original training.

The difference in the degree of conditioned fear in Groups A and B evident during the test sessions is significant because these two groups showed similar losses of conditioned fear during the extinction phase. The fact that conditioned fear was renewed in Group B indicates that the loss of suppression evident during the extinction phase did not reflect the unlearning of the conditioned fear response. (For more recent studies of the renewal effect in aversive Pavlovian conditioning, see Harris, Jones, Bailey, & Westbrook, 2000; Rosas & Bouton, 1997; Williams & Sly, 1999.)

Since its original demonstration, the renewal effect has been observed not only in Pavlovian fear conditioning but also in Pavlovian appetitive conditioning (for example, Bouton & Peck, 1989; Goddard, 1999), in conditioned inhibition (Fiori, Barnet, & Miller, 1994), and in various instrumental conditioning situations (for example, Nakajima, Tanaka, Urushihara, & Imada, 2000). Interestingly, the phenomenon is evident not just with external contextual cues but with contextual cues created by drug states (for example, Bouton, Kenney, & Rosengard, 1990; Cunningham, 1979). Renewal can also occur if the subject is removed from the context of extinction to an alternate context that is not the context of original acquisition (Bouton & Ricker, 1994). However, this type of renewal is not as robust as the renewal that occurs when the context of original acquisition is reinstated.

A simple and rather uninteresting explanation of the renewal effect is that it is due to excitatory properties conditioned to the renewal context. This interpretation readily comes to mind if original acquisition is conducted in one context (A), extinction is conducted in another context (B), and the subjects are then returned to Context A. Because the US was presented in Context A during acquisition, Context A presumably acquired excitatory properties. If these excitatory properties summate with any residual excitation remaining to the CS, responding to the CS will be greater in Context A than Context B. A number of control experiments, however, have ruled out this kind of simple summation explanation of the renewal effect. In one study (Harris et al., 2000, Experiment 1), for example, original acquisition with two different conditioned stimuli was conducted in Context C. One CS was then extinguished in Context A and the other was extinguished in Context B. Subsequent tests revealed that responding to the CS extinguished in Context A was renewed if this CS was tested in Context B. This outcome cannot be attributed to possible excitatory properties of the Context B because the US was never presented in Context B. (For additional experiments that rule out context excitation, see Bouton & Ricker, 1994.)

The preponderance of evidence indicates that the renewal effect occurs because the memory of extinction is specific to the cues that were present during the extinction phase. Therefore, a shift away from the context of extinction disrupts retrieval of the memory of extinction, with the result that extinction performance is lost. But why should this restore behavior characteristic of the original acquisition? To account for that, one has to make the added assumption that original acquisition performance generalizes from one context to another more easily than does extinction performance. This is indeed the case. For example, in the experiment by Bouton and King (1983) I described earlier, acquisition for all subjects occurred in Context A. Half the subjects were then shifted to Context B for extinction. Figure 9.4 shows that these subjects performed the same way during the extinction phase as subjects that remained in Context A during extinction. Thus, a shift in context did not disrupt the originally acquired conditioned suppression.

Why is it that original acquisition is less disrupted (if at all) by a change in context when extinction performance is highly context-specific? Bouton (1993, 1994) has suggested that contextual cues serve to disambiguate the significance of a conditioned stimulus. This function is similar to the function of semantic context in disambiguating the meaning of a word. Consider the word *cut.* Cut could refer to the physical procedure of creating two pieces, as in "The chef cut the carrots." Alternatively, it could refer to dropping a player from a team, as in "Johnny was cut from the team after the first game." The meaning of the word cut depends on the semantic context. A CS that has undergone excitatory conditioning and then extinction also has an ambiguous meaning, in that the CS could signify an impending US (acquisition) or the absence of the US (extinction). This ambiguity allows the CS to come under contextual control more easily. After acquisition training alone, the CS is not ambiguous because it signifies only one thing (impending US delivery). Therefore, such a CS is not as susceptible to contextual control.

The renewal effect has important implications for behavior therapy, and unfortunately these implications are rather troubling. It suggests that even if a therapeutic procedure is effective in extinguishing a pathological fear or phobia in the relative safety of a therapist's office, the conditioned fear may easily return when the client encounters the fear CS in a different context. Equally problematic is the fact that the effects of excitatory conditioning readily generalize from one context to another (see, for example, the left panel of Figure 9.4). Thus, if you acquire a pathological fear in one situation, the fear is likely to plague you in a variety of other contexts. But if you overcome your fear in a particular context, that benefit will not generalize as readily. The renewal effect suggests that problems created by conditioning will have much more widespread effects than the solutions or remedies for those problems.

Troubled by the above dilemma, investigators have explored ways to reduce the renewal effect. One procedure that shows promise is to conduct extinction in a variety of different contexts. Extinction performance is less context-specific if extinction training is carried out in several different alternative contexts (Chelonis, Calton, Hart, & Schachtman, 1999; Gunther, Denniston, & Miller, 1998). Other techniques for reducing the renewal effect involve conditioned inhibition training, differential conditioning, and presenting the CS explicitly paired with the US (Rauhut, Thomas, & Ayres, 2001). (For further discussion of the implications of the renewal effect for behavior therapy, see Bouton, 1988; Bouton & Nelson, 1998.)

Restoration of Extinction Performance

The renewal effect involves reactivating the memory of original excitatory conditioning by shifting the subject out of contextual cues that were present during extinction. More generally, this represents reactivating a previously learned behavior by changing the context to better approximate conditions present when that behavior was previously acquired. This general strategy has been applied to a variety of situations in which something learned is then altered by a second learning experience (Bouton, 1991, 1993). In particular, the strategy can be applied to extinction—that is, extinction performance can be restored by introducing contextual cues that reactivate the memory of extinction. This has been examined within the framework of the phenomenon of spontaneous recovery.

As I described earlier, spontaneous recovery involves the recovery of originally conditioned behavior following extinction if a sufficient period of time passes after the extinction phase. Extinction-like behavior can be restored (thus counteracting spontaneous recovery) by presenting cues that were present during the extinction phase. Such renewal of extinction has been observed in taste-aversion learning (Brooks, Palmatier, Garcia, & Johnson, 1999) as well as in appetitive conditioning preparations (Brooks, 2000; Brooks & Bouton, 1993). Various control experiments have encouraged the conclusion that extinction cues counteract spontaneous recovery because they reactivate the memory of extinction. These results are consistent with the hypothesis that spontaneous recovery is due to a deterioration of the contextual cues of extinction with the passage of time (Bouton, 1993).

Reinstatement of Conditioned Excitation

Another procedure that serves to restore responding to an extinguished conditioned stimulus is called **reinstatement.** Reinstatement refers to the recovery of excitatory responding to an extinguished stimulus produced by exposures to the unconditioned stimulus. Consider, for example, learning an aversion to french fries because you got sick after eating some on a trip. Your aversion is then extinguished by nibbling on french fries without getting sick on a number of occasions. You may actually regain your enjoyment of french fries because of this extinction experience. The phenomenon of reinstatement suggests that if you were to become sick again for some reason, your aversion to french fries would return even if your illness had nothing to do with eating this particular food. (For an analogous study with laboratory rats, see Schachtman, Brown, & Miller, 1985.)

As with renewal, reinstatement is a troublesome phenomenon for behavior therapy. Behavior therapy often involves trying to get clients to stop doing things that are problematic for them. Extinction may be one of the techniques for reducing behavior. Because of reinstatement, responses that are successfully extinguished during the course of therapeutic intervention can recur if the individual encounters the unconditioned stimulus again. Fear and anxiety that are acquired during the course of being in an abusive relationship or living with an abusive parent can return even after years of therapy if the individual encounters similar forms of abuse later in life.

In the initial experiments on the reinstatement effect (for example, Rescorla & Heth, 1975), excitatory conditioning, extinction, and subsequent reinstatement US exposures were all conducted in the same experimental context. As was the case with the renewal effect, it is important to consider whether the reinstatement effect may be a result of context conditioning. Context conditioning is a possible contributor because the US presentations that occurred during the reinstatement phase can result in conditioning of the contextual cues of the experimental situation. That context conditioning could then summate with any excitation remaining to the CS at the end of extinction, to produce the reinstatement of conditioned responding.

A great deal of research has been done on the reinstatement effect in the past 20 years (see Bouton, 1993, 1994; Bouton & Nelson, 1998). The results have indicated that contextual conditioning is important but not because it permits summation of excitation. Furthermore, as was the case with renewal, the role of context is to disambiguate the significance of a stimulus that has a mixed history of conditioning and extinction. Context has relatively little effect on stimuli that have a history of only conditioning.

These conclusions are supported by the results of an early study by Bouton (1984). The experiment was conducted in the conditioned suppression preparation with rats. The procedure is summarized in Table 9.1. For half the subjects, reinstatement was conducted after conditioning a CS with a weak shock that produced only moderate levels of conditioned

TABLE 9.1

EFFECTS OF REINSTATEMENT AFTER ACQUISITION ALONE OR AFTER BOTH ACQUISITION AND EXTINCTION (Bouton, 1984)

PHASE 1	PHASE 2	REINSTATEMENT	TEST
CS → Weak shock	No treatment	Shock same	CS
CS → Weak shock	No treatment	Shock different	CS
CS → Strong shock	Extinction	Shock same	CS
CS → Strong shock	Extinction	Shock different	CS

suppression. The remaining subjects were initially conditioned with a strong shock that resulted in substantially more conditioned suppression. However, extinction was then provided so that by the time the reinstatement procedure was introduced, the level of suppression in these subjects was similar to the suppression in the first group. Thus, reinstatement was introduced when responding to the CS was similar in all subjects; but some of them got to that point by receiving only conditioning, whereas for the others the CS was both conditioned and extinguished. Reinstatement consisted of delivering four unsignaled shocks either in the context of testing or in an alternate context. The results of tests conducted after the reinstatement USs are presented in Figure 9.5.

For subjects that did not receive extinction (left side of Figure 9.5), it did not make any difference whether the reinstatement shocks occurred in the test context (shock same) or elsewhere (shock different). This outcome shows that contextual conditioning did not summate with the suppression elicited by the target CS. In contrast, for subjects that received extinction (right side of Figure 9.5), reinstatement shocks given in the same context as test-

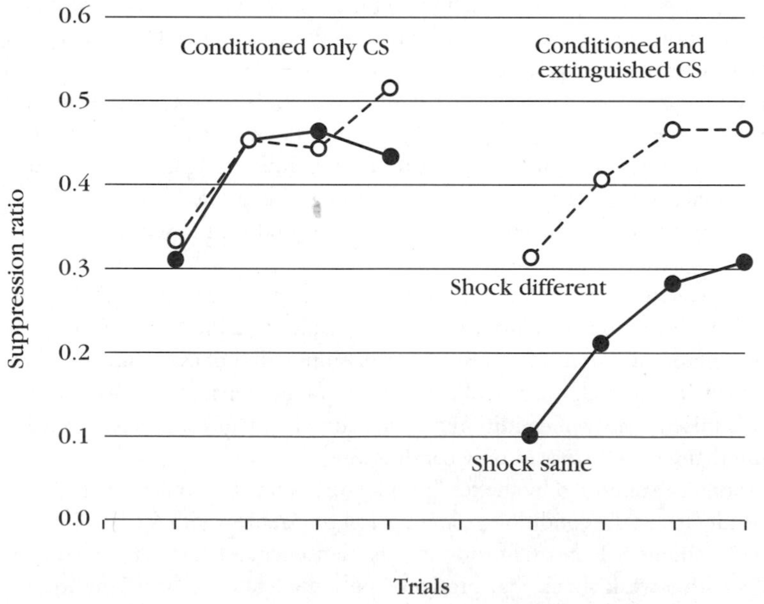

Figure 9.5 Demonstration of reinstatement of conditioned suppression. Four reinstatement shocks were delivered either in the training and test context (Shock same) or in a different context (Shock different) after just excitatory conditioning (Conditioned only CS) or after conditioning and extinction (Conditioned and extinguished CS). (From William O'Donohue, ed., *Learning and Behavior Therapy.* Copyright 1998 by Allyn & Bacon. Reprinted by permission.)

ing produced significantly more response suppression than shocks given in a different context. This outcome shows that context conditioning facilitates the reinstatement effect. (For additional research on the role of context conditioning in the reinstatement effect, see Richardson, Duffield, Bailey, & Westbrook, 1999.)

Results such as those presented in Figure 9.5 have encouraged Bouton to think about reinstatement as a form of renewal. According to this interpretation, conditioned contextual cues provide some of the contextual cues for excitatory responding under ordinary circumstances. These contextual cues become extinguished when the CS is presented by itself during extinction. Reinstatement US presentations in the test context serve to restore the excitatory properties of the contextual cues and thereby enable those cues to be more effective in reactivating the memory of excitatory conditioning of the CS.

Sensitivity to Reinforcer Devaluation

The persistence of original learning despite extinction can also be examined by evaluating the effects of reinforcer devaluation. As I described in Chapter 4, reinforcer or US devaluation in Pavlovian conditioning disrupts performance of the conditioned response if the CR was the product of S-S rather than S-R learning. Rescorla has used the US devaluation technique to determine whether the CS-US association established through Pavlovian conditioning persists through extinction. If extinction does not disrupt a CS-US association, then US devaluation will disrupt responding to an extinguished CS, just as it disrupts responding to a CS that has not undergone extinction.

The outline of one experiment (Rescorla, 1996a, Experiment 2) is presented in Table 9.2. Rats received appetitive conditioning with food and sucrose as the US. For each subject a light was paired with one of the USs and a tone was paired with the other. Which CS was paired with which US was counterbalanced across subjects, and each CS was always paired only with its own US. As conditioning progressed, each subject came to insert its head in

TABLE 9.2 EFFECTS OF US DEVALUATION ON A PAVLOVIAN CS FOLLOWING EXTINCTION (Rescorla 1996a, Experiment 2)

PHASE 1	PHASE 2	US DEVALUATION	TEST
	Group Ext		
CS → US1	CS1 Ext		CS1
and	and	US1 → LiCl	and
CS2 → US2	CS2 Ext		CS2
	Group NotExt		
CS → US1			CS1
and		US1 → LiCl	and
CS2 → US2			CS2

CS1 and CS2 were a light and a tone (counterbalanced across subjects). US1 and US2 were sucrose and food pellets (counterbalanced across subjects and CSs). Before the US Devaluation phase, both CS1 and CS2 were conditioned with a third US (polycose).

the food magazine as the conditioned response (goal tracking). The rate of goal tracking during each CS was about 20 responses/minute at the end of the acquisition phase. Following acquisition, group Ext received extinction trials with both CS1 and CS2. This reduced their responding to CS1 and CS2 to about 1 response/minute. The control group (NotExt) was placed in the experimental chamber during the extinction phase but did not get either CS1 or CS2 trials.

The extinction phase was followed by training in which all subjects had CS1 and CS2 paired with a new US (US3: polycose). This was done to make sure all subjects would show some responding to the CSs during the final test session. US3 was deliberately selected for retraining to be sure that retraining would not influence whatever associations each CS still had with US1 and US2. All of the subjects then had the value of US1 reduced by taste-aversion conditioning. Presentations of US1 in the experimental chamber were followed by an injection of lithium chloride that served to make the rats feel sick. After US devaluation, each subject was tested with CS1 and CS2.

The results of the first two presentations of CS1 and CS2 during the test session are summarized in Figure 9.6. Despite retraining with polycose as the US, responding to CS1 and CS2 in the extinction group was a bit lower than responding in the control group (NotExt). Nevertheless, the two groups showed equal sensitivity to US devaluation. In each group, responding to the CS whose associated US had been devaluated was lower than responding to the CS whose associated US had not been devalued. This pattern of results could have occurred only if extinction allowed the original CS-US associations to remain intact. Thus, this pattern of results indicates that a CS-US association remains intact despite extinction of the CS.

One might argue that the conditioned stimuli in this experiment remained sensitive to devaluation of their associated US because not enough extinction trials had been conducted. Six extinction sessions were conducted, with each CS presented eight times during each ses-

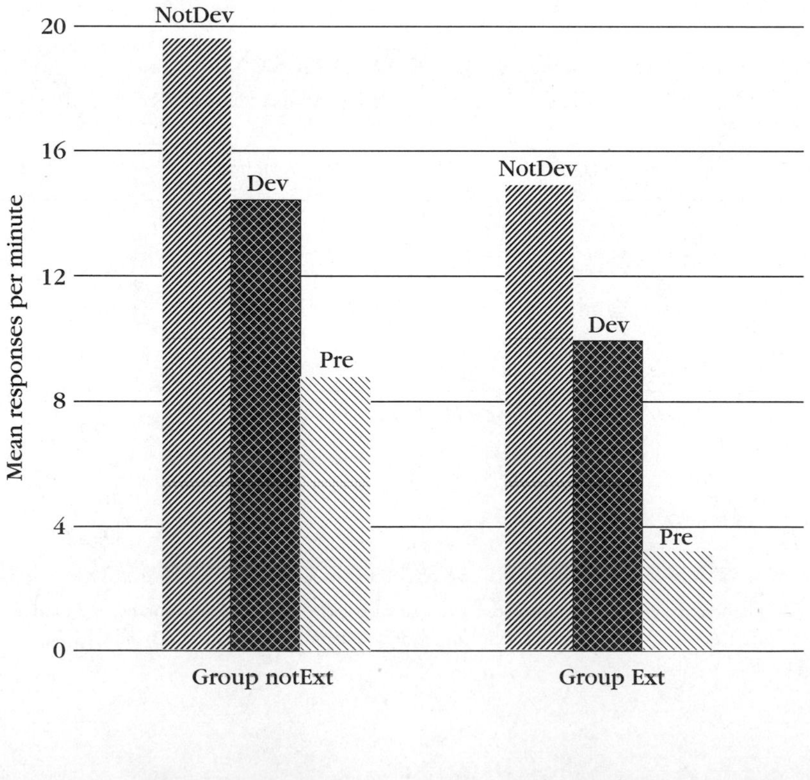

Figure 9.6 Susceptibility of a Pavlovian conditioned stimulus to the effects of US devaluation as a function of whether the CS had (or had not) undergone extinction previously. (Procedures are summarized in Table 9.2. Adapted from Rescorla, 1996a.)

sion. This was clearly enough to produce a major extinction effect because, as I noted above, responding declined from about 20 responses/minute to about 1 response/minute. Thus, extinction had a large impact. It is remarkable that despite this large effect of extinction on conditioned responding, the extinction manipulation did not reduce the sensitivity of the subjects to US devaluation, indicating that the CS-US association remained intact. (For additional related studies, see Delamater, 1996; Rescorla, 2001a.)

Experiments similar to the above study of US devaluation have also been conducted using instrumental conditioning procedures, in which subjects have to perform a specified response to obtain a reinforcer outcome (R → O). As I discussed in Chapter 7, if the instrumental conditioning procedure results in the learning of an R-O association, then devaluation of the reinforcer will produce a decline in the instrumental response. Rescorla has examined whether this susceptibility of instrumental behavior to reinforcer devaluation remains intact through extinction. The procedure for one experiment is summarized in Table 9.3.

Rats were trained to make four different instrumental responses (pressing a lever, pulling a chain, pulling a handle below the grid floor, and nosing a response key) with two different types of food (sucrose and food pellets) serving as the reinforcers. Training procedures were arranged so that within each of a pair of responses, one response (R1 or R3) was reinforced by one of the food types (O1) and the other response (R2 or R4) was reinforced by the second reinforcer (O2), as indicated in Table 9.3. One pair of responses (R1 and R2) was then extinguished. This was then followed by devaluation of the first food type (O1) using a taste-aversion conditioning procedure. As in the Pavlovian conditioning study, the extinguished responses (R1 and R2) were retrained with a third reinforcer (polycose) before the devaluation procedure to make sure that some responding would be evident during the final test.

The results of the experiment are summarized in Figure 9.7. The usual finding with responses that have not been extinguished is that devaluation of a reinforcer reduces the rate of its associated response. This was indeed the case when the subjects were tested with the two responses (R3 and R4) that had not undergone extinction. When given a choice between R3 and R4, the subjects exhibited fewer of the responses whose reinforcer had been devalued (see left panel of Figure 9.7). The primary question in the study was whether this effect would also occur with responses R1 and R2 that had undergone extinction. This was indeed the case (see right panel of Figure 9.7). Although the overall level of responding was

TABLE 9.3 EFFECTS OF REINFORCER DEVALUATION ON INSTRUMENTAL RESPONDING FOLLOWING EXTINCTION (Rescorla 1993a, Experiment 3)

PHASE 1	PHASE 2	US DEVALUATION	TEST
R1 → O1	R1 Ext		R1 vs. R2
R2 → O2	R2 Ext	O1 → LiCl	and
R3 → O1			R3 vs. R4
R4 → O2			

R1, R2, R3, and R4 were four different instrumental responses (counterbalanced across subjects). O1 and O2 were sucrose and food pellets (counterbalanced across subjects and responses). Before the US Devaluation phase both R1 and R2 were reconditioned with a third reinforcer (O3: polycose).

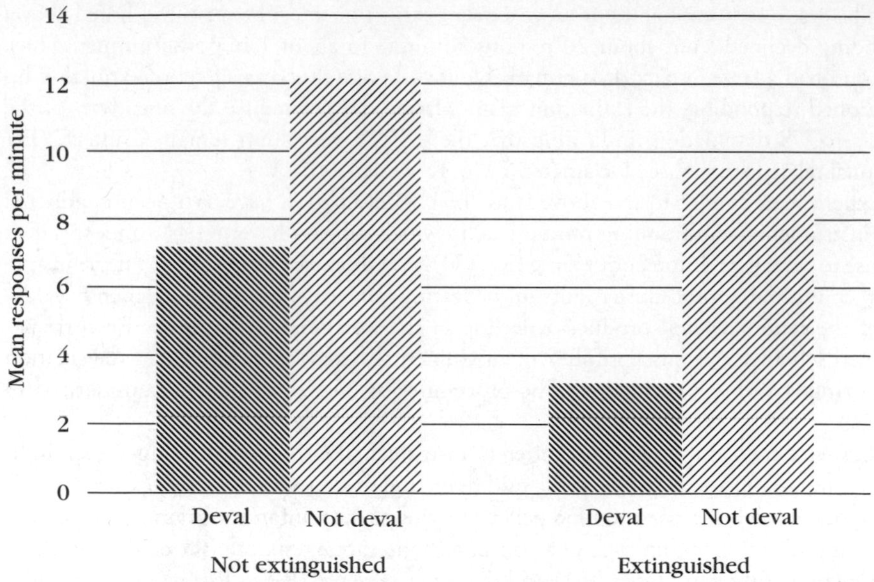

Figure 9.7 Effects of reinforcer devaluation (Deval) evaluated with two responses that have not been extinguished and two responses that previously underwent extinction. (From Figure 4, p. 242, in R. A. Rescorla, *Animal Learning & Behavior,* Vol. 21a. Copyright 1993 Psychonomic Society, Inc. Reprinted with permission.)

less for the responses that had undergone extinction, the devaluation effect was still very much in evidence.

The findings presented in Figure 9.7 and other similar studies have encouraged the conclusion that extinction does not eliminate the R-O and S-O associations that are learned during the course of instrumental conditioning. Rescorla (1993a), for example, has commented that "R-O associations, once trained, are relatively impervious to modification" (p. 244). (For related studies, see Rescorla, 1992, 1993b, 1996, 2001a.)

WHAT IS LEARNED IN EXTINCTION?

The evidence reviewed in the preceding section emphasized that extinction does not involve "unlearning" and that extinction leaves R-O and S-O associations pretty much intact. If these critical associations remain intact, why does responding decline in extinction procedures? In discussing Pavlovian conditioning, I reviewed evidence indicating that S-S associations or S-S learning is more important than S-R learning (see Chapter 4). In discussing instrumental conditioning, I reviewed evidence indicating that S-O and R-O associations are more important than the S-R association that Thorndike emphasized (see Chapter 7). These discussions reflected the major shift away from S-R mechanisms that has occurred in contemporary learning theory during the last quarter of the twentieth century. But this emphasis on S-S and R-O associations creates a dilemma for theories of extinction.

Inhibitory S-R Associations

If conditioned behavior is supported primarily by S-S and R-O associations and these associations are not degraded during the course of extinction, why does extinction produce a decline in responding? In trying to answer this question, investigators have resurrected the importance of S-R associations. However, instead of focusing on excitatory S-R associations, as Thorndike originally did, contemporary investigators have come to the conclusion that nonreinforcement produces an inhibitory S-R association. That is, nonreinforcement of a response in the presence of a specific stimulus produces an inhibitory S-R association that serves to suppress that response whenever S is present. Consistent with the renewal effect, this hypothesis predicts that the effects of extinction will be highly specific to the context in which the response was extinguished.

Why should nonreinforcement produce an inhibitory S-R association? In answering this question, it is important to keep in mind that extinction involves a special type of nonreinforcement. It involves nonreinforcement after a history of reinforcement. Nonreinforcement without such a prior history is not extinction but more akin to habituation. This is an important distinction because nonreinforcement is aversive only after a history of reinforcement. Thus, the emotional effects of nonreinforcement depend critically on the subject's prior history. If your partner never made you coffee in the morning, you will not be disappointed if the coffee is not ready when you get up. If you never received an allowance, you will not be disappointed when you don't get one. It is only the omission of an expected reward that creates disappointment or frustration. Furthermore, these emotional effects are presumed to play a critical role in the behavioral decline that occurs in extinction.

As I mentioned at the outset of the chapter, extinction involves both behavioral and emotional effects. The emotional effects stem from the frustration that is triggered when an expected reinforcer is not forthcoming. Nonreinforcement in the face of the expectation of reward is assumed to trigger an unconditioned aversive frustrative reaction (Amsel, 1958). This aversive emotion serves to discourage responding during the course of extinction through the establishment of an inhibitory S-R association (Rescorla, 2001a).

The establishment of an inhibitory S-R association during the course of extinction is illustrated by an experiment whose procedures are outlined in Table 9.4. The subjects first received discrimination training in which a common response (Rc) was reinforced with food pellets whenever a light or noise stimulus (L or N) was present. This training was conducted so that nonreinforcement in the presence of L or N would elicit frustration when extinction was introduced. The targets of extinction were a lever press and a chain pull response (designated as R1 and R2, counterbalanced across subjects). To allow extinction of these responses, they were first reinforced, again with food pellets. Notice that the reinforcement of R1 and R2 did not occur in the presence of the light and noise stimuli. Therefore, this reinforcement training was not expected to establish any S-R associations involving the light and noise stimuli.

Extinction was conducted in the third phase and consisted of presentations of L and N (to create the expectancy of reward) with either R1 or R2 available but nonreinforced. The

TABLE 9.4

DEVELOPMENT OF AN INHIBITORY S-R ASSOCIATION IN INSTRUMENTAL EXTINCTION (Rescorla 1993b, Experiment 3)

PHASE 1	PHASE 2	EXTINCTION	TEST
N: Rc → P	R1 → P	N: R1–	N: R1, R2
L: Rc → P	R2 → P	L: R2–	L: R1, R2

N and L were noise and light discriminative stimuli. Rc was a common response (nose poking) for all subjects, P represents the food pellet reinforcer, R1 and R2 were lever press and chain pull, counterbalanced across subjects.

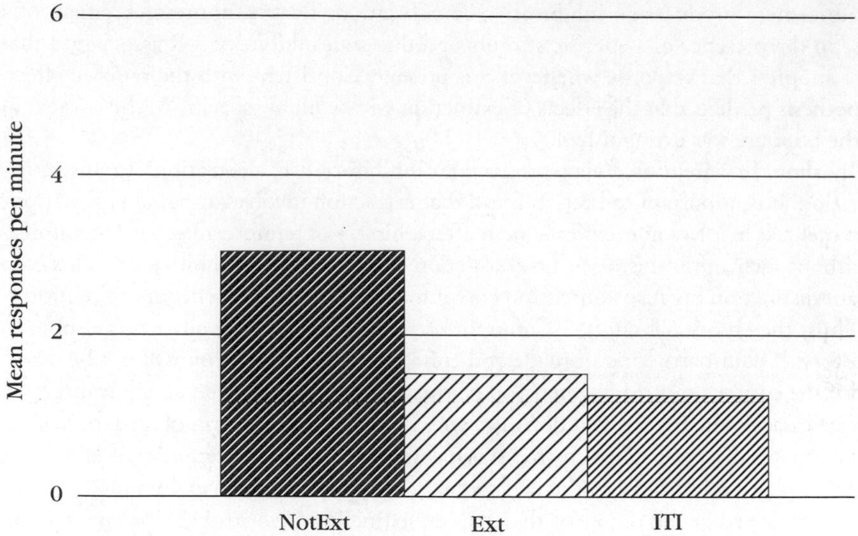

Figure 9.8 Demonstration that extinction involves the acquisition of an inhibitory S-R association that is specific to the stimulus in the presence of which the response is nonreinforced (see procedure summarized in Table 9.4). A particular response occurred less often during the stimulus with which the response had been extinguished than during an alternate stimulus. (From Rescorla, 1993b.)

extinction phase presumably established inhibitory S-R associations involving N-R1 and L-R2. The presence of these associations was tested by measuring the rate of R1 and R2 in the presence of the L and N stimuli. If an inhibitory N-R1 association was established during extinction, the subjects were predicted to make fewer R1 than R2 responses when tested with N. In a corresponding fashion, they were expected to make fewer R2 than R1 responses when tested with L. Notice that this differential response outcome cannot be explained in terms of changes in R-O or S-O associations because such changes should have affected R1 and R2 equally.

The results of the experiment are presented in Figure 9.8. Responding is shown for the intertrial interval (ITI) and in the presence of the stimulus (L or N) with which the response had been extinguished or not. Responding during the stimulus with which the response had been extinguished was significantly less than responding during the alternate stimulus. Furthermore, the extinction stimulus produced responding not significantly higher than what occurred during the intertrial interval. These results indicate that the extinction procedure produced an inhibitory S-R association that was specific to a particular stimulus and response. (For related studies, see Rescorla, 1997a, 1997c.)

The proposition that extinction involves the learning of an inhibitory association is contrary to conventional wisdom that considered conditioned inhibition and extinction to be different phenomena. In previous editions of this text, for example, I emphasized that extinction should not be considered a case of conditioned inhibition because an extinguished stimulus does not pass the conventional summation and retardation-of-acquisition tests for conditioned inhibition (for example, Domjan & Burkhard, 1982, 1986; Domjan, 1993, 1998). However, the distinction between extinction and inhibition is becoming increasingly difficult to maintain in light of data such as those presented in Figure 9.8. Some studies have also demonstrated that extinguished stimuli can pass both of the conventional tests for conditioned inhibition. For example, Carlton, Mitchell, and Schachtman (1996) reported that in a taste-aversion conditioning preparation, an extinguished CS is slower to reacquire excitatory properties than a novel flavor. In addition, an extinguished CS can attenuate responding to a previously established excitatory stimulus, in a summation test (see also Schachtman, Threlkeld, & Meyer, 2000). Evidence that an extinguished CS passes the retardation-of-acquisition test of inhibition has also been reported by Bouton (1986) and Bouton and Swartzentruber (1989). (For additional consideration of retardation of acquisition following extinction, see Bouton & Nelson, 1998; Hart, Bourne, & Schachtman, 1995; Ricker & Bouton, 1996; Rescorla, 2001b). Few published studies of the summation test following extinction are available, and it remains to be seen whether the type of inhibition that is involved in extinction is the same as more traditional forms of Pavlovian conditioned inhibition.

"Paradoxical" Reward Effects

If the decline in responding in extinction is due to the frustrative effects of an unexpected absence of reinforcement, then one would expect more rapid extinction following training that establishes greater expectations of reward. This is indeed the case and has led to a number of paradoxical effects. For example, the more training that is provided with reinforcement, the stronger will be the expectancy of reward, and therefore the stronger will be the frustration that occurs when extinction is introduced. If the decline in responding is due to the frustrative effects of nonreward, more extensive reinforcement training should produce more rapid extinction. This prediction has been confirmed and is called the **overtraining extinction effect** (Ishida & Papini, 1997; Senkowski, 1978; Theios & Brelsford, 1964).

The overtraining extinction effect is "paradoxical" because it represents fewer responses in extinction after more extensive reinforcement training. Thinking casually, an observer might think that more extensive training should create a "stronger" response that would be more resistant to extinction. But the opposite is the case, especially when training involves continuous reinforcement.

Another paradoxical reward effect that reflects similar mechanisms is the **magnitude reinforcement extinction effect.** This phenomenon refers to the fact that responding declines more rapidly in extinction following reinforcement with a larger reinforcer. This phenomenon is also most commonly observed if training involves continuous reinforcement (Hulse, 1958; Wagner, 1961), and is readily accounted for in terms of the frustrative effects of nonreward. Nonreinforcement is apt to be more frustrative if the individual has come to expect a large reward than if the individual has come to expect a small reward. Consider two scenarios: In one, you receive $100/month from your parents to help with incidental expenses at college; in the other, you get only $20/month. In both cases, your parents stop the payments when you drop out of school for a semester. This nonreinforcement will be more aversive if you had come to expect the larger monthly allowance.

The most extensively investigated paradoxical reward effect is the **partial reinforcement extinction effect.** A key factor that determines the magnitude of both the behavioral and the emotional effects of an extinction procedure is the schedule of reinforcement that was in effect before the extinction procedure was introduced. Various subtle features of reinforcement schedules can influence the extinction of instrumental responses. But the dominant schedule characteristic that determines extinction effects is whether the instrumental response was reinforced every time it occurred (**continuous reinforcement**) or only some of the times it occurred (**intermittent,** or *partial,* **reinforcement**). The general finding is that extinction is much slower and involves fewer frustration reactions if partial reinforcement rather than continuous reinforcement was in effect before introduction of the extinction procedure. This phenomenon is called the *partial reinforcement extinction effect,* or PREE.

In one interesting study, the emergence of the PREE during the course of infant development was examined with infant rats serving as subjects (Chen & Amsel, 1980). The rat pups were permitted to run down an alley for a chance to suckle, and they obtained milk as the reinforcer. Some pups were reinforced each time (continuous reinforcement), whereas others were reinforced only some of the time (partial reinforcement). Following training, all of the subjects were tested under conditions of extinction. The experiment was repeated with rat pups of two different ages. In one replication, the experiment began when the pups were 10 days of age. In another, the experiment began when the subjects were 12 days old—just 2 days later. The results are presented in Figure 9.9.

All of the rat pups acquired the runway instrumental response. As might be expected, the 12-day-old pups ran faster than the 10-day-olds, but the 10-day-olds also increased their running speeds with training. This increase in the speed of running was due to the instrumental reinforcement, not to getting older, because when extinction was introduced, all of the subjects slowed down. However, a difference in extinction between continuous reinforcement and partial reinforcement developed only for the pups that began the experiment at 12 days of age. Thus, the PREE was evident in 12-day-old rat pups but not in 10-day-old pups. On the basis of a variety of different lines of evidence, Amsel (1992) has concluded that this developmental difference in the emergence of the PREE is related to the rapid maturation of the hippocampus during this stage of life in rat pups.

The persistence in responding that is created by intermittent reinforcement can be remarkable. Habitual gamblers are at the mercy of intermittent reinforcement. Occasional winnings encourage them to continue gambling during long strings of losses. Intermittent reinforcement can also have undesirable consequences in parenting. Consider, for example, a child riding in a grocery cart while the parent is shopping. The child asks the parent to buy a piece of candy for him. The parent says no. The child asks again and again and then begins to throw a temper tantrum because the parent continues to say no. At this point, the parent is likely to give in to avoid public embarrassment. By finally buying the candy, the parent will have provided intermittent reinforcement for the repeated demands for candy. The parent will also have reinforced the tantrum behavior. The intermittent reinforcement of the requests for candy will make the child very persistent in asking for candy during future shopping trips.

Although most studies of the partial reinforcement extinction have employed instrumental conditioning procedures, the PREE has also been demonstrated in Pavlovian conditioning (for recent examples, see Pearce, Redhead, & Aydin, 1997; Rescorla, 1999). In early studies, the PREE was found only in studies that compared the effects of continuous and partial reinforcement training in different groups of subjects. Recent studies have demonstrated that the PREE can also occur in the same subjects if they experience continuous reinforcement in the presence of one set of cues and intermittent reinforcement in the presence of other stimuli (for example, Pearce, Redhead, & Aydin, 1997; Rescorla, 1999c; Svartdal, 2000; Zarcone, Branch, Hughes, & Pennypacker, 1997). This within-subject PREE presents theoretical challenges that so far have not been completely worked out.

Mechanisms of the Partial Reinforcement Extinction Effect

Perhaps the most obvious explanation of the PREE is that the introduction of extinction is easier to detect after continuous reinforcement than after partial reinforcement. If you don't receive the reinforcer after each response during training, you may not immediately notice when reinforcers are omitted altogether. The absence of reinforcement is presumably much

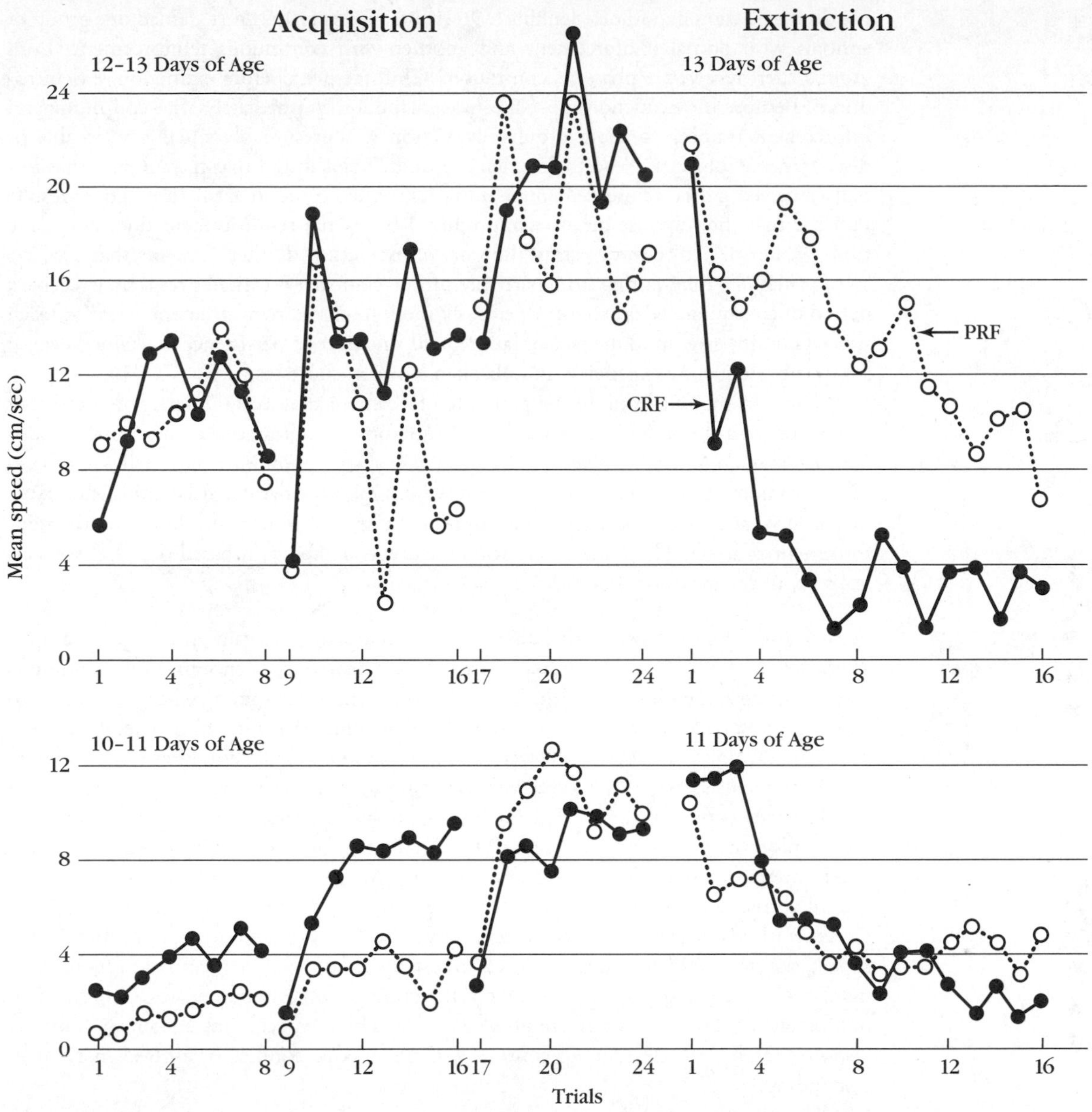

Figure 9.9 Emergence of the partial reinforcement extinction effect between the 10th and 12th day of life in infant rat pups. During acquisition, the pups were reinforced with a chance to suckle milk after running down an alley on either a continuous or a partial reinforcement schedule. Extinction was introduced after 3 sessions of reinforcement training. (From Figure 1, p. 484, J. S. Chen & A. Amsel, in *Developmental Psychobiology,* Vol. 13. © John Wiley & Sons. Reprinted by permission of John Wiley & Sons, Inc.)

easier to detect after continuous reinforcement. This explanation of the partial reinforcement extinction effect is called the **discrimination hypothesis.**

Although the discrimination hypothesis provides an intuitively reasonable explanation, the partial reinforcement extinction effect is not so straightforward. In an ingenious test of the discrimination hypothesis, Jenkins (1962) and Theios (1962) first trained one group of animals with partial reinforcement and another with continuous reinforcement. Both groups then received a phase of continuous reinforcement before extinction was introduced. Because the extinction procedure was introduced immediately after continuous reinforcement training for both groups, extinction was presumably equally noticeable or discriminable for both. Nevertheless, Jenkins and Theios found that the subjects that initially received partial reinforcement training responded more in extinction. These results indicate that the response persistence produced by partial reinforcement does not come from greater difficulty in detecting the start of extinction. Rather, it seems that subjects learn something long-lasting from partial reinforcement that is carried over if they receive a period of continuous reinforcement before extinction. Partial reinforcement seems to teach subjects to not give up in the face of failure, and this learned persistence is retained even if subjects subsequently experience an unbroken string of successes.

What do subjects learn during partial reinforcement that makes them more persistent in the face of a run of bad luck or failure? Numerous complicated experiments have been performed in attempts to answer this question. These studies indicate that partial reinforcement promotes persistence in two different ways. One explanation, **frustration theory,** is based on what subjects learn about the emotional effects of nonreward during partial reinforcement training. The other explanation, **sequential theory,** is based on what subjects learn about the memory of nonreward.

Courtesy of A. Amsel

A. Amsel

Frustration Theory. Frustration theory was developed by Abram Amsel (for example, 1958, 1962, 1967, 1992). According to frustration theory, persistence in extinction results from learning something paradoxical, namely, to continue responding when you expect to be nonreinforced or frustrated. Frustration theory assumes that intermittent reinforcement results in learning to respond in the face of expected nonreinforcement. However, this learning requires considerable experience with intermittent reinforcement.

Frustration theory characterizes the learning that occurs during the course of intermittent reinforcement in terms of stages. Intermittent reinforcement involves both rewarded and nonrewarded trials. Rewarded trials lead individuals to expect reinforcement, and nonrewarded trials lead them to expect the absence of reward. Consequently, intermittent reinforcement leads to the learning of expectations of both reward and nonreward. At first, the expectation of reward encourages subjects to respond, and the anticipation of nonreinforcement discourages responding. Thus, early in training, subjects trained with intermittent reinforcement are in a conflict about what to do. Their expectations encourage opposite response tendencies. As training continues, however, this conflict is resolved in favor of responding.

The resolution of the conflict occurs because reinforcement is not predictable in the typical partial reinforcement schedule. The instrumental response ends up being reinforced some of the times when the subject expects nonreward. Because of such experiences, the instrumental response becomes conditioned to the expectation of nonreward. According to frustration theory, this is the key to persistent responding in extinction. With sufficient training, *intermittent reinforcement results in learning to make the instrumental response as a reaction to the expectation of nonreward.* Once the response has become conditioned to the expectation of nonreward, responding persists when extinction is introduced. By contrast, there is nothing about the experience of continuous reinforcement that encourages subjects to respond when they expect nonreward. Continuous reinforcement does not produce persistence in extinction.

Sequential Theory. Sequential theory was proposed by Capaldi (for example, 1967, 1971) and is stated in terms of memory concepts. It assumes that subjects can remember whether they were reinforced for performing the instrumental response in the recent past. They remember both recent rewarded and nonrewarded trials. The theory assumes further that during intermittent reinforcement training, the memory of nonreward becomes a cue for performing the instrumental response. According to sequential theory, this produces persistence in extinction. Precisely how this happens depends greatly on the sequence of rewarded (R) and nonrewarded (N) trials that are administered in the intermittent reinforcement schedule. That is why the theory is labeled "sequential."

Consider the following sequence of trials: RNN<u>R</u>RRN<u>R</u>. The subject is rewarded on the first trial, not rewarded on the next two trials, then rewarded twice, then not rewarded, and then rewarded again. The fourth and last trials are critical in this schedule and are therefore underlined. On the fourth trial, the subject is reinforced after receiving nonreward on the preceding two trials. It is assumed that the subject remembers the two nonrewarded trials when it is reinforced on the fourth trial. Because of this, the memory of two nonrewarded trials becomes a cue for responding. Responding in the face of the memory of nonreward is again reinforced on the last trial. On the last trial, the animal is reinforced for responding during the memory of one nonreinforced trials. With enough experiences of this type, the subject learns to respond whenever it remembers not having been reinforced on the preceding trials. This learning creates persistence of the instrumental response in extinction. (For more recent studies of this mechanism, see Capaldi, Alptekin, & Birmingham, 1996; Capaldi, Alptekin, Miller, & Barry, 1992; Haggbloom, Lovelace, Brewer, Levins, & Owens, 1990.)

E. J. Capaldi

Some have regarded frustration theory and sequential theory as competing explanations of the partial reinforcement extinction effect. However, since the two mechanisms were originally proposed, a large and impressive body of evidence has been obtained in support of each theory. Therefore, neither theory can be regarded as correct and the other as incorrect. Rather, the two theories point out two different ways in which partial reinforcement can promote responding during extinction. Memory mechanisms may make more of a contribution when training trials are not separated by long intertrial intervals (thus, reducing the difficulty of remembering the outcome of the preceding trial). In contrast, the emotional learning described by frustration theory is less sensitive to intertrial intervals and thus provides a better explanation of the PREE when widely spaced training trials are used. The prudent conclusion is that both mechanisms contribute to persistence in most situations.

RESISTANCE TO CHANGE AND BEHAVIORAL MOMENTUM

Another way to think about response persistence in extinction is that it represents resistance to the change in reinforcement contingencies that occurs when the extinction procedure is introduced. Nevin and his colleagues have focused on resistance to change more generally and have proposed the concept of **behavioral momentum** to characterize the susceptibility of behavior to disruptions (Nevin, 1992, 1998; Nevin & Grace, 2000). The term *behavioral momentum* is based on the concept of momentum in Newtonian physics. The momentum of a physical object is the product of its weight (or mass) and its speed. A fast-moving bullet and a slow-moving freight train both have tremendous momentum, and because of that both are hard to stop. The bullet is not heavy but it moves very fast, making the product of its weight and speed high. A freight train moves slower than a bullet but is much heavier. As a consequence, the product of its weight and speed is also high. By analogy (and a detailed mathematical model), the behavioral momentum hypothesis predicts that behavior that has a great deal of momentum will also be hard to "stop" or disrupt by various manipulations.

Research on behavioral momentum has been conducted using multiple schedules of reinforcement. As I described in Chapter 8, a multiple schedule has two (or more) components. Each component is identified by a distinctive stimulus and its accompanying schedule of reinforcement. Multiple schedules are popular in studies of behavioral momentum because they enable investigators to compare the susceptibility of behavior to disruption under two different conditions in the same session. One observer may be interested, for example, in whether responding maintained by a continuous reinforcement schedule is more (or less) susceptible to disruption than responding maintained on a variable ratio schedule. Such a question can be answered by using a multiple CRF-VR schedule.

A number of different sources of disruption have been examined in studies of behavioral momentum. These have included providing extra food before the experimental session, providing extra food during intervals between components of the multiple schedule, and extinction. Although most of the research has employed laboratory animals, experiments have also been conducted with human subjects (for example, Mace, Lalli, Shea, Lalli, West, Roberts, & Nevin, 1990).

The basic behavioral momentum experiment is illustrated by a recent study that was conducted with two individuals who had severe mental retardation (Dube & McIlvane, 2001). One of the participants, HCB, was a 17-year-old woman whose mental age score was lower than 3 years. Two different instrumental tasks (A and B) were presented on a computer monitor, and pieces of food served as the reinforcer. In one task, a white square with a black cross appeared in one of the four corners of the computer screen, and HCB had to touch the square to get reinforced. In the other task, HCB had to touch one of two pictures that was the same as a picture that had been presented briefly at the start of the trial. The two tasks were alternated in blocks of 15 trials (either ABAB or BABA), with a 3-second pause between components. In the first phase of the experiment, responding on task A was reinforced on a CRF schedule, and responding on task B was reinforced on a variable ratio 4 schedule (VR4). After responding stabilized in each component (the baseline condition), tests of behavioral momentum were conducted. During the momentum test sessions, the CRF and VR4 components remained in effect, but HCB received some food before the session as well as during the pause between task components. In addition, HCB could see Disney cartoons on a TV screen near by, play with a toy displaying colored patterns, and hear an audiotape with various sound effects.

The results obtained in the first phase of the experiment are presented in the left panel of Figure 9.10. The rate of responding during the momentum test is shown as a proportion of the rate of responding during the baseline sessions when the disruptors were not presented. As expected, introducing the various sources of distraction during the test sessions resulted in a decrease in responding. More important, responding during the VR component was disrupted much more than responding during the CRF component. These results suggest that VR responding had less behavioral momentum than CRF responding.

During the second phase of the experiment, responding in each component of the multiple schedule was reinforced on a CRF schedule. The momentum test conducted with this multiple schedule is shown in the middle panel. This time, responding was equally disrupted in each of the components of the multiple schedule. The right panel of Figure 9.10 shows data from a third phase of the experiment, in which the multiple CRF-VR4 schedule was reintroduced. As in Phase 1, responding on the CRF component was less susceptible to disruption than responding on the VR4 component.

The results obtained with HCB illustrate two of the common (but not universal) outcomes of studies of behavioral momentum (see Nevin & Grace, 2000). The first is that

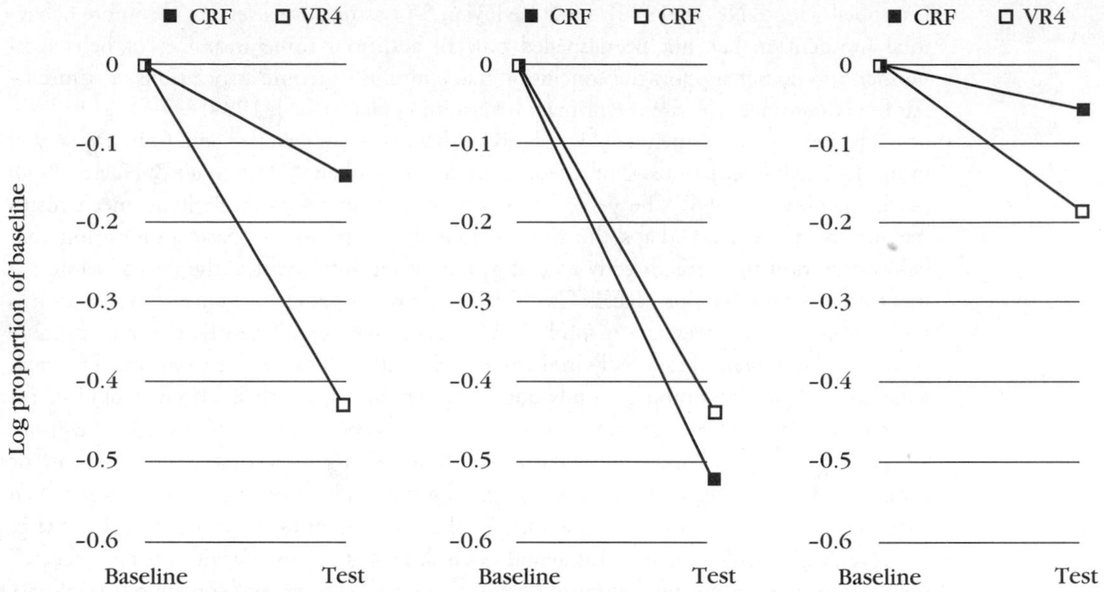

Figure 9.10 Responding on a multiple schedule by a mentally retarded individual (HCB) during baseline and behavioral momentum tests. In Phase 1, responding on components of the multiple schedule was reinforced on CRF and VR4 schedules. In Phase 2, responding in both components was reinforced on a CRF schedule. Phase 3 involved return to the CRF-VR4 multiple schedule. (After Dube & McIlvane, 2001.)

behavioral momentum is directly related to the rate of reinforcement. A higher rate of reinforcement produces behavior that has greater momentum and is less susceptible to disruption. Analyses of rates of reinforcement obtained by HCB indicated that she received a higher rate of reinforcement during the CRF component of the multiple schedule than during the VR component in Phases 1 and 3 of the experiment. In accordance with the generalization that behavioral momentum is directly related to rate of reinforcement, HCB's responding during the CRF component displayed greater momentum in Phases 1 and 3. When both components of the multiple schedule involved CRF (Phase 2), rates of reinforcement were similar in the two components, and measures of behavioral momentum were also similar.

Another common (but not universal) finding is that behavioral momentum is unrelated to response rate. Although this is not shown in Figure 9.10, HCB responded at similar rates on the CRF and VR4 components of the multiple schedule on Phases 1 and 3 of the experiment. Nevertheless, she showed differences in behavioral momentum in those two components. Thus, two behaviors that occur at similar rates do not necessarily have similar degrees of behavioral momentum (for example, Nevin, Mandell, & Atak, 1983). Nevin (1998; see also Nevin & Grace, 2000) has emphasized reinforcement rate rather than response rate as the primary determinant of behavioral momentum. This conclusion is further confirmed by studies showing that schedules that provide similar rates of reinforcement but different rates of responding have similar momentum or resistance to change (for example, Fath, Fields, Malott, & Grossett, 1983).

The primacy of reinforcement rate rather than response rate as the determinant of behavioral momentum has encouraged Nevin and Grace (2000) to attribute behavioral momentum primarily to Pavlovian conditioning or S-O associations (for example, McLean,

Campbell-Tie, & Nevin, 1996). How Pavlovian S-O associations serve to promote behavioral momentum has not been spelled out. In addition, some instances of behavioral momentum do not support the conclusion that stimulus-outcome associations or stimulus-reinforcer contingencies are the primary determining factor (Bell, 1999).

The behavioral momentum hypothesis has helped to characterize data from a variety of multiple schedule situations. (For recent examples, see Cohen, 1998; Grace & Nevin, 2000; Nevin & Grace, 1999.) The generality of the effects and their underlying mechanisms remain controversial. Perhaps the most serious challenge to the basic proposition that behavioral momentum is directly related to rate of reinforcement is the partial reinforcement extinction effect, or PREE. The PREE is a case in which resistance to extinction is greater following a lower rate or probability of reinforcement. The PREE is a commonly observed phenomenon, especially in discrete-trial studies conducted in runways. The challenge to the behavioral momentum hypothesis posed by the PREE has been recognized for more than a decade (for example, Nevin, 1988; see also Harper & McLean, 1992) without adequate resolution. Nevin and Grace (2000) have suggested that the PREE can be explained by assuming that extinction is less discriminable after intermittent rather than continuous reinforcement. This is essentially the discrimination hypothesis of the PREE. However, as I described earlier, this hypothesis is difficult to reconcile with the fact that partial reinforcement increases resistance to extinction even if a stage of continuous reinforcement is provided before the extinction procedure (Jenkins, 1962; Theios, 1962).

The idea of behavioral momentum is intriguing because it attempts to capture in a single concept the resistance of behavior to a variety of sources of change. A related overarching concept that has been entertained periodically is "response strength" (see Killeen & Hall, 2001, for a recent discussion). It remains to be seen whether a single concept can characterize behavioral persistence in the face of various sources of disruption. Some have suggested that the concept of behavioral momentum be applied only to sources of disruption that cause changes in performance rather than to ones that also produce new learning. This restriction is promising because it includes manipulations such as satiation and pre-session feeding, whose effects appear to be consistent with the behavioral momentum hypothesis. At the same time, the restriction excludes manipulations such as extinction, which produce data that are difficult to explain in terms of behavioral momentum.

CONCLUDING COMMENTS

In many ways, studies of extinction illustrate the enduring nature of certain issues in behavior theory. Early studies of extinction focused on the partial reinforcement extinction effect and other "paradoxical" reward effects and were conducted in the Hullian tradition that emphasized S-R learning. S-R mechanisms fell in disrepute with growing evidence that Pavlovian and instrumental conditioning involve S-O and R-O associations and are controlled or modulated by contextual cues. This body of evidence was part of the "cognitive revolution" that swept over psychology in the last quarter of the twentieth century. It gave us a better understanding of spontaneous recovery and led to the discovery of new phenomena such as renewal and reinstatement. However, these phenomena represent the failures of extinction rather than extinction itself. As I have described, understanding extinction itself has required a return to S-R concepts, this time in the form of inhibitory S-R associations. Investigators remain interested in what makes behavior resistant to change. Such resistance or behavioral momentum creates special challenges for behavior therapy.

SAMPLE QUESTIONS

1. Describe the basic behavioral and emotional consequences of extinction.
2. Describe the various ways in which control of behavior by contextual cues is relevant to the behavioral effects of extinction.
3. Describe evidence that identifies the development of inhibitory S-R associations in extinction.
4. Describe the partial reinforcement extinction effect and major explanations of the phenomenon.
5. Describe the concept of behavioral momentum. What are the advantages and disadvantages of the concept?

KEY TERMS

behavioral momentum The susceptibility of responding to disruption by manipulations such as pre-session feeding, delivery of free food, or a change in the schedule of reinforcement.

continuous reinforcement A schedule of reinforcement in which every occurrence of the instrumental response produces the reinforcer. Abbreviated CRF.

discrimination hypothesis An explanation of the partial reinforcement extinction effect, according to which extinction is slower after partial reinforcement than continuous reinforcement because the onset of extinction is more difficult to detect following partial reinforcement.

extinction (in classical conditioning) Reduction of a learned response that occurs because the conditioned stimulus is no longer paired with the unconditioned stimulus. Also, the procedure of repeatedly presenting a conditioned stimulus without the unconditioned stimulus.

extinction (in instrumental conditioning) Reduction of the instrumental response that occurs because the response is no longer followed by the reinforcer. Also, the procedure of no longer reinforcing the instrumental response.

forgetting A reduction of a learned response that occurs because of the passage of time, not because of particular experiences.

frustration An aversive emotional reaction that results from the unexpected absence of reinforcement.

frustration theory A theory of the partial reinforcement extinction effect, according to which extinction is retarded after partial reinforcement because the instrumental response becomes conditioned to the anticipation of frustrative nonreward.

intermittent reinforcement A schedule of reinforcement in which only some of the occurrences of the instrumental response are reinforced. The instrumental response is reinforced occasionally, or intermittently. Also called *partial reinforcement.*

magnitude reinforcement extinction effect Less persistence of instrumental behavior in extinction following training with a large reinforcer than following training with a small or moderate reinforcer.

overtraining extinction effect Less persistence of instrumental behavior in extinction following extensive training with reinforcement (overtraining) than following only moderate levels of reinforcement training.

partial reinforcement extinction effect The term used to describe greater persistence in instrumental responding in extinction after partial (intermittent) reinforcement training than after continuous reinforcement training. Abbreviated PREE.

reinstatement Recovery of excitatory responding to an extinguished stimulus produced by exposures to the unconditioned stimulus.

renewal Recovery of excitatory responding to an extinguished stimulus produced by a shift away from the contextual cues that were present during extinction.

sequential theory A theory of the partial reinforcement extinction effect according to which extinction is retarded after partial reinforcement because the instrumental response becomes conditioned to the memory of nonreward.

CHAPTER

10

AVERSIVE CONTROL: AVOIDANCE AND PUNISHMENT

Chapter 10 deals with how behavior can be controlled by aversive stimulation. The discussion focuses on two types of instrumental aversive control—avoidance and punishment. Avoidance conditioning increases the performance of a target behavior, and punishment decreases the target response. In both cases, individuals learn to minimize their exposure to aversive stimulation. Because of this similarity, theoretical analyses of avoidance and punishment share some of the same concepts. Nevertheless, experimental analyses of avoidance and punishment have, for the most part, proceeded independently of each other. In this chapter, I describe the major theoretical puzzles and empirical findings in both areas of research.

Aversive stimulation is a fact of life and influences much of what we do. Fear, pain, and disappointment are an inevitable part of living. It is therefore understandable that we should be interested in how behavior is controlled by aversive stimuli. Two procedures have been extensively investigated in studies of aversive control—avoidance and punishment. In an avoidance procedure, the individual has to make a specific response to prevent an aversive stimulus from occurring. For example, grabbing a handrail to avoid slipping on the stairs is an avoidance response. An avoidance procedure involves a negative contingency between an instrumental response and the aversive stimulus. If the response occurs, the aversive stimulus is not presented. If you grab the handrail, you will not suffer the pain of falling. By contrast, a punishment procedure involves a positive contingency between the response and the aversive stimulus. In punishment, the aversive stimulus occurs if the specified response is made. For example, if you cut in line at a ticket window, you are likely to be reprimanded by others waiting in the line.

Avoidance procedures increase the occurrence of instrumental behavior, whereas punishment procedures suppress instrumental responding. With both procedures, the behavior that develops serves to minimize contact with the aversive stimulus. The critical difference is that, in avoidance, taking specific action prevents the aversive stimulus whereas, in punishment, refraining from action minimizes contact with the aversive stimulus. Because of this, avoidance behavior is sometimes referred to as *active avoidance* and punishment is sometimes referred to as *passive avoidance.* Both terms emphasize the fact that both avoidance and punishment involve minimizing contact with an aversive stimulus.

Despite the similarities between them, avoidance and punishment have been the subjects of different investigative approaches. Research on avoidance behavior has focused primarily on theoretical issues. Investigators focused on avoidance behavior have been working hard to determine what mechanisms are responsible for behavior whose primary consequence is the absence of aversive stimulation. By contrast, investigators interested in punishment have focused on practical and ethical considerations, such as what procedures are effective in suppressing behavior, and under what circumstances is it justified to use these procedures?

AVOIDANCE BEHAVIOR

Origins of the Study of Avoidance Behavior

One cannot understand the study of avoidance behavior without understanding its historical roots. Experimental investigations of avoidance behavior originated in studies of classical conditioning. The first avoidance conditioning experiments were conducted by the Russian psychologist Vladimir Bechterev (1913) as an extension of Pavlov's research. Unlike Pavlov, however, Bechterev was interested in studying associative learning in human subjects. In one situation, participants were instructed to place a finger on a metal plate. A warning stimulus (the CS) was then presented, followed by a brief shock (the US) through the metal plate. As you might predict, the participants quickly lifted their finger off the plate upon being shocked. After a few trials, they also learned to make this response to the warning stimulus.

Although Bechterev's experiment was viewed as a standard example of classical conditioning, the participants themselves determined whether or not they were exposed to the US. If they lifted their finger in response to the CS, they did not experience the shock delivered through the metal plate on that trial. This aspect of the procedure constitutes a signifi-

Figure 10.1 Modern running wheel for rodents.

cant departure from Pavlov's methods, because in standard classical conditioning exposure to the US does not depend on the participant's behavior.

The fact that Bechterev did not use a standard classical conditioning procedure went unnoticed for many years. However, starting in the 1930s, several investigations focused attention on the difference between a standard classical conditioning procedure and a procedure that had an instrumental avoidance component added (for example, Schlosberg, 1934, 1936). One of the most influential of these studies was performed by Brogden, Lipman, and Culler (1938).

Brogden et al. tested two groups of guinea pigs in a rotating wheel apparatus (see Figure 10.1). A tone served as the CS, and a shock served as the US. The shock stimulated the guinea pigs to run and thereby rotate the wheel. For the classical conditioning group, the shock was always presented 2 seconds after the beginning of the tone. For the avoidance conditioning group, the shock also followed the tone when the animals did not make the conditioned response (a small movement of the wheel). However, if the avoidance animals moved the wheel during the tone CS before the shock occurred, the scheduled shock was omitted. Figure 10.2 shows the percentage of trials on which each group made the conditioned response. The avoidance group quickly learned to make the conditioned response and was responding on 100% of the trials within 8 days of training. In contrast, the classical conditioning group never achieved this high level of performance.

The results obtained by Brogden and his collaborators proved that avoidance conditioning is different from standard classical conditioning and ushered in several decades of active research on avoidance learning.

The Discriminated Avoidance Procedure

Although avoidance behavior is not just another case of classical conditioning, the classical conditioning heritage of the study of avoidance behavior has greatly influenced its experimental and theoretical analysis to the present day (for example, Ayres, 1998). Investigators have been concerned with the importance of the warning signal in avoidance procedures and with how such warning signals are related to the aversive US and the instrumental response. Experimental issues of this type have been extensively investigated with procedures similar to that used by Brogden and his colleagues. This method is called **discriminated,** or **signaled, avoidance.** The standard features of the discriminated avoidance procedure are diagrammed in Figure 10.3.

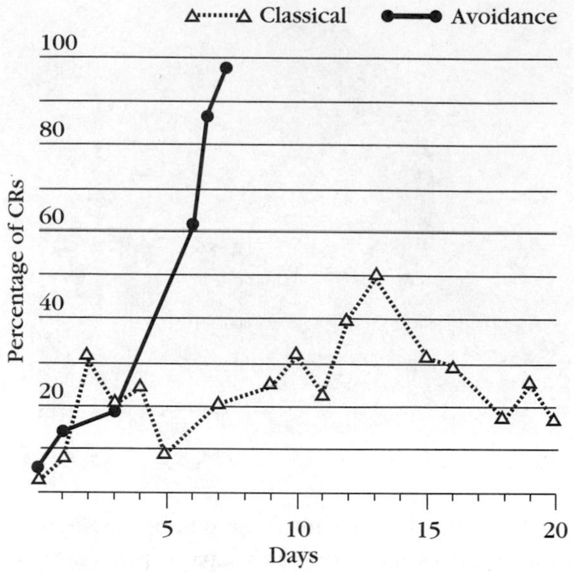

Figure 10.2 Percentage of trials with a conditioned response on successive days of training. The conditioned response prevented shock delivery for the avoidance group but not for the classical group. (From "The Role of Incentive in Conditioning and Extinction," by W. J. Brogden, E. A. Lipman, and E. Culler, 1938. *American Journal of Psychology, 51,* pp. 109–117.)

The first thing to note about the discriminated avoidance procedure is that it involves discrete trials. Each trial is initiated by the CS or warning stimulus. The events that occur after that depend on what the participant does. There are two possibilities. If the subject makes the response required for avoidance during the CS but before the shock is delivered, the CS is turned off and the US is omitted on that trial. This is a successful **avoidance trial.** If the subject fails to make the required response during the CS-US interval, the scheduled shock is presented and remains on until the response occurs, whereupon both the CS and the US are terminated. In this case, the instrumental response results in escape from the shock; hence, this type of trial is called an **escape trial.** During early stages of training, most of the trials are escape trials; but as training progresses and the subject starts making the avoidance response, avoidance trials come to predominate.

Discriminated avoidance procedures are often conducted in a shuttle box like that shown in Figure 10.4. The shuttle box consists of two compartments separated by an open-

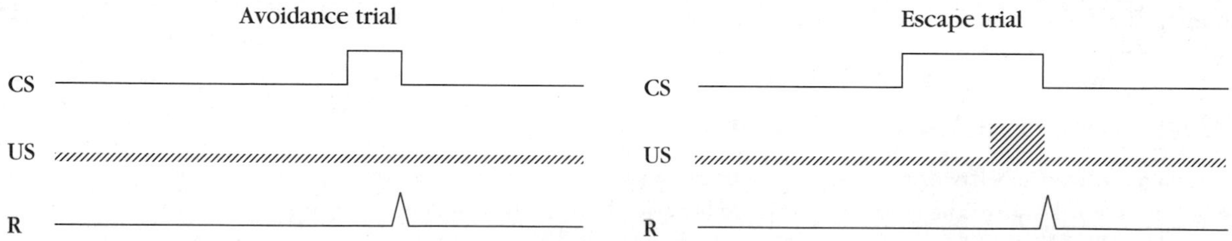

Figure 10.3 Diagram of the discriminated, or signaled, avoidance procedure. *Avoidance trial:* If the participant makes the response required for avoidance during the CS (the signal) but before the US (for example, shock) is scheduled, the CS is turned off, and the US is omitted on that trial. *Escape trial:* If the participant fails to make the required response during the CS-US interval, the scheduled shock is presented and remains on until the response occurs, whereupon both the CS and the US are terminated.

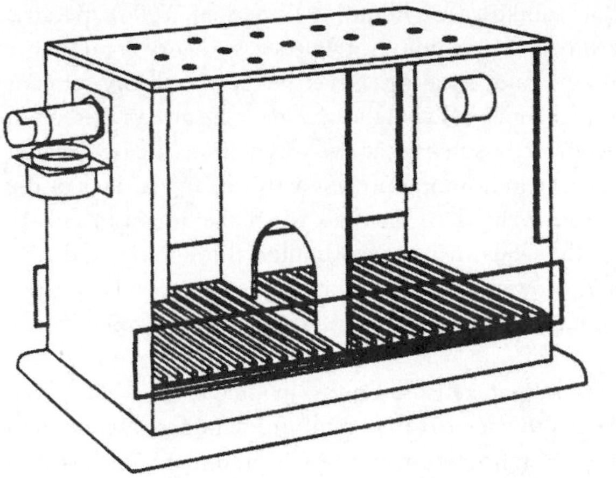

Figure 10.4 A shuttle box. The box has a metal grid floor and is separated into two compartments by an archway. The instrumental response consists of crossing back and forth (shuttling) from one side of the box to the other.

ing at floor level. The animal is placed on one side of the apparatus. At the start of a trial, the CS is presented (a light or a tone, for example). If the subject crosses over to the other side before the shock occurs, no shock is delivered and the CS is turned off. At the end of the intertrial interval, the next trial can be administered starting with the animal in the second compartment. With this procedure, the animal shuttles back and forth between the two sides on successive trials. The response is therefore called **shuttle avoidance.**

There are two types of shuttle avoidance procedures: In the one just described, the animal moves from left to right on the first trial, and from right to left on the second trial. This type is technically called *two-way shuttle avoidance,* because the animal moves in different directions on successive trials. In *one-way shuttle avoidance,* the animal starts each trial on the same side of the apparatus and always moves in the same direction, to the other side. One-way avoidance is generally easier to learn than the two-way procedure.

Two-Process Theory of Avoidance

Avoidance procedures involve a negative contingency between a response and an aversive stimulus. If you make the appropriate avoidance responses, you will not fall, bump into things, or drive off the road. No particular pleasure is derived from these experiences. You simply do not get hurt. The absence of the aversive stimulus is presumably the reason that avoidance responses are made. However, how can the absence of something provide reinforcement for instrumental behavior? This is the fundamental question in the study of avoidance.

Courtesy of Donald A. Dewsbury

N. E. Miller

Mowrer and Lamoreaux (1942) pointed out more than a half century ago that "not getting something can hardly, in and of itself, qualify as rewarding" (p. 6). Since then, much intellectual effort has been devoted to figuring out what subjects "get" in avoidance conditioning procedures that might provide reinforcement for the avoidance response. In fact, the investigation of avoidance behavior has been dominated by this theoretical problem. The first and most influential solution to the puzzle, proposed by Mowrer (1947) and elaborated by Miller (for example, 1951) and others, is known as the **two-process theory of avoidance.**

In one form or another, two-process theory has been the dominant theoretical viewpoint on avoidance learning for many years and continues to enjoy success and support (Levis, 1989; Levis & Brewer, 2001; D. E. McAllister & W. R. McAllister, 1991; W. R.

McAllister & D. E. McAllister, 1995; Zhuikov, Couvillon, & Bitterman, 1994). Because other approaches deal more directly with certain findings, two-process theory is no longer viewed as a complete explanation of avoidance learning. Nevertheless, the theory remains the standard against which all other explanations of avoidance behavior are always measured.

As the name implies, two-process theory assumes that two mechanisms are involved in avoidance learning. The first is a classical conditioning process activated by pairings of the warning stimulus (CS) with the aversive event (US) on trials when the organism fails to make the avoidance response. Because the US is an aversive stimulus, through classical conditioning the CS also becomes aversive. Mowerer (1947) assumed that because it is aversive, it comes to elicit fear. Thus, the first component of two-process theory is the *classical conditioning of fear to the CS.*

Fear is an emotionally arousing unpleasant state. As I noted in Chapter 5, the termination of an unpleasant or aversive event provides negative reinforcement for instrumental behavior. Since fear is elicited by the CS, termination of the CS presumably results in a reduction in the level of fear, and this can be a source of negative reinforcement. The second process in two-process theory is based on this negative reinforcement. Mowrer assumed that learning of the instrumental avoidance response occurs because the response terminates the CS and thereby reduces the conditioned fear elicited by the CS. Thus, the second component in two-process theory is *instrumental reinforcement of the avoidance response through fear reduction.*

There are several noteworthy aspects of two-process theory. First, and perhaps most important, the classical and instrumental processes are assumed to depend on each other. Instrumental reinforcement through fear reduction is not possible until fear has become conditioned to the CS. Therefore, the classical conditioning process has to occur first. After that, the instrumental conditioning process may create extinction trials for the classical conditioning process. This occurs because each successful avoidance response prevents the occurrence of the US. Thus, two-process theory predicts repeated interplay between classical and instrumental processes.

Another important aspect of two-process theory is that it explains avoidance behavior in terms of escape from conditioned fear rather than in terms of the prevention of shock. The fact that the avoidance response prevents shock is seen as a by-product in two-process theory, not as the critical event that motivates avoidance behavior. Escape from conditioned fear provides the critical reinforcement for avoidance behavior. Thus, according to two-process theory, the instrumental response is reinforced by a tangible event (fear reduction) rather than merely the absence of something (aversive stimulation).

Experimental Analysis of Avoidance Behavior

Avoidance learning has been the subject of many experiments. Much of the research has been stimulated by efforts to prove or disprove two-process theory. Space does not permit reviewing all the evidence. However, several important findings must be considered in any effort to fully understand the mechanisms of avoidance behavior.

Acquired-Drive Experiments. In the typical avoidance procedure, classical conditioning of fear and instrumental reinforcement through fear reduction occur intermixed in a series of trials. If these two processes make separate contributions to avoidance learning, it should be possible to demonstrate their operation in a situation where the two types of conditioning are not intermixed. This is the goal of *acquired-drive experiments.*

The basic strategy is to first condition fear to a CS with a "pure" classical conditioning procedure in which the CS is paired with the US regardless of what the subject does. In the

BOX 10.1

FEAR AND THE AMYGDALA

Much of what we do is motivated by fear. Because fear serves a defensive and protective function, organisms seem biologically prepared to learn about stimuli that signal danger (for example, snakes, heights). While such learning is generally adaptive, fear can grow out of proportion to the danger, producing a phobic response that undermines the person's ability to function.

Neuroscientists have discovered that a small region of the brain, the amygdala, plays a central role in fear-mediated behavior (for a review, see Fendt & Fanselow, 1999; LeDoux, 1996). The amygdala (Latin for "almond") is part of the limbic system, a subcortical region of the brain that has been implicated in the processing of emotional stimuli. In humans, brain scans have revealed that processing fear-related stimuli (for example, pictures of a fearful expression) activates the amygdala. Damage to the amygdala disrupts a person's ability to recognize signs of fear, and electrical stimulation of this region produces feelings of fear and apprehension.

The neural circuit that underlies conditioned fear has been explored in laboratory animals using a variety of physiological techniques, including selective lesions, localized stimulation, and physiological recording (see Box 3.2). In animals, electrical stimulation of the amygdala produces a range of behavioral and physiological responses indicative of fear, including freezing, enhanced startle to a loud acoustic stimulus, and a change in heart rate. Conversely, lesioning the amygdala produces a fearless creature that no longer avoids dangerous situations. Rats normally show signs of fear in the presence of a predator (for example, a cat). After having the amygdala lesioned, a rat will approach a cat as if it's a long-lost friend.

Lesioning the amygdala also disrupts learning about cues (CSs) that have been paired with an aversive event (for example, a shock US) in a Pavlovian paradigm. As discussed earlier, animals can associate many different types of stimuli with shock. In some cases, the cue may be relatively simple, such as a discrete light or tone; in others, a constellation of cues, such as the context in which shock occurs, may be associated with shock. In both cases, pairing the stimulus with shock produces conditioned fear, as indicated by a CS-induced increase in freezing and startle.

Evidence suggests that in fear conditioning, the neural signals elicited by the CS and US converge within the amygdala (see Figure 10.5). Information about the US is provided by two distinct neural circuits, each of which is sufficient to support conditioning (Shi & Davis, 1999). Information about the CS is provided by three functionally distinct systems, each of which may represent a distinct type of stimulus quality. One CS path to the amygdala is fairly direct, a path that sacrifices stimulus detail for speed. This pathway allows for a rapid response and primes neural activity. Additional CS inputs arrive from the cortex and likely provide a slower, but more precise, representation of the CS features. In the absence of this cortical input, subjects can acquire a conditioned response to a discrete cue (for example, a tone). They cannot, however, learn to discriminate two auditory cues in a differential conditioning paradigm, where only one of the stimuli is paired with shock. Normally, rats will freeze only during the cue that has been paired with shock. Rats with lesions of the auditory cortex do not respond differentially, but instead show signs of fear to both the paired and the unpaired tones.

The third CS pathway conveys information that has been processed within the hippocampus, a structure that binds together unique sets of stimuli (Fanselow, 1999). For example, in everyday life, we associate the cues that occur together with a temporal code, providing a unique memory that encodes a particular episode in time (for example, what you had for breakfast yesterday). A similar type of learning is required to encode the constellation of cues that distinguish environmental contexts. Both types of memory are disrupted by damage to the hippocampus, a deficit that contributes to the memory dysfunction observed with Alzheimer's and Korsakoff's disease. In animal subjects, hippocampal lesions have no effect on a rat's ability to learn and remember that a discrete cue (for example, tone) predicts shock. But this same rat appears unable to associate a distinct context with shock. It seems that the

(continued)

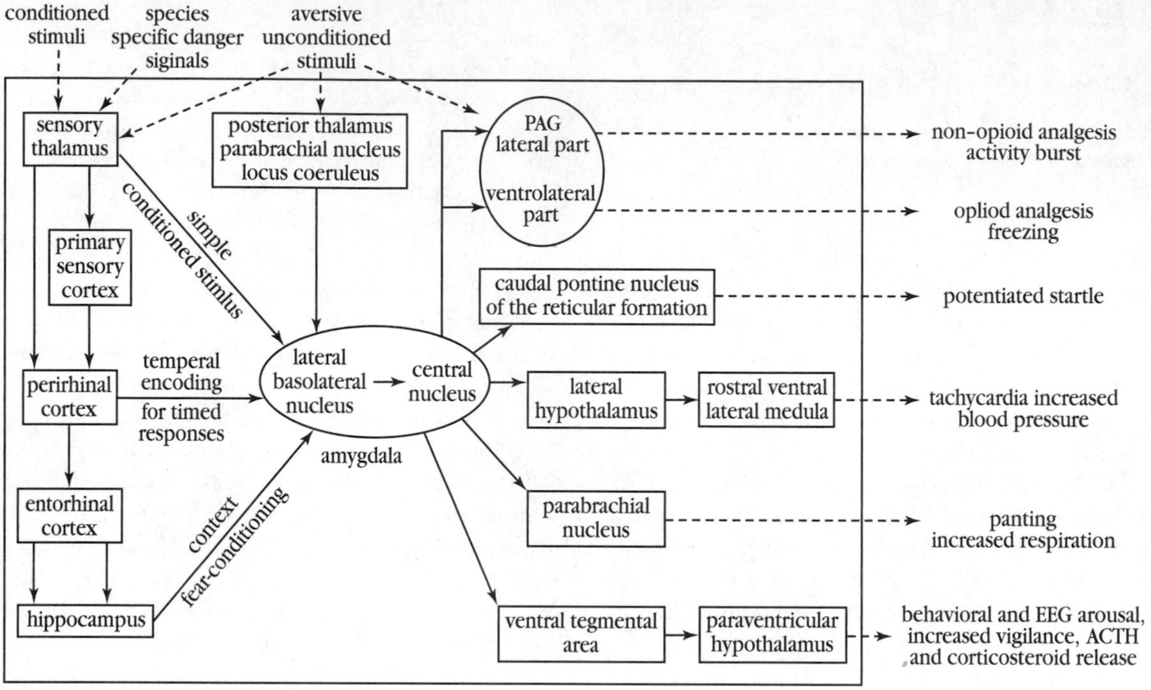

Figure 10.5 A block diagram illustrating some of the neural components that mediate fear and defensive behavior. An aversive US engages parallel pathways that project to the lateral/basolateral amygdala. Information about the CS is conveyed from the sensory thalamus, the cortex, or by means of a hippocampal-dependent process. Output is channeled through the central nucleus of the amygdala, which organizes the expression of fear-mediated behavior. Distinct behavioral outcomes are produced by projections to various brain structures. (Adapted from Fendt and Fanselow, 1989.)

hippocampus plays an essential role in processing complex stimuli. Somehow, the hippocampus helps package the components of a stimulus together, producing a kind of configural representation that can be associated with shock.

Interestingly, the role of the hippocampus changes over time. When the organism is first exposed to a complex stimulus, the hippocampus appears to be necessary to process the interrelated features of the stimulus. Over time, however, the new representation seems to be consolidated and stored elsewhere, presumably within the cortex. Once the configural nature of a stimulus has been established, which takes about a month in rats, the new representation can function on its own without the hippocampal. As a result, lesion of the hippocampus has less effect if the lesion is administered during later stages of learning. If the lesion is conducted within a few days of context exposure, it eliminates the animal's ability to associate the context with shock. In contrast, if rats are exposed to a novel context a month earlier, an enduring memory trace is established that survives the hippocampal lesion. These rats can associate the previously experienced context with shock, but are unable to learn about new contexts. It seems that the hippocampal lesion has eliminated the animal's ability to form a lasting configural representation.

The neural circuits activated by the CS and US converge within the amygdala in the lateral (toward the sides) and basal (lower) lateral region. Here, stimulus inputs may compete for association with the US, with the most predictive cues laying down a form of long-term potentiation (LTP) that helps encode the CS-US relation (Fanselow, 1999). LTP is thought to underlie information storage in other brain regions (see Box 11.1) and depends on the activation of the NMDA receptor. Microinjecting into the basolateral amygdala a drug that blocks the NMDA receptor disrupts the acquisition of conditioned fear. In addition, LTP-like changes have been observed in the CS-input pathways, suggesting that multiple sources of synaptic plasticity contribute to the development of a conditioned response (LeDoux, 1996).

The output of the fear circuit is channeled through the central nucleus of the amygdala, which organizes the expression of conditioned fear. This structure produces a wide range of behavioral and physiological effects, the outcome of which depends on the neural system engaged. For example, enhanced startle is mediated by a neural projection to a region of the brainstem reticular formation (the pontine nucleus). Slightly above this brainstem structure, in the midbrain, is a region known as the periaqueductral gray (PAG). This structure plays a crucial role in organizing defensive behavior. The portion that lies along the upper sides (dorsolateral) organizes active defensive behaviors needed for fight and flight. These circa-strike behaviors are engaged by direct, or inevitable, contact with a noxious, or life-threatening, stimulus. The lower (ventral) portion of the PAG mediates CS-elicited freezing behavior. Rats that have received lesions limited to the ventral PAG appear afraid on a variety of measures but do not freeze.

A CS that predicts shock also elicits a reduction in pain reactivity. This conditioned analgesia is thought to help the organism cope with a painful US. The analgesia is mediated by an internally manufactured (endogenous) opioid that, like morphine, decreases behavioral reactivity to noxious stimuli. Like freezing, this physiological response depends on neurons within the ventral PAG. This conditioned analgesia could provide a form of negative feedback that decreases the effectiveness of an expected aversive US. It is well established that learning that one cue predicts an aversive event can block learning about other cues. This blocking effect can be eliminated by the administration of a drug (an opioid antagonist) that prevents the opioid analgesia, providing a physiological explanation for why an expected US receives less processing (Bolles & Fanselow, 1980; Fanselow, 1999).

—J. W. Grau

next phase of the experiment, the subjects are periodically exposed to the fear-eliciting CS and allowed to perform an instrumental response that is effective in terminating the CS (and thereby reducing fear). No shocks are scheduled in this phase. Therefore, the instrumental response is not required to avoid shock. If escape from a fear-eliciting CS can reinforce instrumental behavior, then the instrumental response should become conditioned in the second phase of the experiment. This type of experiment is called an **acquired-drive** study because the drive to perform the instrumental response (fear) is learned through classical conditioning. (It is not an innate drive, such as hunger or thirst.)

One of the first definitive acquired-drive experiments was performed by Brown and Jacobs (1949), who tested rats in a shuttle box. During the first phase of the experiment, the opening between the two shuttle compartments was blocked. The rats were individually placed on one side of the apparatus and a pulsating light/tone CS was presented, ending in shock through the grid floor. Twenty-two such Pavlovian conditioning trials were conducted, with the rats confined on the right and left sides of the apparatus on alternate trials. The control group received the same training except that no shocks were delivered.

Instrumental conditioning was conducted during the next phase of the experiment. Each animal was placed on one side of the shuttle box, and the center barrier was removed. The CS was then presented and remained on until the rat turned it off by crossing to the other side. The animal was then removed from the apparatus until the next trial. No shocks were delivered during the instrumental conditioning phase. Brown and Jacobs wanted to determine whether the rats would learn to cross rapidly from one side to the other when the only reinforcement for crossing was termination of the previously conditioned light/tone CS.

How long the rats took to cross the shuttle box and turn off the CS was measured for each trial in the instrumental conditioning phase. Figure 10.6 summarizes these response latencies for both the shock-conditioned group and the control group. The two groups had similar response latencies at the beginning of instrumental training. As training progressed, the shock-conditioned animals learned to cross the shuttle box faster (and thus turn off the CS sooner) than the control group. This outcome shows that termination of a fear-conditioned stimulus is sufficient to provide reinforcement for an instrumental response. This basic finding has since been replicated in a variety of experimental situations (for example, Dinsmoor, 1962; McAllister & McAllister, 1971; see also Delprato, 1969; Israel, Devine, O'Dea, & Hamdi, 1974; Katzev, 1967, 1972). These results provide strong support for two-process theory.

Courtesy of Donald A. Dewsbury

S. Mineka

Independent Measurement of Fear during Acquisition of Avoidance Behavior. Another important strategy that has been used in investigations of avoidance behavior involves independent measurement of fear and instrumental avoidance responding. This approach is based on the assumption that if fear motivates and reinforces avoidance responding, then the conditioning of fear and the conditioning of instrumental avoidance behavior should go hand in hand. Contrary to this prediction, however, conditioned fear and avoidance responding are not always highly correlated (Mineka, 1979).

Fairly early in the investigation of avoidance learning, it was noted that animals become less fearful as they become more proficient in performing the avoidance response (Solomon, Kamin, & Wynne, 1953; Solomon & Wynne, 1953). Since then, more systematic measurements of fear have been used. One popular behavioral technique for measuring fear involves the conditioned suppression procedure described in Chapter 3. In this technique, animals are first conditioned to press a response lever for food reinforcement. A shock-conditioned CS is then presented while the animals are responding to obtain food. In general, the CS

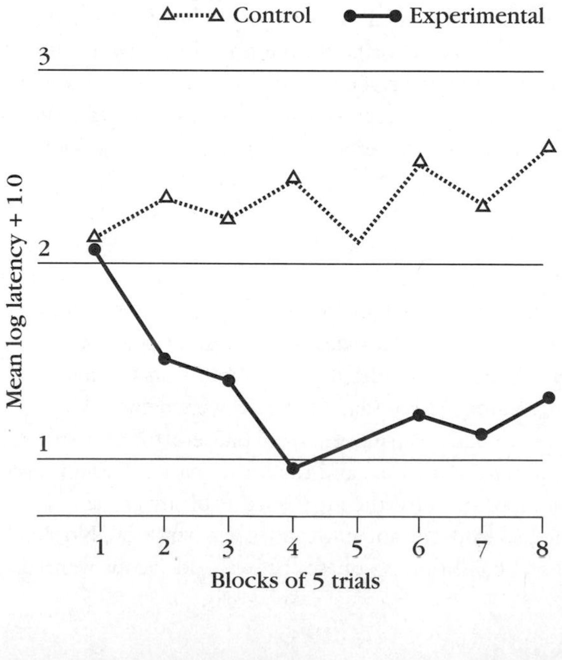

Figure 10.6 Mean latencies to cross from one side to the other in the shuttle box for control and experimental groups. The shuttle crossing resulted in termination of the CS on that trial. For the experimental group, the CS was previously conditioned with shock. Such conditioning was not conducted with the control group. (From "The Role of Fear in the Motivation and Acquisition of Responses," by J. S. Brown and A. Jacobs, 1949, *Journal of Experimental Psychology, 39,* pp. 747–759.)

produces suppression of the lever-press behavior, and the extent of this response suppression is assumed to reflect the amount of fear elicited by the CS.

If the warning signal in an avoidance procedure comes to elicit fear, then presentation of that warning stimulus in a conditioned suppression procedure should result in suppression of food-reinforced behavior. This prediction was tested for the first time in a famous experiment by Kamin, Brimer, and Black (1963). The rats in the experiment were initially trained to press a response lever for food reinforcement on a variable interval schedule. The animals were then trained to avoid shock in response to an auditory CS in a shuttle box. Training was continued for independent groups of animals until they successfully avoided shock on 1, 3, 9, or 27 consecutive trials. The animals were then returned to the Skinner box for lever pressing. The auditory CS that had been used in the shuttle box was periodically presented to see how much suppression of lever pressing it would produce.

The results are summarized in Figure 10.7. Lower values of the suppression index indicate greater disruptions of lever pressing by the shock-avoidance CS. Increasing degrees of response suppression were observed among groups of rats that had received avoidance training until they successfully avoided shock on 1 to 9 successive trials. With more extensive avoidance training, however, response suppression declined. Animals trained until they avoided shock on 27 consecutive trials showed less conditioned suppression to the avoidance CS than those trained to a criterion of 9 consecutive avoidances. This outcome indicates that fear, as measured by conditioned suppression, decreases during extended avoidance training and is at a minimal level after extensive training (see also Cook, Mineka, & Trumble, 1987; Neuenschwander, Fabrigoule, & Mackintosh, 1987; Starr & Mineka, 1977). Interestingly, however, the decrease in fear is not accompanied by a decrease in the strength of the avoidance response (Mineka & Gino, 1980).

The decline in fear to the CS with extended avoidance training presents a puzzle for two-process theory. However, recent evidence and theoretical argument suggest that the scope of two-process theory can accommodate this finding. Although it is well accepted

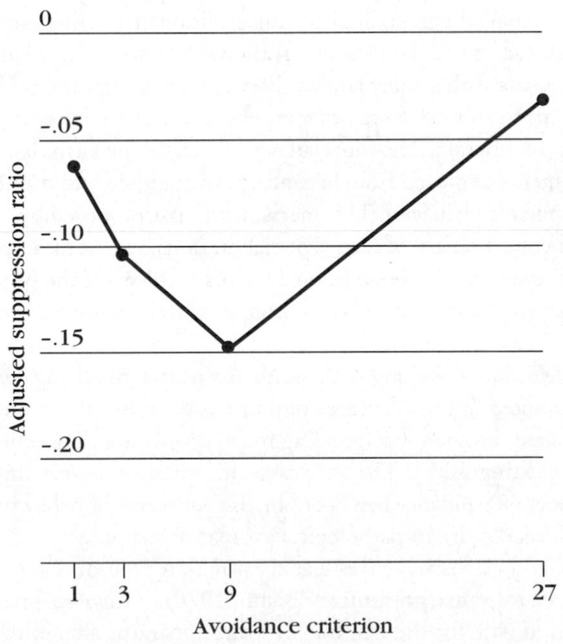

Figure 10.7 Suppression of lever pressing for food during a CS that was previously conditioned in a shock-avoidance procedure. Independent groups received avoidance training until they met a criterion of 1, 3, 9, or 27 consecutive avoidance responses. The suppression scores were adjusted for the degree of suppression produced by the CS before avoidance conditioning. Lower values of the adjusted ratio indicate greater suppression of lever pressing. (From "Conditioned Suppression as a Monitor of Fear of the CS in the Course of Avoidance Training," by L. J. Kamin, C. J. Brimer, and A. H. Black, 1963, *Journal of Comparative and Physiological Psychology, 56,* pp. 497–501.)

that fear declines as avoidance conditioning proceeds, the CS continues to elicit some fear—that is, fear does not decline to zero. D. E. McAllister and W. R. McAllister (1991) pointed out that as long as the CS elicits some degree of fear, CS termination can result in fear reduction and hence reinforcement of the avoidance behavior. Furthermore, as the avoidance response becomes well learned, a small degree of fear reduction may be sufficient to maintain the response. (For additional factors that can lead to a dissociation between avoidance responding and fear elicited by the warning stimulus, see Levis, 1989; Levis & Brewer, 2001; McAllister & McAllister, 1995.)

Asymptotic Avoidance Performance. Two-process theory not only specifies mechanisms responsible for the acquisition of avoidance behavior but also makes predictions about the nature of performance once the response has been well learned. More specifically, it predicts that the strength of the avoidance response will fluctuate in cycles.

Whenever a successful avoidance response occurs, the shock is omitted on that trial. This is an extinction trial for the conditioned fear response. Repetition of the avoidance response (and thus the CS-alone extinction trials) should lead to extinction of fear. As the CS becomes extinguished, there will be less reinforcement resulting from the reduction of fear, and the avoidance response should also become extinguished. However, when shock is not avoided, the CS is paired with the US. This pairing should reinstate fear to the CS and reestablish the potential for reinforcement through fear reduction, thereby reconditioning the avoidance response. Thus, the theory predicts that after initial acquisition, the avoidance response will go through cycles of extinction and reacquisition.

Although evidence of cyclic avoidance responding at asymptote has been obtained (for example, Sheffield, 1948), such findings are not always observed. Some researchers have argued that one of the hallmarks of avoidance behavior is its persistence. Avoidance responding may continue for many trials after shocks are discontinued, as long as the response continues to be effective in terminating the CS. In one experiment (Solomon et al., 1953), for example, a dog was reported to have performed the avoidance response on 650 successive trials after only a few shocks.

In terms of two-process theory, there are several approaches to explaining instances in which avoidance behavior persists after the unconditioned aversive stimulus is no longer delivered. One approach is based on the observation that once an avoidance response has been well learned, it occurs with a short latency. Because the animal responds quickly to turn off the CS, later segments of the CS are never experienced and therefore do not have the opportunity to undergo extinction. The short latency of well-learned avoidance responses serves to protect later segments of the CS from becoming extinguished and thereby contributes to the persistence of avoidance behavior. This mechanism, first proposed by Solomon and Wynne (1953), is called **conservation of fear.** (For elaborations on this idea, see Levis, 1981, 1989, 1991; Levis & Brewer, 2001. For additional factors involved in the persistence of avoidance behavior, see Soltysik, Wolfe, Nicholas, Wilson, & Garcia-Sanchez, 1983.)

Extinction of Avoidance Behavior through Response-Blocking and CS-Alone Exposure. As I have noted, if the avoidance response is effective in terminating the CS and no shocks are presented, avoidance responding may persist for a long time. How might avoidance behavior be extinguished? The answer to this question is very important not only for theoretical analyses of avoidance behavior but also for forms of behavior therapy whose goal is to extinguish maladaptive or pathological avoidance responses.

An effective and extensively investigated extinction procedure for avoidance behavior is called **flooding,** or **response prevention** (Baum, 1970). It involves presenting the CS in the avoidance situation without the US, but with the apparatus altered in such a way that the participant is prevented from making the avoidance response. Thus, the organism is exposed to the CS without being permitted to terminate it. In a sense, it is "flooded" with the CS. (For discussion of a related procedure, called *implosive therapy*, see Levis, 1995; Levis & Brewer, 2001.)

One of the most important variables determining the effects of a flooding procedure is the duration of the forced exposure to the CS. This was convincingly illustrated in an experiment by Schiff, Smith, and Prochaska (1972). Rats were trained to avoid shock in response to an auditory CS by going to a safe compartment. After acquisition, the safe compartment was blocked off by a barrier and the rats received various amounts of exposure to the CS without shock. Different groups received 1, 5, or 12 blocked trials, and on each of these trials the CS was presented for 1, 5, 10, 50, or 120 seconds. The barrier blocking the avoidance response was then removed, and the animals were tested for extinction. At the start of each extinction trial, the animal was placed in the apparatus and the CS was presented until it crossed into the safe compartment. Shocks never occurred during the extinction trials, and each animal was tested until it took at least 120 seconds to cross into the safe compartment on 3 consecutive trials. The strength of the avoidance response was measured by the number of trials required to reach this extinction criterion.

The results of the experiment are summarized in Figure 10.8. As expected, blocked exposure to the CS facilitated extinction of the avoidance response. Furthermore, this effect was determined mainly by the total duration of exposure to the CS. The number of flooding trials administered (1, 5, or 12) facilitated extinction only because each trial added to the total amount of inescapable exposure to the CS. Increases in the total duration of blocked exposure to the CS resulted in more rapid extinction (see also Baum, 1969; Weinberger, 1965).

Two-process theory predicts that flooding will extinguish avoidance behavior because exposure to the CS without the US will produce extinction of fear. The fact that more extensive exposure to the CS results in more rapid extinction is consistent with this view.

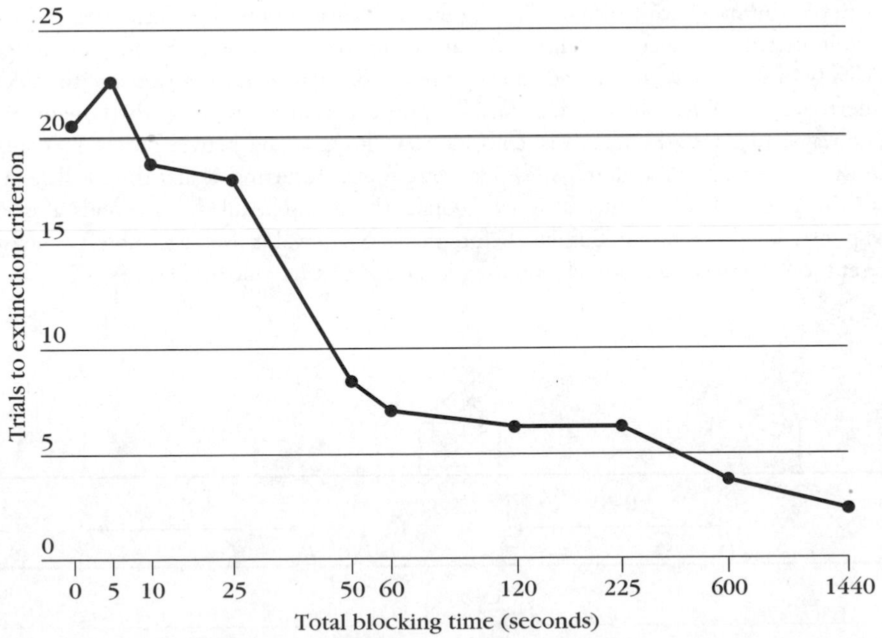

Figure 10.8 Trials to extinction criterion for independent groups of animals that previously received various durations of blocked exposure to the CS. (From "Extinction of Avoidance in Rats as a Function of Duration and Number of Blocked Trials," by R. Schiff, N. Smith, and J. Prochaska, 1972, *Journal of Comparative and Physiological Psychology, 81,* pp. 356–359. Copyright © 1972 by the American Psychological Association. Reprinted by permission.)

However, detailed investigations of the role of fear in flooding procedures have also provided evidence contrary to two-process theory. Independent measurements of fear (with the conditioned suppression technique, for example) have shown that in some situations flooding extinguishes avoidance behavior more rapidly than it extinguishes fear, whereas in other situations the reverse holds (see, for example, Coulter, Riccio, & Page, 1969; Mineka & Gino, 1979; Mineka, Miller, Gino, & Giencke, 1981). These results suggest that extinction of fear is only one factor responsible for the effects of flooding procedures. Other variables may be related to the fact that, during flooding, organisms not only receive forced exposure to the CS but are prevented from making the avoidance response. (For further discussion, see Baum, 1970; Katzev & Berman, 1974; Mineka, 1979.)

Nondiscriminated (Free-Operant) Avoidance. As I have described, two-process theory places great emphasis on the role of the warning signal, or CS, in avoidance learning. Can individuals also learn to avoid shock if there is no external warning stimulus in the situation? Within the context of two-factor theory, this is a heretical question. However, progress in science requires posing bold questions, and Sidman (1953a, 1953b) did just that. He devised an avoidance conditioning procedure that did not involve a warning stimulus. The procedure has come to be called **nondiscriminated,** or **free-operant, avoidance.**

In a free-operant avoidance procedure, a brief shock is scheduled to occur periodically without warning—say, every 3 seconds. Each time the participant makes the avoidance response, it obtains a period of safety—say, 10 seconds—during which shocks do not occur. Repetition of the avoidance response before the end of the shock-free period serves to start the safe period over again.

A free-operant avoidance procedure is constructed from two time intervals (see Figure 10.9). One of these is the interval between shocks in the absence of a response. This is called the **S-S** (shock-shock) **interval.** The other critical time period is the interval between the avoidance response and the next scheduled shock. This is called the **R-S** (response-shock) **interval.** The R-S interval is the period of safety created by each response. In my example, the S-S interval was 3 seconds and the R-S interval was 10 seconds.

In addition to lacking a warning stimulus, the free-operant avoidance procedure differs from discriminated avoidance in allowing for avoidance responses to occur at any time. In discriminated avoidance procedures, the avoidance response is effective in preventing the delivery of shock only if it is made during the CS. Responses in the absence of the CS (the intertrial interval) have no effect. In fact, in some experiments (particularly those involving one-way avoidance), the subject is removed from the apparatus between trials. By contrast, in the free-operant procedure, an avoidance response occurring at any time will reset the R-S interval. If the R-S interval is 10 seconds, shock is scheduled 10 seconds after each response. By always responding just before this R-S interval is over, the subject can always reset the R-S interval and thereby prolong its period of safety indefinitely.

Figure 10.9 Diagram of the nondiscriminated, or free-operant, avoidance procedure. Each occurrence of the response initiates a period without shock, as set by the R-S interval. In the absence of a response, the next shock occurs a fixed period after the last shock, as set by the S-S interval. Shocks are not signaled by an exteroceptive stimulus and are usually brief and inescapable

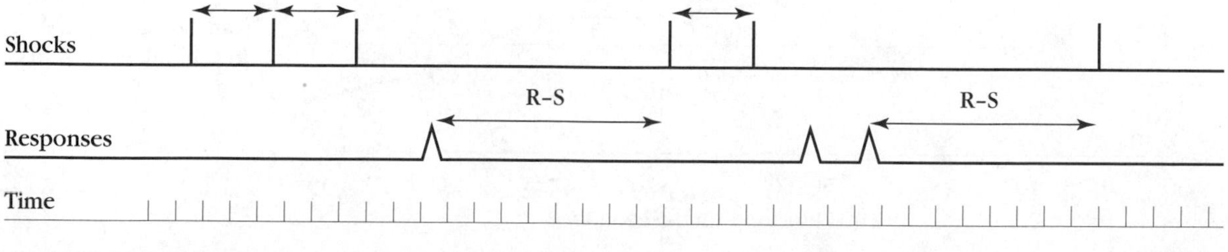

Demonstrations of Free-Operant Avoidance Learning. Most research on free-operant avoidance learning has been conducted with laboratory rats and has used brief footshock as the aversive stimulus. Experiments have also been conducted with human participants and more "natural" aversive stimuli. In one study, for example, four college students served as subjects, and exposure to carbon dioxide (CO_2) was used as the aversive stimulus (Lejuez, O'Donnell, Wirth, Zvolensky, & Eifert, 1998). CO_2 rather than shock was used because the investigators wanted to produced symptoms related to panic attacks. CO_2 inhalation produces respiratory distress, increased heart rate (tachycardia), and dizziness similar to what is experienced during a panic attack.

Potential subjects for the experiment were first screened to make sure they did not have a history of respiratory problems. During the experiment, the students were asked to wear a mask that usually provided room air. To deliver the aversive stimulus, the room air was switched to 20% CO_2 for 25 seconds. Each CO_2 delivery was followed by a 65-second rest period to permit resumption of normal breathing. The instrumental response was operating a plunger. Three seconds after the rest period, a hit of CO_2 was provided without warning if the subject did not pull the plunger (S-S interval = 3 seconds). Following a response, the next CO_2 delivery was scheduled 10 seconds later (R-S interval = 10 seconds). Furthermore, each occurrence of the avoidance response reset the R-S interval. If the subjects never responded, they could get as many as 22 CO_2 deliveries in each avoidance conditioning session. If they responded before the end of the first S-S interval and then before the end of each R-S interval, they could avoid all CO_2 deliveries. Sessions during which the avoidance contingency was in effect were alternated with control sessions during which responding had no effect and the subjects received a CO_2 delivery on average every 6 minutes.

The results of the experiment are summarized in Figure 10.10. The left side of the figure shows the response rates of the four students during the avoidance and control sessions. The right side of the figure shows the number of CO_2 deliveries the subjects received during the two types of sessions. Notice that response rates were higher during the avoidance sessions than during the control sessions. Furthermore, as the subjects acquired the avoidance response, the number of CO_2 presentations they received declined. And these behavior changes (and consequences) occurred even though the CO_2 presentations were not signaled by an explicit warning stimulus.

No explicit instructions about the response plunger were provided at the beginning of the experiment. Subjects S1 and S2 "discovered" the avoidance contingency without much difficulty on their own. In contrast, subjects S3 and S4 had a bit of trouble at first and were given a hint before their 6th and 7th sessions, respectively. The hint was, "The only thing that you can do by pulling the plunger is sometimes change the number of times you receive carbon-dioxide-enriched air. It is even possible for you to sometimes receive no deliveries of carbon dioxide." This hint was enough to get subjects S3 and S4 to respond effectively during subsequent avoidance sessions. Notice, however, that the instructions did not provide clues about the difference between the avoidance and control sessions. Nevertheless, subjects S3 and S4 responded more vigorously during the avoidance sessions than during the control sessions by the end of the experiment. Thus, the difference in response levels (and CO_2 presentations) that occurred during avoidance versus control sessions cannot be attributed to "following instructions" for any of the subjects. They all had to discover without help when the avoidance contingency was in effect when it was not in effect.

Free-operant avoidance behavior has been investigated in numerous other studies, primarily with rats serving as subjects and brief shock as the aversive stimulus (see Hineline, 1977; Sidman, 1966). Because nonverbal subjects were used, observers did not have to worry about the possible role of instructions. These experiments have shown that the rate of responding is controlled by the length of the S-S and R-S intervals. The more frequently

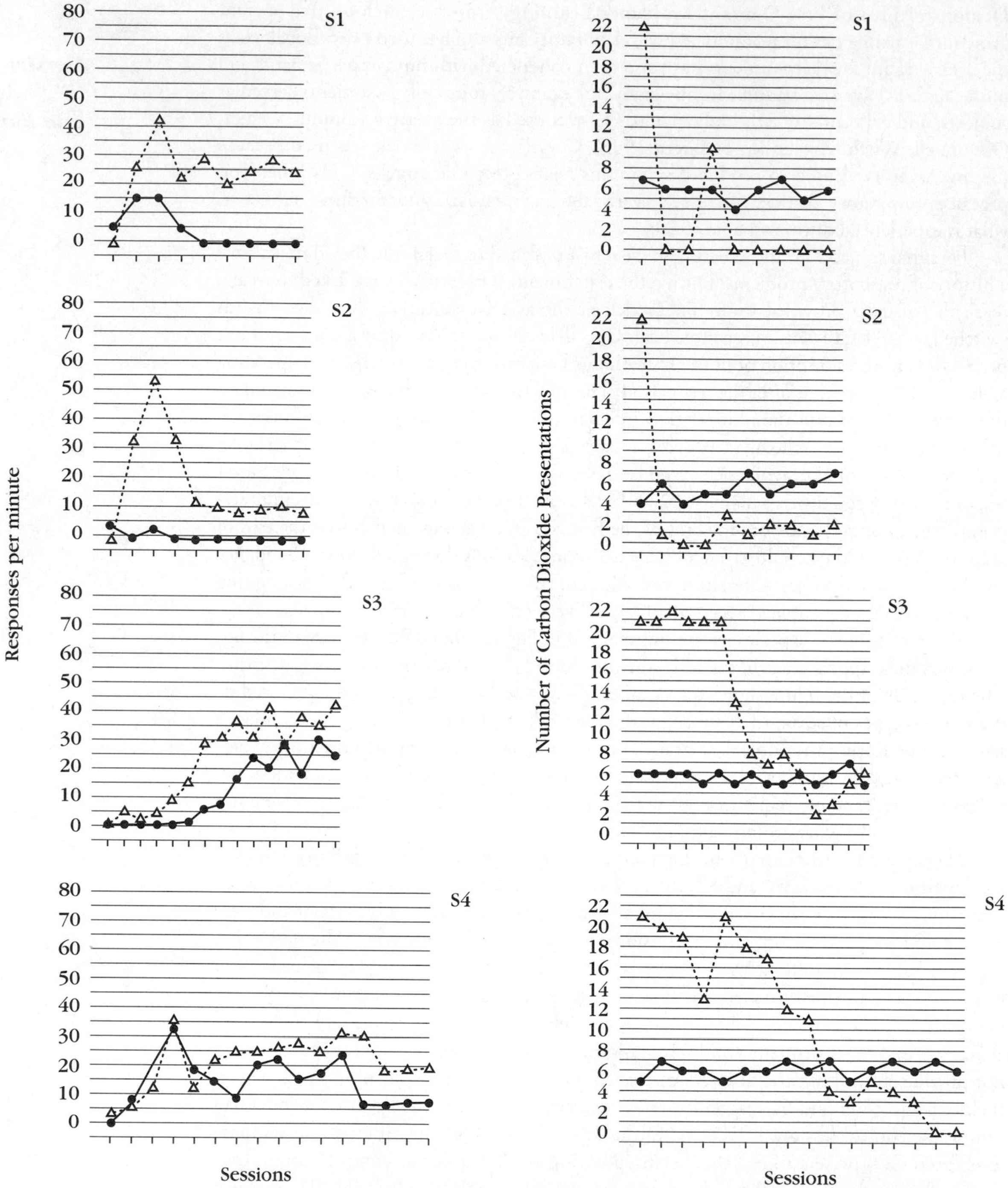

Figure 10.10 Rate of responding and rate of CO_2 presentations for four college students in a study of free-operant avoidance. Open symbols represent data obtained during sessions when the avoidance contingency was in effect. Closed symbols represent data obtained during control sessions when the avoidance response was not effective and the subjects received a CO_2 delivery every 6 minutes. (After Lejuez et al., 1998.)

shocks are scheduled in the absence of responding (the S-S interval), the more likely the subject is to learn the avoidance response. Increasing the periods of safety produced by the response (the R-S interval) also promotes the avoidance behavior. In addition, the relative value of the S-S and R-S intervals is important. Responding is not likely to develop if the R-S interval is shorter than the S-S interval.

Free-Operant Avoidance and Two-Process Theory. Free-operant avoidance behavior presents a challenge for two-process theory because there is no explicit CS to elicit conditioned fear and it is not clear how the avoidance response reduces fear. However, two-process theory has not been entirely abandoned in attempts to explain free-operant avoidance (see Anger, 1963). The S-S and R-S intervals used in effective procedures are usually rather short (less than 1 minute). Furthermore, they remain fixed during an experiment, so that the intervals are highly predictable. It is not unreasonable to suggest that the animals might learn to respond to the passage of time as a signal for shock. This assumption of temporal conditioning permits application of the mechanisms of two-process theory to free-operant avoidance procedures.

According to the two-process explanation of free-operant avoidance, the passage of time after the last shock (in the case of the S-S interval) or after the last response (in the case of the R-S interval) becomes conditioned to elicit fear. Since the timing starts over again with each avoidance response, the response effectively removes the fear-eliciting temporal cues. Termination of these time signals can then reinforce the avoidance response through fear reduction. Thus, the temporal cues that predict shock are assumed to have the same role in free-operant avoidance procedures as the explicit CS has in discriminative avoidance.

The preceding analysis predicts that organisms will not distribute their responses randomly in a free-operant avoidance procedure. They will concentrate their responses at the end of the R-S interval because it is here that the temporal cues presumably elicit the greatest amount of fear. Results consistent with this prediction have been obtained. However, many animals successfully avoid a great many shocks without distributing their responses in the manner predicted by two-process theory. Furthermore, the predicted distribution of responses often develops only after extensive training—after the participants are avoiding a great many of the scheduled shocks (see Sidman, 1966). In addition, avoidance behavior has been successfully conditioned with the use of free-operant procedures in which the S-S and R-S intervals are varied throughout the experiment (for example, Herrnstein & Hineline, 1966). Making the S-S and R-S intervals unpredictable makes it more difficult to use the passage of time as a signal for shock. These types of results have discouraged some investigators from accepting two-process theory as an explanation of free-operant avoidance learning. (For further discussion, see Herrnstein, 1969; Hineline, 1977, 1981.)

Courtesy of Donald A. Dewsbury

P. N. Hineline

Alternative Theoretical Accounts of Avoidance Behavior

In the preceding discussion of experimental investigations of avoidance behavior, I used two-process theory to provide the conceptual framework. This was reasonable because many of the research questions were stimulated in one way or another by two-process theory. However, alternative approaches to the analysis of avoidance learning also have been proposed, as investigators have gradually moved away from using traditional discrete-trial discriminated avoidance procedures. I will now discuss some of the more important of these alternative theories.

In two-process theory, reinforcement for the avoidance response is assumed to be provided by the reduction of fear. This is a case of negative reinforcement—reinforcement due to removal of an aversive stimulus. Several subsequent theoretical treatments have proposed that avoidance procedures also provide for positive reinforcement of the avoidance response, whereas others have suggested that neither negative reinforcement nor positive reinforcement is important in avoidance learning.

Positive Reinforcement through Conditioned Inhibition of Fear or Conditioned Safety Signals. Performance of an avoidance response always results in distinctive feedback stimuli, such as spatial cues involved in going from one side to the other in a shuttle box or tactile and other external stimuli involved in pressing a response lever. Because the avoidance response produces a period of safety in all avoidance conditioning procedures, response feedback stimuli may acquire conditioned inhibitory properties and become signals for the absence of aversive stimulation. Such stimuli are called **safety signals.** Because a shock-free period is desirable, a conditioned inhibitory stimulus for shock may serve as a positive reinforcer. Thus, according to the *safety-signal hypothesis,* the stimuli that accompany avoidance responses may provide positive reinforcement for avoidance behavior.

In most avoidance experiments, no special steps are taken to ensure that the avoidance response is accompanied by vivid feedback stimuli that could acquire conditioned inhibitory properties. Spatial, tactile, and proprioceptive stimuli that are not specifically programmed but inevitably accompany the avoidance response serve this function (Dinsmoor, 2001a). However, any avoidance procedure can easily be modified to provide a distinctive stimulus, such as a brief light or tone, after each occurrence of the avoidance response. The safety-signal hypothesis predicts that introducing an explicit feedback stimulus will facilitate the learning of an avoidance response. Numerous experiments have found this to be true (for example, Bolles & Grossen, 1969; Cándido, Maldonado, & Vila, 1991; D'Amato, Fazzaro, & Etkin, 1968; Keehn & Nakkash, 1959; see also McAllister & McAllister, 1992).

Other studies have shown that during the course of avoidance training, a response feedback stimulus becomes a conditioned inhibitor of fear (for example, Morris, 1974; Rescorla, 1968a). There is also direct evidence that a feedback stimulus that has been conditioned to inhibit fear during avoidance training is an effective positive reinforcer for new responses (Morris, 1975; Weisman & Litner, 1972; see also Dinsmoor & Sears, 1973). Thus, there is considerable evidence for safety signals as sources of positive reinforcement in avoidance learning. (For a review, see Dinsmoor, 2001b, and ensuing commentary.)

There are important similarities and differences between positive reinforcement of avoidance behavior through conditioned inhibition and the negative reinforcement process assumed by two-process theory. Both mechanisms involve a reduction of fear, but the manner in which this occurs is different in the two cases. Whereas a conditioned inhibitor actively inhibits fear, CS termination is assumed to lead to the passive dissipation of fear. Because both mechanisms involve fear reduction, the operation of both processes depends on the existence of fear. However, the conditioned inhibition reinforcement process is less restrictive about the source of the fear. The fear may be elicited by an explicit warning stimulus or by contextual cues or cues of the environment in which the avoidance procedure is conducted.

The fact that fear elicited by situational cues can provide the basis for conditioned inhibition reinforcement makes the safety-signal hypothesis particularly well suited to explain free-operant avoidance behavior. Participants often experience numerous shocks during acquisition of free-operant avoidance behavior. This and the absence of an exteroceptive warning stimulus make it highly likely that the entire experimental situation becomes conditioned to elicit fear. Because shocks never occur for the duration of the R-S interval after a response is made, the proprioceptive and tactile stimuli that accompany the response can become conditioned inhibitors of fear. Thus, response-associated feedback cues can come to

BOX 10.2

OBSERVATIONAL LEARNING OF FEARS AND PHOBIAS

Excessive fears and phobias can be debilitating and may require therapeutic intervention. Some of the most successful treatment procedures, such as flooding and systematic desensitization, were designed on the basis of conditioning principles. A persistent problem for theoretical analyses of such fears is that people with clinically significant fear and anxiety often have no known history of conditioning with traumatic events. Many people, for example, have an intense fear of snakes even though they have never been bitten by a snake.

How might an individual who has no known experience with traumatic events have acquired a fear or phobia? Research with rhesus monkeys (*Macaca mulatta*) suggests that significant fears may be acquired through observational learning (Mineka & Cook, 1988). Rhesus monkeys reared in the wild have an intense fear of snakes. In response to the sight of a snake, they exhibit a variety of fear responses, including fear grimacing, ear flapping, clutching the cage, averting their eyes, and piloerection (erection of the hair follicles). Fear is also evident in their reluctance to reach over the snake to obtain a food treat. By contrast, monkeys reared in the laboratory do not show these behaviors. Mineka and Cook investigated whether laboratory-reared monkeys could acquire a fear of snakes by observing the fear reactions of wild-reared monkeys in response to a snake.

A discriminative observational conditioning procedure was used. During preliminary training, the demonstrator monkeys were taught to reach over a clear plastic container to obtain a food treat. Observer monkeys were then given the opportunity to watch the reactions of the demonstrator monkeys. On some trials, a live or toy snake was placed in the plastic container. During other trials, the plastic container held a neutral object (a block of wood, for example). The demonstrators showed intense fear of the snake stimuli but not of the neutral objects. After as few as two fear-observation trials, most of the observer monkeys showed similar fear reactions to the snake stimuli. The level of fear they acquired was closely related to the level of fear shown by the demonstrator monkeys. Furthermore, once the observers became fearful of the snakes, they could serve effectively as demonstrators in the observational conditioning of other rhesus monkeys. These results indicate that observational learning could be the basis for wide social transmission of fear among members of a monkey troupe or other social group (see also Cook & Mineka, 1990).

provide positive reinforcement for the free-operant avoidance response (Dinsmoor, 1977, 2001a, 2001b; Rescorla, 1968a).

It is important to realize that the conditioned inhibition reinforcement mechanism is not incompatible with or necessarily a substitute for the negative reinforcement process assumed by two-process theory. That is, negative reinforcement through CS termination and positive reinforcement through conditioned inhibitory feedback cues could well be operative simultaneously, both processes contributing to the strength of the avoidance behavior (see Cicala & Owen, 1976; Owen, Cicala, & Herdegen, 1978).

Reinforcement of Avoidance through Reduction of Shock Frequency. As I have described, positive reinforcement through conditioned inhibition can occur alongside the negative reinforcement mechanism of two-process theory. In contrast, another reinforcement mechanism, **shock-frequency reduction,** has been proposed as an alternative to two-process theory (deVilliers, 1974; Herrnstein, 1969; Herrnstein & Hineline, 1966; Hineline, 1981). By definition, avoidance responses prevent the delivery of shock and thereby reduce the frequency of shocks an organism receives. The theories of avoidance I have discussed so far have viewed the reduction of shocks almost as an incidental by-product of avoidance responses rather than as a primary cause of avoidance behavior. By contrast, the shock-frequency reduction hypothesis views the avoidance of shock as critical to the reinforcement of avoidance behavior.

Shock-frequency reduction as the cause of avoidance behavior was first entertained by Sidman (1962) to explain results he obtained in a concurrent free-operant avoidance experiment. Rats were exposed to two free-operant avoidance schedules at the same time. Responses on one response lever prevented shocks on one of the schedules, and responses on the other lever prevented shocks on the second schedule. Sidman concluded that the animals distributed their responses between the two levers in order to reduce the overall frequency of shocks they received. The idea that shock frequency reduction can serve to reinforce avoidance behavior was later encouraged by evidence of learning in a free-operant avoidance procedure specifically designed to minimize the role of fear-conditioned temporal cues (Herrnstein & Hineline, 1966). Studies of the relative importance of various components of the discriminated avoidance procedure have also shown that the avoidance component significantly contributes to the learning (for example, Bolles, Stokes, & Younger, 1966; see also Bolles, 1972a; Kamin, 1956).

Courtesy of Donald A. Dewsbury

R. C. Bolles

Although the evidence just cited clearly indicates that avoidance of shock is important, the mechanisms responsible for these results are debatable. Several experiments have shown that animals can learn to make an avoidance response even if the response does not reduce the frequency of shocks delivered (Gardner & Lewis, 1976; Hineline, 1970; see also Hineline, 1981). Responding in these studies delayed the onset of the next scheduled shock but did not prevent its delivery. Thus, overall shock frequency was unchanged by the instrumental response. Such results can be explained in terms of the shock-frequency reduction hypothesis by assuming that organisms calculate shock frequencies over only a limited period following an avoidance response. However, once this possibility is allowed, the shock-frequency reduction hypothesis becomes difficult to differentiate from conditioned inhibition reinforcement. If a response reduces the frequency of shocks in the short term, external and proprioceptive stimuli involved in making the response will come to signal this shock reduction and become conditioned inhibitors of fear. The conditioned inhibitory properties of these stimuli can then reinforce the avoidance behavior (Dinsmoor, 2001a, 2001b).

Avoidance and Species-Specific Defense Reactions (SSDRs). In the theories discussed so far, the main emphasis has been on how the events that precede and follow the avoidance response control avoidance behavior. The exact nature or form of the response itself was not a concern to these theories. In addition, the reinforcement mechanisms assumed by the theories all required some time to develop. Before fear reduction can be an effective reinforcer, fear first must be conditioned to the CS; before response feedback cues can come to serve as reinforcers, they must become signals for the absence of shock; and before shock-frequency reduction can work, organisms must experience enough shocks to be able to "calculate" shock frequencies. Therefore, these theories tell us little about what determines the organism's behavior during the first few trials of avoidance training.

Lack of concern with what an organism does during the first few trials of avoidance conditioning is a serious weakness. For an avoidance mechanism to be useful under natural conditions, the mechanism has to generate successful avoidance responses quickly. Consider, for example, an animal trying to avoid a predator. An avoidance mechanism that requires numerous training trials is of no use in this case. If the animal fails to avoid being eaten by the predator during its initial encounter, it will not be around for future training trials. Bolles (1970, 1971) recognized this problem and focused on what controls an organism's behavior during the early stages of avoidance training.

Bolles assumed that aversive stimuli and situations elicit strong unconditioned, or innate, responses. These innate responses are assumed to have evolved because they are successful in defense against pain and injury. Therefore, Bolles called these **species-specific defense reactions (SSDRs).** In rats, for example, prominent SSDRs include flight (running), freezing (remaining vigilant but motionless, except for breathing), and defensive fighting. Other reactions to danger include thigmotaxis (approaching walls), defensive burying (covering up the source of aversive stimulation), and seeking out dark areas.

Bolles proposed that the configuration of the environment determines which particular SSDR occurs. For example, flight may predominate when an obvious escape route is available, and freezing may predominate if there is no way out of the situation. This is indeed the case (Blanchard, 1997; Sigmundi, 1997). Defensive fighting, for example, is not possible without an opponent; and defensive burying is not possible unless a medium, such as sand, is available in which to bury the source of danger. Even freezing, a response that you might think does not require stimulus supports, occurs only in relatively safe places (near a wall or in a corner) rather than in the middle of an arena. If a rat finds itself in the middle of an arena when it encounters danger, it will move to a wall or a corner before freezing.

The SSDR theory of avoidance behavior states that species-specific defense reactions predominate during the initial stages of avoidance training. If the most likely SSDR is successful in preventing shocks, this behavior will persist as long as the avoidance procedure is in effect. If the first SSDR is not effective, it will be followed by shock, which will suppress the behavior through punishment. The animal will then make the next most likely SSDR. If shocks persist, this second SSDR will also become suppressed by punishment, and the organism will make the third most likely SSDR.

The response-selection process is assumed to end when a response is found that is effective in avoiding shocks, so that the behavior will not be suppressed by punishment. Thus, according to the SSDR account, *punishment is responsible for the selection of the instrumental avoidance response* from other activities of the organism. Reinforcement, be it positive or negative, is assumed to have a minor role, if any, in avoidance learning. According to SSDR theory, the correct avoidance response is not strengthened by reinforcement; rather, it occurs because other SSDRs are suppressed by punishment.

One obvious prediction of the SSDR theory is that some types of responses will be more easily learned in avoidance experiments than others. Consistent with this prediction, Bolles (1969) found that rats can rapidly learn to run in a running wheel to avoid shock. By contrast, their performance of a rearing response (standing on the hind legs) did not improve much during the course of avoidance training. Presumably, running was learned faster because it was closer to the rat's species-specific defense reactions in the running wheel (see also Grossen & Kelley, 1972).

SSDR theory made significant contributions to the understanding of avoidance learning by calling attention to the importance of species-typical behavior in aversive situations. However, it has not been entirely successful in explaining experimental findings. For example, contrary to SSDR theory, defensive responses that are ineffective in avoiding aversive stimulation are not necessarily suppressed by punishment. Instead, punishment sometimes facilitates the occurrence of species-specific defense responses (for example, Bolles & Riley, 1973; Melvin & Ervey, 1973; Walters & Glazer, 1971).

Predatory Imminence and the Distinction between Defensive and Recuperative Behavior. Shortcomings of SSDR theory have stimulated alternative formulations that have introduced the concept of predatory imminence (Fanselow & Lester, 1988; Fanselow,

1989, 1997). These formulations also make a distinction between defensive responses that presumably reflect the anticipation of a painful event or injury and recuperative responses that are assumed to be performed after the aversive or injurious stimulus (Bolles & Fanselow, 1980).

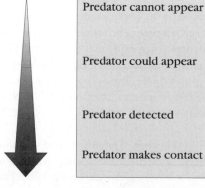

Courtesy of UCLA Department of Psychology

M. S. Fanselow

The concept of **predatory imminence** can be illustrated by considering the circumstances faced by a small rodent (a rat, for example) that is a potential source of food for cats, coyotes, snakes, and other predators. The rat is presumably safest in its nest in a burrow, but it has to go out periodically to forage for food. When it is out foraging, it is not in much danger as long as no cats or snakes are around. When a snake appears, the rat's level of danger increases, but not by much if the snake is far away. As the snake gets closer, the level of danger rises. The situation is very dangerous when the snake is about to strike, and maximally dangerous when the strike actually occurs. This progression of increasing levels of danger is called the predatory-imminence continuum and is illustrated in Figure 10.11.

Different species-typical defense responses are assumed to occur at different levels of predatory imminence. If a rat is forced to forage for food in a location where it periodically encounters snakes, it is likely to leave its burrow to get food less often but eat larger meals during each excursion (Fanselow, Lester, & Helmstetter, 1988). Thus, the response to a low level of predatory imminence is an adjustment in meal patterns. When a snake appears but is not yet about to strike, the rat's defensive behavior is likely to change to freezing. Freezing will reduce the chance that a predator will see or hear the rat. Many predators will strike only at moving prey. Freezing by the prey also may result in the predator shifting its attention to something else (Suarez & Gallup, 1981).

When the snake actually touches the rat, the rat is likely to leap into the air. It is as if the rat's prior freezing behavior prepares it to explode into the air when it is touched. This is called the *circa strike response.* If the rat does not successfully escape the predator at this point, it is likely to engage in defensive aggressive activities. If the defensive behavior is successful and the rat manages to get away from the snake, the rat is likely to engage in grooming and other recuperative responses that should promote healing from its injuries.

The predatory-imminence hypothesis differs from the SSDR theory in two important respects. First, as the scenario illustrates, species-specific defense responses such as freezing, fleeing, and aggression are most likely to occur in anticipation of injury rather than in response to the injury itself. The actual injury stimulates recuperative responses. Thus, unlike the SSDR theory, the predatory-imminence hypothesis makes a distinction between defensive and recuperative responses to aversive stimulation. Second, in the predatory-imminence hypothesis, the primary determinant of the particular defense response that is

Figure 10.11 The predatory-imminence continuum. (From "A Functional Behavioristic Approach to Aversively Motivated Behavior: Predatory Imminence as a Determinant of the Topography of Defensive Behavior," by M. S. Fanselow and L. S. Lester. In R. C. Bolles and M. D. Beecher [Eds.], 1988, *Evolution and Learning,* pp. 185–212. Copyright © 1988 by Lawrence Erlbaum and Associates. Reprinted by permission.)

Status of the predator	*Status of the prey*
Predator cannot appear	Nonaversively motivated behavior and recuperative behavior due to a previous attack
Predator could appear	Preencounter defensive behavior (e.g., modification of foraging patterns)
Predator detected	Postencounter defensive behavior (e.g., freezing)
Predator makes contact	Strike-defensive behavior (leap-jump, defensive aggression)

observed is assumed to be the level of predatory imminence rather than the configuration of the environment. Thus, selection among possible SSDRs is not through suppression of ineffective SSDRs by punishment, as the SSDR theory proposes, but by different levels of perceived danger.

Despite these differences, both the SSDR theory and the predatory-imminence hypothesis assume that defensive behavior initially occurs as unconditioned responding. Stimuli that become associated with an aversive event can come to elicit a defensive response as well. The available evidence suggests that in rats the defensive response that comes to be elicited by a conditioned stimulus is usually one level lower on the predatory-imminence scale than the response elicited by the unconditioned stimulus (Fanselow, 1989). Thus, if the unconditioned stimulus elicits the leap and jump (circa strike) characteristic of peak predatory imminence, the conditioned stimulus is likely to elicit the freezing behavior of the level just below.

Another important similarity between the predatory-imminence hypothesis and the SSDR theory is that neither of them assumes that positive reinforcement is involved in the development of avoidance behavior. The predatory-imminence hypothesis takes a more radical position than the SSDR theory in rejecting the importance of instrumental conditioning altogether, since it does not even include a punishment mechanism. However, the predatory-imminence hypothesis was developed as an explanation of defensive behavior—not as an explanation of the diverse findings that have been obtained in avoidance learning experiments. Therefore, it was not intended to serve as a complete account of what happens in avoidance conditioning experiments.

The Avoidance Puzzle: Concluding Comments

We have learned a great deal about avoidance behavior since Mowrer and Lamoreaux (1942) puzzled about how "not getting something" can motivate avoidance responses. As I described, numerous ingenious answers to this puzzle have been provided. Two-process theory, conditioned inhibition reinforcement, and shock-frequency reduction reinforcement all provide different views of how the avoidance response may be reinforced. By contrast, the SSDR account focuses on unconditioned aspects of defensive behavior, a theme that is further elaborated through the concept of predatory imminence.

None of the major theories can explain everything that occurs in aversive conditioning situations, but each provides ideas that are useful for understanding various aspects of avoidance behavior. For example, two-process theory is uniquely suited to explain the results of the acquired-drive experiments. The safety-signal theory is particularly useful in explaining free-operant avoidance learning, the role of response feedback stimuli in avoidance conditioning, and the maintenance of avoidance behavior in the absence of an explicit warning stimulus. The concept of predatory imminence provides the most useful account of what happens during early stages of avoidance training. Given the complexities of the various avoidance learning paradigms, it is not surprising that several conceptual frameworks are needed to explain all of the available data.

PUNISHMENT

Although most of us engage in avoidance behavior of one sort or another every day, there is little public awareness of it. As a society, we are not particularly concerned about what is involved in making avoidance responses. This may be because procedures that generate active avoidance are rarely used in organized efforts to change or control someone's behavior. By contrast, **punishment** has always been of great concern to people. Sometimes punishment is used as a form of retribution or as a price extracted for undesirable behavior. Punishment is also frequently used to encourage adherence to religious and civil codes of conduct. Many institutions and rules have evolved to ensure that punishment will be administered in ways that are deemed ethical and acceptable to society. What constitutes acceptable punishment in the criminal justice system, in childrearing, in schools, or in the treatment of individuals with psychiatric disorders or mental retardation is a matter of continual debate.

Despite long-standing societal concerns about punishment, for many years experimental psychologists devoted little attention to the topic. On the basis of a few experiments, Thorndike (1932) and Skinner (1938, 1953) concluded that punishment was not a very effective method for controlling behavior and that it had only temporary effects at best (see also Estes, 1944). This claim was not seriously challenged until the 1960s, when punishment processes began to be investigated more extensively (Azrin & Holz, 1966; Campbell & Church, 1969; Church, 1963; Solomon, 1964). We now know that punishment can be an effective technique for modifying behavior (Dinsmoor, 1998). Given several behavioral options, punishment produces a response bias away from the punished behavior (McAdie, Foster, & Temple, 1996). With appropriate procedural parameters, responding can be suppressed nearly totally in just one or two trials. With less severe parameters, the suppression of behavior may be incomplete, and responding may recover.

Courtesy of N. H. Azrin

N. H. Azrin

Experimental Analysis of Punishment

The basic punishment procedure involves presenting an aversive stimulus after a specified response. If the procedure is effective, the specified response becomes suppressed. By not making the punished response, the organism avoids the aversive stimulation. Because punishment involves the suppression of behavior, it can be observed only with responses that are likely to occur in the absence of punishment. To ensure occurrence of the behavior, experimental studies of punishment usually also involve reinforcement of the punished response with something such as food or water. This sets up a conflict between responding to obtain positive reinforcement and withholding responding to avoid punishment. The degree of response suppression that occurs is determined by variables related both to presentation of the aversive stimulus and to the availability of positive reinforcement.

Characteristics of the Aversive Stimulus and Its Method of Introduction. A great variety of aversive stimuli have been used in punishment experiments, including electric shock, a sudden burst of air, loud noise, verbal reprimands, a physical slap, a squirt of lemon juice in the mouth, and a cue previously conditioned with shock (Azrin, 1958; Hake & Azrin, 1965; Hall, Axelrod, Foundopoulos, Shellman, Campbell, & Cranston, 1971; Masserman, 1946; Sajwaj, Libet, & Agras, 1974; Skinner, 1938). Other response-suppression procedures have involved the loss of positive reinforcement, time out from positive reinforcement, overcorrection, and manual restraint (Foxx & Azrin, 1973; Lerman, Iwata, Shore, & DeLeon, 1997; Thomas, 1968; Trenholme & Baron, 1975).

Time out refers to removal of the opportunity to obtain positive reinforcement. Time out is often used to punish children, as when a child is told "Go to your room" after doing something bad. **Overcorrection** involves requiring a person not only to rectify what was done badly but to overcorrect for the mistake. For example, a child who has placed an object in his mouth may be asked to remove the object and also to wash out his mouth with an antiseptic solution.

A convenient aversive stimulus in human studies of punishment is point loss. In one recent study (O'Donnell, Crosbie, Williams, & Saunders, 2000), college students were reinforced for pressing a response lever by points that could be exchanged for money at the end of the experiment. Two discriminative stimuli (lines of different lengths) were used. During the baseline phase, only the S^D was presented, and responses were reinforced on a variable interval schedule. After that, the S^D was alternated with the other discriminative stimulus, the $S^D{}_P$. Responding continued to be reinforced according to the VI schedule during the $S^D{}_P$, but now a point-loss punishment contingency was also in effect. With each response, a certain number of points was subtracted from the total the subject had obtained.

The results of the experiment are summarized in Figure 10.12. Responding was well maintained during S^D in the baseline phase. In the subsequent punishment phase, responding continued at substantial levels during S^D but was suppressed during $S^D{}_P$.

The response suppression produced by punishment depends in part on features of the aversive stimulus. The effects of various characteristics of the aversive event have been most extensively investigated with shock because the duration and intensity of shock can be precisely controlled. The general finding has been that more intense and longer shocks are

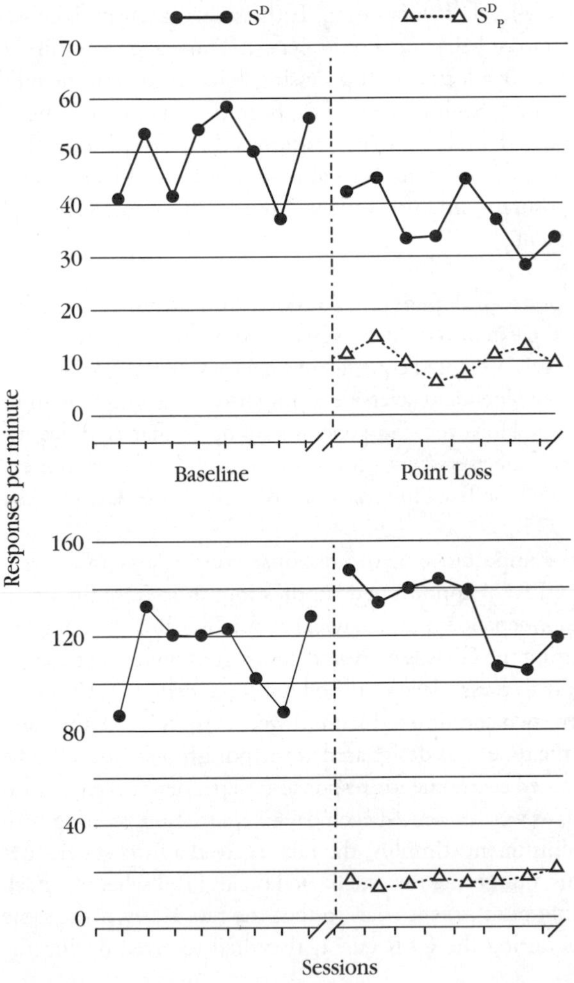

Figure 10.12 Lever-press responding of college students reinforced on a variable interval schedule with points that could be exchanged for money at the end of the experiment. During the baseline phase only the reinforced discriminative stimulus (S^D) was presented. During the next phase the S^D was presented in alternation with a punishment stimulus ($S^D{}_P$), during which the VI schedule remained in effect but each response was also punished by point loss. The top and bottom panels present data for different students. (After O'Donnell et al., 2000.)

more effective in suppressing responding (see reviews by Azrin & Holz, 1966; Church, 1969; Walters & Grusec, 1977). Low-intensity aversive stimulation produces only moderate suppression of responding, and responding may recover with continued exposure to the mild punishment procedure (for example, Azrin, 1960). By contrast, if the aversive stimulus is sufficiently intense, responding will be completely suppressed for a long time. In one experiment, for example, high-intensity punishment completely suppressed the instrumental response for 6 days (Azrin, 1960).

Another very important factor in punishment is how the aversive stimulus is introduced. If a high intensity of shock is used from the outset of punishment, the instrumental response will be severely suppressed. Much less suppression of behavior will occur if the shock intensity is gradually increased during the course of continued punishment training (Azrin, Holz, & Hake, 1963; Miller, 1960; see also Banks, 1976). This finding is very important because it shows that an organism becomes resistant to the effects of intense punishment if it is first exposed to lower levels of shock that do not produce much response suppression. Spending two weeks in jail is not a disturbing experience for someone who has become accustomed to shorter periods of incarceration.

The preceding findings suggest that how organisms respond during their *initial exposure* to punishment determines how they will respond to subsequent punishment (Church, 1969). This idea has an interesting implication. Suppose an individual is first exposed to intense shock that results in a very low level of responding. If the shock intensity is subsequently reduced, the severe suppression of behavior should persist. Thus, after exposure to intense shock, mild shock should be more effective in suppressing behavior than if the mild shock had been used from the beginning. Such findings have been obtained by Raymond (reported in Church, 1969). Taken together, the evidence indicates that initial exposure to mild aversive stimulation that does not disrupt behavior reduces the effects of later intense punishment. By contrast, initial exposure to intense aversive stimulation increases the suppressive effects of later mild punishment.

Response-Contingent versus Response-Independent Aversive Stimulation. Another important variable that determines the extent to which aversive stimulation suppresses behavior is whether the aversive stimulus is presented contingent on a specified response or independently of behavior. Response-independent aversive stimulation can result in some suppression of instrumental behavior. However, the general finding is that significantly more suppression of behavior occurs if the aversive stimulus is produced by the instrumental response (for example, Azrin, 1956; Bolles, Holtz, Dunn, & Hill, 1980; Camp, Raymond, & Church, 1967; Frankel, 1975).

In one study demonstrating the importance of the response contingency in punishment, Goodall (1984) compared a CER, or conditioned suppression, procedure (in which footshock during a CS was delivered independent of behavior) and a discriminative punishment procedure (in which shock during the CS was delivered contingent on lever pressing). One group of rats was trained initially to press a lever for food reinforcement on a VI 60-sec schedule. After responding stabilized, two conditioned stimuli were introduced, a tone and a light. One of the stimuli (let's say the tone) was designated as the punishment cue, and the other stimulus (the light) was designated as the cue for response-independent aversive stimulation. Two trials with each of the CSs were presented each day in alternation, starting with the punishment cue. During the punishment stimulus, the rats received a brief shock after every third lever-press response. Thus, punishment was delivered on an FR 3 schedule. Each CER trial was yoked to the preceding punishment trial, so that the rats received the same number and distribution of shocks during the CER cue as they had received during the

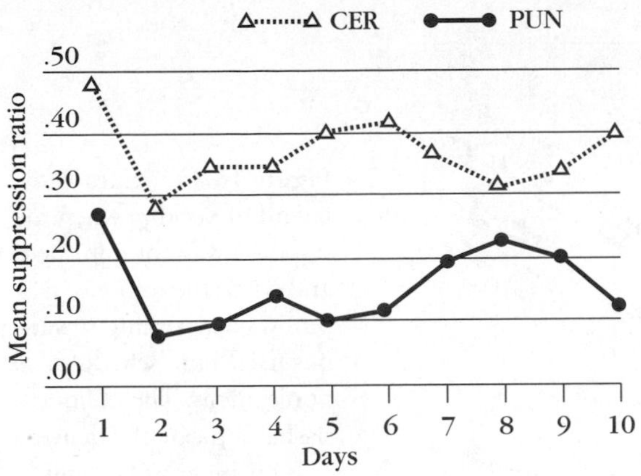

Figure 10.13 Suppression of lever pressing during punishment and CER stimuli during 10 successive sessions. During the punishment cue, lever pressing was punished on an FR 3 schedule. During the CER cue, the same number and distribution of shocks was delivered independent of behavior. (From "Learning Due to the Response-Shock Contingency in Signalled Punishment," by G. Goodall, 1984, *The Quarterly Journal of Experimental Psychology, 36B,* pp. 259–279. Copyright © 1984 by Lawrence Erlbaum and Associates. Reprinted by permission.)

immediately preceding punishment trial. However, shocks during the CER cue were always delivered independent of the lever-press behavior.

The results of the experiment are presented in Figure 10.13 in terms of suppression of lever pressing during the CER and punishment cues. Given the brief and mild shocks that were used (0.5 mA, 0.5 sec), not much suppression of behavior was evident during the CER stimulus. By contrast, the same number and distribution of shocks substantially suppressed responding during the punishment stimulus. This difference illustrates that delivering shocks contingent on an instrumental response is more effective in suppressing that response than delivering aversive stimulation independent of behavior.

Effects of Delay of Punishment. Another important factor in punishment is the interval between the instrumental behavior and the aversive stimulation. The general finding is that increasing the delay of punishment results in less suppression of behavior (for example, Baron, 1965; Camp et al., 1967). This relation is particularly important in practical applications of punishment. Inadvertent delays may occur if the undesired response is not detected right away, if it takes time to investigate who is actually at fault for an error, or if preparing the aversive stimulus requires time. Such delays can make punishment totally ineffective in modifying the undesired behavior.

Effects of Schedules of Punishment. Just as positive reinforcement does not have to be provided for each occurrence of the instrumental response, punishment may also be delivered only intermittently. This was the case in the experiment by Goodall. In the Goodall study, punishment was delivered on an FR 3 schedule. More systematic studies have shown that the degree of response suppression produced by punishment depends on the proportion of responses that are punished.

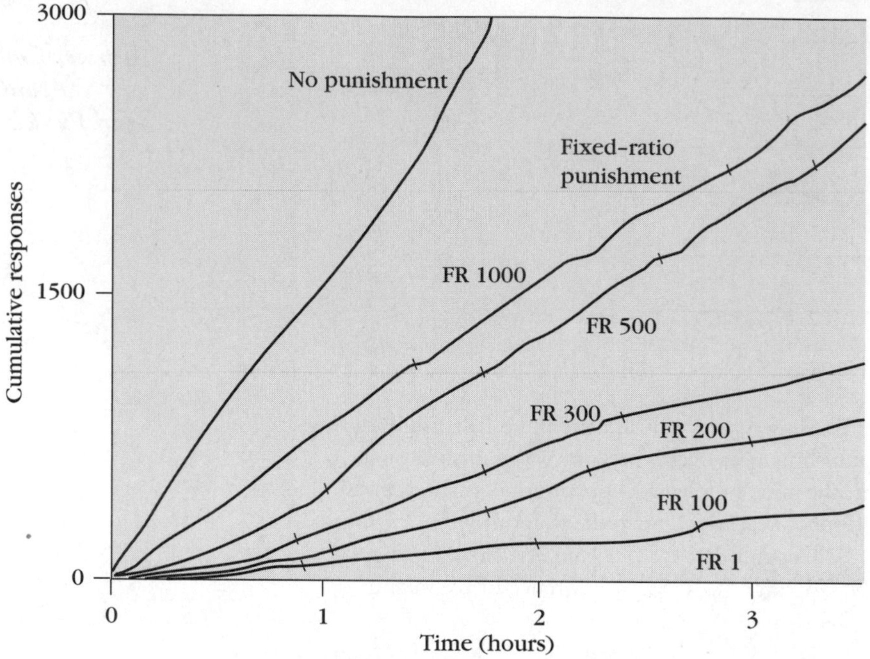

Figure 10.14 Cumulative record of pecking when the response was not punished and when the response was punished according to various fixed-ratio schedules of punishment. The oblique slashes indicate the delivery of punishment. Responding was reinforced on a variable interval 3-min schedule. (From "Fixed-Ratio Punishment," by N. H. Azrin, W. C. Holz, and D. R. Hake, 1963, *Journal of the Experimental Analysis of Behavior, 6,* pp. 141–148.)

In a study of fixed ratio punishment by Azrin and his colleagues (1963), pigeons were first reinforced with food on a variable interval schedule for pecking a response key. Punishment was then introduced. Various fixed ratio punishment procedures were tested while food reinforcement continued to be provided for the pecking behavior. The results are summarized in Figure 10.14. When every response was shocked (FR 1 punishment), key pecking ceased entirely. With the other punishment schedules, the rate of responding depended on the frequency of punishment. Higher fixed ratio schedules allowed more responses to go unpunished. Not surprisingly, therefore, higher rates of responding occurred when higher fixed ratio punishment schedules were used. However, some suppression of behavior was observed even when only every thousandth response was followed by shock.

Effects of Schedules of Positive Reinforcement. As I noted earlier, in most studies of punishment the instrumental response is simultaneously maintained by a positive reinforcement schedule so that some level of responding is available to be punished. The effects of a punishment procedure are in part determined by this positive reinforcement. When behavior is maintained by either a fixed or a variable interval schedule of positive reinforcement, punishment produces a decrease in the overall rate of responding. However, the temporal distribution of the behavior is not disturbed. That is, during the punishment procedure, variable interval positive reinforcement produces a suppressed but stable rate of responding (see Figure 10.14), whereas fixed interval positive reinforcement produces the typical scalloped pattern of responding (for example, Azrin & Holz, 1961).

The outcome is different if the behavior is maintained by a fixed ratio schedule of positive reinforcement. As noted in Chapter 6, fixed ratio schedules produce a pause in responding just after reinforcement (the postreinforcement pause), followed by a high and steady rate of responding to complete the number of responses necessary for the next reinforcer (the ratio run). Punishment usually increases the length of the postreinforcement pause but has little effect on the ratio run (Azrin, 1959; see also Church, 1969; Dardano & Sauerbrunn, 1964).

Availability of Alternative Sources of Positive Reinforcement. Punishment has dramatically different outcomes depending on whether the subject is able to obtain reinforcement by engaging in some other activity. This is particularly important in practical applications of punishment. If the punished response is the only activity available to the subject for obtaining reinforcement, punishment will be much less effective than if an alternative source of reinforcement is provided along with punishment.

The importance of alternative sources of reinforcement was demonstrated by an early study of adult male smokers conducted by Herman and Azrin (1964). The subjects were seated facing two response levers. Pressing either lever was reinforced with a cigarette on a variable interval schedule. After the behavior was occurring at a stable rate, responding on one of the levers was punished by a brief obnoxious noise. In one experimental condition, only one response lever was available during the punishment phase. In another condition, both response levers were available, but responding on one of the levers was punished with the loud noise. Figure 10.15 shows the results. When the punished response was the only way to obtain cigarettes, punishment produced a moderate suppression of behavior. By contrast, when the alternative response lever was available, responding on the punished lever ceased altogether. Thus, the availability of an alternative response for obtaining positive reinforcement greatly increased the suppressive effects of punishment. Similar results have been obtained in other situations. For example, children punished for playing with certain toys are much less likely to play with these if they are allowed to play with other toys instead (Perry & Parke, 1975). Reinforcement for alternative behavior also increases the effectiveness of mild punishment in suppressing self-injurious behavior in individuals with profound mental retardation (Thompson, Iwata, Conners, & Roscoe, 1999).

Effects of a Discriminative Stimulus for Punishment. As discussed in Chapter 8, if positive reinforcement is available for responding in the presence of a distinctive stimulus but is not available in its absence, the organism will learn to respond only when the stimulus is present. The suppressive effects of punishment can also be brought under stimulus control.

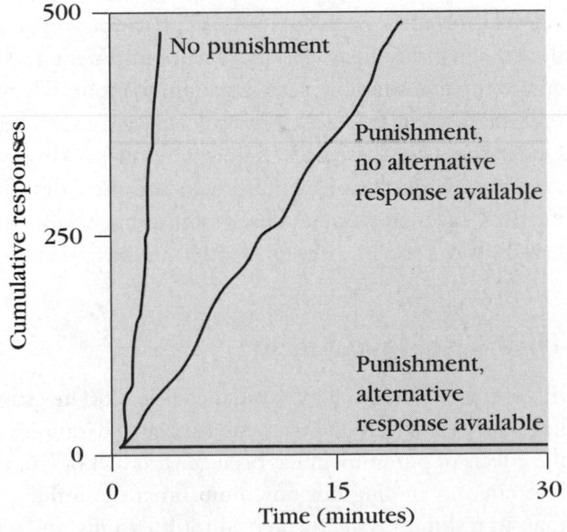

Figure 10.15 Cumulative record of responding when responses are not punished, when responses are punished and there is no alternative source of reinforcement, and when responses are punished but an alternative reinforced response is available. (From "Punishment," by N. H. Azrin and W. C. Holz. In W. K. Honig [Ed.], 1966, *Operant Behavior.* Copyright © 1966 by Prentice-Hall.)

This occurs if responding is punished in the presence of a discriminative stimulus but is not punished when the stimulus is absent. Such a procedure is called **discriminative punishment.** With continued exposure to discriminative punishment, the suppressive effects of punishment will come to be limited to the presence of the discriminative stimulus (Dinsmoor, 1952).

Discriminative punishment was used in the study whose results were summarized in Figure 10.12. The college students who served in this experiment could earn points for responding during one discriminative stimulus, the S^D. In the presence of another discriminative stimulus, the $S^D{}_P$, responding was also punished by loss of points. As Figure 10.12 illustrates, the suppressive effects of punishment were largely limited to the $S^D{}_P$.

The fact that the suppressive effects of punishment can be limited to the presence of a discriminative stimulus is often problematic in applications of punishment. In many situations, the person who administers the punishment also serves as a discriminative stimulus for punishment, with the result that the undesired behavior is suppressed only as long as the monitor is present. For example, children learn which teachers are strict about discipline and learn to suppress their rambunctious behavior in those classes more than in other classes. As another example, a highway patrol car is a discriminative stimulus for punishment for speeding. Drivers are more likely to obey speed laws in areas where they see patrol cars than in unpatrolled stretches of highway.

Punishment as a Signal for the Availability of Positive Reinforcement. Punishment does not always suppress behavior. In fact, in certain situations people seem to seek out punishment. Does this represent a breakdown of the normal mechanisms of behavior, or can such behavior be explained by the principles I have discussed so far? Experimental evidence suggests that conventional behavioral mechanisms may lead to such seemingly abnormal behavior. Punishment seeking can result if positive reinforcement is available only when the instrumental response is also punished. In such circumstances, punishment may become a signal, or discriminative stimulus, for the availability of positive reinforcement. If this occurs, punishment will increase rather than suppress responding.

In one demonstration of the discriminative stimulus properties of punishment, pigeons were first trained to peck a response key for food reinforcement on a variable interval schedule (Holz & Azrin, 1961). Each response was then punished by a mild shock sufficient to reduce the response rate by about 50%. In the next phase of the experiment, periods in which the punishment procedure was in effect were alternated with periods in which punishment was not scheduled. In addition, the pecking response was reinforced with food only during the punishment periods. The punishment and safe periods were not signaled by an environmental stimulus, such as a light or a tone. Therefore, the only way for the pigeons to tell whether reinforcement was available was to see whether they were punished for pecking. Under these circumstances, higher rates of pecking occurred during punishment periods than during safe periods. Punishment became a discriminative stimulus for food reinforcement. (For other examples of self-punitive behavior, see Brown, 1969; Brown & Cunningham, 1981; Dean & Pittman, 1991; Melvin, 1971.)

Theories of Punishment

In contrast to the study of avoidance behavior, investigations of punishment, by and large, have not been motivated by theoretical considerations. Most of the evidence available about the effects of punishment has been the product of empirical curiosity. The investigators were interested in finding out how punishment is influenced by various manipulations rather than in testing specific theoretical formulations. In fact, few systematic theories of punish-

BOX 10.3

WHEN PUNISHMENT DOESN'T WORK

Sometimes children are brought to a therapist because their behavior is out of control. A child may be unruly and unresponsive to the disciplinary practices of parents or teachers. Punishment may be tried as a procedure of last resort, but without much success. The parents or teachers may note that punishing the child only makes the behavior worse. It is not uncommon for children with a severe problem of this type to be diagnosed as hyperactive or emotionally disturbed. These labels suggest there is something fundamentally wrong with the child. Behavior therapists, however, have found that in some cases the problem may be nothing more than the result of mismanaged discipline. The parents or teachers may have inadvertently established punishment as a discriminative stimulus for positive reinforcement. Instead of decreasing some undesirable behavior, punishment increases it. How can this happen?

Take the hypothetical situation of Johnny, who lives in a home with two busy parents. Johnny, like most children, is rather active. If he is quietly playing in his room, the parents are likely to ignore him and engage in activities of their own. By contrast, if Johnny behaves badly or makes demands, the parents are forced to pay attention to him. The parents may be giving Johnny attention only when he is misbehaving or making demands. Any time he is not being a problem, the parents may be thankfully relieved to have a moment's peace. Thus, rather than reinforcing cooperative or peaceful behavior, the parents may be ignoring Johnny at these times. What we have then is a vicious circle. The more Johnny misbehaves, the less attention he is given for nondisruptive behavior, because the parents increasingly come to cherish quiet moments as a chance to do something on their own. Misbehavior becomes Johnny's main means of obtaining attention. The punishments and reprimands that go with the behavior signal to him that his parents are caring and attending.

In actuality, the therapist does not have the opportunity to observe how behavior problems of this type originate. The "discriminative value of punishment" explanation is supported by the outcome of attempts to change the situation. The hypothesis suggests that if one changes the attention patterns, the behavior problem can be alleviated. Indeed, clinical psychologists often show parents how to attend to appropriate and constructive activities and how to administer punishment with a minimum of attention directed toward the child. In many cases dramatic improvement ensues when parents are able to positively reinforce cooperative behavior with their attentions and ignore disruptive activities as much as possible.

ment exist, and most were formulated in some form about 50 years ago. I will describe three of the most prominent theories.

The Conditioned Emotional Response Theory of Punishment. One of the first theories of punishment was proposed by Estes (1944) and is based on the observation by Estes and Skinner (1941) that a conditioned stimulus that has been paired with shock will suppress the performance of food-reinforced instrumental behavior. I discussed this conditioned suppression, or conditioned emotional response, procedure earlier in this chapter as well as in Chapters 3. Conditioned suppression involves a suppression of ongoing behavior elicited by a stimulus that has been associated with aversive stimulation. The behavioral suppression occurs primarily because a fear-conditioned stimulus elicits freezing, which then interferes with other activities.

Estes (1944) proposed that punishment suppresses behavior through the same mechanism that produces response suppression to a fear-conditioned stimulus (see also Estes, 1969). In contrast to the usual conditioned suppression experiment, however, punishment procedures usually do not involve an explicit CS that signals the impending delivery of an aversive stimulus. Estes suggested that the various stimuli an individual experiences just before making the punished response serve this function. Consider for example, how an "invisible" fence works to keep a dog in its yard. An invisible or electronic fence detects when the dog goes to the edge of its yard and administers a brief shock to the dog through a remote sensing collar if the dog steps beyond this boundary. The punished response (going too far) is associated with various cues of the boundary of the yard. When the dog is punished, the various visual and other spatial cues of the yard boundary become paired with shock. With repetition of the punishment episode, the boundary stimuli become strongly conditioned by the shock. According to the conditioned emotional response theory, as these cues acquire conditioned aversive properties, they will come to elicit freezing, which is incompatible with the punished behavior. Thus, the punished response will become suppressed.

The conditioned emotional response theory can explain many punishment effects. For example, the fact that more intense and longer duration shocks produce more response suppression can be explained by assuming that the stimuli conditioned by these aversive events elicit more vigorous conditioned emotional responses. The theory can also explain why response-contingent aversive stimulation produces more response suppression than response-independent delivery of shock. If shock is produced by the instrumental response, the stimuli that become conditioned by the shock are more likely to be closely related to performance of this behavior. Therefore, the conditioned emotional responses are more likely to interfere with the punished response.

The Avoidance Theory of Punishment. An alternative to the conditioned emotional response theory regards punishment as a form of avoidance behavior. This theory is most closely associated with Dinsmoor (1954, 1977, 1998) and follows the tradition of two-process theory of avoidance. Dinsmoor accepted the idea that the stimuli that accompany the instrumental response acquire aversive properties when the response is punished. Dinsmoor went on to propose that organisms learn to escape from the conditioned aversive stimuli related to the punished response by engaging in some other behavior that is incompatible with the punished activity. Since this other behavior is incompatible with the punished response, performance of the alternative activity results in suppression of the punished behavior. Thus, the avoidance theory explains punishment in terms of the acquisition of incompatible avoidance responses.

The avoidance theory of punishment is an ingenious proposal. It suggests that all changes produced by aversive instrumental conditioning, be they increases or decreases in the likelihood of a response, can be explained by the same avoidance learning mechanisms. Suppression of behavior is not viewed as reflecting the weakening of the punished response. Rather, it is explained in terms of the strengthening of competing avoidance responses.

Despite its cleverness and parsimony, the avoidance theory of punishment has been controversial. Because it explains punishment in terms of avoidance mechanisms, all the theoretical problems that have been troublesome in the analysis of avoidance behavior become problems in the analysis of punishment as well. Another challenge for the theory is that its critical elements are not stated in a way that makes them easily accessible to experimental proof (Rachlin & Herrnstein, 1969; Schuster & Rachlin, 1968). The stimuli that are assumed to acquire conditioned aversive properties are not under the direct control of the experimenter. Rather, they are events that an organism is assumed to experience when it is about to make the punished response. The avoidance responses that are presumably acquired are also ill specified. The theory does not tell us what these responses will be in a given situation or how one might look for them.

Punishment and the Negative Law of Effect. This third and last explanation of punishment is also the oldest. Thorndike (1911) originally proposed that positive reinforcement and punishment involve symmetrically opposite processes. Just as positive reinforcement strengthens behavior, so punishment weakens it. In later years Thorndike abandoned the idea that punishment weakens behavior because he failed to find supporting evidence in some of his experiments (Thorndike, 1932). However, the belief that there is a negative law of effect that is comparable to but the opposite of a positive law of effect has retained favor with some investigators (for example, Azrin & Holz, 1966; Rachlin & Herrnstein, 1969).

One approach to the analysis of the negative law of effect was initiated by Premack and his colleagues. As I discussed in Chapter 7, Premack proposed that positive reinforcement occurs when the opportunity to engage in a highly valued activity is made to depend on the prior performance of an activity of lower value. According to Premack, the punishment contingency reverses this relation. In punishment, a low-valued activity is made to occur contingent on the performance of a higher-valued behavior. Exposing oneself to shock, for example, has a much lower probability than pressing a lever for food. Hence, shock can punish lever pressing. (For further discussion, see Premack, 1971a; Weisman & Premack, 1966.)

With a reinforcement procedure, the instrumental response is increased and the reinforcing response is decreased relative to a baseline free-responding situation. With a punishment procedure, the instrumental response is decreased and the reinforcing or punishing response is increased relative to a baseline condition. Moreover, in both cases the response that increases is the low-valued behavior and the one that decreases is the higher-valued behavior (see Table 10.1). Viewed in this way, the procedures of reinforcement and punishment produce the same effects. Operationally, there is only one significant difference. In punishment, the individual must be forced to engage in the lower-valued activity. Individuals do not ordinarily expose themselves to aversive stimuli. In reinforcement, the individual is "induced" to engage in the lower-valued activity by the contingency itself.

The similarity between punishment and reinforcement assumed by the Premack was tested in an interesting experiment involving toy-playing behavior in children (Burkhard, Rachlin, & Schrader, 1978). In a baseline phase, the children were observed playing with three toys. The toys were ranked high, medium, and low on the basis of how much time the children spent with each one. The children were assigned to reinforcement and punishment groups. For the reinforcement group, 1 minute of playing with the high-ranked toy was allowed after 1 minute of play with the low-ranked toy. For the punishment group, 1 minute of play with the low-ranked toy was required after 1 minute of play with the

TABLE 10.1 COMPARISON OF RESPONSE REALLOCATION IN POSITIVE REINFORCEMENT AND PUNISHMENT

PROCEDURE	RESPONSE-REINFORCER CONTINGENCY	RESULTANT BEHAVIOR CHANGE
Positive reinforcement	$L \rightarrow H$	L increases H decreases
Punishment	$H \rightarrow L$	L increases H decreases

(L = low-valued activity; H = high-valued activity)

high-ranked toy. In both cases, the toy ranked as medium provided background activity and could be used freely. If Premack's punishment hypothesis is correct, the reinforcement and punishment procedures should have produced the same new distribution of time among the three toys. This, in fact, was the result. The reinforcement and punishment groups were indistinguishable in how much time they ended up playing with each toy. Playing with the low-ranked toy increased and playing with the high-ranked toy decreased to comparable levels for the two groups.

Premack's perspective suggests that punishment is similar to positive reinforcement in that it imposes a restriction against which behavior has to be adjusted. The negative law of effect is a statement of the way behavior changes under these restrictions: a low-valued activity produces a decrease in a higher-valued activity. Economically minded theorists propose, as in the case of positive reinforcement (see Chapter 7), that organisms respond so as to maximize overall value. The maximization process, with both reinforcement and punishment procedures, involves an increase in a low-valued activity balanced against a decrease in a high-valued activity.

Punishment outside the Laboratory

As I have described, punishment can be a highly effective procedure for rapidly suppressing behavior. However, the effectiveness of punishment in laboratory studies is not sufficient to justify its application outside the laboratory. Punishment procedures are easily misused, and even if the procedures are administered appropriately, there are serious ethical constraints on their application and they can have troublesome side effects.

Punishment is typically not applied in an effective manner. Often, punishment is first introduced at low intensities (a reprimand for the first offense, for example). The aversive stimulus may not be administered rapidly after the target response but delayed until it is convenient to administer it ("Wait until I tell your parents about this"). Punishment is usually administered on an intermittent schedule, and the chances of getting "caught" may not be high. Appropriate alternative behavior may not be recognized and positively reinforced at the same time that transgressions are punished. Often, there are clear discriminative stimuli for punishment. The undesired behavior may be monitored only at particular times or by a particular person, making it likely that the punished response will be suppressed only at those times. Finally, punishment may be the only source of attention for someone, making punishment a discriminative stimulus for positive reinforcement.

The preceding problems with the uses of punishment outside the laboratory can be overcome, but it is difficult to guard against these pitfalls in common interpersonal interactions. People who punish others may do so because they are frustrated and angry. A frustrative act of punishment is likely to violate many of the guidelines for effective use of punishment. Punishing someone in an act of anger and frustration is a form of abuse—not a form of systematic training.

The use of punishment in parenting has been the subject of extensive research. Consistent with the implications of laboratory research, a recent review of the literature on parental corporal punishment concluded that punishment is strongly associated with increased immediate compliance on the part of a child. The same analysis showed, however, that corporal punishment is also associated with increases in aggression and delinquent and anti-social behavior on the part of the children (Gershoff, 2002). In addition, parental punishment is associated with deterioration in the relationship between the parent and the child, poorer child mental health, and increased incidence of aggressive behavior in adulthood. Precise conclusions about the causal role of parental punishment in these effects are difficult to justify because the data were provided by correlational studies.

Parental use of corporal punishment has been outlawed in Austria, Croatia, Cyprus, Denmark, Finland, Germany, Israel, Italy, Latvia, Norway, and Sweden. Although corporal punishment by parents is not against the law in the United States, 27 states have adopted laws limiting the use of corporal punishment by teachers and guardians. Corporal punishment is sometimes used as a procedure of last resort in the treatment of severe behavior problems when other procedures have been unsuccessful.

In one study, for example, punishment was used to suppress recurrent vomiting by a 9-month-old infant (Linscheid & Cunningham, 1977). The recurrent vomiting had resulted in excessive weight loss and malnutrition. Without treatment, the infant risked potentially fatal medical complications. Brief (0.5-second) shocks sufficient to elicit a startle response, but not sufficient to elicit crying, were used as the aversive stimulus. Within 3 days, vomiting was nearly totally suppressed by the punishment procedure. The suppression of vomiting persisted after discharge from the hospital. The infant started gaining weight again and was soon within normal range.

Cases such as the preceding one illustrate that punishment can be beneficial, but even in such instances, serious ethical dilemmas have to be resolved. There is an ongoing debate about when, if ever, punishment is justified as a treatment procedure, and therapists are continuing their search for alternative ways to deal with potentially life-threatening behavior problems (see Repp & Singh, 1990.) Many states have adopted stringent procedures to review and monitor the use of aversive control procedures in therapeutic settings and have banned certain forms of aversive control altogether. Professional and patient rights organizations also have adopted detailed and restrictive guidelines for the therapeutic uses of aversive control. Fewer restrictions apply to punishment involving time out from reinforcement rather than the administration of a physically painful aversive stimulus.

SAMPLE QUESTIONS

1. What is the fundamental problem in the analysis of avoidance behavior, and how is this problem resolved by two-process theory?
2. Compare and contrast discriminated and free-operant avoidance procedures.
3. How can the concept of a safety signal be used to explain free-operant avoidance learning?
4. Describe factors that enhance the effectiveness of punishment in suppressing behavior.
5. In what ways is punishment similar to positive reinforcement; in what ways is it different?

KEY TERMS

acquired-drive A source of motivation for instrumental behavior caused by the presentation of a stimulus that was previously conditioned with a primary, or unconditioned, reinforcer.

avoidance An instrumental conditioning procedure in which the participant's behavior prevents the delivery of an aversive stimulus.

avoidance trial A trial in a discriminated avoidance procedure in which the occurrence of the avoidance response prevents the delivery of the aversive stimulus.

conservation of fear The assumption that conditioned fear is maintained in a signaled avoidance procedure if participants respond rapidly to turn off the CS because later segments of the CS are not experienced.

discriminated avoidance An avoidance conditioning procedure in which occurrences of the aversive stimulus are signaled by a conditioned stimulus. Responding during the conditioned stimulus terminates the CS and prevents the delivery of the aversive unconditioned stimulus. Also called *signaled avoidance.*

discriminative punishment A procedure in which responding is punished in the presence of a particular stimulus and not punished in the absence of that stimulus.

escape trial A type of trial during avoidance training in which the required avoidance response is not made and the aversive unconditioned stimulus is presented. Performance of the instrumental response during the aversive stimulus results in termination of the aversive stimulus. Thus, the organism is able to escape from the aversive stimulus.

flooding A procedure for extinguishing avoidance behavior in which the conditioned stimulus is presented while the participant is prevented from making the avoidance response. Also called *response prevention.*

free-operant avoidance Same as *nondiscriminated avoidance.*

nondiscriminated avoidance An avoidance conditioning procedure in which occurrences of the aversive stimulus are not signaled by an external stimulus. In the absence of avoidance behavior, the aversive stimulus is presented periodically, as set by the S-S interval. Each occurrence of the avoidance response prevents delivery of aversive stimulation for a fixed period (the R-S interval). Also called *free-operant avoidance*; originally called *Sidman avoidance.*

overcorrection A procedure for discouraging behavior in which the participant is required not only to correct or rectify a mistake but to go beyond that by, for example, extensively practicing the correct response alternative.

predatory imminence The perceived likelihood of being attacked by a predator. Different species-typical defense responses are assumed to be performed in the face of different degrees of predatory imminence.

punishment An instrumental conditioning procedure in which there is a positive contingency between the instrumental response and an aversive stimulus. If the participant performs the instrumental response, it receives the aversive stimulus; if the participant does not perform the instrumental response, it does not receive the aversive stimulus.

R-S interval The interval between the occurrence of an avoidance response and the next scheduled presentation of the aversive stimulus in a nondiscriminated avoidance procedure.

response prevention Same as *flooding.*

safety signal A stimulus that signals the absence of an aversive event.

shock-frequency reduction A hypothesis according to which reduction in the frequency of shock serves to reinforce avoidance behavior.

shuttle avoidance A type of avoidance conditioning procedure in which the required instrumental response consists in going back and forth (shuttling) between two sides of an experimental apparatus.

signaled avoidance Same as *discriminated avoidance.*

species-specific defense reactions (SSDRs) Species-typical responses that animals perform in an aversive situation. The responses may involve freezing, fleeing, or fighting.

S-S interval The interval between successive presentations of the aversive stimulus in a nondiscriminated avoidance procedure when the avoidance response is not performed.

time out A period during which the opportunity to obtain reinforcement is removed. This may involve removal of the participant from the situation where reinforcers may be obtained.

two-process theory of avoidance A theory originally developed to explain discriminated avoidance learning that presumes the operation of two mechanisms: (1) classical conditioning of fear to the warning signal, and (2) instrumental reinforcement of the avoidance response through termination of the warning signal and consequent fear reduction.

CHAPTER

11 ANIMAL COGNITION I: MEMORY MECHANISMS

In Chapter 11, I turn to a more focused consideration of animal cognition. The study of animal cognition dates back to Darwin's writings about the evolution of intelligence and the subsequent research on learning in nonhuman animals. However, the best research on animal cognition has been done in the past 30 years. Chapter 11 begins with a definition of animal cognition and a brief discussion of some cognitive effects I have already described in earlier sections of this book. The rest of the chapter is devoted to one of the most important cognitive processes—memory. I describe the relationship between learning and memory and the distinction between working memory and reference memory. I then discuss several prominent paradigms for the study of working memory in nonhuman animals and describe research relevant to three different stages of memory—acquisition, retention, and retrieval. The chapter ends with a discussion of different sources of forgetting or memory failure.

As I noted in Chapter 1, interest in animal cognition dates back to the founding of the field of animal learning in the second half of the nineteenth century. Early experimental efforts to study animal cognition employed animal learning paradigms. Studies of animal learning soon came to have a life of their own. Through much of the twentieth century, learning processes in animals have been investigated for what they told us about behavior in general rather than about animal cognition or animal intelligence in particular. However, the past 30 years have witnessed a resurgence of interest in animal cognition and animal intelligence (for example, Griffin, 1976; Hulse, Fowler, & Honig, 1978; Ristau, 1991; Roitblat, Bever, & Terrace, 1984; Shettleworth, 1998; Spear & Riccio, 1994; Zentall, 1993).

The renewed focus on issues relevant to animal cognition is part of the "cognitive revolution" that has swept many areas of psychology. These developments have stimulated considerable theoretical debate (for example, Amsel, 1989; Hintzman, 1991). Regardless of that debate, an important consequence of contemporary interest in animal cognition has been the extension of the study of animal learning to numerous new paradigms. These extensions have raised many new and interesting questions about behavior—questions that were not explored in conventional studies of classical and instrumental conditioning. I describe some of these developments in this chapter and in Chapter 12.

In addition to providing important new information about learning and memory processes, studies of animal cognition address the kind of theoretical questions about the evolution of intelligence that captivated Darwin. Exploring the cognitive skills of animals tells us about the uniqueness of various human cognitive skills, just as exploring other planets can reveal the uniqueness of our terrestrial habitat. As Wasserman (1993, p. 211) put it, "comparing the intelligence of many species of animals may help us know better what it means to be human." Studies of animal cognition are also important because they provide model systems for the investigation of the neurophysiological bases of cognitive functions. Memory-enhancing drugs, for example, cannot be developed without first developing animal model systems for the study of memory mechanisms. Studies of the mechanisms of cognition in animals may also help us in designing intelligent machines and robots (Meyer, Berthoz, Floreano, Roitblat, & Wilson, 2000; Meyer & Wilson, 1991; Roitblat & Meyer, 1995).

WHAT IS ANIMAL COGNITION?

The word *cognition* comes from the Latin meaning "knowledge or thinking" and is commonly used to refer to thought processes. In casual discourse, we regard thinking as voluntary, deliberate, and conscious reflection on some topic, usually involving language. When we "think out loud," we say the words loud enough for someone else to hear. The casual inference is that silent thinking involves similar verbal behavior.

The second prominent characteristic of thinking is that it can lead to actions that cannot be explained on the basis of the external stimuli a person experiences at the time. For example, on your way to work, you may start thinking that you did not lock the door to your apartment when you left home. This thought may stimulate you to return home to check whether the door is locked. Your returning cannot be explained by the external stimuli to which you are exposed on your way to work. You encounter these same stimuli every day, but usually they do not make you return home. Rather, your behavior is attributed to the thought of the unlocked door.

There is some controversy about what the domain of animal cognition should be. Advocates of **cognitive ethology** claim that animals are capable of conscious thought and intentionality (Griffin, 1992; Ristau, 1991). According to cognitive ethologists, animal cognition should encompass the full range of issues that are included in considerations of human cognition. The claim that nonhuman animals are capable of consciousness and intentionality is based on the complexity, flexibility, and cleverness of various examples of animal behavior. The argument is that conscious intent is the likely source of such complex, flexible, and apparently clever behavior. This is basically an argument from design, an argument that has been debated and rejected by philosophers for centuries (Blumberg & Wasserman, 1995). In addition to such philosophical arguments, it is also important to consider recent studies showing the limitations of conscious intent as an adequate explanation of human behavior (Bargh & Chartrand, 1999; Wegner & Wheatley, 1999). If conscious intent cannot adequately characterize important features of human behavior, why should we assume that the concept will be useful in explaining the behavior of nonhuman organisms?

In contrast to cognitive ethologists, experimental psychologists use the term *animal cognition* in a more restricted sense. They follow H. S. Jennings (1904–1976) who argued a century ago that "objective evidence cannot give a demonstration either of the existence or of the non-existence of consciousness, for consciousness is precisely that which cannot be perceived objectively." Jennings went on to say that "no statement concerning consciousness in animals is open to refutation by observation and experiment." To make sure that their cognitive concepts can be refuted by observation, contemporary experimental psychologists tie cognitive mechanisms closely to behavioral predictions. Experimental psychologists make inferences about the internal or cognitive machinery that mediates behavior in cases where simple S-R or reflex mechanisms are insufficient. They are careful, however, to accept only those hypothesized cognitive processes that lead to unambiguous behavioral predictions (Zentall, 2001). Thus, for experimental psychologists, animal cognition does not imply anything about awareness, consciousness, or verbal reasoning. As Terrace (1984) pointed out nearly 20 years ago, "The rationale for the study of cognitive processes in animals requires no reference to animal consciousness" (p. 8). Rather **animal cognition** refers to theoretical constructs and models used to explain aspects of behavior that cannot be readily characterized in terms of simple S-R or reflex mechanisms.

= non S-R / reflex mechanisms

A common feature of cognitive mechanisms is that they involve an internal representation or "mental" record of something and rules for manipulating these mental records. Internal representations may encode various types of information, such as particular features of stimuli or relations between stimuli. Internal representations and their manipulations cannot be investigated directly by looking into the brain. Rather, they have to be inferred from behavior. Thus, a cognitive mechanism is a theoretical construct inferred from behavior, just as gravity is a theoretical construct inferred from the behavior of falling objects.

Research on animal cognition is concerned with questions like how representations are formed, what aspects of experience they encode, how the information is stored, and how it is used later to guide behavior. I have already discussed research relevant to such questions in analyses of classical and instrumental conditioning. For example, I noted in Chapter 4 that classical conditioning involves the learning of an association between a CS and a US. As a result of this association, presentation of the CS activates a representation ("mental image") of the US, and the conditioned response is performed because of this representation. In Chapter 7, I noted that instrumental conditioning results in the establishment of S-O and R-O associations. Because of these associations, an internal representation of the reinforcer O is activated by the stimuli of the conditioning situation (S) as well as by the instrumental response (R). Additional evidence suggests that S can also activate the R-O association. Another area that clearly involves cognitive processes is the study of memory (Spear & Riccio, 1994).

ANIMAL MEMORY PARADIGMS

The term **memory** is commonly used to refer to the ability to respond to or recount information that was experienced earlier. We are said to remember what happened in our childhood if we talk about our childhood experiences, and we are said to remember someone's name if we call that person by the correct name. Unfortunately, such tests of memory are impractical with nonhuman animals. We cannot ask a pigeon to tell us what it did last week. Instead, we have to use the bird's nonverbal responses as clues to its memory.

If your cat goes down the street but finds its way back to your house, you might conclude that it remembers where you live. If your dog greets you with unusual exuberance after a long vacation, you might conclude that it remembers you. These and similar examples illustrate that the existence of memory in animals is identified by the fact that *their current behavior is based on some aspect of their earlier experiences.* Any time an animal's behavior is determined by past events, we can conclude that some type of memory is involved.

This definition of memory is very similar to the definition of learning stated in Chapter 1. There, learning was defined as an enduring change in how an organism might respond to a particular situation because of prior experience with that type of situation. Evidence of learning is also identified on the basis of changes in behavior due to earlier experiences. Indeed, learning is not possible without memory.

How, then, are studies of memory to be distinguished from studies of learning? The differences may be clarified by considering the components that are common to both learning and memory experiments (see Table 11.1). The first thing that happens in both types of experiments is that the participants are exposed to certain kinds of stimuli or information. This phase is termed **acquisition.** The information that was acquired is then retained for a period called the **retention interval.** At the end of the retention interval, the participants are tested for their memory of the original experience, which requires **retrieval** or reactivation of the information encountered during acquisition. Thus, studies of learning and studies of memory all involve three basic phases: acquisition, retention, and retrieval.

Consider, for example, riding a bicycle. Skilled bicyclists initially had to be trained to balance, pedal, and steer the bike (acquisition). They have to hold onto the information they acquired (retention). And when they get on a bicycle again, they have to reactivate their knowledge of bike riding (retrieval).

In studies of learning, the focus is on the acquisition phase. Learning experiments deal with the kind of information we acquire and the ways in which we acquire it. Thus, *learning experiments involve manipulations of the conditions of acquisition.* The retention interval is always fairly long (a day or longer), because short-term changes in behavior are not considered to be instances of learning. Furthermore, the retention interval typically is not varied within the experiment. Because the emphasis is on the conditions of acquisition, the conditions of retrieval are also kept constant. All participants in a given experiment are tested for their knowledge using the same test procedures.

In contrast, *studies of memory focus on the retention and retrieval phases.* Acquisition is of interest only to the extent that it is relevant to retention and retrieval. The retention interval is often varied to determine how the availability of the acquired information changes with time. Unlike studies of learning, which employ only long retention intervals, studies of memory can employ retention intervals of any duration. In fact, many studies of animal memory involve short retention intervals.

Studies of memory also focus on the circumstances of retrieval. Consider, for example, taking a vocabulary test on a set of technical terms in a college course. You may miss many items if the test consists of a series of fill-in-the-blank questions for which you have to pro-

TABLE 11.1 COMPARISON OF LEARNING AND MEMORY EXPERIMENTS

PHASE	STUDIES OF LEARNING	STUDIES OF MEMORY
Acquisition	Varied	Constant
Retention	Constant (long)	Varied (short and long)
Retrieval	Constant	Varied

vide the technical terms. In contrast, you are likely to do much better if you are provided with a list of the technical terms and are merely required to match up each term with its definition. These different forms of the test involve different conditions of retrieval.

Memory mechanisms have been classified in various ways depending on what is remembered (the contents of memory), how long the memory lasts (the retention interval), and the mechanisms involved in the memory. Schachter and Tulving (1994), for example, identified five types of human learning and memory: *procedural memory, perceptual memory, semantic memory, primary or working memory,* and *episodic or declarative memory.* Not all these forms of memory have their counterparts in research with nonhuman subjects.

Much of the research on classical and instrumental conditioning that I described in earlier chapters corresponds to **procedural memory.** This type of memory often reflects knowledge about invariant relationships in the environment and mediates the learning of behavioral and cognitive skills that are performed automatically, without the requirement of conscious control. However, investigators of memory in nonhuman animals have not emphasized the distinction between procedural and other forms of memory. Rather, they have emphasized the distinction between working memory and reference memory.

Working Memory and Reference Memory

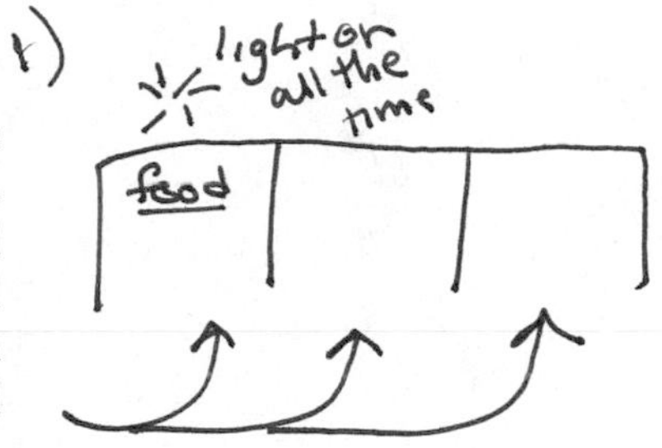

One of the earliest experimental investigations of animal memory was conducted by the American psychologist Walter S. Hunter (1913). Hunter tested rats, dogs, and raccoons in a simple memory task. The apparatus consisted of a start area from which the animals could enter any one of three goal compartments. Only one of the goal compartments was baited with a piece of food on each trial, and the baited compartment was marked by turning on a light above that compartment at the start of the trial. Which compartment was baited (and marked by the light) was varied from trial to trial.

After the animals learned to always choose the compartment whose light was turned on, Hunter made the task a bit more difficult. Now the light marking the baited goal compartment remained on for only a short time. After the signal was turned off, the animal was detained in the start area for various lengths of time before being allowed to choose among the three compartments. The animal had to somehow remember which light had been on in order to find the food. The longer the animals were delayed before being allowed to make a choice, the less likely they were to go to the correct compartment. The maximum delay rats could handle was about 10 seconds. The performance of dogs did not deteriorate until the delay interval was extended past 5 minutes. Raccoons performed well as long as the delay was no more than 25 seconds.

2) light turned on & off, animal must wait until light is off before getting food → tests if animal can remember where light flashed.

The species also differed in what they did during the delay interval. Rats and dogs were observed to maintain a postural orientation toward the correct compartment during the delay interval. No such postural orientations were observed in the raccoons. Since the raccoons did not maintain a postural orientation during the delay interval, their behavior required some type of internal memory mechanism.

With the delay procedure, the animals had to remember which compartment had been illuminated at the start of that trial. Once the trial was finished, however, this information was no longer useful because the food could be in any of the three goal compartments on the next trial. Thus, memory for which compartment had been recently illuminated was required only to complete the work during a given trial. This type of memory is called **working memory.**

Working memory is operative when information has to be retained only long enough to complete a particular task, after which the information is best discarded because it is not needed or (as in Hunter's experiment) because it may interfere with successful completion of the next trial. A mechanic changing the oil and lubricating a car has to remember which steps of the job he has finished, but only as long as he is servicing that particular car. In cooking a good stew, you have to remember which spices you have already put in before adding others, but once the stew is finished, you can forget this information. All these illustrate instances of working memory.

Working memory is often short-lasting. In Hunter's experiment, the memory lasted for only 10 seconds in rats and for 25 seconds in raccoons. In some situations, working memory may last for several hours or days.

Examples of working memory illustrate the retention, for a limited duration, of recently acquired information. However, such information is useful only in the context of more enduring knowledge. In Hunter's experiment, for example, remembering which compartment had been illuminated at the start of a trial was not enough to obtain food. This information was useful only in the context of the knowledge that the light marked the baited compartment. In contrast to information in working memory that was disposed of after each trial, information about the relation between the light and food had to be remembered on all trials. Such memory is called **reference memory** (Honig, 1978).

Reference memory is *long-term retention of information necessary for successful use of incoming and recently acquired information.* Information about what a mechanic has done recently is useless without more general knowledge about cars and lubrication procedures. Knowing which spices you have already added to a stew is useful only if you know the basics of cooking and flavoring food. All successful uses of working memory require appropriate reference memories.

Since Hunter's research, increasingly sophisticated techniques have been developed for the study of working memory, such as the two I now describe. The first procedure, delayed matching to sample, is a laboratory procedure that was developed without much regard for the behavioral predispositions of animals and can be adapted to the study of how animals remember a variety of different events. The second technique, the radial maze, tests spatial memory or memory for particular locations.

Delayed Matching to Sample

The delayed-matching-to-sample procedure is perhaps the most versatile technique available for the study of working memory and is a substantial refinement of Hunter's original procedure. As in Hunter's procedure, the participant is exposed to a cue that identifies the correct response on a particular trial. This stimulus is then removed before the animal is permitted to perform the designated behavior. In the typical experiment with pigeons, for ex-

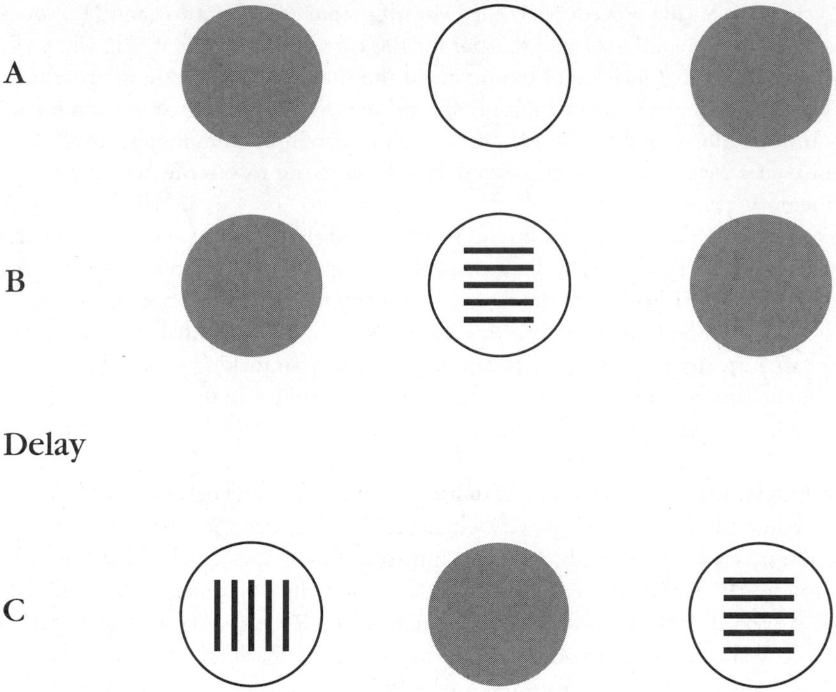

Figure 11.1 Diagram of the delayed-matching-to-sample procedure for pigeons. The experimental chamber has three response keys arranged in a row. At the start of a trial, the center key is illuminated with a white light, the start cue (row A). After the pigeon pecks the start cue, the sample stimulus (horizontal) is projected on the center key (row B). This stimulus is then removed, and after a delay two choice stimuli (horizontal and vertical) are presented on the side keys (row C). Pecks at the choice stimulus that matches the sample are reinforced.

ample, the experimental chamber contains three response keys arranged in a row, as in Figure 11.1. The cue that identifies the correct response is called the *sample* and is presented on the center key. After a delay, the pigeon is given a choice between the sample and an alternative stimulus, and pecks on the test stimulus that matches the sample are reinforced.

The stimuli used in an experiment might include arrays of horizontal and vertical lines projected on the response keys from the rear. The start of a trial is signaled by illumination of the center key with a white light, the start cue (see row A in Figure 11.1). The pigeon is first required to peck the start cue, to make sure it is facing the pecking keys. Then, the sample for that trial—the horizontal array, for example—is projected on the center key (row B in Figure 11.1). Usually several pecks at the sample stimulus are required, after which the sample is turned off and the two side keys are lit up. One of the side keys is illuminated with the sample for that trial (horizontal), and the other key is illuminated with the alternative pattern (vertical) (row C in Figure 11.1). If the pigeon pecks the test stimulus that matches the sample (in this case horizontal), it is reinforced with access to grain. If it pecks the other stimulus, no reinforcement is provided. Thus, to obtain reinforcement, the pigeon has to select the test stimulus that matches what was the sample on that trial—hence the term *matching to sample.*

Whether the horizontal or vertical grid pattern serves as the sample is randomly varied from one trial to the next. In addition, the matching stimulus is equally likely to be presented on the right or left key during the choice component of the trial. Therefore, the pigeon cannot predict which stimulus will be the sample on a given trial or where the matching stimulus will appear during the choice test.

During the initial stages of matching-to-sample training, the sample stimulus remains visible until the pigeon has made the correct choice. Thus, in my example, the horizontal pattern on the center key would remain illuminated until the bird correctly pecked the horizontal side key. Such a procedure is called **simultaneous matching to sample.** It does not require working memory because the cue for the correct response is visible when the choice response is made. Once a bird has mastered the simultaneous matching procedure, the sample stimulus can be presented just briefly and removed before the choice stimuli are provided. Introduction of a delay between exposure to the sample stimulus and availability of the choice cues changes the procedure to **delayed matching to sample,** which requires working memory.

As I mentioned, the matching stimulus is equally likely to appear on the left or the right choice key at the end of a trial. Because of this, the participant cannot make the correct response merely by orienting to the right or left when the sample appears on the center key and holding this body posture until the choice stimuli are presented. In contrast to Hunter's procedure, simple postural orientations do not help in making the correct choice. The participants are forced to use more sophisticated memory processes. (For an especially effective matching-to-sample procedure for use with pigeons, see Wright & Delius, 1994.)

Courtesy of D. S. Grant

D. S. Grant

Procedural Determinants of Delayed Matching to Sample. The delayed-matching-to-sample procedure has been used extensively with a variety of species, including monkeys, pigeons, dolphins, sea lions, goldfish, rats, and humans (Baron & Menich, 1985; Blough, 1959; D'Amato, 1973; D'Amato & Colombo, 1985; Forestell & Herman, 1988; Jarrard & Moise, 1971; Iversen, 1993a; Kastak & Schusterman, 1994; Roberts & Grant, 1976; Steinert, Fallon, & Wallace, 1976). In addition, the procedure has been adapted to investigate how animals remember a variety of stimuli, including visual shapes, numbers of responses performed, presence or absence of reward, the spatial location of stimuli, the order of two successively presented events, or which particular response the subject recently performed (for example, D'Amato, 1973; Maki, Moe, & Bierley, 1977; MacDonald, 1993; Mercado, Murray, Uyeyama, Pack, & Herman, 1998; Wilkie & Summers, 1982).

Several aspects of the matching-to-sample procedure are critical in determining the accuracy of performance. One of these is the nature of the stimulus that serves as the sample. Some types of stimuli are more effective than others (for example, Wilkie & Summers, 1982). Other important factors are the duration of exposure to the sample stimulus at the start of the trial and the delay interval after the sample. In one experiment, for example, Grant (1976) tested pigeons in a standard three-key apparatus after they had received extensive training on delayed matching to sample with visual stimuli. Two pairs of colors—red/green and blue/yellow—served as sample and comparison stimuli on alternate trials. At the start of each trial, the center key was illuminated with a white light. After the pigeon pecked the start cue, the sample color for that trial was presented on the center key for 1, 4, 8, or 14 seconds. This was followed by delay intervals of 0, 20, 40, or 60 seconds, after which the two side keys were illuminated, one with the sample-matching color and the other with the paired alternative color. After the bird made its choice, all the keys were turned off for a 2-minute intertrial interval.

The results of the experiment are summarized in Figure 11.2. If pigeons had pecked the choice keys randomly, they would have been correct 50% of the time. Better than chance performance indicates the use of working memory. For each sample duration, the accuracy of matching decreased as longer delays were introduced between exposure to the sample and opportunity to make the choice response. In fact, if the sample was presented for only 1 second and the opportunity to make a choice was delayed 40 seconds or more, the pigeons responded at chance level. Performance improved if the birds were exposed to the sample for longer periods. When the sample was presented for 4, 8, or 14 seconds, the birds performed above chance levels even when the delay interval was as long as 60 seconds. Thus, accuracy in the delayed-matching-to-sample procedure decreased as a function of the

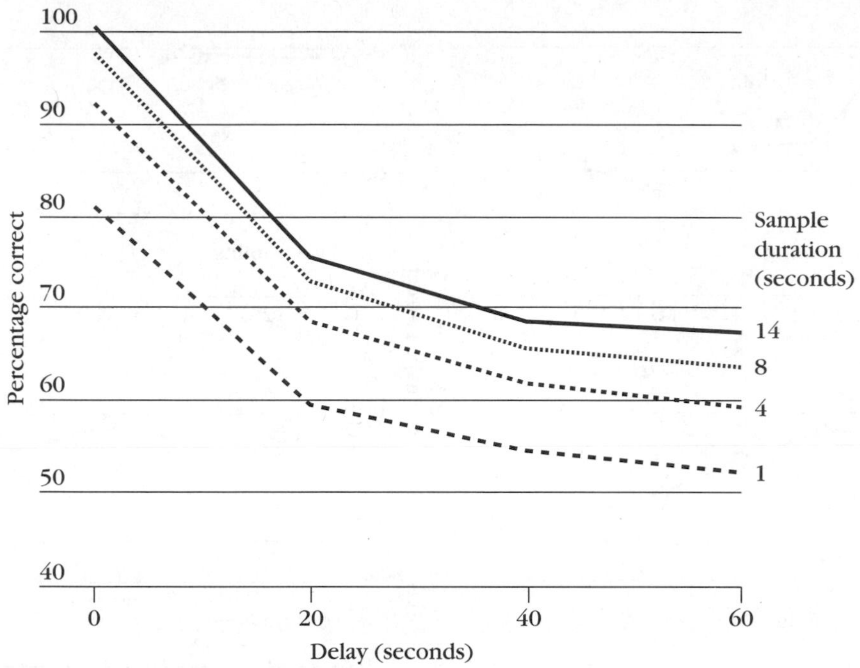

Figure 11.2 Percentage of correct responses in a delayed-matching-to-sample task as a function of the duration of the sample stimulus (1–14 seconds) and the delay between the sample and the choice stimuli (0–60 seconds). (From "Effect of Sample Presentation Time on Long Delay Matching in the Pigeon," by D. S. Grant, 1976, *Learning and Motivation, 7,* pp. 580–590. Copyright © 1976 by Academic Press. Reprinted by permission.)

delay interval and increased as a function of the duration of exposure to the sample stimulus (see also Blough, 1996; Hunt, Parr, & Smith, 1999; Guttenberger & Wasserman, 1985).

Results such as those in Figure 11.2 can be explained by the **trace decay hypothesis,** the oldest and simplest account of memory (and memory loss) (Roberts & Grant, 1976). This hypothesis assumes that presentation of a stimulus produces changes in the nervous system that gradually dissipate, or decay, after the stimulus has been removed. The initial strength of the stimulus trace is assumed to reflect the physical energy of the stimulus. Thus, longer or more intense stimuli are presumed to result in stronger stimulus traces. No matter what the initial strength of the trace, it is assumed to decay at the same rate after the stimulus ends.

According to the trace decay hypothesis, the extent to which the memory of an event controls behavior depends on the strength of the stimulus trace at that moment. The stronger the trace, the stronger is the effect of the past stimulus on the organism's behavior. The trace decay model predicts results exactly like those summarized in Figure 11.2. Increasing the delay interval in the matching-to-sample procedure reduces the accuracy of performance presumably because the trace of the sample stimulus is weaker after longer delays. By contrast, increasing the duration of exposure to the sample improves performance presumably because longer stimulus exposures establish stronger stimulus traces.

The trace decay hypothesis assumes that forgetting functions like those presented in Figure 11.2 reflect fairly directly the strength of memory for the sample stimulus at different delay intervals. Unfortunately, no behavioral test permits a "direct" readout of the strength of memory. Performance on memory tests also depends a great deal on the conditions of training. In a key recent experiment, Sargisson and White (2001) asked whether the forgetting function would be influenced by the delay between the sample and the choice stimuli that was in effect during training.

Sargisson and White trained separate groups of pigeons on a matching-to-sample procedure with different sample-choice delays. For one group, the delay between the sample

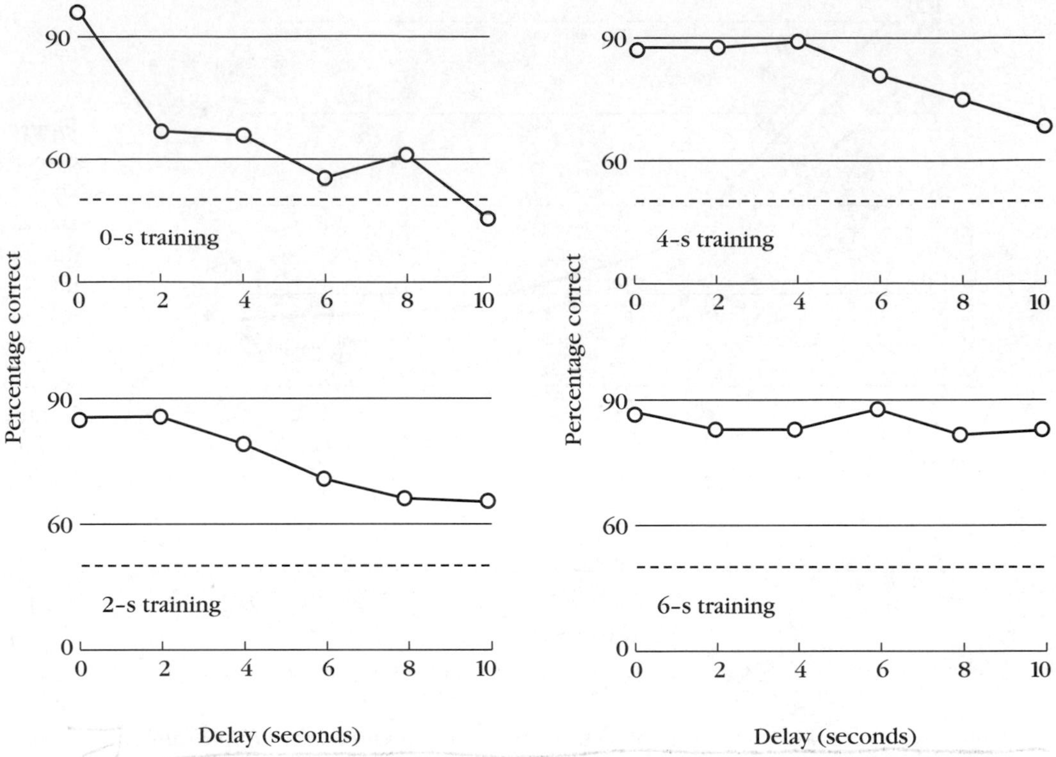

Figure 11.3 Accuracy of matching-to-sample performance as a function of delay between the sample and choice stimuli for independent groups of pigeons that were previously trained with delays of 0, 2, 4, or 6 seconds. (After Sargisson & White, 2001.)

Courtesy of M. Spetch

M. Spetch

and choice stimuli was always 0 seconds during training. For other groups, this delay was 2, 4, or 6 seconds. Training was continued until each group performed correctly on at least 80% of the trials. All of the birds were then tested with delays ranging from 0 to 10 seconds to determine the forgetting function. The results of these tests are presented in Figure 11.3.

The group that had been trained with a 0-second sample-choice delay showed the standard forgetting function. They made more errors as the delay between the sample and choice stimuli was increased from 0 to 10 seconds. In contrast, no such decline was evident in pigeons that had been trained with a 6-second delay between the sample and choice stimuli. These birds performed equally well at all test delays. The other groups showed results between these two extremes. It is important to note that for all groups the most accurate performance occurred when the delay used in the test was the same as the delay that they received during training. These results clearly show that forgetting functions do not directly reflect the decay or fading of memory for the sample stimulus as a function of time. Rather, test performance depends on the similarity between the conditions of testing and the conditions of training (see also Spetch, 1987). The common finding that memory gets worse with the passage of time may simply reflect the fact that subjects are unfamiliar with long delay intervals.

The delay interval used in training is just one training variable that influences delayed-matching-to-sample performance. Matching is basically instrumental behavior motivated by the reinforcer provided at the end of the trial. Therefore, it should not be surprising that matching behavior is also influenced by the relation between the sample stimulus and the reinforcer. In general, subjects perform more accurately on a matching task under conditions in which the sample stimulus is a better signal for reinforcement. Matching accuracy is greater when the interval between the sample stimulus and the reinforcer is shorter (Weavers, Foster, & Temple, 1998). Matching accuracy is also improved if the sample stimulus signals a greater reduction in delay to reinforcement (Hartl, Dougherty, & Wixted, 1996; Urcuioli, DeMarse, & Lionello, 1999). Both of these factors presumably make the sample stimulus a better signal for reinforcement or a more effective conditioned reinforcer. (For a discussion of additional reinforcement variables that influence accuracy in delayed matching memory tasks, see White & Wixted, 1999.)

Response Strategies in Matching to Sample. The matching-to-sample procedure is analogous to a discrimination problem in that the participant has to respond to the correct stimulus and refrain from responding to the incorrect one to get reinforced. As I described in discussions of what is learned in discrimination training in Chapter 8, such a two-alternative task can be solved in several ways. The participant can make the correct choice by focusing on the correct stimulus, by inhibiting behavior to the incorrect stimulus, or by using both these response strategies. In discrimination learning (which establishes a reference memory), participants appear to use the combined response strategy. By contrast, participants in matching to sample appear to focus primarily on the correct choice.

Courtesy of Donald A. Dewsbury

A. A. Wright

One interesting experiment supporting this conclusion used a three-key apparatus for pigeons that was specially constructed so that the stimulus projected on a response key was visible only if the pigeon was standing directly in front of that key (Wright & Sands, 1981). This apparatus enabled the experimenters to determine which response keys the pigeons looked at before making their choice. The results showed that the birds focused on the correct alternative. If they saw the matching stimulus, they pecked it without bothering to check what stimulus was presented on the other side (see also Roitblat, Penner, & Nachtigall, 1990; Wright, 1990, 1992; Zentall, Edwards, Moore, & Hogan, 1981).

General versus Specific Rule Learning. The evidence just reviewed indicates that animals focus on the correct choice in matching to sample. What leads them to identify a stimulus as correct? One possibility is that they learn a general "same as" rule. The rule may be, "Choose the choice stimulus that is the same as the sample." Another possibility is that the animals learn a series of specific rules or stimulus-response relations. In the experiment by Grant (1976), for example, pairs of colors were used—red/green and blue/yellow. The pigeons may have learned a series of specific stimulus-response relations: "Select red after exposure to red," "Select green after exposure to green," and so on. Most matching-to-sample procedures can be solved either by learning a general "same as" rule or by learning a series of specific stimulus-response relations.

The two alternative strategies can be evaluated by testing transfer of matching performance to new stimuli. After training with one set of stimuli, another matching problem is presented with a new set of stimuli. Specific stimulus-response learning predicts little positive (or negative) transfer of matching behavior to the new stimuli because the new task requires learning a new set of stimulus-response relations. By contrast, general-rule learning predicts considerable positive carryover, because the general "same as" rule can be used to solve any matching-to-sample problem. Thus, in tests of transfer from one matching-to-sample problem to another, general-rule learning should produce better performance than specific-rule learning.

In a study with infant chimpanzees, Oden, Thompson, and Premack (1988) first provided training on a matching-to-sample task with just one pair of stimulus objects, a stainless steel measuring cup and a brass bolt lock. One of the objects was presented at the start of the trial, followed by a choice of both objects. If the chimp selected the matching object, it was reinforced with effusive praise, tickling, cuddling, or an edible treat, depending on its preference. After the animals learned the task with the two training stimuli, they were tested with a variety of other stimulus objects. Remarkably, with most of the test objects, the transfer performance was better than 80% accurate. Thus, the chimps seemed to have learned a general "same as" rule with just two training stimuli.

Chimpanzees are more likely to show evidence of generalized matching than pigeons and other species. However, the preponderance of evidence suggests that both general-rule learning and specific stimulus-response learning can occur as a result of matching-to-sample training in a variety of species. Which type of learning predominates appears to be related to the size of the stimulus set used in the matching-to-sample procedure. A study such as Grant's (1976), in which sample and comparison stimuli were selected from two pairs of colors, is likely to favor the learning of specific stimulus-response relations. By contrast, procedures that employ a wide range of stimuli are more likely to favor the learning of a general rule. The extreme of a procedure of this type is the **trials-unique procedure.**

In a trials-unique procedure, a different stimulus serves as the sample on each trial and is paired with another stimulus during the choice phase. Because a given sample stimulus is not presented on more than one trial, accurate performance with a trials-unique procedure is possible only if the participant learns to respond on the basis of a general "same as" rule. Successful learning of the "same as" concept has been obtained with the trials-unique procedure with visual stimuli in pigeons and auditory stimuli in monkeys (Wright, Cook, Rivera, Sands, & Delius, 1988; Wright, Shyan, & Jitsumori, 1990). (For another approach to learning the concept "same as," see Wright, 1997.)

Spatial Memory in a Radial Maze

The matching-to-sample procedure can be adapted to investigate how animals remember a variety of stimuli. The next technique I describe has more limited applicability but focuses on a very important type of memory—memory for places.

To move about their habitat efficiently, animals have to remember how their environment is laid out—where open spaces, sheltered areas, and potential food sources are located. In many environments, once food has been eaten at one location, it is not available there again for some time until it is replenished. Therefore, animals have to remember where they last found food and avoid that location for a while. For example, the amakihi (*Loxops virens*), a species of Hawaiian honeycreeper, feeds on the nectar of mamane flowers (Kamil, 1978). After feeding on a cluster of flowers, these birds have to avoid returning to the same flowers for about an hour. By delaying their return to clusters they have recently visited, the birds increase the chance that they will find nectar in the flowers they search. They appear to remember the spatial location of recently visited flower clusters (see also Healy & Hurly, 1995).

Courtesy of Donald A. Dewsbury

D. S. Olton

Memory for locations in space—spatial memory—has been studied in the laboratory with the use of complex mazes (for example, Olton, 1979). One popular technique uses an elevated radial arm maze (see Figure 11.4). Olton and Samuelson (1976) tested rats in an elevated maze that had eight arms radiating from a central choice area, with a food cup at the end of each arm. Before the start of each trial, a pellet of food was placed in each food cup. The rat was then placed in the center of the maze and was allowed to go from one arm

Figure 11.4 Rat foraging on an elevated radial maze.

to another and pick up all the food. Once a food pellet had been consumed, that arm of the maze remained without food for the rest of the trial.

How could the rat have gone about finding food in this situation? It could have randomly selected which alley to enter each time. Thus, the rat might have entered an alley, eaten the food there, returned to the center area and then randomly selected another arm of the maze to enter next. With such a strategy, however, the rat would have ended up going down alleys from which it had already removed the food. A more efficient strategy would have been to enter only those arms of the maze that had not yet been visited and therefore still had food. This is in fact what the animals learned to do.

The results of the experiment are summarized in Figure 11.5. Entering an arm that had not been visited previously was considered to be a correct choice. Figure 11.5 summarizes the number of correct choices the rats made during the first eight choices of successive tests. During the first five test runs after familiarization with the maze, the rats made a mean of nearly seven correct choices during each test. With continued practice, the mean number of correct choices was consistently above seven, indicating that the animals rarely entered an arm they had previously chosen on that trial.

Rats do not require much training to perform efficiently in the radial maze. The radial maze task appears to take advantage of a preexisting tendency of rats to move about without returning to recently visited places. This tendency is so strong that the failure of rats to return to a place where they recently have obtained food may not be related to having obtained food there (Gaffan & Davies, 1981). Several investigators have found that rats tend to stay away from recently visited arms in a radial maze whether or not the maze arms are baited with food (FitzGerald, Isler, Rosenberg, Oettinger, & Battig, 1985; Timberlake & White, 1990; see also Maki, 1987).

There are several mechanisms by which rats could choose to enter only previously unchosen arms of a maze without necessarily remembering which arms they had already

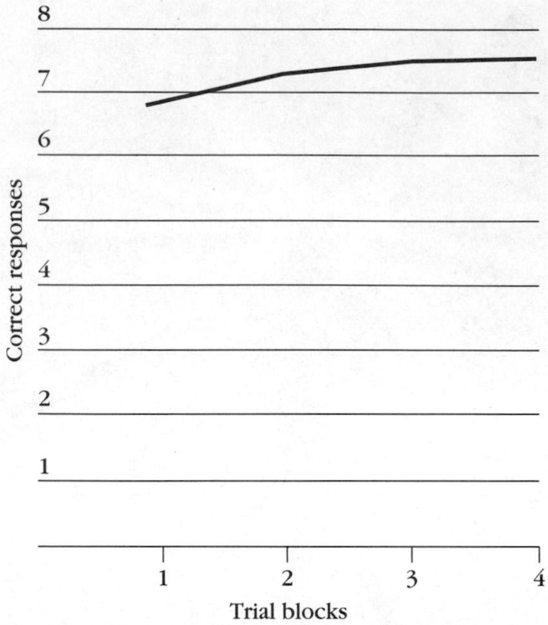

Figure 11.5 Mean number of correct responses rats made in the first eight choices during blocks of five test trials in the eight-arm radial maze. (Adapted from Olton, 1978.)

visited. For example, they could mark each arm they visit with a drop of urine, and then avoid maze arms that had this odor marker. Alternatively, they could select arms in a fixed sequence, such as always entering successive arms in a clockwise order. However, they do not appear to use either of these tactics.

Various procedures have convincingly ruled out the use of odor cues in the selection of maze arms (for example, Olton, Collison, & Werz, 1977; Olton & Samuelson, 1976; Zoladek & Roberts, 1978). The available evidence also indicates that rats in a radial maze experiment can perform efficiently without using response chains or entering maze arms in a fixed order from one trial to the next. As long as the central choice area is small enough for the rats to reach all the arms easily from anywhere in the central area, they do not choose arms in a fixed order (Olton & Samuelson, 1976; see also Olton et al., 1977). Furthermore, rats select previously unvisited arms even if procedures are introduced that should disrupt response chains (for example, Beatty & Shavalia, 1980a, 1980b).

The studies cited have been important in ruling out various potential cues for radial maze performance and suggest that spatial stimuli are critical. What are spatial cues and how are they identified? Spatial cues are stimuli that identify the location of an object in the environment. Rats appear to use distinctive features of the environment, such as a window, a door, a corner of the room, or a poster on the wall, as landmarks and locate maze arms relative to these landmarks. Movement of landmarks relative to the maze causes the rats to treat the maze arms as being in new locations (Suzuki, Augerinos, & Black, 1980). Thus, under ordinary circumstances, spatial location is identified relative to distal room cues, not to local stimuli inside the maze (see also Morris, 1981). However, rats are able to use intra-maze cues to guide their choices if access to extra-maze cues is blocked (Brown & Bing, 1997; Brown & Moore, 1997).

Because radial maze performance usually depends on memory for recently visited locations, the radial maze procedure has become a popular technique for the study of memory processes, both at the behavioral level and the physiological level. The memory capacity

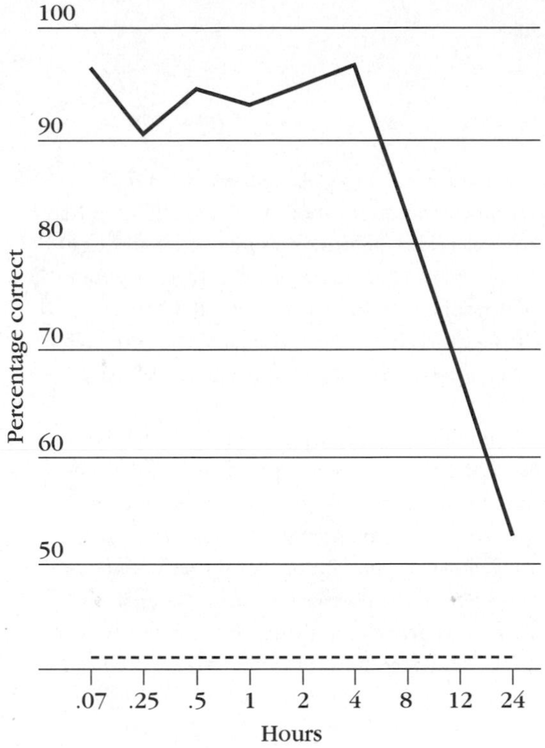

Figure 11.6 Percentage correct responses on choices 5–8 in an eight-arm radial maze. Between choices 4 and 5 the animals were returned to their home cages for varying intervals ranging from .07 to 24 hours. The dashed line indicates chance performance (41%). (From "Rat Spatial Memory: Resistance to Retroactive Interference at Long Retention Intervals," by W. W. Beatty and D A. Shavalia, 1980, *Animal Learning & Behavior, 8,* pp. 550–552. Copyright © 1980 by the Psychonomic Society. Reprinted by permission.)

revealed by the technique is impressive. For example, rats and gerbils have been observed to perform well in radial mazes with as many as 17 arms (Olton et al., 1977; Wilkie & Slobin, 1983), and this probably does not represent the limit of their spatial memory (Roberts, 1979). The duration of spatial working memory is also remarkable.

In a test of the limits of spatial memory, Beatty and Shavalia (1980b) allowed rats to make four choices in the eight-arm radial maze in the usual manner. The subjects were then detained in their home cages for various periods up to 24 hours. After the delay interval, they were returned to the maze and allowed to make choices 5–8. As usual, an entry into an alley they had not previously visited was considered a correct choice.

Figure 11.6 shows the percentage of correct choices as a function of the delay interval between the first four and last four choices. Delays of up to 4 hours after the first four choices did not disrupt performance. Longer periods of confinement in the home cage produced progressively more errors. These data show that spatial memory is not permanent. However, the memory can last for several hours (see also Maki, Beatty, Hoffman, Bierley, & Clouse, 1984; Spetch, 1990; Strijkstra & Bolhuis, 1987; Willson & Wilkie, 1991).

Results such as those presented in Figure 11.6 illustrate that rats have excellent spatial memory. How do they use this memory to guide their search responses? On an elevated maze, the rats have little choice but to run along the arms of the maze. There are no other places to go. In a highly creative experiment, Hoffman, Timberlake, Leffel, and Gont (1999) repeated the radial-arm maze experiment, but instead of having the maze raised off the floor to restrict the rats to the maze arms, they put the maze on the floor so that the rats could easily step off and go from one food cup to another without returning to the central choice area. Hoffman et al. used a six-arm maze. With the maze on the floor, the rats could

BOX 11.1

LEARNING AS SYNAPTIC PLASTICITY: LONG-TERM POTENTIATION (LTP) AND LONG-TERM DEPRESSION (LTD)

It is estimated that the human brain contains more than a 100 billion neurons. Each neuron may be coupled through a chemical synapse to thousands of other neurons, forming a complex neural network. If we assume that each of these connections can store just one bit of information, the brain can hold the computer equivalent of 100,000 gigs!

How can experience bring about a change within this network? Many assume that experience modifies the strength of the synaptic connections. If this is true, when are the connections modified, and what are the molecular mechanisms that mediate this synaptic plasticity?

An answer to the first question was suggested by Donald Hebb a half century ago (Hebb, 1949). He argued that neural connections are strengthened when two cells are active at the same time, an idea that is sometimes summarized with the mnemonic "cells that fire together wire together." Modern theorists have extended this notion to address decreases in synaptic strength, arguing that this will occur when cellular activity is uncorrelated.

In a classic experiment, Bliss and Lomo (1973) provided neural evidence for Hebb's hypothesis. They examined how neural activity within the hippocampus alters the strength of synaptic connections. To induce neural activity, they lowered an electrode into a bundle of neurons known as the perforant path and applied an electrical current (see Figure 11.7). The cells that form the perforant path synapse on neurons are called mossy fibers. By recording neural activity through electrodes placed near the mossy fiber cell bodies, Bliss and Lomo obtained a measure of synaptic strength. As we would expect, applying a moderate electrical stimulus to the perforant path elicited moderate neural activity in the mossy fibers, and this response changed little over time. But if a strong input was provided—one that caused a very strong response in the mossy fibers—subsequent inputs produced a much larger response. This phenomenon is called *long-term potentiation* (LTP). It appears that a strong input can effectively strengthen synaptic connections. The converse phenomenon, *long-term depression* (LTD), can weaken synaptic connections. Both LTP and LTD can last for days to weeks. This enduring feature of LTP and LTD has encouraged researchers to suggest that these phenomena may represent a kind of neurobiological memory—a way in which cells can store the consequences of experience (for a recent review, see Martin, Grimwood, & Morris, 2000).

Cells communicate at a synapse through the release of neurotransmitters that engage a response in the adjoining (postsynaptic) neuron by activating specialized receptors. A strong input could alter the strength of a chemical synapse by increasing either the amount of transmitter released or the responsiveness of the postsynaptic cell. Research suggests that LTP is largely due to the latter possibility. One of the most important ways in which a postsynaptic cell can become more responsive involves specialized receptors (NMDA receptors) that lie on the surface of the cell. NMDA receptors act as coincidence detectors. Their activation depends on both the release of transmitter and a strong response in the postsynaptic cell. If these two conditions are met, the NMDA receptors initiate a biochemical cascade that awakens silent AMPA receptors. The AMPA receptors mediate the propagation of the neural signal from one neuron to the next. Awakening more of these receptors increases the magnitude of the response elicited in the postsynaptic cell. As a result, the postsynaptic cell exhibits a stronger response even though the amount of neurotransmitter released has not changed.

LTP has a number of properties that suggest it plays a role in learning and memory. The most obvious is *its enduring nature.* Another important quality is *input specificity*—the modification is limited to those synapses that are concurrently active. LTP also exhibits a kind of *cooperativity.* The induction of LTP requires a strong response in the postsynaptic cell. This strong response does not have to come from just one input. A number of inputs can work together to drive the postsynaptic cell to the threshold for learning, and all the contributing inputs can benefit. A variation of this cooperativity yields the final, and most interesting, property—*associativity* (Figure 11.7). If a weak input is paired with a strong input; the latter will be sufficient to engage LTP at both connections. As a result, the weak input will acquire the capacity to drive a response in

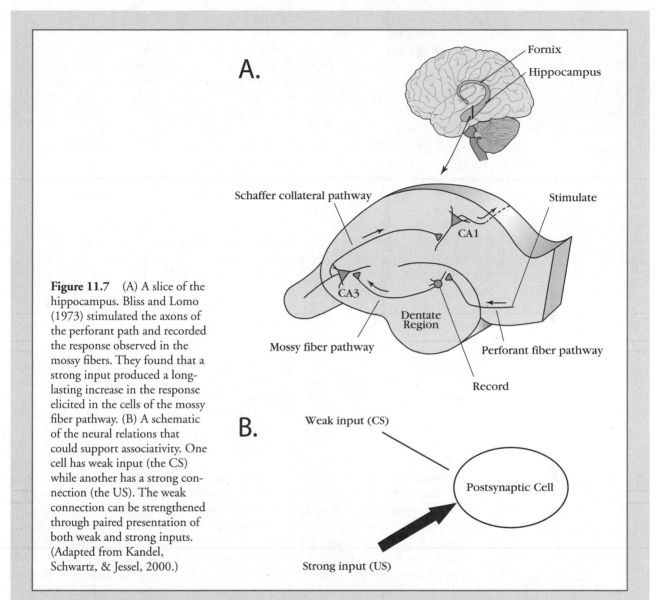

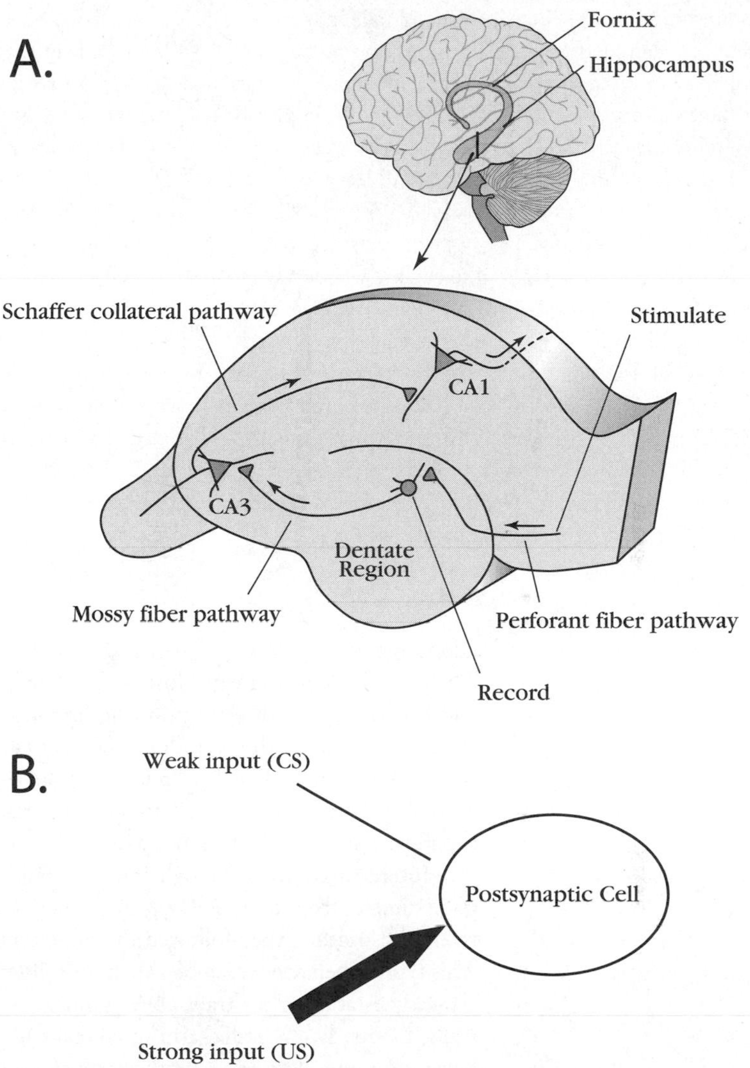

Figure 11.7 (A) A slice of the hippocampus. Bliss and Lomo (1973) stimulated the axons of the perforant path and recorded the response observed in the mossy fibers. They found that a strong input produced a long-lasting increase in the response elicited in the cells of the mossy fiber pathway. (B) A schematic of the neural relations that could support associativity. One cell has weak input (the CS) while another has a strong connection (the US). The weak connection can be strengthened through paired presentation of both weak and strong inputs. (Adapted from Kandel, Schwartz, & Jessel, 2000.)

the postsynaptic cell, in much the same way that a CS acquires the ability to generate a CR as a result of being paired with a US.

To explore whether hippocampal LTP plays a role in learning and memory, researchers have used a number of behavioral tasks that are known to depend on the hippocampus. One of the most popular involves learning about spatial cues. R. G. Morris developed a simple way to study such learning using a water maze. The maze consists of a large tank filled with a milky liquid. Just under the surface of the liquid lies a hidden platform on which the rat can stand. Subjects are gently lowered into the pool from various locations along the edge of the tank. Normally, rats quickly learn to swim to the location of the

(continued)

Box 11.1 (continued)

platform, which they climb upon to rest. Rats with lesions to the hippocampus do not remember where the platform is located from one test to the next and take far longer to find the hidden platform. Lesioned rats do not have any problem swimming to a visible platform, which suggests that their sensory and motor functions are not impaired. Rather, hippocampal lesions produce a more selective deficit that interferes with the capacity to learn about spatial cues.

Developing a behavioral assay that is sensitive to hippocampal lesions gives us a tool to explore whether synaptic modification (NMDA-mediated plasticity) is involved in learning. To explore this issue, researchers have tested the impact of drugs that disrupt NMDA receptor activity (for example, APV and MK-801). These drugs bind to the NMDA receptor and prevent it from working normally. Physiological studies have shown that pretreatment with an NMDA antagonist blocks the induction of LTP. Significantly, the same drug manipulation also disrupts spatial learning in the water maze (Morris, Anderson, Lynch, & Baudry, 1986).

Similar experiments conducted in other learning paradigms have indicated that synaptic plasticity mediated by the NMDA receptor is not limited to spatial learning. For example, encoding the cues that represent a context, a new object, or a new conspecific (a form of social learning) all depend on the hippocampus, and evidence suggests that each of these forms of learning depends on NMDA-mediated plasticity (Martin et al., 2000).

Researchers have also shown that LTP occurs in many other regions of the brain. Even neurons within the spinal cord exhibit LTP. When you get a sunburn, neurons within the spinal cord become sensitized (Willis, 2001). This increases the level of pain you feel when the skin is stimulated. This heightened pain appears to reflect a form of LTP, a cellular memory within the spinal cord that heightens the pain signal sent to the brain.

—J. W. Grau

adopt one of four strategies to visit all of the food cups. These are illustrated in Figure 11.8. The most efficient strategy, illustrated in Panel "a" of Figure 11.8, minimizes travel distance and involves going directly from the first food cup to the next by stepping off the maze. Panel "b" illustrates the path the rats would take if they used the arms of the maze as guides to following a trail. Panel "c" represents the path the rats might take if they walked about randomly. Panel "d" represents the path the rats might take if they followed the walls of the experimental chamber (thigmotaxis).

Interestingly, even though the rats could have easily stepped off the maze arms and gone directly from one food cup to the next (and thereby minimized travel distance), they rarely did. Rather, they followed the maze arms, with only occasional forays off the maze. This type of behavior resembles the trail-following behavior of rats in the wild. Rat colonies typically establish clear trails above ground and go from place to place by following those trails. Evidently, the radial-arm maze takes advantage of this propensity for trail-following behavior in rats. The rats treat the arms of the maze as trails even if the maze is on the floor so that the rats are not confined to the maze arms (see also Timberlake, Leffel, & Hoffman, 1999). Rats may show rapid learning and impressive memory on a radial-arm maze because this experimental paradigm is particularly well suited to their behavioral propensities.

MEMORY MECHANISMS

In the preceding section I described several prominent techniques for the study of memory processes in animals and some results of that research. I now discuss factors that determine what we remember and how well we remember it. As I noted earlier, memory processes in-

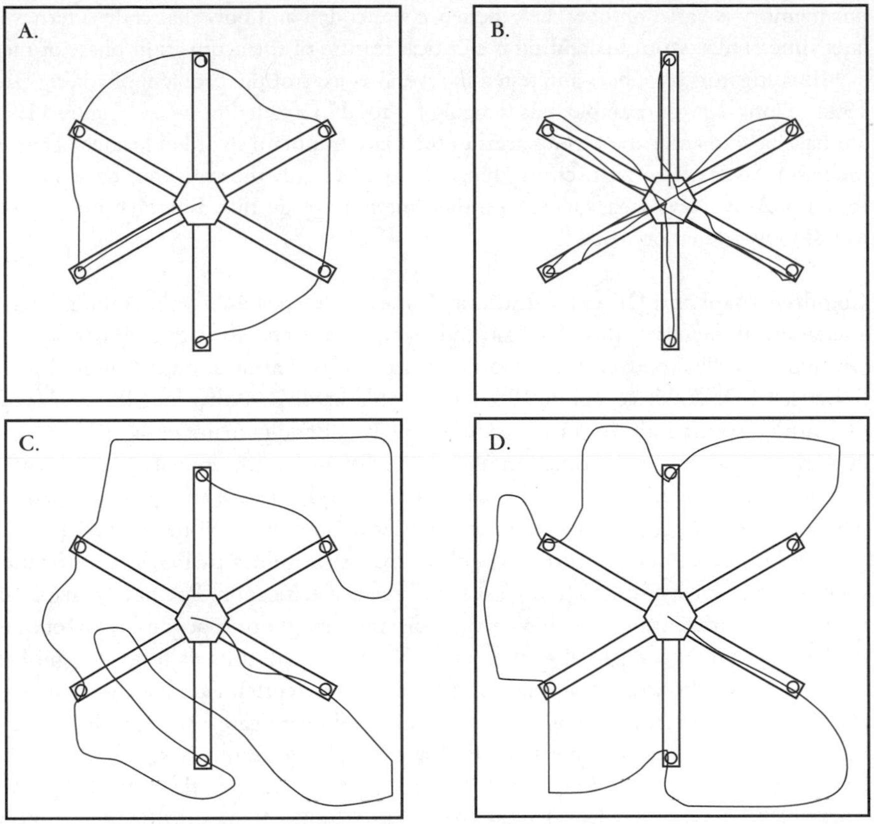

Figure 11.8 Possible routes a rat might take to obtain food from food cups at the ends of a radial-arm maze that is placed on the floor. Panel "a" shows route that minimizes travel distance. Panel "b" shows trail following behavior. Panel "c" shows random search. Panel "d" shows travel along the walls or thigmotaxis. (From Hoffman, Timberlake, Leffel, & Gont, 1999.)

volve three phases: acquisition, retention, and retrieval (see Table 11.1). What we remember and how well we remember it depend on all three of these phases, often in combination with each other. In this part of the chapter, I also discuss research with nonhuman animals relevant to each of the three phases of memory processes.

Acquisition and the Problem of Stimulus Coding

Obviously, we cannot remember something (the winning play in a championship game, for example) if we were not exposed to it in the first place. Memory depends on our having experienced an event and having made some kind of record of that experience. However, even when our memory is excellent, it is not because we have retained a perfect or literal record of the earlier experience.

Experiences cannot be recorded in a literal sense, even by machines. A movie camera can do an excellent job recording the sights and sounds of the winning play in a championship game. The visual aspects of the event are recorded in a series of stationary images; the auditory aspects are recorded in a pattern of magnetized particles on the film. The winning play is coded in terms of still photographs and magnetic patterns for the purposes of retention, but the coded record (a strip of film with a soundtrack) bears little resemblance to the actual event.

In a similar fashion, we do not have a literal record of a past experience in memory. The experience is coded in the nervous system in some way for the purposes of retention, and our memory is based on how the experience was coded and how that code is retrieved at a later time. Thus, **stimulus coding** is a critical feature of the acquisition phase of memory.

Investigators have been interested in several aspects of the problem of coding (Zentall, 1993). Consider, for example, rats foraging for food in a radial maze (see Figure 11.4). The animals have to enter the various arms of the maze to obtain the food located at the end of each arm. So as not to waste effort, they have to select only the arms they have not yet tried that day. As we have seen, rats rely on their memory to do this. But what do they keep in mind? How is memory coded?

D. Wilkie

Cognitive Maps and Other Navigational Codes. One possibility is that the animals make a serial list of the maze arms they visit, adding an item to the list with each new arm visited. Given the excellent performance of rats on mazes with 17 arms or more (Olton et al., 1977; Roberts, 1979; Wilkie & Slobin, 1983), this would involve a rather long list. Such extensive list learning seems unlikely, since even humans have difficulty maintaining 17 items or more in working memory at one time. Another possibility is that the animals form a mental map or mental representation of how the maze and the food cups are arranged and then use this "cognitive map" to decide which arm of the maze to enter next (Roberts, 1984).

The idea that animals form a cognitive map that guides their spatial navigation has been an attractive hypothesis, but it calls for further specification. Potentially, maps can represent many different types of information (distance, height or topography, presence of particular landmarks, compass direction, etc.). To claim that animals form a cognitive map does not tell us precisely what kinds of information are contained in such a map and how animals use this information. Such questions have led investigators to focus on more specific mechanisms that enable subjects to find a particular location in space (see reviews by Biegler, 2000; Cheng, 2000; Gallistel, 1990; Roberts, 1998; Shettleworth, 1998). Shettleworth (1998), for example, advocated that "discussion of cognitive mapping should be abandoned in favor of more operational discussion of how animals get from place to place" (p. 311). A number of mechanisms have been examined.

Figure 11.9 illustrates three possible navigational mechanisms. The goal is located near a rock. There is a tree to the left of the rock and a bush to the right. An animal could find the goal location by looking at the rock and aiming for it. This represents *beacon following.* The rock serves as a beacon that marks the location of the goal object. Beacon following is a fairly simple navigational tactic, requiring little more than the formation of an association between the beacon and the goal object. Sign tracking behavior described in Chapter 3 is an example of beacon following (see especially Figure 3.5). Given the cues present in Figure 11.9, the animal could also find the goal by going to the right of the tree or to the left of the bush. In these cases, it would be using the tree and the bush as landmarks to guide its navigation. A *landmark* is a distinctive stimulus that is not at the goal location but has a fixed relation to the goal ("to the left of" or "to the right of"). A third navigation tactic is to find the goal by using the *relation between the landmarks.* The goal is located midway between the tree and bush landmarks.

Animals can encode spatial information by using beacons, landmarks, and the relation between landmarks. Depending on the demands of a particular spatial task, animals may use one or another spatial coding mechanism, or may rely on several mechanisms at the same time.

Retrospective and Prospective Coding. So far I have discussed the kinds of spatial information animals may use in finding particular food locations. Another interesting question is which food locations are encoded as a rat goes about foraging on a radial-arm maze. Perhaps the most obvious possibility is that the animals keep in mind where they have al-

Figure 11.9 Diagram of a spatial task in which the goal (a patch of food, for example) is located near a rock, with a tree to the left of the goal and a bush to the right. An animal can find the goal by going to the rock (beacon following), or by responding to the tree and bush as landmarks.

ready been. This is called **retrospective memory,** or *retrospective coding.* An equally effective memory strategy is for the animals to keep in mind which maze arms they have yet to visit. This strategy is called **prospective memory,** or *prospective coding.* Because animal memory paradigms typically have a limited range of outcomes, they can be solved successfully either by remembering a past event (retrospection) or by remembering a plan for future action (prospection). This distinction has become a major focus of research (Honig & Thompson, 1982; Wasserman, 1986; Grant, 1993).

Consider going shopping at a mall. Let's assume that to complete your shopping, you have to visit six stores: a shoe store, a record store, a bookstore, a bakery, a clothing store, and a pharmacy. What memory strategy could you use to avoid going to the same place twice? One possibility would be to form a memory code for each store after visiting that store. This would be a retrospective code. You could then decide whether to enter the next store on the list based on whether you remembered already having gone there. With such a retrospective strategy, the contents of your working memory would increase by one item with each store you visit. Thus, how much you have to remember (the memory load) would increase as you progressed through the task (see Figure 11.10).

An alternative would be to memorize a list of all the stores you intended to visit before you start your trip. Such memory would involve prospection, because it would be memory for what you intended to do. After visiting a particular store, you could delete that store from your memory. Thus, in this scheme, a visit to a store would be "recorded" by having that store removed from the prospective memory list. Because you would be keeping in

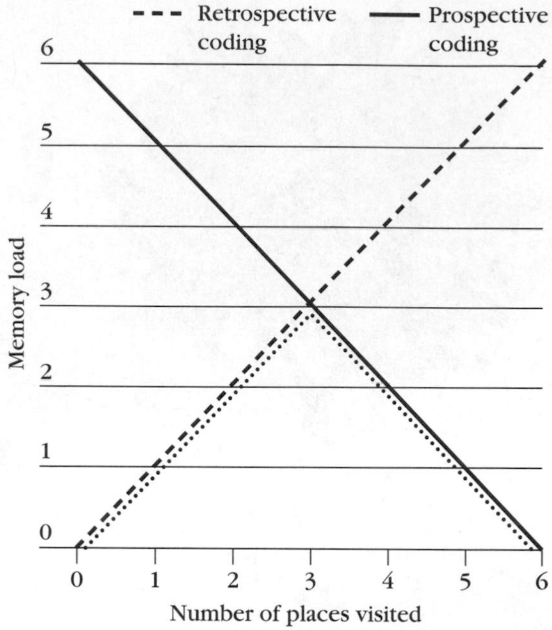

Figure 11.10 Memory load following different numbers of places visited, out of a possible total of six, given retrospective and prospective coding strategies. The dotted line represents memory load when the coding strategy is changed from retrospection to prospection halfway through the task. (Based on Cook, Brown, & Riley, 1985.)

mind only which stores you still had to visit, the memory load would decrease as you progressed through your shopping, as shown in Figure 11.10.

P. Urcuioli

Numerous ingenious experiments have been conducted to determine whether animals use retrospective or prospective memory. Many of these have involved variations of the matching-to-sample procedure with pigeons. The experiments have demonstrated that animals use both retrospective and prospective memory, but under different circumstances (Santi, Musgrave, & Bradford, 1988; Zentall, Jagielo, Jackson-Smith, & Urcuioli, 1987; Zentall, Urcuioli, Jagielo, & Jackson-Smith, 1989). Such experiments illustrate that coding strategies are flexible, with different strategies adopted in response to different task demands. (For other evidence of coding flexibility, see Ducharme & Santi, 1993; Grant, 1991; Grant & Spetch, 1993.)

Coding Strategies and Task Demands. To illustrate how coding strategies might change as a function of task demands, return to the example of having to shop in six different stores in a mall. As I have noted, with a retrospective coding strategy the demands on working memory increase as you progress through the shopping trip. In contrast, with a prospective coding strategy the demands on working memory decrease as you progress through the six stores (see Figure 11.10). How might you minimize the demands on your memory? Is there a way to keep the demands on working memory to three items or fewer throughout the shopping trip? There is, if you change your memory strategy halfway through the task.

At the start of the shopping trip, memory load is least if you use a retrospective strategy. Therefore, you should start with retrospective coding. Remembering where you have been works well for the first three stores you visit. After that, the memory load for retrospection begins to exceed the memory load for prospection (see Figure 11.10). Therefore, after having visited three stores, you should switch to a prospective code and keep in mind only which stores remain to be visited. By switching coding strategies halfway through, you minimize how much you have to remember at any one time. If you use retrospection followed by prospection, memory load will at first increase and then decrease as you complete the task, as illustrated by the dashed line in Figure 11.10.

Do animals (including people) use coding strategies so flexibly, and if so how could researchers prove that? The results of several experiments indicate that coding strategies change from retrospection to prospection as one goes through a list of places or items. Early in the list, individuals keep in mind what has already happened. Later, they remember what remains to be done (Cook, Brown, & Riley, 1985; Zentall, Steirn, & Jackson-Smith, 1990; see also Brown, Wheeler, & Riley, 1989).

In one study, Kesner and DeSpain (1988) compared the coding strategies of rats and college students in spatial memory tasks. If individuals switch from retrospection to prospection in the course of remembering a series of places, memory load should first increase and then decrease. Memory load was estimated from the rate of errors the participants made on a test that was conducted after they had visited different numbers of places (see Figure 11.11).

The rats in Kesner and DeSpain's study were first trained to forage for food on a 12-arm radial maze in the standard manner. Once they had become proficient at obtaining food by going to each maze arm, a series of test trials was conducted. On each test trial, the rats were allowed to make a certain number of arm entries. They were then removed from the maze for 15 minutes. At the end of the delay, they were returned to the maze and allowed to enter one of two alleys selected by the experimenter. One was an alley they had entered earlier; the other was a previously unchosen alley. Selecting the new alley was judged to be the correct response. The rate of errors the rats made during the test phase is presented in the left graph of Figure 11.11. As the number of visited locations before the test increased from 2 to 8 arms of the maze, the error rate increased. This finding is consistent with the hypothesis that the rats were using a retrospective coding strategy during the first 8 arm entries. Interestingly, however, when the rats were tested after having entered 10 arms, they

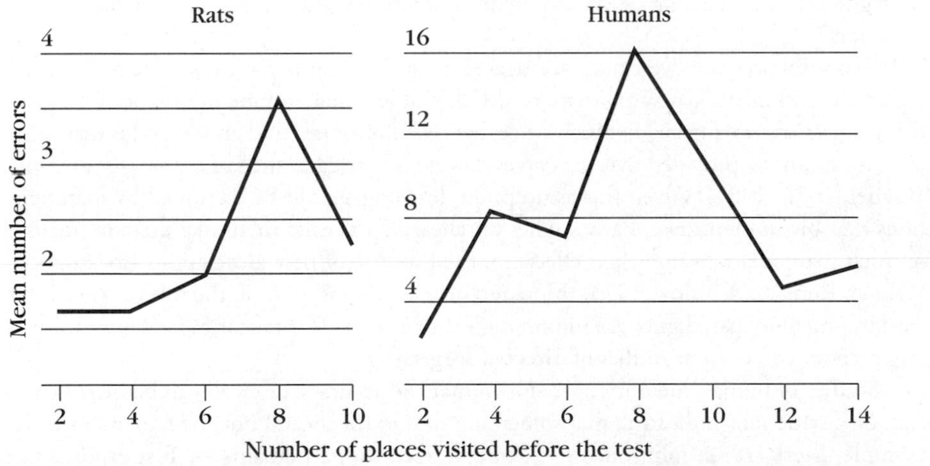

Figure 11.11 Error rate of rats (left) and college students (right) on spatial memory tasks requiring identification of a new place after a delay. The delay was imposed after the participants had "visited" various numbers of locations. (From "Correspondence Between Rats and Humans in the Utilization of Retrospective and Prospective Codes," by R. P. Kesner and M. J. DeSpain, 1988, *Animal Learning and Behavior, 16,* pp. 299–302. Copyright © 1988 by the Psychonomic Society. Reprinted by permission.)

made fewer errors. This improvement in performance toward the end of the series suggests that the animals switched to a prospective coding strategy.

The college students in the study were presented with a grid with 16 squares (corresponding to 16 places in a maze). During the course of a trial, the symbol X traveled from one square to another in an irregular order, simulating movement from one place to another in a maze. After the X had been presented at various locations, a delay of 5 seconds was introduced, followed by a test of two test locations. One test location was a place where the X had been; the other was a new square. The participants had to identify which was the new square.

The rate of errors the young adults made is presented in the right graph of Figure 11.11 as a function of the number of places the X had been before the test. The results were strikingly similar to the pattern of errors obtained with the rats. The error rate initially increased, consistent with a retrospective coding strategy. After the target stimulus had been in 8 places, however, the error rate decreased, consistent with a prospective coding strategy.

These results illustrate that memory performance is a function of coding strategies and that coding strategies may vary as a function of task demands. Given alternative possible coding strategies, participants switch from one to another so as to reduce memory load and thereby improve response accuracy. (For evidence of the flexibility of coding strategies in a matching-to-sample task, see Clement & Zentall, 2000b.)

Courtesy of T. Zentall

T. Zentall

Retention and the Problem of Rehearsal

The second phase of memory processes is retention. With working-memory tasks, a prominent issue involving retention is **rehearsal.** Rehearsal refers to keeping information in an active state, readily available for use. If someone tells you a phone number, you may rehearse the number by repeating it to yourself over and over again until you get to a phone. If someone is giving you directions for getting to the post office, you may try to create a mental image of the route and imagine yourself following the route a number of times. Such rehearsal strategies facilitate keeping newly acquired information readily at hand, available to guide behavior.

Rehearsal processes were first investigated in animal memory as they relate to the learning or establishment of new associations. Models of learning and memory typically assume that associations are formed between two events (a conditioned and an unconditioned stimulus, for example) provided that the two events are rehearsed at the same time (for example, Wagner, 1976, 1981). Given this assumption, learning should be disrupted by manipulations that disrupt rehearsal. Early studies of rehearsal processes in animal memory focused on such manipulations and their effects on the learning of new associations (for example, Wagner, Rudy, & Whitlow, 1973). More recent research has been on the role of rehearsal in working-memory paradigms. An important line of evidence for rehearsal processes in working memory comes from studies of **directed forgetting.**

Studies of human memory have shown that the accuracy of recall can be modified by cues or instructions indicating that something should (or should not) be remembered (for example, Bjork, 1972; Johnson, 1994). In this research, participants are first exposed to a list of items. Some of the items are accompanied by a remember cue (R-cue), indicating that the item will appear later in a test of memory. Other items are accompanied by a forget cue (F-cue) indicating that the item will not be included in the memory test. Occasionally, probe trials are included in which memory is tested for an item that was accompanied by the F-cue. The results of these probe trials indicate that memory is disrupted by the forget cues.

Demonstrations of directed forgetting are important because they provide evidence that memory is an active process that can be brought under stimulus control. Research on directed forgetting in people has sparked interest in finding analogous effects with nonhuman animals (Rilling, Kendrick, & Stonebraker, 1984.) How might researchers devise a procedure to study directed forgetting in animals?

One possibility is to use a variation of the delayed-matching-to-sample procedure. In a matching task, each trial begins with exposure to a sample stimulus (a horizontal grid, for example). The animal is then presented with both the sample (horizontal grid) and a distracter stimulus (vertical grid). Responses to the sample are reinforced; responses to the distracter stimulus do not produce reinforcement. In this paradigm, cues to remember or forget can be introduced into the matching task after the sample stimulus, as is shown in Figure 11.12. On R-cue trials, the animals are tested for their memory of the sample; on F-cue trials, such a memory test is not conducted; the F-cue ends the trial and nothing else happens until the next trial begins.

Early research on directed forgetting in animals used procedures similar to that outlined in Figure 11.12. After extensive training on such a procedure, probe trials were introduced that tested for memory of the sample after an F-cue. As in the human research, these probe trials indicated that memory was disrupted by the F-cue. Why might such a disruption occur? One possibility is that the F-cue disrupts rehearsal and thereby leads to poorer memory performance. Unfortunately, however, the procedure outlined in Figure 11.12 allows other possibilities as well (see Roper & Zentall, 1993; Zentall, Roper, Kaiser, & Sherburne, 1997). Notice, for example, that during training, the animals cannot earn reinforcement on F-cue trials. Therefore, the F-cue may become a signal for nonreinforcement and may elicit

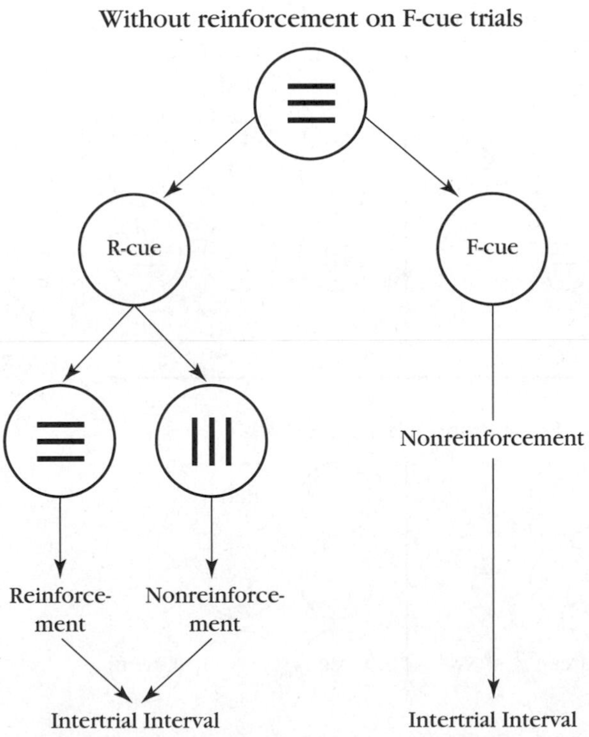

Figure 11.12 A simple but inadequate procedure for studying directed forgetting in the context of delayed matching to sample. Each trial begins with a sample stimulus. This is then followed by either a remember cue (R-cue) or a forget cue (F-cue). Subjects are tested with the sample versus a distracter stimulus at the end of R-cue trials but not at the end of F-cue trials.

negative emotions or frustration. Poor performance on F-cue probe trials may be due to the expectation of nonreward elicited by the F-cue rather than to poor memory (Zentall, Roper, & Sherburne, 1995).

Poor performance on F-cue probe trials may also be due to attentional factors. During training, the subjects may learn that once they have seen the F-cue, there is no reason to pay attention to anything else that happens on that trial. This lack of attention may result in low accuracy on F-cue probe trials.

To overcome the problems identified above, the procedure should permit subjects to obtain reinforcement on F-cue trials and should also maintain attention. These goals are met by the procedure outlined in Figure 11.13. Devised by Roper, Kaiser, and Zentall (1995), it involves two remember cues (White and Blue) and two forget cues (filled circle and open circle). At the end of R-cue trials, the subjects are asked to chose between the sam-

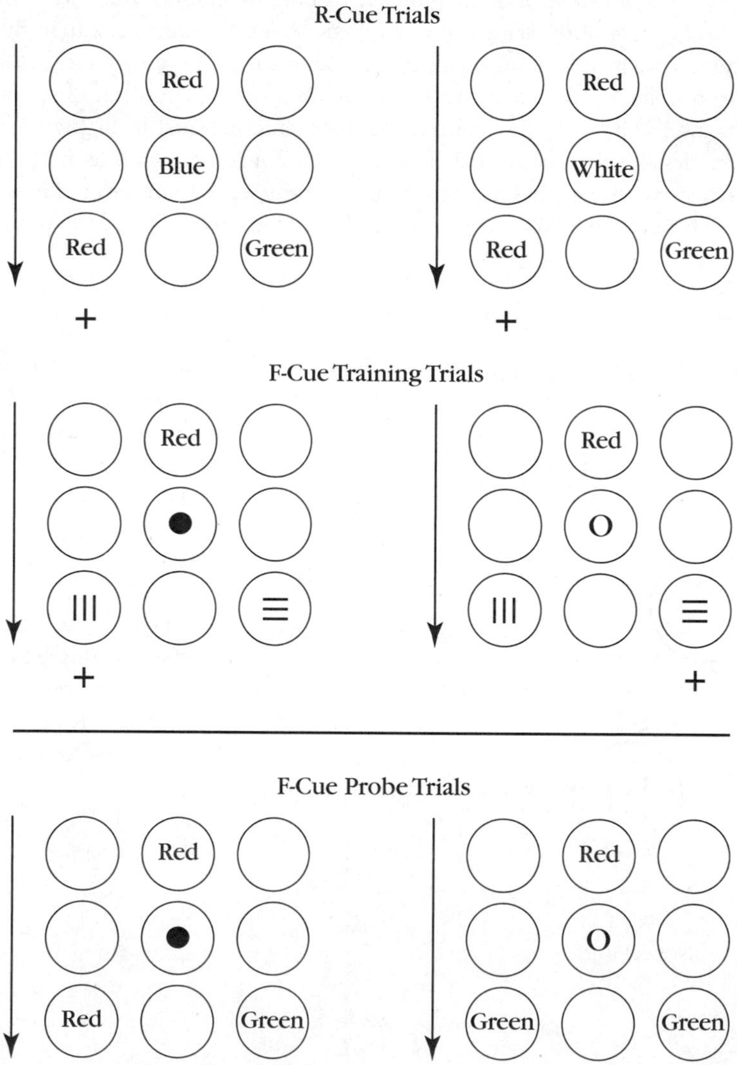

Figure 11.13 Procedures used by Roper, Kaiser, and Zentall (1995) to demonstrate directed forgetting in pigeons. On R-cue training (and test) trials, a color sample (Red) was followed by one of two remember cues (Blue or White). At the end of a 4-second delay interval, the subjects were presented with the sample (Red) and a distracter (Green) stimulus, and responding to the sample was reinforced. On F-cue training trials, the sample was followed by one of two forget cues, which in turn were followed by vertical and horizontal lines. If the forget cue was a filled circle, responding to the vertical lines was reinforced. If the forget cue was an open circle, responding to the horizontal lines was reinforced. On F-cue probe trials, the sample and distractor color stimuli (Red and Green) appeared after the forget cues.

ple stimulus (Red) and a distractor (Green). In contrast, the sample stimulus (and its distractor) do not appear at the end of F-cue trials during training. Rather, the subjects are given a choice between vertical and horizontal lines. If the F-cue was the filled circle, pecking the vertical lines is reinforced. If the F-cue was the open circle, pecking the horizontal lines is reinforced. Thus, the subjects can earn reinforcement on both R-cue and F-cue trials. In addition, they cannot afford to stop paying attention as soon as they have seen the F-cue because they have to select between the vertical and horizontal lines on F-cue trials. On F-cue probe trials, the subjects are tested with the color sample stimuli instead of the vertical or horizontal lines following presentation of the F-cue.

Roper et al. (1995) tested six pigeons with the procedures outlined in Figure 11.13. All of the pigeons showed evidence of directed forgetting on the F-cue probe trials. On R-cue trials, the mean accuracy for selecting the sample stimulus at the end of the 4-sec delay was 86%. In contrast, mean accuracy on F-cue probe trials was just 73%. Furthermore, each of the six pigeons tested in the experiment responded more accurately on R-cue trials than on F-cue probe trials (see also Kaiser, Sherburne, & Zentall, 1997).

Retrieval

In the third phase of memory processes, retrieval, stored information is recovered so that it can be used to guide behavior. Whereas problems of coding and rehearsal are primarily being investigated in working-memory paradigms, research on retrieval has focused on reference memory and, more specifically, on memory for learned associations. Retrieval processes are of special interest because many instances of memory failure reflect deficits in the recovery of information—**retrieval failure**—rather than loss of the information from the memory store.

During the course of our daily lives, we learn many things, all of which are somehow stored in the brain. Which aspect of our extensive knowledge we think of at a particular time depends on which pieces of information are retrieved from our long-term memory store. At any moment, we recall only a minute proportion of what we know. Retrieval processes are triggered by reminders, or **retrieval cues.** If you are discussing summer camp experiences with your friends, the things they say will serve as retrieval cues to remind you of things you did at summer camp.

Retrieval cues are effective in reminding you of a past experience because they are associated with the memory for that experience. A song may remind you of the concert you attended on your first date. Balancing on a bicycle will remind you of what you have to do to ride a bicycle. The sensations of sinking in a swimming pool will remind you of what you learned about swimming, and the voice of a friend you have not seen for a long time will stimulate retrieval of memories for the things you used to do together.

Retrieval Cues and Memory for Instrumental Behavior in Human Infants. Various stimuli that are present during acquisition of a memory can come to serve as retrieval cues for that memory. Borovsky and Rovee-Collier (1990), for example, investigated retrieval of the memory for instrumental conditioning in 6-month-old infants. The infants were trained in their own homes in playpens whose sides were covered with a cloth liner. Some of these liners were striped and others had a square pattern. The investigators were interested in whether the cloth liner might serve as a retrieval cue for the instrumental response.

A mobile was mounted above the playpen. Each infant was seated in the playpen in a reclining baby seat so that he or she could see the mobile. One end of a satin ribbon was

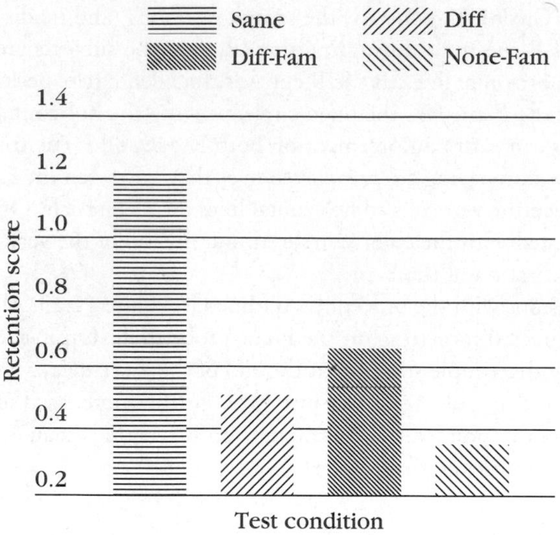

Figure 11.14 Retention scores of 6-month-old infants in a test of instrumental conditioning. Group Same was tested in a playpen with the same cloth liner that had been present during conditioning. Group Diff was tested with a new cloth liner. Group Diff-Fam was tested with a familiar cloth liner that was different from the one in the playpen during conditioning. Group None-Fam was tested without a cloth liner but in a familiar playpen in a familiar room. (From "Contextual Constraints on Memory Retrieval at Six Months," by D. Borovsky and C. Rovee-Collier, 1990, *Child Development, 61,* pp. 1569–1583. Copyright © 1990 by University of Chicago Press. Reprinted by permission.)

C. Rovee-Collier

looped around the infant's ankle and the other end was attached to the stand that supported the mobile. With this arrangement, each kick by the infant made the mobile move. The instrumental response was kicking the leg, and the reinforcer was movement of the mobile. The kicking response first was conditioned in two short training sessions. The infants then received a test session 24 hours later.

The cues present during the test session were varied for different groups of infants. Some of the babies were tested in a crib with the same cloth liner that had been present during the training sessions (Group Same). Others were tested with the alternate cloth liner that was new to them (Group Diff). For a third group, the alternate cloth liner was familiar, but it had not been present during the training trials (Group Diff-Fam). A fourth group of babies was tested without a liner and could look around their familiar playroom (None-Fam).

The results of the experiment are summarized in Figure 11.14. The best retention performance was evident in the group that was tested with the same playpen liner that had been present during conditioning. Each of the other groups showed significantly poorer memory performance. Infants tested with a novel liner (Group Diff) may have shown poor performance because novelty somehow disrupted their behavior (Thomas & Empedocles, 1992). However, the poor performance of Group Diff-Fam indicates that novelty was not entirely responsible for the disruptions of memory that occurred. A change in the crib liner from conditioning to testing resulted in poor performance even if the liner used during testing was familiar. The inferior performance of Group Diff-Fam as compared to group

Same provides strong evidence that the cloth liner served as a retrieval cue for the instrumental kicking behavior. (For related research with human infants, see Bhatt, Rovee-Collier, & Shyi, 1994; Rovee-Collier & Bhatt, 1993; Hartshorn & Rovee-Collier, 1997. For other examples of context effects in memory retrieval, see Smith & Vela, 2001; Zhou & Riccio, 1996.)

Contextual Cues and the Retrieval of Conflicting Memories. Changing the cloth pattern on the playpen liner changed the contextual cues of the playpen. Thus, the study by Borovsky and Rovee-Collier was a study of the role of contextual cues in memory retrieval. I described other examples of contextual cues in memory retrieval in the discussion of contextual stimulus control in Chapter 8 and in connection with extinction, in Chapter 9. A particularly striking example was presented in Figure 8.13, which showed data from an experiment by Thomas, McKelvie, and Mah (1985). Pigeons in this experiment first learned to peck when a vertical line (S+ = 90°) was projected on the response key and to not peck when a horizontal line (S– = 0°) appeared. The contextual cues were then changed (by altering the sounds and lighting in the chamber), and the pigeons were trained on the reversal of the original discrimination. Now, the horizontal line (0°) was S+ and the vertical line (90°) was S–.

Subsequent generalization tests in each context indicated that responding to the vertical and horizontal lines depended on the context in which the lines were tested. Which discrimination was retrieved depended on which set of contextual cues was presented. The study illustrates that organisms can retain memories of diametrically opposing response tendencies. (For other examples of involving the retrieval of conflicting memories, see Bouton, 1993, 1994; Dekeyne & Deweer, 1990; Fiori, Barnet, & Miller, 1994; Haggbloom & Morris, 1994.)

The Generality of Reminder Treatments. Much has been learned about the facilitation of memory retrieval by reminder treatments (see Gordon, 1981; Spear, 1978, 1981; Spear & Riccio, 1994). As I have described, contextual cues are especially effective in stimulating memory retrieval (Gordon & Klein, 1994; Hitchcock & Rovee-Collier, 1996; Zhou & Riccio, 1996). In addition, various other reminder procedures have been found to facilitate recall, including exposure to the *unconditioned stimulus* (Hunt, 1997; MacArdy & Riccio, 1995; Miller, Jagielo, & Spear, 1991; Quartermain, McEwen, & Azmitia, 1970), exposure to the *reinforced conditioned stimulus* (CS+) (Gisquet-Verrier & Alexinsky, 1990; Gordon & Mowrer, 1980), and exposure to a *nonreinforced conditioned stimulus* (CS–) that was present during training (Campbell & Randall, 1976; Miller, Jagielo, & Spear, 1990a, 1991, 1992).

Reminder treatments can be used to reverse many instances of memory loss. (For a review, see Miller, Kasprow, & Schachtman, 1986.) For example, reminder treatments have been used to facilitate memory retrieval from short-term memory (Feldman & Gordon, 1979; Kasprow, 1987). They can remind older animals (and babies) of forgotten early-life experiences (for example, Campbell & Randall, 1976; Fagen & Rovee-Collier, 1983; Haroutunian & Riccio, 1979; Galluccio & Rovee-Collier, 1999; Richardson, Riccio, & Jonke, 1983). Reminder treatments can counteract stimulus-generalization decrements that occur when learned behavior is tested in a new situation (Gordon, McCracken, Dess-Beech, & Mowrer, 1981; Mowrer & Gordon, 1983). They also have been observed to increase the low levels of conditioned responding that typically occur in latent inhibition, overshadowing, and blocking procedures (Kasprow, Cacheiro, Balaz, & Miller, 1982; Kasprow, Catterson, Schachtman, & Miller, 1984; Miller, Jagielo, & Spear, 1990b; Schachtman, Gee, Kasprow, & Miller, 1983; see also Gordon, McGinnis, & Weaver, 1985).

Courtesy of N. E. Spear

N. E. Spear

Courtesy of W. C. Gordon

W. C. Gordon

BOX 11.2

GENES AND LEARNING

The nervous system is composed of billions of neurons interconnected by chemical connections called synapses. In Box 11.1, I described how learning can alter behavior by producing a change in the way a synapse operates. In some cases, learning may bring about a lasting increase in synaptic strength, yielding a form of long-term potentiation (LTP). In other cases, experience will result in a downregulation known as long-term depression (LTD).

The mechanisms that mediate changes in synaptic strength operate in phases. Initially, local molecular mechanisms produce short-term and rapid changes in synaptic strength. Additional processes are then activated that result in lasting memories. Establishing a long-term memory depends on the activation of genes that manufacture new protein products that produce a lasting change in how a synapse works.

Using drugs that block protein synthesis, researchers demonstrated many years ago that the manufacture of new proteins contributes to the formation of long-term memories (Davis & Squire, 1984). More recently, it has been established that the same is true for the lasting forms of LTP and LTD (Mayford & Kandel, 1999). Even learning in the invertebrate *Aplysia* (see Box 2.3) depends on gene expression.

Modern molecular biology has given us a host of new techniques that allow researchers to uncover the genes involved in learning. These studies have revealed that a variety of learning mechanisms depend on the induction of common genetic codes, genes that encode some biological universals that have been well conserved through evolution. Just as the mechanisms that underlie the generation of a neural signal (the action potential) are well conserved across species, so too may be the mechanisms that underlie synaptic plasticity.

Modern genetics has also given us new tools for studying the role of gene expression in learning. We can read the genetic code, identify the locus of the relevant genes, and experimentally manipulate how those genes operate. If we believe that a particular protein plays an essential role in learning, we can test this by using mice in which the relevant gene has been knocked out. This provides a new and unique window into the molecular mechanisms that underlie learning.

Silva and his colleagues have been at the forefront of this new technology, creating genetically engineered mice that exhibit specific deficits in the way they learn and remember (see review by Silva & Giese, 1998). One of the earliest experiments focused on the role of a protein known as CaMKII. One way a synapse can be strengthened is by allowing calcium (Ca^{++}) into the cell. Ca^{++} is an electrically charged particle that normally has a higher concentration outside of the neuron than inside. When Ca^{++} is allowed into the neuron by the NMDA receptor (see Figure 11.15), it engages CaMKII, which enhances synaptic efficacy by activating the AMPA receptors that mediate the neural signal. Silva created mice that lacked the gene that underlies the production of CaMKII within the hippocampus. From other studies, Silva knew that the hippocampus plays a critical role in learning about spatial relations. He reasoned that if CaMKII is critical for learning, then knockout mice that lack this gene should have difficulty remembering where a hidden platform is in a Morris water maze. That is precisely what occurred, providing a link between learning and a particular protein product.

A difficulty with studies of knockout mice is that the mice may not develop normally. When a gene is missing, other biochemical mechanisms can be enlisted that help the organism compensate for its deficiency. This could yield a brain that differs in a variety of ways from a normal brain. The abnormal neural environment may make it difficult to interpret the consequences of the genetic manipulation. Neuroscientists are solving this problem by making mice in which the expression of a gene can be experimentally controlled. An interesting application of this technology involves the creation of a transgenic mouse. Instead of losing a gene (a knockout), the transgenic mouse has an extra gene that makes a new protein product.

In one example, mice were engineered that made a mutant version of CaMKII that did not work properly. These mice did not exhibit normal LTP and exhibited a learning deficit in the Morris water maze (Mayford, Bach, Huang,

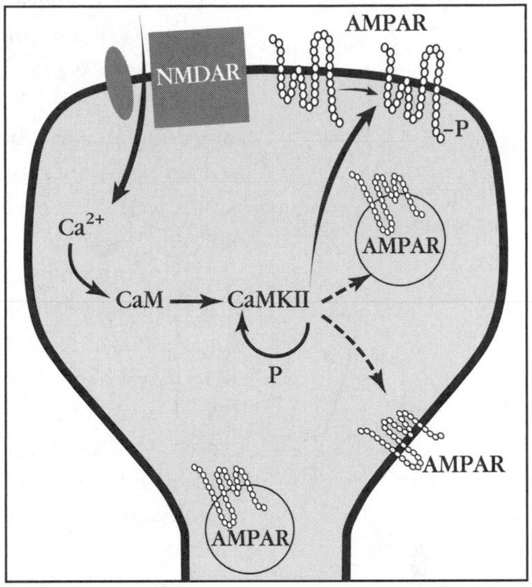

Figure 11.15 The molecular mechanisms that underlie long-term potentiation. The NMDA receptor allows CA++ to enter the cell, which engages the enzyme CaMKII. CaMKII plays a critical role in strengthening the synaptic response. It does so, in part, by awakening silent AMPA receptors. (Adapted from Malenka & Nicoll, 1999.)

Wang, Hawkins, & Kandel, 1996). The expression of the added gene in these mice was controlled by a molecular switch. This switch, which had been added by the researchers, was controlled by a novel chemical (doxycycline). To turn the switch off, and stop production of the mutant CaMKII, all the researchers had to do was add some doxycycline to the diet of the mice. When this was done, the mice once again exhibited normal LTP. They also recovered their ability to learn and remember spatial locations. As long as doxycycline was present, their brains worked normally. Only when this chemical was removed, and the mutant gene was expressed, was LTP and learning disrupted.

All of the genetic manipulations I described so far produced deficits in memory. Researchers are also exploring the possibility that modifying gene expression might improve memory. A good example is provided by a genetically engineered mouse named Doogie, after the ficticious TV boy genius, Doogie Howser. As I discussed in Box 11.1, the induction of LTP depends on the NMDA receptor. This receptor is formed from components (subunits), one of which changes with development. Early in development, animals have a subunit called NR2B that appears to promote the induction of LTP. In adults, this subunit is replaced by an alternative form (NR2A) that downregulates LTP. The change from the juvenile form (NR2B) to the adult form (NR2A) could make it more difficult for an adult animal to learn about new environmental relations. To explore this possibility, Tsien and his colleagues created mice that continued to make the juvenile form of the subunit (NR2B) into adulthood (Tang et al., 1999). As expected, these mice showed stronger LTP as adults. The mice also exhibited enhanced learning on an object recognition task and improved spatial memory in the Morris water maze. Across a range of tests, Doogie mice seemed smarter.

If the juvenile form of the NMDA receptor works better, why would nature replace it with one that undermines learning and memory? The answer is still being debated. Perhaps this change helps to protect some early memories that are crucial to survival. For example, once we have learned the words of our language, this information should not be readily unlearned. By enabling learning early in development, nature may open a critical window, only to close it later in life to help protect what was learned.

—J. W. Grau

FORGETTING

Forgetting is the flip side of memory. We are said to exhibit forgetting when memory fails and we don't respond in accordance with past experience or learning, but as Kraemer and Golding (1997) have argued, forgetting should not be viewed simply as the absence of remembering. Forgetting should instead be considered an important phenomenon in its own right (see also White, 2001). Forgetting can be adaptive because it increases behavioral variability. That behavioral variability is not a welcome experience when you cannot remember something on a test, but it can be useful when you move to a new job or a new city and have to learn new skills. Forgetting can also reduce the context specificity of learning and thereby permit learned behavior to occur in a broader range of situations (Riccio, Rabinowitz, & Axelrod, 1994).

The common experience is that failures of memory become more likely as time passes after a learning episode. However, it is not informative to view time as a "cause" of forgetting. As Piaget is reputed to have said, "Time is not a cause but a vehicle of causes." And there may be a variety of causes of forgetting. As I have described, memory mechanisms involve many different factors. Some of these concern coding and the acquisition of information. Others involve rehearsal and the retention of information. Still others involve processes of retrieval. Things can go wrong at any point along the way. Therefore, failures of memory, or forgetting, can occur for a variety of reasons.

Forgetting has been extensively investigated in the context of two types of phenomena—interference effects and retrograde amnesia. In the concluding sections of this chapter, I describe these phenomena in turn.

Proactive and Retroactive Interference

The most common sources of memory disruption arise from exposure to prominent stimuli either before or after the event that one is trying to remember. Consider meeting people at a party, for example. If the only new person you meet is Alice, chances are you will not have much trouble remembering her name. However, if you are introduced to a number of new people before and/or after meeting Alice, you may find it much harder to remember her name.

There are numerous well-documented and well-analyzed cases of **proactive interference**—situations in which memory for something is disrupted by earlier exposure to other information. In these cases, the interfering of information acts forward to disrupt the memory of a future target event. In cases of **retroactive interference,** memory for something is disrupted by subsequent exposure to other information. In these situations, the interfering stimulus acts backward to disrupt the memory of a preceding target event.

The mechanisms of proactive and retroactive interference have been extensively investigated in studies of human memory (Postman, 1971; Slamecka & Ceraso, 1960; Underwood, 1957). Proactive and retroactive interference have been also investigated in various animal memory paradigms. For examples of proactive interference, see Grant (1982, 2000), and Edhouse and White (1988a, 1988b). For examples of retroactive interference, see Harper and Garry (2000), Killeen (2001b), and Terry (1996).

Retrograde Amnesia

A sad and too frequent source of memory failure is severe head injury. For example, people who receive a concussion in a car accident often suffer memory loss. However, the amnesia is likely to be selective. They may forget how the injury occurred, where the accident took place, or who else was in the car at the time. But they will continue to remember their name and address, where they grew up, and what they prefer to eat for dessert. Thus, there is a gradient of memory loss, with forgetting limited to events that occurred close to the accident. This phenomenon is called **retrograde amnesia** (Russell & Nathan, 1946).

The clinical significance of retrograde amnesia resulting from closed-head injury received in traffic and sports accidents has encouraged investigators to develop techniques to study this phenomenon in laboratory animals. One experiment with laboratory rats, for example, examined the effects of closed-head injury on memory for a passive avoidance task (Zhou & Riccio, 1995). The rats received a single training trial in an experimental chamber that had two compartments, one white and the other black, separated by a sliding door. The rats were first confined in the white compartment for 15 seconds. The door was then opened allowing them to enter the black compartment. But as soon as the rats entered the black compartment, they encountered shock through the grid floor. The results of this single training trial were evaluated several days later, when the rats were again placed in the white compartment of the apparatus. This time when the door to the black compartment was opened, the rats were much slower to enter the black compartment. This hesitation was used as evidence of passive avoidance learning.

Courtesy of D. C. Riccio

D. C. Riccio

To evaluate the effects of closed-head injury, different groups of rats received a concussion at various times after the single conditioning trial. For one group, the concussion occurred 1 minute after the conditioning trial. For other groups, it occurred 6 hours, 1 day, 3 days, or 5 days later. Each of these groups was tested two days after the head injury. Two control groups did not receive a concussion and were tested at the same time as the 1-minute and 5-day experimental groups. The results of the experiment are summarized in Figure 11.16. The two control groups showed the maximum latencies (300 seconds) to enter the black compartment, indicating strong memory for the passive avoidance training trial. Strong learning was also evident in the subjects that received a concussion 5 days after the training trial. In contrast, a gradient of performance was evident in the other experimental

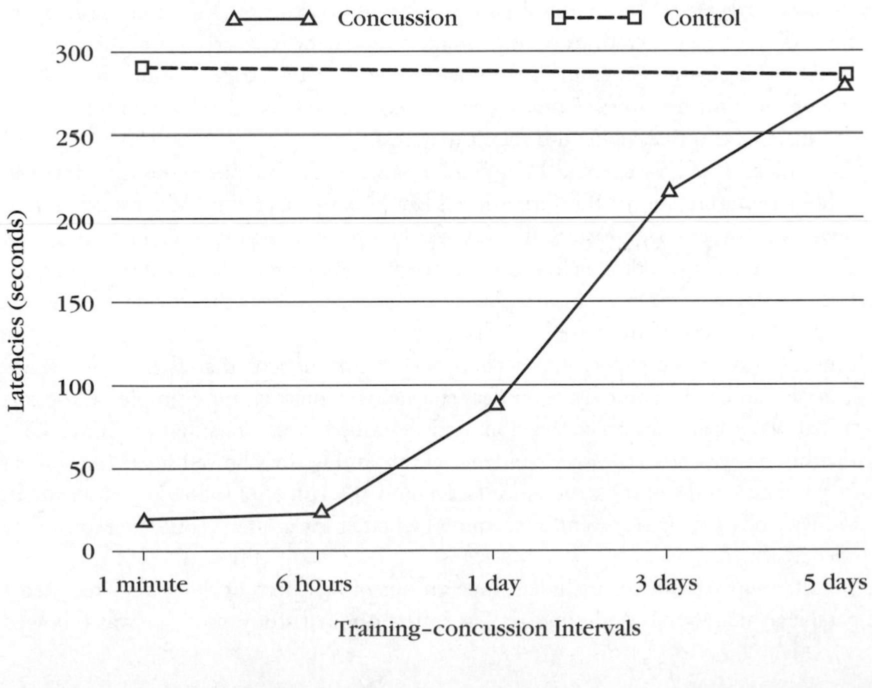

Figure 11.16 Median latencies to enter the black compartment after a passive avoidance conditioning trial. Control groups did not receive a concussion after the training trial. In contrast, each of the other groups received a concussion at intervals ranging from 1 minute to 5 days after conditioning. The concussion resulted in a retrograde amnesia for the passive avoidance task. (From Zhou & Riccio, 1995.)

groups. In general, less passive avoidance behavior occurred during the test session in groups that received shorter intervals between the training trial and the concussion. This illustrates the phenomenon on retrograde amnesia.

Many studies have provided convincing evidence of experimentally induced retrograde amnesia in a variety of learning tasks (for reviews, see McGaugh & Herz, 1972; Spear, 1978; Spear & Riccio, 1994). In addition, experiments have shown that retrograde amnesia can be produced by many different treatments that affect the nervous system, including anesthesia (McGaugh & Petrinovich, 1965); temporary cooling of the body, or hypothermia (Riccio, Hodges, & Randall, 1968); and injection of drugs that inhibit protein synthesis (Flexner, Flexner, & Stellar, 1963).

Why do various neural insults produce a graded loss of memory? The traditional explanation of retrograde amnesia involves the concept of **memory consolidation** (see McGaugh & Herz, 1972). According to the memory-consolidation hypothesis, when an event is first experienced, it enters a short-term, or temporary, memory store. While in short-term memory, the information is vulnerable and can be lost because of interfering stimuli or other disruptive events. However, if the proper conditions are met, the information gradually becomes consolidated into a relatively permanent form.

Memory consolidation is assumed to be a physiological process by which information is gradually transformed into a long-term or permanent state. Neurophysiological disturbances such as electroconvulsive shock, anesthesia, and body cooling are assumed to interfere with the consolidation process and thereby disrupt the transfer of information to long-term memory. Disruption of consolidation produces amnesia only for information stored in short-term memory. Once information has been transferred to long-term memory, it cannot be lost because of disruptions of consolidation. Amnesic agents presumably lead to loss of memory only for recently experienced events because only recent events are in short-term memory, and are thus susceptible to disruptions of consolidation.

Disruptions of performance caused by amnesic agents can also be explained in a very different way. According to this alternative account, amnesia results not from loss of the memory but from inability to retrieve or reactivate the memory (Lewis, 1979; Miller & Springer, 1973; Riccio & Richardson, 1984; Spear, 1973). This explanation is called the *retrieval-failure hypothesis.* The retrieval-failure hypothesis assumes that an amnesic agent alters the coding of new memories so as to make subsequent recovery of the information difficult. Thus, unlike the memory-consolidation view, the retrieval-failure hypothesis assumes that the information surrounding an amnesic episode is acquired and retained in memory, but in a form that makes it difficult to access.

What kinds of evidence would help decide between the memory-consolidation and retrieval-failure interpretations? If information is lost because of a failure of consolidation, it cannot ever be recovered. By contrast, the retrieval-failure view assumes that amnesia can be reversed if the proper procedure is found to reactivate the memory. To decide between the alternatives, researchers have to find techniques that can reverse the effects of amnesic agents. Several such procedures have been discovered.

Numerous experiments have shown that the memory deficits that characterize retrograde amnesia can be overcome by reminder treatments. Consider, for example, retrograde amnesia that was produced by a concussion. As I described earlier, rats that received a concussion within 3 days of their passive avoidance conditioning trial showed significant loss of memory for their conditioning experience (see Figure 11.16). In a follow-up experiment, Zhou and Riccio (1995, Experiment 3) examined whether the amnesia could be reversed by a reminder treatment.

The follow-up experiment included three groups of rats. Two of the groups received a single passive avoidance conditioning trial, as in the original study, and this was followed

1 minute later by a concussion. The third group was a "pseudo-training" group and received shock in another apparatus. All of the subjects were tested for their passive avoidance behavior 3 days later. However, shortly before this test, a brief shock was administered to one of the experimental groups in a novel environment to see if this US-alone reminder treatment would reverse the course of their amnesia. (The reminder treatment was also given to the pseudo-training group, but this was not expected to facilitate their recall since they did not learn the original task in the first place.)

The results of the experiment are summarized in Figure 11.17. The group that received a concussion after its training trial showed no evidence of learning. They stepped into the black compartment just as quickly during the test trial as they had during the training trial. This result confirms that the concussion produced amnesia. However, the amnesia was reversible. Subjects that received the concussion and were then given a US-alone reminder before the test showed strong passive avoidance performance. The results obtained with the pseudo-learning control group show that the strong passive avoidance performance of the second group was not due to new learning produced by the reminder treatment. The pseudo-learning group also received the reminder treatment but did not show evidence of passive avoidance behavior.

Results such as those in Figure 11.17 indicate that retrograde amnesia can be reversed by reminder treatments. Numerous similar studies have been conducted with similar results (see reviews by Gordon, 1981; Riccio & Richardson, 1984; Spear, 1978; Spear & Riccio, 1994). This body of evidence seriously calls into question the validity of consolidation failure as an explanation of retrograde amnesia. Rather, retrograde amnesia appears to be due to retrieval failure—the inability to retrieve information that was learned shortly before an amnesic treatment.

Interest in the consolidation hypothesis has been rekindled by recent findings that indicate that a recently activated memory is susceptible to the same kind of retrograde amnesia

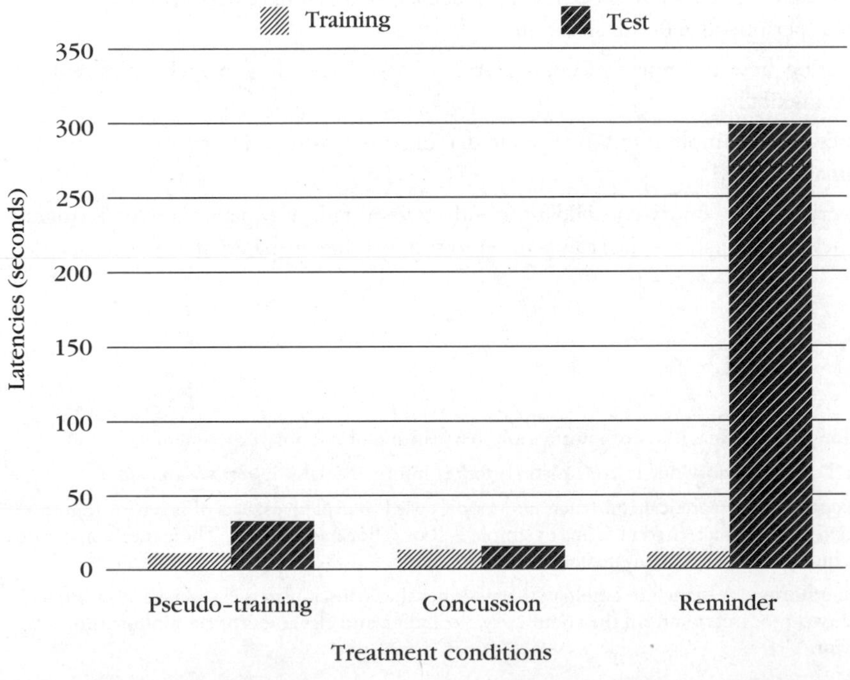

Figure 11.17 Effects of US-alone reminder treatment on recovery from amnesia for a passive avoidance training trial induced by a concussion. An increase in the response latency from training to testing is evidence of passive avoidance behavior. (Based on Zhou & Riccio, 1995.)

that can disrupt original learning (Nader, Schafe, & LeDoux, 2000). These data have been used to argue that memories have to be reconsolidated after each time that they are activated. As a number of commentators have pointed out, however, evidence contrary to the original consolidation hypothesis also presents problems for this reconsolidation hypothesis (for example, Miller & Matzel, 2000; Millin, Moody, & Riccio, 2001; Sara, 2000; see also Nader, Schafe, & LeDoux, 2000).

CONCLUDING COMMENTS

The study of memory processes is central to the understanding of animal cognition. Memory processes involve acquisition and coding of information, rehearsal and retention, and retrieval. Difficulties in any of these phases, or problems involving interactions among the phases, can result in failures of memory, or forgetting. Several ingenious techniques for the study of memory processes in animals have been developed in the past 30 years. These techniques have told us much about the coding of information, rehearsal processes, and retrieval processes. This information has, in turn, allowed us to better understand failures of memory that occur in interference paradigms and in retrograde amnesia.

SAMPLE QUESTIONS

1. Compare and contrast working memory and reference memory.
2. Describe the delayed-matching-to-sample procedure and alternative strategies that can be used to respond accurately in such a procedure. How can these response strategies be distinguished experimentally?
3. Describe the radial maze procedure and mechanisms that have been used to explain efficient performance in this situation.
4. Describe how retrospective coding and prospective coding may be differentiated experimentally?
5. Describe the complications involved in demonstrating directed forgetting in laboratory animals.
6. Describe the memory-consolidation and retrieval-failure explanations of retrograde amnesia and what evidence can be used to support one or the other hypothesis.

KEY TERMS

acquisition The original input of information in a learning or memory experiment.

amnesia Loss of memory due to concussion or other injury. (See also *retrograde amnesia.*)

animal cognition Theoretical constructs and models used to explain aspects of behavior that cannot be readily characterized in terms of simple S-R or reflex mechanisms. These mechanisms do not require consciousness, awareness, or intentionality.

cognitive ethology A branch of ethology that assumes that consciousness, awareness, and intentionality can be inferred from the complexity, flexibility, and cleverness of certain forms of behavior.

delayed matching to sample A procedure in which participants are reinforced for responding to a test stimulus that is the same as a sample stimulus that was presented some time earlier.

directed forgetting Forgetting that occurs because of a stimulus (a forget cue) that indicates that working memory will not be tested on that trial. Directed forgetting is an example of the stimulus control of memory.

memory A term used to characterize instances in which an organism's current behavior is determined by some aspect of its previous experience.

memory consolidation The establishment of a memory in relatively permanent form, or the transfer of information from short-term to long-term memory.

proactive interference Disruption of memory caused by exposure to stimuli before the event to be remembered.

procedural memory Memory that mediates the learning of behavioral and cognitive skills that are performed automatically, without conscious control, often reflecting knowledge about invariant relationships in the environment, such as CS-US contiguity (classical conditioning) or response-reinforcer contiguity (instrumental conditioning).

prospective memory Memory for an expected future event or response.

reference memory Long-term retention of background information necessary for successful use of incoming and recently acquired information. (Compare with *working memory.*)

rehearsal A theoretical process whereby information is maintained in an active state, available to influence behavior and/or the processing of other information.

retention interval The time between acquisition of information and a test of memory for that information.

retrieval The recovery of information from a memory store.

retrieval cues A stimulus related to an experience that facilitates the recall of other information related to that experience.

retrieval failure A deficit in recovering information from a memory store.

retroactive interference Disruption of memory caused by exposure to stimuli following the event to be remembered.

retrograde amnesia A gradient of memory loss going back in time from the occurrence of a major injury or physiological disturbance. Amnesia is greatest for events that took place closest to the time of injury.

retrospective memory Memory for a previously experienced event. Also called *retrospection.*

simultaneous matching to sample A procedure in which participants are reinforced for responding to a test stimulus that is the same as a sample stimulus. The sample and the test stimuli are presented at the same time. (Compare with *delayed matching to sample.*)

stimulus coding How a stimulus is represented in memory.

trace decay hypothesis The theoretical idea that exposure to a stimulus produces changes in the nervous system that gradually and automatically decrease after the stimulus has been terminated.

trials-unique procedure A matching-to-sample procedure in which different sample and comparison stimuli are used on each trial.

working memory Short-term retention of information that is needed for successful responding on the task at hand but not on subsequent (or previous) similar tasks. (Compare with *reference memory.*)

CHAPTER 12

ANIMAL COGNITION II: SPECIAL TOPICS

Chapter 12 explores a diversity of contemporary research areas in animal cognition involving the processing of various types of information. In each of these areas, it is important to consider basic conditioning mechanisms before accepting more complex cognitive interpretations of the behavior. This principle is nicely illustrated with transitive inference, the first area of research I discuss here. Transitive inference was initially thought to reflect complex cognitive processes, but recent research has provided a simpler associative account. Next, I describe a more specialized cognitive skill, memory (especially episodic memory) in food-storing birds. I then describe more widespread phenomena of animal cognition, including timing, serial pattern learning, and perceptual concept formation. In the last section of the chapter, I return to a more specialized form of cognition—namely, language—which is actually a collection of cognitive skills, some of which are clearly evident in a number of nonhuman species.

The various aspects of behavior discussed in Chapter 12 are not all reflections of a common underlying mechanism, nor are they all involved in the solution of a common behavioral problem or challenge to survival. However, they all involve major contemporary areas of research in animal cognition that have stimulated a great deal of interest. This interest has come in part because until recently the cognitive processes involved were considered to be characteristic primarily of human behavior. In addition, each of these areas of research has stimulated considerable controversy.

The controversies have centered on whether complex cognitive processes had to be postulated to explain the various behaviors that were observed. Opponents of cognitive interpretations have argued that the phenomena could be explained by traditional learning principles. By contrast, proponents of cognitive interpretations have argued that cognitive mechanisms provide simpler explanations for the phenomena and are more productive in stimulating new research. The work in this area has amply borne out this latter justification. Without a cognitive perspective, much of the research I describe in this chapter would never have been done, and many of the phenomena would never have been discovered. But, as the research on transitive inference has shown, not all cases of "intelligent" behavior require complex cognitive processes.

TRANSITIVE INFERENCE AND VALUE TRANSFER

Transitive inference refers to inferring that a set of stimuli is organized in a sequential order based on exposure to only two stimuli at a time. Consider, for example, the following puzzle. You have to figure out how to put five cards in order from "best" to "worst," but you are only given information about the cards in pairs. The five cards are labeled A, B, C, D, and E. During training trials, you are allowed to look at one pair of cards at a time. The training pairs are A-B, B-C, C-D, and D-E. Which stimulus is presented on the right or the left each time is varied randomly across trials, to prevent you from using position as a clue. With each stimulus pair, you are told that the card closer to the beginning of the alphabet is the better one. Thus, in a choice between A and B, you are told A is better than B (A+B–), but in a choice of B and C, you are told B is better than C (B+C–). In a choice between C and D, C is better than D (C+D–), and in a choice between D and E, D is better than E (D+E–). Could you figure out the order of the five cards from these paired trials, and what test would reveal your learning?

The critical test after training involves determining how a participant would respond during a test trial when she or he encountered the novel pair of stimuli, B versus D. Notice that during the training phase, cards B and D appeared equally often as "better" and "worse" cards. (The training pairs with these stimuli were A+B–, B+C–, C+D–, and D+E.) Based on how often cards B and D were "better" during training, there should be no basis for selecting between them. However, if during training you formed a mental representation of the sequence A through E, you should select B over D. This would be a transitive inferential choice.

Evidence of transitive inference was first obtained with chimpanzees (Gillan, 1981). Pairs of stimuli (AB, BC, CD, and DE) were presented at the same time to the chimpanzees. Which stimulus was "better" was indicated by providing food reinforcement for responding to that stimulus. Responding to the alternate ("worse") stimulus was not reinforced. Thus, just as in the card puzzle described above, the trials for the chimpanzees can be described as A+B–, B+C–, C+D–, and D+E–. After the subjects learned to perform with good accuracy on the stimulus pairs, they were tested in a choice between B and D.

They responded more to B than to D and this was considered evidence of "transitive inference," a form of complex cognition.

Since the chimpanzee experiment, transitive inference has also been demonstrated in pigeons. Furthermore, investigators have come to question the phenomenon as evidence of complex cognition. They have suggested that the phenomenon can be explained by the fairly elementary associative mechanism of *value transfer* (Couvillon & Bitterman, 1992; von Fersen, Wynne, Delius, & Staddon, 1991; Zentall & Sherburne, 1994). According to value transfer, a nonreinforced stimulus gains some "value" or excitatory strength through stimulus generalization if the stimulus is presented at the same time as another cue that is reinforced. Thus, when responding to A is reinforced in a choice between A and B, some generalized excitation also develops to B. That is, there is positive transfer from A+ to B– when these appear together. D will also gain some generalized excitation (or value transfer) on C+D– trials. However, C will have less value to transfer to D than A has to transfer to B. This is because C is reinforced only half the time it appears during training (B+C– and C+D–), whereas A is reinforced every time it appears (only in A+B–). Because B receives more value transfer than D during training, subjects will pick B over D during the test. (For additional studies of value transfer, see Clement & Zentall, 2000a; Dorrance, Kaiser, & Zentall, 1998; Lonon & Zentall, 1999; Zentall, Weaver, & Sherburne, 1996.)

The development of research on transitive inference is instructive because it illustrates that observers have to be careful in interpreting seemingly clever behavior as evidence of "complex" cognitive processes. On the face of it, transitive inference appears to require that subjects create a mental ordering of a series of stimuli based on their exposure to just pairs of stimuli. If that were in fact required to solve the task, it would represent fairly sophisticated cognitive activity. As the value transfer explanation indicates, however, a much simpler account of the behavior is available (and supported by experimental evidence). The concept of value transfer requires simply that the associative value of one stimulus generalize to a second stimulus that is present at the same time. Such generalization of associative value does not require sophisticated cognitive mechanisms.

MEMORY IN FOOD-STORING BIRDS

Memory in food-storing birds is another feat of cognition. A number of avian and mammalian species hoard food in various places during times of plenty and visit these caches later to recover the stored food items (for example, Barkley & Jacobs, 1998; Sherry, 1985, 1992; Shettleworth, 1995). One remarkable example of cache recovery is provided by the Clark's nutcracker (*Nucifraga columbiana*) (Balda & Turek, 1984; Kamil & Balda, 1990b). These birds live in alpine areas of the western United States and harvest seeds from pine cones in late summer and early autumn. They hide the seeds in underground caches and recover them months later in the winter and spring when other food sources are scarce. A Clark's nutcracker may store as many as 33,000 seeds in caches of 4 or 5 seeds each and recover several thousand of these during the next winter. Cache recovery also has been extensively investigated in the marsh tit (*Parus palustris*), a small, lively bird found in England, and in its North American relative, the chickadee (Shettleworth, 1983; Sherry, 1988). Marsh tits and chickadees store several hundred food items and recover them within a few days.

What mechanisms might food-storing birds use to recover food they previously placed in caches? One possibility is that they remember where they stored each food item and subsequently return to the remembered cache locations. However, before researchers can accept a memory interpretation, they have to rule out other possibilities. The possible alternatives to a memory interpretation are similar to those I discussed in the analysis of spatial memory in a radial maze. One possibility is that birds find caches by searching randomly among possible cache sites. Another possibility is that they store food only in particular types of locations and then go around to these favored places to recover the food items. They also may mark food-storage sites somehow and then look for these marks when it comes time to recover the food. Yet another possibility is that they are able to smell or see the stored food and identify caches in that way.

Ruling out nonmemory interpretations has required laboratory studies of the food-storing and retrieval behavior of the birds (for example, Kamil & Balda, 1990a, 1990b; Sherry, 1984; Sherry, Krebs, & Cowie, 1981; Shettleworth & Krebs, 1986). In one such laboratory study, for example, Kamil and Balda (1985) tested nutcrackers in a room that had a special floor with 180 recessed cups of sand (see left panel of Figure 12.1). After habituation to the experimental situation and while they were hungry, the birds were given three sessions during which they could store pinyon pine seeds in the sand cups. During each caching session, only 18 cups were available; the rest of the cups were covered with lids. This procedure forced the birds to store food in cups selected by the experimenter rather than in cups or locations the birds might have found especially attractive.

Starting 10 days after the seeds had been stored by the nutcrackers, four recovery sessions were conducted on successive days. During recovery sessions none of the 180 sand cups was covered with a lid, but seeds were located only in the cups where the birds had previously stored seeds. The results are summarized on the right side of Figure 12.1. Notice that on average the birds performed much better than chance in going to the sand cups where they had previously stored food. The correct locations could not be identified by disturbed sand because the experimenters raked the sand smooth at the start of each recovery session. Other tests showed that the correct locations were not identified by the smell of the

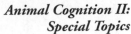

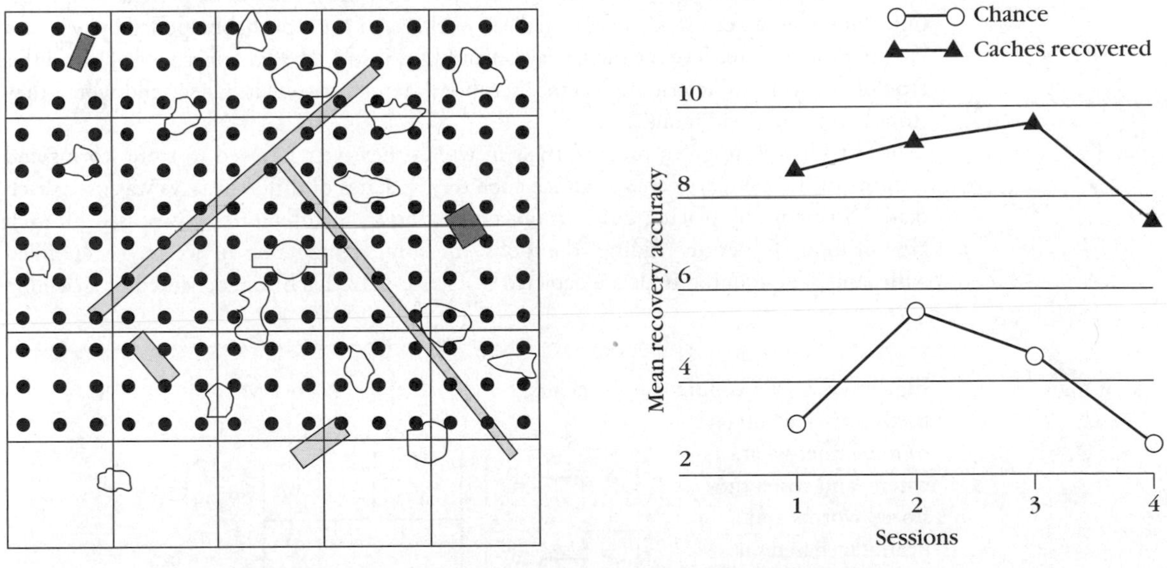

Figure 12.1 Left panel: Floor plan of the apparatus used by Kamil and Balda (1985) to test the spatial memory of Clark's nutcrackers. Filled circles represent sand cups. Other symbols represent rocks, logs, and a feeder in the middle. Right panel: Recovery accuracy, compared to chance, during four successive recovery sessions started 10 days after the birds stored pine seeds. (After Kamil & Balda, 1985.)

seeds buried in the sand because the birds visited places where they had previously stored food even if the food was removed before the test session. These control studies indicate that cache recovery reflects long-lasting spatial memory.

Having established that memory mechanisms are responsible for the cache-recovery behavior of food-storing birds, investigators turned their attention to identifying exactly what kinds of information are retained about a food-caching episode. It is clear that the birds remember *where* they previously stored food items, because without that information they could not return to the location of the stored items. How animals manage to return to locations where they previously stored or found food is the subject of studies of *spatial navigation.* Recent experiments have shown that Clark's nutcrackers use landmarks and the geometric relations between landmarks to guide their spatial navigation (Gibson & Kamil, 2001; Jones & Kamil, 2001; Kamil & Jones, 2000; for similar studies with rats, see Brown & Terrinoni, 1996; Brown, DiGello, Milewski, Wilson, & Kozak, 2000; Greene & Cook, 1997).

In addition to remembering *where* they stored food, do the birds also remember *what* type of food they stored, and *when* they stored it? Clayton and Dickinson have been examining these questions in a series of experiments with scrub jays. If you store several different food items in a number of places, why should you care about which type of food is stored where? If you find all of the food items equally acceptable, then there is no reason to keep track of where specific food items are located. However, if you prefer one food over another, then knowing the location of each type of food will be useful. If you know where each type of food is located, you can retrieve the foods you like best before retrieving the less preferred items.

Why might it be useful to know *when* you stored a particular type of food? Information about the time of storage is useful if the food is likely to spoil or deteriorate the longer it is in storage. Without refrigeration, meat spoils much faster than nuts, for example. If you like meat better than nuts, which food you retrieve will depend on how long each has been stored. If both foods were stored less than an hour ago, the meat will be preferable over the nuts. However, if both foods were stored last week, the meat is probably spoiled by now and you might as well retrieve the nuts. Clayton and Dickinson (1999a, Experiment 1) used this type of situation to determine whether scrub jays remember what, when, and where they stored particular food items.

The birds were given practice trials in which they were allowed to store worms and peanuts in the compartments of an ice cube tray. A series of different trays was used, each made distinctive by placing different objects around it. A different tray was used for each type of food. To permit "hiding" the foods, the compartments of the ice trays were filled with sand. The training trials are depicted in Figure 12.2. Each trial consisted of a caching

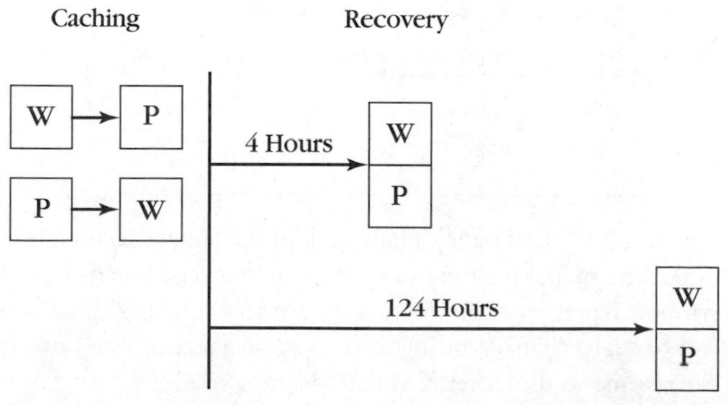

Figure 12.2 Procedure used to train scrub jays to remember what, where, and when they stored worms and peanuts. (Based on Clayton & Dickinson, 1999a.)

period, followed by a recovery period that occurred either 4 hours or 124 hours later. During the caching episodes one type of food was available at a time, and the order of the two foods was counterbalanced. During the recovery period, both foods were available simultaneously. On training trials with a 4-hour delay between caching and recovery, neither food deteriorated by the time the recovery or choice period occurred. In contrast, on training trials with the 124-hour delay between caching and recovery, the worms were in pretty bad shape by the time the recovery occurred.

As training progressed, the birds learned to select the worms during the recovery period if recovery was permitted after the 4-hour delay. If the recovery period was delayed 124 hours, the birds selected the peanuts instead. However, this behavior could have been cued by the smell of the peanut and worm caches during the recovery period. To prevent responding on the basis of olfactory cues, test trials were conducted at the end of the experiment during which fresh sand was put in the trays and all food was removed. The results of those test trials are summarized in Figure 12.3. Data for the scrub jays that learned that worms deteriorate if stored for 124 hours are presented in the left panel. (This was the "deteriorate" group.) As expected, these birds searched more in the worm tray than the peanut tray if the choice test occurred 4 hours after caching of the worms. In contrast, they searched more in the peanut tray than in the worm tray if the worms had been stored 124 hours earlier.

The right panel shows the results for a second group of scrub jays ("replenish") that received a different training history. For the "replenish" group, the fresh worms were always provided during the recovery or choice periods during training. Therefore, these birds did not get a chance to learn that worms deteriorate with time. Consistent with their training

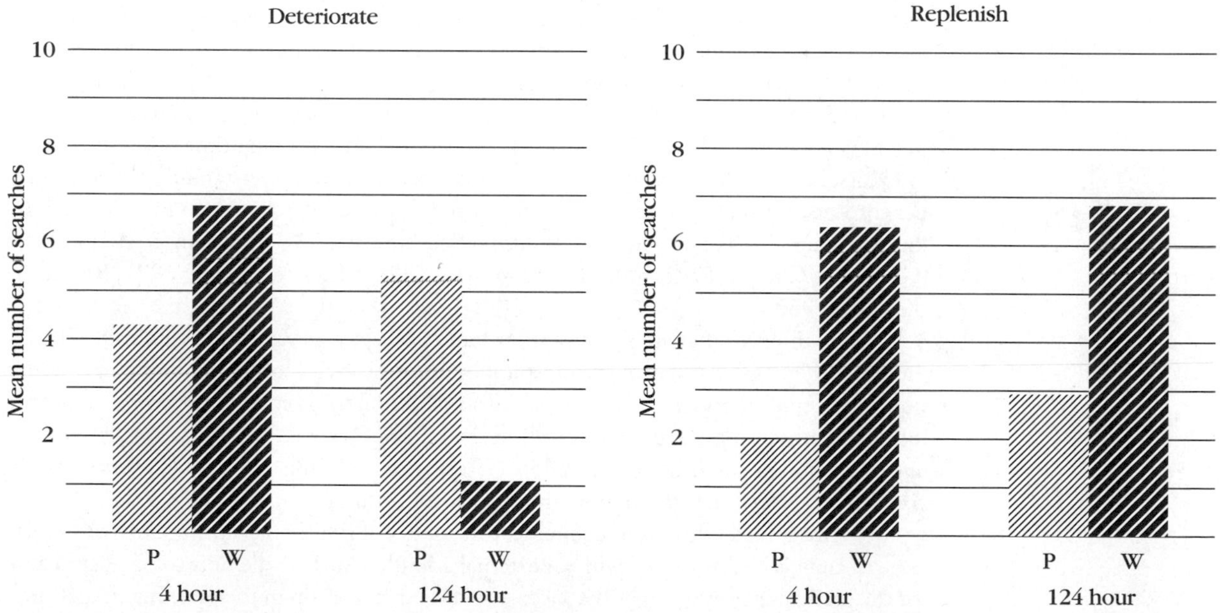

Figure 12.3 Searching for worms versus peanuts in scrub jays that previously learned that worms deteriorate with time ("deteriorate" group, top panel) and scrub jays for which worms were always replenished ("replenish" group, bottom panel). The choice tests were conducted 4 hours or 124 hours after the caching of worms. (Based on Clayton & Dickinson, 1999a.)

history, the "replenish" group showed a preference for worms whether caching had occurred 4 hours or 124 hours before the recovery or choice period.

The scrub jays in the Clayton and Dickinson study could not have returned to the compartments in which food had been stored if they had not remembered *where* they had stored the foods. The fact that the birds distinguished between the worm and peanut storage sites indicates that they remembered *what* type of food was stored in each site. The fact that the "deteriorate" group changed its choice depending on how long ago the worms had been stored indicates that they also remember *when* the food had been stored. These results indicate that scrub jays are able to remember not only *what* food items they stored, but *where* and *when* they stored them (see also Clayton & Dickinson, 1998, 1999b; Clayton, Yu, & Dickinson, 2001). Evidently scrub jays can remember many of the specifics of a particular caching episode. This is analogous to human episodic or declarative memory (Griffiths, Dickinson, & Clayton, 1999).

TIMING

Cache recovery is a highly specialized type of behavior, exhibited by a limited number of species. Timing, in contrast, is universally relevant. Everything occurs across time. All experience is embedded in a temporal context. Some events occur closely together; others are separated by longer intervals. In either case, the effects of stimuli are determined by their durations and distribution in time.

I have described numerous aspects of conditioning and learning that reflect the timing of events. Habituation, sensitization, and spontaneous recovery (Chapter 2) are all time-dependent effects. Pavlovian conditioning critically depends on the temporal relation between conditioned and unconditioned stimuli (Chapter 3), instrumental conditioning depends on the temporal relation between response and reinforcer (Chapter 5), and some schedules of reinforcement involve important temporal factors (Chapter 6). There are also important time-dependent effects in avoidance learning (Chapter 10) and memory (Chapter 11). These and related phenomena have been known for a long time. Only in the past 30 years, however, has substantial progress been made toward understanding the psychological processes that are responsible for the temporal control of behavior in human and nonhuman animals. (For reviews, see Bradshaw & Szabadi, 1997; Gibbon & Allan, 1984; Gibbon & Church, 1992; Killeen & Fetterman, 1988; Maier & Church, 1991; Richelle & Lejeune, 1980.)

Time intervals that are significant for biological systems vary greatly in scale. The 24-hour day/night cycle is one of the most important time cycles for biological systems. Other important time intervals operate on the order of fractions of a second (different components of the heartbeat, for example). Intervals in the range of seconds (and occasionally minutes) are important in conditioning procedures. Timing on this order, referred to as *interval timing*, has captivated the attention of investigators of learning.

A critical methodological requirement in studies of timing is to make sure that the passage of time is not correlated with an external stimulus, such as the noise of a clock ticking or the gradual increase in light that occurs as the sun comes up in the morning. Experimental situations have to be set up carefully to eliminate time-related external stimuli that might inadvertently "tip off" the organism and permit accurate responding without the use of an internal timing process. This methodological requirement is similar to that encountered in tests for memory. Like tests for memory, tests for timing have to make sure that the behavior is mediated by the internal cognitive process of interest rather than external cues or signals.

Techniques for the Measurement of Timing Behavior

Various powerful techniques have been developed to investigate timing in human and nonhuman animals (see review by Killeen, Fetterman, & Bizo, 1997). Some tasks involve **duration estimation.** A duration estimation task is basically a discrimination procedure in which the discriminative stimulus is the duration of an event. One study (Fetterman, 1995), for example, employed a modified matching-to-sample procedure. Pigeons were trained in an experimental chamber that had three pecking keys arranged in a row. The sample stimulus at the start of the trial was an amber light presented on the center key for either 2 seconds or 10 seconds. The sample was followed by illumination of one side key with a red light and the other side key with a green light. If the sample on that trial had been short (the 2-second stimulus), pecks on the red key were reinforced. If the sample had been long (the 10-second stimulus), pecks on the green key were reinforced. Pigeons and rats can learn to perform accurately in such tasks without too much difficulty (see also Church, Getty, & Lerner, 1976; Wasserman, DeLong, & Larew, 1984; for studies of duration estimation with people, see, for example, Wearden & Ferrara, 1996; Ferrara, Lejeune, & Wearden, 1997).

Other useful techniques for the study of timing have involved duration production instead of duration estimation. One popular technique, called the **peak procedure,** involves a discrete-trial variation of a fixed interval schedule. (Fixed interval schedules were described in Chapter 6.) Each trial begins with the presentation of a discriminative stimulus, a noise or a light. A specified duration after the start of the trial stimulus, a food pellet is set up, or made ready for delivery. Once the food pellet has been set up, the subject can obtain it by performing a specified instrumental response.

A study by Roberts (1981) nicely illustrates use of the peak procedure to investigate timing in laboratory rats. The subjects were tested in a standard lever-press chamber housed in a sound-attenuating enclosure to minimize extraneous stimuli. Some trials began with a light; others began with a noise. In the presence of the light, food was set up after 20 seconds; in the presence of the noise, food was set up after 40 seconds. Most of the trials ended when the rats responded and obtained the food pellet. However, some of the trials were designated as test trials and continued for 80 seconds or more and ended without food reward. These extralong trials were included to see how the participants would respond after the usual time of reinforcement had passed.

Figure 12.4 summarizes the results of the experiment in terms of rates of responding at various points during the test trials. The figure shows that during the 20-second signal, the highest rate of responding occurred around 20 seconds into the trial. By contrast, during the 40-second signal, the highest rate of responding occurred around 40 seconds into the

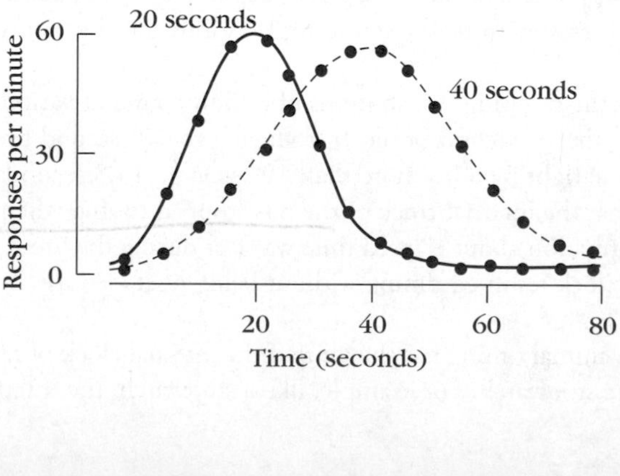

Figure 12.4 Rate of responding at various times during nonreinforced test trials. During training, food became available for delivery after 20 seconds in the presence of one stimulus (solid line) and after 40 seconds in the presence of another stimulus (dashed line). (From "Isolation of an Internal Clock," by S. Roberts, 1981, *Journal of Experimental Psychology: Animal Behavior Processes, 7,* pp. 242–268. Copyright © 1981 by the American Psychological Association. Reprinted by permission.)

trial. The results were remarkably orderly. The peak response rates occurred near the times that food became available during training, with lower response rates evident before and after that point. These features make the peak procedure especially useful in animal studies of timing. It should be noted, however, that results like those shown in Figure 12.4 emerge only after extensive training that includes numerous nonreinforced test trials that extend beyond the time when the reinforcer is usually set up (Kirkpatrick-Steger, Miller, Betti, & Wasserman, 1996; Papini & Hollingsworth, 1998; see also Cheng & Westwood, 1993; Cheng, Westwood, & Crystal, 1993; Church, Miller, Meck, & Gibbon, 1991; Church, Meck, & Gibbon, 1994).

The Concept of an Internal Clock

Results like those presented in Figure 12.4 also have been obtained with human participants (Rakitin, Gibbon, Penney, Malapani, Hinton, & Meck, 1998; Wearden & McShane, 1988) and clearly indicate that behavior can be exquisitely tuned to the passage of time. How might such findings be interpreted? An almost irresistible interpretation has been to assume that organisms use an internal clock and respond differentially based on the readings of this internal clock. Although the assumption of an internal clock may seem a bit fanciful at first glance, the suggestion is not that animals have a pocket watch that they can pull out and read now and then. Rather, the suggestion is that organisms have a timing mechanism localized somewhere in the nervous system that has clocklike properties.

Why should we entertain the possibility that organisms have an internal clock? The advantage of such a hypothesis is that it helps organize research. As Church (1978) pointed out, the concept of an internal clock may simplify explanation and discussion of instances of behavior controlled by time cues. The concept of a clock can also stimulate questions about animal timing that we would not be likely to ask otherwise, as I discuss shortly. Finally, an internal clock may be a physiological reality. We are more likely to find a biological clock if we first postulate its existence and investigate its properties at a behavioral level (for example, Hinton & Meck, 1997; Matell & Meck, 2000).

Characteristics of the Internal Clock

Courtesy of R. M. Church

R. M. Church

If the concept of an internal clock is useful in explaining results of the peak procedure and other timing situations, we should be able to use the concept to generate interesting research questions. We may ask, for example, whether the clock can be stopped and restarted without loss of information about how much time has already elapsed. Roberts (1981) designed an experiment to answer this question (see also Roberts & Church, 1978). The experimental chamber used was ordinarily dark. Each trial started with the presentation of a light, and food was set up 40 seconds after the start of the trial. On special test trials without food reinforcement, the light was turned off for 10 seconds, beginning 10 seconds after the start of the trial. Roberts was interested in how the interruption influenced when the rats showed their peak responding.

Figure 12.5 shows the resulting distributions of response rates at various times during trials with and without the 10-second break. Introducing the 10-second break shifted the peak response rate to the right by a bit more than 10 seconds (13.3 seconds, to be exact). These results suggest that the internal clock of the rats stopped timing when the break was introduced. Some information about elapsed time was lost during the break, but when the stimulus resumed, the clock resumed timing without being reset (see also de Vaca, Brown, & Hemmes, 1994).

Other research on animal timing has shown that the internal clock of rats has many of the same properties as a stopwatch. For example, like a stopwatch, the internal clock mea-

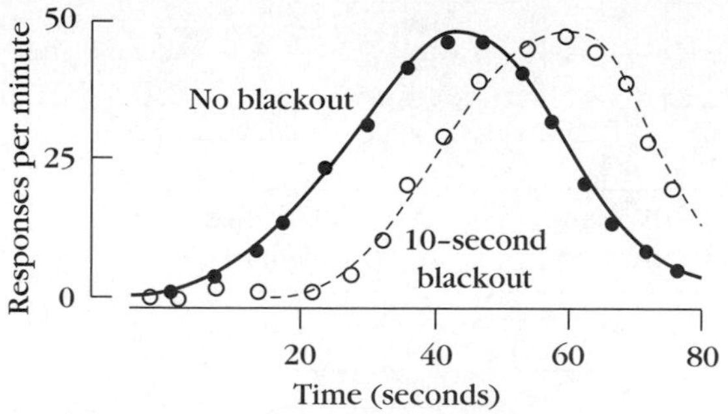

Figure 12.5 Rate of responding as a function of time during a signal in the presence of which food was set up after 40 seconds. On some trials, the signal was interrupted for a 10-second blackout period (dashed line). On other trials, no blackout occurred (solid line). (From "Isolation of an Internal Clock," by S. Roberts, 1981, *Journal of Experimental Psychology: Animal Behavior Processes, 7,* pp. 242–268. Copyright © 1981 by the American Psychological Association. Reprinted by permission.)

sures how much time has elapsed from the start of a stimulus (rather than how much time remains until the stimulus usually ends). Rats seem to use the same internal clock to measure the duration of stimuli from different sensory modalities (visual and auditory); they also use the same clock and clock speed to measure intervals of different durations (Meck & Church, 1982; Roberts, 1981, 1982; Roberts & Church, 1978). In contrast to rats, pigeons appear to use different clocks to measure the duration of visual and auditory stimuli (Brown, Hemmes, & de Vaca, 1992; Roberts, Cheng, & Cohen, 1989; Santi, Stanford, & Coyle, 1998).

Investigators have also started studying what determines the speed and accuracy of the internal clock. Increasing the rate of food reinforcement appears to increase the speed of the internal clock (Bizo & White, 1994, 1995a, 1995b; MacEwen & Killeen, 1991). The speed of the clock is also altered by diet (Meck & Church, 1987b), body temperature (Wearden & Penton-Voak, 1995), and psychoactive drugs. For example, methamphetamine has been observed to increase the speed of the internal clock, whereas other drugs, such as haloperidol, have been noted to decrease clock speed (see Maricq, Roberts, & Church, 1981; Meck, 1983; Meck & Church, 1987a).

Models of Timing

So far I have considered the notion of an internal clock somewhat loosely. What might be the details of a mechanism that permits organisms to respond on the basis of temporal information? This has been one of the thorniest theoretical questions in behavior theory. Time is not a physical reality. It is a human invention that helps us characterize certain aspects of our environment. We cannot see time; we can only see events that are distributed in time. Given that time itself is a conceptual abstraction, models of how organisms tell and use time are even more abstract.

Information Processing Model of Timing. The first and most influential detailed account of timing is the information processing model proposed by Gibbon and Church (1984) (see also Gibbon, Church, & Meck, 1984; Church, Meck, & Gibbon, 1994). The model (also known as *scalar expectancy theory* or SET) is depicted in Figure 12.6. It assumes

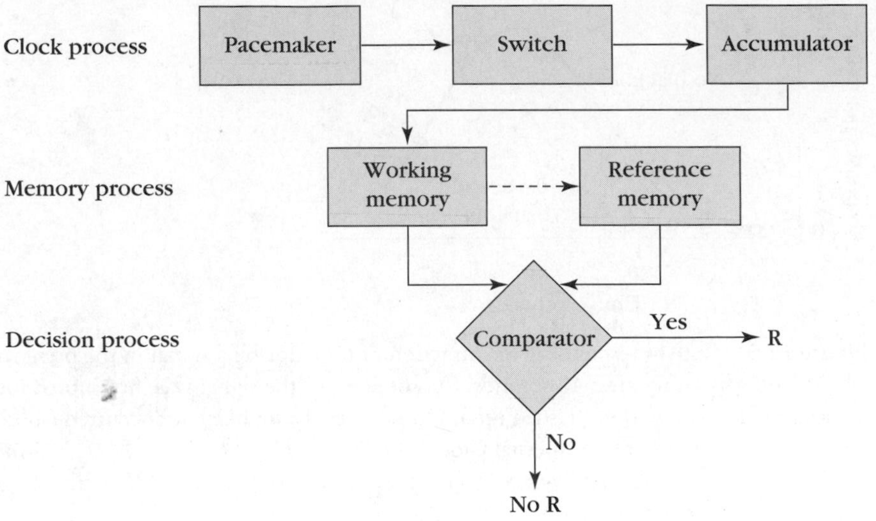

Figure 12.6 Diagram of an information processing model of timing. (From "Sources of Variance in an Information Processing Theory of Timing," by J. Gibbon and R. M. Church. In H. L. Roitblat, T. G. Bever, and H. S. Terrace [Eds.], 1984, *Animal Cognition.* Copyright © 1984 Lawrence Erlbaum and Associates. Reprinted by permission.)

that interval timing is the product of three independent processes: a clock process, a memory process, and a decision process.

The clock process provides information about the duration of elapsed time. A key component of the clock process is a pacemaker that generates pulses at a certain rate (something like the beating of a metronome). The pacemaker pulses are fed to a switch, which is opened by the start of the interval to be timed. Opening the switch allows the pacemaker pulses to go to an accumulator that counts the number of pulses that come through. When the interval to be timed ends, the switch closes, thereby blocking any further accumulations of pacemaker pulses. Thus, the accumulator adds up the number of pulses that occurred during the timed interval. The greater the number of accumulated pulses, the longer the interval.

The number of accumulated pulses is then relayed to the memory process. The memory process thereby obtains information about the duration of the current stimulus. This information is stored in working memory. The memory process is also assumed to have information about the duration of similar stimuli in reference memory from past training. The contents of working and reference memory are then compared in the decision process, and this comparison provides the basis for the individual's response. For example, in the peak procedure, if the time information in working memory matches the information in reference memory concerning availability of reinforcement, the decision is to respond. If information in working and reference memory does not match closely enough, the decision is to not respond. This mechanism produces a peak response rate close to the time when reinforcement is set up.

A detailed hypothetical model of timing is necessary to guide analyses of fine-grained details of timing behavior (see Church, Meck, & Gibbon, 1994; Gibbon & Church, 1984). The model also helps explain different ways in which timing behavior can be altered. Evidence, for example, suggests that certain drugs alter timing behavior by changing the speed of the internal clock (altering the frequency of impulses generated by the pacemaker). By contrast, other drugs change timing behavior by altering the memory process, the remembered duration of past time intervals (Meck, 1983). These contrasting influences on timing behavior would be difficult to interpret without a model that distinguishes a clock process from a memory process.

The information processing model of timing has been useful in guiding our thinking about how timing might be accomplished and has been successfully applied to many experimental results. However, the theory has not been without its critics. The most vigorous challenge has come from Staddon and Higa (1999) who argued that key predictions of the model do not require a pacemaker and accumulator process (see also Staddon & Higa, 1996). The resultant discourse (for example, Donahoe & Burgos, 1999; Gallistel, 1999; Gibbon, 1999; Staddon, Higa, & Chelaru, 1999; Zeiler, 1999) has helped to identify critical theoretical issues and has also increased the range of explanatory models that are being considered in efforts to explain timing. It is unclear how these controversies will be resolved, but one can be sure that the debate will stimulate important new research and theoretical development.

Behavioral Theory of Timing. A prominent alternative to the Gibbon-Church information processing model was offered by Killeen and Fetterman (1988, 1993; see also Killeen, 1991; Killeen, Fetterman, & Bizo, 1997; Machado, 1997) who characterized the timing process in more behavioral terms. This behavioral theory of timing (BeT) follows the Gibbon-Church model in postulating the existence of a pacemaker. However, the role of the pacemaker in BeT is quite different. BeT also characterizes the memory and decision processes differently (see especially Machado, 1997).

Arizona State University photo

P. R. Killeen

The behavioral theory of timing is based on the observation that situations in which the primary basis for the delivery of a reinforcer is the passage of time produce systematic time–related activities. These activities are akin to the pacing or finger tapping that people engage in during periods of forced waiting. In experimental situations these activities have been called **adjunctive behaviors** because they are not specifically required to pass the time but seem to emerge automatically when organisms are forced to wait for something important.

Clear examples of adjunctive behavior are evident in situations in which food is presented periodically at predictable intervals, say every 15 seconds. As I described in Chapter 5 (see discussion of "Skinner's superstition experiment" in Chapter 5), the feeding system (and its accompanying foraging responses) is activated in food-deprived animals that are periodically given small portions of food. Behavior under these circumstances reflects preorganized species-typical foraging and feeding activities (Silva & Timberlake, 1998; Timberlake, 2001). Different behaviors occur depending on when food was last delivered and when food is going to occur again. Just after the delivery of food, the organism is assumed to display *postfood focal search* responses that involve activities near the food cup. In the middle of the interval between food deliveries (when the subjects are least likely to get food), *general search* responses are evident that take the subject away from the food cup. As time for the next food delivery approaches, subjects exhibit *prefood focal search* responses that bring the subject back to the food cup. (General search and prefood focal search responses have been also called **interim** and **terminal** responses [Staddon & Simmelhag, 1971].)

The behavioral theory of timing focuses on the successive behavioral states that are activated by periodic presentations of food. Because different responses emerge at different intervals in a forced waiting period, these contrasting responses can be used to tell time. The successive adjunctive responses are assumed to reflect a pacemaker or clock process. According to the behavioral theory of timing, participants in a timing experiment learn to use their adjunctive responses as discriminative stimuli for the experimentally required timing responses. Thus, instead of reading an internal clock, participants are assumed to "read" their adjunctive behavior to tell time.

If reading a clock basically consists of reading one's own adjunctive behavior, then we should be able to observe the timing mechanism by carefully observing an organism's adjunctive behaviors in a timing task. Thus, the behavior theory of timing should be easy to prove or disprove by direct observation. Based on this, one might argue that the behavioral theory of timing is preferable over the information processing model because more of its mechanisms are accessible to direct observation. Unfortunately, this apparent transparency is illusory. BeT is no easier to prove or disprove than the information processing theory. As Fetterman, Killeen, and Hall (1998) pointed out, if an investigator fails to find the adjunctive responses that are consistent with the theory, one can argue that the investigators did not look carefully enough. On the other hand, if the postulated adjunctive responses are found in a particular experiment, that does not prove that adjunctive responses are necessary for timing in other situations. Nevertheless, careful observations of the behavior of subjects in timing tasks have provided data supportive of BeT (for example, Lejeune, Cornet, Ferreira, & Wearden, 1998). In addition, in some cases adjunctive responses are better predictors of timing behavior than the actual passage of time (Fetterman et al., 1998).

SERIAL PATTERN LEARNING

Time is one ubiquitous characteristic of events in the environment. Another is serial order. Stimuli rarely occur randomly or independently of each other. Rather, many aspects of the environment involve orderly sequences of events. One thing leads to the next in a predictable fashion. Stimuli are arranged in orderly sequences as you walk from one end of a street to the other, as you work to open a package, or as you eat dinner, from the appetizer to the dessert. Stimulus order is also very important in language. "The hunters ate the bear" is very different from "The bear ate the hunters." Investigators of animal cognition have been interested in whether animals recognize order in a series of stimuli, whether they can form a representation of the serial order of stimuli, and what mechanisms they use to respond correctly to a series of stimuli.

Possible Bases of Serial Pattern Behavior

There are several possible ways in which to respond to a series of stimuli. By way of illustration, consider playing through a six-hole miniature golf course, a schematic of which is shown to the left in Figure 12.7. Each hole involves a unique set of stimuli and may be represented by letters of the alphabet: A, B, C, D, E, and F. Each hole also requires a unique response—a unique way in which the ball must be hit to get it into the hole. Let's label the responses R1, R2, . . . , R6. In playing the course, you have to go in order from the first to the last hole, A→F. In addition, you have to make the correct response on each hole: R1 on hole A, R2 on B, and so on.

How might you learn to play the course successfully? The simplest way would be to learn which response goes with which stimulus. This would involve learning a set of S-R associations: A-R1, B-R2, . . . , F-R6. In the presence of A, you would automatically make R1, which would get you to stimulus B; in the presence of B, you would automatically make R2, which would get you to C; in the presence of C, you would automatically make R3, which would get you to D, and so on. Such a mechanism is called a **response chain.** In a response chain, each response produces the stimulus for the next response in the sequence, and correct responses occur because the organism has learned a series of S-R associations.

Although a response chain can result in responding appropriately to a series of stimuli, it does not require learning the stimulus sequence or forming a mental representation of the order in which the stimuli or responses occur. Response chains do not require cognitive

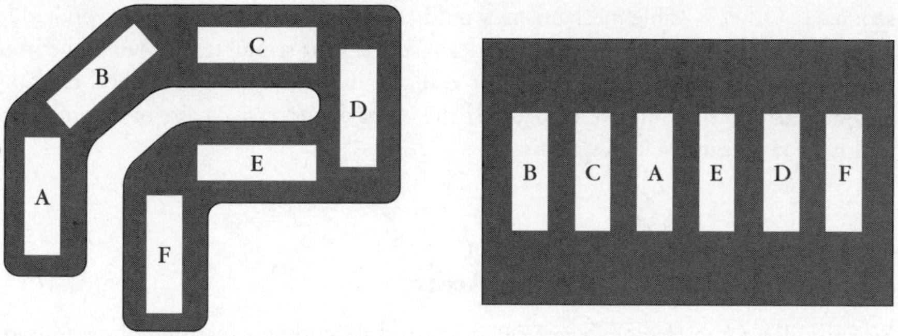

Figure 12.7 Two possible layouts of a six-hole miniature golf course. A sequential arrangement is shown on the left, and a simultaneous arrangement is shown on the right.

mechanisms any more complex than S-R associations. A response-chain strategy works perfectly well on the usual miniature golf course, because the successive holes are laid out so that you are forced to go through them in the correct sequence, A→F.

Now, consider a course with a different layout. The rules are the same in that you have to play in order from A to F, but this course is laid out in such a way that you are not forced to go in that order. Imagine having the holes lined up next to each other in a random order on a playing field, as shown to the right in Figure 12.7. After having played hole A, for example, your movement would not be restricted to hole B. You could go to any other hole next. To earn points, however, you would still have to play B after having finished with A, and then go to C, then D, and so on. Learning a series of stimulus-response associations (A-R1, B-R2, and so on) would not be enough to succeed on such a course. Even if someone got you started at A, after playing hole A, you would not know where to go next because you would be confronted with the full array of possibilities, not just B.

What would you have to learn to respond in the correct sequence with a simultaneous stimulus array? This time, you would be forced to learn something about the order of the stimuli. You could get by with just knowing the order of successive pairs of stimuli. You could learn that A is followed by B, B is followed by C, and so forth. These would be a set of independent stimulus-stimulus associations (A-B, B-C, C-D, and so on). This type of mechanism is called **paired-associate learning.** Once you know the correct independent paired associates, having played hole A, you would know to go to B; having played B, you would know to go to C; and so on until you had completed the course.

Obviously, learning more than just the order of successive pairs of stimuli would also enable you to perform the task accurately. At the extreme, you might form a mental representation of the entire sequence: A-B-C-D-E-F. This alternative is called **serial representation learning.** A serial representation can be formed in different ways. One possibility is to string together a series of paired associates, such that A activates the representation of B, which in turn activates the representation of C, and so forth. Thus, a serial representation could consist of a chain of paired associates. Alternatively, you could learn the particular ordinal position of each stimulus. This would involve learning that stimulus A is in position 1, B is in position 2, and so forth.

How might we decide among possible mechanisms of serial pattern behavior? An especially powerful technique involves presenting carefully constructed test trials after training. Returning to the simultaneous layout of the miniature golf course (right side of Figure 12.7), consider being given a choice between holes C and E after having learned to respond to the entire sequence, A→F, in the correct order. In a choice between C and E, which hole would you play first? If you had learned a representation of the entire stimulus sequence, you could respond without difficulty because you would know that C occurs before E in the sequence. Other possible mechanisms would create errors. For example, if you had learned a response chain in which one response leads to the next stimulus, you would be in trouble because the response preceding C is not available in a choice of only C and E. You would also be in trouble if you had learned just the order of successive pairs of stimuli because C and E do not form a successive pair.

Courtesy of Donald A. Dewsbury

H. S. Terrace

Tests with Subsets after Training with a Simultaneous Stimulus Array

Several different techniques have been developed to study the learning of serial representations in animals (for example, Hulse, 1978; Roitblat, Bever, Helweg, & Harley, 1991; Roitblat, Scopatz, Bever, 1987; Terrace, 1986a, 1986b). Straub and Terrace (1981) introduced the technique of training animals with a set of stimuli presented in a simultaneous array and then testing them with subsets of those stimuli (see also Terrace, 1987). This technique was then adopted by D'Amato and Colombo (1988) in a study with cebus monkeys (*Cebus apella*).

The monkeys were trained on a five-stimulus sequence, A→B→C→D→E. The stimuli were various visual patterns (dots, circles, and the like), which could be projected on any of five square panels. Which pattern appeared on which panel varied from one trial to the next, but all five stimuli were presented at the same time on each training trial. The task was to press the panels in the prescribed order, A→B→C→D→E. Training started with just stimulus A. After the monkeys learned to press A, B was added. After they learned the A→B sequence, C was added, and so forth. (For an alternative training strategy, see Swartz, Chen, & Terrace, 2000.)

Once the monkeys became proficient at responding to the simultaneous array with the correct sequence of responses, they were tested with subsets of the pattern that included just two or three of the stimuli. Two-element subsets could start with A, B, C, or D. Three-element subsets could start with A, B, or C. The monkeys performed with above-chance accuracy on all the subset test trials, including those that included only stimuli in the middle of the series (BC, CD, BD, and BCD). These results indicate that the monkeys learned the prescribed order of the five stimuli.

D'Amato and Colombo also measured the latencies of the correct responses during the tests with subsets of the five-element series. These results were particularly interesting and are shown in Figure 12.8. The left-hand graph shows the latency of responding to the first item of subsets of stimuli. Some of these subsets started with A (as in the subset AC, for example); some started with B (as in the subset BC or BD); some started with C (as in CD); and one started with D (DE).

When the first item of the subset was A, the monkeys responded rapidly. When the first item was B, responding was slower. Responding was slower still when the first item was C or D. Loosely speaking, these latencies suggest that at the start of a trial the monkeys started to walk through the sequence mentally. When they came to one of the stimuli presented on that trial, they responded to that stimulus. Since they encountered A first in this mental walk through the sequence, they responded to A quickest. Longer latencies occurred with items that came up later in their mental progression.

Additional evidence for mental scanning of the stimulus sequence was provided by how long it took for the subjects to respond to the second item in the subset tests. Some of the subsets involved adjacent items in the list, such as subset BC. Others involved one missing item, such as subset BD or CE. Still others involved two missing items (BE) or three missing items (AE). If the monkeys were walking through the list mentally as they performed

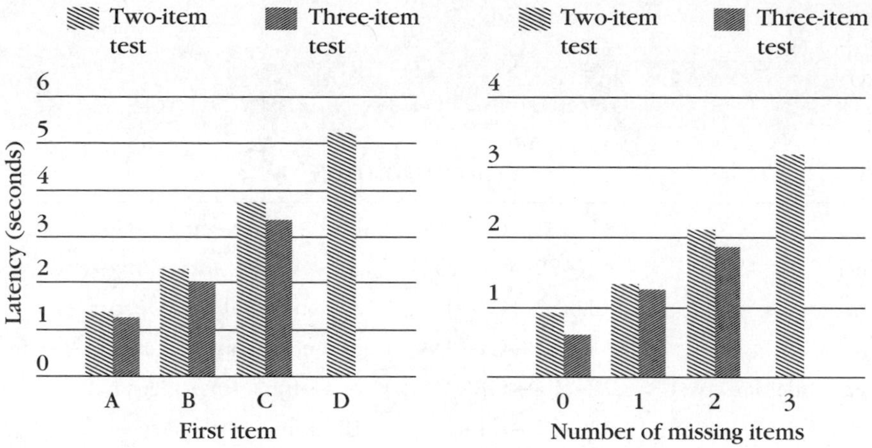

Figure 12.8 Latency of correct responses during tests of two- and three-item subsets of a five-item list with cebus monkeys. Left: Latency of responding to the first item of the subset as a function of the position of that item in the original sequence. Right: Latency of responding to the second item of the subset as a function of the number of items missing between the first and second items. (From "Representation of Serial Order in Monkeys (*Cebus apella*)," by M. R. D'Amato and M. Colombo, 1988, *Journal of Experimental Psychology: Animal Behavior Processes, 14,* pp. 131–139. Copyright © 1988 by the American Psychological Association. Reprinted by permission.)

the subset tests, how long they took to respond between the first and second items would depend on the number of missing items. With more missing items between stimuli in a subset, the monkeys should take longer to respond to the second item. This is exactly what occurred (see Figure 12.8, right). (For additional studies of the nature of that mental representation, see D'Amato and Colombo, 1989, 1990.)

Evidence of the Learning of Ordinal Position

The data presented in Figure 12.8 strongly indicates that the monkeys formed a mental representation of the prescribed order in which to respond to the stimuli presented in the simultaneous array. This mental representation no doubt included the knowledge that stimulus A was in position 1. However, the mental representation did not have to include knowing the specific ordinal position of each of the other stimuli. Once the monkeys started with stimulus A, they could have gotten through the sequence in the correct order if they just learned to associate stimulus A with B, B with C, C with D, and D with E. That is, a series of paired associates could have gotten them through the series correctly after they got started correctly with A.

More convincing evidence of the learning of ordinal positions was obtained in an experiment with two rhesus monkeys conducted by Chen, Swartz, and Terrace (1997). A simultaneous stimulus array was again used, but it included only four rather than five items. The items were color photographs of various objects and were presented in any of 9 positions on a stimulus display. As usual, the position of each stimulus was varied across trials. The subjects were first trained on one 4-item sequence, and then another, and another, until over the course of several years they became proficient on 15 different sequences.

TABLE 12.1 COMPOSITION OF STIMULUS ARRAYS IN A TEST OF ORDINAL POSITION LEARNING

ARRAY	COMPOSITION	
Original 1	A1→B1→C1→D1	bird→flower→frog→shells
Original 2	A2→B2→C2→D2	tree→weasel→dragonfly→water
Original 3	A3→B3→C3→D3	elk→rocks→leaves→person
Original 4	A4→B4→C4→D4	mountain→fish→monkey→tomato
Derived: Order Preserved	A2→B4→C1→D3	tree→fish→frog→person
Derived: Order Preserved	A3→B1→C4→D2	elk→flower→monkey→water
Derived: Order Changed	B3→A1→D4→C2	rocks→bird→tomato→dragonfly
Derived: Order Changed	D1→C3→B2→A4	shells→leaves→weasel→mountain

Source: Based on Chen, Swartz, & Terrace, 1997.

Four of the original sequences the subjects learned are represented in Table 12.1. The letters A, B, C, and D represent the order of the stimuli in each array. (To obtain reinforcement, the subjects had to respond to stimulus A first, then B, then C, and finally D.) The number associated with each stimulus represents the array in which the item appeared. Thus, the first array involved stimuli A1→B1→C1→D1. The second array involved stimuli A2→B2→C2→D2, and so on.

The critical aspect of the experiment involved training subjects on new stimulus arrays that were constructed from earlier ones in special ways. In some of the new arrays, the correct ordinal positions of the stimuli were the same as in original training (order preserved), but stimuli from different arrays were selected. One such derived array was A2→B4→C1→D3. A2 was the first stimulus from array #2, B4 was the second stimulus from array #4, C1 was the third stimulus from array #1, and D3 was the fourth stimulus from array #3. In other derived arrays, the correct ordinal positions of the stimuli were changed compared with original training (order changed). B3→A1→D4→C2 is an example of such an array. Here the subjects had to respond first to the second item from list 3, then pick the first item in array 1, then the fourth item from array 3, and finally the third item from array 2.

How might the subjects perform on the derived stimulus arrays? If they learned a series of paired associates, they would treat the derived arrays as entirely new problems because none of the adjacent stimuli in the derived arrays had occurred after one another in the original problems. Thus, the subjects would treat A2→B4→C1→D3 as a new problem because they never had to pick B4 after A2 or C1 after B4 during original training. Prior paired associate learning would not help the subjects deal with the new A2→B4→C1→D3 array. In contrast, if the subjects previously learned the specific ordinal position of each stimulus, they would do very well on the new A2→B4→C1→D3 array. If the subjects previously learned the ordinal position of each stimulus, they would know that A2 was in the first position, B4 in the second position, C1 in the third, and D3 in the fourth, even though these particular stimuli were never presented in the same array before.

The results obtained by Chen, Swartz, and Terrace showed dramatically that the monkeys had learned the ordinal position of the stimuli during original training. They responded to the new A2→B4→C1→D3 array almost perfectly the first time even though they had never seen these stimuli together before. In contrast, they treated derived arrays in which the order of the stimuli was changed (B3→A1→D4→C2) as if these were entirely new problems.

It is important to keep in mind that the monkeys in this study were highly proficient in serial pattern learning. Their extensive training history was probably critical for their learning the ordinal position of the stimuli. Paired associate learning may characterize the serial pattern learning of novice subjects, with a shift toward ordinal position learning with the acquisition of expertise.

PERCEPTUAL CONCEPT LEARNING

Organisms experience a great variety of stimuli during their lifetime. However, as I have pointed out, they do not have to respond to stimuli as independent and isolated events. Serial pattern learning represents one type of cognitive organization of stimuli. An even more basic form of cognitive organization involves perceptual concept learning. Consider, for example, seeing a chair. You may note some of its specific features: its color, shape, height, and firmness. You would also immediately identify it as a "chair." We can all agree on which things are chairs and which things are not chairs even though chairs come in a variety of shapes, sizes, and colors. "Chair" is an example of a perceptual concept.

We rely on perceptual concepts in much of our interaction with the world. We have perceptual concepts of physical objects, such as chairs, houses, trees, water, cats, and cars. We also have perceptual concepts of events, such as rain and wind or day and night. Perceptual concepts are important because they help us organize or categorize the wide variety of stimuli that we encounter during the course of normal experience. Perceptual concepts are also important in language. Words are often labels for perceptual concepts.

In the rough and tumble of life, nothing occurs exactly the same way twice. Even the same tree viewed from the same vantage point appears slightly different each time you look at it. The sun may be shining on it from a different angle, clouds may be casting a different pattern of shadows, and a breeze may be moving the branches and leaves. Perceptual concepts help organisms navigate through the maze of ever-changing stimuli in the world.

Through perceptual concepts, certain variations among stimuli are ignored. For example, you recognize your cat as the same animal, even though, strictly speaking, the visual image the cat projects on your retina is different every time you see it. You also recognize various objects as chairs, even though they may differ in color, size, and firmness. By contrast, other differences are emphasized. You distinguish your cat from your neighbor's cat and from your parakeet. You also distinguish between things that are called chairs and things that are called tables. As these examples illustrate, perceptual concepts have two important and complementary characteristics, *generalization within a category* or set of stimuli and *discrimination between categories* or sets of stimuli.

The typical perceptual concept learning experiment involves instrumental discrimination training. Each trial begins with a stimulus. If the stimulus belongs to the category of interest (S+), responding is reinforced. If the stimulus does not belong to the target category (S–), responding is not reinforced. As training progresses, subjects come to respond more to the S+ stimuli than to the S– stimuli.

In one study with pigeons (Herrnstein, Loveland, & Cable, 1976), for example, color slides of various scenes were projected on one wall of the experimental chamber near a response key. If the scene included a tree or some part of a tree, the pigeons were reinforced with food for pecking the response key. If the picture did not include a tree or any part of one, pecking was not reinforced. Each experimental session consisted of 80 slide presentations, about 40 of which included a tree. During training, the stimuli for any given day were randomly selected from 500–700 pictures depicting various scenes from all four seasons of the year in New England. The same photographs were only occasionally used more than once. The reinforced stimuli included trees (or parts of trees) of all descriptions, but the trees were not necessarily the main point of interest in the pictures. Some slides showed a tree far in the distance, others showed trees that were partly obstructed so that only some of the branches were visible, for example.

The pigeons learned the requirements of the task without much difficulty. Soon they were pecking at a much higher rate in the presence of pictures that included a tree than in the presence of pictures without trees. What might have been responsible for the accuracy of their performance? One possibility is that the pigeons memorized what the reinforced and nonreinforced pictures looked like without paying particular attention to the presence or absence of trees. Although this may seem to be an unlikely possibility, it has to be seriously considered because pigeons are able to memorize several hundred pictures (Vaughan & Greene, 1984).

A common tactic for ruling out the role of memorization of the training exemplars is to test for transfer of performance to stimuli that did not appear during training. Herrnstein et al. (1976) did this by presenting a new set of photos that did and did not include trees. The pigeons performed nearly as accurately on the new pictures as on those used during prior training. Much higher rates of pecking occurred in the presence of new slides that included a tree (or part of one) than in the presence of new slides without trees. Such evidence of *generalization to novel exemplars* is critical for demonstrations of perceptual concept learning.

Courtesy of E. A. Wasserman

E. A. Wasserman

Much research has been done on the learning of perceptual concepts since this area of research was initiated by Herrnstein and Loveland (1964) nearly 40 years ago (for example, Commons, Herrnstein, Kosslyn, & Mumford, 1990; Herrnstein, 1984, 1990; Lea, 1984; Macintosh, 1995; Pearce, 1994a; Wasserman & Astley, 1994). In the tradition set by Herrnstein, much of the research has been done with pigeons responding to complex visual stimuli. Studies have demonstrated the learning of numerous different visual perceptual concepts. Pigeons have learned to respond to the presence or absence of water in various forms (lakes, oceans, puddles, and so on) and to the presence or absence of a particular person (in various types of clothing, in various situations, and engaged in various activities) (Herrnstein et al., 1976). In other studies, pigeons have been conditioned to respond to the presence or absence of fish in underwater photographs (Herrnstein & deVilliers, 1980), to the presence of the letter A as opposed to other letters of the alphabet in various fonts (Morgan, Fitch, Holman, & Lea, 1976), to various views of a particular location on campus (Honig & Stewart, 1988; Wilkie, Willson, & Kardal, 1989), and to video images of certain actions performed by other pigeons (Dittrich, Lea, Barrett, & Gurr, 1998; Jitsumori et al., 1999). As I noted in Chapter 8, pigeons have also been conditioned to distinguish samples of the music of Bach from that of Stravinsky (Porter & Neuringer, 1984) and to discriminate pictures of Monet from those of Picasso (Watanabe et al., 1995).

Studies have also demonstrated perceptual concept learning in other species, including monkeys, quail, rats, and dolphins (for example, D'Amato & Van Sant, 1988; Helweg, Roitblat, Nachtigall, & Hautus, 1996; Jitsumori, 1994; Kluender, Diehl, & Killeen, 1987; Martin-Malivel & Fagot, 2001; Roberts & Mazmanian, 1988; Schrier & Brady, 1987). In all of these cases, the participants learned to respond similarly to stimuli belonging to the category in question even though members of the category differed in numerous respects. As I noted in Chapter 8, perceptual concept learning is a form of stimulus equivalence learning. Because responding to various examples of the target category has the same (or equivalent) reinforcing consequence, physically different stimuli come to be treated in the same (or equivalent) manner by the organism. Stimulus equivalence training produces generalization within a set of stimuli (Astley & Wasserman, 1998, 1999).

Discrimination between Perceptual Categories

In many of the studies of perceptual concept learning, the participants had to discriminate between stimuli that contained an exemplar of the concept from stimuli that did not—pictures of trees versus pictures without trees, for example. However, there was no common or unifying theme for the nonreinforced stimuli. The experiments demonstrated how one comes to discriminate stimuli that belong to a category from those that do not belong. However, the studies did not show how one comes to distinguish one category from another—how one learns to tell the difference between instances of oak trees from instances of pine trees, for example.

How one comes to discriminate between one concept and another depends not only on the reinforced category but also on the nonreinforced stimuli. Roberts and Mazmanian (1988), for example, found that both pigeons and monkeys had difficulty learning to discriminate pictures of birds from pictures of other types of animals. However, the participants had little trouble learning to distinguish pictures of birds from pictures not containing animals. Other aspects of their study demonstrated that the failure to discriminate birds from other animals was not due to a general inability to distinguish between two categories. Rather, the difficulty was related to the level of abstractness of the concepts. The pigeons and monkeys easily learned to discriminate various views of a particular bird, the common kingfisher, from pictures of other types of birds (see also Aitken, Bennett, McLaren, & Mackintosh, 1996; Macintosh, 1995; Wasserman, Kiedinger, & Bhatt, 1988).

Mechanisms of Perceptual Concept Learning

Perceptual concept learning is a well-established phenomenon. How animals do this, however, remains a lively topic of debate. The empirical analysis of perceptual categorization has turned out to be very difficult because of the complexity of the stimuli that are involved. Consider, for example, the learning of the concept "tree" by the pigeons that Herrnstein et al. (1976) tested. Photographs of natural scenes that do and do not include a tree (or part of a tree) are highly complex visual stimuli. Figuring out how the pigeons accomplish the categorization task requires closely examining not only their behavior but also the nature of the stimuli that control their behavior. What aspect(s) of the tree photographs led the pigeons to classify those photographs differently from the nontree photographs? Was it something about the color, shape, or texture of the photographs, and how were these (or some other) features used by the birds to make correct decisions?

Progress in categorization research was stymied by the stimulus problem for nearly a quarter century. However, this obstacle is finally being overcome by advances in computer image analysis and image production. Some investigators are examining perceptual categorization using computer-generated artificial images. The primary advantage of this approach is that the statistical properties of images can be perfectly specified. Unfortunately, however, researchers cannot be sure whether the mechanisms revealed in these experiments can be generalized to categorization involving complex natural stimuli. An alternative strategy has been to use computer image analysis (and complex statistical analyses of responses to these stimuli) to identify the features of complex natural stimuli that control categorization behavior. The tension between highly controlled studies with artificial stimuli and statistically more noisy studies of natural stimuli is not unique to categorization research. Ultimate progress will no doubt depend on both approaches.

Explanations of perceptual categorization have focused on three major alternatives: feature theory, exemplar theory, and prototype theory.

Feature Theory. The first and perhaps most obvious account of perceptual categorization is based on the concept of stimulus features. Feature theory assumes that members of a perceptual category have certain features in common—features to which the instrumental response becomes conditioned when the organism is reinforced. A chair, for example, is something that you can sit on. Therefore, it might be concluded that the property of supporting someone's sitting is a feature that defines a chair. Unfortunately, however, an individual feature such as this is rarely necessary or sufficient for membership in a category. The property of supporting someone's sitting, for example, is not sufficient to define a chair. You can also sit on the floor, but floors are not chairs. The property of being able to sit on the chair is also not a necessary feature. A chair suspended on the tip of a pole in the circus is still a chair, even though no one can sit on it.

Investigators of perceptual concept learning have argued against a simple feature-analysis explanation because a single feature common to all positive instances of natural perceptual concepts is often difficult (and sometimes impossible) to identify. Instead of focusing on a single critical feature, feature theorists have argued that category membership depends on an object having a number of features, no one of which is either necessary or sufficient for category membership. For example, features that are relevant to the concept of chair include having four legs, a back, a platform about 18 inches above the floor, a surface big enough to sit on, and a structure that will support the weight of a person. Exceptions to each of these features can be found, and no one of these features alone serves to identify a chair. However, if something has enough of these features, most of us would agree that it is a chair. This kind of reasoning involves a **polymorphic rule** (Herrnstein, 1984; Lea & Harrison, 1978; von Fersen & Lea, 1990).

According to a polymorphic rule, no one stimulus feature is necessary or sufficient for membership in a perceptual category. Rather, category membership is based on having a certain number of relevant features. For example, if something has three or four features that are relevant to chairs, one would conclude that it belongs in the chair category. Although polymorphic rules do not require a single critical feature, they still depend on stimulus features for perceptual categorization.

Research relevant to feature theory has been conducted using both artificial and natural stimuli. Huber and Lenz (1993), for example, used simple line drawings of faces, like those shown in Figure 12.9. Four features of the drawings were varied: the distance between the eyes, the height of the forehead, the length of the nose, and the size of the chin. Each of these features could take on one of three values, designated as −1, 0, and +1. Two categories were created from the resultant drawings by adding the values of the four features. One category (called "positive") was composed of drawings that had feature sums greater than zero; another category (called "negative") was made of drawings that had feature sums less than zero.

The drawing on the left in Figure 12.9 represents the face with the highest negative sum of the features, and the drawing on the right represents the face with the highest positive sum of the features. The pigeons were reinforced for pecking in the presence of faces with a positive feature sum and were not reinforced for pecking in the presence of faces with a negative feature sum. The birds learned the concept discrimination in about 20 sessions, and detailed analyses of their performance indicated that their behavior was controlled by the four features that were manipulated. Responding of each pigeon was highly correlated with the sum of the features that appeared in a test stimulus. Greater feature sums produced proportionately greater rates of responding. (For feature analysis of categorization of natural

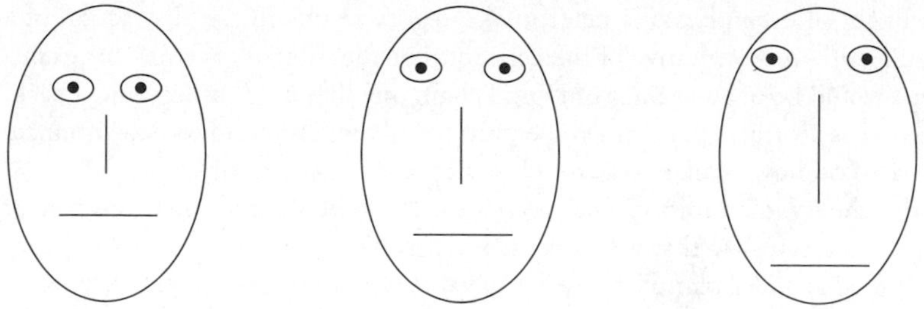

Figure 12.9 Examples of drawings of faces used by Huber and Lenz (1993). The face on the left represents the highest negative sum of facial features. The face in the middle has a feature sum of zero, and the face on the right has the highest positive feature sum. (From "A Test of the Linear Feature Model of Polymorphous Concept Discrimination with Pigeons," by L. Huber and R. Lenz, 1993, *The Quarterly Journal of Experimental Psychology, 46B,* pp. 1–18. Copyright © 1993 by the Experimental Psychology Society. Reprinted by permission.)

face stimuli by pigeons and baboons, see Aust & Huber, 2001; Huber, Troje, Loidolt, Aust, & Grass, 2000; Jitsumori & Yoshihara, 1997; Martin-Malivel & Fagot, 2001.)

Exemplar Theory. The simplest, and in some ways the most successful, explanation of perceptual concept learning is the exemplar theory (Wasserman & Astley, 1994). This theory is based on conventional concepts of discrimination learning and stimulus generalization, such as those I described in Chapter 8. Reinforcement for responding in the presence of a stimulus is assumed to result in the conditioning of excitation to that stimulus. In contrast, nonreinforcement is assumed to result in the absence of excitation and perhaps the conditioning of inhibition to the stimulus. Both conditioned excitation and inhibition are assumed to generalize to other stimuli, with the degree of generalization determined by the degree of similarity between the new and old stimuli.

The basic ideas of exemplar theory are consistent with many aspects of perceptual concept learning. The theory explains generalization of a perceptual concept to new exemplars by assuming that the new test stimuli are in some ways similar to the stimuli that were used when the perceptual concept was originally trained. If the perceptual concept is that of a tree, for example, new pictures that include trees are treated as members of the category presumably because they resemble the pictures with trees that were reinforced during training. On the other hand, new pictures that do not include a tree are rejected because they have less in common with the reinforced stimuli that were used in training, and may even resemble some of the nonreinforced training stimuli.

Although exemplar theory is highly successful in explaining many aspects of perceptual concept learning, it should be pointed out that this theory may well operate in combination with the mechanisms of feature theory. In fact, exemplar theory is difficult to distinguish from feature theory in situations where organisms respond to examples of a perceptual concept in terms of the salient features that those examples have in common. The advantage of exemplar theory, however, is that it can predict various aspects of categorization behavior without first identifying which stimulus features are important to a perceptual category (for further details, see Wasserman & Astley, 1994).

Prototype Theory. Of the three theories of perceptual categorization, prototype theory relies most heavily on higher-order cognitive mechanisms. According to prototype theory, exposure to a number of exemplars of a perceptual category results in the abstraction of a **prototype** or "standard" representative of the concept. For the category "chair," for example, the prototype would be of an average or typical chair, one that has four legs and a back. Once the organism has abstracted or formed the prototype, it will respond to new instances of the category based on how similar these new instances are to the prototype.

In tests of this theory, the prototype has been assumed to be the arithmetic average of all of the examples of a category that are presented to a subject. Tests of prototype theory have typically involved artificial stimuli whose mean value can be computed relatively easily. Jitsumori (1996), for example, conducted a test of prototype theory with butterfly-like stimuli. The stimuli varied in the complexity of the pattern on the forewings, the shape of the hind wings, and the shading of the butterfly. Each of these features could take on one of six values.

To test prototype theory, Jitsumori (1996) created two sets of butterflies. The pigeons were reinforced for pecking in the presence of stimuli from one set (S+) and were not reinforced in the presence of stimuli from the contrasting set (S–). The S+ and S– stimuli were carefully selected so that they surrounded different average or prototype images. However, the actual average images were never presented during training. Thus, the pigeons were never explicitly reinforced for responding to the S+ prototype (and never received nonreward in the presence of the S– prototype). Despite never having seen the prototypes during training, the subjects responded most during a postconditioning test when the S+ prototype was presented. (For other evidence in support of prototype theory, see Huber & Lenz, 1996; Aydin & Pearce, 1994; Pearce, 1994a.)

Although evidence in support of prototype theory has been obtained, it has not been easy to differentiate predictions of this theory from predictions of other accounts, particularly exemplar theory. The differentiation between these two theories will require additional theoretical work.

LANGUAGE LEARNING IN NONHUMAN ANIMALS

Perhaps the most complex cognitive skill is linguistic competence. In fact, many have argued that linguistic skill is so complex and specialized that it is uniquely human. According to this view, the ability to use language depends on certain innate processes that have evolved only in our own species (for example, Chomsky, 1972; Lennenberg, 1967). By contrast, others have proposed that human beings are able to use language because they are especially intelligent and have experiences that permit language acquisition. This second view suggests that nonhuman organisms may also acquire language skills if they are sufficiently intelligent and encounter the requisite experiences. Encouraged by this possibility, investigators have tried to teach language skills to various species.

Early language training efforts attempted to determine whether nonhuman animals are capable of language. However, it has become evident that this is not an answerable question (Roitblat, Harley, & Helweg, 1993). Language is not a unitary entity that one either does or does not have; rather, it consists of component skills. A human infant's language abilities, for example, improve gradually as the infant acquires and integrates increasingly sophisticated language skills. In this developmental sequence, there is no one point at which the young child graduates from not having language to having it.

Some theoreticians remain interested in whether human-like language is possible in other species. Kako (1999), for example, recently proposed four elements of syntax that should be present to justify concluding that a particular species has human-like language.

However, investigators who have been on the front lines actually collecting the relevant data reject the value of trying to meet criteria that define human linguistic competence. Some have become impatient with this approach because the criteria keep changing. For example, E. Sue Savage-Rumbaugh, who has probably spent more effort studying language learning in apes than anyone else, recently commented (with two colleagues), "The history of comparative studies in animal learning and behavior has been marked by the constantly shifting demands made by those who want to preserve some species-specific attribute that will distinguish human behavior from all other primates" (Shanker, Savage-Rumbaugh, & Taylor, 1999).

If the goal is no longer to demonstrate human-like linguistic competence in nonhuman species, what is the goal of this type of research? There are several goals. One is to use language training as a vehicle to study the cognitive abilities of nonhuman species. This is the basic objective of the program of work directed by Irene Pepperberg (1999), who has been studying the cognitive abilities of a Grey parrot, Alex, since 1977. A related sentiment is expressed by Louis Herman, who directed language studies in dolphins: "The animal language work can help us to identify with more surety those processes in humans that may derive from general cognitive structures rather than from language-specific structures" (Herman & Uyeyama, 1999, p. 22). Research on language learning in nonhuman species can tell us a great deal about the cognitive prerequisites and components of language competence. Such research can also provide information about how best to teach linguistic skills. This information can then be put to good use in language instruction for persons with cognitive disabilities (Sevcik, Romski, & Wilkenson, 1991).

Early Attempts at Language Training

Most efforts to teach animals language have involved chimpanzees because chimpanzees have many characteristics in common with human beings. Despite these similarities, however, chimpanzees do not learn to speak when they are given the same types of experiences that children have as they learn to speak. Nadezhda Kohts, of the Darwinian Museum in Moscow, raised a chimpanzee in her home from 1913 to 1916 without once having it imitate the human voice or utter a word of Russian (see Premack, 1976). More detailed accounts of life with a chimpanzee are available from the experiences of Winthrop and Louise Kellogg, who raised a baby chimpanzee along with their baby boy (Kellogg, 1933). Their adopted charge also did not learn to speak like a person. Undaunted by this evidence, Cathy and Keith Hayes raised a chimpanzee named Viki with the explicit intent of teaching her to talk (Hayes & Hayes, 1951). Despite several years of training, Viki learned to say only three words: mama, papa, and cup.

The failure of the Hayeses to teach Viki to talk despite their great efforts discouraged others from trying again. However, people remained intrigued with the possibility that animals might acquire some language skills. The search for linguistic competence in chimpanzees got a big boost from the innovative work of Allen and Beatrice Gardner and their students (Gardner & Gardner, 1969, 1975, 1978). Instead of trying to teach their chimpanzee, Washoe, to talk using vocal speech, the Gardners taught her American Sign Language.

American Sign Language consists of manual gestures in place of words. Chimpanzees are much more adept at making hand movements and gestures than they are at making the vocal-laryngeal movements required for the production of speech sounds. Washoe was a good student. She learned to sign well over 100 words. Washoe's success suggested that earlier efforts to teach speech to chimpanzees may have failed not because of the inability of the chimpanzee to learn linguistic skills but because an inappropriate response medium (vocalization) was used. Washoe held out the promise that animals would acquire linguistic competence with the appropriate response medium.

The success of the Gardners with Washoe encouraged other language training efforts with chimpanzees as well as with other species. These included a gorilla (Patterson, 1978); dolphins (Herman, 1987); sea lions (Gisiner & Schusterman, 1992; Schusterman & Gisiner, 1988); and an African Grey parrot (Pepperberg, 1990). Some investigators followed the approach of the Gardners in using American Sign Language to train chimpanzees (see Gardner, Gardner, & Van Cantfort, 1989) and gorillas (Patterson, 1978). Others adopted alternative procedures.

Courtesy of I. M. Pepperberg

I. M. Pepperberg, with Alex

Language Training Procedures

A variety of procedures have been employed to train language skills. For example, the program of research on African Grey parrots directed by Irene Pepperberg (for example, 1990, 1993, 1999) employed an observational learning procedure known as the **model-rival technique.** The first subject trained by Pepperberg was Alex. The model-rival technique involves two people interacting with the subject. One research assistant acts as a trainer and the other acts as a rival student who competes with Alex for the attention of the trainer. The trainer may present an object of interest to Alex and ask what color it is. The person acting as the student then responds, sometimes correctly and sometimes incorrectly. An incorrect response results in a reprimand from the trainer and temporary removal of the object. A correct response results in praise and a chance to manipulate the object. Alex observes these interactions and attempts to gain the attention of the trainer (and obtain the object) by responding correctly before the rival human "student" does so.

In the dolphin and sea lion language training projects, more conventional stimulus discrimination procedures have been used (for example, Herman, Pack, & Morrel-Samuels, 1993; Schusterman & Krieger, 1986). The instructional stimuli were provided by a person making a particular gesture (arms crossed against the chest, for example) at the edge of the pool. The correct response on the part of the marine mammal to the gesture was reinforced with food; incorrect responses were not reinforced. Thus, the training procedures used with the African Grey parrot and the marine mammals differ in numerous respects, including opportunities for observational learning and the reinforcers employed. These differences complicate comparisons between the species.

Starting with the pioneering work of the Gardners in training sign language to Washoe, language training has been conducted with more than a dozen chimpanzees. Sign language training was usually conducted within the context of an established social relationship between the trainers and the chimpanzees. The chimpanzees lived in a rich homelike environment and were cared for by a small number of people throughout the day, each of whom was adept in sign language. Every effort was made to engage the chimpanzees in active conversation (through signing) during their waking hours. New signs were learned during games, in the course of getting dressed, or in going from place to place. The intent was to teach language to the chimpanzees in the way that children presumably learn to talk during the normal course of interacting with parents and other children.

Although the naturalistic context for teaching sign language used by the Gardners seemed to facilitate learning, the informality of the approach made it difficult to document the course of language acquisition in detail. In an effort to gain greater control, other investigators developed artificial languages for use with chimpanzees. One artificial language, developed and used by David Premack and his associates, consists of various shapes made of plastic in place of words (Premack, 1971b, 1976). Another artificial language developed by Duane Rumbaugh and his colleagues at the Language Research Center associated with

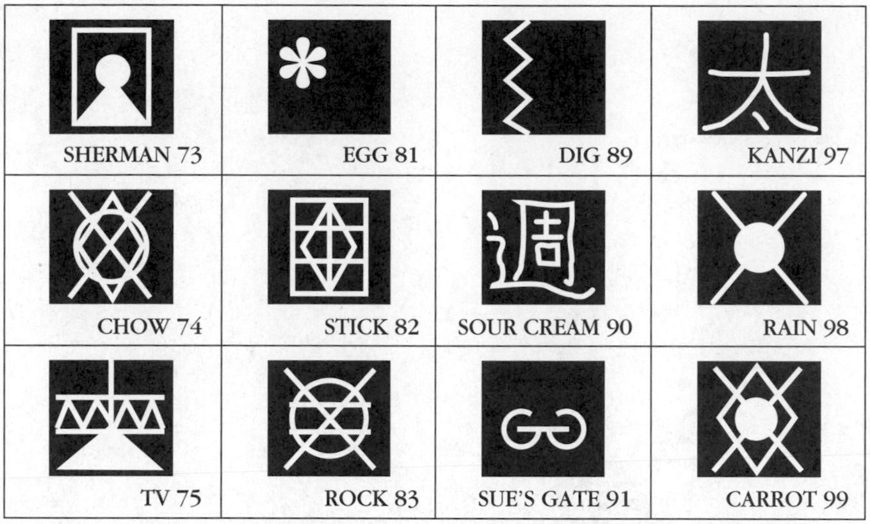

Courtesy of Duane Rumbaugh, Language Research Center, Georgia State University

Figure 12.10 Examples of lexigrams used at the Language Research Center of Georgia State University.

Georgia State University used simple designs of various shapes and colors to represent words (Rumbaugh, 1977; see also Savage-Rumbaugh, 1986). These symbols, called lexigrams, are presented on a board (see Figure 12.10). The chimpanzee can select a word by pointing to or pressing the corresponding lexigram on the board. Computer records of these lexigram responses provide detailed information about the linguistic performance of the research participant.

The first chimpanzee trained with lexigrams was Lana (Rumbaugh, 1977). The lexigrams appeared on a modified keyboard hooked up to a computer. Lana could "talk" to the computer and make various requests. The computer, in turn, was programmed to reply with lexigrams presented on a display console.

Lana's training emphasized the naming of objects and the learning of short sequences of symbols. After Lana, two other chimpanzees, Austin and Sherman, entered the research program at the Georgia State University Language Research Center (see Savage-Rumbaugh, 1986). In contrast to Lana, Austin and Sherman were reared with more extensive human contact, and, perhaps more important, they learned language within the context of interacting not only with humans but also with each other. However, they were trained with the same lexigram language system that had been used in training Lana rather than American Sign Language. Austin and Sherman interacted with caretakers and with each other by pointing to or pressing lexigrams on a stimulus board. Portable versions of the lexigram board were available to extend training to a variety of settings.

The most sophisticated demonstrations of language competence to date have been obtained with Kanzi, a bonobo great ape (*Pan paniscus*) (Savage-Rumbaugh, Murphy, Sevcik, Brakke, Williams, & Rumbaugh, 1993; Savage-Rumbaugh, Sevcik, Brakke, & Rumbaugh, 1990). Bonobos are more similar to human beings than are chimpanzees, but they are rare both in the wild and in captivity. Kanzi's experience was unusual in comparison to previous language-trained chimpanzees in that Kanzi did not receive formal language training. During the first 2.5 years of his life, he lived with his mother, Matata, who was born in the wild and started language training at the Language Research Center of Georgia State University when Kanzi was 6 months old.

Matata was trained with standard procedures in which she had to indicate the lexigram names of food objects to obtain those foods. She progressed slowly, however, and never

Courtesy of Duane Rumbaugh, Language Research Center, Georgia State University

Figure 12.11 Kanzi working with a lexigram board.

attained the language competence of Austin and Sherman. For several years, Kanzi observed these training sessions but did not participate in them. Matata was then removed for a period for breeding purposes. During this separation Kanzi began to interact with the lexigram board spontaneously (see Figure 12.11). The investigators took advantage of this spontaneous use of the lexigram board and allowed Kanzi to continue to use it in addition to communicating with manual gestures. They also allowed Kanzi to continue to learn language skills by listening to spoken English and observing humans communicating with gestures and lexigrams.

Every effort was made to provide Kanzi with as rich and as natural an environment as possible. He was allowed to go on excursions in a 50-acre wooded area adjacent to the laboratory. The woods were provisioned with food stations at fixed locations. Excursions in the woods provided numerous opportunities for conversation concerning which food site to visit, what to take along, and so on. Kanzi was also allowed to visit various areas of the laboratory, including areas in which other apes were housed, and periodically he was taken on car rides.

Spoken and lexical language were incorporated into Kanzi's daily activities, such as diaper changes, food preparation, and various games. The hope was that Kanzi would acquire language incidentally during his normal daily activities, as children do. No explicit language training sessions were conducted, and Kanzi's use of language was not explicitly reinforced with food. However, the reinforcement contingencies inherent in social interactions were probably important in Kanzi's language learning (Sundberg, 1996).

Documenting Language Skills

Documenting acquired language skill requires special test procedures because language training typically involves extensive interactions with the participant under conditions in which hints or prompts might be provided, or conditions in which a trainer might give the animal "the benefit of the doubt" and credit the animal with more intelligent behavior than is warranted. Terrace and his colleagues (Terrace, 1979; Terrace, Petitto, Sanders, & Bever, 1979), for example, studied videotaped records of the sign language behavior of their chimpanzee, Nim, and found that Nim often imitated signs previously made by the trainer. Imitative signing was poor evidence of language skill.

Not only must test procedures preclude inadvertent prompts, they must also be constructed to allow for objective measurement of behavior. In a test of sign language vocabulary, for example, Gardner and Gardner (1984), presented pictures to Washoe for her to identify by signing. Two observers recorded the signs Washoe made. To minimize the possibility of prompting, neither observer could see the picture Washoe was trying to name. To ensure objective independent observations, the observers also could not see each other. With these elaborate procedures, Washoe could not be given hints about the correct sign by the observers. Since the observers did not know what the correct sign was on each trial, they also could not give her credit for incorrect responses. Despite these precautions, Washoe responded correctly about 80% of the time.

Washoe's vocabulary test was a test of word production. Another important aspect of vocabulary is comprehension of words presented or spoken by others. An interesting opportunity for testing comprehension arose in the work that Savage-Rumbaugh and her colleagues were doing with Kanzi. In addition to learning lexigrams spontaneously, Kanzi also seemed to have learned to recognize spoken English words. Kanzi, like other chimpanzees, could not produce the sounds of English words, but he appeared to know their meaning. Savage-Rumbaugh decided to evaluate this comprehension in several systematic tests. In one test (Savage-Rumbaugh, McDonald, Sevcik, Hopkins, & Rubert, 1986), English words were "spoken" by a speech synthesizer to make sure Kanzi was not responding to the intonation of human speech. After each word, Kanzi was asked to select the lexical symbol for that word from a selection of three lexigrams (see Figure 12.12). The experimenter did not see the possible choices, and thus could not inadvertently indicate which was correct. The

Courtesy of Duane Rumbaugh, Language Research Center, Georgia State University

Figure 12.12 The bonobo chimpanzee Kanzi participating in a test of English comprehension. Words were presented to him through the earphones, and he had to respond by pressing lexigrams on the panel in the background.

choice alternatives were presented by a second experimenter who then did not observe Kanzi's choices, so that she also could not prompt the correct response. Each of 66 words was presented three times. Kanzi responded correctly each time 51 of the words was presented. In a similar test with spoken human speech, Kanzi erred on only on one of the 66 words. Thus, synthesized speech was more difficult for Kanzi to comprehend, as it is for human listeners sometimes.

Components of Linguistic Competence

As I noted earlier, research on language learning has come to focus on various components of linguistic competence rather than on whether nonhuman animals are capable of language. Let us consider those components of linguistic competence in greater detail.

Learning a Vocabulary. One of the undisputed results of language training programs is that animals can learn to associate arbitrary symbols (be they manual signs or lexigrams) with objects. They can learn to name correctly a large number of different objects. To what extent does this skill represent having learned what we call words in human language?

A word in human language is an abstract representation that can be used in a variety of ways. One can use the word as a label for its referent object (as in saying "tomato" when presented with an example of the vegetable). One can also identify the referent object in response to the word (as in picking out a tomato when asked, "Which is the tomato?"). One can also use the word in relation to other words (as in saying "tomato" when asked to name examples of "vegetables").

Strong evidence of multiple uses of words was obtained with the chimpanzees Austin and Sherman (Savage-Rumbaugh, Rumbaugh, Smith, & Lawson, 1980). In one study, for example, Austin and Sherman were trained to label lexigrams of various foods (beancake, orange, and bread) and tools (key, money, and stick) as "food" and "tool." They were then tested with a variety of symbols of new tools (magnet, sponge, lever, string, for example) and foods (M&M, banana, corn, for example). They had previously learned the lexigrams for each of these new tools and foods. However, they had not been explicitly trained to categorize or label these items in terms of their uses ("tool" and "food"). Nevertheless, Austin and Sherman performed with nearly perfect accuracy in categorizing these new lexigrams. Thus, they were able to use words to label and categorize other words.

Evidence of "Grammar" in Great Apes. Although it is agreed that great apes (and Grey parrots, dolphins, and sea lions) can learn a vocabulary, language is more than just a collection of words. Language also involves arrangement of words into sequences according to certain rules set forth by the grammar or syntax of the language. Hence, a major issue in language research has been whether the subjects display evidence of using grammatical rules. There has been considerable debate about this and the debate is ongoing (for example, Kako, 1999).

The smallest word sequence contains two words. However, the utterance of a pair of words does not prove that the participant is using grammar to create the sequence. An often-recounted incident involving a two-word sequence occurred when the chimpanzee Washoe saw a swan in the water. She had never seen a swan before. When asked "What is that?" she signed "Water bird." In this sequence, was Washoe using "water" as an adjective to specify the kind of bird she saw? Perhaps. However, an equally plausible interpretation is that she signed "water" because she saw the water and "bird" because she saw a bird. That is, she may have signed "water bird" as two independent words rather than as an utterance of two words related to each other as adjective and noun (Terrace et al., 1979).

Early detailed studies of language production in the chimpanzee failed to provide convincing evidence of responding on the basis of some kind of grammar or set of rules for word combinations (Terrace, 1979; Terrace et al., 1979). The chimpanzee Nim, who was taught sign language by Terrace and his associates, performed sequences of signs, but these appeared to be imitations of the trainer and included meaningless repetitions. For example, Nim's most common four-sign combination was "eat-drink-eat-drink."

Convincing evidence of the development of grammatical word sequences has been obtained in studies with the bonobo ape Kanzi (Greenfield & Savage-Rumbaugh, 1990; see also Savage-Rumbaugh et al., 1990). Data for the analysis of the possible existence of grammatical structure in Kanzi's language production were first obtained when Kanzi was 5.5 years old (Greenfield & Savage-Rumbaugh, 1990). Over a 5-month period of observations, Kanzi communicated 13,691 "words." Of these, about 10% contained more than one element or "word." The analysis of word sequences was limited to spontaneous communications. Thus, responses to directed questions were excluded from the analyses, as were responses that Kanzi performed to obtain something that was otherwise withheld, or responses that involved some degree of imitation. Unlike Nim, Kanzi rarely repeated himself or combined words that did not make sense together. Analyses of the multiple-word communications revealed a structure indicative of rules for word order.

Kanzi's word combinations could be categorized according to the types of words that were involved. By way of example, Table 12.2 summarizes data from three different types of two-word combinations. The first type involves a word for an action and a word for an agent. A total of 132 such action/agent combinations were observed. Of these, in 119 instances the word identifying the action preceded the word identifying the agent. In only 13 of the 132 cases did the word for the agent precede the word for the action. A similar bias in favor of a particular word order is evident with the other types of two-word combinations, action/object and goal/action. Notice that the "grammatical" rule is not a simple one. One of the words in all three of these types of two-word combinations involved an action. However, the action word did not come first predominantly in all three types of two-word combinations. When talking about an action and a goal, Kanzi tended to state the goal first.

TABLE 12.2 FREQUENCY OF VARIOUS TWO-ELEMENT COMMUNICATIONS BY KANZI*

WORD ORDER	FREQUENCY	EXAMPLE OF DOMINANT ORDER
Action→Agent	119	CARRY→gesture to Phil, who agrees to carry Kanzi
Agent→Action	13	
Action→Object	39	KEEP AWAY BALLOON→wanting to tease Bill with
Object→Action	15	a balloon and start a fight
Goal→Action	46	COKE CHASE→researcher chases Kanzi to place
Action→Goal	10	in woods where Coke is kept

*Lexigram responses are indicated by small capital letters.
Source: Adapted from Greenfield and Savage-Rumbaugh, 1990.

Some of the rules for word order that were manifest in Kanzi's word combinations were probably learned by observing his human caretakers. However, other grammatical rules appeared to be Kanzi's original inventions. Perhaps the most prominent of these concerned word combinations that Kanzi made involving a lexigram and a hand gesture. In such cases, Kanzi nearly always performed the lexigram response first, followed by the gesture. For example, in requesting to be carried, Kanzi would press the lexigram for CARRY, followed by a gesture pointing to the caretaker. Kanzi faithfully followed the rule of making the lexigram response before any manual gestures, but the caretakers usually performed such word sequences in the opposite order.

Language Comprehension versus Production. Historically, studies of ape language have focused on whether apes can learn to produce orderly linguistic responses, be those words or word sequences. Starting with the findings obtained with Kanzi, the focus has shifted toward investigations of language comprehension. The initial observations of Kanzi's language competence were incidental and serendipitous. Recall that Kanzi was not in an organized language training program but was present while his mother received explicit language training. Savage-Rumbaugh and her colleagues noticed that Kanzi seemed to understand the words that were being used with his mother. This incidental observation led them to investigate language comprehension rather than production in a systematic fashion. The shift in emphasis has provided dramatic results (for example, Brakke & Savage-Rumbaugh, 1995; Savage-Rumbaugh et al., 1993).

Comprehension precedes the ability to speak a language in human language learning. Individuals learning a second language, for example, can often understand more of that language than they are able to speak. This raises the possibility that studies of language comprehension may reveal sophisticated aspects of linguistic competence that are not evident in language production.

A prominent feature of human language is its variety and flexibility. A limited set of words can be combined to form a great variety of different sentences, and you can understand a new sentence even if you have never seen that particular sequence of words before. It has been difficult to prove that animals can use language in as flexible a fashion as human beings (see, for example, Thompson & Church, 1980). Tests of comprehension conducted with Kanzi provided promising results.

Savage-Rumbaugh et al. (1993) conducted detailed evaluations of the language comprehension of Kanzi when he was 8 years old and compared his performance to that of a 2-year-old child, Alia. Alia's mother, Jeannine Murphy, was one of Kanzi's caretakers. She worked with Kanzi in the mornings and spent the afternoons with Alia in a double-wide mobile home at the Language Research Center that was set up like Kanzi's laboratory. Alia participated in games and other activities similar to those that were used with Kanzi and received similar exposure to lexigrams and spoken English.

The test sentences involved instructions to manipulate various objects that were familiar and available to Kanzi and Alia. Kanzi faced up to 12 objects, and Alia was given up to 8. In the critical test phase, the sentences were spoken by an experimenter hidden by a one-way mirror so that the experimenter could not make gestures that might prompt the correct response. All trials were recorded on videotape. Usually two or three other people were present in the room so that sentences involving interactions with these people could be included in the test. However, the additional individuals wore headphones that played loud music so that they could not hear the instructions given Kanzi or Alia. To further preclude inadvertent influences on the data, the results of tests with Kanzi were not known to the person conducting the tests with Alia, and vice versa.

Kanzi was tested with 415 sentences, and Alia was tested with 407. The sentences were distributed among seven different types. Some were fairly simple, such as "Put object X in object Y," "Give object X to person A," "Do action A on object X," and "Take object X to location Y." Others were more complicated, such as "Make pretend animate A do action A on recipient Y." (For example, "Make the [toy] doggie bite the [toy] snake.") Both Kanzi and Alia did remarkably well. Each responded correctly more than 50% of the time on all but one sentence type. Overall, Kanzi did a bit better than Alia. Kanzi responded correctly on 74% of the trials, and Alia responded correctly on 65% of the trials.

Both Kanzi and Alia responded correctly when tested with sentences involving the same words but in different orders. For example, they responded correctly to the sentences "Take the umbrella outdoors," and "Go outdoors and get the umbrella"; "Take the potato to the bedroom," and "Go to the bedroom and get the potato"; "Put some water on the carrot," and "Put the carrot in the water"; and "Kanzi/Alia is going to chase Liz/Nathaniel," and "Liz/Nathaniel is going to chase Kanzi/Alia." Kanzi was more accurate on sentence pairs involving the same words in different orders. Kanzi made the correct response on 66% of such pairs of sentences, whereas Alia was correct on 38% of them.

Kanzi and Alia also responded correctly to sentences involving unusual instructions that they had not previously encountered. For example, on one occasion the objects available to Kanzi included a tomato and a sponge ball. The ball was shaped in the form of a head, with eyes, a nose, and a mouth. One of Kanzi's test sentences was, "Feed your ball some tomato." Before this test item, the word "feed" had never been used with "ball." Nevertheless, in response to "Feed your ball some tomato," Kanzi took the tomato and put it into the mouth on the sponge ball (see Figure 12.13).

Both Kanzi and Alia also came up with some unusual solutions to the instructions they were given. Both had seen food washed in the kitchen sink. Therefore, in response to "Wash

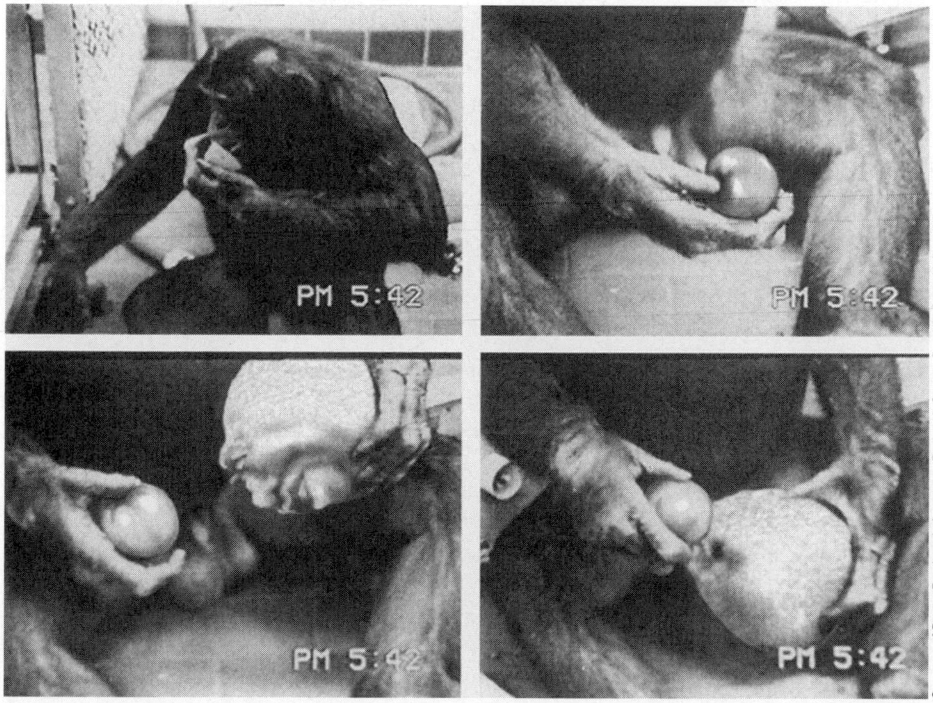

Figure 12.13 Video sequence showing Kanzi's response to the instruction, "Feed your ball some tomato."

the hot dogs," the experimenters expected that they would take the hot dogs to the sink. But, neither did so. Rather, they responded in a way that did not require going to the sink. Kanzi washed the hot dogs with a hose that was in the room to clean the floor. Alia, in contrast, rubbed the hot dogs with a sponge that was close at hand.

Kanzi's performance provides the best evidence available so far that a nonhuman mammal can acquire sophisticated linguistic skills. Kanzi acquired a substantial vocabulary and also showed evidence of syntax in language production. In addition, he mastered some of the flexibility of language. He could understand differences in meaning created by different word orders and new messages created by combining familiar words in unfamiliar sentences. The language sophistication of Kanzi proves that many important linguistic skills are not uniquely human attributes. Thus, these findings vindicate Darwin's belief that seemingly unique human abilities and skills do not reflect a discontinuity in the animal kingdom. (For a discussion of the broader philosophical implications of this research, see Savage-Rumbaugh, Shanker, & Taylor, 1998.)

SAMPLE QUESTIONS

1. Describe the phenomenon of transitive inference, and explain how it could occur through simple associative mechanisms.
2. Describe how the behavior of food-storing birds can be used to provide evidence of episodic memory.
3. Describe the peak procedure and how results obtained with the peak procedure may be explained by an information processing model.
4. Compare and contrast the information processing model of timing and the behavioral theory of timing.
5. Explain why tests with subsets of items from a simultaneous array are useful in assessing the mechanisms of serial pattern learning.
6. Compare and contrast three different theories of perceptual concept learning.
7. Describe how responsiveness to word order may be evaluated in the language comprehension of chimpanzees and children.

KEY TERMS

adjunctive behaviors Systematic activities or responses that occur when reinforcers are delivered at fixed intervals.

duration estimation A discrimination procedure in which the discriminative stimulus is the duration of an event.

interim response A response that increases in frequency after the delivery of a periodic reinforcer and then declines as time for the the next reinforcer approaches.

model-rival technique An observational learning procedure in which the participant observes a trainer teaching a student and tries to compete with that student for the trainer's attention.

paired-associate learning Learning of associations between successive pairs of an ordered list of stimuli.

peak procedure A discrete-trial variation of a fixed interval schedule used to study timing in animals.

polymorphic rule A criterion for membership in a perceptual category, according to which categorization is determined by the exemplar having a certain number of stimulus features that are relevant to the category. However, no one feature alone (or in combination with other features) is assumed to be necessary or sufficient for category membership.

prototype An exemplar of a category that is the average, typical, or "standard" representation of that category.

response chain A consecutively ordered series of responses in which each response produces the cue for the next response in the sequence.

serial representation learning The learning of a mental representation of the order of an entire list or series of stimuli.

terminal response A response that is most likely to occur at the end of the interval between successive reinforcements that are presented at fixed intervals.

REFERENCES

Abramson, L. Y., Metalsky, G. I., & Alloy, L. B. (1989). Hopelessness depression: A theory-based subtype of depression. *Psychological Review, 96,* 358–372.

Acediano, F., Matute, H., Miller, R. R. (1997). Blocking of Pavlovian conditioning in humans. *Learning & Motivation, 28*(2), 188–199.

Aitken, M. R. F., Bennett, C. H., McLaren, I. P. L., & Mackintosh, N. J. (1996). Perceptual differentiation during categorization learning by pigeons. *Journal of Experimental Psychology: Animal Behavior Processes, 22,* 43–50.

Akins, C. K. (1998). Context excitation and modulation of conditioned sexual behavior. *Animal Learning & Behavior, 26,* 416–426.

Akins, C. K. (2000). Effects of species-specific cues and the CS-US interval on the topography of the sexually conditioned response. *Learning and Motivation, 31,* 211–235.

Akins, C. K., & Domjan, M. (1996). The topography of sexually conditioned behaviour: Effects of a trace interval. *Quarterly Journal of Experimental Psychology, 49B,* 346–356.

Akins, C. K., Domjan, M., & Gutiérrez, G. (1994). Topography of sexually conditioned behavior in male Japanese quail (*Coturnix japonica*) depends on the CS-US interval. *Journal of Experimental Psychology: Animal Behavior Processes, 20,* 199–209.

Albert, M., & Ayres, J. J. B. (1997). One-trial simultaneous and backward excitatory fear conditioning in rats: Lick suppression, freezing, and rearing to CS compounds and their elements. *Animal Learning & Behavior, 25,* 210–220.

Allan, R. W., & Zeigler, H. P. (1994). Autoshaping the pigeon's gape response: Acquisition and topography as a function of reinforcer type and magnitude. *Journal of the Experimental Analysis of Behavior, 62,* 201–223.

Allison, J. (1983). *Behavioral economics.* New York: Praeger.

Allison, J. (1989). The nature of reinforcement. In S. B. Klein & R. R. Mowrer (Eds.), *Contemporary learning theories: Instrumental conditioning and the impact of biological constraints on learning* (pp. 13–39). Hillsdale, NJ: Erlbaum.

Allison, J. (1993). Response deprivation, reinforcement, and economics. *Journal of the Experimental Analysis of Behavior, 60,* 129–140.

Allison, J., Buxton, A., & Moore, K. E. (1987). Bliss points, stop lines, and performance under schedule constraint. *Journal of Experimental Psychology: Animal Behavior Processes, 13,* 331–340.

Amsel, A. (1958). The role of frustrative nonreward in noncontinuous reward situations. *Psychological Bulletin, 55,* 102–119.

Amsel, A. (1962). Frustrative nonreward in partial reinforcement and discrimination learning. *Psychological Review, 69,* 306–328.

Amsel, A. (1967). Partial reinforcement effects on vigor and persistence. In K. W. Spence & J. T. Spence (Eds.), *The psychology of learning and motivation* (Vol. 1, pp. 1–65). New York: Academic Press.

Amsel, A. (1989). *Behaviorism, neobehaviorism, and cognitivism in learning theory.* Hillsdale, NJ: Erlbaum.

Amsel, A. (1992). *Frustration theory.* Cambridge, England: Cambridge University Press.

Anderson, D. C., Crowell, C. R., Cunningham, C. L., & Lupo, J. V. (1979). Behavior during shock exposure as a determinant of subsequent interference with shuttle box escape-avoidance learning in the rat. *Journal of Experimental Psychology: Animal Behavior Processes, 5,* 243–257.

Anderson, M. C., & Shettleworth, S. J. (1977). Behavioral adaptation to fixed-interval and fixed-time food delivery in golden hamsters. *Journal of the Experimental Analysis of Behavior, 25,* 33–49.

Anger, D. (1963). The role of temporal discrimination in the reinforcement of Sidman avoidance behavior. *Journal of the Experimental Analysis of Behavior, 6,* 477–506.

Anisman, H., de Catanzaro, D., & Remington, G. (1978). Escape performance following exposure to inescapable shock: Deficits in motor response maintenance. *Journal of Experimental Psychology: Animal Behavior Processes, 4,* 197–218.

Anisman, H., Hamilton, M., & Zacharko, R. M. (1984). Cue and response-choice acquisition and reversal after exposure to uncontrollable shock: Induction of response perseveration. *Journal of Experimental Psychology: Animal Behavior Processes, 10,* 229–243.

Aparicio, C. F. (2001). Overmatching in rats: The barrier choice paradigm. *Journal of the Experimental Analysis of Behavior, 75,* 93–106.

Arcediano, F., Ortega, N., & Matute, H. (1996). A behavioural preparation for the study of human Pavlovian conditioning. *Quarterly Journal of Experimental Psychology, 49B,* 270–283.

Astley, S. L., & Wasserman, E. A. (1998). Novelty and functional equivalence in superordinate categorization by pigeons. *Animal Learning & Behavior, 26,* 125–138.

Astley, S. L., & Wasserman, E. A. (1999). Superordinate category formation in pigeons: Association with a common delay or probability of food reinforcement makes perceptually dissimilar stimuli functionally equivalent. *Journal of Experimental Psychology: Animal Behavior Processes, 25,* 415–432.

Aust, U., & Huber, L. (2001). The role of item- and category-specific information in the discrimination of people versus nonpeople images by pigeons. *Animal Learning & Behavior, 29,* 107–119.

Aydin, A., & Pearce, J. M. (1994). Prototype effects in categorization by pigeons. *Journal of Experimental Psychology: Animal Behavior Processes, 20,* 264–277.

Ayres, J. J. B. (1998). Fear conditioning and avoidance. In W. O'Donohue (Ed.), *Learning and behavior therapy* (pp. 122–145). Boston: Allyn and Bacon.

Ayres, J. J. B., Haddad, C., & Albert, M. (1987). One-trial excitatory backward conditioning as assessed by suppression of licking in rats: Concurrent observations of lick suppression and defensive behaviors. *Animal Learning & Behavior, 15,* 212–217.

Azorlosa, J. L., & Cicala, G. A. (1986). Blocking of conditioned suppression with 1 or 10 compound trials. *Animal Learning & Behavior, 14,* 163–167.

Azrin, N. H. (1956). Some effects of two intermittent schedules of immediate and non-immediate punishment. *Journal of Psychology, 42,* 3–21.

Azrin, N. H. (1958). Some effects of noise on human behavior. *Journal of the Experimental Analysis of Behavior, 1,* 183–200.

Azrin, N. H. (1959). Punishment and recovery during fixed ratio performance. *Journal of the Experimental Analysis of Behavior, 2,* 301–305.

Azrin, N. H. (1960). Effects of punishment intensity during variable-interval reinforcement. *Journal of the Experimental Analysis of Behavior, 3,* 123–142.

Azrin, N. H., & Holz, W. C. (1961). Punishment during fixed-interval reinforcement. *Journal of the Experimental Analysis of Behavior, 4,* 343–347.

Azrin, N. H., & Holz, W. C. (1966). Punishment. In W. K. Honig (Ed.), *Operant behavior: Areas of research and application* (pp. 380–447). New York: Appleton-Century-Crofts.

Azrin, N. H., Holz, W. C., & Hake, D. F. (1963). Fixed-ratio punishment. *Journal of the Experimental Analysis of Behavior, 6,* 141–148.

Azrin, N. H., Hutchinson, R. R., & Hake, D. F. (1966). Extinction-induced aggression. *Journal of the Experimental Analysis of Behavior, 9,* 191–204.

Babkin, B. P. (1949). *Pavlov: A biography.* Chicago: University of Chicago Press.

Baer, D. M., & Wolf, M. M. (1970). The entry into natural communities of reinforcement. In R. Ulrich, T. Stachnik, & J. Mabry (Eds.), *Control of human behavior* (Vol. 2, pp. 319–324). Glenview, IL: Scott, Foresman.

Baerends, G. P. (1988). Ethology. In R. C. Atkinson, R. J. Herrnstein, G. Lindzey, & R. D. Luce (Eds.), *Stevens' handbook of experimental psychology* (Vol. 1, pp. 765–830). New York: Wiley.

Baerends, G. P., & Drent, R. H. (Eds.). (1982). The herring gull and its egg. Part II. The responsiveness to egg features. *Behaviour, 82,* 1–417.

Baker, A. G., & Baker, P. A. (1985). Does inhibition differ from excitation? Proactive interference, contextual conditioning, and extinction. In R. R. Miller & N. E. Spear (Eds.), *Information processing in animals: Conditioned inhibition* (pp. 151–183). Hillsdale, NJ: Erlbaum.

Baker, T. B., & Tiffany, S. T. (1985). Morphine tolerance as habituation. *Psychological Review, 92,* 78–108.

Balaz, M. A., Kasprow, W. J., & Miller, R. R. (1982). Blocking with a single compound trial. *Animal Learning & Behavior, 10,* 271–276.

Balda, R. P., & Turek, R. J. (1984). The cache-recovery system as an example of memory capabilities in Clark's nutcracker. In H. L. Roitblat, T. G. Bever, & H. S. Terrace (Eds.), *Animal cognition* (pp. 513–532). Hillsdale, NJ: Erlbaum.

Balleine, B. W. (2001). Incentive processes in instrumental conditioning. In R. R. Mowrer and S. B. Klein (Eds.), *Handbook of contemporary learning theories* (pp. 307–366). Mahwah, NJ: Erlbaum.

Balsam, P. D. (1985). The functions of context in learning and performance. In P. D. Balsam & A. Tomie (Eds.), *Context and learning* (pp. 1–21). Hillsdale, NJ: Erlbaum.

Balsam, P. D. (1988). Selection, representation, and equivalence of controlling stimuli. In R. C. Atkinson, R. J. Herrnstein, G. Lindzey, & R. D. Luce (Eds.), *Stevens' handbook of experimental psychology: Vol. 2. Learning and cognition* (pp. 111–166). New York: Wiley.

Balsam, P. D., & Tomie, A. (Eds.). (1985). *Context and learning.* Hillsdale, NJ: Erlbaum.

Balsam, P. D., Deich, J. D., Ohyama, T., & Stokes, P. D. (1998). Origins of new behavior. In W. O'Donohue (Ed.), *Learning and behavior therapy* (pp. 403–420). Boston: Allyn and Bacon.

Banks, R. K. (1976). Resistance to punishment as a function of intensity and frequency of prior punishment experience. *Learning and Motivation, 7,* 551–558.

Bargh, J. A., & Chartrand, T. L. (1999). The unbearable automaticity of being. *American Psychologist, 54,* 462–479.

Barker, L. M., Best, M. R., & Domjan, M. (Eds.). (1977). *Learning mechanisms in food selection.* Waco, TX: Baylor University Press.

Barkley, C. L., & Jacobs, L. F. (1998). Visual environment and delay affect cache retrieval accuracy in a food-storing rodent. *Animal Learning & Behavior, 26,* 439–447.

Barnet, R. C., & Miller, R. R. (1996). Second-order excitation mediated by a backward conditioned inhibitor. *Journal of Experimental Psychology: Animal Behavior Processes, 22,* 279–296.

Barnet, R. C., Arnold, H. M., & Miller, R. R. (1991). Simultaneous conditioning demonstrated in second-order conditioning: Evidence for similar associative structure in forward and simultaneous conditioning. *Learning and Motivation, 22,* 253–268.

Barnet, R. C., Cole, R. P., & Miller, R. R. (1997). Temporal integration in second-order conditioning and sensory preconditioning. *Animal Learning & Behavior, 25,* 221–233.

Baron, A. (1965). Delayed punishment of a runway response. *Journal of Comparative and Physiological Psychology, 60,* 131–134.

Baron, A., & Herpolsheimer, L. R. (1999). Averaging effects in the study of fixed-ratio response patterns. *Journal of the Experimental Analysis of Behavior, 71,* 145–153.

Baron, A., & Leinenweber, A. (1994). Molecular and molar analyses of fixed-interval performance. *Journal of the Experimental Analysis of Behavior, 61,* 11–18.

Baron, A., & Menich, S. R. (1985). Reaction times of younger and older men: Effects of compound samples and a prechoice signal on delayed matching-to-sample performances. *Journal of the Experimental Analysis of Behavior, 44,* 1–14.

Barrett, J. E., & Hoffmann, S. M. (1991). Neurochemical changes correlated with behavior maintained under fixed-interval and fixed-ratio schedules of reinforcement. *Journal of the Experimental Analysis of Behavior, 56,* 395–405.

Barton, L. E., Brulle, A. R., & Repp, A. C. (1986). Maintenance of therapeutic change by momentary DRO. *Journal of Applied Behavior Analysis, 19,* 277–282.

Bashinski, H., Werner, J., & Rudy, J. (1985). Determinants of infant visual attention: Evidence for a two-process theory. *Journal of Experimental Child Psychology, 39* 580–598.

Batsell, W. R., Jr., & Batson, J. D. (1999). Augmentation of taste conditioning by a preconditioned odor. *Journal of Experimental Psychology: Animal Behavior Processes, 25,* 374–388.

Batsell, W. R., Jr., & Brown, A. S. (1998). Human flavor-aversion learning: A comparison of traditional aversions and cognitive aversions. *Learning and Motivation, 29,* 383–396.

Batsell, W. R., Jr., Paschall, G. Y., Gleason, D. I., & Batson, J. D. (2001). Taste preconditioning augments odor-aversion learning. *Journal of Experimental Psychology: Animal Behavior Processes, 27,* 30–47.

Batson, J. D., & Batsell, W. R., Jr. (2000). Augmentation, not blocking, in an A+/AX+ flavor-conditioning procedure. *Psychonomic Bulletin & Review, 7,* 466–471.

Baum, M. (1969). Extinction of avoidance response following response prevention: Some parametric investigations. *Canadian Journal of Psychology, 23,* 1–10.

Baum, M. (1970). Extinction of avoidance responding through response prevention (flooding). *Psychological Bulletin, 74,* 276–284.

Baum, W. M. (1974). On two types of deviation from the matching law: Bias and undermatching. *Journal of the Experimental Analysis of Behavior, 22,* 231–242.

Baum, W. M. (1975). Time allocation in human vigilance. *Journal of the Experimental Analysis of Behavior, 23,* 45–53.

Baum, W. M. (1979). Matching, undermatching, and overmatching in studies of choice. *Journal of the Experimental Analysis of Behavior, 32,* 269–281.

Baum, W. M. (1981). Optimization and the matching law as accounts of instrumental behavior. *Journal of the Experimental Analysis of Behavior, 36,* 387–403.

Baum, W. M. (1993). Performances on ratio and interval schedules of reinforcement: Data and theory. *Journal of the Experimental Analysis of Behavior, 59,* 245–264.

Baum, W. M., & Aparicio, C. F. (1999). Optimality and concurrent variable-interval variable-ratio schedules. *Journal of the Experimental Analysis of Behavior, 71,* 75–89.

Baum, W. M., & Kraft, J. R. (1998). Group choice: Competition, travel, and the ideal free distribution. *Journal of the Experimental Analysis of Behavior, 69,* 227–245.

Baxter, D. J., & Zamble, E. (1982). Reinforcer and response specificity in appetitive transfer of control. *Animal Learning & Behavior, 10,* 201–210.

Beatty, W. W., & Shavalia, D. A. (1980a). Rat spatial memory: Resistance to retroactive interference at long retention intervals. *Animal Learning & Behavior, 8,* 550–552.

Beatty, W. W., & Shavalia, D. A. (1980b). Spatial memory in rats: Time course of working memory and effects of anesthetics. *Behavioral and Neural Biology, 28,* 454–462.

Bechterev, V. M. (1913). *La psychologie objective.* Paris: Alcan.

Beck, C. D. O., & Rankin, C. H. (1997). Long-term habituation is produced by distributed training at long ISIs and not by massed training or short ISIs in *Caenorhabditis elegans. Animal Learning & Behavior, 25,* 446–457.

Bee, M. A. (2001). Habituation and sensitization of aggression in bullfrogs (*Rana catesbeiana*): Testing the dual-process theory of habituation. *Journal of Comparative Psychology, 115,* 307–316.

Belke, T. W. (1992). Stimulus preference and the transitivity of preference. *Animal Learning & Behavior, 20,* 401–406.

Belke, T. W. (1998). Qualitatively different reinforcers and parameters of Herrnstein's (1970) response-strength equation. *Animal Learning & Behavior, 26,* 235–242.

Belke, T. W., & Heyman, G. M. (1994a). A matching law analysis of the reinforcing efficacy of wheel running in rats. *Animal Learning & Behavior, 22,* 267–274.

Belke, T. W., & Heyman, G. M. (1994b). Increasing and signaling background reinforcement: Effect on the foreground response-reinforcer relation. *Journal of the Experimental Analysis of Behavior, 61,* 65–81.

Belke, T. W., & Spetch, M. (1994). Choice between reliable and unreliable reinforcement alternatives revisited: Preference for unreliable reinforcement. *Journal of the Experimental Analysis of Behavior, 62,* 353–366.

Bell, M. C. (1999). Pavlovian contingencies and resistance to change in a multiple schedule. *Journal of the Experimental Analysis of Behavior, 72,* 81–96.

Bernstein, I. L. (1978). Learned taste aversions in children receiving chemotherapy. *Science, 200,* 1302–1303.

Bernstein, I. L. (1991). Aversion conditioning in response to cancer and cancer treatment. *Clinical Psychology Review, 11,* 185–191.

Bernstein, I. L., & Borson, S. (1986). Learned food aversion: A component of anorexia syndromes. *Psychological Review, 93,* 462–472.

Bernstein, I. L., & Webster, M. M. (1980). Learned taste aversions in humans. *Physiology and Behavior, 25,* 363–366.

Berridge, K. C. (2001). Reward learning: Reinforcement, incentives, and expectations. In D. L. Medin (Ed.), *The psychology of learning and motivation* (Vol. 40, pp. 223–278). San Diego: Academic Press.

Berridge, K. C., & Schulkin, J. (1989). Palatability shift of a salt-associated incentive during sodium depletion. *Quarterly Journal of Experimental Psychology, 41B,* 121–138.

Best, M. R., Dunn, D. P., Batson, J. D., Meachum, C. L., & Nash, S. M. (1985). Extinguishing conditioned inhibition in flavour-aversion learning: Effects of repeated testing and extinction of the excitatory element. *Quarterly Journal of Experimental Psychology, 37B,* 359–378.

Bevins, R. A., & Ayres, J. J. B. (1994). Factors affecting rats' location during conditioned suppression training. *Animal Learning and Behavior, 22,* 302–308.

Bevins, R. A., Delzer, T. A., & Bardo, M. T. (1996). Second-order conditioning detects unexpressed morphine-induced salt aversion. *Animal Learning & Behavior, 24,* 221–229.

Bhatt, R. S., Rovee-Collier, C., & Shyi, G. C.-W. (1994). Global and local processing of incidental information and memory retrieval at 6 months. *Journal of Experimental Child Psychology, 52,* 141–162.

Bickel, W. K., DeGrandpre, R. J., Hughes, J. R., & Higgins, S. T. (1991). Behavioral economics of drug self-administration. II. A unit-price analysis of cigarette smoking. *Journal of the Experimental Analysis of Behavior, 55,* 145–154.

Bickel, W. K., Green, L., & Vuchinich, R. E. (1995). Behavioral economics. *Journal of the Experimental Analysis of Behavior, 64,* 257–262.

Bickel, W. K., Madden, G. J., & DeGrandpre, R. J. (1997). Modeling the effects of combined behavioral and pharmacological treatment on cigarette smoking: Behavioral-economic analyses. *Experimental and Clinical Psychopharmacology, 5,* 334–343.

Bickel, W. K., Odum, A. L., & Madden, G. J. (1999). Impulsivity and cigarette smoking: Delay discounting in current, never, and ex-smokers. *Psychopharmacology, 146,* 447–454.

Biegler, R. (2000). Possible uses of path integration in animal navigation. *Animal Learning & Behavior, 28,* 257–277.

Bitterman, M. E. (1964). Classical conditioning in the goldfish as a function of the CS-US interval. *Journal of Comparative and Physiological Psychology, 58,* 359–366.

Bitterman, M. E. (1988). Vertebrate-invertebrate comparisons. In H. J. Jerison & I. Jerison (Eds.), *Intelligence and evolutionary biology* (NATO ASI Series, Vol. G17, pp. 251–276). Berlin: Springer.

Bitterman, M. E. (1996). Comparative analysis of learning in honeybees. *Animal Learning & Behavior, 24,* 123–141.

Bizo, L. A., Bogdanov, S. V., & Killeen, P. R. (1998). Satiation causes within-session decreases in instrumental responding. *Journal of Experimental Psychology: Animal Behavior Processes, 24,* 439–452.

Bizo, L. A., Kettle, L. C., & Killeen, P. R. (2001). Rats don't always respond faster for more food: The paradoxical incentive effect. *Animal Learning & Behavior, 29,* 66–78.

Bizo, L. A., & Killeen, P. R. (1997). Models of ratio schedule performance. *Journal of Experimental Psychology: Animal Behavior Processes, 23,* 351–367.

Bizo, L. A., & White, K. G. (1994). Pacemaker rate in the behavioral theory of timing. *Journal of Experimental Psychology: Animal Behavior Processes, 20,* 308–321.

Bizo, L. A., & White, K. G. (1995a). Biasing the pacemaker in the behavioral theory of timing. *Journal of the Experimental Analysis of Behavior, 64,* 225–235.

Bizo, L. A., & White, K. G. (1995b). Reinforcement context and pacemaker rate in the behavioral theory of timing. *Animal Learning & Behavior, 23,* 376–382.

Bjork, R. A. (1972). The updating of human memory. In G. H. Bower (Ed.), *The psychology of learning and motivation* (Vol. 12, pp. 235–259). New York: Academic Press.

Black, A. H. (1971). Autonomic aversive conditioning in infrahuman subjects. In F. R. Brush (Ed.), *Aversive conditioning and learning* (pp. 3–104). New York: Academic Press.

Black, A. H. (1977). Comments on "Learned helplessness: Theory and evidence" by Maier and Seligman. *Journal of Experimental Psychology: General, 106,* 41–43.

Blackman, D. (1977). Conditioned suppression and the effects of classical conditioning on operant behavior. In W. K. Honig & J. E. R. Staddon (Eds.), *Handbook of operant behavior* (pp. 340–363). Englewood Cliffs, NJ: Prentice-Hall.

Blaisdell, A. P., Gunther, L. M., & Miller, R. R. (1999). Recovery from blocking achieved by extinguishing the blocking CS. *Animal Learning & Behavior, 27,* 63–76.

Blakely, E., & Schlinger, H. (1988). Determinants of pausing under variable-ratio schedules: Reinforcer magnitude, ratio size, and schedule configuration. *Journal of the Experimental Analysis of Behavior, 50,* 65–73.

Blakemore, C., & Cooper, G. F. (1970). Development of the brain depends on visual environment. *Science, 228,* 477–478.

Blanchard, D. C. (1997). Stimulus, environmental, and pharmacological control of defensive behaviors. In M. E. Bouton & M. S. Fanselow (Eds.), *Learning, motivation, and cognition* (pp. 283–303). Washington, DC: American Psychological Association.

Blass, E. M., Ganchrow, J. R., & Steiner, J. E. (1984). Classical conditioning in newborn humans 2–48 hours of age. *Infant Behavior and Development, 7,* 223–235.

Bliss, T. V. P., & Lomo, T. (1973). Long-lasting potentiation of synaptic transmission in the dentate area of the anesthetized rabbit following stimulation of the perforant path. *Journal of Physiology, 232,* 331–356.

Blough, D. S. (1959). Delayed matching in the pigeon. *Journal of the Experimental Analysis of Behavior, 2,* 151–160.

Blough, D. S. (1996). Error factors in pigeon discrimination and delayed matching. *Journal of Experimental Psychology: Animal Behavior Processes, 22,* 118–131.

Blumberg, M. S., & Wasserman, E. A. (1995). Animal mind and the argument from design. *American Psychologist, 50,* 133–144.

Boakes, R. A. (1984). *From Darwin to behaviourism.* Cambridge: Cambridge University Press.

Boakes, R. A., & Halliday, M. S. (Eds.). (1972). *Inhibition and learning.* London: Academic Press.

Boakes, R. A., Westbrook, R. F., Elliott, M., & Swinbourne, A. L. (1997). Context dependency of conditioned aversions to water and sweet tastes. *Journal of Experimental Psychology: Animal Behavior Processes, 25,* 324–333.

Boice, R. (1973). Domestication. *Psychological Bulletin, 80,* 215–230.

Boice, R. (1977). Burrows of wild and albino rats: Effects of domestication, outdoor raising, age, experience, and maternal state. *Journal of Comparative and Physiological Psychology, 91,* 649–661.

Boice, R. (1981). Behavioral comparability of wild and domesticated rats. *Behavior Genetics, 11,* 545–553.

Bolles, R. C. (1969). Avoidance and escape learning: Simultaneous acquisition of different responses. *Journal of Comparative and Physiological Psychology, 68,* 355–358.

Bolles, R. C. (1970). Species-specific defense reactions and avoidance learning. *Psychological Review, 71,* 32–48.

Bolles, R. C. (1971). Species-specific defense reaction. In F. R. Brush (Ed.), *Aversive conditioning and learning* (pp. 183–233). New York: Academic Press.

Bolles, R. C. (1972a). The avoidance learning problem. In G. H. Bower (Ed.), *The psychology of learning and motivation* (Vol. 6, pp. 97–145). New York: Academic Press.

Bolles, R. C. (1972b). Reinforcement, expectancy, and learning. *Psychological Review, 79,* 394–409.

Bolles, R. C., & Fanselow, M. S. (1980). A perceptual defensive-recuperative model of fear and pain. *Behavioral and Brain Sciences, 3,* 291–323.

Bolles, R. C., & Grossen, N. E. (1969). Effects of an informational stimulus on the acquisition of avoidance behavior in rats. *Journal of Comparative and Physiological Psychology, 68,* 90–99.

Bolles, R. C., Holtz, R., Dunn, T., & Hill, W. (1980). Comparisons of stimulus learning and response learning in a punishment situation. *Learning and Motivation, 11,* 78–96.

Bolles, R. C., & Riley, A. L. (1973). Freezing as an avoidance response: Another look at the operant-respondent distinction. *Learning and Motivation, 4,* 268–275.

Bolles, R. C., Stokes, L. W., & Younger, M. S. (1966). Does CS termination reinforce avoidance behavior? *Journal of Comparative and Physiological Psychology, 62,* 201–207.

Bonardi, C. (1996). Transfer of occasion setting: The role of generalization decrement. *Animal Learning & Behavior, 24,* 277–289.

Bonardi, C., Rey, V., Richmond, M., & Hall, G. (1993). Acquired equivalence of cues in pigeon autoshaping: Effects of training with common consequences and with common antecedents. *Animal Learning & Behavior, 21,* 369–376.

Borovsky, D., & Rovee-Collier, C. (1990). Contextual constraints on memory retrieval at six months. *Child Development, 61,* 1569–1583.

Borszcz, G. S., Cranney, J., & Leaton, R. N. (1989). Influence of long-term sensitization on long-term habituation of the acoustic startle response in rats: Central gray lesions, preexposure, and extinction. *Journal of Experimental Psychology: Animal Behavior Processes, 15,* 54–64.

Bouton, M. E. (1984). Differential control by context in the inflation and reinstatement paradigms. *Journal of Experimental Psychology: Animal Behavior Processes, 10,* 56–74.

Bouton, M. E. (1986). Slow reacquisition following the extinction of conditioned suppression. *Learning and Motivation, 17,* 1–15.

Bouton, M. E. (1988). Context and ambiguity in the extinction of emotional learning: Implications for exposure therapy. *Behaviour Research and Therapy, 26,* 137–149.

Bouton, M. E. (1991). Context and retrieval in extinction and in other examples of interference in simple associative learning. In L. Dachowski & C. F. Flaherty (Eds.), *Current topics in animal learning* (pp. 25–53). Hillsdale, NJ: Erlbaum.

Bouton, M. E. (1993). Context, time, and memory retrieval in the interference paradigms of Pavlovian learning. *Psychological Bulletin, 114,* 80–99.

Bouton, M. E. (1994). Conditioning, remembering, and forgetting. *Journal of Experimental Psychology: Animal Behavior Processes, 20,* 219–231.

Bouton, M. E. (2001). Classical conditioning and clinical psychology. In N. J. Smelser & P. B. Baltes (Eds.), *Encyclopedia of the social and behavioral sciences.* (Vol. 3, pp. 1942–1945). Oxford: Elsevier Science.

Bouton, M. E., & Bolles, R. C. (1980). Conditioned fear assessed by freezing and by the suppression of three different baselines. *Animal Learning & Behavior, 8,* 429–434.

Bouton, M. E., Kenney, F. A., & Rosengard, C. (1990). State-dependent fear extinction with two benzodiazepine tranquilizers. *Behavioral Neuroscience, 104,* 44–55.

Bouton, M. E., & King, D. A. (1983). Contextual control of the extinction of conditioned fear: Tests for the associative value of the context. *Journal of Experimental Psychology: Animal Behavior Processes, 9,* 248–265.

Bouton, M. E., Mineka, S., & Barlow, D. H. (2001). A modern learning theory perspective on the etiology of panic disorder. *Psychological Review, 108,* 4–32.

Bouton, M. E., & Nelson, J. B. (1998). The role of context in classical conditioning: Some implications for behavior therapy. In O'Donohue, W. (Ed.), *Learning and behavior therapy* (pp. 59–84). Boston: Allyn and Bacon.

Bouton, M. E., & Peck, C. A. (1989). Context effects on conditioning, extinction, and reinstatement in an appetitive conditioning preparation. *Animal Learning & Behavior, 17,* 188–198.

Bouton, M. E., & Ricker, S. T. (1994). Renewal of extinguished responding in a second context. *Animal Learning & Behavior, 22,* 317–324.

Bouton, M. E., & Swartzentruber, D. (1986). Analysis of the associative and occasion-setting properties of contexts participating in a Pavlovian discrimination. *Journal of Experimental Psychology: Animal Behavior Processes, 12,* 333–350.

Bouton, M. E., & Swartzentruber, D. (1989). Slow reacquisition following extinction: Context, encoding, and retrieval mechanisms. *Journal of Experimental Psychology: Animal Behavior Processes, 15,* 43–53.

Bowe, C. A., Miller, J. D., & Green, L. (1987). Qualities and locations of stimuli and responses affecting discrimination learning of chinchillas (*Chinchilla laniger*) and pigeons (*Columbia livia*). *Journal of Comparative Psychology, 101,* 132–138.

Bradshaw, C. M., & Szabadi, E. (Eds.). (1997). *Time and behaviour: Psychological and neurobiological analyses.* Oxford: Elsevier Science.

Brakke, K. E., & Savage-Rumbaugh, E. S. (1995). The development of language skills in bonobo and chimpanzee. I. Comprehension. *Language & Communication, 15,* 121–148.

Branch, M. N., & Hackenberg, T. D. (1998). Humans are animals, too: Connecting animal research to human behavior and cognition. In W. O'Donohue (Ed.), *Learning and behavior therapy* (pp. 15–35). Boston: Allyn and Bacon.

Braveman, N. S., & Bronstein, P. (Eds.). (1985). *Annals of the New York Academy of Sciences: Vol. 443. Experimental assessments and clinical applications of conditioned food aversions.* New York: New York Academy of Sciences.

Breland, K., & Breland, M. (1961). The misbehavior of organisms. *American Psychologist, 16,* 681–684.

Brener, J., & Mitchell, S. (1989). Changes in energy expenditure and work during response acquisition in rats. *Journal of Experimental Psychology: Animal Behavior Processes, 15,* 166–175.

Brogden, W. J., Lipman, E. A., & Culler, E. (1938). The role of incentive in conditioning and extinction. *American Journal of Psychology, 51,* 109–117.

Brooks, D. C. (2000). Recent and remote extinction cues reduce spontaneous recovery. *Quarterly Journal of Experimental Psychology, 53B,* 25–58.

Brooks, D. C., & Bouton, M. E. (1993). A retrieval cue for extinction attenuates spontaneous recovery. *Journal of Experimental Psychology: Animal Behavior Processes, 19,* 77–89.

Brooks, D. C., Palmatier, M. I., Garcia, E. O., & Johnson, J. L. (1999). An extinction cue reduces spontaneous recovery of a conditioned taste aversion. *Animal Learning & Behavior, 27,* 77–88.

Brown, B. L., Hemmes, N. S., & de Vaca, S. C. (1992). Effects of intratrial stimulus change on fixed-interval performance: The roles of clock and memory processes. *Animal Learning & Behavior, 20,* 83–93.

Brown, B. L., Hemmes, N. S., & de Vaca, S. C. (1997). Timing of the CS-US interval by pigeons in trace and delay autoshaping. *Quarterly Journal of Experimental Psychology, 50B,* 40–53.

Brown, J. S. (1969). Factors affecting self-punitive behavior. In B. Campbell & R. M. Church (Eds.), *Punishment and aversive behavior.* New York: Appleton-Century-Crofts.

Brown, J. S., & Cunningham, C. L. (1981). The paradox of persisting self-punitive behavior. *Neuroscience & Biobehavioral Reviews, 5,* 343–354.

Brown, J. S., & Jacobs, A. (1949). The role of fear in the motivation and acquisition of responses. *Journal of Experimental Psychology, 39,* 747–759.

Brown, M. F., & Bing, M. N. (1997). In the dark: Spatial choice when access to spatial cues is restricted. *Animal Learning & Behavior, 25,* 21–30.

Brown, M. F., DiGello, E., Milewski, M., Wilson, M., & Kozak, M. (2000). Spatial pattern learning in rats: Conditional control by two patterns. *Animal Learning & Behavior, 28,* 278–287.

Brown, M. F., & Moore, J. A. (1997). In the dark II: Spatial choice when access to extrinsic spatial cues is eliminated. *Animal Learning & Behavior, 25,* 335–346.

Brown, M. F., & Terrinoni, M. (1996). Control of choice by the spatial configuration of goals. *Journal of Experimental Psychology: Animal Behavior Processes, 22,* 438–446.

Brown, M. F., Wheeler, E. A., & Riley, D. A. (1989). Evidence for a shift in the choice criterion of rats in a 12–arm radial maze. *Animal Learning & Behavior, 17,* 12–20.

Brown, P. L., & Jenkins, H. M. (1968). Auto-shaping the pigeon's key peck. *Journal of the Experimental Analysis of Behavior, 11,* 1–8.

Bruner, D., Gibbon, J., & Fairhurst, S. (1994). Choice between fixed and variable delays with different reward amounts. *Journal of Experimental Psychology: Animal Behavior Processes, 20,* 331– 346.

Budzynski, C. A., & Bingman, V. P. (1999). Time-of-day discriminative learning in homing pigeons, *Columba livia. Animal Learning & Behavior, 27,* 295–302.

Burkhard, B., Rachlin, H., & Schrader, S. (1978). Reinforcement and punishment in a closed system. *Learning and Motivation, 9,* 392–410.

Burns, M., & Domjan, M. (1996). Sign tracking versus goal tracking in the sexual conditioning of male Japanese quail (*Coturnix japonica*). *Journal of Experimental Psychology: Animal Behavior Processes, 22,* 297–306.

Burns, M., & Domjan, M. (2000). Sign tracking in domesticated quail with one trial a day: Generality across CS and US parameters. *Animal Learning & Behavior, 28,* 109–119.

Burns, M., & Domjan, M. (2001). Topography of spatially directed conditioned responding: Effects of context and trial duration. *Journal of Experimental Psychology: Animal Behavior Processes, 27,* 269–278.

Cadieu, N., El Ghadraoui, L., & Cadieu, J. C. (2000). Egg-laying preference for ethanol involving learning has adaptive significance in *Drosophila melanogaster. Animal Learning & Behavior, 28,* 187–194.

Cameron, J., & Pierce, W. D. (1994). Reinforcement, reward, and intrinsic motivation: A meta-analysis. *Review of Educational Research, 64,* 363–423.

Camhi, J. M. (1984). *Neuroethology.* Sunderland, MA: Sinauer.

Camp, D. S., Raymond, G. A., & Church, R. M. (1967). Temporal relationship between response and punishment. *Journal of Experimental Psychology, 74,* 114–123.

Campbell, B. A., & Church, R. M. (Eds.). (1969). *Punishment and aversive behavior.* New York: Appleton-Century-Crofts.

Campbell, B. A., & Randall, P. K. (1976). The effect of reinstatement stimulus conditions on the maintenance of long-term memory. *Developmental Psychobiology, 9,* 325–333.

Cándido, A., Maldonado, A., & Vila, J. (1991). Effects of duration of feedback on signaled avoidance. *Animal Learning & Behavior, 19,* 81–87.

Capaldi, E. D., Hunter, M. J., & Lyn, S. A. (1997). Conditioning with taste as the CS in conditioned flavor preference learning. *Animal Learning & Behavior, 25,* 427–436.

Capaldi, E. J. (1967). A sequential hypothesis of instrumental learning. In K. W. Spence & J. T. Spence (Eds.), *The psychology of learning and motivation* (Vol. 1, pp. 67–156). New York: Academic Press.

Capaldi, E. J. (1971). Memory and learning: A sequential viewpoint. In W. K. Honig & P. H. R. James (Eds.), *Animal memory* (pp. 115–154). New York: Academic Press.

Capaldi, E. J., Alptekin, S., & Birmingham, K. M. (1996). Instrumental performance and time between reinforcements: Intimate relation to learning or memory retrieval? *Animal Learning & Behavior, 24,* 211–220.

Capaldi, E. J., Alptekin, S., Miller, D. J., & Barry, K. (1992). The role of instrumental responses in memory retrieval in a T-maze. *Quarterly Journal of Experimental Psychology, 45B,* 65–76.

Carew, T. J., Hawkins, R. D., & Kandel, E. R. (1983). Differential classical conditioning of a defensive withdrawal reflex in *Aplysia californica. Science, 219,* 397–400.

Carlton, J. L., Mitchell, K. G., Schachtman, T. R. (1996). Conditioned inhibition produced by extinction of a conditioned stimulus. *Learning and Motivation, 27,* 335–361.

Carr, D., & Blackman, D. E. (2001). Relations among equivalence, naming, and conflicting baseline control. *Journal of the Experimental Analysis of Behavior, 75,* 55–76.

Carr, D., Wilkinson, K. M., Blackman, D., & McIlvane, W. J. (2000). Equivalence classes in individuals with minimal verbal repertoires. *Journal of the Experimental Analysis of Behavior, 74,* 101–114.

Carrell, L. E., Cannon, D. S., Best, M. R., & Stone, M. J. (1986). Nausea and radiation-induced taste aversions in cancer patients. *Appetite, 7,* 203–208.

Carroll, M. E., Carmona, G. G., & May, S. A. (1991). Modifying drug-reinforced behavior by altering the economic conditions of the drug and nondrug reinforcer. *Journal of the Experimental Analysis of Behavior, 56,* 361–376.

Carroll, M. E., & Overmier, J. B. (2001). *Animal research and human health.* Washington, DC: American Psychological Association.

Carter, M. M., Hollon, S. D., Carson, R., & Shelton, R. C. (1995). Effects of a safe person on induced distress following a biological challenge in panic disorder with agoraphobics. *Journal of Abnormal Psychology, 104,* 156–163.

Caspy, T., & Lubow, R. E. (1981). Generality of US preexposure effects: Transfer from food to shock or shock to food with and without the same response requirements. *Animal Learning & Behavior, 9,* 524–532.

Catania, A. C. (1999). Thorndike's legacy: Learning, selection, and the law of effect. *Journal of the Experimental Analysis of Behavior, 72,* 425–428.

Cerutti, D., & Catania, A. C. (1997). Pigeons' preference for free choice: Number of keys versus key area. *Journal of the Experimental Analysis of Behavior, 68,* 349–356.

Chance, P. (1999). Thorndike's puzzle boxes and the origins of the experimental analysis of behavior. *Journal of the Experimental Analysis of Behavior, 72,* 433–440.

Charlop, M. H., Kurtz, P. F., & Casey, F. G. (1990). Using aberrant behaviors as reinforcers for autistic children. *Journal of Applied Behavior Analysis, 23,* 163–181.

Chelonis, J. J., Calton, J. L., Hart, J. A., & Schachtman, T. R. (1999). Attenuation of the renewal effect by extinction in multiple contexts. *Learning and Motivation, 30,* 1–14.

Chen, J.-S., & Amsel, A. (1980). Learned persistence at 11–12 but not at 10–11 days in infant rats. *Developmental Psychobiology, 13,* 481–491.

Chen, S., Swartz, K. B., & Terrace, H. S. (1997). Knowledge of the ordinal position of list items in rhesus monkeys. *Psychological Science, 8,* 80–86.

Cheng, K. (2000). How honeybees find a place: Lessons from a simple mind. *Animal Learning & Behavior, 28,* 1–15.

Cheng, K., & Spetch, M. L. (1995). Stimulus control in the use of landmarks by pigeons in a touch-screen task. *Journal of the Experimental Analysis of Behavior, 63,* 187–201.

Cheng, K., Spetch, M. L., & Johnson, M. (1997). Spatial peak shift and generalization in pigeons. *Journal of Experimental Psychology: Animal Behavior Processes, 23,* 469–481.

Cheng, K., & Westwood, R. (1993). Analysis of single trials in pigeons' timing performance. *Journal of Experimental Psychology: Animal Behavior Processes, 19,* 56–67.

Cheng, K., Westwood, R., & Crystal, J. D. (1993). Memory variance in the peak procedure of timing in pigeons. *Journal of Experimental Psychology: Animal Behavior Processes, 19,* 68–76.

Cherot, C., Jones, A., & Neuringer, A. (1996). Reinforced variability decreases with approach to reinforcers. *Journal of Experimental Psychology: Animal Behavior Processes, 22,* 497–508.

Chomsky, N. (1972). *Language and mind.* New York: Harcourt Brace Jovanovich.

Church, R. M. (1963). The varied effects of punishment on behavior. *Psychological Review, 70,* 369–402.

Church, R. M. (1969). Response suppression. In B. A. Campbell & R. M. Church (Eds.), *Punishment and aversive behavior* (pp. 111–156). New York: Appleton-Century-Crofts.

Church, R. M. (1978). The internal clock. In S. H. Hulse, H. Fowler, & W. K. Honig (Eds.), *Cognitive processes in animal behavior* (pp. 277–310). Hillsdale, NJ: Erlbaum.

Church, R. M., Getty, D. J., & Lerner, N. D. (1976). Duration discrimination by rats. *Journal of Experimental Psychology: Animal Behavior Processes, 2,* 303–312.

Church, R. M., Meck, W. H., & Gibbon, J. (1994). Application of scalar timing theory to individual trials. *Journal of Experimental Psychology: Animal Behavior Processes, 20,* 135–155.

Church, R. M., Miller, K. D., Meck, W. H., & Gibbon, J. (1991). Symmetrical and asymmetrical sources of variance in temporal generalization. *Animal Learning & Behavior, 19,* 207–214.

Cicala, G. A., & Owen, J. W. (1976). Warning signal termination and a feedback signal may not serve the same function. *Learning and Motivation, 7,* 356–367.

Clark, R. E., & Squire, L. R. (1998). Classical conditioning and brain systems: The role of awareness. *Science, 280,* 77–81.

Clark, R. E., & Squire, L. R., (1999). Human eyeblink classical conditioning: Effects of manipulating awareness of the stimulus contingencies. *Psychological Science, 10,* 14–18.

Clayton, N. S., & Dickinson, A. (1998). Episodic-like memory during cache recovery by scrub jays. *Nature, 395,* 272–274.

Clayton, N. S., & Dickinson, A. (1999a). Scrub jays (*Aphelocoma coerulescens*) remember the relative time of caching as well as the location and content of their caches. *Journal of Comparative Psychology, 113,* 403–416.

Clayton, N. S., & Dickinson, A. (1999b). Memory for the content of caches by scrub jays (*Aphelocoma coerulescens*). *Journal of Experimental Psychology: Animal Behavior Processes, 25,* 82–91.

Clayton, N. S., Yu, K. S., & Dickinson, A. (2001). Scrub jays (*Aphelocoma coerulescens*) form integrated memories of the multiple features of caching episodes. *Journal of Experimental Psychology: Animal Behavior Processes, 27,* 17–29.

Cleaveland, J. M. (1999). Interresponse-time sensitivity during discrete-trial and free-operant concurrent variable-interval schedules. *Journal of the Experimental Analysis of Behavior, 72,* 317–330.

Cleland, G. G., & Davey, G. C. L. (1982). The effects of satiation and reinforcer devaluation on signal centered behavior in the rat. *Learning and Motivation, 13,* 343–360.

Cleland, G. G., & Davey, G. C. L. (1983). Autoshaping in the rat: The effects of localizable visual and auditory signals for food. *Journal of the Experimental Analysis of Behavior, 40,* 47–56.

Clement, T. S., & Zentall, T. R. (2000a). Determinants of value transfer and contrast in simultaneous discriminations by pigeons. *Animal Learning & Behavior, 28,* 195–200.

Clement, T. S., & Zentall, T. R. (2000b). Development of a single-code/default coding strategy in pigeons. *Psychological Science, 11,* 261–264.

Cohen, L. B. (1988). An information processing view of infant cognitive development. In L. Weiskrantz (Ed.), *Thought without language* (pp. 211–228). Oxford: Oxford University Press.

Cohen, S. L. (1998). Behavioral momentum: The effect of the temporal separation of rates of reinforcement. *Journal of the Experimental Analysis of Behavior, 69,* 29–47.

Cole, M. R. (1994). Response-rate differences in variable-interval and variable-ratio schedules: An old problem revisited. *Journal of the Experimental Analysis of Behavior, 61,* 441–451.

Cole, M. R. (1999). Molar and molecular control in variable-interval and variable-ratio schedules. *Journal of the Experimental Analysis of Behavior, 71,* 319–328.

Cole, R. P., Barnet, R. C., & Miller, R. R. (1995a). Effect of relative stimulus validity: Learning or performance deficit? *Journal of Experimental Psychology: Animal Behavior Processes, 21,* 293–303.

Cole, R. P., Barnet, R. C., & Miller, R. R. (1995b). Temporal encoding in trace conditioning. *Animal Learning & Behavior, 23,* 144–153.

Cole, R. P., Barnet, R. C., & Miller, R. R. (1997). An evaluation of conditioned inhibition as defined by Rescorla's two-test strategy. *Learning and Motivation, 28,* 323–341.

Cole, R. P., & Miller, R. R. (1999). Conditioned excitation and conditioned inhibition acquired through backward conditioning. *Learning and Motivation, 30,* 129–156.

Cole, R. P., Oberling, P., & Miller, R. R. (1999). Recovery from one-trial overshadowing. *Psychonomic Bulletin & Review, 6,* 424–431.

Collier, G., & Johnson, D. F. (1997). Who is in charge? Animal vs. experimenter control. *Appetite, 29,* 159–180.

Collier, G., & Johnson, D. F. (2000). Sucrose intake as a function of its cost and the cost of chow. *Physiology & Behavior, 70,* 477–487.

Collier, G., Johnson, D. F., & Morgan, C. (1992). The magnitude-of-reinforcement function in closed and open economies. *Journal of the Experimental Analysis of Behavior, 57,* 81–89.

Colwill, R. M. (1994). Associative representations of instrumental contingencies. *The psychology of learning and motivation* (Vol. 31, pp. 1–72). San Diego: Academic Press.

Colwill, R. M., & Delameter, B. A. (1995). An associative analysis of instrumental biconditional discrimination learning. *Animal Learning & Behavior, 23,* 218–233.

Colwill, R. M., Goodrum, K., & Martin, A. (1997). Pavlovian appetitive discriminative conditioning in *Aplysia californica. Animal Learning & Behavior, 25,* 268–276.

Colwill, R. M., & Motzkin, D. K. (1994). Encoding of the unconditioned stimulus in Pavlovian conditioning. *Animal Learning & Behavior, 22,* 384–394.

Colwill, R. M., & Rescorla, R. A. (1986). Associative structures in instrumental learning. In G. H. Bower (Ed.), *The psychology of learning and motivation* (Vol. 20, pp. 55–104). Orlando, FL: Academic Press.

Colwill, R. M., & Rescorla, R. A. (1990). Evidence for the hierarchical structure of instrumental learning. *Animal Learning & Behavior, 18,* 71–82.

Commons, M. L., Herrnstein, R. J., Kosslyn, S. M., & Mumford, D. B. (Eds.). (1990). *Quantitative analyses of behavior: Vol. 8. Behavioral approaches to pattern recognition and concept formation.* Hillsdale, NJ: Erlbaum.

Commons, M. L., Herrnstein, R. J., & Rachlin, H. (Eds.). (1982). *Quantitative analyses of behavior: Vol. 2. Matching and maximizing accounts.* Cambridge, MA: Ballinger.

Conger, R., & Killeen, P. (1974). Use of concurrent operants in small group research. *Pacific Sociological Review, 17,* 399–416.

Conn, P. M., & Parker, J. (1998). Animal rights: Reaching the public. *Science, 282,* 1417.

Cook, M., & Mineka, S. (1990). Selective associations in the observational conditioning of fear in rhesus monkeys. *Journal of Experimental Psychology: Animal Behavior Processes, 16,* 372–389.

Cook, M., Mineka, S., & Trumble, D. (1987). The role of response-produced and exteroceptive feedback in the attenuation of fear over the course of avoidance learning. *Journal of Experimental Psychology: Animal Behavior Processes, 13,* 239–249.

Cook, R. G., Brown, M. F., & Riley, D. A. (1985). Flexible memory processing by rats: Use of prospective and retrospective information in the radial maze. *Journal of Experimental Psychology: Animal Behavior Processes, 11,* 453–469.

Coulter, X., Riccio, D. C., & Page, H. A. (1969). Effects of blocking an instrumental avoidance response: Facilitated extinction but persistence of "fear." *Journal of Comparative and Physiological Psychology, 68,* 377–381.

Couvillon, P. A., & Bitterman, M. E. (1992). A conventional conditioning analysis of "transitive inference" in pigeons. *Journal of Experimental Psychology: Animal Behavior Processes, 18,* 308–310.

Craig, W. (1918). Appetites and aversions as constituents of instinct. *Biological Bulletin, 34,* 91–107.

Craske, M. G., Glover, D., & DeCola, J. (1995). Predicted versus unpredicted panic attacks: Acute versus general distress. *Journal of Abnormal Psychology, 104,* 214–223.

Crespi, L. P. (1942). Quantitative variation in incentive and performance in the white rat. *American Journal of Psychology, 55,* 467–517.

Critchfield, T. S., & Lattal, K. A. (1993). Acquisition of a spatially defined operant with delayed reinforcement. *Journal of the Experimental Analysis of Behavior, 59,* 373–387.

Cronin, P. B. (1980). Reinstatement of post response stimuli prior to reward in delayed-reward discrimination learning by pigeons. *Animal Learning & Behavior, 8,* 352–358.

Crossman, E. K., Bonem, E. J., & Phelps, B. J. (1987). A comparison of response patterns on fixed-, variable-, and random-ratio schedules. *Journal of the Experimental Analysis of Behavior, 48,* 395–406.

Crown, E. D., & Grau, J. W. (2001). Preserving and restoring behavioral potential within the spinal cord using an instrumental training paradigm. *Journal of Neurophysiology, 86,* 845–855.

Cumming, W. W. (1999). A review of Geraldine Jonçich's *The sane positivist: A biography of Edward L. Thorndike. Journal of the Experimental Analysis of Behavior, 72,* 429–432.

Cunningham, C. L. (1979). Alcohol as a cue for extinction: State dependency produced by conditioned inhibition. *Animal Learning & Behavior, 7,* 45–52.

Cunningham, C. L. (1998). Drug conditioning and drug-seeking behavior. In W. O'Donohue (Ed.) *Learning and behavior therapy.* (pp. 518–544). Boston: Allyn and Bacon.

Cusato, B., & Domjan, M. (1998). Special efficacy of sexual conditioned stimuli that include species typical cues: Tests with a conditioned stimulus preexposure design. *Learning and Motivation, 29,* 152–167.

Cusato, B., & Domjan, M. (2000). Facilitation of appetitive conditioning with naturalistic conditioned stimuli: CS and US factors. *Animal Learning & Behavior, 28,* 247–256.

Cusato, B., & Domjan, M. (2001). *CS-US similarity effects in sexual conditioning.* Paper presented at meetings of the Psychonomic Society, Orlando, FL, November, 2001.

Dallery, J., McDowell, J. J., & Lancaster, J. S. (2000). Falsification of matching theory's account of single-alternative responding: Herrnstein's K varies with sucrose concentration. *Journal of the Experimental Analysis of Behavior, 73,* 23–43.

D'Amato, M. R. (1973). Delayed matching and short-term memory in monkeys. In G. H. Bower (Ed.), *The psychology of learning and motivation* (Vol. 7, pp. 227–269). New York: Academic Press.

D'Amato, M. R., & Colombo, M. (1985). Auditory matching-to-sample in monkeys (*Cebus apella*). *Animal Learning & Behavior, 13,* 375–382.

D'Amato, M. R., & Colombo, M. (1988). Representation of serial order in monkeys (*Cebus apella*). *Journal of Experimental Psychology: Animal Behavior Processes, 14,* 131–139.

D'Amato, M. R., & Colombo, M. (1989). Serial learning with wild card items by monkeys (*Cebus apella*): Implications for knowledge of ordinal position. *Journal of Comparative Psychology, 103,* 252–261.

D'Amato, M. R., & Colombo, M. (1990). The symbolic distance effect in monkeys (*Cebus apella*). *Animal Learning & Behavior, 18,* 133–140.

D'Amato, M. R., Fazzaro, J., & Etkin, M. (1968). Anticipatory responding and avoidance discrimination as factors in avoidance conditioning. *Journal of Comparative and Physiological Psychology, 77,* 41–47.

D'Amato, M. R., & Salmon, D. P. (1982). Tune discrimination in monkeys (*Cebus apella*) and in rats. *Animal Learning & Behavior, 10,* 126–134.

D'Amato, M. R., & Van Sant, P. (1988). The person concept in monkeys (*Cebus apella*). *Journal of Experimental Psychology: Animal Behavior Processes, 14,* 43–55.

Dardano, J. F., & Sauerbrunn, D. (1964). An aversive stimulus as a correlated block counter in FR performance. *Journal of the Experimental Analysis of Behavior, 7,* 37–43.

Darwin, C. (1897). *The descent of man and selection in relation to sex.* New York: Appleton-Century-Crofts.

Davey, G. C. L. (1995). Preparedness and phobias: Specific evolved associations or a generalized expectancy bias? *Behavioral and Brain Sciences, 18,* 289–325.

Davey, G. C. L., & Cleland, G. G. (1982). Topography of signal-centered behavior in the rat: Effects of deprivation state and reinforcer type. *Journal of the Experimental Analysis of Behavior, 38,* 291–304.

Davey, G. C. L., Phillips, S., & Cleland, G. G. (1981). The topography of signal-centered behaviour in the rat: The effects of solid and liquid food reinforcers. *Behaviour Analysis Letters, 1,* 331–337.

Davidson, T. L., Aparicio, J., & Rescorla, R. A. (1988). Transfer between Pavlovian facilitators and instrumental discriminative stimuli. *Animal Learning & Behavior, 16,* 285–291.

Davidson, T. L., Flynn, F. W., & Jarrard, L. E. (1992). Potency of food deprivation intensity cues as discriminative stimuli. *Journal of Experimental Psychology: Animal Behavior Processes, 18,* 174–181.

Davis, D. G., Staddon, J. E., Machado, A., & Palmer, R. G. (1993). The process of recurrent choice. *Psychological Review, 100,* 320–341.

Davis, E. R., & Platt, J. R. (1983). Contiguity and contingency in the acquisition and maintenance of an operant. *Learning and Motivation, 14,* 487–512.

Davis, H. (1968). Conditioned suppression: A survey of the literature. *Psychonomic Monograph Supplements, 2* (14, Whole No. 30), 283–291.

Davis, H. P., & Squire, L. R. (1984). Protein synthesis and memory: A review. *Psychological Bulletin, 96,* 518–559.

Davis, M. (1974). Sensitization of the rat startle response by noise. *Journal of Comparative and Physiological Psychology, 87,* 571–581.

Davis, M. (1989). Sensitization of the acoustic startle reflex by footshock. *Behavioral Neuroscience, 103,* 495–503.

Davis, M., Hitchcock, J. M., & Rosen, J. B. (1987). Anxiety and the amygdala: Pharmacological and anatomical analysis of the fear-potentiated startle paradigm. In G. H. Bower (Ed.), *The psychology of learning and motivation* (Vol. 21, pp. 263–304). Orlando, FL: Academic Press.

Davis, R. L. (1996). Physiology and biochemistry of *Drosophila* learning mutants. *American Physiological Society, 76,* 299–317.

Davison, M. (1991). Choice, changeover, and travel: A quantitative model. *Journal of the Experimental Analysis of Behavior, 55,* 47–61.

Davison, M., & Jones, B. M. (1995). A quantitative analysis of extreme choice. *Journal of the Experimental Analysis of Behavior, 64,* 147–162.

Davison, M., & McCarthy, D. (1988). *The matching law: A research review.* Hillsdale, NJ: Erlbaum.

Davison, M., & Nevin, J. A. (1999). Stimuli, reinforcers, and behavior: An integration. *Journal of the Experimental Analysis of Behavior, 71,* 439–482.

Dawson, G. R., & Dickinson, A. (1990). Performance on ratio and interval schedules with matched reinforcement rates. *Quarterly Journal of Experimental Psychology, 42B,* 225–239.

Dean, S. J., & Pittman, C. M. (1991). Self-punitive behavior: A revised analysis. In M. R. Denny (Ed.), *Fear, avoidance and phobias* (pp. 259–284). Hillsdale, NJ: Erlbaum.

DeCarlo, L. T. (1985). Matching and maximizing with variable-time schedules. *Journal of the Experimental Analysis of Behavior, 43,* 75–81.

DeCola, J. P., & Rosellini, R. A. (1990). Unpredictable/uncontrollable stress proactively interferes with appetitive Pavlovian conditioning. *Learning and Motivation, 21,* 137–152.

DeCola, J. P., Rosellini, R. A., & Warren, D. A. (1988). A dissociation of the effects of control and prediction. *Learning and Motivation, 19,* 269–282.

DeGrandpre, R. J., Bickel, W. K., Rizvi, S. A. T., & Hughes, J. R. (1993). Effect of income on drug choice in humans. *Journal of the Experimental Analysis of Behavior, 59,* 483–500.

Deich, J. D., Allan, R. W., & Zeigler, H. P. (1988). Conjunctive differentiation of gape during food-reinforced key pecking in the pigeon. *Animal Learning & Behavior, 16,* 268–276.

DeKeyne, A., & Deweer, B. (1990). Interaction between conflicting memories in the rat: Contextual pretest cuing reverses control of behavior by testing context. *Animal Learning & Behavior, 18,* 1–12.

Delameter, A. R. (1996). Effects of several extinction treatments upon the integrity of Pavlovian stimulus-outcome associations. *Animal Learning & Behavior, 24,* 437–449.

Delprato, D. J. (1969). Extinction of one-way avoidance and delayed warning signal termination. *Journal of Experimental Psychology, 80,* 192–193.

DeMarse, T. B., & Urcuioli, P. J. (1993). Enhancement of matching acquisition by differential comparison-outcome associations. *Journal of Experimental Psychology: Animal Behavior Processes, 19,* 317–326.

Denniston, J. C., Blaisdell, A. P., & Miller, R. R. (1998). Temporal coding affects transfer of serial and simultaneous inhibitors. *Animal Learning & Behavior, 26,* 336–350.

Denniston, J. C., Cole, R. P., & Miller, R. R. (1998). The role of temporal relationships in the transfer of conditioned inhibition. *Journal of Experimental Psychology: Animal Behavior Processes, 24,* 200–214.

Denniston, J. C., Savastano, H. I., & Miller, R. R. (2001). The extended comparator hypothesis: Learning by contiguity, responding by relative strength. In R. R. Mowrer & S. B. Klein (Eds.), *Handbook of contemporary learning theories* (pp. 65–117). Mahwah, NJ: Erlbaum.

deVaca, S. C., Brown, B. L., & Hemmes, N. S. (1994). Internal clock and memory processes in animal timing. *Journal of Experimental Psychology: Animal Behavior Processes, 20,* 184–198.

Devenport, L. D. (1998). Spontaneous recovery without interference: Why remembering is adaptive. *Animal Learning & Behavior, 26,* 172–181.

deVilliers, P. A. (1974). The law of effect and avoidance: A quantitative relationship between response rate and shock-frequency reduction. *Journal of the Experimental Analysis of Behavior, 21,* 223–235.

DeVito, P. L., & Fowler, H. (1987). Enhancement of conditioned inhibition via an extinction treatment. *Animal Learning & Behavior, 15,* 448–454.

Dewsbury, D. A. (1998). Celebrating E. L. Thorndike a century after *Animal intelligence. American Psychologist, 53,* 1121–1124.

Dickinson, A. (2001). Causal learning: Association versus computation. *Current Directions in Psychological Science, 10,* 127–132.

Dickinson, A., & Balleine, B. (1994). Motivational control of goal-directed behavior. *Animal Learning & Behavior, 22,* 1–18.

Dickinson, A., & Dearing, M. F. (1979). Appetitive aversive interactions and inhibitory processes. In A. Dickinson & R. A. Boakes (Eds.), *Mechanisms of learning and motivation* (pp. 203–231). Hillsdale, NJ: Erlbaum.

Dickinson, A., Nicholas, D. J., & Macintosh, N. J. (1983). A re-examination of one-trial blocking in conditioned suppression. *Quarterly Journal of Experimental Psychology, 35,* 67–79.

Dickinson, A., Watt, A., & Griffiths, W. J. H. (1992). Free-operant acquisition with delayed reinforcement. *The Quarterly Journal of Experimental Psychology, 45B,* 241–258.

Dickinson, A., Watt, A., & Varga, Z. I. (1996). Context conditioning and free-operant acquisition under delayed reinforcement. *Quarterly Journal of Experimental Psychology, 49B,* 97–110.

Didden, R., Prinsen, H., & Sigafoos, J. (2000). The blocking effect of pictorial prompts on sight-word reading. *Journal of Applied Behavior Analysis, 33,* 317–320.

Dinsmoor, J. A. (1952). A discrimination based on punishment. *Quarterly Journal of Experimental Psychology, 4,* 27–45.

Dinsmoor, J. A. (1954). Punishment: I. The avoidance hypothesis. *Psychological Review, 61,* 34–46.

Dinsmoor, J. A. (1962). Variable-interval escape from stimuli accompanied by shocks. *Journal of the Experimental Analysis of Behavior, 5,* 41–48.

Dinsmoor, J. A. (1977). Escape, avoidance, punishment: Where do we stand? *Journal of the Experimental Analysis of Behavior, 28,* 83–95.

Dinsmoor, J. A. (1995). Stimulus control: Part I. *The Behavior Analyst, 18,* 51–68.

Dinsmoor, J. A. (1998). Punishment. In W. O'Donohue (Ed.), *Learning and behavior therapy* (pp. 188–204). Boston: Allyn and Bacon.

Dinsmoor, J. A. (2001a). Still no evidence for temporally extended shock-frequency reduction as a reinforcer. *Journal of the Experimental Analysis of Behavior, 75,* 367–378.

Dinsmoor, J. A. (2001b). Stimuli inevitably generated by behavior that avoids electric shock are inherently reinforcing. *Journal of the Experimental Analysis of Behavior, 75,* 311–333.

Dinsmoor, J. A., & Sears, G. W. (1973). Control of avoidance by a response-produced stimulus. *Learning and Motivation, 4,* 284–293.

Dittrich, W. H., Lea, S. E. G., Barrett, J., & Gurr, P. R. (1998). Categorization of natural movement by pigeons: Visual concept discrimination and biological motion. *Journal of the Experimental Analysis of Behavior, 70,* 281–299.

Dobrzecka, C., Szwejkowska, G., & Konorski, J. (1966). Qualitative versus directional cues in two forms of differentiation. *Science, 153,* 87–89.

Dollard, J., & Miller, N. E. (1950). *Personality and psychotherapy.* New York: McGraw-Hill.

Dollard, J., Miller, N. E., Doob, L. W., Mowrer, O. H., & Sears, R. R. (1939). *Frustration and aggression.* New Haven, CT: Yale University Press.

Domjan, M. (1980). Ingestional aversion learning: Unique and general processes. In J. S. Rosenblatt, R. A. Hinde, C. Beer, & M. Busnel (Eds.), *Advances in the study of behavior* (Vol. 11, pp. 275–336). New York: Academic Press.

Domjan, M. (1983). Biological constraints on instrumental and classical conditioning: Implications for general process theory. In G. H. Bower (Ed.), *The psychology of learning and motivation* (Vol. 17, pp. 215–277). New York: Academic Press.

Domjan, M. (1987). Animal learning comes of age. *American Psychologist, 42,* 556–564.

Domjan, M. (1993). *The principles of learning and behavior* (3rd ed.). Pacific Grove, CA: Brooks/Cole.

Domjan, M. (1997). Behavior systems and the demise of equipotentiality: Historical antecedents and evidence from sexual conditioning. In M. E. Bouton & M. S. Fanselow (Eds.), *Learning, motivation, and cognition* (pp. 31–51). Washington, DC: American Psychological Association.

Domjan, M. (1998). Going wild in the laboratory: Learning about species typical cues. In D. L. Medin (Ed.), *The psychology of learning and motivation* (Vol. 38, pp. 155–186). San Diego: Academic Press.

Domjan, M. (2000). Learning: Overview. In A. E. Kazdin (Ed.), *Encyclopedia of psychology* (Vol. 5, pp. 1–3). New York: Oxford University Press.

Domjan, M., Blesbois, E., & Williams, J. (1998). The adaptive significance of sexual conditioning: Pavlovian control of sperm release. *Psychological Science, 9,* 411–415.

Domjan, M., & Burkhard, B. (1982). *The principles of learning and behavior.* Pacific Grove, CA: Brooks/Cole.

Domjan, M., & Burkhard, B. (1986). *The principles of learning and behavior* (2nd ed.). Pacific Grove, CA: Brooks/Cole.

Domjan, M., Cusato, B., & Villarreal, R. (2000). Pavlovian feed-forward mechanisms in the control of social behavior. *Behavioral and Brain Sciences, 23,* 235–249.

Domjan, M., & Hollis, K. L. (1988). Reproductive behavior: A potential model system for adaptive specializations in learning. In R. C. Bolles & M. D. Beecher (Eds.), *Evolution and learning* (pp. 213–237). Hillsdale, NJ: Erlbaum.

Domjan, M., & Holloway, K. S. (1998). Sexual learning. In G. Greenberg & M. M. Haraway (Eds.), *Comparative psychology: A handbook* (pp. 602–613). New York: Garland.

Domjan, M., & Mahometa, M. (2001). Learning and fertilization success in the domesticated quail. Paper presented at meetings of the Winter Conference on Learning and Behavior, Winter Park, CO, January, 2001.

Donahoe, J. W., & Burgos, J. E. (1999). Timing without a timer. *Journal of the Experimental Analysis of Behavior, 72,* 257–263.

Donahoe, J. W., & Burgos, J. E. (2000). Behavioral analysis and reevaluation. *Journal of the Experimental Analysis of Behavior, 74,* 331–346.

Donahoe, J. W., Palmer, D. C., & Burgos, J. E. (1997). The S-R issue: Its status in behavior analysis and in Donahoe and Palmer's *Learning and complex behavior. Journal of the Experimental Analysis of Behavior, 67,* 193–211.

Dorrance, B. R., Kaiser, D. H., & Zentall, T. R. (1998). Value transfer in a simultaneous discrimination by pigeons: The value of the S+ is not specific to the simultaneous discrimination context. *Animal Learning & Behavior, 26,* 257–263.

Dougherty, D. M., & Lewis, P. (1991). Stimulus generalization, discrimination learning, and peak shift in horses. *Journal of the Experimental Analysis of Behavior, 56,* 97–104.

Dragoi, V., & Staddon, J. E. R. (1999). The dynamics of operant conditioning. *Psychological Review, 106,* 20–61.

Dreyfus, L. R., DePorto-Callan, D., & Pesillo, S. A. (1993). Changeover contingencies and choice on concurrent schedules. *Animal Learning & Behavior, 21,* 203–213.

Dube, W. V., & McIlvane, W. J. (2001). Behavioral momentum in computer-presented discriminations in individuals with severe mental retardation. *Journal of the Experimental Analysis of Behavior, 75,* 15–23.

Ducharme, M. J., & Santi, A. (1993). Alterations in the memory code for temporal events induced by differential outcome expectancies in pigeons. *Animal Learning & Behavior, 21,* 73–81.

Dudai, Y. (1989). *The neurobiology of memory: Concepts, findings, trends.* Oxford: Oxford University Press.

Dudley, R. T., & Papini, M. R. (1995). Pavlovian performance of rats following unexpected reward omissions. *Learning and Motivation, 26,* 63–82.

Dudley, R. T., & Papini, M. R. (1997). Amsel's frustration effect: A Pavlovian replication with control for frequency and distribution of rewards. *Physiology & Behavior, 61,* 627–629.

Dugdale, N., & Lowe, C. F. (2000). Testing for symmetry in the conditional discriminations of language-trained chimpanzees. *Journal of the Experimental Analysis of Behavior, 73,* 5–22.

Durkin, M., Prescott, L., Furchtgott, E., & Cantor, J. (1993). Concomitant eyeblink and heart rate classical conditioning in young, middle-aged, and elderly human subjects. *Psychology and Aging, 8,* 571–581.

Dweck, C. S., & Wagner, A. R. (1970). Situational cues and correlation between conditioned stimulus and unconditioned stimulus as determinants of the conditioned emotional response. *Psychonomic Science, 18,* 145–147.

Dworkin, B. R. (1993). *Learning and physiological regulation.* Chicago and London: University of Chicago Press.

Edgerton, V. R., Roy, R. R., & de Leon, R. D. (2001). Neural Darwinism in the mammalian spinal cord. In M. M. Patterson & J. W. Grau (Eds.), *Spinal cord plasticity: Alterations in reflex function* (pp. 185–206). Boston: Kluwer Academic Publishers.

Edhouse, W. V., & White, K. G. (1988a). Cumulative proactive interference in animal memory. *Animal Learning & Behavior, 16,* 461–467.

Edhouse, W. V., & White, K. G. (1988b). Sources of proactive interference in animal memory. *Journal of Experimental Psychology: Animal Behavior Processes, 14,* 56–70.

Ehrman, R. N., Robbins, S. J., Childress, A. R., & O'Brien, C. P. (1992). Conditioned responses to cocaine-related stimuli in cocaine abuse patients. *Psychopharmacology, 107,* 523–529.

Eisenberger, R., & Adornetto, M. (1986). Generalized self-control of delay and effort. *Journal of Personality and Social Psychology, 51,* 1020–1031.

Eisenberger, R., & Cameron, J. (1996). Detrimental effects of reward: Reality or myth? *American Psychologist,* 51, 1153–1166.

Eisenberger, R., Karpman, M., & Trattner, J. (1967). What is the necessary and sufficient condition for reinforcement in the contingency situation? *Journal of Experimental Psychology, 74,* 342–350.

Elliffe, D., & Alslop, B. (1996). Concurrent choice: Effects of overall reinforcer rate and the temporal distribution of reinforcers. *Journal of the Experimental Analysis of Behavior, 65,* 445–463.

Ellins, S. R., Cramer, R. E., & Martin, G. C. (1982). Discrimination reversal learning in newts. *Animal Learning & Behavior, 10,* 301–304.

Ellison, G. D. (1964). Differential salivary conditioning to traces. *Journal of Comparative and Physiological Psychology, 57,* 373–380.

Emmerton, J. (1998). Numerosity differences and effects of stimulus density on pigeon's discrimination performance. *Animal Learning & Behavior, 26,* 243–256.

English, J. A., Rowlett, J. K., & Woolverton, W. L. (1995). Unit-price analysis of opioid consumption by monkeys responding under a progressive-ratio schedule of drug injection. *Journal of the Experimental Analysis of Behavior, 64,* 361–371.

Epstein, L. H., Rodefer, J. S., Wisniewski, L., & Caggiula, A. R. (1992). *Physiology & Behavior, 51,* 945–950.

Escobar, M., Matute, H., & Miller, R. R. (2001). Cues trained apart compete for behavioral control in rats: Convergence with the associative interference literature. *Journal of Experimental Psychology: General, 130,* 97–115.

Estes, W. K. (1943). Discriminative conditioning: I. A discriminative property of conditioned anticipation. *Journal of Experimental Psychology, 32,* 150–155.

Estes, W. K. (1944). An experimental study of punishment. *Psychological Monographs, 57* (3, Whole No. 263).

Estes, W. K. (1948). Discriminative conditioning: II. Effects of a Pavlovian conditioned stimulus upon a subsequently established operant response. *Journal of Experimental Psychology, 38,* 173–177.

Estes, W. K. (1969). Outline of a theory of punishment. In B. A. Campbell & R. M. Church (Eds.), *Punishment and aversive behavior* (pp. 57–82). New York: Appleton-Century-Crofts.

Estes, W. K., & Skinner, B. F. (1941). Some quantitative properties of anxiety. *Journal of Experimental Psychology, 29,* 390–400.

Fagen, J. W., & Ohr, P. S. (2001). Learning and memory in infancy: Habituation, instrumental conditioning, and expectancy information. In L. T. Singer & P. S. Zeskind (Eds.), *Biobehavioral assessment of the infant* (pp. 233–273). New York: Guilford.

Fagen, J. W., & Rovee-Collier, C. (1983). Memory retrieval: A time-locked process in infancy. *Science, 222,* 1349–1351.

Falls, W. A. (1998). Extinction: A review of theory and the evidence suggesting that memories are not erased with nonreinforcement. In W. O'Donohue (Ed.),

Learning and behavior therapy (pp. 205–229). Boston: Allyn and Bacon.

Falls, W. A., & Davis, M. (1994). Fear-potentiated startle using three conditioned stimulus modalities. *Animal Learning & Behavior, 22,* 379–383.

Fanselow, M. S. (1989). The adaptive function of conditioned defensive behavior: An ecological approach to Pavlovian stimulus-substitution theory. In R. J. Blanchard, P. F. Brain, D. C. Blanchard, & S. Parmigiani (Eds.), *Ethoexperimental approaches to the study of behavior* (NATO ASI Series D, Vol. 48, pp. 151–166). Boston: Kluver Academic Publishers.

Fanselow, M. S. (1991). Analgesia as a response to aversive Pavlovian conditioned stimuli: Cognitive and emotional mediators. In M. R. Denny (Ed.), *Fear, avoidance and phobias* (pp. 61–86). Hillsdale, NJ: Erlbaum.

Fanselow, M. S. (1997). Species-specific defense reactions: Retrospect and prospect. In M. E. Bouton & M. S. Fanselow (Eds.), *Learning, motivation, and cognition.* (pp. 321–341). Washington, DC: American Psychological Association.

Fanselow, M. S. (1999). Learning theory and neuropsychology: Configuring their disparate elements in the hippocampus. *Journal of Experimental Psychology: Animal Behavior Processes, 25,* 275–283.

Fanselow, M. S., & Lester, L. S. (1988). A functional behavioristic approach to aversively motivated behavior: Predatory imminence as a determinant of the topography of defensive behavior. In R. C. Bolles & M. D. Beecher (Eds.), *Evolution and learning* (pp. 185–212). Hillsdale, NJ: Erlbaum.

Fanselow, M. S., Lester, L. S., & Helmstetter, F. J. (1988). Changes in feeding and foraging patterns as an antipredator defensive strategy: A laboratory simulation using aversive stimulation in a closed economy. *Journal of the Experimental Analysis of Behavior, 50,* 361–374.

Farley, J., & Alkon, D. L. (1980). Neural organization predicts stimulus specificity for a retained associative behavioral change. *Science, 210,* 1373–1375.

Fath, S. J., Fields, L., Malott, M. K., & Grossett, D. (1983). Response rate, latency, and resistance to change. *Journal of the Experimental Analysis of Behavior, 39,* 267–274.

Feldman, D. T., & Gordon, W. C. (1979). The alleviation of short-term retention decrements with reactivation. *Learning and Motivation, 10,* 198–210.

Felton, M., & Lyon, D. O. (1966). The post-reinforcement pause. Journal of the *Experimental Analysis of Behavior, 9,* 131–134.

Fendt, M., & Fanselow, M. S. (1999). The neuroanatomical and neurochemical basis of conditioned fear. *Neuroscience and Biobehavioral Reviews, 23,* 743–760.

Ferguson, E., & Job, R. F. S. (1997). Uncontrollable water deliveries and subsequent finickiness. *Animal Learning & Behavior, 25,* 62–67.

Ferrara, A., Lejeune, H., & Wearden, J. H. (1997). Changing sensitivity to duration in human scalar timing: An experiment, a review, and some possible explanations. *Quarterly Journal of Experimental Psychology, 50B,* 227–237.

Ferster, C. B., & Skinner, B. F. (1957). *Schedules of reinforcement.* New York: Appleton-Century-Crofts.

Fetterman, J. G. (1995). The psychophysics of remembered duration. *Animal Learning & Behavior, 23,* 49–62.

Fetterman, J. G. (1996). Dimensions of stimulus complexity. *Journal of Experimental Psychology: Animal Behavior Processes, 22,* 3–18.

Fetterman, J. G., Killeen, P. R., & Hall, S. (1998). Watching the clock. *Behavioural Processes, 44,* 222–224.

Field, D. P., Tonneau, F., Ahearn, W., & Hineline, P. N. (1996). Preference between variable-ratio and fixed-ratio schedules: Local and extended relations. *Journal of the Experimental Analysis of Behavior, 66,* 283–295.

Fiori, L. M., Barnet, R. C., & Miller, R. R. (1994). Renewal of Pavlovian conditioned inhibition. *Animal Learning & Behavior, 22,* 47–52.

FitzGerald, R. E., Isler, R., Rosenberg, E., Oettinger, R., & Battig, K. (1985). Maze patrolling by rats with and without food reward. *Animal Learning & Behavior, 13,* 451–462.

Flaherty, C. F., Grigson, P. S., & Lind, S. (1990). Chlordiazepoxide and the moderation of the initial response to reward reduction. *Quarterly Journal of Experimental Psychology. B, Comparative & Physiological Psychology, 42,* (B-1) 87–105.

Flaherty, C. F. (1982). Incentive contrast: A review of behavioral changes following shifts in reward. *Animal Learning & Behavior, 10*(4), 409–440.

Flaherty, C. F. (1991). Incentive contrast and selected animal models of anxiety. In L. Dachowski & C. F. Flaherty (Eds.) *Current topics in animal learning: Brain, emotion, and cognition* (pp. 207–243). Hillsdale, NJ: Erlbaum.

Flaherty, C. F. (1996). *Incentive relativity.* New York: Cambridge University Press.

Flaherty, C. F., Greenwood, A., Martin, J., & Leszczuk, M. (1998). Relationship of negative contrast to animal models of fear and anxiety. *Animal Learning & Behavior, 26,* 397–407.

Flaten, M. A., & Blumenthal, T. D. (1999). Caffeine-associated stimuli elicit conditioned responses: An experimental model of the placebo effect. *Psychopharmacology, 145,* 105–112.

Flexner, J. B., Flexner, L. B., & Stellar, E. (1963). Memory in mice as affected by intracerebral puromycin. *Science, 141,* 57–59.

Foa, E. B., Zinbarg, R., & Rothbaum, B. O. (1992). Uncontrollability and unpredictability in post-traumatic stress disorder: An animal model. *Psychological Review, 112,* 218–238.

Foltin, R. W. (1991). An economic analysis of "demand" for food in baboons. *Journal of the Experimental Analysis of Behavior, 56,* 445–454.

Foltin, R. W. (1994). Does package size matter? A unit-price analysis of "demand" for food in baboons. *Journal of the Experimental Analysis of Behavior, 62,* 293–306.

Foltin, R. W. (1997). Food and amphetamine self-administration by baboons: Effects of alternatives. *Journal of the Experimental Analysis of Behavior, 68,* 47–66.

Foltin, R. W. (1999). Food and cocaine self-administration by baboons: Effects of alternatives. *Journal of the Experimental Analysis of Behavior, 72,* 215–234.

Foree, D. D., & LoLordo, V. M. (1973). Attention in the pigeon: The differential effects of food-getting vs. shock avoidance procedures. *Journal of Comparative and Physiological Psychology, 85,* 551–558.

Forestell, P. H., & Herman, L. M. (1988). Delayed matching of visual materials by a bottlenosed dolphin aided by auditory symbols. *Animal Learning & Behavior, 16,* 137–146.

Forzano, L. B., & Corry, R. J. (1998). Self-control and impusiveness in adult human females: Effects of visual food cues. *Learning and Motivation, 29,* 184–199.

Foster, T. M., Blackman, K. A., & Temple, W. (1997). Open versus closed economies: Performance of domestic hens under fixed-ratio schedules. *Journal of the Experimental Analysis of Behavior, 67,* 67–89.

Foster, T. M., Temple, W., Robertson, B., Nair, V., & Poling, A. (1996). Concurrent-schedule performance in dairy cows: Persistent undermatching. *Journal of the Experimental Analysis of Behavior, 65,* 57–80.

Fowler, H., Kleiman, M., & Lysle, D. (1985). Factors controlling the acquisition and extinction of conditioned inhibition suggest a "slave" process. In R. R. Miller & N. E. Spear (Eds.), *Information processing in animals: Conditioned inhibition* (pp. 113–150). Hillsdale, NJ: Erlbaum.

Fowler, H., Lysle, D. T., & DeVito, P. L. (1991). Conditioned excitation and conditioned inhibition of fear: Asymmetrical processes as evident in extinction. In M. R. Denny (Ed.), *Fear, avoidance and phobias* (pp. 317–362). Hillsdale, NJ: Erlbaum.

Foxx, R. M., & Azrin, N. H. (1973). The elimination of autistic self-stimulatory behavior by overcorrection. *Journal of Applied Behavioral Analysis, 6,* 1–14.

France, K. G., & Hudson, S. M. (1990). Behavior management of infant sleep disturbance. *Journal of Applied Behavior Analysis, 23,* 91–98.

Frankel, F. D. (1975). The role of response-punishment contingency in the suppression of a positively reinforced operant. *Learning and Motivation, 6,* 385–403.

Frankland, P. W., & Yeomans, J. S. (1995). Fear-potentiated startle and electrically evoked startle mediated by synapses in rostrolateral midbrain. *Behavioral Neuroscience, 109,* 669–680.

Friedman, B. X., Blaisdell, A. P., Escobar, M., & Miller, R. R. (1998). Comparator mechanisms and conditioned inhibition: Conditioned stimulus preexposure disrupts Pavlovian conditioned inhibition but not explicitly unpaired inhibition. *Journal of Experimental Psychology: Animal Behavior Processes, 24,* 453–466.

Gaffan, E. A., & Davies, J. (1981). The role of exploration in win-shift and win-stay performance on a radial maze. *Learning and Motivation, 12,* 282–299.

Galbicka, G. (1988). Differentiating the behavior of organisms. *Journal of the Experimental Analysis of Behavior, 50,* 343–354.

Gallistel, C. R. (1990). *The organization of behavior.* Cambridge, MA: MIT Press.

Gallistel, C. R. (1999). Can a decay process explain the timing of conditioned responses? *Journal of the Experimental Analysis of Behavior, 72,* 264–272.

Gallistel, C. R., & Gibbon, J. (2000). Time, rate, and conditioning. *Psychological Review, 107,* 289–344.

Gallistel, C. R., & Gibbon, J. (2001). Computational versus associative models of simple conditioning. *Current Directions in Psychological Science, 10,* 146–150.

Galluccio, L., & Rovee-Collier, C. (1999). Reinstatement effects on retention at 3 months of age. *Learning and Motivation, 30,* 296–316.

Gallup, G. G., Jr., & Suarez, S. D. (1985). Alternatives to the use of animals in psychological research. *American Psychologist, 40,* 1104–1111.

Gamzu, E. R., & Williams, D. R. (1971). Classical conditioning of a complex skeletal act. *Science, 171,* 923–925.

Gamzu, E. R., & Williams, D. R. (1973). Associative factors underlying the pigeon's key pecking in autoshaping procedures. *Journal of the Experimental Analysis of Behavior, 19,* 225–232.

Gantt, W. H. (1966). Conditional or conditioned, reflex or response? *Conditioned Reflex, 1,* 69–74.

Garb, J. J., & Stunkard, A. J. (1974). Taste aversions in man. *American Journal of Psychiatry, 131,* 1204–1207.

Garber, J., & Seligman, M. E. P. (Eds.). (1980). *Human helplessness: Theory and application.* New York: Academic Press.

Garcia, J., Ervin, F. R., & Koelling, R. A. (1966). Learning with prolonged delay of reinforcement. *Psychonomic Science, 5,* 121–122.

Garcia, J., & Koelling, R. A. (1966). Relation of cue to consequence in avoidance learning. *Psychonomic Science, 4,* 123–124.

Gardner, E. T., & Lewis, P. (1976). Negative reinforcement with shock-frequency increase. *Journal of the Experimental Analysis of Behavior, 25,* 3–14.

Gardner, R. A., & Gardner, B. T. (1969). Teaching sign language to a chimpanzee. *Science, 165,* 664–672.

Gardner, R. A., & Gardner, B. T. (1975). Early signs of language in child and chimpanzee. *Science, 187,* 752–753.

Gardner, R. A., & Gardner, B. T. (1978). Comparative psychology and language acquisition. *Annals of the New York Academy of Science, 309,* 37–76.

Gardner, R. A., & Gardner, B. T. (1984). A vocabulary test for chimpanzees (*Pan troglodytes*). *Journal of Comparative Psychology, 98,* 381–404.

Gardner, R. A., Gardner, B. T., & Van Cantfort, T. E. (Eds.). (1989). *Teaching sign language to chimpanzees.* Albany: State University of New York Press.

Gawley, D. J., Timberlake, W., & Lucas, G. A. (1987). System-specific differences in behavior regulation: Overrunning and underdrinking in molar nondepriving schedules. *Journal of Experimental Psychology: Animal Behavior Processes, 13,* 354–365.

Gemberling, G. A., & Domjan, M. (1982). Selective association in one-day-old rats: Taste-toxicosis and textureshock aversion learning. *Journal of Comparative and Physiological Psychology, 96,* 105–113.

George, J. T., & Hopkins, B. L. (1989). Multiple effects of performance-contingent pay for waitpersons. *Journal of Applied Behavior Analysis, 22,* 131–141.

Gershoff, E. T. (2002). Parental corporal punishment and associated child behaviors and experiences: A meta-analytic and theoretical review. *Psychological Bulletin,* in press.

Gewirtz, J. C., Brandon, S. E., & Wagner, A. R. (1998). Modulation of the acquisition of the rabbit eyeblink conditioned response by conditioned contextual stimuli. *Journal of Experimental Psychology: Animal Behavior Processes, 24,* 106–117.

Gharib, A., Derby, S., & Roberts, S. (2001). Timing and the control of variation. *Journal of Experimental Psychology: Animal Behavior Processes, 27,* 165–178.

Gibbon, J. (1999). Multiple time scales is well named. *Journal of the Experimental Analysis of Behavior, 72,* 272–275.

Gibbon, J., & Allan, L. (Eds.). (1984). Time and time perception. *Annals of the New York Academy of Sciences, 423.*

Gibbon, J., & Balsam, P. (1981). Spreading association in time. In C. M. Locurto, H. S. Terrace, & J. Gibbon (Eds.), *Autoshaping and conditioning theory* (pp. 219–253). New York: Academic Press.

Gibbon, J., & Church, R. M. (1984). Sources of variance in an information processing theory of timing. In H. L. Roitblat, T. G. Bever, & H. S. Terrace (Eds.), *Animal cognition.* Hillsdale, NJ: Erlbaum.

Gibbon, J., & Church, R. M. (1992). Comparison of variance and covariance patterns in parallel and serial theories of timing. *Journal of the Experimental Analysis of Behavior, 57,* 393–406.

Gibbon, J., Church, R. M., & Meck, W. H. (1984). Scalar timing in memory. *Annals of the New York Academy of Sciences, 423,* 52–77.

Gibbon, J., & Fairhurst, S. (1994). Ratio versus difference comparators in choice. *Journal of the Experimental Analysis of Behavior, 62,* 409–434.

Gibson, B. M., & Kamil, A. C. (2001). Search for a hidden goal by Clark's nutcrackers (*Nucifraga columbiana*) is more accurate inside than outside a landmark array. *Animal Learning & Behavior, 29,* 234–249.

Giftakis, J., & Tait, R. W. (1998). Blocking of the rabbit's classically conditioned nictitating membrane response: Effects of modifications of context associative strength. *Learning and Motivation, 29,* 23–48.

Gillan, D. J. (1981). Reasoning in the chimpanzee: II. Transitive inference. *Journal of Experimental Psychology: Animal Behavior Processes, 7,* 150–164.

Gillan, D. J., & Domjan, M. (1977). Taste-aversion conditioning with expected versus unexpected drug treatment. *Journal of Experimental Psychology: Animal Behavior Processes, 3,* 297–309.

Gillette, K., Martin, G. M., & Bellingham, W. P. (1980). Differential use of food and water cues in the formation of conditioned aversions by domestic chicks (*Gallus gallus*). *Journal of Experimental Psychology: Animal Behavior Processes, 6,* 99–111.

Gisiner, R., & Schusterman, R. J. (1992). Sequence, syntax, and semantics: Responses of a language-trained sea lion (*Zalophus californianus*) to novel sign combinations. *Journal of Comparative Psychology, 106,* 78–91.

Gisquet-Verrier, P., & Alexinsky, T. (1990). Facilitative effect of a pretest exposure to the CS: Analysis and implications for the memory trace. *Animal Learning & Behavior, 18,* 323–331.

Goddard, M. J. (1996). Effect of US signal value on blocking of a CS-US association. *Journal of Experimental Psychology: Animal Behavior Processes, 22,* 258–264.

Goddard, M. J. (1999). Renewal to the signal value of an unconditioned stimulus. *Learning and Motivation, 30,* 15–34.

Goddard, M. J., & Holland, P. C. (1996). Type of feature affects transfer in operant serial feature-positive discriminations. *Animal Learning & Behavior, 24,* 266–276.

Goldshmidt, J. N., Lattal, K. M., & Fantino, E. (1998). Context effects on choice. *Journal of the Experimental Analysis of Behavior, 70,* 301–320.

Goodall, G. (1984). Learning due to the response-shock contingency in signalled punishment. *Quarterly Journal of Experimental Psychology, 36B,* 259–279.

Goodall, G., & Mackintosh, N. J. (1987). Analysis of the Pavlovian properties of signals for punishment. *Quarterly Journal of Experimental Psychology, 39B,* 1–21.

Gordon, W. C. (1981). Mechanisms for cue-induced retention enhancement. In N. E. Spear & R. R. Miller (Eds.), *Information processing in animals: Memory mechanisms.* Hillsdale, NJ: Erlbaum.

Gordon, W. C., & Klein, R. L. (1994). Animal memory: The effects of context change on retention performance. In N. J. Mackintosh (Ed.), *Animal learning and cognition* (pp. 255–279). San Diego: Academic Press.

Gordon, W. C., McCracken, K. M., Dess-Beech, N., & Mowrer, R. R. (1981). Mechanisms for the cueing phenomenon: The addition of the cueing context to the training memory. *Learning and Motivation, 12,* 196–211.

Gordon, W. C., McGinnis, C. M., & Weaver, M. S. (1985). The effect of cuing after backward conditioning trials. *Learning and Motivation, 16,* 444–463.

Gordon, W. C., & Mowrer, R. R. (1980). An extinction trial as a reminder treatment following electroconvulsive shock. *Animal Learning & Behavior, 8,* 363–367.

Gormezano, I. (1966). Classical conditioning. In J. B. Sidowski (Ed.), *Experimental methods and instrumentation in psychology.* New York: McGraw-Hill.

Gormezano, I., Kehoe, E. J., & Marshall, B. S. (1983). Twenty years of classical conditioning research with the rabbit. In J. M. Prague & A. N. Epstein (Eds.), *Progress in psychobiology and physiological psychology* (Vol. 10). New York: Academic Press.

Gosling, S. D. (2001). From mice to men: What can we learn about personality from animal research? *Psychological Bulletin, 127,* 45–86.

Gosling, S. D., John, O. P., Craik, K. H., & Robins, R. W. (1998). Do people know how they behave? Self-reported act frequencies compared with on-line codings by observers. *Journal of Personality and Social Psychology, 74,* 1337–1349.

Grace, R. C. (1994). A contextual model of concurrent-chains choice. *Journal of the Experimental Analysis of Behavior, 61,* 113–129.

Grace, R. C. (1995). Independence of reinforcement delay and magnitude in concurrent chains. *Journal of the Experimental Analysis of Behavior, 63,* 255–276.

Grace, R. C. (1999). The matching law and amount-dependent exponential discounting as accounts of self-control choice. *Journal of the Experimental Analysis of Behavior, 71,* 27–44.

Grace, R. C., & Nevin, J. A. (2000). Response strength and temporal control in fixed-interval schedules. *Animal Learning & Behavior, 28,* 313–331.

Graham, J. M., & Desjardins, C. (1980). Classical conditioning: Induction of luteinizing hormone and testosterone secretion in anticipation of sexual activity. *Science, 210,* 1039–1041.

Graham, N. J., Barnet, R. C., Gunther, L. M., & Miller, R. R. (1994). Latent inhibition as a performance deficit resulting from CS-context associations. *Animal Learning & Behavior, 22,* 395–408.

Grant, D. S. (1976). Effect of sample presentation time on long-delay matching in the pigeon. *Learning and Motivation, 7,* 580–590.

Grant, D. S. (1982). Intratrial proactive interference in pigeon short-term memory: Manipulation of stimulus dimension and dimensional similarity. *Learning and Motivation, 13,* 417–433.

Grant, D. S. (1991). Symmetrical and asymmetrical coding of food and no-food samples in delayed matching in pigeons. *Journal of Experimental Psychology: Animal Behavior Processes, 17,* 186–193.

Grant, D. S. (1993). Coding processes in pigeons. In T. R. Zentall (Ed.), *Animal cognition* (pp. 193–216). Hillsdale, NJ: Erlbaum.

Grant, D. S. (2000). Influence of intertrial interval duration on the intertrial agreement effect in delayed matching-to-sample with pigeons. *Animal Learning & Behavior, 28,* 288–297.

Grant, D. S., & Spetch, M. L. (1993). Analogical and nonanalogical coding of samples differing in duration in a choice-matching task in pigeons. *Journal of Experimental Psychology: Animal Behavior Processes, 19,* 15–25.

Grau, J. W., & Joynes, R. L. (2001). Spinal cord injury: From animal research to human therapy. In M. E. Carroll & J. B. Overmier (Eds.), *Animal research and human health: Advancing human welfare through behavioral science* (pp. 209–226). Washington, DC: American Psychological Association.

Green, J. T., Ivry, R. B., & Woodruff-Pak, D. S. (1999). Timing in eyeblink classical conditioning and timed-interval tapping. *Psychological Science, 10,* 19–23.

Green, L., & Freed, D. E. (1993). The substitutability of reinforcers. *Journal of the Experimental Analysis of Behavior, 60,* 141–158.

Green, L., & Freed, D. E. (1998). Behavioral economics. In W. O'Donohue (Ed.), *Learning and behavior therapy* (pp. 274–300). Boston: Allyn and Bacon.

Greene, C. M., & Cook, R. G. (1997). Landmark geometry and identity controls spatial navigation in rats. *Animal Learning & Behavior, 25,* 312–323.

Greenfield, P. M., & Savage-Rumbaugh, E. S. (1990). Grammatical combination in *Pan paniscus:* Processes of learning and invention in the evolution and development of language. In S. T. Parker & K. R. Gibson (Eds.), *Language and intelligence in monkeys and apes* (pp. 540–578). Cambridge: Cambridge University Press.

Greenough, W. T., & Black, J. E. (2000). In A. E. Kazdin (Ed.), Learning: Molecular and Cellular Aspects. *Encyclopedia of psychology* (Vol. 5, pp. 3–5). New York: Oxford University Press.

Grice, G. R. (1948). The relation of secondary reinforcement to delayed reward in visual discrimination learning. *Journal of Experimental Psychology, 38,* 1–16.

Griffin, D. R. (1976). *The question of animal awareness.* New York: Rockefeller University Press.

Griffin, D. R. (1992). *Animal minds.* Chicago: University of Chicago Press.

Griffiths, D., Dickinson, A., & Clayton, N. (1999). Episodic memory: What can animals remember about their past? *Trends in Cognitive Sciences, 3,* 74–80.

Grossen, N. E., & Kelley, M. J. (1972). Species-specific behavior and acquisition of avoidance behavior in rats. *Journal of Comparative and Physiological Psychology, 81,* 307–310.

Groves, P. M., & Thompson, R. F. (1970). Habituation: A dual-process theory. *Psychological Review, 77,* 419–450.

Gunther, L. M., Denniston, J. C., & Miller, R. R. (1998). Conducting exposure treatment in multiple contexts can prevent relapse. *Behaviour Research and Therapy, 36,* 75–91.

Gunther, L. M., Miller, R. R., & Matute, H. (1997). CSs and USs: What's the difference? *Journal of Experimental Psychology: Animal Behavior Processes, 23,* 15–30.

Gunther, M. (1961). Infant behavior at the breast. In B. Foss (Ed.), *Determinants of infant behavior.* London: Wiley.

Gutiérrez, G., & Domjan, M. (1996). Learning and male-male sexual competition in Japanese quail (*Coturnix japonica*). *Journal of Comparative Psychology, 110,* 170–175.

Guttenberger, V. T., & Wasserman, E. A. (1985). Effects of sample duration, retention interval, and passage of time in the test on pigeons' matching-to-sample performance. *Animal Learning & Behavior, 13,* 121–128.

Guttman, N., & Kalish, H. I. (1956). Discriminability and stimulus generalization. *Journal of Experimental Psychology, 51,* 79–88.

Haggbloom, S. J., & Morris, K. M. (1994). Contextual cues and the retrieval of competing memories of goal events. *Animal Learning & Behavior, 22,* 165–172.

Haggbloom, S. J., Lovelace, L., Brewer, V. R., Levins, S. M., Owens, J. D. (1990). Replacement of event-generated memories of nonreinforcement with signal-generated memories of reinforcement during partial reinforcement training: Effects on resistance to extinction. *Animal Learning & Behavior, 18,* 315–322.

Hailman, J. P. (1967). The ontogeny of an instinct. *Behaviour Supplements, 15,* 1–159.

Hake, D. F., & Azrin, N. H. (1965). Conditioned punishment. *Journal of the Experimental Analysis of Behavior, 8,* 279–293.

Hall, G. (1991). *Perceptual and associative learning.* Oxford, England: Clarendon Press.

Hall, G. (1994). Pavlovian conditioning. In N. J. Mackintosh (Ed.), *Animal learning and cognition* (pp. 15–43). San Diego: Academic Press.

Hall, G., & Honey, R. C. (1989). Contextual effects in conditioning, latent inhibition, and habituation: Associative and retrieval functions of contextual cues. *Journal of Experimental Psychology: Animal Behavior Processes, 15,* 232–241.

Hall, G., Kaye, H., & Pearce, J. M. (1985). Attention and conditioned inhibition. In R. R. Miller & N. E. Spear (Eds.), *Information processing in animals: Conditioned inhibition* (pp. 185–207). Hillsdale, NJ: Erlbaum.

Hall, G., Ray, E., & Bonardi, C. (1993). Acquired equivalence between cues trained with a common antecedent. *Journal of Experimental Psychology: Animal Behavior Processes, 19,* 391–399.

Hall, R. V., Axelrod, S., Foundopoulos, M., Shellman, J., Campbell, R. A., & Cranston, S. S. (1971). The effective use of punishment to modify behavior in the classroom. *Educational Technology, 11*(4), 24–26.

Hall, S. M., Hall, R. G., & Ginsberg, D. (1990). Pharmacological and behavioral treatment for cigarette smoking. In M. Hersen, R. M. Eisler, & P. M. Miller (Eds.), *Progress in behavior modification* (Vol. 25, pp. 86–118). Newbury Park, CA: Sage.

Hallam, S. C., Grahame, N. J., Harris, K., & Miller, R. R. (1992). Associative structures underlying enhanced negative summation following operational extinction of a Pavlovian inhibitor. *Learning and Motivation, 23,* 43–62.

Hammond, L. J. (1968). Retardation of fear acquisition by a previously inhibitory CS. *Journal of Comparative and Physiological Psychology, 66,* 756–759.

Hanson, H. M. (1959). Effects of discrimination training on stimulus generalization. *Journal of Experimental Psychology, 58,* 321–333.

Hanson, J., & Green, L. (1986). Time and response matching with topographically different responses. *Animal Learning & Behavior, 14,* 435–442.

Hanson, S. J., & Timberlake, W. (1983). Regulation during challenge: A general model of learned performance under schedule constraint. *Psychological Review, 90,* 261–282.

Harlow, H. F. (1969). Age-mate or peer affectional system. In D. S. Lehrman, R. H. Hinde, & E. Shaw (Eds.), *Advances in the study of behavior* (Vol. 2). New York: Academic Press.

Haroutunian, V., & Riccio, D. C. (1979). Drug-induced "arousal" and the effectiveness of CS exposure in the reinstatement of memory. *Behavioral and Neural Biology, 26,* 115–120.

Harper, D. N., & Garry, M. (2000). Postevent cues bias recognition performance in pigeons. *Animal Learning & Behavior, 28,* 59–67.

Harper, D. N., & McLean, A. P. (1992). Resistance to change and the law of effect. *Journal of the Experimental Analysis of Behavior, 57,* 317–337.

Harris, J. A., Jones, M. L., Bailey, G. K., & Westbrook, R. F. (2000). Contextual control over conditioned responding in an extinction paradigm. *Journal of Experimental Psychology: Animal Behavior Processes, 9,* 248–265.

Hart, B. L. (1973). Reflexive behavior. In G. Bermant (Ed.), *Perspectives in animal behavior.* Glenview, IL: Scott, Foresman.

Hart, J. A., Bourne, M. J., & Schachtman, T. R. (1995). Slow reacquisition of a conditioned taste aversion. Animal Learning & Behavior, 23, *297–303.*

Hartl, J. A., Dougherty, D. H., & Wixted, J. T. (1996). Separating the effects of trial-specific and average sample-stimulus duration in delayed matching to sample in pigeons. *Journal of the Experimental Analysis of Behavior, 66,* 231–242.

Hartshorn, K., & Rovee-Collier, C. (1997). Infant learning and long-term memory at 6 months: A confirming analysis. *Developmental Psychobiology, 30,* 71–85.

Hastjarjo, T., & Silberberg, A. (1992). Effects of reinforcer delays on choice as a function of income level. *J*ournal of the Experimental Analysis of Behavior, 57, *119–125.*

Hastjarjo, T., Silberberg, A., & Hursh, S. R. (1990). Quinine pellets as an inferior good and a Giffen good in rats. *Journal of the Experimental Analysis of Behavior, 53,* 263–271.

Haug, M., & Whalen, R. E. (Eds.). (1999). *Animal models of human emotion and cognition.* Washington, DC: American Psychological Association.

Hayes, K. J., & Hayes, C. (1951). The intellectual development of a home-raised chimpanzee. *Proceedings of the American Philosophical Society, 95,* 105–109.

Healy, S. D., & Hurly, R. A. (1995). Spatial memory in rufous hummingbirds (*Selasphorus rufus*): A field test. *Animal Learning & Behavior, 23,* 63–68.

Hearst, E. (1968). Discrimination learning as the summation of excitation and inhibition. *Science, 162,* 1303–1306.

Hearst, E. (1969). Excitation, inhibition, and discrimination learning. In N. J. Mackintosh & W. K. Honig (Eds.), *Fundamental issues in associative learning.* Halifax: Dalhousie University Press.

Hearst, E. (1975). Pavlovian conditioning and directed movements. In G. Bower (Ed.), *The psychology of learning and motivation* (Vol. 9, pp. 215–262). New York: Academic Press.

Hearst, E. (1989). Backward associations: Differential learning about stimuli that follow the presence versus the absence of food in pigeons. *Animal Learning & Behavior, 17,* 280–290.

Hearst, E., & Franklin, S. R. (1977). Positive and negative relations between a signal and food: Approach withdrawal behavior to the signal. *Journal of Experimental Psychology: Animal Behavior Processes, 3,* 37–52.

Hearst, E., & Jenkins, H. M. (1974). *Sign-tracking: The stimulus-reinforcer relation and directed action.* Austin, TX: Psychonomic Society.

Hebb, D. O. (1949). *The organization of behavior.* New York: Wiley.

Hefner, H. E. (1999). The symbiotic nature of animal research. *Perspectives in Biology and Medicine, 43,* 128–139.

Heiligenberg, W. (1974). Processes governing behavioral states of readiness. In D. S. Lehrman, J. S. Rosenblatt, R. Hinde, & E. Shaw (Eds.), *Advances in the study of behavior* (Vol. 5, pp. 173–200). New York: Academic Press.

Helweg, D. A., Roitblat, H. L., Nachtigall, P. E., & Hautus, M. J. (1996). Recognition of aspect-dependent three-dimensional objects by an echolocating Atlantic bottlenose dolphin. *Journal of*

Experimental Psychology: Animal Behavior Processes, 22, 19–31.

Hendersen, R. W., Patterson, J. M., & Jackson, R. L. (1980). Acquisition and retention of control of instrumental behavior by a cue signaling airblast: How specific are conditioned anticipations? *Learning and Motivation, 11,* 407–426.

Hepper, P. G., & Shahidullah, S. (1992). Habituation in normal and Down's syndrome fetuses. *Quarterly Journal of Experimental Psychology, 44B,* 305–317.

Herman, L. M. (1987). Receptive competencies of language-trained animals. In J. S. Rosenblatt, C. Beer, M.-C. Busnel, & P. J. B. Slater (Eds.), *Advances in the study of behavior* (Vol. 17, pp. 1–60). Orlando, FL: Academic Press.

Herman, L. M., Pack, A. A., & Morrel-Samuels, P. (1993). Representational and conceptual skills of dolphins. In H. L. Roitblat, L. M. Herman, & P. E. Nachtigall (Eds.), *Language and communication: Comparative perspectives* (pp. 403–442). Hillsdale, NJ: Erlbaum.

Herman, L. M., & Uyeyama, R. K. (1999). The dolphin's grammatical competency: Comments on Kako. *Animal Learning & Behavior, 27,* 18–23.

Herman, R. L., & Azrin, N. H. (1964). Punishment by noise in an alternative response situation. *Journal of the Experimental Analysis of Behavior, 7,* 185–188.

Herrnstein, R. J. (1961). Relative and absolute strength of response as a function of frequency of reinforcement. *Journal of the Experimental Analysis of Behavior, 4,* 267–272.

Herrnstein, R. J. (1969). Method and theory in the study of avoidance. *Psychological Review, 76,* 49–69.

Herrnstein, R. J. (1970). On the law of effect. *Journal of the Experimental Analysis of Behavior, 13,* 243–266.

Herrnstein, R. J. (1984). Objects, categories, and discriminative stimuli. In H. L. Roitblat, T. G Bever, & H. S. Terrace (Eds.), *Animal cognition* (pp. 233–261). Hillsdale, NJ: Erlbaum.

Herrnstein, R. J. (1990). Levels of stimulus control: A functional approach. *Cognition, 37,* 133–166.

Herrnstein, R. J. (1997). *The matching law.* (H. Rachlin and D. I. Laibson, Eds.). New York: Russell Sage; and Cambridge: Harvard University Press.

Herrnstein, R. J., & deVilliers, P. A. (1980). Fish as a natural category for people and pigeons. In G. H. Bower (Ed.), *The psychology of learning and motivation* (Vol. 14, pp. 60–97). New York: Academic Press.

Herrnstein, R. J., & Heyman, G. M. (1979). Is matching compatible with reinforcement maximization on concurrent variable interval, variable ratio? *Journal of the Experimental Analysis of Behavior, 31,* 209–223.

Herrnstein, R. J., & Hineline, P. N. (1966). Negative reinforcement as shock-frequency reduction. *Journal of the Experimental Analysis of Behavior, 9,* 421–430.

Herrnstein, R. J., & Loveland, D. H. (1964). Complex visual concept in the pigeon. *Science, 146,* 549–551.

Herrnstein, R. J., Loveland, D. H., & Cable, C. (1976). Natural concepts in pigeons. *Journal of Experimental Psychology: Animal Behavior Processes, 2,* 285–301.

Herrnstein, R. J., & Vaughan, W., Jr. (1980). Melioration and behavioral allocation. In J. E. R. Staddon (Ed.), *Limits to action.* New York: Academic Press.

Herzog, H. A., Jr. (1988). The moral status of mice. *American Psychologist,* 43, 473–474.

Heyman, G. M. (1983). Optimization theory: Close but no cigar. *Behaviour Analysis Letters, 3,* 17–26.

Heyman, G. M., & Herrnstein, R. J. (1986). More on concurrent interval-ratio schedules: A replication and review. *Journal of the Experimental Analysis of Behavior, 46,* 331–351.

Heyman, G. M., & Monaghan, M. M. (1994). Reinforcer magnitude (sucrose concentration) and the matching law theory of response strength. *Journal of the Experimental Analysis of Behavior, 61,* 505–516.

Hilgard, E. R., & Marquis, D. G. (1940). *Conditioning and learning.* New York: Appleton.

Hilliard, S. H., Domjan, M., Nguyen, M., & Cusato, B. (1998). Dissociation of conditioned appetitive and consummatory sexual behavior: Satiation and extinction tests. *Animal Learning & Behavior, 26,* 20–33.

Hineline, P. N. (1977). Negative reinforcement and avoidance. In W. K. Honig & J. E. R. Staddon (Eds.), *Handbook of operant behavior* (pp. 364–414). Englewood Cliffs, NJ: Prentice-Hall.

Hineline, P. N. (1981). The several roles of stimuli in negative reinforcement. In P. Harzem & M. D. Zeiler (Eds.), *Predictability, correlation, and contiguity* (pp. 203–246). Chichester, England: Wiley.

Hinson, J. M., & Cannon, C. B. (1999). Stimulus spacing, attention, and dimensional contrast. *Animal Learning & Behavior, 27,* 472–480.

Hinson, J. M., Cannon, C. B., & Tennison, L. R. (1999). Orthogonal stimulus variation and attention in dimensional contrast. *Animal Learning & Behavior, 27,* 181–189.

Hinson, J. M., & Staddon, J. E. R. (1983a). Hill-climbing by pigeons. *Journal of the Experimental Analysis of Behavior, 39,* 25–47.

Hinson, J. M., & Staddon, J. E. R. (1983b). Matching, maximizing, and hill-climbing. *Journal of the Experimental Analysis of Behavior, 40,* 321–331.

Hinton, S. H., & Meck, W. H. (1997). The "internal clocks" of circadian and interval timing. *Endeavour, 22,* 82–87.

Hintzman, D. L. (1991). Twenty-five years of learning and memory: Was the cognitive revolution a mistake? In D.E. Meyer & S. Kornblum (Eds.), *Attention and performance XIVP.* Hillsdale, NJ: Erlbaum.

Hitchcock, D. F. A., & Rovee-Collier, C. (1996). The effect of repeated reactivations on memory specificity in infancy. *Journal of Experimental Child Psychology, 62,* 378–400.

Ho, M.-Y., Wogar, M. A., Bradshaw, C. M., & Szabadi, E. (1997). Choice between delayed reinforcers: Interaction between delay and deprivation level. *Quarterly Journal of Experimental Psychology, 50B,* 193–202.

Hoffman, C. M., Timberlake, W., Leffel, J., & Gont, R. (1999). How is radial arm maze behavior in rats related to locomotor search tactics? *Animal Learning & Behavior, 27,* 426–444.

Hoffman, H. S., & Solomon, R. L. (1974). An opponent-process theory of motivation: III. Some affective dynamics in imprinting. *Learning and Motivation, 5,* 149–164.

Holland, P. C. (1977). Conditioned stimulus as a determinant of the form of the Pavlovian conditioned response. *Journal of Experimental Psychology: Animal Behavior Processes, 3,* 77–104.

Holland, P. C. (1980). Influence of visual conditioned stimulus characteristics on the form of Pavlovian appetitive conditioned responding in rats. *Journal of Experimental Psychology: Animal Behavior Processes, 6,* 81–97.

Holland, P. C. (1984). Origins of behavior in Pavlovian conditioning. In G. H. Bower (Ed.), *The psychology of learning and motivation* (Vol. 18, pp. 129–174). Orlando, FL: Academic Press.

Holland, P. C. (1985). The nature of conditioned inhibition in serial and simultaneous feature negative discriminations. In R. R. Miller & N. E. Spear (Eds.), *Information processing in animals: Conditioned inhibition* (pp. 267–297). Hillsdale, NJ: Erlbaum.

Holland, P. C. (1986). Temporal determinants of occasion setting in feature-positive discriminations. *Animal Learning and Behavior, 14,* 111–120.

Holland, P. C. (1989a). Feature extinction enhances transfer of occasion setting. *Animal Learning & Behavior, 17,* 269–279.

Holland, P. C. (1989b). Occasion setting with simultaneous compounds in rats. *Journal of Experimental Psychology: Animal Behavior Processes, 15,* 183–193.

Holland, P. C. (1989c). Transfer of negative occasion setting and conditioned inhibition across conditioned and unconditioned stimuli. *Journal of Experimental Psychology: Animal Behavior Processes, 15,* 311–328.

Holland, P. C. (1991). Acquisition and transfer of occasion setting in operant feature positive and feature negative discriminations. *Learning and Motivation, 22,* 366–387.

Holland, P. C. (1992). Occasion setting in Pavlovian conditioning. In D. L. Medin (Ed.), *The psychology of learning and motivation* (Vol. 28, pp. 69–125). San Diego, CA: Academic Press.

Holland, P. C. (2000). Trial and intertrial durations in appetitive conditioning in rats. *Animal Learning & Behavior, 28,* 121–135.

Holland, P. C., & Rescorla, R. A. (1975a). The effect of two ways of devaluing the unconditioned stimulus after first- and second-order appetitive conditioning. *Journal of Experimental Psychology: Animal Behavior Processes, 1,* 355–363.

Holland, P. C., & Rescorla, R. A. (1975b). Second-order conditioning with food unconditioned stimulus. *Journal of Comparative and Physiological Psychology, 88,* 459–467.

Holland, P. C., & Straub, J. J. (1979). Differential effect of two ways of devaluing the unconditioned stimulus after Pavlovian appetitive conditioning. *Journal of Experimental Psychology: Animal Behavior Processes, 5,* 65–78.

Holliday, M., & Hirsch, J. (1986). Excitatory conditioning of individual *Drosophila melanogaster. Journal of Experimental Psychology: Animal Behavior Processes, 12,* 131–142.

Hollis, K. L. (1997). Contemporary research on Pavlovian conditioning: A "new" functional analysis. *American Psychologist, 52,* 956–965.

Hollis, K. L., Cadieux, E. L., & Colbert, M. M. (1989). The biological function of Pavlovian conditioning: A mechanism for mating success in the blue gourami (Trichogaster trichopterus). *Journal of Comparative Psychology, 103,* 115–121.

Hollis, K. L., Pharr, V. L., Dumas, M. J., Britton, G. B., & Field, J. (1997). Classical conditioning provides paternity advantage for territorial male blue gouramis (*Trichogaster trichopterus*). *Journal of Comparative Psychology, 111,* 219–225.

Holloway, K. S., & Domjan, M. (1993). Sexual approach conditioning: Tests of unconditioned stimulus devaluation using hormone manipulations. *Journal of Experimental Psychology: Animal Behavior Processes, 19,* 47–55.

Holman, J. G., & Mackintosh, N. J. (1981). The control of appetitive instrumental responding does not depend on classical conditioning to the discriminative stimulus. *Quarterly Journal of Experimental Psychology, 33B,* 21–31.

Holz, W. C., & Azrin, N. H. (1961). Discriminative properties of punishment. *Journal of the Experimental Analysis of Behavior, 4,* 225–232.

Honey, R. C., Good, M., & Manser, K. L. (1998). Negative priming in associative learning: Evidence from a serial-habituation procedure. *Journal of Experimental Psychology: Animal Behavior Processes, 24,* 229–237.

Honey, R. C., & Hall, G. (1989). Acquired equivalence and distinctiveness of cues. *Journal of Experimental Psychology: Animal Behavior Processes,* 15, 338–346.

Honey, R. C., & Hall, G. (1991). Acquired equivalence and distinctiveness of cues using a sensory-preconditioning procedure. *Quarterly Journal of Experimental Psychology, 43B,* 121–135.

Honey, R. C., & Watt, A. (1998). Acquired relational equivalence: Implications for the nature of associative structures. *Journal of Experimental Psychology: Animal Behavior Processes, 24,* 325–334.

Honey, R. C., & Watt, A. (1999). Acquired relational equivalence between contexts and features. *Journal of Experimental Psychology: Animal Behavior Processes, 25,* 324–333.

Honey, R. C., Willis, A., & Hall, G. (1990). Context specificity in pigeon autoshaping. *Learning and Motivation, 21,* 125–136.

Honig, W. K. (1978). Studies of working memory in the pigeon. In S. H. Hulse, H. Fowler, & W. K. Honig (Eds.), *Cognitive processes in animal behavior* (pp. 211–248). Hillsdale, NJ: Erlbaum.

Honig, W. K., Boneau, C. A., Burstein, K. R., & Pennypacker, H. S. (1963). Positive and negative generalization gradients obtained under equivalent training conditions. *Journal of Comparative and Physiological Psychology, 56,* 111–116.

Honig, W. K., & Stewart, K. E. (1988). Pigeons can discriminate locations presented in pictures. *Journal of the Experimental Analysis of Behavior, 50,* 541–551.

Honig, W. K., & Thompson, R. K. R. (1982). Retrospective and prospective processing in animal working memory. In G. H. Bower (Ed.), *The psychology of learning and motivation* (Vol. 16, pp. 239–283). Orlando, FL: Academic Press.

Honig, W. K., & Urcuioli, P. J. (1981). The legacy of Guttman and Kalish (1956): 25 years of research on stimulus generalization. *Journal of the Experimental Analysis of Behavior, 36,* 405–445.

Horne, P. J., & Lowe, C. F. (1996). On the origins on naming and other symbolic behavior, *Journal of the Experimental Analysis of Behavior, 65,* 185–241.

Horne, P. J., & Lowe, C. F. (1997). Toward a theory of verbal behavior. *Journal of the Experimental Analysis of Behavior, 68,* 271–296.

Hoyert, M. S. (1992). Order and chaos in fixed-interval schedules of reinforcement. *Journal of the Experimental Analysis of Behavior, 57,* 339–363.

Huber, L., & Lenz, R. (1993). A test of the linear feature model of polymorphous concept discrimination with pigeons. *The Quarterly Journal of Experimental Psychology, 46B,* 1–18.

Huber, L., & Lenz, R. (1996). Categorization of prototypical stimulus classes by pigeons. *Quarterly Journal of Experimental Psychology, 49B,* 111–133.

Huber, L., Troje, N. F., Loidolt, M., Aust, U., & Grass, D. (2000). Natural categorization through multiple feature learning in pigeons. *Quarterly Journal of Experimental Psychology, 53B,* 341–357.

Hull, C. L. (1930). Knowledge and purpose as habit mechanisms. *Psychological Review, 30,* 511–525.

Hull, C. L. (1931). Goal attraction and directing ideas conceived as habit phenomena. *Psychological Review, 38,* 487–506.

Hulse, S. H. (1958). Amount and percentage of reinforcement and duration of goal confinement in conditioning and extinction. *Journal of Experimental Psychology, 56,* 48–57.

Hulse, S. H. (1978). Cognitive structure and serial pattern learning by animals. In S. H. Hulse, H. Fowler, & W. K. Honig (Eds.), *Cognitive processes in animal behavior* (pp. 311–340). Hillsdale, NJ: Erlbaum.

Hulse, S. H., Fowler, H., & Honig, W. K. (Eds.). (1978). *Cognitive processes in animal behavior.* Hillsdale, NJ: Erlbaum.

Hulse, S. H., Page, S. C., & Braaten, R. F. (1990). Frequency range size and the frequency range constraint in auditory perception by European starlings (*Sturnus vulgaris*). Animal Learning & Behavior, 18, *238–245.*

Hunt, M., Parr, W. V., & Smith, P. (1999). Local and global sources of control in pigeon delayed matching-to-sample performance. Quarterly Journal of Experimental Psychology, 52B, *203–233.*

Hunt, P. S. (1997). Retention of conditioned autonomic and behavioral responses in preweanling rats: Forgetting and reinstatement. *Animal Learning & Behavior, 25,* 301–311.

Hunter, W. S. (1913). The delayed reaction in animals and children. *Behavior Monographs, 2,* serial #6.

Hursh, S. R. (1984). Behavioral economics. *Journal of the Experimental Analysis of Behavior, 42,* 435–452.

Hursh, S. R. (1991). Behavioral economics of drug self-administration and drug abuse policy. *Journal of the Experimental Analysis of Behavior, 56,* 377–393.

Hursh, S. R., Raslear, T. G., Shurtleff, D., Bauman, R., & Simmons, L. (1988). A cost-benefit analysis of demand for food. *Journal of the Experimental Analysis of Behavior, 50,* 419–440.

Hutt, P. J. (1954). Rate of bar pressing as a function of quality and quantity of food reward. *Journal of Comparative and Physiological Psychology, 47,* 235–239.

Innis, N. K., Reberg, D., Mann, B., Jacobson, J., & Turton, D. (1983). Schedule-induced behavior for food and water: Effects of interval duration. *Behaviour Analysis Letters, 3,* 191–200.

Innis, N. K., Simmelhag-Grant, V. L., & Staddon, J. E. R. (1983). Behavior induced by periodic food delivery: The effects of interfood interval. *Journal of the Experimental Analysis of Behavior, 39,* 309–322.

Irwin, J., Suissa, A., & Anisman, H. (1980). Differential effects of inescapable shock on escape performance and discrimination learning in a water escape task. *Journal of Experimental Psychology: Animal Behavior Processes, 6,* 21–40.

Ishida, M., & Papini, M. R. (1997). Massed-trial overtraining effects on extinction and reversal performance in turtles (*Geoclemys reevesii*). *Quarterly Journal of Experimental Psychology, 50B,* 1–16.

Israel, A. C., Devine, V. T., O'Dea, M. A., & Hamdi, M. E. (1974). Effect of delayed conditioned stimulus termination on extinction of an avoidance response following differential termination conditions during acquisition. *Journal of Experimental Psychology, 103,* 360–362.

Ito, M., & Nakamura, K. (1998). Human's choice in a self-control choice situation: sensitivity to reinforcer amount, reinforcer delay, and overall reinforcement density. *Journal of the Experimental Analysis of Behavior, 69,* 87–102.

Iversen, I. H. (1993a). Acquisition of matching-to-sample performance in rats using visual stimuli on nose keys. *Journal of the Experimental Analysis of Behavior, 59,* 471–482.

Iversen, I. H. (1993b). Techniques for establishing schedules with wheel running as reinforcement in rats. *Journal of the Experimental Analysis of Behavior, 60,* 219–238.

Ivkovich, D., Collins, K. L., Eckerman, C. O., Krasnegor, N. A., & Stanton, M. E. (1999). Classical delay eyeblink conditioning in 4– and 5–month-old human infants. *Psychological Science, 10,* 4–8.

Jackson, R. L., & Minor, T. R. (1988). Effects of signaling inescapable shock on subsequent escape learning: Implications for theories of coping and "learned helplessness." *Journal of Experimental Psychology: Animal Behavior Processes, 14,* 390–400.

Jackson, R. L., Alexander, J. H., & Maier, S. F. (1980). Learned helplessness, inactivity, and associative deficits: Effects of inescapable shock on response choice escape learning. *Journal of Experimental Psychology: Animal Behavior Processes, 6,* 1–20.

Janssen, M., Farley, J., & Hearst, E. (1995). Temporal location of unsignaled food deliveries: Effects on conditioned withdrawal (inhibition) in pigeon signtracking. *Journal of Experimental Psychology: Animal Behavior Processes, 21,* 116–128.

Jarrard, L. E., & Moise, S. L. (1971). Short-term memory in the monkey. In L. E. Jarrard (Ed.), *Cognitive processes of non-*

human primates. New York: Academic Press.

Jenkins, H. M. (1962). Resistance to extinction when partial reinforcement is followed by regular reinforcement. *Journal of Experimental Psychology, 64,* 441–450.

Jenkins, H. M. (1977). Sensitivity of different response systems to stimulus-reinforcer and response-reinforcer relations. In H. Davis & H. M. B. Hurwitz (Eds.), *Operant-Pavlovian interactions* (pp. 47–62). Hillsdale, NJ: Erlbaum.

Jenkins, H. M., Barnes, R. A., & Barrera, F. J. (1981). Why autoshaping depends on trial spacing. In C. M. Locurto, H. S. Terrace, & J. Gibbon (Eds.), *Autoshaping and conditioning theory* (pp. 255–284). New York: Academic Press.

Jenkins, H. M., & Harrison, R. H. (1960). Effects of discrimination training on auditory generalization. *Journal of Experimental Psychology, 59,* 246–253.

Jenkins, H. M., & Harrison, R. H. (1962). Generalization gradients of inhibition following auditory discrimination learning. *Journal of the Experimental Analysis of Behavior, 5,* 435–441.

Jenkins, H. M., & Moore, B. R. (1973). The form of the autoshaped response with food or water reinforcers. *Journal of the Experimental Analysis of Behavior, 20,* 163–181.

Jennings, H. S. (1976). *Behavior of the lower organisms.* Bloomington: Indiana University Press. (Original work published 1904)

Jitsumori, M. (1994). Discrimination of artificial polymorphous categories by rhesus monkeys (*Macaca mulatta*). *The Quarterly Journal of Experimental Psychology, 47B,* 371–386.

Jitsumori, M. (1996). A prototype effect and categorization of artificial polymorphous stimuli in pigeons. *Journal of Experimental Psychology: Animal Behavior Processes, 22,* 405–419.

Jitsumori, M., Natori, M., & Okuyama, K. (1999). Recognition of moving video images of conspecifics by pigeons: Effects of individuals, static and dynamic motion cues, and movement. *Animal Learning & Behavior, 27,* 303–315.

Jitsumori, M., & Yoshihara, M. (1997). Categorical discrimination of human facial expressions by pigeons: A test of the linear feature model. *Quarterly Journal of Experimental Psychology, 50B,* 253–268.

Job, R. F. S. (1987). Learned helplessness in an appetitive discrete-trial T-maze discrimination test. *Animal Learning & Behavior, 15,* 342–346.

Job, R. F. S. (1989). A test of proposed mechanisms underlying the interference effect produced by noncontingent food presentations. *Learning and Motivation, 20,* 153–177.

Johnson, H. M. (1994). Processes of successful intentional forgetting. *Psychological Bulletin, 116,* 274–292.

Jordan, W. P., Strasser, H. C., & McHale, L. (2000). Contextual control of long-term habituation in rats. *Journal of Experimental Psychology: Animal Behavior Processes, 26,* 323–339.

Kaiser, D. H., Sherburne, L. M., & Zentall, T. R. (1997). Directed forgetting in pigeons resulting from reallocation of memory-maintaining processes on forget-cue trials. *Psychonomic Bulletin & Review, 4,* 559–565.

Kaiser, L., & De Jong, R. (1995). Induction of odor preference in a specialist insect parasitoid. *Animal Learning & Behavior, 23,* 17–21.

Kako, E. (1999). Elements of syntax in the systems of three language-trained animals. *Animal Learning & Behavior, 27,* 1–14.

Kamil, A. C. (1978). Systematic foraging by a nectarfeeding bird, the amakihi (*Loxops virens*). *Journal of Comparative and Physiological Psychology, 92,* 388–396.

Kamil, A. C., & Balda, R. P. (1985). Cache recovery and spatial memory in Clark's nutcrackers (Nucifraga columbiana). *Journal of Experimental Psychology: Animal Behavior Processes, 11,* 95–111.

Kamil, A. C., & Balda, R. P. (1990a). Differential memory for different cache sites by Clark's nutcrackers (*Nucifraga columbiana*). *Journal of Experimental Psychology: Animal Behavior Processes, 16,* 162–168.

Kamil, A. C., & Balda, R. P. (1990b). Spatial memory in seed-caching corvids. In G. H. Bower (Ed.), *The psychology of learning and motivation* (Vol. 26, pp. 1–25). San Diego: Academic Press.

Kamil, A. C., & Jones, J. E. (2000). Geometric rule learning by Clark's nutcrackers (*Nucifraga columbiana*). *Journal of Experimental Psychology: Animal Behavior Processes, 26,* 439–453.

Kamin, L. J. (1956). The effects of termination of the CS and avoidance of the US on avoidance learning. *Journal of Comparative and Physiological Psychology, 49,* 420–424.

Kamin, L. J. (1965). Temporal and intensity characteristics of the conditioned stimulus. In W. F. Prokasy (Ed.), *Classical conditioning* (pp. 118–147). New York: Appleton-Century-Crofts.

Kamin, L. J. (1968). "Attention-like" processes in classical conditioning. In M. R. Jones (Ed.), *Miami Symposium on the Prediction of Behavior: Aversive stimulation* (pp. 9–31). Miami: University of Miami Press.

Kamin, L. J. (1969). Predictability, surprise, attention, and conditioning. In B. A. Campbell & R. M. Church (Eds.), *Punishment and aversive behavior* (pp. 279–296). New York: Appleton-Century-Crofts.

Kamin, L. J., & Brimer, C. J. (1963). The effects of intensity of conditioned and unconditioned stimuli on a conditioned emotional response. *Canadian Journal of Psychology, 17,* 194–198.

Kamin, L. J., Brimer, C. J., & Black, A. H. (1963). Conditioned suppression as a monitor of fear of the CS in the course of avoidance training. *Journal of Comparative and Physiological Psychology, 56,* 497–501.

Kamin, L. J., & Schaub, R. E. (1963). Effects of conditioned stimulus intensity on the conditioned emotional response. *Journal of Comparative and Physiological Psychology, 56,* 502–507.

Kandel, E. R. (1976). *Cellular basis of behavior.* San Francisco: Freeman.

Kandel, E. R., & Schwartz, J. H. (1982). Molecular biology of learning: Modulation of transmitter release. *Science, 218,* 433–443.

Kandel, E. R., Schwartz, J. H., & Jessell, T. M. (Eds.). (1991). *Principles of neural science.* New York: Elsevier.

Kandel, E. R., Schwartz, J. H., & Jessell, T. M. (Eds.). (2000). *Principles of neural science.* New York: McGraw-Hill.

Kaplan, P. S., Goldstein, M. H., Huckeby, E. R., & Cooper, R. P. (1995). Habituation, sensitization, and infants' responses to motherese speech. *Developmental Psychobiology, 28,* 45–57.

Kaplan, P. S., & Hearst, E. (1982). Bridging temporal gaps between CS and US in autoshaping: Insertion of other stimuli before, during, and after the CS. *Journal of Experimental Psychology: Animal Behavior Processes, 8,* 187–203.

Kaplan, P. S., Werner, J. S., & Rudy, J. W. (1990). Habituation, sensitization, and infant visual attention. In C. Rovee-Collier & L. P. Lipsitt (Eds.), *Advances in infancy research* (Vol. 6, pp. 61–109). Norwood, NJ: Ablex.

Karpicke, J. (1978). Directed approach responses and positive conditioned suppression in the rat. *Animal Learning & Behavior, 6,* 216–224.

Kasprow, W. J. (1987). Enhancement of short-term retention by appetitive-reinforcer reminder treatment. *Animal Learning & Behavior, 15,* 412–416.

Kasprow, W. J., Cacheiro, H., Balaz, M. A., & Miller, R. R. (1982). Reminder-induced recovery of associations to an overshadowed stimulus. *Learning and Motivation, 13,* 155–166.

Kasprow, W. J., Catterson, D., Schachtman, T. R., & Miller, R. R. (1984). Attenuation of latent inhibition by post-acquisition reminder. *Quarterly Journal of Experimental Psychology, 36B,* 53–63.

Kasprow, W. J., Schachtman, T. R., & Miller, R. R. (1987). The comparator hypothesis of conditioned response generation: Manifest conditioned excitation and inhibition as a function of relative excitatory strengths of CS and conditioning context at the time of testing. *Journal of Experimental Psychology: Animal Behavior Processes, 13,* 395–406.

Kastak, D., & Schusterman, R. J. (1994). Transfer of visual identity matching-to-sample in two California sea lions (*Zatophus californianus*). *Animal Learning & Behavior, 22,* 427–435.

Kastak, D., & Schusterman, R. J. (1998). Low-frequency amphibious hearing in pinnipeds: Methods, measurement, noise, and ecology. *Journal of the Acoustical Society of America, 103,* 2216–2228.

Kastak, D., Schusterman, R. J., Southall, B. L., & Reichmuth, C. J. (1999). Underwater temporary threshold shift induced by octave-band noise in three species of pinniped. *Journal of the Acoustical Society of America, 106,* 1142–1148.

Katzev, R. D. (1967). Extinguishing avoidance responses as a function of delayed warning signal termination. *Journal of Experimental Psychology, 75,* 339–344.

Katzev, R. D. (1972). What is both necessary and sufficient to maintain avoidance responding in the shuttle box? *Quarterly Journal of Experimental Psychology, 24,* 310–317.

Katzev, R. D., & Berman, J. S. (1974). Effect of exposure to conditioned stimulus and control of its termination in the extinction of avoidance behavior. *Journal of Comparative and Physiological Psychology, 87,* 347–353.

Kaufman, L. W., & Collier, G. (1983). Cost and meal pattern in wild-caught rats. *Physiology and Behavior, 30,* 445–449.

Keehn, J. D., & Nakkash, S. (1959). Effect of a signal contingent upon an avoidance response. *Nature, 184,* 566–568.

Keen, R., & Machado, A. (1999). How pigeons discriminate the relative frequency of events. *Journal of the Experimental Analysis of Behavior, 72,* 151–175.

Kehoe, E. J., Cool, V., & Gormezano, I. (1991). Trace conditioning of the rabbit's nictitating membrane response as a function of CS-US interstimulus interval and trials per session. *Learning and Motivation, 22,* 269–290.

Kelly, M. J. (1986). Selective attention and stimulus reinforcer interactions in the pigeon. *Quarterly Journal of Experimental Psychology, 38B,* 97–110.

Kellogg, W. N. (1933). *The ape and the child.* New York: McGraw-Hill.

Kesner, R. P., & DeSpain, M. J. (1988). Correspondence between rats and humans in the utilization of retrospective and prospective codes. *Animal Learning & Behavior, 16,* 299–302.

Kessler, R. C., McGonagle, K. A., Zhao, S., Nelson, C. B., Hughes, M., Eshleman, S., Wittchen, H.-U., & Kendler, K. S. (1994). Lifetime and 12-month prevalence of DSM-III-R psychiatric disorders in the United States: Results from the National Comorbidity Survey. *Archives of General Psychiatry, 51,* 8–19.

Khallad, Y., & Moore, J. (1996). Blocking, unblocking, and overexpectation in autoshaping with pigeons. *Journal of the Experimental Analysis of Behavior, 65,* 575–591.

Killeen, P. R. (1991). Behavior's time. In G. H. Bower (Ed.), *The psychology of learning and motivation* (Vol. 27, pp. 295–334). San Diego: Academic Press.

Killeen, P. R. (1995). Economics, ecologics, and mechanics: The dynamics of responding under conditions of varying motivation. *Journal of the Experimental Analysis of Behavior, 64,* 405–431.

Killeen, P. R. (2001a). The four causes of behavior. *Current Directions in Psychological Science, 10,* 136–140.

Killeen, P. R. (2001b). Writing and overwriting short-term memory. *Psychonomic Bulletin & Review, 8,* 18–43.

Killeen, P. R., & Fetterman, J. G. (1988). A behavioral theory of timing. *Psychological Review, 95,* 274–295.

Killeen, P. R., & Fetterman, J. G. (1993). The behavioral theory of timing: Transition analyses. *Journal of the Experimental Analysis of Behavior, 59,* 411–422.

Killeen, P. R., Fetterman, J. G., & Bizo, L. A. (1997). Time's causes. In C. M. Bradshaw & E. Szabadi (Eds.), *Time and behaviour: Psychological and neurobiological analyses* (pp. 79–139). Amsterdam: Elsevier Science.

Killeen, P. R., & Hall, S. S. (2001). The principal components of response strength. *Journal of the Experimental Analysis of Behavior, 75,* 111–134.

Kim, J. J., D. J. Krupa, et al. (1998). Inhibitory cerebello-olivary projections and blocking effect in classical conditioning. *Science, 279,* 570–573.

Kim, S. D., Rivers, S., Bevins, R. A., & Ayres, J. J. B. (1996). Conditioned stimulus determinants of conditioned response form in Pavlovian fear conditioning. *Journal of Experimental Psychology: Animal Behavior Processes, 22,* 87–104.

Kimble, G. A. (1961). *Hilgard and Marquis' conditioning and learning* (2nd ed.). New York: Appleton.

Kirby, K. N., Petry, N. M., & Bickel, W. K. (1999). Heroin addicts have higher discount rates for delayed rewards than non-drug-using controls. *Journal of Experimental Psychology: General, 128,* 78–87.

Kirkpatrick, K., & Church, R. M. (2000). Independent effects of stimulus and cycle duration in conditioning: The role of timing processes. *Animal Learning & Behavior,* 28, 373–388.

Kirkpatrick-Steger, K., Miller S. S., Betti, C. A., & Wasserman, E. A. (1996). Cyclic responding by pigeons on the peak timing procedure. *Journal of Experimental Psychology: Animal Behavior Processes, 22,* 447–460.

Klein, B. G., LaMon, B., & Zeigler, H. P. (1983). Drinking in the pigeon (*Columba livia*): Topography and spatiotemporal organization. *Journal of Comparative Psychology, 97,* 178–181.

Klein, M., & Rilling, M. (1974). Generalization of free operant avoidance behavior in pigeons. *Journal of the Experimental Analysis of Behavior, 21,* 75–88.

Kluender, K. R., Diehl, R. L., & Killeen, P. R. (1987). Japanese quail can learn phonetic categories. *Science, 237,* 1195–1197.

Köhler, W. (1939). Simple structural functions in the chimpanzee and in the chicken. In W. D. Ellis (Ed.), *A source book of Gestalt psychology* (pp. 217–227). New York: Harcourt Brace Jovanovich.

Koob, G. F., Caine, S. B., Parsons, L., Markou, A., & Weiss, F. (1997). Opponent-process model and psychostimulant addiction. *Pharmacology Biochemistry and Behavior, 57,* 531–521.

Kraemer, P. J., & Golding, J. M. (1997). Adaptive forgetting in animals. *Psychonomic Bulletin & Review, 4,* 480–491.

Kraemer, P. J., Hoffmann, H., Randall, C. K., & Spear, N. E. (1992). Devaluation of Pavlovian conditioning in the 10-day-old rat. *Animal Learning & Behavior, 20,* 219–222.

Kraemer, P. J., & Roberts, W. A. (1985). Short-term memory for simultaneously presented visual and auditory signals in the pigeon. *Journal of Experimental Psychology: Animal Behavior Processes, 11,* 13–39.

Kremer, E. F. (1978). The Rescorla-Wagner model: Losses in associative strength in compound conditioned stimuli. *Journal of Experimental Psychology: Animal Behavior Processes, 4,* 22–36.

Kriekhaus, E. E., & Wolf, G. (1968). Acquisition of sodium by rats: Interaction of innate and latent learning. *Journal of Comparative and Physiological Psychology, 65,* 197–201.

Kruse, J. M., Overmier, J. B., Konz, W. A., & Rokke, E. (1983). Pavlovian conditioned stimulus effects upon instrumental choice behavior are reinforcer specific. *Learning and Motivation, 14,* 165–181.

Lansdell, H. (1988). Laboratory animals need only humane treatment: Animal "rights" may debase human rights. *International Journal of Neuroscience, 42,* 169–178.

Lashley, K. S., & Wade, M. (1946). The Pavlovian theory of generalization. *Psychological Review, 53,* 72–87.

Lattal, K. A. (1998). A century of effect: Legacies of E. L. Thorndike's *Animal intelligence* monograph. *Journal of the Experimental Analysis of Behavior, 70,* 325–336.

Lattal, K. A., & Abreu-Rodrigues, J. (1997). Response independent events in the behavior stream. *Journal of the Experimental Analysis of Behavior, 68,* 375–398.

Lattal, K. A., & Gleeson, S. (1990). Response acquisition with delayed reinforcement. *Journal of Experimental Psychology: Animal Behavior Processes, 16,* 27–39.

Lattal, K. A., & Metzger, B. (1994). Response acquisition by Siamese fighting fish (*Betta spendens*) with delayed visual reinforcement. *Journal of the Experimental Analysis of Behavior, 61,* 35–44.

Lattal, K. A., & Neef, N. A. (1996). Recent reinforcement-schedule research and applied behavior analysis. *Journal of Applied Behavior Analysis, 29,* 213–230.

Lattal, K. A. Reilly, M. P., & Kohn, J. P. (1998). Response persistence under ratio and interval reinforcement schedules. *Journal of the Experimental Analysis of Behavior, 70,* 165–183.

Lattal, K. M. (1999). Trial and intertrial durations in Pavlovian conditioning: Issues of learning and performance. *Journal of Experimental Psychology: Animal Behavior Processes, 25,* 433–450.

Lattal, K. M., & Nakajima, S. (1998). Overexpectation in appetitive Pavlovian and instrumental conditioning. *Animal Learning & Behavior, 26,* 351–360.

Lavin, M. J. (1976). The establishment of flavor-flavor associations using a sensory preconditioning training procedure. *Learning and Motivation, 7,* 173–183.

Lawler, C. P., & Cohen, P. S. (1992). Temporal patterns of schedule-induced drinking and pawgrooming in rats exposed to periodic food. *Animal Learning & Behavior, 20,* 266–280.

Lea, S. E. G. (1978). The psychology and economics of demand. *Psychological Bulletin, 85,* 441–466.

Lea, S. E. G. (1984). In what sense do pigeons learn concepts? In H. L. Roitblat, T. G. Bever, & H. S. Terrace (Eds.), *Animal cognition* (pp. 263–276). Hillsdale, NJ: Erlbaum.

Lea, S. E. G., & Harrison, S. N. (1978). Discrimination of polymorphous stimulus sets by pigeons. *Quarterly Journal of Experimental Psychology, 30,* 521–537.

Leaton, R. N. (1976). Long-term retention of the habituation of lick suppression and startle response produced by a single auditory stimulus. *Journal of Experimental Psychology: Animal Behavior Processes, 2,* 248–259.

LeDoux, J. (1996). Emotional networks and motor control: A fearful view. *Progress in Brain Research, 107,* 437–446.

Lee, R. K. K., & Maier, S. F. (1988). Inescapable shock and attention to internal versus external cues in a water discrimination escape task. *Journal of Experimental Psychology: Animal Behavior Processes, 14,* 302–310.

Leinbach, M. D., & Fagot, B. I. (1993). Categorical habituation to male and female faces: Gender schematic processing in infancy. *Infant Behavior and Development, 16,* 317–332.

Lejeune, H., Cornet, S., & Ferreira, M. A., & Wearden, J. H. (1998). How do Mongolian gerbils (*Meriones unguiculatus*) pass the time? Adjunctive behavior during temporal differentiation in gerbils. *Journal of Experimental Psychology: Animal Behavior Processes, 24,* 352–368.

Lejeune, H., & Wearden, J. H. (1991). The comparative psychology of fixed-interval responding: Some quantitative analyses. *Learning and Motivation, 22,* 84–111.

Lejuez, C. W., O'Donnell, J., Wirth, O., Zvolensky, M. J., & Eifert, G. H. (1998). Avoidance of 20% carbon dioxide–enriched air with humans. *Journal of the Experimental Analysis of Behavior, 70,* 79–86.

Lennenberg, E. H. (1967). *Biological foundations of language.* New York: Wiley.

Lepper, M. R., Greene, D., & Nisbett, R. E. (1973). Undermining children's intrinsic interest with extrinsic reward: A test of the "overjustification" hypothesis. *Journal of Personality & Social Psychology, 28*(1), 129–137.

Lerman, D. C., Iwata, B. A., Shore, B. A., & DeLeon, I. G. (1997). Effects of intermittent punishment on self-injurious behavior: An evaluation of schedule thinning. *Journal of Applied Behavioral Analysis, 30,* 187–201.

Lerman, D. C., Iwata. B. A., & Wallace, M. D. (1999). Side effects of extinction: Prevalence of bursting and aggression during the treatment of self-injurious behavior. *Journal of Applied Behavior Analysis, 32,* 1–8.

Leslie, J. C., Boyle, C., & Shaw, D. (2000). Effects of reinforcement magnitude and ratio values on behaviour maintained by a cyclic ratio schedule of reinforcement. *Quarterly Journal of Experimental Psychology, 53B,* 289–308.

Levenson, D. H., & Schusterman, R. J. (1999). Dark adaptation and visual sensitivity in shallow and deep-diving pinnipeds. *Marine Mammal Science, 15,* 1303–1313.

Levis, D. J. (1976). Learned helplessness: A reply and alternative S-R interpretation. *Journal of Experimental Psychology: General, 105,* 47–65.

Levis, D. J. (1981). Extrapolation of two-factor learning theory of infrahuman avoidance behavior to psychopathology. *Neuroscience & Biobehavioral Reviews, 5,* 355–370.

Levis, D. J. (1989). The case for a return to a two-factor theory of avoidance: The failure of non-fear interpretations. In S. B. Klein & R. R. Mowrer (Eds.), *Contemporary learning theories: Pavlovian conditioning and the status of learning theory* (pp. 227–277). Hillsdale, NJ: Erlbaum.

Levis, D. J. (1991). A clinician's plea for a return to the development of nonhuman models of psychopathology: New clinical observations in need of laboratory study. In M. R. Denny (Ed.), *Fear, avoidance and phobias* (pp. 395–427). Hillsdale, NJ: Erlbaum.

Levis, D. J. (1995). Decoding traumatic memory: Implosive theory of psychopathology. In W. O'Donohue & L. Krasner (Eds.), *Theories of behavior therapy* (pp. 173–207). Washington, DC: American Psychological Association.

Levis, D. J., & Brewer, K. E. (2001). The neurotic paradox: Attempts by two-factor fear theory and alternative avoidance models to resolve the issues associated with sustained avoidance responding in extinction. In R. R. Mowrer & S. B. Klein (Eds.), *Handbook of contemporary learning theories* (pp. 561–597). Mahwah, NJ: Erlbaum.

Lewis, D. J. (1979). Psychobiology of active and inactive memory. *Psychological Bulletin, 86,* 1054–1083.

Lewis, M., Alessandri, S. M., & Sullivan, M. W. (1990). Violation of expectancy, loss of control, and anger expression in young infants. *Developmental Psychology, 26,* 745–751.

Lieberman, D. A., & Thomas, G. V. (1986). Marking, memory and superstition in the pigeon. *Quarterly Journal of Experimental Psychology, 38B,* 449–459.

Lieberman, D. A., Davidson, F. H., & Thomas, G. V. (1985). Marking in pigeons: The role of memory in delayed reinforcement. *Journal of Experimental Psychology: Animal Behavior Processes, 11,* 611–624.

Lieberman, D. A., McIntosh, D. C., & Thomas, G. V. (1979). Learning when reward is delayed: A marking hypothesis. *Journal of Experimental Psychology: Animal Behavior Processes, 5,* 224–242.

Lieberman, D. A., Sunnucks, W. L., & Kirk, J. D. J. (1998). Reinforcement without awareness: I. Voice level. *Quarterly Journal of Experimental Psychology, 51B,* 301–316.

Limebeer, C. L., & Parker, L. A. (1999). Delta-9–tetrahydrocannabinol interferes with the establishment and the expression of conditioned rejection reactions produced by cyclophosphamide: A rat model of nausea. *NeuroReport, 10,* 3769–3772.

Limebeer, C. L., & Parker, L. A. (2000). The antiemetic drug ondansetron interferes with lithium-induced conditioned rejection reactions, but not lithium-induced taste avoidance in rats. *Journal of Experimental Psychology: Animal Behavior Processes, 26,* 371–384.

Lindberg, J. S., Iwata, B. A., Kahng, S. W., & DeLeon, I. G. (1999). DRO contingencies: An analysis of variable-momentary schedules. *Journal of Applied Behavior Analysis, 32,* 123–136.

Linscheid, T. R., & Cunningham, C. E. (1977). A controlled demonstration of the effectiveness of electric shock in the elimination of chronic infant rumination. *Journal of Applied Behavior Analysis, 10,* 500.

Lipp, O. V., Sheridan, J., & Siddle, D. A. T. (1994). Human blink startle during aversive and nonaversive Pavlovian conditioning. *Journal of Experimental Psychology: Animal Behavior Processes, 20,* 380–389.

Lockard, R. B. (1968). The albino rat: A defensible choice or a bad habit? *American Psychologist, 23,* 734–742.

Locurto, C. M., Terrace, H. S., & Gibbon, J. (Eds.). (1981). *Autoshaping and conditioning theory.* New York: Academic Press.

Loeb, J. (1900). *Comparative physiology of the brain and comparative psychology.* New York: G. P. Putman.

Logue, A. W. (1985). Conditioned food aversion learning in humans. *Annals of the New York Academy of Sciences, 433,* 316–329.

Logue, A. W. (1988a). A comparison of taste aversion learning in humans and other vertebrates: Evolutionary pressures in common. In R. C. Bolles & M. D. Beecher (Eds.), *Evolution and learning* (pp. 97–116). Hillsdale, NJ: Erlbaum.

Logue, A. W. (1988b). Research on self-control: An integrating framework. *Behavioral and Brain Sciences, 11,* 665–709.

Logue, A. W. (1995). *Self-control: Waiting until tomorrow for what you want today.* Englewood Cliffs, NJ: Prentice-Hall.

Logue, A. W. (1998a). Laboratory research on self-control: Applications to administration. *Review of General Psychology, 2,* 221–238.

Logue, A. W. (1998b). Self-control. In W. O'Donohue (Ed.), *Learning and behavior therapy* (pp. 252–273). Boston: Allyn and Bacon.

Logue, A. W., Forzano, L. B., & Ackerman, K. T. (1996). Self-control in children: Age, preference for reinforcer amount and delay, and language ability. *Learning and Motivation, 27,* 260–277.

Logue, A. W., Ophir, I., & Strauss, K. E. (1981). The acquisition of taste aversions in humans. *Behaviour Research and Therapy, 19,* 319–333.

LoLordo, V. M. (1971). Facilitation of food-reinforced responding by a signal for response-independent food. *Journal of the Experimental Analysis of Behavior, 15* 49–55.

LoLordo, V. M. (1979). Selective associations. In A. Dickinson & R. A. Boakes (Eds.), *Mechanisms of learning and motivation* (pp. 367–398). Hillsdale, NJ: Erlbaum.

LoLordo, V. M., & Fairless, J. L. (1985). Pavlovian conditioned inhibition: The literature since 1969. In R. R. Miller & N. E. Spear (Eds.), *Information processing in animals: Conditioned inhibition* (pp. 1–49). Hillsdale, NJ: Erlbaum.

LoLordo, V. M., Jacobs, W. J., & Foree, D. D. (1982). Failure to block control by a relevant stimulus. *Animal Learning & Behavior, 10,* 183–193.

LoLordo, V. M., McMillan, J. C., & Riley, A. L. (1974). The effects upon food-reinforced pecking and treadle-pressing of auditory and visual signals for response-independent food. *Learning and Motivation, 5,* 24–41.

LoLordo, V. M., & Taylor, T. L. (2001). Effects of uncontrollable aversive events: Some unsolved puzzles. In R. R. Mowrer & S. B. Klein (Eds.), *Handbook of contemporary learning theories* (pp. 469–504). Mahwah, NJ: Erlbaum

Lonon, A. M., & Zentall, T. R. (1999). Transfer of value from S+ to S– in simultaneous discriminations in humans. *American Journal of Psychology, 112,* 21–39.

Losey, G. S., & Sevenster, P. (1995). Can three-spined sticklebacks learn when to display? Rewarded displays. *Animal Behaviour, 49,* 137–150.

Lovibond, P. F. (1983). Facilitation of instrumental behavior by a Pavlovian appetitive conditioned stimulus. *Journal of Experimental Psychology: Animal Behavior Processes, 9,* 225–247.

Lubow, R. E. (1989). *Latent inhibition and conditioned attention theory.* Cambridge, England: Cambridge University Press.

Lubow, R. E., & Gewirtz, J. C. (1995). Latent inhibition in humans: Data, theory, and implications for schizophrenia. *Psychological Bulletin, 117,* 87–103.

Lubow, R. E., Weiner, I., & Schnur, P. (1981). Conditioned attention theory. In G. H. Bower (Ed.), *The psychology of learning and motivation* (Vol. 15, pp. 1–49). Orlando, FL: Academic Press.

Lucas, G. A., Timberlake, W., & Gawley, D. J. (1988). Adjunctive behavior of the rat under periodic food delivery in a 24–hour environment. *Animal Learning & Behavior, 16,* 19–30.

Lyon, D. O. (1968). Conditioned suppression: Operant variables and aversive control. *Psychological Record, 18,* 317–338.

Lysle, D. T., & Fowler, H. (1985). Inhibition as a "slave" process: Deactivation of conditioned inhibition through extinction of conditioned excitation. *Journal of Experimental Psychology: Animal Behavior Processes, 11,* 71–94.

MacArdy, E. A., & Riccio, D. C. (1995). Time-dependent changes in the effectiveness of a noncontingent footshock reminder. *Learning and Motivation, 26,* 29–42.

MacDonald, S. E. (1993). Delayed matching-to-successive-samples in pigeons: Short-term memory for item and order information. *Animal Learning & Behavior, 21,* 59–67.

MacDonall, J. S. (1998). Run length, visit duration, and reinforcers per visit in concurrent performance. *Journal of the Experimental Analysis of Behavior, 69,* 275–293.

MacDonall, J. S. (1999). A local model of concurrent performance. *Journal of the Experimental Analysis of Behavior, 71,* 57–74.

MacDonall, J. S. (2000). Synthesizing concurrent interval performances. *Journal of the Experimental Analysis of Behavior, 74,* 189–206.

Mace, F. C., Lalli, J. S., Shea, M. C., Lalli, E. P., West, B. J., Roberts, M., & Nevin, J. A. (1990). The momentum of human behavior in a natural setting. *Journal of the Experimental Analysis of Behavior, 54,* 163–172.

MacEwen, D., & Killeen, P. (1991). The effects of rate and amount of reinforcement on the speed of the pacemaker in pigeons' timing behavior. *Animal Learning & Behavior, 19,* 164–170.

Machado, A. (1989). Operant conditioning of behavioral variability using a percentile reinforcement schedule. *Journal of the Experimental Analysis of Behavior, 52,* 155–166.

Machado, A. (1992). Behavioral variability and frequency-dependent selection. *Journal of the Experimental Analysis of Behavior, 58,* 241–263.

Machado, A. (1994). Polymorphic response patterns under frequency-dependent selection. *Animal Learning & Behavior, 22,* 53–71.

Machado, A. (1997). Learning the temporal dynamics of behavior. *Psychological Review, 104,* 241–265.

Machado, A., & Cevik, M. (1997). The discrimination of relative frequency by pigeons. *Journal of the Experimental Analysis of Behavior, 67,* 11–41

Machado, A., & Cevik, M. (1998). Acquisition and extinction under periodic reinforcement. *Behavioural Processes, 44,* 237–262.

Machado, A., & Keen, R. (1999). The learning of response patterns in choice situation. *Animal Learning & Behavior, 27,* 251–271.

Mackintosh, N. J. (1974). *The psychology of animal learning.* New York: Academic Press.

Mackintosh, N. J. (1975). A theory of attention: Variations in the associability of stimuli with reinforcement. *Psychological Review, 82,* 276–298.

Mackintosh, N. J. (1995). Categorization by people and pigeons: The twenty-second Bartlett memorial lecture. *The Quarterly Journal of Experimental Psychology, 48B,* 193–214.

Mackintosh, N. J., Bygrave, D. J., & Picton, B. M. B. (1977). Locus of the effect of a surprising reinforcer in the attenuation of blocking. *Quarterly Journal of Experimental Psychology, 29,* 327–336.

Mackintosh, N. J., & Dickinson, A. (1979). Instrumental (Type II) conditioning. In A. Dickinson & R. A. Boakes (Eds.), *Mechanisms of learning and motivation* (pp. 143–169). Hillsdale, NJ: Erlbaum.

Madden, G. J., & Bickel, W. K. (1999). Abstinence and price effects on demand for cigarettes: A behavioral-economic analysis. *Addiction, 94,* 577–588.

Madden, G. J., Bickel, W. K., & Jacobs, E. A. (1999). Discounting of delayed rewards in opioid-dependent outpatients: Exponential or hyperbolic discounting functions? *Experimental and Clinical Psychopharmacology, 7,* 284–293.

Madden, G. J., Bickel, W. K., & Jacobs, E. A. (2000). Three predictions of the economic concept of unit price in a choice context. *Journal of the Experimental* Analysis of Behavior, *73, 45–64.*

Madden, G. J., Petry, N. M., Badger, G. J., & Bickel, W. K. (1997). Impulsive and self-control choices in opioid-dependent patients and non-drug-using control participants: Drug and monetary rewards. *Experimental and Clinical Psychopharmacology, 5,* 256–262.

Maier, S. F. (1990). Role of fear in mediating shuttle escape learning deficit produced by inescapable shock. *Journal of Experimental Psychology: Animal Behavior Processes, 16,* 137–149.

Maier, S. F., & Church, R. M. (Eds.). (1991). Special issue on animal timing. *Learning and Motivation, 22,* 1–252.

Maier, S. F., & Jackson, R. L. (1979). Learned helplessness: All of us were right (and wrong): Inescapable shock has multiple effects. In G. H. Bower (Ed.), *The psychology of learning and motivation* (Vol. 13, pp. 155–218). New York: Academic Press.

Maier, S. F., Jackson, R. L., & Tomie, A. (1987). Potentiation, overshadowing, and prior exposure to inescapable shock. *Journal of Experimental Psychology: Animal Behavior Processes, 13,* 260–270.

Maier, S. F., Rapaport, P., & Wheatley, K. L. (1976). Conditioned inhibition and the UCS-CS interval. *Animal Learning and Behavior, 4,* 217–220.

Maier, S. F., & Seligman, M. E. P. (1976). Learned helplessness: Theory and evidence. *Journal of Experimental Psychology: General, 105,* 3–46.

Maier, S. F., Seligman, M. E. P., & Solomon, R. L. (1969). Pavlovian fear conditioning and learned helplessness. In B. A. Campbell & R. M. Church (Eds.), *Punishment and aversive behavior* (pp. 299–342). New York: Appleton-Century-Crofts.

Maier, S. F., & Warren, D. A. (1988). Controllability and safety signals exert dissimilar proactive effects on nociception and escape performance. *Journal of Experimental Psychology: Animal Behavior Processes, 14,* 18–25.

Maki, W. S. (1987). On the nonassociative nature of working memory. *Learning and Motivation, 18,* 99–117.

Maki, W. S., Beatty, W. W., Hoffman, N., Bierley, R. A., & Clouse, B. A. (1984). Spatial memory over long retention intervals: Nonmemorial factors are not necessary for accurate performance on the radial arm maze by rats. *Behavioral and Neural Biology, 41,* 1–6.

Maki, W. S., Moe, J. C., & Bierley, C. M. (1977). Short-term memory for stimuli, responses, and reinforcers. *Journal of Experimental Psychology: Animal Behavior Processes, 3,* 156–177.

Malenka, R. C., & Nicoll, R. A. (1999). Long-term potentiation—A decade of progress? *Science, 285,* 1870–1874.

March, J., Chamizo, V. D., & Mackintosh, N. J. (1992). Reciprocal overshadowing between intra-maze and extra-maze cues. *Quarterly Journal of Experimental Psychology, 45,* 49–63.

Marchand, A. R., & Kamper, E. (2000). Time course of cardiac conditioned responses in restrained rats as a function of the trace CS-US interval. *Journal of Experimental Psychology: Animal Behavior Processes, 26,* 385–398.

Marchant, H. G., III, Mis, F. W., & Moore, J. W. (1972). Conditioned inhibition of the rabbit's nictitating membrane response. *Journal of Experimental Psychology, 95,* 408–411.

Maricq, A. V., Roberts, S., & Church, R. M. (1981). Methamphetamine and time estimation. *Journal of Experimental Psychology: Animal Behavior Processes, 7,* 18–30.

Marsh, G. (1972). Prediction of the peak shift in pigeons from gradients of excitation and inhibition. *Journal of Comparative and Physiological Psychology, 81,* 262–266.

Martens, B. K., Lochner, D. G., & Kelly, S. Q. (1992). The effects of variable-interval reinforcement on academic engagement: A demonstration of matching theory. *Journal of Applied Behavior Analysis, 25,* 143–151.

Martin, S. J., Grimwood, P. D., & Morris, R. G. M. (2000). Synaptic plasticity and memory: An evaluation of the hypothesis. *Annual Review of Neuroscience, 23,* 649–711.

Martin-Malivel, J., & Fagot, J. (2001). Perception of pictorial human faces by baboons: Effects of stimulus orientation on discrimination performance. *Animal Learning & Behavior, 29,* 10–20.

Masserman, J. H. (1946). *Principles of dynamic psychiatry.* Philadelphia: Saunders.

Mast, M., Blanchard, R. J., & Blanchard, D. C. (1982). The relationship of freezing and response suppression in a CER situation. *Psychological Record, 32,* 151–167.

Matell, M. S., & Meck, W. H. (2000). Neuropsychological mechanisms of interval timing behaviour. *BioEssays, 22,* 94–203.

Matthews, T. J., Bordi, F., & Depollo, D. (1990). Schedule induced kinesic and taxic behavioral stereotypy in the pigeon. *Journal of Experimental Psychology: Animal Behavior Processes, 16,* 335–344.

Matzel, L. D., Gladstein, L., & Miller, R. R. (1988). Conditioned excitation and conditioned inhibition are not mutually exclusive. *Learning and Motivation, 19,* 99–121.

Mayford, M., Bach, M. E., Huang, Y.-Y., Wang, L., Hawkins, R. D., & Kandel, E. R. (1996). Control of memory formation through regulated expression of a CaMKII transgene. *Science, 274,* 1678–1683.

Mayford, M., & Kandel, E. R. (1999). Genetic approaches to memory storage. *Trends in Genetics, 15,* 463–470.

Mazur, J. E. (1987). An adjusting procedure for studying delayed reinforcement. In M. L. Commons, J. E. Mazur, J. A. Nevin, & H. Rachlin (Eds.), *Quantitative analyses of behavior: Vol. 5. The effect of delay and intervening events on reinforcement value* (pp. 55–73). Hillsdale, NJ: Erlbaum.

Mazur, J. E. (1991). Choice with probabilistic reinforcement: Effects of delay and conditioned reinforcers. *Journal of the Experimental Analysis of Behavior, 55,* 63–77.

Mazur, J. E. (1998). Choice with delayed and probabilistic reinforcers: Effects of prereinforcer and postreinforcer stimuli. *Journal of the Experimental Analysis of Behavior, 70,* 253–265.

Mazur, J. E. (2000). Two- versus three-alternative concurrent-chain schedules: A test of three models. *Journal of Experimental Psychology: Animal Behavior Processes, 26,* 286–293.

Mazur, J. E. (2001). Hyperbolic value addition and general models of animal choice. *Psychological Review, 108,* 96–112.

Mazur, J. E., & Romano, A. (1992). Choice with delayed and probabilistic reinforcers: Effects of variability, time between trials, and conditioned reinforcers. *Journal of the Experimental Analysis of Behavior, 58,* 513–525.

McAdie, T. M., Foster, T. M., & Temple, W. (1996). Concurrent schedules: Quantifying the aversiveness of noise. *Journal of the Experimental Analysis of Behavior, 65,* 37–55.

McAllister, D. E., & McAllister, W. R. (1991). Fear theory and aversively motivated behavior: Some controversial issues. In M. R. Denny (Ed.), *Fear, avoidance and phobias* (pp. 135–163). Hillsdale, NJ: Erlbaum.

McAllister, W. R., & McAllister, D. E. (1971). Behavioral measurement of fear. In F. R. Brush (Ed.), *Aversive conditioning and learning* (pp. 105–179). New York: Academic Press.

McAllister, W. R., & McAllister, D. E. (1992). Fear determines the effectiveness of a feedback stimulus in aversively motivated instrumental learning. *Learning and Motivation, 23,* 99–115.

McAllister, W. R., & McAllister, D. E. (1995). Two-factor fear theory: Implications for understanding anxiety-based clinical phenomena. In W. O'Donohue & L. Krasner (Eds.), *Theories of behavior therapy* (pp. 145–171). Washington, DC: American Psychological Association.

McDevitt, M. A., & Williams, B. A. (2001). Effects of signaled versus unsignaled delay of reinforcement on choice. *Journal of the Experimental Analysis of Behavior, 75,* 165–182.

McDowell, J. J. (1982). The importance of Herrnstein's mathematical statement of the law of effect for behavior therapy. *American Psychologist, 37,* 771–779.

McDowell, J. J., & Dallery, J. (1999). Falsification of matching theory: Changes in the asymptote of Herrnstein's hyperbola as a function of water deprivation. *Journal of the Experimental Analysis of Behavior, 72,* 251–268.

McDowell, J. J., & Wixted, J. T. (1988). The linear system theory's account of behavior maintained by variable ratio schedules. *Journal of the Experimental Analysis of Behavior, 49,* 143–169.

McFarland, D., & Bösser, T. (1993). *Intelligent behavior in animals and robots.* Cambridge, MA: MIT Press.

McGaugh, J. L., & Herz, M. J. (1972). *Memory consolidation.* San Francisco: Albion.

McGaugh, J. L., & Petrinovich, L. F. (1965). Effects of drugs on learning and memory. *International Review of Neurobiology, 8,* 139–196.

McGee, G. G., Krantz, P. J., & McClannahan, L. E. (1986). An extension of incidental teaching procedures to reading instruction for autistic children. *Journal of Applied Behavior Analysis, 19,* 147–157.

McLaren, I. P. L., & Mackintosh, N. J. (2000). An elemental model of associative learning: I. Latent inhibition and perceptual learning. *Animal Learning & Behavior, 28,* 211–246.

McLean, A. P., & Blampied, N. M. (2001). Sensitivity to relative reinforcer rate in concurrent schedules: Independence from relative and absolute reinforcer duration. *Journal of the Experimental Analysis of Behavior, 75,* 25–42.

McLean, A. P., Campbell-Tie, P., & Nevin, J. A. (1996). Resistance to change as a function of stimulus-reinforcer and location-reinforcer contingencies. *Journal of the Experimental Analysis of Behavior, 66,* 169–191.

McMillan, D. E., & Li, M. (1999). Drug discrimination under a concurrent fixed-ratio fixed-ratio schedule. *Journal of the Experimental Analysis of Behavior, 72,* 187–204.

McMillan, D. E., & Li, M. (2000). Drug discrimination under two concurrent fixed-interval fixed-interval schedules. *Journal of the Experimental Analysis of Behavior, 74,* 55–77.

McMillan, D. E., Li, M., & Hardwick, W. C. (1997). Drug discrimination under a concurrent fixed-interval fixed-interval schedule. *Journal of the Experimental Analysis of Behavior, 68,* 193–217.

McNish, K. A., Betts, S. L., Brandon, S. E., & Wagner, A. R. (1997). Divergence of conditioned eyeblink and conditioned fear in backward Pavlovian training. *Animal Learning & Behavior, 25,* 43–52.

McPhee, J. E., Rauhut, A. S., & Ayres, J. J. B. (2001). Evidence for learning-deficit versus performance-deficit theories of latent inhibition in Pavlovian fear conditioning. *Learning & Motivation, 32*(3), 274–305.

McSweeney, F. K., Hinson, J. M., & Cannon, C. B. (1996). Sensitization-habituation may occur during operant conditioning. *Psychological Bulletin, 120,* 256–271.

McSweeney, F. K., & Melville, C. L. (1993). Behavioral contrast for key pecking as a function of component duration when only one component varies. *Journal of the Experimental Analysis of Behavior, 60,* 311–343.

McSweeney, F. K., Melville, C. L., Buck, M. A., & Whipple, J. E. (1983). Local rates of responding and reinforcement during concurrent schedules. *Journal of the Experimental Analysis of Behavior, 40,* 79–98.

McSweeney, F. K., & Roll, J. M. (1998). Do animals satiate or habituate to repeatedly presented reinforcers? *Psychonomic Bulletin & Review, 5,* 428–442.

McSweeney, F. K., & Swindell, S. (1999). General-process theories of motivation revisited: The role of habituation. *Psychological Bulletin, 125,* 437–457.

Meck, W. H. (1983). Selective adjustment of the speed of internal clock and memory processes. *Journal of Experimental Psychology: Animal Behavior Processes, 9,* 171–201.

Meck, W. H., & Church, R. M. (1982). Abstraction of temporal attributes. *Journal of Experimental Psychology: Animal Behavior Processes, 8,* 226–243.

Meck, W. H., & Church, R. M. (1987a). Cholinergic modulation of the content of temporal memory. *Behavioral Neuroscience, 101,* 457–464.

Meck, W. H., & Church, R. M. (1987b). Nutrients that modify the speed of internal clock and memory storage processes. *Behavioral Neuroscience, 101,* 465–475.

Meisch, R. A., & Spiga, R. (1998). Matching under nonindependent variable-ratio schedules of drug reinforcement. *Journal of the Experimental Analysis of Behavior, 70,* 23–34.

Mellgren, R. L. (1972). Positive and negative contrast effects using delayed reinforcement. *Learning and Motivation, 3,* 185–193.

Melvin, K. B. (1971). Vicious circle behavior. In H. D. Kimmel (Ed.), *Experimental psychopathology.* New York: Academic Press.

Melvin, K. B., & Ervey, D. H. (1973). Facilitative and suppressive effects of punishment of species-typical aggressive display in *Betta splendens. Journal of Comparative and Physiological Psychology, 83,* 451–457.

Mercado, E., III, Murray, S. O., Uyeyama, R. K., Pack, A. A., & Herman, L. M. (1998). Memory for recent actions in the bottlenosed dolphin (*Tursiops truncates*): Repetition of arbitrary behaviors using an abstract rule. *Animal Learning & Behavior, 26,* 210–218.

Meyer, J.-A., & Wilson, S. W. (Eds.). (1991). *From animals to animats: Proceedings of the first international conference on simulation of adaptive behavior.* Cambridge, MA: MIT Press.

Meyer, J.-A., Berthoz, A., Floreano, D., Roitblat, H., & Wilson, S. W. (Eds.). (2000). *From animals to animats 6.* Cambridge, MA: MIT Press.

Midgley, M., Lea, S. E. G., & Kirby, R. M. (1989). Algorithmic shaping and misbehavior in the acquisition of token deposit by rats. *Journal of the Experimental Analysis of Behavior, 52,* 27–40.

Mikulincer, M. (1994). *Human learned helplessness.* New York: Plenum.

Miller, H. L. (1976). Matching-based hedonic scaling in the pigeon. *Journal of the Experimental Analysis of Behavior, 26,* 335–347.

Miller, J. S., Jagielo, J. A., & Spear, N. E. (1990a). Alleviation of short-term forgetting: Effects of the CS– and other conditioning elements in prior cueing or as context during test. *Learning and Motivation, 21,* 96–109.

Miller, J. S., Jagielo, J. A., & Spear, N. E. (1990b). Changes in the retrievability of associations to elements of the compound CS determine the expression of overshadowing. *Animal Learning & Behavior, 18,* 157–161.

Miller, J. S., Jagielo, J. A., & Spear, N. E. (1991). Differential effectiveness of various prior-cuing treatments in the reactivation and maintenance of memory. *Journal of Experimental Psychology: Animal Behavior Processes, 17,* 249–258.

Miller, J. S., Jagielo, J. A., & Spear, N. E. (1992). The influence of the information value provided by prior-cuing treatment on the reactivation of memory in preweanling rats. *Animal Learning & Behavior, 20,* 233–239.

Miller, N. E. (1951). Learnable drives and rewards. In S. S. Stevens (Ed.), *Handbook of experimental psychology.* New York: Wiley.

Miller, N. E. (1960). Learning resistance to pain and fear: Effects of overlearning, exposure, and rewarded exposure in context. *Journal of Experimental Psychology, 60,* 137–145.

Miller, N. E., & Dollard, J. (1941). *Social learning and imitation.* New Haven, CT: Yale University Press.

Miller, R. R., Barnet, R. C., & Grahame, N. J. (1992). Responding to a conditioned stimulus depends on the current associative status of other cues present during training of that specific stimulus. *Journal of Experimental Psychology: Animal Be*havior Processes, 18, *251–264.*

Miller, R. R., Barnet, R. C., & Grahame, N. J. (1995). Assessment of the Rescorla–Wagner model. *Psychological Bulletin, 117,* 363–386.

Miller, R. R., & Escobar, M. (2001). Contrasting acquisition-focused and performance-focused models of acquired behavior. *Current Directions in Psychological Science, 10,* 141–145.

Miller, R. R., Hallam, S. C., & Grahame, N. J. (1990). Inflation of comparator stimuli following CS training. *Animal Learning & Behavior, 18,* 434–443.

Miller, R. R., Kasprow, W. J., & Schachtman, T. R. (1986). Retrieval variability: Sources and consequences. *American Journal of Psychology, 99,* 145–218.

Miller, R. R., & Matute, H. (1996). Animal analogues of causal judgment. In G. H. Bower (Ed.), *The psychology of learning and motivation* (Vol. 34, pp. 133–166). San Diego, CA: Academic Press.

Miller, R. R., & Matzel, L. D. (1988). The comparator hypothesis: A response rule for the expression of associations. In G. H. Bower (Ed.), *The psychology of learning and motivation* (Vol. 22, pp. 51–92). Orlando, FL: Academic Press.

Miller, R. R., & Matzel, L. D. (1989). Contingency and relative associative strength. In S. B. Klein & R. R. Mowrer (Eds.), *Contemporary learning theories: Pavlovian conditioning and the status of learning theory* (pp. 61–84). Hillsdale, NJ: Erlbaum.

Miller, R. R., & Matzel, L. D. (2000). Memory involves far more than consolidation. *Nature Reviews Neuroscience, 1,* 214–216.

Miller, R. R., & Spear, N. E. (Eds.). (1985). *Information processing in animals: Conditioned inhibition.* Hillsdale, NJ: Erlbaum.

Miller, R. R., & Springer, A. D. (1973). Amnesia, consolidation, and retrieval. *Psychological Review, 80,* 69–79.

Miller, V., & Domjan, M. (1981). Selective sensitization induced by lithium malaise and footshock in rats. *Behavioral and Neural Biology, 31,* 42–55.

Millin, P. M., Moody, E. W., & Riccio, D. C. (2001). Interpretations of retrograde amnesia: Old problems redux. *Nature Reviews Neuroscience, 2,* 68–70.

Mineka, S. (1979). The role of fear in theories of avoidance learning, flooding, and extinction. *Psychological Bulletin, 86,* 985–1010.

Mineka, S., & Cook, M. (1988). Social learning and the acquisition of snake fear in monkeys. In T. Zentall & B. G. Galef, Jr. (Eds.), *Social learning* (pp. 51–73). Hillsdale, NJ: Erlbaum.

Mineka, S., & Gino, A. (1979). Dissociative effects of different types and amounts of nonreinforced CS exposure on avoidance extinction and the CER. *Learning and Motivation, 10,* 141–160.

Mineka, S., & Gino, A. (1980). Dissociation between conditioned emotional response and extended avoidance performance. *Learning and Motivation, 11,* 476–502.

Mineka, S., & Henderson, R. (1985). Controllability and predictability in acquired motivation. *Annual Review of Psychology, 36,* 495–530.

Mineka, S., Miller, S., Gino, A., & Giencke, L. (1981). Dissociative effects of flooding on a multivariate assessment of fear reduction and on jump-up avoidance extinction. *Learning and Motivation, 12,* 435–461.

Mineka, S., Suomi, S. J., & DeLizio, R. (1981). Multiple separations in adolescent monkeys: An opponent-process interpretation. *Journal of Experimental Psychology: General, 110,* 56–85.

Minor, T. R., Dess, N. K., & Overmier, J. B. (1991). Inverting the traditional view of "learned helplessness." In M. R. Denny (Ed.), *Fear, avoidance and phobias* (pp. 87–133). Hillsdale, NJ: Erlbaum.

Minor, T. R., Trauner, M. A., Lee, C.-Y., & Dess, N. K. (1990). Modeling signal features of escape response: Effects of cessation conditioning in "learned helplessness" paradigm. *Journal of Experimental Psychology: Animal Behavior Processes, 16,* 123–136.

Mitchell, S. H., & Brener, J. (1991). Energetic and motor responses to increasing food requirements. *Journal of Experimental Psychology: Animal Behavior Processes, 17,* 174–185.

Morgan, C. L. (1903). *Introduction to comparative psychology* (rev. ed.). New York: Scribner.

Morgan, L., & Neuringer, A. (1990). Behavioral variability as a function of response topography and reinforcement contingency. *Animal Learning & Behavior, 18,* 257–263.

Morgan, M. J., Fitch, M. D., Holman, J. G., & Lea, S. E. G. (1976). Pigeons learn the concept of an "A." *Perception, 5,* 57–66.

Morris, C. J. (1987). The operant conditioning of response variability: Free-operant versus discrete-response procedures. *Journal of the Experimental Analysis of Behavior, 47,* 273–277.

Morris, R. G. M. (1974). Pavlovian conditioned inhibition of fear during shuttlebox avoidance behavior. *Learning and Motivation, 5,* 424–447.

Morris, R. G. M. (1975). Preconditioning of reinforcing properties to an exteroceptive feedback stimulus. *Learning and Motivation, 6,* 289–298.

Morris, R. G. M. (1981). Spatial localization does not require the presence of local cues. *Learning and Motivation, 12,* 239–260.

Morris, R. G. M., Anderson, E., Lynch, G. S., & Baudry, M. (1986). Selective impairment of learning and blockade of long-term potentiation by an N-methyl-D-aspartate receptor antagonist, AP5. *Nature, 319,* 774–776.

Mowrer, O. H. (1947). On the dual nature of learning: A reinterpretation of "conditioning" and "problem-solving." *Harvard Educational Review, 17,* 102–150.

Mowrer, O. H. (1960). *Learning theory and behavior.* New York: Wiley.

Mowrer, O. H., & Lamoreaux, R. R. (1942). Avoidance conditioning and signal duration: A study of secondary motivation and reward. *Psychological Monographs, 54* (Whole No. 247).

Mowrer, R. R., & Gordon, W. C. (1983). Effects of cuing in an "irrelevant" context. *Animal Learning & Behavior, 11,* 401–406.

Mowrer, R. R., & Klein, S. B. (Eds.). (2001). *Handbook of contemporary learning theories.* Mahwah, NJ: Erlbaum.

Moye, T. B., & Thomas, D. R. (1982). Effects of memory reactivation treatments on postdiscrimination generalization performance in pigeons. *Animal Learning & Behavior, 10,* 159–166.

Murkerjee, M. (1997, February). Trends in animal research. *Scientific American,* 86–93.

Myers, H. H., & Siegel, P. S. (1985). The motivation to breastfeed: A fit to the opponent-process theory? *Journal of Personality and Social Psychology, 49,* 188–193.

Myers, K. M., Vogel, E. H., Shin, J., & Wagner, A. R. (2001). A comparison of the Rescorla–Wagner and Pearce models in a negative patterning and summation problem. *Animal Learning & Behavior, 29,* 36–45.

Nader, K., Schafe, G., & LeDoux, J. E. (2000). Reconsolidation: The labile nature of consolidation theory. *Nature Reviews Neuroscience, 1,* 216–219.

Nakajima, S. (1997a). Failure of inhibition by B over C after A+, AB–, and ABC+ training. *Journal of Experimental Psychology: Animal Behavior Processes, 23,* 482–490.

Nakajima, S. (1997b). Transfer testing after serial feature-ambiguous discrimination in Pavlovian keypeck conditioning. *Animal Learning & Behavior, 25,* 413–426.

Nakajima, S. (1998). Further investigation of responding elicited by BC and C after A+, AB–, and ABC+ training. *Quarterly Journal of Experimental Psychology, 51B,* 289–300.

Nakajima, S., Tanaka, S., Urushihara, K., & Imada, H. (2000). Renewal of extinguished lever-press responses upon return to the training context. *Learning and Motivation, 31,* 416–431.

Nakajima, S., & Urushihara, K. (1999). Inhibition and facilitation by B over C after A+, AB–, and ABC+ training with multimodality stimulus combinations. *Journal of Experimental Psychology: Animal Behavior Processes, 25,* 68–81.

Nation, J. R., & Cooney, J. B. (1982). The time course of extinction-induced aggressive behavior in humans: Evidence for a stage model of extinction. *Learning and Motivation, 13,* 95–112.

Neill, J. C., & Harrison, J. M. (1987). Auditory discrimination: The Konorski quality-location effect. *Journal of the Experimental Analysis of Behavior, 48,* 81–95.

Neuenschwander, N., Fabrigoule, C., & Mackintosh, N. J. (1987). Fear of the warning signal during overtraining of avoidance. *Quarterly Journal of Experimental Psychology, 39B,* 23–33.

Neuringer, A. (1991). Operant variability and repetition as functions of interresponse time. *Journal of Experimental Psychology: Animal Behavior Processes, 17,* 3–12.

Neuringer, A. (1992). Choosing to vary and repeat. *Psychological Science, 3,* 246–250.

Neuringer, A. (1993). Reinforced variation and selection. *Animal Learning & Behavior, 21,* 83–91.

Neuringer, A., Deiss, C., & Olson, G. (2000). Reinforced variability and operant learning. *Journal of Experimental Psychology: Animal Behavior Processes, 26,* 98–111.

Neuringer, A., Kornell, N., & Olufs, M. (2001). Stability and variability in extinction. *Journal of Experimental Psychology: Animal Behavior Processes, 27,* 79–94.

Nevin, J. A. (1969). Interval reinforcement of choice behavior in discrete trials. *Journal of the Experimental Analysis of Behavior, 12,* 875–885.

Nevin, J. A. (1979). Overall matching versus momentary maximizing: Nevin (1969) revisited. *Journal of Experimental Psychology: Animal Behavior Processes, 5,* 300–306.

Nevin, J. A. (1988). Behavioral momentum and the partial reinforcement extinction effect. *Psychological Bulletin, 103,* 44–56.

Nevin, J. A. (1992). An integrative model for the study of behavioral momentum. *Journal of the Experimental Analysis of Behavior, 57,* 301–316.

Nevin, J. A. (1998). Choice and momentum. In W. O'Donohue (Ed.), *Learning and behavior therapy* (pp. 230–251). Boston: Allyn and Bacon.

Nevin, J. A., & Grace, R. C. (1999). Does the context of reinforcement affect resistance to change? *Journal of Experimental Psychology: Animal Behavior Processes, 25,* 256–268.

Nevin, J. A., & Grace, R. C. (2000). Behavioral momentum and the law of effect. *Behavioral and Brain Sciences, 23,* 73–130.

Nevin, J. A., Mandell, G., & Atak, J. R. (1983). The analysis of behavioral momentum. *Journal of the Experimental Analysis of Behavior, 39,* 49–59.

Noll, J. P. (1995). The matching law as a theory of choice in behavior therapy. In W. O'Donohue & L. Krasner (Eds.), *Theories of behavior therapy* (pp. 129–144). Washington, DC: American Psychological Association.

O'Donnell, J., Crosbie, J., Williams, D. C., & Saunders, K. J. (2000). Stimulus control and generalization of point-loss punishment with humans. *Journal of the Experimental Analysis of Behavior, 73,* 261–274.

O'Donohue, W. (1998). Conditioning and third-generation behavior therapy. In W. O'Donohue (Ed.), *Learning and behavior therapy* (pp. 1–14). Boston: Allyn and Bacon.

Oades, R. D., Roepcke, B., & Schepker, R. (1996). A test of conditioned blocking and its development in childhood and adolescence: Relationship to personality and monoamine metabolism. *Developmental Neuropsychology, 12,* 207–230.

Oberling, P., Gosselin, O., & Miller, R. R. (1997). Latent inhibition in animals as a model of acute schizophrenia: A reanalysis. In M. Haug & R. E. Whalen (Eds.), *Animal models of human emotion and cognition* (pp. 97–102). Washington, DC: American Psychological Association.

Oden, D. L., Thompson, R. K. R., & Premack, D. (1988). Spontaneous transfer of matching by infant chimpanzees (*Pan troglodytes*). *Journal of Experimental Psychology: Animal Behavior Processes, 14,* 140–145.

Odum, A. L., Madden, G. J., Badger, G. J., & Bickel, W. K. (2000). Needle sharing in opioid-dependent outpatients: Psychological process underlying risk. *Drug and Alcohol Dependence, 60,* 259–266.

Öhman, A., Dimberg, U., & Öst, L. G. (1985). Animal and social phobias: Biological constraints on learned fear responses. In S. Reiss & R. R. Bootzin (Eds.), *Theoretical issues in behavior therapy.* Orlando, FL: Academic Press.

Ohyama, T., Gibbon, J., Deich, J. D., & Balsam, P. (1999). Temporal control during maintenance and extinction of conditioned keypecking in ring doves. *Animal Learning & Behavior, 27,* 89–98.

Olton, D. S. (1978). Characteristics of spatial memory. In S. H. Hulse, H. Fowler, & W. K. Honig (Eds.), *Cognitive processes in animal behavior* (pp. 341–374). Hillsdale, NJ: Erlbaum.

Olton, D. S. (1979). Mazes, maps, and memory. *American Psychologist, 34,* 583–596.

Olton, D. S., Collison, C., & Werz, M. A. (1977). Spatial memory and radial arm maze performance of rats. *Learning and Motivation, 8,* 289–314.

Olton, D. S., & Samuelson, R. J. (1976). Remembrance of places passed: Spatial memory in rats. *Journal of Experimental Psychology: Animal Behavior Processes, 2,* 97–116.

Ost, J. W. P., & Lauer, D.W. (1965). Some investigations of salivary conditioning in the dog. In W. F. Prokasy (Ed.), *Classical conditioning* (pp. 192–207). New York: Appleton-Century-Crofts.

Overmier, J. B. (1999). On the nature of animal models of human behavioral dysfunction. In M. Haug & R. E. Whalen (Eds.), *Animal models of human emotion and cognition* (pp. 15–24). Washington, DC: American Psychological Association.

Overmier, J. B., & Lawry, J. A. (1979). Pavlovian conditioning and the mediation of behavior. In G. H. Bower (Ed.), *The psychology of learning and motivation* (Vol. 13, pp. 1–55). New York: Academic Press.

Overmier, J. B., & LoLordo, V. M. (1998). Learned helplessness. In W. O'Donohue (Ed.), *Learning and behavior therapy* (pp. 352–373). Boston: Allyn and Bacon.

Overmier, J. B., & Seligman, M. E. P. (1967). Effects of inescapable shock upon subsequent escape and avoidance learning. *Journal of Comparative and Physiological Psychology, 63,* 23–33.

Owen, J. W., Cicala, G. A., & Herdegen, R. T. (1978). Fear inhibition and species specific defense reaction termination may contribute independently to avoidance learning. *Learning and Motivation, 9,* 297–313.

Page, S., & Neuringer, A. (1985). Variability as an operant. *Journal of Experimental Psychology: Animal Behavior Processes, 11,* 429–452.

Palya, W. L. (1993). Bipolar control in fixed interfood intervals. *Journal of the Experimental Analysis of Behavior, 60,* 345–359.

Papadouka, V., & Matthews, T. J. (1995). Motivational mechanisms and schedule-induced behavioral stereotypy. *Animal Learning & Behavior, 23,* 461–469.

Papini, M. R. (2002). Pattern and process in the evolution of learning. *Psychological Review, 109,* 186–201.

Papini, M. R., & Bitterman, M. E. (1990). The role of contingency in classical conditioning. *Psychological Review, 97,* 396–403.

Papini, M. R., & Bitterman, M. E. (1993). The two-test strategy in the study of inhibitory conditioning. *Journal of Experimental Psychology: Animal Behavior Processes, 19,* 342–352.

Papini, M. R., & Dudley, R. T. (1997). Consequences of surprising reward omissions. *Review of General Psychology, 1,* 175–197.

Papini, M. R., & Hollingsworth, P. R. (1998). Role of nonreinforcement in the fixed-interval performance of pigeons. *Psychonomic Bulletin & Review, 5,* 84–90.

Parker, B. K., Serdikoff, S. L., Kaminski, B. J., & Critchfield, T. S. (1991). Stimulus control of Pavlovian facilitation. *Journal of the Experimental Analysis of Behavior, 55,* 275–286.

Patterson, F. G. (1978). The gestures of a gorilla: Language acquisition in another pongid. *Brain and Language, 5,* 56–71.

Patterson, M. M., & Grau, J. W. (2001). *Spinal cord plasticity: Alterations in reflex function.* Boston: Kluwer Academic Publishers.

Pavlov, I. P. (1927). *Conditioned reflexes* (G. V. Anrep, trans.). London: Oxford University Press.

Pear, J. J., & Legris, J. A. (1987). Shaping by automated tracking of an arbitrary operant response. *Journal of the Experimental Analysis of Behavior, 47,* 241–247.

Pearce, J. M. (1987). A model for stimulus generalization in Pavlovian conditioning. *Psychological Review, 94,* 61–73.

Pearce, J. M. (1994a). Discrimination and categorization. In N. J. Mackintosh (Ed.), *Animal learning and cognition* (pp. 109–134). San Diego: Academic Press.

Pearce, J. M. (1994b). Similarity and discrimination: A selective review and a connectionistic model. *Psychological Review, 101,* 587–607.

Pearce, J. M., Aydin, A., & Redhead, E. S. (1997). Configural analysis of summation in autoshaping. *Journal of Experimental Psychology: Animal Behavior Processes, 23,* 84–94.

Pearce, J. M., & Bouton, M. E. (2001). Theories of associate learning in animals. *Annual Review of Psychology, 52,* 111–139.

Pearce, J. M., & Dickinson, A. (1975). Pavlovian counterconditioning: Changing the suppressive properties of shock by association with food. *Journal of Experimental Psychology: Animal Behavior Processes, 1,* 170–177.

Pearce, J. M., & Hall, G. (1980). A model for Pavlovian learning: Variations in the effectiveness of conditioned but not of unconditioned stimuli. *Psychological Review, 87,* 532–552.

Pearce, J. M., Redhead, E. S., & Aydin, A. (1997). Partial reinforcement in appetitive Pavlovian conditioning in rats. *Quarterly Journal of Experimental Psychology, 50B,* 273–294.

Pecoraro, N. C., Timberlake, W. D., & Tinsley, M. (1999). Incentive downshifts evoke search repertoires in rats. *Journal of Experimental Psychology: Animal Behavior Processes, 25,* 153–167.

Pedreira, M. E., Romano, A., Tomsic, D., Lozada, M., & Maldonado, H. (1998). Massed and spaced training build up different components of long-term habituation in the crab *Chasmagnathus. Animal Learning & Behavior, 26,* 34–45.

Pelchat, M. L., & Rozin, P. (1982). The special role of nausea in the acquisition of food dislikes by humans. *Appetite, 3,* 341–351.

Pepperberg, I. M. (1990). Some cognitive capacities of an African grey parrot (Psittacus erithacus). In P. J. B. Slater, J. S. Rosenblatt, & C. Beer (Eds.), *Advances in the study of behavior* (Vol. 19, pp. 357–409). San Diego: Academic Press.

Pepperberg, I. M. (1993). Cognition and communication in an African Grey parrot (*Psittacus erithacus*): Studies on a non-human, nonprimate, nonmammalian subject. In H. L. Roitblat, L. M. Herman, & P. E. Nachtigall (Eds.), *Language and communication: Comparative perspectives* (pp. 221– 248). Hillsdale, NJ: Erlbaum.

Pepperberg, I. M. (1999). *The Alex studies: Cognitive and communicative abilities of Grey Parrots.* Cambridge, MA: Harvard University Press.

Pérez, C., Fanizza, L. J., & Sclafani, A. (1999). Flavor preferences conditioned by intragastric nutrient infusions in rats fed chow or a cafeteria diet. *Appetite, 32,* 155–170.

Perry, D. G., & Parke, R. D. (1975). Punishment and alternative response training as determinants of response inhibition in children. *Genetic Psychology Monographs, 91,* 257–279.

Peterson, C., Maier, S. F., & Seligman, M. E. P. (1993). *Learned helplessness: A theory for the age of personal control.* New York: Oxford University Press.

Peterson, C., & Seligman, M. E. P. (1984). Causal explanations as a risk factor for depression: Theory and evidence. *Psychological Review, 91,* 347–374.

Peterson, G. B., Ackil, J. E., Frommer, G. P., & Hearst, E. S. (1972). Conditioned approach and contact behavior toward signals for food and brain-stimulation reinforcement. *Science, 177,* 1009–1011.

Peterson, G. B., & Trapold, M. A. (1980). Effects of altering outcome expectancies on pigeons' delayed conditional discrimination performance. *Learning and Motivation, 11,* 267–288.

Petry, N. M., & Bickel, W. K. (1998). Polydrug abuse in heroin addicts: A behavioral economic analysis. *Addiction, 93,* 321–335.

Petry, N. M., & Heyman, G. M. (1994). Effects of qualitatively different reinforcers on the parameters of the response-strength equation. *Journal of the Experimental Analysis of Behavior, 61,* 97–106.

Petry, N. M., & Heyman, G. M. (1995). Behavioral economics of concurrent ethanol-sucrose and sucrose reinforcement in the rat: Effects of altering variable-ratio requirements. *Journal of the Experimental Analysis of Behavior, 64,* 331–359.

Pilz, P. K., & Schnitzler, H.-U. (1996). Habituation and sensitization of the acoustic startle response in rats: Amplitude, threshold, and latency measures. *Neurobiology of Learning and Memory, 66,* 67–79.

Pisacreta, R. (1982). Some factors that influence the acquisition of complex, stereotyped, response sequences in pigeons. *Journal of the Experimental Analysis of Behavior, 37,* 359–369.

Platt, J. R. (1973). Percentile reinforcement: Paradigms for experimental analysis of response shaping. In G. H. Bower (Ed.), *The psychology of learning and motivation* (Vol. 7, pp. 271–296). Orlando, FL: Academic Press.

Ploog, B. O. (2001). Net amount of food affects autoshaped response rate, response latency, and gape amplitude in pigeons. *Learning and Motivation, 32,* 383–400.

Ploog, B. O., & Zeigler, H. P. (1996). Effects of food-pellet size on rate, latency, and topography of autoshaped key pecks and gapes in pigeons. *Journal of the Experimental Analysis of Behavior, 65,* 21–35.

Plous, S. (1991). An attitude survey of animal rights activists. *Psychological Science, 2,* 194–196.

Plous, S. (1998). Signs of change within the animal rights movement: Results from a follow-up survey of activists. *Journal of Comparative Psychology, 112,* 48–54.

Poling, A., Nickel, M., & Alling, K. (1990). Free birds aren't fat: Weight gain in captured wild pigeons maintained under laboratory conditions.*Journal of the Experimental Analysis of Behavior, 53,* 423–424.

Porter, D., & Neuringer, A. (1984). Music discrimination by pigeons. *Journal of Experimental Psychology: Animal Behavior Processes, 10,* 138–148.

Postman, L. (1971). Transfer, interference, and forgetting. In J. W. Kling & L. A. Riggs (Eds.), *Woodworth and Schlosberg's experimental psychology* (3rd ed.). New York: Holt, Rinehart and Winston.

Poulos, C. X., & Cappell, H. (1991). Homeostatic theory of drug tolerance: A general model of physiological adaptation. *Psychological Review, 98,* 390–408.

Premack, D. (1962). Reversibility of the reinforcement relation. *Science, 136,* 255–257.

Premack, D. (1965). Reinforcement theory. In D. Levine (Ed.), *Nebraska symposium on motivation* (Vol. 13, pp. 123–180). Lincoln: University of Nebraska Press.

Premack, D. (1971a). Catching up with common sense, or two sides of a generalization: Reinforcement and punishment. In R. Glaser (Ed.), *The nature of reinforcement.* New York: Academic Press.

Premack, D. (1971b). Language in chimpanzee? *Science, 172,* 808–822.

Premack, D. (1976). *Intelligence in ape and man.* Hillsdale, NJ: Erlbaum.

Puente, G. P., Cannon, D. S., Best, M. R., & Carrell, L. E. (1988). Occasion setting of fluid ingestion by contextual cues. *Learning and Motivation, 19,* 239–253.

Quartermain, D., McEwen, B. S., & Azmitia, E. C., Jr. (1970). Amnesia produced by electroconvulsive shock or cycloheximide: Conditions for recovery. *Science, 169,* 683–686.

Rachlin, H. (1989). *Judgement, decision, and choice.* New York: Freeman.

Rachlin, H. (1995). Behavioral economics without anomalies. *Journal of the Experimental Analysis of Behavior, 64,* 397–404.

Rachlin, H. C., Battalio, R., Kagel, J., & Green, L. (1981). Maximization theory in behavioral psychology. *Behavioral and Brain Sciences, 4,* 371–417.

Rachlin, H. C., & Green, L. (1972). Commitment, choice, and self-control. *Journal of the Experimental Analysis of Behavior, 17,* 15–22.

Rachlin, H. C., Green, L., Kagel, J. H., & Battalio, R. C. (1976). Economic demand theory and studies of choice. In G. H. Bower (Ed.), *The psychology of learning and motivation* (Vol. 10, pp. 129–154). New York: Academic Press.

Rachlin, H. C., & Herrnstein, R. L. (1969). Hedonism revisited: On the negative law of effect. In B. A. Campbell & R. M. Church (Eds.), *Punishment and aversive behavior* (pp. 83–109). New York: Appleton-Century-Crofts.

Raia, C. P., Shillingford, S. W., Miller, H. L., Jr., & Baier, P. S. (2000). Interaction of procedural factors in human performance on yoked schedules. *Journal of the Experimental Analysis of Behavior, 74,* 265–281.

Rakitin, B. C., Gibbon, J., Penney, T. B., Malapani, C., Hinton, S. C., & Meck, W. H. (1998). Scalar expectancy theory and peak-interval timing in humans. *Journal of Experimental Psychology: Animal Behavior Processes, 24,* 25–33.

Ramirez, I. (1997). Carbohydrate-induced stimulation of saccharin intake: Yoked controls. *Animal Learning & Behavior, 25,* 347–356.

Ramsey, D. S., & Woods, S. C. (1997). Biological consequences of drug administration: Implications for acute and chronic tolerance. *Psychological Review, 104,* 170–193.

Randell, T., & Remington, B. (1999). Equivalence relations between visual stimuli: The functional role of naming. *Journal of the Experimental Analysis of Behavior, 71,* 395–415.

Randich, A. (1981). The US preexposure phenomenon in the conditioned suppression paradigm: A role for conditioned situational stimuli. *Learning and Motivation, 12,* 321–341.

Randich, A., & LoLordo, V. M. (1979). Associative and non-associative theories of the UCS preexposure phenomenon: Implications for Pavlovian conditioning. *Psychological Bulletin, 86,* 523–548.

Rashotte, M. E., Griffin, R. W., & Sisk, C. L. (1977). Second-order conditioning of the pigeon's keypeck. *Animal Learning & Behavior, 5,* 25–38.

Rauhut, A. S., Thomas, B. L., & Ayres, J. J. B. (2001). Treatments that weaken Pavlovian conditioned fear and thwart its renewal in rats: Implications for treating human phobias. *Journal of Experimental Psychology: Animal Behavior Processes, 27,* 99–114.

Raymond, J. L., Lisberger, S. G., & Mauk, M. D. (1996). The cerebellum: A neuronal learning machine? *Science, 272,* 1126–1131.

Reberg, D., Innis, N. K., Mann, B., & Eizenga, C. (1978). "Superstitious" behavior resulting from periodic response-independent presentations of food or water. *Animal Behaviour, 26,* 506–519.

Reed, P. (1991). Multiple determinants of the effects of reinforcement magnitude on free-operant response rates. *Journal of the Experimental Analysis of Behavior, 55,* 109–123.

Reed, P. (1999). Role of stimulus filling an action-outcome delay in human judgements of causal effectiveness. *Journal of Experimental Psychology: Animal Behavior Processes, 25,* 92–102.

Reed, P., Soh, M., Hildebrandt, T., DeJongh, J., & Shek, W. Y. (2000). Free-operant performance on variable interval schedules with a linear feedback loop: No evidence for molar sensitivities in rats. *Journal of Experimental Psychology: Animal Behavior Processes, 26,* 416–427.

Reed, P., & Wright, J. E. (1989). Effects of magnitude of food reinforcement on free-operant response rates. *Journal of the Experimental Analysis of Behavior, 49,* 75–85.

Reid, A. K., Chadwick, C. Z., Dunham, M., & Miller, A. (2001). The development of functional response units: The role of demarcating stimuli. *Journal of the Experimental Analysis of Behavior, 72,* 81–96.

Repp, A. C., & Singh, N. N. (Eds.). (1990). *Perspectives on the use of nonaversive and aversive interventions for persons with developmental disabilities.* Sycamore, IL: Sycamore.

Rescorla, R. A. (1967a). Inhibition of delay in Pavlovian fear conditioning. *Journal of Comparative and Physiological Psychology, 64,* 114–120.

Rescorla, R. A. (1967b). Pavlovian conditioning and its proper control procedures. *Psychological Review, 74,* 71–80.

Rescorla, R. A. (1968a). Pavlovian conditioned fear in Sidman avoidance learning. *Journal of Comparative and Physiological Psychology, 65,* 55–60.

Rescorla, R. A. (1968b). Probability of shock in the presence and absence of CS in fear conditioning. *Journal of Comparative and Physiological Psychology, 66,* 1–5.

Rescorla, R. A. (1969a). Conditioned inhibition of fear resulting from negative CS-US contingencies. *Journal of Comparative and Physiological Psychology, 67,* 504–509.

Rescorla, R. A. (1969b). Pavlovian conditioned inhibition. *Psychological Bulletin, 72,* 77–94.

Rescorla, R. A. (1973). Effect of US habituation following conditioning. *Journal of Comparative and Physiological Psychology, 82,* 137–143.

Rescorla, R. A. (1980a). *Pavlovian second-order conditioning.* Hillsdale, NJ: Erlbaum.

Rescorla, R. A. (1980b). Simultaneous and successive associations in sensory preconditioning. *Journal of Experimental Psychology: Animal Behavior Processes, 6,* 207–216.

Rescorla, R. A. (1982a). Effect of a stimulus intervening between CS and US in autoshaping. *Journal of Experimental Psychology: Animal Behavior Processes, 8,* 131–141.

Rescorla, R. A. (1982b). Some consequences of associations between the excitor and the inhibitor in a conditioned inhibition paradigm. *Journal of Experimental Psychology: Animal Behavior Processes, 8,* 288–298.

Rescorla, R. A. (1985). Conditioned inhibition and facilitation. In R. R. Miller & N. E. Spear (Eds.), *Information processing in animals: Conditioned inhibition* (pp. 299–326). Hillsdale, NJ: Erlbaum.

Rescorla, R. A. (1986). Extinction of facilitation. *Journal of Experimental Psychology: Animal Behavior Processes, 12,* 16–24.

Rescorla, R. A. (1987). Facilitation and inhibition. *Journal of Experimental Psychology: Animal Behavior Processes, 13,* 250–259.

Rescorla, R. A. (1988a). Facilitation based on inhibition. *Animal Learning & Behavior, 16,* 169–176.

Rescorla, R. A. (1988b). Pavlovian conditioning: It's not what you think it is. *American Psychologist, 43,* 151–160.

Rescorla, R. A. (1990a). Evidence for an association between the discriminative stimulus and the response-outcome association in instrumental learning. *Journal of Experimental Psychology: Animal Behavior Processes, 16,* 326–334

Rescorla, R. A. (1990b). The role of information about the response-outcome relation in instrumental discrimination learning. *Journal of Experimental Psychology: Animal Behavior Processes, 16,* 262–270.

Rescorla, R. A. (1991). Associative relations in instrumental learning: The eighteenth Bartlett memorial lecture. *Quarterly Journal of Experimental Psychology, 43B,* 1–23.

Rescorla, R. A. (1992). Association between an instrumental discriminative stimulus and multiple outcomes. *Journal of Experimental Psychology: Animal Behavior Processes, 18,* 95–104.

Rescorla, R. A. (1993a). Preservation of response–outcome associations through extinction. *Animal Learning & Behavior, 21,* 238–245.

Rescorla, R. A. (1993b). Inhibitory associations between S and R in extinction. *Animal Learning & Behavior, 21,* 327–336.

Rescorla, R. A. (1996a). Preservation of Pavlovian associations through extinction. *Quarterly Journal of Experimental Psychology, 49B,* 245–258.

Rescorla, R. A. (1996b). Response-outcome associations remain functional through interference treatments. *Animal Learning & Behavior, 24,* 450–458.

Rescorla, R. A. (1996c). Spontaneous recovery after training with multiple outcomes. *Animal Learning & Behavior, 24,* 11–18.

Rescorla, R. A. (1997a). Response-inhibition in extinction. *Quarterly Journal of Experimental Psychology, 50B,* 238–252.

Rescorla, R. A. (1997b). Spontaneous recovery after Pavlovian conditioning with multiple outcomes. *Animal Learning & Behavior, 25,* 99–107.

Rescorla, R. A. (1997c). Spontaneous recovery of instrumental discriminative responding. *Animal Learning & Behavior, 25,* 485–497.

Rescorla, R. A. (1997d). Spontaneous recovery of instrumental discriminative responding. *Animal Learning & Behavior, 27,* 485–497. (b)

Rescorla, R. A. (1997e). Summation: Assessment of a configural theory. *Animal Learning Behavior, 25,* 200–209.

Rescorla, R. A. (1999a). Associative changes in elements and compounds when the other is reinforced. *Journal of Experimental Psychology: Animal Behavior Processes, 25,* 247–255.

Rescorla, R. A. (1999b). Summation and overexpectation with qualitatively different outcomes. *Animal Learning & Behavior, 27,* 50–62.

Rescorla, R. A. (1999c). Within-subject partial reinforcement extinction effect in autoshaping. *Quarterly Journal of Experimental Psychology, 52B,* 75–87.

Rescorla, R. A. (2000a). Associative changes with a random CS-US relationship. *Quarterly Journal of Experimental Psychology, 53B,* 325–340.

Rescorla, R. A. (2000b). Extinction can be enhanced by a concurrent excitor. *Journal of Experimental Psychology: Animal Behavior Processes, 26,* 251–260.

Rescorla, R. A. (2001a). Experimental extinction. In R. R. Mowrer & S. B. Klein (Eds.), *Contemporary learning theories* (pp. 119–154). Mahwah, NJ: Erlbaum.

Rescorla, R. A. (2001b). Retraining of extinguished Pavlovian stimuli. *Journal of Experimental Psychology: Animal Behavior Processes, 27,* 115–124.

Rescorla, R. A., & Durlach, P. J. (1981). Within-event learning in Pavlovian conditioning. In N. E. Spear & R. R. Miller (Eds.), *Information processing in animals: Memory mechanisms* (pp. 81–112). Hillsdale, NJ: Erlbaum.

Rescorla, R. A., Durlach, P. J., & Grau, J. W. (1985). Contextual learning in Pavlovian conditioning. In P. Balsam & A. Tomie (Eds.), *Context and learning* (pp. 23–56). Hillsdale, NJ: Erlbaum.

Rescorla, R. A., & Furrow, D. R. (1977). Stimulus similarity as a determinant of Pavlovian conditioning. *Journal of Experimental Psychology: Animal Behavior Processes, 3,* 203–215.

Rescorla, R. A., & Heth, C. D. (1975). Reinstatement of fear to an extinguished conditioned stimulus. *Journal of Experimental Psychology: Animal Behavior Processes, 104,* 88–96.

Rescorla, R. A., & Solomon, R. L. (1967). Two-process learning theory: Relationships between Pavlovian conditioning and instrumental learning. *Psychological Review, 74,* 151–182.

Rescorla, R. A., & Wagner, A. R. (1972). A theory of Pavlovian conditioning: Variations in the effectiveness of reinforcement and nonreinforcement. In A. H. Black & W. F. Prokasy (Eds.), *Classical conditioning II: Current research and theory* (pp. 64–99). New York: Appleton-Century-Crofts.

Revusky, S. H., & Garcia, J. (1970). Learned associations over long delays. In G. H. Bower & J. T. Spence (Eds.), *The psychology of learning and motivation* (Vol. 4, pp. 1–84). New York: Academic Press.

Reynolds, G. S. (1961). Attention in the pigeon. *Journal of the Experimental Analysis of Behavior, 4,* 203–208.

Reynolds, G. S. (1975). *A primer of operant conditioning.* Glenview, IL: Scott, Foresman.

Riccio, D. C., Hodges, L. A., & Randall, P. R. (1968). Retrograde amnesia produced by hypothermia in rats. *Journal of Comparative and Physiological Psychology, 3,* 618–622.

Riccio, D. C., MacArdy, E. A., & Kissinger, S. C. (1991). Associative processes in adaptation to repeated cold exposure in rats. *Behavioral Neuroscience, 105,* 599–602.

Riccio, D. C., Rabinowitz, V. C., & Axelrod, S. (1994). Memory: When less is more. *American Psychologist, 49,* 917–926.

Riccio, D. C., & Richardson, R. (1984). The status of memory following experimentally induced amnesias: Gone, but not forgotten. *Physiological Psychology, 12,* 59–72.

Richardson, R., Duffield, T. Q., Bailey, G. K., & Westbrook, R. F. (1999). Reinstatement of fear to an extinguished conditioned context. *Animal Learning & Behavior, 27,* 399–415.

Richardson, R., Riccio, D. C., & Jonke, T. (1983). Alleviation of infantile amnesia in rats by means of a pharmacological contextual state. *Developmental Psychobiology, 16,* 511–518.

Richelle, M., & Lejeune, H. (1980). *Time in animal behavior.* New York: Pergamon.

Ricker, S. T., & Bouton, M. E. (1996). Reacquisition following extinction in appetitive conditioning. *Animal Learning & Behavior, 24,* 423–436.

Riley, A. L., & Simpson, G. R. (2001). The attenuating effects of drug preexposure on taste aversion conditioning: Generality, experimental parameters, underlying mechanisms, and implications for drug use and abuse. In R. R. Mowrer & S. B. Klein (Eds.), *Handbook of contemporary learning theories* (pp. 505–559). Mahwah, NJ: Erlbaum.

Riley, A. L., & Tuck, D. L. (1985). Conditioned food aversions: A bibliography. *Annals of the New York Academy of Sciences, 433,* 381–437.

Rilling, M., Kendrick, D. F., & Stonebraker, T. B. (1984). Directed forgetting in context. In G. H. Bower (Ed.), *The psychology of learning and motivation* (Vol. 18). New York: Academic Press.

Ristau, C. A. (Ed.). (1991). *Cognitive ethology.* Hillsdale, NJ: Erlbaum.

Robbins, S. J. (1988). Role of context in performance on a random schedule of autoshaping. *Journal of Experimental Psychology: Animal Behavior Processes, 14,* 413–424.

Robbins, S. J. (1990). Mechanisms underlying spontaneous recovery in autoshaping. *Journal of Experimental Psychology: Animal Behavior Processes, 16,* 235–249.

Roberts, A. D. L., & Pearce, J. M. (1999). Blocking in the Morris swimming pool. *Journal of Experimental Psychology: Animal Behavior Processes, 25,* 225–235.

Roberts, S. (1981). Isolation of an internal clock. *Journal of Experimental Psychology: Animal Behavior Processes, 7,* 242–268.

Roberts, S. (1982). Cross-modal use of an internal clock. *Journal of Experimental Psychology: Animal Behavior Processes, 8,* 2–22.

Roberts, S., & Church, R. M. (1978). Control of an internal clock. *Journal of Experimental Psychology: Animal Behavior Processes, 4,* 318–337.

Roberts, W. A. (1979). Spatial memory in the rat on a hierarchical maze. *Learning and Motivation, 10,* 117–140.

Roberts, W. A. (1984). Some issues in animal spatial memory. In H. L. Roitblat, T. G. Bever, & H. S. Terrace (Eds.), *Animal cognition* (pp. 425–443). Hillsdale, NJ: Erlbaum.

Roberts, W. A. (1998). *Animal cognition.* Boston: McGraw-Hill.

Roberts, W. A., Cheng, K., & Cohen, J. S. (1989). Timing light and tone signals in pigeons. *Journal of Experimental Psychology: Animal Behavior Processes, 15,* 23–35.

Roberts, W. A., & Grant, D. S. (1976). Studies of short-term memory in the pigeon using the delayed matching to sample procedure. In D. L. Medin, W. A. Roberts, & R. T. Davis (Eds.), *Processes of animal memory.* Hillsdale, NJ: Erlbaum.

Roberts, W. A., & Mazmanian, D. S. (1988). Concept learning at different levels of abstraction by pigeons, monkeys, and people. *Journal of Experimental Psychology: Animal Behavior Processes, 14,* 247–260.

Rodd, Z. A., Rosellini, R. A., Stock, H. S., & Gallup, G. G., Jr. (1997). Learned helplessness in chickens (*Gallus gallus*): Evidence for attentional bias. *Learning and Motivation, 28,* 43–55.

Rogers, R. F., Schiller, K. M., & Matzel, L. D. (1996). Chemosensory-based contextual conditioning in *Hermissendra crassicornis. Animal Learning & Behavior, 24,* 28–37.

Roitblat, H. L., Bever, T. G., & Terrace, H. S. (Eds.). (1984). *Animal cognition.* Hillsdale, NJ: Erlbaum.

Roitblat, H. L., Bever, T. G., Helweg, D. A., & Harley, H. E. (1991). On-line choice and the representation of serially structured stimuli. *Journal of Experimental Psychology: Animal Behavior Processes, 17,* 55–67.

Roitblat, H. L., Harley, H. E., & Helweg, D. A. (1993). Cognitive processing in artificial language research. In H. L. Roitblat, L. M. Herman, & P. E. Nachtigall (Eds.), *Language and communication: Comparative perspectives* (pp. 1–23). Hillsdale, NJ: Erlbaum.

Roitblat, H. L., & Meyer, J.-A. (Eds.). (1995). *Comparative approaches to cognitive science.* Cambridge, MA: MIT Press.

Roitblat, H. L., Penner, R. H., & Nachtigall, P. E. (1990). Matching-to-sample by an echo locating dolphin (*Tursiops truncatus*) *Journal of Experimental Psychology: Animal Behavior Processes, 16,* 85–95.

Roitblat, H. L., Scopatz, R. A., & Bever, T. G. (1987). The hierarchical representation of three-item sequences. *Animal Learning & Behavior, 15,* 179–192.

Romanes, G. J. (1882). *Animal intelligence.* New York: Appleton.

Romaniuk, C. B., & Williams, D. A. (2000). Conditioning across the duration of a backward conditioned stimulus. *Journal of Experimental Psychology: Animal Behavior Processes, 26,* 454–461.

Roper, K. L., Kaiser, D. H., & Zentall, T. R. (1995). True directed forgetting in pigeons may occur only when alternative working memory is required on forget-cue trials. *Animal Learning & Behavior, 23,* 280–285.

Roper, K. L., & Zentall, T. R. (1993). Directed forgetting in animals. *Psychological Bulletin, 113,* 513–532.

Rosas, J. M., & Bouton, M. E. (1996). Spontaneous recovery after extinction of a conditioned taste aversion. *Animal Learning & Behavior, 24,* 341–348.

Rosas, J. M., & Bouton, M. E. (1997). Additivity of the effects of retention interval and context change on latent inhibition: Toward resolution of the context forgetting paradox. *Journal of Experimental Psychology: Animal Behavior Processes, 23,* 283–294.

Rosas, J. M., & Bouton, M. E. (1997). Renewal of a conditioned taste aversion upon return to the conditioning context after extinction in another one. *Learning and Motivation, 28,* 216–229.

Rose, S. A., & Orlian, E. K. (2001). Visual information processing. In L. T. Singer and P. S. Zeskind (Eds.), *Biobehavioral assessment of the infant* (pp. 274–292). New York: Guilford.

Rosellini, R. A., & DeCola, J. P. (1981). Inescapable shock interferes with the acquisition of a low-activity response in an appetitive context. *Animal Learning & Behavior, 9,* 487–490.

Rosellini, R. A., DeCola, J. P., & Shapiro, N. R. (1982). Cross-motivational effects of inescapable shock are associative in nature. *Journal of Experimental Psychology: Animal Behavior Processes, 8,* 376–388.

Rosellini, R. A., DeCola, J. P., Plonsky, M., Warren, D. A., & Stilman, A. J. (1984). Uncontrollable shock proactively increases sensitivity to response-reinforcer independence in rats. *Journal of Experimental Psychology: Animal Behavior Processes, 10,* 346–359.

Rosellini, R. A., Warren, D. A., & DeCola, J. P. (1987). Predictability and controllability: Differential effects upon contextual fear. *Learning and Motivation, 18,* 392–420.

Ross, R. T. (1983). Relationships between the determinants of performance in serial feature-positive discriminations. *Journal of Experimental Psychology: Animal Behavior Processes, 9,* 349–373.

Ross, R. T., & Holland, P. C. (1981). Conditioning of simultaneous and serial feature-positive discriminations. *Animal Learning & Behavior, 9,* 293–303.

Rovee-Collier, C., & Bhatt, R. S. (1993). Evidence of long-term memory in infancy. In R. Vasta (Ed.), *Annals of child development* (Vol. 9, pp. 1–45). London: Jessica Kingsley.

Rozin, P., & Zellner, D. (1985). The role of Pavlovian conditioning in the acquisition of food likes and dislikes. *Annals of the New York Academy of Sciences, 443,* 189–202.

Rumbaugh, D. M. (Ed.). (1977). *Language learning by a chimpanzee: The Lana project.* New York: Academic Press .

Russell, M. S., & Burch, R. L. (1959). *The principles of humane experimental technique.* London: Methuen.

Russell, W. R., & Nathan, P. W. (1946). Traumatic amnesia. *Brain, 69,* 280–300.

Sahley, C., Rudy, J. W., & Gelperin, A. (1981). An analysis of associative learning in a terrestrial mollusc: I. Higher-order conditioning, blocking, and a transient US-pre-exposure effect. *Journal of Comparative Physiology-A, 144,* 1–8.

Sajwaj, T., Libet, J., & Agras, S. (1974). Lemon-juice therapy: The control of life-threatening rumination in a six-month-old infant. *Journal of Applied Behavior Analysis, 7,* 557–563.

Saladin, M. E., ten Have, W. N., Saper, Z. L., Labinsky, J. S., & Tait, R. W. (1989). Retardation of rabbit nictitating membrane conditioning following US preexposures depends on the distribution and numbers of US presentations. *Animal Learning & Behavior, 17,* 179–187.

Santi, A., Musgrave, S., & Bradford, S. A. (1988). Utilization of cues signaling different test stimulus dimensions in delayed matching to sample by pigeons. *Learning and Motivation, 19,* 87–98.

Santi, A., Stanford, L., & Coyle, J. (1998). Pigeons' memory for event duration: Differences between visual and auditory signals. *Animal Learning & Behavior, 26,* 163–171.

Sara, S. J. (2000). Reconsolidation: Strengthening the shaky trace through retrieval. *Nature Reviews Neuroscience, 1,* 212–213.

Sargisson, R. J., & White, K. G. (2001). Generalization of delayed matching to sample following training at different delays. *Journal of the Experimental Analysis of Behavior, 75,* 1–14.

Saunders, R. R., & Green, G. (1999). A discrimination analysis of training structure effects on stimulus equivalence outcomes. *Journal of the Experimental Analysis of Behavior, 74,* 117–137.

Savage-Rumbaugh, E. S. (1986). *Ape language.* New York: Columbia University Press.

Savage-Rumbaugh, E. S., McDonald, K., Sevcik, R. A., Hopkins, W. D., & Rubert, E. (1986). Spontaneous symbol acquisition and communicative use by pigmy chimpanzees (*Pan paniscus*). *Journal of Experimental Psychology: General, 115,* 211–235.

Savage-Rumbaugh, E. S., Murphy, J., Sevcik, R. A., Brakke, K. E., Williams, S. L., & Rumbaugh, D. M. (1993). Language comprehension in ape and child. *Monographs of the Society for Research in Child Development,* Vol. 58 (Nos. 3–4), Serial No. 233.

Savage-Rumbaugh, E. S., Rumbaugh, D. M., Smith, S. T., & Lawson, J. (1980). Reference: The linguistic essential. *Science, 210,* 922–925.

Savage-Rumbaugh, E. S., Sevcik, R. A., Brakke, K. E., & Rumbaugh, D. M. (1990). Symbols: Their communicative use, comprehension, and combination by bonobos (*Pan paniscus*). In C. Rovee-Collier & L. P. Lipsitt (Eds.), *Advances in infancy research* (Vol. 6, pp. 221–278). Norwood, NJ: Ablex.

Savage-Rumbaugh, S., Shanker, S. G., & Taylor, T. J. (1998). *Apes, language, and the human mind.* New York: Oxford University Press.

Savastano, H. I., Cole, R. P., Barnet, R. C., & Miller, R. R. (1999). Reconsidering conditioned inhibition. *Learning and Motivation, 30,* 101–127.

Savastano, H., & Fantino, E. (1994). Human choice in concurrent ratio-interval schedules of reinforcement. *Journal of the Experimental Analysis of Behavior, 61,* 453–463.

Savastano, H. I., & Fantino, E. (1996). Differences in delay, not ratios, control choice in concurrent chains. *Journal of the Experimental Analysis of Behavior, 66,* 97–116.

Savastano, H. I., & Miller, R. R. (1998). Time as content in Pavlovian conditioning. *Behavioural Processes, 44,* 147–162.

Sawa, K., Nakajima, S., & Imada, H. (1999). Facilitation of sodium aversion learning in sodium-deprived rats. *Learning and Motivation, 30,* 281–295.

Scavio, M. J., Jr., & Gormezano, I. (1974). CS intensity effects on rabbit nictitating membrane conditioning, extinction and generalization. *Pavlovian Journal of Biological Science, 9,* 25–34.

Schaal, D. W., McDonald, M. P., Miller, M. A., & Reilly, M. P. (1996). Discrimination of methadone and cocaine by pigeons without explicit discrimination training. *Journal of the Experimental Analysis of Behavior, 66,* 193–203.

Schaal, D. W., Shahan, T. A., Kovera, C. A., & Reilly, M. P. (1998). Mechanisms underlying the effects of unsignaled delayed reinforcement on key pecking of pigeons under variable interval schedules. *Journal of the Experimental Analysis of Behavior, 69,* 103–122.

Schachter, D. L., & Tulving, E. (1994). What are the memory systems of 1994? In D. L. Schachter & E. Tulving (Eds.), *Memory systems* (pp. 1–38). Cambridge, MA: MIT Press.

Schachtman, T. R., Brown, A. M., Gordon, E. L., Catterson, D. A., & Miller, R. R. (1987). Mechanisms underlying retarded emergence of conditioned responding following inhibitory training: Evidence for the comparator hypothesis. *Journal of Experimental Psychology: Animal Behavior Processes, 13,* 310–322.

Schachtman, T. R., Brown, A. M., & Miller, R. R. (1985). Reinstatement-induced recovery of a taste-LiCl association following extinction. *Animal Learning & Behavior, 13,* 223–227.

Schachtman, T. R., Gee, J.-L., Kasprow, W. J., & Miller, R. R. (1983). Reminder-induced recovery from blocking as a function of the number of compound trials. *Learning and Motivation, 14,* 154–164.

Schachtman, T. R., Kasprow, W. J., Meyer, R. C., Bourne, M. J., & Hart, J. A. (1992). Extinction of the overshadowing CS after overshadowing in conditioned taste aversion. *Animal Learning & Behavior, 20,* 207–218.

Schachtman, T. R., Threlkeld, R., & Meyer, K. (2000). Retention of conditioned inhibition produced by extinction. *Learning and Motivation, 31,* 283–300.

Schiff, R., Smith, N., & Prochaska, J. (1972). Extinction of avoidance in rats as a function of duration and number of blocked trials. *Journal of Comparative and Physiological Psychology, 81,* 356–359.

Schindler, C. W., & Weiss, S. J. (1982). The influence of positive and negative reinforcement on selective attention in the rat. *Learning and Motivation, 13,* 304–323.

Schlinger, H., Blakely, E., & Kaczor, T. (1990). Pausing under variable-ratio schedules: Interaction of reinforcer magnitude, variable-ratio size, and lowest ratio. *Journal of the Experimental Analysis of Behavior, 53,* 133–139.

Schlosberg, H. (1934). Conditioned responses in the white rat. *Journal of Genetic Psychology, 45,* 303–335.

Schlosberg, H. (1936). Conditioned responses in the white rat: II. Conditioned responses based upon shock to the foreleg. *Journal of Genetic Psychology, 49,* 107–138.

Schmajuk, N. A., & Holland, P. C. (Eds.). (1998). *Occasion setting: Associative learning and cognition in animals.* Washington, DC: American Psychological Association.

Schneider, A. M., Tyler, J., & Jinich, D. (1974). Recovery from retrograde amnesia: A learning process. *Science, 184,* 87–88.

Schneiderman, N., & Gormezano, I. (1964). Conditioning of the nictitating membrane of the rabbit as a function of CS-US interval. *Journal of Comparative and Physiological Psychology, 57,* 188–195.

Schreibman, L., Koegel, R. L., Charlop, M. H., & Egel, A. L. (1990). Infantile autism. In A. S. Bellack, M. Hersen, & A. E. Kazdin (Eds.), *International handbook of behavior modification and therapy* (pp. 763–789). New York: Plenum.

Schreurs, B. G. (1998). Long-term memory and extinction of rabbit nictitating membrane trace conditioning. *Learning and Motivation, 29,* 68–82.

Schrier, A. M., & Brady, P. M. (1987). Categorization of natural stimuli by monkeys (*Macaca mulatta*): Effects of stimulus set size and modification of exemplars. *Journal of Experimental Psychology: Animal Behavior Processes, 13,* 136–143.

Schultz, L. A., Collier, G., & Johnson, D. F. (1999). Behavioral strategies in the cold: Effects of feeding and nesting costs. *Physiology & Behavior, 67,* 107–115.

Schuster, R. H., & Rachlin, H. (1968). Indifference between punishment and free shock: Evidence for the negative law of effect. *Journal of the Experimental Analysis of Behavior, 11,* 777–786.

Schusterman, R. J., & Gisiner, R. (1988). Artificial language comprehension in dolphins and sea lions: The essential cognitive skills. *Psychological Record, 38,* 311–348.

Schusterman, R. J., & Kreiger, K. (1986). Artificial language comprehension and size transposition by a California sea lion (*Zalophus californianus*). *Journal of Comparative Psychology, 100,* 348–355.

Schwartz, B. (1976). Positive and negative conditioned suppression in the pigeon: Effects of the locus and modality of the CS. *Learning and Motivation, 7,* 86–100.

Schwartz, B. (1980). Development of complex, stereotyped behavior in pigeons. *Journal of the Experimental Analysis of Behavior, 33,* 153–166.

Schwartz, B. (1981). Reinforcement creates behavioral units. *Behavioural Analysis Letters, 1,* 33–41.

Schwartz, B. (1985). On the organization of stereotyped response sequences. *Animal Learning & Behavior, 13,* 261–268.

Schwartz, B. (1988). The experimental synthesis of behavior: Reinforcement, behavioral stereotypy, and problem solving. In G. H. Bower (Ed.), *The psychology of learning and motivation* (Vol. 22, pp. 93–138). Orlando, FL: Academic Press.

Schweitzer, J. B., & Sulzer-Azaroff, B. (1988). Self-control: Teaching tolerance for delay in impulsive children. *Journal of the Experimental Analysis of Behavior, 50,* 173–186.

Sclafani, A. (1997). Learned controls of ingestive behaviour. *Appetite, 29,* 153–158.

Seligman, M. E. P. (1971). Phobias and preparedness. *Behavior Therapy, 2,* 307–320.

Seligman, M. E. P. (1975). *Helplessness: On depression, development and death.* San Francisco: W. H. Freeman.

Seligman, M. E. P., & Maier, S. F. (1967). Failure to escape traumatic shock. *Journal of Experimental Psychology, 74,* 1–9.

Senkowski, P. C. (1978). Variables affecting the overtraining extinction effect in discrete-trial lever pressing. *Journal of Experimental Psychology: Animal Behavior Processes, 4,* 131–143.

Sevcik, R. A., Romski, M. A., & Wilkenson, K. (1991). Roles of graphic symbols in the language acquisition process for persons with severe cognitive disabilities. *Journal of Augmentative and Alternative Communication, 7,* 161–170.

Sevenster, P. (1973). Incompatibility of response and reward. In R. A. Hinde & J. Stevenson-Hinde (Eds.), *Constraints on learning* (pp. 265–283). London: Academic Press.

Shah, K., Bradshaw, C. M., & Szabadi, E. (1991). Relative and absolute reinforcement frequency as determinants of choice in concurrent variable interval schedules. *Quarterly Journal of Experimental Psychology, 43,* 25–38.

Shanker, S. G., Savage-Rumbaugh, E. S., & Taylor, T. J. (1999). Kanzi: A new beginning. *Animal Learning & Behavior, 27,* 24–25.

Shanks, D. R., & Dickinson, A. (1987). Associative accounts of causality judgment. In G. H. Bower (Ed.), *The psychology of learning and motivation* (Vol. 21, pp. 229–261). San Diego, CA: Academic Press.

Shapiro, K. L., & LoLordo, V. M. (1982). Constraints on Pavlovian conditioning of the pigeon: Relative conditioned reinforcing effects of red-light and tone CSs paired with food. *Learning and Motivation, 13,* 68–80.

Shapiro, K. L., Jacobs, W. J., & LoLordo, V. M. (1980). Stimulus-reinforcer interactions in Pavlovian conditioning of pigeons: Implications for selective associations. *Animal Learning & Behavior, 8,* 586–594.

Sheffield, F. D. (1948). Avoidance training and the contiguity principle. *Journal of Comparative and Physiological Psychology, 41,* 165–177.

Sheffield, F. D., Roby, T. B., & Campbell, B. A. (1954). Drive reduction versus consummatory behavior as determinants of reinforcement. *Journal of Comparative and Physiological Psychology, 47,* 349–354.

Sherburne, L. M., & Zentall, T. R. (1998). The differential outcomes effect in pigeons is not reduced by eliminating response-outcome associations: Support for a two-process account. *Animal Learning & Behavior, 26,* 378–387.

Sherry, D. F. (1984). Food storage by black-capped chickadees: Memory for the location and contents of caches. *Animal Behaviour, 32,* 451–464.

Sherry, D. F. (1985). Food storage by birds and mammals. *Advances in the Study of Behavior, 15,* 153–188.

Sherry, D. F. (1988). Learning and adaptation in food-storing birds. In R. C. Bolles & M. D. Beecher (Eds.), *Evolution and learning* (pp. 79–95). Hillsdale, NJ: Erlbaum .

Sherry, D. F. (1992). Memory, the hippocampus, and natural selection: Studies of food-storing birds. In L. R. Squire & N. Butters (Eds.), *Neuropsychology of memory* (2nd ed., pp. 521–532). New York: Gilford.

Sherry, D. F., Krebs, J. R., & Cowie, R. J. (1981). Memory for the location of stored food in marsh tits. *Animal Behaviour, 29,* 1260–1266.

Shettleworth, S. J. (1975). Reinforcement and the organization of behavior in golden hamsters: Hunger, environment, and food reinforcement. *Journal of Experimental Psychology: Animal Behavior Processes, 1,* 56–87.

Shettleworth, S. J. (1983). Memory in food-hoarding birds. *Scientific American, 248,* 102–110.

Shettleworth, S. J. (1995). Comparative studies of memory in food storing birds. In E. Alleva, A. Fasolo, H. Lipp, L. Nadel, & L. Ricceri (Eds.), *Behavioral brain research in natural and semi-natural settings: Possibilities and perspectives* (pp. 159–192). Dordrecht: Kluwer.

Shettleworth, S. J. (1998). *Cognition, evolution, and behavior.* New York: Oxford University Press.

Shettleworth, S. J., & Krebs, J. R. (1986). Stored and encountered seeds: A comparison of two spatial memory tasks in marsh tits and chickadees. *Journal of Experimental Psychology: Animal Behavior Processes, 12,* 248–257.

Shi, C., & Davis, M. (1999). Pain pathways involved in fear conditioning measured with fear-potentiated startle: Lesion studies. *Journal of Neuroscience, 19,* 420–430.

Shimp, C. P. (1966). Probabilistically reinforced choice behavior in pigeons. *Journal of the Experimental Analysis of Behavior, 9,* 443–455.

Shimp, C. P. (1969). Optimum behavior in free-operant experiments. *Psychological Review, 76,* 97–112.

Shurtleff, D., & Ayres, J. J. B. (1981). One-trial backward excitatory fear conditioning in rats: Acquisition, retention, extinction, and spontaneous recovery. *Animal Learning & Behavior, 9,* 65–74.

Sidman, M. (1953a). Avoidance conditioning with brief shock and no exteroceptive warning signal. *Science, 118,* 157–158.

Sidman, M. (1953b). Two temporal parameters of the maintenance of avoidance behavior by the white rat. *Journal of Comparative and Physiological Psychology, 46,* 253–261.

Sidman, M. (1962). Reduction of shock frequency as reinforcement for avoidance behavior. *Journal of the Experimental Analysis of Behavior, 5,* 247–257.

Sidman, M. (1966). Avoidance behavior. In W. K. Honig (Ed.), *Operant behavior* (pp. 448–498). New York: Appleton-Century-Crofts.

Sidman, M. (1990). Equivalence relations: Where do they come from? In D. E. Blackman & H. Lejeune (Eds.), *Behavioral analysis in theory and practice: Contributions and controversies* (pp. 93–114). Hillsdale, NJ: Erlbaum.

Sidman, M. (1994). *Equivalence relations and behavior: A research story.* Boston: Authors Cooperative.

Sidman, M. (2000). Equivalence relations and the reinforcement contingency. *Journal of the Experimental Analysis of Behavior, 74,* 127–146.

Sidman, M., & Tailby, W. (1982). Conditional discrimination vs. matching to sample: An expansion of the testing paradigm. *Journal of the Experimental Analysis of Behavior, 37,* 5–22.

Siegel, S. (1983). Classical conditioning, drug tolerance, and drug dependence. In Y. Israel, F. B. Glaser, H. Kalant, R. E. Popham, W. Schmidt, & R. G. Smart (Eds.), *Research advances in alcohol and drug problems* (Vol. 7). New York: Plenum.

Siegel, S. (1989). Pharmacological conditioning and drug effects. In A. J. Goudie & M. W. Emmett-Oglesby (Eds.), *Psychoactive drugs: Tolerance and sensitization* (pp. 115–180). Clifton, NJ: Humana Press.

Siegel, S. (1999). Drug anticipation and drug addiction. The 1998 H. David Archibald lecture. *Addiction, 94,* 1113–1124.

Siegel, S., & Allan, L. G. (1996). The widespread influence of the Rescorla–Wagner model. *Psychonomic Bulletin & Review, 3,* 314–321.

Siegel, S., & Allan, L. G. (1998). Learning and homeostasis: Drug addiction and the McCollough effect. *Psychological Bulletin, 124,* 230–239.

Siegel, S., Baptista, M. A. S., Kim, J. A., McDonald, R. V., & Weise-Kelly, L. (2000). Pavlovian psychopharmacology: The associative basis of tolerance. *Experimental and Clinical Psychopharmacology, 8,* 276– 293.

Siegel, S., & Domjan, M. (1971). Backward conditioning as an inhibitory procedure. *Learning and Motivation, 2,* 1–11.

Sigmundi, R. A. (1997). Performance rules for problem-specific defense reactions. In M. E. Bouton & M. S. Fanselow (Eds.), *Learning, motivation, and cognition* (pp. 305–319). Washington, DC: American Psychological Association.

Sigmundi, R. A., & Bolles, R. C. (1983). CS modality, context conditioning, and conditioned freezing. *Animal Learning & Behavior, 11,* 205–212.

Silberberg, A., Warren-Bouton, F. R., & Asano, T. (1987). Inferior-good and Giffen-good effects in monkey choice behavior. *Journal of Experimental Psychology: Animal Behavior Processes, 13,* 292–301.

Silva, A. J., & Giese, K. P. (1998). Gene targeting: A novel window into the biology of learning and memory. In J. L. Martinez & R. P. Kesner (Eds.), *Neurobiology of learning and memory* (pp. 89–142). San Diego: Academic Press.

Silva, F. J., & Timberlake, W. (2000). A clarification of the nature of backward excitatory conditioning. *Learning and Motivation, 31,* 67–80.

Silva, F. J., Timberlake, W., & Cevik, M. O. (1998). A behavior systems approach to the expression of backward associations. *Learning and Motivation, 29,* 1–22.

Silva, K. M., & Timberlake, W. (1997). A behavior systems view of conditioned states during long and short CS-US intervals. *Learning and Motivation, 28,* 465–490.

Silva, K. M., & Timberlake, W. (1998). The organization and temporal properties of appetitive behavior in rats. *Animal Learning & Behavior, 26,* 182–195.

Simons, R. C. (1996). *Boo! Culture, experience, and the startle reflex.* New York: Oxford University Press.

Singh, N. N., & Solman, R. T. (1990). A stimulus control analysis of the picture-word problem in children who are mentally retarded: The blocking effect. *Journal of Applied Behavior Analysis, 23,* 525–532.

Skinner, B. F. (1938). *The behavior of organisms.* New York: Appleton-Century-Crofts.

Skinner, B. F. (1948). "Superstition" in the pigeon. *Journal of Experimental Psychology, 38,* 168–172.

Skinner, B. F. (1953). *Science and human behavior.* New York: Macmillan.

Skinner, D. M. (2000). Modulation of taste aversions by a pentobarbital drug state: An assessment of its transfer properties. *Learning and Motivation, 31,* 381–401.

Slamecka, N. J., & Ceraso, J. (1960). Retroactive and proactive inhibition of verbal learning. *Psychological Bulletin, 57,* 449–475.

Small, W. S. (1899). An experimental study of the mental processes of the rat: I. *American Journal of Psychology, 11,* 133–164.

Small, W. S. (1900). An experimental study of the mental processes of the rat: II. *American Journal of Psychology, 12,* 206–239.

Smith, J. C., & Roll, D. L. (1967). Trace conditioning with X-rays as an aversive stimulus. *Psychonomic Science, 9,* 11–12.

Smith, M. C., Coleman, S. R., & Gormezano, I. (1969). Classical conditioning of the rabbit's nictitating membrane response at backward, simultaneous, and forward CS-US intervals. *Journal of Comparative and Physiological Psychology, 69,* 226–231.

Smith, S. M., & Vela, E. (2001). Environmental context-dependent memory: A review and meta-analysis. *Psychonomic Bulletin & Review, 8,* 203–220.

Smotherman, W. P., & Robinson, S. R. (1992). Habituation in the rat fetus. *Quarterly Journal of Experimental Psychology, 44B,* 215–230.

Snodgrass, S. H., & McMillan, D. E. (1996). Drug discrimination under a concurrent schedule. *Journal of the Experimental Analysis of Behavior, 65,* 495–512.

Solomon, R. L. (1964). Punishment. *American Psychologist, 19,* 239–253.

Solomon, R. L. (1977). An opponent-process theory of acquired motivation: The affective dynamics of addiction. In J. D. Maser & M. E. P. Seligman (Eds.), *Psychopathology: Experimental models* (pp. 66–103). San Francisco: W. H. Freeman.

Solomon, R. L., & Corbit, J. D. (1973). An opponent-process theory of motivation: II. Cigarette addiction. *Journal of Abnormal Psychology, 81,* 158–171.

Solomon, R. L., & Corbit, J. D. (1974). An opponent-process theory of motivation: I. The temporal dynamics of affect. *Psychological Review, 81,* 119–145.

Solomon, R. L., Kamin, L. J., & Wynne, L. C. (1953). Traumatic avoidance learning: The outcomes of several extinction procedures with dogs. *Journal of Abnormal and Social Psychology, 48,* 291–302.

Solomon, R. L., & Wynne, L. C. (1953). Traumatic avoidance learning: Acquisition in normal dogs. *Psychological Monographs, 67* (Whole No. 354).

Soltysik, S. S., Wolfe, G. E., Nicholas, T., Wilson, W. J., & Garcia-Sanchez, L. (1983). Blocking of inhibitory conditioning within a serial conditioned stimulus conditioned inhibitor compound: Maintenance of acquired behavior without an unconditioned stimulus. *Learning and Motivation, 14,* 1–29.

Spear, N. E. (1973). Retrieval of memory in animals. *Psychological Review, 80,* 163–194.

Spear, N. E. (1978). *The processing of memories: Forgetting and retention.* Hillsdale, NJ: Erlbaum.

Spear, N. E. (1981). Extending the domain of memory retrieval. In N. E. Spear & R. R. Miller (Eds.), *Information processing in animals: Memory mechanisms* (pp. 341– 378). Hillsdale, NJ: Erlbaum.

Spear, N. E., & Riccio, D. C. (1994). *Memory: Phenomena and principles.* Boston: Allyn and Bacon.

Spence, K. W. (1936). The nature of discrimination learning in animals. *Psychological Review, 43,* 427–449.

Spence, K. W. (1937). The differential response in animals to stimuli varying within a single dimension. *Psychological Review, 44,* 430–444.

Spence, K. W. (1956). *Behavior theory and conditioning.* New Haven, CT: Yale University Press.

Spetch, M. L. (1987). Systematic errors in pigeons' memory for event duration: Interaction between training and test delays. *Animal Learning & Behavior, 15,* 1–5.

Spetch, M. L. (1990). Further studies of pigeons' spatial working memory in the open-field task. *Animal Learning & Behavior, 18,* 332–340.

Spetch, M. L. (1995). Overshadowing in landmark learning: Touch-screen studies with pigeons and humans. *Journal of Experimental Psychology: Animal Behavior Processes, 21,* 166–181.

Spetch, M. L., Mondloch, M. V., Belke, T. W., & Dunn, R. (1994). Determinants of pigeons' choice between certain and probabilistic outcomes. *Animal Learning & Behavior, 22,* 239–251.

Spetch, M. L., Wilkie, D. M., & Pinel, J. P. J. (1981). Backward conditioning: A reevaluation of the empirical evidence. *Psychological Bulletin, 89,* 163–175.

Spetch, M. L., Wilkie, D. M., & Skelton, R. W. (1981). Control of pigeons' keypecking topography by a schedule of alternating food and water reward. *Animal Learning & Behavior, 9,* 223–229.

Staddon, J. E. R. (1979). Operant behavior as adaptation to constraint. *Journal of Experimental Psychology: General, 108,* 48–67.

Staddon, J. E. R. (1983). *Adaptive behavior and learning.* Cambridge: Cambridge University Press.

Staddon, J. E. R., & Higa, J. (1996). Multiple time scales in simple habituation. *Psychological Review, 203,* 720–733.

Staddon, J. E. R., & Higa, J. J. (1999). Time and memory: Towards a pacemaker-free theory of interval timing. *Journal of the Experimental Analysis of Behavior, 72,* 225–252.

Staddon, J. E. R., Higa, J. J., & Chelaru, I. M. (1999). Time, trace, memory. *Journal of the Experimental Analysis of Behavior, 72,* 293–302.

Staddon, J. E. R., & Simmelhag, V. L. (1971). The "superstition" experiment: A reexamination of its implications for the principles of adaptive behavior. *Psychological Review, 78,* 3–43.

Staddon, J. E. R., Wynne, C. D. L., & Higa, J. J. (1991). The role of timing in reinforcement schedule performance. *Learning and Motivation, 22,* 200–225.

Stafford, D., & Branch, M. N. (1998). Effects of step size and break point criterion on progressive-ratio performance. *Journal of the Experimental Analysis of Behavior, 70,* 123–138.

Stanhope, K. J. (1992). The representation of the reinforcer and the force of the pigeon's keypeck in first- and second-order conditioning. *The Quarterly Journal of Experimental Psychology, 44B,* 137–158.

Starr, M. D. (1978). An opponent-process theory of motivation: VI. Time and intensity variables in the development of separation-induced distress calling in ducklings. *Journal of Experimental Psychology: Animal Behavior Processes, 4,* 338–355.

Starr, M. D., & Mineka, S. (1977). Determinants of fear over the course of avoidance learning. *Learning and Motivation, 8,* 332–350.

Steinert, P., Fallon, D., & Wallace, J. (1976). Matching to sample in goldfish (*Carassuis auratus*). *Bulletin of the Psychonomic Society, 8,* 265.

Steinmetz, J. E. (1999). A renewed interest in human classical eyeblink conditioning. *Psychological Science, 10,* 24–25.

Steinmetz, J. E., Gluck, M. A., & Solomon, P. R. (2001). *Model systems and the neurobiology of associative learning: A festschrift in honor of Richard F. Thompson.* Hillsdale, NJ: Erlbaum.

Stephenson, D., & Siddle, D. (1983). Theories of habituation. In D. Siddle (Ed.), *Orienting and habituation: Perspectives in human research* (pp. 183–236). Chichester, England: Wiley.

Stevens, S. S. (1951). Mathematics, measurement and psychophysics. In S. S. Stevens (Ed.), *Handbook of experimental psychology* (pp. 1–49). New York: Wiley.

Stewart, J., & Eikelboom, R. (1987). Conditioned drug effects. In L. L. Iversen, S. D. Iversen, & S. H. Snyder (Eds.), *Handbook of psychopharmacology* (Vol. 19, pp. 1–57). New York: Plenum.

Stokes, P. D. (2001). Variability, constraints, and creativity: Shedding light on Claude Monet. *American Psychologist, 56,* 355–359.

Stokes, P. D., & Balsam, P. D. (1991). Effects of reinforcing preselected approximations on the topography of the rat's bar press. *Journal of the Experimental Analysis of Behavior, 55,* 213–231.

Stokes, P. D., Mechner, F., & Balsam, P. D. (1999). Effects of different acquisition procedures on response variability. *Animal Learning & Behavior, 27,* 28–41.

Stokes, T. F., & Baer, D. M. (1977). An implicit technology of generalization. *Journal of Applied Behavior Analysis, 10,* 349–367.

Straub, R. O., & Terrace, H. S. (1981). Generalization of serial learning in the pigeon. *Animal Learning & Behavior, 9,* 454–468.

Strijkstra, A. M., & Bolhuis, J. J. (1987). Memory persistence of rats in a radial maze varies with training procedure. *Behavioral and Neural Biology, 47,* 158–166.

Suarez, S. D., & Gallup, G. G. (1981). An ethological analysis of open-field behavior in rats and mice. *Learning and Motivation, 12,* 342–363.

Sumpter, C. E., Temple, W., & Foster, T. M. (1998). Response form, force, and number: Effects on concurrent-schedule performance. *Journal of the Experimental Analysis of Behavior, 70,* 45–68.

Sumpter, C. E., Temple, W., & Foster, T. M. (1999). The effects of differing response types and price manipulations on demand measures. *Journal of the Experimental Analysis of Behavior, 71,* 329–354.

Sundberg, M. L. (1996). Toward granting linguistic competence to apes: A review of Savage-Rumbaugh et al.'s *Language comprehension in ape and child. Journal of the Experimental Analysis of Behavior, 65,* 477–492.

Suomi, S. J., Mineka, S., & Harlow, H. F. (1983). Social separation in monkeys as viewed from several motivational perspectives. In E. Satinoff & P. Teitelbaum (Eds.), *Handbook of neurobiology: Vol. 6. Motivation.* New York: Plenum.

Susswein, A. J., & Schwarz, M. (1983). A learned change of response to inedible food in Aplysia. *Behavioral and Neural Biology, 39,* 1–6.

Sutphin, G., Byrne, T., & Poling, A. (1998). Response acquisition with delayed reinforcement: A comparison of two-lever procedures. *Journal of the Experimental Analysis of Behavior, 69,* 17–28.

Suzuki, S., Augerinos, G., & Black, A. H. (1980). Stimulus control of spatial behavior on the eight-arm maze in rats. *Learning and Motivation, 11,* 1–18.

Svartdal, F. (2000). Persistence during extinction: Conventional and reversed PREE under multiple schedules. *Learning and Motivation, 31,* 21–40.

Swartz, K. B., Chen, S., & Terrace, H. S. (2000). Serial learning by rhesus monkeys: II. Learning four-item lists by trial and error. *Journal of Experimental Psychology: Animal Behavior Processes, 26,* 274–285.

Swartzentruber, D. (1993). Transfer of contextual control across similarly trained conditioned stimuli. *Animal Learning & Behavior, 21,* 14–22.

Swartzentruber, D. (1995). Modulatory mechanisms in Pavlovian conditioning. *Animal Learning & Behavior, 23,* 123–143.

Swartzentruber, D. (1997). Modulation by the stimulus properties of excitation. *Journal of Experimental Psychology: Animal Behavior Processes, 23,* 434–440.

Symonds, M., & Hall, G. (1997). Contextual conditioning with lithium-induced nausea as the US: Evidence from a blocking procedure. *Learning and Motivation, 28,* 200–215.

Tait, R. W., & Saladin, M. E. (1986). Concurrent development of excitatory and inhibitory associations during backward conditioning. *Animal Learning & Behavior, 14,* 133–137.

Tang, Y.-P., Shimizu, E., Dube, G. R., Rampon, C., Kerchner, G. A., Zhuo, M., Liu, G., & Tsien, J. Z. (1999). Genetic enhancement of learning and memory in mice. *Nature, 401,* 63–69.

Terrace, H. S. (1979). *Nim.* New York: Knopf.

Terrace, H. S. (1984). Animal cognition. In H. L. Roitblat, T. G. Bever, & H. S. Terrace (Eds.), *Animal cognition* (pp. 7–28). Hillsdale, NJ: Erlbaum.

Terrace, H. S. (1986a). A nonverbal organism's knowledge of ordinal position in a serial learning task. *Journal of Experimental Psychology: Animal Behavior Processes, 12,* 203–214.

Terrace, H. S. (1986b). Positive transfer from sequence production to sequence discrimination in a nonverbal organism. *Journal of Experimental Psychology: Animal Behavior Processes, 12,* 215–234.

Terrace, H. S. (1987). Chunking by a pigeon in a serial learning task. *Nature, 325,* 149–151.

Terrace, H. S., Petitto, L. A., Sanders, R. J., & Bever, T. G. (1979). Can an ape create a sentence? *Science, 206,* 891–1201.

Terry, W. S. (1996). Retroactive interference effects of surprising reward omission on serial spatial memory. *Journal of Experimental Psychology: Animal Behavior Processes, 22,* 472–479.

Theios, J. (1962). The partial reinforcement effect sustained through blocks of continuous reinforcement. *Journal of Experimental Psychology, 64,* 1–6.

Theios, J., & Brelsford, J. (1964). Overlearning-extinction effect as an incentive phenomena. *Journal of Experimental Psychology, 67,* 463–467.

Thomas, B. L., & Papini, M. R. (2001). Adrenalectomy eliminates the extinction spike inn autoshaping with rats. *Physiology & Behavior, 72,* 543–547.

Thomas, D. R. (1993). A model for adaptation-level effects on stimulus generalization. *Psychological Review, 100,* 658–673.

Thomas, D. R., Cook, S. C., & Terrones, J. P. (1990). Conditional discrimination learning by pigeons: The role of simultaneous versus successive stimulus presentations. *Journal of Experimental Psychology: Animal Behavior Processes, 16,* 390–401.

Thomas, D. R., Curran, P. J., & Russell, R. J. (1988). Factors affecting conditional discrimination learning by pigeons: II. Physical and temporal characteristics of stimuli. *Animal Learning & Behavior, 16,* 468–476.

Thomas, D. R., & Empedocles, S. (1992). Novelty vs. retrieval cue value in the study of long-term memory in pigeons. *Journal of Experimental Psychology: Animal Behavior Processes, 18,* 22–23.

Thomas, D. R., McKelvie, A. R., & Mah, W. L. (1985). Context as a conditional cue in operant discrimination reversal learning. *Journal of Experimental Psychology: Animal Behavior Processes, 11,* 317–330.

Thomas, G. V., & Lieberman, D. A. (1990). Commentary: Determinants of success and failure in experiments on marking. *Learning and Motivation, 21,* 110–124.

Thomas, J. R. (1968). Fixed ratio punishment by timeout of concurrent variable-interval behavior. *Journal of the Experimental Analysis of Behavior, 11,* 609–616.

Thompson, C. R., & Church, R. M. (1980). An explanation of the language of a chimpanzee. *Science, 208,* 313–314.

Thompson, R. F. (1986). The neurobiology of learning and memory. *Science, 233,* 941–947.

Thompson, R. F. (1993). *The brain: A neuroscience primer.* New York: W. H. Freeman.

Thompson, R. F., Groves, P. M., Teyler, T. J., & Roemer, R. A. (1973). A dual-process theory of habituation: Theory and behavior. In H. V. S. Peeke & M. J. Herz (Eds.), *Habituation.* New York: Academic Press.

Thompson, R. H., Iwata, B. A., Conners, J., & Roscoe, E. M. (1999). Effects of reinforcement for alternative behavior during punishment of self-injury. *Journal of Applied Behavior Analysis, 32,* 317–328.

Thompson, R. F., & Spencer, W. A. (1966). Habituation: A model phenomenon for the study of neuronal substrates of behavior. *Psychological Review, 73,* 16–43.

Thorndike, E. L. (1898). Animal intelligence: An experimental study of the association processes in animals. *Psychological Review Monograph, 2* (Whole No. 8).

Thorndike, E. L. (1911). *Animal intelligence: Experimental studies.* New York: Macmillan.

Thorndike, E. L. (1932). *The fundamentals of learning.* New York: Teachers College, Columbia University.

Tierney, K. J. (1995). Molar regulatory theory and behavior therapy. In W. O'Donohue & L. Krasnerr (Eds.), *Theories of behavior therapy* (pp. 97–128). Washington, DC: American Psychological Association.

Tierney, K. J., & Bracken, M. (1998). Stimulus equivalence and behavior therapy. In W. O'Donohue (Ed.), *Learning and behavior therapy* (pp. 392–402). Boston: Allyn and Bacon.

Tierney, K. J., Smith, H. V., & Gannon, K. N. (1987). Some tests of molar models of instrumental performance. *Journal of Experimental Psychology: Animal Behavior Processes, 13,* 341–353.

Timberlake, W. (1980). A molar equilibrium theory of learned performance. In G. H. Bower (Ed.), *The psychology of learning and motivation* (Vol. 14, pp. 1–58). New York: Academic Press.

Timberlake, W. (1983a). The functional organization of appetitive behavior: Behavior systems and learning. In M. D. Zeiler & P. Harzem (Eds.), *Advances in analysis of behavior: Vol. 3. Biological factors in learning* (pp. 177–221). Chichester, England: Wiley.

Timberlake, W. (1983b). Rats' responses to a moving object related to food or water: A behavior-systems analysis. *Animal Learning & Behavior, 11,* 309–320.

Timberlake, W. (1984). Behavior regulation and learned performance: Some misapprehensions and disagreements. *Journal of the Experimental Analysis of Behavior, 41,* 355–375.

Timberlake, W. (1990). Natural learning in laboratory paradigms. In D. A. Dewsbury (Ed.), *Contemporary issues in comparative psychology* (pp. 31–54). Sunderland, MA: Sinauer.

Timberlake, W. (1994). Behavior systems, associationism, and Pavlovian conditioning. *Psychonomic Bulletin & Review, 1*(4), 405–420.

Timberlake, W. (1995). Reconceptualizing reinforcement: A causal-system approach to reinforcement and behavior change. In W. O'Donohue & L. Krasnerr (Eds.), *Theories of behavior therapy* (pp. 59–96). Washington, DC: American Psychological Association.

Timberlake, W. (2001). Motivational modes in behavior systems. In R. R. Mowrer & S. B. Klein (Eds.), *Handbook of contemporary learning theories* (pp. 155–209). Mahwah, NJ: Erlbaum.

Timberlake, W., & Allison, J. (1974). Response deprivation: An empirical approach to instrumental performance. *Psychological Review, 81,* 146–164.

Timberlake, W., & Farmer-Dougan, V. A. (1991). Reinforcement in applied settings: Figuring out ahead of time what will work. Psychological Bulletin, 110, *379–391.*

Timberlake, W., & Grant, D. S. (1975). Auto-shaping in rats to the presentation of another rat predicting food. *Science, 190,* 690–692.

Timberlake, W., Leffel, J., & Hoffman, C. M. (1999). Stimulus control and function of arm and wall travel by rats on a radial arm floor maze. *Animal Learning & Behavior, 27,* 445–460.

Timberlake, W., & Lucas, G. A. (1985). The basis of superstitious behavior: Chance contingency, stimulus substitution, or appetitive behavior? *Journal of the Experimental Analysis of Behavior, 44,* 279–299.

Timberlake, W., & Lucas, G. A. (1989). Behavior systems and learning: From misbehavior to general principles. In S. B. Klein & R. R. Mowrer (Eds.), *Contemporary learning theories: Instrumental conditioning and the impact of biological constraints on learning* (pp. 237–275). Hillsdale, NJ: Erlbaum.

Timberlake, W., & Lucas, G. A. (1991). Period water, interwater interval, and adjunctive behavior in a 24–hour multiresponse environment. *Animal Learning & Behavior, 19,* 369–380.

Timberlake, W., Wahl, G., & King, D. (1982). Stimulus and response contingencies in the misbehavior of rats. *Journal of Experimental Psychology: Animal Behavior Processes, 8,* 62–85.

Timberlake, W., & Washburne, D. L. (1989). Feeding ecology and laboratory predatory behavior toward live and artificial moving prey in seven rodent species. *Animal Learning & Behavior, 17,* 2–11.

Timberlake, W., & White, W. (1990). Winning isn't everything: Rats need only food deprivation and not food reward to efficiently traverse a radial arm maze. *Learning and Motivation, 21,* 153–163.

Tinbergen, N. (1951). *The study of instinct.* Oxford: Clarendon Press.

Tinbergen, N., & Perdeck, A. C. (1950). On the stimulus situation releasing the begging response in the newly hatched herring gull chick (*Larus argentatus argentatus Pont.*). *Behaviour, 3,* 1–39.

Todes, D. P. (1997). From the machine to the ghost within: Pavlov's transition from digestive physiology to conditioned reflexes. *American Psychologist, 52,* 947–955.

Tomie, A., Brooks, W., & Zito, B. (1989). Sign-tracking: The search for reward. In S. B. Klein & R. R. Mowrer (Eds.), *Contemporary learning theories: Pavlovian conditioning and the status of learning theory* (pp. 191–223). Hillsdale, NJ: Erlbaum.

Tomie, A., Carelli, R., & Wagner, G. C. (1993). Negative correlation between tone (S–) and water increases target biting during S– in rats. *Animal Learning & Behavior, 21,* 355–359.

Tomsic, D., Pedreira, M. E., Romano, A., Hermitte, G., & Maldonado, H. (1998). Context-US association as a determinant of long-term habituation in the crab *Chasmagnathus. Animal Learning & Behavior, 26,* 196–209.

Tracy, J. A., Ghose, S. S., Stecher, T., McFall, R. M. & Steinmetz, J. E. (1999). Classical conditioning in a nonclinical obsessive-compulsive population. *Psychological Science, 10,* 9–13.

Trenholme, I. A., & Baron, A. (1975). Immediate and delayed punishment of human behavior by loss of reinforcement. *Learning and Motivation, 6,* 62–79.

Turkkan, J. S. (1989). Classical conditioning: The new hegemony. *The Behavioral and Brain Sciences, 12,* 121–179.

Twitmyer, E. B. (1974). A study of the knee jerk. *Journal of Experimental Psychology, 103,* 1047–1066.

Tzeng, O. C. S., & Gomez, M. (1992). Physiological paradigm of love. In O. C. S. Thzeng (Ed.), *Theories of love development, maintenance, and dissolution: Octagonal cycle and differential perspectives* (pp. 102–116). New York: Praeger.

Underwood, B. J. (1957). Interference and forgetting. *Psychological Review, 64,* 49–60.

Ungless, M. A. (1998). A Pavlovian analysis of food-attraction conditioning in the snail *Helix aspersa. Animal Learning & Behavior, 26,* 15–19.

United States Department of Agriculture, National Agricultural Statistics Service, 2001.

United States Department of Health and Human Services. (1996). *Smoking cessation: Clinical practice guideline.* AHCPR Publication No. 96–0692.

Urcuioli, P. J., & DeMarse, T. (1996). Associative processes in differential outcome discriminations. *Journal of Experimental Psychology: Animal Behavior Processes, 22,* 192–204.

Urcuioli, P. J., DeMarse, T. B., & Lionello, K. M. (1999). Sample duration effects on pigeons' delayed matching as a function of predictability of durations. *Journal of the Experimental Analysis of Behavior, 72,* 279–297.

Urcuioli, P. J., & Kasprow, W. J. (1988). Long-delay learning in the T-maze: Effects of marking and delay-interval location. *Learning and Motivation, 19,* 66–86.

Vaughan, W., Jr. (1981). Melioration, matching, and maximizing. *Journal of the Experimental Analysis of Behavior, 36,* 141–149.

Vaughan, W., Jr. (1985). Choice: A local analysis. *Journal of the Experimental Analysis of Behavior, 43,* 383–405.

Vaughan, W., Jr., & Greene, S. L. (1984). Pigeon visual memory capacity. *Journal of Experimental Psychology: Animal Behavior Processes, 10,* 256–271.

Viken, R. J., & McFall, R. M. (1994). Paradox lost: Implications of contemporary reinforcement theory for behavior therapy. *Current Directions in Psychological Science, 4,* 121–125.

Vollmer, T. R., & Bourret, J. (2000). An application of the matching law to evaluate the allocation of two- and three-point shots by college basketball players. *Journal of Applied Behavior Analysis, 33,* 137–150.

von Fersen, L., & Lea, S. E. G. (1990). Category discrimination by pigeons using five polymorphous features. *Journal of the Experimental Analysis of Behavior, 54,* 69–84.

von Fersen, L., Wynne, C. D. L., Delius, J. D., & Staddon, J. E. R. (1991). Transitive inference in pigeons. *Journal of Experimental Psychology: Animal Behavior Processes, 17,* 334–341.

Vyse, S. A., & Belke, T. W. (1992). Maximizing versus matching on concurrent variable-interval schedules. *Journal of the Experimental Analysis of Behavior, 58,* 325–334.

Wagner, A. R. (1961). Effects of amount and percentage of reinforcement and number of acquisition trials on conditioning and extinction. *Journal of Experimental Psychology, 62,* 234–242.

Wagner, A. R. (1976). Priming in STM: An information processing mechanism for self-generated or retrieval generated depression in performance. In T. J. Tighe & R. N. Leaton (Eds.), *Habituation: Perspectives from child development, animal behavior, and neurophysiology* (pp. 95–128). Hillsdale, NJ: Erlbaum.

Wagner, A. R. (1981). SOP: A model of automatic memory processing in animal behavior. In N. E. Spear & R. R. Miller (Eds.), *Information processing in animals: Memory mechanisms* (pp. 5–47). Hillsdale, NJ: Erlbaum.

Wagner, A. R., & Brandon, S. E. (2001). A componential theory of Pavlovian conditioning. In R. R. Mowrer & S. B. Klein (Eds.), *Handbook of contemporary learning theories* (pp. 23–64). Mahwah, NJ: Erlbaum.

Wagner, A. R., Logan, F. A., Haberlandt, K., & Price, T. (1968). Stimulus selection in animal discrimination learning. *Journal of Experimental Psychology, 76,* 171–180.

Wagner, A. R., & Rescorla, R. A. (1972). Inhibition in Pavlovian conditioning: Application of a theory. In R. A. Boakes & M. S. Halliday (Eds.), *Inhibition and learning.* London: Academic Press.

Wagner, A. R., Rudy, J. W., & Whitlow, J. W. (1973). Rehearsal in animal conditioning. *Journal of Experimental Psychology, 97,* 407–426.

Walters, E. T. (1994). Injury related behavior and neuronal plasticity: An evolutionary perspective on sensitization, hyperalgesia, and analgesia. *International Review of Neurobiology, 36,* 325–427.

Walters, G. C., & Glazer, R. D. (1971). Punishment of instinctive behavior in the Mongolian gerbil. *Journal of Comparative and Physiological Psychology, 75,* 331–340.

Walters, G. C., & Grusec, J. F. (1977). *Punishment.* San Francisco: W. H. Freeman.

Ward-Robinson, J., & Hall, G. (1996). Backward sensory preconditioning. *Journal of Experimental Psychology: Animal Behavior Processes, 22,* 395–404.

Ward-Robinson, J., & Hall, G. (1998). Backward sensory preconditioning when reinforcement is delayed. *Quarterly Journal of Experimental Psychology, 51,* 349–362.

Ward-Robinson, J., & Hall, G. (1999). The role of mediated conditioning in acquired equivalence. *Quarterly Journal of Experimental Psychology, 52B,* 335–350.

Wasserman, E. A. (1986). Prospection and retrospection as processes of animal short-term memory. In D. F. Kendrick, M. E. Rilling, & M. R. Denny (Eds.), *Theories of animal memory* (pp. 53–75). Hillsdale, NJ: Erlbaum.

Wasserman, E. A. (1990). Detecting response-outcome relations: Toward an understanding of the causal texture of the environment. In G. H. Bower (Ed.), *The psychology of learning and motivation* (Vol. 26, pp. 27–82). San Diego, CA: Academic Press.

Wasserman, E. A. (1993). Comparative cognition: Beginning the second century of the study of animal intelligence. *Psychological Bulletin, 113,* 211–228.

Wasserman, E. A., & Astley, S. L. (1994). A behavioral analysis of concepts: Its application to pigeons and children. In D. L. Medin (Ed.), *The psychology of learning and motivation* (Vol. 31, pp. 73–132). San Diego: Academic Press.

Wasserman, E. A., DeLong, R. E., & Larew, M. B. (1984). Temporal order and duration: Their discrimination and retention by pigeons. *Annals of the New York Academy of Sciences, 423,* 103–115.

Wasserman, E. A., Franklin, S. R., & Hearst, E. (1974). Pavlovian appetitive contingencies and approach versus withdrawal to conditioned stimuli in pigeons. *Journal of Comparative and Physiological Psychology, 86,* 616–627.

Wasserman, E. A., Kiedinger, R. E., & Bhatt, R. S. (1988). Conceptual behavior in pigeons: Categories, subcategories, and pseudocategories. *Journal of Experimental Psychology: Animal Behavior Processes, 14,* 235–246.

Wasserman, E. A., & Miller, R. R. (1997). What's elementary about associative learning? *Annual Review of Psychology, 48,* 573–607.

Watanabe, S., Sakamoto, J., & Wakita, M. (1995). Pigeons' discrimination of paintings by Monet and Picasso. *Journal of the Experimental Analysis of Behavior, 63,* 165–174.

Watson, J. B., & Rayner, R. (1920). Conditioned emotional reactions. *Journal of Experimental Psychology, 3,* 1–14. Reprinted in *American Psychologist, 55,* 313–317.

Wearden, J. H., & Burgess, I. S. (1982). Matching since Baum (1979). *Journal of the Experimental Analysis of Behavior, 38,* 339–348.

Wearden, J. H., & Clark, R. B. (1988). Interresponse-time reinforcement and behavior under aperiodic reinforcement schedules: A case study using computer modeling. *Journal of Experimental Psychology: Animal Behavior Processes, 14,* 200–211.

Wearden, J. H., & Ferrara, A. (1996). Stimulus range effects in temporal bisection by humans. *Quarterly Journal of Experimental Psychology, 49B,* 24–44.

Wearden, J. H., & McShane, B. (1988). Interval production as an analogue of the peak procedure: Evidence for similarity of human and animal timing processes. *Quarterly Journal of Experimental Psychology, 40B,* 363–375.

Wearden, J. H., & Penton-Voak, I. S. (1995). Feeling the heat: Body temperature and the rate of subjective time, revisited. *The Quarterly Journal of Experimental Psychology, 48B,* 129–141.

Weavers, R., Foster, T. M., & Temple, W. (1998). Reinforcer efficacy in a delayed matching-to-sample task. *Journal of the Experimental Analysis of Behavior, 69,* 77–85.

Wegner, D. M., & Wheatley, T. (1999). Apparent mental causation: Sources of the experience of will. *American Psychologist, 54,* 480–492.

Weinberger, N. (1965). Effect of detainment on extinction of avoidance responses. *Journal of Comparative and Physiological Psychology, 60,* 135–138.

Weisman, R. G., & Litner, J. S. (1972). The role of Pavlovian events in avoidance training. In R. A. Boakes & M. S. Halliday (Eds.), *Inhibition and learning.* London: Academic Press.

Weisman, R. G., & Premack, D. (1966). *Reinforcement and punishment produced by the same response depending upon the probability relation between the instrumental and contingent responses.* Paper presented at the meeting of the Psychonomic Society, St. Louis.

Weiss, S. J., Kearns, D. N., Cohn, S. I., Schindler, C. W., & Panlilio, L. V. (in press). Stimulus control of cocaine self-administration. *Journal of the Experimental Analysis of Behavior.*

Weiss, S. J., & Panlilio, L. V. (1999). Blocking a selective association in pigeons. *Journal of the Experimental Analysis of Behavior, 71,* 13–24.

Weiss, S. J., Panlilio, L. V., & Schindler, C. W. (1993a). Selective associations produced solely with appetitive contingencies: The stimulus-reinforcer interaction revisited. *Journal of the Experimental Analysis of Behavior, 59,* 309–322.

Weiss, S. J., Panlilio, L. V., & Schindler, C. W. (1993b). Single-incentive selective associations produced solely as a function of compound-stimulus conditioning context. *Journal of Experimental Psychology: Animal Behavior Processes, 19,* 284–294.

Weiss, S. J., & Schindler, C. W. (1981). Generalization peak shift in rats under conditions of positive reinforcement and avoidance. *Journal of the Experimental Analysis of Behavior, 35,* 175–185.

Weiss, S. J., & Weissman, R. D. (1992). Generalization peak shift for autoshaped and operant key pecks. *Journal of the Experimental Analysis of Behavior, 57,* 27–143.

Wernig, A., Muller, S., Nanassy, A., & Cagol, E. (1995). Laufband therapy based on "rules of spinal locomotion" is effective in spinal cord injured persons. *European Journal of Neuroscience, 7,* 823–829.

Westbrook, R. F., Jones, M. L., Bailey, G. K., & Harris, J. A. (2000). Contextual control over conditioned responding in a latent inhibition paradigm. *Journal of Experimental Psychology: Animal Behavior Processes, 26,* 157–173.

White, K. G. (2001). Forgetting functions. *Animal Learning and Behavior, 29,* 193–207.

White, K. G., & Wixted, J. T. (1999). Psychophysics of remembering. *Journal of the Experimental Analysis of Behavior, 71,* 91–113.

Whitlow, J. W., Jr., & Wagner, A. R. (1984). Memory and habituation. In H. V. S. Peeke & L. Petrinovich (Eds.), *Habituation, sensitization, and behavior.* New York: Academic Press.

Wilkie, D. M., & Slobin, P. (1983). Gerbils in space: Performance on the 17–arm radial maze. *Journal of the Experimental Analysis of Behavior, 40,* 301–312.

Wilkie, D. M., & Summers, R. J. (1982). Pigeons' spatial memory: Factors affecting delayed matching of key location. *Journal of the Experimental Analysis of Behavior, 37,* 45–56.

Wilkie, D. M., Willson, R. J., & Kardal, S. (1989). Pigeons discriminate pictures of a geographic location. *Animal Learning & Behavior, 17,* 163–171.

Williams, A. M., & Lattal, K. A. (1999). The role of the response-reinforcer relation in delay-of-reinforcement effects. *Journal of the Experimental Analysis of Behavior, 71,* 187–194.

Williams, B. A. (1983). Another look at contrast in multiple schedules. *Journal of the Experimental Analysis of Behavior, 39,* 345–384.

Williams, B. A. (1988). Reinforcement, choice, and response strength. In R. C. Atkinson, R. J. Herrnstein, G. Lindzey, & R. D. Luce (Eds.), *Stevens' handbook of experimental psychology: Vol. 2. Learning and cognition* (pp. 167–244) New York: Wiley.

Williams, B. A. (1990). Pavlovian contingencies and anticipatory contrast. *Animal Learning & Behavior, 18,* 44–50.

Williams, B. A. (1991). Marking and bridging versus conditioned reinforcement. *Animal Learning & Behavior, 19,* 264–269.

Williams, B. A. (1992a). Dissociation of theories of choice via temporal spacing of choice opportunities. *Journal of Experimental Psychology: Animal Behavior Processes, 18,* 287–297.

Williams, B. A. (1992b). Inverse relations between preference and contrast. *Journal of the Experimental Analysis of Behavior, 58,* 303–312.

Williams, B. A. (1993). Molar versus local reinforcement probability as determinants of stimulus value. *Journal of the Experimental Analysis of Behavior, 59,* 163–172.

Williams, B. A. (1994a). Conditioned reinforcement: Neglected or outmoded explanatory construct? *Psychonomic Bulletin & Review, 1,* 457–475.

Williams, B. A. (1994b). Reinforcement and choice. In N. J. Mackintosh (Ed.), *Animal learning and cognition* (pp. 81–108). San Diego: Academic Press.

Williams, B. A. (1997a). Conditioned reinforcement dynamics in three-link chained schedules. *Journal of the Experimental Analysis of Behavior, 67,* 145–159.

Williams, B. A. (1997b). Varieties of contrast: A review of *Incentive relativity* by Charles F. Flaherty. *Journal of the Experimental Analysis of Behavior, 68,* 133–141.

Williams, D. A., Butler, M. M., & Overmier, J. B. (1990). Expectancies of reinforcer location and quality as cues for a conditional discrimination in pigeons. *Journal of Experimental Psychology: Animal Behavior Processes, 16,* 3–13.

Williams, D. A., & Hurlburt, J. L. (2000). Mechanisms of second-order conditioning with a backward conditioned stimulus. *Journal of Experimental Psychology: Animal Behavior Processes, 26,* 340–351.

Williams, D. A., & Overmier, J. B. (1988a). Backward inhibitory conditioning with signaled and unsignaled unconditioned stimuli: Distribution of trials across days and intertrial interval. *Journal of Experimental Psychology: Animal Behavior Processes, 14,* 26–35.

Williams, D. A., & Overmier, J. B. (1988b). Some types of conditioned inhibitors carry collateral excitatory associations. *Learning and Motivation, 19,* 345–368.

Williams, D. A., Overmier, J. B., & LoLordo, V. M. (1992). A reevaluation of Rescorla's early dictums about Pavlovian conditioned inhibition. *Psychological Bulletin, 111,* 275–290.

Williams, D. A., & Sly, C. A. (1999). Recovery of conditioned suppression after backward pairings. *Animal Learning & Behavior, 27,* 152–167.

Willis, W. D. (2001). Mechanisms of central sensitization of nociceptive dorsal horn neurons. In M. M. Patterson & J. W. Grau (Eds.), *Spinal cord plasticity: Alterations in reflex function* (pp. 127–161). Boston: Kluwer Academic Publishers.

Wills, S., & Mackintosh, N. J. (1998). Peak shift on an artificial dimension. *Quarterly Journal of Experimental Psychology, 51B,* 1–31.

Willson, R. J., & Wilkie, D. M. (1991). Discrimination training facilitates pigeons' performance on one-trial-per-day delayed matching of key location. *Journal of the Experimental Analysis of Behavior, 55,* 201–212.

Wilson, S. W. (1991). The animal path to AI. In J. A. Meyer & S. W. Wilson (Eds.), *From animals to animats: Proceedings of the first international conference on simulation of adaptive behavior.* Cambridge, MA: MIT Press.

Winter, J., & Perkins, C. C. (1982). Immediate reinforcement in delayed reward learning in pigeons *Journal of the Experimental Analysis of Behavior, 38,* 169–179.

Witcher, E. S., & Ayres, J. J. B. (1984). A test of two methods for extinguishing Pavlovian conditioned inhibition. *Animal Learning & Behavior, 12,* 149–156.

Wolpe, J. (1990). *The practice of behavior therapy* (4th ed.). New York: Pergamon.

Woodworth, R. S., & Schlosberg, H. (1954). *Experimental psychology.* New York: Holt, Rinehart and Winston.

Wright, A. A. (1990). Markov choice processes in simultaneous matching-to-sample at different levels of discriminability. *Animal Learning & Behavior, 18,* 277– 286.

Wright, A. A. (1992). Learning mechanisms in matching to sample. *Journal of Experimental Psychology: Animal Behavior Processes, 18,* 67–79.

Wright, A. A. (1997). Concept learning and learning strategies. *Psychological Science, 8,* 119–123.

Wright, A. A., Cook, R. G., Rivera, J. J., Sands, S. F., & Delius, J. D. (1988). Concept learning by pigeons: Matching-to-sample with trial-unique video picture stimuli. *Animal Learning & Behavior, 16,* 436–444.

Wright, A. A., & Delius, J. D. (1994). Scratch and match: Pigeons learn matching and oddity with gravel stimuli. *Journal of Experimental Psychology: Animal Behavior Processes, 20,* 108–112.

Wright, A. A., Shyan, M. R., & Jitsumori, M. (1990). Auditory same/different concept learning by monkeys. *Animal Learning & Behavior, 18,* 287–294.

Wright, A. A., & Sands, S. F. (1981). A model of detection and decision processes during matching to sample by pigeons: Performance with 88 different wavelengths in delayed and simultaneous matching tasks. *Journal of Experimental Psychology: Aminal Behavior Process, 7,* 191–216.

Wynne, C. D. L., Staddon, J. E. R., & Delius, J. D. (1996). Dynamics of waiting in pigeons. *Journal of the Experimental Analysis of Behavior, 65,* 603–618.

Yerkes, R. M., & Morgulis, S. (1909). The method of Pavlov in animal psychology. *Psychological Bulletin, 6,* 257–273.

Yin, H., Barnet, R. C., & Miller, R. R. (1994). Second-order conditioning and Pavlovian conditioned inhibition: Operational similarities and differences. *Journal of Experimental Psychology: Animal Behavior Processes, 20,* 419–428.

Zamble, E., Hadad, G. M., Mitchell, J. B., & Cutmore, T. R. H. (1985). Pavlovian conditioning of sexual arousal: First- and second-order effects. *Journal of Experimental Psychology: Animal Behavior Processes, 11,* 598–610.

Zarcone, T. J., & Ator, N. A. (2000). Drug discrimination: stimulus control during repeated testing in extinction. *Journal of the Experimental Analysis of Behavior, 74,* 283–294.

Zarcone, T. J., Branch, M. N., Hughes, C. E., & Pennypacker, H. S. (1997). Key pecking during extinction after intermittent or continuous reinforcement as a function of the number of reinforcers delivered during training. *Journal of the Experimental Analysis of Behavior, 67,* 91–108.

Zeiler, M. D. (1984). The sleeping giant: Reinforcement schedules. *Journal of the Experimental Analysis of Behavior, 42,* 485–493.

Zeiler, M. D. (1999). Time without clocks. *Journal of the Experimental Analysis of Behavior, 72,* 288–292.

Zentall, T. R. (Ed.). (1993). *Animal cognition.* Hillsdale, NJ: Erlbaum.

Zentall, T. R. (1998). Symbolic representation in animals: Emergent stimulus relations in conditional discrimination learning. *Animal Learning & Behavior, 26,* 363–377.

Zentall, T. R. (2001). The case for a cognitive approach to animal learning and behavior. *Behavioural Processes, 54,* 65–78.

Zentall, T. R., Edwards, C. A., Moore, B. S., & Hogan, D. E. (1981). Identity: The basis for both matching and oddity learning in pigeons. *Journal of Experimental Psychology: Animal Behavior Processes, 7,* 70–86.

Zentall, T. R., Jagielo, J. A., Jackson-Smith, P. & Urcuioli, P. J. (1987). Memory codes in pigeon short-term memory: Effects of varying the number of sample and comparison stimuli. *Learning and Motivation, 18,* 21–33.

Zentall, T. R., Roper, K. L., Kaiser, D. H., & Sherburne, L. M. (1997). A critical analysis of directed-forgetting research in animals. In J. M. Golding & C. MacLeod (Eds.), *Interdisciplinary approaches to intentional forgetting* (pp. 265–287). Hillsdale, NJ: Erlbaum.

Zentall, T. R., Roper, K. L., & Sherburne, L. M. (1995). Most directed forgetting in pigeons can be attributed to the absence of reinforcement of forget trials during training or to other procedural artifacts. *Journal of the Experimental Analysis of Behavior, 63,* 127–137.

Zentall, T. R., & Sherburne, L. M. (1994). Transfer of value from S+ to S– in a simultaneous discrimination. *Journal of Experimental Psychology: Animal Behavior Processes, 20,* 176–183.

Zentall, T. R., & Smeets, P. M. (Eds.). (1996). *Stimulus class formation in humans and animals. Advances in Psychology* Vol. 117. New York: North-Holland (Elsevier Science).

Zentall, T. R., Steirn, J. N., & Jackson-Smith, P. (1990). Memory strategies in pigeons' performance of a radial-arm-maze analog task. *Journal of Experimental Psychology: Animal Behavior Processes, 16,* 358–371.

Zentall, T. R., Urcuioli, P. J., Jagielo, J. A., & Jackson-Smith, P. (1989). Interaction of sample dimension and sample comparison mapping on pigeons' performance of delayed conditional discriminations. *Animal Learning & Behavior, 17,* 172–178.

Zentall, T. R., Weaver, J. E., & Sherburne, L. M. (1996). Value transfer in concurrent-schedule discriminations by pigeons. *Animal Learning & Behavior, 24,* 401–409.

Zhou, Y., & Riccio, D. C. (1995). Concussion-induced retrograde amnesia in rats. *Physiology & Behavior, 57,* 1107–1115.

Zhou, Y., & Riccio, D. C. (1996). Manipulation of components of context: The context shift effect and forgetting of stimulus attributes. *Learning and Motivation, 27,* 400–407.

Zhuikov, A. Y., Couvillon, P. A., & Bitterman, M. E. (1994). Quantitative two-process analysis of avoidance conditioning in goldfish. *Journal of Experimental Psychology: Animal Behavior Processes, 20,* 32–43.

Zimmer-Hart, C. L., & Rescorla, R. A. (1974). Extinction of Pavlovian conditioned inhibition. *Journal of Comparative and Physiological Psychology, 86,* 837–845.

Zoladek, L., & Roberts, W. A. (1978). The sensory basis of spatial memory in the rat. *Animal Learning & Behavior, 6,* 77–81.

NAME INDEX

SUBJECT INDEX

PHOTO CREDITS

Chapter 1: 4, Bettmann / CORBIS **8,** Sovfoto **10,** Bettmann / CORBIS **20,** Robert W. Allan, Lafayette College **Chapter 2: 31,** Courtesy of Allen Zak **33,** Courtesy of G. P. Baerends **51,** Courtesy of Donald A. Dewsbury **Chapter 3: 62,** Bettmann Archive **65,** Courtesy of the author **67,** Courtesy of I. Gormezano **73,** Courtesy of Donald A. Dewsbury **82,** Courtesy of Donald A. Dewsbury **87,** Courtesy of Donald A. Dewsbury **88,** Courtesy of Donald A. Dewsbury **Chapter 4: 102,** Courtesy of Donald A. Dewsbury **107,** Courtesy of C. K. Akins **110,** Courtesy of L. J. Kamin **112,** Courtesy of Donald A. Dewsbury **117,** Courtesy of Donald A. Dewsbury **118,** Courtesy of J. Gibbon **119,** top, Courtesy of M. Burns; bottom, Courtesy of Donald A. Dewsbury **120,** Courtesy of R. R. Miller **Chapter 5: 130,** Bettmann Archive **131,** Omikron / Photo Researchers, Inc. **138,** Courtesy of A. Neuringer **140,** Courtesy of Donald A. Dewsbury **141,** top, Animal Behavior Enterprises; bottom, Courtesy of Courtesy of Donald A. Dewsbury **144,** Courtesy of Donald A. Dewsbury **145,** Courtesy of Donald A. Dewsbury **147,** Courtesy of D. A. Lieberman **150,** Courtesy of Donald A. Dewsbury **153,** top, Courtesy of Donald A. Dewsbury; bottom, Courtesy of M. E. P. Seligman **155,** Courtesy of N. K. Dess **156,** Courtesy of UCLA Department of Psychology **Chapter 6: 174,** Courtesy of Donald A. Dewsbury **176,** Courtesy of W. M. Baum **179,** Courtesy of B. A. Williams **184,** top, Courtesy of Donald A. Dewsbury; bottom, Courtesy of L. Green **185,** Courtesy of A.W. Logue **Chapter 7: 204,** top, Courtesy of W. Timberlake; bottom, Courtesy of J. Allison **Chapter 8: 224,** Courtesy of the author **225,** Courtesy of Donald A. Dewsbury **229,** Courtesy of Donald A. Dewsbury **240,** Courtesy of Donald A. Dewsbury **Chapter 9: 272,** Courtesy of A. Amsel **273:** Courtesy of E. J. Capaldi **Chapter 10: 283,** Courtesy of Donald A. Dewsbury **288,** Courtesy of Donald A. Dewsbury **295,** Courtesy of Donald A. Dewsbury **298,** Courtesy of Donald A. Dewsbury **300,** Courtesy of UCLA Department of Psychology **302,** Courtesy of N. H. Azrin **Chapter 11: 322,** Courtesy of D. S. Grant **324,** Courtesy of M. Spetch **325,** Courtesy of Donald A. Dewsbury **327,** Courtesy of Catherine Green, from Patricia Sharp Lab, Department of Psychology, Yale University **334,** Courtesy of Dr. D. M. Wilkie **336,** Courtesy of P. Urcuioli **338,** Courtesy of T. Zentall **342,** Courtesy of C. Rovee-Collier **343,** top, Courtesy of N.E. Spear; bottom, Courtesy of W. C. Gordon **347,** Courtesy of D. C. Riccio **Chapter 12: 360,** Courtesy of R. M. Church **363,** Arizona State University photo **366,** Courtesy of Donald A. Dewsbury **370,** Courtesy of E. A. Wasserman **376,** Courtesy of I. M. Pepperberg **378,** Courtesy of Duane Rumbaugh, Language Research Center, Georgia State University **379,** Courtesy of Duane Rumbaugh, Language Research Center, Georgia State University **383,** Courtesy of Duane Rumbaugh, Language Research Center, Georgia State University

TO THE OWNER OF THIS BOOK:

I hope that you have found *The Principles of Learning and Behavior*, Fifth Edition, useful. So that this book can be improved in a future edition, would you take the time to complete this sheet and return it? Thank you.

School and address: ____

Department: ____

Instructor's name: ____

1. What I like most about this book is: ____

____

____

2. What I like least about this book is: ____

____

____

3. My general reaction to this book is: ____

____

4. The name of the course in which I used this book is: ______________________________

____

5. Were all of the chapters of the book assigned for you to read? ____________________

If not, which ones weren't? ____

6. In the space below, or on a separate sheet of paper, please write specific suggestions for improving this book and anything else you'd care to share about your experience in using the book.

____

____

____

____

Optional:

Your name: ______________________________ Date: ______________________________

May Wadsworth quote you, either in promotion for *The Principles of Learning and Behavior,* Fifth Edition, or in future publishing ventures?

Yes: __________ No: __________

Sincerely,

Michael Domjan

FOLD HERE

NO POSTAGE
NECESSARY
IF MAILED
IN THE
UNITED STATES

BUSINESS REPLY MAIL

FIRST CLASS PERMIT NO. 358 PACIFIC GROVE, CA

POSTAGE WILL BE PAID BY ADDRESSEE

ATT: *Michael Domjan*

Wadsworth
511 Forest Lodge Road
Pacific Grove, California 93950-9968

FOLD HERE

Habituation

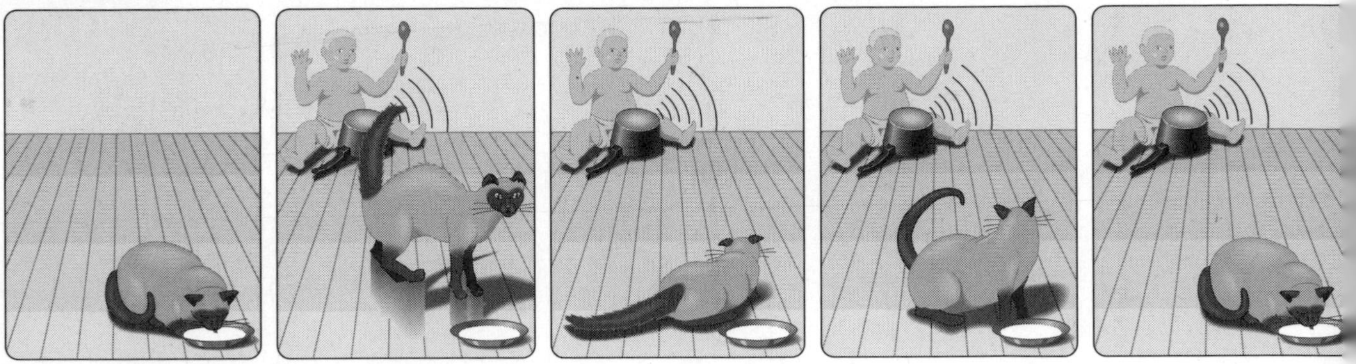

Banging on the pot startles the cat at first and disrupts its drinking.
After the startle response has become habituated, the cat resumes drinking.

Classical conditioning

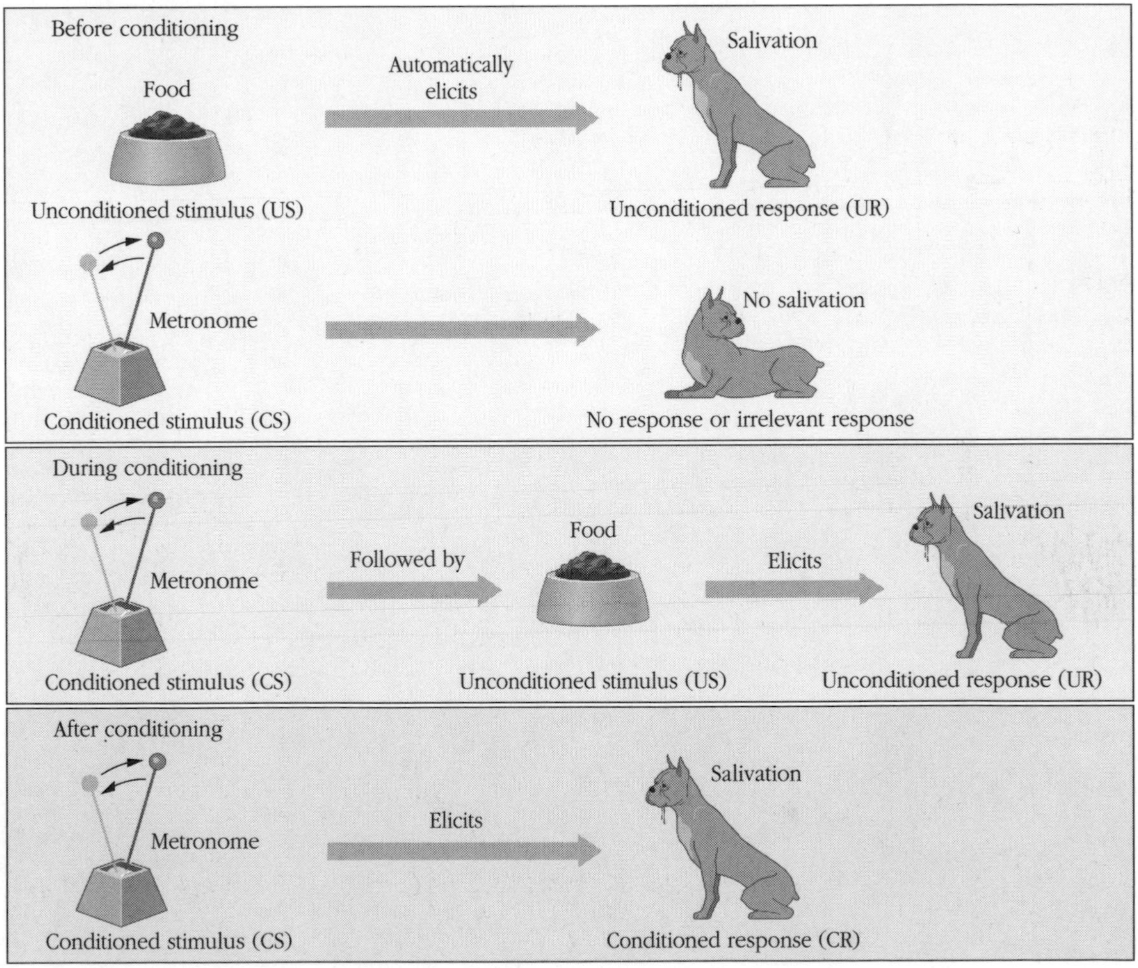

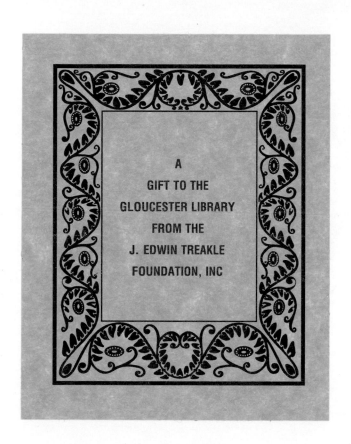

THE

WILD ROSE

ALSO BY JENNIFER DONNELLY

The Tea Rose

The Winter Rose

A Northern Light

Revolution

THE

WILD ROSE

JENNIFER DONNELLY

HYPERION

NEW YORK

Library of Congress Cataloging-in-Publication Data

Donnelly, Jennifer.
The wild rose / Jennifer Donnelly. — 1st ed.
p. cm.
ISBN 978-1-4013-0104-0
1. World War, 1914–1918—England—Fiction.
2. Upper class families—England—Fiction.
3. Domestic fiction. I. Title.
PS3604.O563W55 2011
813'.6—dc22
2011013278

Hyperion books are available for special promotions and premiums. For details contact the HarperCollins Special Markets Department in the New York office at 212-207-7528, fax 212-207-7222, or email spsales@harpercollins.com.

Design by Fritz Metsch

FIRST EDITION
10 9 8 7 6 5 4 3 2 1

SUSTAINABLE FORESTRY INITIATIVE
Certified Fiber Sourcing
www.sfiprogram.org

THIS LABEL APPLIES TO TEXT STOCK

We try to produce the most beautiful books possible, and we are also extremely concerned about the impact of our manufacturing process on the forests of the world and the environment as a whole. Accordingly, we've made sure that all of the paper we use has been certified as coming from forests that are managed, to ensure the protection of the people and wildlife dependent upon them.

FOR

SIMON LIPSKAR

AND

MAJA NIKOLIC

It is not the mountain we conquer, but ourselves.

—SIR EDMUND HILLARY

THE

WILD ROSE

PROLOGUE

August 1913—Tibet

DID ALL ENGLISH girls make love like a man? Or was it only this one?

Max von Brandt, a German mountaineer, wondered this as he stroked the hair out of the face of the young woman lying next to him in the dark. He'd been with many women. Soft, pliant women, who clung to him afterward, extorting promises and endearments. This woman wasn't soft, and neither was her lovemaking. It was hard and quick and without preliminaries. And when it was over, as it was now, she would turn away, curl into herself, and sleep.

"I don't suppose there is anything I can say. To make you stay with me," he said.

"No, Max, there isn't."

He lay on his back in the dark, listening as her breath slowed and deepened, as she drifted off to sleep. He couldn't sleep. He didn't want to. He wanted to make this night last. To remember it always. He wanted to remember the feel of her, the smell of her. The sound of the wind. The piercing cold.

He had told her he loved her. Weeks ago. And he'd meant it. For the first time in his life, he'd meant it. She'd laughed. And then, seeing that she'd hurt him, she'd kissed him and shaken her head no.

The night passed quickly. Before the sun rose, the woman did. As Max stared ahead of himself, into the darkness, she dressed, then quietly left their tent.

He never found her beside him when he woke. She always left the tent or cave or whatever shelter they'd found while it was still dark. He'd searched for her in the beginning, and always he'd found her perched somewhere high, somewhere solitary and still, her face lifted to the dawn sky and its fading stars.

"What are you looking for?" he would ask, following her gaze.

"Orion," she would answer.

In only a few hours, he would say good-bye to her. In the time he had left, he would think of their first days together, for it was those memories he would hold on to.

They'd met about four months ago. He'd been traveling in Asia for five months prior. A renowned Alpine climber, he'd decided he wanted to see the Himalayas. To see if it was possible to conquer Everest; to take the world's highest mountain for Germany, for the fatherland. The kaiser wanted conquests, and better to satisfy him with a beautiful mountain in Asia than a wretched war in Europe. He'd left Berlin for India, traveled north through that country, then quietly entered Nepal, a country closed to Westerners.

He'd made it all the way to Kathmandu before he was apprehended by Nepalese authorities and told to leave. He promised he would, but he needed help, he told them; a guide. He needed someone to take him through the high valleys of the Solu Khumbu and into Tibet over the Nangpa La pass. From there he wanted to trek east, exploring the northern base of Everest on his way to Lhasa, the City of God, where he hoped to ask permission of the Dalai Lama to climb. He had heard about a place called Rongbuk, and hoped he might find an approach there. He'd heard of one who might be able to help him—a woman, another Westerner. Did they know anything about her?

The authorities said that they did know her, though they had not seen her in several months. He gave them presents: rubies and sapphires he'd bought in Jaipur, pearls, a large emerald. In return, they gave him permission to wait for her. For a month.

Max had first heard of the woman when he'd arrived in Bombay. Western climbers he'd met there told him of her—an English girl who lived in the shadow of the Himalayas. She'd climbed Kilimanjaro—the Mawenzi peak—and had lost a leg on Kili in a horrible accident. She'd almost died there. Now, they said, she was photographing and mapping the Himalayas. She was trekking as high as she could, but the difficult climbs were beyond her. She lived among the mountain people now. She was strong like them, and had earned their respect and their liking. She did what almost no European could—moved over borders with goodwill, receiving hospitality from Nepalese and Tibetans alike.

But how to find her? Rumors abounded. She had been in China and India, but was in Tibet now, some said. No, Burma. No, Afghanistan. She was surveying for the British. Spying for the French. She'd died in an avalanche. She'd gone native. She'd taken a Nepalese husband. She traded horses. Yaks. Gold. He heard more talk as he made his way northeast across India. In Agra. Kanpur. And then, finally, he'd found her. In Kathmandu. Or at least he'd found a hut she used.

"She's in the mountains," a villager told him. "She'll come."

"When?"

"Soon. Soon."

Days passed. Then weeks. A month. The Nepalese were growing impatient. They wanted him gone. He asked the villagers again and again when she was coming, and always he was told soon. He thought it must be a ruse by the wily farmer with whom he was staying to get a few more coins out of him.

And then she'd arrived. He'd thought her a Nepalese at first. She was dressed in indigo trousers and a long sheepskin jacket. Her shrewd green eyes were large in her angular face. They assessed him from beneath the furry fringe of her cap. Turquoise beads hung from her neck and dangled from her ears. She wore her hair in a long braid ornamented with bits of silver and glass as the native women did. Her face was bronzed by the Himalayan sun. Her body was wiry and strong. She walked with a limp. He found out, later, that she wore a false l- made of yak bone, carved and hollowed for her by a villager.

"*Namaste,*" she'd said to him, bowing her head slightly, a- farmer had told her what he wanted.

Namaste. It was a Nepalese greeting. It meant: The me bows to the light within you.

He'd told her he wished to hire her to take him into Tibet. She told him she'd just returned from Shigatse and was tired. She would sleep first, then eat, and then they would discuss it.

The next day she prepared him a meal of rice and curried mutton, with strong black tea. He'd sat with her on the rug-covered floor of her hut and they'd talked, sharing a pipeful of opium. It killed the pain, she said. He'd thought then that she was referring to her damaged leg, but later he realized that the pain she spoke of went much deeper, and the opium she smoked did little to dull it. Sadness enfolded her like a long black cape.

He was astonished by the depth and breadth of her knowledge of the Himalayas. She had surveyed, mapped, and photographed more of the range than any Westerner had ever done. She kept herself by guiding and by publishing papers on the topography of the mountains for Britain's Royal Geographical Society. The RGS would soon publish a book of her Himalayan photographs, too. Max had seen some of them. They were astonishingly good. They captured the fierce magnificence of the mountains, their beauty and cold indifference, like no other images ever had. She never went to the RGS in person, for she would not leave her beloved mountains. Instead she sent her work to be presented there by Sir Clements Markham, the RGS's president.

Max had exclaimed over her photographs and the precision of her maps, amazed by both. She was younger than he—only twenty-nine—and yet she'd accomplished so much. She had shrugged his praise off, saying there was so much more to do, but she couldn't do it—couldn't get high enough to do it—because of her leg.

"But you've had to climb in order to do this much," he said.

"Not so high, really. And not on anything tricky. No ice fields. No cliffs or crevasses," she replied.

"But, it's all tricky," he said. "How do you climb at all? Without . . . without both legs, I mean."

"I climb with my heart," she replied. "Can you?"

When he had proved to her that he could do that, that he could climb with love and awe and respect for the mountains, she agreed to take him to Lhasa. They'd left Kathmandu with two yaks to carry a tent and supplies, and had trekked through mountain villages and valleys and passes that only she and a handful of sherpas knew. It was hard and exhausting and unspeakably beautiful. It was brutally cold, too. They slept close to each other in a tent, under skins for warmth. On the third night of the trek he told her he loved her. She laughed and he'd turned away, upset. He'd meant it, and his pride had been deeply wounded by her rejection.

"I'm sorry," she said, placing a hand on his back. "I'm sorry, I can't . . ."

He asked if there was someone else and she said yes, and then she took him in her arms. For comfort and warmth, for pleasure, but not for love. It was the first time in his life his heart had been broken.

They'd arrived three weeks ago at a bleak Tibetan village at the base of Everest—Rongbuk, where she lived. They waited there while the woman, who was known and well connected, used her influence to get him papers from Tibetan officials which would allow him to enter Lhasa. He stayed with her in her house—a small whitewashed stone structure, with a smaller building tacked on that she used to house her animals.

She'd taken photographs during those days. Once he'd seen her try to climb. She attempted an ice field when she thought he wasn't watching, with her camera strapped to her back. She was not bad even with only one leg. But then she suddenly stopped dead and did not move for a solid ten minutes. He saw her struggling with herself. "Damn you!" she suddenly screamed. "Damn you! Damn you!" until he feared she would start an avalanche. At whom was she yelling? he wondered. At the mountain? Herself? At someone else?

His papers had finally come through. The day after he received them, he and the woman left Rongbuk with a tent and five yaks. Yesterday, they'd reached the outskirts of Lhasa. It had been their last day together. Last night, their last night. In a few hours, he would begin the trek to the holy city alone. He planned to stay for some months, studying and photographing Lhasa and its inhabitants, while he tried to obtain an audience with the Dalai Lama. He knew his chances were slim. The Dalai Lama tolerated one Westerner—the woman. It was said that on occasion he would drink with her, sing Tibetan songs with her, and swap bawdy stories. She was not going into Lhasa this time, however. She wanted to get back to Rongbuk.

Max wondered now, as he rose in the cold gray dawn, if he would ever see her again. He quickly dressed, packed a few things into his rucksack, buttoned his jacket, and walked out of the tent. Four yaks, presents for the governor of Lhasa, were stamping and snorting, their breath white in the morning air, but the woman was nowhere to be seen.

He looked around and finally spotted her sitting on a large, jutting rock, silhouetted against the sky. She sat still and alone, one knee hugged to her chest, her face lifted to the fading stars. He would leave now. With morning breaking. With this image of her forever in his mind.

"*Namaste*, Willa Alden," he whispered, touching his steepled hands to his forehead. "*Namaste*."

Part One

MARCH
1914

LONDON

CHAPTER ONE

"AUNT EDDIE, STOP! You can't go in there!"

Seamus Finnegan, sprawled naked across his bed, opened one eye. He knew that voice. It belonged to Albie Alden, his best friend.

"For heaven's sake, why not?"

"Because he's asleep! You can't just barge in on a sleeping man. It's not decent!"

"Oh, bosh."

Seamie knew that voice, too. He sat up, grabbed the bedcovers, and pulled them up to his chin.

"Albie! Do something!" he yelled.

"I tried, old chap. You're on your own," Albie shouted back.

A second later, a small, stout woman dressed in a tweed suit threw open the door and greeted Seamie loudly. It was Edwina Hedley. She was Albie's aunt, but Seamie had known her since he was a boy and called her Aunt Eddie, too. She sat down on the bed, then immediately jumped up again when the bed squawked. A young woman, tousled and yawning, emerged from under the covers.

Eddie frowned. "My dear," she said to the girl, "I earnestly hope you have taken preventive measures. Otherwise, you'll find yourself with a baby on the way and the father en route to the North Pole."

"I thought it was the South Pole," the woman said sleepily.

"It was," Seamie replied.

"Has he told you about all the children?" Eddie asked the girl, lowering her voice conspiratorially.

Seamie started to protest. "Eddie, don't . . ."

"Children? What children?" the woman asked, her sleepy look gone now.

"You know he has four children, don't you? All illegitimate. He sends the mothers money—he's not a complete bounder—but he won't marry any of them. They're completely ruined, of course. London girls, all of them. Three left for the country. Couldn't show their faces anymore. The fourth went to America, the poor dear. Why do you think the whole thing with Lady Caroline Wainwright ended?"

The girl, a pretty brunette with a short bob, turned to Seamie. "Is this true?" she asked indignantly.

"Entirely," Eddie said, before Seamie could even open his mouth.

The girl wrapped the duvet around herself and got out of bed. She picked her clothes up off the floor and huffed out of the room, slamming the door on her way.

"*Four* children, Aunt Eddie?" Seamie said, after she'd gone. "Last time it was two."

"A gold digger through and through," Eddie sniffed. "I saved you just now, but I won't always be around at times like these, you know."

"What a pity," Seamie said.

Eddie leaned over and kissed his cheek. "It's good to see you."

"Likewise. How was Aleppo?"

"Absolutely splendid! Stayed in a palace. Dined with a pasha. Met the most extraordinary people. A Tom Lawrence among them. He traveled back to London with me. He's staying in the Belgravia place and—"

There was a loud, resounding boom as the house's heavy front door slammed shut.

Eddie smiled. "Well, that's the end of that one. Won't be seeing her again. What a tomcat you are."

"More of a stray dog, I'd say," Seamie said ruefully.

"I heard about Lady Caroline. It's all over London."

"So I gathered."

Seamie had come to Highgate, Eddie's beautiful Georgian brick house in Cambridge, to recuperate from a brief and heady love affair that had soured. Lady Caroline Wainwright was a privileged young woman—wealthy, beautiful, spoiled—and used to getting what she wanted. And what she wanted was him—for her husband. He'd told her it would never work. He wasn't good husband material. He was too independent. Too used to his own ways. He traveled too much. He told her any bloody thing he could think of—except the truth.

"There's someone else, isn't there?" Caroline had said tearfully. "Who is she? Tell me her name."

"There's no one else," he'd said. It was a lie, of course. There was someone else. Someone he'd loved long ago, and lost. Someone who'd ruined him, it seemed, for any other woman.

He'd finished with Caroline, and then he'd hightailed it to Cambridge to hide out with his friend. He had no home of his own to go to, and when he was in England, he tended to bounce between Highgate, his sister's house, and various hotels.

Albie Alden, a brilliant physicist, taught at King's College and lived in his aunt's house. He was constantly being offered positions by universities all over the world—Paris, Vienna, Berlin, New York—but he wanted to stay in Cambridge. Dull, sleepy Cambridge. God knew why. Seamie certainly didn't. He'd asked him many times, and Albie always said he liked it best here. It was peaceful and quiet—at least when Eddie was away—and he needed that for his work. And Eddie, who was rarely home, needed someone to look after things. The arrangement suited them both.

"What happened?" Eddie asked Seamie now. "Lady Caroline break your heart? Didn't want to marry you?"

"No, she *did* want to marry me. That's the problem."

"Mmm. Well, what do you expect? It's what happens when you're a dashing and handsome hero. Women want to get their claws into you."

"Turn around, will you? So I can get dressed," Seamie said.

Eddie did so, and Seamie got out of bed and grabbed his clothing off the floor. He was tall, strong, and beautifully made. Muscles flexed and rippled under his skin as he pulled his pants on, then shrugged into his shirt. His hair, cut short on the sides, long and wavy on the top, was a dark auburn with copper glints. His face was weathered by the sun and the sea. His eyes were a frank and startling blue.

At thirty-one years of age, he was one of the world's most renowned polar explorers. He'd attempted the South Pole with Ernest Shackleton when he was still a teenager. Two years ago, he'd returned from the first successful expedition to the South Pole, led by the Norwegian Roald Amundsen. In demand all over the world, he'd embarked on a lecture tour shortly after returning from Antarctica and had traveled nonstop for nearly two years. He'd come back to London a month ago and already he felt it, and everyone in it, to be dull and gray. He felt restless and confined, and couldn't wait to be gone again on some new adventure.

"How long have you been in town? How are you liking it? Are you going to stay for a bit this time?" Eddie asked him.

Seamie laughed. Eddie always talked this way—asking a question, and before you could answer it, asking ten more.

"I'm not sure," he said, combing his hair in the mirror above the bureau. "I may be off again soon."

"Another lecture tour?"

"No. An expedition."

"Really? How exciting! Where to?"

"Back to Antarctica. Shackleton's trying to get something together. He's quite serious. He announced it in the *Times* last year, and he's already drawn up some very detailed timetables. All he has to do now is scare up some funds."

"What about all the war talk? Doesn't that worry him?" Eddie asked. "People talked about nothing else on board the ship. In Aleppo, too."

"It doesn't worry him a bit," Seamie replied. "He doesn't give much credence to it. Says it'll all blow over, and wants to sail by summer's end, if not earlier."

Eddie gave him a long look. "Aren't you getting a bit old for the lad's life? Shouldn't you settle down? Find a good woman?"

"How? You chase them all away!" Seamie said teasingly. He sat down on the bed again to put his socks on.

Eddie flapped a hand at him. "Come downstairs when you've finished dressing. I'll make us all some breakfast. Eggs with harissa sauce. I bought pots of the stuff back with me. Wait till you taste it. Simply marvelous! I'll tell you and Albie and his boffin friends about all my adventures. And then we'll go to London."

"To London? When? Right after breakfast?"

"Well, perhaps not right after," Eddie conceded. "Maybe in a day or two. I've got the most fascinating man staying in my town house whom I want you to meet. Mr. Thomas Lawrence. I was telling you about him just a moment ago, before your paramour nearly slammed my door off its hinges. I met him in Aleppo. He's an explorer, too. And an archaeologist. He's traveled all around the desert, knows all the most powerful poohbahs, and speaks flawless Arabic." Eddie suddenly stopped speaking and lowered her voice. "Some people say he's a *spy*." Eddie said this last word in a whisper, then resumed her normal, booming tone. "Whatever he is, he's thoroughly amazing."

Eddie's words were punctuated by a sudden clap of thunder, followed by the pattering of rain against the mullioned windows, one of which had a cracked pane.

"Water's coming in," she said. "I must call the glazier." She sat watching the rain for another minute. "I never thought I'd miss the English weather," she added, smiling wistfully. "But that was before I'd seen the Arabian desert. It's good to be back. I do love my creaky old house. And creaky old Cambridge." Her smile faded. "Though I do wish the circumstances of my return were different."

"He'll be all right, Eddie," Seamie said.

Eddie sighed heavily. "I hope so," she said. "But I know my sister. She wouldn't have asked me to come home if she wasn't terribly worried."

Seamie knew that Mrs. Alden, Albie's mother and Eddie's sister, had wired Eddie at Aleppo, asking her to return to England. Admiral Alden, her husband, had taken ill with some sort of stomach complaint. His doctors had not yet figured out what was wrong with him, but whatever it was, it was bad enough to keep him in bed and on pain medication.

"He's made of tough stuff," Seamie said. "All the Aldens are."

Eddie nodded and tried to smile. "You're right, of course. And anyway, that's about enough moping for one morning. There's breakfast to attend to and then I must call the glazier. And the gardener. And the chimney man, too. Albie's done nothing in my absence. The house is dusty. My mail is up to the rafters. And there's not one clean plate in the entire kitchen. Why doesn't he get that girl from the village up here to do some cleaning?"

"He says she disturbs him."

Eddie snorted. "I really don't see how she could. He never comes out of his study. He was in it when I left two months ago. And he's in it now, working harder than ever, even though he's supposed to be on sabbatical. He's got two more boffins in there with him. I just met them. Dilly Knox, one's called. And Oliver Strachey. They've got blackboards and charts and books strewn all over. What on earth can they be doing in there? What can possibly be so fascinating?"

"Their work?"

"Hardly. It's all just numbers and formulas," Eddie said dismissively. "That boy needs a wife. Even more than you do, I daresay. He's far too odd and absentminded to continue without one. Why is it that you have more women after you than you can possibly cope with and poor Albie hasn't any? Can't you push some of your admirers in his direction? He needs a good woman. And children. Oh, I would so love to hear the happy noise of little ones in my home again. How wonderful those years were when Albie and Willa were little and my sister would bring them here and they'd swim in the pond and swing from that old tree—that one right there," Eddie said, pointing at the huge oak outside the bedroom window. "Willa would climb so high. My sister would plead with her to come down, but she wouldn't. She'd only climb higher and—"

Eddie suddenly stopped talking. She turned and looked at Seamie. "Oh, crumbs. I shouldn't have spoken of her. Do forgive me."

"It's all right, Eddie," Seamie said.

"No, it isn't. I . . . I don't suppose you've had a letter from her recently, have you? Her own mother hasn't. Not for the last three months anyway. And she's been writing to Willa twice a week. Trying to get word to her about her father. Well, I suppose getting letters to and from Tibet is a rather tricky business."

"I suppose it is. And no, I haven't heard from her," Seamie said. "But I never have. Not since she left Africa. I only know as much as you do. That she nearly died in Nairobi. That she traveled through the Far East afterward. And that she's in the Himalayas now, looking for a way to finish the job."

Eddie winced at that. "You're still pining for her, aren't you?" she said. "That's why you go through women like water. One after another. Because you're looking for someone who can take Willa's place. But you never find her."

And I never will, Seamie said to himself. He had lost Willa, the love of his life, eight years ago, and though he'd tried, he'd never found a woman to come close to her. No other woman had Willa's lust for life, for adventure. No other woman possessed her bravery or her passionate, daring soul.

"It's all my fault," Seamie said now. "She wouldn't be there, a million miles away from her family, her home, if it hadn't been for me. If I'd handled things properly on Kilimanjaro, she'd be here."

He would never forget what had happened in Africa. They'd been climbing Kilimanjaro, he and Willa, hoping to set a record by being the first to climb the Mawenzi peak. Altitude sickness had plagued them both, but it had hit Willa especially hard. He'd wanted her to go down, but she'd refused. So they went up instead, summitting much later than they should have. There on Mawenzi, he'd told her something he'd felt for years, but had kept to himself—that he loved her. "I love you, too," she said. "Always have. Since forever." He still heard those words. Every day of his life. They echoed in his head and in his heart.

The sun was high by the time they'd begun their descent, too high, and its rays were strong. An ice-bound boulder, loosened by the sun's heat, came crashing down on them as they were heading down a couloir. It hit Willa and she fell. Seamie would never forget the sound of her screams, or the twisting blur of her body as it flew past him.

When he finally got to her, he saw that her right leg was broken. Jagged bone stuck through her skin. He went down the mountain to their base camp to get help from their Masai guides, only to find they'd been murdered by hostile tribesmen. He'd had to carry her off the mountain, and through jungle and plains, alone. After days of walking, he'd found the train tracks that run between Mombasa and Nairobi. After flagging down a train, he managed to get Willa to a doctor in Nairobi, but by the time they got there, the wound had turned gangrenous. There was no choice, the doctor had said; it would have to be amputated. Willa begged and pleaded with him not to let the man cut her leg off. She knew she'd never climb without it. But Seamie hadn't listened to her pleas. He'd let the doctor amputate to save her life, and she'd never forgiven him for it. As soon as she was able, she left the hospital. And him.

I wake up every morning in despair and go to sleep the same way, she'd written in the note she left for him. *I don't know what to do. Where to go. How to live. I don't know how to make it through the next ten minutes, never mind the rest of my life. There are no more hills for me to climb, no more mountains, no more dreams. It would have been better to have died on Kilimanjaro than to live like this.*

Eddie reached for his hand and squeezed it. "Stop blaming yourself, Seamie, it's not your fault," she said resolutely. "You did everything a human being could have done on that mountain. And when you got her to Nairobi, you did the only thing you could do. The right thing. Imagine had you not done it. Imagine standing in my sister's drawing room and telling her that you did nothing at all, that you let her child die. I understand, Seamie. We all do."

Seamie smiled sadly. "That's the hard thing of it, though, Eddie," he said. "Everyone understands. Everyone but Willa."

CHAPTER TWO

"PARDON ME, MR. Bristow," Gertrude Mellors said, poking her head around the door to her boss's office, "but Mr. Churchill's on the telephone, the *Times* wants a comment from you on the trade secretary's report on child labor in East London, and Mr. Asquith's requested that you join him for supper at the Reform Club this evening. Eight o'clock sharp."

Joe Bristow, member of Parliament for Hackney, stopped writing. "Tell Winston if he wants more boats, he can pay for them himself. The people of East London need sewers and drains, not dreadnoughts," he said. "Tell the *Times* that London's children must spend their days in schools, not sweatshops, and that it's Parliament's moral duty to act upon the report swiftly and decisively. And tell the prime minister to order me the guinea hen. Thanks, Trudy luv."

He turned back to the elderly man seated on the other side of his desk. Nothing, not newspapers, not party business, not the prime minister himself, was more important to him than his constituents. The men and women of East London were the reason he'd become a Labor MP back in 1900, and they were the reason why, fourteen years later, he remained one.

"I'm sorry, Harry. Where were we?" he said.

"The water pump," Harry Coyne, resident of number 31 Lauriston Street, Hackney, said. "As I was saying, about a month ago the water started tasting funny. And now everyone on the street's ill. Lad I talked to works down the tannery says they're dumping barrels of lye on the ground behind the building at night. Says the foreman don't want to pay to have the waste carted away. Water lines run under that building and I think the waste from the tannery's getting into them. Has to be. There's no other explanation."

"Have you told the health inspector?"

"Three times. He don't do nothing. That's why I came to you. Only one who ever gets anything done is you, Mr. Bristow."

"I have to have names, Harry," he said. "Of the tannery. The man in charge. The lad who works there. Anyone who's been ill. Will they speak to me?"

"I can't answer for the tannery man, but the rest will," Harry said. "Here, give us that pen." As Harry wrote down names and addresses, Joe poured two cups of tea, pushed one over to Harry, and downed the other. He'd been seeing constituents since eight o'clock that morning, with no break for lunch, and it was now half past four.

"Here you are," Harry said, handing the list to Joe.

"Thank you," Joe said, pouring more tea. "I'll start knocking on doors tomorrow. I'll pay a personal visit to the health inspector. We'll get this solved, Harry, I promise you. We'll—" Before he could finish his sentence, the door to his office was wrenched open. "Yes, Trudy. What, Trudy?" he said.

But it wasn't Trudy. It was a young woman. She was tall, raven-haired, blue-eyed—a beauty. She wore a smartly tailored charcoal gray coat and matching hat, and carried a reporter's notebook and fountain pen in her gloved hands.

"Dad! Mum's been arrested again!" she said breathlessly.

"Bloody hell. *Again?*" Joe said.

"Katie Bristow, I've told you a hundred times to knock first!" Trudy scolded, hot on her heels.

"Sorry, Miss Mellors," Katie said to Trudy. Then she turned back to her father. "Dad, you've got to come. Mum was at a suffrage march this morning. It was supposed to be peaceful, but it turned into a donnybrook, and the police came, and she was arrested and charged, and now she's in jail!"

Joe sighed. "Trudy, call the carriage, will you? Mr. Coyne, this is my daughter, Katharine. Katie, this is Mr. Coyne, one of my constituents," he said.

"Very pleased to meet you, sir," Kate said, extending a hand to Mr. Coyne. To her father she said, "Dad, come on! We've got to go!"

Harry Coyne stood. He put his hat on and said, "You go on, lad. I'll see meself out."

"I'll be on Lauriston Street tomorrow, Harry," Joe said, then he turned to his daughter. "What happened, Katie? How do you know she's in jail?" he asked her.

"Mum sent a messenger to the house. Oh, and Dad? How much money have you got on you? Because Mum says you need to post bail for her and Auntie Maud before they can be released, but you can do it at the jail, because they were taken straight there, not to the courts, and crikey but I'm parched! Are you going to finish that?"

Joe handed her his teacup. "Did you come all the way over here alone?" he asked sternly.

"No, I have Uncle Seamie with me and Mr. Foster, too."

"Uncle Seamie? What's he doing here?"

"He's staying with us again. Just for a bit while he's in London. Didn't Mum tell you?" Katie said, between gulps of tea.

"No," Joe said, leaning forward in his wheelchair and peering out of his office. Amid five or six of his constituents sat Mr. Foster, his butler, upright, knees together, hands folded on top of his walking stick. Upon seeing Joe looking at him, he removed his hat and said, "Good afternoon, sir."

Joe leaned farther and saw his usually brisk, no-nonsense secretary fluttering madly around someone. She was blushing and twisting her necklace and giggling like a schoolgirl. The someone was his brother-in-law. Seamie looked up, smiled, and gave him a wave.

"I wish Mum had let me go to the march. I wanted to. Would have, too, but she said I had to stay put in school," Katie said.

"Too right," Joe said. "This is the third school we've put you in this year. If you get thrown out of this one, it won't be so easy to find another that will take you."

"Come *on,* Dad!" Katie said impatiently, ignoring his warning.

"Where were they taken?" he asked.

"Holloway," Katie said. "Mum wrote in her note that over a

hundred women were arrested. It's so unfair! Mum and Dr. Hatcher and Dr. Rosen—they're all so accomplished and smart. Smarter than a lot of men. Why won't Mr. Asquith listen to them? Why won't he give them the vote?"

"He feels it won't go over well with the Liberal Party's voters, all of whom are men, and most of whom are not yet ready to acknowledge that women are every bit as smart, if not smarter, than they are," Joe said.

"No, I don't think so. That's not it."

Joe raised an eyebrow. "It isn't?"

"No. I think Mr. Asquith knows that if women get the vote, they'll use it to throw him out on his bum."

Joe burst into laughter. Katie scowled at him. "It's not funny, Dad. It's true," she said.

"It is indeed. Stuff those folders in my briefcase and bring it along, will you?"

Joe watched her as she put her pad and pen down and then collected his things, and as he did, his heart filled with love. He and Fiona had six children now: Katie, fifteen; Charlie, thirteen; Peter, eleven; Rose, six; and the four-year-old twins, Patrick and Michael. Looking at Katie now, so tall and grown-up, so beautiful, he remembered the day she was put into his arms, the day he became a father. From the moment he held her, and looked into her eyes, he was a changed man. He'd held that tiny girl in his arms that moment; he would hold her in his heart forever.

Joe loved all his children fiercely, and delighted in their differences, their passions, their opinions and abilities, but Katie, his first-born, was more truly his child than any of the others. In looks, she was a younger version of her mother. She had Fiona's Irish loveliness, her slender build and her grace, but Katie had got her driving passion—politics—from him. She was determined to go up to Oxford, read history, and then go into politics. She'd declared that once women were fully enfranchised, she would run for office on the Labour ticket and become the country's first female member of Parliament, and already her ambitions had gotten her into hot water.

Six months ago, she'd been asked to leave the Kensington School for Young Ladies after she'd single-handedly got the school's cleaners and groundsmen into a labor union. He and Fiona had found her a place at another school—Briarton—and then, three months ago, she was asked to leave that school, too. That time, it was three unexplained absences from her afternoon French and deportment classes that had gotten her into trouble. After the third infraction, the headmistress—Miss Amanda Franklin—had called Katie into her office. There, she asked Katie why she had missed her classes and what could possibly be more important than French and deportment.

For a reply, Katie had proudly handed her a single sheet newspaper, printed front and back. On the front, at the top, were the words *Battle Cry,* in twenty-two-point type. Followed by KATHARINE BRISTOW, EDITOR-IN-CHIEF, in eighteen-point.

"I should have told you about it, Miss Franklin. I would have, but I wanted to wait until it was finished, you see," she said proudly. "And here it is, hot off the presses."

"And what exactly is it, may I ask?" Miss Franklin had asked, raising an eyebrow.

"My very own newspaper, ma'am," Katie replied. "I just started it. I used my allowance money to get the first edition printed. But money from advertisements will help with the next one. I intend for it to be a voice for working men and women, to chronicle their struggle for fair working conditions, higher wages, and a stronger voice in government."

Katie's newspaper featured a story about the prime minister's refusal to meet with a delegation of suffragists, another about the appalling work conditions at a Milford jam factory, and a third about the enormous turnout for a Labour rally held in Limehouse.

"Who wrote these stories?" Miss Franklin asked, her hand going to the brooch at her neck, her voice rising slightly.

"I did, ma'am," Katie said brightly.

"You spoke with factory workers, Miss Bristow? And with radicals? You sat in upon debates in the Commons?" Miss Franklin said. "By yourself?"

"Oh, no. I had our butler with me—Mr. Foster. He always goes with me. Do you see those there?" Katie asked, pointing at advertisements for men's athletic supporters and bath salts for women's troubles. "I got those by myself, too. Had to knock on quite a few doors on the Whitechapel High Street to do it. Would you like to buy a copy, Miss Franklin?" Katie asked her eagerly. "It's only three pence. Or four shillings for a year's subscription. Which saves you one shilling and two pence over the newsstand price. I've already sold eleven subscriptions to my fellow students."

Miss Franklin, whose students included many privileged and sheltered daughters of the aristocracy—girls who had no idea that men had bits that needed supporting, or that women had troubles only bath salts could solve—went as white as a sheet.

She declined Katie's offer, and promptly wrote to her parents to inquire if their daughter's extracurricular activities might be more fully fostered at another school.

Joe supposed he should have been stern with Katie after she was sent down for a second time—Fiona certainly was—but he hadn't been able to. He was too proud of her. He didn't know many fifteen-year-old girls who could organize a labor force—a small one granted, but still—or publish their very own newspapers. He'd found her a new school, one that offered no deportment lessons and that prided itself on its progressive teaching methods. One that didn't mind if she missed French to attend Prime Minister's Questions—as long as she made up her homework and did well on her tests.

"Here you are, Dad. All packed," Katie said now, handing Joe his briefcase. Joe put it on his lap and wheeled himself out from behind his desk. Katie picked up her pad and pen and followed him.

Joe had been paralyzed by a villain's bullet fourteen years ago and had lost the use of his legs. An East End man by the name of Frank Betts, hoping to discredit Fiona's brother Sid—then a villain himself—had dressed like Sid, appeared in Joe's office, and shot him twice. One of the bullets lodged in Joe's spine. He'd only barely survived and spent several weeks in a coma. When he finally came to, his doctors gave him no hope of a normal, productive life. They said he would be bedridden, an invalid. They said he might well lose both his legs, but Joe had defied them. Six months after the shooting, he was healthy and strong. He'd had to give up the Tower Hamlets seat he'd won just before he'd been shot, but in the meantime, the MP for Hackney had died and a by-election had been called. Joe went out campaigning again, this time in a wheelchair. He won the seat for Labour handily and had held it ever since.

Joe rolled himself into his waiting room now and explained to his constituents what had happened to his wife. He apologized and asked them to please come back first thing in the morning. All agreed to his request, except a group of church ladies outraged over the posters they'd found plastered all over Hackney advertising a racy new musical revue—*Princess Zema and the Nubians of the Nile*.

"Lass has got about as much clothing on her as she had the day she was born!" one indignant lady—a Mrs. Hughes—said.

"I have to cover me grandkiddies' eyes when they walk down the very street we live on!" another—Mrs. Archer—exclaimed. "We've got the kaiser making ructions, and Mrs. Pankhurst and her lot throwing bricks through windows. Our young girls are smoking and driving, and to top it all off, we've now got naked Egyptians in Hackney! I ask you, Mr. Bristow, what's the world coming to?"

"I don't know, Mrs. Archer, but I give you my word that I will personally see to it that the posters are removed by the end of the week," Joe said.

After he'd mollified the women, and they'd left his office, Joe, together with Katie, Seamie, and Mr. Foster, took the elevator to the street, where Joe's driver and carriage were stationed. Another carriage, the one Katie and her escorts had traveled in, waited behind his.

"Thanks for coming to get me, luv," he said to Katie, squeezing her hand. "I'll see you at home."

"But I'm not going home. I'm going with you," Katie said.

"Katie, Holloway is a prison. It's not a Labour rally, or a jam factory. It's a terrible place and it's not fit for a fifteen-year-old girl,"

Joe said firmly. "Go with your uncle and Mr. Foster. Your mother and I will be home shortly."

"Come on, Kate the Great," Seamie said.

"No! I won't go home! You're treating me like a child, Dad!" Katie said hotly. "The suffrage movement is something that will affect me. It's politics. And women's rights. It's history in the making. And you're putting me on the sidelines! I want to write about the march and the arrests and Holloway itself for my paper and you're going to make me miss the whole thing!"

Joe was about to order Katie home when Mr. Foster cleared his throat. "Sir, if I may make an observation," he began.

"As if I could stop you, Mr. Foster," Joe said.

"Miss Katharine does present a most persuasive argument—a skill, I might add, which will serve her well in Parliament one day. What a remarkable boon for the country's first female MP to be able to say she was on the front lines of the fight for women's suffrage."

"You've got *him* in your pocket, too, haven't you?" Joe said to his daughter.

Katie said nothing. She just looked at her father hopefully.

"Come on, then," Joe said. She clapped her hands and kissed him.

"We'll see if you're so happy once you're inside Holloway," he said. "Don't say I didn't warn you."

"Can you use a hand, Joe?" Seamie asked. "I'm feeling a bit useless here."

"I could," Joe said. "And an extra bit of dosh, too. Since it seems I'm expected to liberate half the prison. Have you got any?"

Seamie checked his wallet, said that he did, and handed Joe twenty pounds. Joe asked Mr. Foster to take the second carriage home.

"I will, sir," Mr. Foster replied. "And I shall have the maid ready a pot of tea."

"Good man," Joe said.

He, Seamie, and Katie got into his carriage, a vehicle custom made to accommodate his chair. The driver carefully urged his pair of bay horses into traffic, then headed west, toward the prison. In only a few minutes they were at London Fields, the park where the suffrage march was to have terminated. The three passengers had been talking during the ride, but they all fell silent as the carriage rolled past the green.

"Blimey," Joe said, looking out one of the windows.

Wherever they looked, they saw devastation. The windows of a local pub and several houses were broken. Costers' carts were upended. Apples, oranges, potatoes, and cabbages had rolled everywhere. Banners, torn and tattered, hung limply from lampposts. Trampled placards littered the ground. Residents, costermongers, and the publican were trying their best to restore order to the square, sweeping up glass and debris.

"Dad, I'm worried about Mum," Katie said quietly.

"Me, too," Joe said.

"What happened here?" Seamie asked

Joe could hear a note of alarm in his voice. "I'm not sure," he replied, "but I don't think it was good."

As the carriage rolled out of the square, Joe saw the publican throw a bucket of water over the cobbles in front of his pub. He was washing something red off them.

"Was that—" Seamie started to say.

"Aye," Joe said curtly, cutting him off. He didn't want his daughter to hear the word, but it was too late.

"Blood," she said.

"Blood?" Seamie said, shocked. "Whose blood?"

"The marchers'," Joe said quietly.

"Wait a minute . . . you're telling me that women—*women*—are being beaten up on the streets of London? For marching? For asking for the vote?" Seamie shook his head in disbelief, then said, "When did this start happening?"

"You've been off tramping across icebergs for quite a few years, mate," Joe said wryly. "And then off on your lecture tours, too. If you'd stayed in London, you'd know that no one's *asking* for much of anything anymore. The have-nots—whether they're the poor of

Whitechapel, or national labor unions, or the country's suffragists—are all demanding reform now. Things have changed in dear old England."

"I'll say they have. What happened to the peaceful marches?"

Joe smiled mirthlessly. "They're a thing of the past. The struggle for suffrage has turned violent," he said. "We've now two factions pushing for the vote. There's the National Union of Women's Suffrage Societies—led by Millicent Fawcett, with Fiona a member—which wants to work constitutionally to achieve its aims. And then there's the Women's Social and Political Union, let by Emmeline Pankhurst, which has become fed up with Asquith's foot-dragging and has turned militant. Christobel, Emmeline's daughter, is a firebrand. She's chained herself to gates. Thrown bricks through windows. Heckled the PM in public. Set things on fire. The Pankhursts' activities get a lot of press coverage. Unfortunately, they also get the Pankhursts—and anyone who happens to be near them—arrested."

Joe glanced at Katie as he spoke, and saw that she'd gone pale. "It's not too late, luv. I can still get you home," he told her. "I'll have the driver take us there first, then Uncle Seamie and I can continue on to Holloway."

"I'm not afraid, Dad. And I'm not going home," Katie said quietly. "This is my battle, too. Who's Mum doing this for? You? Charlie? Peter? No. For me. For me and Rose, that's who. The least I can do is go with you to fetch her. And write about what I see for my paper."

Joe nodded. Brave girl. Just like your mother, he thought. Bravery was good and bravery was noble, but bravery couldn't protect one from horses and batons. He was anxious about his wife, worried she might've been hurt.

"I guess that old dear was right," Seamie said.

"What old dear?" Joe asked.

"The one in your office. The one complaining about the musical revue. She asked you, 'What's the world coming to?' I thought she was just a cranky old bat, going on about naked Egyptians, but now I'm wondering if maybe she had a point. England, London . . . they're not the same places that I left back in 1912. I sound like an old dear myself, but stone me, Joe—roughing up women? What *is* the world coming to?"

Joe looked at his brother-in-law, whose expression was still one of astonishment. He thought of his wife and her friends in some dank holding cell in Holloway. He thought of the strikes and labor marches that were nearly a daily occurrence in London now. He thought of the latest volley of threats from Germany, and of Winston Churchill's telephone call, which had almost certainly been about garnering support for the financing of more British battleships.

And he found that he had no answer.

CHAPTER THREE

SEAMIE FINNEGAN THOUGHT he knew about prisons. He'd been in one for a few days once, years ago in Nairobi. His brother Sid had been incarcerated there for a crime he had not committed. Seamie and Maggie Carr, a coffee plantation owner and Sid's boss, had contrived to break him out, which had involved Seamie and Sid trading places. It hadn't been a difficult thing to do. There had only been one guard on duty and the building itself was, as Mrs. Carr had put it, "a two-bit ramshackle chicken coop of a jail."

Now, however, as he gazed at the building looming in front of him, Seamie realized he knew nothing about prisons, for Holloway was like nothing he'd ever seen.

It looked like a dark medieval fortress, one with a keep, an iron gate, and crenellated turrets. A pair of gryphons flanked the entrance—an arched passage wide enough to permit carriages—and through it he could see the cell blocks—long, rectangular structures with row upon row of small, high windows.

He felt suffocated just looking at it. His explorer's soul craved the vast, open places of the world—the snowy expanses of Antarctica and the soaring peaks of Kilimanjaro. To him, the mere thought of being confined behind Holloway's ugly stone walls was crushing.

"Uncle Seamie, this way. Come on," Katie said, tugging on his hand.

Joe had already rolled through the passage in his wheelchair and was halfway across the lawn and heading toward an inner building marked RECEIVING. Seamie and Katie quickly caught up with him.

The scene inside the receiving area was chaos. As Joe counted out Fiona's and her friend Maud Selwyn Jones's bail money to a uniformed man seated behind a desk, and Katie interviewed a woman holding a bloodstained handkerchief to her head, other women—many wearing torn and bloodied clothing, some with cuts and bruises—angrily denounced the wardresses and the warden. Family members and friends who'd come to collect them pleaded with them, trying to convince them to leave, but they would not.

"Where's Mrs. Fawcett?" one of them shouted. "We won't leave until you release her!"

"Where are Mrs. Bristow and Dr. Hatcher?" another yelled. "What are you doing with them? Let them go!"

The chant was taken up. Scores of voices rang out as one. "Let them go! Let them go! Let them go!"

The noise was immense. Over it, a wardress yelled that they must all leave, right now, but she was soon shouted down. Seamie saw an older man in a black suit and white collar going from guard to guard, a worried expression on his face.

Joe saw him, too. He called to him. "Reverend Wilcott? Is that you?"

The man turned around. He wore spectacles, was clean-shaven, and looked to be in his fifties. His hair was graying, his expression kindly and befuddled.

He squinted at them, lifted his glasses, and said, "Ah! Mr. Bristow. Well met in Islington, eh?"

"Hardly, Reverend. Jennie's been arrested, too, then?"

"Indeed she has. I've come to collect her, but she doesn't appear to be here. I'm most concerned. The warden has released many of the women to family members, but not Jennie. I've no idea why. I spotted Mr. von Brandt a moment ago, looking for Harriet. Ah! Here he is now."

A tall, well-dressed man with silvery blond hair joined them. Introductions were made and Seamie learned that Max von Brandt—German and from Berlin originally, but currently living in London—was Dr. Harriet Hatcher's cousin and had been sent by Harriet's anxious mother to fetch her.

"Have you found her?" Joe asked him.

"No, but I did see the warden briefly, and he told me that Harriet and several other officers from the National Union of Women's Suffrage Societies are being held elsewhere in the prison."

"Why?" Joe asked.

"He said it was for their own safety. He told me that he'd had to separate officers of Mrs. Fawcett's group from those of Mrs. Pankhurst's. There were some harsh words between them, apparently, and he feared further hostilities would take place. He said they would be released shortly, but that was an hour ago and there's still no sign of them."

Joe, frustrated, wheeled himself over to a harried wardress to try to find out more. Max went with him. Katie continued to interview marchers and scribble notes. Seamie and the Reverend Wilcott attempted to make polite conversation. The reverend knew Seamie's name and asked about his adventures in Antarctica. Seamie learned that the reverend headed a parish in Wapping and that his daughter Jennie, who lived in the rectory with him, ran a school for poor children in the church.

"It's also a de facto soup kitchen," the Reverend Wilcott explained. "As Jennie always says, 'Children who are hungry cannot learn, and children who cannot learn will always be hungry.'"

As Reverend Wilcott was talking, a gate at the far end of the receiving room was opened and a group of dazed and weary-looking women walked through it. Seamie recognized his sister immediately, but his relief at seeing her soon turned to dismay. Fiona's face was bruised. There was a cut on her forehead and blood in her hair. Her jacket was torn.

As the women entered the receiving area, a cheer went up from their fellow marchers—those who had been released but had refused to leave. There were hugs and tears and promises to march again. Joe and Katie hurried to collect Fiona. Seamie followed them. Women's voices swirled around him as he made his way across the room. Seamie didn't know most of the women, but he recognized a few of them.

"God, but I need a cigarette," one woman said loudly. Seamie knew her. She was Fiona's friend Harriet Hatcher. "A cigarette and a tall glass of gin," she said. "Max, is that you? Thank God! Give us a fag, will you?"

"Hatch, is that a cigarette? Have you got an extra?" Seamie knew that voice, too. It belonged to Maud Selwyn Jones, the sister of India Selwyn Jones, who was married to his and Fiona's brother Sid.

"You all right, Fee?" Seamie asked his sister when he finally got to her. Joe and Katie were already on either side of her, fussing over her.

"Seamie? What are you doing here?" Fiona asked.

"I was at home when your message arrived. I accompanied Katie."

"Sorry, luv," Fiona said.

"No, don't apologize. I'm glad I came. I had no idea, Fiona. None. I . . . well, I'm so glad you're all right."

He was upset to see the marks of violence on her. Fiona had raised him. They'd lost both parents when she was seventeen and he was four, and she'd been both sister and mother to him. She was one of the most loving, loyal, unselfish human beings he had ever known, and to think that someone had hurt her . . . well, he only wished he had that someone here now, right in front of him.

"What happened?" Joe asked her.

"Emmeline and Christabel happened," Fiona said wryly. "Our group was marching peacefully. There were crowds there, and police constables, but very little heckling or baiting. Then the Pankhursts showed up. Christabel spat at a constable. Then she lobbed a rock through a pub window. Things went downhill from there. There was a great deal of shouting. Fights broke out. The publican's wife was furious. She walloped Christabel, and went after other marchers, too. The police started making arrests. Those of us who had been marching peacefully resisted and, as you can see, paid for it quite dearly."

"The warden told us you were being held downstairs for your safety," Joe said. "That there was scuffling between the two factions here at the prison."

Fiona laughed wearily. "Is that what he told you?"

"It's not true, Mum?" Katie asked.

"No, luv, it's not. The warden held us downstairs, but not for our safety. There was no scuffling between us. The warden wanted to scare us, and he did. But he didn't scare us off. He'll never succeed in doing that."

"What do you mean, scare you off?" Seamie asked.

"He put us all in a cell next to one in which a woman, another suffragist on a hunger strike, was being force-fed. He did it on purpose. So we would hear it. It was terrible. We had to listen to the poor thing scream and struggle, and then she was violently sick. So they did the whole thing over again. And again. Until she kept the food down. They made sure we saw her, too. Afterward. They marched her right by our cell when it was over. She could hardly walk. Her face was bloodied. . . ."

Fiona paused, overcome by emotion. When she could finally speak again, she said, "We were all quite undone, sickened ourselves, and cowed, every one of us. Except Jennie Wilcott. She was the only one amongst us with any presence of mind. She was magnificent. As the woman was marched by us, Jennie started to sing. She sang 'Abide with Me,' and the woman heard her. Her head was hanging down, but when Jennie sang, she looked up. And then she smiled. Through the blood and the tears, she smiled. And then we all started singing. I think the whole prison must have heard us and taken heart. And it was all because of Jennie."

"Fiona, what exactly is force—" Seamie had started to ask, when a young woman suddenly stumbled and bumped into him. She was small and blond, about twenty-five or so, he guessed, and she had the ugliest black eye he'd ever seen.

"Pardon me! I'm ever so sorry," she said, embarrassed. "It's this eye. I can't see terribly well with only one." She was holding tightly to the Reverend Wilcott's arm.

"There's no need to apologize," Seamie said. "None at all."

"Mr. Finnegan, this is my daughter Jennie Wilcott," the Reverend said. "Jennie, this is Seamus Finnegan, Fiona's brother and a very famous explorer. He found the South Pole."

"Very pleased to meet you, Miss Wilcott," Seamie said.

"Likewise, Mr. Finnegan. How on earth did you get from the South Pole to Holloway? Some great misfortune must have befallen you."

Before Seamie could answer her, Katie tugged on his arm. "Uncle Seamie, we're leaving now. Are you coming?"

Seamie said he was, then turned back to the Wilcotts. "Please, take my arm, too, Miss Wilcott. It'll be easier for you with someone on either side of you. I know it will. I went snowblind once. On my first trip to Antarctica. Had to be led around like a lamb."

Jennie took Seamie's arm. Together, Seamie and the Reverend Wilcott walked her out of the receiving area, toward the long, gloomy passageway that led from the prison to the street.

"Fiona's just been telling us about your ordeal," Seamie said as they walked. "You must be the same Jennie who sang 'Abide with Me'?"

"Did you now, Jennie?" the Reverend Wilcott said. "You told me about the force-feeding but you didn't tell me that. I'm glad you sang that one. It's a lovely old hymn. It must have given that poor woman a great deal of comfort."

"My motivation had more to do with defiance than comfort, I'm afraid, Dad," Jennie said. "I sang to that woman, yes. But also to her tormentors. I wanted them to know that no matter what they do to us, they will not break us."

"What is force-feeding?" Seamie asked. "And why were the wardresses force-feeding a prisoner?"

"Do you not read the London papers, Mr. Finnegan?" Jennie asked. There was an edge to her voice.

"Indeed I do, Miss Wilcott," Seamie replied. "But they are hard to come by in New York, Boston, or Chicago. To say nothing of the South Pole. I only returned to London a month ago."

"Forgive me, Mr. Finnegan. For the second time. It has been a very trying day," Jennie said.

"Once again, there is nothing to forgive, Miss Wilcott," Seamie said. He turned toward her as he spoke. Her eye was horribly swollen. He knew it had to be very painful.

"It was a fellow suffragist the wardresses were force-feeding," Jennie said slowly. "One who'd been arrested for damaging Mr. Asquith's carriage. She's been in prison for a month now and is in the process of starving herself."

"But why would she do that?"

"To protest her imprisonment. And to call attention to the cause of women's suffrage. A young woman starving herself to death in prison makes for a good news story and elicits a great deal of sympathy from the public—which makes Mr. Asquith and his government very unhappy."

"But surely you can't force a person to eat if she doesn't wish to."

Jennie, who'd been looking straight ahead as she walked, turned her head, appraising him with her good eye. "Actually, you can. It's a very dreadful procedure, Mr. Finnegan. Are you sure you wish to know about it?"

Seamie bristled at her question, and at her appraisal of him. Did she think he couldn't handle it? He'd handled Africa. And Antarctica.

He'd handled scurvy, snowblindness, and frostbite. He could certainly handle this conversation. "Yes, Miss Wilcott, I am sure," he said.

"A female prisoner on hunger strike is subdued," Jennie began. "She is wrapped in a sheet to prevent her from flailing and kicking. Of course she does not wish to cooperate with the wardresses, or the prison doctor, and so clamps her mouth shut. Sometimes, a metal gag is inserted between her lips to force her mouth open and she is fed that way. At other times, a length of rubber tubing is forced into her nose and down her gullet. Needless to say, that is very painful. The doctor pours nourishment through the tube—usually milk mixed with powdered oats. If the woman is calm enough, she can breathe during the procedure. If she is not . . . well, if she is not, then there are difficulties. When the allotted amount of milk has been fed, the tube is removed and the woman is released. If she vomits it up, the doctor begins again."

Seamie's stomach turned. "You were right, Miss Wilcott," he said, "it *is* a dreadful thing." He caught her glance and held it. She knew a great deal about the procedure. He shuddered as he guessed the reason why. "It's been done to you, hasn't it?" he asked. As soon as the words were out of his mouth, he regretted them. It was not the sort of thing one asked a woman one had only just met.

"Yes, it has. Twice," Jennie said, unflinchingly. Her frankness surprised him.

"Perhaps we should find a pleasanter subject to talk about with Mr. Finnegan, my dear," the Reverend Wilcott said gently. "Look! Here we are. Out of the lion's den and into the light. Just like Daniel."

Seamie looked ahead of himself. They'd come to the end of the long stone passageway and were now outside of the prison. He saw that his family had preceded him to the street. Darkness was coming down and the streetlamps were glowing.

Fiona was sitting on a bench, her eyes closed. Katie sat next to her scribbling in her notepad. Joe, Seamie guessed, had gone off in search of the carriage. The street had been filled with carriages when they'd arrived, and his driver had not been able to park in front of the prison. Harriet Hatcher, standing next to the bench, had found a fresh cigarette. Max and Maud were with her. Maud was laughing throatily over something Max had just said.

"I must find a hackney cab. Mr. Finnegan, would you be so good as to stay with Jennie while I do?" the Reverend Wilcott asked.

Seamie said that he would. "Let's get you to a bench, Miss Wilcott," he said.

They passed under a streetlight on their way, and Seamie, glancing once again at Jennie's face, let out a low whistle. He examined the puffed and blackened flesh in the lamplight and winced.

"Is it very bad?" Jennie asked.

"It is. It's awful."

"Why, thank you," Jennie said, laughing. "Thank you very much! Ever hear of something called tact?"

Seamie laughed, too. He had seen something else when he'd looked at her just now—that she was very pretty, even with a black eye. A few seconds of awkward silence followed, and Seamie found he didn't want their conversation to end. He quickly thought of something to say to make sure it didn't.

"Your father mentioned that he heads a church in the East End."

"Yes, that's right. In Wapping. St. Nicholas's. Are you familiar with the saint?"

"No," Seamie said, suddenly worried that she would give him some dull, proselytizing description of the saint and all his miraculous doings, and then admonish him to start attending church on Sundays, but again she surprised him.

"He's the patron saint of sailors, thieves, and prostitutes," she said. "Which means he's perfect for us, really, since we have plenty of all three in Wapping. You should see the High Street on a Saturday night."

Seamie laughed again. "Have you been in Wapping a long time?" he asked her.

"We've been there for twenty-five years now. Well, my father has," Jennie said. "Dad took over a poorly attended church and made it vital again. My mother opened a school for neighborhood children about twenty years ago. I took it over six years ago. One hundred percent of our children stay until they're fourteen. And twenty percent of our graduates go on to a vocational school," Jennie said. "Of course, we don't do it alone," she continued. "That the school is still open is due mostly to the generosity of your sister and brother-in-law, Mr. Finnegan. It is their school as much as mine. In fact, they just gave us money for ten more desks and a blackboard."

Seamie found that he was very interested in the work she was doing. He wanted to ask her more about it, but they'd reached the bench. Fiona and Katie moved over to make room for Jennie. Harriet, Max, and Maud, having finished their cigarettes, walked over to join them.

"Were you just talking about your school, Jennie?" Fiona asked, opening her weary eyes.

"I was," Jennie replied. "In fact, I was just telling your brother about yours and Joe's contributions."

Fiona smiling tiredly, pointed at a poster stuck to the side of an idling omnibus. "I was just thinking about the school myself. I see that one of your former students, little Josie Meadows, has done quite well for herself," she said. " 'Princess Zema, Ancient Egypt's Most Mysterious Enigma.' Mysterious *and* an enigma. Top that if you can!"

Jennie, looking at the poster now, too, sighed. "I suppose she has. If you call dancing around half-naked and carrying on with villains doing well."

"Villains?" Fiona echoed.

"Half-naked?" Seamie said.

"Princess Zema?" Harriet said. "Why do I know that name?"

"Because it's on every billboard, every telephone pole, and every bus in London," Jennie said, shaking her head. "Josie Meadows, a girl I used to teach, is the lead."

"In *Princess Zema*," Fiona said. "Eighty exotic dancers, twenty peacocks, two panthers, and a python bring to life the story of an

Egyptian princess, stolen from her palace bed on the eve of her wedding, sold into slavery by a false, fierce, and felonious pharaoh."

"Sounds fantastically fabulous," Max joked.

"My goodness, Fiona, how do you know all that? You haven't seen it, have you?" Jennie said.

Fiona shook her head. "Charlie, my eldest boy, had the poster. God knows where he got it. I took it away from him. It's rather risqué, as you can see."

"Josie was actually more than just a student of mine," Jennie explained to Seamie and the others. "She was like a sister to me. I'd taught her since she was ten years old. She's nineteen now. She desperately wanted to be on stage. And now she is. As an exotic dancer. She does a number with veils, I'm told, that leaves very little to the imagination."

"What's this about villains?" Fiona asked.

"Rumor has it that Billy Madden's taken a fancy to her," Jennie said quietly.

"Billy Madden," Fiona said grimly. "My god, what a foolish girl. She doesn't know what she's gotten herself into."

She traded glances with Seamie. They both knew who Billy Madden was—the most powerful crime lord in all of London. Sid, their brother, and once the boss of the entire East End crime world, had told them Madden was one of the most brutal, vicious men he'd ever known.

"Oh, I think she does know," Jennie said sadly. "I saw her the other day. Diamonds on her fingers and bruises on her face."

"Yegads, how ghastly," Maud said. "As if today wasn't depressing enough already. Let's change the subject. Or better yet, let's have another smoke. Harriet, darling, care to join me? Max?"

"I guess I had better, Miss Selwyn Jones," Max said. "Since I'm the one with the cigarettes."

As Maud, Max, and Harriet headed to the curb so as not to blow smoke all over the others, Fiona turned back to Jennie. "Never mind Josie and her villains. Tell Seamie about one of our successes," she said. "Tell him about Gladys."

But before Jennie could tell him, Joe arrived with his carriage. Fiona and Katie said their good-byes and offered to take Maud with them and drop her at her home. Maud thanked them, but said she would go to the Hatchers' house with Harriet and Max. Seamie said he would wait with Miss Wilcott until her father returned, and then get his own cab to Fiona and Joe's house.

"I'd love to hear about the other girl," he said to Jennie, when they'd left. He was glad the others had gone—glad for the chance to talk with her alone.

"The other girl?" Jennie repeated.

"The success story. You were starting to tell me about her when Joe came with the carriage."

Jennie smiled. "Yes, I was. Gladys Bigelow *is* a success story," she said. "Truly. She was a student at our school. A very bright girl. Came from a dreadful situation—a drunken, violent father, who's since died, and a very poorly mum. She was destined for some dreadful job in a factory, but instead she's working for Sir George Burgess, second in command under Mr. Churchill at the Admiralty."

Seamie watched Jennie's expression change as she talked about her former student. Her face became radiant.

"She attended our little school, then went on to secretarial studies. I'd originally asked Fiona and Joe if they might have a place for her. They didn't at the time, but Joe knew Sir George was looking for a capable girl and he gave him Gladys's name. And Sir George hired her."

"That's a wonderful story, Miss Wilcott," a voice said from behind them. It was Max von Brandt. Seamie hadn't been aware that Max was listening. He hadn't even known Max was there. He'd thought he was still out by the curb, smoking.

"Yes, it is, Mr. von Brandt," Jennie said, turning toward Max. "That job has changed her life. Gladys was a bit shy. A bit withdrawn, you see. All she had in her life was her sick mother and her Thursday-night knitting group. And now, because of her studies, she also has a job she loves. At the Admiralty, no less! She has purpose and independence, and they mean the world to her. Why, she's even become a suffragist. She attends the evening meetings. Isn't it amazing? These are the things an education can do."

"Jennie! Over here, my dear!"

It was the Reverend Wilcott. He'd finally found a cab.

"Take my arm," Seamie said. "I'll walk you to the street." Jennie did so. She said good-bye to Max, waved at Maud and Harriet, then Seamie led her toward the cab.

"I wonder, Mr. Finnegan . . . I wonder if I might ask you to come and speak to the children. At the school," she said as they walked. "Perhaps next week? You're a very dashing figure, you know. You've achieved so much, done so many amazing things. I know they would be so excited to see you. And so grateful. And so would I."

Seamie had speaking engagements planned for the week, and a meeting with Sir Clements Markham at the Royal Geographical Society. Markham had rung him up at Fiona's house and told him he wanted to speak with him about a position at the RGS. In addition, Seamie had long-standing plans with his friend George Mallory to go on a pub crawl. They were all reasons for saying no—but they weren't the main reason. The main reason he wanted to say no to Jennie Wilcott was that he was afraid to say yes. He was afraid to see her again. She stirred something in him. Admiration, he quickly told himself. But it was deeper than that, and he knew it and it scared him. The other women he'd been with over the last few years . . . they'd stirred something in him, too—his lust. This was a different feeling. Jennie Wilcott, in just the few moments he'd known her, had touched his heart. No woman had touched that part of him for a very long time.

Don't do it, he told himself. You've just finished with Caroline. The last thing you need right now is some new entanglement. "I'm not sure I can, Miss Wilcott. I'll have to look at my schedule," he said to Jennie.

"I understand, Mr. Finnegan," she said, trying to hide her disappointment. "You must be incredibly busy." She tried for a smile, but winced instead. "Oh! Ouch!" she exclaimed. "This eye's so big and fat, it hurts to even smile now."

"That shiner's getting worse, I'm afraid," Seamie said. And then without thinking, he gently touched the bruised skin around her eye. "It's going to swell a bit more and then, in a day or so, it'll start to go down, though the bruising will last a bit longer, I'm afraid."

"I take it you've had a few black eyes yourself," Jennie said.

"One or two," he admitted. "Good night, Miss Wilcott," he said, handing her into the carriage,

"Good night, Mr. Finnegan," Jennie said. She sat down, then leaned toward the door before he could close it. "You will try to visit our school, won't you? You'll think about it at least?"

Seamie looked at her, at her poor eye, nearly swollen shut now, at her blouse stained with blood. He thought of what she had endured in her fight to obtain the vote—beatings, imprisonment, force-feeding. He remembered how only days ago, at Cambridge, he'd felt that London, and everyone in it, was dull and gray, and wondered now if he'd been mistaken.

"Yes, Miss Wilcott," he finally said. "I will."

CHAPTER FOUR

WILLA ALDEN STOPPED her heavily laden yak. For several long minutes she did nothing but stare at the sight before her. She'd seen it too many times to count. She'd looked at it through a camera lens, a telescope, a theodilite, and a sextant. She'd photographed it, sketched it, mapped it, measured it. And still, it took her breath away.

"Oh, you beauty," she whispered. "You cold, impossible beauty."

Rising before her, all peaks, ridges, and sheer cliff faces, was Everest. A white plume swirled around the summit. Willa knew it was high winds blowing the snow around, but she liked instead to think it was the mountain spirit dancing around her high, remote home. *Chomolungma* the Tibetans called Everest—Goddess Mother of Mountains.

From where she stood, a few miles south of Rongbuk village, on the Rongbuk Glacier, Willa could see the mountain's north face rising. Time after time, her head told her there was no way up that bloody mountain, and time after time, as she looked at the north face, all forbidding rock and snow, her heart wouldn't listen. What about that ridge? Or that spur? it said to her. And that cliff . . . it looks like a tough nut from here, but maybe if a very experienced climber were to tackle it, in good weather, a very gifted climber, one equipped with an oxygen tank . . . what then?

There was no way up Everest, no way at all, without oxygen—of this she was certain. She had suffered badly from altitude sickness climbing Kilimanjaro's Mawenzi peak, and that was only about seventeen thousand feet. What would happen to a human being at twenty-nine thousand feet?

Willa knew the first symptoms of altitude sickness—the ceaseless nausea and vomiting; the swelling of the face, hands, and feet; and the crucifying difficulty of pulling air in and out of your lungs. She had suffered all of them. And as one climbed higher, the symptoms became more serious. Altitude sickness often attacked the lungs. A dry, hacking cough would set in, and then fever—both of which signaled fluid in the lungs. A climber might then find himself coughing up bright red froth. If the height didn't get the lungs, it often got the brain. A nagging headache became a crashing one. Confusion followed, and then blurred vision. The climber started losing control over his hands and feet. If he didn't get down, and fast, paralysis and coma were next. Then death.

"Why?" people asked her, unable to understand that which made alpinists risk everything to achieve a summit.

If only I could show them this sight, this magnificent Everest soaring into the blue sky. Untouched, pristine, wild, and fearsome, she thought. If only I could show them that, they'd never ask why again.

And soon she would. Soon her pictures of the Himalayas would be published. She had almost all the shots she needed. Soon the world would see for itself what mere words could never adequately describe.

"Come on, old stick," she said to her yak.

She pulled her fur cap down tightly around her ears and clapped her mittened hands together. A small, thin grimace stiffened her features as she and her animal started walking again. Her leg was playing up. Just a bit. But a bit often turned into something more, and she had no time for it today. She wanted to be well upon the Rongbuk Glacier and have her camp set up by early afternoon. She had a great deal of work to do.

During the time she'd been in the Far East, she'd sent the Royal Geographical Society photographs—shots of India, of her temples and cities and villages. Of her mighty rivers, arid plains, her lush hills and valleys. She'd sent pictures of China and its Great Wall. Of Marco Polo's Silk Road and Genghis Khan's Mongolia. Sir Clements Markham had shown her pictures at the RGS. He'd turned them into books—books that had made her a bit of money.

Two years ago, she'd written Markham with a new proposal—a book of photographs on the Himalayas. Of Annapurna. The Nilgiris. And Everest.

A few months later, she'd received his one-line reply—*Himalayas. Yes. How soon?*—and ever since, she'd been working nonstop, pushing herself mercilessly in the pursuit of the perfect shot—a shot that would be stunning and beautiful, so good it would make people gasp, or quiet them into a reverent awe. She now had more than two hundred images for her Himalayas book—of the mountains in all their moods, the villages that surrounded them, the people who lived at their feet.

And the route. She had that.

She had pictures of what might be a way up Everest.

And they would make her famous. Cement her reputation as an Alpine explorer. They would sell a great deal of books and make her money, which was something she desperately needed now. Her aunt

Eddie had given her five thousand pounds when she was younger, but she'd already spent a good deal of it. On a passage to Africa. And then one to India. On her travels throughout the Far East. On bribes to officials to let her cross borders. On food and tea and shelter. On cameras and film, darkroom equipment, tents and cots, and the animals needed to carry it all.

The route, the path, the way, she thought now, squinting up at the mountain as she trekked along. Markham wanted it. The Germans wanted it. The Italians and the French and the Americans, too. Alpinists were a competitive lot; being first was all that mattered to them. And being first up the highest mountain in the world—well, there was no prize greater than that. Willa knew that well enough. She'd been first once. First up the Kilimanjaro's Mawenzi peak. It had cost her her leg and nearly her life. It had cost her her heart.

"Hup, hup!" she said to her yak, urging him up the snowy shoulders of the glacier.

They walked on, over the white vastness, for an hour, then two, until Willa had what she wanted—an unobstructed view of the north col. She stopped then, hammered an iron stake into the snow, and tied the yak. Slowly, methodically, she unloaded her animal and set up camp.

It took her an hour to unpack her gear, pitch her tent, and build a fire pit. She always traveled and worked alone. She preferred it that way, but even if she hadn't, there was no other choice. There were not many women who wished to live as she did, in a cold, foreign, and forbidding environment. Without any domestic comforts. Without a husband or children. Without any guarantee of safety or protection.

And as for men . . . Willa would have gladly signed on to any number of expeditions sponsored by the RGS, but they would not have her. Their expeditions were conceived and executed by men, and it was still unthinkable for a woman to be included in an exploratory party to the North Pole or the South Pole, or down the Nile, or up Everest, because she would have to trek, climb, eat, and sleep with men. And that was unacceptable. Not to herself or the men she might be climbing with, but to British society, and it was British society that was footing the bill. They were the ones contributing monies to the RGS, and they were the ones financing its expeditions.

When Willa finished setting up camp, she loaded her rifle and placed it on the ground beside her cot. The rifle was protection against wolves; the kind that went around on four legs and the kind that went around on two. When she was satisfied that everything was in its proper place, she fed her yak and then fixed herself a small meal of hot tea and sampa—a mixture of barley flour, sugar, and a pungent butter made from yak's milk. She deliberately ate little to keep herself thin. The thinner her body, the less likely she was to suffer her menses—an encumbrance at the best of times, and even more so when one was a world away from flush toilets and running water.

When she'd finished her meal, she decided to do a bit of trekking. It was late afternoon, she still had two, maybe three hours of light. She stood up to wash her dishes, and gave a small gasp. The yak bone prosthetic was lighter and more comfortable than the wooden one she'd had made in Bombay, when she'd first arrived in India, but after a long day's trekking, it still hurt her. The pain was growing stronger now. She knew what was coming and she dreaded it. People talked of the feeling of a phantom limb, of the odd, unsettling sensation that the lost arm or leg was still there—people who hadn't lost a limb, that was. Those who had knew of something different. They knew of the dull, hard aches that often turned into an unbearable agony. They knew of the lost days, the restless nights.

How many times had she screamed herself awake? How many nights had she torn her sheets to bits, wept and shrieked and banged her head against the wall, nearly blind from pain? Too many to count. Dr. Ribiero, the man who'd amputated her leg, had given her morphine in the days following her surgery. She'd left Nairobi on crutches only a few days after her amputation, with a few bottles of the drug, and had traveled east. And there, after her morphine supply had run out, she'd discovered opium. She'd bought it in the markets of Morocco and Marrakech, from farmers in Afghanistan, and from peddlers in India, Nepal, and Tibet. It dulled the pain in her leg, and it dulled a pain that was even sharper—the one in her heart.

She took some now. She reached into her coat pocket, for she always kept it close, drew out a small hardened chunk of brown paste, cut a piece off, and proceeded to smoke it in a pipe. Within minutes, the drug had beaten back the pain and she could walk again. She quickly cleaned her dishes, checked that her yak was tied securely, then set off.

Untethered and alone, trekking across the pristine snows of the glacier, she felt as wild and free as a falcon circling, a winter fox loping across the snow, a wolf howling at the moon. As she approached the lower foothills of Everest, the trek became a climb, but still she went on over an ice field, across some jagged moraine. The terrain became more challenging, and her artificial leg more of a hindrance, but she could not stop. Everest, soaring high above the glacier, was glorious. It pulled at her, cast its spell upon her, and she was powerless to resist it.

The low foothill became a proper slope, and still she pressed on, heedless and unaware, seduced by the mountain, refusing to remember that she could no longer climb. She used her good leg to push herself up the slope, and she used her bad one, too—jamming the carved, unfeeling toes into cracks and crevices, using the foot to pivot and the leg to hold her weight. She used her strong, sinewy arms to pull herself up to a hold, and her powerful hands to keep her there.

Up she went, higher and higher, intoxicated by the cold whiteness, the sound of her own breath, the incredible feeling of ascending. Of gaining the slope. She was climbing, well and fast, and then it happened. She lost a handhold and slipped. Down she hurtled, screaming, as the fall jammed the edge of her false leg into her flesh. Ten feet. Twenty. Thirty. At forty, she managed to arrest the fall, clawing at the side of the slope. She ripped off two nails doing so, but she'd only feel those later.

She clung there, shaking and sobbing, her face pressed into the snow. The pain of her injuries was terrible, but it wasn't that pain that was making her cry. It was the terrifying memories of Mawenzi. This fall had woken them up and they rushed at her now, paralyzing her. They were so intense, so harrowing, that she could not move an inch, she could only clutch at the slope, eyes closed, sick with fear.

She remembered the fall and the impact. She remembered Seamie getting her down off the mountain and then pulling her shattered leg straight. She remembered him carrying her for miles and miles. And the pain—she remembered the red, ragged, unspeakable pain.

She'd been out of her mind from it—and from fever—by the time Seamie got her to Nairobi. The doctor there had taken one look at her and decided to amputate immediately. She'd begged him not to, begged Seamie not to let him. But the doctor had taken her leg anyway, right below the knee.

Seamie had told her she would've died if he hadn't allowed the operation. What he hadn't understood is that she *had* died, at least a part of her had. She would never climb high again. She couldn't. Her artificial leg didn't allow the flexibility, the stability, and the fluid physical finesse that were required to undertake challenging ascents. In some ways, what had happened to her was worse than death, for all that was left to her now was working to ensure that others would one day climb the highest mountain in the world. It was a leftover life. A second best. She hated it, but it was all she had.

She had hated Seamie, too. Almost as much as she loved him. She'd cursed him, and her useless leg. She'd blamed him, too. Because it was easier that way—having somebody to blame for what had happened to her, someone other than herself.

She remembered leaving Nairobi, and taking a boat from Mombasa. Her wound was still seeping blood; she could barely hobble on her new crutches, but she was so wild with grief and anger, so overwhelmed by the conflicting emotions she felt for Seamie, that she'd wanted to put as much distance between herself and him as possible. She'd managed to get herself all the way to Goa, where she'd taken a small house on the coast. She'd stayed there for half a year, waiting for her leg to heal properly and mourning her lost life. When she'd gotten her strength back, she traveled to Bombay, where she'd found a doctor who could fit her with an artificial leg. She allowed herself a month in that city to learn how to walk properly on the new leg, and then, loaded with cameras, a few pieces of clothing, a chunk of her aunt's money, and little else, she left Bombay. She could never climb again, but she could still explore, and she was determined to do so. She left the civilized world, hoping to leave her heartbreak behind as well, but it followed her. Wherever she went, whatever she saw, or heard, or felt—it was Seamie she ached to share it with—whether it was the breathtaking vastness of the Gobi desert, the sound of a hundred camel bells announcing the arrival of a merchant's caravan, or the sun rising over the Potala Palace in Lhasa. She had tried to run away from him and had failed, for he was in her head and in her heart, always.

There had been times—so many of them—when, longing for him, she would impulsively decide to return to London. And to him. If he would have her. As she began to pack, she would imagine seeing him again, talking to him, holding him in her arms—but then just as quickly, she would stop packing and tell herself that she was a fool because surely Seamie wouldn't even wish to see her, much less talk to her or take her in his arms. She had left him eight years ago. She'd run away. Blamed him. Broken his heart. What man could forgive those things?

A strong wind blew down upon Willa now, making her shiver, whirling away her memories of Mawenzi and of all she had lost there. She stopped trembling, stopped crying, and got herself down the last thirty feet of the climb.

Dusk was falling by the time she made it back to the glacier. She didn't have her gun with her, but she wasn't afraid. Camp was not far. She knew she would make it there before the light faded entirely. She was limping. Her leg was bleeding; she could feel it. Her hands, too. Opium would dull the pain of those wounds, and the wound to her heart as well.

Willa walked slowly across the snow, the sun setting behind her—a small, broken figure, lost in the shadows of the soaring, ageless mountain, and in the shadows of her own broken dreams.

CHAPTER FIVE

SEAMIE HAD BEEN a guest in Edwina Hedley's London house on many occasions. He should have been familiar with it, but every time he set foot in it, it looked completely different. Eddie was forever traveling and forever bringing home plunder from her adventures with which to redecorate it.

There might be a new bronze Buddha in the dining room. Or a stone carving of Kali. Or a Thai demon, a dragon from Peking, a beaded fertility goddess from the Sudan. There might be Indian silks draping the windows, or Afghan suzanis, or fringed shawls from Spain. Once when he'd visited, a massive Russian icon was hanging from the foyer's ceiling. Right now, a huge, ornate mosaic fountain was burbling in the middle of its floor.

"It looks like Ali Baba's cave," he said, turning around in circles.

"It looks like a bloody souk," Albie muttered. "How can anyone move with all this rubbish strewn about?"

"Good evening, my dears!" a voice boomed from the drawing room.

A few seconds later, Eddie was kissing them hello. She wore a flowing turquoise silk tunic over a long, beaded skirt, and heavy necklaces of amber and lapis. Her thick gray hair was piled high on her head, held in place by two silver combs. Bracelets of silver studded with onyx jangled on her wrists.

"I like the new decor, Eddie," Seamie said. "That fountain's a smasher."

"Oh, that's nothing!" Eddie replied. "Most of what I bought is still on a boat in the middle of the Mediterranean. I can't wait until it arrives. I bought an entire Bedouin tent! I shall have it installed in the backyard. And furnish it with rugs, skins, and pillows. And we shall have the most wonderful garden parties in it. I shall have to find some belly dancers, however, for the proper effect."

"Might take some doing here in Belgravia," Seamie said.

Albie handed her a box. "From Mum," he said.

Eddie peered inside. "An almond sponge! What a darling! She knows it's my favorite. But she shouldn't have taken the time to make it for me. Not with all that's going on. How is your father, dear?"

"About the same, Aunt Eddie. No change, I'm afraid," Albie said. Then he quickly changed the subject.

The admiral was not well, not at all. Seamie and Albie had visited him that afternoon. He was gaunt and gray-faced and barely had the energy to sit up in bed. Seamie knew that his old friend didn't like talking about his father's illness; he knew that it worried him terribly.

The admiral's illness had changed Albie. In fact, Seamie barely recognized his friend these days. Albie's entire personality had changed. He'd always been the befuddled academic—even when he was ten years old. He'd always been bookish and distracted, dreaming of formulas and theories. But he was more than distracted now. He was tense. He was haggard-looking and short-tempered. And how could he not be? Seamie wondered. He never stopped working. Seamie thought the constant work was likely Albie's way of coping with his fears for his father's health, but he wished he wouldn't push himself so hard. Albie spent almost all of his time poring over documents with Strachey and Knox and other Cambridge lads. They were already at work when Seamie rose in the morning, and were still at it when he went to bed at night. Seamie didn't know exactly what they were all doing—dreaming up more incomprehensible equations, he imagined—but whatever it was, it was damaging Albie. He barely ate or slept. Seamie had had to drag him out of his office and practically push him onto the train to London today. He was certain that if Albie kept up this punishing pace, he would soon find his own health broken.

"Come in, my dears! Come in and meet my other guest," Eddie said now, taking Seamie's arm and Albie's hand and leading them into her drawing room. Seamie saw that she'd gotten rid of her furniture and replaced it with low, painted wooden beds, each topped with bright silk cushions. The place looked like an opium den.

"Tom, this is my nephew Albie Alden, and his friend Seamus Finnegan, the dashing Antarctic explorer," Eddie said, as a young man, holding a glass of champagne, stood up to greet them. "Albie and Seamie, may I present Tom Lawrence. He's an explorer, too, but he prefers the warmer climes. He's just returned from the deserts of Arabia. We met onboard a steamer out of Cairo. Spent some lovely days together."

Seamie and Albie shook hands with Tom, then Eddie handed them glasses of champagne. Seamie guessed that Lawrence was in his mid-twenties. His skin was bronzed. His eyes were a light, Wedgwood blue; his hair was blond. He stood awkwardly in Eddie's overdone drawing room and looked so uncomfortable in his suit—as if he would like nothing better than to chuck it off, pull on some trousers and boots, and head back to the desert. Seamie liked him immediately.

"I believe we've met, Mr. Alden," Lawrence said. "I was visiting friends at Cambridge several years ago. The Stracheys. George Mallory. I met you and Miss Willa Alden, too. In the Pick. Do you remember?"

"Why, yes. Yes, I do," Albie said. "One of the Stephen girls was with you. Virginia."

"Yes, that's right," Lawrence said.

"I'm very pleased to see you again, Tom," Albie said. "I wouldn't have recognized you. The desert's turned you from a pasty English lad to a golden boy."

Lawrence laughed warmly. "You should have seen me a year ago," he said. "Not golden at all, but as red as a radish and peeling like an onion. How is Miss Alden? I've seen her photographs of India and China. They're quite remarkable. Superb, actually. Is she well?"

Albie shook his head. "I wish I could tell you. Unfortunately, I have no idea."

"I don't understand," Lawrence said, puzzled.

"She had an accident. About eight years ago. On Kilimanjaro. She was there with Mr. Finnegan," Eddie said, her eyes resting on Seamie as she spoke. "She took a fall and broke her leg. It had to be amputated. The fall broke her heart, too, I fear, for she never came back home. Took off to the East instead, the headstrong girl. To Tibet. Lives there with the yaks and the sheep and that bloody great mountain."

Seamie looked away. The conversation pained him.

Lawrence noticed. "I see. I fear I've treaded rather harshly on tender ground," he said. "Please forgive me."

Eddie flapped a hand at him. "Don't be silly. There's nothing to forgive. We've all moved past it. Well, most of us have."

Seamie looked out of a window. Most of the time he appreciated Eddie's honest nature, her candid words, but there were times he wished she could at least *try* to be subtle.

"Why is everyone still standing? Sit down," Eddie said. "Albie, you take those pillows . . . yes, those right there. Seamie, you sit here, next to Tom." Eddie's voice dropped to a whisper. "He's a spy, you know. I'm certain of it."

"What rubbish, Eddie," Lawrence said.

"What do you talk about with all those Arab sheiks, then, Tom? Camels? Pomegranates? I doubt it. You talk uprisings. Rebellion. Freedom from their Turkish masters."

"We talk about their lives, their ancestry, and their customs. I take photographs, Eddie. Of ruins and tombs and vases and pots. I make notes and sketches."

"You make maps and alliances, my dear," Eddie said knowingly.

"Yes. Well. Turkish delight, anyone?" Lawrence asked, passing a plate of sugared rosewater jellies.

"Tell me, Mr. Lawrence, how did you come to find yourself in Arabia?" Seamie asked diplomatically.

"Archaeology. I love digging up old things. Went to Syria while I was an undergraduate. Studied the crusaders' castles there and did my thesis on them. After I left university, I was offered work with

D. G. Hogarth, an archaeologist with the British Museum. I took it. Did quite a bit of digging in the ancient Hittite city of Carchemish. In fact, I think we dug up both banks of the Euphrates," Lawrence said happily.

"I don't know if I could take the desert," Seamie said. "All that heat and sand. I need snow and ice."

Lawrence laughed. "I understand your love of all things pristine and cold, Mr. Finnegan. I enjoy mountains, and Alpine scenery, but the desert, Mr. Finnegan . . . oh, the desert."

Lawrence stopped speaking for a few seconds and smiled helplessly, and suddenly his was the face of a man in love.

"I wish you could see it," he said. "I wish you could hear the sound of the muezzins calling the faithful to prayer. And see the rays of the sun coming through the minarets. I wish you could taste the dates and the pomegranates, picked in a lush desert garden. And sit in a Bedouin tent at night listening to their stories. If you could meet the people—the imperious sheiks and sharifs. The veiled harem women. If you could meet Hussein, the sharif of Mecca, and his sons. If you could feel their hunger for independence, for freedom." He shook his head suddenly, as if embarrassed by the depth of his feeling. "If you could do these things, Mr. Finnegan, you would turn your back on Antarctica in a heartbeat."

"Oh, I don't know, Mr. Lawrence," Seamie said, baitingly. "I don't think your sand dunes can live up to my icebergs. To say nothing of my seals and penguins." His voice turned serious. He matched Lawrence's poetry with his own. "I wish you could see the sun rising on the Weddell Sea, its rays striking the ice and exploding into a million shards of light. I wish you could hear the song the wind sings to you at night and the shrieking of the ice floes shifting and shattering on the restless seas. . . ."

Tom listened raptly as Seamie spoke. They were talking about such vastly different parts of the world, and yet their kinship was immediate, for each understood the passion in the other. They were explorers, and each felt the force that called one into the great unknown. They knew the pull that made one give up the comforts of hearth and home, the nearness of friends and family. It was no accident that they were both unmarried, Seamie and Lawrence. They belonged to their passion, their yearning to see, to discover, to know. They belonged to their quest, and to nothing else.

For a few seconds after he finished speaking, Seamie's heart clenched with sorrow. It was so good to sit with these people. So few understood what drove him, but they did. There was another who understood. But she wasn't here and he wished—with his heart and his soul and everything inside him—that she was.

"I'm going back as soon as I can," Lawrence said, breaking the silence, giving voice to the urge they were both feeling. To get out of this gray, smothering London and back into the wild, beckoning world. "I'm going back to Carchemish. I've been working under William Ramsey most recently, the renowned New Testament scholar. He's with the British Museum. I'm back here to give a report on our findings. It has to be done, of course, but as soon as I've finished, I'm heading back to the desert. There's so much more to do. And you, Mr. Finnegan? Have you any further adventures planned?"

"Yes," Seamie said. "And no. And . . . well, *possibly* I guess."

"That's a strange answer," Lawrence said.

Seamie admitted that it was. "Ernest Shackleton is getting up another expedition to Antarctica, and I'm very interested in going," he explained. "But I have a compelling reason to stay in London now, too."

"Really?" Eddie said, raising an eyebrow. "Who is she?"

Seamie ignored her. "Clements Markham offered me a position at the RGS. Just yesterday in fact. He wants me to help with the money-raising efforts for new expeditions. I'd have an office and a fancy brass plaque on the door and a salary, and he tells me I'd be a fool not to take it."

"He's right," Albie said. "You would be. You're getting too old for this *Boy's Own* adventure stuff."

"Why, thank you for pointing that out, Alb," Seamie said.

A melancholy quiet descended on both Seamie and Lawrence at those words. Perhaps he is thinking himself too old for further adventures, too, Seamie thought. Or perhaps, he—like me—travels the world because he's lost someone and hopes that if he goes far enough afield, if he's cold enough or hot enough, in deep enough danger, hungry enough or sick enough, he might just forget that person. He never does, of course, but he always keeps trying. The strange, sad mood persisted until Lawrence said, "And what do you do, Mr. Alden?"

"I'm a physicist," Albie said. "I teach at Cambridge."

"He writes the most horrible, inscrutable, incomprehensible equations you've ever seen," Eddie interjected. "On a blackboard in his office. All day long. He's supposed to be on sabbatical, taking it a bit easy. Instead, he's working all hours. It's absolutely inhuman."

"Aunt Eddie . . . ," Albie protested, smiling embarrassedly.

"It's true, Albie. You never rest. Never have a nice long lunch. Never go for a ramble. You're as washed-out-looking as a pair of old knickers. You need a holiday. I know you're the country's leading and most exalted boffin, Albie dear, but surely England can wait another month or two for whatever it is that you're working on?"

"No, Aunt Eddie, England can't," Albie said. He was still smiling, but there was suddenly an edge to his voice and a grim look in his eyes. Seamie stared at his old friend, startled. Albie never spoke in anything but polite and measured tones.

As quickly as it had come, though, the hard edge was gone, and Albie's voice was mild again. No one else seemed to have noticed the lapse and Seamie wondered if he'd only imagined it. Frowning slightly, he decided he would get Albie out of the house this week for a hike across the fens, no matter how much he protested.

Prodded by his aunt, Albie told them all a bit about his work, and about the current preoccupation of physics professors the world over: the rumor that Albert Einstein would soon publish a set of ten field equations that would support a new theory of general relativity. Albie was in the process of trying to explain geodesic equations when the butler appeared in the doorway and said, "Beg your pardon, ma'am, but dinner is served."

"Oh, thank God!" Eddie said. "My head is spinning!"

The party rose. Eddie led the way out of the drawing room and down the hallway to the dining room.

As they reached the dining room, Lawrence stopped suddenly and placed a hand on Seamie's arm. "Never mind Clements Markham," he said to him quietly and with feeling. "Come out and visit me, Mr. Finnegan. You're not too old for adventures; you can't be. Because if you are, then I am, too. And if I was, I shouldn't know what to do. I shouldn't know how to live, and, frankly, I wouldn't wish to. Do you understand that feeling?"

Seamie nodded. "I do, Mr. Lawrence. All too well."

"Then do come. Bake your cold bones in Arabia's desert heat for a while."

Eddie, who'd been standing inside the doorway to the dining room listening, said, "Tom's right, Seamie. Sod Markham and Shackleton, too. Go to the desert. Bake your bones in Arabia." She smiled, then added, "And thaw your heart while you're at it."

CHAPTER SIX

"FOURPENCE, MISTER. YOU won't regret it," the girl in the red shawl said, smiling seductively. Or trying to.

Max von Brandt, head down, shoulders hunched against the cold, shook his head.

"Two, then. I'm clean, I swear. Only been on the game a week." The false brazenness was gone. She sounded desperate now.

Max glanced at her face. She couldn't have been more than fourteen. A child. Thin and shivering. He pulled a sixpence from his pocket and tossed it to her. "Go home," he said.

The girl looked at the coin, then at him. "God bless you, mister. You're a good man, you are."

Max laughed. *Hardly*, he thought. He opened the door to the Barkentine, hoping the girl had not seen his face, or that she would not remember it if she had. The Barkentine, a den of thieves in Limehouse, on the north bank of the Thames, was the sort of place Max von Brandt occasionally had to visit but was careful never to be seen doing so.

He had done his best to blend in. He'd worn the rough clothes of a workingman, he hadn't shaved for three days, and he'd hidden his silvery blond hair under a flat cap, but it was harder to hide his height, his sun-bronzed skin, or the fact that his legs weren't bowed from rickets. These things came from good food and fresh air, and in the East End of London, there was precious little of either.

Once inside the pub, Max approached the bartender. "I need to see Billy Madden," he said to him.

"No one here by that name," the man said, not bothering to look up from the day's racing sheet.

Max looked around. He knew what Madden looked like; he had a picture. He knew what Madden was, too: a thief with a boatyard—which was exactly what he needed. He inspected the faces in the room. Many had scars. Some ignored him, others eyed him insolently. He saw a woman, young, blond, and pretty—despite the faded bruises on her face—sitting alone by a window. Finally, he spotted Madden at the back, playing a game of solitaire, and walked up to his table.

"Mr. Madden, I'd like to speak with you," he said.

Billy Madden looked up. He wore a bright scarf knotted around his neck and a gold hoop in one ear. A scar puckered his brow. His mouth was filled with decaying teeth. He was a large man, physically imposing, but most unsettling were his eyes. They were predator's eyes—dark, soulless, and keen.

"Who the fuck are you?" Madden growled, his free hand going to a large flick knife on top of the table.

Max knew he would have to tread carefully. He'd been warned that Madden was violent and unstable. He wished he didn't have to deal with him, but he had no choice. The boys from Cambridge were hot on the scent. He had to find some new way of evading them, and fast, or everything would be ruined.

"My name is Peter Stiles. I'm a businessman. I would like to make a deal with you," he said, in a perfect London accent.

"You're a dead man, is what you are," Madden said. "You've a lot of bloody cheek. Maybe I'll cut some off. Throw it in the river. Throw you in after it. What's to stop me, eh?"

"A good deal of money," Max said. "I need your help, Mr. Madden. I'm prepared to pay you well for it. If you kill me, we can't do business."

Madden sat back in his chair. He gave a curt nod. He kicked a chair out from under the table. Max sat down.

"I've heard you've a boatyard," Max said. "I need a boat. A motorized one."

"For what?" Madden asked.

"To take a man from London to the North Sea. To certain coordinates there. Every fortnight. I also need a man who can pilot that boat. A man who is well known to the river authorities, who has been seen coming and going on the Thames for years, and whose movements will raise no eyebrows."

"Why do you need all this?"

"I have something that needs passing into other hands."

"Swag?" Madden asked.

"I would prefer not to say," Max said.

"If I'm risking my boat, and my man, I've a right to know," Billy said.

"Jewels, Mr. Madden. Valuable ones. I need to get them out of England, to the continent," Max said. He took his money clip out of his pocket, peeled off five twenty-pound notes from it, and laid them on the table. He rested his hand on top of them. "I'm prepared to make generous terms with you," he said.

Madden's small eyes lit up. He reached for the money, but Max did not release it.

"I'm paying you for your boat, your man, and your silence. Are we clear on this? If one word of this gets out, our deal is off."

"I hardly go looking for publicity in my line of work. Your secret's safe with me," Madden said.

Max nodded. He pushed the money over to him. "This is a down payment only. My man will bring more each time. His name is Hutchins. He will be on the dock behind the Barkentine two weeks from tonight. At midnight. Have your man meet him here."

Max stood up. He tipped his cap to Madden, then left. Madden was a grim and horrible man, and Limehouse a grim and horrible place. He was glad to be leaving both, but the meeting had been productive. Very productive.

He had something to pass into other hands, yes—but it wasn't jewelry. And he needed a chain to do it. A strong, unbreakable one stretching between London and Berlin.

And tonight, the first link had been forged.

CHAPTER SEVEN

"VOTES FOR WOMEN NO?" Seamie said, reading aloud the words on a huge banner stretched across his sister's dining room table. "That's not going to help your case, Fee," he added, as he kissed her cheek.

Fiona laughed. She had a needle in her hand and was bent over the banner, stitching. "I still have to add the W," she said. "Get yourself some breakfast, Seamie, luv."

"I think I will, thank you," Seamie said, sitting down at the table. A maid was clearing dirty plates, smeared with egg and jam, where the younger children had been sitting. They'd just gotten up from the table and had run past Seamie in the hallway. Only Katie and Joe remained at the table.

"Good morning all," Seamie said, but he got no response. Katie, her eggs untouched, her tea going cold, was shifting photographs around on a mocked-up layout of the *Battle Cry*. Joe, sitting at the head of the table, was writing furiously. The morning's newspapers lay open on the table near him. Crumpled sheets of paper littered the floor all around him.

"Pass us those kippers, Joe, will you?" Seamie said, as he put his napkin in his lap. "Joe? Oi! *Joe!*"

Joe looked up, blinking. "Sorry, lad," he said. "What is it?"

"Can I have the kippers?" Seamie said. Joe passed them over. "What are you doing?" Seamie asked him.

"Working on the speech I'm due to deliver in the Commons asking Parliament for more money for schools."

"Will you get it?" Seamie asked, spearing a fish from the platter Joe had handed him.

"It's doubtful," Katie said, before Joe could reply and without looking up from her newspaper. "Mr. Churchill's speaking, too. Right after Dad. He wants more boats and he has a good deal of support for them from both benches. Germany's saber rattling has many in England eager to build up our military. Calls are being made for monies to fund a new fleet of dreadnoughts and Dad thinks they'll be heeded—based on precedent. Five years ago, Lloyd George tried to cut naval spending—back when he was chancellor of the exchequer—and was roundly defeated."

Seamie shook his head, laughing. "Is that so, Kitkat?" he said, calling Katie by a nickname he'd given her—one that he knew she hated. "Don't you ever talk about anything other than politics?

You're fifteen years old, and a girl, for goodness' sake. Don't you ever talk about dances or dresses or boys?"

Katie looked up at him, narrowing her eyes. Seamie laughed. He liked to spar with her.

"You really oughtn't to tease her," Fiona said, still stitching. "She gives as good as she gets. You know that."

"Come on, Kitkat," Seamie said, not heeding his sister's warning. "I'll buy you a new dress. From Harrods. A frilly pink one with bows on it. And a hat to match. We'll go today."

"Yes, let's," Katie said, smiling like a shark. "And while we're there, let's buy a suit, too. For you, Uncle Seamie. A gray worsted cut nice and tight with miles of buttons. We'll get a tie, too. To keep your shirt collar nice and tight around your throat. Just like a noose. Today a desk job at the RGS, tomorrow a nice little wife who'll darn your socks for you, and next week a semidetached in Croydon." She sat back in her chair, crossed her arms over her chest, and started humming Chopin's Funeral March.

"Tomboy," Seamie said, bested and genuinely annoyed by it.

"Pencil pusher," Katie retorted.

"Hoyden."

"Office boy."

"I haven't even taken the job yet!" Seamie said defensively.

"Oi, you two!" Joe said. "That's enough."

Seamie, still glowering—for Katie had touched a nerve—speared himself a broiled tomato from a platter.

"I warned you," Fiona said to him.

"Can you take me to the *Clarion*'s printing presses tomorrow afternoon, Uncle Seamie? Please? I need to get the next edition of the *Battle Cry* printed and Mum and Dad are busy and they won't let me go alone," Katie said.

"I don't see why I should," Seamie said, huffily.

Katie smiled again. It was a real smile this time, broad and engaging. "Because you're my uncle and you love me to bits," she said.

"*Did*," Seamie said. "I did love you to bits."

Katie's face fell.

"Oh, I'm just joking. Of course I'll take you," Seamie quickly said. He couldn't stand to see her sad, even if she was just putting it on.

"Thank you, Uncle Seamie!" Katie said. "I was just joking, too. You'd never take that job, I know you wouldn't. And you'd never move to Croydon, either."

Katie went back to her paper. Joe continued to write, Fiona to stitch. The younger children's voices carried to Seamie from another part of the house—they were shrieking and laughing and undoubtedly having fun.

Seamie stopped piling food on his plate and looked at them—Fiona, Joe, and Katie. He was happy, being here with his sister and her family, but it struck him now that it was her family, not his. As much as they loved him, and as much as he loved them, he was an uncle—not a father, not a husband. And he had never felt that distinction as keenly as he did right now. He had no idea why. Perhaps it was Katie teasing him about having a little wife who would darn his socks. She was right, of course—he wouldn't take the RGS job, much less move to Croydon—but as he looked at his sister and her family—together around the table, busy and contented, always happy to spend time in one another's company—he wished, just for a moment, that he had someone in his life who could make him *want* to move to Croydon. An image of Jennie Wilcott popped into his head, but he quickly pushed it out again. Connecting her to this odd, uncharacteristic longing for domestic bliss was madness; he barely knew her.

"Give us a paper, will you?" he suddenly said to Joe, wanting to dispel his strange mood.

Joe handed him one. Seamie spread it out next to his plate, picked up his fork, and glanced at the headline. KAISER'S DREADNOUGHT LAUNCHED, it read. And below it, CHILL WIND BLOWS ACROSS BELGIUM AND FRANCE.

Neither the ominous headline nor the story that followed it did anything to dampen Seamie's appetite. He was starving. He added broiled mushrooms, bacon, poached eggs, and buttered toast to the herring and tomato already on his plate, then poured himself a cup of tea. It was an Assam, bright, brick red, and strong enough to bring the dead back to life. He needed that. George Mallory was in town. They'd gone out on a pub crawl last night and he hadn't gotten home until three A.M.

It was nine o'clock now on a clear and crisp March Saturday. Seamie was spending a long weekend with Joe and Fiona at their Greenwich estate. Easter was only a month away, and Fiona had come out especially to check on the progress the painters were making. She had invited fifty people for Easter dinner and wanted several rooms freshened up before the holiday.

"The post, madam," Foster said now, placing a silver tray piled high with letters on the table.

"Thank you, Mr. Foster," Fiona said, not bothering to look up from her work.

"I believe that a missive from California is included among the invitations and tradesmen's bills, madam. I believe the cancellation reads Point Reyes Station."

"Point Reyes? How wonderful!" Fiona said. She put her needle down, dove into the mail, and fished out a large, stiff envelope.

"How are the painters faring, Mr. Foster?" Joe asked.

"Quite well, sir. They've finished in the drawing room and have moved on to the foyer."

"Oh, Joe! Seamie! Look!" Fiona said with emotion. "India's sent us a beautiful likeness of herself, Sid, and the children. How lovely they are!"

Seamie snorted. "Our brother? Lovely?" he said.

"Well, his children are," Fiona said, laughing. "Just look at Charlotte. What a beauty. And the baby. And Wish, who looks just like his father." She paused for a few seconds, then softly said, "And ours."

Seamie tried to read his sister's expression as her eyes traveled over the images in the photograph. He saw love in it, and happiness, and loss.

He knew she still grieved for their parents. Their father, Paddy, had been killed back in 1888 at the docks where he worked. His death had looked like an accident, but it had been the work of his employer, William Burton. Paddy, a union organizer, had been trying to get his fellow dockers at Burton Tea to join the dockworkers union. Burton, together with an East London thug named Bowler Sheehan, had arranged the so-called accident to put an end to Paddy's unionizing. And Kate, their mother, had been murdered the same year by a madman known as Jack the Ripper.

Their baby sister, ill and weak, had died shortly thereafter. And then they'd lost their brother Charlie. He hadn't died. He'd been driven mad by the sight of his mother dying in the street by their house. He'd run away, and then killed another lad in self-defense. Too afraid to return to his family, he'd taken the dead boy's name—Sid Malone—and descended into a life of crime.

Years later, Fiona had met up with him again. They had a falling out, and Sid disappeared back into the dark streets of East London. Heartbroken over what he'd become, Fiona made the decision never to tell Seamie what had really happened to the brother he'd loved.

He had found out anyway, though—years later, in the most horrible way. Joe, the newly elected MP for Whitechapel, had sought out Sid, to warn him to stay on the straight and narrow or there would be consequences. Joe hadn't been able to see Sid, but he'd seen his henchman—Frankie Betts. They got into a terrible fight, and Frankie, worried that Sid would desert him and the other hard men who worked for him, had shot Joe and blamed the shooting on Sid—hoping to make it impossible for him to return to the straight world.

Sid, on the run and wounded by a detective's bullet, had come to Fiona's house late one night to tell her that he hadn't shot her Joe. She'd taken him in and hidden him until it was safe for him to get out of London. He'd gotten himself hired on the first ship he could find, a cargo ship bound for Africa. He'd left everything behind: his life, his family, and the woman he loved—a young, aristocratic doctor named India Selwyn Jones. He'd left her because he believed she'd abandoned him to marry a man of her class—a corrupt and heartless politician named Freddie Lytton. India only married Freddie, however, because she believed Sid was dead, and because she was carrying Sid's child and wanted a father, if only on paper, for that child.

Sid and India met again in Africa. Sid was living there under an assumed last name—Baxter—and Freddie, a rising star in the Colonial Office, had been sent there on government business. When he realized that Sid was still alive, he had him arrested and thrown in jail, in hopes of having him hanged. And then Freddie had nearly killed both India and the child—a girl named Charlotte—by abandoning them in the African bush. He'd been killed himself, however, by hyenas as he was on his way back to the bungalow where they'd all been staying. With Seamie's help—for he had been in Africa himself at the time, at Kilimanjaro—Sid escaped from jail, barely in time to save India and Charlotte. He brought them to safety, and then, still fearing arrest, he rode off, leaving them with only a note telling them to meet him in America, in California, where India owned land. They would begin again there. He promised them that. At Point Reyes on the coast, where he and India had once dreamed of going, where the sea met the sky.

"I wouldn't believe it if I wasn't seeing it," Seamie said now, as Fiona handed him the photograph. He looked at the faces of the beaming children, the beautiful woman, and the man, tanned and smiling. "Our brother—married, happy, and raising cows."

"Steers," Joe said.

"Cow, steers . . . does it matter? I couldn't be more surprised if he was raising daffodils," Seamie said.

"He's so fortunate," Fiona said. "To have survived that journey, all those miles across Africa, and then the passage to New York, and the trek to the west."

Seamie nodded. He remembered waiting desperately for news of his brother. They had all waited, and worried, and suffered, for the better part of a year, until finally they'd had a letter from India in Point Reyes telling them that Sid had come home to her and Charlotte, and that he was all right. Or would be, in time.

He had journeyed west across the entire continent of Africa with a horse and little else—including little money. He'd had his gun with him and so was able to hunt his food. His horse grazed. And water was free wherever he could find it. Halfway across, he'd come down with malaria. Tribesmen found him and doctored him. He pulled through, and when he got his strength back—about a month later—he continued on to Port Gentil. There, he sold his horse and worked the docks until he'd saved up enough money for a passage to New York. He worked the docks again when he arrived in the States, this time in Brooklyn, until he'd earned enough money for train fare to San Francisco.

He almost made it, too, but he was coshed and robbed in Denver one night as he made his way to a cheap hotel where he'd planned to spend the night before catching a train west the next morning. He'd had to hunt for work again and found it in a slaughter yard. He worked there for two months, and nearly had his fare earned, when he was injured. A steer got loose, trampled him, and broke his leg. A man in the tenement where he lived—an orderly at a pauper's hospital—set his leg to save him the doctor's fee, which was why he walked with a cane. He'd gotten five dollars out of the yard's foreman. That, together with the money he'd saved, got him to San Francisco, and then up the coast. He'd arrived at Point Reyes with forty-six cents in his pocket.

Seamie had asked him once, in a letter, if he'd ever had a moment where he wondered if he should be making the journey. He hadn't spoken to India since he deposited her, half-delirious, back at the bungalow in Kenya, where she had been staying. What the hell would he have done if she hadn't been there?

Sid wrote back that the thought had never crossed his mind. Of course she'd be there. And he'd have made a hundred such journeys, if that's what it took to get to her and Charlotte.

"I know some people might think I'm mad," he wrote. "But I'm not, I'm lucky. So bloody lucky."

Seamie had smiled at that and folded the letter away. Sid had married India only days after he arrived. They'd had another child, a boy, in 1908. They named him Aloysius—Wish for short—for India's cousin. And then baby Elizabeth had arrived four months ago. She was named for Elizabeth Garrett Anderson and Elizabeth Blackwell, two of the first women doctors. They were happy, Sid and India. Seamie hadn't been to visit them yet, but Fiona and Joe and their children had. Fiona said that their house was filled with light and love and laughter, and that one could see and smell and hear the ocean from every room.

Seamie thought now that both his sister and his brother had had lives that seemed as if they'd come from a fairy story, complete with happy endings. He thought it must be nice to have those things. Not everyone got to have them. He hadn't. His happy ending had run away from him, all the way to the other side of the world.

"Oh, Joe, we must go to California again next year. I miss them all so much," Fiona said, still gazing longingly at the photograph. "The baby's already four months old, and we've never even seen her. Well, Maud's going at the end of the summer. That's something."

Maud Selwyn Jones was India's sister and now Seamie's, Fiona's, and Joe's sister-in-law. She was also Fiona's good friend. The two women had worked together for years on women's suffrage, and a close bond had developed between them. A widow and enormously wealthy, Maud scandalized British society by doing exactly what she pleased, when she pleased—whether it involved traveling to unsuitable places, indulging in unsuitable substances, or dallying with unsuitable men.

"I'm going to give Maud a trunk filled with presents for the children to take with her. She said she'd be happy to do it. I saw her the other day, you know. We talked about the trip, and how much she was looking forward to seeing her nieces and nephew. She joked that she's finally become the thing she most feared—an old spinster aunt." Fiona laughed. "Hardly! She's still very beautiful. She must've been something else when she was younger. Well, weren't we all?"

Seamie looked at Joe. He looked mortified. Seamie knew Joe and Maud had been lovers once, many years ago, before Fiona and Joe were married.

"Oh, sorry, luv!" Fiona said sheepishly, noticing Joe's expression. "Forgot about all that. I suppose I should be jealous, shouldn't I? I would be, Joe, but the problem is, good women friends are so hard to find." She reached over and patted his hand. "Almost as hard to find as good husbands. And anyway, Maud's not after you anymore. I think she's quite taken with Harriet's cousin, that handsome Max von Brandt. She told me he's too young for her, but then again, Jennie Churchill married a man twenty years her junior, didn't she? It's the fashion now, and why not? Men have been doing it for ages. I saw Lady Nevill in the park the other day. She's in her eighties now and as wicked as ever. She was walking amongst a whole gaggle of children. I asked her what she was doing there, and she said, 'Well, if you want to know, my dear, I am searching in the perambulators for *my* next husband!' "

Joe rolled his eyes. Seamie laughed. He poured himself a second cup of tea, downed it, finished the last of his kipper, then said, "Well, I'm off, Fee. I've a busy morning. I'm going to visit Admiral Alden again."

"How is he?" Fiona asked.

"Worsening, I'm afraid," Seamie said.

"I'm so sorry to hear it. We'll go to visit him soon. In the meantime, please give him and Mrs. Alden our best."

"I will, Fee. And after I've seen him, there's a lunch at the Royal Geographical Society. Shackleton's going to be there."

"Oh, no," Fiona said, frowning. "Not again! We just got you back."

"Very possibly," Seamie said, grinning. "Rumor has it his latest expedition's actually coming together. Don't wait for me for tea. I'll be back late."

Fiona was looking at him thoughtfully as he spoke. He knew his sister well enough to be worried when she did that.

"Seamie, luv . . ."

"Yes, Fiona?"

"Since you're going into the city anyway, would you do me a favor?"

"Uh-oh."

"What? Why uh-oh? All I wanted you to do was to drop off a check at the Wilcotts'. Joe and I are making a donation to Jennie's school."

Katie looked up, giggling. "Croydon, here I come!" she said.

Seamie ignored his niece. He gave his sister a long look. "Ever heard of a post office, Fee?"

"In fact, yes. I have. I thought you taking it would be safer, that's all."

"Fine. I'll take it. All I have to do is slide it through the Reverend Wilcott's mail slot, right?"

"Well, it *would* be nice if you could give it to the Wilcotts in person. It's for a rather large amount, you know. I wouldn't want it to go missing."

Joe, still working on his speech, snorted. "You're about as subtle as a freight train, lass," he said.

"What?" Fiona said, feigning innocence. "You don't . . . you *can't* think I'm matchmaking?"

"Yes, I can," Seamie and Joe said together.

Fiona made a face at them. "All right, then," she admitted. "I am. So what? Jennie Wilcott's a lovely young woman. Any man in his right mind would be madly interested in her."

"Stop, Fiona," Seamie said. "Just stop."

"I'm only concerned about you, you know. Concerned about your happiness."

"I'm perfectly happy," Seamie said. "Deliriously happy."

"How could you be? With no home of your own? With no wife and family? I don't worry about Sid anymore—"

"Lucky sod," Seamie said under his breath.

"—but I do worry about you. I wish you had what he had. You can't spend your best years alone at the South Pole with only icebergs and penguins for company, you know. What kind of life is that?"

Seamie sighed.

"I just want you to be happy, Seamie. Truly happy, I mean. As happy as Sid and India are. As happy as Joe and I are. I just want—"

Fiona's words were cut off by the sound of a loud and terrible crash. It was followed by shouting, swearing, barking, and crying.

"Bloody hell," Joe said.

Two seconds later, the dogs, Tetley and Typhoo, came tearing into the dining room, yipping and covered in paint. Six-year-old Rose, eleven-year-old Peter, and the twins, Patrick and Michael, who were four, followed, clutching on to their thirteen-year-old brother, Charlie. All five were also covered in paint. The three painters came next, covered in paint, followed, most alarmingly, by Mr. Foster, also covered in paint.

Rose stamped her foot and sobbed that it was all Peter's fault and he'd ruined her favorite dress. Peter blamed Charlie. Charlie just blinked through the blobs of white paint dripping off his head onto his clothing. Patrick and Michael, howling, blamed no one. They just sought comfort—in their father's lap. Joe tried to fight them off, but in no time at all he, too, was covered in paint. The dogs trotted about, tracking paint everywhere. Then one of them shook himself, spraying paint all over Fiona. The head painter swore he wouldn't come back, not ever.

Seamie shook his head in disbelief. He had sailed to Antarctica, often on rough seas, in a small ship with men and dogs and livestock, but that had been a peaceful stroll through the park compared to the noise and commotion he was witnessing now. He poured himself another cup of tea, drank it, then said, "You lot can keep Croydon. I'll take the South Pole any day of the week!"

CHAPTER EIGHT

THE LONDON OMNIBUS turned onto Wapping's High Street. It bumped and banged over the rutted cobblestones, belched and sputtered as it picked up speed, then careened dangerously around the bends and turns of the narrow and winding dockside thoroughfare.

Seamie, sitting on the bus's open top deck, lifted his face to the sky. It was a fair day, but the locals wouldn't have known it. The sun didn't shine on the streets of Wapping; the warehouses, dark and looming, blocked it out. A stiff breeze carried the smell of the Thames on it, muddy and low, with a tang of salt.

An image suddenly shimmered across Seamie's mind, a quick, fleeting picture of a handsome man with black hair and blue eyes. They were sitting together on a flight of stone steps at the river's edge. He was small, only a tiny boy, and the man had his arm around him. The man's voice was low and beautiful and full of the music of his native Ireland. He was telling him the names of all the ships in the river and what they were carrying and where they were from.

And then the picture faded. As it always did. Seamie tried to call it back, but he couldn't. He wished he remembered more about the man, his father. He was only four when his father died and his memories of him were few, but he knew he'd been happy then, sitting by the river. He knew even then, at the age of four, that he loved ships and the water, but not nearly as much as he loved his father.

The bus slowed, coughed, and came to a stop at the Prospect of Whitby, an old riverside public house. Seamie hopped off. Fiona had told him that the Reverend Wilcott's church was on Watts Street, just north of the pub. He planned to say a quick hello to the Wilcotts, drop off the check, and be on his way.

He'd just come from visiting the Aldens and would have to go all the way back west again to get to the dinner at the Royal Geographical Society. He was running late, too, for he'd stayed at the Aldens' house longer than he'd planned.

Seamie was no doctor, but he didn't need to be to see that the admiral's condition was worsening. His face was waxen and he was in a great deal of pain. He'd been happy to see Seamie and eager to hear about Ernest Shackleton's plans for another trip to Antarctica, but he'd needed morphine twice in the scant hour that Seamie had been with him.

"It's cancer of the stomach," Mrs. Alden had said tearfully, as he'd sat with her in the drawing room afterward. "We've known it for a while, but we haven't talked about it much. I suppose we should have. But we're not terribly good at talking about such things, Albie and I. Dogs and the weather, those are our preferred topics."

"Does Willa know?" he asked.

Mrs. Alden shook her head. "If she does, she's given us no word. I've written her. Albie has, too. Several times. But I've received nothing from her. Nothing at all."

"She'll come," Seamie said. "I know she will."

He'd promised Mrs. Alden to call again soon, given her Fiona's and Joe's regards, and then left for Wapping. It was too much for him, seeing the admiral suffering so, and seeing all the photographs of Willa in Mrs. Alden's drawing room.

He tried to shake the sadness off now, as the church of St. Nicholas came into sight. It was old and unlovely, as was most everything in Wapping. Seamie first tried the door to the rectory—a sooty stone building built cheek-by-jowl to the church, but it was locked. He then tried the church door. It was open. He went inside, hoping he might find the Reverend Wilcott in there, tidying the altar or some such thing. Instead, he found Jennie Wilcott and two dozen children.

They weren't in the classroom he passed, but were all seated—some on chairs, some on tea chests—around a small black stove in the sacristy, reading words chalked on a portable blackboard. Jennie looked up at the sound of his footsteps, startled. He was startled, too—startled to see how pretty she was. She looked so different from the last time he'd seen her. Her eye was no longer swollen; the bruising around it had faded some. Her blond hair was neatly combed and pinned up in a twist. Her clothes, a white cotton blouse and blue twill skirt, were clean and pressed and showed off her lovely curves and tiny waist.

She's more than pretty, he thought. She's beautiful.

"Hello, again, Miss Wilcott," he said. "I'm Seamus Finnegan. Fiona Bristow's brother. We met a few weeks ago. At the . . . um . . . well, at the prison."

Jennie Wilcott's face lit up. "Yes, of course! What a pleasure it is to see you again, Mr. Finnegan!" she said.

"Cor, miss, was you sent down *again*?" a little boy asked.

"It's '*Were* you sent down again?,' Dennis. And yes, I was."

"You're in the clink more than me dad, miss!" a girl said.

"Do you think so? I'd say it's pretty close. Luckily, I had Mr. Finnegan to help get me out last time. Boys and girls, do you know who Mr. Finnegan is?"

"No, miss," twenty-four voices said in unison.

"Then I shall tell you. He is one of our country's heroes—a real, live explorer!"

There were cries of "Get out of it, miss!" and "Blimey!" and "Pull the other one, it's got bells on."

"Yes, he is. He went with Mr. Amundsen to the South Pole in Antarctica, and he's here now to tell you all about it. He promised me that he would come and here he is!"

Jennie's voice was excited. Her eyes, as she looked at the children seated all around her, shone.

Seamie had quite forgotten about the promise he'd made. "Actually, Miss Wilcott, I came to give you this," he said, pulling an envelope from his breast pocket. "It's from Fiona and Joe. It's a donation."

"Oh. Oh, I see," Jennie said, disappointment in her voice. "Forgive me, Mr. Finnegan, I thought . . ."

Twenty-four little faces, upturned and eager, suddenly fell.

"Is he not going to talk to us, miss?" one boy asked.

"Miss, won't he stay?"

"Won't he tell us about Ann Tartika?"

"Now, children. Mr. Finnegan is very busy and—" Jennie began to say.

"Of course I'll stay," Seamie said hastily, finding that he couldn't bear the disappointment in the children's faces. Or Jennie Wilcott's.

He hastily stuffed the envelope back into his pocket, then sat down among the children. One boy stood to give him his seat, which was close to the stove, but Seamie told him to sit down again. The child was poorly dressed for a March day.

Seamie began by telling them about his first expedition. He'd gone to the Royal Geographical Society one night to hear Ernest Shackleton speak about his upcoming trip to Antarctica, and his quest to find the South Pole. He'd been so impressed with Shackleton, and so determined to be a part of his expedition, that he'd followed the man home and stood outside his house for thirty-three hours, never moving, never so much as flinching, not when night fell, not when it poured rain, until Shackleton invited him in. He'd impressed the explorer with his enthusiasm and his steadfastness, and Shackleton had taken him on.

The children's eyes grew wide as Seamie told them what it had been like to set off for the South Pole at the age of seventeen. He told them of the endless seas, the vast night skies, the lashing storms. He told them of life on board the *Discovery*—Shackleton's vessel—and of the hard work, the discipline, and the tedium of being cooped up for months in such a small space with so many men. He told them about his more recent journey to the pole with Amundsen. He told them what it was like to finally feel the air turn frigid and see ice in the water. To be watched by seals and penguins and whales. To work at twenty below zero, to set up camp, run dog sleds, take measurements and readings, to trek over treacherous pack ice, to force the body to perform miracles of physical endurance when it hurt just to breathe.

And he told them that it was worth it. The long voyage, the

loneliness, the bad food, the agony of cold—it was worth every second of pain and doubt, just to stand where no one had ever stood before, in a pristine wilderness of snow and ice. To be the first.

He talked to the children for nearly two hours. He didn't notice the time passing. He never did when he talked about Antarctica. He forgot time, and he forgot himself. He was aware of only one thing—his desire to make his audience feel the passion he felt for Antarctica and to see—if only in their imaginations—the beauty he'd seen there.

When he finished, the children applauded loudly. Seamie smiled at their enthusiasm, at the curiosity and excitement in their faces. They had a million questions for him, and he did his best to answer them. But suddenly it was four o'clock and time for them to go home. They thanked him and begged him to come back, and he said he would. They readied themselves to leave, and as they did, Jennie said, "There's one more thing, children. One thing Mr. Finnegan forgot to tell you. Do any of you know where Mr. Finnegan was born?"

They all shook their heads.

"Who can guess?"

"Buckingham Palace!"

"Blackpool!"

"Harrods!"

"He was born in East London," Jennie finally said. "Just like you. He lived with his sister and brother in Whitechapel."

There were expressions of disbelief, then searching glances and shy smiles—all evidence of some small, secret hope held in each heart.

"I'm so sorry, Mr. Finnegan," Jennie said, when the children were gone. "I didn't mean to put you on show. I didn't know you'd come to bring a donation. I thought you'd come to speak with the children."

"Please don't apologize. I enjoyed it. Really."

"Then thank you. It was very kind of you."

"It was nothing, Miss Wilcott. I hope I gave them a bit of entertainment."

"You gave them more than entertainment," Jennie said, with a sudden intensity. "You gave them hope. Their lives are very hard, Mr. Finnegan. Very hard. Everything and everyone conspires against them. Every voice they hear—a weary mother's, a drunken father's, a grasping employer's—tells them that the bright and shining things of this world are for others, not for them. Today, you silenced those voices. If only for a few hours."

Jennie turned away then, as if embarrassed by her emotion, and busied herself with banking the coals in the stove. "I don't know why I bother," she said. "It's a useless stove. It heats nothing. But at least it's a stove. We don't have any heat at all in our actual classroom."

"It's Saturday, Miss Wilcott."

"Yes, it is," she said, raking the embers into a pile with a poker.

"You hold school on Saturdays?"

"Yes, of course. It's a day when I can actually persuade the children's parents to send them to me. Most of the factories and warehouses close at half day on Saturdays, you see. There's no work to be had in the afternoons, so they can come here."

"Don't they go to regular schools?"

"In theory, yes," Jennie said, closing the stove's door.

"In theory?"

"Families must eat, Mr. Finnegan. They must pay their rent. Pay for coal. Children can do piecework at factories. They can stuff tickings with straw. They can scrub floors." She gave him a wry smile. "When you weigh a pound of sausages bought with a child's wages against maths equations or writing out Tennyson, the sausages always win."

Seamie laughed. Jennie took her coat off a hook, shrugged into it, and put her hat on. She pulled a pair of leather gloves from her coat pocket, and as she did, Seamie saw that a long, faded scar ran across the back of one hand. He wondered what had caused it, but thought it rude to ask.

"I'm off to the market," she said, picking up a willow basket off the floor. "There's one on Cable Street on Saturday evenings."

Seamie said he was going that way, too. Which he wasn't, of course. Until now. They left the church, leaving the doors unlocked.

"Aren't you worried about robberies?" he asked.

"I am. But my father's more worried about people's souls. So we leave the doors open," she said.

They set off north.

"Your life sounds so exciting, Mr. Finnegan," Jennie said, as they walked together.

"It's Seamie. Please."

"All right, then. And you must call me Jennie. As I was saying, your life sounds amazing. What incredible adventures you've had."

"Do you think so? You should go exploring," Seamie said.

"Oh, no. Not me. I can't bear the cold. I wouldn't last two seconds at the South Pole."

"What about India then? Or Africa? The dark continent," Seamie said, echoing an expression used by mapmakers about Africa, because so much of it was unknown and hence left dark on the maps.

Jennie laughed. "*England* is the dark continent. Take a walk in Whitechapel, down Flower and Dean Street, or Hanbury, or Brick Lane, if you need convincing. I've always felt that British politicians and missionaries should make certain their own house is in order before marching off to set the Africans to rights." She paused, then looked up at him from under her hat brim. "I sound terribly righteous, don't I?"

"Not at all."

"Liar."

It was Seamie's turn to laugh.

"It's just that I feel there are such important discoveries to be made right here, Mr. Finnegan."

"Seamie."

"Seamie. One doesn't have to travel far. Watching the children who come to my school learn their letters and numbers, watching them read pages of Kipling or Dickens and thrilling at the worlds and the people those books contain, watching their small faces light up as they make their own discoveries . . . well, I know it's not mountains or rivers, but there's nothing more exciting. To me, at least."

Seamie noticed the way Jennie's own face lit up as she talked about the children. The sparkle in her eyes, the flush on her cheeks, made her look even prettier.

They arrived at Cable Street, where the bustling and noisy Saturday market was in full swing. Costers of all stripes sang their wares. A greengrocer juggled last autumn's apples. Butchers hefted chops for their customers' appreciation. Fishmongers cleaved the heads off salmon, plaice, and haddock. At a clothes stall, women tussled over secondhand shoes for their children.

"That's an awful lot of potatoes for two people," Seamie said, as Jennie bought five pounds from a greengrocer.

"Oh, it's not just for my father and me, it's for the children, too."

Seamie felt puzzled. "The children?" he said, trying to keep the surprise from his voice.

"Oh, yes. I cook for them. Cornish pasties usually. They're very partial to them."

"I didn't know you had children," Seamie said.

"I don't," Jennie said. "I meant for the schoolchildren. They're always hungry. There are times when the pasties are all they get to eat in a day."

"Oh, right. Of course," Seamie said. He'd felt an unwelcome twinge of jealousy at the thought of her with children—and a husband.

Jennie finished loading the potatoes into her basket, paid the coster, then struggled to lift the basket.

"Please, Miss Wil—Jennie. May I carry that for you?"

"You don't mind? It would be a great help."

"Not at all," he said, taking the basket. He also took a loaf of bread from a baker, two pounds of lamb from a butcher, and nutmeg from a spice seller, and put them all in her basket. He noticed how expertly she negotiated with the costers, shaving pennies off prices at every stall. He wondered what sort of salary a minister made. It couldn't be much. And he was willing to bet a good deal of it went on food and books for the children and coal for the church stove.

"I believe I'm finally finished," Jennie said, after tucking a half pound of butter into the basket. She looked at her watch. "My goodness,

I'd better be getting back. The reverend will be home shortly and expecting his tea. He'll be tired, my dad. Today's his day to visit the sick of his parish. There was a rumor of a cholera outbreak on Kennet Street. I hope it's only a rumor."

"*Cholera?*" Seamie said. "That must be very dangerous work."

Jennie smiled sadly. "Very. It's how my mother died. She caught typhoid on one of her visits to a parish family. That was ten years ago."

"I'm sorry," Seamie said.

"Thank you. You would think it might've stopped my father, wouldn't you? Losing his wife and all. But it didn't. He believes God is watching over him." She shook her head. "His faith is so strong. So absolute. I wish I had it, but I don't. I'm afraid I spend more time arguing with God than I do praising Him."

Jennie took a deep breath, then blew it back out again. She looked as if she was trying to gather her composure. Seamie wondered what it was like to tend mortally ill people. To visit slum houses that most doctors were afraid to set foot in. To lose one's mother to typhoid. To brave ignorance and poverty every day of one's life. Looking at Jennie, Seamie realized that courage took many forms.

"I'm sure I've taken enough of your time," she said. "Thank you again for talking to the children and for carrying my marketing. You've gone above and beyond the call of duty today."

She reached for her basket, but Seamie didn't give it to her. "Don't be silly. It's far too heavy," he said. "I'll carry it for you."

"No, really. I couldn't ask you to."

"You didn't," Seamie said. "I offered."

Twenty minutes later, they arrived at the rectory. The Reverend Wilcott was already home. "Come in! Come in!" he said, opening the door for them. "Why, Mr. Finnegan, is that you?"

"I'm afraid so, Reverend," Seamie said, taking the man's outstretched hand.

"It's wonderful to see you again, my boy! Have you come to join us for tea?"

"No, sir, I haven't. I was just helping Jen—Miss Wilcott with her marketing," Seamie said, suddenly formal again in front of the reverend.

"Nonsense! Stay and have a bite of something with us. There's plenty. Jennie's had a hotpot simmering on the stove all day."

"Won't you stay?" Jennie said. "It's the least I could do after all you've done for me today."

Seamie knew he was supposed to be at the RGS. At a talk. And a dinner. And the interminable drinks session that was bound to follow. "All right, then. Yes. I'd love to," he said.

Jennie led the way through a short, narrow hallway, into a brightly lit kitchen. The reverend took a seat by the hearth. Seamie put the heavy basket on a bench under a window, then stood around feeling foolish. He looked out of a window and saw a small yard.

"Our garden," Jennie said, smiling. "Such as it is. It looks much nicer in summer." She took his jacket and told him to sit down next to her father. The next thing he knew, she was handing him a cup of tea, hot and reviving.

He looked around the little kitchen as he sipped his tea. It was tidy and warm. White lace curtains hung in the window. Bright rag rugs dotted the floor. A little earthen pot, filled with purple crocuses, sat atop the table. The fire gave off a delicious heat, and whatever Jennie had in the oven gave off a delicious smell.

"Did you put the parsley in, Dad?" Jennie asked her father, laying a gentle hand on his shoulder.

"Hmm? What was that?" the Reverend said, taking her hand in his.

"Did you put any parsley into the hotpot? You were supposed to. To finish it off."

"I'm sorry, my dear. I quite forgot."

"Oh, you." She scolded him fondly.

He patted her hand, bade her sit down beside him. "It will be a wonderful dish, parsley or no." To Seamie he said, "Jennie is a marvelous cook."

"I look forward to it," Seamie said. "My bachelor existence doesn't allow me home-cooked meals very often."

"How were the children today?" the reverend asked Jennie.

"Just wonderful!" she said. "Mr. Finnegan came to talk to them. He told them all about his expeditions. Oh, you should have seen their faces, Dad. They were so excited!"

"Did you now, lad? That was very good of you," the reverend said.

"How were your visits? Is it as bad as you feared?" Jennie asked.

The Reverend Wilcott shook his head. "Thankfully, the cholera scare was only that—a scare—and I pray to God it stays that way. Cholera moves like lightning through the slums, Mr. Finnegan. It's the closeness that does it, of course. Too many people jammed into too little space. Sharing rooms and beds and privies. Water lines running close to the sewers. Bad air. All it takes is one person, and before you know it, the entire street's down. But for today at least, we are spared."

Jennie squeezed his hand, then went back to her stove.

"Can I help you with anything?" Seamie asked.

"No, thank you. I can manage," Jennie said.

"I'm quite handy. I cooked onboard the *Discovery*, you know," Seamie said.

"Did you?"

"Yes. For the sled dogs."

Jennie narrowed her eyes. "Are you making comparisons, Mr. Finnegan?" she asked.

"What? No. No! Oh, blast. I just meant that I know my way around a kitchen. It was one of the most important jobs on the entire expedition. If the dogs hadn't been well fed and healthy when we made land, we would have gone nowhere."

"Well, *I* won't be needing your help, but perhaps you can go with my father on his visits. You could feel his parishioners' noses. See if they're cold and wet," Jennie said.

The reverend laughed out loud. "Did you say you're a bachelor, lad? Can't imagine why!"

"At least let me set the table," Seamie said sheepishly, trying to make good.

"That would be helpful. The feed bowls are above the sink," Jennie said.

She teased Seamie a bit more, then served the dinner—a Lancashire hotpot—a casserole of lamb chops, potatoes, and onions—with hunks of crusty brown bread and fresh, sweet butter. They all sat down, and the reverend gave the blessing. Seamie bowed his head. He knew he should close his eyes, but he didn't. Instead he looked at Jennie. Her color was high from the heat of the stove. The light from the lamps picked out the threads of pure gold in her hair. When the blessing ended, she opened her eyes and saw him looking at her, and she did not look away.

"This is delicious," he said as he tucked into his meal. "Truly."

Jennie thanked him and didn't make any more dog jokes, and Seamie realized as he ate that he was hungry—for something other than food. He was hungry for the warmth and ease he felt here, in Jennie Wilcott's tiny kitchen.

There was something about her—something lovely and comfortable. He felt contented in her presence. Peaceful. Not stirred up. Not wild. Not angry and sad and desperate, the way he felt every time he thought of Willa Alden.

He liked the home she had made for herself and her father. He liked the ticking of the mantel clock, the smell of furniture polish and the freshly washed tablecloth. He found himself wishing, to his great surprise, that he had such a thing himself—a home, a real home.

After Seamie and the Wilcotts had finished their meal, and topped it off with a dish of apple crumble doused with cream, the reverend declared he would pour everyone a sherry, but Seamie said he was not to do it until he—Seamie—had done the washing up. He made Jennie take a seat by the fire, then he rolled up his sleeves and got busy. He didn't sit down again until every plate, glass, and piece of cutlery was clean and dry.

He stayed with the Wilcotts, sipping his sherry, until the clock struck eight, and then he said he must be going. He knew tomorrow was Sunday and that both the reverend and Jennie would have an early start in the morning. He didn't want to leave, though. He didn't want to go out in the cold, dark night alone, always alone, and make his way across the river, to his sister's house, to the empty room, and the empty bed, that awaited him there.

"Thank you," he said to the Wilcotts as he took his leave. "For the supper and for your company. I enjoyed both immensely."

Jennie and the reverend both walked him to the door. He had just put his hat on, and was buttoning his jacket, when something crinkled in his front pocket.

"Oh, the check!" he said, laughing. It was the only reason he'd come here, and he'd forgotten it completely. He gave it to Jennie and told her it was for her school. She thanked him and said she would thank Fiona in person.

"You'll come back and see us again soon, won't you, my boy?" the reverend said, seeing him to the steps.

And Seamie, who, earlier in the day, had found himself so annoyed that Fiona had asked him to come here at all, said, "Yes, Reverend Wilcott. I will. Very soon."

CHAPTER NINE

MAX VON BRANDT checked his watch: 8:05 P.M. The bus he was waiting for would be here any minute now. He'd been standing under the awning of a tobacco shop on the Whitechapel Road for the last fifteen minutes to make certain he didn't miss it.

A chill crept up his spine. He hunched his shoulders against the cold, damp night. He hated the filthy English weather, but he was glad it was raining. It served his purpose.

A few feet away from him, a hissing gas lamp cast its weak glow over the slick black cobbles, the dreary shop fronts, the sooty brick buildings. Nowhere was there a pot of flowers, a green park, a cheerful coffee shop. If ever he had a mind to commit suicide, he thought, he would do it here in Whitechapel. It was made for it.

Max was not wearing his usual uniform tonight—a beautifully tailored suit, crisp white shirt, and silk tie. Instead, he wore a navy sailor's jacket, a cap, canvas trousers, heavy boots, and wire-rimmed spectacles with fake glass inserts.

Another minute passed. Two. And then he heard it, the sputter and pop of an omnibus engine. The sound grew louder as the bus rounded a bend. The engine grumbled as the driver stopped at a bus shelter across the street and waited for a handful of passengers to step off. Max watched them as they did, inspecting their faces.

There she is, he thought, watching as the last passenger—a young woman—stepped into the street. She had a plain, round face, framed by dark, wavy hair. Her eyes were small behind her glasses, her teeth large and rabbity. Looking at her, he knew his plan would succeed. In fact, it would be easy. The knowledge made him feel a deep and dreadful regret. He quickly quashed the feeling, though, for he could not afford to indulge it. There was work to be done, another link to be forged.

He waited. Until she was on the pavement, struggling with her umbrella. Until the conductor had rung his bell. Until the bus had pulled away from the curb, spewing black exhaust. And then he crossed the street and started walking toward her, hands in his pockets, head down against the rain.

He knew she would walk toward him. From a window high above the street he'd watched her take the exact same path for four nights in a row. He heard her steps coming closer and closer, his head still down. He waited until he could feel her. Smell her. Not yet, he told himself, not yet . . . hold on . . . *now.*

With a quick, fluid motion, he clipped her hard with his shoulder, knocking her satchel out of her arms and her glasses off her face.

"By gum, I'm sorry!" he exclaimed, in a flawless Yorkshire accent, quickly bending to pick up her things. "I didn't see you. Are you all right?"

"I . . . I think so," she said, squinting at him from under her umbrella. "Do you see my glasses anywhere?"

"Right here," he said, giving them to her.

She put them on with shaking hands, then took her satchel back from him.

"I'm very sorry. What an oaf I am. I feel terrible about this," he said.

"It's all right, really," the woman said.

"I'm afraid I'm a bit lost. I'm coming from Wapping. My ship just docked an hour ago. I'm looking for a lodging house by the name of Duffin's."

"Oh, I know Duffin's," the woman said. "It's just that way," she pointed east, "two streets down. On the left. But Duffin's is dear, you know. You might've been better off finding a lodging house closer to the river. Wapping's full of them."

Max shook his head. "I can't imagine you've ever stopped in one, miss. They're terrible, no better than a doss-house. I have a few days until my ship sails again, and I want to be in a decent place. One near a church."

He noticed the girl's eyes widen a bit at that.

"I'd actually been looking up at the street signs. Just before I smacked into you. I still feel terrible about it. Could I make it up to you? Buy you a cup of tea in a nice tea shop? Is there one around here?"

"No, everything's closed now," the girl said. She bit her lip.

It started raining harder. Perfect, Max thought. He pulled his collar up around his neck and shivered visibly.

"Here . . . ," she said, holding her umbrella so that it covered them both.

Max made a show of looking around. "There's a pub," he said. "The Blind Beggar. Would you accompany me there?"

The girl shook her head. "I don't frequent pubs," she said.

"There might be a ladies' area in that one," Max said hopefully.

The girl still hesitated, but her eyes looked hungry and sad. She was lonely, as he'd known she would be from the way Jennie Wilcott had described her when they'd all been waiting for cabs and carriages outside Holloway: a single woman with a poorly mother, a knitting group, suffrage work. She was desperate for a man's company. He could see that. Anyone could.

"Right. Well, I won't keep you," he said, tugging on the brim of his cap. "Good night, miss."

"Maybe just one drink," she suddenly said. "A lemonade or some such. My mother waits up for me. But I don't think she'll miss me. Not just yet. I sometimes get home a bit late from my knitting circle."

Max smiled. "That's wonderful. I'm glad you changed your mind. Just one drink, then. It's the least I could do after nearly knocking you down. I'm Peter, by the way. Peter Stiles," Max said, offering her his arm.

The woman's glasses had slid down her nose. She pushed them back up and gave him a shy smile.

"I didn't get *your* name," he said.

"Oh! Right. Silly me," she said, with a nervous laugh. "It's Gladys. Gladys Bigelow. Very pleased to meet you."

CHAPTER TEN

"THE STOVE GOES where, guv? *There?* Are you quite certain? It's a church," Robbie Barlow, the deliveryman, said.

"It's a very cold church," Seamie said.

"Is the door open? This thing's bloody heavy, you know. Once we get it off the cart, we'll want to get it straight inside."

Seamie nodded. "It's always open. The reverend keeps it that way." He jumped off the cart, trotted up the church steps, opened the door, and called out, "Hello? Anyone here? Reverend Wilcott? Jennie?"

There was no answer, so he went inside and tried again.

"Hello? Is there anyone here?"

He heard footsteps, and then a young woman, a very pretty young woman in an ivory blouse and beige skirt, came out of a room off the church's vestibule.

"Seamie Finnegan? Is that you?" she said.

"Jennie! You're here!"

"Yes, of course. I finished with the children a few minutes ago. I was just tidying up."

"I was hoping you'd be here."

Hope had nothing to do with it. It was a Saturday, the day Jennie taught school. He knew she would be here.

Just then the church door opened again. "Pardon me, missus, but where's the stove going?" Robbie said. He and another man had just carried it inside and were straining under its weight.

"What stove?" Jennie asked.

"I've brought you a new stove," Seamie said. "To replace the old one. You said it didn't work. And the children looked so cold the other day."

"I can't believe you did this," Jennie said.

"It's nothing. Really," Seamie said. "I just wanted to help."

It was true. Mostly. What he'd really wanted was to see her again. Very much. He hadn't stopped thinking about her since he'd said good-bye to her a week ago. He hadn't wanted to think about her. Hadn't wanted to remember the color of her eyes, the curve of her waist, or the sound of her laughter, but he couldn't help it. It was a bit crazy—coming here like this with a delivery wagon and a stove—he knew it was, but he didn't care. It gave him a reason to see her again.

"I don't know what to say. Thank you. Thank you so much," Jennie said now, visibly moved by his gift.

"Oi, missus!" Robbie wheezed. "Save the thank-yous for later. Where the devil do you want this thing?"

"I'm so sorry!" Jennie said. "This way, please."

She turned and led the men into the small sacristy that served as her classroom. They put the stove down with a bang, then stood bent over, hands on knees, chests heaving.

"Is the old stove hot?" Robbie asked when he'd caught his breath.

"No, it isn't. We couldn't use it today. I couldn't get it to work. I think the flue's finally broken."

"Do you want it removed?"

Seamie said they did. The two men detached it from its vent pipe and took it to their cart.

"I . . . I don't know what to say," Jennie said after they'd left. "It's far too kind of you."

Seamie waved her thanks away, took off his jacket, and rolled up his sleeves. He opened the bag of tools he'd brought with him from Joe's house and got busy installing the new stove. He'd tinkered with Primus stoves and the stove on board the *Discovery* so often that hooking up this one was no great challenge. Half an hour after he started, he was finished.

"There!" he said, crawling out from behind the stove. "You'll all be warm as toast in here now."

Jennie looked at him and burst into laughter.

"What?" he asked, looking back at her.

"You're black as a chimney sweep! You should see your face. You look like you fell down a coal hatch. Wait there. I'll get a basin and some water."

She was back in a few minutes with water, soap, and a flannel. She bade him sit down, then scrubbed at the soot on his cheeks and neck. He closed his eyes as she washed him. Her hands were soft and gentle and he liked the feeling of them. So much so that he let his feelings get the better of him. He'd planned to be very proper, very formal. He'd planned to go to her house and speak with her father first. Instead, he reached up, caught her hand in his, and said, "Jennie, come walking with me."

"Yes. All right. I'd like a walk. I've got to go to the market, and—"

"No. I mean tomorrow. After services. In Hyde Park."

"Oh," she said softly. "That sort of a walk." She looked down at their hands and did not pull hers away.

"I'd call for you in a carriage. All proper."

She looked up at him then and smiled. "Yes, all right, then. That would be lovely."

"Good."

"Yes. Good."

"I'll . . . um . . . I'll walk you home."

"My home is right next door, Seamie."

"I know that. I'd like a word with your father."

"About the stove?"

"No."

"You don't have to. He doesn't expect it. I'm twenty-five, you know. All grown up."

"I know. I still want to talk to him, though."

She laughed. "All right, then. If you insist."

The Reverend Wilcott was seated at the kitchen table with a pot of tea, working on his sermon. He looked up when Jennie and Seamie came in.

"Seamus! Good to see you again, my boy! Will you have a cup of tea?"

"No, Reverend. No, thank you."

"What brings you our way?"

And Seamie, who'd braved uncharted seas, howling gales, and subzero temperatures, suddenly found that his nerve had deserted him. He felt like a six-year-old lad in short pants asking for tuppence to spend at the fair. He'd never asked permission to take a woman walking. The women he'd been with in the last few years—well, walking wasn't in it—and he found now that he didn't know how.

"I . . . uh . . . well, sir I . . . I want . . . I mean I'd *like* to ask your permission to take Jennie walking tomorrow."

The Reverend Wilcott blinked at him, but didn't say a word.

"Unless that would be a problem, Reverend," Seamie said nervously.

"No, no! It's not that at all," the reverend said, laughing. "It's just that I'm not used to being consulted, that's all. My Jennie does what she likes. She always has. She's a very independent girl. But if it makes you happy, then yes, you have my permission to take her walking tomorrow."

"Thank you, sir," he said. "I'll call at two, shall I?"

"Call whenever you like," the reverend said.

"Two would be lovely," Jennie said.

Seamie bid the reverend good day, and Jennie walked him to the door.

"You didn't need to do that," she said, before she opened it.

"Yes, I did."

"Next you'll be insisting on a chaperone."

He hadn't thought of that. "It would be all right. If you want one, I mean," he quickly said.

"No, I don't," she said. And then she went up on her tiptoes and kissed him.

Before he even had time to respond, she'd opened the door. "Until tomorrow," she said.

"Right. Yes. Until tomorrow," he said.

She closed the door then and he knew he should go. But he didn't. Not right away. For a few seconds, he just stood there, touching the place she'd kissed, touching his fingers to his cheek, wonderingly.

CHAPTER ELEVEN

"DARLING, HAVE YOU seen my new German?"

"No, Elinor, I haven't. Have you misplaced him?" Maud Selwyn Jones asked.

"Cheeky girl," Elinor Glyn said. "Do come. He's playing piano across the hall and making all the ladies swoon. You'll adore him. He's positively glorious. His name is Max von Brandt. He came with his cousin, Harriet Hatcher. The lady doctor. Do you know her?"

"I do. And him, too."

"Wonderful! The Hatchers were great friends with the Curzons, of course. Mrs. Hatcher and Mary Curzon were like sisters, I'm told."

A servant walked by carrying a tray of crystal goblets filled with champagne. "Here," Elinor said, plucking one. "You look parched."

"I am. Thank you," Maud said.

"Drink up. We've plenty. I found twelve cases in George's cellar this afternoon," Elinor said, winking. And then she was off, trailing silks and perfume. "We're just across the way, darling!" she trilled over her shoulder.

Maud smiled. Across the way was no short distance at Kedleston Hall, the sprawling ancestral home of George Nathaniel Curzon, First Marquess Curzon of Kedleston, and a widower. She had come up for a weekend party at Elinor's urging, and though she'd been at Kedleston several times, she never failed to marvel at the size and beauty of the Adam-designed house. It was very old and very beautiful and quite excessive, and she loved it.

Elinor adored it, too, Maud knew, and would love nothing more than to become its mistress. She was already Curzon's mistress, and made no secret of her desire to become his wife as well. But there were impediments. Her reputation, for one. She was a scandalous lady novelist whose books included *It*, *Three Weeks*, and *Beyond the Rocks*—racy stories no respectable woman would be caught dead reading. And then there was her husband—Sir Richard. Once wealthy, he had become a spendthrift and a debtor. Elinor had started writing back in 1900 and churned out a book a year now to pay the bills. They sold by the lorry load.

Maud didn't particularly feel like music tonight. She was bored by George and the other politicians who were visiting Kedleston for the weekend. Even her good friend Asquith, the prime minister, bored her tonight. She'd been feeling awfully restless, actually, and had been thinking about taking a stroll through Kedleston's gardens, or simply going to bed with a book. But now Max von Brandt was here and that changed things. She remembered him. Very well. A woman never forgot a man with a face like his. In fact, she'd thought about him ever since she'd met him that day at Holloway.

She placed her empty champagne glass on a table, took a cigarette from her purse, and lit it. It was a special cigarette, one with a touch of opium mixed into the tobacco—courtesy of a Limehouse drug lord named Teddy Ko. She'd visited him a few days ago for a fresh supply. She'd improved over the years. She didn't frequent the East London opium dens anymore, and she didn't even smoke as many of these things as she used to, but she still allowed herself the odd one. Every now and again.

She inhaled deeply, blew out a plume of smoke, then walked to the music room. It was enormous, of course, like every other room at Kedleston, and filled with a thousand distracting things—paintings, porcelain, furniture, and people—but even so, she spotted Max immediately.

He was seated at the piano playing "In the Shadows." His silver-blond hair was brushed back from his forehead. He was beautifully dressed in a black tuxedo and every bit as impossibly handsome as she'd remembered.

He looked up suddenly and smiled at her, and she felt herself go weak in the knees. Like some silly sixteen-year-old girl. It had been a long time since a man had had that effect on her.

He sang the next few songs to her, all songs she loved—"Destiny," "*Mon Coeur S'ouvre a ta Voix*," "*Songe d'Automne*"—never taking his eyes off her, and to her dismay, she found herself looking away and, worse yet, blushing.

As the last notes of "*Salut d'Amour*" rose and faded, he declared himself exhausted and in need of a drink and abruptly left the room. There was applause and shouts of "Bravo!" but Maud felt as if the whole world had suddenly gone dark.

"Do get hold of yourself," she whispered.

She walked out of the music room and down the hall to the ballroom. It was empty, but a pair of French doors was open, and she quickly walked through them, badly in need of some air. Kedleston's marble terrace was bathed in moonlight. No one else was outside.

"Thank God," she sighed.

The quiet and the coolness of the night calmed her, but her hands still trembled slightly as she fished another cigarette from her purse.

"I wonder at you. I really do," she told herself. She was too old for this sort of schoolgirl behavior. At least, she thought she was.

"Ah. There you are," a voice said from behind her. A warm, rich voice, colored by a German accent. Maud slowly turned. Max was standing a few feet away. He held a bottle of champagne in one hand. "I thought you'd left. I thought all I'd find was your glass slipper," he said.

"I . . . I went outside. To take the air," she said.

Max smiled. "Yes, I see that. May I?" he asked, reaching for her cigarette.

"What? This? No, you don't want this," Maud said, hiding the cigarette behind her back.

"Yes, I do," Max replied. He leaned close, so that his face was only inches from her own. She could smell him—champagne and sandalwood and leather. He reached behind her and pulled the cigarette from her fingers. He took a deep drag and blew the smoke out slowly. His brown eyes widened. "You must tell me the name of your tobacconist," he said, coughing.

"Give that back," she said.

"Oh, no. Not yet," he said. He took another drag, smiling at her. "It's so nice to see you again. I didn't expect to."

"Nor I you," Maud said. "I enjoyed your playing. It was beautiful."

"I enjoyed you. Your dress is beautiful."

She didn't reply. He was playing with her. Teasing her. Mocking her. He must be.

"Fortuny, no?" he said.

"Very good," she replied. "Most men wouldn't know Fortuny from a tuba."

"Amethyst is your color. You should only ever wear amethyst.

I'll buy you a dozen amethyst dresses. A rare jewel should only have the very best setting."

Maud burst into laughter. She couldn't help it. "Oh, Max. How absolutely full of shit you are!"

Max laughed, too. "Yes, I am, and it's a relief to hear you say so." He took a slug from the champagne bottle. "So you're a woman who likes to hear the truth, eh?" He handed her the bottle, motioned for her to take a drink. "Here it is then: I want to make love to you. I have since I laid eyes on you. I won't be happy until I do."

Maud nearly choked on the champagne. She wasn't shocked by much, but she was shocked by that.

"Cheeky sod," she said, wiping bubbly off her chin. She handed him the bottle, then turned to go back inside.

"I see," Max called after her. "Like most women, you only thought you wanted the truth. Should I have lied to you? Sent you roses? Chocolates? Spouted poetry?"

She stopped.

"You *are* poetry, Maud."

Slowly, she turned around again. And then she walked back to him, took his face in her hands, and kissed him. Hard. Hungrily. She felt his hands on her waist, her back. He pulled her close and she felt the heat inside him, and inside herself, and suddenly she wanted him as she had never wanted a man. Wildly. Desperately.

"Where?" she whispered.

"My room," he said. "In half an hour."

He pressed a key into her hand. It had a number on it. All the bedrooms in Kedleston were numbered. She kissed him again, biting his lip, and then she quickly left him, her heels clicking against the marble tiles as she walked across the terrace, her heart pounding in her chest.

She didn't look back. Not once. So she did not see the smile that played upon Max von Brandt's lips. A smile tinged with sorrow. A smile that did not touch his eyes.

CHAPTER TWELVE

"ORDER! ORDER!" THE speaker of the house boomed, pounding his gavel. "Order, please!"

No one listened. On both sides of the aisle, MPs cheered and jeered.

"You've done it again, Joe," Lewis Mead, a Labour MP for Blackheath, whispered to him. "Can't you ever take the easy road? Suggest something uncontentious for a change? New flower boxes at Hackney Downs? More benches at London Fields?"

Joe laughed. He leaned back in his wheelchair, knowing it would take several minutes for the speaker to restore the peace. He looked around the room as he waited, taking in its soaring ceiling, its graceful Gothic windows and paneled galleries. These, plus the room's high, leaded windows and long, raked benches, always made him feel he was in a cathedral. It was an association that pleased him, for there was no place in all of Britain as sacred to him as this one, the House of Commons' chamber, and no calling as holy to him as that of member of Parliament.

Politics was Joe's religion, and this chamber his pulpit, and only moments ago, he had been speaking with all the zeal and eloquence of a fiery evangelist preacher. He wished now that he had some brimstone to hurl as well, for he saw he would need it.

"This is my last warning!" the speaker bellowed. "I ask the honorable gentlemen to sit down immediately! Or I shall have them removed!"

One by one those who had been standing sat—Conservatives, Liberals, and Labourites. Joe saw that Churchill was glowering. Henderson and MacDonald were beaming. Asquith was rubbing his brow.

Joe had opened today's session by introducing his new education bill with its demands upon the state to enlarge existing schools, build seventy new ones, raise the leaving age, and inaugurate education programs in ten of His Majesty's prisons. It had been given quite a reception.

"This is preposterous!" Sir Charles Mozier, owner of five clothing factories, had sputtered, as soon as Joe had finished speaking. "Government cannot afford this bill. It will bankrupt the state."

"Government *can* afford it. The question is—can capital?" Joe shot back. "Educated children become smart children and smart children ask questions. We can't have our seamstresses suddenly asking, 'Why am I paid seven pence to make a blouse Sir Charles sells for two quid?' They might take it in their heads to strike. And then it will be you, Sir Charles, not the state, who is bankrupt."

That had gotten half the room bellowing. What came next finished the job.

"Perhaps we can mandate tea and crumpets in the prisons, too," shouted John Arthur, whose Welsh mines had lucrative contracts to supply coal to prisons and Borstals. "We can have china teapots brought to the convicts on silver trays! Tell me, sir, have you any idea what such a program would cost?"

"Nothing," Joe replied.

"I beg your pardon?"

"I said, 'Nothing.' In fact, it'll save the state money. Educate every man in Wandsworth, every woman in Holloway. Give them the opportunities education brings, help them lift themselves out of poverty, and you can close those hellholes forever," Joe had said.

He waited now, until every man had sat down, until it was quiet once more. He looked at the faces he knew so well, faces of friends and adversaries. He looked up at the Strangers' Gallery, where his mother, Rose, his wife, Fiona, and his daughter Katie sat. Looking at them, he thought how easily they could not be sitting there. How easily he and his family could be shivering in some dank room in East London, with little to eat, not enough coal for a warm fire, or enough money to pay their rent. They had escaped that life, he and

Fiona. But so many hadn't. He thought about all the ones who were still there, still working for pennies an hour, still hungry, still cold. And then he started speaking again.

"Prime Minister, Mr. Speaker, honorable colleagues, it is time. Time to educate every child in Britain to the fullest of his or her potential. Time to bring every girl and every boy in Whitechapel, in the Gorbals, in the Liverpool courts, out of destitution and hopelessness. Only education can accomplish this. Only education can empty the workhouses and prisons, the slums and rookeries.

"Our government is, at last, beginning to recognize the dire plight of working people. It is beginning to work on behalf of the many, not the few. Look how far we have come in the last decade alone. Look at our accomplishments: better protection for children against abuse and exploitation, pensions for the aged, and national unemployment insurance—to name but a few.

"The naysayers said these things could never be. They called those who proposed the Children's Act and the National Insurance Act dreamers. As some of you—the kinder ones among you—have called me. If it is the dreamers who keep six-year-olds out of mills, if it is the dreamers who strive to end illiteracy and ignorance—then I am proud to be called a dreamer."

Joe paused for a few seconds, then delivered the closing lines of his speech.

"We now come to a crossroads in Britain's history," he said. "Do we proceed down the new and shining path, and in so doing, secure the future for *all* of Britain's children? Or do we turn back? Back to business as usual. Back to failure. Back to deprivation and despair. I cannot tell you how to vote. I can only tell you this: It is time to set aside self-interest, it is time to set aside politics, and it is time to consider the very ones who put you in the seats you now occupy. Look to your constituents, gentlemen, and to your consciences."

It was quiet when Joe finished speaking, so quiet that he could hear the chamber clock ticking. And then the applause began. And the cheering. Labour MPs to a man stood and clapped. Many of their Liberal colleagues joined them. Only the Tory benches were quiet.

The applause lasted for two minutes straight, and then the speaker once again called for order.

When the vote was called, enough ayes were counted to get Joe's bill to a second reading. The ayes were not unanimous, not by a long shot. The bill still had a long way to go before it became a law, but at least it had passed its first reading; it had not been killed. It was as much as Joe could have hoped for today.

As he wheeled himself back to his customary place near the front benches, he glanced up at the gallery. Fiona and Rose were smiling triumphantly. Katie, notepad in hand, gave him a quick wave.

There was a brief break, and then the speaker called upon the Honorable Winston Churchill, first lord of the admiralty and head of Britain's navy.

"What's Winston after now?" a man seated behind Joe whispered.

"More bloody boats," Lewis Mead replied.

As Churchill began to speak, it became clear that it was not mere boats he was after, but dreadnoughts.

Britain's first dreadnought had been launched in 1906. An entirely new breed of battleship—one armed with enormous guns and driven by steam turbines—the fearsome dreadnought had sparked an arms race with Germany.

After the kaiser had built two similar such ships, Parliament—in 1909—voted to fund the construction of four more dreadnoughts, with provisions for another four to follow in 1910.

Authorizing the battleships had pitted the Liberals against the Conservatives in an epic battle. The Liberals, hoping to reduce military spending, had wanted to fund only four ships. The Tories would have none of it. Joe well remembered the scene in the Commons when the number had been debated, with the Tories yelling, "We want eight and we won't wait!" until they'd defeated the Liberal chancellor, David Lloyd George, and won their boats. And now Winston wanted even more.

Churchill spoke at length now, with great command of figures and facts, and in his usual impatient tone, about Germany's increasingly aggressive stance toward France and Belgium. He raised the possibility of a coming conflict and the possibility of Turkey aligning itself with Germany should that conflict actually occur.

"What would such an alliance mean for our ally Russia?" he asked the chamber. "For the Balkan states? And most importantly, what would it mean for Britain's continued access to her Persian oil supplies and her Indian colonies?"

He paced the chamber for a moment, letting those dark scenarios hang in the mind of every man in the room, and then he quietly said, "The country with the superior naval fleet is the country that will control the Dardanelles, gentlemen. And the country that controls the Dardanelles controls passage to the Middle East, to Russia, and to the Orient. I ask you today to authorize a new dreadnought to make absolutely certain that that country is Britain, not Germany."

The Conservative benches were not quiet at the end of Churchill's speech, as they had been at the end of Joe's. Instead, they positively erupted. Tory MPs whistled, cheered, shouted, and applauded. Joe expected them to burst into the chorus of "Rule Britannia" any second. The speaker nearly splintered his hammer trying to quiet them.

"Hmm . . . slum rats or ships? Which will it be?" Lewis Mead said to Joe. "I know which one my money's on."

"Mine, too," Joe said. "When it comes to a second reading, Winston's bill will pass and mine will be killed. Winston's got everyone convinced that the Germans are two seconds away from marching on Buckingham Palace. My schools won't stand a chance, Lewis. Not against his ships."

A vote was taken, and Churchill's bill, too, passed its first reading. The speaker then called a recess for lunch and the members stood up to leave.

Joe, of course, could not stand, but as he wheeled himself out of the chamber, he could see. Quite clearly. He could see the writing on the wall. He could hear the conversations of the men around him. The chill wind he had read of in the papers only days ago was strengthening. A storm was gathering, blowing west from Germany across Europe and the Channel, all the way to London.

Several MPs came up to congratulate him on his speech. Among them was the former Tory prime minister A. J. Balfour.

"Fancy a spot of lunch, old boy?" he asked Joe. "Yes? Excellent! Brilliant speech you gave, I must say. Not that any of them gives a toss. They've all got a raging case of war fever. Time to give the kaiser a black eye and all that. Next thing you know, Winston will have them all marching up and down Trafalgar Square with saucepans on their heads."

Joe nodded solemnly. Balfour might joke, but they both knew he was right.

"Now, now, old boy. Don't look so glum," Balfour said. "It's all saber-rattling, really. We'll stay well out of it, mark my words. You know as well as I do that a strong military is the best way to avoid a war."

"Not this time, Arthur," Joe said, with a bitter laugh. "Not with that madman in Berlin," he said. "In fact, I'm quite certain it's the best way to start one."

CHAPTER THIRTEEN

"MUM'S BEEN ASKING me about you, Peter. 'What's he like, Gladys?' and 'What does he do, Gladys?' and 'Why don't you bring him home, all proper like, Gladys?' and I thought . . . well, hoped really . . . that maybe you could come for tea next Sunday."

Max von Brandt looked down at his hands, then back up at the dowdy young woman sitting across from him. He hesitated for a few seconds—just long enough to terrify her—then said, "I'd like that, Gladys. Very much."

"You would?" she whispered, her voice incredulous. "I mean, you would! How wonderful! Mum'll be ever so pleased." She looked at him shyly, her brown eyes blinking behind her thick glasses, then added, "I know I am."

Max smiled at her. "How about another shandy?" he said. "To celebrate."

"I shouldn't. I've had two already," Gladys said, biting her lip.

"No, you're absolutely right, pet, you shouldn't," Max said. "A moment like this deserves something better—champagne."

"Oh, Peter! Champagne!" Gladys said. "I love champagne, me. But we shouldn't, really. It's awfully dear."

"Nonsense. Nothing's too good for my girl," Max said, patting her hand.

He stood, walked to the bar, and ordered a bottle of plonk and two glasses. As he waited for the publican to bring it, he watched Gladys in the mirror above the bar. She was fussing with her hair. Her cheeks were flushed. She was smiling. This was almost too easy.

Tonight was the fifth time he had taken her out. They'd gone for drinks twice. A stroll in Greenwich once. To the music hall another time. And now they were here again, back to the pub where he'd taken her the night he'd staged their first encounter.

He'd been a perfect gentleman on each outing. Solicitous, polite, happy to pay for everything. He'd taken her hand to help her on or off the omnibus, asked about her mother, talked of his work and his church and his parents up north in Bradford. He'd made sure to disappear now and again for several days at a time, as a seaman on a run north to Hull or south to Brighton would be expected to.

"Here we are!" he said, bringing the champagne back to their table.

He poured two glasses, then made a toast.

As he leaned toward Gladys, her eyes flickered to his neck.

"My goodness! What happened to you?" she asked.

"It's nothing," Max said.

Gladys hooked a finger in his collar, pulled it open. "It looks terrible," she said.

Max knew it did. It was a deep scratch, and livid.

"I was carrying a trunk for the captain," he said. "It had a rough edge. Caught me in the neck."

"Poor thing. Let me make it better," Gladys said coyly.

She kissed her the tip of her finger, touched it to his neck, then giggled behind her hand. She always held her hand over her mouth; she was embarrassed by her large, crooked teeth.

He caught her other hand in his and kissed it. "That's much better. Thank you, darling Glad," he said.

Gladys blushed a deep, unbecoming shade of red. "Naughty boy," she said, giggling again. "Don't be going and getting any ideas, now."

Max felt leaden inside. It was awful to watch this sad, plain dumpling of a woman, with her thick stockings and her sensible shoes, trying to be flirtatious and gay. It was cruel what he was doing, and he suddenly wanted to stop this charade, to apologize to her, bundle her into a hackney, and send her home. But he did not. There were times he hated what he did—times when he hated himself for doing it—but he would no more run from his duties than his father would have in 1870 on the battlefield at Metz. Duty had always come first, for every generation of von Brandts, and it did now for Max.

He closed his collar, wincing as the cloth rubbed against the wound, and feigned interest in Gladys's chatter. He had lied to her about the wound, as he had lied to her about everything else. It was no trunk that had caused that scratch, or the ones on his back. It was his lover who had done it, Maud Selwyn Jones.

As Gladys burbled on about the dinner she would cook for him on Sunday, Max remembered making love to Maud.

The first time, in his room at Kedleston, they'd knocked over a table and broken a vase.

The second time, at Wickersham Hall, her Cotswold estate, he'd had her in the woods. Or maybe it had been the other way around. He'd simply leaned over to kiss her as they stopped to rest the horses, and the next thing he knew, they were tumbling onto the ground. She'd somehow kept her riding hat on the whole time, and her silk stockings. Her teasing smile, just visible under the hat's black net veil, had driven him mad with desire. They'd certainly frightened the horses.

The third time, they'd been on their way to his flat after the opera. Just as the hackney driver had pulled away from the curb and into the dark London night, she'd kicked off her shoes, then lifted the hem of her dress, slowly, teasingly, an inch at a time, until it was quite apparent that she was wearing nothing under her gown. That time, they'd frightened the driver.

And then there was last night. At her flat. She'd had what seemed like a hundred candles burning in her bedroom when he arrived. Champagne in a silver cooler. Oysters on ice. She'd trailed a chunk of that ice down his body when they started, and had held another chunk to the scratches on his skin when they finished. The memory alone made him hard as stone now. She was everything he craved in a woman—exciting, exhausting, beautiful, and wild. She gave him what he wanted most—a few hours in which he could forget what he was, and the things he did.

". . . or a Victoria sponge? Which one do you think, Peter? Peter?"

Gott verdammt noch mal. He'd been miles away.

"Yes, Gladys?" he said, quickly putting Maud out of his mind. Thoughts of her made it impossible to concentrate on Gladys, and that would not do. He had things to accomplish this evening.

"I asked you which pudding you'd like," she said anxiously. "For tea on Sunday. Weren't you listening?"

"No, not entirely."

"Oh," she said, looking upset. "I'm sorry. I must be boring you, talking of puddings. How stupid of me. I don't know why I rabbit on so, I just—"

He took her hand in his. "If you must know, Gladys, I was thinking about how much I want to kiss you. It's something I think about a lot. Much more than I think about puddings."

Gladys blushed again, visibly flustered. "Oh, Peter, I . . . I don't know what to say."

"Say you'll give me a kiss, Glad. Just one."

Gladys looked around nervously, then gave him a quick peck on the cheek. He caught the scent of her as she did—wet wool, talcum powder, and camphor.

"That's much nicer than Victoria sponge," he said. "Now, let me give you one."

He leaned forward and kissed her mouth, lingering slightly. She could barely look at him afterward. He looked at her though, and saw that her chest was heaving and her hands were trembling. Good. He poured her more champagne. Several times. And half an hour later, Gladys Bigelow was drunk.

"Oh, Peter, this champagne is delicious!" she said. "Let's have some more."

"I think you've had plenty, pet. It's time we got you home."

Gladys pouted. "Don't want to go home."

"Yes, you do. Come on now, upsy-daisy, there's a good girl. . . ."

Max got her up on her feet, into her coat, and out of the pub. She swayed a bit on the sidewalk. He had to take her arm as they walked toward the bus stop. Before they'd gone five steps, she tripped, and he only just managed to stop her falling flat on her face.

Things were going perfectly.

"Gladys, dear," he said. "I think you've had a bit too much. You can't go home like this. We've got to get some coffee into you first. Only there's no place around here for tea or coffee, is there?" he said, pretending to look up and down the street.

"Kiss me, Peter," Gladys said. Only it came out sounding like *Kish me*.

He sighed deeply. "I'd love to," he said. "Only what sort of cad would I be, then? Kissing a girl who's had too much champagne?"

"Oh, Peter, you're not a cad," Gladys said, with feeling. "You're the most wonderful, wonderful, *wonderful* man I've ever met."

Max smiled. "Now I know you're drunk, Gladys. Listen, this is what we're going to do. I'm going to take you back to my room."

"I . . . I don't think that's a good idea," Gladys said, worriedly.

"Just for a bit. Just until you sober up a little. I can make you a pot of coffee there."

"No, I'm all right. I can get home. Really."

Max shook his head. "I can't let you go on a bus all by yourself in this state, Gladys. And I can't take you home to your mother like this, either. What on earth will she think of me? She'll never let me come to tea on Sunday. Never."

At these words, Gladys's eyes grew wide. "All right then," she said anxiously. "I'll go with you. But just long enough to drink some coffee. I've got to get home right after."

"Of course," Max said. "Just for a few minutes. Then I'll walk you to the bus."

Max put an arm around Gladys and led her down the dark cobbled streets to Duffin's, his lodging house. He helped her up the stoop, then unlocked the front door and poked his head inside to make sure no one was hanging about in the hallways. As he'd expected, no one was, for Mrs. Mary Margaret Duffin did not tolerate smoking, swearing, spitting, or loitering. He hurried Gladys inside, locked the door, then held a finger to his lips. She nodded, giggled, tried to kiss him again, then allowed herself to be helped up the stairs.

"Oh, Peter, my head's spinning," she said, when they were inside his room. "I don't feel very well."

"Lie down for a minute," he said, leading her to his bed.

"I shouldn't. I should go," she protested.

"Gladys, it's all right," he said easing her down onto the mattress. "Just lie back and close your eyes. The spinning will stop soon, I promise."

Gladys did as she was told. She sank back against his pillow, moaning slightly. Max lifted her legs onto the mattress, unlaced her boots, and took them off. He wasn't surprised that she felt awful. After all, he'd made sure that she drank most of the bottle.

He talked to her soothingly, telling her that the coffee would be ready in a minute. And it would be. He needed it to be there when she woke up. Later, he would tell her she'd drunk some and then fallen asleep. After a few minutes had elapsed, he called her name and got a mumbled response. He waited a bit, then called her again. Nothing. She was out.

Moving quickly, Max went to the one closet in the room, opened the door, and took out a tripod and camera. He had it set up in seconds. There was no need to pull the blind down; he'd done that earlier. He took the shade off the gas lamp on the wall, then lit two kerosene lamps, positioning them close to the bed. When he was satisfied with the light, he moved the camera close to the bed, then turned his attention to Gladys.

He sat her up and started to undress her. It was heavy going. She had layers of clothing on. Her thick wool jacket had to be unbuttoned and pulled from under her. There was also a suit jacket and skirt. A high-necked blouse. And a corset. He had just got it unlaced and was pulling it off her when her eyes suddenly opened and she sleepily protested. For a few seconds, he was worried that she was coming round, but then her eyelids fluttered and she was out again.

Max was relieved. He didn't want to have to use chloral hydrate on her. It kept people under for hours, and he didn't have hours. If he didn't get her back to her mother by ten at the latest, the old woman might worry and ask a neighbor to fetch the police.

He threw her corset on the floor, then quickly unbuttoned her camisole and bloomers and pulled them off. She stirred again, murmuring slightly, but did not waken. By the time he got her stockings off, he was sweating, but he didn't pause to catch his breath. Instead, he arranged her hands behind her head, tucked a fake flower behind her ear and turned her face toward the camera. He stood back to take in his handiwork, hesitating for a few seconds, then brusquely pushed her legs apart. It wasn't a pretty picture, but then again, it wasn't meant to be.

Max dropped a dry plate into the camera. He glanced at the naked woman on his bed one more time, focused his lens, and started to shoot.

CHAPTER FOURTEEN

"BLOODY HELL, BUT she's beautiful," Seamie said.

He stood on the dock, head back, eyes wide and full of wonder as he took in every proud and graceful inch of the ship in front of him. She was a three-hundred-and-fifty-ton barkentine, with her forward mast square-rigged and the other two masts rigged for fore and aft sails, like a schooner's. The subtle curves of her hull, the thrust of her prow, the soaring height of her mainmast—they all took his breath away.

"She's more than beautiful, lad," said the man standing next to him. "She's the strongest wooden ship ever built."

Seamie raised a skeptical eyebrow.

"The *Fram* comes close, I'll give you that, but this one's stronger."

Seamie knew the *Fram*, every inch of her. He'd sailed in her, with Roald Amundsen, to the South Pole. That ship had been specially designed to cope with pack ice. Built stouter, its hull more rounded, it rose up on top of the ice when the ice closed in, almost floating on it, instead of being crushed by it. It was an ingenious design and an effective one, but not beautiful. Compared to the ship in front of him, the *Fram* looked like a washtub.

"She won't do as well in the ice," Seamie said.

"She won't need to. She's to be used for loose pack only."

"Is that so? What do you call her?"

"Her name's *Polaris*, but I'm thinking of calling her *Endurance*. After my family motto: *Fortitudine vincimus*—'By endurance we conquer.' "

"*Endurance*," Seamie said. "It's a perfect name. Perfect for anyone, or anything, connected with you, sir."

Ernest Shackleton laughed loudly, his shrewd eyes sparkling. "Come aboard her, lad," he said. "Let's see what you think. Still have your sea legs?" Before he'd even finished speaking, Shackleton was halfway up the rope ladder dangling down the ship's side.

Seamie shook his head, smiling. He could see where this was leading. Shackleton hadn't said too much over the telephone. He hadn't needed to.

"How are you, Seamus, lad?" he'd bellowed. Seamie had recognized the voice on the other end of the line immediately. He'd heard it daily for more than two years in the Antarctic, when he made his first polar expedition aboard another of Shackleton's vessels, the *Discovery*.

Before he'd even give Seamie time to answer his question, Shackleton had launched into the reason for his call. "I need your help," he said. "There's this ship I'm thinking about. Norwegian built, but currently in dock at Portsmouth. Could you come out and take a look? I'd love to know what you make of her." He'd paused for a breath then, and Seamie could hear the teasing note in his voice as he added, "If you aren't too busy sipping tea and nibbling biscuits with Clements Markham at the RGS, that is."

"You heard about the job offer?" Seamie said.

"I did. And I assume you turned him down."

"Not yet."

"Why not?"

"It's a good job, doing good work on behalf of the RGS, a place that means a great deal to me and to us all," Seamie said. "I may take it. Why not? I haven't had any better offers," he added pointedly.

After they'd sounded each other out a bit more, Seamie had agreed to meet his old captain in Portsmouth and give him his frank opinion of the boat, quite certain that Shackleton would ask him to sign on.

But would he agree to go? A few weeks ago, he would have had no hesitation, but that was before he'd met Jennie. Before he'd started courting her. Before he'd taken her hand as they walked, talking about her life and his. Before he'd held her close and kissed her lips and felt her heart beating against his own. Before he'd started to think—for the first time in his life—that there might be another woman for him besides Willa Alden.

Seamie looked at the ship again now. He climbed up the rope ladder and stood next to Shackleton on the deck.

"Her keel's seven feet thick. Sides are anywhere from one-and-a-half-feet to two-and-a-half-feet thick. She's got twice the number of frames any other ship her size has. Bow's over four feet thick where it meets the ice," Shackleton said, answering Seamie's questions before he could even ask them.

Seamie nodded, impressed—even though he didn't want to be. He almost wished there was something wrong with the ship. He wished it had some terrible flaw in its design or construction—something that would give him a reason not to go. To stay in London and take the job at the RGS. To stay with Jennie.

"And her engine?" he asked.

"Coal-fired steam. She'll do just over ten knots," Shackleton said.

He talked on, telling Seamie about the ship's many qualities and how it was purposely built to handle polar conditions. He went on about the oak, Norwegian fir, and greenheart wood that was used in her construction. He talked for over an hour, leading Seamie up and down her deck, then below it to the crew's and captain's quarters, the engine room, the kitchen, and the hold. When he'd finished the tour, he brought Seamie abovedecks again.

He lit a cigarette, offered it to Seamie, then lit another for himself. He took a deep drag, blew the smoke out, then said, "Well, lad, I might as well tell you, I didn't bring you to the seaside for a box of taffy."

"No, I don't expect you did, sir."

"I'm getting up another expedition."

"I'd heard as much."

"You lot found the South Pole, but that doesn't mark the end of exploration in the Antarctic. I want to do another journey—a transcontinental trek. Two parties. Two ships. The *Endurance* will sail to the Weddell Sea and put a party ashore at Vahsel Bay, where they will begin a trek to the Ross Sea, via the pole."

"What about supplies?" Seamie cut in, remembering how crucial the proper planning of food, drink, shelter, and warmth was to Amundsen's success in obtaining the pole. "The Weddell Sea party won't be able to carry enough to get them all the way across."

Shackleton smiled. "That's where the second party comes in. As the first party heads to the Weddell Sea, a second ship will take a second party to McMurdo Sound in the Ross Sea, where they'll establish a base camp. From that camp, they'll trek toward the Ross Sea, laying down caches of food and fuel across the Ross Ice Shelf to the Beardmore Glacier, supplies that will sustain the first party as they complete the crossing. The Weddell Sea group eventually joins the Ross Sea group, and there you have it—the first land crossing of Antarctica."

Seamie mulled Shackleton's plan. "It could work," he said at length.

"*Could?* There's no could about it. It *will* work!" Shackleton bellowed.

Seamie heard the excitement in the man's voice. He'd heard that same excitement the first time he'd met him—at a lecture at the Royal Geographical Society, right before he'd talked Shackleton into taking him along on his *Discovery* expedition.

He smiled now. "You're never happier than when you have a quest, sir," he said.

"The quest is all, lad," Shackleton said. "You know it as well as I do. So what's it going to be? I'd love to have you with me. Are you in? Or are you going to let Clements make a file clerk out of you?"

Seamie laughed, but then found, to his consternation, that he had no answer.

Am I in? he wondered.

He remembered the *Discovery* expedition and the South Pole trek. He remembered the stark, aching beauty of Antarctica—the steel gray seas, the ice-blasted landscape, and the vastness of the night sky. It was nothing like London's sky, or New York's, where man-made light and smog obscured the stars. It was so clear there, so unspeakably still, that he'd felt as if he was seeing the heavens for the very first time. On so many of those nights, he'd felt as if he could reach up and touch the stars, as if he could gather them in his hands like diamonds.

Most of all, he remembered the life-threatening push to the pole. The first time, with Shackleton, they'd had to turn back only a hundred miles away from it. If they hadn't, they would have died. The second time, with Amundsen, they'd made it. He remembered how much each of the expeditions had taken out of him. He remembered the hunger, cold, and exhaustion. Two years had elapsed since the South Pole expedition, and he was only just now getting back to any sort of a real life, and the expedition Shackleton had outlined for him would take two more. Maybe even three. He'd be that much older when he returned. And what about Jennie? Would she wait for him? Was he sure he wanted her to?

"Well, lad?" Shackleton pressed.

Seamie shrugged helplessly. "Can I think about it, sir? I'm afraid I just don't know."

"You don't know?" Shackleton said, disbelief in his voice. "How can you not know? For God's sake, where's your heart, lad?"

Good question, Seamie thought. Where, indeed? Had he left it at Kilimanjaro? Was it lost somewhere out in the icy oceans of the Antarctic? Was it in London with Jennie Wilcott?

As he looked out over the harbor, past Shackleton, past all the ships moored nearby, he realized, with an aching sadness, that he knew the answer. He didn't want to admit it, because it was so painful to always long for something you would never have, but he knew it nonetheless. His heart was where it had always been—in the keeping of a wild and fearless girl, a girl he'd never see again. How he wished it wasn't.

Shackleton sighed. "It's a woman, isn't it?"

Seamie nodded. "Yes, it is."

"Wed her, bed her, then come sailing with me."

Seamie laughed. "I wish it was that simple, sir."

Shackleton softened. "Look, lad, it's only March. I won't be sailing until August, at the earliest. Take your time. Think it over. I want you with me. You know that. But you must do the thing that's right for you."

"I know that, sir. Thank you. I will," he said to Shackleton.

And to himself, he added, "If I only knew what the right thing was."

CHAPTER FIFTEEN

MAX VON BRANDT took a deep drag on his cigarette, then exhaled slowly. He was glad of the plume of smoke that hung about him. It helped mask the stench.

Max was sitting on the one and only chair in his room at Duffin's. Across from him, on the bed, sat Gladys Bigelow. She was sobbing and shaking. She'd already vomited twice, all over his bed, and she looked as if she would soon be sick again. He'd gathered up the quilt, the sheets and the pillows, and had taken them downstairs to the rubbish bin, but the smell still lingered.

Spread out on a table in the center of the room was the cause of Gladys's tears—a set of photographs, ugly and obscene. They showed a woman lying in a bed, naked, her legs splayed. The woman's face was clearly visible. Max knew the photos well. He had taken them himself, only a few days ago.

"Please," Gladys sobbed. "I can't. I can't do it. Please."

Max took another drag on his cigarette, then said, "You have no choice. If you refuse, I'll send the pictures to George Burgess. You'll lose your position immediately and the resulting disgrace will ensure you don't find another. That job is your life, Gladys. You told me so yourself. On several occasions. What else do you have? A family? A husband? No. And you're not likely to. Not if I make these photographs public."

"I'll kill myself," Gladys said in a choked voice. "I'll walk to Tower Bridge and jump off."

"Who would look after your ailing mother if you did?" Max asked. "Who would pay her doctor's bills? Buy her food? Pay her rent? Who would take her to the park on Sunday in her wheelchair? You know how much it means to her. She looks forward to it all week. Do you think the orderlies in the institution where she'll end up will do it? She'll be lucky if they remember to feed her."

Gladys covered her face with her hands. A low, animal moan of anguish escaped her. She retched again, but there was nothing left inside her.

Max rested his cigarette on the edge of an ashtray and crossed his arms over his chest. He wished he was not here in this filthy place, breathing in the smell of vomit and despair. He closed his eyes briefly, summoning an image in his mind of the place he did want to be—a place that was wild and free and untouched by men.

It was white and pure and cold this place, it was Everest, the rooftop of the world, and the hope that he would go back there one day when all of this was over, and that he might find her—Willa Alden—still living there, as wild and beautiful as the mountain itself, sustained him.

Thinking of that place, and that woman, made him want to stand up and leave. Leave the wretched room he was sitting in. And the wretched woman nearby. And wretched, ugly Whitechapel. He'd put his life in danger every time he came here. He knew he had. He'd heard that the Cambridge lads were on to him, that it was only a matter of time. Well, that was as it must be, and to leave before the job was done was to put other people's lives in danger. Millions of them. And so he stayed.

He waited a few more minutes, giving Gladys a little more time to recover, then he said, "Will you do it? Or do I send the pictures?"

"I'll do it," she replied, in a hollow voice.

"I knew you'd see reason," Max said. He stubbed his cigarette out, then leaned forward in his chair. "I want copies of every letter that leaves George Burgess's office."

"How? How am I to do that?" she said. "He's in and out of my office. So are other people."

"Carbons. You make a copy of every letter for his files, don't you?"

Gladys nodded.

"Use a second carbon. One for each letter. The carbons are all placed in a special basket, dumped into an incinerator at the end of the day, are they not? It's a tremendous waste and expense, but necessary for security. At least, that's what you told me."

"Yes."

"Make sure the second carbon does not go into the basket."

"*How?*" Gladys asked. "I told you that people—"

"I would suggest you fold each one twice and tuck it into the top of your stockings. Wait until you are alone. Or pretend to reach under your desk for a dropped pencil. Use your good mind, Gladys. Your bag is searched every night, but you are not because Burgess trusts you completely. That's another thing you told me. I also want notes on the documents you can't copy. Incoming correspondence, for example. Blueprints. Maps. Tell me what they are and what they contain. Leave nothing out, I warn you. If I hear about naval plans or acquisitions from other sources, the pictures go in the mail. Do you understand?"

"Yes."

"Every Wednesday, my agent will meet you on the bus you take home from work. He'll board at Tower Hill and sit next to you. You will be sitting on the top deck. He'll be wearing a suit and carrying a doctor's bag. He'll also be holding a copy of that day's *Times*. So will you. Inside your paper will be the carbons you've obtained for me. You will put your paper on the seat between you. The man will exchange yours for his. Afterward, you'll get off the bus at your usual stop. That's all you have to do. Do anything else, Gladys, anything at all, and you know what will happen."

Gladys nodded. Her face was gray. Her eyes were dull and expressionless. She looked dead inside.

"May I go now?" she asked.

"Yes," Max said. "This is the last you will see of me unless you give me some reason to doubt you."

He stood then and pulled an envelope from his pocket.

"This is from the kaiser," he said. "To show his appreciation for your efforts. It contains one hundred pounds. To help with your mother's medical bills."

Gladys took the envelope from him and tore it to bits, letting the pieces flutter to the floor. When she was finished, she staggered out of the room, slamming the door behind her. Max listened as the sound of her shoes on the stairs faded, then disappeared, and as he did, an expression of almost unbearable pain crossed his face. He knelt down, picked the pieces up off the floor, and fed them into the fire.

CHAPTER SIXTEEN

"ARE YOU COLD?" Seamie asked Jennie, as he pushed the punt they were in up the River Cam.

"Not at all. It's so warm today, it feels more like June than April. It's glorious, isn't it? After that dreary, endless winter," she said, smiling at him from under the brim of her straw hat.

She was wearing a dress of robin's egg blue faille. A sash of ivory silk set off her tiny waist. Her color was high and her eyes were sparkling. Fetching, he thought, as he looked at her. That's the perfect word. That's exactly what she is.

They'd come up to Cambridge together on a train last night, along with Albie Alden and Aunt Eddie, and were spending a long weekend at Eddie's house. Eddie had taken to Jennie immediately and, in typical Eddie fashion, had made all sorts of inappropriate comments during the train ride, such as "You'd be stark raving mad to let this one go, old chap." And "Best get a ring on her finger, before she finds out what you're really like." And Seamie couldn't forget this one—delivered sotto voce, or Eddie's best attempt at sotto voce, which meant only half the train heard it: "If you take my advice, you won't trifle with this girl. She's not a gin-swilling, gold-digging hussy like all the rest of them."

By the time the train had pulled into the Cambridge station, Seamie had been utterly mortified, but he also knew deep down that Eddie was right. He'd been seeing Jennie for nearly two months now. They'd done something together every weekend—whether it was walking in Hyde Park, or seeing a show, eating fish and chips at Blackheath, or taking tea at the Coburg Hotel. Jennie was undoubtedly wondering what his intentions were. Her father, too. He would gladly tell them, if only he knew.

"I'm a bit worried about the clouds over there," he said now, pointing ahead of them. "It was a bit of a mad idea, this. People don't usually go punting until high summer."

"Mad ideas are often the best ones," Jennie said. "I love being here, Seamie. Truly. I love being on a river. My father used to take us punting on the Cherwell all the time when I was a girl. My mother's father left her a cottage at Binsey. We would holiday there, and often go into Oxford and rent a punt at the Cherwell Boathouse. It's mine now, the cottage. My mother left it to me. Though I don't go there nearly enough."

"You'll have to show it to me someday," Seamie said, expertly guiding the boat around a downed tree limb.

"I don't know if you'd like it. It's very small. Lots of antimacassars and teacups and pictures of the royal family."

Seamie laughed.

"How did it go with Sir Clements?" Jennie asked him. "You never told me."

Seamie had met with Clements Markham at the RGS yesterday

morning to talk further about the position Markham was offering him.

"Well, there's an office," he said flatly.

"What's wrong?" Jennie said. "Is it not a nice one?"

"It's very nice, actually. Grand. Spacious. With a desk in it. And a chair. And filing cabinets and rugs. And views of the park from the window. And a secretary sitting outside waiting who'll bring me tea and biscuits anytime I like."

"It sounds rather splendid."

"It is rather splendid. That's the whole problem."

"No icebergs or penguins," Jennie said.

"No," he said ruefully. "No icebergs or penguins."

No sunrises that stop you dead with their unspeakable beauty, either, he thought. No whales breaching only yards from the ship, showering your awestruck self with a cold ocean rain. No songs and whiskey belowdecks at night while the wind plucks at the ship's rigging and the ice beats against her hull.

He thought these things but didn't say them, because he thought they might be hurtful to Jennie and he did not wish to distress her. She wanted him to stay here, to take the job at the RGS. He knew she did. She had never said so, had never once pressured him, but he'd felt it in her touch. In the kisses she gave him. He'd heard it in her words—how she would talk about wanting to visit Brighton with him over the summer, or the Lake District, or some such thing, then suddenly stop herself, realizing he would not be here over the summer if he signed on for Shackleton's expedition.

She turned away from him now, feigning interest in a pair of ducks, but the unspoken words lay heavily between them. He had a choice to make: take the position Markham had offered him and stay here in London, or go on another Antarctic expedition with Shackleton, one that would take him away for years. Much depended on that choice and they both knew it.

"What do you think about that barn over there for our picnic?" Seamie said, nodding at a small tumbledown stone building at the edge of a field. "It's looks a bit ramshackle, but I bet it's dry inside. Drier than the bare ground, at least."

"It looks perfect," Jennie said.

Seamie poled the boat over to the bank, jumped out, and pulled it ashore. He helped Jennie out and then reached for their picnic basket and the tarpaulin.

They'd planned to go into town for Sunday lunch at a pub, but as they walked across the Silver Street bridge, Seamie had glimpsed Scudamore's, which hired out punts—narrow, flat-bottomed boats that were not rowed, but rather pushed along the river by long, thin poles. Workmen had taken a few out to repair them, and Seamie, never able to resist the intoxicating combination of boats and water, asked Jennie if she'd like to go punting. She'd agreed immediately but the Scud's proprietor had been a bit hesitant. The boats weren't officially out yet, he said, and the Cam was high just now from all the spring rain. But then he'd recognized Seamie and said he reckoned if a man could get himself to the South Pole and back, he could get himself up the Cam.

Seamie had ducked into the nearby Anchor pub and arranged a picnic lunch. He'd placed the basket in the boat and asked the Scud's proprietor for a tarp to put on what would surely be sodden ground. Then he handed Jennie into the punt, and they were off, poling through the ancient village, past the colleges, and into the countryside.

Jennie led the way now, up the riverbank toward the field. Seamie trailed behind her with their lunch. He nearly crashed into her when she stopped suddenly.

"Oh, Seamie! Snowbells!" she exclaimed. "Look at them all!"

His eyes followed where she was pointing. To the right of them, on the crest of the bank, were clumps of small white flowers, their tiny blooms dangling above slender green stalks.

"Oh, what a lovely sight," Jennie said. She went closer to the flowers, taking great care not to step on any, and bent down to touch one of the blooms. "It's been such a dreadful winter," she went on, all in a rush. "So cold and long. And I've been so worried about so many things. About my father doing too much. About some of the children—a little boy in particular whose own father is far too handy with his belt. About a friend of mine, a lovely girl caught up with the wrong people." She turned to him and he saw a shimmer of tears in her eyes. "I'm sorry. It's daft, I know, but snowbells always make me cry. They're so tiny and fragile, yet they push themselves through the cold, hard soil. They're so brave. They give me hope."

Seamie looked at her, at her beautiful face turned up to his, at the tears in her eyes, at the smile on her lips despite them. She was so good, this woman. So gentle and kind. She worried about others always, never herself. His heart clenched inside him, full of emotion. It wasn't what he'd felt before—the blind, tearing, wild yearning he'd felt for Willa—but it must be love all the same, he thought. It must be.

Overcome by his feelings, he put the picnic things down, knelt beside her, and kissed her. Her lips were sweet and yielding and he would have kept on kissing them, but it started to rain. He looked up, saw that the dark clouds he'd spotted earlier were now directly over them, and knew there would soon be a downpour.

"Come on," he said, picking up the basket and tarp. "We'll have to make a run for it."

They dashed across the field—Jennie pressing her hat to her head—and made it inside the barn just as the skies opened. The barn wasn't much—only three of its walls were standing—but it still had most of its roof and would do to keep the rain off them.

"It must've been abandoned some time ago," Jennie said, spreading the tarp over the earthen floor. "Seamie, would you hand me the basket? I'll set the luncheon out and . . . Oh!"

Seamie didn't give a toss about the lunch or the basket or any of it. He had taken Jennie into his arms and was kissing her again. He wanted to feel what he'd felt only moments ago. He wanted to savor that feeling and know it for love. He wanted that so much.

Jennie kissed him back. Shyly at first, then more passionately. And then she sank down onto the tarp, pulling him with her. "Make love to me, Seamie," she whispered.

He had not expected that. "Jennie, I . . . ," he started to say.

"Shh," she whispered, taking off her jacket. "I want you to." She unbuttoned her blouse and shrugged out of it. Seamie could see the shape of her breasts through her camisole, full and round, and before he knew what he was doing, he was unbuttoning it, and then fumbling with her skirts. She was beautiful and he wanted her. Very badly.

He put his jacket on the tarp and laid her down. He began to kiss her, his lips traveling over her neck, her breasts, down to her belly, and then he saw it—a long, jagged scar running from the bottom of her rib cage, across her belly to her opposite hip.

"My God, Jennie . . . what happened?"

He heard her take a deep breath, then let it out again. "An accident. When I was a child. I was hit by a carriage."

"Were you in hospital?" he asked.

"For six months," she said. "I don't remember the accident. I was nine. I remember the recovery, though."

"My poor girl," he said, tracing the long jagged line with his fingers.

"Don't look at it. Please," Jennie said, stopping his hand. "It's so ugly."

He took her hand in his and kissed it. "Nothing about you is ugly, Jennie Wilcott. You're beautiful. In every way. God, but you're beautiful." He lost himself then, in the sweet softness of her body. In the depth of her lovely eyes. In the taste and smell of her. In the sound of her voice, whispering his name.

It was over too fast. He hadn't meant it to be, but he couldn't help himself. "I'm sorry," he said smiling sheepishly. "Couldn't help myself. I'll make it up to you. I swear," he said, nibbling on her earlobe and making her giggle. "It'll be wonderful. Simply fantastic. So good, you won't be able to stand it. You'll be begging me for mercy." She was laughing now. He loved the sound of her laughter. Loved knowing that he was making her happy. He bit her shoulder gently, making her laugh even more, then kissed her throat, the place between her breasts, her hip. He put his hand between her legs, wanting to kiss her there, too, until he looked down and saw the blood on her thighs.

Oh, hell. Bugger. Damn it all, he thought.

"Jennie . . . are you . . . You're not . . . ," he started to say.

"A virgin?" She laughed. "Not anymore."

A wave of remorse washed over him. He had wanted her so much, he hadn't stopped to consider whether she might or might not have had a lover before him. He shouldn't have done it. Not with her. He'd only ever bedded experienced women. He was a blackguard. A cad. An utter bounder. She was a reverend's daughter, for God's sake. Upright and upstanding, and all those sorts of things. Of course she was a virgin. How could he have been so thoughtless and stupid?

"I'm sorry, Jennie. I didn't know or I wouldn't have done it. Truly," he said, expecting tears and remonstrance.

But Jennie surprised him. Just as she'd done that day at Holloway.

"Sorry? Why? I'm not," she said, laughing. "I've wanted you since the day I first saw you, Seamus Finnegan." And then she kissed his mouth and pressed her body against his, making him want her, too. Again.

He went slowly the second time, holding himself back until he heard her breath hitch, felt her twine her legs around his and shudder against him, and then he came again, hard and fast and calling her name. He was in thrall to her beauty. To her sweet face. To her body—so full and lush and achingly lovely. She looked like something the old masters had carved, a flawless Galatea come to life. The curve of her breast, so softly heavy in his hand now. Her tapered waist. The generous flare of her hips. The unspeakable softness of her thighs, and what lay between them.

Willa had not looked like this. She had not felt like this. She was muscular and thin, not lush. They had never made love, he and

Willa, but he had held her close and kissed her. Right before her accident. He'd felt the bones of her hips pressed against him. The strong, thumping beat of her fearless heart. And after the accident, he'd set her hopelessly broken leg. Carried her injured body for miles, through African jungle and veldt, feeling her fever-racked cheek against his. He'd made her eat and drink. Held her when she vomited. Cleaned the blood and pus from her wounds. He knew her body. Better than he knew Jennie's. He knew her soul. Her spirit. Her heart.

Willa. Again, he thought, his heart suddenly heavy. Always Willa. Even now as he lay naked next to Jennie. Would he never be free of her? Of the memories? The longing? The torment? He wished he could rip her out of his head. And his heart.

By God, he would rip her out of himself. He'd do it. He'd rid himself of her. Break her hold over him. End the misery he felt whenever he thought of her. Here. Now. Forever.

He propped himself up on one elbow. "I love you, Jennie," he said.

Jennie, who'd been drowsing, opened her eyes. "What?" she whispered.

"I love you," he said, hoping she couldn't hear the desperation in his voice. "I do."

I do love her, he told himself. I do. Because she's beautiful and wonderful and I'd be completely mad not to.

Jennie blinked at him. She looked as if she wanted to say something but couldn't get the words out. Seamie's heart sank. He'd said too much. Or maybe he hadn't said enough. Yes, that was the most likely thing. He should've followed up his mad declaration with a proposal. He'd just made love to her, taken her virginity. He should be on bended knee now, asking her to marry him. But he couldn't do it. Because it wasn't her lovely hazel eyes he saw when he imagined asking that question, it was Willa's green ones. Still. Always.

"I'm a fool, Jennie," he quickly said. "You don't have to answer. I understand," he said. "I probably shouldn't have said anything. I—"

"You're not a fool, Seamie," she said. "Not at all. I . . . I . . ." She took a deep breath, then said, “I love you, too. Madly.” A tear rolled down her cheek, and then another.

Seamie brushed her tears away. “Don’t cry. Please don’t cry. I don’t know what I’m doing, Jennie. I don’t know if I’m going to be on a ship bound for Antarctica in a few months, or behind a desk at the RGS. I don’t know if . . .”

He wanted to be honest with her. He wanted to tell her that he wished he knew what to do. Whether to go or to stay. He wanted to tell her that he loved her, he did, as best he could. He wanted to ask her, to beg her, to somehow make him love her more. Enough to make him forget Willa Alden forever. But he didn’t know how to say those things, not without hurting her. He tried. He stuttered and stammered, until she finally stopped him.

“Shh,” she said, touching her finger to his lips. “It’s all right, Seamie.”

“Please don’t be sad,” he said. “I can’t bear to see you sad.”

She shook her head and kissed him. “I’m not sad. Not at all. I’m happy. Very, very happy. I have your love. It’s all that I want and more than I ever thought I’d have.”

He wondered at her words. How could a woman as beautiful and good and smart as Jennie have thought for a second that a man’s love was more than she’d ever have? Jennie Wilcott could have a thousand men, and every last one of them would have counted himself beyond lucky to have won her. Why on earth didn’t he love her as much as he loved Willa? Why couldn’t he ever get over Willa—the woman who’d smashed his heart and left him to pick up the pieces? What was wrong with him?

These questions hounded Seamie now; they tortured him. He wanted to get up, to get dressed, and go walking in the rain-soaked fields. He wanted to walk until the anger was out of him. Until the despair was gone. Until he had his answers.

But Jennie didn’t let him. She kissed him softly and pulled him down to her.

“It’s all right,” she said again.

And in her arms, for a few sweet hours, it was.

CHAPTER SEVENTEEN

"AH! THERE SHE is! My green-eyed heretic!"

Willa Alden smiled. She stood up and bowed to the man who'd just walked into Rongbuk's one and only public house—a corner of an enterprising villager's yak barn.

"*Namaste, Rinpoche,*" she said warmly, greeting him—an elder and a lama—first, as tradition demanded. She addressed him not by his name but by the honorific *Rinpoche*—"precious one."

"*Namaste,* Willa Alden," the lama replied. "I should've known to look for you in Jingpa's. Have I not often told you that alcohol obscures the path to enlightenment?" His words were chiding, but his eyes were kind.

Willa lifted the bamboo cup she was holding. It was filled with chang, an ale-like drink made from barley. "Ah, *Rinpoche,* I am in error!" she said. "I thought Jingpa's chang *was* the path to enlightenment."

The lama laughed. He pulled up a low wooden stool and sat down at Willa's table—a plank stretched across two tea chests, placed close to the fire. He pulled off his sheepskin hat and mittens and unbuttoned his coat. The night was brutally cold, and the wind was howling outside, but inside Jingpa's stone barn it was warm, for his fire and his animals gave off a great deal of heat.

"Will you have a sip of something hot, *Rinpoche*?" Willa asked. "The night is cold and the body desires warmth."

"My body desires little, Willa Alden. I have mastered my desires, for desire is the enemy of enlightenment."

Willa suppressed a smile. It was a game they played, she and this wily old man. He was the village's spiritual leader, head of the

Rongbuk Buddhist monastery, and must not be seen to be enjoying himself in a public house. Tomorrow Jingpa, a gossip, would talk to the entire village of the lama's visit. If he stayed to drink with her, he must be seen to be doing it for her sake only.

"Ah, *Rinpoche*, have pity on me. I am not as fortunate as you. Enlightenment eludes me. My desires control me. Even now, for I greatly desire the pleasure of your esteemed company. Will you deny a poor heretic the comfort of your light and knowledge?"

The lama sniffed. "Since you ask it, I will take a small cup of tea," he said.

"Jingpa! Po cha, please," Willa called out.

Jingpa nodded. He began whisking together the ingredients for the restorative drink—hot black tea, salt, yak milk, and butter. When he was finished, he poured the steaming mixture into a bamboo cup and brought it over. The lama held the hot cup in his hands, warming them, then took a sip and smiled. Jingpa bowed.

"What brings you here, *Rinpoche*?" Willa asked.

"A group of men, traders from Nepal, has just come through the pass on their way to Lhasa. They are staying overnight in the village. There is one among them—a Westerner—who is asking for you," the lama said.

Willa felt her heart leap at his words. For a wild, hopeful second, she allowed herself to believe that it was him—Seamie Finnegan—here somehow and wanting to see her. Then she silently scolded herself for her foolishness. Seamie wanted nothing to do with her. Why would he? She had left him, told him to live his life without her.

"His name is Villiers. He is a Frenchman, I believe," the lama continued. "A heretic like yourself. Determined to climb that which cannot be climbed, our holy mountain mother. He wishes to hire you as a guide. Shall I tell him where to find you? And endanger your soul? Or shall I say that there is no such person in Rongbuk and, by doing so, bring you closer to the Buddha?"

"I thank you for your concern, *Rinpoche*, and though my soul longs for transcendence, my body longs for sampa, po cha, and a warm fire at night. I must have the money I earn from guiding to buy these things, and so I will meet your Frenchman now, and the Buddha not quite yet, but soon."

"Soon. Always soon. Never now," the lama sighed. "As you wish, Willa Alden."

The lama finished his drink quickly and readied himself to return to the monastery.

"Will you please tell the man to meet me at my hut, *Rinpoche*?" Willa asked him as he pulled his mittens on.

The lama said he would. Willa thanked him, then asked Jingpa to fill an earthen bowl with hot chang and cover it with a plate. She knew the Frenchman would need it after trekking over the pass. She put her outer things on, paid Jingpa, and took the pot from him. She walked home through the village holding the pot close to her body, warming it as it warmed her.

As she passed by the monastery, she could smell the incense, smoky and thick, wafting from under the door and through cracks in the shutters. Under the wind's banshee howl, she could hear the monks chanting, their strong voices carrying through the monastery's walls. She loved the deep-voiced chants and was greatly moved by them. They sounded older than time, like the mountain itself speaking.

Willa stopped for a minute to listen. She had been inside the temple often and knew the saffron-robed monks would be seated to either side of their Buddha, eyes closed, palms turned up. She knew the Buddha would be gazing down on them, his face radiant with kindness, acceptance, and serenity.

She remembered the lama's words now and how he had wished to bring her closer to the Buddha. He wanted her to accept the Buddhist way. To detach herself from desire, to transcend it.

Willa knew the lama meant well for her, but what he was asking . . . well, it was like asking her to transcend the need to breathe. She simply could not do it. Her desire, her drive, they were what kept her going. They got her up and out in the morning when it was twenty below. They kept her working, photographing, trying to find a route up the mountain, even though she was hobbled by the loss of her leg. They kept her here year after year, though she was lonely and often longed for her family. She *was* her desire. To not want Everest, to not want to explore as much as she could of this magnificent mountain, was inconceivable to her. To stop desiring, to stop questing, was to die.

The lama called her, and all those who came to Rongbuk wishing to climb Everest, heretics. The mountain was holy, he said, and must be left undefiled by man. Yet he was kind, and though he tried his best to convert Willa and the other Westerners who made their way to Rongbuk, he also allowed them to stay in the village. He made sure they were provided for and prayed for their acceptance of the Buddha.

Willa walked on, certain the lama had worn out many beads praying for her, and certain he would wear out many more. She continued toward her home, more than a bit reluctant to meet the stranger who waited for her there. She needed his money—for food and drink and supplies, as she'd told the lama, and also for opium. Her leg was playing up something fierce. Her supply had dwindled and she would need to buy a fresh stock of the drug from the trading party that had stopped in Rongbuk, if they had any.

Willa always needed money, but solitude was what she wanted now, not visitors and their money, for she was finishing up her photographs and maps of her proposed route up Everest, and she needed to keep that route a secret. She didn't want anyone—and certainly not this man Villiers—to go back to Europe and claim her findings as his own.

Hopefully he wouldn't be too much trouble. He'd likely been trekking for weeks, and would need a few days to rest and recover from his exertions. That would give her the time she needed to do the climbing she wanted to do, finish taking notes, and write up her findings. Then she'd have to post them to Clements Markham at the RGS, which meant surrendering them to the first trading party heading to India and the British post office at Darjeeling.

As Willa neared her small, one-roomed hut at the eastern edge of the village, she spotted him, standing by her door, stamping his feet and clapping his hands to keep warm. As she got closer to him, she saw that he was gaunt and trembling. His lips were puffy and blue. There were white patches on his nose and chin.

"Miss Alden?" he called out.

"Mr. Villiers, I presume," she replied.

"Yes. M-M-Maurice Villiers. From France. I'm . . . I'm an alpinist, Miss Alden, and h-h-have heard of your f-f-familiarity with the north face of Everest. I w-w-wish to retain a guide and was w-w-wondering if you would consent—"

Willa laughed. The man was shivering so hard he could barely speak. "Stop talking and come inside," she said. "Before you drop dead."

She pushed her door open, then pushed him in, shaking her head as she did. She had begun to see Europeans as the Tibetans did. This man would insist on formalities and politenesses and the proper form of address even as he was freezing to death.

"Sit down. There," she said, pointing to a chair by the hearth. He did as he was told, putting his pack down first, while Willa immediately set about warming the room. She built up the fire she'd banked earlier, then lit a lamp. Then she pulled off her guest's hat, inspecting his ears, cheeks, and chin. Next she took off his mittens and turned his blue, swollen hands over in her own.

"They look worse than they are. You won't lose any fingers," she said. She poured a cup of Jinpa's chang, still steaming, from the earthen bowl and handed it to him. He took it gratefully, drank it quickly, and asked for more.

"In a minute," Willa said. "First let's see about your toes."

The fire had thawed his frozen laces. She untied them, opened his boots, and took them off. He made no protest. Not when his boots came off. And not when his socks wouldn't—because they were frozen to his swollen, blackened toes. She waited until the socks had thawed, too, then carefully peeled them off.

"How bad is it?" he asked her, not looking.

"I don't know. We'll have to wait and see."

"Am I going to lose my toes?"

"One or two."

He swore and raged. Willa waited for him to stop, then gave him a bowl of sampa. He was still shivering convulsively even after he'd finished eating, which worried her greatly. She quickly took his coat off and then his clothing. His underwear was sodden. She took a pair of scissors and cut the legs of it so that she could ease it over his damaged feet. He didn't want to take it off, but she made him.

"It's wet," she said. "You can't get in my bed in wet underwear. Here, put these on. I won't look," she added, giving him a tunic and a pair of wide-leg trousers. She turned away. When he'd dressed himself, she wrapped him in a wool robe and helped him hobble to her bed. The bed was piled high with sheepskins and furs.

"Get in and turn on your side," she said. He did. She got in next to him, pressed her body to his, and wrapped her arms around him.

He turned suddenly and kissed her violently, then grabbed her breast.

She slapped his hand away. "Do that again," she said, "and I shall beat you with the poker."

"But . . . but you touched me . . . you held me . . . ," Maurice said, through his blue lips.

"You're hypothermic, you bloody fool," Willa said. "I'm trying to save your life. Turn around now. Unless you want to be buried in Rongbuk."

Maurice Villiers did as he was told, and Willa put her arms back around him, holding him tightly, giving him her warmth. The heavy pelts held the heat around them. After an hour or so, his shivering stopped. A little while later, he fell asleep. When Willa heard his breathing deepen and even out, and felt his chest rising and falling steadily, she got out of bed and stoked the fire. She hoped he would sleep until morning. He needed it. She knew that eventually the pain in his thawing feet would wake him, and when that happened, she would give him some of her opium.

Willa was tired herself. She quickly tidied up the room—hanging up her visitor's wet things and opening up his boots so that they would dry properly. She was just about to douse the lamp and go to bed herself when Maurice Villiers rolled over in bed.

"The letters," he said groggily. "I forgot them. . . ."

"Go to sleep, Mr. Villiers," Willa said, not bothering to look at him, certain he was talking in his sleep.

". . . letters . . . in my pack."

Willa turned to look at him. "What letters?"

"For you. In my pack," he said, blinking at her. "Postman in Darjeeling gave them to me. I told him I was coming here." Then he rolled over again and went back to sleep.

Willa crossed the room, unbuckled his pack, and rooted through it. At the very bottom, bundled together with twine, was a thick stack of letters. The top one had a British stamp. She pulled the bundle out and flipped through the envelopes. Most were addressed in her mother's hand. Some were in her brother's. There were so many of them—too many of them. The post was dependent on traders and travelers coming and going, and was often delayed on its way north from Darjeeling, but even allowing for that, there were still too many letters here. Looking at them all, she was suddenly gripped by fear. Something was wrong, she knew it. Whatever news these letters contained, it was not good.

Willa pulled the top letter out of the stack. With trembling hands, she opened it and started to read.

CHAPTER EIGHTEEN

"MAUD?" THE PRIME minister said.

"Hmm?"

"It's your turn."

"My turn for what, darling?"

"Your turn to play! Ye gads, woman, where are you?" Asquith said petulantly.

"Here, Henry. Right here." She quickly looked at her cards, couldn't make heads or tails of them, and said, "No bid."

The turn passed to Margot, Asquith's wife, who made a whacking great bid, then Max.

Asquith oughtn't to have asked me "Where are you?" Maud thought. But rather "Where were you?" Because in her head, she was back in the Coburg, in Max's room. She was in Max's bed, naked. He'd tied a silk cravat around her eyes, tied her wrists to the headboard.

"We'll miss the train," she'd said.

"I don't care," he'd said.

"Max, he's the prime minister."

"So what?"

He'd kissed her mouth, then proceeded to nibble his way down her body, slowly and gently, biting her earlobe, her neck, her breast, her hip. He pushed her legs apart and kissed the place between them.

"Now, Max," she'd whispered throatily. "Now."

"No," he'd said, kissing her knee, biting her calf. "Not now."

She'd moaned and twined against him, wishing she could get her hands free and pull him to her, pull him inside of her. "Bastard," she'd hissed. But he'd only laughed and nibbled her toes. Her belly. Her shoulder.

He went on like that, teasing her with his lips and his tongue, until she was nearly mad with her need of him. And then suddenly he was inside of her, and her release, when it finally came, was so strong, so hot and violent, that it frightened her. She'd cried out, she remembered that. Actually, she'd screamed. It was amazing the manager hadn't come knocking on the door. Or the police. Never had a man made her feel so good. She was addicted to Max von Brandt. Her body craved him like a drug. He was all she could think about.

They'd drunk champagne afterward, made love again, and missed the damned train. They had to take Max's motorcar to Sutton Courtenay in Oxfordshire, where the Asquiths had their country home, and where the PM had invited them both for the weekend. Max had driven like a demon and they'd only been half an hour late.

Maud knew Asquith well. She was friends with his wife Margot and with his grown daughter, Violet. Violet's mother had died when she and her brothers were young, and Asquith had later married Margot, one of the beautiful and vivacious Tennant sisters.

Maud and Max had had a spot of tea with Margot and Violet, and the Asquiths' other weekend guests, when they arrived, then they'd bathed and changed for dinner. After they'd dined, Asquith suggested bridge. Maud and Max had been paired with the prime minister and his wife. The other guests played against one another at tables nearby. Maud was a good, competitive player and usually enjoyed the game, but memories of the afternoon's activities had her so hot and bothered tonight, that she could barely keep her cards straight.

"It's your turn *again*, Maud," Asquith said, a note of irritation in his voice. "What's distracting you? You usually go for your opponent's throat at the bridge table."

"Millicent Fawcett," Maud said abruptly.

Millicent and the suffragists were actually the farthest thing from her mind, but she was the best Maud could come up with. She could hardly tell the PM what she'd really been thinking about.

"She's making noises about going over to Labour. Doing her all to support and campaign for their candidates. She feels the Labour Party will be more sympathetic to the cause of women's suffrage," Maud said. "You'd best not ignore her, Henry. She may not have got us the vote—*yet*—but she does have clout, you know."

"Are you trying to rattle me, old girl? If so, it's very unsporting of you and it won't work."

"All's fair in bridge and war," Maud said. "Seriously though, you would be well advised not to underestimate Millicent. She is not altogether what she seems. She is polite and reserved, but she is also resolute, tough, and relentless."

Asquith raised his eyes from his cards. "I would say that no one, and nothing, is as it seems," he said, and Maud noticed it was not herself he was looking at as he spoke these words, but her partner, and that his expression had become most somber. "Wouldn't you agree, Mr. von Brandt?" he added.

"I would, yes," Max said, meeting Asquith's steely gaze unwaveringly.

For the briefest second, Maud had the inexplicably unsettling feeling that the two men were not still talking about bridge, but about something else completely. Then Margot started chattily asking questions, and as quickly as it had come, the strange feeling was gone.

"Maud tells me you've been to Everest, Mr. von Brandt," Margot said.

"I have, yes. I spent most of last year in Nepal and Tibet," Max replied.

Margot was about to say more, when the door to the drawing room opened.

"Excuse me, sir. . . ." It was Asquith's secretary.

"Mmm? What is it, man?"

"A telephone call, sir. From Cambridge."

Asquith was silent for a few seconds, then he turned in his chair. "Cambridge, you say?"

"Yes, sir."

The prime minister nodded. He turned back to the table and looked at Max, and Maud noticed, again, that the look in his eyes had become a hard one.

"I believe it's your turn now, Mr. von Brandt. I wonder . . . how will you play your hand this time? A bold move, perhaps?"

Max shook his head and smiled tightly. "With so many seasoned players about me, I must be cautious," he said. "I think I will play it safe for the present."

Asquith nodded. He rose from his chair.

"Will you take the call in your study, sir?" his secretary asked.

"I suppose I shall have to, to spare everyone my wittering," Asquith said, placing his cards facedown on the table. "Wish the blasted study wasn't so far away, but I shan't be a moment." He stood up, wagging a finger at Maud as he did. "No peeking, old girl. Margot, see that she doesn't."

It felt to Maud as if Asquith had suddenly remembered he had guests and must be genial toward them. She found the man's mood odd and hard to follow, but she chalked it up to the pressures of his office and the bother of having to take what were very likely difficult phone calls at all hours.

"Is the study so far?" Max asked.

"No, it's upstairs. Right above us. Henry's just being cross," Margot said.

Max nodded, then stood. "Would anyone like a top-up?" he asked.

"I would, darling," Maud said. "Claret, please."

Max took her glass. He smiled at her seductively, and Maud found herself wondering what sort of excuse she could come up with to get herself out of this beastly card game. She didn't want to be sitting here in the drawing room, concentrating on suits and trumps and tricks. She wanted to be lying in bed, reveling in Max's glorious body.

Margot had seen Max's smile, too. As he crossed the room to a cabinet containing decanters of spirits and wines, she gave Maud a mischievous look. "Is it just me? Or is it warm in here?" she whispered, fanning herself with her cards. Maud swatted her.

As they whispered and laughed together, neither woman saw Max glance up at the ceiling, his smile gone, a grim, determined look in his eyes.

CHAPTER NINETEEN

"YOU WANT TO break it off. That's it, isn't it?" Seamie said quietly, a stricken expression on his face. "That's why you wrote me." He was sitting on a blue silk settee in the Wilcotts' parlor.

Jennie, who'd been pacing back and forth, stopped and turned to him. "No!" she quickly said. "That's not it at all, Seamie. Would you let me finish, please?"

"Well, what is it, then? Something must be wrong. I can't imagine you asked me to come here in such a big fat hurry for a cup of tea."

"No, I didn't," Jennie said. She opened the parlor door, glanced down the hallway to make sure her father was nowhere near, then shut it again. Seamie was right—there was something wrong. She'd written to him last night, at his sister's Mayfair address, asking him to come this morning because she had something she needed to tell him, something urgent. It had been worrying at her for days. Ever since she'd been to see Harriet Hatcher. He was here now, and she had to tell him. She couldn't keep it to herself any longer.

"Seamie," she said quietly, "I'm pregnant."

Seamie's eyebrows shot up. "Pregnant? You mean you're going to have a baby?"

"Yes. That's what pregnant means—that one is going to have a baby."

Seamie, ashen-faced, slowly stood up.

Jennie looked down at her clasped hands. "I know it's a shock," she said. "And I know you have many plans, some of which do not include me. I've looked into homes for unwed mothers. Places where I could go to have the baby. Places that would find a good home for the child—"

"Never," Seamie said swiftly and harshly, cutting her words off. "Don't speak of it, Jennie. Don't even think of it." He crossed the room to where she stood, took her hand in his, and went down on one knee. "Marry me, Jennie," he said.

Jennie stopped speaking. She looked down at him, her eyes wide and searching.

"Marry me," he said again. "I want a life with you. A home. I want this child, and many more children. Lots of them. Three or four. Six. Ten. I want you to be my wife."

"But, Seamie," she said softly, "what about Ernest Shackleton and the expedition?"

"Shackleton will just have to trek off across Antarctica without me. My place is here now. With you and with our child. Marry me, Jennie. Say yes."

Jennie shook her head. In a small, anguished voice she said, "Seamie, I . . . I need to tell you . . ."

"What? Need to tell me what? Do you not want me? Is there someone else?" he asked, a mixture of hurt and surprise in his voice.

She raised her head. "*Someone else?*" she said, wounded. "No, there isn't. How could you say such a thing? There's only you, Seamie. And yes . . . yes, I *do* want you. So very much. That's what I wanted to tell you. Only that." She took a deep breath, then said, "Yes, Seamie. I *will* marry you. Yes. Oh, yes." And then she burst into tears.

Seamie brought her over to the settee, pulled her onto his lap, and kissed her. "I'm so happy about this, Jennie. Really. This is what I want—you, me, our children. I love you, Jennie. I do. I told you that in Cambridge and nothing's changed. I love you as much this very second as I did then."

Jennie let out a long, deep breath that it felt like she'd been holding for days. "You're not upset, then?" she said.

"Upset? I'm delighted! Why? Are you?"

"Well, no, not exactly. But, well, you see . . . I'm only a few weeks along. That's what Harriet—Dr. Hatcher—says. So for now, everything's well and good. But in a few months it won't be."

Seamie grinned at her mischievously. "You're worried about

waddling down the aisle with a big fat belly and everyone in the church knowing we had it off long before our wedding night?"

"Yes," Jennie said, coloring. "I am."

"It's nothing to worry about," Seamie said.

"It isn't?"

"No. If anyone says anything, I'll just tell them that we *did* have it off . . ."

"Seamie!"

". . . in an old cow barn by the Cam." He kissed her mouth. "I'll tell them how you lured me inside in a rainstorm and took advantage of me," he said, undoing the top buttons of her blouse. "I'll tell them I was completely helpless and . . . ," he hooked a finger in her camisole and peeked down it, ". . . and good God, woman, if they could see these, they'd believe me, too."

"For goodness' sake!" Jennie said, pulling her camisole closed.

"They get bigger, don't they? When you're pregnant, I mean. That's what I've heard. I hope so. I love too much of a good thing."

"Seamie, don't joke!"

"Why not?" he said, looking up at her. "What's the matter?"

"What's the matter? Have you not been listening to me? I can't walk down the aisle of a church with a huge belly!"

"I have been listening. I've heard every word. Let's get married tomorrow."

"*Tomorrow?*"

"Yes, tomorrow. We can take a train to Scotland. To Gretna Green. Spend the night there. Get married in the morning."

Jennie knew she should feel relieved. Even grateful to him for suggesting such a quick solution. Instead she began to cry again.

"Jennie . . . darling, what's wrong now?"

"I can't go to Gretna Green, Seamie. I can't get married without my father there."

"No worries, then. We'll have our wedding here. We'll post the bans this Sunday, all right? How long do we have to post them before we can have the actual ceremony?"

"For three weeks."

"Then we'll have our wedding three weeks from this coming Sunday. Your father can do the honors and I'm sure my sister will want to do something, too—a breakfast, a luncheon, something." Seamie was excited. He was speaking quickly. "I'm going to go to an estate agent's as soon as I leave here. I'll find us a nice flat. Near Hyde Park. And then I'm going to a furniture shop and find a bed. With a big cushy mattress. So I can throw you in it and make love to you again the very second we're married," he said.

He undid more buttons on her blouse as he spoke, then pulled open her camisole and cupped her breasts. He kissed them, and then her throat, her mouth, and the soft hollow beneath her ear. Jennie surrendered to his hands and his lips. She wanted him, too. So much. She couldn't wait until they were married and in a home of their own, in a bed of their own. She wanted to feel him reach for her in the darkness, to hear him whispering her name, and know he was hers, truly hers.

Seamie suddenly broke the kiss. "Oh, no," he said. "Oh, bloody hell."

"What is it?" Jennie asked him, pulling the sides of her camisole together.

"It's just dawned on me that I'm going to have to go and tell your father that you're pregnant. After I promised him I'd take good care of you in Cambridge."

"Don't worry . . . ," Jennie started to say, buttoning her blouse.

"Don't worry? I *am* worried. I'm flipping terrified!" he said. "Icebergs, leopard seals, blizzards—none of those things ever scared me. Telling the Reverend Wilcott that I've put his daughter up the spout—now, that scares me."

"Let's not tell him. Not right away," Jennie said, biting her lip.

"No, we have to. *I* have to. It's the right thing to do." He stood up, and Jennie did, too, smoothing her skirts and her hair. "No, you stay here," he told her. "This is a conversation between your father and me. I'll be back. Sit down."

Jennie smiled at him as he left the room, but as soon as the door closed behind him, her face crumpled. She put her head in her hands.

She was happy, she was, but she was also sick with worry. This pregnancy—it was more than she could have hoped for. It was nothing short of a miracle, actually, and Seamie had no idea. Because she hadn't told him the truth. Not about the scar running down the right side of her body. And not about the accident that caused it.

They'd been playing, she and her friends. Their ball had gone into the street and she'd run after it. She never saw the carriage, and thankfully, she didn't remember it striking her, didn't remember her body going under the front wheel. It had nearly crushed her. After a long, risky surgery, the doctor—Dr. Addison—told her parents that the carriage had broken five of her ribs, ruptured her spleen, collapsed a lung, destroyed an ovary, and punctured her uterus. He also told them that he had done his very best for her, but that they must prepare themselves for the likelihood of losing her. If the trauma her body had suffered did not kill her, infection probably would.

"We put stock in his opinion, of course," her mother had told her, months after she'd recovered, "but we put our faith in God."

Jennie was in the hospital for six long months, and though she didn't remember the accident, she remembered the recovery. It was an agony to her—the pain of the injuries, the infections and raging fevers, the bedsores and boredom, and the endless process of healing.

When she finally left the hospital, she was weak, pale, and horribly gaunt, but she was alive. It took another six months for her to put on a few pounds, and even longer for her to regain her strength, but with her parents' help she did it. The doctor came to visit her several times over the course of her convalescence. The last time he saw her, he brought her a beautiful china baby doll. A consolation prize, she'd thought as she grew older, for the real baby she would never have. The doctor had said good-bye to her in the parlor, then he'd taken her mother out in the hallway to speak privately. Jennie wasn't supposed to hear what he said, but she listened at the door.

"Her uterus is still inside her, Mrs. Wilcott, but it was badly damaged. She may have her menses, but she will never carry a child. I'm sorry. It's a blow to you now, and it will be a cross for Jennie later, but not all women need husbands to be happy. Jennie is a very bright girl. She would do well to enter the teaching profession or indeed my own. There is always a need for good nurses."

She'd hadn't understood his words then, for she was nine years old and innocent and could not imagine ever needing a husband for anything, never mind happiness. But when she was thirteen, and her menses started, and her mother sat her down and explained the facts of life and how they no longer applied to her, she then understood what Dr. Addison had been trying to say: that no man would ever want her, for she would not be able to bear children.

As she grew older, she told herself it did not matter. If she could not marry, she would find satisfaction in her work. If she could not have children of her own, she would love the little ones she taught at her school. Once, a young man, a deacon in her father's church, wanted to court her. He was fair and slender and kind. She did not love him, but she could have liked him well. Because she did not love him, she was honest with him, and when he learned that she could not give him a family, he thanked her for her frankness and promptly transferred his affections to a cloth merchant's daughter.

There had been two others—a teacher like herself and a young minister. She had been honest with them, too, and had lost them both. It had hurt a little, but not too terribly much, for she had not been in love with them, either.

And then she'd met Seamie Finnegan and had fallen in love, deeply and passionately.

That afternoon, in the cow barn on the River Cam, she had asked him to make love to her and she had not been worried about any repercussions, for she knew there could be none. She knew, too, that once she told him the truth about her scar, he would leave her, just as the others had, for she was damaged and could not give him what a normal woman could. And so she had not told him the truth.

I'll tell him afterward, she'd silently promised God before she gave herself to Seamie, but let me have him first. Let me have love, just this once, she'd prayed, and I'll never ask for anything more.

And when it was over, and she was lying there, happy and sated, loving the smell of him on her skin, the taste of him on her lips, she had remembered her promise and begun to frame the words, to think of the right thing to say, when out of the blue, he'd told her that he loved her. And she found she could not say the words she knew she ought to. Because she could not bear to lose him. The others, yes—but not him.

So she'd said nothing.

Not during their trip on the River Cam. And not moments ago, when he'd proposed to her. She'd tried. Very hard. She'd almost got the words out, but she'd failed.

"I want a life with you. A home. Children. Lots of them. Three or four. Six. Ten. I want you to be my wife," he'd told her. At those words, her resolve had deserted her and she'd said yes. She'd let him believe she could give him the sons and daughters he wanted. She'd lied to him. Not by what she'd said, but by what she hadn't.

She'd told herself she would tell him the truth about herself. Over and over again. Weeks ago, on their way back to Cambridge. Then at Aunt Eddie's house. On the train back to London. But she hadn't. Every morning after their trip, when she first woke up, she told herself that today was the day she would tell Seamie the truth, no matter what it cost her. And every day he made it harder and harder for her to say anything.

And then, she realized her monthlies had not come. She'd thought little of it at first. They'd always been a little off—early one month, late the next. But then she'd started to hope. Could it be? What if Dr. Addison had been wrong? What if she *could* carry a child?

Hoping against hope, she'd gone to see Harriet Hatcher. Harriet had examined her and then said the words Jennie Wilcott never thought she would hear: "You're pregnant." Of course Harriet, who was Jennie's doctor and knew of her injuries, warned her not to get her hopes up. "You've conceived, yes," she said, "and that's wonderful, but it doesn't change the damage that was done to your reproductive organs. We don't know if your womb can carry a child to term."

Seamie had not hesitated to do the right thing when she told him she was pregnant. Though he'd been torn during the last few weeks, he now wanted to settle down. He wanted children. Many children. He'd said so. Why would he marry a woman who couldn't give them to him? No man would. Least of all a man like him—a man who was young and handsome and famous. A man who could have any woman. Who'd had many women, including the dazzling Willa Alden.

Jennie knew who Willa was. The magazines sometimes published photographs she'd taken in the East. They always mentioned how she and Seamie had set a record together, years ago on Kilimanjaro. They said how a terrible accident on the mountain had taken her leg and that she hadn't returned to England, but had gone instead to Nepal and Tibet.

Jennie had asked Seamie about her once. She asked if he still had feelings for Willa. He'd assured her that he did not, and that what he and Willa had had was firmly in the past. But his face had changed as he spoke about her, and the look in his eyes had not been one of indifference. He wasn't over Willa. He loved her still. Of that Jennie was certain.

Willa was like him, and she, Jennie, was not. And she wondered now, as she had so many times in the past few weeks, exactly what Seamie was doing with her. She who was not daring and bold and had not even explored west London, never mind the South Pole. She couldn't offer him what Willa could—the shared passion for discovery, for taking risks and setting records. What she could offer was the domestic pleasures—a comfortable home life, a family. And if she couldn't even give him these things, what then?

"I love you, Jennie. I do," he'd said to her when he'd proposed. It had almost sounded desperate to her. As if he very much wanted to love her and was trying to convince himself that he *did* love her. Her, not Willa. If she lost the child she was carrying, if he ever found out the truth about her, he *would* leave her. She was certain of it.

Tears threatened to overwhelm her again. Instinctively, her hands went to her belly. "Can you hear me?" she whispered. "Stay with me, little one. Please, please stay."

Footsteps came toward the parlor. Jennie quickly brushed her tears away. The door opened and her father stepped inside. He gave her a stormy look at first, then he crossed the room, took her by her shoulders, and quietly said, "I wish this had happened after the wedding, I must say, but I'm happy it's happened at all. I'm glad for you, Jennie. Truly. There is no greater joy than a child. I know this, for I know what joy you've given me."

"Thank you, Dad," she said, her voice breaking.

"Yes. Well. Come in, lad!" the Reverend Wilcott bellowed. The door opened and Seamie walked into the parlor. "I've some sherry in the kitchen," the Reverend said. "I'll fetch it and some glasses, too. I think we could all use a nip."

As soon as he was gone, Seamie gathered Jennie into his arms. "He didn't kill me!" he whispered to her. "He'll post the bans this Sunday and marry us in three weeks."

"Oh, Seamie! That's wonderful!" Jennie said.

"It is. I'm so relieved. He was much better about it than I would have thought. Much better than I would have been in the circumstances." He put his hand on Jennie's belly. "If this baby is a girl, I'll make sure to protect her from the likes of me." He laughed, then said, "I can't wait to become your husband. And our child's father. It's everything I want, Jennie. Truly."

Jennie smiled weakly. A feeling of dread gripped her as she looked at him. She tried to shake it off. Tried to tell herself to stop being silly and to be grateful instead for the tiny life growing inside her. For the miracle she'd been given.

Nine months, she thought. That's all I need. Nine months from now, he'll be holding our child and he'll be happy. Happy with the baby. Happy with his life. Happy with me.

CHAPTER TWENTY

"THREE MILLION POUNDS. For boats," Joe Bristow said. He was sitting behind his desk in the study of his Mayfair home. "How many do we get for that? Two? Three?"

"Eight. And they're ships not boats," said the man sitting across from him. "The finest warships ever built." He drained the glass of whiskey he was holding, stood up, and walked to the window.

George Burgess never sat still for long, Joe thought as he watched him. Pale and freckled, his reddish-blond hair already receding, Burgess, at the tender age of twenty-nine, was a war hero, an acclaimed author, and had already held the offices of MP and secretary of state for the colonies. It was in his current role as second lord of the Admiralty that he'd paid a visit to Joe this evening, to harangue him into supporting Churchill's call for more dreadnoughts.

Joe was supposed to be downstairs at a family dinner. It was a lovely April evening, and Fiona had invited Joe's parents; his brothers and their families; her brother Seamie, and his fiancée, Jennie Wilcott; and a dozen close friends to dine with them. Jennie and Seamie were to be married in two weeks' time, and a great deal of planning was taking place tonight. Just as Joe had sat down, Burgess had arrived, saying he had urgent state business to discuss with him, and adding that another man from the Admiralty would be joining them shortly. Joe had excused himself and taken George upstairs in the elevator to his study, where the two men had engaged in a tense and heated discussion, for over an hour now, with George adamant on the need for Britain to acquire not one new dreadnought, as Churchill had originally asked of Parliament, but a whole new fleet of dreadnoughts, and

Joe intransigent on the idea of government releasing three million pounds with which to do the acquiring.

"I don't care how fine they are, George," he said now. "My constituents don't need warships. They don't want them. They want schools, hospitals, and parks. And jobs. Jobs would be very nice."

"Oh, they'll get them," Burgess retorted. "In the kaiser's munition factories. He plans to build several on the Thames docks as soon as he invades England."

"This is war-mongering, pure and simple," Joe said hotly. "You say you want to head off military aggression by making a show of strength, yet you take every opportunity to stir up feeling for the very war you wish to avoid!"

"I do not need to stir up feeling. It is already there. Furthermore—"

Burgess's words were cut off by a knock at Joe's door. "Come in!" Joe barked.

The door opened, and then Albie Alden, Seamie's friend from Cambridge, was suddenly standing in the room.

"Hello, Albie lad," Joe said. "The dinner's downstairs. Seamie and Jennie—"

Burgess cut him off. "He's here to see us," he said.

"Hold on," Joe said. "Albie's your man from the Admiralty? Albie Alden?"

"Finally, the other shoe drops," Burgess replied. He motioned impatiently at Albie. "Do come in, old boy," he said. "And lock the door, will you?"

Albie did as he was asked, then crossed the room, opened his briefcase, and handed Burgess a thick dossier. Burgess opened it, paged through its contents, snorting and nodding and sometimes swearing, then slapped it down on Joe's desk.

"Read that," he said. "Read it, *then* tell me we can't have our ships."

Joe looked at Burgess, then at Albie, wondering what could possibly be in the dossier. He opened it. The documents it contained were all stamped with the seal of the Secret Service Bureau, a department within the Admiralty whose presence was known to very few.

By the second or third page, Joe realized what he was reading: reports on various men and women, German nationals all, whom the SSB suspected of spying. One name in particular caught Joe's eyes—Max von Brandt. Joe knew the man; he'd met him a few weeks ago, after a suffragists' march at Holloway prison. He'd seen him several times since in the company of Maud Selwyn Jones.

Joe was greatly relieved to read that while von Brandt's name had been put forward as a possible spy, the author of the report had concluded that it was unlikely he was one. He had an independent income, family in England, and no ties to the German military other than carrying out his compulsory service.

Furthermore, Max had had a public falling-out with his industrialist uncle—his father's older brother—over the kaiser's aggressiveness. The argument had occurred in a Berlin restaurant. Both men ended up shouting at each other. Max's uncle had thrown a plate at him. The event was reported by three different, reliable eyewitnesses, and Max had left Germany for England a week later. Reportedly, his uncle was pleased about Max's departure. He openly accused him of being an embarrassment to the family and of costing him, the uncle, business. Max von Brandt, the report concluded, was an accomplished alpinist, a playboy, and a philanderer, but he was not a spy. Others were, though. Dozens of them. Joe flipped past page after page of names and grainy gray photographs. When he'd gone through them all, he looked up.

"How did you find all of these people?" he asked Albie.

Burgess answered. "Albie here, together with Alfred Ewing, Dilly Knox, Oliver Strachey, and various other Cambridge geniuses, has been very busy cracking codes over the last year. They've confirmed the existence of a widespread and effective German espionage ring in the UK, and as you can see, they've identified many of its foot soldiers."

"Then why haven't you arrested them?" Joe asked, alarmed.

"Because we are hoping the foot soldiers will lead us to the spymaster himself," Burgess said. "He's the one we dearly want to catch. Our own agents in Germany tell us that he's very effective.

Frighteningly so. He's already gathered and conveyed a great deal of very valuable information to Berlin. Our agents also tell us that Germany will invade France at the first possible opportunity and that they will do it via Belgium."

"It's nonsense, George," Joe said. "It can't be true. Even if the Germans wanted to invade France, they can't do it by going through Belgium. It's a treaty violation. Belgium's a neutral country."

"Why don't you ring up the kaiser and tell him so?" Burgess said. "Others—plenty of them—have already tried. To no avail."

He crossed the room now and sat down across from Joe. He poured himself another scotch, sat back in his chair, and said, "I am worried about Germany, Joe. Extremely so. I am also worried about the Middle East. About Germany's growing friendship with Turkey and about England's Persian oil fields and our ability to defend them should war be declared. We've got spies there, too. Some rather unlikely ones—a Mr. Thomas Lawrence among them. They've been mapping the whole bloody desert, forging bonds with many Arab leaders. Lawrence was debriefed only a fortnight ago."

"Lawrence? The young man who just gave a presentation at the RGS?"

"The very same. It was an important presentation, that one. Not so much for the ruins and rocks and bits of pottery he was nattering on about, but to keep the impression going that he's simply an impassioned archaeologist and nothing more."

Joe closed the dossier and pushed it across his desk. "Why are you doing all this?" he asked him. "Why all the cloak-and-dagger? Bringing Albie here? Showing me the dossier? Telling me about German spies in London and British spies in the desert?"

Burgess put his glass down. He leaned forward. When he spoke, his voice was low and urgent. "In the desperate hope that by doing so, I can underscore for you the dire seriousness of the German military threat and the very pressing need for Britain to counteract it. Now."

Joe went silent. He knew George wanted an answer from him, but he could not give it. He knew George wanted his support in his bid to build up Britain's military defenses. All efforts, all funds,

George felt, should go to strengthening the navy, the army, and the nascent air force. He wanted Joe to stop fighting him, to stop calling for funds for social reform programs.

As if reading his mind, Burgess spoke. "We in government must present a united front to the voters," he said. "I, and many others in the Liberal Party, are very aware of your influence with the workingman, and frankly, we wish to harness it to our cause. We need the weight of public opinion with us, not against us. Help me in this, Joe, and I will help you. I will back your calls for social reform, and for funding for your schools and hospitals."

Joe raised an eyebrow. "When?" he asked.

"After the war is over and won," Burgess said.

Joe knew what this request meant—that the things that mattered so dearly to him, and to his constituents, would be swept away in a mad burst of war fever. The suffrage question would be pushed aside. Monies for his projects—for the soup kitchens, the libraries, the orphanages—would dry up. And who would suffer when they did? Who would go hungry and cold? Not the children of the rich. Not the Asquiths and the Cecils and the Churchills, no. It would be the children of East London. As always. Men would go to war and would not come home. Women would lose their husbands, children their fathers.

After some time, Joe finally spoke. "I do not want this war, George, and you must promise me that you will do everything in your power to keep us from it. Everything. Use our diplomats. Use trade sanctions. Embargoes. Buy your boats. Buy ten of them. Twenty. If having more of them makes the kaiser draw back, then it will have been worth the cost. It's better to lose money than human lives."

Burgess nodded, then he said, "And if, even then, even after we have made every effort, war still cannot be avoided . . . then what is your choice?"

"Then there is no choice, George," Joe said. "And there never was."

CHAPTER TWENTY-ONE

JENNIE WILCOTT WAS helping her father get ready for his weekly parish visits. "Do you have your scarf, Dad?" she asked him.

"I don't need it, my dear. It's a sunny day."

"And a blustery one. You do need it. Here, put it on. And wear your other coat. It's warmer."

The Reverend Wilcott smiled. He took her face in his hands. "Ah, my darling Jennie. You take such good care of your old father. What will I do when you go?"

"Don't, Dad. You'll start me crying again," she said.

He kissed her cheek. "Only tears of joy, I hope. You'll make such a beautiful bride. I only hope I can get through the ceremony without crying myself. And speaking of the ceremony, did my best suit come back from the tailor's? I'm worried they won't get it back to me in time."

"It's in your wardrobe, Dad. A man from the shop brought it yesterday."

"Good. Well, I'm off then." He stopped in the doorway and turned around. "You're not to do too much today. You must rest yourself. Promise me you will."

"I promise," Jennie said, smiling.

As soon as she closed the door behind him, she went to the parlor, where she'd begun to make a list of all the errands she needed to run and notes she needed to write and gifts she needed to buy before Sunday.

"Why is it that lists only get longer, never shorter?" she wondered aloud. The wedding, which would be held at Seamie's sister's home in Greenwich, was only five days away and there was still so much to do. After the reception, they would leave for Cornwall for a honeymoon—a short one only, as Seamie was due to begin at the RGS the following Monday. When they returned from Cornwall, they would take up residence in a lovely, spacious flat in Belsize Park. Seamie had found it for them, just as he'd said he would, but they had very little furniture in it and no carpets or curtains whatsoever.

Jennie had been to see a seamstress about the curtains, and had even selected fabric, but it would be weeks before they were finished. Whenever she fretted about all that they still needed, Seamie would kiss her and shush her and tell her not to worry herself or the baby. He had means and would provide whatever they needed.

And he did. All she had to do was mention something, and he was off to the shops and back a few hours later with cutlery, towels, a mop bucket—whatever she wanted. He didn't mind doing these things one bit, he would tell her. He'd never gone shopping before—not for lamps and antimacassars, at least—and he found it all very interesting. He was always so good to her. So cheerful and willing. Excited about their wedding. He was always so happy. Too happy.

She thought now, as she looked out her parlor window, that he reminded her at times of the drunks who came to her father—men and women broken by alcohol. They'd lost everything—jobs, homes, their families. They shook and wept and promised to do anything, even swear off the demon drink forever, if only he would help them. He always did. He got them cleaned up, let them sleep on a cot in the sacristy, and tried to find them work. He prayed with them and made them take the pledge. And his efforts always succeeded—for a little while. They tried hard, all of them. They were eager, bright-eyed, and willing, full of good intentions. Happy to tell anyone and everyone that their drinking days were behind them. But deep inside, they struggled. They thought about drink constantly. Dreamed about it. Craved it. And many, unable to resist the ever-present temptation, went back to it.

Seamie was the same way. He wanted so much to embrace his new life. He talked excitedly about his new position at the RGS. He'd leased a flat, bought a bed, a set of sheets, cutlery, and a box of crockery. But

Jennie knew that underneath the bluff good cheer, under all the protestations of happiness, he still dreamed about his old life.

She had seen him unpack a box of his belongings in their new flat one evening when he wasn't aware she was watching him. He'd taken photographs out of the box. Field glasses, book, maps, an old, battered compass. He'd held the compass in his palm, then closed his fingers around it. And then he'd gone to the window and stood there, just stood there, gazing up at the night sky.

He was thinking about past adventures, Jennie was sure of it. And about Willa Alden. Looking at him, she had been convinced that if, at that very moment, the compass in his hands could have shown him the way back to Willa, he would have followed it.

Jennie's hands went to her belly, as they did all the time now when she was nervous or worried. As always, she prayed for the tiny life inside to stay with her. A fortnight had passed since she'd told Seamie she was pregnant. She was two weeks closer to being the mother of his child. The love of a wife, of a child, these were good things, too, Jennie told herself, the very best things. And in time, as Seamie got older, as they had more children, he would grow to want them—and her—more than he wanted other things and other people.

A knock on the door startled her out of her thoughts.

"Dad? Is that you? What've you forgotten now?" Jennie shouted, trotting out of the parlor and down the hallway. "It's your specs, isn't it?" she said as she opened the door. "How many times . . ."

Her words died away. It wasn't her father who was standing on the stoop. It was Josie Meadows, a young woman whom she used to teach. Josie had no coat on. The front of her dress was bloodied and torn. More blood dripped onto it from a cut on her cheek. Her eyes were bruised and swollen.

"Hello, duck," Josie said.

"Josie?" Jennie whispered. "My God, is that you?"

"Aye. I'm afraid so. Can I come in?"

"Of course!" Jennie said, ushering her inside and closing the door. "I'm sorry, I . . . I just . . . Josie, what on earth happened to you?"

"Billy Madden happened to me," the girl said, walking past Jennie, down the hallway to the kitchen. She went to the sink, stoppered it, and turned on the taps. "Can I clean myself up?" she asked. "Borrow a dress? I've got to get out of here before he twigs where I've gone. Bastard's threatened to kill me."

Jennie saw that Josie was shaking. The cut on her cheek was still dripping blood. Her nose had started to bleed, too. Most women in Josie's shape would have been weeping. Not Josie. Josie Meadows was a Wapping girl, and Wapping girls did not cry. They were hard, loud, and tough as nails. Jennie had taught many of them and knew that the lives they led—the lives they endured—made them so. Josie would shake. She would drink, smoke, shout, and swear, but she would never, ever cry.

"Sit down," Jennie said, turning the taps off.

"Can't, luv. Haven't the time."

"Josie Meadows, you sit down. Right now."

Josie smiled, though it made her wince. "Yes, miss," she said. "You always get your way when you use your teacher voice, don't you?"

"Let me help you, Josie. We'll get everything sorted. Only sit down, please, before you fall down."

Josie took a seat at the kitchen table and Jennie put the kettle on. Then she got a bowl of hot water, some clean rags, and a bottle of rubbing alcohol and set about cleaning Josie's face. She tried not to let her emotions show on her own face—the shock she felt, the anger that a man could hurt a woman as badly as Billy Madden had hurt Josie. The kettle sang just as she was finishing up. She made the tea, then got two cups and saucers off a shelf and put them on the table. As she set a pitcher of milk and a sugar bowl down, she asked Josie what had happened.

"He put me up the spout, didn't he?" Josie said bitterly. "Man's bloody insatiable. Always got his cock out. Fucks me nine ways to Sunday—in bed, in the bath, up against the wall . . . Oh, sorry, luv! Forgot where I was. Well, anyway, he does me right and proper two, three, four times a day, and then he has the nerve to get angry at me—me!—when I tell him there's a little Billy Junior on the way." She reached into her dress pocket, pulled out a cigarette and a box of matches, and lit up. She took a drag, let out a long plume of smoke, then said, "Tells me I'm to get rid of it. Doesn't want his wife to find out, you see. He's scared to death of her. Doesn't want his three sons to know, either. Thinks the world of them three. I tell him I'm not getting rid of it. Been down that road a few times already. First time, I had no money, so the doctor who did it took his payment in kind, if you know what I mean. Last time, I had a woman. She was old. Her hands shook. She cut me up so, I almost bled to death. I'm finished with those butchers. I'm having this baby, Jennie. I swear to God I am. I'll give him up to a good home when he comes, but I'm damn well having him. I can't go through that again." She paused to take another drag, then continued. "So when I tell Billy all this, what does he do, the gobshite? He hits me. Hard. In the stomach. I bend over, like this," she curled up, arms crossed over her stomach, "so he can't get at my belly again, and I catch it in the face. He's yelling at me. Hitting me. Trying to kick me. Telling me he'll get rid of it himself. Well, I managed to get away from him. I had a few quid in my pocket and I ran out of the Bark, found a hackney, and paid the driver to bring me here. And here I am. I'm sorry to drag you into it. I didn't know where else to go. If I can just borrow a dress, any old thing, I'll be on me way."

Jennie, too upset to speak, said nothing. Instead she poured the tea. Josie picked up a spoon and tried to shovel some sugar into her cup, but her hands were still shaking so badly, she got more on the table than she did in her tea.

Jennie looked at those small hands, at the pretty rings on them, and the bitten nails, and her heart ached. Josie was only nineteen. She was bright. She was lively and funny and pretty. She could have done so many things with her life, but instead of studying to be a nurse, or taking a secretarial course, she'd taken to the stage and fallen in with a fast lot—chorus girls on the make, prostitutes, wide boys, married men, and finally, Billy Madden. Billy had set her up with her own flat and carriage, with diamonds and clothing, but as Josie soon learned, Madden did no favors. People paid for what they got from him. One way or the other.

"Where are you going to go?" Jennie finally asked her.

"Paris. To the Moulin Rouge. I'll get work there. I can sing and dance with the best of them."

"Now you can, but what about when you're seven months along?"

"Hadn't thought of that."

"And what about money?"

"I've got some squirreled away in a bank. My wages from the halls. Billy don't know about it."

"Is it enough to get you to Paris? To keep yourself until you find work?"

"I don't know," Josie said. "Probably not. I've got jewels. Plenty of them. But I can't get them. They're in my flat and Billy'll have his lads watching it. I don't know what I'm going to do, but I'll figure something."

"Stay here, Josie."

"It's good of you to offer, and I thank you for it," Josie said, "but I can't. I couldn't go outside, you see. Wouldn't dare risk being seen. So I'd have to stay inside. For months. I'd go mad."

Jennie went quiet again. She racked her brains trying to think up the best way to help Josie. She had to help her. She could not let the girl go out on her own. From her description of the beating Madden had given her, Jennie was quite sure he'd finish the job if he found her. She thought of friends she had in the south, near Bristol. And others in Leeds and Liverpool. They would help her if she asked them to, but what if she ended up endangering them, too? She needed a hotel, a house, a cottage . . . someplace private and quiet, but neither Josie nor she had the money required to rent a house or cottage. And then, suddenly, she had the answer. "Binsey!" she said, quite loudly.

"What's that?" Josie asked.

"You can go to Binsey."

"Where the flippin' hell is Binsey?"

"In Oxfordshire. Not too far, but far enough. I have a cottage there, Josie. It was my mother's. I barely ever go there anymore. You can stay there as long as you need to. It's not far from the village. You can buy everything you need. You can have the baby; then, when you're recovered and strong again, you can go to Paris. I could help you with the boat fare."

"Could you really? I'll pay you back. Every bleedin' penny. I swear I will."

"I know you will, Josie. I'm not worried about that. What I'm worried about is getting you there. Quickly. Let me think for a minute." She looked at the clock on the wall. "It's still early. Not even ten." She bit her lip. "We could do it, I think. In fact, I'm sure we could."

"Do what?"

"Make it to Binsey."

"Today?"

"Yes, today. We'd have to get you changed. And pack a few things for you. But if we could get to Paddington by eleven, and then get a train out by noon, we could be at the cottage by two at the latest. It's only a short walk from the station. I could settle you there, then come right back." She went quiet, then started thinking out loud again, almost unaware that she was talking. "My father will be home before I get home, and he'll wonder where I've gone. I'll have to leave a note. Say I went out to do some errands for the wedding. I'll pick up some cards on my way back. Nip into the florist's. So it's not entirely a lie."

"What wedding? Who's getting married?"

"Oh . . . um . . . I am," Jennie said.

"That's wonderful news! When is it?"

"This Sunday," Jennie said, hoping that the conversation would end. But it didn't.

"This Sunday," Josie echoed. Then she smiled cheekily. "That's awfully sudden, isn't it? I didn't even know you were engaged."

Jennie colored. "Yes, well, it is, but . . ." She stammered, at a loss for a convincing lie.

Josie gave her a close look, then said, "Oh, Jennie, you didn't! Not you!"

"Well . . . um . . . yes. I'm rather afraid I did," Jennie said.

Josie screeched laughter. "You little hussy," she said. "Sitting here like butter wouldn't melt in your mouth, and all the time you've a bun in the oven yourself. Same as me."

"Josie, we really have to get going if we're to make the train."

But Josie paid her no attention. "Is he nice?" she asked.

"Very nice."

"Handsome? Strong?"

"Yes, both of those."

"Is he a good kisser?"

"Josie Meadows," Jennie scolded. Then she laughed. "Yes. Yes, he is."

"Good," Josie said. "I'm glad he's nice. You deserve a nice one, miss. It's nice when they're nice, isn't it? In bed, I mean. When they've washed and shaved and they've brought you flowers and champagne. When they say sweet things and take their time. Cor, I do like the feel of a man in my bed. Makes me half-mad sometimes, the wanting of them." She dropped her voice to a whisper. "Does it make you feel that way, too?"

Jennie was about to tell her no, to tell her to hurry and change for they had a train to catch. But then she thought of that afternoon on the River Cam. And how it had felt to lie in Seamie's arms. She thought of how much she loved him, and how that love had made her do things she never thought she would, and hope for things she never should have.

And so she didn't tell Josie no. Instead she smiled and, with a rueful note in her voice, said, "Yes, Josie. It does."

CHAPTER TWENTY-TWO

"THERE'S NOT ENOUGH champagne. We'll run out. I just know it. I should've ordered more," Fiona whispered tersely.

"Are you mad, lass?" Joe whispered back. "There's enough champagne in the house to drown all of London."

"And the ice creams, Joe. I should've ordered four flavors. Not three. Four. How could I have been so daft?"

Joe took her hand in his. "Stop now. There's more than enough of everything. The luncheon will be beautiful. The house is beautiful. The day is beautiful." He smiled and kissed her cheek. "Most of all, you're beautiful."

Fiona smiled and kissed him back. Then she frowned again. "You do think he'll show up?" she said. "He won't do a runner or some such thing?"

Joe laughed. "I've just seen him. He's right inside the conservatory looking as happy as a sand boy."

Fiona sighed with relief. "Good. Maybe this will all go off without a hitch after all."

"Of course it will," Joe said. "Stop worrying and enjoy the day."

Fiona nodded. She turned her head and, smiling at this one and waving at that one, she looked at the people seated behind her in neat rows of white rattan chairs. The chairs had been divided into two groups and arranged with a little aisle between them. In ten minutes or so, at precisely one o'clock, her brother Seamus would walk down that aisle, to the bower the florists had made, turn around, and wait for his bride. It almost felt unreal to her. She couldn't quite believe that this day had come, that wild and reckless Seamie had given up roaming, found himself a job in London and a wife, and was ready to settle down. For so long he had mourned the loss of Willa Alden. No woman had ever been able to replace her.

And then he'd met Jennie Wilcott, who was as different from Willa as chalk was from cheese. Perhaps that was what had been needed all along to break Willa's spell. Jennie was blond and pink-cheeked, soft and feminine. She had a marvelous womanly figure and a quiet but determined way about her. Yet for all her sweetness and light, Jennie had tamed Seamie somehow. God knew how. Well, actually, they all did, Fiona thought, smiling—and the evidence would arrive in about eight months' time. She didn't think that Seamie was marrying Jennie because he had to, though. He wanted to marry her. So much. He'd told her so. Over and over again.

So many times that it unsettled her, if the truth were known. It made her uneasy, this sudden change on Seamie's part. Had Seamie really changed? Was he really over Willa?

Fiona had confided her doubts to Joe just a few days ago. He'd thrown up his hands in frustration and said, "For years, all I've heard from you is how much you want Seamie to meet a good woman and settle down. Now he has. He's met a very good woman. And you're still worrying. There's no pleasing you, Fiona!"

Maybe Joe was right. Maybe there was no pleasing her. And yet she could not quell the niggling little voice, deep down inside, the one that was always right, the one that was saying now that it had all happened so fast.

She looked at her watch—only ten more minutes to go—then felt an arm twine around her shoulders and lips upon her cheek. She looked up. It was Maud. Max von Brandt, tall, charming, and stylishly dressed, was with her. Fiona kissed Maud back, greeted Max, and then Maud and Max went to find chairs.

Fiona noticed that a few more late arrivals had seated themselves—the Shackletons, George Mallory and his fiancée, Ruth Turner, Mrs. Alden. She looked again at all the faces of her family and friends—Joe's parents, Peter and Rose; his brothers and sisters; all their children. Her own beautiful children. The Rosens, the Moskowitzes, Harriet Hatcher and her parents, Mr. Foster, friends of Seamie's—men whom he'd sailed with—and friends of Jennie's, so fetching in their spring dresses and hats.

A soft breeze caressed Fiona's cheek. She looked up, hoping it was not a harbinger of rain—it was May, but still early in the month, and the English weather could be so changeable—but no, the sun was still shining. The sky was blue. And all around them, buds were bursting into life. She was suddenly overcome by the beauty of it all and found herself wishing that she could stop time, that she could keep this perfect spring day forever. She saw suddenly, with a piercing clarity, that instead of worrying so much, instead of always looking for problems, she should feel deeply blessed, and deeply grateful, to be surrounded by so many dear people on such a joyous day. For joyous days were not always so plentiful.

She had lost loved ones years ago. Once, she had nearly lost Joe. Those losses, the terrible grief they had caused her, had made her ever fearful of losing another person she loved. It made her think dark thoughts too often, made her dwell on the bad—real and imagined—and blinded her to the good.

And today was good. Seamie had found someone wonderful. And if he was a little overexcited about marrying her, well, he had every right to be. She was the sort of woman any man would be excited to marry. Fiona told herself that she was being silly for worrying, and she resolved, once and for all, to stop it.

A few minutes later, the string quartet that she'd hired began to play the wedding processional. Everyone stood. Albie Alden, Seamie's best man, came striding down the aisle, smiling. He was followed by Seamie, looking so handsome in a gray morning suit. Next came the ring bearer and the flower girl—Joe's sister Ellen's two youngest—a maid of honor, and then the bride herself, lovely and radiant on her father's arm.

A moment in time, Fiona thought again, as she watched the Reverend Wilcott kiss his daughter and place her hand in Seamie's.

"Let it last forever," she murmured. "Please let it last."

CHAPTER TWENTY-THREE

"I ALWAYS WONDER how the sun can shine on days like today," Seamie said sadly.

"I wondered the same thing the day my mother died," Jennie said, slipping her hand into his. "My father says it's to remind us that brightness follows darkness, and that happiness will one day follow our grief."

They were in the Aldens' parlor, standing by a coffin. Admiral Alden had lost his battle with cancer two days ago, and Seamie was paying his last respects before the admiral's body was taken to Westminster Abbey for a funeral service, and then to the cemetery for a small, private burial.

"He was one of the old breed," Seamie said. "Duty and service above all. He was one of the finest men I have ever known." He paused to master his emotion, then said, "I used to sail with him and his family. As a lad. He gave me my first lessons in navigation. He saw how much I loved the sea and loved to explore, and he encouraged that. He was like a father to me."

Jennie leaned her head against his arm. "Would you like a few minutes alone with him?" she asked.

Seamie nodded, unable to speak.

"Take all the time you need," she said, kissing his cheek. "I'll be with Fiona and Joe."

Seamie took a handkerchief from his pocket. He wiped his eyes with it and blew his nose. He knew he should join the others, but he couldn't. Not yet. His feelings were still too close to the surface. So he walked around the parlor instead, looking at the books on the shelves, at paintings and family mementoes.

Seamie remembered this house so well. He remembered sliding down its banister, chasing Albie through its halls, drinking hot chocolate and eating biscuits in its warm and cozy kitchen. But he remembered this parlor best of all. He and Albie had built teepees here out of Mrs. Alden's sheets and blankets too many times to count. They'd sat by the fire at night as the admiral told them of his adventures on the high seas. Played draughts on the rug. Sung along to songs Mrs. Alden played on the piano.

He touched an ivory key now, listening as the sound it made faded. He looked at the photographs standing on top of the piano. Photos of ships the admiral had commanded, of boats he'd sailed and raced. There were family pictures, many taken on the water. Pictures of the Aldens, and Seamie with them, on the admiral's yacht *Tradewind*. One from July of '91, another from August of '92, a third from June of '93—all the endless summers of his youth.

There were pictures of Albie as a boy and as a young man. There was one of him receiving his doctoral degree at Cambridge. And there were pictures of Willa. As a toddler in braids and a pinafore. As a girl in trousers, standing on top of a boulder, or at *Tradewind*'s wheel. As a fetching young woman in an ivory dress and stockings.

Seamie picked that photo up and gazed at it. He remembered that dress, remembered that night. They'd been teenagers then. He'd been seventeen years old. The Aldens had had a party, that was why Willa was dressed up. They were in the backyard, the three of them, lying on a blanket and gazing up at the sky. He'd been about to leave, in just a few days, on his first expedition. It would be years before he saw his two friends again. Albie had gone inside to get them something to eat, and then Willa had kissed him, and told him to meet her one day again, under Orion.

He remembered how they'd met again. Years later in the Pickerel, a Cambridge pub. She'd challenged him to a climb—up the side of St. Botolph's Church—and bet him he couldn't beat her. If he won, she was to buy him a new pair of hiking boots. If she won, he was to accompany her to Africa, to Kilimanjaro. She'd won. She'd won the bet, the wager, the summit, and his heart.

And then he remembered coming home from Africa without her. He remembered standing here, in this very room, and telling her parents what had happened. He thought they would blame him for it—he blamed himself—but they didn't. Instead, they'd guessed his feelings for their daughter and said they were sorry that things had ended up as they had. Both the admiral and Mrs. Alden had taken Willa's decision to travel east instead of coming home very hard.

"How could you do it?" he asked the girl in the photograph now. "How could you not come home? Not once in all this time?"

The admiral had loved his daughter and she had loved him. She'd looked up to him and sought his respect and admiration in everything she did. How on earth could she have ignored her mother's and brother's many letters of the past few weeks begging her to return to London and see her father before it was too late? How could she be so cruel? She had certainly been cruel to him, true—but he was only her brokenhearted lover; Admiral Alden was her father.

Seamie put the photograph back, knowing he would never have an answer to that question. Willa should've come. She should've said good-bye to her father. She should've been here to help her mother mourn the loss of the man she'd been married to for more than forty years. She should've been here for Albie, her brother, who had struggled manfully to comfort his devastated mother, organize the wake and funeral service, the burial and the mourners' luncheon, all while trying to cope with his own grief. Willa should've been here, but she was not.

Seamie walked back to the coffin. He reached into his pocket, pulled out a pebble, and placed it under the admiral's folded hands. It was one of a handful he'd brought back from the icy shores of the Weddell Sea—a place he would never have got to if it hadn't been for this man. He swallowed hard, snapped the admiral a smart salute, then left the parlor for the drawing room.

There, he found Jennie again, sitting on a settee. She was talking with Mrs. Alden, who was seated in the chair across from her. Seamie took the empty spot next to her on the settee. As he sat down, Jennie wordlessly reached for his hand, and her gentle touch made his grief a bit easier to bear. He thought, as he had so many times over the last few weeks, how very good to him she was and how glad he was that he had married her.

He smiled to himself now, though, as he recalled that he'd been something other than glad when she'd told him she was pregnant. He'd been shocked, actually. In fact, he'd seen his life flash before his eyes, as men sometimes said they did when they thought they were going to die. But he'd also immediately seen what he must do. Jennie was pregnant and he had made her so; he could not possibly take off to the Antarctic and leave her in London, alone and unmarried, to bear their child. Only an utter blackguard could have done that. And so he had done the right thing, the honorable thing, the only thing—he had proposed to her.

He'd felt afraid as he spoke the words to her, and painfully torn. By asking her to marry him, he knew he was finally saying goodbye to Willa, once and for all. But to his great surprise, Jennie's acceptance had made him happy. The fear had left him as soon as she said yes, and in the days that followed, he'd felt only contentment and relief.

The thing was done, his decision made. In fact, all his decisions were made. He would stay in London. He would take the RGS job and leave exploring to other men—men who were younger, or crazier. Men who had nothing but themselves to lose. He'd been mistaken, he told himself, in his belief that Willa Alden was the only woman he could ever love, and he resolved to let go of the sad, destructive love he felt for her and to embrace the love Jennie offered. He took his memories of Willa—the sound of her laughter, the way she looked when she climbed, the taste of her lips—and locked them in a strongbox in the deepest recesses of his memory—a box that was never to be opened again.

For the first time in many years, he felt at peace with himself—calm, contented, light and easy. Not restless, not churned up. Not feeling as if he was always bleeding inside from a wound that never healed.

Yes, he told himself now, as he squeezed Jennie's hand, I was mistaken all those years ago. He'd found love, at last, he knew he had. And happiness, too. With the woman sitting next to him. Willa Alden belonged to the past. And the past was where she would stay. His future was with Jennie Wilcott.

Mrs. Alden excused herself and rose to greet some distant cousins who'd just arrived, and Jennie asked Seamie if he'd like another cup of tea.

"No, thank you, my darling," he said. "I've had three already and I'm bursting. I'm going to head to the loo. I'll be right back."

On his way there, he passed the parlor, where Admiral Alden lay, and as he did, he heard voices coming from it—a man's and a woman's. They sounded strained. They rose, then quickly fell again. He hurried past, thinking that whatever was being discussed, it was none of his business, and that whoever was doing the discussing would soon finish and leave.

But he was wrong. As he passed the parlor again on his way back from the loo, he discovered that the voices had only grown louder. Well, one of them had—the man's. To his surprise, he realized he knew that voice—it belonged to Albie.

Worried for his friend, Seamie stuck his head in the doorway. He saw Albie pacing back and forth. There was another man with him—an odd-looking chap who was tall and thin and dressed in loose trousers and a red cotton jacket and had a scarf wound round his head. Seamie could only see the man's back, but he looked dusty and rumpled, as if he'd traveled a long way. Seamie wondered where the woman was. He could've sworn that he'd heard a woman's voice, too.

The discussion continued, only it sounded more like an argument now, and Albie was doing all the talking. Seamie could see that he was angry but trying to contain himself.

Why was this person bothering him? Now? In a time of such distress? Seamie stepped inside the room, very concerned now. As he did, the strange man took a few faltering steps toward the coffin and Seamie saw that he walked with a slight limp.

With a sharp, gut-wrenching suddenness, Seamie realized who the man was. He tried to back up quickly, to get out of the room before he was seen, but in his haste he backed into a pedestal with a heavy Chinese vase on it. The vase teetered and, before he could catch it, fell. It hit the floor and shattered. The man turned around. Her huge green eyes, swollen with tears, widened in recognition, and pain.

"Hello, Seamie," Willa Alden said.

CHAPTER TWENTY-FOUR

SEAMIE STOOD STOCK still, emotions ripping through him like a howling arctic wind. He felt sorrow and anger for what she'd done to him, to them. Pity and guilt for what had happened to her. And love. Most of all, he felt love.

He loved her. Still. As much as he did when he'd first told her so, on top of Kilimanjaro. As much as he did when she'd told him goodbye.

"Hello, Willa," he said quietly, unable to take his eyes off her.

Willa's face worked as she looked at him; tears slipped down her cheeks. She took a few hesitant steps toward him, then stopped.

"The prodigal has returned," Albie said acidly, breaking the silence.

Willa winced at that, stung. Albie looked like he didn't care that he'd hurt her. Instead of embracing the sister he hadn't seen for years, he stood apart from her.

Seamie remembered that last time they were all together, in the Pick. It felt like a lifetime ago. Seamie and Albie had been drinking there. Willa and George had come in unexpectedly. She'd been dressed in men's clothes—tweed trousers and a bulky sweater. Her wavy brown hair had been cut short, setting off her long fawn's neck and high cheekbones. Her eyes had been merry and challenging and full of life.

The Willa standing before him now looked very different from the girl in his memory. This Willa looked gaunt. Haunted. Her face was tanned and weathered. Her hair, under her cap, was no longer short but gathered into a long, thick braid. She was still beautiful, though. Her eyes had lost none of their challenging intensity. Looking into them now, Seamie saw what he had always seen inside them—the same restless, questing soul that lived inside him.

He opened his mouth, wanting to tell her what he was feeling, wanting to say something that would make things right, that would bridge the gulf between them, all three of them, but all that would come out was "Well, then. Shall we have a cup of tea?"

"No, we shall not," Albie said, giving him a filthy look. "This isn't bloody Epsom and I don't want a bloody cup of tea on the bloody lawn!" And then he stormed out, slamming the door behind him, leaving Seamie and Willa alone.

Willa wiped the tears from her cheeks with her sleeve. "He's so angry with me. He called me cruel," she said in a choked voice. "I never meant to come so late. I didn't even know my father was ill. The letters were delayed—the ones from Albie and my mother. I set out the day they arrived—six weeks ago—and got here as quickly as I could." She shook her head. "It doesn't matter to Albie, though. My mother's already forgiven me, but he won't." She smiled sadly. "Well, at least I made the funeral," she added. "It's still a good-bye of sorts, isn't it? Not the one I'd have wanted, but the one I've got, it seems." She went silent for a long moment, gazing at the coffin, then said, "I never thought he'd die. Not him. He was so strong. So full of life." And then she broke down, covering her face with her hands.

Seamie went to her, wanting to comfort her. The man in the coffin was her beloved father, this house was her home. And yet she seemed so utterly out of place here, so totally alone. He put a tentative hand on her back. "I'm sorry, Willa," he said. "I'm so sorry."

She turned to him, helpless and heartbroken. "Oh, Seamie, I wish I could have said a real good-bye," she said, sobbing piteously.

"I wish I could have told him what he meant to me and how much I loved him. If only I'd got here sooner!"

Her grief was so deep, so harrowing, that tears came to Seamie's eyes for her. He forgot himself entirely, folded her into his arms, and held her close. Her sorrow came out of her in great, wrenching torrents. He could feel her chest heaving, her hands clutching bunches of his shirt. He held her as she wept agonizing tears, until she was spent and limp in his arms. And then he kept holding her, overwhelmed by their shared grief, overwhelmed by her nearness. Willa—whom he thought he'd never see again, whom he'd loved and sometimes hated.

"I miss him, Seamie. I miss him so much," she whispered, when she could speak again.

"I know. I miss him, too."

They both heard the door open at the same time, heard the voice, a woman's, say "Seamie? Are you in here . . . Oh! Pardon me, I . . . Seamie?"

It was Jennie.

Bloody hell, Seamie thought. He released Willa immediately.

"Miss Alden?" Jennie said, uncertainly, looking first at him, then at Willa.

Seamie was mortified. He felt terrible. Jennie would be hurt when she found out that the woman he'd been holding was indeed Willa Alden. She'd be furious. He only hoped that she would not make a scene. Not here. He hoped that whatever she had to say to him could wait until they were in their carriage.

He cleared his throat, expecting the worst. "Jennie, this is Albie's sister and my old friend, Willa Alden," he said. "Willa, may I introduce Jennie Finnegan, my wife."

He waited then, watching Jennie's face, expecting fireworks and tears. But Jennie indulged in neither. Instead, she walked up to Willa, took her hand, and said, "My condolences, Miss Alden. My husband has told me something of the admiral, enough for me to know that he was a wonderful man. I cannot imagine your pain and am so very sorry for your loss."

Willa nodded, unable to speak, and wiped her face on her sleeve again. Jennie opened her purse, took out a lace-edged handkerchief, and handed it to her.

"Thank you, Mrs. Finnegan," Willa said. "Forgive me, please. I wish we were meeting under better circumstances."

"I wish it, too," Jennie said, "and there is nothing to forgive." She looked at Seamie. "The hearse has arrived. We are expected to leave for the abbey in ten minutes' time."

"I'll get our coats," Seamie said.

Jennie shook her head. "Perhaps you should stay with Miss Alden for a few more minutes." She turned to Willa. "Pardon me, Miss Alden, but you do not look to be in a fit state to travel. May I bring you a cup of tea? And perhaps a damp facecloth?"

Willa nodded gratefully. Jennie bustled out of the room, and Seamie watched her go, marveling at her goodness and compassion. Another woman might've shouted and carried on. Not Jennie. She saw the best in people always. The most noble explanation for what she'd just seen was that her husband was simply comforting a grieving friend, and that was the only explanation she could accept. Seamie was touched, and not for the first time, at her faith in him, and in most everyone else. And he resolved, then and there, to always be deserving of that faith. To never hurt the good woman he had married. Whatever he had felt moments ago belonged to the past, and that was where it would stay.

"She is very kind and very beautiful. You are lucky," Willa said, sitting down tiredly on an overstuffed chair.

"Yes, I am," Seamie replied.

Willa looked at her hands. "I'm happy for you. Happy you found such a wonderful person," she said quietly.

"Are you?" he said. The words came out bitingly harsh. He hadn't meant them to.

Willa looked up at him, a stricken expression on her face, and the promise Seamie had made to himself, only seconds ago, was lost in a rush of emotion. "Why?" he said. "Why did you—"

But then the undertaker's men were suddenly in the parlor,

excusing themselves and closing the coffin, and Jennie was right behind them.

"Here you are, Miss Alden," she said, handing Willa a facecloth and putting a cup of tea down on the table beside her.

Seamie turned away from Willa and Jennie and feigned interest in an old sailing trophy. What am I doing? he wondered. I'm letting my feelings get the better of me. Stop it, he told himself. Now. It's utter madness.

"Thank you," he heard Willa say to Jennie. "I probably need more than a cat lick with a facecloth, though. I should change my clothes before we leave for the abbey. I've been in them for weeks."

"Was the journey very arduous?" Jennie asked.

"Yes, and very long," Willa said.

"Will you be going right back or staying in London for a while?" Jennie asked lightly.

Seamie closed his eyes, willing her to say she was going back east tomorrow. For his sake. For all of their sakes.

"I don't know. I actually hadn't thought about it," Willa said, and Seamie could hear the weariness in her voice. "I left in such a hurry, you see. I'll be here for a few weeks I should think. Perhaps a month or two. I shall have to do something to earn my fare back. I spent almost all I have getting here."

"Perhaps we can help you," Jennie said. "With the fare, I mean. Seamie, darling, could we?"

The realization of exactly what was occurring here hit him like a bolt of lightning. Oh, Jennie, he thought, you might be kind and good, but you're no fool, are you? He'd thought that she saw only the best in everyone, and that's why she behaved so generously to a rival. Well, he was wrong. She'd seen exactly what was going on between him and Willa, but had behaved generously anyway. He thought then that she was the most admirable human being he'd ever met, and told himself once more that he must never do anything that would hurt her.

"Of course, Jennie," he said. He'd gladly pay Willa's entire fare back. First class all the way if she liked. Anything. As long as she would go and leave him in peace and let him forget the feeling of her in his arms, the smell of her, the sound of her voice. As long as she'd leave him to the life he now had—a life with Jennie and their child.

"Thank you—you are both very kind—but that won't be necessary," Willa said. "I'm due to publish a book of photographs with the RGS. On Everest. I brought all the photos with me. I'm handing the materials all in a bit sooner than expected, and I'm hoping Sir Clements will pay up a bit earlier. I shall also speak at the RGS about Everest." She smiled tiredly, then added, "For a fee, of course. I brought my maps with me. Couldn't risk leaving them in Rongbuk. They might not be there when I returned."

Albie stuck his head in the door. "The hearse is leaving," he said. "Mother wants you to ride with us, Willa." And then he was gone again.

"So much for changing my clothes," Willa sighed. She stood up and looked from Seamie to Jennie. An uncomfortable silence descended, and Seamie found himself wishing to be at the abbey, where they would not have to talk. Where Willa would sit with her mother and brother, and he would sit with Jennie, far away from her.

"Well, thank you again, both of you, for your kindnesses to me," Willa said awkwardly. "And you'll come, won't you? If I speak at the RGS? Please say you will."

Jennie, smiling brightly, said they would make every effort to be there. Then she excused herself to fetch their things.

Willa started walking toward the door, and Seamie followed her. Before she reached it, she stopped, turned, and put a hand on his arm. "Seamie, wait. About before . . . I . . . I'm sorry. I never meant—" she began to say.

He smiled politely, the master of his emotions again. "Don't, Willa. There's no need to speak of it. Once again, my condolences. I'm so sorry for your loss."

He paused slightly, then ruefully added, "And for mine."

CHAPTER TWENTY-FIVE

IT WAS CLOSE to midnight. Joe Bristow had been working at his office in the House of Commons since three o'clock that afternoon. He was tired and wanted to go home, to his wife, to his bed. But he could not. Because George Burgess was sitting across from him, drinking his whiskey and talking about airplanes.

Most of London was asleep, but not Sir George. He'd been working late, too, going over facts and figures for a speech he was to deliver at the Commons tomorrow, on the need for the Royal Naval Air Service to be brought under the wing of the Admiralty as part of the Royal Navy's military branch.

First Churchill and his boats, Joe thought. Now Sir George and his planes. Every day there was some new call for increased military spending, usually fueled by the latest petulant remark, naval acquisition, or military parade put on by the kaiser.

"You simply cannot imagine it, old man," Burgess said. "The speed and maneuverability are unparalleled. And to be up in the clouds, safely able to see the exact position of an enemy encampment, the number of troops and cannon, well, the implications for reconnaissance are nothing less than staggering, to say nothing of the potential for the deployment of aerial munitions. I'll take you up myself, Joe. I can witter on about it all day, but you must see a war plane's capabilities for yourself."

"I'm going to hold you to it, George," Joe said. "We can fly right over Hackney. I'll show you where I plan to build a new school."

"I shall put it in my calendar," Burgess said, ignoring the arch note in Joe's tone. "We'll go to Eastchurch during the August recess, to the navy's flying school there. I'll take you up in a Sopwith and you'll be convinced. The Service is only in its infancy now," he added, "and it must grow up quickly. It has only forty airplanes, fifty seaplanes, and a hundred or so pilots, and it must be enlarged. We're being left behind. The Italians, the Greeks and Bulgarians, even the Americans are miles ahead of us with the development of combat planes, and—"

Burgess's words were interrupted by a battering on Joe's door.

"Does no one in this city sleep anymore?" Joe said. "Come in!" he bellowed.

"Sir George? Thank goodness I've found you. Hello, Mr. Bristow." It was Albie Alden, breathless and disheveled. He'd clearly been running.

"What is it, man?" Burgess asked.

Albie struggled to catch his breath. "We've had a bit of bother at the SSB," he said, glancing at Joe uncertainly.

"Speak plainly," Burgess said impatiently. "This man's as loyal to his country as the king."

"Two German spies were nearly apprehended tonight."

"Nearly? What do you mean by nearly?"

"Sit down, Albie," Joe said, pouring another glass of whiskey and pushing it across his desk.

Albie took the empty chair next to Burgess. He knocked the drink back in one gulp, wiped his mouth with the back of his hand, then continued speaking.

"Four days ago, our code work, plus intelligence from a paid informant, revealed that a man named Bauer—Johann Bauer—has been working at Fairfields."

Burgess, who'd been shaking his head as Albie spoke, suddenly swore. Joe knew why. Fairfields was a shipyard in Scotland. On the River Clyde. They built ships for the Royal Navy.

"Johann Bauer?" Burgess thundered. "That name's as German as sauerkraut! How the hell did a man with a name like Johann Bauer get work on the Clyde?"

"By changing it to John Bowman," Albie said. "He had all the documents. A forged birth certificate from an Edinburgh hospital. School leaving papers. A reference from an iron monger's. Nobody suspected a thing."

"But his voice," Burgess said. "His voice would have given him away."

Albie shook his head. "His accent's impeccable. *Was* impeccable."

"What happened?" Joe asked, pouring Albie another drink.

"As I said, we were on to Bauer, but we didn't move right away. We wanted to watch him for a few days first, to see if he might lead us to anyone else. I think he figured out we were on to him, though, because he suddenly left Govan last night and took a train to London. He was followed, of course. By one of our men from the SSB. When he got off the train, he traveled to East London, to a pub called the Blind Beggar."

"I know that pub. It's in Whitechapel," Joe said.

Albie nodded. "Bauer met another man there, Ernst Hoffman—he goes by the name of Sam Hutchins. They ate supper together, then left the pub and walked to Duffin's, a boardinghouse. Our man slipped in after them and watched them go upstairs to one of the rooms—a room we later found out had been let to a man called Peter Stiles. That's when our man—Hammond's his name—decided he had to act. He went to the police to get help, then he and five constables moved in. Hammond banged on the door to the room where Bauer and Hoffman were. A man answered. He yelled 'Who's there?' and when Hammond said it was the police, he said he'd be right there, he just had to put his trousers on."

Albie took a swallow of his drink, then continued. "Immediately after that, two gunshots were heard. The constables broke the door down, but it was too late. When they got inside the room, they found Bauer and Hoffman dead on the floor and the dormer window wide open. The third man—Stiles—apparently shot both of them in the head, then climbed out of the window to the roof and escaped. Hammond immediately went to the fireplace. Papers were burning in it. Stiles must've been worried that he might be caught and didn't want to be caught with the papers on him. Hammond managed to pull a few of them out before they were completely burned."

"What were they?" Burgess asked, his voice somber.

"Blueprints."

"Not the *Valiant*," Burgess said.

"I'm afraid so," Albie said.

Burgess picked up his own whiskey glass. For a few seconds, Joe thought he would fling it across the room, but he restrained himself.

"What's the *Valiant*?" Joe asked.

"Our best hope," Burgess replied. "A new and very advanced class of warship."

"One of the dreadnoughts?" Joe asked.

"A super-dreadnought. Only four are being made, and they're supposed to outdo anything the Germans have come up with."

"We must look on the positive side," Albie said.

"I didn't realize there was one," Burgess shot back.

"Two enemy spies are dead. Their plans to pass the blueprints to Berlin have failed."

"We were lucky this time, damned lucky," Burgess said. "The next time we might not be." He stood up and started pacing the room. "We have to find the other man—Stiles. He's the spymaster. I know it. I feel it in my bones."

"We are working on it, sir. We've gone through the contents of the room, and we're questioning the Duffin's landlady, and each one of her tenants, trying to get descriptions of Stiles—his habits, his movements, everything we possibly can."

"Good man," Burgess said.

"Can you get him?" Joe asked, alarmed at the thought of this vicious man at large in East London.

Burgess didn't reply at first. Big Ben's chimes, loud and somber, were sounding the hour—midnight.

When the last echoing tone finally faded away, he spoke. "Oh, we'll get him, the wily bird," he said, his voice hard. "We shall stalk him, carefully and patiently. We shall flush him out, and when he tries to fly back to Berlin . . . *bang!* We shall send a bullet straight through his black and treacherous heart."

CHAPTER TWENTY-SIX

SEAMIE FINNEGAN, STANDING wide-eyed in the foyer of 18 Bedford Square, a tall Georgian town house, turned to his friend, Albie.

"Does one *have* to be exotic and stylish to be here?" he asked him, watching a young man with kohl-rimmed eyes swan by, all perfume and silk scarves.

"No, or we wouldn't be here," Albie said. "You just have to know the hostess, Lady Lucinda Allington."

"And how, exactly, does a nearsighted swot like yourself know such people?" Seamie asked, smiling awkwardly as a girl with short hair, rouged lips, and a cigarette in a holder blew smoke rings at him and giggled.

"I was at Cambridge with Lulu's brother Charles. He died some years ago now, poor bastard. Typhoid. It was a terrible blow to the family. I've remained friends with his sister. Come on, let's see if we can find her."

Seamie and Albie hung their coats and set off in search of their hostess. They wound their way through the high-ceilinged rooms of the house, each painted a shockingly bold hue—peacock blue, crimson, chartreuse—past all sorts of equally colorful people talking, drinking, or dancing to the songs played on a gramophone. Albie pointed out various painters, musicians, and actors, telling Seamie that if he didn't know who they were, he should. They found their hostess—Lulu—in the dining room, having her palm read by a stunning Russian ballet dancer named Nijinksy. He was wearing a silk turban, a fur-trimmed jacket, and red silk trousers tucked inside brown suede boots.

Lulu was slender, with a swan's neck, red hair, and hazel eyes. Her voice was deep and dramatic, her face intelligent and lively.

"Albie Alden," she said, taking Albie's hand with her free one. "Why on earth are you here?"

"Lovely to see you, too, Lu," Albie said, bending to kiss her cheek.

"Why aren't you at your sister's lecture?" she asked. "Everyone I know is there. Virginia and Leonard, Lytton, Carrington . . ."

"Everyone?" Albie asked. "What are all of these people doing here, then?"

Lulu looked around the room. "Oh, these," she said. "They're not people. They're actors, most of them. Or dancers. They've all just come off one stage or another and are looking to cadge as much free champagne as they possibly can. But you . . . why aren't you at the RGS?"

"Have I introduced my friend, Seamus Finnegan?" Albie said.

"Finnegan? The explorer? I'm quite honored to meet you," Lulu said to Seamie. "Though I would have thought that you would be at the RGS, too. Aren't you interested in Everest? Having been to the South Pole, I should think that—"

Albie took Lulu's hand from the palm-reading dancer. "I say, old boy, what have you got there? Ah! Her tact line. Damned short, isn't it?"

Lulu looked from Albie to Seamie. "Oh, dear. Am I being tedious? Is Willa not a good topic?"

Albie smiled ruefully. "Most people would have figured out by my reticence on the subject and by my Herculean efforts to change it that no, she is not."

"I'm sorry. I had no idea. I'll make it up to you by telling you where I've stashed the champagne." She lowered her voice. "It's in the oven."

Albie thanked her and started to move off. "I'll want to know why!" she called after them. "You'll have to tell me everything." Then she turned back to the handsome dancer. "Now, Vaslav," she said. "Tell me if I've got a chance with that delicious Tom Lawrence."

Seamie followed Albie into the kitchen. A beautiful and bored woman was sitting on the kitchen table, smoking, as a man spouted poetry to her. Across the room, a wiry young man was balancing a plate on top of a wooden spoon, the end of which was positioned on his chin, while he stood on one leg. A group was egging him on in Russian.

Seamie was glad they'd got away from Lulu and her talk of Willa. He had resolved to put Willa out of his mind the day of her father's funeral, and he was doing his best to stick to that resolution. He thought now, as Albie opened the oven door, took out a bottle of Bolly, and poured two glasses, that maybe he shouldn't have come to this party at all. Maybe he should have just stayed home. It had been a last-minute decision. Albie had dropped by to visit with the Finnegans at their new flat. He said he'd been going mad cooped up at his mother's house.

"Where's Jennie?" he'd asked, after Seamie ushered him into the living room and started to open a bottle of wine.

"She's gone to the country. To her cottage in the Cotswolds," Seamie said. "Felt in need of a bit of quiet."

"The baby tiring her?" Albie asked.

"Yes," Seamie said.

"Why didn't you go with her?"

"She wanted to go for the week."

"So?"

"So I've work. At the RGS."

"Oh, yes. Forgot about that. You've become an upstanding and respectable member of society, haven't you?"

Snorting, Seamie chucked the wine cork at him. Work *had* kept him from going to Binsey, but the truth was, there was another reason he hadn't gone, one that he did not share with Albie: He'd sensed that Jennie had not wanted him to.

"Seamie, darling," she'd said to him two days ago, "I hope you don't mind, but I won't be able to attend Miss Alden's presentation at the RGS with you. I'm feeling a bit weary, and I thought I might go to Binsey for a few days. To my mother's cottage. For a bit of a rest."

"Are you not well?" Seamie had asked her, immediately worried.

"I'm fine. Just tired. It's completely normal. Harriet says so."

"I'll come with you," he said. "We'll go at the weekend. I've never seen the cottage and I'd like to. Besides, you shouldn't make the trip alone."

"You are so sweet to me," she said, smiling, but her voice had a slight edge of something in it—anxiousness? nervousness? He wasn't quite sure. "I think that's a lovely idea, of course I do, but I don't want to drag you all the way there just so you can watch me nap. It's a beautiful place, but it is rather dull. I don't plan on doing much while I'm there. Just a bit of reading, I should think. I'll also catch up on some correspondence, and perhaps I'll arrange for a man to come and look at the roof. The last time I went, I noticed some shingles were missing."

Seamie didn't know much about pregnant women, but he knew they could be moody and odd, prone to frets and tears. Maybe Jennie needed a break from noisy London, he thought, from all the demands of her life: checking in on her father, supervising the new teacher she'd hired to take over her duties at the school, attending suffrage meetings. Maybe she needed a break from him but did not know how to tell him—a break from running their home and cooking his meals and attending an endless number of RGS dinners.

"Of course," he'd said, not wanting to press her any further. "You must do what you think best, but you must write to me. Every day. So that I know you're safe and well."

She kissed him and said of course she'd write and that she would miss him terribly. He'd put her on the train just this morning at Paddington Station and promised to pick her up again next Saturday evening.

"Well, since you're a bachelor again, let's go live it up," Albie had said later. "We can head to a pub—there must be something decent around here—and then a party. Some friends of mine who live on Bedford Square are having a do."

"Live it up, Alb? Since when do *you* live it up?" Seamie asked him.

"Every single day of my life," Albie said, looking at him over the top of his glasses.

Seamie laughed. "Really? And since when do you like parties?"

"I love parties. Quantum physics is one big endless party," Albie said.

They'd finished their drinks, gone to a pub for a few more, then made their way to Bedford Square. Seamie noticed that no matter how much he might be joking, or talking about parties, Albie looked weary, yet again. Seamie had told him so and asked him if there was anything wrong.

"The funeral . . . work . . . it's all got to me," Albie replied. "I shall take a holiday at Easter. Go to Bath or some such place and restore myself, but for now, I must rely on Theakston's Bitter, and old friends, to do the job."

Seamie had nodded, but had been unconvinced. He knew that the death of a parent, combined with a heavy workload, would be enough to exhaust anyone, but deep down, he still felt there was more to Albie's ever-present air of nervous strain than his old friend was letting on. Perhaps it's Willa, he thought, and Albie—considerate fellow that he is—isn't mentioning her out of tact. He knew that Willa and Albie were both staying at their mother's house. Perhaps they still weren't getting on. Seamie thought about pressing Albie on it, but he didn't wish to speak of Willa either, so he decided against it.

"Shall we mingle?" Albie asked him now, glancing about the room.

"After you," Seamie said, sweeping his hand before him, still wondering at his friend's newfound sociability.

As they moved through the various rooms of the house, Seamie met a writer named Virginia Stephen, her sister Vanessa Bell, who was a painter, and Vanessa's husband Clive, a critic. He met the poet Rupert Brooke, bumped into Tom Lawrence, who'd come from the

RGS, and whom he was glad to see again, then chatted with an economist named John Maynard Keynes.

Albie had explained to him, on the way over, that Lulu was at the center of a colorful coterie of artists and intellectuals called the Bloomsbury Group. "It's a very forward-thinking bunch," Albie had said. "Not terribly mindful of proprieties, morals, or much of anything else, as far as I can see."

Seamie enjoyed meeting these people, enjoyed their dramatic clothes and gestures, but for some reason, when they found out who he was and what he'd done, the talk always turned to Willa and the RGS lecture. Time and time again, he'd found himself explaining that no, he had not gone to hear it, but he was certain it must've been fascinating.

An hour had passed this way when Seamie decided he could take no more. He decided to find Albie—who'd earlier said he was going to make the acquaintance of two painters he'd heard about, young Germans visiting from Munich—and let him know he was leaving. The only problem was, he couldn't find him anywhere. It was getting on; the party had become loud and crowded. More people were arriving by the minute, making it difficult to move through the rooms.

A woman wearing a long silk kimono and ropes of pearls around her neck made her way over to him, cornering him by the dining room mantel. "You're Seamus Finnegan, aren't you?" she said. "I recognize you from your pictures. Were you at the Royal Geographical Society tonight? I've just come from there. Saw that smashing girl, Willa Alden. The one who's mapping Everest. She gave a marvelous presentation. Completely spellbinding."

"Good God," Seamie muttered. Desperate to get away from the chatterbox, he excused himself. The only place in the whole house where people were not congregating was on the staircase, which was across from the foyer. He made his way to it, getting jostled as he did, and nearly knocking over a marble bust of Shakespeare with green laurels on his head. When he got to the stairs, he climbed halfway up them and sat down. This was a good vantage point. And a quiet one. He would wait for Albie to walk by, tell him good-bye, then make his way home.

As he waited, finishing off the champagne still in his glass, the front door banged open yet again. A new, and noisy, group had just come in—two men and a handful of women. The men, in suits and overcoats, were tipsy. The women, in long, slim-cut silk dresses with ropes of glass beads around their necks, were laughing at something. One of them, Seamie noticed, was not wearing a dress. She was wearing trousers and a long silk coat.

He couldn't quite see her face. Her head was down because she was unbuttoning her coat. But his heart started to hammer nonetheless.

"No," he said to himself. "It's not her. It just looks like her, but it's not. It's just a coincidence. A bloody great coincidence. Everyone here dresses strangely."

"All hail our conquering hero!" one of the men suddenly shouted, grabbing the laurel wreath off Shakespeare's head and placing it on the woman's.

"Oh, do stop, Lytton," the woman said, looking up and laughing. "You're embarrassing me."

"Fucking hell," Seamie said.

It was Willa.

CHAPTER TWENTY-SEVEN

A VOLLEY OF cheers rang out. Applause echoed in the foyer. Willa Alden looked around herself shyly, mortified by the attention. She gave a quick bow and tried to back out of the foyer into the dining room, but a drunken man swooped down on her, lifted her up, and deposited her on the table in the center of the hallway, banging her false leg against the table as he did. She clamped down on a groan of pain as she struggled to find her balance. The leg was throbbing. If she didn't get some laudanum down her throat quickly, she was going to be in trouble.

She tried to get down, but some silly woman was throwing roses she'd swiped from a vase. Guests in the other rooms craned their necks to see what was happening, or ran into the foyer to join in the applause.

"I give you the mountain goddess Cholmolungha!" Lytton Strachey shouted, bowing and salaaming. Willa had known Lytton, a brilliant, acerbic writer, before she'd left London, known he could be a bit dramatic. His antics had amused her in the past, but now she very much wished he would stop.

"Thank you," Willa said awkwardly, to the people who were clapping for her. "Thank you so much." Then she turned to Lytton and hissed, "Get me down!"

Lytton did as she asked, taking her hand as she jumped off the table. The leg sometimes made such jumps tricky. The last thing she wanted to do was to knock the damn thing off in front of so many people. That would be quite the party piece.

"Willa Alden," Lulu said, striding into the foyer and enfolding her in an embrace. "Leonard Woolf just came to fetch me. He saw you at the RGS. He said you'd just arrived, and here you are! I thought so often that I'd never see you again." Lulu released her. "Oh, just look at you. You're positively swashbuckling."

"It's so good to see you, Lu," Willa said, forcing herself to smile and be charming. "It's been ever so long. You are impossibly ethereal and more beautiful than ever. You look as if you exist on air alone."

"Air and champagne," Leonard Woolf said. He was Virginia Stephen's fiancé and a literary critic. He was clever and bookish, like the Stephen girls and all their friends. He'd come to the RGS with Lytton tonight. Willa had met him after her lecture.

A man, tanned and blond and handsome, came up to them. "Lulu, I just wanted to say thank you and good night," he said.

Thank God, Willa thought. While Lulu was talking to him, she could slip off and take her pills. But no such luck.

"Tom, you're not leaving, are you?" Lulu cried. "You can't! Not until you've met Miss Alden. She's another adventurer, just like you."

Willa smiled at him. She was in such terrible pain. She'd just given an hour-long presentation, then fielded questions for another hour and a half. She had thought this was going to be a small gathering of friends, where she might be able to quickly take some medicine, get a bite to eat, and then collapse in a soft chair. She had not expected this—a large and noisy party. There would be so many people to meet. So many hands to shake. So much chattering.

"It's an honor, Miss Alden," Lawrence said. "I was at the RGS tonight. Your lecture was wonderful. There is much I would still like to know, but I will not keep you. I'm sure you're quite spent. I've given one or two talks at the RGS myself and I know how draining they can be."

"On what topic, Mr. Lawrence?" Willa asked, struggling not to show her pain, to be interested and polite. She wanted no one to think about her leg or guess at her pain. She wanted no one's pity.

"Carchemish. The Hittites. That sort of thing," Lawrence replied. "I would just like to say that you must come to the desert. There's so much to be discovered there, and you won't have to suffer altitude sickness to do it."

"Oh, the desert won't do for our girl," Strachey said. "She prefers her quests to be impossible. She likes to chase that which she can never have. It's so hopelessly noble. So impossibly romantic."

"Are we still talking about a mountain, Lytton? Or your newest boyfriend?" Lulu asked archly.

They all laughed. Lulu invited Tom to lunch; Tom accepted and then invited Willa to supper. Lytton swanned off in pursuit of a drink. Leonard said that Willa must be famished, and then he and Virginia went off to the kitchen to make her up a plate, and Willa found herself suddenly alone in the midst of the huge roiling party.

Thank God, she thought. The pain was nearly blinding now. She reached into her jacket pocket and pulled the pill bottle out. She spotted a half-empty bottle of champagne on the floor by Shakespeare's pedestal and grabbed it to wash the pills down. She knew she should join the party and be a sociable guest, but she couldn't, not until she got the pain under control. She decided to sit down on Lulu's staircase. Just for a few minutes. Just long enough to swallow a few pills and rest her leg.

She walked over to the steps stiffly, trying not to limp, and saw that someone had beaten her to them. A man was sitting halfway up the stairs, looking at her. Her heart leapt as she recognized him—Seamie Finnegan, the man she'd once loved. And still did.

"Seamie?" she said softly.

He raised his glass to her. "Congratulations, Willa," he said. "I hear the lecture was quite a success."

"You didn't come," she said.

"No. I didn't."

"Why?"

"I was busy."

She flinched, feeling as if she'd been slapped, but quickly recovered. She wouldn't show him her hurt feelings. She had no right to. She was the one who'd left; she wasn't allowed to have hurt feelings.

"Yes," she said, trying to keep her voice steady and light. "I can see how busy you are. Well, the lecture was a success. I met some fascinating people, too. Quite a few of them, in fact. I see more people here in an hour than I do in a month in Rongbuk." She paused, then smiled and said, "If you'll excuse me, I must get by you. Have to freshen up a bit."

Seamie moved over on the step to let her pass.

"Lovely seeing you again," Willa said.

"Yes," he said tersely. "Lovely."

Willa, who'd been resting her weight on her good leg, took a step forward now onto her false one. As she did, a white-hot bolt of pain shot up into her hip. She cried out, stumbled, and fell. She hit the steps hard, losing her grip on the champagne bottle and her pills. Immediately, Seamie was at her side, lifting her back onto her feet.

"What's wrong?" he asked her, alarm in his voice.

"My leg," she gasped, nearly blinded by the pain. "Where the hell are my pills?" she said, desperately looking about herself. "Do you see them anywhere?"

"They're here. I've got them."

"I need them. Please," she said, her voice ragged with pain.

"Hold on, Willa. This is no good," Seamie said. "If your leg is that bad, you should be lying down, not standing on it."

She felt him pick her up and carry her upstairs. He knocked on a door, opened it, then carried her inside a room. It was someone's bedroom. He put her down on the bed and lit a lamp. He disappeared for a few agonizing seconds, then reappeared with a glass of water.

"Here," he said, handing her the glass, then opening the pill bottle. "How many?"

"Four," she said.

"That's a lot. Are you certain that—"

"Give me the bloody pills!" she shouted.

He did. She swallowed them down then fell back against the pillows, desperately hoping they would do their work quickly.

Seamie walked down to the foot of the bed and started unlacing her boots. She didn't want that. She didn't want anything from him; she remembered his cutting words to her on the stairs.

"Don't. I'm all right. Just go," she said fiercely.

"Shut up, Willa."

She felt his hands pulling her boots off, rolling up one of her trouser legs. Felt him undoing the buckles and straps of her fake leg. Then she heard him swear. She knew why. She knew what the flesh below her knee looked like when she overdid it.

"Look at you," he said. "Your leg's a mess. It's swollen and bleeding." He looked up at her. "This is what you've been wearing?" he said angrily, holding the leg up. "What is it? Animal bone? It's barbaric."

"Yes, well, there aren't many prosthetic factories at the base of Everest," she snapped.

"There are in London. You have to see a doctor and have something proper built for yourself. You're going to lose more of your leg if you don't. Your body can't take this kind of punishment. No one's can."

And then he was gone. Willa looked at the ceiling, teeth clenched, as she waited for her pills to kick in. They weren't as good as the thick brown opium paste that she smoked in the East, but she'd run out of that weeks ago, somewhere around Suez, and had to make do with what she could buy aboard the ship, and then laudanum pills from London chemists.

A few minutes later, Seamie returned carrying a basin of warm water, clean rags, carbolic, salve, and bandages.

"I'm sorry I shouted at you," she said, her voice more civil now, for the pain had backed off a little.

"It's all right," he said, placing the basin on the night table and sitting down next to her on the bed.

"No, it isn't. I . . . Ouch! Blimey! What are you doing?" Willa said, as Seamie dabbed at her leg.

"Cleaning up this mess."

"It hurts. Can't you just leave it alone?"

"No, I can't. You'll get an infection."

"I won't. I haven't in Rongbuk."

"Probably because it's so bloody cold there. Germs can't survive. This is London, remember? It's warmer. And dirtier. So . . . how have you been?"

"How have I been?" Willa asked incredulously.

"Since the funeral, I mean," Seamie said. "How's your mother? Your family?"

She saw what he was doing—making conversation to take her mind off the pain, but steering away from anything contentious, from anything smacking of the past.

"Mother and I get along as well as can be expected. Albie and I don't. He barely speaks to me."

"He'll get over it," Seamie said.

And what about you, Seamus Finnegan? she wondered, looking at him, at his handsome face. How have you been? But she did not ask him that question. She thought, again, that she had no right to.

Instead she talked about her father's funeral, and about all the people who'd come to the abbey to pay their respects.

"The burial was the hardest part," she said. "Going through the tall black gates of that cemetery, so gray and dreary. With the hearse all draped in black, and the horses with their ghastly black plumes. All I could think about as they carried my father's coffin to the grave site was the Tibetan sky burial ceremony, and how I wished he could have had one."

"What is it?" Seamie asked, ripping a length of gauze with his teeth and tying it around the dressing he'd made for her leg.

"When someone dies in Tibet, the family takes the body to their priests and the priests take it to a holy place. There, they cut the flesh into bits and crush the bones. Then they feed it all—flesh, bones, organs, everything—to the vultures. The birds take the bodily remains, and the soul, liberated from its earthly prison, goes free."

"It must be a hard thing to watch," Seamie said, rolling her trouser leg back down over her knee.

"It was at first, not anymore," Willa said. "Now I prefer it to our own burials. I hate to think of my father, who so loved the sea and the sky, buried in the cold, sodden ground." She stopped talking for a bit, as her emotions got the better of her; then she laughingly said, "Though I can't quite imagine how I'd convince my very proper mother to feed her husband to a pack of vultures."

Seamie laughed, too. "He was a good man, your father," he said. "Proud of you, I can tell you. Proud of your climbing. Of what you'd achieved on Kili. He was so distraught to hear of your accident, but even so, he was proud you'd summitted. I remember that, I remember—" He suddenly stopped talking, as if he'd forgotten himself and now regretted what he'd said.

Willa, anxious herself not to bring up what had happened on Kilimanjaro, quickly started talking, desperate to fill the awkward, painful silence.

"You must tell me about the South Pole," she said. "It must've been so wonderful, to be part of that expedition. I can't even imagine it. To do what you've done. See what you've seen. To have been the first party to ever reach the South Pole. How amazing. You've achieved so much, Seamie, really. You've got everything, haven't you? Everything you ever wanted."

Seamie looking at the roll of gauze he still held in his hand and didn't reply immediately. Then he said, "No, Willa. Not everything. I don't have you."

Willa, stricken by the sadness in his voice, could not speak.

"I promised myself not to see you again," he said. "Not to ever talk about this. But here you are. And I need to know. For eight long years, I've needed to know how you could do it, Willa. How you could tell me you love me, and then walk away from me."

Willa felt as if he'd seared her with his words. His pain—the pain in his voice and in his heart—hurt her more than her leg, more than the fall at Kili had. It hurt her more deeply than any pain she'd ever felt. "I was angry," she said quietly. "I blamed you for what had happened, for the loss of my leg. And I was jealous. You could still climb. I couldn't."

"Blamed me?" he said, his voice rising. "*Blamed* me?" He stood up, anger contorting his face. "What was I supposed to do?" he yelled at her. "What the hell was I supposed to do? Let you die?" Furious now, he threw the wad of gauze across the room, then smacked the basin off the night table, sending bloodied water everywhere.

"What was *I* supposed to do?" Willa yelled back. "Pretend everything was rosy? Return to England? Have a nice church wedding? Cook and sew and play housewife while you went off to the South Pole? I'd rather have died!"

"No," Seamie said brokenly. "You weren't supposed to do any of those things. But you could have talked to me. That's all. Just talked to me. Instead of leaving and ripping my heart out."

Willa balled her hands into fists. She pressed them against her eyes. The pain inside her had become an agony. She reached for her prosthesis and started to put it back on, desperate to get away from Seamie.

"Go, Willa. Run away again. That's what you do best," he said, watching her.

Willa turned to him, tears of anger and grief in her eyes. "I was wrong! All right?" she shouted. "I know that. I've known it for the past eight years. I knew I'd made a mistake the minute I set foot on the train out of Nairobi, but I couldn't turn around. It was too late. I was afraid—afraid you wouldn't have me back after what I'd done."

Seamie shook his head. "Oh, Willa," he said, his voice cracking. "I loved you, for God's sake. I still love you."

Willa began to cry. "I love you, too, Seamie," she said. "I never stopped loving you. I've missed you every day since I got on that train."

Seamie crossed the room, took her tearstained face in his hands, and kissed her. She pulled him down on the bed next to her. They sat there, facing each other. Willa started laughing. Then she cried again. Then she kissed him hard, twining her fingers in his hair. To have him in her arms again, to feel him so close to her, it was nothing short of joy. A joy she had not felt for eight long years—mad, intoxicating, and dangerous.

"I love you, Seamus Finnegan," she said. "I love you, I love you, I love you."

Seamie kissed her back hard, as she'd kissed him. He slid his hands under the tunic she was wearing, and the sweet shock of his touch made her gasp. He pulled the tunic off her, cupped her small breasts and kissed them. She fought with the buttons of his shirt, fumbling with them, until she got them undone, then she pulled him down to her, loving the feeling of his skin against hers, the warm, heavy weight of him on top of her.

She wanted this. Wanted him close to her. So much. She caught one of his hands in hers and kissed his palm. And as she did, she saw it—his wedding ring, gold and shining.

"Oh, God," she said in a choked voice. "Seamie, wait . . . stop. . . . I can't do this. We can't do this. It's not right. There's another person involved now, not just us. There's Jennie. Your wife. You can't betray her."

Seamie rolled onto his back. He stared into the gloom of the small, lamplit room, then said, "I already have. I betrayed her when

I first saw you again. In the parlor of your parents' house. And I'm going to keep on betraying her. Every day of my life. A hundred times a day. By wishing I was with you."

Willa rested her head against his shoulder. "What are we going to do?" she whispered.

"I don't know, Willa," he said. "I wish to God I did."

CHAPTER TWENTY-EIGHT

"YOU CAN'T GO back to London, Jennie. I won't let you. Who will I talk to? There's nothing here but squirrels and cows. I've only been here for three weeks and that was enough to drive me barmy. How am I going to manage for another seven months?" Josie Meadows wailed.

Jennie, sitting by the cozy fireplace of her Binsey cottage with a pile of knitting and a pot of tea, gave Josie a stern look. "Would you like to go back to London?" she asked her. "I hear Billy Madden's in quite a state over your departure."

Josie paled. She quickly shook her head no.

"I didn't think so," Jennie said. "You'll find things to occupy yourself. You can knit. I know you can. I taught you myself. Knit something for the baby. She'll need a few things. And you can read, too. Improve your mind. You can even study a bit of French for when you go to Paris. I'll find a lesson book and post it to you." Josie nodded miserably and Jennie softened toward her. "It's only a few months, you know, and then you'll have the baby, and I'll take her to an orphanage, and you'll be free to go to Paris and start a new life."

Jennie thought Josie might smile at her words—she'd tried to make them sound encouraging—but Josie did not.

"She'll go to an orphanage then, my baby?" she said quietly.

"Yes. Where else would she go?"

"I don't like orphanages. Me mum was in an orphanage. Back in Dublin. And cor, the stories she tells. They make your hair stand on end. I don't want that for her, Jennie. I don't. Can't we find her a family to go to? A good one, with a sweet mum and a kind dad? With people who will love her and care for her?"

Jennie put her knitting down and thought about this. "We could try," she said. "I'm not sure how to go about it, but I can ask some friends. Some doctor friends who care for expectant mothers. They might know how to make inquiries."

"Would you?" Josie asked. "She can't go to an orphanage, my baby. She just can't."

"I'll do it as soon as I get back. Don't fret about it, Josie. We'll figure something out. We've got time. The most important thing right now is that you're safe and well and far away from Billy Madden."

"You're right. Of course you are. Only, I still wish you weren't leaving tomorrow," Josie said, suddenly petulant again.

"I'll be back again in a fortnight. I promise," Jennie said.

"A fortnight?" Josie said. "I can't take another two weeks here all by myself. I just can't!" She started to cry.

"Now, Josie," Jennie said soothingly.

"'Now Josie' my arse!" Josie raged. "It's not you stuck here. I wish it was you instead of me. I wish I was you. You're so lucky. You can go back to London tomorrow. You're married to a good man and carrying a baby you both want. You've a wonderful, wonderful life and no worries at all!"

Jennie almost laughed out loud. No worries? She had nothing but worries. She worried Billy Madden would find out where Josie had gone. She worried Seamie would find out what she was really doing at Binsey. She worried he was going to find out the truth about her accident. She worried, with every twinge and ache and cramp, that she was going to lose the baby. And she worried that he was going to leave her for Willa Alden. She had seen his face when he was holding Willa. In the parlor at her father's funeral. She had seen that he loved her. Still. It was in his eyes, in the softness of his expression, in the tender way he'd rested his cheek against hers.

"We all have worries, Josie," she said now softly.

Josie cried even harder. "Oh, Jennie, I'm so sorry. What a selfish git I am. Of course you have worries. You're due the same time as me, and you've got to worry about me and my baby as well as your own. Can you forgive me?" She got up from her chair, knelt down, and put her head in Jennie's lap.

"Don't be silly. There's nothing to forgive," she said, stroking Josie's hair. "I know it's hard on you. I do. But you've only seven more months to go. It's not so long. You'll see."

Josie snuffled and nodded. And Jennie, still stroking her hair, raised her head and looked out of the sitting room window, at the evening's gathering gloom.

Only seven more months, for you, too, she said to herself. It's not so long. You'll see. Only seven more months.

CHAPTER TWENTY-NINE

"WELL, WELL, IF it ain't Mr. Stiles. Always a pleasure," Billy Madden said, looking up from his newspaper.

"I need to speak with you," Max said tersely. "Alone."

Billy gave a curt nod, and the three men sitting with him stood up and made their way to the bar. Max sat down with Billy.

"You see this?" Billy said, pointing to a story on the front page of his paper. "Two blokes in Whitechapel shot each other over a few quid a few nights ago. One of 'em was called Sam Hutchins. Wasn't he one of yours? The one who was taking your swag out to meet the boat in the North Sea?"

"Yes, he was," Max said tersely. "The other one worked for me, too. Apparently, they fought over payment for a job I had them do. It's buggered everything for me. That's why I'm here."

It was not a total lie. The papers hadn't printed the real story about the mess at Duffin's. Max knew the government would never have allowed it. They'd printed what they were told—that two friends had been drinking and started to argue violently over money. One man pulled a gun out and shot his rival. When he realized what he'd done, he shot himself.

There was no mention about the third man who'd been there. The man who'd realized they'd been followed, shot the others, then escaped through a window. No, nothing about him.

Max remembered the horrible scene. He remembered pulling the pistol out. The look of horror on Bauer's face. The stoic resignation on Hoffman's. It had been quick, at least. He was an excellent marksman and had hit them both squarely between the eyes. And then he'd run, managing to elude the police and the man from the SSB, but only barely.

Two agents gone. The chain to Berlin hopelessly broken. And all because that fool Bauer had panicked and come to London when he should have stayed in Govan, at the shipyard. It was unspeakably frustrating. The system Max had set up had worked like a perfectly calibrated piece of machinery—Gladys to Hoffman, Hoffman to the boatyard, and then a quick trip to the ship waiting in the North Sea. And now that machine was smashed. Berlin desperately wanted the information from the Admiralty in London, and from the shipyards on the Clyde, that Max had been supplying to them, and now he no longer had any way of doing so.

Max had received a message from Bauer two days before the shooting. In it, Bauer had said that they were on to him; he was certain of it. He'd said he had something for Berlin, something big, and he had to get it to London. Now. Max had sent word that he was to stay put and wait for a courier. But he hadn't. He'd got on a train and shown up on Hoffman's doorstep—Hoffman, of all people—Max's most valuable courier. Hoffman had got word to him, Max, that Bauer had arrived in London, and Max had told Hoffman to bring Bauer to Duffin's.

Bauer must've been followed the entire way to Duffin's, for the knock on the door and the constable telling them to open up had happened only moments after he and Hoffman arrived. Max had had only seconds in which to execute the two men, throw Bauer's documents into the fire, and flee. That he had not been caught was a miracle. They'd shot at him, and one bullet had come uncomfortably close. They would've killed him if they could have.

"The boat is off," Max said to Billy now. "That's what I came to tell you."

"For how long?"

"I don't know," Max said. "As long as it takes me to find a new courier."

"Why can't you get your swag to the boat yourself?" Billy asked. "Business as usual."

"It wouldn't be wise right now."

"The busies are making things a bit hot?"

"Yes," Max said. "They are."

That, too, was not completely a lie. It wasn't the London constabulary Max was worried about, though. It was the British SSB. Max was a German in London and, as such, was under suspicion. He knew that he'd been followed on more than one occasion. He also knew that he was in the clear, for among all the documents Gladys had brought to him were letters bound for his own dossier, all of which showed that the SSB did not consider him a threat.

He must remain above suspicion, though, and that meant making no unusual movements. It wouldn't look right for a West End playboy, one accustomed to staying at the Coburg and dining in London's most stylish clubs and homes, to suddenly be seen hanging around a ramshackle East End boatyard.

Billy, who'd been blowing smoke rings, now said, "Could you get yourself to Whitechapel? Or Wapping? At night?"

"Why?" Max asked. He'd gone to Whitechapel many times, but it would be risky now after what had happened. He couldn't afford to be seen and identified by Mrs. Duffin or any of her boarders.

"The tunnels, lad," Billy said, stubbing his cigarette out.

"What tunnels?" Max asked, his interest piqued.

"The ones that run under East London. From Whitechapel to Wapping to Limehouse and all the way under the river to Southwark."

Max sat forward in his chair. "I had no idea such tunnels existed," he said.

"They do. They're a right maze. Very dangerous if you don't know your way through them, but very handy if you do. For avoiding the busies and for moving swag."

"Where, exactly, are they, Billy?"

"All over. One even runs from the basement in a church—St. Nicholas's—right to my boatyard. If you could get yourself to the church and drop the goods there, I could send my man Harris through. He'd pick them up and get them to your man in the North Sea. Many's the time one of my lads has hidden something in St. Nick's and another's picked it up by coming through the tunnels. Couldn't be easier."

"Doesn't the Reverend Wilcott mind this?"

"Oh, you know him, do you? Nah, he's a daft old git. Leaves the doors open all day long just in case someone's soul needs saving. Easy as can be to nip down to the basement."

"But doesn't he see the things you put down there?"

"He doesn't have a clue about any of it. Doesn't even know there's a door down there, or where it leads. I don't think he ever goes down himself. There's no reason to. It's a right nasty place. Dark and damp. Only thing down there is rats. Some old, rotted church pews. And a broken statue of St. Nicholas. It fell and smashed several years ago, when some yobs dropped it as they were trying to steal it. It's all in pieces now. Good thing is, the head's hollow. Makes a great place to hide guns and jewels and other smalls. Or forget Wapping and go into the tunnels in Whitechapel. At the Blind Beggar. Then walk to the boatyard from there. It's a longer walk, but my men have done it loads of times. You want to give it a go?"

Max thought about what Billy had said. There was something in it. He liked the idea of moving the documents underground, away from prying eyes, but he couldn't quite figure out how to make it work. At least, not yet.

"It's a good idea. But I can't do the trip myself. I still need a new courier."

A man, thick-browed, bald, and built like a barrel, came over to Billy. Billy looked up at him. "Any word?"

"No, guv. There's no sign of her. Nothing whatsoever."

Billy slammed his fist on the table. "Fucking cunt!" he shouted. "I'm going to gut her when I find her!"

"Lady troubles?" Max asked.

"It's this tart I was shagging. Little actress from the halls. A blonde named Josie Meadows. You ever see her here?"

Max nodded. He recalled a young, blond woman with bruises on her face, sitting by a window. "Once, I think," he said.

"She disappeared on me."

"Actresses are thick on the ground in London. Can't you find another one?"

"This one took something with her that belongs to me," he said.

Max had the feeling there was more to the story than Billy was telling him, but he didn't push him for the details.

"You know, I'm thinking you might come across her," Billy said. "Might see her skulking around somewhere."

"It's possible," Max said, hesitantly.

"You don't have to get your hands dirty, if that's what you're worried about," Billy said. "All I'm asking is that you let me know if you see anything or hear anything. I'd be grateful."

Billy smiled his horrible, black smile. Looking at it, and at the cruel, soulless eyes above it, Max thought that this girl, this Josie Meadows, would do well to get out of London. Max had known men like Billy before, men who took pleasure in hurting and killing, and he knew that if Billy ever found this girl, she would sorely wish that he hadn't.

Well, that wasn't his worry. Reestablishing the links in the chain, that was his worry. That and staying alive. He took an envelope from his jacket and put it on the table.

"Keep the boat ready for me," he said.

Billy nodded. He picked the envelope up and tucked it inside his jacket.

"I'll be in touch again when I can," Max said, standing up to leave. He thought about Duffin's again, about his narrow escape, and the bullet whizzing past his cheek. "*If* I can," he added.

CHAPTER THIRTY

SEAMIE TOOK A swallow of the whiskey he'd poured for himself. It burned his throat. Made his eyes water. He took another.

Glass in hand, he walked to the window of his hotel room, at the Coburg, and looked out of it. Night had come down. The street lamps were all aglow. He gazed at the street below but did not see the person he was looking for. He turned from the window, caught sight of himself in a mirror, and quickly looked away.

"Leave," he said out loud. "Now. Get out of here before it's too late."

He could do it. He still had time. He *would* do it. He put his glass down and grabbed his jacket. He was across the room in a few quick strides, had his hand on the doorknob—and then he heard it: a knock at his door. He stood there, frozen. Ran a hand through his hair. The knock came again. He took a deep breath and opened the door.

"I didn't know if you'd really be here," Willa said.

"Neither did I," he replied.

"Can I come in?" she asked.

He laughed. "Yes, of course," he said. "Sorry."

He took her jacket and hat and placed them on a chair with his own jacket. She was wearing a cream silk blouse under it and a navy skirt. He commented on her outfit and she told him she hated it, but had worn it to blend in. She didn't want to be recognized here.

He offered her tea, but she wanted whiskey. He was so jittery, he sloshed some on her as he handed it to her.

"It's all right, Seamie," she said. "We can just talk, you know. Like adults. We can try to sort things out."

That's what they'd decided to do at Lulu's party. They hadn't made love. Instead, they decided they would meet in a private place, at a time when emotions were not running as high, and there they would put the old ghosts to rest. They would talk about Africa, and about what had happened there, and when they'd finished, they would go their separate ways. They would part friends—not enemies and not lovers, but friends.

Seamie laughed mirthlessly now. "I told myself that, too, Willa. On my way over. I told myself all we would do tonight was talk. But I knew if I came here, I'd do more than talk. And I think you knew that, too."

He had booked a suite—a room with settees and chairs and a desk—so that the large, inviting hotel bed would be firmly out of sight. He'd hoped that would help. It hadn't. He wanted her so badly right now, it was all he could do not to take her on the floor.

She nodded at his words, looking at him as she did. Her eyes were frank and unflinching. He could see the love in them, and the longing.

"One time, then, all right?" she said quietly. "Just this one time and never again."

As she spoke, she put her drink down and started undoing the buttons of her blouse. She shrugged it off and let it fall to the floor. She had nothing on underneath it. She undid her boots and stockings. Then unbuttoned the waistband of her skirt and let that fall, too.

She stood before him, unashamed of her nakedness, or of the scars on her body, and he moved toward her as if in a trance. He knew what he was doing was wrong, and he knew, too, that he would pay a heavy price for his sins. The memories of this night would torture him for the rest of his life.

But he would pay that price. He'd pay any price to be with her.

He didn't take her in his arms. He would, but not yet. He wanted to see her, to discover and know every inch of her. And so he went slowly, taking his time.

He kissed her gently on the lips. Then on her neck. He took her hand, held her arm out, and kissed his way from her shoulder to her palm, brushing his lips along her muscled upper arm, the hollow of her elbow, over the veins and sinews of her forearm, to her hand, scarred and strong.

He kissed her throat, the bronzed skin of her chest. His mouth moved to her breasts, and he felt her arch against him as he teased her small, hard nipples with his tongue and teeth.

He turned her around and kissed the nape of her neck, ran his hand over the graceful flare of her back. He traced the knotted pearls of her spine one by one, kissed the jutting bones of her hips. He knelt down then and turned her once more. Toward him.

He slid his hands to her bum and pulled her hard against him. He kissed the place between her legs, and touched her there. She was soft, so soft. And warm and wet. He felt her fingers dig into his shoulders, felt her shudder against him, heard her cry his name.

That sound, the sound of her crying his name, maddened him with desire. He wanted to have her, to possess her body and soul. He wanted to hear her call his name again. His name. He'd wanted it for so long.

He picked her up and carried her into the bedroom. He had his own clothes off in seconds. And then he was on top of her. She pulled his face down to hers and kissed him. Then she pushed him off of her.

"No," she said in a rough, husky voice, her green eyes glittering. "It's my turn."

She pushed him down on the bed, onto his back, then lay next to him on her side. He grabbed her hips, wanting only to be inside her again, but again she told him no. She took hold of his wrists and pinned them to the pillows. Then she kissed his mouth, biting his bottom lip. She kissed his forehead and his chin. Bit his shoulder. She kissed his chest, trailing her tongue down his torso. Bit his hip and made him shiver, as he'd done to her. She went lower, tormenting him with her mouth. "Jesus, woman," he groaned.

And then she was kissing his mouth again, taking him inside her, moving with him, her eyes closed. He cupped her face in one hand, touched his forehead to hers.

"Tell me, Willa," he said, his voice barely more than a gasp. "Tell me."

She opened her eyes and he saw that they were bright with tears. "I love you, Seamie," she said. "I love you so."

He came then. Wildly. Helplessly. Overwhelmed by lust and love and sorrow and pain. And she did, too. When it was over, he held her close. He kissed her, brushed a stray tendril of hair from her sweaty cheek.

There was a vase of roses on the bedside table, lush and bright, their perfume strong and enticing. They were no scentless, lifeless hothouse blooms. They'd been cut for their perfume and their color, cut from a hedgerow in the country where they'd grown wild and brought to London. They didn't belong here in this hotel room, in this gray city. Neither did Willa. Seamie took one out and tucked it behind her ear. "A wild rose for my wild rose," he whispered to her. He smoothed a piece of hair out of her face, then said, "Why did you come back into my life, Willa? You've ruined it. Ruined me. You're the best thing that ever happened to me, and the worst."

"I told myself it would only be once," she said. "I told you that, too. But it can't be, Seamie. I can't leave here tomorrow morning knowing I'll never have this again. Never be with you like this again.

What are we going to do?" she asked desolately. Just as she had at Lulu's party. "What on earth are we going to do?"

"Love each other," Seamie said.

"For how long?" she asked, her eyes searching his.

He took her in his arms and held her close. "For as long as we possibly can," he whispered. "As long as we can."

CHAPTER THIRTY-ONE

MAUD HURRIED ALONG the third-floor corridor of the Coburg, the key to Max's suite of rooms in her hand. She'd just bribed a bellboy handsomely to get it. In her other hand, she carried a small, beautifully made traveling case. It contained two tickets to Bombay, a compass, and a pair of field glasses. They would go in the autumn, after she returned from visiting India in Point Reyes. Bombay was only the first leg of the journey, of course. Once there, they'd have to make their way north to Darjeeling, then to Tibet. And Everest.

It was a birthday surprise for Max, one she'd been planning for ages. He would turn thirty-four tomorrow and she wanted him to find the gift when he came home today. He'd been away in Scotland for a few days. "Shooting with friends, darling," he'd said. "Men only, I'm afraid. I'll miss you horribly."

Maud smiled now, as she fit the key into the lock, imagining the look on his face when he opened the case. He adored Everest. He was forever talking about it, and always with such passion, such longing. In fact, if Everest had been a woman instead of a mountain, she would have been quite jealous. She opened the door and quickly went inside. The plush, luxurious rooms were dark and silent. She could hear the echo of her heels as she walked across the foyer's marbled floor.

Now . . . where should I leave the gift? she wondered. Here in the foyer? No, he might trip over it. On the sitting room table, perhaps. That wouldn't do either. He'd likely walk right by it.

She decided to leave it on his bed. He'd be sure to see it there. She walked into the bedroom and laid the case on his pillow. It looked a bit lonely there, so she decided to leave a note as well. She sat down at his desk, placed her large silk clutch purse down next to the blotter, and shrugged out of her fur coat. Then she pulled open one of the desk drawers and rooted about for a pen and a sheet of paper. She found the first, but not the second. She opened another drawer, and then another, but still no paper. Frustrated, she picked up the leather desk blotter, to see if there might be a few sheets under it, but there was nothing. She'd tilted it slightly as she'd lifted it, and when she went to put it back on the desk, she noticed that something had slid partially out of it—out of a thin slit, one that had been cut almost invisibly into the bottom edge of the blotter.

It looked like the corner of a photograph. She tugged it all of the way out and saw that it was a black-and-white photo of a naked woman. "Why, Max, you dirty little bugger," she said aloud. She had no idea he collected pornography.

She shook the blotter and the edges of more photographs slipped out. Five in all. A whole collection. Maud looked at them, expecting something seductive and erotic, but there was nothing alluring about these pictures. They were wretched. Disgusting. The girl in them looked drunk or drugged. Her legs were spread. Her hands were behind her head. And her face . . .

Her face. Maud gasped. She recognized it. She knew this woman. "My God," she said out loud. "It's Gladys. Gladys Bigelow."

She knew Gladys from suffrage meetings. She'd been one of Jennie Wilcott's students and was now Sir George Burgess's secretary. What was she doing in these horrible photographs?

Maud scrabbled in Max's drawers until she found a letter opener. She poked it into the blotter, widening the slit. There was something else inside, she could see it. She wedged her fingers in, expecting to pull out another awful photograph. Instead she pulled out a thin sheaf of folded carbon papers.

She held one up to the light. It took her a minute to read the backward type, but as soon as she did, she realized she was holding a letter from George Burgess to Winston Churchill regarding the acquisition of fifty Sopwith airplanes. Another, from Burgess to Asquith, requested further funds for something called Room 40.

The horrible pictures of Gladys, the carbons of sensitive letters written by her employer—Maud put the two together and realized that Gladys was being blackmailed by Max.

There were more letters from Burgess, but she didn't read them all. With her heart in her mouth, she reached into the blotter again, dreading what she would find.

She pulled out a folded blueprint of what seemed to be a submarine. All the words on it were written in German. She found more carbons, but these, too, were written in German. They were addressed to a man whose name she recognized—Bismarck.

The blood froze in her veins as she pulled out the last item inside the blotter—a white card, with printing on the front, measuring about five by seven inches. She recognized it—it was the invitation Max had received to the Asquiths' country home, the Wharf. She had received one just like it, and they'd gone there together about a fortnight ago.

She turned it over. There was handwriting on the back—Max's. The words were in German. Maud spoke and read some German, enough to understand what she was seeing: Asquith's name and the names of French, Belgian, Russian, and American diplomats, as well as place names, times, and dates.

With horror, she remembered their first evening at the Wharf. She remembered Asquith's secretary coming into the room and telling the prime minister that there was a telephone call for him. Asquith had decided to take the call in his study. He'd left them, and after he had, Max had asked where the study was.

It's upstairs. Right above us. Henry's just being cross. He doesn't like stairs, Margot had replied.

"He's a spy," Maud whispered now. "My God, he's a German spy. And he used me, and my friendship with Margot, to get to Asquith."

The names and dates—they were notations of meetings the prime minister had had with foreign diplomats, or was going to have, Maud thought. They were very likely secret meetings, or else why had Max bothered to note them down? If they weren't secret, they'd be reported on in the daily papers, where anyone could read about them. Max must've gone to Asquith's study later that night, riffled through his diary and his papers, and written the information down.

But why, if he was passing British information to the Germans, did he also have a blueprint of a German submarine and carbons of letters written to Bismarck?

Maud didn't have an answer for that, and she knew she had no time to find one. With shaking hands, she shuffled together the papers she'd pulled out of the blotter into a stack, folded them over, tucked the photos inside, and put the whole bundle into her purse. She had to get out of here. Now. She didn't know exactly when Max was returning to London. He could arrive at the Coburg at any minute. She decided to take the traveling case with her so he'd never know she'd been here. Once she was outside of the hotel, she'd flag down a hackney cab and tell the man to take her to Downing Street. To Number 10. There, she would tell Asquith where she'd just been and give him the papers. He would know what to do.

Maud positioned the blotter exactly as she'd found it, then made certain all the desk drawers were closed. She stood, pulled her coat on, and was about to grab the traveling case off the bed, when a sudden movement in the doorway startled her. She gasped out loud. It was Max.

"Max, darling, you gave me such a fright!" she said, pressing a hand to her chest.

Max smiled, but his eyes were cold. "What are you doing here, Maud?" he asked her.

Maud was terrified, but knew she mustn't show it. She must appear simply to be flustered, and to use that to her advantage. It was her only chance.

"Well, if you must know, I was trying my hardest to surprise you. For your birthday. I was just trying to write you a note, but I can't seem to find any bloody paper in your desk."

"You were trying to surprise me?"

"Yes. Seems I've failed miserably though. There it is," she said, pointing to his bed. "Go on, open it."

Max looked past her. He smiled again. It was a real smile this time, warm and engaging.

"I can't wait to see what it is," he said. "But let's make it a proper celebration. Hold on . . . stay right there. I'll bring some wine."

He disappeared into another room and Maud let out a ragged breath. A few seconds later, she heard him pull a cork. She'd fooled him, she was sure of it. Why wouldn't he believe her? The present was on his pillow. He'd open it in a few minutes, and thank her, and then she'd suggest they go out for dinner. As soon as she was downstairs, in the lobby, she'd say that she forgot something in his room and would he be a dear and run back up for it. When he did, she would make a dash for it.

"Here we are," he said, returning with two glasses of red wine. He handed her one. "A Pomerol. 1894. I had one just last night. It was wonderful."

She touched her glass to his and smiled. "Happy birthday, darling," she said, kissing him for good measure. She took a generous swallow for courage, then licked her lips and said, "You're right. This *is* wonderful."

"I'm glad you like it. Drink up. I've plenty more."

She took another sip, then said, "Go on, then. Open your present."

"All I really want is you," he said, sitting down on the bed.

"You already have me," she said, laughing and taking another large gulp of wine. She must steady her nerves. He mustn't see her hands shaking. "Open your present," she said again, sitting down next to him.

"All right, then, I will." He reached behind himself for the case.

As Maud watched him opening the locks, she began to feel dizzy.

She suddenly saw two cases on his lap. Then one again. A low buzzing started in her ears. She looked away from Max, at the floor, trying to clear her head. But it didn't work. The dizziness only got worse. Was she drunk? On half a glass of wine?

"Max, darling . . . I feel rather strange," she said, putting her wineglass down.

She looked at him. He wasn't holding the box anymore. He'd put it down. He was watching her.

She tried to get up, tried to stand, but her legs went out from under her and she hit the floor. She closed her eyes, tried to take a deep breath. When she opened them again, Max was standing over her.

"I'm so sorry, Maud," he said quietly.

"No, Max," she said, though it was difficult to speak. "It's my . . . it's my fault. Too much wine, I think. Can you . . . can you help me? I . . . I can't seem . . ."

"Don't fight it," he said. "It's easier if you just let go."

Let go? Let go of what? Hadn't she put the wineglass down already?

The wineglass. He'd put something in her drink.

She tried once more to get up, but her arms and legs seemed as if they were made of lead. The room was whirling. Her vision began to fade.

"Max, please . . . ," she said, reaching a hand out to him.

He looked at her, but did not move to help her. There was a strange expression on his face. Maud didn't recognize it at first, but then suddenly she did; it was grief.

"Let go," he whispered.

"Oh, God," she pleaded. "Somebody help me . . . somebody, please help me. . . ."

CHAPTER THIRTY-TWO

"BEG YOUR PARDON, ma'am," Mr. Foster said, stepping inside Fiona's study. "I'm terribly sorry to intrude. I did knock."

Fiona looked up from the plans she'd been studying—blueprints for a new tearoom to be built in Sydney. She'd been so deeply absorbed by them she hadn't heard him.

"What is it now, Mr. Foster?" she asked. "No, let me guess . . . Katie's led a march on the House of Commons, Rose has taken a necklace without asking and now she's in tears because she can't find it, and the twins have jumped off the roof."

"I wish it was so, madam. All except for the twins jumping off the roof, of course. But I fear it is something of a graver nature."

"What's happened?" Fiona said, instantly alarmed. "The children . . . are they—"

"The children are well, madam. It's Dr. Hatcher. She is most distressed. She's in the drawing room and would like to see you."

Fiona was out of her chair immediately. She hurried by Foster and ran down the stairs. Harriet Hatcher was never distressed. She was rarely so much as perturbed. Nothing fazed her—not the blood and gore she dealt with on a daily basis, not the constant threats hurled at her when she took part in suffrage marches, not even the harsh treatment she received when she was arrested. Whatever it was that had upset her, it had to be grave indeed.

"Harriet?" Fiona called out as she opened the door to the drawing room. "What's the matter? What's happened?"

Harriet was sitting on a settee, ashen and trembling. Her eyes were red from crying. Fiona quickly closed the door and sat down beside her. "What is it?" she said, taking her hand.

"Oh, Fiona. I have the most terrible news. Maud is dead and the police are saying it's a suicide."

Fiona shook her head, stunned. She thought that perhaps she had not heard her correctly. "You must be mistaken," she said. "Do you know what you're saying? You're saying that Maud . . . our Maud . . . that she—"

"Killed herself," Harriet said. "I know how it sounds, Fiona. I can't believe it myself, but it's true."

"How do you know this?" Fiona asked.

"A police constable. He came to my house a few hours ago. He told me that Maud was found dead in her bed this morning by Mrs. Rudge, her housekeeper. The police questioned Mrs. Rudge, then asked her for names and addresses of Maud's family and her friends. They're going to question everyone. I imagine they'll come here. They've already been to see Max. He's in an awful way."

"I can imagine he would be. The poor man," Fiona said woodenly, still in shock.

"He's beyond distraught. He blames himself completely."

"Blames himself? Why?" Fiona asked.

"They'd had some kind of row, apparently, he and Maud, and he'd broken it off with her."

"Oh, no."

"Oh, yes. And it gets worse. The police believe that he was the last person to see her alive. So not only has he been questioned by a constable, but a detective inspector is going to question him again. Later today."

"I still can't believe this. Not any of it. How could Maud take her own life?" Fiona said. "Harriet, how . . . how did she—"

"An overdose," Harriet said. "Morphine. She injected herself. The police found two bottles and a hypodermic on her night table. The coroner found marks on her arm."

"I had no idea she even knew how to do something like that," Fiona said. The shock of Harriet's news had receded a little, and Fiona felt as if she could think straight again. She was trying to reason now, to make sense of it all.

"It's not hard to use a hypodermic, Fiona. You don't have to be a doctor. Anyone can do it," Harriet said.

"But I thought it was all over with, her drug use," Fiona said. "I know that she used to visit opium dens. In Limehouse. Years ago. And she used to smoke opium-laced cigarettes. She had mostly stopped, though. She still had the odd cigarette, but the trips to Limehouse were a thing of the past. India saw to that. It made her furious that Maud went there, and . . . and—oh, Harriet!"

Fiona's voice cracked, she covered her face with her hands and started to weep. Now that her mind had cleared a bit, she'd realized that there was someone else who must be told. Someone else who would be devastated by Maud's death, even more so than she and Harriet were.

"What is it, Fiona?" Harriet asked, putting an arm around her.

"How am I going to tell her, Harriet? How?"

"Tell who?"

Fiona lowered her hands. "How am I going to tell India that her sister is dead?"

CHAPTER THIRTY-THREE

"DO YOU MIND if I smoke?" Max asked the man seated across from him.

"Not at all," the man, Detective Inspector Arnold Barrett, said. "Nice place," he added, looking around Max's spacious receiving room, at the luxurious furnishings, the silver tea tray on the table, the blazing logs in the fireplace.

"Yes, it's very comfortable," Max said, sitting back in his chair.

They were in Max's hotel suite. Barrett had arrived a few minutes before. Max had offered him tea, which he'd gratefully accepted, and then they'd sat down.

"Thank you for seeing me, Mr. von Brandt," Barrett said, taking out a notebook and fountain pen. "I know this has been a very difficult day for you and I won't take up any more of your time than I have to."

Max nodded.

"Now, then, according to P.C. Gallagher, the man who interviewed you this morning, you believe you were the last person to see Miss Selwyn Jones alive," Barrett said.

"Yes, I believe so," Max replied.

"I would like to go over the events leading up to Miss Selwyn Jones's death. To begin with, the doorman here at the hotel, one William Frazier, remembers seeing you helping Miss Selwyn Jones into a hackney cab. Mr. Frazier has said that Miss Selwyn Jones appeared to be inebriated."

"Yes, that's correct," Max said. "Maud was very drunk."

"Alfred Ludd, the cabdriver, has stated that he heard Miss Selwyn Jones crying at times during the cab ride to her flat, and saying, and I quote, 'Please, Max. Please don't do this.' "

"That is also correct."

Barrett gave Max a long look. "You're hardly helping yourself here, Mr. von Brandt."

"There is no help for me, Detective Inspector. As I told P.C. Gallagher, and will now tell you, it was all my fault."

Barrett paused, weighing Max's words, then he resumed his questioning. "According to Ludd, when he arrived at Miss Selwyn Jones's building, you paid him, then helped Miss Selwyn Jones out of the cab and into her house."

"Yes."

"You yourself told P.C. Gallagher that you then carried Miss Selwyn Jones to her bedroom and laid her down on her bed. You covered her, then left the premises via the front door, locking it behind you."

"Yes. Maud had given me a key. I gave it to P.C. Gallagher this morning."

"A note was found on the deceased's bedside table, in what appears to be her handwriting. In it, she wrote that she was distraught over her breakup with 'Max.' That would be you."

Max nodded and took a deep drag of his cigarette.

"The note was hard to read," Barrett said. "It was scrawled more than it was written, but then again, Miss Selwyn Jones, as everyone seems to agree, was drunk. However, we could make it out well enough. It went on to say that she was sorry for doing what she was about to do, but she couldn't live without you."

Max rubbed at his forehead with one hand. The other hand, still holding his cigarette, shook slightly.

"Miss Selwyn Jones was found facedown in her bed, a tourniquet around her arm. An empty syringe and two empty morphine bottles were found nearby her," Barrett said, watching Max closely.

"I'm to blame," Max said in a choked voice. "If it wasn't for me, she would still be alive."

"What exactly happened last evening, Mr. von Brandt?" Barrett asked, his keen eyes on Max. "Why did Miss Selwyn Jones leave here so drunk she could barely stand? Why did she kill herself?"

Max lowered his hand. He brushed at his eyes awkwardly. "We had a fight," he began. "She had come here to give me a birthday present. A trip to India. With her."

"A very nice gift," Barrett said.

"Yes, it was. It was a very lovely gesture. But it was too much."

"The gift was?"

"No, her expectations."

"I don't understand."

"The relationship we had . . . our romance, if you will . . . well, for me it was only ever intended to be a short-lived thing. A fling between two grown, unattached people. I thought Maud understood that, but she didn't. She wanted more from me and I couldn't give it to her."

"Why not?" Barrett asked.

"Because expectations have been placed upon me. Family obligations. Maud was older than I. She had been married before. . . ."

"Not the kind of girl to bring home to Mama," Barrett said.

"No, not at all the kind of girl. I'd recently had a falling out with my uncle, you see. He now runs the company my grandfather started. I came to London to cool off, but I know that eventually I will have to return home, take my place in the family business, and marry a suitable girl—a respectable girl from a good family who will give me many children. My mother has several candidates picked out for me," Max said, with a bitter smile. "Maud knew this. I never lied to her. I was honest from the beginning. She said it didn't matter to her, and for while, it did not seem to. We had a very good time together, but lately she'd become unreasonable."

"How so?" Barrett asked.

"She began to pressure me constantly. She wanted me to not return to Germany. To stay in London. She wanted to get married. She told me I didn't need to go back, to join the family firm. She said she had plenty of money, more than enough to keep us both in a very high style. The gift was the last straw."

"Why?"

"She suggested it could be our honeymoon trip. I refused to accept it. I told her it was over between us. She got very upset with me. She yelled and screamed and started drinking. Quite a lot, in fact."

"You're an odd duck, Mr. von Brandt. Some men would have had no hesitation in marrying a very wealthy woman. A woman whose company, and whose bed, they happened to like."

"You are quite right, Detective Inspector. Some men would have no hesitation. They are called gigolos," Max said coldly.

Barrett held up a hand. "Now, now, Mr. von Brandt," he said. "I didn't mean to offend you. Tell me what happened next."

"Maud became very drunk. I couldn't listen to her anymore and I thought the best thing would be to take her home. So I did. And the rest you know." Max paused for a few seconds, then he said, "She told me I'd be sorry. She was right. I am. Very sorry. I shouldn't have broken it off with her. I wouldn't have if I'd known how fragile she was."

"Do you have any idea where she got the morphine? It was a very strong concentration. Stronger than you can buy at a chemist's."

"No. I know she used the drug, somewhat frequently, but I don't know where she got it," he said. He hesitated, then said, "Detective Inspector Barrett?"

"Yes?"

"I do know that she sometimes smoked cigarettes with opium in them. She told me once that she got them in a place called Limehouse. Does that help you?"

Barrett laughed. "Mr. von Brandt, there are a hundred places in the place called Limehouse where Miss Selwyn Jones could've bought those cigarettes. And the morphine, too." He capped his pen and closed his notebook. "Thank you for your time, Mr. von Brandt. We won't be bothering you again."

Barrett stood up. Max stood, too. He walked Barrett to the door and opened it for him.

"Now, if you'd married Miss Selwyn Jones, and then she ended up dead, her being such a rich woman, then we'd have more questions," Barrett said, pausing in the doorway. "But as things are, you've got no motive. None whatsoever. Miss Selwyn Jones's death was suicide, plain and simple. The papers won't be happy. They always like a good story—some sort of nefarious motive, some mystery novel nonsense—but sometimes death is just what it looks like—sad and sorry. Nothing else. My condolences on your loss, Mr. von Brandt. Good day."

"Thank you, Detective Inspector," Max said. "Good day."

As he was about to close the door behind him, Barrett turned and said, "Mr. von Brandt?"

"Yes?"

"A piece of advice . . . if I may."

"Of course."

"Don't be so hard on yourself. If breaking hearts was a crime, every jail in London would be full."

Max smiled sadly. Detective Inspector Arnold tipped his hat and then he was gone. Max closed the door, poured himself a glass of wine, and sat down heavily. Dusk was starting to fall, but he did not turn on a light. He sat staring into the fireplace, and as he did, a tear rolled down his cheek, and then another.

This was no false emotion, put on for a police officer's benefit. His sorrow was real. He had felt something for Maud. He had enjoyed her company and her humor and her bed, and he missed her. She did not deserve what had happened to her. And he was full of remorse for it.

But he had had no choice. He'd known she was in his room the minute he opened the door. He'd smelled her perfume. He'd prayed then, that she had come to welcome him home, that she was merely waiting for him, naked in his bed. His heart had clenched in sadness and anger when, having quietly walked to the doorway of his bedroom, he saw the photographs and documents spread out over his desk. He watched as she put the papers into her purse, and he knew what she was going to do with them, knew she would go to the police, or to somebody she knew in the government. Joe Bristow, perhaps. Or Asquith himself. And in so doing, she would have brought his carefully constructed house of cards crashing down.

He'd known, too, what he would have to do, and he'd done it unflinchingly. Indeed, he kept a small supply of the necessary drugs on hand for such occasions. And yet it had hurt him terribly, far more than he'd thought it would, to drug her, bring her to her home, stick a needle repeatedly into the soft skin inside her elbow, and empty two bottles of morphine into her veins.

As he sat in his chair now, still staring into the fireplace, unmoving, he heard a small, soft, sliding noise. He raised his head and looked toward his door. An envelope had been pushed under it.

"Further orders," he said to himself, wondering if it would be written in German or in English. Regardless, the envelope would have no return address, no postmark. It never did.

For a few seconds, a violent anger possessed him. He stood up, shaking with rage, grabbed a vase from a table, and hurled it against a wall. It shattered explosively, raining glass everywhere.

Maud didn't matter to them. She was expendable. Bauer, Hoffman—they were expendable, too. He himself was expendable; he knew that. No one mattered to them.

"One life," they would say. "What is one life against millions?"

He had cared for this one life, though. He'd almost loved this one woman. But he realized now, as he mastered his emotion once more, that getting close to Maud, letting himself feel things for her, had been a stupid mistake—one he must be sure never to repeat. Had he not gotten so close to her, she might never have come to his room, and might never have found what she shouldn't have.

Max toed the larger shards of glass into a pile, then telephoned to the concierge to have a maid come clean the mess up. He crossed the room, picked up the envelope, and read the letter inside it. It was time to get to work again.

Maud was gone. His heart was heavy with grief for her. And he knew it didn't matter. No one's cover had been blown. That was what mattered. That was all that mattered.

Love is dangerous, he told himself now. Far too dangerous. You learned that lesson already, but you chose not to remember it.

Max walked over to the fireplace. As he fed the letter, and its envelope, into the flames, he made himself a promise never to forget again.

CHAPTER THIRTY-FOUR

SEAMIE STARED OUT of the hotel room's window. The sun was in the western sky. It was probably five o'clock already. He looked at the light coming in the window, slanting across the bed, across Willa's naked body as she lay next to him, dozing. He knew this light well now. It was the sad, gray light of unfaithfulness. Married people—

well, the happy ones, at least—did not know it. They made love in the darkness, or in the clear and hopeful light of morning.

He pulled Willa close now and kissed the top of her head. She mumbled sleepily.

"I've got to go soon, my love," he said.

Willa looked up at him. "Already?" she said.

He nodded. There was a dinner at the RGS tonight. For donors. He was expected to attend, and Jennie, too. He had told her he would be talking with possible donors all day long, and that he would meet her there, at the RGS. He wanted to get there before she did. He wanted to not give her any reason to suspect he was lying. He and Willa worried all the time that she would find out. Or that Albie would.

"Let me see your photos before I go," he said to Willa now.

"Oh, yes. The photos. Forgot about those," she said. "I forget everything when I'm with you."

He did, too. He forgot so many things he shouldn't have—that he was married, that his wife loved him, that she was carrying their child.

It can't last, this, he thought, as he watched Willa get up and shrug into her shirt. He knew it couldn't. They both did. But he couldn't bear to let it go. Not yet.

She rummaged in a large satchel she'd brought with her, then got back into bed, carrying a pile of black-and-white photographs. They were of Everest. He hadn't seen them because he hadn't gone to her lecture at the RGS. But he wanted to. Very much. He wanted to see her work, to see Everest and Rongbuk, where she lived. He'd asked her to bring them with her today.

"I'm going to use this lot in my book," she said, depositing the stack in his lap. "The text is finished. The RGS has put an editor onto the project. It should be ready to be printed in three months or so."

"That's wonderful, Willa. Congratulations," Seamie said. "I'm sure it'll be a smashing success. Let's have a look." He held up the first picture and immediately fell silent, stunned by the beauty and clarity of the photograph, by the unspeakable majesty of Everest.

"That's the north face," Willa explained. "Taken from on top of the glacier. I'd been camping there for two weeks. Trying to get a clear shot. But I couldn't. There were always clouds. On the last day, in the morning as I was making tea, the clouds suddenly broke. I knew it wouldn't last. Knew I had about thirty seconds. The camera was set up, thank God. I fumbled a plate into it, and just before the clouds closed again, I got the picture."

"It's incredible," Seamie said.

He looked at the next shot. And the next. Of the mountain and the glacier and the clouds and Rongbuk and its people. Of Lhasa. Of Everest's south face, shot from Nepal. He saw the streets of Kathmandu. Peddlers and priests. Traders coming over a treacherous pass. Imperious nobles in their tribal dress. Shy and bright-eyed children, peering out at the camera from tent doorways.

And all the while, Willa told him stories. Stories of how she got the shot. Or what the laughing priest in the photo was like. How beautiful the mayor's wife was. And what an absolute bugger the Zar Gama Pass was.

He asked about Everest, and she told him that she was convinced the south face—in Nepal—was the easier way up, but the Nepalese were not at all amenable to Westerners messing about on their mountain. The Tibetans were slightly more welcoming. Any serious European climber would have to come into Tibet from Darjeeling and attempt the north face, if a climber were to attempt the mountain at all.

"Can you imagine it?" Seamie said. "To be the first up that mountain? The first up Everest? Everyone at the RGS wants that mountain for England."

"England's going to have to move fast, then," Willa said. "Germany and France want Everest, too. Success is going to depend on preparation, not only on technical skill. Stamina, too. You've got to set up a good base camp, and then a string of camps after that. Half the party does the setting up and provisioning with the help of sherpas. Then they come down and rest, before the altitude kills them. Then the other half goes up—the best climbers. The best and the toughest. They have to get up incredibly fast, and get down just as fast. And the weather, the wind, and the temperature all have to be on their side."

She pointed out the places on the north face that she thought would be best for the camps. Seamie listened, nodded, asked her question after question. He felt excited as he had not since his expedition with Amundsen, carried away by the very idea of climbing the world's tallest mountain. For a few brief and happy moments, they were once again as they had been in Africa, when they'd traveled together, camped together, planned their assault on Kili together. They were one.

Seamie looked at her now, as she pointed out a dark spot below a col and said she couldn't work out if it was a shadow from a passing cloud or a crevasse, and his heart ached with love for her. He craved her body, thought about making love to her all the time, but he craved this—this union of their souls—even more.

He looked away, unable to bear the intensity of his longing for her, and picked up the first photograph again. "It's so beautiful," he said.

Willa shook her head. "It's beyond beautiful, Seamie. My pictures don't do it justice. They don't begin to capture the beauty of that mountain. Oh, if only you could see it. I wish I could show it to you. I wish I could see your face as you first glimpse it. I wish—"

She stopped talking suddenly.

"What? What's wrong?" he asked her.

"We never will, though, will we? See Everest together."

He looked away. The light from the window was fading. Evening was coming down. He would have to leave now. To go to the RGS, where he was expected. And then home, where he belonged.

As if sensing what he was feeling, what he was thinking, Willa leaned her head against his. "We have to stop this," she said softly.

He laughed sadly. "I would, Willa," he said. "If only I knew how."

CHAPTER THIRTY-FIVE

"THIS WILL PROVE to be the spark in the tinderbox," Churchill said hotly. "There can be no denying it."

A chorus of voices rose in enthusiastic support.

"And we can fan the spark or douse it," Joe said, just as vehemently. "This is the twentieth century, not the tenth. We must solve our disputes in staterooms, not on battlefields."

A volley of "Hear! Hear!"s went up in response.

Joe was sitting in a private room at the Reform Club, the political headquarters of the Liberal Party. He loved the venerable old building, with its marble and its mirrors, its palazzo-like gallery and impossible crystal roof, and he usually took time to admire it when he visited, lingering in its many rooms and corridors, gazing at portraits of past Whig leaders or perusing volumes in the vast library.

Tonight, however, he was in no mood to admire the architecture.

Only hours ago, Archduke Franz Ferdinand, heir to the Austro-Hungarian throne, had been assassinated, together with his wife, in Sarajevo. The royal couple's killer was a young Serbian nationalist by the name of Gavrilo Princip.

News of the archduke's death had sent shock waves of alarm through both the Commons and the Lords. The day had been dreadful, with the government publicly promising a calm and considered response to the calamitous event, and privately scrambling to head off an international disaster. Austria-Hungary had immediately demanded justice from Serbia, and Germany was raging, promising to rush to the defense of its wronged neighbor. Sir Edward Gray, Britain's secretary for foreign and commonwealth affairs, had been quickly dispatched on a diplomatic mission of the utmost delicacy.

And now, at eleven o'clock, the prime minister had adjourned to the Reform Club with members of his cabinet and a small group of key frontbenchers from all parties to discuss further response to Austria-Hungary, Serbia, and Germany.

"Sarajevo is exactly what Germany has been looking for," Churchill thundered, "and the kaiser will use it, by God. He'll use it to march right into France and trample Belgium on the way. We must inform Germany immediately and in no uncertain terms that their interference will not be tolerated in this affair."

"Can we not wait until they tell us they wish to interfere?" Joe asked, to jeers and laughter.

Winston waited until the noise died down, then he said, "The honorable member for Whitechapel is blind. He cannot see the consequences of hesitating."

"No, I cannot," Joe shot back. "I can, however, see the consequences of rushing. I can see the consequences of hotheaded, blundering responses when patience and forbearance are required. I can see the consequences of forcing Germany's hand. I can the see the bodies of hundreds of thousands of dead Englishmen."

"Can you? I cannot. I can only see the Hun defeated. Belgium spared. The women and children of France throwing flowers at our brave lads' feet."

Joe tried to respond, but his words were drowned out by cheers and calls for God to save the King. He gave up. He recognized war fever when he saw it. He turned to Asquith, who was seated at his right, and said, "Henry, you can see what's coming, can't you? You must do all that you can to hold out against the dogs of war."

Asquith shook his head slowly. "I can control my own dogs, Joe—even that hothead Winston. What I cannot control is the pack across the channel."

"You think it's unavoidable, then?"

"I do. We will go to war. All of Europe will," he said. "It's no longer a case of if, but of when."

"I don't believe that, Henry. I can't."

Asquith sighed deeply. "Believe what you like, Joe. But be glad your sons are too young to fight and pray that it all ends quickly."

CHAPTER THIRTY-SIX

MAX STEPPED OUTSIDE of the elevator into the Coburg's sumptuous lobby. He thanked the operator, smiled at a woman waiting to enter the elevator, and made his way to the front desk. His tanned, handsome face looked smooth and untroubled.

Only because he wanted it to.

Inside, he was jittery and rattled. His nerves were frayed. Everything was going badly. Bauer, Hoffman, Maud . . . and now this new catastrophe—Sarajevo.

He had just received orders from Berlin, brought to his room hidden in a stack of freshly laundered shirts by a hotel maid on the kaiser's payroll. They wanted as much information as he could possibly get them on British ships, planes, and cannon—and what could he get them? Not a bloody thing.

The chain was still broken, and until he could forge a link between Gladys Bigelow and John Harris—Billy Madden's man—he had no way of fixing it. What had that lunatic in Sarajevo been thinking? What had he and his fellow anarchists hoped to do? Set the world on fire? If that was the goal, they might well succeed.

Lost in his thoughts, Max did not the see the woman walking toward him, her head down, until it was too late. He collided with her, knocking her hat and her purse to the ground.

"My goodness," he said, horrified. "How incredibly clumsy of me. I'm so sorry. Please let me get your things." He bent down, picked up the hat and purse, and handed them to her. "Again, please accept my . . ." He stopped talking, stunned. He took a step back, recovered himself, and said, "Willa Alden? Is that you?"

Willa looked up at him. "Max? Max von Brandt?"

"Yes!" he said excitedly. "What a pleasure it is to see you." He embraced her, then released her and looked at her, shaking his head. "I hardly recognize you in your Western outfit," he said.

Willa laughed. "I hardly recognize myself. You're looking well, Max. What are you doing in London? The last time I saw you, you were headed to Lhasa."

"Yes, I was. I got there, too. And was granted an audience with the Dalai Lama, thanks to your influence," he said. He then explained the falling out he'd had with his uncle, and that he'd come to London to get away from his family for a bit. "You look well, too, Willa," he said, when he'd finished. "What are you doing here? I didn't think anything could tempt you away from your mountain."

Willa told him about her father.

"I'm so sorry," he said, taking her hand and squeezing it.

She squeezed back. "Thank you, Max. That's very kind of you," she said. "It's still so hard for me to accept that he's gone."

They talked more, and as Max looked into her large, expressive eyes and listened to her voice, so full of life, everything he'd felt for her in the Himalayas came flooding back. His heart was full of emotion. He wanted to take her in his arms, right here in the lobby, to hold her close and tell her what he felt.

Stop it. Now. Before it goes too far, a voice inside him said. It's too dangerous. You know that. This woman, these feelings . . . they'll be the end of you.

He ignored the voice. As Willa started to say good-bye, as she told him she must be going, he pressed her to stay.

"But you haven't even told me what you're doing here," he asked her. "What brings you to the Coburg?"

"I'm . . . um . . . I'm meeting an old friend," she said. "For lunch."

She was lying; he knew she was. She suddenly seemed agitated and nervous. Max was experienced in identifying the tells that betrayed liars—the too-quick laugh, the darting eyes, the rising voice—and Willa was exhibiting all of them.

"Join me for a drink first," Max said. "You must. I insist. And your friend, too. Where is she?"

"I . . . I'm afraid I can't. I'm meeting her in her room, you see, and I'm late as it is."

"I understand," he said. "But you must give me your address, and you must allow me to take you to supper while you're in London."

Willa looked at him, her green eyes frank and appraising. "I don't know if that's such a good idea, Max," she said.

Max held his hands up, stopping her protests. "It will just be two old trekking companions catching up, that's all. I promise you, I've no ulterior motives," he said, smiling warmly.

Willa smiled back. "All right, then," she said. "Supper it is. I look forward to it."

"Tomorrow?"

"I can't tomorrow, I'm afraid. I already have plans. I'm meeting Thomas Lawrence."

"Ah, yes. The archaeologist. I've heard of him. Sounds like a fascinating chap. How about next week, then?"

They set a date—Monday—and a place—Simpson's. Then he kissed her cheek and walked her to the elevator. The smell of her, the marble smoothness of her cheek thrilled him. How did she do this to him?

"Good-bye, Willa," he said, working to keep his voice even. "Until Monday."

"Until Monday," she said, and then the elevator doors closed.

He stood there, watching the hand on the floor indicator until it stopped on five. Another elevator had just stopped next to this one. The doors opened. The occupants stepped out and Max quickly stepped in.

"Hold the door!" a man bellowed from across the lobby.

"Ignore him," Max said, handing the operator a pound note. "Get me to five. Now."

The man did as he was told, whisking Max to the fifth floor in seconds. He stepped out quietly, in case she was nearby, and the elevator doors closed silently behind him. He looked left, then right, and spotted Willa walking down a long corridor. Her back was to him. He pressed himself against the elevator doors in case she turned around. But she did not. She stopped halfway down the corridor, turned to her right, and knocked twice on a door. The door opened and she stepped inside. As soon as Max heard it close and lock behind her, he made his way down the corridor.

She had come here to be with a man. Max felt it in his bones. Why else would she have acted the way she did—so odd and skittish? Jealousy seared him. He knew it was a childish and stupid emotion, and he tried to damp it down, but he could not. He wanted her for himself and hated to think of her in the arms of another man, but at the same time, he had to know who the other man was. He reached the door that she'd entered, glanced quickly at the number, and kept on walking. To the end of the corridor and the fire stairs.

When he was back downstairs in the lobby, he collared a bellhop, a lad he'd tipped generously on many occasions. "I need you to do me a favor," he said quietly.

"Anything, Mr. von Brandt."

"Find out the name of the man in room 524. I'll be over there." He pointed to a group of plush chairs.

The bellhop nodded. A few minutes later, he was standing by Max's chair, bending to his ear. "It's a Mr. O. Ryan, sir," he said. "But I think that's a false name."

"Is it?"

"Aye. Pete, my mate, gave the bloke his key. Said he knew him instantly and he wasn't no Mr. Ryan."

"Who is he, then?"

"He's that famous explorer. The one who went to the South Pole. Finnegan's his name. Seamus Finnegan."

CHAPTER THIRTY-SEVEN

"I COULD EAT every berry in Binsey, me," Josie said, plucking another strawberry from her basket and popping it into her mouth. "Blimey, but they're good."

"If you don't stop, we'll have nothing for our tea," Jennie said, laughing. "We haven't even got ourselves outside of the village yet. Wait until we get back to the cottage before you eat any more."

They had just come from the village square, where a market was held every Monday. They'd bought strawberries freshly picked that morning, a pint of clotted cream, rich and crumbly scones, a wedge of sharp cheddar, another of Caerphilly, a loaf of brown bread, some smoked trout, and a pound of pale yellow butter.

Jennie knew she would only pick at the feast, for her stomach was upset most of the time now. Josie, on the other hand, would devour it. She had not been troubled by nausea in the least and was hungry all the time.

Jennie looked at her as they walked along. Josie was the picture of health. Her cheeks were pink and her eyes were sparkling. Her belly had already begun to pop out. Jennie, whose due date was three weeks later than Josie's, had not begun to show. She couldn't wait until she did. It would make it more real. It would show her—and Seamie, too—that the baby was healthy and growing. She had just seen Harriet Hatcher last week and was due to see her again in a few days' time. Harriet said that she'd heard a heartbeat and that so far all seemed well, but she'd still reminded Jennie of the delicate nature of her pregnancy and cautioned her against too much hope.

"What shall we do today?" Josie asked, swinging her basket. "Pick flowers? Make jam? God knows we bought enough berries. I know! Let's go to the river and dip our toes in. It's already beastly hot and it's only nine o'clock."

"The river . . . that sounds like a wonderful idea," Jennie said. It *was* hot, far too hot for June. Jennie was perspiring heavily. Her cheeks were flushed. A wade in the river would be just the thing to cool them both off. "Let's just put the marketing away, and then we'll go."

Jennie had come up from London the day before. It was her third trip to Binsey in two months. She'd told Seamie, yet again, that she needed some quiet time—time to rest and relax. He had been agreeable to the trip and had not questioned her or protested.

But then again, why would he? Her absence meant he could spend more time with Willa Alden.

Jennie didn't know where he was seeing her, or when, because he was always home at night, but she knew in her heart that he was.

He was always preoccupied now. He spent more time in his study. And even when he was in the very same room with her, he was miles away. He was still kind to her, though—solicitous of her health, concerned about the baby, anxious that she was overtaxing herself. But he didn't kiss her much anymore. Not like he used to. And at night, in their bed, he would turn out the light, roll on his side, and go right to sleep. They hadn't made love in weeks. She had tried to interest him a few times, but he had said they shouldn't. He didn't want to do anything to hurt the baby.

She thought of them together sometimes, Seamie and Willa—she couldn't help it. In her mind's eye, she saw him in bed with her, saw him kissing her and caressing her, and the images made her feel sick. There were days when she was so distraught that she vowed she would confront him. She would ask him about Willa. Ask him if they'd been together, if he was still in love with her.

But what would she do if he said, *Yes, Jennie, I am*?

And so she pretended. She pretended to him that she didn't know. Pretended to herself that she didn't care. That it didn't matter. And she hoped and prayed that one day it wouldn't. That one day soon, Willa would leave London and go back to the East. And that

Seamie would come back to her, Jennie. To their home. Their life. Their bed.

"We could go fishing," Josie said suddenly, as they passed a small sporting goods shop. "I saw fishing rods in the coat closet."

Jennie laughed, grateful for Josie's companionship, for her cheerfulness, and for the distraction Josie provided from her own dark thoughts.

"Yes, we could," she said. "If either one of us knew the first thing about fishing."

"All we would need are some worms," Josie said. "And hooks. We could get the hooks here. Right inside this shop."

"And line. I think we need some sort of fishing line. I think we need . . ." Jennie gasped suddenly, as a pain—dark and horrible—gripped her deep inside.

"Jennie? What is it?" Josie asked.

"Nothing, I . . ." She stopped talking as another cramp, stronger than the one before, shuddered through her.

She took a few more steps, and then she felt something warm and wet between her legs. It was coming out of her, seeping into her underthings. She didn't have to see it to know what it was—blood.

"Oh, no," she said, in a small, scared voice. "Please, no."

"Jennie," Josie said, her eyes large and worried. "What's wrong?"

"I think it's the baby . . . I . . . I'm bleeding," Jennie said. She started to cry.

"Come on," Josie said, taking her arm. "There's a surgery at the edge of the village. It's not far. Dr. Cobb's the man's name. I saw the shingle once. When I first got here. I made a point to remember it. Just in case something happened and I needed someone. It's not far."

"No!" Jennie said, shaking Josie off. "I'm not going to any doctor."

"Are you mad? You need help. The baby needs help."

"I won't go," Jennie said. "He can't know. Nobody can know."

"Who can't know?" Josie asked. "The doctor?"

"Seamie. My husband. He can't know," Jennie said, her voice rising. She was becoming hysterical, she couldn't help it. "If the cramps don't stop, if I keep bleeding," she said wildly, "I'll lose the baby, and him, too."

Josie looked at her with pity and understanding. "That's how it is between you, eh?" she said softly.

"Yes, that's how it is," Jennie said miserably. She didn't want to be telling Josie these things, but she couldn't seem to stop herself. "He's got someone . . . another woman. And all I've got is this baby. It's the only thing keeping him with me. I'm sure of it."

Josie nodded. "All right, luv. Calm down. Nobody's losing anybody," she said. Her voice was soothing, but her eyes were hard and determined. "We won't tell Seamie about this, right? Because they'll be nothing to tell. But we are going to see Dr. Cobb now. If you want those cramps to stop, we've got to see him. We'll just nip in, you and I. He'll check you over and give you something, and half an hour from now, you'll be right as rain again. Here we go now, you and me . . . just a few more steps . . . come on now, duck."

Josie took her arm once more and Jennie started walking again, desperately hoping that her friend was right, that there was something Dr. Cobb could do to stop the bleeding and the pain, but then another cramp gripped her.

"Oh, God," she sobbed. "It's no use, Josie. I'm going to lose this baby."

"Now, you listen to me," Josie said fiercely. "I'll sort it for you, Jennie, don't you worry. I'll take care of you. I'll take care of everything."

"How, Josie?" Jennie sobbed. "How? You can't! No one can!"

"Oh, but I can. You'd have to be a right git to have spent as much time around villains as I have and not pick up a trick or two," she said.

"I . . . I don't understand," Jennie said.

"You don't have to. All you have to do is remember something when we get to Dr. Cobb's. Just one small thing. Can you do that for me, Jennie? Jennie, luv, can you do that?"

"Yes," Jennie said. "What is it?"

"That my name is Jennie Finnegan," Josie said. "And that yours is Josie. Josie Meadows."

CHAPTER THIRTY-EIGHT

"HARRIET, MY DEAR," Max said, as he entered her office.

"My, goodness, Max. Is it noon already?" Harriet Hatcher asked, looking up from a patient's file. She closed the file. Her expression was troubled. "Sit down, won't you? Just clear the things off that chair."

Max did so, shifting a copy of the *Battle Cry* and a VOTES FOR WOMEN banner from the chair to a credenza. "How goes the struggle?" he asked.

"Well, and not so well," Harriet said. "You heard about the by-election in Cumbria, I'm sure. Labour won a seat that had long been held by the Liberals. So there's another MP sympathetic to our cause, which is wonderful, of course. . . ."

"But . . ." Max prompted.

"There's always a but, isn't there?" Harriet said wryly. "In this case, the but is the sudden bout of war fever that's gripped government. We in the movement fear that the push for women's suffrage will take a backseat to military concerns."

"Even if it does," Max said, "you must keep fighting."

Harriet nodded, a determined smile on her face now. "Oh, we will. Millicent Fawcett is like a glacier—slow but implacable. There is no stopping her. She will not give up and neither will the rest of us."

"Then you must be well fortified for the fight," Max said. "Where shall we dine tonight? I was thinking of the Eastern."

"It's a bit far and I don't have long today. I've lots of appointments to get through this afternoon. What about something closer? There's a nice pub only a street away."

Max feigned interest in her suggestions, pretending he was game for anything, but really, the very last thing he wanted to be doing right now was swanning off to lunch.

A war of words was heating up between Austria-Hungary and Serbia. The kaiser had signaled his readiness to jump into the fray. Berlin was waiting on Max for crucial information, and yet he could get nothing to them, for he still could not come up with a way to get the documents from Gladys Bigelow to the North Sea.

He had risked one meeting with her, on her bus, to tell her to keep bringing carbons out of Burgess's office, but to hold them in her home for now, until she received further instructions. There were times when he'd felt so desperate, he'd nearly decided to put on his old disguise, the one he'd used to seduce Gladys, and get the papers from her himself. But he knew that would be foolish. He must not be seen in those clothes anywhere near Duffin's again.

Max knew he had to be patient, as hard as that was. He had always dined with Harriet on Thursdays, and so he must continue to dine with Harriet on Thursdays. He must appear to be as predictable as the English rain after the disaster with Bauer and Hoffman, and the one with Maud, in case he was now being watched.

"And there's always the Moskowitzes' cafe, of course," Harriet said. "What do you think of that? Max? Max?"

"I think it's a fine idea," he said quickly, hoping she hadn't noticed that he'd been miles away.

"Good," Harriet said. She closed the file she'd been reading and put it on top of a stack of folders on her desk. He glanced at the name on the file—Jennie Finnegan. "Suzanne!" she called out.

A few seconds later, Harriet's receptionist stuck her head in. Harriet handed her the stack of folders. "After you go to lunch, could you file these, please?" she asked. "But don't file the three on top—Mrs. Finnegan's, Mrs. Erikson's, and Mrs. O'Rourke's. Put those in my briefcase. They're all coming in for appointments tomorrow, and I want to study my notes at home tonight." Suzanne nodded, took the stack of folders, and returned to her office.

Max had seen the slight frown on Harriet's face as she'd read Jennie Finnegan's file. Her reaction piqued his interest, accustomed as he was to reading people's facial cues. Something in Jennie Finnegan's file was especially bothering her. He remembered seeing Willa at the Coburg—how could he forget?—and discovering that it was Seamus Finnegan—Jennie's husband—whom she'd gone there to see. He wondered what it was that was troubling Harriet about Jennie, and he wondered if it had any connection to what was going on at the Coburg. He decided to press Harriet, ever so subtly, to see if he could find out more. Other people's private matters often proved useful.

"Mrs. Finnegan . . . ," he said now. "Would that be the former Jennie Wilcott? I haven't seen her, or her husband, since their wedding. What a lovely bride she was. What a perfect day that was. Blue skies. Flowers. All of us together. Who would think that only weeks later . . ." He let his voice trail off, swallowed hard, then picked up a wooden rattle that was lying on Harriet's desk and fiddled with it.

Harriet reached across her desk and covered his hand with her own. "It's not your fault, Max. You know that. Everyone knows that."

He nodded, then said, "We should talk of happier things." He held up the rattle, shook it, and smiled. "Like babies. What could be happier than a baby? Jennie and her husband must be very excited to have a little one due soon. How is she? Is she well?"

"As far as I know, yes," Harriet said, a bit distractedly.

What an odd answer, Max thought, but he decided to push it no further. He knew Harriet was a stickler for doctor-patient confidentiality. He didn't want to make her uncomfortable. Or suspicious.

"Perhaps we should get going," he said. "Before Moskowitzes' gets crowded."

"Yes, I think we should. Let's have a glass of wine while we're there, Max, shall we? Let's forget about struggles and sadnesses for an hour. Excuse me for a moment. I'm just going to go freshen up," Harriet said, disappearing down the hall.

As soon as he heard the door to the loo open and close, Max rushed out of Harriet's office and into her receptionist's, hoping that the woman had already gone to lunch. Luckily, she had—and she'd left all the folders Harriet had given her on her desk. Jennie Finnegan's was on top. Max flipped it open and began to read its contents.

He learned that Jennie Wilcott Finnegan's due date was a bit less than eight months after her wedding. Eight, not the usual nine. Furthermore, he learned that she had been horribly injured in an accident as a child, an accident that had damaged several of her organs, including her uterus. There were diagrams of Jennie's scars, sketches of what looked to him like a misshapen womb. There was a note that Jennie was taking time to rest quietly at her cottage in Binsey, Oxfordshire.

And finally, Max learned that his cousin, Dr. Harriet Hatcher, did not expect Jennie's due date to be reached. She had written in her notes that she did not believe the pregnancy would advance to full-term and that she had counseled Jennie on this very concern, telling her that she should prepare herself for the very real possibility of a miscarriage.

As Max put the folder back exactly as he'd found it and hurried back into Harriet's office, he found himself feeling newly optimistic.

He'd learned so many valuable things in the past few days—and they all centered on Jennie Finnegan, the Reverend Wilcott's daughter. He'd learned that she was pregnant before she was married, that she would likely never have the child she was carrying, and that her husband was making secret trips to the Coburg, where he was meeting Willa Alden. It was true—people's private matters *did* prove useful.

"Are you ready?" Harriet asked, as she walked back into her office.

"I am," he said, rising from the chair.

He helped Harriet into her coat—a linen duster—and complimented her on her hat, a pretty straw affair trimmed with silk flowers. When they got outside, they discovered that it had started to drizzle. Max quickly put his umbrella up and took Harriet's arm.

"Of course," she sighed. "How perfect. Dreary skies to match our dreary moods. I think we should cheer up, Max. What do you say? I think we should endeavor to enjoy our afternoon despite the gray clouds."

"Ah, my dear, Harriet," Max said, smiling, "I'm enjoying it already."

CHAPTER THIRTY-NINE

JOSIE PUT ANOTHER shovelful of coal on the fire. The summer evening had turned cool. She stoked the flames until they were burning brightly, leaned the shovel against the wall, and turned to look at her friend.

Jennie was sitting in a nearby chair. Her eyes were open, but dull. Her face was gray. She had stopped weeping—that was something—but now she just sat lifelessly, staring into the fire, not speaking.

The little life inside her had died this morning. And it seemed to Josie as if Jennie had died along with it. She was wrung out. Empty. A shell. There was no spark left in her.

It hurt Josie terribly to see her this way. Jennie had been like a second mother to her. She'd made sure Josie had learned how to read and write. She'd coached her on how to speak properly. At least, she'd tried to. She'd encouraged her love of music and singing. When Josie's father drank his wages, leaving nothing for food, Jennie had fed her. When he came home from the pub and started hammering on Josie's mother, and Josie ran away because she could not bear it, Jennie had taken her in and let her sleep in her bed.

Jennie was the only reason Josie was on stage. She'd saved her, years ago, from a life of drudgery in the factories of Wapping or Whitechapel, and she'd saved her again, just a few weeks ago, when Madden had put her up the pole. There wasn't anything Josie wouldn't do for Jennie—if only Jennie would let her.

Josie took a deep breath now and pulled a wooden chair over to where Jennie was sitting. She sat down in it, so close to Jennie that their knees were touching, then she took Jennie's hands in hers and said, "We can do this. I know we can. The two of us together."

Jennie shook her head. "It'll never work," she said.

"Yes, it will. If we want it to. If *you* want it to."

Jennie said nothing, but her eyes flickered from the fire to Josie's face and back to the fire again. Josie took this as a hopeful sign.

She'd hatched a plan—a plan that was clever and perfect. She'd thought it up as she was rushing Jennie into Dr. Cobb's, and then she'd refined it that afternoon, after she'd got Jennie home from the doctor's and into bed. She'd made herself a pot of tea, sat down at the kitchen table, and thought the whole thing through once more, carefully and slowly, testing it for flaws, just as she'd seen Madden and his men do when they were planning some new piece of villainy.

Only this wasn't villainy. This plan wouldn't hurt anyone. It would only help.

Jennie, out of her mind with both grief and laudanum, had told Josie everything after they'd come home from Dr. Cobb's. She told her about the accident and how it meant she couldn't have children. She told her about meeting Seamus Finnegan and falling in love with him and marrying him without having told him the truth about herself. And she told her about Willa Alden.

Josie knew her plan would solve both Jennie's problems and her own, but she hadn't been able to convince Jennie of that. She'd tried to explain it to her earlier, but Jennie, distraught and inconsolable, refused to listen, telling her it was impossible. Josie decided now to try one more time.

"The hardest bit's already taken care of, the rest will be a doddle," she said. "Dr. Cobb thinks you're Josie Meadows and I'm Jennie

Finnegan. He's written it all down and has his notes all safely tucked away in a file."

Josie had done all the talking at Dr. Cobb's. She'd told him that her friend Mrs. Meadows was visiting her at her cottage for the week and had started experiencing terrible pains.

It hadn't taken Dr. Cobb long to confirm Jennie's greatest fear—that she was indeed miscarrying her baby. He did only a cursory exam, gave her laudanum, and told her to expect cramping and bleeding for the next few hours, as her uterus expelled its contents. He told her that this was an unfortunate occurrence, but not an uncommon one, and that she would surely conceive again within the year.

"All we have to do now is go on exactly as we have been," Josie said to her.

"How, Josie? I lost the baby. Even if I don't tell a soul, everyone will know. My belly won't be growing," Jennie said.

"Yes, it will. Because you'll stuff a pillow under your skirt."

Jennie shook her head. "Josie, it's impossible. It won't work," she said.

"No, listen to me! It *will* work. We do it all the time at the music hall. For a gag. A girl goes off stage left, hand in hand with some rake, then comes back stage right crying and carrying on with a big fat belly. You start with a small pillow and change it for bigger ones as the weeks go by. I'll show you how to do it. The only tricky part will be your husband. If he wants relations, I mean. You'll have to put him off. Say you're poorly and it's bad for the baby. Doctor's orders."

"That won't be a problem at all," Jennie said bitterly. "My husband doesn't want relations. Not with me, at least."

"All right, then. So that part won't be hard. You keep the act going for a few months, and you come here when you need to take a break from it. In a few months, my baby comes. Dr. Cobb delivers it and writes out a birth certificate for baby Finnegan. Just make sure to figure out a name well in advance, right? I'll get word to you when the baby arrives. You come to Binsey immediately. You don't write home for a day or two, then you ring your husband from the pub, tell him what's happened—that you stumbled and fell, and your pains came on, and the baby came a little earlier than expected. He'll probably throw a wobbly and say that he wants to come to Binsey straightaway to collect you, but you tell him that the baby came easily and that you feel fine, and that you've engaged a girl from the village to travel to London with you and help you with your bags."

"A girl from the village? What girl?" Jennie asked.

"Me, of course," Josie said. "I'll get some sort of frumpy farm girl outfit together, put on a bonnet, and ride to London with you. I've never met your husband, so he won't know who I really am. There's always a chance he saw the *Zema* posters, but I had a wig on in those and not much else. I'm sure he wouldn't recognize me. Before you ring off, you tell him what time the train's arriving at Paddington and ask him to collect you. He does. I say hello and good-bye, then pretend I'm getting on a return train to Binsey, get on a train to the coast instead, and then on the ferry to Calais."

Josie paused to let her words sink in, then she said, "When your husband sees his baby, the baby he wanted so much, he'll be happy, and maybe he'll remember his wedding vows. And then you've got your child and your husband. And I escape to Paris, far away from Billy Madden, knowing my child won't grow up in some horrible orphanage, that she will grow up with the best woman in the world for a mother."

"Do you really think it could work?" Jennie said, her voice a whisper.

"I do."

"What if the baby looks nothing like me? Or Seamie?"

"We're both blond, you and I," Josie said. "And we both have hazel eyes. So if the baby looks like me, she'll look like you, too."

"It's ever so risky. So much could go wrong," Jennie said.

"No, luv," Josie said. "So much could go right."

Jennie looked Josie in the eye then, and for the first time since they left the market, Josie saw a spark there—faint and struggling, but a spark nonetheless. “Well?” she said hopefully, squeezing her friend’s hands.

Jennie nodded, and squeezed back.

CHAPTER FORTY

“GOOD NIGHT, MR. Bristow. Safe trip home,” Sir David Erskine, sergeant at arms for the House of Commons, said to Joe.

“Good night to you as well, Sergeant,” Joe said, as he wheeled himself down St. Stephen’s Hall, out the door, and toward Cromwell Green.

Outside, the air was soft and warm and the sky twinkled with a million stars. It was a beautiful summer night—a night to make anyone feel glad to be alive. But Joe didn’t even notice it. He’d just come from another late session in the Commons. Earlier that day, Austria-Hungary had declared war on Serbia. Fearing the worst—Germany’s imminent involvement—a wary Britain was now in constant contact with France and Russia, its Triple Entente allies, trying to determine a plan of containment should the kaiser actually declare war. Fortunately, the *Entente* had been put in place long before Franz Ferdinand’s assassination.

France, who’d suffered a bruising defeat in the Franco-Prussian War of 1870 and had seen her territories of Alsace-Lorraine annexed to Germany, had aligned with Russia at the end of the last century, both countries finding common ground in their shared mistrust of the kaiser. Russia was especially concerned about Germany’s warm relationship with Turkey. The tsar feared that if Germany gained a foothold in Turkey, the kaiser would try to take control of the Dardanelles and Bosporus straits—waterways that connected the Mediterranean to the Black Sea and which were crucial to Russia' s ability to trade with the rest of the world.

Britain—already aligned with France as the result of the Entente Cordiale, a treaty signed in 1904 after both countries had settled their skirmishes over colonial territories in Africa—saw an alliance with Russia as also advantageous, and so the Anglo-Russian Entente had been signed in 1907. Britain had pledged to come to the defense of both France and Russia should they be threatened by Germany, and they had pledged the same for her.

In addition to strategizing with his country's allies, the prime minister had also approached Britain's own Field Marshal Horatio Kitchener—a soldier and statesman who'd distinguished himself on several major battlefields—and asked him to become secretary of state for war.

Joe had spoken with Kitchener and had learned that, unlike many of Asquith's advisors, the field marshal did not expect a war with Germany to be quickly fought and won. On the contrary, he had made the dire and unpopular prediction that such a war would last at least three years and would result in enormous casualties—a prediction that gave Joe renewed energy with which to argue against the warmongers in the Commons.

But his arguments were all to no avail. Joe could see that. Everyone could. Kitchener himself had come up to Joe in the Commons dining room, after he had spent the day giving a speech in the House and listening to many more. "Save your breath, old chap," he'd counseled Joe. "It doesn't matter what I say. It wouldn't matter what God said, had He the patience to sit in the Commons and endure Churchill's endless harangues. They will have their war."

It would be soon, Kitchener felt. Perhaps as soon as the coming autumn.

Weary and dispirited now, Joe wheeled himself across Cromwell Green to the line of carriages waiting just past it on the street. He saw his carriage in the queue and knew that Tom, his driver, would be nearby—fetching water for the horses or talking to one of the other drivers. As Joe drew up to his carriage, he saw a flower girl walking up and down the queue, trying to sell bouquets of roses. She was having little luck.

Joe stopped to watch her. He watched as people walked by her, deaf to her entreaties, blind to the holes in her shoes and the hollows in her cheeks. And he felt as if his heart was breaking. For he knew that while this child—she couldn't have been more than ten years old—walked the dark streets of London, desperately trying to make a few bob, men who had been raised in great homes and palaces, who had all the privileges wealth and power conferred, swept their make-believe armies across maps of the world. While she shivered and pulled her threadbare shawl around her thin shoulders, they poured more port into their crystal glasses and lit cigars.

They thought of borders broken and territories taken, these men. They thought of victories won and of medals gleaming, but they did not think—not once—of the struggle this child endured, every day, to simply survive. And they did not think to wonder what would become of this child and of every child like her, poor children in every town and every village in Britain and Europe, if they lost their fathers to bullets, their houses to cannons, their fields and animals to the pillaging of foreign invaders.

It was this child I fought for, Joe said to himself. And it's this child I've failed.

He wanted to go to her now. He wanted to tell her that he'd tried. But she would think him mad if he did that. So instead he wheeled himself over to her and told her that he wanted to buy all her flowers, everything she had.

"What? All of them?" she asked, stunned.

"Yes," Joe said. He turned to Tom, who had joined him now. "Tom, could you put these in the carriage, please?"

"Right away, sir," Tom replied, picking up the child's heavy basket.

Joe gave the child more than the price of the flowers. "You keep the extra for yourself," he said.

"Thank you, sir! Oh, thank you!"

"You're welcome," Joe replied.

Tom gave the child her basket back, and Joe watched as she hurried off, her money still clutched in her hand.

"That was good of you, sir. To help that child," Tom said.

"I didn't help her, Tom," Joe said. "A year from now, she'll likely be worse off than she is. With her father at the front. Her brothers, too, if she has any. Men earn a lot more than women do. It'll be her and her mum and her sisters, all shifting for themselves on factory wages and what they can make selling flowers. Poor little thing should be in school, learning how to read and write. Not out on the streets at all hours."

"Can't fix the entire world, sir. Not even you. Not tonight, leastways," Tom said.

Joe watched the child as she turned the corner and disappeared into the night. "Ah, Tom," he said, shaking his head. "Why did I tell her 'You're welcome'? When I should've told her 'I'm sorry.' "

CHAPTER FORTY-ONE

MAX VON BRANDT loved churches.

Churches were quiet and peaceful. Sometimes they had magnificent works of art to look at or wonderful choirs to listen to. But what he loved best about churches was that they were full of good people and good people were so easily used.

He opened the door of St. Nicholas's, in Wapping, removed his hat, and went inside. He moved quietly through the foyer into the nave. The church was empty, except for one person—a young blond woman. Gladys Bigelow had told him the woman would be here, that she cleaned the altar and brought fresh flowers for it every Wednesday.

She wasn't cleaning now, though. She was kneeling in a church pew near a statue of the Virgin Mary, her blond head bent, praying. He could see her belly, looking rounder. How interesting. It had not looked that way last week, when he'd seen her hanging out the washing at the back of her cottage at Binsey.

Max had decided to take a look around the village after learning from notes Harriet had written in her file that Jennie was staying there. He'd had to stay out of sight for most of the time he was there—skulking in the woods behind the cottage during the day, listening at the window at night, cooling his heels in his room at the pub—but even so, it had been such a productive trip. He'd discovered so much.

As he stood patiently now, waiting for Jennie to finish her prayers, he heard a sob escape her. And then another. She was weeping. Max was certain he knew why. He was certain, too, that her tears—and the reason behind them—would make his present task easier.

My God, he thought watching her, what havoc love wreaks. What damage it does. And had done. To Gladys Bigelow. Maud. Jennie. To Seamie. And Willa. And to him.

Even he had not escaped love's destruction, try as he might. He'd had his dinner with Willa. She had been friendly and lovely, but that was all, for she was in love with another man. And he? He had sat next to her for two hours, tortured the whole time by his feelings for her—feelings he knew she did not return. Afterward, he had made a vow, again, never to be so dangerously moved by his emotions.

He walked up the aisle to where Jennie was seated. "Mrs. Finnegan?" he said, gently touching her arm.

Jennie quickly sat up and wiped her eyes. "Mr. von Brandt . . . this . . . this is very unexpected," she stammered.

"Forgive me, Mrs. Finnegan, I didn't mean to disturb you. I tried the rectory first, but no one was there," Max said. He paused, then hesitatingly continued, "It grieves me to see you so upset. If I may be so bold . . . what is troubling you? Tell me. Perhaps I can be of help."

"Nothing. Nothing at all, really," Jennie said, trying hard to smile.

"It's my condition, I'm afraid. It makes me rather prone to moods and tears."

Max looked down at his hat. He fingered its brim, then said, "I don't believe you, Mrs. Finnegan." He looked up again and said, "Is it Willa Alden?"

Jennie paled. She looked as if she wanted to be sick. "Willa?" she said, working to keep her voice even. "No. Of course not. Why do you ask?"

Max affected a flustered look. "No reason," he said. "I misspoke. Please forgive me."

But Jennie pressed him, as he'd known she would, until finally, with feigned reluctance, he said, "I thought you knew. I shouldn't have said anything. It's just that I was so certain that's why you were crying."

"Mr. von Brandt . . . please," Jennie said, her voice strained. She made room for him in the pew, and he sat down next to her. "What do you know about Willa Alden?"

"I know that Willa and your husband are having an affair," Max said. Jennie said nothing. It was very quiet inside the church. Max could hear horses clopping past the open window, hear their traces jingling and their driver shouting at someone to get out of his way. "I'm sorry," he said.

Jennie nodded. She sat back in the pew. Then she put her head in her hands and wept again. Max patted her hand. He waited until she composed herself, then he said, "I'm sure that I can help you."

"How?" Jennie asked miserably.

"I'm acquainted with Miss Alden. I may be able to prevail upon her to stop seeing your husband."

Jennie laughed unhappily. "But will my husband stop seeing her?" she said.

"I will convince her to leave London."

"She might not wish to."

"I think she will."

He knew she would. He'd met Willa's brother at Jennie and Seamie's wedding. Albie was still in London. Max would contrive to meet him, seemingly by chance, and make sure to mention that he'd bumped into both his sister and his good friend Seamus at the Coburg recently.

Jennie looked at Max with anguished eyes now. "If you could do that, Mr. von Brandt, if you could get Willa to leave London, I would be forever in your debt." She wiped her eyes again, and then, as if remembering herself, she said, "I'm certain you did not come here today with the intention of discussing my marital problems."

Max smiled. "No, I didn't actually. I came here to ask for your help."

Jennie looked surprised. "I cannot imagine how I could be of help to you, Mr. von Brandt."

"It's very simple," he said. "I need you to help me pass along some information. Some rather crucial information. If you decide to help me, every fortnight Gladys Bigelow will give you an envelope containing documents. She will do this at your women's suffrage meetings. You would bring them here to the church during your Wednesday visits. You would go into the church, just as you always do, then go down to the basement. There's a statue of St. Nicholas down there. It's broken. All you would have to do is put the envelope inside the statue's head."

Jennie's expression changed from one of surprise to one of anger. "Do you take me for a fool, Mr. von Brandt?" she said.

"I do not," Max said.

"I know where Gladys works," Jennie said. "And for whom she works. What will be in those envelopes? Secrets? Information for your government?"

Max had anticipated this question and was prepared for it.

"Forgeries will be in those envelopes, Mrs. Finnegan," he said earnestly. "Fake travel papers, fake histories. Fake work contracts. Fake lives. They are to be delivered to dissidents in Germany—high-ranking professors, scientists, and ministers—pacifists all. Men who have been vocal critics of Germany's militarization. We are trying to help them and their families get out. Now. Before it's too late. We've already lost some. A physicist, a professor at one of our universities, tried to leave the country two days ago. His papers were confiscated. No one has heard from him or seen him since. Two ministers were jailed last week for speaking out against war. We are doing our best to get to them quickly, but sometimes we are not quick enough."

"Who is 'we'?"

"Britain's Secret Service. I am a spy, Mrs. Finnegan. A double agent. The kaiser thinks I am working for Germany. I am not. I am working against her. Germany is trying to start a war. An unjust war. I am doing all I can to stop it."

Jennie looked as if she was wavering, just a little. "And Gladys . . . is she a willing participant in this?" she asked.

"She is," Max replied. "But you must never discuss it with her. You must simply accept the envelope she gives you, put it in your own bag, and then bring it to St. Nicholas's basement. Everyone is watched. Gladys, too."

"But why me?" Jennie asks. "Why couldn't you get someone else?"

"Because you had the misfortune to be perfectly placed."

"I don't understand."

"We needed a friend of Gladys Bigelow's, someone whom Gladys sees regularly and has for years. If Gladys suddenly changed her daily patterns—if she suddenly started meeting a new person and traveling to a new place to do so—it would raise suspicions."

"Whose suspicions?"

"My fellow spies. Both British and German. There are double-agents everywhere. There are British agents who are feeding secrets to Germany as we speak. For money. If they figure out what Gladys is doing, the people we're trying to help are lost."

"Surely Gladys has other friends besides me," Jennie says.

"Yes, of course, but none with ties to this church. There is a network of tunnels under Wapping, Mrs. Finnegan. And under St. Nicholas's. Our man will be using them to move the documents. So you see, you are the critical link. Of course you must say nothing of this to anyone. Not your husband. Your father. No one. The more people who know about this, the more dangerous it becomes for all involved."

"I cannot do it, Mr. von Brandt. I cannot keep secrets from my husband," Jennie said resolutely, shaking her head.

Max had thought that perhaps he had her, but no, he'd lost her. No matter, he would get her back. He'd hoped it wouldn't come to this, but it had.

"I understand your reservations, Mrs. Finnegan," he said. He was no longer feigning earnestness, concern, or anything else. His voice was quiet now and deadly serious. "Let us discuss it with your husband, then. Perhaps he would like to join us—all of us—you, myself, and Miss Meadows, in that lovely cottage of yours in Binsey. I took the train there last week. What a beautiful little village. I stayed at the King's Head."

Jennie's eyes widened. Her hand came up to her mouth. "No," she said. "Stop. Please, stop."

But Max didn't stop. "Of course, if we were to do that," he said, "we might have to explain more than my request, mightn't we? We might have to explain Miss Meadows's presence at your cottage. We might also have to explain the contents of your file—the one I read a few weeks ago in Harriet Hatcher's office while Harriet was in the loo. And we might have to explain what, exactly, you have up under your skirts. I don't think it's a baby, is it, Mrs. Finnegan? Not anymore. At least, that's what Mrs. Cobb, Dr. Cobb's wife, said to Mrs. Kerrigan, the publican's wife, as Mrs. Kerrigan was doing her washing last week. I'm sure they thought no one could hear them, but my window faced the yard. Of course, Mrs. Cobb thinks it was Josie Meadows who lost her baby. Which, I must say, was an exceedingly clever idea. Tell me, was it yours? Or Josie's?"

"My God," Jennie said, a look of horror on her face. "You are a monster. A *monster*."

"Your husband will be leaving the RGS in about a half hour's time, I believe. I shall ask you one more time, Mrs. Finnegan . . . will you help me? Or do I tell him what's been going on at Binsey?"

Jennie looked at the altar, at the statue of Christ on the crucifix. Then she looked at her hand, the one with her wedding ring on it.

"I will help you," she said. "And God help me."

"Thank you, Mrs. Finnegan. Regarding the other matter we discussed, I shall do all that I can. Immediately. Good day."

"Good day, Mr. von Brandt," Jennie said woodenly.

Max moved quickly once he was outside of the church. He headed west, toward the Katharine Docks, where he hoped to hire a hackney cab. He did not want to be seen and recognized in Wapping.

He thought of Sarajevo as he walked. Of the kaiser's determination to go to war. Of the armaments on both sides. War was coming, of this he was certain. He had seen war, and what it did, and he wanted a quick and decisive battle, with as few lives lost as possible.

He thought of all the young German men ready and willing to fight, and of all the young men in England and France and Russia and Austria ready to do the same. They had no idea what they were in for. Young men never did. They thought it was all a great adventure. Which made it that much easier for old men to send them to the slaughter.

By the time Max found a cab, he felt good—better than he'd felt in many weeks. He'd finally been able to reestablish the chain of communication to Berlin, and not before time. Berlin was getting restive. They were doubting him, and that was not good.

Thank God for good people, Max thought again, as he climbed into the cab and shut the door behind him. Good people were loving and kind and charitable. They had the best intentions. Like Jennie Finnegan. She only wanted to save her marriage, to give her husband a child so that he might love her. Max closed his eyes. He leaned back in his seat and sighed. How very odd, he thought, that it's always people's best intentions, not their worst, that bury them.

CHAPTER FORTY-TWO

"MADAM, I BELIEVE—"

Mr. Foster didn't get to finish his sentence. Fiona was already out of her chair, out of the drawing room, and racing down the hallway to the foyer of her home.

The front door was open. The driver and the under-butler were carrying bags. Miss Simon, the governess, was corralling the excited children. In the midst of it all stood a weary-looking blond woman holding a small boy by the hand and a baby in her arms. A willowy, beautiful girl, blond with huge gray eyes, stood next to her.

Wordlessly, Fiona ran to them. She threw one arm around the woman's neck, enfolding her and the baby. With her other arm, she gathered the girl and the little boy into her embrace. The blond woman hugged her back. Fiona could feel her tense, hitching breaths, and knew that she was trying hard not to cry. Tears ran down Fiona's own cheeks.

"Oh, India," she said, releasing her. "I'm so happy to see you. Thank God you and the children made it here safely."

India Baxter nodded. She tried to speak, but burst into tears. "I'm so sorry, Fiona. I promised myself I wouldn't cry about Maud anymore. Not in front of the children," she said.

India's small son looked at his mother, saw that she was crying, and promptly burst into tears, too. The baby, tired and flushed, followed suit.

"I'm sure he's wet," India said tiredly. "And hungry. I'll just go change him and then—"

"No, India, you must sit down. Miss Simon, where's Pillowy?" Fiona asked.

"Right here, ma'am!" a large voice boomed.

It was the children's nurse. Her real name was Mrs. Pillower, but when Katie was tiny, she had christened her Pillowy because she was large, soft, and comforting.

"I've just drawn baths—one for Miss Charlotte and another for Mrs. Baxter's wee ones," she said. "I'll get them washed and dressed in fresh clothes, and then we'll pop down to the kitchen for a nice meal."

"Come on, Charlotte," Katie said, taking her cousin's hand. The two girls were almost the same age. "You're sleeping in my room. I'll show you where it is, and then you can have your bath."

Charlotte followed her cousin, and Mrs. Pillower offered her hand to six-year-old Wish, but he shook his head.

"I don't want a bath and I'm not hungry," he said, hiding behind his mother's skirts.

Mrs. Pillower put her hands on her large hips and shook her head sadly. "You aren't? What a pity! Cook's just made the loveliest berry pudding and a big dish of whipped cream to go with it. I suppose I shall have to eat it all myself now."

"No, Pillowy! Don't!" Patrick, one of Fiona's twin boys, said. "We want some!"

"And I would love to let you have some, my ducks, but I can't, you see. I've got to get Master Aloysius here bathed, and I can't very well let you two loose in the kitchen on your own. Cook will have my head."

"Oh, come on, Wish!" Patrick said. "Just get your bath, will you? It'll only take a minute and then we can all have pudding!"

"Pudding! Pudding! We want pudding!" Michael, the other twin, started chanting.

"Pudding," Wish said solemnly, taking a tentative step out from behind his mother. "Pudding!" he said again, with more conviction.

"That's the spirit, old son," Mrs. Pillower said. "Now, tell me, do you like a little demerara sugar sprinkled on top of your cream? I do. Gives it a bit of crunch. Sometimes I like to put a few fresh raspberries on top, too."

"I like raspberries," Wish said shyly.

"Course you do! Who doesn't? Nutters, that's who." Mrs. Pillower paused and affected a worried look, as if she'd just thought of something disturbing. "You're not a nutter, are you?" she asked Wish.

The little boy giggled. He quickly shook his head no.

"Didn't think so," Mrs. Pillower said. "But it pays to ask. You can't be too careful these days." She gently took Elizabeth from India's arms, and when she started to fuss, Mrs. Pillower produced a rattle from her pocket, which made the baby smile again. "Oh, you're damp as a mop, you," Mrs. Pillower said. Then she turned to India and added, "I'll have them back in an hour, washed, fed, and good as new."

India smiled. "Thank you, Mrs. Pillower," she said. "I'm very grateful to you."

As Mrs. Pillower disappeared upstairs with Wish and Elizabeth, the twins and Charlotte following her, Fiona led India into the drawing room, where a pot of tea and a tray of scones, cakes, and biscuits had been thoughtfully set out.

"Mr. Foster, no doubt," India said when she saw it. "How is he?"

"Well," Fiona said. "Getting on a bit, as we all are. The under butler's doing more of the heavy work, but Mr. Foster is still captain of the ship. Thank God. It would be utter chaos without him."

The two women sat down on a settee. India rested her head against the back of it as Fiona poured the tea. She handed India a cup. "This will knit body and soul back together," she said. "Sarah, the maid, is unpacking your things. After you've rested a bit, I'll have her draw you a bath."

"Thank you," India said. "It's so good to finally be here, Fiona. There were days when I thought we'd never make it. Two weeks to get from California to New York," she said. "And then three more on the ship from New York to Southampton. I don't ever want to see a train, a boat, or a hackney cab again. At least not until the children are grown. I had no idea Wish would be seasick. Charlotte isn't. I think it's because she's constantly out with Sid on his boat."

"How is my brother?" Fiona asked.

India smiled. "Happy and well. Delivering a calf one minute, off to meet the fishing boats to collect our supper the next. I've never seen anyone take to a new life so quickly. It's as if he'd been born at Point Reyes. We all miss him, of course. It's been weeks and weeks since we've seen him, and it'll be months before we return home."

"I wish he could have come," Fiona said.

"He wishes it, too. We all do," India said. "But it's not safe for him in London, given his past."

Fiona nodded. Her brother had spent many years in London's underworld, as one of the East End's leading crime bosses. Many of the people he'd known were dead, but many were still alive—and possessed of long memories.

She looked at India, who was too thin and too pale, and had dark smudges under her eyes, and said, "And how are you?"

India shook her head. "I don't know, Fiona. I'm heartbroken, of course. But I think I'm mostly still in shock, really. Maud died nearly six weeks ago now, and yet I still cannot get her death through my head. It makes no sense to me. Suicide, of all things. That's something I'd never thought she'd do in a million years. Not Maud."

"But if she was addicted to morphine, perhaps she was not in her right mind," Fiona said.

"That makes no sense, either," India said. "She used to smoke opium, quite frequently, but she'd stopped. For the most part. I think she still indulged in the odd doctored-up cigarette, but that was all."

"Perhaps she'd started again," Fiona said gently. "Max von Brandt—the man she was seeing at the time of her death—seemed to think that she had."

"That must be it, then," India said. "She must've started taking drugs, and more heavily than she ever had before. There's no other way her death can be explained. I can't imagine Maud killing herself over anything, least of all a man, if she was in her right mind."

India drained her teacup. Fiona poured her more.

"She left everything to me," India said. "The London flat, the Oxford estate. I'll have to sell them both, and most of her things. And I can't bear to even think about it. The thought of going into her house, and her not being there, is too painful."

"No, don't think about it right now," Fiona said. "I've already engaged an estate lawyer to help you. You can meet him in a few days, after you've rested and recovered from your journey. I'll help you with Maud's belongings, too. I'll go with you, if you like, to sort through them."

"Would you?" India said. "I feel like it's too much to ask of you. I've already descended upon you with the children, when I should probably just have gone to Maud's house. You have enough on your plate without us moving in."

"Don't be silly, and don't you dare say another word about going to Maud's house. Joe and I want you here, and so do the children. They were wild with excitement when they heard you were coming."

India looked down at her teacup. "I think I'll go to her grave site first, before anything else," she said.

"I'll go with you. We'll take the train," Fiona said. Maud had been buried in Oxford. In a small churchyard on her estate.

India looked at her, her eyes suddenly fierce and full of tears. "And I'm going to the police, too," she said. "I'm going to look at the coroner's pictures. I want to see her for myself. See the needle marks on her arms. See the bruises. Maybe that will make it real for me. Maybe that will help me make some sense of it."

Fiona shuddered at the idea of India doing any such thing. How could cold, black-and-white photographs of Maud's lifeless body offer her any comfort? It was her grief speaking—mad and wild and searching for answers.

Fiona put an arm around her. "I know you are very upset, India, but are you certain you want to do that?" she asked her. "Wouldn't it be better to remember Maud the way she was—beautiful and funny and full of life?"

India leaned her head against Fiona and gave vent to her grief.

"Full of life," she sobbed. "That was my sister. My God, Fiona, what went wrong?"

CHAPTER FORTY-THREE

WILLA SAT AT a table for two at the Dorchester, fiddling with her napkin.

The tearoom, with its low tables and silver trays and overstuffed chintz chairs, had been Albie's idea. She would never have chosen to come here. But then again, the idea to have afternoon tea together, out of their mother's house, was his idea, too.

"Why, Albie? Why can't we talk in the parlor, for God's sake?" she'd asked him earlier this morning, after he'd proposed the idea.

"We need to talk, Willa, and it will be easier without Mother nearby," he'd said.

He was right about that. They were still not on the best of terms, and their frequent silences or brusque exchanges upset their mother.

Willa was relieved her brother finally wanted to talk, and she hoped he would say what he had to say, get it off his chest, and get over it. He was mad about their father's funeral—and her coming home so late—but there was nothing else she could have done. She had loved their father, too. She hadn't meant to be away from him when he was ill, and as soon as she'd found out about his condition, she'd tried to get home as quickly as possible. It wasn't her fault letters took as long as they did to reach her in Rongbuk. She hoped she could make Albie understand that.

Willa checked her watch again. Albie was late and she wished he'd get here. She planned to see Seamie after she'd finished with her brother, and she didn't want to miss even one minute of the precious little time she had to spend with him. She would see him tonight and then, a few days later . . . in Scotland. They'd made plans to go to Ben Nevis next week, she and Seamie, and she was counting the hours.

"I can get away, Willa. For a whole week," he'd told her a few nights ago, in bed at the Coburg. "Come to Scotland with me. To Ben Nevis. Let's try for a climb."

He told her that Jennie often went to a cottage she owned in Binsey to rest and relax and that she'd be going the following week. It was August now, and people were taking their holidays. He himself was entitled to a bit of time off from the RGS. He planned to say that he was going to Scotland on a climbing trip. It was nothing out of the ordinary; he often went hiking or climbing.

He would rent a cottage, a tiny place situated somewhere wild and remote. They would travel up separately, avoiding any risk of being seen together. They'd each buy some provisions and meet at the cottage. And then they would spend an entire week together. Seven glorious days. Of hiking and climbing. Of eating every meal together. Talking. Going to bed in the dark together. Waking up in the light.

"Please come, Willa. Say you will," he said.

She'd tried to say no. She'd tried to do the right thing, and once again she'd failed. She wanted to be with him, and more than anything, she wanted to climb with him again. And she would.

On Seamie's advice, Willa had spent a good deal of her time in London investigating artificial limbs. Her inquiries had finally led her to Marcel and Charles Desoutter, two brothers who'd recently invented something called the duralumin alloy leg—a prosthetic leg made from light metal. It was half the weight of a wooden leg and had a frictional knee control that would allow Willa to manage the speed and length of her stride. Best of all, it had a feature called a cushion-joint foot, which moved and flexed in the manner of a real human foot.

Willa had tried one and had been so excited by its possibilities that she'd had one made for herself immediately, using the advance she had from Clements Markham for her Everest book to pay for it.

The new leg was nothing like her old one. Its comfort and lightness left her less fatigued and bruised at the end of the day and its flexibility broadened her range of movement considerably. She was hopeful now that it might even allow her to attempt a climb. A real one. She couldn't wait to try it out on Ben Nevis.

Willa looked at her watch now. It was a quarter past four already. Maybe Albie had got caught up in work and wasn't coming. She would give him ten more minutes. In the meantime, she went back to fiddling with her napkin. She'd just made a rabbit's head out of it, when she heard a voice say, "Hello, Willa."

Willa looked up. "Albie?" she said, confused.

He looked flushed and a little disheveled. He looked like a man who'd been drinking, and he was, in fact, carrying two glasses of scotch. He put one down in front of her, then sat down across the table from her and knocked his back in one gulp.

"Albie, what are you doing?" she asked him.

"Drinking," he replied.

"Yes, I can see that. But why?"

"What do you intend to do, Willa?" he asked her.

Willa felt even more confused. "About what?" she said.

"Are you planning on returning to Everest?"

"I'm not sure. Not yet. Why—" she began.

"Because I think you should. Father's funeral is over. Mother is coping now. And I think you should go back. As soon as possible."

Willa was taken aback—by her brother's questions and his tone and the smell of scotch coming off him. Her confusion turned to anger.

"Albie, just what do you mean by coming in here and speaking to me so rudely? I've explained over and over why I couldn't get home before Father died and—"

"I know, Willa," he said, cutting her off.

"You know? Know what?" she asked.

"What the hell do you think? About Seamie."

Willa felt as if he'd struck her. "How do you know?" she asked in a small voice.

"I figured it out. After I found out you've been visiting the Coburg. And Seamie, too."

"Who told you that?"

"I'm not going to tell you, so don't bother asking."

Willa continued to press him, but he would not reveal who'd told him. And then it hit her. How could she have been so stupid? "It was Max von Brandt, wasn't it?" she said, knowing that Max and Albie had met.

Albie didn't reply right away, but Willa could see from his expression that she was right, and she said so.

"Yes. All right, then. It was him," Albie said. "He didn't do it on purpose, though. I bumped into him on the street. He told me that he'd seen you in the lobby of his hotel, and that you'd had dinner together and he'd had such a nice time. He said he'd seen Seamie at the Coburg once, too. Max might have thought it a coincidence, but I didn't. I waited in the lobby one afternoon. I saw Seamie come in, saw him take the elevator to the fifth floor. You were about ten minutes behind him. You also went to the fifth floor."

Willa, stricken, said nothing.

"The next evening, I went to Seamie's flat, intending to have it out with him. He wasn't there. Jennie was, though. She was upset. She'd been crying. I sat down with her and we talked. She knows, too, Willa."

"But that's not possible. She couldn't know," Willa says. "We've been so careful."

"Not careful enough, apparently," Albie said. "Jennie's distraught. She isn't sleeping or eating properly, which is not good for her baby." He leaned forward in his chair, his eyes hard with anger. "Did you ever think about that, Willa? Either of you? Did you ever think about the damage it would do to other people? To Jennie? To me? To our mother, if she ever found out?"

"Stop it, Albie. Please."

"No, I won't stop. I can't imagine either of you did think about anyone else. You never do. You never have. You've always done just as you pleased. Doesn't matter who gets hurt, does it? Doesn't matter who worries, who suffers, who gets left behind. All that matters is the bloody quest. Being first. Getting to the top. Getting what you want. Or, in this case, whom you want. And icebergs and mountains, and people—yes, even people—are all just obstacles to be got round."

Willa's defenses crumbled. Albie was right. All along, she had been so wrong, so selfish. She'd wanted Seamie so badly, and so she'd taken him, with no thought for the woman he'd married, the woman who was going to have his child. Shame and remorse engulfed her now.

"I never meant to hurt her, Albie. Or you. I love him, that's all. I love him more than my own life and I wanted to be with him. Oh, God," she whispered, covering her face with her hands. "What have I done?"

Albie must've heard the sorrow in her voice, for he softened slightly. "You have to stop this, Willa. For Jennie's sake. And Seamie's. And their child's. And for your own sake, too. It's an impossible situation, can't you see that?"

Willa lowered her hands and nodded. Tears were running down her cheeks. She was frightened suddenly. She, who had climbed Kilimanjaro and nearly died, who'd journeyed to one of the most forbidding places on the planet and made it her own. She was terrified, because she knew now what the worst thing was that could ever happen to her—and it wasn't losing a leg, or not being able to climb. It was losing the one she loved most in this world. Again.

"What will I do?" she asked her brother, though she already knew the answer.

"You have to leave, Willa," he said. "You have to leave Seamie. You have to leave London. There's nothing else you can do."

CHAPTER FORTY-FOUR

SEAMIE POURED HIMSELF another glass of wine. His third. If he didn't stop, he'd be tipsy when Willa arrived.

He walked to the window and looked out over the rooftops of London. Where was she? She was supposed to have been here an hour ago. It was already six o'clock. They had so little time together, he didn't want to miss a second spent with her, never mind an entire hour.

He had a surprise for her—a key to their cottage near Ben Nevis. He'd finalized the arrangements just this afternoon and the agent had given it to him. They would leave for Scotland in a few days' time. Seven days they would have together. Seven days of walking and climbing. Of looking up at the stars at night and searching for Orion. Of sitting by the fire. Cooking breakfast together. Reading. Doing the washing up. Six nights of making love to her without watching the clock, of lying next to her in the dark and listening to her breathe.

Jennie had looked unhappy this morning when he'd told her of his plans to climb Ben Nevis. She'd looked as if she were about to protest, but then she'd forced a smile and wished him a wonderful trip. He'd wondered then, just for a moment, if she suspected. How could she? They'd always been so careful, he and Willa. They'd never taken chances.

He told himself he was being foolish, and yet something still nagged at him. Something in Jennie's eyes as he'd put her on the train to Oxford. Not suspicion exactly, no. It was more like sadness. It *would* have to stop one day. What he and Willa were doing. And likely the day would come soon. One day, yes, he thought. But not yet, he begged the fates. Please, not yet.

He heard a knock at the door. Finally, he thought. But when he opened it, a bellhop was standing there, not Willa.

"Letter for you, sir," the man said, handing Seamie an envelope. There was no name on it, just his room number.

"A letter? When did it arrive?" Seamie asked.

"Just a few minutes ago."

"Who brought it?"

"I didn't see, sir."

Seamie reached into his pocket, gave the man a tip, and closed the door. He opened the envelope and unfolded the sheet of paper inside. It was covered with Willa's handwriting.

My dearest Seamie,

I cannot do this anymore. It's not right and it never was. Jennie deserves better. Your child deserves better. I am sorry for leaving a note—again. But if I come upstairs right now, and say good-bye to you in person, I will do what is wrong, not what is right. I love you, Seamie. I always have and I always will. Wherever you go in this wide world, and whatever you do, never forget that.

Willa

"Well," he said aloud. "It looks like the day has come. Sooner rather than later."

He folded the note, put it back in its envelope, and tucked it in his jacket pocket, next to his heart. He was not angry. Not this time. He knew that Willa was right—that she'd somehow found the courage to do what he could not.

He knew, too, that he must try to forget her now. That he must go back to the woman he'd married and try his best to love her again. To be a proper husband to her and a good father to their child. She needed him. He had made her a promise, had taken a vow.

A long time ago, Willa had lost her leg, and she had learned to live without it. He had lost his heart. Twice now. He would have to learn to live without that. And without her—the woman who shared his soul.

He poured himself another glass of wine, emptying the bottle, and took his time in drinking it. He didn't have to be home at any particular hour tonight. Jennie was in the country. When he'd finished his drink, he collected his things and left a few coins on a table for the maid. He settled his bill downstairs and told the receptionist that he would not be needing the room again.

Dusk was coming down by the time he left the hotel. The doorman asked him if he required a hackney and he told him no. It was a mild night—warm and overcast. He would walk. He took off his jacket, slung it over his shoulder, and set off. He looked up at the sky once as he walked London's dark streets, but he could not see the stars.

CHAPTER FORTY-FIVE

"ALL THAT'S LEFT for tonight is the sleeper to Edinburgh . . . or the ferry train," the man in the ticket booth said.

"What time does that one leave?" Willa asked.

"Nine-twenty. Which one will it be, luv?"

"I . . . I don't know. How much is the Edinburgh fare? And the other one? The fare to Calais?"

The ticketing agent patiently explained the different prices, depending on whether she wanted a berth and, if so, whether she wanted it in first, second, or third class.

Willa was standing at a ticket window in Kings Cross Station, dazed and heartbroken, two large suitcases nearby. She had left the note for Seamie at the Coburg, then hailed a hackney cab back to her home, where she'd quickly packed her bags, said good-bye to her brother and tearful mother, and promised to write soon.

"But why are you leaving so suddenly, Willa?" her mother asked. "You only just got here."

"Now, Mother, that's not true. I've been here for quite a while," Willa said. "I've done my presentations. Finished the text for my book and turned it in. It's time I went back east. I've so much more to do. I've got to get back to my work."

"But we should have a going-away dinner. You can't just leave."

"I must, and anyway, I hate long good-byes. I'll write. I promise. And with any luck, the letters will go back and forth between us more speedily than they have been. Oh, please don't cry, Mum. You're making it even more difficult than it already is."

Albie had put a hand on their mother's shoulder. "We mustn't be selfish, Mother," he'd said. "We must think of Willa and let her get back to her mountain."

But Willa wasn't going back to her mountain. Not just yet. She couldn't bear to get there and look at yet something else she loved and could never have. She would go to Paris instead. Or Edinburgh. And knock around either place for a few days until she figured out what to do next. The important thing was that she put distance between herself and Seamie.

"Have you decided yet, miss?" the ticketing agent asked her. "Where will it be?"

She was just about to say Edinburgh, when she heard a voice calling her name. She turned around and saw Tom Lawrence hurrying toward her. He was wearing a linen suit and looked handsome and dashing.

"I say, Willa, I thought that was you!" he said cheerfully. "How are you? Where are you headed? I hope you're on my train—the ferry train to Calais. I'm going to visit Paris for a few days, then head to Italy."

"Whatever will you do there, Tom?"

"I'm taking a steamer across the Mediterranean to Turkey, then it's through the Straits to Cairo. I hope, at least. If the Germans haven't got hold of them by then. I've officially joined up, you see. I'm working under General Murray at the Bureau of Arab Affairs. I do hope you're on my train. I'd love to have a spot of tea with you en route. Hear more about Everest and Tibet."

"Miss? What train do you want?" the ticketing agent asked impatiently. "There are people behind you waiting."

Willa suddenly got an idea—a mad, impossible idea.

"Take me with you, Tom," she said.

Lawrence blinked at her. "I beg your pardon?"

"Take me to Cairo with you. I don't want to go back to Tibet. Not just yet, at least. I want to do something else. I can pay my way. I have enough money. And once I'm there, I'd be happy to work for the place you mentioned—the Bureau of Arab Affairs."

"Willa, you can't be serious. It's a bloody long way, you know. And I can't guarantee you any sort of employment once we arrive."

"Couldn't you find me something? I can survey. Make maps. Ride a camel. Type letters. Mop floors. Empty rubbish bins. Anything, Tom. Anything at all. Just please, please take me with you."

"You *are* a damned good surveyor," Lawrence said. "Good navigator, too. I'm sure Arab Affairs could find some way to make you useful." He frowned thoughtfully. "Well, General Murray will have my head, but what the devil." He turned to the ticketing agent and said, "Good evening, sir. We'll take two for Calais, please."

CHAPTER FORTY-SIX

MAX VON BRANDT sat in his hotel room, smoking.

He was attending a supper at the Asquiths' tonight. The PM would not be there, of course. He had things other than dinner parties to occupy him just now. But many others would be. Margot was a shimmering social butterfly, and her circle was not limited to politicians. There would be writers and artists, people who knew people. He was sure to learn things there. He always made it a point to learn things.

He would have to leave shortly, but not just yet. He would relax for a little while longer, savoring both his cigar and the moment.

The chain was whole. The information so critical to Berlin was moving along it smoothly once more. Just in the nick of time.

Gladys was handing copies of everything that went in and out of Burgess's office to Jennie. Jennie was hiding it all in the basement of her father's church. And a new man, one who'd come up to London from Brighton—Josef Fleischer, also known as Jack Flynn—was picking the material up every fortnight and taking it through the tunnels to Billy Madden's man, John Harris. Together Fleischer and Harris were sailing out of London with the documents twice monthly, on the fifteenth and the thirtieth, to meet the boat in the North Sea.

All the links were sound. John Harris would do what Billy Madden told him to. Gladys would do what he, Max, told her to, or some very unsavory pictures would be sent to her boss, and Jennie . . . Jennie would also continue to do as he wished, if she didn't want her husband to find out that his child, the one that Max guessed would happen to be born in Binsey, was really Billy Madden's bastard.

Of course, Jennie's continued tractability depended a great deal upon her husband. She wanted him. And he wanted Willa. If he had left Jennie for Willa, Jennie might well have given up her charade of a pregnancy and Max would have had no leverage over her. So he'd removed *that* particular impediment as well—by enlisting Albie Alden's help.

Willa Alden was gone. Nobody knew where, not even her brother, for Max had questioned him.

"Willa's left London," Albie had said to him, at a party they'd both attended, after Max had asked how she was.

"That was rather sudden, no?" he said. "I assume she's gone back east?"

"I suppose so," Albie had said. "To be truthful, though, I actually don't know where she's gone. We'll have a letter at some point. Or perhaps not. Willa follows her own rules."

"Indeed she does," Max said to himself now. He had no doubt that Willa would turn up again—in a place that was just like she was—beautiful, desolate, and wild.

For a moment, Max felt a heaviness in his heart, and he wished—desperately—that things had been different. He wished that he and Willa had been different people and that she could have been his. She was the only woman he'd ever truly loved, and he wished he could have spent his life with her in a place like Tibet—far away from Europe and its madmen.

He stubbed out his cigar and stood. He smoothed his lapels, tugged his cuffs straight, boxed his feelings away. It was eight o'clock, time to get going. Margot Asquith started her evenings punctually.

Max smiled grimly as he thought about Margot. They had formed a sudden and close bond, he and the prime minister's wife, having found themselves united in their sorrow over Maud's death.

Max had let her find him sitting alone in the drawing room at Maud's Oxford estate after the funeral, staring down at a ruby ring he was holding in his palm—a ring he'd found only moments before on the mantel.

"Max? Is that you? Whatever are you doing in here all alone?" Margot had asked him.

"She asked me to marry her once, Margot. Did you know that? She took this ring off her hand and put it on my little finger and said we were engaged." He had smiled sadly, then said, "She tried to say she was only joking and that she wanted it back, but I wouldn't give it to her. I'd . . . I'd hoped to find a way, you see . . ." His voice broke. He brushed at his eyes.

"Max, darling. Don't," Margot said, hurrying to his side.

"The thing that hurts me, the thing that is so hard to bear, is that no one knows the truth," he said.

"What is the truth? Tell me."

"The truth is that I cared for her a great deal. And if things had been different, if I hadn't had the family obligations that I do, I would never have broken it off. I would have married her."

Margot, greatly moved by this admission of love, had taken him to her heart then. She rang him up constantly, invited him to all her soirees and weekends, made sure he was not too much alone. He was spending every weekend, and many weeknights, in the homes of politicians, military men, cabinet ministers. Which made Berlin very happy.

A man's tears were a powerful enticement to a woman, he knew. Women could not resist them. Let a woman see you cry and she thought she owned you. But actually, you owned her—heart and soul.

Dusk was just beginning to fall as Max walked out of the Coburg's lobby. He waited patiently as one doorman hailed a cab for him, and watched with interest as two more took down the Union Jack that always flew above the hotel.

He wondered, as he watched them fold the flag with care and respect, if the Union Jack would always fly over the Coburg. And the Houses of Parliament. Buckingham Palace. He wondered if one day the kaiser's troops would march down Pall Mall. Germany's army and her navy were unsurpassed now in size and strength. The kaiser had put it about that he'd be in Paris in a week or two and in London shortly thereafter. Max was not quite so optimistic.

It would begin soon, though—in a mere matter of days, if his sources were to be trusted—a war that would span all of Europe, if not the entire globe. Sarajevo had merely been a convenient excuse. If it had not happened, the kaiser would have found another one.

Max's cab arrived. He climbed inside and gave the driver the Asquiths' address. Then he sat back in his seat and opened the window. He wanted to smell the air. It was a warm night, and beautiful in a fragile, fleeting way—as only English summer nights could be.

It was the first of August today. Already, Max thought. Summer would soon be over. For a very long time.

As the carriage skirted Hyde Park, so full of leafy trees and lush flowers and couples enjoying an evening stroll, Max's heart, hidden and unknowable, clenched. He was suddenly very glad that Willa had left London. He hoped she climbed to the top of Everest and stayed there, far away from what was about to come. He was glad, too, that he had nothing and no one now—no wife, no children—to love.

For the world was about to change. Suddenly, violently, and forever.

And love had no place in it.

CHAPTER FORTY-SEVEN

FIONA, BUSILY PUTTING the finishing touches on a birthday cake for Rose Bristow, her mother-in-law, glanced out of the dining room window of her and Joe's Greenwich estate and groaned.

"Katie, luv," she said, "can you get your brothers down out of the tree? And can you tell your little sister to get out of my dressing room? I know she's in there, spraying perfume all around. I can smell it. The whole house stinks. This cake is going to taste like Narcisse Noir."

Katie put an arm around her mother and kissed her cheek. "Calm down, Mum. Everything's fine. Nothing stinks and Gran's in no hurry for her cake. She's only just finished her supper and she's having a wonderful time. Auntie India gave her Elizabeth to hold and you know she's never happier than when she's got a baby on her lap."

"And your grandfather? He's all right?" Fiona asked fretfully.

"He's having a better time than anyone. Who do you think bet the twins they couldn't get up that tree?" Katie said, laughing. "Don't worry so much, Mum. Come outside and enjoy the party."

Fiona smiled. "All right, then. I will," she said. Then she walked through the dining room's huge French doors into a gloriously beautiful summer evening.

Her smile broadened and her blue eyes sparkled as she regarded the scene before her. A huge table had been set up on the lawn and decorated with a white lace cloth and masses of tea roses, all clipped from her gardens. Seated around it talking and laughing—or racing up and down the lawn, or hanging from trees, or playing croquet—was her large and boisterous family. Nearly every one of them.

Her children. Her brother Seamie and his wife, whose first child would soon arrive. Joe's sisters and brothers and their many children. Rose and Peter Bristow, Joe's parents. And Fiona's sister-in-law India and her three children. Fiona wished, with a deep pang of longing, that her brother Sid was here, too. But it could not be.

They were all here to celebrate Rose's birthday, and looking at them now, Fiona felt her heart swell with love and gratitude. And she, who had spent so much of her life arguing with God, sent Him a quick and heartfelt thank-you—thank you for these people, thank you for this incredible day, and thank you for not letting the twins fall out of the tree onto their heads.

She talked for a bit with Rose, who was completely taken with Elizabeth, allowed the twins to tie a serviette over her eyes for a game of blindman's buff, admired the latest edition of Katie's newspaper, which Katie had passed out to nearly everyone present, and then sat down to drink a glass of punch with India. As she did, Sarah, the maid, came up to Fiona and said, "Excuse me, ma'am, the supper dishes have all been cleared. Shall I bring the cake now?"

"Oh, my goodness. I'd quite forgotten about the cake. Yes, Sarah, do. No! Hold on a moment," she said, looking around. "Where's Mr. Bristow? He should be here."

Fiona realized she hadn't seen Joe for quite some time—at least an hour.

"Have you seen him, Ellen?" she asked his sister. But Ellen had not. No one had. Not since the party began.

"He must be in his study working, as always," Fiona said. "I'll drag him out. Wait on the cake, please, Sarah, until I return."

Fiona hurried into the house and up the stairs to Joe's study, but he was not there. She checked their bedroom, thinking perhaps he'd tired himself and gone to lie down for a few minutes, but he wasn't there, either.

As she was walking back downstairs, she happened to glance out the huge round window at the top of the second-floor landing and spotted him. He was in the orchards. Sitting in his wheelchair. Alone.

"What is he doing all the way down there?" she wondered aloud, a bit put out. It was just like her husband to go off and admire his fruit trees when his mother's cake was about to be served.

She hurried back down the stairs, over the east lawn, and down the gently sloping hill that led to the orchards. Joe had planted the trees long ago, years ago, before he and Fiona were married. Their limbs were dotted with ripening fruit. In another month or so, she and the children would be picking pippin apples and rosy Anjou pears.

Joe was sitting at the far end of the orchard, where the trees gave way to another hill and the River Thames beyond it. Fiona could just see him from where she stood. He was gazing out over the water, his face lifted to the flawless evening sky. It was nearly eight o'clock. The soft summer light had begun to wane. Dusk would come down soon and, with it, the night's first silvery stars. Fiona would have stopped and left Joe to his enjoyment, if she hadn't been so irritated with him.

"Joe!" she called loudly, waving at him. He must've heard her, but he didn't answer. He didn't even turn around.

Red-faced and flushed now, she hoisted up her skirts and started running, making her way between two rows of pear trees. When she was ten or so yards from him, she called to him again.

"Joseph Bristow! Have you not heard me calling you? Your mother's cake is about to be served, and—"

Joe turned to her now and her words fell away. His face was a picture of devastation. She saw that he held a piece of paper in his hand. It looked like a telegram.

"Joe, what is it? What's wrong?" she asked.

"It's all going to change soon, Fee. It's all going to end," he said softly.

"What will, luv? What's going to change?"

"This. Our lives. Others' lives. England. Europe. All of it. It's begun," he said. "Three days ago, Germany declared war on Russia and France."

"I know that," Fiona said. "The whole world knows it. It's been in all the papers. But England's not involved in it. We still have hope, Joe. The war is only on the continent. It's a European war and there's still a chance of containing it."

Joe shook his head. "The Germans invaded Belgium this morning," he said, "a neutral country. All our diplomatic efforts have failed." He held the paper he'd been holding out to her. "It's from Downing Street," he said. "A messenger brought it about an hour ago."

"Asquith needed to send a messenger? He couldn't have rung?" Fiona asked.

"No. Not for this."

Fiona took it from him.

Classified, the first line read.

3 August 1914, the second line read.

And then the third line, and Fiona knew that Joe was right, that their lives would never be the same.

At 1900 hours this evening, Great Britain declared war on Germany.

Part Two

FEBRUARY
1918

HEJAZ, ARABIA

CHAPTER FORTY-EIGHT

WILLA ALDEN SPOKE loudly and heatedly to the man kneeling down by the railroad tie, pointing at him for emphasis with the slender red cylinder she was holding.

"You know what pictures like that could do for the cause, Tom," she said. "They'll bring interest, support, and money. You need all three. Especially now with the push to Damascus."

"I won't hear of it. It's far too dangerous. You're to stay behind the dunes with the rest of us."

"I can't get the shot from behind a bloody sand dune!"

"You also can't get shot behind a bloody sand dune," Lawrence said matter-of-factly. "Stop waving that dynamite around, please, and hand it to me."

Willa did so, sighing. "I suppose you'll want the charges next?" she said.

"Rather difficult to blow up a train without them," Lawrence replied, carefully placing the dynamite next to several other sticks in the hollow he'd dug underneath the tie.

Willa crouched down by a wooden box, carefully lifted out two gelatin charges, and handed them to him. One slip and they'd both be blown sky high. She should've been frightened by the thought, but she'd long ago learned that only those with something to lose were afraid of dying.

Lawrence connected the charges to a pair of wires stretching away from the tracks, across the sands, and over the nearest dune, then carefully positioned them. Willa helped him as he worked, handing him wire strippers, screwdrivers, whatever he asked for. Sweat, caused by the brutal Arabian sun, poured down his deeply tanned face. His blue eyes, made even bluer by the white head scarf he wore, were focused on his task.

They were on a raid, Lawrence and his men. They were rigging explosives just north of Al-'Ula, under the tracks of the Hejaz Railway, a line that ran from Damascus to Medina and had been built by the Turks to strengthen their hold over their Arab domains. Lawrence's mission was to blow up a train known to be carrying Turkish soldiers, guns, and gold, for a strike against Turkey was a strike against Germany and Austria-Hungary, Turkey's Central Powers allies. It was also a strike for Arabia's independence from its Turkish masters.

Willa was there to document the raid, as she had many times before. Her images, and the copy she wrote to accompany them, were couriered to Cairo, where Lawrence's commanding officer—General Allenby—reviewed them, then released them to Downing Street, who, in turn, released them to the press.

This time, however, Willa didn't want to stay behind the dunes during the action, photographing only the befores and afters. She'd got her hands on a Bell & Howell, a small motion picture camera—she'd been hounding Allenby for it for more than a year—and she wanted to shoot live footage as the raid was happening.

She wanted to capture the victories, as she'd told Lawrence, because victories would rally support, but there was another, equally urgent reason why Willa wanted to film the raid—she desperately wanted to show the West the brutal, beautiful place that was Arabia, and to document its people's fierce struggle for autonomy.

Large swaths of Arabia had been—and still were—under the control of the Ottoman Empire, but Britain wanted to change that, for the British had seen an advantage in helping the native tribes rise up and throw off the Turks. If Turkish troops were engaged fending off guerrilla fighters in Arabia, they could not attack the Suez Canal and attempt to take it from the British, as they had already tried to do. Furthermore, with the Turks gone from Arabia, and the Arabs their allies, the British would have new access to, and greater influence in, the Middle East.

To achieve this aim, the British had cultivated ties with Hussein, sharif of Mecca, and his son, Faisal. Faisal, it was determined, would lead the revolt against the Turks, and Britain would help fund it. Lawrence, who had spent his postgraduate years traveling in Arabia, digging among its ruins and studying the people, their customs, and their language, was made advisor to Faisal. With Lawrence's help, and the use of guerrilla tactics, the desert fighters—known as the Arab irregulars—had already taken a number of garrison towns. They were also able to tie up Turkish troops by blowing up sections of the Hejaz Railway—preferably when a Turkish train was passing over them—thereby forcing the Turks to defend it constantly.

Willa had been in the desert for three years now, and she had come to love this wild, impossible place, and its wild, impossible people. She loved the proud and fierce Bedouin men, the tribal women with their blue robes, their veils and jewels, their language and songs. She loved the shy, darting children. And she loved Tom Lawrence.

She didn't love him as she loved Seamus Finnegan. Seamie had her heart and her soul, and he always would. She loved him, still, even though she knew she could never again have him. The pain of that knowledge tortured her every day, as did the pain of her remorse for loving a man who belonged to someone else. There had been times, during the long passage to Cairo, that she'd sat alone in her cabin, pills in one hand, a glass of water in the other, ready to take her own life. She hadn't been able to do it, though. Suicide was the cowardly way out. She deserved her pain, deserved to suffer for what she'd done.

Lawrence she loved as friend and brother, for he was both those things to her. Back in 1914, when she'd left Seamie and was leaving London, brokenhearted, guilt-ridden, and despairing, Lawrence had brought her to Cairo, to the Intelligence Department's Arab Bureau, and had found her work in the Maps Department. It was her job to alter and expand the map of the Arabian Peninsula as information on the Turks' movements and encampments, and those of the various desert tribes, became known.

The position Tom Lawrence had secured for her was an important one, one that kept her so inundated with work during the day that she had no time to think of anything else. No time to remember and grieve. He'd helped her forget, if only for a few hours a day, that she had lost Seamie Finnegan forever. The opium she bought in the back streets of Cairo helped her forget at night. And that was the only thing she wanted now—a way to forget. A way to forget Seamie and what they'd had. A way to forget she'd ever loved him, for their love was not a good thing, it was dangerous and destructive. To them and everyone around them.

When Lawrence had left Cairo to go into the desert and fight with Arab troops under the command of Emir Faisal, Willa had followed him. She had resigned her position, cut her hair off, donned britches and a head scarf, packed her cameras, and set out into the desert on a camel. Everyone at the Arab Bureau said Tom was going to get himself killed out there. Maybe he could get her killed, too. Dying in service of one's country was an honorable death, she thought, a far better death than suicide.

Lawrence was furious with her when she caught up with him, at a rough campsite near Medina. General Allenby was furious with her, too. He sent word from Cairo telling her that she couldn't be at a campsite with men. She couldn't be a lone woman in the desert. She couldn't stay. She would have to return to Cairo. Both Lawrence and Allenby badgered her and would not stop.

Until they saw her pictures.

Pictures of the blond, blue-eyed Lawrence, striking in white Arab robes, a golden dagger at his waist, and of the dark-haired, handsome Faisal, with his shrewd and piercing eyes. Pictures of Auda Abu Tayi, a fierce Bedouin, a Howeitat chief who fought with Lawrence, and of the defiant desert fighters—the Arab irregulars. Pictures of the Bedouin encampments. The red cliffs of Wadi Rum, the Valley of the Moon. The endless dunes. The shimmering waters of the Red Sea.

"So?" she'd said to Allenby as she slapped a stack of them down on his desk back in Cairo. She'd returned with him under the pretense of cooperating with his demands, but really she'd only gone back to develop her film.

The general had picked the photographs up, one after the other, and though he'd tried his best to hide it, Willa saw that he was impressed. And that he saw the possibilities the images presented.

"Mmm. Yes. Quite nice," he said.

"They're better than nice, sir, and you know it. They'll capture people's imaginations. Their sympathies. Their hearts. Everyone in the world will be rooting for Lawrence and for Arabia. He'll become a hero. I'll write dispatches to go with them. Reports from the desert front."

Allenby looked out of his window, brow furrowed, saying nothing.

"Can I go back?" Willa asked him.

"For now," he replied.

That was in 1915. Willa had ridden with Lawrence and his men ever since. She'd photographed them and written about them, and her reports had been published in every major newspaper in the world. Because Allenby was worried about the public's reaction to a woman riding with soldiers, Willa filed her reports under a pseudonym: Alden Williams. Because of her, Tom Lawrence was now Lawrence of Arabia. Every man who read about him admired him. Every woman fell in love with him. Every schoolboy wanted to be him.

Against all odds, Lawrence and his desert fighters had pulled off some stunning victories against the much stronger Turkish Army, but the final routing of the Turks hinged on the Arabs' ability to push northward and capture Aqaba, and then the biggest prize: Damascus. Willa had followed Lawrence this far, and she would follow him farther yet, until they won the fight and gained independence for Arabia, or died in the attempt.

As she watched him now, finishing with the charges, her hands unconsciously went to her camera, and before she knew what she was doing, she was shooting him again.

"Trying to get footage of me blowing myself up?" he asked her.

"Let me do it, Tom. Let me shoot the whole thing," she said, "the train coming, the explosion, the heat of the battle, and the victory.

What amazing footage that would be. Cairo will send it to London and London will give it to Pathé and it will be on every newsreel in the world and Allenby will get more funds."

"You'll spook them, Willa," Lawrence said. "If the Turks see you, they'll know something's up. They'll stop the train, search for our device, and disable it. Then they'll search for us."

"I won't spook them. I'll wait until the countdown and run out on three. Three seconds are all I need. I know it. I've timed myself. Out on three and not before. No one can stop a locomotive in three seconds. You know that."

"He is right, *Sidi*," a voice behind her said, using a very respectful term of address. "You should let him do this thing. If anyone can do it, he can. He is the bravest man I know."

It was Auda abu Tayi. Auda called Willa "him" because he refused to believe she was a woman. Even now after years together in the desert. No woman could handle camels as she did, or shoot a rifle. No woman could navigate as well.

"It's *Sidi* now, it is, Auda?" Lawrence said. "That makes a change. Usually you roar at me like I was your camel boy."

"You must let him do this. His pictures bring money from Cairo. We need money for the push to Damascus. My men must eat."

"Victories are important, Tom," Willa said quietly.

"Yes, Willa, they certainly are," Lawrence said.

"I meant to the people back home. It keeps up their morale. Gives them hope. Lets them know that their sons and brothers and fathers have not died in vain."

Lawrence turned his blue eyes, troubled and searching now, upon her. "What happened to you?" he asked her. "What are you trying to forget? Or whom?"

Willa looked away. "I don't know what you mean," she said.

"Something must've happened. Something terrible. Why else do you insist on taking such chances? None of us is mad enough to go over the dune before the charge goes off. None but you."

"He is a warrior, *Sidi*. He is brave," Auda said.

Lawrence shook his head. "No, Auda. Bravery is feeling fear but doing the thing anyway. Willa Alden feels no fear."

"Let me do it, Tom," Willa said stubbornly.

Lawrence looked away from her, down the track, deliberating. "Out on three," he finally said. "Not one tenth of one second before."

Willa nodded. She was excited. She'd never filmed a full attack, start to finish. "How much longer have we got?" she asked.

"By the best of my calculations, a half hour," he replied. "How are the men coming with the wires?"

"They are almost done," Auda said.

"Good," Lawrence said. "All we've got to do now is connect the wires to the plunger box. Then wait."

Willa looked at the tall sand dune. Close to the top of it, men were scooping out a shallow trench in the sand with their hands. More were laying wires in it, then smoothing the sand back over them. They stayed close together as they worked, so as not to make footprints all over the dune.

Lawrence was still speaking, asking Auda if the men behind the dune, about a hundred in all, were ready, when he abruptly stopped speaking and placed his hand on the iron rail. He was perfectly still, listening, it seemed, with his entire being.

Willa looked down the track. She could see nothing, only the two iron rails stretching away into the desert.

"They're coming," Lawrence said crisply. "Auda, get the men in position. Willa, brush our tracks away. I'll take care of the wires. Go!"

As Lawrence and Auda picked up the boxes of dynamite and charges and hurried over the dune with them, Willa stuffed her camera into the carrying case dangling from her neck and grabbed the broom lying on the tracks. Moving quickly, she swept sand over the hole Lawrence had dug for the dynamite, then began working her way backward up the dune, brushing away all evidence of their presence, taking care not to disturb the wires lying only inches under the sand. She was panting by the time she finished. Sand, with its constant shifting, was hard on her artificial leg and took more effort to maneuver in.

As soon as she got over the top of the dune, she threw the broom down, crouched low, and pulled her camera from its case. She tossed the case aside and started shooting. She panned over the men crouched only a few feet below her, rifles ready, then focused in on Lawrence, who was feverishly attaching the wires to the plunger box. She could see the tension in his face. They could hear the train now. It was traveling fast.

There was no guarantee any of this would work and they all knew it. The connection might be bad. The charges, or dynamite, might be faulty. Their work, the deadly risks they were taking, might all be for nothing.

Lawrence finished with the wires. He readied his own rifle, slung it over his back, then bent his head, listening. They could chance no lookout at the top of the dune. The Turks were wary. They'd have their own lookout, and very likely a sharpshooter, in the front of the train. Lawrence would start his countdown when he heard the engine pass them by. By the time he got to one, the middle of the train would be over the dynamite. That's when he'd press the plunger. There would be a tremendous explosion. Train cars would be blown apart. Those that remained would likely tumble off the tracks. Then Lawrence, Auda, and the men would rush down the dune, rifles raised, to complete the attack.

They waited silently now, nerves taut, as the train drew closer. Lawrence with one hand on the box, the other on the plunger.

"Ten, nine, eight, seven . . . ," he began.

The men closed their eyes, took deep breaths, and prayed.

Willa inched closer to the top of the dune, her camera ready. Please let this work, she said silently. Please. For Lawrence. For Arabia. For the whole wretched war-torn world.

". . . six, five, four, three . . ."

Like a racehorse out of its gate, Willa shot over the top of the dune. She knelt in the sand, trained her camera on the section of track where the dynamite lay buried, and started her film rolling. For what seemed like an eternity, there was nothing, just the train . . . wary faces in its windows . . . a mouth opening in surprise . . . a rifle barrel pointed at her . . . and then it came—the explosion.

There was a blinding light and then a sound like the end of the world, as the force of the explosion tore two cars apart and sent three more tumbling down the embankment. Willa felt herself pushed violently back into the dune. She felt sand, sharp as needles, driven into her hands and face. Felt shrapnel raining down around her. A piece of charred wood hit her arm, tearing her shirt and ripping her skin. She barely felt it; she was only relieved it hadn't hit her camera.

And then there was smoke, thick and black, and the shouts and screams of the injured. A battle cry went up behind her, a lone voice. It was joined by others, and then the men were streaming down the dune past her, already firing on the train.

Willa raced down with them, stumbling in the shifting sand, nearly falling, righting herself, all the while keeping her film rolling.

She heard the sound of bullets flying past her—felt the impact of one lodging itself in the sand only inches from her left foot. A man next to her fell, his head blown off. She felt his blood, warm and wet, on her cheek. And still she ran on, panning over the train, focusing in on the skirmishing, capturing the expression of a tribesman as he thanked Allah that his bullet had found its mark.

The battle raged for nearly an hour. And then it was over. The Turkish commander surrendered. Prisoners were taken. Loot plundered. The remaining train cars were set on fire. Auda had lost eight men. The Turks, many more. And Willa had got it all on film, stopping only once, when the shooting was over, to load a new roll.

Lawrence would later say that it had been a close battle, that the Turks had nearly won it. They all knew what that meant. If they'd lost, they'd be dead now. The Turks might've taken Lawrence prisoner, but they'd likely have shot everyone else.

Willa didn't care. She'd never felt fear, not for a second. She'd felt only a mad determination to film Lawrence and his men at battle. And a wild and raw hope that for a few moments there would be no pain, no sorrow, no guilt, just the sweet nothingness of forgetting.

CHAPTER FORTY-NINE

CAPTAIN SEAMUS FINNEGAN, standing on the bridge of his destroyer, *Hawk*, looked out over the sparkling waters of the southeast Mediterranean with a pair of binoculars. The expression on his deeply tanned face was troubled.

They were out there. Under the calm blue waters, German U-boats were gliding, as dark and silent as sharks. He could feel them, and he would find them.

As he lowered his binoculars, his lieutenant, David Walker, appeared by his side. "They want to draw us out. Away from the coast," he said.

"I am aware of that, Mr. Walker," Seamie said. "They cannot hit us unless they do. Nor, however, can we hit them."

"Our orders, sir, are clearly stated. They say we are to patrol the coastline for German vessels."

"Our orders, Mr. Walker, are to win this war," Seamie said curtly. "And I, and this crew, of which you are a part, will do our utmost to carry them out. Is that clear?"

"Eminently. Sir," Walker said tightly.

Seamie raised his binoculars again, ending the conversation. David Walker was a coward, and Seamie could not abide cowards. Walker constantly tried to couch fear for his own personal safety in a feigned concern for protocol. Seamie had been trying to have him transferred off the *Hawk* for the last four months. He made a mental note now to redouble his efforts.

Unlike Walker, Seamie, a heavily decorated naval captain, had been personally responsible for sinking three German warships and had been a member of various crews on dreadnoughts and destroyers that had together sunk another eight. It was an impressive record, and one that had not been achieved by fretting over his own safety.

He had joined the Royal Navy a day after Britain declared war on Germany. Because of his extensive seafaring experience and knowledge, and the courage he'd demonstrated on two Antarctic expeditions, he was made an officer—a sublieutenant—directly upon enlisting. His courageous conduct during the hellish Battle of Gallipoli in 1915, when the Allies tried and failed to force their way through the Dardanelles to Istanbul, had gained him the rank of full lieutenant, and his bravery during the Battle of Jutland, off the coast of Denmark in the North Sea, in which his ship had sunk two German battle cruisers, had made him a captain.

Many called him brave; some, like Walker, called him reckless—behind his back, of course. But Seamie knew that he wasn't reckless. He took risks, yes, but that was what one did in a war, and the risks he took were very carefully calculated. He knew his crew and what they could do, and he knew his ship—every nut and bolt of her. The *Hawk* was no great tub of a battleship, a sitting duck for U-boats. Lighter and faster than the dreadnoughts, she was made for patrolling, for raiding enemy harbors, harrying minelayers, and ferreting out U-boats. The *Hawk*'s bow had been specially fortified for ramming surfacing submarines. Her shallow draft made it difficult for their torpedoes to hit her. She'd been equipped with hydrophones for detecting submerged U-boats and depth charges for destroying them.

Seamie lowered his glasses again, mulling the question. They were only half a mile out from Haifa, a port town in western Arabia. They could play it safe and travel north or south along the coastline, searching for suspicious-looking vessels, or they could make for the open water—a more dangerous proposition.

The Germans had an effective intelligence-gathering force, for too often they knew the exact positions of British ships in the Mediterranean. It was as if they had some shadowy phantom of a chess master, constantly moving his pieces closer and closer to the *Hawk* and her sister ships. Seamie often wondered where this master was. In Berlin? London? Arabia? He thought it most likely that the man, whoever he was, was here. He had to be. Seamie and the other ships' captains rarely relayed messages on their ships' whereabouts by radio, fearing they would be intercepted. For someone to know so much about their movements, that someone—or his sources—had to be nearby. Watching the ships. Overhearing talk in the port towns, the bazaars, the officers' messes.

Thanks to Britain's own highly effective Secret Service Bureau, Seamie and the Allied captains often knew where Germany's ships were, too, but not her U-boats. The U-boats were a different thing completely, much harder to track—even with the advantage of intercepted German messages.

Seamie well understood the consequences of failing to find a U-boat before it found them. He had seen the devastation a submarine's torpedoes could wreak. He'd seen the explosions and the fires, heard the screams of dying men, had helped recover the broken and charred bodies. He had read, as had the entire world, of the sinking of the *Lusitania*, and the deaths of nearly twelve hundred of its passengers, civilians all—an act so reviled, it had pulled the United States, a country reluctant to sacrifice its sons on foreign battlefields, into the war.

But he did not allow himself to think about those consequences. He did not think about the possibility of his death, or his men's. He did not think about the wives and children his crew had left back in England. He did not think of his own child, James, the young son whom he loved so dearly, or his wife, Jennie, whom he did not. He did not think of the woman he did love, Willa Alden. All he thought of was the necessity of sending enemy sailors to their graves before they sent him, and his crew, to theirs.

"Mr. Ellis," he said now to his quartermaster, "set a course bearing three hundred degrees north."

"Aye, aye, sir," Ellis said.

"Open waters, sir?" Walker asked.

"Yes, Mr. Walker. Open waters."

"But sir, the report from SSB said—" Walker began.

Seamie knew what report Walker meant. The SSB had received intelligence that Germany had increased the number of U-boats in the southeastern Mediterranean, with an eye toward wiping out the Allied naval presence there and, by so doing, weakening Britain's grip on the important strongholds of Port Said, Cairo, Jaffa, and Haifa.

"The reports are only that—reports," he said now. "They may have been planted by the Germans to keep us close to shore. They may be entirely false."

"And they may be entirely real," Walker said.

Seamie gave the man an icy, dismissive glance. "Cold feet, Mr. Walker? Perhaps we should stay right here and knit. We'll knit you some socks to warm them," he said.

Walker flushed red. "No, sir. Of course not. I just—"

But Seamie had already turned his back on the man.

"Full speed ahead," he said.

CHAPTER FIFTY

FIONA, DRESSED IN a handsome cream silk suit and standing in an ornate and cavernous room in Buckingham Palace, held her breath as Britain's sovereign, King George V, raised his pen.

For a few seconds, a strong, dizzying feeling of unreality gripped her. For a few seconds, she simply could not believe that this was happening, that she was here, with Joe and Katie, with the prime minister, with Millicent Fawcett and Sylvia Pankhurst and other suffragist leaders, watching the king giving his royal assent to the Representation of the People Act of 1918, the Fourth Reform Act.

Joe, at her side in his wheelchair, took her hand. Katie, on her other side, whispered, "Are you all right, Mum?"

She nodded, tears glistening in her eyes. She had worked for this, fought for this, spent time in Holloway prison for this, and now here she was, watching the king signing an act of Parliament that would grant voting rights to a large segment of British women.

Fiona had read the bill many times. She practically knew it word for word. It decreed that women over the age of thirty, who were married, or who were single but met certain basic property requirements, could vote in Parliamentary elections. A separate act had additionally decreed that women over the age of twenty-one could stand for Parliament.

Fiona knew that the act had come about because Millicent Fawcett and her group—to which Fiona belonged—had quietly, but forcefully, continued to nonviolently petition government for the vote all during the war, at the same time that the Pankhursts and the WSPU had stopped their violent protests and supported the war effort. In addition, the young women of Britain had made a splendid example of themselves as they took up the jobs British men left when they enlisted, especially jobs in the munitions factories.

Fiona knew that the women of Britain had earned this day, and yet she could still barely comprehend it. It was a proud day, a historic day, and as the king bent over the document, she was filled with emotion that the dream had become reality, that she, at the age of forty-seven, finally had the vote, and that her daughters would have it, too. It was not enough, she knew that—the voting age for women must be lowered—but it was a start, and a very sweet victory after such a long and bitter struggle.

As she watched the king scribble his signature across the document, a million memories raced through her mind. For a moment, she was not a wife and mother, not a successful tea merchant; she was a seventeen-year-old girl, a poor tea-packer in Whitechapel, struggling to make ends meet. Then, after her father's and mother's murders, she was a young woman on the run, struggling to survive.

She remembered her early battles—to get herself and Seamie out of London, to get to America and start a business there. She remembered how she'd fought to make her first shop—a shop she shared with her uncle Michael, her father's brother—a success. She remembered fighting for her first husband's—Nicholas Soames's—health, and his life. For justice against William Burton, her father's killer.

She'd fought for her own life after William Burton had threatened to kill her and had tried to make good on that threat. She'd fought for her brother Sid's life after he'd been wrongly accused of murdering Gemma Dean, an East London actress. She'd fought for Joe's life after he'd nearly been murdered himself at the hands of the villain Frankie Betts.

And she continued to fight now, she and Joe both. Together they'd set up two hospitals—one in France and one in Oxfordshire, at Wickersham Hall, Maud's old and sprawling estate, which now belonged to India—for wounded British veterans, and they fought constantly for funding.

Katie, now nineteen, fought, too. She was reading history at Magdalene College and hoped to graduate with a first this coming spring, when she would promptly leave the dreaming spires of Oxford for the teeming streets of Whitechapel. There she planned to set up a proper office and print shop for the Labour newspaper she'd started four years ago, the *Battle Cry*. Her circulation was two thousand strong now and growing. Though still only an undergraduate, she routinely got interviews from leading political figures, keen to put their policies and arguments across to the young readership the *Battle Cry* served. She'd been arrested several times at suffragette marches, had had her eye blackened, and had even had the windows of her room at the college put out by thugs working for an Oxfordshire factory owner whose abusive practices she'd publicized. Not easily intimidated, Katie shrugged these damages off, considering them mere bumps and bruises from the rough-and-tumble of politics and journalism.

And then there was Charlie, Fiona's eldest boy. He fought every day of his life now—on the front lines in France. He'd enlisted two years ago at the age of fifteen. He'd told his parents he was going on a camping trip with some mates, but he'd gone to see a recruiting sergeant instead. He'd lied about his age, joined the army, and three days later, he was shipped off to the Somme. Fiona and Joe found out from a postcard he sent them from Dover. And by then it was too late; he was gone. Fiona had wanted him found and brought back, but Joe said it was pointless—even if they managed to bring him home, he'd just slip off again the first chance he got. She worried about him constantly now and dreaded every unexpected knock on the door, every telegram, every official-looking envelope that arrived in the post.

Three and a half horrible years had passed since August of 1914. The jaunty, boisterous mood that had greeted the declaration of war had quickly changed with the first reports of heavy fighting in Belgium and then that brave country's defeat. The ones who had said there would be a few quick, decisive battles and then the Germans would limp back home defeated had been dead wrong. The Germans had pressed on through Belgium into France, and the resulting carnage had been unspeakable. Millions had been killed, soldiers and civilians. Lives, towns, entire countries had been ripped apart. Every day, Fiona hoped to hear that it was ending, hoped to hear of some decisive victory that would tip the scales in the Allies' favor. And every day passed without one.

It seemed to her sometimes as if the struggles never ended. She had come so far in her life, she and Joe both, and she'd tried to bring others with her—through her charitable endeavors, through the East End schools she and Joe funded, and through her fight for women's suffrage. And today, for one brief, shining moment, it seemed as if she'd finally won a battle—she and the other women who'd fought so hard for the right to vote. For once, they'd won. The knowledge of the victory they'd achieved at home gave her hope that victory could be achieved abroad as well. America was now involved in the fighting. With her men, money, and might added to the Allies' side, the war would end soon. It had to. Before there were no men left to fight it.

The king finished signing. He raised his pen. There was applause—some polite, some, like Fiona's, a bit more boisterous—and then there were photographs and tea and cakes and champagne.

Joe was buttonholed by another MP. Katie hurried off to try to get a quick interview with the new prime minister, Mr. Lloyd George. Millicent and Sylvia were busily giving interviews, and Fiona, overwhelmed by her emotion, slipped away for a few minutes, to a corner of the huge state room, to collect herself.

She pulled a handkerchief from her purse, dabbed at her eyes, discreetly blew her nose, then stood by a window, staring out at the wintery February day until she felt she could converse once more without bursting into tears. She was just about to turn around and join the rest of the king's audience when she felt a soft cheek pressed against her own and an arm around her shoulders. It was Katie.

"Mum, are you really all right?" she asked.

"I'm fine, luv."

"Then why aren't you with everyone else? You should be clinking champagne glasses with the king and Mr. Lloyd George, instead of moping in a corner."

Fiona smiled. "You're absolutely right. And I will. I was just feeling a little tired, that's all. As you do at the end of big things," she said.

Kate took hold of Fiona by both shoulders now. Her excitement was palpable. "But, Mum," she said, "it's not the end of anything. Not at all."

"It isn't?" Fiona said, looking at her daughter's bright, beautiful face, looking into her fierce, intelligent blue eyes.

"No. I've decided that I'm going to stand for Parliament on the Labour ticket. I can't wait until I'm thirty to participate in my own government. I just can't. Mr. Lloyd George might've placed a high age bar on voting—he couldn't have us women wielding too much influence in government, now, could he? But he set a lower one on standing for Parliament. I can't vote for eleven more years, but I can run as soon as I turn twenty-one—which is less than two years away. And I will. As soon as I'm out of university, I'm going to start planning my campaign."

"Oh, Katie," Fiona said, her eyes shining. "That's the most wonderful news. I'm so excited. And so proud."

"Thank you, Mum. I hoped you would be. Oh, look! The king's free. Be right back!"

"The king? Katie, you're not going to . . ." Her voice trailed off. It was too late. Katie was making her way over to the monarch.

Fiona felt someone take her hand and squeeze it. It was Joe. "Looks like she's gone off to buttonhole old King George," he said.

"You don't think she's going to give him a copy of this week's *Battle Cry*, do you?" Fiona said. "She's got articles by Ben Tillet, Ella Rosen, Annie Besant, and Millicent Fawcett in there. Every firebrand in London. She'll give him heart palpitations."

"She's already giving him heart palpitations," Joe said, "and it's not because of her newspaper."

Fiona laughed. The king was looking at Katie, motioning for her to come forward. He was smiling at her. Of course he was, Fiona thought. Katie had that effect on men. With her black hair, blue eyes, and slender figure, she was a beauty.

"Have you heard her news, then?" Joe asked.

"I have," Fiona said. "You wouldn't have had anything to do with it, would you now?" she added, raising an eyebrow.

Joe shook his head. "Katie makes her own decisions. She's her own girl, you know that."

"I certainly do."

Joe smiled roguishly. "I *will* say I'm pleased she's going into the family business, though," he said.

"Politics, the family business," Fiona said wonderingly. "It used to be barrows and the docks. Who'd have thought it, Joe? Back when we were our children's ages, I mean. Who'd ever have believed it?"

Katie dropped a curtsy to the king, then stood up straight, squared her shoulders, and started talking. Joe and Fiona couldn't hear what she was saying, but they both watched as the king, nodding his head, leaned in closer to listen.

"Poor sod," Joe said. "He has no idea what he's in for."

Fiona shook her head, then she said, "You know, luv, earlier tonight, I thought it was ended. I thought the struggle—at least one of them—was over. I thought . . ."

Joe was about to answer, but his words died away also, as he and Fiona, both incredulous, watched their daughter pull a folded copy of the *Battle Cry* from her purse and hand it to the king.

"Yes, Fee? What were you saying?" Joe said, when he could find his voice again.

"Forget what I was saying," Fiona said, laughing. "Nothing's over. Nothing's ended. With our Katie in the fray, it's only just beginning."

"Joe! There you are!" a familiar voice said. Fiona turned. David Lloyd George was at Joe's side. "Greetings, Mrs. Bristow. How are you today? Well, I trust. I must tell you both, that daughter of yours is a firecracker of a girl. Just had the most fascinating conversation with her. All about her newspaper. She gave me a copy and made me promise to subscribe. She's an excellent saleswoman, and as smart as a whip!"

"Takes after her mum, she does," Joe said proudly.

"She also told me that she planned to run for Parliament just as soon as she turned twenty-one," Lloyd George said. He smiled at Joe and added, "I think you'd better watch out for your job, old boy."

Joe smiled back and said, "Actually, Prime Minister, I think you'd better watch out for *yours*!"

CHAPTER FIFTY-ONE

"THEY SAY NOW that the Yanks are in, it'll be over soon," Allie Beech said.

"I heard it might be as soon as this year," Lizzie Caldwell said.

"Wouldn't that be wonderful? Having them all home again?" Jennie Finnegan said.

"I remember when my Ronnie enlisted. It was all a big lark, wasn't it? The boys were going off to give old Gerry a big black eye. They'd be home in two months, three at the most. It would all be over before we knew it," Peg McDonnell said.

"And here we are, March of 1918, going on four years," Nancy Barrett said.

"And millions dead. And so many others badly injured and in hospital," Peg said.

"Peg, dear, pass me the teapot, won't you? I'm parched," Jennie said, wanting to stop any talk about dead and injured men before it got started.

Jennie was sitting in the kitchen of her father's house, the rectory house of St. Nicholas's parish. She'd moved back here to be with her father after Seamie had enlisted. He'd wanted that. He hadn't wanted her to be alone in their flat with a new baby. He'd felt it would be good for all of them—herself, the reverend, and little James—to be together during this long, hard, horrible war.

She put her knitting needles in her lap now, poured herself another cup of tea, then set the pot on the table. She and half a dozen women from the parish were knitting socks for British soldiers. They met here every Wednesday evening at seven o'clock.

It had been Jennie's idea to start this knitting circle. She knew the women of her father's parish and knew that many of them were suffering greatly. They were lonely for their men and worried they'd never see them again. They were raising their children alone, without enough money, and—thanks to the German U-boats that prevented supply ships from getting to Britain—without enough food, either. Rationing had made them all thin. Jennie scrimped on her own rations to provide a pot of tea and a few thin biscuits for these evenings. But she did it gladly, for their lives—and hers—were difficult and uncertain and it bolstered all their spirits to spend an evening sitting together and talking, to make socks and send them off and feel that they were contributing, if only in a small way, to the comfort and well-being of the men on the front lines.

"Gladys, can I pour you more tea?" Jennie asked the woman sitting on her right.

"No, thank you," Gladys Bigelow said, never taking her eyes off her knitting.

Jennie set the pot down on the low tea table in front of her, frowning with concern. Gladys no longer lived in the parish, but Jennie had asked her to join them anyway. She was worried about her. As the years of the war had dragged on, she'd watched Gladys turn into a shadow. Once plump and bubbly, she'd become thin, pale, and withdrawn. Jennie had asked her several times what was troubling her, but Gladys would only smile wanly and say that her work was demanding.

"Sir George is always the first to hear what ship was torpedoed and how many were lost," she'd explained. "It takes a toll on him. Takes a toll on us all, doesn't it? But I mustn't complain. So many have it so much worse."

Jennie had taken her hand then and had quietly said to her, "At least we have the comfort of knowing that we're doing our part, along with Mr. von Brandt, to help save innocent lives. And perhaps even hasten the end of this dreadful war."

Perhaps she'd only imagined it, but it had seemed to her then that Gladys, already pale, had gone even whiter at the mention of Max's name.

"Yes, Jennie," she'd said, pulling her hand away. "We always have that."

Jennie had not mentioned Max again, but she had continued to take the envelope Gladys gave her, after every Tuesday night suffrage meeting, just as Max von Brandt had asked her to do three and a half years ago.

This very evening, before the women had arrived, while her father was busy giving James his bath, Jennie had quietly slipped down to the church's basement to tuck this week's envelope inside the broken statue of St. Nicholas.

She had often wondered if the man who took the envelope was nearby when she placed it under the statue. Was he in the tunnel, waiting for her to leave? Was he in the basement itself, watching her? The thought made her shiver. She was quick about her work, never tarrying, and felt glad only when she'd climbed back up the steps and closed the basement door behind her.

Jennie had never opened the envelopes, not once, though she had been tempted. Sometimes, on a long, sleepless night, she would lie quietly in her bed and wonder if Max von Brandt had told her the truth, if he was really on the side of peace. She would remember how he'd mentioned Binsey to her, and the cottage there, and how her heart had stuttered inside her at his ugly threat. And then she would resolve to open the very next envelope Gladys gave her, to find out the truth once and for all.

But then the night would give way to day, and her resolve would give way with it, and she would tell herself she must not open it. Max von Brandt had told her not to and he'd likely had a reason. Perhaps to do so might somehow breach security. Perhaps the envelope might not be accepted if it was opened. Perhaps she might even endanger an innocent person's life with her foolish curiosity.

Jennie told herself these things, because to believe otherwise—to believe that Max was not what he said he was, that he was using her to aid Germany and harm Britain—was simply unthinkable. And so she refused to do so. She had become very practiced, over the last few years, at not thinking about difficult things.

"I hear that a lot of soldiers are coming down with the influenza," Lizzie said now, diverting Jennie's thoughts from Max and Gladys. "The new one . . . the Spanish flu. Supposed to be worse than any other kind. I've heard it can kill you in a day."

"As if there wasn't enough to worry about," Allie sighed. "Now that."

"Allie, how's your Sarah doing at the secretarial school?" Jennie asked, trying, yet again, to steer the conversation away from worrisome topics.

"Oh, she's getting on like a house on fire!" Allie said, brightening. "Her teacher says she's top of the class and that she's going to put her name in for a position at Thompson's—it's a boot factory in Hackney—in the Accounts Department."

"Oh, I'm so pleased!" Jennie said. She'd taught Sarah at her school.

"She always was a bright one, your Sarah," Lizzie said approvingly.

As the talk drifted to other children and their doings, Jennie finished the sock she was working on. She had cast it off her needles and was just starting the second of the pair, when she heard the sound of small feet in the hallway and a little voice calling, "Mummy! Mummy!"

She looked up and saw a blond, hazel-eyed, pink-cheeked boy run into the kitchen—her son, James. Her face broke into a radiant smile. She felt her heart swell with love, as it always did at the sight of him. He stopped a few feet past the doorway and said, "May I please have a biscuit, Mummy? Grandpa says I might have milk and a biscuit if I ask nicely."

Jennie never got the chance to answer him. The others beat her to it.

"Of course you may, my duck!" Peg said.

"Come here and sit with your auntie Liz, you little dumpling!" Lizzie said.

"Wait your turn, you lot. I'm closest and I get him first," Nancy said.

James, giggling, allowed himself to be squeezed and kissed, passed around and cuddled and fed too many biscuits. He'd single-handedly managed to do what Jennie could not—take the women's minds off the war and their absent men and their worries.

"Look at the color of his hair. And those eyes!" Nancy exclaimed. "Why, he's the spitting image of his mother."

Jennie forced a smile. "Yes, he is," she said aloud, silently adding, His real mother—Josie Meadows.

Anyone glancing at her and then at three-year-old James would think them mother and child. They both had blond hair, hazel eyes, and porcelain skin. But if that same person were to look closer, he would notice differences.

Jennie looked at James now, as the women around her continued to fuss and chatter, and she saw Josie in the shape of the eyes, the tilt of his nose, and the curve of his smile. She remembered, with a sudden, startling clarity, the day the letter had arrived from Binsey—the letter from Josie telling her that she'd had the baby, that Dr. Cobb from the village had delivered him, and that he'd written Jennie Finnegan's name on the child's birth certificate, for that was what Josie had told the doctor her name was. When Dr. Cobb had asked Josie who the father was, she'd smiled and said, "My husband, of course. Seamus Finnegan."

Jennie, still faking her own nonexistent pregnancy, had left for Binsey that very same day. She'd met Josie at the cottage that evening, and then she'd met her son—James.

Josie was holding him and cooing to him, but as soon as she saw Jennie, she put the baby in her arms. Then she put her jacket on.

"You're not leaving, are you?" Jennie said, surprised. "I only just got here. You have to stay. At least for a day or two. And you said you'd travel to London with me. That we'd say you were a girl from the village."

Josie, her eyes bright with tears, had shaken her head no. "I'm sorry, Jennie. I can't," she said. "It gets harder every second I'm with him. If I don't go now, I never will."

Jennie looked into her friend's eyes, and in them she saw what it cost to surrender a child. "I can't do it," she said. "I can't take him from you. He's your baby."

"You have to take him. I can't stay here. You know that," Josie said. "Billy Madden doesn't forget and he doesn't forgive. He'll beat me within an inch of my life and put the baby into an orphanage—and that's if he's in a good mood. This is the best thing, Jennie. The only thing." She'd buttoned her jacket, put on her hat, and picked up her suitcase. "I'll write. Under a different name. Once I have a flat and get myself settled," she said. "Write me back and tell me about him. Send a picture now and again, if you can."

"I will. I promise. He'll be loved, Josie. Loved and cared for. Always. I promise you that."

"I know he will," Josie said. She kissed baby James and then Jennie, and then she left, suitcase in hand, never once looking back.

Jennie had spent a strange and terrifying and wonderful week alone with her new son, and then she'd got on a train back to London. She told her father and her friends and Seamie's family that the baby had come a bit early. There was some surprise, and she'd had to endure a bit of scolding for going off to the country on her own so close to her due date, but mostly there was joy and delight in the tiny new life in their midst. No one suspected her of passing off another woman's child as her own—why would they? Only her father and Harriet knew the exact nature of the injuries her accident had caused. Her father, being a man of faith, simply accepted James's birth as yet another of God's miracles. Harriet Hatcher, being a woman of science, had posed a bigger problem, but Jennie had got round it by telling Harriet that as she was spending so much time in Binsey, she had decided to see the doctor there, Dr. Cobb, for her check-ups. Harriet said she understood and told Jennie to come back to her after the baby was born, but Jennie never did. And never would.

It would have been a far trickier thing to pull off had Seamie been in London. He would have seen that her body had not changed during her pregnancy, and that her breasts were not full of milk, and would likely have wanted to know why. She told any woman friend who asked if she was nursing James that her milk was scanty and so she'd decided to bottle-feed him instead. Seamie might also have wanted to go to Binsey, to see Dr. Cobb and thank him for delivering his son, but Seamie had been hundreds of miles away on a British warship when James arrived, so that had not happened.

Jennie'd had a photograph taken of the baby, which she'd enclosed in a letter to Seamie, informing him he was now the father of a strapping son. She'd written that she hoped he didn't mind, but she'd named the boy James, after him. When he'd come home on furlough, nearly a year later, he'd fallen in love with the child at first sight and made Jennie promise to send him photos of James every month.

And so, amazingly, Josie's mad plan had worked—perfectly. Josie herself was safely away from London, working as a chorus girl in Paris under a stage name. Her child was safely in Jennie Finnegan's care. And no one was the wiser.

Jennie should have been happy. She had the child she'd desperately wanted. James was hers. He was her pride and her joy, her beautiful, golden boy. And she loved him fiercely. She had her handsome, war-hero husband. She had the love of family and friends.

But she was not happy. She was tortured and miserable, for her happiness had all been built upon lies. She had lied to Seamie about her ability to have children. She hadn't told him about her miscarriage. And she'd lied again by telling him James was their son. And though she'd got away with those lies, she knew that God was nonetheless punishing her for them, because Seamie, her beloved husband, no longer loved her.

He had never said as much. He was good to her. Concerned about her. He signed all his letters to her with love. He tried his best to love her, but he did not. There was no fire in his touch anymore. His eyes, when he looked at her, were kind, but distant. There was a sadness and a heaviness to him always, as if the fire that had burned so brightly inside of him, the fire that had carried him to places like Kilimanjaro and the South Pole, that had made him brave and daring, that had kept him always on a quest, had gone out forever.

She had found the letter Willa had written to him, the one in which she told him good-bye. It was crumpled in the pocket of one of his jackets. And she'd found one he started to write to her after she left—torn into pieces at the bottom of the rubbish bin in his study. In it, he'd told her that she'd done the right thing by leaving, that she'd been stronger than he had. He told her that he was sorry for being unfaithful to his wife and that he was going to spend the rest of his life being a good husband to her and a good father to their child, but that he wanted her, Willa, to know that no matter what happened, no matter how many years passed, even if he never laid eyes on her again, he loved her and he always would. She was his heart and his soul.

Jennie had cried when she'd read those words. For her sorrow and for his. Knowing that he was sorry for what he'd done, that he wanted to try to be a good husband even at the expense of his own happiness, didn't make anything better. It just made it sadder and harder. Willa Alden—not she, Jennie—was Seamie Finnegan's heart and his soul, and Willa had left him. And the loss of her, for the second time in his life, had gutted him. Emptied him. Turned him into a shell.

"Come on, you little monkey," her father said to James now. "We have to leave these ladies to their work. Our boys can't march without nice warm socks."

James finished the biscuit he was holding and kissed Jennie good night. She pressed him close and held him tightly, inhaling his little boy smell. He was all she had to love now, the best and brightest thing in her life.

"Ow, Mummy! You're squoooshing me!" he squeaked.

The women all laughed. Jennie kissed his cheek one more time, then released him. She watched him take his grandfather's hand as they walked out of the kitchen, and for a few seconds, the depth of her feeling for him completely overcame her. She desperately hoped he would never find out what she'd done. She imagined him doing so, when he was older, and hating her for it. The thought alone caused her a deep and terrible anguish. She closed her eyes and put a hand to her temple.

Lizzie noticed immediately. "Are you all right, Jennie?" she asked her.

Jennie opened her eyes again. She nodded and smiled. "I'm fine, thank you. Just a bit tired, that's all."

Peg grinned wickedly. "Maybe you're expecting again," she said.

"Peg McDonnell! What a terrible thing to say. Her husband's away!" Lizzie scolded her.

"Oh, keep your knickers on, will you? I was only joking," Peg said.

Jennie smiled, pretending she thought the women's ribbing was all good fun. Deep down, though, she knew it wouldn't have mattered if Seamie had never left, for she'd never be expecting his child. Never. Even if he still wanted to make love to her, which he did not, she couldn't have given him a child.

"At least Jennie's husband writes to her. I haven't heard from Ronnie for over a week now," Peg said, and her voice, usually loud and boisterous, had gone quiet. Now that James was gone, Peg's mind had returned to its anxious thoughts.

Looking at her, Jennie thought she saw a shimmer of tears in her eyes. Allie must've seen them, too, because she suddenly said, "He hasn't written because he's thrown you over and taken up with a French girl. Her name's Fifi LaBelle."

The women all screeched laughter. Peg wiped her eyes and scowled. Allie winked at her, then elbowed her in the ribs, jollying her out of her tears. Allie knew, as they all did, that Peg wasn't worried about her Ronnie taking up with a French girl. She was worried he'd been shot and was lying dead on the cold, hard ground somewhere far away.

"Fifi LaBelle has bubs as big as melons and feathers in her hair and she wears pink silk knickers with diamonds on them," Allie added.

"Fine by me," Peg sniffed. "Fifi's welcome to him. Randier than a goat, that man. Never gives me a minute's peace." She sighed deeply, then added, "Oh, how I miss him."

There was more laughter at that, followed by more bawdy chatter. Jennie watched them as they talked, and listened to them, and envied them. She knew that French girls were not her problem. Her husband was not in love with a French girl. He was in love with an English girl and he always would be.

CHAPTER FIFTY-TWO

WILLA SAT, HER bare feet tucked discreetly beneath her, on a soft, woven rug in a *bayt char,* or house of hair—a black Bedouin tent woven of goat's hair. The tent was enormous and richly decorated with exquisite rugs and hangings—all signs of its owner's wealth and power—but Willa barely noticed. Her attention was focused on the glass of hot tea in her hands, flavored with mint and sweetened with sugar. She, Lawrence, and Auda had been riding across the desert for five days, with nothing to sustain them but water, dates, and dried goat's meat. The tea tasted so good to her, and was so restoring, she had to remind herself to sip it politely, not gulp it like a glutton, for she knew well that the Bedouin placed a high value on mannerly conduct and would not treat with those they deemed boorish and rude.

Lawrence had been searching for the Beni Sakhr, the sons of the rock, a Bedouin tribe, and their sheik, Khalaf al Mor. Earlier today, they had found his encampment. Khalaf had sent an emissary to meet them and inquire after their purpose.

"*Salaam aleikum,*" Lawrence said to the man, bowing slightly, his hand upon his heart. "Peace be upon you."

"*Wa aleikum salaam,*" the man replied. "Peace be upon you, too." He told them his name was Fahed.

"I come with greetings from Faisal ibn Hussein," Lawrence said in Arabic. "I wish to speak with your sheik. To ask him for his counsel and his aid in our war against the Turks. I am Lawrence, from England. This is Auda abu Tayi, a Howeitat chief. This is Willa Alden, my secretary."

Fahed's eyes widened. He looked Willa up and down, frowning. Willa had never so much as typed a letter for Lawrence, but in Bedouin culture, where women were kept apart from the public life of men, it was the most easily accepted explanation for her presence at Lawrence's side, and the one most likely to gain her admittance to the sheik's tent, instead of banishment to his wives' quarters. Willa didn't give a damn what the sheik thought of her, or of any other woman; all she cared about was getting photographs of these remarkable people, their homes, their lands, their animals, their way of life.

Fahed frowned a bit more, then he said, "I will bring this news to the sheik," giving them no promises and no commitments. He showed them where to water and rest their camels, and had water brought to them as well, and then beetled off to the largest tent in the encampment.

Half an hour later, he returned. "Sheik Khalaf al Mor instructs me to tell you that you may attend him in his tent this evening."

Lawrence bowed. "Please tell the sheik he does us a great honor."

Fahed then took Lawrence and Auda to one tent to wash themselves, and Willa to another. Clean robes were unpacked from their satchels. It would not do to appear before a sheik in dusty ones. Willa was grateful for the bath. It was only April, but already the days were warm, and she was sweaty and dirty after her long ride through the desert. While they waited for evening and the sheik's summons, Lawrence and Auda talked of strategy and how best to win Khalaf al Mor to their cause, while Willa took photographs of the Beni Sakhr women and children. The women were shy, but the children were as curious about her as she was about them. They pulled up her sleeves to see her skin, pulled off her head scarf to touch her hair. They felt her artificial leg, then demanded to see how it attached to her body. They clasped her face between their hands so that they could look more closely at her green eyes. As they touched and inspected her, Willa laughed, marveling at how these desert children were so different from English children, and yet—with their shy giggles, their curiosity, their mischievous smiles—they were so very much the same.

Willa asked them in their language if any of them belonged to Khalaf al Mor. They went silent then and looked at one another. She asked what was wrong, if she had given offense. And then one, a boy of ten or so, Ali, told her in a hushed voice that the sheik's children, and their mothers, were all in his first wife's tent. Her eldest child—the sheik's firstborn son—was very ill and not expected to live. The sheik's entire family was praying for him, beseeching Allah to spare his life.

Willa was gravely concerned when she heard this—for the child first and foremost, and for Lawrence's petition. How could Khalaf al Mor even listen to them, much less favor them with counsel and men, when his child was dying?

As the sun was beginning to set, Fahed came for them. Willa had told Lawrence and Auda of Ali's news. It had made them both solemn. They went along nonetheless, all three of them, carrying gifts—pearl-handled revolvers, daggers in intricately worked sheaths, compasses in brass cases, plus beautifully worked dog collars and jesses with golden bells for hunting birds—for Khalaf was known to keep salukis and hawks.

Greetings and bows were made, gifts were presented and warmly accepted. The guests were welcomed by Khalaf. He was charming and gracious, and betrayed no sign that anything was troubling him, but Willa could see the worry deep within his eyes. She knew, too, that his Bedouin pride would not allow him to share his private grief with strangers.

Instead, he expressed a jovial curiosity at her presence. "Is your sheik Lawrence so poor he cannot afford a proper secretary?" he asked her jestingly. "And must make do with a woman?"

"Ah, *Sidi*! My sheik is so clever that for me he pays half what he would pay a man, yet gets twice the work . . . and ten times the brains!" she replied.

Khalaf laughed uproariously at that, his worries forgotten for a moment, and beckoned Willa to sit beside him. Lawrence was invited to sit at his right, and Auda was seated next to Lawrence. *Day'f Allah,* Khalaf called them—"guests of God." Finger bowls were brought, then a delicious minted tea, which Willa was now sipping. She knew that a lavish dinner would be laid on as well. The Bedouin code of hospitality demanded it. To offer guests anything less than a feast would have been unthinkable.

There was talk of superficial things to begin with—weather and camels, mainly—for to launch directly into the purpose of their visit would have been seen as awkward and unsubtle. After an hour or so, the meal was brought.

It was mansaf, a Bedouin dish of stewed lamb in yogurt sauce, spiced with baharat—a mixture of black pepper, allspice, cinnamon, and nutmeg—cooked over an open fire, sprinkled with pine nuts and almonds, and served on a bed of rice on a large, communal platter. It was one of Willa's favorites.

Well versed now in Bedouin etiquette, Willa washed her hands in the nearest finger bowl, then rolled up her right sleeve. Only the right hand was used for eating, never the left, for the left was the hand one wiped one's backside with.

Everyone knew why they were here, but as the desert saying advised, "It is good to know the truth, but it is better to speak of palm trees."

"*Al-hamdu illah,*" Khalaf said—"Thanks be to God"—and the dining began. Willa moistened a portion of the mansaf with jamid, the yogurt sauce, then used her right hand to delicately fashion it into a small ball. She lifted the ball to her mouth and popped it in, careful not to touch her lips, or to drop any of the rice or meat from her hand or her mouth. She was careful, too, to keep her feet well tucked away beneath her robe, for showing the sole of your foot to an Arab was the very height of rudeness.

After the meal, sweets were served, and Khalaf had his prize salukis and his favorite hawk brought out to be admired. Auda, a Bedouin, too, was much moved by the beauty of the hawk and pronounced it an exceptional bird. Lawrence inquired after the dogs' bloodlines. And then they got down to the reason for their visit.

"Faisal ibn Hussein has asked us to convey his respectful greetings, and to petition you and your men to join with him in the battle for Arabia's independence," Lawrence said. "We have four thousand men ready and willing to march north upon the Turks in Aqaba, and then Damascus. I need more. I need the men of the Beni Sakhr."

Khalaf made no reply. Instead he gave Auda a long, assessing look. "And my Howeitat brothers?" he asked him. "Have they joined with Faisal?"

"We have," Auda said.

Willa held her breath, waiting for Khalaf's reaction. Auda's reply might have brought favor, or it might not have. The Bedouin could be extremely distrustful of one another. Allegiances between tribes often went back for generations, but so did rivalries and feuds.

Khalaf opened his mouth to speak, but before he could, a long and piercing wail ripped through the walls of the tent—a woman's cry of grief. All heard it, but none remarked it. Khalaf al Mor's stony look forbade it.

The cry shook Willa terribly. She was certain it had come from the sheik's wife, the mother of his very ill son. She longed to go to the woman, to help her care for her dying child. She had Western medicines with her—quinine, aconite, and morphine. She always carried them. People who trekked across glaciers at the foot of Everest, who rode for days in the desert, she had learned, had to be their own doctors. If the first two medicines did no good, the third would at least ease the child's suffering. She could not go, however—not without the sheik's permission. If she asked him for it, he might grant it—or he might be gravely insulted. He might take her request as her suggesting that his own efforts to care for his child were inadequate. If that happened, if she offended Khalaf, here in his own tent, among his own men, he would never agree to join with Lawrence and Faisal.

"The Turks are very powerful," Khalaf said now, still evasive. "Faisal may win a few battles, but they will win the war."

"That is true, *Sidi* . . . unless you were to help us," Lawrence said.

"Why should the Bedouin fight for Hussein? For the English?

The Bedouin do not belong to Hussein, or to the English, or to the Turks. We belong to no man. We belong only to the desert."

"Then you must fight for that desert. You must expel the Turks."

"What will Faisal give?"

"Gold."

"And the English?"

"More gold."

"Why?"

"Because we have interests in Arabia," Lawrence said. "We have our Persian oil fields to defend, and access to our colonies in India to protect. We wish also to tie up the armies of the Turks and the Germans, to draw their resources away from the western front."

"What guarantees have I that once our Turkish masters are ousted, the English will not try to replace them?"

"You have my guarantee. And that of Mr. Lloyd George, England's great sheik. England wishes to have only influence in the region, not control."

Khalaf nodded. "And what of—" he started to say, but his words were cut off by yet another wail. He rose quickly, crossed the floor of his tent, and feigned interest in his hawk, perched in a large cage behind him, in order to hide his face and the despair etched upon it.

Damn these men and their wars, Willa thought angrily. She could sit still no longer. She rose and approached Khalaf.

"*Sidi,*" she began. "I have medicines with me—strong, good medicines. Allow me please to go to your son."

Khalaf looked at her. The pain in his eyes was searing. He shook his head no. "It is Allah's will," he said quietly.

Willa had expected this response. It was the only one he knew how to give. She understood the hardship of his life, of all the Bedouins' lives. Death stalked them always. They died of disease, of battle wounds, or in childbirth. How many times had she seen a Bedouin man walk into the desert with the shrouded body of a wife or child in his arms? She had expected the response, yes, but she could not accept it.

"Great sheik," she said, humbly bowing her head before him, "is it not also Allah's will that I am here this night? He, who with infinite care painted every speckle on every feather of this magnificent hawk? He, who sees the sparrow fall. Does He not also know that I am here with you now? Did He not will that, too?"

It was dead quiet inside the tent. Willa, a woman, had just countered the decree of a sheik. She had been heard to do it by every man there. She might well have just ruined any chance Lawrence had to secure Khalaf al Mor's support. She raised her head slowly and looked at Khalaf. She did not see a great sheik before her then, but a heartbroken father.

He nodded. "*Inshallah,*" he said softly. "If Allah wills it."

Fahed was sitting nearby. She hurried to him. "Please," she said, "take me to the child."

Willa gasped as she saw the boy. He was so dehydrated, he looked like an old man. He was burning with fever, delirious, and in a great deal of pain from the violent spasms that gripped his gut. She laid a gentle hand on his chest. His small heart was racing. It was cholera. She was sure of it. She'd seen enough cases of it in India and Tibet to recognize its symptoms.

"You will help him, please. Please. Allah in his goodness has sent you here to help him, I know He has. Please help my child," the boy's mother said. Her name was Fatima. She was weeping so hard now that Willa could barely understand her.

"I'll do my best," Willa said. "I need tea. Mint tea. Cooled. Can you get me some right away?"

She knew that the child needed liquids inside him, immediately. His mother had been giving him water, but Willa didn't want to give him any more. Cholera was a waterborne disease. He might have got it from a tainted well here. Or he might have got it at the last encampment. There was no way to tell. The Bedouin traveled frequently, staying in no one place longer than a fortnight. The tea would be safe, though, for it had been boiled. She would give him some with sugar in it and a few drops of the aconite tincture she always carried with her. She'd learned about aconite in the East. It was used there against cholera. It helped to diminish a fever and slow a too-rapid heartbeat.

The tea was brought, dosed, and administered. The boy fought against it, splashing it everywhere, but Willa thought she'd managed to get at least half a pint down him. A few minutes later, however, it all came gushing out of him. Willa asked for more tea and gave him a few more ounces. Again, spasms racked his small body, and again the life-giving liquid came out of him.

Willa changed tactics. She used what tea she had left to bathe him. The liquid evaporating from his skin, and the cooling properties of mint, helped to take some heat from him, but he was still delirious, still moaning with pain. When she was finished washing him, she asked for more tea to be brought and gave him, yet again, a few ounces of it. She waited. Two minutes. Four. Ten. There were no spasms. No diarrhea. Had some of the aconite she'd put in the first cup of tea been absorbed by his body? Willa desperately hoped so. Stopping his body from trying to expel every drop of liquid she tried to put in it was his only chance. His bones poked through his skin. His breathing was labored. She touched her fingers to his neck, underneath his ear. His pulse fluttered. He was truly on death's doorstep. They would have to fight, very hard, to pull him back.

"Might I have a pot of coffee?" she suddenly asked Fatima.

Fatima's eyes widened. "Coffee? But it's so strong. Will it help him?"

"No, it will help me," she said. "It's going to be a long night."

Hours passed, then the night, and then the following day. Willa refused to sleep. Over and over again, she raised the boy's head, held the glass of tea to his lips, and coaxed him to drink. Over and over again, she bathed his thin body. And somehow the child, Daoud was his name, hung on. He did not open his eyes. His fever did not break. But his diarrhea stopped, and somehow, he held on. Willa gave him another dose of aconite. And then one of quinine. She drank more coffee, ate flatbread and roasted goat, and waited.

They talked, she and Fatima, while they kept vigil. About the sheik. About the desert. About camels and goats. About Lawrence. About Willa's accident. About Fatima's wedding day. About their lives.

"There is a sadness in you," Fatima said, as the first night gave way to day. "I see it in your eyes."

"I'm not sad, I'm tired," Willa said.

"Why have you no husband? No child of your own?"

Willa didn't answer, so Fatima pressed.

"There was someone once. A man. I loved him very much. I still do. But he's with another," Willa finally said.

Fatima shook her head. "But why can he not marry you both? This other woman and you. He would have to give his first wife more jewels, of course. And a better tent. That is her due. But you would be his second wife and that is not so bad."

Willa smiled wearily. "I'm afraid it doesn't work that way where I'm from," she said. "They don't let men have more than one wife in London, and there's no place to pitch a tent."

"I do not understand these English."

"Neither do I," Willa said.

"Fatima," she said later, as the day lengthened into night again and still Daoud would not open his eyes. "Do you and the other women of the Beni Sahkr ever mind your lot in life? Do you ever long for something different?"

"No," Fatima said slowly, as if she'd only just now—for the first time—even considered having a different life. "Why would I? This is the life Allah ordained for me. This is my fate. Do you mind your life?"

"No, but that's the whole point, isn't it? I've nothing to mind. I have my freedom."

Fatima laughed out loud. "Is that what you think?

"Yes, that's what I think. What on earth is so funny?" Willa asked.

"You are. You might have your freedom, Willa Alden, but you are not free," Fatima said. "You are a driven creature. Possessed by something. What, I do not know. But whatever it is, it haunts you. It takes you from your home, causes you to chase phantoms in the desert with madmen like Auda abu Tayi and the sheik Lawrence."

"It's called a war, Fatima. I'm fighting for my country. It will be different when it's over. I'll go home then. I'll buy myself a nice little house in the country and be peaceable and contented and sew by the fire."

"No, I do not think so," Fatima said.

"But I thought you *did* think so!" Willa chided her. "I thought I was supposed to find a husband and have children. Isn't that what you told me last night? Isn't that what you want me to do?"

"Yes, but what I want is of no consequence. It is Allah's will that matters, and He has much work for you yet, and it does not involve sewing."

Willa was just about to tell Fatima that she was an impossible woman, when they both heard a small, raspy voice say, "Mama?"

It was Daoud. His eyes were open and clear. He was gazing at his mother. Fatima, who'd been pouring tea into a glass, dropped both the pot and the glass and flew to him, praising Allah as she embraced him.

"I'm thirsty, Mama," he said, still weak and confused.

Willa got the child more tea, and then she ran to find his father. They hurried back to Fatima's tent together, and then Willa left the family to themselves. For some reason, the sight of the fierce Bedouin sheik sitting on his child's bed and kissing his small hands made her cry.

"He's out of the woods," she told Lawrence. Then she staggered back to the Khalaf's sixth wife's tent—where she'd gone to wash when she first arrived at the encampment—sank down on some cushions, and slept for fifteen hours straight.

When she awoke, Fatima was sitting across from her, smiling. "He is doing well," she said.

Willa smiled back. She sat up. "I'm so happy, Fatima," she said.

"Khalaf wishes to see you once you have eaten. But I wanted to see you first," she said. She stood up, crossed the small room, and knelt down by Willa. She drew a necklace from the folds of her robe, and before Willa could protest, she fastened it around her neck.

"Khalaf gave it to me when Daoud was born. A present for the woman who gave life to his first son. You gave my child life again, Willa Alden. Now you are his mother, too."

Willa, speechless, looked down at the necklace lying against her chest. It was made of gold medallions set with turquoise and strung together with red amber and agates. Fatima picked the necklace up off Willa's chest and shook it. The medallions made a soft jingle.

"Do you hear that? It is to ward off evil spirits."

The necklace was very valuable. Willa wanted to give it back, she wanted to tell Fatima that it was too great a gift. But she could not. To refuse a gift gave great offense to the Bedouin.

She embraced Fatima. "Thank you," she said, her voice husky with emotion. "I will wear it always, and think of the one who gave it to me."

Willa washed, dressed herself in clean clothes, and went to Khalaf al Mor's tent. The sheik smiled when he saw her. His smile broadened when he saw the gift his wife had given her. He bowed to her, then thanked her for the life of his son.

Two days later, with promises of five hundred men and two hundred camels from Khalaf for the march on Damascus, she, Lawrence, and Auda said their good-byes. They had a long ride ahead of them back to Lawrence's own camp.

"I wish you would stay with us, Willa Alden," Khalaf said as he stood outside his tent, watching them mount their camels and bidding them farewell. "I must tell you, I tried to buy you from Lawrence, but he will not part with you. Not even for twenty thousand dinars. I do not blame him."

"Twenty thousand dinars?" Auda thundered. "*I* blame him! Twenty thousand dinars would buy us all the guns we need!" He stuck his chin out at Willa. "I would have parted with you for five," he said. Then he snapped his crop against his camel's haunch and rode off.

Laughing, Willa and Lawrence said a final good-bye to Khalaf, then set off after Auda.

"Twenty thousand dinars," Willa said, as they rode out of the Beni Sakhr encampment. "My word, but that's an awful lot of money. And you didn't take it. I think you like me, Tom. I really do."

"No, that's not it all," Lawrence said, looking at her, mischief sparkling in his eyes.

"It isn't? Then why didn't you sell me to Khalaf?"

"Because I'm holding out for thirty."

CHAPTER FIFTY-THREE

BEN COTTON, TWENTY-ONE years old, from the city of Leeds, and a patient at Wickersham Hall, a hospital for injured veterans, sat on the edge of his bed, hands clasped, head down. A new artificial leg, complete with flexible knee joint, lay on the floor next to him where he'd thrown it only moments before.

Sid Baxter, standing in the doorway to Ben's room, his cane in one hand, a pile of clothing in the other, looked at the fake leg and then at Ben. Tough nut, this one, he thought. Ever since he'd arrived, the lad had barely eaten, barely spoken, and had refused to wear his new leg. Dr. Barnes, the head psychiatrist, had given up. He couldn't do a thing with him, he said, so he'd asked Sid to have a go.

"Ben Cotton, is it?" Sid said now.

"Aye," Ben said, not raising his head.

"I brought some clothes for you. A pair of trousers. Shirt and tie. A jumper," Sid said. He got no response.

"I thought you might need them," he continued. "There's a girl down in the visitors' room who wants to see you. Says she came all the way from Leeds. Says she's staying in a little inn in the village but she can't stay much longer. It's costing her quite a bit, you see. She's been coming here every day for a week, hoping to see you. I figure you haven't gone down yet, because all you've got to wear is that silly bloody nightshirt."

"I told Dr. Barnes to tell her to go home," Ben said.

"Who is she?"

"My fiancée."

"A bit rude of you to stay in your room when she's come all this way to see you, wouldn't you say so, lad? It's a beautiful June evening. Sun's still out. Birds are singing. Why don't you go down and sit out in the garden?"

Ben picked his head up and looked at him then, and Sid saw that his eyes were filled with anger.

"Just waltz downstairs on my one good leg and say hello, will I? Maybe have a nice stroll round the grounds and a spot of tea while I'm at it?"

Sid shrugged. "Why not?"

"Why not? *Why not?* How can I go down to her? How can I let her see me?" he said bitterly, gesturing at his missing leg. "I'm not even a man anymore."

"You're not?" Sid said. "Why's that? Did Gerry blow your nuts off, too?"

Ben blinked. His mouth dropped open.

"I guess he must've. It's the only thing that might explain why you're sitting up here on your bed whinging and moaning and feeling sorry for yourself instead of going to see that pretty little lass of yours."

Ben scowled; he started to tell Sid off, but then burst into laughter instead. The laughter grew until it became hysterical, and then it turned into great, wrenching sobs. Sid had seen it before. The doctors here were a fine and educated lot, but they didn't speak to the men as bluntly as he did. And sometimes bluntness was exactly what was needed to draw them out.

Sid sat down on the bed, patted Ben's back, and waited patiently for his emotion to subside. "You finished?" he said when the lad had gone quiet.

Ben nodded. He wiped his eyes on his sleeve.

"I know your story," Sid said. "I read your records. You signed up right away. Fought for your country. You spent over three years on the front in France, earning yourself some nice commendations for bravery while you were at it, until one of Gerry's bombs took your leg. You almost bled to death in the mud. Then an infection almost took you. The field doctor who fixed you up wrote that it was a miracle you didn't die. 'One of the toughest, bravest lads I've ever seen,' he wrote. You're a man all right, Ben Cotton. You're more of a man on one leg than most are on two."

Ben said nothing, but Sid could see his jaw working. He reached down, picked the artificial leg up off the floor, and handed it to Ben, hoping he'd take it. Ben did. He started to buckle it on.

"I can't walk on it properly," he said. "I hobble around on it like an old man."

"You can't walk on it properly *yet,*" Sid said. "It takes a bit of practice. Give it some time."

"What happened to your leg?" Ben asked. "I've seen you around here. You walk with a limp. Was it the war?"

"No, it was a steer. And a bad doctor. Years ago. In Denver. I broke it in a slaughterhouse. Steer rushed at me and knocked me down. Doctor set it badly. It didn't heal right. Mostly I can manage. Sometimes, if it's paining me, I need a cane."

"You're married, aren't you?" Ben asked. "To the lady doctor?"

Sid could hear the worry in his voice. "I am," he replied. "She liked me before my leg was broken. And she liked me after, too."

Ben nodded.

"Here's the clothing I brought," Sid said. "The docs have you lot running around in these bloody nightshirts all the time, I don't understand it. No wonder you don't feel like a man. You've got no trousers on."

Ben thanked him. He reached for the clothes, pulled them on, then stood up. He took a few clumsy steps, then turned around in the doorway, fists clenched, and looked back at Sid. "I'm afraid," he said.

"I don't blame you, lad. Women are scarier than anything in Gerry's whole bloody arsenal."

Ben smiled bravely. Then he squared his shoulders, turned around again, and started walking.

Sid waited for a few minutes, then he followed him downstairs, casting a quick, casual glance into the visitors' room. The girl, Amanda was her name, was crying, but she was laughing, too, and Sid could see that her tears were tears of joy.

As Sid ducked out of the doorway, Dr. Barnes walked by, wearing his overcoat and hat, and carrying his briefcase. He, too, peered into the visitors' room, then ducked out again, smiling.

"Well done, Mr. Baxter! Bravo!" he said quietly.

Sid smiled. "I expect we'll see Ben eating and talking a bit more. Maybe even trying a bit harder with the new leg. Amazing, isn't it, how women make us want to buck ourselves up?"

Dr. Barnes laughed. "What's amazing is your effect on the hard cases," he said.

"I suppose it takes one to know one," Sid said.

Dr. Barnes told Sid he was leaving for the night and asked if he was heading home, too.

"Soon," Sid replied. "But I thought I might visit Stephen first. If you've no objection."

"Of course not," Dr. Barnes said. He frowned, then added, "Any signs of life there?"

"Maybe," Sid said cautiously.

"Really?" Dr. Barnes said eagerly.

"Don't get excited, mate. I said *maybe,* didn't I? I really don't know. I thought I saw something. Yesterday, when I took him into the stables. I found out his people are farmers, you see. . . ."

"How did you find that out? Stephen doesn't speak."

"I wrote his da. Asked him to tell me as much as he could about Stephen's life. Before the war, I mean."

Dr. Barnes nodded, impressed.

"Anyway," Sid continued, "I got the idea to take him into the stables and walk with him past the horses and the cows, and I thought—like I said, maybe I only imagined it—but I thought I felt the trembling subside a little, and I saw his eyes go to Hannibal, the big plow horse. Just for a second. I thought I'd take him again this evening. When they've all come inside from the fields and the cows are being milked."

"You've a most unorthodox method, but please, by all means, keep it up. Good night, Sid."

"Ta-ra, Doc."

Sid made his way down a long hallway to a set of rooms at the back of the hospital, rooms that had padded walls and no beds, only mattresses—rooms for men suffering from the horrors of shell shock. Many of them had no physical signs of injury, and yet Sid knew that of all the patients at Wickersham Hall, these men were the most damaged, and the hardest to reach.

He remembered now how he and India had barely any idea of what shell shock was when they'd opened the hospital. They'd been prepared for amputees, for men who'd been badly burned, even brain-damaged by bullets or shrapnel to the skull, but they'd been woefully unprepared for the wretches who came to them shaking and trembling, or sitting in wheelchairs, impossibly still. Some came with their eyes screwed shut, others with eyes downcast and blank, or impossibly wide open, as if still staring at the carnage that had driven them mad.

Dr. Barnes had wanted them to talk about their experiences on the battlefield, to share what had happened to them and not keep it inside. Sometimes the talking cure worked, sometimes it didn't. Sid observed the doctor's method, and knew that his intentions were the best, but privately he wondered how reliving the hell that these men had suffered through was supposed to help them.

"Who'd want to talk about it over and over again?" he'd asked India. "Wouldn't a geezer just want to forget it all? To look at a tree or pat a dog and forget he'd ever set foot in a trench? At least until he regained a bit of strength and could cope with the memories?"

"Sounds like you have an idea," India said.

"Maybe I do," Sid replied. "Maybe I do."

The next day, he'd gone to see Dr. Barnes and asked if he might take some of the men outside, for a stroll around the grounds. He said he thought the fresh air might do them good. Dr. Barnes, overwhelmed as he was by the needs of his patients and desperate for any helpful measures, quickly agreed to Sid's request.

Sid had started with a nineteen-year-old boy named Willie McVeigh. Willie's entire unit had been slaughtered on the Somme. Willie himself had been shot in the side and had lain on the battlefield, next to his dead and dying comrades, for two days before a field doctor had found him. When he'd arrived at Wickersham Hall, his body was rigid and his eyes were as wide, and as wild, as a frightened horse's.

Sid had taken Willie by the arm that April morning, and they'd set off around Wickersham Hall's grounds—all three hundred acres of them. As they walked—slowly, for Sid had a cane and Willie's gait was stiff—Sid had pointed out the daffodils and tulips poking through the ground. He'd showed Willie the new green willow leaves and the lilac buds about to burst open. He'd sat him down in the freshly tilled kitchen garden and put his clenched hands into the rich, wet dirt.

He did these things for five weeks straight, with no discernible effect whatsoever. And still he persisted, until, after two months of strolls and hikes and nature walks, Willie suddenly bent down in the garden, picked a strawberry from one of the plants growing there, ate it, and asked if he might have another.

Sid gave Willie another strawberry. He gave him a whole basketful. He'd have picked every strawberry in the garden if the lad had asked him to. He stood there watching Willie eat them, wanting to whoop and twirl and click his heels together.

The next day, he asked Henry the gardener if Willie might help hoe weeds between the plants.

"What if he throws a wobbly? Hacks me plants to bits?" Henry asked unhappily.

"He won't, Henry. I know he won't," Sid said.

He knew no such thing. In fact, he half expected Willie to try to hack *him* to bits, but Willie didn't. Sid sat in a chair at the edge of the garden, watching Willie as anxiously as a new mother watches her darling infant take its first steps. And Willie did marvelously. He hoed the weeds, carefully hilled the soil around the base of the plants, and then helped Henry harvest the berries.

When, at the end of the day, Henry complimented him, Willie simply said, "Me dad had an allotment. I used to help him with it." It was the most he had said since he'd arrived.

They'd had setbacks, of course. A thunderstorm had sent Willie diving under a bench, and it had taken Sid and Henry two hours to coax him out again. A backfiring motorcycle sent him running inside, howling in fear, and he'd refused to go out again for three whole days. But there was more progress now than there were setbacks. With Willie and with others, too. With Stanley, who, Sid had discovered, liked to knead bread, for the repetitious motion calmed him. He now helped Mrs. Culver, the hospital's cook, with her baking. And Miles, who refused to stop playing an imaginary piano until Sid bought him a real one, and who now played Brahms, Chopin, and Schubert for the other patients.

But not with Stephen. Poor, mad Stephen, who'd arrived at the hospital six months ago with red, raw marks around his neck from trying to hang himself.

Stephen was Sid's greatest challenge. Sid had worked with him day in and day out, trying everything he could think of. When nothing had had any effect, he'd hit upon the idea of writing to Stephen's father, to ask about his life at home. His father had written back, telling him all about their farm and their fields and livestock, and Bella, their huge workhorse, an ornery creature that had only ever been tractable for Stephen.

Immediately Sid had thought of Hannibal—Wickersham Hall's own plow horse, a very large and very cross animal, whom only Henry could handle, and even Henry had trouble with him. Sid had asked Henry if he could leave Hannibal in the pasture a little longer tonight, instead of putting him in his stall, for Hannibal was better behaved outside and Sid needed him in an amenable mood. He planned to coax Hannibal to the fence with some carrots, then to place Stephen's hand on the horse's withers.

As he reached Stephen's room, he paused and took a deep breath—to calm himself. He was excited, but he didn't want to betray his excitement to Stephen or Hannibal, in case he spooked either of them. He thought his plan might actually work, that Hannibal might offer a way to break through to Stephen. Then again, Hannibal, the little bleeder, might just kick them both straight into the next county.

Sid hurried across the meadow that separated the hospital from the house where he was now living—the Brambles, the caretaker's cottage on Wickersham Hall's grounds.

It was dark. India would certainly scold him for missing his tea—again. He hadn't meant to be so late, but he'd had a breakthrough with Stephen and he'd lost track of the time. He was so excited, so happy about it, that he couldn't wait to tell India. She was concerned about Stephen. She asked for him, or visited him herself, nearly every day.

Sid saw her now, his wife, as he drew closer to the cottage, through the mullioned windows of the kitchen. She was sitting at the table, reading. He stopped for a moment and stood still in the darkness, watching her. Just as he had once, long ago, outside her flat in Bloomsbury. Before she was his wife. Before their children were born. Before he'd ever imagined that he could know the kind of happiness she'd given him.

She was leaning her head on one hand, turning the pages of whatever she was reading with the other—the *Lancet*, no doubt. She was a new doctor when he'd first met her, a woman dedicated and driven to improve the health of her patients, and she hadn't changed. She'd only grown more dedicated as the years passed.

Wickersham Hall had been her idea. When the first injured men started coming home, she'd volunteered to care for them at Barts Hospital, in London. She'd soon seen that a busy city hospital could not address the long-term needs of wounded veterans, and that something more was needed. She'd written him.

My darling Sid,
I've had the most marvelous idea today. I don't want to sell Wickersham Hall anymore. I want to make it into a hospital—a hospital for those wounded in the war. A place where they can receive the very best of care, and stay, in comfort, for as long as is needed to make them whole again. It is a way to turn a sad, unhappy place into something useful and hopeful. I can't think of a better way to honor the memory of my sister, and I know in my heart that this is what Maud would want. . . .

That had been back in January of 1915. They'd been apart for months. After she'd received news of Maud's death, India and the children had gone to London, so she could try to find out why her sister had taken her own life and also settle her affairs. Maud had left everything to India, and India, who had no use for Maud's Oxford estate and couldn't even bear to be in her London house, had decided to sell them. She thought she'd stay for two months, three at the most, then return to their home in Point Reyes, California.

But things hadn't quite worked out as they'd planned. War broke out. India had managed to sell Maud's London town house, but it was more difficult to sell Wickersham Hall. People were anxious and uncertain and not eager to spend on large estates.

With European navies engaged in battles and blockades, ocean travel became perilous. Sid cabled India shortly after Britain declared war on Germany and told her that under no circumstances were she and the children to travel back to the United States—not until the war was over. At that point, Sid, like most of the rest of the world, thought it would take a few months, possibly a year, for the fighting to end, but it had not. The Germans had taken Belgium, then France, and it looked as if Italy and Russia would fall, too. For a few months, the kaiser looked to be unstoppable. Sid realized that he might well invade England, and that his wife and children were in London, without him to protect them. He left his ranch in the hands of his capable foreman and began the long journey to Southampton. He didn't tell India he was coming, for he knew she would worry. He simply showed up one day—having crossed America by train and the Atlantic Ocean by steamer—on Joe and Fiona's doorstep.

India was furious at him for coming. "Haven't you heard that German U-boats are targeting civilian ships?" she angrily asked him, but she kissed him and hugged him and told him how very glad she was that he was there.

By the time he arrived, she'd already made Maud's estate into a hospital. She'd staffed it and supplied it herself. She already had a great deal of her own money, and Maud had left her another very large fortune. Joe and Fiona also contributed to the hospital's upkeep. When India suggested that they leave London for the hospital, because she wanted to work there, Sid quickly agreed. London was not a good place for him. He had long ago been cleared of any wrongdoing regarding Gemma Dean's death, a former girlfriend for whose murder he'd once been blamed, but that was not his only worry—there were those in the London underworld who undoubtedly remembered him—and not with great fondness. The sooner he left the city, the better.

As they journeyed to Oxford on the train, he wondered how he would occupy himself while India was busy doctoring all day long. He had thought of enlisting when he arrived in England, but he knew he'd never be accepted—not with his dodgy leg and not with the scars on his back, the ones the screws had put there with a cat-o'-nine-tails when, as a young man, he'd done hard time. Those scars said *prison* loud and clear, and the recruiting sergeants were not terribly fond of ex-convicts.

Sid hadn't had to wonder how to make himself useful for long, however. Every spare pair of hands was needed at the hospital. He helped dig the hospital's kitchen garden—an absolute necessity in a time of rationing. He helped drive ice, crates of eggs, sacks of flour, and sides of meat from markets and shops and farms into the kitchen.

He helped feed, wash, and dress the damaged bodies of soldiers and sailors and airmen, and as he did, he talked with them, to calm them and reassure them and try to lift their spirits, as well.

Young, working-class lads—boys who were uncomfortable talking to educated medical men with their clipped accents and soft hands—heard Sid's voice, still full of East London even after so many years away from it. They saw his rough worker's hands, and they recognized him as one of their own. They trusted him, felt comfortable with him, and they talked to him. They told him about their lives, about their injuries, about their fears—things they would not tell their doctors.

And Sid, to his great surprise, discovered that he liked the talking and the listening and that he was very good at it. His life, the part of it he'd spent in England, had been all about taking—taking money, and jewels, and many other things that hadn't belonged to him. Now he was giving, and he found it the most rewarding thing he'd ever done.

"Ever think of medical school, Mr. Baxter?" India had asked him one day, as she watched him work his magic on yet another broken body, broken mind.

"Nah, I hear it's a doddle. Got better things to do, me," he said, teasing her. "I'm getting a football team together. The lads are all mad for it. I figure it'll get them all out and running around. Excuse me, luv, will you?" And then, a clipboard in hand, he'd tried to hurry off to the gymnasium, which had been set up in one of the stables, but before he could, India grabbed his sleeve, pulled him close, and whispered, "You're a good man, Sid, and I love you."

He loved her, too. More than his life. And he thought now, as he looked at her, silhouetted in the warm light of the kitchen, that his heart would surely burst, it was so full of emotion.

He went into the house, took off his jacket and boots and left them in the mudroom, then made his way into the kitchen.

She looked up at him, smiling, happy to see him. "There's rabbit stew on the stove. Mrs. Culver made it. She made biscuits, too."

"Ta, luv. Where are the children?"

"In bed, you daft man. It's after nine."

"Is it? I'd no idea." Sid shoveled some of the stew onto a plate. As he did, he told her all about Stephen.

He'd taken the lad to the pasture to see Hannibal, the workhorse. Hannibal, true to his ornery nature, had flattened his ears and stamped ominously the very second Sid had approached him, but before he could start snorting or kicking or any other horsely nonsense, he'd spotted Stephen. His eyes had widened and his ears had gone up. Sid didn't know if horses were capable of curiosity, but at that moment, that's how Hannibal had looked—curious.

Stephen wouldn't raise his eyes, he wouldn't make direct contact with Hannibal, and yet he saw him. Sid knew he did; he could feel it. Stephen saw the horse with something inside of him—his heart, his soul maybe—Sid didn't know. What he did know was that for the first time in six months, Stephen's trembling had stopped.

Hannibal trotted over to the fence, ignoring Sid, looking only at Stephen. For a few seconds, Sid's heart was in his throat, so certain was he that Hannibal was going to open that huge mouth of his and take a chunk out of the lad; but he didn't. He sniffed Stephen. He whickered and blew. Then he pushed his great velvety nose against Stephen's cheek. Once, twice, three times. Until slowly, miraculously, Stephen raised his hand and placed it on Hannibal's neck.

The look on that lad's face at that moment . . . well, it was something Sid would never forget as long as he lived. He'd seen that look before, on the faces of men coming home on furlough and embracing the wives and children, the ones they hadn't seen for years and had often thought they'd never see again.

Stephen was too young to have a wife or a child, but he'd had a horse once. Long ago. In another, better, lifetime.

They stood that way, the boy and the horse, silent and still, for five, and then ten minutes, and then Stephen said, "He should be in his stall now. It's damp out tonight."

"Right. Yes. He will be, Stephen. Straightaway. Henry's coming for him," Sid said, trying to keep his voice even.

"Henry led Hannibal to the stables," he said to India now, "and I took Stephen back to his room. I told him we'd go see the horse again tomorrow night. He didn't say anything to that, but I saw that his trembling hadn't come back."

"Sid, that's wonderful news!" she exclaimed. "Oh, I'm so pleased to hear it!"

"We've still a long, long way to go," he said. "But it's a start." He grabbed a biscuit and sat down at the table across from her. As he did he saw that her eyes were red. "Can't you put that away now?" he asked her. "Give medicine a rest for the night?"

"It's nothing," India said. "Just a bit of eyestrain."

Sid glanced at the journal lying open in front of her. "The *Lancet*, is it?"

"Yes," she said. "There's a very disturbing report in it, about the new strain of influenza—the Spanish flu. It says that it's killing thousands in America and has started moving into Europe. Soldiers on all the European fronts are being hit heavily, and now it's supposedly started cropping up in Scotland and in some of the northern English cities."

"It's bad?" Sid said, between bites of stew.

"Very," India replied. "It starts out as a typical flu. The patient becomes very ill, seems to rally, but then grows worse. Bleeding from the nose and eyes may occur, followed by a virulent pneumonia. It's the pneumonia that's actually killing people. And oddly enough it's not the usual victims who are succumbing to it—babies and the elderly. It's carrying off young, healthy men and women. The United States already has quarantines in place. I just pray it doesn't hit the hospital. The men here have been through so much already."

She closed the journal then, and Sid saw that there was something underneath it. He recognized it. It was a photo album that had belonged to Maud. It contained pictures of Maud and India when they were children.

"It's not the *Lancet* that's made your eyes red, it is, luv?" he said quietly.

India looked down at the photo album. She shook her head. "No, it isn't," she said. "I shouldn't have got it out, but I couldn't help it. It's her birthday today. Or rather, it would have been."

Sid reached across the table for her hand and squeezed it. "I'm sorry," he said. She nodded and squeezed back.

He remembered how shattered India had been when the letter arrived from Fiona telling them that Maud was dead. She'd cried in his arms, sobbing "Why, Sid? Why?" over and over again.

She hadn't accepted the coroner's verdict on Maud's death. She simply could not believe that her sister would take her own life. Other people, yes; Maud, never. When she'd arrived in London, she immediately went to see the officer who'd investigated Maud's death. She asked the man—Arnold Barrett—for the mortuary photographs. He tried hard to talk her out of looking at them, but she would not be swayed. She steeled herself, made herself view them as a doctor, not a sister.

Holding a magnifying glass over the photos, India had examined the puncture wounds inside Maud's elbow. They had definitely been made by a hypodermic needle, but they were all fresh-looking wounds, not old.

"Yes, of course they are," Barrett said. "A hypodermic only holds so much and she'd injected herself several times, to make sure the dosage she received was lethal."

"But her lover, von Brandt . . . you told me that he said she was using morphine regularly. Someone who was an addict, who was getting and using morphine regularly, would have had old bruises where she'd injected the drug on previous occasions—not just fresh needle marks. There are no faded bruises anywhere on her. No old, scabbed punctures. And furthermore, Detective Inspector, my sister hated needles. She hated blood. She nearly fainted at my medical school graduation because she thought there were cadavers on the premises. How could she, of all people, have injected herself repeatedly?"

"Drug addiction forces its victims to do things neither they nor anyone else ever thought them capable of," Barrett said. "And hadn't

Miss Selwyn Jones had a past history of visiting Limehouse opium dens?"

"At one point in her life, yes," India said. "But my sister was not an addict. Not at the time of her death. She doesn't look overly thin in these pictures, as addicts do. No one who'd seen her or been with her in the last few weeks of her life—except for von Brandt—ever described anything that matched the behavior of a drug addict." India had paused for a few seconds, and then she'd said, "I want you to reopen the case, Detective Inspector. My sister did not kill herself. I am certain of that. Which means someone else did kill her."

Barrett had leaned forward in his chair and in a kindly voice told her that he could not possibly do what she was asking.

"I'm afraid there simply isn't enough to warrant a reopening of the case," he told her. "I know that she was your sister, and that this is terribly hard for you to accept, but if you go home now and think it over, I believe you will see, as I do, that your suspicions sound, well . . . a little bit mad."

India had bristled at that.

"Hear me out . . . listen to me . . . think carefully about what I'm about to ask you: Who on earth would have wanted to kill your sister?"

"What about the man she was seeing . . . Max von Brandt?" India asked.

Barrett had shaken his head. "If anything, I believe Miss Selwyn Jones might have wanted to kill him," he said. "I interviewed von Brandt. The very next day. I've been at this for thirty years, and I can tell you that he was genuinely and deeply upset. Furthermore, he had corroboration for all of his movements leading up to her death. He was seen with Miss Selwyn Jones leaving his hotel. The cabdriver who took them to your sister's home backed up von Brandt's story one hundred percent. At no time did Mr. von Brandt attempt to conceal his movements. Are these the actions of a criminal trying to cover his tracks, Doctor?"

India had found she could not answer him.

He had given her a kind smile and said, "It's a very bitter thing, suicide. The ones left behind always look for another explanation. But I am convinced that Miss Selwyn Jones's death was just that—a suicide."

"I miss her, Sid," India said now, in a small, choked voice. "I miss her so much."

Sid stood up and pulled India up out of her seat. He put his arms around her and held her close and let her cry. Her cousin Aloysius had been killed several years ago and now her sister was gone. They were the only members of her family she had been close to. If only he could do something for her. She was not getting over Maud's death. She was still sad, still grieving.

"I wish I could just believe what Barrett told me," she said now, wiping her eyes. "If I could believe it, I could let it go. Let her go. But I can't."

Sid wished she could let it go, too. He wished *he* could, but like India, he couldn't quite believe Maud had killed herself, either. And yet perhaps Barrett was right. Perhaps she'd become an addict, and the morphine, combined with the loss of her lover, had caused her to behave irrationally.

If Maud was an addict, though, someone had to have supplied her with the drugs, Sid thought. He wondered, for the briefest of seconds, if it could possibly have been his old colleague, the East End drug lord Teddy Ko. It was Ko's establishment that Maud used to frequent. It was at Ko's that Sid had first met India, as she was trying to convince Maud—and every other poor sod in the place—to leave it.

As he thought about those sad, smoke-filled rooms, Sid knew what he had to do; he knew how he could help his wife. He would go to see Teddy Ko and ask him if he'd sold drugs to Maud, or if anyone he knew had. He and Teddy went back a long way. If Teddy knew something, he might tell him. Then again, he might not. Either way, though, Sid had to try. He wanted to get answers for India, to give her some peace over her sister's death.

He would go back. Not right away; Stephen and the other lads needed him too much right now, but before the summer was out. He'd been steering clear of London, and India knew it, so he would have to cook up a story about why he was suddenly going—maybe he'd say that he was after supplies for the hospital—so that she wouldn't worry about him. It was the last place he wanted to go, but he would do it for her.

Back to the East End. Back to the past. Back to the scene of so many crimes.

CHAPTER FIFTY-FOUR

"MAKE IT QUICK, Wills, or Johnny Turkey'll blow us both to hell!" Dan Harper shouted over the noise of his biplane's propeller.

Willa gave him a thumbs-up to signal that she'd heard him. He gave her one back, then the biplane banked sharply right. Willa unfastened her safety belt, raised her camera, leaned as far out of her seat as she dared, and started to film.

Bedouin raiders had told Lawrence about the Turkish Army encampment in a valley to the west of the Jabal ad Duruz hills. Lawrence had no idea if they were telling the truth or if they'd been paid by the Turks to spread false information. He immediately sent a messenger to Amman, where the British had troops garrisoned and two biplanes, and asked the commander to undertake aerial reconnaissance for him. Willa had gone with the messenger. She'd never filmed from the air and thought this would be the perfect opportunity to start. For once, Lawrence had taken little convincing. The Bedouins' reports troubled him, and he knew she would bring back good pictures. The rumored encampment was close to Damascus. Had the Turks got wind of Lawrence's plan to march on the city? Were they building up troops to defend it? It was early August now, and Lawrence and his troops had taken Aqaba last month without too much difficulty, but Damascus, which was well defended, and which Lawrence wanted in British hands before autumn, would be a much harder nut to crack.

Willa saw now that the Bedouins had got the camp's position right—it lay roughly a hundred and fifty miles southeast of Damascus, in a shallow valley, but they'd vastly underestimated its size. Canvas tents covered at least fifty acres of ground. Soldiers were drilling—at least a thousand of them. There was a huge livestock pen full of the goats and sheep needed to feed the men. Another pen held camels—which would undoubtedly be used by the Turks for reconnaissance missions of their own.

Luckily there were no airplanes on the ground. The Germans had far fewer aircraft in the desert than the British did. Consequently, their air reconnaissance wasn't as good as Britain's, and their air attacks were less frequent. There were guns on the ground though: two large antiaircraft guns. She and Dan had seen them immediately, and both had known that they had only minutes to get the film they needed and get gone. The Turks obviously did not want their position discovered, or if it was, they wanted to make sure the discoverers did not live to make their findings public.

As Willa looked through her viewfinder, she saw soldiers running out to man those guns. Only seconds later, the barrels had been aimed—at them.

"Go, Dan!" she shouted, still filming. "Get us out of here!"

Dan was way ahead of her. The plane, a Sopwith Strutter, was quick and maneuverable, and he now put it through its paces, swooping down suddenly, then banking left, climbing again, flying fast and erratically in a bid to evade the guns.

Willa heard them blasting and hoped—because she still had not put her camera down—that she'd caught it all on film.

Only a minute or so later, though it felt much longer, the plane shot over the first of the Jabal ad Duruz hills, out of range of the guns.

Dan whooped loudly, raising his thumb again, and Willa leaned back in her seat, eyes closed, relief flooding through her. They'd done it. She'd got her film, Dan had got them out alive, and Lawrence would get the recon information he so desperately needed.

Willa wondered, as Dan passed over the hills completely, what the Turkish troops were doing. If they were meant to defend Damascus, why weren't they garrisoned there? She felt the plane bank sharply left and knew they were heading south now, to Lawrence's camp. Dan would drop her there then continue back to Amman. She had just started to breathe a little easier, when—about seventy miles south of the hills—she heard Dan suddenly swear, panic in his voice.

"What is it?" she shouted.

"Sandstorm!" he shouted back. "Out of bloody nowhere! I'm going to try to set us down!"

Two minutes later, the storm hit them, buffeting the plane badly, driving sharp, stinging grains of sand everywhere. Willa felt them against her face. Her goggles protected her eyes from being scratched, but they afforded her no vision. The winds were so wild, and the sand was whirling so thickly, she could barely see a foot in front of her.

She felt the plane descending, felt it bucking and jumping as it did. She heard Dan swear again and again as he struggled to control it, and then she heard nothing—nothing but the fierce screaming of the wind—for the propeller had stopped.

"It's jammed!" Dan shouted. "Sand's got inside it. Hang on!"

"How high are we?" Willa shouted, refastening her safety belt. If they'd got down low enough, they might have a chance.

But Dan didn't answer her. He couldn't. He was struggling to keep the plane level, so he could bring it down like a glider. Willa felt the plane lurch and then dive, level itself, and then dive again.

The film, she thought. The camera. No matter what happened to her, the film had to survive. She put the camera on her lap, then curled her torso over it, head down, hoping to cushion it from the impact of the landing—or the crash—with her body.

She heard screaming—she didn't know if it was coming from

her, Dan, or the wind. And then there was a roaring noise as the plane went down. It hit the ground hard, knocking the landing gear off. It skidded along at speed, hit a large rock, and flipped over, tearing its wings and propeller off, tearing its pilot apart.

Willa felt the plane roll over and over. She felt sand and rock pelt against her, felt the plane's body crush in against her. The belt that held her in her seat felt as if it would cut her in two. The plane rolled over a few more times, then stopped and toppled onto its left side.

Willa spat sand from her mouth. "Dan!" she cried out hoarsely, but she got no answer.

Dazed and shaking, hardly daring to believe she was alive, Willa raised her head. There was no more wind, no more driving sand. The storm had stopped. There was sand in her eyes, though. Blood, too. Her goggles had been ripped off. She lowered her head again, horribly dizzy, and felt for her camera, but it was gone. She was taking a few deep breaths, trying to clear her head, to make the spinning stop, when she smelled something, something acrid—smoke. The plane was on fire.

"Dan . . . Dan, are you there?" she called again, more weakly. And again there was no answer. He must've been knocked out, she thought.

She sat up all the way, gasping from a horrible pain in her side, and tried to pull herself out but could not. She remembered her restraints and unbuckled them, then crawled out of her seat. It was difficult. The harness on her artificial leg had been damaged in the crash and the leg was hard to control. When she was finally out of the plane, she turned around—ready to pull Dan out—and screamed.

Dan Harper had been decapitated by the impact.

She didn't have long to mourn him, for smoke from the burning engine, thick and choking, enveloped her. She stood up, panting with pain, and staggered away from the plane.

It was then that she saw them—four Bedouin men, their faces wrapped protectively against the storm. They were about ten yards away. Staring at her. They must have seen the plane go down, she thought.

They spoke among themselves in a dialect she couldn't understand. Then they shouted at her. In Turkish.

Oh, God, she thought. Oh, no. They were in the employ of the Turks. No matter what, they must not get her camera, for they would take it to their masters, and the Turks would see what was on it and know that the English had seen the Jabal ad Duruz camp. But where was it? She looked around frantically, then spotted it on the ground, about halfway between herself and the Bedouins.

Willa knew she only had seconds. She started hobbling toward the camera, as fast as she could go, but one of the men, seeing her intent, got to it first. The others started moving toward her.

Willa was trapped. She knew she must not let them take her, for they would bring her to their masters, along with the camera, and she well knew what the Turks were capable of. They had captured Lawrence once, when he was spying in Amman. They had thrown him in prison, beaten him, and raped him.

She pulled up her right trouser leg. She was reaching for the knife she always wore strapped to her calf when the first man got to her. He backhanded her hard and sent her reeling. She hit the ground; the knife went flying from her hand. She tried to get up, to go after it, but the man who'd hit her grabbed the back of her shirt and flipped her over. She felt his rough hands on her, tearing her shirt open. Felt him rip Fatima's necklace from her.

Again she lunged for the knife, but a second man kicked it away. Two other men grabbed her arms and hoisted her to her feet. She struggled and fought ferociously, hoping to make them angry enough to kill her. She screamed insults at them, shouted curses at them. Begged for death.

Until a fist, aimed to the side of her head, finally silenced her.

CHAPTER FIFTY-FIVE

"FUCKING HELL! IT *is* you!" Teddy Ko bellowed.

Teddy was standing in the doorway of his Limehouse office, wearing a gold ring, diamond cuff links, and a striped flannel suit—one that all but shouted *wide boy.*

"Couldn't believe me ears when Mai here said Sid Malone wants to see me. Fucking Sid Malone! I thought you was dead, Sid. Last I heard, you was floating facedown in the Thames."

Sid forced a smile. "Can't believe everything you hear, Teddy."

"Come in! Come in!" Teddy said, waving Sid into his office. "Mai!" he shouted at his secretary. "Bring us some whiskey. Cigars, too. Hurry up!"

That's our Teddy, Sid thought. Always a charmer.

Teddy sat down at a huge desk, fashioned from ebony and embellished with paintings of dragons, and motioned for Sid to take one of the chairs across from him.

As he did, Sid looked around the large and opulently appointed room. On the walls hung richly embroidered ceremonial robes from China, crossed swords with jeweled hilts, and hand-colored photographs of Peking. Tall blue and white urns stood in the corners of the room. Thick rugs with more dragons on them covered the floor.

Sid remembered when Teddy worked out of a room in one of his laundries. Back when he paid Sid protection money. Back when Sid was the governor—the biggest, most feared crime lord in all of London.

"You've come up in the world, Teddy," he said.

Teddy chuckled, pleased by the compliment. "Got fifty-eight

laundries now, me. All over London. A big importing business, too—porcelain, furniture, artworks, silk, parasols, you name it—direct from Shanghai to London." His voice dropped. "That's the legit side. I'm still going gangbusters with the drugs. Branched off into prostitution, too. Got whorehouses in the East End and the West. Twenty-three and counting."

"That's wonderful, Teddy," Sid said. He couldn't quite muster a warm *Congratulations*.

"What about you? Where have you been? What have you been doing with yourself all these years?"

"It's a long story," Sid said. "I've been out of the country."

Teddy nodded knowingly. "Busies made it too hot for you here, did they?" he said. "Had to go farther afield? Well, I imagine the villainy's just as good in Dublin or Glasgow or wherever it is you are now."

Sid smiled. It was fine with him if Teddy thought he was up to no good elsewhere. He was not about to tell Teddy Ko, or anyone else from his old life, about his new life or his new last name. His wife, his children, America—it was all off-limits.

Teddy's secretary entered his office. She placed a silver tray on the table. On it was a bottle of scotch, a bucket of ice, two crystal glasses, and a small wooden humidor. She poured the men their whiskey, trimmed and lit their cigars, then quietly disappeared again. Sid didn't want either the drink or the smoke, but he felt it would be rude to refuse them.

"So, Sid," Teddy said, glancing at his watch, "what can I do for you? What brings you here? Business or pleasure?"

"Neither," Sid said. "I'm here as a favor to a friend."

Teddy, puffing away on his cigar, raised an eyebrow. "Go on," he said.

"A few years ago, right before the war started, a former customer of yours, Maud Selwyn Jones, overdosed on morphine."

"I remember. It was a shame, that."

"Did she get it from you?"

Teddy leaned forward in his chair. His smile was gone. "Maybe she did, maybe she didn't. Either way, why the fuck would I tell you?" he said. "You've been gone a long time, Sid. Things have changed. You're not the guv anymore. You want something from me now, you can pay for it. Just like everyone else."

Sid had anticipated this. He reached inside his jacket. He pulled out an envelope and pushed it across the desk to Teddy.

Teddy opened the envelope, counted its contents—which came to a hundred pounds—then said, "I didn't sell the morphine to Maud. I barely sold her anything anymore. She'd quit coming to the dens years ago. After that bloody doctor, her sister or whatever the hell she was, tried to drag her out. Meddling bitch, she was. Bent on wrecking my business."

Sid's jaw tightened at that, but he said nothing. A bust-up with Teddy wouldn't serve his purposes. "Did she look like an addict to you?" he asked. "The last time you saw her?"

Teddy shook his head. "No, she didn't. She was thin, but she was always thin. She didn't have the hop-fiend look. You know, all pale skin and dark circles under the eyes and desperate. I know a lot of addicts. Maud didn't look like one."

"Did you hear anything about it at the time? From anyone else in the business? Did anyone else you know sell Maud any morphine?" he asked.

Teddy shook his head. "Not that I know of. But I hardly went round asking, did I?"

"Can you ask now?"

Teddy shrugged. "For a hundred quid I can do a lot of things," he said. "But it was over four years ago, wasn't it? I'm not sure how much I can find out. Why is it so important to you?"

"I'd appreciate anything you can do, Teddy," Sid said, stubbing out the rest of his cigar.

"Where can I get hold of you? If I find out anything?" Teddy asked.

"I'll get hold of you."

"When? I'm a busy man."

"How about we meet right here again? In a month's time. Same day. In September."

"I'll try me best," Teddy said.

Sid rose to take his leave.

"You're not leaving already, are you?" Teddy said. "You only just got here. Let me show you round the place."

Sid noted that Teddy looked at his watch again as he spoke. He'd said he was a busy man. Undoubtedly he had places to go and things to do, but oddly, it seemed to Sid that Teddy wanted to keep talking, to hold him here. Sid didn't want to stay. He couldn't wait to get out of the East End, to get away from all the memories and all the ghosts.

Teddy wouldn't hear of his leaving, though. He had to at least see the warehouse first. Sid agreed, reluctantly. He wanted Teddy to do him a favor, and if admiring the warehouse was what it took to get Teddy's goodwill, he would do it.

They walked out of Teddy's two-story office building, to the four-story warehouse that abutted it. As he stepped inside, Sid felt as if he'd stepped into a giant, sprawling Chinese bazaar. There were huge brightly painted beds. Tables inlaid with mother-of-pearl, ebony, and ivory. Giant blue-glazed statues of lions and dogs. Urns large enough to plant trees in. There were vases and teapots and gongs. Rolled up rugs were propped against the walls. Bolts of silks and satins were stacked on shelves. There were open crates containing beaded necklaces, bracelets carved of cinnabar, and tiny jade figurines. Teddy reached into one crate, pulled out a small carved Buddha, no taller than two inches, and gave it to Sid.

"For good luck," he said, winking.

"Thank you, Teddy," Sid said, putting the figurine in his jacket pocket.

"Here, this'll interest you. Come take a look," Teddy said.

He led Sid upstairs to the second floor. It was filled with tea chests. Teddy pried the lid off one, dug deep down into the rich black tea that filled it, and pulled up a large, dark brown lump, roughly the shape and size of a cannonball.

"Chinese opium. The purest. The very best. It comes in buried in tea chests. Stuffed inside statues. Teapots. Furniture. And it goes out through my laundries, cut up and wrapped in brown paper like a bundle of napkins or shirts. And Old Bill's none the wiser."

"You were always a clever one, Teddy. Always going places," Sid said. "I've got to hand it to you."

Teddy didn't give a damn about the people the drug enslaved. He didn't care whether they could afford it or not. Whether they went without shoes, or clothes, or food to fund their habit. Or whether their children did. He'd made himself a bundle in the opium trade, stood to make a lot more, and that's all that counted. Sid knew this, for he'd been the same as Teddy once, done the same things. A long time ago. In another life. Before he'd met India.

Teddy held the fat brown lump out to Sid now. "You want a taste? I'll have Mai fix us a pipe. Get us a couple of girls, too. Just like old times."

"Thanks, Teddy, but I have to be off."

Out on the sidewalk, Sid said his good-byes. Teddy shook his hand, glancing up the street as he did, and said, "I'll start asking around on the other thing. Hopefully I'll get something for you. Same day next month, right?"

"Right-o," Sid said. He hunched his shoulders against a sudden August rain shower and started walking west. He passed by several small, dreary shops, a rope-maker's, and two dingy pubs. On the corner, three little girls, not one of whom was dressed for the weather, were jumping rope and singing a morbid rhyme.

There was a little bird, her name was Enza.
I opened the window and in flew Enza.

The Spanish flu had already cropped up in Scotland, India had said. Sid shuddered to think what would happen if it hit the East End. The area, with its notorious overcrowding and poor sanitation, would provide an ideal breeding ground for the disease. It would move through the slums like wildfire.

Five minutes later, he found a hackney cab, climbed inside, and told the driver to take him to Paddington Station. He was well on his way out of Limehouse by the time a carriage, sleek and black, pulled up in front of Teddy's offices, so he did not see the two men step out of it—one wearing the rough clothes of a riverman, the other in a flash suit, tugging on a gold earring and smiling with a mouthful of black, rotted teeth.

CHAPTER FIFTY-SIX

"HELLO, MAI, DARLING," Billy Madden said. "Where's that boss of yours?"

"He's in his office, Mr. Madden," Mai said. "He's expecting you. What may I get for you? Tea? Whiskey?"

Billy put his hands on Mai's desk. He leaned in close to her and smiled horribly. "How about yourself, you lovely little lotus flower? Buck naked on a bed in the back? I've always wanted to see what's under those pretty silk dresses of yours."

The man with Billy looked away, clearly uncomfortable. Mai colored, but her polite smile didn't falter. "If you would like, Mr. Madden, I can arrange a girl for you when your are finished with Mr. Ko," she said.

Billy's smile faded. His eyes turned hard. "I told you what I would like. You. On your back. Now get up and get your knickers off, you useless . . ."

Teddy, hearing Billy's voice, stepped out of his office and saw what was going on.

"Oh, for fuck's sake, Billy, you don't want her," he said, trying to defuse the situation. "She's got smaller tits than you do. Why do you think she's here doing my typing instead of working in one of my whorehouses?"

"Is that so?" Billy said.

He walked around Mai's desk, behind Mai herself. Then he reached around her and cupped her small breasts, weighing them in his hands. Mai stiffened. She swallowed hard, stared straight ahead, and did not make a sound.

Anger rose in Teddy. He liked Mai. She was a nice girl, not a tart. She was good at her job. She didn't deserve this. But Billy was the guv'nor. He took what he wanted. If he wanted Mai, he'd have her, and there wasn't a damn thing Teddy or anyone else could do about it.

"You're right, Teddy," Billy finally said. "Not enough here to keep me happy. Back to your typing, darlin'."

Mai picked up a pencil. Teddy saw that her hands were shaking. He swore under his breath. Scenes like this were becoming more frequent. Billy Madden was a bastard and always had been, but he was getting worse. Bothering women. Losing his temper. Starting fights for no good reason. He'd bashed a lad's skull in a month ago at the Bark because he thought he was laughing at him. He'd got this mad, wild look in his eyes, then did for the poor sod.

"Come have a glass of whiskey with me, Billy," Teddy said now. "You and John, both. Afterward, I'll fix you up with a girl who's worth your while. Two girls, if you like. From Shanghai. They'll have you begging for mercy. Come on, come inside now, I've got things I need to discuss with you."

"And I've got things to discuss with you, Edward," Billy said, sitting down behind Teddy's desk. "You were short. Two weeks in a row." Billy's man, John, stood behind him.

"I wasn't short. That was twenty-five percent. Same as always. Your cut was less because I sold less. My supplies were low. Got another shipment in at Millwall as we speak. Soon as I get it, and get selling it—"

Billy cut him off. "John here is going with you to unload your tea from the *Ning Hai* tonight. Him and three more of my men."

"Tonight? Why tonight? It's supposed to be unloaded tomorrow afternoon," Teddy asked.

"Because the next high tide's at two A.M.," John Harris said.

"And because I don't want you offloading any of the cargo before tomorrow," Billy said, picking his nails with Teddy's letter opener. "John and the others are going to get it, bring it here to the warehouse, open it, and see just how much hop you're bringing in. So I can figure out myself what you should be paying me."

"You think I'm cheating you out of your cut," Teddy said.

The anger Billy had kindled in Teddy flamed into a hot fury. Billy was the guv'nor, yes, but even so, he was taking a few too many liberties. Accusing him, Teddy, of cheating him out of money, the cheek of it. Teddy *was* cheating him, of course, but still—he shouldn't just come in here, rough up his help, and make Teddy look small on his own turf.

"I'm just keeping my eye on things, that's all," Billy said.

"Is that so? Well, you know what, Billy? You might want to start keeping both eyes on things," Teddy said hotly

Billy leaned forward. "Oh, aye? And just what do you mean by that?"

"Sid Malone's back in town."

Billy stopped picking his nails. He looked up at Teddy, and Teddy saw, to his satisfaction, that Billy had paled. Teddy knew that there was only one thing Billy hated more than another villain cheating him out of money, and that was another villain making a play for his manor—a manor they both knew used to belong to Sid.

"What did you say?"

"I said Sid Malone's back in town."

"Now I know where all your hop's gone, Teddy. You've been smoking it yourself."

"He was here. Right in this office. Not ten minutes ago."

"Sid Malone was fished out of the Thames years ago. He's dead."

"Not anymore he isn't."

"Are you sure, Teddy?"

"I'm sure. I know him. I used to work for him. Remember? It was Sid Malone in my office, sure as I'm standing here."

Billy glowered at him. Then he slammed his fists on the desk and stood up. "Why didn't you tell me that?" he shouted.

"I wanted to!" Teddy shouted back. "But you were too busy interfering with my girl, and with my business! I even tried to keep him here until you came. Tried to stall. But he said he had to be off."

"What the fuck was he doing here?" he said. "What did he want?"

"He wanted information on that woman's death—Selwyn Jones. The rich one. The one who topped herself a few years back. He wanted to know if I'd sold her the drugs."

"What? Why the hell would he want to know that?"

"I asked him. He didn't tell me."

"You tell him about Stiles?"

Teddy shook his head.

A man named Peter Stiles had bought quite a bit of morphine from Teddy only days before Maud Selwyn Jones died. Billy knew about it; he was the one who'd sent Stiles to Teddy. Both Billy and Teddy had wondered at the time if there was any connection between Stiles and the Selwyn Jones woman's death.

"Why is he nosing into this?" Billy asked. "What's this Jones woman's suicide to him?"

"I have no idea," Teddy said. "It makes no sense."

Billy made no response at first, then, at length, he said, "Yes, it does. Sid Malone's back and he wants his old manor back. He has to get me out of the way first, though, and he's looking to see if there's any way he can land me in the shit with Old Bill. He's trying to do it through you. Wants to have me sent down for the Selwyn Jones woman. Do it all nice and clean-like. No violence. No blood. At least not to begin with, that is."

Billy lit up a cigarette as he spoke, and started pacing the room. Teddy wasn't quite sure that Billy had it right. Sid Malone certainly hadn't acted like a man planning to launch a big turf war. But Teddy also knew that once Billy Madden got an idea into his head, there was no getting it out.

"Did you tell him anything at all?"

"I said I'd dig around, see what I could come up with. We're supposed to meet again next month. Right here."

"Good. Well done, Teddy lad."

"What do you want me to do when he comes back? Give him something? Give him nothing?"

"Just keep him here, Teddy. Keep him talking."

"You're going to do for him," Teddy said.

Billy Madden shook his head. His eyes had that mad look in them. The one Teddy knew all too well, and wished he didn't.

"No," Billy said, "I'm going to beat him bloody first. Make him tell me what he's got on me. Who he's working with. And then I'm going to do for him."

CHAPTER FIFTY-SEVEN

WILLA OPENED HER eyes.

The world, bright and sand-colored, spun sickeningly beneath her. She tried to move, but pain, breathtaking and horrible, shot through her side. She tried to right herself, tried to sit up, but she could not make her arms and legs work.

She wondered, for a few seconds, if she was dead.

She managed to pick her head up, but was seized by a dizziness so strong that she was sick. Her stomach heaved again and again, but nothing came up. She lowered her head. Her cheek pressed into something thick and soft. It seemed to be moving. She seemed to be moving.

"Water," she moaned, closing her eyes. Her throat was parched. It felt like it was on fire. Her lips were cracked. "Water, please . . . ."

A voice was yelling. A man's voice. The words sounded like Bedouin, but she couldn't understand them.

She opened her eyes again, and this time they focused. She saw rocks and sand going by. She saw a camel's leg. And her own hands, tied at the wrists by a length of rope, hanging down in front of her.

She realized she was lying across the back of a camel, bound fast against the back of the rider's saddle. How long had she been like this? Hours? Days?

She struggled, trying again to right herself, to sit up. The rider must have felt her movements, or heard them, for he turned around to shout at her. He was telling her to stop, to lie still, but she did not understand him, and would not have heeded him if she had. Frenzied by pain and fear, she kept struggling, kept pleading for water.

The camel driver was angered by this, for her movements were spooking his animal. He shouted once more for her to be still, then he struck her where he could easily reach her—on her side. Willa screamed with pain as her damaged ribs received his blows.

Pain filled her senses. She could see nothing, hear nothing, feel nothing but it's awful suffocating blackness. She cried out once more, and then she was still.

CHAPTER FIFTY-EIGHT

"COME ON, ALBIE. What's the news? Did Lawrence take Damascus yet? Are Gerry and Johnny Turkey chasing him all around the sand dunes?" Seamie Finnegan said. He was sitting in a chair in Albie's office in the building that housed the Bureau of Arab Affairs in Haifa.

"I could tell you," Albie Alden said, not looking up from the document he was reading—a telegram, taken from a stack that his secretary had just delivered. "But then I'd have to kill you."

Seamie shook his head. "I still can't believe it: Albie Alden, spy catcher. The Secret Service Bureau. Room 40. And you cool as a cucumber the whole time. Never said a word."

Albie looked at Seamie over the top of his spectacles. "Stop pestering me and let me get these telegrams read. Or else I'll have the guards come and escort you back to hospital. Where you should be. In your bed. Recovering."

"Bugger that. I can't stand it anymore. I'm going mad in hospital. I shouldn't be there at all. I'm fit enough to take command of another vessel right now, but the bloody doctors won't let me. I'm getting a new ship, the *Exeter*, but not for another five weeks."

"Fit? Didn't you just take a two-inch chunk of shrapnel to the torso? Lift up your shirt. No, go on. Lift it up. . . ." Albie stared at Seamie's torso, shaking his head. "Your dressings haven't even come off yet," he said. "They're covering your entire right side. What happened anyway? You still haven't told me the whole story."

"My ship, *Hawk*—she was a destroyer—tangled with a German gunboat about twenty miles west of here. We took a hit to the hull, just above the waterline. And then another to the foredeck. I caught a piece of it."

"Bloody hell," Albie said.

"Yes, it was," Seamie said, with a sardonic smile. "The shrapnel missed my ribs and my vitals, but it took a chunk of flesh out of my side. Luckily, we'd sited the gunboat and were able to radio one of our own boats about fifteen minutes before we were hit. They got there too late to stop the attack, but in time to rescue us." His smile faded. "Well, most of us. I lost five men."

"I'm sorry," Albie said.

Seamie nodded. "I am, too. The gunboat got us back to Haifa and the hospital here, but I swear, if I'd known they were going to keep hold of me for so long, I'd have stayed in the water. I'm going off my nut with boredom. I was so happy when I heard you'd arrived in Haifa. I still can't believe it."

"How *did* you hear about it? I'm supposed to be keeping a low profile here."

"Completely by chance. I overheard one of the nurses talking to her friend about you. Seems you were in for some sort of stomach trouble."

Albie made a face. "Yes. Dysentery. Picked it up in Cairo. Bloody awful thing."

"Anyway, I guess she gave you some medicine and fell in love at the same time. God knows why. The heat must be affecting her head. When I heard your name, I asked her to describe you. When she had, I knew it was you. Couldn't possibly be two gangly, four-eyed boffins in the world with the name of Albie Alden."

Albie laughed. "Can you keep quiet for two more minutes so I can finish reading these telegrams?"

"I'll do my best," Seamie said, picking up a folder and fanning himself with it, for the August heat was brutal.

He had knocked on Albie's door about half an hour ago. His old friend had been so surprised to see him. He'd invited him in and had him sit down, and Seamie had learned that Albie had arrived in Haifa two days ago. After Albie had sworn him to secrecy, he'd also learned that Albie had been posted from London, where he'd been working since 1914 for Room 40, a group of code breakers under the aegis of the Royal Navy, to head intelligence and espionage in western Arabia.

Seamie was astonished to learn that his shy, quiet friend was part of Room 40. He remembered Albie back in 1914, remembered how weary and tense he'd been. He'd thought it had all been caused by his father's illness and by overwork. Now he knew that Albie and a team of brilliant Cambridge academics had been working feverishly, before the war had even begun, to intercept and unravel German intelligence communications. He had always admired Albie greatly; he admired him even more now, knowing how relentlessly he had worked—literally night and day—even when he had lost his beloved father.

Albie, finished with the stack of telegrams now, rose and called for his secretary. He asked her to file them all before she left, then he picked up his briefcase.

"Sorry to be so distracted. It's been a bit hectic. I just have to gather some things for an early meeting tomorrow and then we can go," he said. He stopped shuffling papers for a few seconds, looked at Seamie, and earnestly said, "It's ever so good to see you here. Truly."

"It's good to see you, too, Alb," Seamie replied. "Haifa . . . who'd have guessed it?"

Neither man said, for it was not in either's nature to be overly emotional, but they both knew what their words really meant—not so much that they had never expected to see each other in Haifa, but that they had never expected to see each other anywhere again. Ever.

The war had taken millions of lives, including those of many of their friends—men they'd known as boys, men they'd gone to school with, grown up with, sailed and hiked and climbed and drunk with. Sometimes it seemed everyone they'd ever known was gone.

"You hear much about Everton?" Seamie said now.

"Dead. The Marne."

"Erickson?"

"The Somme."

Seamie rattle off another dozen names. Albie told him that ten had been killed and the other two had been injured.

"Gorgeous George?" Seamie asked hesitantly, afraid of the answer.

"Mallory's still with us. Last I heard."

"I'm so glad," Seamie said. "Someday, when this whole damn thing is over, we're going climbing again, Alb. All of us. On Ben Nevis. Or Snowdon."

"Wouldn't that be lovely?" Albie said wistfully. "We could rent a cottage. In Scotland or Wales. Or maybe the Lake District."

"Anywhere, as long as there's a good pub close by."

"Oh, for a plate of cheese sandwiches with Branston pickle."

"You're a madman, Albie. You really are," Seamie said, laughing. "Ask any man here what he misses and he'll say women. A pint of good ale. Roast beef with gravy. Not you. You want Branston pickle." Seamie suddenly stopped laughing and turned serious. "We'll do it, Albie. We will. All of us together again. You and I, and George, and . . . well, maybe not quite all of us." He was quiet for a bit, then he said, "Do you . . . do you ever hear anything from her?"

Albie sighed. "Very little," he said. "Mother received a letter, late in 1914, from Cairo. A few more in 1915. Not much since."

"Cairo? You mean here in the Mideast?"

"I do," Albie said. "She'd followed Tom Lawrence out here, if you can believe it."

"Yes, I can."

"She arrived here in September of '14. Just after the war broke out. Lawrence got her a job under Allenby. She was working on maps. I've seen some of them. They're bloody good. Then she resigned her position. Left Cairo. Right about the same time Lawrence went into the desert. Wrote to Mother and said she was traveling east. That was the last we heard from her. I imagine she went back to Tibet, but I really have no idea."

Albie's expression was pained as he spoke.

"I shouldn't have mentioned her," Seamie said. "I'm sorry."

Albie smiled ruefully. "It's all right, old mole," he said.

No more was said about it. No more needed to be. Seamie knew Albie's relationship with his sister was a difficult one. He was glad, however, that Albie knew nothing about the relationship he and Willa had had in London, shortly after he'd married Jennie.

"Now, if I can just find those figures . . . ," Albie said, digging under a pile of papers on his desk.

"Albie, you didn't tell me . . . why the devil did London post you all the way out here, anyway? Why Haifa? Are you being sent down? Did you bugger something up? Get a code wrong?"

Albie laughed unhappily. "I only wish it was that," he said. "I'd be having myself a holiday. Buy myself a nice pair of field glasses and see the sights."

Seamie, who'd gotten out of his chair and walked over to the window, turned around, worried by the grim note in his friend's voice.

"What is it, then?" he asked him.

Albie gave Seamie a long look, then gravely said, "I shouldn't tell you this either, but I will because your life may well depend on it and because you may be able to help me. However, you must keep the information to yourself."

"Of course."

"We have a German mole in London. A very effective one. Somewhere in the Admiralty."

"What?" Seamie said. "How can that be?"

"We don't know. We've taken great pains to ferret him out—for years—but we've not been successful. I can tell you, though, that we're almost certain someone has been feeding information on our ships to German high command and that it's been happening for years. At the beginning of the war, they received intelligence on the design and capabilities of our dreadnoughts. Now they're getting information on deployment of our ships. In the European theater. And here, in the Mediterranean."

Seamie's blood ran cold.

"For a long time, Germany was not overly concerned about the eastern front," Albie said. "Now that Lawrence is making such headway in the desert—and now that it actually looks like he has a crack at Damascus—they are paying more attention. Messages appear to be going from London to a contact in Damascus. We don't know how. Or to whom. But we do know why—the Germans and the Turks want to keep hold of the city at all costs. They plan to strongly defend it—which means putting paid to Lawrence and his band. When they've done that, they want to retake Aqaba, then advance on Cairo. This entails added ground troops, of course, but they've also begun to step up their naval presence here."

"My God. The *Hawk,*" Seamie said, stricken. "My men."

Albie nodded. "We don't believe it was luck that led that German gunboat to you. They knew where you were. We lost two more ships in the last three days as well. One off the coast of Tripoli, the other south of Cyprus. The Admiralty wants it stopped. Now."

"But how?" Seamie said. "You haven't been able to find the mole in London, you said. And he's been operating for years."

Albie nodded. "Captain Reginald Hall, the head of Room 40, thinks that if we can't nab him, perhaps we can nab his counterpart here. It's a long shot, admittedly, but a great deal of intelligence comes and goes through Cairo, Jaffa, and Haifa. People here hear things and see things. I'm hopeful that we can collect enough pieces to put the puzzle together. We're cultivating a lot of sources—Bedouin traders who move between Cairo and Damascus, and who courier goods and parcels. Brothel owners whose girls service Europeans. Hotel owners. Waiters. Barmen. I'm not sure whom the information is going to come from, but I'm chasing down every lead I can think of. We have to find the man and soon. Before it's too late. Before he does any more damage."

"How can I help, Albie?"

"You can keep your ear to the ground," Albie said. "It's amazing who these people are. He could be the man who cuts your hair. The one who serves your lunch. You never know how close you might be."

"Excuse me, Mr. Alden. . . ." A young woman was standing in the doorway. She was small and pretty and serious. She wore a white blouse and gray skirt. Her hair was neatly pulled back.

"Yes, Florence?"

"One more thing . . . this just arrived classified from General Allenby's office," she said, handing him an envelope.

"Thank you, Florence," Albie said. "That will be all. I shall see you tomorrow. I expect to be back here by ten o'clock."

"Very well. Good night, sir."

"Good night."

"I'll just take a quick look at this and we'll be off. Grab our jackets, will you?" Albie said to Seamie.

As Albie opened the envelope and pulled out a typed memo,

Seamie took their jackets off the coat stand in Albie's office. He was glad they were finally leaving for the officers' mess. Never mind bed rest, a tall cool gin and tonic would be just what the doctor ordered.

"You ready?" he said, turning back to Albie.

But Albie didn't answer him. One hand was over his face, covering his eyes. The other, the one holding whatever had come in the envelope from Allenby, was at his side.

"Albie?" Seamie said, alarmed. "Albie, what is it?"

Albie didn't answer him. Instead, he held the document out to him. Seamie quickly took it and started to read.

He skimmed the lines that warned the reader that this was classified information, and quickly came to the subject of the memo. A British plane doing reconnaissance in the Jabal ad Duruz hills had gone down in the desert four days ago. The pilot, Dan Harper, was killed in the crash. The plane was carrying one passenger—the photographer Alden Williams. Williams, whose body was not found at the crash site and who was presumed dead, might have been captured by Bedouin raiders, or by Turkish troops, who held the area. The wreckage was thoroughly searched, but Williams's camera was not found. Whatever information Williams was able to gain about the size and movements of Turkish troops near Damascus had been lost. There was concern that if the Turks had Williams, they might try to extract sensitive information from their prisoner. And then, at the bottom of the note, was a hand-scrawled message from General Allenby.

"No," Seamie said as he read it. "Dear God, no."

Dear Alden,

As this event concerns reconnaissance, and may come under your bailiwick, I wish to apprise you of some particulars.

Alden Williams, as you likely know, was the photographer attached to Lawrence and his camp. Williams is a pseudonym used to obscure the fact that the photographer is a woman. It is highly doubtful that the British public would approve of a woman's presence on the battlefield. Equally unpalatable to the public would be the idea of a British woman taken prisoner by the Turkish—some of whom, as you also know, have been known to treat their prisoners with the utmost brutality. Please keep me posted of any and all intelligence gathered on this particular topic.

Alden Williams's real name is Willa Alden. Same surname as your own. Is she any relation to you?

Please keep these details confidential.

Yours,
Allenby

CHAPTER FIFTY-NINE

INDIA FROWNED. SHE sat back in her chair and regarded Lindy Summers, her head nurse. "What about the new one? The blond boy who came in yesterday . . . Matthews? Any changes in his condition?" she asked her.

Lindy shook her head. "No, there isn't, Dr. Jones. Which is both good and bad. Good because I'm still convinced he has bronchitis, not the flu, but bad because he's so weak, I'm worried the bronchitis alone will be enough to finish him off." Lindy fished out a folder from the stack she'd just placed on India's desk and handed it to her. "Here's the latest on his vitals. Another lad, Abbott . . . now, he has me worried."

"Tall lad? Red hair and freckles? Facial burns?" India asked.

"That's the one. He came in feverish, complaining of headache. Now he's coughing. And his lungs sound wet."

India's expression became grim. "We have to set up a quarantine for possible flu victims. Right now," she said. "We simply cannot afford to take any chances. These men are so weak as it is that if the flu gets hold of them, they won't stand a chance. Gather the staff, tell them to go ahead and set up the ward in the attic."

"The attic?" Lindy said uncertainly.

"We had four men arrive this morning, and we're due to get another seven tomorrow. We're out of room. The attic's cramped but it's clean. It's hardly ideal, but it's all we've got," India said. She had long ago learned that when it came to medicine, ideal situations existed only in textbooks.

"Yes, Dr. Jones," Lindy said. "I'll get started right away."

At that moment, the door to India's office opened and Sid stepped inside. A visit from him during the day was very unusual. He was often so busy with the shell-shocked patients that she was lucky if she and the children saw him at suppertime.

"Sid! I'm so glad you're here. Lindy and I were just talking about the quarantine ward and . . . ," she began.

And then she stopped speaking. For as he sat down across from her, she saw that his face was ashen and his eyes were red. She had only ever seen her husband cry once. A long time ago. She could not imagine what had upset him enough to make him weep.

And then a terrifying thought gripped her. "Sid, the children . . . ," she started to say, her heart in her throat.

"They're fine. All fine," he said. "Lindy, if I could have a minute?"

"Of course. Please excuse me," Lindy Summers said. She quickly stood up, left the room, and closed the door behind her.

India got up, came around to the front of her desk, and sat down next to her husband.

"What is it? What's happened?" she asked him. "Is it Seamie? Did he take a turn for the worse?" India knew, as did the rest of the family, about the destruction of the *Hawk*, and Seamie's resulting injuries, for Jennie had received a telegram and had told them, but those injuries—the telegram said—were not life-threatening.

Sid tried to answer her and found he could not.

"You're scaring me," India said.

He swallowed hard and tried again. "Some new patients came in this morning," he said.

"Yes, I know. Four of them."

"One of them is badly shell-shocked," Sid said. "In fact, it's the worst case I've ever seen. He's gone. Totally gone. Does nothing but shake and stare straight ahead of himself." He paused, and then his voice broke as he said, "India . . . it's Charlie. My nephew. My namesake. And he doesn't know me. He doesn't even know me."

It took a minute for Sid's words to sink in. "I'm so sorry, Sid," she finally said, in a choked voice, leaning her head against his. "Is there no hope? None at all? You can do something, I know you can. I've seen what you've done with the other lads."

Sid shook his head. "Come with me," he said, standing up.

India followed him downstairs. He led her to the last room on the hall where the shell-shocked men lived. She looked through the open door and saw a young man seated on the bed, shaking horribly. He was skeletally thin, just skin over bones. His eyes were open, but they had a dead and empty look to them.

India went to him. She sat down on the bed next to him and gave him a quick examination. She talked to him as she did, trying to make some contact, trying to elicit a response, a flicker of recognition. But her efforts were in vain. There was nothing there. Nothing. It was as if all the things inside of him—his heart and his soul, his bright mind and quick sense of humor—had been ripped out, and all that was left was a shell.

"He's only seventeen, India," Sid said. "He's only seventeen years old."

India heard her husband's choked sobs then. She thought of what she had to do next—call Fiona and Joe and tell them that their precious child was here, in her hospital. That he was wounded, not dead—but he might as well be.

And then India, who had learned long ago not to cry over her patients, covered her face with her hands and wept.

CHAPTER SIXTY

"WALK!" THE MAN shouted in Turkish. "Walk or I'll kick the hell out of you!"

Willa had fallen onto her side in the dirt. Her legs didn't work. Nothing worked. She was dizzy and disoriented. Her eyes wouldn't focus.

"Walk, I said!" the man yelled.

His boot in her ribs made her scream, but it did not bring her to her feet. Nothing could do that. She was going to die here. In the dirt. In the crucifying heat. And she didn't care. She had heard the Bedouin talking to the Turks, and had understood enough of their conversation to know she'd been traveling for five days. After five days of crossing the desert, bound and slung over the back of a camel, after nights spent tied like an animal to a stake in the ground, after enduring dehydration, hunger, and excruciating pain, dying would be a mercy.

Her clothes were caked with dirt, blood, and vomit. She had soiled herself. One of her captors had tried to rape her three nights ago, but had been so repulsed by her condition that he'd turned away from her in disgust.

It didn't matter anymore. None of it mattered. It would all be over soon. She closed her eyes and waited for death. She was not frightened; she welcomed it.

But the Turkish Army had other ideas.

There was more yelling, and then Willa felt hands under her arms, hoisting her to her feet. She opened her eyes, saw a man in uniform hand a leather purse—small and heavy—to the Bedouin raiders who'd captured her. Then two men lifted her off the ground and frog-marched her inside a stone building. She had the vague notion she was in some kind of garrison town. But which one? Was it Damascus?

Her new captors continued to half drag, half carry her through the building. They went through a foyer, down a long hallway, and then down a flight of stairs. It was dark, and her vision was still coming and going, but Willa was certain that she was in a prison.

A thick wooden door was opened, and she was dumped inside a small, dark room with an earthen floor. One of the men left, then came back a minute later with a jug of water. He yelled at her again. She thought he wanted her to drink. But she didn't want the water. She'd made up her mind to die. She struggled, trying to shake the man off, but he was far too strong for her. He held her mouth open until he'd poured most of the water into her, then he held it shut so she could not vomit it back out. After a few minutes had passed, he let go of her and she slumped to the ground.

A plate of food was brought and set down on the floor. The door was closed and locked. It was completely dark in the cell. There was no window, no light at all.

Willa did not know where she was. All she knew was that Bedouins had taken her from the crash site, transported her for many miles, and finally sold her to the Turks—who likely thought she was a spy and intended to interrogate her.

She felt very afraid at the thought of an interrogation. She had heard tales of the Turks' methods and knew they would stop at nothing to get information from her. She promised herself then and there that she would tell them nothing, no matter what they did to her. They would tire eventually and would kill her, but she would give them nothing—nothing about Lawrence, nothing about Damascus.

She would need something to get her through the coming ordeal. Something she could think of to keep up her courage and her strength as they beat her bloody.

An image of a face came to her in the darkness, though she did not want it to. With a trembling hand she traced a single letter in the dirt of her cell floor—the letter S.

CHAPTER SIXTY-ONE

"SEAMIE, YOU CAN'T do this. It's madness. Total bloody madness," Albie Alden said.

Seamie, busy tightening the girth strap on his camel's saddle, did not reply.

"Allenby will send men out to hunt for her," Albie said.

"What men? In case you haven't noticed, Albie, there's a war on," Seamie replied. "Allenby's not going to use valuable troops to hunt for one person—a person who's not even supposed to be in the desert."

"But you're wounded! You can't ride with your injuries. And even if you could, you don't know what you're doing. You don't even know where you're going!"

"He does," Seamie said, pointing at a man sitting atop a second camel, his Bedouin guide, Abdul.

Albie shook his head. "The two of you . . . all alone in the desert. You'll be hopelessly lost within a day. And for what, Seamie? Willa's plane crashed. The pilot was killed. It's likely she was badly injured, and it's equally likely that she is now dead."

Seamie sighed. "That's our Albie, ever the optimist."

"What about your ship? You're supposed to take command of a new ship in just under five weeks' time. How are you going to get out to the Jabal ad Duruz hills, search the area around them, and get back to Haifa in time? If you're not at the docks the morning of the day your commission begins, you'll be classed as a deserter. You know what the British military thinks of deserters, don't you? You'll be court-martialed and shot."

"I'll make sure that I hurry then."

As Albie hectored him, Seamie looked inside his saddlebags, double checking that he'd packed both of his pistols, sufficient ammunition, basic medicines and dressings, and his field glasses; then he rechecked his food and water supplies. It was difficult to see in the darkness. The sun had not yet risen over Haifa.

He had made up his mind to find Willa right after he'd finished reading Allenby's memo. The news had devastated him. He couldn't stand the thought of Willa, possibly injured, certainly afraid, in the hands of cruel and vicious men. It nearly drove him mad.

Instead of going to dinner at the officers' mess, as he and Albie had planned, he'd spent most of the night preparing for the trip. He'd found a guide before the sun had even gone down, and they'd spent the following day gathering supplies. When night fell again, he slept for a few hours, then rose at four A.M., dressed, and made his way to the gates of the city. He'd met Abdul by the east wall just after five o'clock.

Albie, who'd been against the plan ever since he'd heard of it, had met them at the wall and was still trying to talk Seamie out of it. He'd used almost every argument he could think of—every argument, that is, except the one that mattered most to him. He hadn't want to use that one, but he saw now that if he wanted to stop his friend from doing something rash, he had no choice.

"Seamie . . . ," he said now, hesitantly.

"Yes?" Seamie said, buckling one of his saddlebags.

"What about Jennie?"

Seamie stopped what he was doing. He stared straight ahead of himself for a few seconds, then turned to Albie. Albie had never broached the topic of Seamie's affair with Willa; he'd never so much as mentioned it. For years, Seamie thought Albie hadn't known anything about it. Now he saw that he was wrong. He saw something else, too.

"It was you, wasn't it, Albie?" he said quietly. "You're the one who told Willa to go. To leave London. And to leave me. I always wondered if somebody had said something to her. Willa's note . . . her decision to go . . . it was all so abrupt."

"I didn't have a choice, Seamie. It was wrong. For you. For Willa. And for Jennie. I went to your flat one night to see you. You weren't there, but Jennie was. She was very upset. She knew, Seamie. And she was carrying your son. You and Willa are the most important people in the world to me. How could I do nothing? How could I let you destroy yourselves and everyone around you?" Albie looked at Seamie. "You're furious with me, aren't you?"

Seamie felt gutted by his friend's revelation, and by the knowledge that he himself had caused Jennie such grief. "No, Albie, I'm not furious with you," he said. "I'm furious with myself. I had no idea that Jennie knew," he said, sadly. "I thought I'd managed to keep it from her."

"I'm sorry. I've only caused more pain by bringing this all up. I made a mistake. I shouldn't have said anything."

"No, Albie. I'm the one who made a mistake. Quite a few of them. I made one when I married Jennie. And another one when I took up again with Willa. And I've tried to set things right. I've tried my best to be a good husband and a good father. And when this war is over, I will try again."

"Is going after Willa your idea of being a good husband?" Albie asked him.

"For God's sake, Albie!" Seamie said angrily. "I'm not riding out into the desert to rekindle a love affair. What do you want me to do? Sit on my backside while she rots in a Turkish prison? While her guards beat her or starve her . . . or worse?"

"Lawrence will search for her. If she is alive, he'll find her."

Seamie laughed joylessly. "And risk giving away his position? The size of his troops? Right before an offensive? I doubt it. Lawrence is a soldier through and through, Albie, and you know it. As much as he might want to rescue Willa, he cannot risk the lives of thousands for the life of one."

"You mustn't do this."

"What the hell is it with you, Albie? Don't you want me to find her?" Seamie said, but he regretted his words as soon as they were out of his mouth. The pain they caused Albie was evident on his face.

"Of course I want her found. She's my sister, Seamie. We have been at odds over the past few years, but I care about her greatly," Albie said quietly, looking at the ground. "But I don't think you can find her. I think all you can do is recover her body. Which is what I will attempt to do from here with the help of local contacts—Bedouin traders, Turkish informants, and the like. I wish you would help me in that. I wish you would stay here and . . ." He faltered.

"What?"

Albie looked at Seamie. "I'm afraid this will be it, the thing that finally kills you. I've always thought you'd do each other in, you and Willa. Always. As children on my father's boat. In Cambridge, when you climbed up buildings. You came damned close on Kilimanjaro. And then in London I thought you'd do it by breaking each other's hearts. You still might. It's a madness what you have between you. Love, I guess you call it. It almost destroyed Willa in Africa. And again in London. She's likely dead now, Seamie. I know it, and you do, too, but you can't accept it. And now you're hell-bent on destroying yourself on this impossible mission. If you're captured by the enemy, well, you know what will happen . . ." His voice trailed off.

"Albie," Seamie said. "I have no choice. Can't you see that? She is my heart and my soul. There's a chance she's still alive, even if it's a slight one, and while there is, I can't abandon her. I can't."

Albie sighed. "I knew I wouldn't dissuade you," he said heavily. He reached into his trousers pocket and pulled out a folded paper. "It's a map of the region. The most current we have. Destroy it if you're taken."

Seamie took the map. Then he pulled Albie close and hugged him tightly.

"I'll be back," he said. "She'll be back, too. In the meantime, get off your skinny, bespectacled arse and find some spies, will you? So my next boat doesn't get blown up like my last one did."

And then Seamie mounted his camel, and he and Abdul were off. As they rode away, Albie heard the song of the muezzin rising from within the walled city, calling the faithful to prayer. He was not a religious man, but he never failed to be moved by the beauty and emotion of the muezzin's voice, and as the sun rose, sending its golden rays across the desert dunes, he sent up a quick prayer of his own.

He asked God to protect Willa and Seamie, these two people whom he cared about so deeply. He asked Him to overlook the mad and reckless love that bound them, and then he asked for one more thing—he asked God to please spare him from ever knowing anything like it.

CHAPTER SIXTY-TWO

FIONA STOPPED DEAD at the front doors of the Wickersham Hall hospital—a hospital she and Joe had helped fund, one they visited often. Never did she think she would one day come here to visit her own son.

She, Joe, and Sid had come up from London early this morning on the train. A carriage had met them at the station and brought them here. She'd alighted, waited until Sid and the driver got Joe's chair down and got Joe into it, and then she'd proceeded with her husband and brother to the hospital doors. Now, however, she found she could go no farther.

Sid had come to London last night to tell her and Joe, and the rest of their family, about Charlie. They were all in the drawing room, sitting by the fire. It was late when they heard the knock on the door, and Fiona had felt her heart falter inside her. She got to her feet immediately, waiting for Mr. Foster to come into the drawing room. With a son in the army, she lived in terror of a knock on the door.

"He's *not* dead. Oh, thank God!" she said, when Sid came into the drawing room where she and Joe had been sitting by the fire. "They send a telegram to tell you when your son's died, not an uncle."

"No one's dead, Fiona," Sid had said, closing the door behind himself.

"It can't be good, though, your news, can it? You wouldn't have come all this way at this hour if it was," she said, steeling herself. "What's happened?"

Sid made her sit down first. She'd known then that whatever he had to tell her would be very bad. People always made you sit down when the news was very bad. And it was. She cried when he told her about Charlie, and then she kept crying—all night long. She wanted to leave for the hospital right away, but Sid was against it.

"He's only just arrived," he said. "Let him sleep. Maybe a good night's rest in a safe, quiet place will help calm him."

The three of them had left for Paddington Station early. They were on the first train out. Fiona left the younger children in Mrs. Pillower's care. Katie was in Oxford.

Fiona looked up at the large doors now. She had walked through them in happier days, years ago, when she'd come to visit Maud. It felt like such a long time ago, like another lifetime. She remembered another set of hospital doors that she'd walked through once. Even farther back in her past. When she was only seventeen years old. She'd walked through those doors, rushed through them, to see her injured father, right before he died.

She shook her head. "No," she said. "I can't do it."

Joe, who was by her side in his wheelchair, took her hand. "You have to, love," he said. "Charlie needs you."

Fiona nodded. "Yes, you're right," she said. She gave him a brave smile, and together they went inside.

India was waiting for them. She hugged and kissed them wordlessly, then she and Sid led them down a long hallway and into a patient's room. Fiona looked at the poor young man sitting on the bed. He was shaking and pale and as thin as a scarecrow. He was staring at the wall. She looked away again, confused.

"Where is he? Where's Charlie?" she asked.

Sid put his arm around her. "Fee . . . that is Charlie."

Fiona felt her heart shatter inside of her. She covered her face with her hands. A low animal moan of pain escaped her. She took a deep breath and then another and then she lowered her hands. "It can't be," she said. "How did this happen? How?" she asked. "Do you know?"

"We know, Fiona," Sid said hesitantly. "India and I read the medical reports yesterday."

"Tell me," she said.

"It was a hard thing to read, Fee," Sid said. "And probably it's a harder thing still to hear. I don't think—"

"Tell her. Tell us. Both of us. We have to know," Joe said.

Sid nodded. He took them out of the room and then he told them.

"According to the reports of the medical officer in the field," he said, "Charlie had been in the trenches, on the front lines, for five straight months prior to the final attack on his unit. He'd held up under terrible conditions and had always conducted himself bravely. He'd rushed enemy lines during the heat of the battle many times. And then, during an attempt on an enemy position early one morning, two shells in succession hit very close to him. One shell deafened him. The other blew his friend, a lad by the name of Eddie Easton, to bits. Charlie was covered in Eddie's blood, and in pieces of his flesh." Sid had to stop speaking for a bit. "I'm sorry," he said, clearing his throat.

"Go on," Fiona whispered, her fists clenched at her sides.

"Charlie lost his mind," Sid continued. "He couldn't stop screaming, and couldn't stop trying to shake the blood and gore off himself. He tried to crawl back into the trench, but his commander wouldn't let him. The man—Lieutenant Stevens—kept screaming at Charlie to get back out to the battlefield, but Charlie couldn't. Stevens called him a coward and threatened to have him shot for desertion if he didn't return to battle. Charlie kept crying and shaking. Another shell exploded nearby. He curled into a ball. Stevens grabbed him and dragged him back to the front lines. He hauled him into no-man's-land and tied him to a tree. He left him there for seven hours. Said it would set him straight, make a man of him. By the time the shelling stopped and Stevens finally gave the order to bring him back, Charlie was catatonic. The two soldiers who went to untie him said they could get no response from him at all. They carried him back to the trench. Stevens had at him again, yelling at him, slapping him—all to no effect. He then ordered him invalided."

When Sid finished speaking, Fiona turned to Joe, but he was facing away from her, from all of them. His head was bent. He was crying. This man, this good, brave man, who'd never cried for himself when he'd been shot, who'd never shed one tear when he'd lost his legs, and very nearly his life, was sobbing.

Reeling, Fiona walked back into Charlie's room. She took a halting step toward her son. And then another, until she was standing next to his bed. She knelt down beside him and gently stroked his arm.

"Charlie? Charlie, love? It's me, it's Mum."

Charlie made no response. He just kept staring at the wall and shaking uncontrollably. Fiona tried again. And again. And again. She squeezed his arm. Touched his cheek. She took his trembling hands in hers and kissed them. And still Charlie gave no sign that he knew her, that he knew himself, that he knew anything at all. Finally, when she could bear it no longer, Fiona leaned her head against her son's legs and wept. She thought that she had been through everything a human being could go through. Losing her family as a young girl. Losing her beloved first husband, Nicholas, and then almost losing Joe to a criminal's bullets. But she discovered now that she had not, for this pain was like nothing she'd ever known. It was new and terrible. It was a mother's pain at seeing her precious child destroyed.

And Fiona realized that for once in her life, she did not know what to do. She did not know how she would ever get off her knees and stand up again. She did not know how she would manage to take her next breath.

She did not know how to bear the unbearable.

CHAPTER SIXTY-THREE

WILLA ALDEN EXPECTED death to come.

She had hoped for it, prayed for it, and sometimes, alone in the darkness of her cell for days on end, she had begged for it. But death did not come.

Loneliness came, along with despair. Hunger came, and the bone-chilling cold of desert nights. Lice came and, with them, fever. But not death.

She learned to tell day from night by the levels of noise and activity outside her cell. Morning was when the warden walked from cell to cell, opening a small sliding hatch, peering in at his prisoners to make sure they were still alive, then closing it and moving on again.

Midday was when her jailers brought her a jug of fresh water and her one and only meal, and emptied the tin pot that served as her toilet.

Evening was when a hush fell over the prison.

Night was when the rats came out. She had learned to leave some food for them on her plate and to push her plate into a corner, so they would fight one another for the scraps and leave her alone.

She kept track of the passing days by scraping marks in the wall with a stone she'd found on the floor of her cell. She thought she'd been locked away for thirteen days.

The jailers worked in teams. They talked as they worked, but only to each other. When she was feverish, which was most of the time, she could do little but lie mute on her filthy cot. On the few occasions when she could muster the strength to sit or stand, she tried to engage her jailers. She tried to find out why they were holding her and what they planned to do with her, but they would tell her nothing. She understood a bit of Turkish, however, and from the snatches of conversation she could hear, she was able to make out the words "Lawrence," "Damascus," and "Germans."

It was still August; she was sure of that. Had Lawrence marched on Damascus so soon? she wondered. Or had the Turks held the city with the help of the Germans? And for God's sake, where was she? And what were her Turkish captors going to do with her?

Willa finally got her answer nearly two weeks after she'd been brought to the prison. Shortly after the warden made his morning rounds, her door was opened again. The warden was standing in it, along with two of his men. One of them carried a lantern. The warden wrinkled his nose at the smell, then barked at Willa to get up. She could not. The fever she'd been running off and on for most of her imprisonment had spiked up the night before. She was weak and delirious and did not have the strength to stand.

"Get her up," the warden said to his men.

One of them swore under his breath. He did not want to touch her, he said. She was filthy and full of fever. The warden shouted something at him, and he smartly did as he was told. Willa was marched out of the cell and down a long corridor. The daylight, coming in at the windows, blinded her. She had been in the dark for so long her eyes could not cope with brightness. They had adjusted somewhat, however, by the time she arrived at her destination—a small, well-lit room at the back of the prison. There was a metal chair in the middle of it. Underneath the chair was a drain. Willa's stomach knotted at the sight of it.

Please, she prayed. Make it quick. "Death rides a fast camel," Auda always said. Willa fervently hoped he was right.

The men sat her down in the chair and tied her arms behind her back. In the light of the room, she could see how filthy she was. Her clothes were in tatters. Her shoes had been taken away weeks ago. Her feet were covered in dirt. A dull red rash covered her ankles.

"What is your name?" the warden asked her. In English.

"Little Bo Peep," Willa said. She'd been asked her name several times since she'd arrived at the prison and had steadfastly refused to reveal it.

The warden slapped her across her face. Hard. Her head snapped back. She slowly raised it again, sat up straight, and stared straight ahead.

There were more questions. More smart answers, or no answers. The questions got louder. And the slaps turned to punches. Willa felt her right eye swell up, tasted blood at the corner of her mouth, and still she gave them nothing. She thought of Seamie. Of Kilimanjaro. Of their time together in London. And she gave her captors nothing.

"Do you know what I'm going to do to you, you filthy bitch?" the warden finally said to her in English. "I'm going to stick my big fat cock up your ass and make you scream. And when I'm done, my men will have a turn."

Willa, her head lolling on her chest now, laughed. "Are you? For your sake, I hope you have a cold," she said. "A bad one. I hope you can't smell a thing."

The warden cursed at her. He turned to one of his men and, forgetting to switch back to Turkish, said, "I'm not touching her. She stinks like a sewer. Her hair's crawling with lice. She probably has typhus. He's here now, isn't he? Go and get him. He can do his own dirty work. From what I hear, he's very good at it."

Typhus, Willa thought woozily. Well, that's me done for. I only wish it had carried me off sooner.

She wondered who the *he* the warden had talked about was and wondered if she would stay conscious long enough to find out. The door opened again. Someone new walked into the room. She heard harsh words. It was a man. He was speaking German. A rough hand grabbed hold of her hair and yanked her head up.

"*Um Gottes Willen!*" the man said. He was close now. His voice sounded strangely familiar.

There was the sound of laughter, mirthless and bitter. And then the man said, "I should've guessed it was you. *Namaste,* Willa Alden. *Namaste.*"

CHAPTER SIXTY-FOUR

SEAMIE STARED AT the sheared and twisted metal of the Sopwith Strutter. How Willa had survived such a violent crash was beyond him. She must have been injured, he thought. Badly. The pilot certainly had been. His headless body still sat in the cockpit, festering in the desert sun.

"What do, Boss?" Abdul, his guide, said in his broken English.

What do, indeed, Seamie thought. If only I knew.

It had taken them twelve days to reach the crash site—twelve days of arduous travel in the blazing desert sun. As Seamie could speak little Arabic, and most tribesmen spoke no English, Albie thought it might be useful for Seamie to have images of Willa. They'd stopped in every village along the way, showing the pictures of Willa. They'd questioned Bedouins on the move, traders, goatherds—anyone they saw—using up precious time in the pursuit of information on Willa's whereabouts, but no one had seen her. No one had heard a thing. They'd stopped to sleep only when it was too dark to see, then risen at dawn's first light to try to gain as much ground as they could.

They'd arrived at the crash site only minutes earlier, and Seamie had been careful to search the perimeter of the site for any tracks left by Willa's abductors, but the wind had swept them away.

He turned around in a circle now, trying to take in the lay of the land, trying to piece together what might have happened to Willa and where she might be. If Turkish soldiers had taken her, she would likely be in a military prison in a garrison town or at an army camp. If tribal raiders had taken her, she could be anywhere.

Seamie told Abdul to rest himself and the animals. As Abdul dismounted, Seamie took his map—the one Albie had given him—out of his saddlebag. The map indicated known Turkish camps in the desert, watering holes frequented by the Bedouin, and desert settlements too small to have names.

Since he had not been able to discover anything during his journey east to the crash site, or from the site itself, Seamie decided that the next thing to do would be to start riding in an ever-widening circle around the site, hoping to spot tracks, a trail, anything.

He was all too aware of how little time he had before he had to be back in Haifa and on his new ship, and how much ground he had to cover before then. How he would ever find Willa in this endless god-forsaken nothingness, he did not know. It was like trying to find a grain of sand in . . . well, a desert.

Abdul, already drowsing in the shade of his camel, did not see the raiding party as it approached from the south. Nor did Seamie, who was carefully studying Albie's map. He was not aware of them at all until one of their camels bellowed, and by then it was too late. All but one of the men had already jumped down from their camels and surrounded them. They wore dusty white robes, head scarves, and daggers in their belts.

Abdul woke up with a start and scrambled to his feet. "Raiders. Six of them. Very terrible news," he said.

"So I gather," Seamie said. "What do you want?" he asked the men. But he got no answer.

One of them went to Seamie's camel, opened his saddlebag, and started digging through it.

"Hey! What are you doing there! Get your hands off that!" Seamie shouted angrily.

He made a move to stop the man and instantly found a dagger at his throat. The raider pulled out a pistol, bullets, and a photograph of Willa that Albie had given Seamie. The raider handed the goods to the sixth man, a tall, fearsome-looking Bedouin who was still seated atop his camel and who seemed to be the leader. The leader examined the gun, then the photographs, and then he shouted at Seamie.

Abdul translated as best he could. "He asks why you have these photographs," Abdul said. "He asks your name."

"Tell him I ask that he kiss my arse!" Seamie yelled. "Tell him to put my things back and take his bloody pack of thieves out of here."

Abdul, wide-eyed, shook his head no.

"Tell him!" Seamie shouted.

The Bedouin shouted at Abdul, too, until Abdul, quaking in his robes, did as he was told. The Bedouin listened to Abdul's words. He nodded, laughed, then barked an order at one of his men.

Seamie never saw the man take the pistol from beneath his robes, never saw him grasp it by its barrel and raise it high, never saw the blow coming.

CHAPTER SIXTY-FIVE

"OH, GRAN! I'M so glad you're here!" Katie Bristow said, rushing down the stairs of her parents' Mayfair house. "Come upstairs, will you?" she said, tugging on her arm.

"Goodness, Katie! Let me get my coat off first!" Rose Bristow said breathlessly. Katie had rung her an hour ago, sounding very upset. Rose had grabbed her things and come as quickly as she could. "What's going on?" she asked Katie now. "You were talking a thousand words to the minute on the blower. I could hardly understand you."

"It's Mum. She's barely eaten since she and Dad came back from hospital, and that was nearly two weeks ago! She doesn't sleep. She barely speaks. She just lies in her bed, all curled up in a ball."

Rose frowned. "Where's your father gone?" she asked.

"He went back to Wickersham Hall. To see Charlie. He's tried everything, Gran. He talked to her. Held her. Brought her cups of tea. He even yelled at her. Nothing worked. Then he called me to come home from school. But nothing I do works, either, and I've done everything I can think of. I don't know what else to do, Gran. I've never seen Mum like this. Never," Katie said, and then she burst into tears.

Rose took her granddaughter in her arms and soothed her. "Hush now, Katie. We'll sort it all out. Your mum's had a terrible shock. She just needs some time to find her feet again, that's all. Go downstairs now and get yourself a cup of tea and I'll go up to her."

Rose took hold of the banister and started up the stairs. She hadn't been to see Charlie yet. Peter, her husband, was very poorly with a chest complaint, and with that terrible influenza going around, she'd hadn't wanted to leave him in case it got worse. Joe had come to see her, though, and had told her what had happened. She'd never seen her son so broken-looking.

Life, Rose well knew, could throw some hard punches at you, but nothing hurt as much as losing a child, or seeing one of your children hurt and suffering. Becoming a parent changed you forever, as nothing else could. Not good or bad fortune. Not friendships. Not even a man or a woman.

Rose remembered how she was before she married and had children, when she was a young woman. She was slim and small, with a pretty face and figure. Several lads had wanted to court her. She had prayed and wished and hoped for all sorts of silly things then. For ribbons. For thick hair and pink cheeks. For a pretty dress. For a husband who was handsome and let her spend the pin money.

After she became a mother, she had only ever prayed for one thing: that no harm would ever come to her children.

She reached the landing now and—huffing and puffing slightly—walked down the hallway to Fiona and Joe's bedroom. She knocked on the door, received no answer, and walked in.

Her daughter-in-law was in her bed, fully clothed, with her back to the door. Rose's heart clenched at the sight of her. She knew Fiona had lost her own mother when she was young. Kate Finnegan had been Rose's close friend. They'd lived on the same street when they were newly married. For the love of Kate, and of Fiona, Rose had tried to be a mother to her daughter-in-law all these years.

"What's all this then, eh, Fiona?" she said gently. "Lolling about in bed all day, are we? That's not the Fiona I know. How about you come downstairs now? And join Katie and me in the kitchen for a nice cup of tea?"

She sat down on the bed next to Fiona and began to rub her back. "You've got both Joe and Katie at their wits' end with worry. The littler ones are running rings around poor old Mrs. Pillower. Mr. Foster's at a loss. Even the dogs look sorry for themselves. No one knows what to do without you to tell them. You've got to get up now."

Rose heard a sob, and then another. Fiona turned around, and Rose saw that her face was swollen and her eyes were red from crying.

"I try to get up, Rose," she said in a small, choked voice. "I try to get out of this bed, but when I do, all I can see are the faces of the men in the veterans' hospital. All the young men who look like old men now because of what's happened to them. And I see a new face among them—my Charlie, who doesn't even know me anymore. He's gone, Rose."

"He's not gone. He's in a good hospital in Oxford with his uncle Sid and auntie India, where he'll get good care. The best. There's no better place for him," Rose said.

Fiona shook her head. "You didn't see him. My beautiful boy is gone. There's a stranger in his place. A hollowed-out, dead-eyed stranger. How could he do it, Rose? The lieutenant . . . Stevens is his name. How could he do what he did to Charlie? Nothing happened to him. No disciplinary action was taken against him. He should be in jail for what he did. He destroyed my son. Charlie will never get better. How can he? There's nothing there anymore. He doesn't have a chance."

Rose let her weep. She let her cry the grief and rage out, and when she had stopped, when the sobs had subsided to silent tears,

Rose said, “Listen to me, Fiona, and listen well. If you really believe that Stevens has destroyed Charlie, then he has. And then you’re right—the poor lad doesn’t have a chance. Not as long as you stay in this bed. Not as long as you’ve given up on him.”

Fiona wiped her eyes. For the first time since Rose had come into the room, Fiona met her eyes.

“He’s still there,” Rose said. “He’s just gone deep inside himself. To someplace quiet and safe. Where the shells can’t get at him. Where he can’t see his dead friend anymore. You’re his mother. If anyone can get to him and pull him back out, you can. But you’ve got to try. You’ve got to fight. I’ve known you since the day you were born, Fiona. You’ve fought your whole life. For God’s sake, don’t stop now.”

“But I don’t know how, Rose. I don’t know what to do,” Fiona said helplessly.

Rose laughed. She took Fiona’s hand and squeezed it tightly. “Do we ever know what to do, we mothers?” she asked her. “Did I know what to do when Joe had his first bout of croup? Did you know what to do when Charlie fell out of a tree and broke his arm? No. You never know what to do. You just figure it all out somehow because you have to. If you don’t, who will?” Rose said.

Fiona nodded.

“All you have to do, lass, is try,” Rose said, patting her arm. “I know you can do that for Charlie. I know you can.”

Fiona sat up. “Can I, Rose? Really?”

“Yes, of course you can,” Rose said. “You’ll find him, Fiona. I know you will. You’ll find him and bring him back to us.”

“Do you promise?” Fiona asked, her voice small and uncertain.

Rose thought about her damaged grandson. She thought about what had happened to him, about the horror of having to wipe his dead friend’s blood off him. She thought about how cruelly he’d been abused and how people had been driven hopelessly mad over less.

And then she thought about the woman sitting next to her, and all that she’d overcome in her life, and how her losses and sorrows had not made her bitter and cruel, they'd only made her stronger, kinder, and more generous.

"I do," Rose said, smiling. "I promise."

CHAPTER SIXTY-SIX

SEAMIE OPENED HIS eyes.

"Where am I?" he muttered. "What's happened?"

He blinked a few times to clear his vision, then tried to sit up, ignoring the pain battering at his skull. Groaning, he lay back down again.

He looked around and realized he was lying on a soft rug, inside a tent. How he'd got here, he did not know. For a few seconds he could remember nothing, and then it all came back to him: He'd been at the crash site with Abdul when the raiders arrived. He'd mouthed off to their leader. One of the raiders must have coshed him.

"Bloody hell," he said. Then he called for Abdul. Loudly.

A woman, alerted by his shouts, came into the tent and looked at him. She quickly went out again, shouting herself. A few minutes later, Abdul came dashing into the tent.

"Where are the camels?" Seamie asked him. "Where are our things?"

Before Abdul could answer him, another man came into the tent. Seamie recognized him; he was the raiders' leader. Behind him came the woman. She was wrapped in robes of indigo blue, with a veil across the lower half of her face.

"This is Khalaf al Mor," Abdul said, in a hushed voice, "sheik of the Beni Sahkr. The woman is Fatima, his first wife."

"I don't care if he's George the fifth, tell him to give me back my gear," Seamie growled.

Abdul ignored him. Khalaf al Mor held up the photograph of Willa. He looked at Abdul, then nodded.

"The sheik wishes to know why you have these photographs," Abdul said.

Khalaf then held up a necklace. Seamie could not know it, but it was the very one Fatima had given Willa, the one her abductors took from her.

"The sheik also wishes you to tell him what you know about this necklace," Abdul said. In a lower voice he added, "I advise you to make no further references to your backside."

Seamie looked at the Bedouin. Why was the man so interested in Willa's photograph? He had asked about it at the crash site, too. Did he know something about her? It suddenly dawned on him that perhaps Khalaf al Mor could help him. For the first time in days, a spark of hope kindled inside of him.

"Tell the sheik my name is Seamus Finnegan and that I'm a captain with the British Navy. Tell him I know nothing about the necklace, but the photographs are of my friend, Willa Alden. She was in a plane crash. Out by the Jabal ad Duruz hills," Seamie said. "Tell him I'm looking for her. I want to find her."

Fatima shrilled at Abdul. It seemed to Seamie that she was desperate to know what he, Seamie, had just said. Abdul translated. Khalaf nodded as he spoke, but his expression—one of mistrust—never changed. Fatima chattered at her husband. Khalaf impatiently waved her away.

"The sheik wishes to know if this woman is so important to you, why is she not your wife?"

"Because I already have a wife," Seamie said. "Back in England."

Abdul related his answer to the sheik and his wife. Fatima let out a loud exclamation. She shrilled at her husband again. He flapped a hand at her then said something to Abdul.

"The sheik says that your explanation is like a cracked pot and will not hold water," Abdul said.

"Why the hell does he say that?" Seamie asked.

"Because a man may have more than one wife," he replied.

"Not in England he can't," Seamie said.

Abdul relayed that information to Khalaf. Fatima, listening, excitedly talked at her husband again, quite loudly. Khalaf barked at her, silencing her. Then he spoke to Abdul again.

"The sheik says he has heard of this custom before," Abdul said. "He admits it may have its advantages. But he wishes to know how one wife alone can give you many sons. A man must have twenty at least."

"Well, I don't have twenty, but I do have one," Seamie said. He held one hand up to show he was not reaching for a weapon, then dug into his back pocket, hoping his wallet was still there. It was. He pulled it out, opened it, and showed Khalaf the photograph of little James standing with Jennie.

Khalaf smiled. He nodded. He and Fatima spoke. Abdul quietly told Seamie what they were saying. "The sheik's wife is telling him that it is exactly as she said—Willa—the woman we are all searching for. She is telling him that you are the one that this woman spoke about. You are the reason she has no husband, no child. The sheik's wife said she told her that you had a wife already, a pretty wife back in England, and a small son, too. She is telling her husband to help you."

As Abdul spoke, a small, beautiful, dark-eyed boy came into the tent and touched the sheik's arm. The Bedouin smiled at the sight of the boy and put an arm around him. Then he grabbed Abdul's arm and spoke rapidly to him.

Abdul nodded, then he turned to Seamie and said, "Khalaf al Mor wishes to tell you that this is Daoud, his firstborn son. He wishes you to know that Willa Alden saved the life of Daoud."

Seamie nodded, alert with excitement. He was certain now that Khalaf al Mor could help him find Willa.

"The sheik also wishes you to know that his wife Fatima gave the necklace he showed you to Willa Alden and that this necklace was found in the possession of some Howeitat raiders who were trying to sell it in Umm al Qittayn, a small village at the base of the Jabal ad

Duruz hills. Some of the sheik's men were there and recognized it. They asked the Howeitat how they had got it, but they would say only that they'd found it—not where or how. The sheik's men were outnumbered, or they would've simply taken the necklace. Since they could not, they paid the Howeitat for it and brought it back here. The sheik's wife saw it and right away knew it for her own."

"Go on, Abdul," Seamie said. "Tell me the rest."

"Khalaf al Mor says that these men call themselves Howeitat, but belong to no tribe, no village. They are known to be robbers and kidnappers. They have sold things—guns, information, sometimes people—to the Turks before. Khalaf al Mor fears they have done the same with Willa Alden."

"Ask him where they are, and how I can find them," Seamie said.

The words went back and forth between Seamie and Khalaf al Mor quickly. Seamie learned that the raiders were thought to live a few miles south of the Jabal ad Duruz hills and that in all likelihood all Seamie would have to do was give them money and they would tell him what they'd done with Willa. But, Khalaf cautioned, they were unpredictable. They were wary and took offense easily, and under no circumstances should Seamie try to approach them on his own.

"But I must approach them," Seamie said. "How else can I find out if they're the ones who took Willa?"

Khalaf told him that he would help him. He would give him ten men, with rifles and camels, and he himself would ride with him, too, to help him hunt for Willa Alden.

Seamie said they must start out right away. Much moved by Khalaf al Mor's kindness, he thanked the sheik for his generosity and concern and for doing so much for him.

The sheik smiled. "I do not do it for you, my friend," he told Seamie through Abdul. "I do it because Willa Alden is beloved of Allah. And beloved of Khalaf al Mor."

CHAPTER SIXTY-SEVEN

WILLA OPENED HER bruised and swollen eyes.

She expected the darkness of her prison cell, but instead there was light. Bright desert sunshine poured in through a window and spilled onto the clean white sheets of the bed in which she lay.

She held her hand up in front of her face. Her skin was clean. Her nails, which had been clotted with dirt and blood, had been trimmed and scrubbed. The filthy, tattered sleeve of the khaki shirt she'd worn for weeks was gone. In its place was a sleeve of cool white cotton.

It's a hallucination, she thought, brought on by my illness. Or perhaps I'm dreaming. Perhaps the warden of the prison has finally beaten me unconscious and I'm only dreaming that I'm in a clean place, wearing clean clothes, and lying in a clean bed. She waited, her eyes still open, for the hallucination to stop, for the dream to be over. To find herself back in her cell, back in the darkness. But it didn't happen.

"Where am I?" she finally murmured.

"Ah, you're awake," a voice said, startling her. It was a woman's voice. It was brisk and businesslike and sounded German.

Willa sat up, gasping with the pain of her broken ribs. She turned her head around and saw that the woman was standing at her left, by a small sink. She was dressed all in white and her hair was tucked up neatly under a white cap.

"You've been very ill," she said, with a smile. "In fact, at one stage I was quite sure we were going to lose you. You have three broken ribs, you know. And you've just come through a terrible case of typhus. Your fever hit one hundred and six a few nights ago."

"Who are you?" Willa asked.

"I'm your nurse," the woman replied.

"But how—"

"Not so much talking. You're still very weak. Here, take this," she said, putting a small white pill in Willa's hand and holding out a glass of water.

"What is it?" Willa asked.

"Morphine. It will help with the pain. Take it, please."

Something in the tone of the woman's voice told Willa she had no choice. She dutifully washed the pill down with some water.

"Very good," the woman said. "Now lie back down. Morphine can make one a bit light-headed. Especially one in a debilitated condition. I'll be right here if you need anything."

Something inside Willa wanted to argue, to ask more questions, to put up a fight, but the drug was already flowing through her, making her feel deliciously warm and drowsy, taking the pain in her chest away, taking all her pain away. It was stronger than the opium she smoked, much stronger. And so she did not fight. She just lay on the bed, feeling as if she was floating along on a soft, hazy cloud.

How long she remained in this state, she did not know. An hour could have passed, or only a minute, before she heard the footsteps in the hallway. They were slow and measured. They stopped at her door, then entered her room.

She tried to open her eyes, to see who it was, but she was so tired now, and so weak, that she could not make even her eyelids do what she wanted.

She felt a hand stroking her hair, then her cheek. It was a man's hand. She knew because he started speaking to her in a man's voice. It was familiar, this voice. She had heard it before, but where?

And then she remembered—in the prison. In the interrogation room. For a few seconds, she was gripped by terror. She wanted to get up. To run. To get out of this room, but she couldn't. It was as if her limbs were made of lead.

"Shh," the voice said. "It's all right, Willa. Everything's all right.

I just have a few questions for you. Just one or two. And then you can sleep." The voice was low and soothing. Not angry, like before.

"Where's Lawrence, Willa?" it said. "I need to know. It's very important that I know. You'll help me with this, won't you? Just like you helped me on the mountain."

Willa tried to nod. She wanted to help. She wanted to sleep.

"No, don't nod. Don't move at all. You need to be still. To rest. Just speak, that's all. Where's Lawrence?"

Willa swallowed. Her mouth suddenly felt so dry. She was about to speak, about to tell him, when suddenly she saw Lawrence—in her mind's eye. He was crouched over a campfire in the desert. He was with Auda. He looked at her, then slowly raised a finger to his lips. And she knew she must protect them—Lawrence and Auda both. She must tell the man nothing.

"Tired . . . ," she said, trying to think clearly through the swirling fog in her head, trying to parry the man's questions.

The hand on her cheek now gripped her chin. Hard.

"Where is Lawrence?" the voice said, not so kindly now.

Willa struggled to keep her wits about her. She dug down deep, mustering her last reserves of strength, in order to think of a good answer, one that would throw the man off.

"Carchemish," she said. "He's at Carchemish, digging. He found a temple there. . . ."

Carchemish was the ancient Hittite site where Lawrence had worked as an archaeologist before the war.

The man released her. She heard him swear under his breath, then he said, "You've given her too much. Between the drugs and the fever, she's out of her mind. A bit less next time, please."

Willa heard the sound of footsteps receding, heard the door close, and then she heard nothing more.

CHAPTER SIXTY-EIGHT

"IT'S MADNESS, ISN'T it, Mr. Foster?"

"Only if it fails, madam. If it works, it's genius."

Fiona, sitting across from her butler on the 8:15 to Oxford, nodded. "Sid said some of them love to garden. Charlie used to help me with the roses. Do you remember?" she asked.

"I do," Foster replied. "I particularly remember one incident when he decided to concoct his own fertilizer. From vegetable scraps, fish heads, and some ale that had gone flat. He mixed it up in the pantry, then forgot about it, and then the scullery maid kicked it over by accident."

"I remember that, too," Fiona said, laughing. "It stunk up the entire house."

"Indeed, it did. The fumes in the kitchen were eye-watering. Cook was furious. She resigned. It took all my powers of persuasion to convince her to stay."

"I had no idea, Mr. Foster," Fiona said. "Thank you."

She looked at Foster and realized there was so much she didn't know, so many problems she'd never had to concern herself with because he was always there, fixing things, smoothing things, making sure that the headaches of running a household never troubled her. And it seemed to her now that he always had been.

He was getting on, he was nearly sixty-five and graying, and he suffered from arthritis in his knees and hands. Five years ago, she and Joe had hired another man—Kevin Richardson—to work with Mr. Foster as under-butler and relieve him of his most arduous duties, but Mr. Foster was still in charge, and that was the way Fiona wanted it. She could not imagine her house, or her life, without him in it.

Fiona and Joe had always been good to Mr. Foster. He was compensated well for his work. He had a spacious set of rooms within their house. He was respected and appreciated. But suddenly, sitting across from him in the rattling train car, a huge basket of gardening clobber on the floor between them, Fiona felt that she hadn't been good enough. That she'd never told him how much he meant to her, how much she valued him.

She cleared her throat now and leaned forward in her seat. "Mr. Foster, I . . . ," she began to say.

"There's no need, ma'am. It's quite all right. I know," Foster said.

"Do you?" Fiona said. "Do you really?"

"I do."

Fiona nodded, knowing that he was not overly fond of emotional displays. In fact, when she had finally worked up the strength and courage she needed to travel back to the veterans' hospital to visit her son, it was Mr. Foster she asked to go with her. Not Joe. With Joe, her beloved husband, the father of her damaged child, she would cry. With Mr. Foster, an ex–army man himself, she would buck up and do what needed to be done.

And what needed to be done, Fiona had decided, was gardening. Maud had kept a rose garden at her Oxford home. It contained some beautiful, blowsy, fragrant old roses, but it was not as well tended as it should be. The hospital gardener and his crew put most of their efforts into the kitchen garden, which was needed to feed both patients and staff.

Fiona had heard her brother Sid talk about the progress he'd made with some of the shell-shocked men by getting them out of their rooms and putting them to work around the hospital. Charlie had shared his father's love of gardens and orchards and had always trailed behind Joe as he rolled down his rows of pear and apple trees in his wheelchair at Greenwich, inspecting his crops. Fiona hoped that caring for Maud's roses might help Charlie recover.

Fiona felt the train slow slightly now. She looked out the window and saw the station approaching. "We're here, Mr. Foster," she said. But Foster was already up and gathering their things.

"There is one thing to keep in mind, ma'am," he said, as she reached to the luggage rack overhead for her carpetbag and umbrella.

"Yes?" Fiona said. "What is it?"

"Rome was not built in a day."

"No, it wasn't, Mr. Foster, and I will keep it firmly in mind," Fiona said.

Sid greeted them when they arrived.

"How is he?" Fiona asked her brother.

"The same, I'm afraid. No change. How are you?"

Worried, Fiona thought. Frightened. Angry. Sorrowful. Uncertain.

"Resolute," she said.

Sid smiled. "I've never known you to be anything but," he said.

"I thought we would get to work on the rose garden straight away," Fiona said. "Could we borrow a barrow?"

Sid got them all set up as Fiona changed into an old work dress. He secured a barrow, some fertilizer, and a few tools that she had been unable to bring. Then he tucked a basket into the barrow, containing sandwiches and tea. When Fiona was ready, he took her and Mr. Foster to Charlie's room.

Charlie was sitting on the bed, in the exact same place he had been the first time Fiona had come to see him. He was still shaking, still staring straight ahead of himself. For a moment, her grief came back and threatened to engulf her, but she heard Rose's voice in her head, telling her she was his mother, telling her to fight for her child. And she heard Foster's voice, right next to her, saying, "Remember Rome, ma'am."

"Hello, Charlie," she said, in a strong, clear voice. "It's me, Mum. I've brought Mr. Foster with me. I thought we'd take a walk today. Get outside for a bit and do a little gardening. It's a beautiful day, you know, and there are roses at the back of the property. August is waning, the hottest weather's over, so some of them should be reblooming. Shall we take a look? Come on, then. There we go."

Together, Sid and Mr. Foster got Charlie to his feet. His legs shook as badly as the rest of him did, and it was slow going getting him down the hallway and out of the building. Once they were outside, the two men continued helping Charlie on the way to the rose garden. Fiona, pushing the wheelbarrow, followed them.

"Oh, Charlie! Look at them all!" she exclaimed, once they'd arrived. The garden, though neglected, was still magnificent. Roses of every size, shape, and color spilled over the willow fences, over the slate stepping-stones, and over one another.

"They all need pruning and a bit of manure turned in. I see black spot on the Maiden's Blush over there. Do you see it, Mr. Foster? And that Cecile Brunner's become very unruly. Let's start with the cleanup, and the fertilizing, and then we'll clip a few dozen blooms. We'll bring them all back to the hospital and fill vases and bottles and jam jars and anything else we can find and put them in all the rooms. Shall we do that?"

Sid said he thought it sounded like a wonderful idea and that the rooms could use some brightening, then he excused himself. He said he had to get Stephen, one of his lads, to the barn to tend to Hannibal, for Hannibal, the surly sod, was needed to harrow a field and now allowed no one but Stephen to harness him.

Fiona and Mr. Foster spread a blanket on the ground and sat Charlie down near a rosebush heavily laden with bright pink blooms. Right after they got him settled, a chattering squirrel, angered by their presence, jumped from the ground into the very same rosebush, shaking the blooms roughly and sending the dew that was still on some of them flying. Droplets of water landed on Charlie. One of the soft blooms flopped down onto his shoulder, brushing his cheek as it did.

And as it did, Fiona saw something. She saw her son's eyes flicker toward the rose. The movement was subtle and small, it happened in the space of a split second, but it happened. For an instant, there was a tiny spark of life in Charlie's dull, dead eyes.

She looked at Mr. Foster. He had seen it, too. She could tell by the excitement on his face. Fiona quickly picked up a pair of secateurs and clipped a rose from high up on the bush. Then she knelt down and put it into her boy's shaking hand. She closed his fingers gently around the stem and held his hand in her own.

"I'm stronger than Lieutenant Stevens, Charlie," she said to him. "Stronger than any bloody bomb. Stronger than all the ghosts wailing in your head. I gave you life once and the war took it away, but I will give it back to you. Do you hear me, lad?" She pressed her lips to his forehead and kissed him. "You do hear me. I know you do."

She stood up then, clapped the dew off her hands, picked up a rake, and got to work.

CHAPTER SIXTY-NINE

SEAMIE LOOKED AT the man standing before him. His name was Aziz. He wore a red head scarf and red robes. He stood, feet planted firmly on the ground, arms crossed over his chest, and demanded to know why he—Seamie—was insulting him with his questions and his presence.

Seamie, Abdul, Khalaf, and Khalaf's men had ridden into the center of the man's village only moments before. From some traders on their way to Haifa they'd learned they would find who they were looking for here. It had taken them four days to find the village.

Looking around from his vantage point atop his camel, Seamie thought that this place could hardly even be called a village. It was little more than a collection of stone hovels, twenty at the most, and some ramshackle animal pens.

Aziz had come out of one of the crumbling houses to speak with them just after they'd arrived. One of Khalaf's men who'd bought Willa's necklace at Umm al Quittan had told Khalaf that this was the man from whom they'd bought it.

"I want information on the woman," Seamie said to Aziz now, for

Aziz spoke some English. "The woman from the airplane. The one you kidnapped. What did you do with her?"

Aziz laughed. He spat. He said nothing.

Seamie reached behind himself into his saddlebag, slowly and carefully to show that he was not reaching for a gun, and pulled out a small leather sack. He shook it so that everyone could hear the coins inside it clink.

"Twenty guineas," he said, looking Aziz in the eye. "It's yours. If you tell me where she is."

Aziz laughed. He let out a cry, sudden and piercing, like that of a falcon, and suddenly two dozen men came out of the houses, each one armed with a rifle.

"Mine if I tell you," he said, nodding at the sack and smiling. "And also if I don't."

CHAPTER SEVENTY

A MINUTE? AN hour? A day? A week?

Willa Alden had no idea how long she had slept. When she woke, she saw a man sitting in the chair near her bed. He was tall and handsome, with silvery blond hair, and Willa wondered, again, if she was seeing things. She closed her eyes, waited for a few seconds, then opened them again. The man was still there.

"Max?" she said. "Max von Brandt?"

The man smiled and nodded. "We meet in the desert this time, instead of in London, or in the Himalayas." He leaned forward in his chair and touched the back of his hand to her cheek. "You feel much cooler," he said. "You look better, too. Then again, you should. You slept for four days straight."

"Max, I must tell you, this is a bit of a surprise," Willa said. She tried to sit up and gasped with pain.

"Be careful, Willa. Your ribs are still healing."

"What are you doing here? What am I doing here? What is this place?" she said, pulling herself upright with the help of her bed-rail. The pain was intense. Tiny beads of sweat broke out on her upper lip.

"To answer your last question first—this place is a hospital. For Turkish and German troops. In Damascus. You are here, in Damascus, because you are a spy. I am here for the very same reason."

"You . . . you're a spy?" Willa said.

"Yes, for the German secret service. I was stationed in London for quite some time, then Paris. Now Damascus. The situation here is critical, as I'm sure you know."

"You're sure I know? Know what, Max?" Willa said, putting a note of irritation in her voice.

She had quickly assessed the situation. She was quite certain now that her Turkish jailers had kept her alive on Max's orders—though he didn't know exactly who he was keeping alive until he'd seen her in the interrogation room. The Turks, simply following commands, hadn't particularly cared if she lived or died, but Max was a different story. He'd had feelings for her once. Now he believed she was a spy, but if she could convince him otherwise, he might let her go.

Max didn't answer her question right away. He looked at her for a bit, frowning slightly, then he said, "I'm being completely truthful with you, Willa. In return, I want you to be truthful with me. . . . Where is Lawrence and when is he planning to attack Damascus?"

Willa laughed. "Max," she said, "you've got it all wrong. I'm not a spy. I'm a photographer, as you know. I needed money so I talked Pathé into footing the bill for me to come out here, and then I badgered General Allenby—I'm sure you know who he is—into letting me follow Lawrence around. I've been taking stills and shooting some film, too. It all goes back to London, gets cleared, and then goes into the newsreels shown at every movie theater in England and America. Hardly top secret spy stuff, is it?"

Willa had shifted in her bed as she spoke, waking up the pain in her ribs again. It was getting worse. She wanted some morphine to dull it.

"Hello?" she said loudly, leaning forward in her bed. "Is anybody there? *Hello?* Crumbs! Where's that nurse?"

"She'll come in a minute," Max said.

His smile was gone. There was a slight hint of menace in his voice. And Willa, sweating, was suddenly chilled by the knowledge that Max had sent the nurse out and that he would bring her back only when he felt like it.

"Listen to me, Willa. Listen very carefully," he said now. "You are in a great deal of trouble. I saved you from being very badly beaten the other day. And probably raped, too. But I cannot save you forever. I have only so much influence. A motion picture camera was found in the wreckage of your plane. The film inside it was of a Turkish camp in the Jabal ad Duruz hills."

Willa's heart sank at that. She'd hoped that the film had been ruined in the crash.

"You and the pilot were very brave," Max continued. "You flew low and got some rather comprehensive footage."

Willa did not answer him. Max stood. He put his hands on her bed rail and leaned in close to her.

"I can help you. I want to help you," he said. "But you have to help me, too. I saved you from those animals in the interrogation room, and I can do more, but only if you give me something. I must have information on Lawrence."

"I have none," Willa said stubbornly. "Yes, you are right. I was on a recon mission, but it failed. As you know. As for Lawrence, he does not share his plans with me. Only with Auda and Faisal."

Max straightened. He nodded. "Perhaps you would like a little more time to think about my request," he said.

He walked out into the hallway and signaled for two orderlies to come into the room. They did. One was pushing a wheelchair.

"Where am I going?" Willa asked Max warily.

"Sightseeing," he replied.

Wordlessly, the two men lifted Willa out of her bed. They were not particularly gentle and they jostled her. Though she tried not to, Willa cried out in pain.

Max dismissed the men, then wheeled Willa out of her room, down the corridor, and out of the hospital. The hot, dusty streets of Damascus sprawled out before her. She had never been to the city before, and she took mental notes now of which way they were heading and what buildings she passed. They traveled for five minutes or so, made two left turns, and then arrived at their destination—the prison.

Willa panicked when she saw it, and tried to climb out of the wheelchair, but a firm hand on her shoulder pressed her back down.

"Don't worry," Max said. "I'm not taking you back to your cell."

He pushed her through the arched entryway, through which camels and horses and vehicles passed, over a cobbled court, past various buildings, to a dirt yard behind the prison. It was enclosed by a high stone wall and it was empty.

"What is this?" Willa asked. "What are we doing here?"

Before Max could answer her, a group of about eight soldiers marched past them. In their midst, shackled, was a Bedouin man.

"Howeitat," Max said. "One of Auda's and a spy."

As Willa watched, the soldiers marched the Bedouin to the far wall. They tied his hands behind him, then blindfolded him.

"No," Willa said, realizing what they were about to do. "Please, Max. No."

"I think you should see this," he said.

The soldiers raised their rifles. Their commander raised his sword. When he lowered it, they fired. The Bedouin arched backward into the wall, then slumped to the ground, twitching. Red stains blossomed across his white robes.

Wordlessly, Max wheeled Willa back to her hospital room, then helped her get back into her bed. She was shaking with pain and sick with shock. Max summoned the nurse and told her to give Willa a pill. She swallowed it immediately, wanting the pain to stop, wanting the images of the slaughtered man to go away, wanting to escape this misery with a deep, narcotic sleep.

When the nurse left, Max fluffed Willa's pillow for her. Then he said, "What you just saw will become your fate. I cannot stop it. Not unless you help me. Not unless you tell me what I need to know."

Max pulled the crisp white sheet over her legs. "I care for you, Willa," he said. "I have since the first day I met you, and I do not want to see you standing in front of a firing squad."

He kissed her cheek, told her he would see her tomorrow, and took his leave. He stopped inside the doorway, turned back to her, and said, "Think about my request, but not for too much longer."

CHAPTER SEVENTY-ONE

SEAMIE RAISED HIS canteen to his lips and took a swig of water. His body swayed slightly as he drank, rising and dipping in the saddle with every plodding step his camel took. He looked ahead of himself, through the shimmering waves of heat rising off the sand, at what looked like an infinite expanse of desert. He'd been traveling across it for three weeks now.

"Do you trust him?" he asked Khalaf al Mor, who was riding next to him.

"No," Khalaf replied, "but I don't have to trust him. I know he will do as we've asked. There's too much gold in it for him not to."

Aziz rode about twenty yards ahead of them, flanked by two of his own men. They were riding north, to Damascus, but would stop at Lawrence's camp first to rest and water their animals. No one knew where Lawrence made his camp—he changed locations frequently to ensure that—but Aziz claimed that he knew where Lawrence was now, and that it was on the way to Damascus. He said there was shade there, and a well that gave plenty of fresh, sweet water.

Seamie hoped Khalaf was right about Aziz. He had been right about many things so far. That they were here, heading to Damascus—that they were here at all, actually—was due entirely to him. Khalaf was the one who'd persuaded Aziz and his village full of armed bandits not to kill them.

Only minutes after Seamie and Khalaf had ridden to the village to ask about Willa, Aziz and his men had taken the bag of gold Seamie offered him for information on Willa, and were about to take everything else from Seamie, Khalaf, and Khalaf's men—including their lives—until Khalaf told Aziz there would be more gold for him if he did not.

"Spare our lives, take us to the girl, and I will give you twice as much gold again upon our safe return," he said.

Instantly the guns were lowered. Warm greetings and apologies for the misunderstanding were offered, and the visitors were invited into Aziz's house for a meal. He told them how he had seen the British plane go down, had ridden to the wreck in search of plunder, found Willa, and taken her to Damascus.

"I almost did not," Aziz explained. "She was badly injured. There was every chance she would die on the way, and then the whole trip, the time, the wear and tear on my camels—all of it would have been for nothing. But she survived. And I got two thousand dinars. So it was a profitable trip after all, thanks be to Allah."

Seamie, enraged by the man's callous cruelty, had nearly lashed out at Aziz. Khalaf's hand on his arm stopped him.

"Do not allow your anger to lead you," he said under his breath. "You can do nothing for Willa if you are dead."

"Why?" Seamie asked Aziz, barely able to keep his voice even. "Why did you sell her to the Turks?"

Aziz looked at him as if he were a simpleton. "Because they pay more than the British," he said.

The following day, Seamie and Khalaf set off again, joined by

Aziz and two of his men. They had been traveling for three days now and were still another three days from where Aziz said Lawrence's camp was. Seamie was weary. His wound was oozing and hurting him. He changed the dressings daily, but the strenuousness and constant motion of desert travel aggravated his stitches and slowed his healing. And getting to Damascus was only part of the battle.

"What will you do once you reach the city, eh?" Aziz had asked him, laughing. "Make an assault on it yourself? You are a fool, Seamus Finnegan, but I like fools. Fools and their money are soon parted."

"He will get us to Damascus," Khalaf al Mor said now, pulling Seamie out of his thoughts. "What we do once we get there, that is the question."

"It's a question I ask myself all the time," Seamie said. "I never get an answer."

"Then do not ask yourself. Ask Allah. With Allah, all things are possible," Khalaf said serenely.

Right, Seamie thought. I'll just ask God. I'll ask Him to help me find the woman I love, the one who isn't my wife. The woman with whom I've caused my wife and my best friend nothing but grief. The one I still dream about and long for, even though I know I shouldn't. I'm sure He'll understand. And oh, by the way, God, it's me and Khalaf and a few of his men against an entire Turkish garrison. Will you see what you can do, old boy?

"Have faith, my friend," Khalaf said. "Have faith."

All right, then, Seamie decided. He'd do it. He'd have faith.

It was better than having nothing.

CHAPTER SEVENTY-TWO

WILLA, DROWSING, HEARD a soft knocking sound. She opened her eyes and saw Max standing in her doorway, smiling, his hands behind his back.

"May I come in?" he asked.

"This is your hospital, Max. I am your prisoner. I should think you can do whatever you like," she replied.

"How are you feeling?" he asked her, ignoring the barb. "Are you still in pain?"

"I am," she said nodding. "You wouldn't happen to have a pill on you, would you? The ribs are still kicking up and I haven't seen the nurse for hours."

"This might help," he said, pulling a bottle of wine out from behind his back. It was a 1907 Château Lafite. In his other hand, he had two wineglasses. He filled both glasses, then handed her one. "I snuck it out of the officers' mess. I hope you like it," he said, sitting on the bed.

Willa's hands shook as she took the glass. Eyeing him warily, she sniffed it, which made him laugh.

"If I wanted to kill you, there are quicker ways. Slower ones, too. Drink up. There's nothing in your glass but wine, I swear it," he said.

Willa took a sip of the rich Bordeaux. She hadn't had anything like it in years. It tasted impossibly good. Like civilization and happiness. Like all the beautiful, peaceful nights she'd squandered. Like life before the war.

"This is wonderful," she said. "Thank you."

"It is good, isn't it? I'm glad I'm drinking it here. With you. Not with some ghastly old major general in the mess, who's reminiscing fondly—and endlessly—about the Franco-Prussian War."

Willa smiled. She swallowed another mouthful of wine, loving the feeling of it coursing through her body, warming her blood, bringing a flush to her cheeks. For a few seconds, it was as if they were back in Tibet again. They hadn't any Lafite to drink there, but they'd had tea, which they'd often drunk together in the warmth of a campfire.

Max refilled her glass. "Have you thought about my offer?" he asked.

Willa took another drink. "Of course I have," she said. "But what can I say about it, Max? What do you want me to do? Be a traitor to my own country? Could you do that?"

Max smiled ruefully. He shook his head. Willa half expected him to call for the firing squad, but he didn't.

"It's amazing how we both ended up here at the same time, isn't it?" he said. "I'd be tempted to say it was fate, if I believed in fate."

"But you don't."

"No. I believe life is what you make it," he said, refilling his own glass. "I don't want to be here, that's for certain. I don't want to be anywhere near this dreadful place, all heat and dust and soldiers." He put the bottle on the floor and looked at her. "I want to be where I was happiest, Willa. Back at Everest. With you. I feel that that's my true country—the Himalayas. It's yours, too, and you know it. It's where we both belong."

Willa didn't say anything. She looked into her wineglass.

"Let's go back there. The two of us together," he said softly.

Willa laughed joylessly. "Just catch the next train east?" she said. "You make it sound so easy."

"I never married, you know," he said, still looking at her. "You ruined me for any other woman."

"Max, I—" Willa began, not liking where the conversation was going. Wanting to stop it. Now. Before he said anything else.

"No, hear me out. At least do that much for me," he said. "I knew then, back in Tibet, that you had feelings for someone else. But

Willa, where is he? All these years later, where is Seamus Finnegan? I shall tell you: not with you. He's married to another woman and they have a little boy together."

Willa broke his gaze. She lowered her head. Tears smarted behind her eyes.

"I don't say these things to hurt you," Max said. "Just to make you see the truth. You're wasting your life longing for something that can never be." Max reached for her hand. "You don't belong with Seamus Finnegan. And you don't belong here, in this desert hell. You don't belong to this war. Neither of us does."

Max leaned in close to her. "For God's sake, Willa, just tell me what I need to know so I can get this all over with sooner rather than later and get you out of here. I've done what I had to do—scare you. I've acted the official. Now I'll protect you. I'll take care of you. Germany is going to win the war. It won't take too much longer before it's all over. And when it is, I'll marry you—if you'll let me—and take you back where you belong, to Everest."

Willa, her head still down, said, "Do you mean that, Max? Or is it just another spy maneuver?"

"I do mean it, Willa. I swear it. I give you my word."

Willa raised her head. Tears spilled from her eyes.

"You're right, Max," she said. "I'm so tired of this damned war. I'm tired of the waste and the loss. Take me there. Promise me you will. Take me back to Everest." She leaned her forehead against his, then raised her lips to his and kissed him fiercely.

He kissed her back, passionately, then with a knowing smile, he pulled away from her.

"Convince me you mean it, Willa," he said. "Tell me where Lawrence is. We know the British want Damascus. How far north has he come?"

"Nablus," Willa said.

"He's that far west?" Max said. "Why?"

"He's moving amongst the tribes. Trying to recruit from them."

"How many man has he got with him?"

"Not many. Only about a thousand or so and he's having difficulty bringing more on board. The Bedouin don't trust Faisal, and they fear the Turks."

Max nodded thoughtfully. "We can fend a thousand off easily. What about Dara?" he asked. "We have reports that say he wants to take that before he takes Damascus."

Willa shook her head. "Lawrence doesn't care about Dara. He's going to bypass it altogether."

Max looked skeptical. "I have difficulty believing that," he said. "Dara's a valuable town on the Hejaz line. The biggest town between Amman and Damascus. In fact, I very much doubt everything you're telling me."

"I'm sure you do," Willa said, "which is exactly why Lawrence is doing it. If you think about it, though, it makes perfect sense. Lawrence has to save his men for the attack on Damascus. He can't afford to lose any fighting over Dara."

"What about Allenby?" Max asked.

"General Allenby has all he can manage with Suez. His orders are to hold that at all costs. He has little faith in Lawrence's ability to gather the troops he needs to take Damascus, and even less in Faisal's."

Max narrowed his eyes. "How do you know Allenby's plans if you've been in the desert with Lawrence?" he said.

"Because I've been working with Lawrence, but for Allenby," Willa replied. "I was at the Cairo office before I went into the desert—but you probably know that already. In fact, my presence in the desert was all Allenby's idea. He wanted me to be his eyes and ears in Lawrence's camp. I've been keeping him apprised of Lawrence's every move."

"How? You've been in the desert. In the middle of nowhere."

Willa smiled. "The airplane. I did more than one recon mission, you know. I did many. And every time I went up, I radioed Allenby in Cairo. We used code of course, but I got many messages through to him."

Max nodded, and Willa saw that the suspicion that had been on his face was gone. "Thank you," he said. "For all the information. For trusting me. And for making me believe in a future again. We will leave this place, Willa," he said. "I promise you that. We'll be together again."

He kissed her once more, pulling her close, taking her in his arms. As he did, Willa gasped. "My ribs," she said.

"I'm sorry," he whispered. "I got carried away and forgot about your injuries. Forgive me. I want you so much, I didn't think. I'll call for the nurse now to give you your pill."

He gathered up the empty bottle and the glasses, kissed her goodbye, and disappeared down the hallway.

Willa watched him go, touched her fingers to her lips, and smiled.

CHAPTER SEVENTY-THREE

SID PULLED his collar up against the filthy weather, marveling at how the rain was always wetter and the sky grayer in East London. It was early September, and a Sunday. A few people, poorly dressed, heads down against the driving wind, hurried past him on the sidewalk.

Sid knew where they were going—to pubs, where they could warm their insides with gin and their outsides by a fire. Or, if they had no money, back to their small, damp, dreary rooms. Where there was no heat, no heart, no hope. He remembered those rooms so well.

Sid hurried himself, wanting to finish his business and leave this place as quickly as he could. He turned a corner, walked halfway down a narrow, winding street, and arrived at Teddy's offices. He greatly hoped that Teddy had been able to dig up some information for him in the month since they'd last met. He didn't relish the thought of making a third trip to Limehouse.

Inside the foyer, he shook the rain off himself and gave Teddy's girl his name.

"Mr. Ko is expecting you," she said, escorting him to Teddy's office. "Would you like some tea, Mr. Malone?"

"I would, darlin', thank you," Sid said.

He greeted Teddy, who was seated at his desk yelling into a telephone in Chinese, and sat down across from him. Teddy yelled for a few more minutes, then slammed the phone down.

"Sorry, Sid," he said. "Business headaches. How are you?"

"Fine, Teddy. Yourself?"

"Fine. Fine. Just found out that one of my ships is late. No one's heard from it, or seen it, and I'm thinking the fucking thing's gone down with half a ton of my opium on board."

Sid gave what he hoped was a sympathetic smile. It was just like Teddy to be worried about his opium, not the ship or its sailors. Teddy kept nattering on, talking about business deals, and Sid had the strange feeling, yet again, that Teddy was stalling for time. Why? Had he not been able to dig up anything on Maud and the morphine?

"Teddy," Sid finally said, interrupting him. "How about our own little business deal? Were you able to find anything out?"

Before Teddy could answer, the door to his office opened and closed. Sid turned around. He figured it was Teddy's girl with the tea. He was glad of it. The rain had wet him through. He felt like he could drink an entire pot of strong, hot tea.

But it wasn't Teddy's girl. It was a ghost from his past, come back to haunt him. Only the ghost was alive and well and flanked by two of the hardest-looking men Sid had ever seen.

"Well, as I live and breathe. If it ain't Sid Malone," said Billy Madden. "What a surprise. I thought you was dead, Sid. I was in the neighborhood, thought I'd pay Teddy here a call—he's always happy to see me, ain't you, Ted?—and here you are."

But Billy didn't seem surprised at all, and Sid doubted very much that his visit was a coincidence. Teddy had told Billy that Sid had been to see him, and Billy, for some reason, didn't like it. Including

Teddy, there were four of them, and one of him. Sid cursed himself. How could he have not seen this coming? He would have to tread very carefully.

"Why'd you leave us so abruptly, Sid? Without even a going away party?" Billy asked, taking the chair next to him. His thugs remained by the door.

"It was getting a bit hot for me here, Billy. Had to make a quick exit," Sid said, keeping his voice even.

"And so you did. But now you're back."

"Indeed I am."

Billy nodded. He smiled. And then he sat forward and said, "What the fuck do you want?"

"Some information from Teddy."

"Information, is it?" Billy spat. "I'll give you some information, Sid: You made a big fucking mistake coming back here. Who are you working with? Fat Patsy Giovanna? The Kenney brothers? Who?"

So that was it—Billy thought he wanted his manor back.

Sid held up his hands. "Easy, Billy," he said. "I'm not working with or for anyone. I'm just looking into a death, a suicide that happened a few years back. For a friend of mine. That's all."

"You expect me to believe that shite? Would you have believed that, Sid? Would you?"

Sid stole a quick glance at Teddy's desk as Madden ranted, desperate to see if there was anything there he could use. A paperweight. A letter opener. Just in case. Billy Madden had always been a bit barmy, but he must've really gone off his nut in the last few years. His eyes were wild. He was nearly frothing as he spoke.

"Billy, I swear to you, I'm not here after my old manor. You can have it. With my blessings," he said.

"Is that so? Then tell me what you're really doing here. Why do you care about some old tart who offed herself years ago?"

Sid could have told Billy the truth. The truth might have saved him. But he didn't. There was no way in the world he was going to tell Billy Madden that he had a wife now, and that Maud was his wife's sister, and that all he wanted to do was find out if she'd truly killed herself, so his wife could have some peace. No matter what happened to him, he was not going to tell Billy Madden a damn thing about India or their children.

"That old tart mattered, Billy. To a friend of mine. That's why I care."

Billy shook his head. "Do for him," he said.

Sid was expecting it. In a flash, he grabbed a stone lion from Teddy's desk and threw it at Teddy. It hit the side of his head hard, taking him out of the fray. Sid turned, then, and faced Billy's men. He wasn't afraid of Billy; Billy was a coward, but Billy's lads were a different matter. If he wanted to get out of here alive, he had to get through them first. Sid got a few good punches in. He split a lip and cracked a nose, but Billy's lads were younger, stronger, and bigger. Their blows bloodied Sid and weakened him. And then a well-aimed punch to the back of his head dropped him.

"Get him up and get him out of here," Billy said, looking at Sid with contempt as he lay on the floor, barely conscious, groaning, his face covered in gore.

"What are you going to do with him?" Teddy asked. He was holding a handkerchief to the gash in his left temple. The white cloth was rapidly turning crimson. The front of his suit was stained with blood.

Billy was calmer now. His eyes were clear and focused; they'd lost their mad look. He took a cigar from the box on Teddy's desk and lit it, tossing the match on the floor.

"I'm taking him to the boatyard. I'll lock him in the basement till John gets back. He's off on his North Sea run, but he'll be back in a few days. Soon as he is, I'll have him take Malone out. Way out. Past Gravesend."

"Dead or alive?" Teddy asked.

"Who cares?" Madden said. "John'll weight him and dump him over the side, and if he's not dead when he goes in the water, he soon will be."

"Good riddance," Teddy said. "Bastard cracked my skull."

"Good riddance is right," Billy growled. "He fooled everyone once, back in 1900, but he won't do it again. It's over for him. This time Sid Malone really is going to rot in the Thames."

CHAPTER SEVENTY-FOUR

THE RACKET OUTSIDE Willa's hospital window was earsplitting. Men were yelling. Camels—it seemed like there must be a thousand of them—were bawling. Noisy motorcycles were sputtering by. A woman was scolding someone at the top of her lungs. An automobile was honking its horn.

"What on earth is going on?" Willa asked Sister Anna, who had just bustled into the room, an angry expression on her face.

"The Sunday souk," Sister Anna said, firmly closing Willa's window. "It's one of the days that animals are traded in the marketplace. The other day is Wednesday. Camels, horses, donkeys, goats . . . they all pass by the hospital on the way to market, and pass by again on their way out of the city with their new owners. The noise and dust and mess are unspeakable. It's disturbing for our patients and a health hazard, too. What you're hearing right now is because a camel broke loose and upended a vegetable cart. Two people were hurt. The hospital's administrators have spoken to the city authorities numerous times, but nothing changes."

"Camels, you say? I should like to buy a camel and go riding. Right this very instant. It's been so long since I was outside," Willa said.

"Camel riding? With broken ribs?" Sister Anna said, raising an eyebrow. "I should think it will be a little while yet before you're ready for that."

"I suppose you're right," Willa said. "I'll stick to my mapmaking for now."

She had paper, pencils, and an eraser on a narrow rolling hospital table that allowed her to work in her bed, as her doctor would not allow her to work out of it. Max had asked her draw a map of the area south of Damascus, indicating what route Lawrence would take to attack the city.

"Mr. von Brandt is very pleased with your work. I overheard him talking to Dr. Meyers, asking him when he might be able to take you out of the hospital for a small jaunt," Sister Anna said. "Wouldn't that be lovely?"

Willa smiled. "I'm pleased that he's pleased," she said. Then she clumsily dropped her pencil, tried to catch it before it fell on the floor, and winced with the effort.

Sister Anna saw her. "Is the pain still bad?" she asked, frowning.

Willa nodded.

"I'm sorry to hear it. A woman with three broken ribs and typhus should not have been kept in a prison cell for even one day, never mind several weeks. The disease has obviously weakened you." She reached into her skirt pocket and drew out a small glass bottle. "Here's another pill," she said. "It's been slightly less time between dosages than I would like, but I do not like to see you in pain."

Willa took the pill. She raised her hand to her mouth and took a drink of water—spilling some because her hand was shaking. Then she sat back against her pillows, her hands folded in her lap.

"Thank you," she said, giving the nurse a weary smile of relief.

"I think you should rest for a bit or you will overdo it," Sister Anna said. "You need to build your strength, not tax your body further. You can continue your work later."

"But Mr. von Brandt's maps . . ." Willa protested.

"They can wait for a bit. And if Mr. von Brandt has any objections, he may speak about them with Dr. Meyers." She wheeled the table away from Willa's bed, then walked to the window and let the blind down. "Sleep now," she said.

Willa, eyes already closed, nodded gratefully. Sister Anna quietly left the darkened room, pulling the door closed after her, and locking it—as she always did.

As soon as she heard the bolt turn, Willa opened her eyes and sat up in bed. Her movements were quicker and surer than any she'd made in front of Max or Sister Anna. She quietly got out of bed and flipped her mattress up. She took the pill Sister Anna had given her—it was still in her hand, she'd only pretended to swallow it—and pushed it into a small hole she'd made in the mattress's welting. Then she felt along the welting to make sure the other pills she'd hidden were still there. They were. No one had discovered them—yet. She lowered the mattress, got back into bed, and smoothed her sheets and blankets, then she closed her eyes to sleep.

Sister Anna was right. She needed to build her strength, for she would need it. Max had talked to Dr. Meyers about a jaunt. She doubted it would happen today, or tomorrow, but she was sure it would happen soon. Very soon. And when it did, she must be ready.

CHAPTER SEVENTY-FIVE

"IS THAT YOU, love?" India called out. She was sitting in the kitchen of the Brambles and had just heard the mudroom door open. She'd been expecting Sid for the last two hours.

"I'm afraid not. It's just me, not my handsome brother," Fiona called back.

India laughed. "Fancy a banger?" she said.

"I could murder a banger. A dozen bangers," Fiona said, walking into the kitchen. "And mash and onion gravy. Have you got any?"

"Enough to feed an army. Sit down and tuck in," India said.

She got up from the kitchen table, where she'd been reading at least twenty British newspapers—some that she'd sent for from as far afield as Glasgow and Leeds—and got a plate, cutlery, and a cup of tea for Fiona.

"Sit, India," Fiona said, rubbing her hands together. "I can see to myself." She gave her sister-in-law a quick kiss on the cheek, took the cup of tea from her hands, and took a seat at the table.

"How did Charlie do today?" India asked. "Any progress?"

"None," Fiona said, shoveling potatoes onto her plate. "We've nearly got through the entire rose garden now, but he's still exactly the same. I'd hoped for something—some small but steady improvement—ever since I saw that spark in his eyes. But there's no change. I'm starting to wonder if I only imagined his reaction to the roses."

"I'm sure you didn't. It takes time. He'll get there," India said. "With a mother like you and an uncle like Sid, he has no choice."

Fiona laughed, but India could see she was tired. She'd been working with Charlie all day long. Worried that Fiona would exhaust herself coming and going, she and Sid had asked her to stay with them at the Brambles—an offer she gladly accepted. Mr. Foster had gone back to London and Fiona had decided to return to London on the weekends, and come up again on Monday mornings. India was glad about the arrangement; she loved her sister-in-law's company.

"It's so quiet in here. Are the children in bed?" Fiona asked now, dousing her sausages and mash with gravy.

"They went up half an hour ago. They wanted to wait up for Sid—he promised them presents when he got back—but it was already eight-thirty and they could barely hold their heads up. I told them he'd give them a kiss when he got in.

"Where did he go?" Fiona asked.

"London. He went yesterday evening and spent the night. He was due back around six-thirty. I don't know what's keeping him."

"London?" Fiona said, with a slight note of concern in her voice. "Why did he go there?"

"You don't like it either, do you?" India said worriedly. "I told him not to go. But he said he had business there."

"What kind of business?"

"He said he wanted to talk to someone about medical supplies for the hospital. Drugs, specifically."

Fiona's expression softened. "Oh, it's just hospital business then, isn't it? Forgive me, India. I was being silly. It's just that given his past, I worry."

"I know," India said, gathering her newspapers into a stack. "I do, too. I'm always afraid someone from his old life will spot him in the city and try to make trouble for him. It's probably a daft notion, but I can't help it."

"Well, I'm sure he'll be back any minute. I bet he missed his train, that's all." Fiona pointed at the newspapers in front of India. "What do you have there? A little light reading?" she asked.

India suspected she was trying to change the subject. "Hardly," she said. "I'm trying to follow any and all reported outbreaks of Spanish flu in Britain. It's certainly getting a foothold here. The numbers of infected are increasing in Glasgow, Edinburgh, Newcastle, and York; holding steady in the Midlands and Wales; and starting to pick up in Weymouth, Brighton, and Dover. I've read that quite a few of the major cities are going to start spraying streets in hard-hit areas with disinfectant."

"Any sign of it in the lads here yet?" Fiona asked.

"Not yet, no. Thank God. We have a quarantine ward set up though, just in case. Harriet wrote me to say that she's seeing it starting in London. South of the river, mostly. I wish I could convince Jennie to leave the city and come here. And to bring James with her."

"Have you spoken with her about it?" Fiona asked.

"I wrote her last week, inviting her to come, but she wrote back that she can't leave her father, and he won't leave his parish. She did say, though, that they aren't seeing a tremendous amount of it in Wapping yet. She said if that changes, she'll send James to me. You must be vigilant, too, Fiona, and send the children—at least the younger ones—if the outbreak grows."

"I certainly will. I won't need telling twice," Fiona said. "You'll have us all camped out with you. Mr. Foster, too."

"That would be lovely," India said, smiling. "I think the Brambles needs a butler. We could use some poshing up around here."

The two women continued to chat as Fiona ate her meal. When she finished, she washed up her dishes, then excused herself. "I'm completely knackered," she said. "I'm going to go up to my room, write Joe a letter, and then fall into bed. Thank you for the supper, India. It was delicious," Fiona said. Then she impishly added, "What's for supper tomorrow night? Pickled whelks? Cockles?"

India laughed. She'd grown up the child of very wealthy parents. They had been served fancy dishes at every meal, she'd once told Fiona, but—being a well-bred young lady—she'd never been expected to learn to cook any of them. She'd only learned her way around a kitchen after she'd married Sid—an East Londoner who liked his native dishes. She could not cook bifteck au poivre, or Dover sole in cream sauce, but she could turn out a perfectly cooked sausage, a wonderful steak and kidney pie, and the most delicious fish and chips Fiona had ever tasted.

"I'll make you eel and mash tomorrow," she said now.

Fiona made a face. "My brother doesn't actually eat that, does he?" she said.

"I'm afraid he does."

Fiona kissed India good night. "It's late," she said. "You should get some sleep, too. He'll be home soon. Don't worry."

India smiled and nodded. "Good night," she said. "Sleep well. Send our love to Joe."

As soon as Fiona left the kitchen, India's smile faded. She reached into her skirt pocket and pulled out a small jade Buddha, about two inches long. She'd found it in the pocket of one of Sid's jackets earlier today, when she'd picked the jacket up off the back of a chair to hang it, and could not imagine where he'd got it or what he was doing with it. She stared at it for a bit longer, then put it back in her pocket. For some reason, she hated the sight of it. It frightened her. It seemed like a bad omen.

Desperate to busy herself, and so distract herself from her anxious thoughts, India rose from the table, put her newspapers away, wiped down the sink, and then went out the back door to shake out the tablecloth.

The night air was chilly, but she lingered for a few minutes, peering into the darkness, hoping to catch a glimpse of Sid coming up the drive. Trying to follow Fiona's advice. Trying not to worry.

CHAPTER SEVENTY-SIX

"OH, MAX! I don't know what to say! It's beautiful, and you shouldn't have, but I'm ever so glad that you did," Willa said happily.

"I'm so pleased you like it," Max said, smiling. "It's time you had something to wear other than a hospital gown."

Willa sat in her bed, amid pink ribbons and tissue paper. Max sat in a chair close by. Moments ago, he had appeared in her doorway carrying an armful of boxes. Inside them were a pair of calfskin shoes, silk stockings, lacy underthings, and a beautifully made lawn dress—all in ivory.

"How did you have time to get to Paris and back? I saw you only two days ago!" Willa said, teasing him.

Max grinned. "The seamstresses here are astonishing. They can copy anything. And some of the shops carry very fine goods from Europe."

"Thank you, Max. Really. You are far too good to me," Willa said. "Shall I change into it? Are we going for another outing?"

Two days ago, Max had come for her with a wheelchair and had taken her for an hour-long ride around the streets of Damascus. They'd gone to the souk, where he'd bought her a lovely necklace, and then they'd had lunch in a cafe. And then Willa's strength had faded and Max had brought her back to the hospital.

"As much as I'd love to take you for a jaunt this instant," he said now, "I can't. I have a meeting with Jamal Pasha in an hour . . ."

Willa knew the name. Jamal Pasha was the Turkish governor of Damascus.

". . . but I was wondering if you would do me the great honor of joining me for dinner at my quarters this evening. If, and only if, you feel up to it."

"I would be delighted to," Willa said.

"Wonderful. I will call for you at eight."

Willa suddenly looked down at her dress, not meeting Max's eyes.

"Is something wrong? Is eight too late?" he asked, concern in his voice.

Willa smiled ruefully. "Nothing's wrong. Nothing at all. It's just that it's so nice to have something to look forward to," she said. "It's been so long since I've had that."

Max rose from his chair and sat on the edge of her bed. He hooked a finger under her chin and lifted her face to his. "You have the rest of your life to look forward to Willa Alden," he said, kissing her mouth. "With me."

Willa kissed him back. He put his arms around her and held her close, releasing her only when he heard footsteps in the hall.

"Sister Anna will scold me," he whispered. "She'll say I'm tiring you."

"I hope you will. Tire me, that is," Willa whispered. "Later."

Max feigned shock at her words. Then, as Sister Anna came into the room, he said, "Until this evening, Miss Alden."

"Until this evening, Mr. von Brandt," Willa said.

"And how is our patient this afternoon?" Sister Anna asked. She had just started her shift.

"Very well, Sister Anna," Willa said, as Max left the room. "I've been invited to Mr. von Brandt's for supper this evening."

"So soon?" Sister Anna asked. "Are you certain you are up to it? You are still taking three doses of morphine daily."

"I will manage. One cannot always give in to pain and weakness.

That is no way to win a war, is it? And Mr. von Brandt and I have much to discuss concerning the war."

"Yes, of course," Sister Anna said. "Is there anything I can get for you? Anything that you require?"

Willa looked at her beautiful new clothes, then said, "Yes, there is. A bath."

Sister Anna smiled. "Of course. I'll run one for you," she said. "I'll fetch you in about fifteen minutes."

Willa nodded and Sister Anna left the room. As soon as she had, Willa's smile faded and her jaw took on a grim and determined set.

So soon, she thought.

She'd hoped she would have a few more days. Her side still hurt. She was still weak from the typhus. She would have to overcome both, for Max was bringing her to his house tonight. Once she was there, it would be now or never. She would do her best to look as good as she possibly could. And she would hope like hell that he had wine to drink. A lot of it.

She suddenly felt terrified. It was such a hopeless long shot, her plan. Most likely it would all go horribly wrong, and then it would be her in the yard of the prison, blindfolded and awaiting the firing squad.

She thought of Lawrence and how he had endured years of hardship and privation in the desert to further the cause of Arab independence. She thought of Khalaf and Fatima and their little son. She thought of Auda and of all the wild, indomitable Bedouin. She heard Auda's voice in her head. "Dwell not upon thy weariness, thy strength shall be according to the measure of thy desire," he told her now, just as he had so many times before in the desert. Willa snaked her hand down under her mattress and felt for the pills she'd hidden.

"Tonight, then," she whispered in the silence of her room. *"Inshallah."*

CHAPTER SEVENTY-SEVEN

WILLA WAS READY.

It was a few minutes before eight. She was washed, combed, and dressed. The gown Max had bought had been made for her. It caressed her slim body beautifully and set off her dramatic coloring—her pale skin and dark hair, her luminous green eyes. She was wearing the necklace he'd bought for her in the souk. One of the younger nurses had put her hair up in a soft, fetching twist and loaned her a tube of lipstick.

"My goodness, Miss Alden," Max said when he came for her. "You are absolutely beautiful."

Willa smiled. She was standing by the foot of her bed. Dr. Meyers had gotten her a new leg, to replace the one battered in the plane crash. It fit her well and allowed her to walk relatively easily—though no one knew that but her.

"Why, thank you, Mr. von Brandt," she said. "You look very handsome yourself."

Max bowed his head at the compliment. Willa took a few slow steps toward him, reaching for his arm.

Max frowned. "I'm going to get you a wheelchair. I saw one downstairs."

"It's not necessary, Max," Willa protested. "I can walk. I should walk."

"We'll only use it to get you to my house. Once you're there, you can walk all you like."

Willa sighed. "If you insist," she said.

As Max pushed her through the city streets, Willa commented on the number of animals in the streets and asked many questions.

Who lived in the splendid stone house? The whitewashed one? The tiled one? Where did Jamal Pasha live? What was Max's house like?

"You can see for yourself," he replied to her last question. "It's right there."

He wheeled her up to a beautiful whitewashed house, one of a row of houses about a half mile from the city square. Its arched windows were framed by intricately painted Arabic designs. The entrance—which was set back slightly from the street—was tiled in squares of blue, green, orange, and yellow. Lush red roses climbed the pillars flanking the door, and a stained-glass lantern hung over it, casting a warm glow.

"Max, it's lovely!" Willa exclaimed.

"I'm glad you like it. I'm renting it from a wealthy Turkish merchant. He and his family decamped to Aleppo."

"Are we close to the souk here?" Willa asked. "I'm afraid I haven't got my bearings yet."

"The souk is about four streets west of us. Southwest, actually. Over that way," Max said, pointing.

"Ah, that explains all the animals in the streets," Willa said.

"Yes, they're sold there on Sundays and Wednesdays. But the traders bring them in the night before, which is why there were so many of them in the streets just now. Tomorrow's Wednesday of course."

Willa knew that already. Sister Anna had told her about the animal markets. But she did not let on. The Wednesday animal market was the reason she had said yes to Max's invitation tonight. Had his offer been made for another night, one that did not precede an animal market, she would have begged off, pleading fatigue.

Max's butler, a tall Damascan in an embroidered robe and silk turban, welcomed them. He told Max that the cook had made a most divine meal and that it would be ready shortly.

"Will you show me the house before we dine?" Willa asked, getting out of the wheelchair and taking Max's arm.

Max said he would be delighted to and began to take her around, walking her from room to room.

They started in the sitting room. Willa marveled at the ornately carved chairs and settees, all upholstered in heavy silks, and the thick, patterned Persian rugs on the floor.

"Did the merchant let the house to you furnished?" she asked.

Max nodded. "He left everything in the house. Furniture, rugs, books, kitchenware. He even left some of his robes in the closet. In case I get the urge to go native, I guess."

In the billiards room, there were zebra rugs underfoot and lion and tiger heads on the walls. Antique swords and pistols were also displayed on the walls, many with jeweled hilts and handles.

"Toys for boys," Willa said, running her hand over one heavily crusted sword handle.

Max laughed. He led her into the study, where the walls were lined with books, some in English, some in Turkish and Arabic. They were all beautifully bound in leather. More books, and magazines and newspapers, were piled haphazardly on tables and chairs. A pair of Max's boots and a riding crop lay on the rug by a settee. His desk was covered by maps and memos, some of which had fallen to the floor. Willa glanced casually at the desk as she passed by it, then turned to Max and said, "Very sloppy, Mr. von Brandt. I think you need a wife."

Max walked to the desk. He shuffled the memos into a pile, then turned them over.

"Any candidates in mind?" he asked her, as he rolled the maps up.

"Let me think about it," Willa said. "Perhaps I can come up with one."

Just then, Max's butler came into the room, bowed, and informed them that dinner was served.

"Are you hungry?" Max asked Willa.

Willa reshelved a book she'd been looking at and turned to him. "Desperately," she said. She took his arm again, then added, "Hungry for good food, good wine, and good company. After years in the desert, I feel like I've suddenly stumbled into Paradise."

"Come," Max said, leading her out of the study and to the dining room. "Let's see what the cook has made for us."

The dining room was beautiful and romantic. Candles in silver holders had been set on the table. They cast a soft glow over the room. Roses in vases perfumed the air. Max seated her on the left of one of the short ends of the dining table—a long, ornate affair, made of ebony and inlaid with ivory, malachite, and lapis lazuli. He took the end seat himself, so they would be close together.

As Willa laid her napkin in her lap, he filled her glass and then his own with wine—again a rare Bordeaux.

"To you," he said, lifting his glass.

Willa shook her head. "No, Max, to us," she said.

Their meal began with mezze—a tantalizing array of appetizers. There were grape leaves stuffed with lamb and rice, chickpea patties, hummus, and a dish of grilled eggplant, sesame seed paste, olive oil, lemon, and garlic that Willa could not get enough of.

"This is so good, Max," she said, savoring a bite of stuffed grape leaf. "I've never had such wonderful food. Your cook is amazing."

Max sat back in his chair, watching her eat and smiling, enjoying her enjoyment of the meal. The mezze was followed by fattoush, a peasant salad made of toasted bits of bread, cucumbers, tomatoes, and mint. Then the butler brought out chicken kabobs and kibbeh—minced lamb balls, stuffed with rice and spices. To go with the meat dishes, there were lentils cooked with rice and garnished with fried onions, a dish of stuffed squash, and another of spiced potatoes.

"Max, did your other dinner guests cancel?" Willa asked halfway through the feast. "Your cook made enough for twenty people!"

Max laughed. He leaned forward and refilled Willa's wineglass and then his own. "It's all for you, Willa," he said. "I want to fatten you up. Make you healthy and hearty and happy again."

As they ate, Max asked her about Lawrence, about the sort of man he was. Willa told him, admiringly, about Lawrence's bravery, his intelligence, and his enormous charisma.

"Were you lovers?" Max asked suddenly.

She looked at him over the top of her wineglass, then teasingly said, "Why? Would you be jealous if we were? I should like you to be."

"Yes, I would," Max admitted.

"We were not," she said. "Lawrence has only one mistress—and it's not me."

"Who is it, then?" Max asked.

"Arabia," Willa replied.

Max nodded. "Well," he said at length, "I fear Lawrence is going to have to learn to get along without his mistress, because she won't be his for very much longer."

Willa forced herself to smile. She asked Max to pass her another chicken kabob. She wanted to eat as much as she could. She did not know when she would find food again after tonight.

"Let's not talk about Lawrence or the war," she said. "Not tonight. Let's talk about Everest instead."

They did. Max told her that as soon as he was finished here at Damascus, he would return to Germany and he would take her with him. He would be needed in Berlin until the war was over, but as soon as he could get away, they would travel east again. They talked about plans for their future for quite some time. Until the bottle of wine had been emptied, and another brought. Until the supper dishes were cleared, and a platter of fresh fruit, dates, and honey pastries had been served. Until the candles burned down and Max had dismissed the servants.

As they sat together in the candlelight, reminiscing about Rongbuk, Max suddenly reached across the table and covered Willa's hand with his own. "I want you, Willa Alden," Max said. "I've wanted you all night. All during the trip from the hospital. All through supper. I want you so much I can't bear it."

"What about dessert?" Willa coyly asked, biting into a date. "Don't you want any?"

"You are dessert," Max said. He rose from his chair then, picked her up, and carried her to his bedroom.

He put her down, kissed her, and gently unbuttoned the back of her dress. It slipped off her arms, down her slender body, to the floor, where it lay—a shimmering silk puddle at her feet. As she stood in her camisole, petticoat, and stockings, he took off his jacket and shirt. Then he stretched out on his bed, took her hand, and pulled her down to him. He kissed her mouth, her throat, the delicate bones of her neck. She buried her hands in his thick blond hair and kissed him back. He was gloriously handsome. His body was hard and smooth. His face, that of a stone god.

I could have loved you, Max, she thought, if things had been different.

She remembered his warm hands, his passionate kisses. She remembered the feel and smell of him. She saw him as he had been on Everest—strong and daring, hard and fearless. He had been her lover then. Now he was her enemy. She must not forget that, not for a second. It would cost her her life if she did—hers and many more besides.

Max untied the string at the top of her camisole. He started working at the buttons down the front of it. She stopped him.

"What's wrong?" he asked her.

"I'm . . . I'm afraid, Max," she said.

"You? Afraid? Of what?"

"I'm afraid you won't want me if you see me. Underneath these beautiful things you gave me, I'm not beautiful. I'm all bones and bruises. I look like . . . well, like I've been through a war."

Max laughed. He propped himself on one elbow and looked into her eyes. "When I first saw you, in Kathmandu, I thought you were the most beautiful woman I'd ever seen. I still do, Willa. I don't give a damn about bones and bruises," he said. "Let me see you."

"All right," she said, pulling his face to hers and kissing him hungrily. "But first, more wine."

Max started to get up, but she stopped him. "No, I can get it. You've indulged me enough this evening. Surely I can walk to the dining room and back."

She left the room walking slowly and deliberately, but as soon as she was out of his sight, she hurried. The seductive smile had fallen away. She had seconds only. Moving as quickly as she could, she hiked up her petticoat, rolled back the top of her stocking, and took out a small, folded square of paper. It contained white powder. She'd ground the pills between the soles of her new shoes earlier that day, when she was supposed to be sleeping, and brushed the powder into a piece of tissue paper from Max's gift boxes. She dumped the paper's contents into one of the wineglasses, poured wine on top of it, then stirred the mixture with her finger, praying it would speedily dissolve. She poured wine into the second glass, then picked up both glasses, careful to note which had the ground pills in it, and carried them to the bedroom.

"Here you are," she said, handing the spiked drink to him. He took a sip, put the glass down on the floor, and reached for her. He had her camisole and petticoat off in a twinkling. Then he finished undressing himself.

Willa smiled and nuzzled him as he did, but inside she was panicking. He had to drink more than a mouthful. She didn't know how strong the mixture was, or how fast it would work, but she was certain that if he became woozy, instead of unconscious, he would figure out what she'd done. And then it would all be over.

She picked up his glass and handed it back to him. "A toast, Max. To the end of this war," she said, taking a sip. Max followed her lead.

"To Everest," she added, taking another mouthful. Max did, too.

"And to us," she said. "To our future. Which begins tonight." She drained her glass then, and Max did the same.

She took his glass and put it, and hers, on the floor. "Make love to me slowly, Max. I don't want to rush this. I want it to last," she said, her voice soft and low. "I want us to take our time tonight, to forget all the bad memories and make new ones. Good ones."

She lay down on the bed and twined her arms around his neck. He kissed her mouth again, then her breasts, her belly. He kissed her hip, then parted her legs.

Willa let out a small sigh of what she hoped sounded like pleasure. She wondered, desperately, how long it would be before the pills took effect. She didn't want to do this.

"My God, but I want you," Max said suddenly, and then he was inside her.

Willa gasped loudly and not from desire. Hot tears stung behind her eyes. What did you do wrong? she silently shouted at herself. Why isn't it working?

She bit her lip as Max pounded against her. Her plan had failed. She would go back to her hospital room after tonight—if by some mercy Max didn't figure out what she'd done. And she would have to pretend, day in and day out, that she adored him; she would have to have dinners with him, and sleep with him, and all the while Faisal, Lawrence, Auda, and their soldiers would be marching to their doom.

And then suddenly, Max stopped. He laughed self-consciously and passed a hand over his sweaty face. "The wine," he said. "It must've gone to my head."

Willa laughed. "I feel tipsy, too. It's wonderful, isn't it?" She kissed him again. "Don't stop, Max. Make love to me. Now. I want you so."

Max rolled off her onto his side. He blinked his eyes a few times, then closed them and shook his head.

Terrified that he'd twigged what she'd done, Willa pretended that she thought he'd only grown tired. "You can rest," she whispered. "It's my turn now." She bent over him, to kiss him, ran a hand over his chest. He opened his eyes, caressed one of her breasts, then quickly closed his eyes again and pressed his hands to his face.

"My head . . . it's spinning," he said. Willa kissed him again. He pushed her off him and sat up, understanding dawning in his eyes. "The wine," he said, swaying slightly. "You put something in the wine." With effort, he swung his feet over the side of the bed and stood up, but his legs gave way and he fell to the floor. "Why, Willa?" he rasped, trying to pull himself up. He fell back on the floor then, toppling over with the bedcover in his hands. He groaned once. His eyes closed. He was still.

Willa was so terrified, she could barely breathe. She nudged him once with her foot, then again, then she jumped out of bed and dressed as quickly as she could. Her injured ribs were protesting, but she ignored them. She was a lot stronger than she'd been letting on.

Glancing nervously at Max, she picked his clothes up off the floor and went through them. She found nothing in his trousers, but there was a wallet in his jacket. She took the paper money from it and threw the wallet on the floor.

Next, she raced to the billiards room and grabbed an antique sword and three pistols off the wall. She ransacked the room's closets and cabinets, looking for bullets, and finally found some. Then she flew down the hall to the study and grabbed the maps she'd seen Max roll up earlier. She didn't stop to look at them, just took them all.

She was at the front door, almost out of the house, when she caught sight of her reflection in a hallway mirror, and saw a woman in a fancy dress, clutching weapons and maps. How far would she get looking like this? Not far at all. She needed different clothes. She would have to go back into the bedroom, and she had no idea how long the effects of the pills would last.

Moving slowly and quietly, she made her way back down the hallway. She peered around the door, her heart crashing in her chest, and saw Max. He was still on the floor, right where she'd left him.

Go, she commanded herself. Now. Hurry.

She put the weapons and maps on the bed then ran to the closet. "Please be here," she whispered. "Please." She rifled through the uniforms, dinner jackets, shirts, and trousers. They weren't what she wanted. "Come on, you have to be in here somewhere," she said. And then she spotted what she was after—the long robes worn by Arab men. She grabbed a blue one and a white one, and two matching head scarves. She quickly put the blue one on over her dress and wrapped a scarf around her head. The garments' dark colors would make her less visible in the city streets.

She looked at Max again; he hadn't moved. Everything inside her was urging her to run, but she knew she couldn't. Not yet. She needed something to put the sword, pistols, and maps in. Saddlebags would have been nice, and would have helped her look inconspicuous in a city where most still rode camels, but she had no time to look for them. Max could wake up at any second. As she tried to decide what to do, her eyes came to rest on the bed. She quickly grabbed a pillow, pulled off its case and stuffed her things inside it. The sword stuck out of the opening, but she would just have to make do. She'd spent too long here already; she should have been gone by now.

Willa was just lifting the case off the bed when Max's hand closed around her ankle. She screamed and tried to break free, but he jerked her leg hard and she lost her balance and fell to the floor. The pillowcase and its contents crashed down next to her.

"Morphine, was it?" Max rasped. "You should've put more in. You should've finished me off."

Willa struggled. She kicked at him with her free leg, but he caught it in his other hand and held it fast against the floor. Max woozily got to his knees and lurched toward her. His hands closed on her arm. He tried to drag her to her feet, but Willa kicked and struggled against him. She had to get free. It was over for her, and for Lawrence, if she didn't.

Max tightened his grip. Willa's hands scrabbled against his, trying to pry his fingers loose, but even though the drugs had made Max slow and clumsy, she was still no match for him. She kicked at him again and her foot caught him in the groin. He roared out in pain, rose up, and slapped her hard. She fell back against the floor, hitting her head. Lights exploded in front of her eyes. Her hands fell away from Max. One of them came down on the pillowcase.

The pillowcase. With every last ounce of her strength, Willa shoved her hand inside of it. Her fingers closed on a pistol barrel. It wasn't loaded, but it didn't need to be. Max was on all fours now, groaning. Willa pulled the pistol out, raised it as high as she could, and brought it down on his head.

Max shouted. Pain and rage contorted his face. His hands went to his head. That was all Willa needed. She hit him again. And again. Until he had stopped yelling, stopped groaning, until he had collapsed against her and was still.

Willa threw the pistol down. A small moan escaped her. Had she killed him? Oh, God, no. She didn't want to kill him. She'd only wanted to escape from him.

"Max? *Max!*" she cried. He gave her no answer. For a few seconds she was paralyzed by the horror of what she'd done.

Get out of here, a voice inside her suddenly said. Go. *Now.*

Sobbing, she pushed him off. His blood had spattered across her face and onto her hands. It had seeped into her robes. She got to her feet and staggered to the bathroom. She quickly washed the blood off her skin and decided not to change her robes. They were blue; the blood wouldn't show in the dark.

She stumbled back to the bedroom, picked up the pillowcase, and ran.

CHAPTER SEVENTY-EIGHT

"SOUTHWEST," WILLA WHISPERED as she ran through the night streets of Damascus. *The souk is about four streets west of us. Southwest, actually*, Max had said.

But which way was southwest? She had tried to walk back the way they'd come, but had become disoriented. It had not yet been dark when they'd arrived at Max's house. Now it was past eleven and pitch-black. There were no streetlights and no moon, and Willa, who'd been running flat out for the last fifteen minutes, realized she was lost.

She stopped, trying to make sense of her surroundings, to get her bearings, but she was unfamiliar with the city and its streets. Her heart was pounding so hard that she could barely breathe. She was panicking.

She had likely just killed a man. And not just any man, but Max von Brandt, a high-ranking German officer. If Max was dead, he would be discovered in a matter of hours when his servants arrived to begin their morning duties. But if he was still alive, if he could move, he would stagger to a neighbor's house for help. The alarm could go up at any minute, and when it did, the whole city would be searching for her. Willa knew she must get as far away from Damascus as she possibly could. As fast as she could.

She fought down her panic, looking left and right, trying to decide which way to go. A cry came from above her. She quickly looked up. A bird startled by something, perhaps a cat on the prowl, flew noisily from its nest into the sky. Willa followed, more by sound than by sight, and then she saw it—the night sky, full of stars.

She nearly laughed out loud. Of course! She'd been in shock, too upset to think straight, or she would have looked up at the stars when she'd first run out of Max's house. The stars were always there for her when she was lost. Picking out Polaris, she gauged southwest by its position, then pressed on, turned right instead of continuing straight as she'd intended to do, and ten minutes later, she was nearing the souk.

She saw the glow of lanterns up ahead, under whitewashed arches, smelled animals, heard the low, murmuring conversation of the traders who were still awake, and knew she was in the right place.

The first group she came to only had goats for sale. The next had horses. She pushed on, her head down, until she found the camel traders. The ones closest to her were Howeitat. She recognized their language and their clothing. Their camels were lying down in the dirt. She addressed the nearest man. He was standing at the edge of the group, facing away from them, eating olives and spitting the pits.

"I need a camel and bridle. Now," she told him, in his own tongue. She lowered her voice, hoping that in her robes and headscarf she would pass for a man.

The man took her to his animals, which were a few yards away, and prodded the beasts into standing. Willa picked one. The man shook his head and regretfully informed her that the camel she'd picked was his very best one and therefore very expensive.

Willa pulled the jeweled sword out of the pillowcase. She noticed for the first time that there was blood on the case. The camel trader noticed it, too.

She turned the bloodstain toward herself and said, "I will trade you this sword for the camel."

The man took the sword from her, inspected it, then handed it back to her. "It is a fake," he said. "Very nice, but a fake. I will take it as partial payment. What else have you got?"

"It is no fake. If you will not take it, perhaps another man will," Willa said, putting the sword back in the pillowcase.

"Perhaps I spoke too quickly," the man said.

"Good. But my offer's changed," Willa said. "I'll still give you the sword, but I want a saddle, a crop, and a skin of water as well."

The man bowed his head. "Very well," he said.

Willa took the sword out of the case again. She handed it to the man. He took it and grabbed her roughly by the wrist. She didn't dare scream. She couldn't afford to attract attention.

"Let me go," she hissed at him.

But he didn't. Instead he pushed up the sleeve of her robe. "Your skin's as white as goat's milk," he said, "just like the great sheik Lawrence." He pushed her scarf back on her head. "And a woman, too." His voice turned menacing. "I wonder, are you the one Lawrence seeks? The one who flew in the sky? What have you done, little bird? How did you come by this sword? Why is there blood upon the sack you carried it in?"

Terror gripped Willa. This man was a trader. He would sell her, and not to Lawrence. Lawrence was too far away. He would hand her back to the Turks. Her only chance was to somehow convince him not to.

"Let me go, Howeitat," she said. "The Turk is no friend to you. Let me go to help Lawrence and Auda abu Tayi return to you and your sons the land the Turks stole. The land of your fathers."

For a few seconds, the man's face softened, but then his eyes narrowed, and he said, "Lawrence cannot win. He has too few men."

"He can win. He *will* win. If you let me go." She shook her pillowcase. "I have information in here. Maps I took from the Turks and the Germans. They will help Lawrence find the best way to

Damascus. A great sheik from Cairo, a great warrior, will come with Lawrence. Together they will take the city."

The camel trader weighed this, and weighed her, Willa felt, and then he let her go.

"Ride due south. Lawrence's camp is past the Jabal al Duruz hills. Just north of Azraq. Well east of Minifir. Six days away, five if you're fast. Stay away from the railway. Turkish battalions are patrolling it daily. Be wary."

Willa, weak with relief, thanked him. She started walking toward the camel she'd picked, but the man stopped her. "That one is lame. Take this other. He name is Attayeh. He is young and healthy," he said, directing her to a larger animal. The trader saddled the camel, gave Willa the water and crop she'd asked for, tied her pillowcase securely to her saddle, and told her to go with Allah.

Seconds later, she was off, riding down the street to the Bab al-Jabiya gate. It wasn't far from the souk. She could see the light from the lanterns positioned at either side of the gate. Willa prayed that the gate was open. If it was closed for the night, she was finished. Willa pulled her scarf down low on her forehead.

As she got closer to the gate, she saw that it was still open. Better yet, there were no guards around it. Her heart leapt. She spurred the camel into a trot, then a canter. She'd have one chance to get through the gate and one chance only, and she wasn't stopping for anybody or anything.

When she was about twenty yards away, a guard suddenly stepped out of a small stone hut that was just to the left of the gate. He saw her and immediately yelled at her to stop. Another guard joined him. Both men had rifles. They raised them and aimed at Willa.

"Keep the gates open!" she yelled at them in Turkish, as manfully as she could. "Jamal Pasha is coming! Jamal Pasha is coming. He is behind me in his automobile! There is an emergency! He must get to Beirut by morning! Make way for Jamal Pasha!"

Surprised, the guards lowered their guns and stepped aside, trying to see past Willa, looking for the governor's car. Their surprise lasted for only a few seconds, but that was all she needed. She was past them in a flash, through the gate, and on the road out of Damascus, riding like the wind.

She heard gunshots behind her and prayed nothing hit her camel, or herself. In that order. She would keep going with a bullet wound, for as long as she could, but her camel might not. Nothing hit either of them, and within a few minutes, the hardpan road gave way to the looser sands of the desert. Willa did not let up on her camel, but kept whipping the creature, yelling at him, keeping him in a canter, afraid that the guards would send someone after her. No one followed, however. Perhaps the guards could not scare up a car or camels at this hour, or perhaps they had no wish to—not wanting anyone to know they had allowed someone through the gates whom they should not have.

Willa chanced a few glances behind her, heartened to see the city falling away. Her camel cantered up a dune and down the other side, and Damascus was gone. Willa whooped for joy and then, her robes flying behind her, disappeared into the desert night.

CHAPTER SEVENTY-NINE

SID SMELLED TEA. He heard voices. And water.

He was afraid. Water was dangerous. Water meant death. He'd heard them talking—Madden and his boys. They were going to put him in the water, dump him into the river. He would drown there. He would never see India again. Never see his children. They would never know what happened to him.

He tried to move, to get up, desperate to get away from the water, but when he did, pain—fierce, hot, and red—slammed into him. It was everywhere. Inside his head. In his gut. His knees. His back. He felt like he was made of pain. He cried out with it. He tried again, to get up, to at least open his eyes, but they wouldn't do what he wanted.

"Shh! Stop it, Sid. You're all right. Everything's all right," one of the voices said.

With great effort, Sid opened his swollen eyes. His vision was blurry. He could see a man's face leaning over him. And a woman's. He didn't know who they were.

"He sees us, John," the woman said. "I don't think he knows us, though. Talk to him, love. Tell him who we are."

"Sid? Sid, can you hear me?"

Sid nodded. He tried to get up.

"No, don't get up. Don't move. You'll start everything bleeding again. Just stay still. I'm John. This is me wife, Maggie. I used to do some work for you. Years ago. Do you remember us?"

Sid tried to think, tried to remember, but the pain wouldn't let him.

"He doesn't know us. Poor sod probably doesn't know his own name right now," Maggie whispered to her husband. "You came to our room one night, Sid. You had a lady doctor with you," she said. "She was asking us questions. About what we eat and what it costs and what John's wages were."

Suddenly Sid remembered. "Maggie Harris," he croaked, through his split lips. "Maggie and John."

"Yes! Yes, that's us," John said.

Sid's mind went back in time. To 1900. Before he'd left London. Before he'd married India. She had been at a Labour rally and had been arrested. He'd got her out of jail, but a reporter had pursued her. She hadn't wanted to speak to the man, so Sid had helped her throw him off. They'd hidden out in the tunnels under Whitechapel, had finally surfaced in the Blind Beggar, a pub, where they'd had a meal. Afterward, he'd taken her to meet the poor of Whitechapel.

One of the homes they'd visited had belonged to John and Maggie Harris, who had six small children and lived in two damp, dreary rooms. Maggie and her children—all but the youngest, who was sleeping under the table—were up late, working. They were gluing matchboxes together. He had fallen in love with India that night.

"Where am I?" Sid asked now.

"You're in the hold of me boat," John said.

"How did I get here?" Sid remembered clocking Teddy Ko and taking a few shots at Madden's men. Nothing else.

"Madden's lads brought you. They gave you one hell of a hiding."

Sid remembered that part.

"Then after you'd blacked out, they slung you into the basement at the boatyard. You've been there for days. This morning, just as I got in from one job, they told me I had another to do—picking up some swag in Margate. They carried you on board, threw you in the hold, and then Madden told me I'm to sail out into open waters before I go to Margate, weight you, and throw you in. I told them I would, but I won't. I made you a bed here. Got some laudanum into you, too."

"Why? Why did you do that?" Sid asked, knowing full well that Madden would kill John if he ever found out he'd disobeyed him.

"Because you always took care of me, Sid. So now it's on me to do you a good turn. And besides, I hate that bastard Madden. He works me to death, pays me nothing. Makes me do things I don't want to do. I mean, thieving's one thing, but murdering blokes, well, that's quite another. I want to leave but I can't. I'd have to go far away, me and me whole family, and I haven't the money. Madden's threatened he'd do for me, and for Maggie, and he'd make me kids watch, if I ever do leave."

"What are you going to tell him?" Sid asked, as he realized the full enormity of the risk John was taking on his behalf.

"I'll tell him I did the job, of course," John said. "He'll believe me. There's no reason not to. I'll take the boat out past Margate. Dump a pile of rubbish off the stern—rocks, old rope, broken tools—all wrapped up in a canvas in case someone's watching. Knowing Billy, someone will be. Then I'll continue on to the job."

"How the hell am I going to get home?" Sid asked, wincing with the effort of talking.

"You're not. Not yet. I should get to Margate after dark tomorrow.

Cargo won't be loaded until the following morning. We'll get you off the boat safely. You'll have to make your own way home from there."

Sid nodded.

John stared at Sid, frowning, as Maggie pressed a cloth to Sid's lip. All the talking had opened it up again. Sid could feel blood running down his chin. He could see the worry in John's eyes.

"You ought to have a doctor," John said. "You're in rough shape, Sid, but you've got to hang on. Do you hear me?"

Sid nodded. His vision was fading. The pain was pulling him under. He thought of India. She would be frantic with worry. He wished he could get word to her, but he'd have to tell John who she was and where she was and he didn't want to tell him—or anyone connected with Madden—that he even had a family, much less where they were.

"You hang on, Sid. . . ."

John's voice was growing fainter. It sounded farther away. Sid heard the water again, lapping at the boat's hull. It wanted to get at him. To fill his nose and mouth. To drown him. He wouldn't let it. He would fight it. There had been another time, long ago, when he'd gone into the water. It was here, on the London river. He'd been doing a job with his men. The robbery had gone wrong. He'd fallen off the dock into the river, hit a piling, and ripped his side open. He'd almost died from the wound. He'd felt, then, that he would die. And he hadn't much cared. But India had saved him. She'd fought for his life.

He pictured her now, held her beautiful face in his mind as the pain racking his damaged body pulled at him, threatening to drag him under. He'd had nothing to live for the last time, and no one to love.

This time he did.

CHAPTER EIGHTY

WILLA LEANED BACK into the furry warmth of her camel. The animal was lying down for a much-needed rest. Willa had driven Attayeh hard, but she knew she couldn't work him too hard. If something happened to him, she would never make it to Lawrence's camp.

Willa had driven herself hard, too. She had ridden all night, and all the next day, ever since she'd escaped from Damascus. It was now eight o'clock of the following night. She was hurting and exhausted, but she did not sleep. Instead, she had pulled all of Max's maps and papers out of the pillowcase and was going through them. What she'd read so far made her see that Max von Brandt had been playing her just as hard as she'd been playing him.

She'd read reports he'd made in which he stated he did not believe what she had told him about the size of Lawrence's army or its location. This disappointed her. She'd given him nothing but false information, hoping it would throw him off Lawrence's scent. In Max's opinion, Lawrence was south of the Jabal ad Duruz hills and he was going to ride due north from there to attack Damascus.

Furthermore, Willa had discovered that the Turkish Army had a second encampment ten miles west of their Jabal ad Duruz camp and directly parallel to it, so that when Lawrence rode north, Turkish troops from both camps would converge on him, making defense all but impossible—and making the slaughter of Tom Lawrence, Faisal, Auda, and the thousands of men with them all but inevitable.

And Lawrence had no idea of the trap that waited for him, not even an inkling. Because her plane had crashed, and she'd been taken prisoner, Willa had not been able to tell him about the first camp, and until this very moment, no one but the Turks had known about the second.

Willa rested her chin on her knee, thinking. Max had indicated on one of his maps exactly where he thought Lawrence might be—at Salkhad. It was well north of where the Bedouin trader in the market had said Lawrence was. According to Max's reports, he'd based the position on recon carried out by Bedouin scouts. But were those scouts reliable? Were they truly in the service of the Turks? Some of the Bedouin were extremely wily and would think nothing of taking Max's money and then taking even more money from Lawrence to feed Max misinformation. Was the trader who'd told her Lawrence's whereabouts reliable? Had Lawrence moved since that man had seen his camp? The area south of Jabal was large and desolate, and Lawrence could be anywhere in it.

Willa knew she had to get him, no matter what. She had to let him know what he was riding into. Should she trust Max's information and ride to the point he'd indicated on his map? Or would she need to ride farther south as the trader had told her to?

"How far do we go, Attayeh?" she said softly. But Attayeh had no answer for her.

She rolled up the maps and put them back in the pillowcase. Thank God she'd thought to take them; she would have no idea where she was going without them. She then gathered the memos and reports, having decided that she would finish reading them later. She was tired and needed to sleep. As she shuffled the scattered papers together, a few slipped from the pile. She picked them up, and a line at the top of one caught her eye.

It was a death warrant. Her own. Telegraphed from Berlin.

Her blood ran cold as she read it. Max, as it turned out, was not going to take her to Germany, or to Everest, but to the prison yard to have her shot. Today. The day after their dinner together. The day after he'd made love to her.

For the first time since she'd beaten him, she thought about the possibility of having killed him and she felt no remorse. He would have killed her. If not last night, when he'd beaten her as she tried to escape, then today.

The Bedouin who'd sold her the camel and given her water and some of his own food had also stashed two cigarettes and a box of matches in her saddlebag. She fished one of the cigarettes out now, lit it with shaking hands, and took a long drag.

She was still days away from Lawrence's camp—wherever it might be. She had little food and water. She had stolen vital military information from the desk of a German officer, information that might well turn the tide of the battle for the Middle East. She had likely killed that same German officer, and by now there would be a price on her head. Every desert bandit would be after her, as would every soldier in the entire Turkish Army.

She had escaped death last night, yes . . . but for how long?

CHAPTER EIGHTY-ONE

SID WINCED AS Maggie pressed a warm, damp cloth to his forehead. He was sitting shirtless, enduring Maggie's efforts to clean him up, at a tiny table in the small space belowdecks that John used for sleeping and eating when he was on the water.

It was nearly ten o'clock at night, and John had just docked at a tumbledown warehouse in Margate. He was on deck right now, pretending to check the lines, but really checking to see if anyone was about—a watchman, perhaps, or any of Madden's crew. Sid was desperate to get off the boat, desperate to get home to India and the children. He knew they'd be out of their minds with worry.

"Hold still, Sid," Maggie scolded. "You can't go out and about with blood all over you. The busies'll be on you quicker than you can blink. Surely you don't need me to tell you that. You must remember one or two things about avoiding Old Bill from your London days."

Sid smiled as best he could. "One or two, Maggs," he said.

It was Wednesday—four days since Madden and his boys had given him a beating, one day since he'd come to in John's boat, but everything still hurt. It was painful to open his eyes. To turn his head. To bend and stand and walk. It hurt to swallow, and when he'd taken a piss off the stern of the boat earlier, his water had been bloody.

"Your clothes are a lost cause," Maggie said. "John brought some of his old things for you. As soon as you're washed, you can put them on."

"You and John have been very good to me, Maggie. I owe you both."

Maggie shook her head. "You owe us nothing, Sid Malone. I couldn't even count the times you saved our bacon. With all those jobs you gave John. There were several times we would have starved without you. I don't know how I would've fed the kids without those wages."

"How are your children?"

Maggie didn't answer right away. "The younger ones are all right," she finally said. "They're still only kiddies. The older ones are a worry. Me eldest girl has trouble with her lungs. And the two boys, well . . . they're boys, aren't they? Starting to run wild. Can't blame them, I suppose, with what they see all round them. But still, once upon a time, I had hopes, you know? Hopes that it might be better for them than it was for us. Madden's already got his eye on our Johnnie. I don't want our lad near that man, but it's hard to keep him away. He gives him booze. Women, too, I've heard. Makes him feel like he's cock of the walk. He's only fifteen, Sid. He don't know any better. He won't know any better until it's too late."

Sid saw that her brow was knit with worry as she spoke. "You can't get him out of London?" he asked her. "Send him off to the country with relatives for a bit?"

"We haven't got any relatives in the country. They're all in London," she said. "As mad as it sounds, I'm thinking of talking to him about enlisting as soon as he's sixteen. If the war's still on. He's safer on the lines, with Gerry shooting at him, then he is in Madden's company."

As Maggie finished speaking, they both heard footsteps above them—two sets. And then voices. Maggie held a finger to her lips. Sid stiffened.

"You all right then, John?" they heard a man say. "All settled in for the night?"

"Aye, Bert. Right as rain," John replied.

"I'm leaving now. Harry's on in the morning. He knows to expect you. Lads should be early. Madden told me to tell them to get the goods here before dawn."

"I'll be ready for them. Ta ra, Bert."

"Ta ra, John. Sleep well."

A minute or so later, John's feet were seen climbing down the narrow wooden ladder that connected the deck to the lighter's hold.

"Coast is clear," he said, closing that hatch above him. "There was only Bert about, and he's leaving." He looked at Sid. "Well, you won't win any beauty contests, not with that face, but you look better than you did," he said.

"I wouldn't have won any beauty contests before Madden got hold of me either," Sid said.

John took a seat across from him. He reached into his jacket pocket, took out some money, and put it on the table. "That's two and six," he said. "It's all I could scrape together. Take it. Get yourself home."

Sid was deeply moved by his friend's generosity. He knew that this money was likely all John had in the world. He didn't want to take it, but he had no choice. Billy's men had gone through his pockets before they'd dumped him off with John. They'd taken all his money.

"Thank you," he said. "I'll get it back to you. I swear."

John nodded. The clothes he'd found for Sid were lying on top of the table. Sid picked up the shirt and put it on. The sleeves were too short, which made them all laugh, but it was better than what he'd had. The trousers and jacket fit. John gave Sid the layout of the town of Margate and told him the best way to go to get out of the town quickly.

When they'd finished talking, Sid readied himself to go. He stood up and tried to thank John and Maggie, but they waved his words away.

"Sid, before you go . . . can I ask you something?" John said.

Sid nodded.

"Why did you go back to Teddy Ko's to ask about that woman—the one who killed herself—Maud Selwyn Jones? Are you really looking to take your manor back, or were you feeling completely barmy that day?"

Sid raised an eyebrow. "Neither, I was just after some information. How do you know about that, anyway?" he asked. He'd told John he was at Teddy Ko's, but not why.

"Because we—me and Madden—arrived at Ko's just after your first visit. I heard everything Billy and Teddy talked about. Enough to know you was digging around for information on the Jones woman. And enough to know that you just being here made Billy furious. Did you get what you was after?" John asked.

"No, I didn't," Sid said.

John and Maggie traded anxious looks.

"What is it?" Sid asked them. "Do you know something? Can you tell me?"

"Aye, I know plenty," John said. "Enough to maybe put Billy Madden in front of a firing squad. Which I'd quite like. And meself as well. Which I wouldn't."

Sid sat back down. "Tell me, John," he said. "I'll keep you out of the shite no matter what. I promise."

John took a deep breath. "Years back, right before the Jones woman's death, a man by the name of Peter Stiles bought morphine and a syringe off Teddy Ko. I was at Ko's that day, picking up his weekly payment to Billy. I saw Stiles come in. I saw him pay Teddy for something in a small brown bag. After he'd gone, I asked Teddy what it was and he told me."

"I don't see the connection," Sid said. "The name Stiles doesn't ring a bell. It's never come up in the police reports on Maud's death," Sid said. "Lots of people buy drugs from Teddy."

"Hear me out," John said. "I knew Stiles. He'd come to the Bark, to see Madden, earlier in the year. This is 1914 I'm talking about. He had made certain arrangements with Madden. . . ." John's voice trailed off. He looked pained. Sid could see that talking about Peter Stiles was difficult for him.

"Go on, John," he said.

"These arrangements concerned taking a mate of Stiles's—a man named Hutchins—out on me boat. Every fortnight. To the North Sea. To certain coordinates, to meet another boat. Stiles was moving swag to the continent. Jewelry. At least that's what he said. Meself? I don't think it was jewels that he was moving. We were always met there by a boat. Hutchins would give a box to the captain. He sounded as English I do, Hutchins that is. The captain of the other boat, though? And the crew. They were speaking German."

"Christ, John," Sid said. "How long did this go on? When did it stop?"

"That's the thing—it didn't," John said. "Hutchins is dead. Another bloke did for him back in '14, but I'm still meeting the boat. With a new man—Flynn. I don't want to do this, Sid. I never wanted to do it. I'm running secrets to the Germans. I know I am. Our boys are dying over there and I'm helping Gerry kill them. I want to stop but I can't. I'm in too deep. Madden'll do for me. And then what happens to me kids?" His voice broke. He looked away from Sid, but before he did, Sid saw the anguish in his eyes—and recognized it. It had been his own once.

"Madden's a bastard, well and truly," Sid said. "We'll get round him, though, John. Don't worry. We'll figure something out. I'll fix this somehow. But first finish your story. Tell me all of it. I still don't understand how this ties in with the death of Maud Selwyn Jones."

John wiped his eyes. "Her death was a big news story, wasn't it? It was in all the papers. HEIRESS TAKES HER OWN LIFE, the headlines said. There were pictures of her. I saw them. And when I saw them, I recognized her. I'd seen her before. And Stiles, too. I saw them together. Only he wasn't Stiles then."

"Hold on, John. Slow down. I'm not following you," Sid said.

"We was casing a house, me and a few more of Madden's crew. In the West End. Belonged to some toff who had lots of silver, paintings, the usual. We was going to knock it off one weekend when he was away. We went in one afternoon—me and another bloke—posing as inspectors from the gas company. Wanted to get a gander round the place—see what was where upstairs, and get the lay of the basement doors and windows. While we was in the foyer, messing about with a gas lamp, I saw them come in—the Selwyn Jones woman and Peter Stiles. Only she called him Max, and she introduced him to the lady of the house as Max von Brandt. After her death, I checked out this Max von Brandt. Found out he was from Germany. He only posed as Stiles, an Englishman, to get the use of Madden's boat. I don't see him anymore—Stiles, that is. And I never told Billy about him being von Brandt. But I still see his man Flynn. Every fortnight. And whatever he's giving the Germans . . . well, it ain't diamond earrings."

Sid sat back in his chair, gobsmacked. So many questions were whirling around in his head, he barely knew which one to ask first.

"John," he said at length. "I believe what you're telling me—that Stiles or von Brandt is passing documents to Germany, but it doesn't follow on that he killed Maud. Max von Brandt's alibi was solid. He was completely cleared of any connection in Maud's death. The police reports said he didn't do it. They said she killed herself with an overdose of morphine."

"I know what the reports said. I read the papers," John said. "But since when do the busies have the last word on anything? What are they now, geniuses? They say he didn't. So what? I say he did."

"How?"

John shook his head. "That's the rub, isn't it? I don't know. Maybe he was quick and injected her right then and there when he took her home. Maybe he paid off the cabbie to say he'd only been in her house a minute or two, when he'd actually been in there longer. Maybe he had a key on him and snuck back later that night. Maybe he didn't need a key. Maybe he went back all nice-like, pretending he wanted to make up, and she let him in. If anyone could've pulled it off, he could've. He's one clever sod."

"But why? Why would he want to kill her? He finished with her, not the other way round."

John thought for a bit, then he said, "Maybe it had nothing to do with their love affair. Maybe she knew something. Maybe she'd seen something she shouldn't have."

"Maybe you're right," Sid said slowly. "Here's another question: Where is von Brandt or Stiles or whatever he calls himself now?"

"I don't know. I haven't seen him since the war started."

"But you're still taking Flynn and the documents out to the North Sea?"

John nodded.

"So Billy's still getting paid," Sid said. "Or else you wouldn't be. He doesn't do anything from the goodness of his heart, not our Billy. Somebody's still sending the money." Sid thought for a minute, then he said, "How does Flynn get the documents?"

"I don't know. He doesn't say much. He just appears at the boatyard every fortnight. Like clockwork. I just took him out this past weekend. Due to go again not this coming Friday, but the next one."

Sid took a deep breath, then blew it out. "Well, John, I have to say . . . this is one fine fucking mess. We could go to the police, tell them all you know about von Brandt and Flynn and Madden. Maybe get you some sort of informant's deal. But then what? Madden just denies everything. There's no proof of any of this, right? It's just your word against his. Old Bill does nothing, much as they'd like to, because they can't. Madden knows you snitched and comes after you. Not what I'd call a good result."

"Nor I," said Maggie.

"We go to the government," Sid said. "Tell them about von Brandt and Flynn. Tell them they can't implicate you. They nab Flynn at the boatyard with the documents on him. He's in the shit. You say you've never seen him before. You have no idea what he's doing in the boatyard. You're in the clear. That way, we put an end to the passing of any secrets to Gerry, but you still belong to Billy. Also not good."

Sid put his elbows on the table and his head in his hands, trying to come up with a solution. After a few minutes, he raised his head and said, "John, Maggie . . . how would you fancy a trip to Scotland, followed by an even longer one to America?"

"What?" John said.

"Listen, what I'm going to tell you now you can't tell a soul."

John and Maggie nodded.

"I have a place. In America. It's a huge ranch in California. Right on the coast. I have a family, too. They came to England right before the war started and then got stuck over here. I got myself over here because I didn't want them here without me for all these years. When this bloody war ends—if this bloody war ever ends—we're all going back. I left the ranch in the hands of my foreman. He's a capable man and I think he's taking good care of it, at least I hope he is, but I'm always looking for good help. What if you were to go to Scotland, to someplace nice and quiet in the country, and stay there for a bit, and then make the trip to California when all this nonsense is over?"

It was John's turn to look gobsmacked. "But how, Sid? We have no money," he said

"I do. I'll pay for it. All of it."

"We couldn't do that," Maggie said, shaking her head. "Couldn't ask that of you."

"Yes, you could. Because of you, my wife's not a widow tonight. My children still have a father. I'm in debt to you the rest of my life for that. Let me start paying you back."

John and Maggie looked at each other. Sid could see that he almost had them.

"Think of it . . . you'd be out of London, away from Madden. Safe. Your kids would grow up in the most beautiful place you can imagine. With green grass and blue skies and the whole Pacific Ocean right there. I'd get your sons ranching instead of breaking heads and thieving. Your daughter will have clean air. Sunshine. Come on, Maggs . . . John . . . what do you say?"

Maggie nodded at John, and then John said, "Can you really do all that? Get us, all of us, all the way to California?"

"I can."

"All right, then. Yes. We'll go. But how? When? And what do we do about Flynn? And Madden?"

"I don't know. Not just yet. But I'll figure it out. We've got to stop Flynn before your next North Sea run, get you away from Madden, and make sure no one twigs any of it until it's too late."

"That's one tall order, Sid," John said.

"Aye, it is, but if anyone can figure out how to get you lot out of London, it's me. I'm a master at disappearing. I've died in the Thames three times already. What's going to take a bit more maneuvering is nabbing Flynn. But we'll worry about that a little later," he said, standing up and scooping the money John had given him off the table. "Right now, my biggest problem isn't Germans or spies or Billy Madden. It's how the hell I'm going to get all the way from Margate to Oxford on two pounds and six shillings."

CHAPTER EIGHTY-TWO

WILLA, SITTING ATOP her camel, leaned over to one side and vomited into the sand. She did not stop the animal while she was sick, but kept him going. The punishing sun beat down upon her, making the desert air shimmer, making her feel a thousand times worse than she already did.

She didn't want to even acknowledge what she was feeling—the nausea, the cramps in her gut and in her legs. They were all signs of cholera. If she acknowledged them, she would dwell on them and worry about them. And she could not afford to do that.

Willa had stopped at an abandoned well yesterday. It was old and disused, and had been left for a reason. The water—what there was—had a dark look to it and a musty smell. She knew better than to drink it, but she'd had no choice. She had already emptied the one skin of water the camel trader had given her. Attayeh had become stubborn and unbiddable, a sure sign that he needed water, too. They'd both drunk their fill, rested for a few hours, then moved on. Twenty-four hours later, Attayeh seemed no worse for the well water, but she was.

She had consulted Max's map a few hours ago. According to it, she would soon come to a small village. She still had Max's money on her, and the remaining two pistols she'd stolen. She hoped to be able to barter something for water and medicine there—if the people there were friendly, if the village wasn't a dwelling place for raiders, or an outpost for Turkish soldiers. If she could rest there for half a day or so, patch herself up a bit, and make sure Attayeh got plenty of water, then she could make Lawrence's camp in a day if it was where Max thought it was, or two days if it was where the camel trader said it was. But those were a lot of ifs, and she knew it.

She leaned over Attayeh's side again, retching violently, her eyes tearing with the force of the spasms. When it was over, she spat into the sand, then wiped her mouth on her sleeve.

Turkish soldiers, Bedouin raiders, the killing sun, cholera, the threat of dehydration if she didn't stop throwing up . . .

Willa wondered, ruefully, which one would get her first.

CHAPTER EIGHTY-THREE

"SEAMIE, YOU CAN'T do it. It's madness. You'll never make it. Damascus is at least five days from here. That's five days to get there, and what? Another eight or nine days to get from Damascus back to Haifa? And that's not including the time it takes to track down news of Willa in the city, while somehow managing to not be recognized. You told me you need to be back in Haifa in eight days. What you're proposing simply cannot be done," Lawrence said.

"Are you certain it's five days to Damascus?" Seamie said. "Has it ever been done faster?"

"Perhaps," Lawrence said, "but you still have to turn around and head south again once you've reached Damascus. Unless, that is, you fancy a court-martial. Even if you got there, and found Willa, what do you plan to do? Do you think the Turkish Army will just allow you to waltz off with her?"

Seamie had no answer for him.

"We start our march on the city in a matter of weeks. If she's in Damascus, I will find her. Let me do it. Let me find her. You must go back to Haifa. It's the only possible course," Lawrence said.

Seamie nodded, defeated. There was nothing else he could do.

He had ridden into Lawrence's camp a day ago, with Khalaf, Aziz, and their men—Lawrence's *new* camp. Spooked by rumors of Turkish patrols, Lawrence had broken his last camp earlier than he'd intended and moved farther east, to a new position. When Seamie and his comrades had found the new camp—thanks to word from a passing cloth merchant—they'd nearly been shot for their troubles. A sentry had spied them and ridden out with fifty men, all of whom had rifles. They were surrounded and led back to camp. Lawrence recognized both Seamie and Khalaf immediately and embraced them warmly. Their animals were seen to, and they were all invited into Lawrence's tent to eat and drink. There, they met Auda, and then explained why they had come. Lawrence had been elated to hear that Willa had survived the plane crash, but furious at Aziz for selling her to the Turks.

"You should have brought her to me!" he thundered at him.

Aziz had merely shrugged. "You should have paid me better for the last hostage," he said.

Seamie had to admit now that his attempt to find Willa had failed. He would return to Haifa tomorrow with no idea where she was, or if she was even still alive. He knew that what Lawrence had said made sense, but it was so hard to turn back to Haifa. He couldn't believe he had ridden all this way, and against all odds found Lawrence's camp, only to have to give up now. And yet if he did not, if he pushed on and got back to Haifa late, he would be accused of desertion.

"I will go to Damascus with Lawrence," Khalaf told him now. "I will find Willa Alden. If she is not there, I will search elsewhere. I will not give up until I have her, and when I do, I will send word to you."

Seamie nodded. He had to accept Lawrence's offer, and Khalaf's. He could do nothing else. As he thanked the two men, they all heard shouts from outside the tent. A minute later, a young man, a Howeitat, was inside the tent, excitedly telling Lawrence, and everyone else, that an airplane was approaching from the west.

"One?" Lawrence asked tersely.

"Just one," the young man said.

"Ours or theirs?"

"Ours, *Sidi*."

Lawrence rose. Outside the tent, he motioned for the young man's field glasses and raised them to his eyes. Seamie was following the plane with his own field glasses. It was circling low now. As they all watched, the pilot brought it down on the flattest, hardest part of the camp's terrain, near the camel pen. Bellowing, spitting camels welcomed both the pilot and his single passenger as they climbed out of their seats.

"Is that . . . ," Lawrence began, his glasses still trained on the two men.

"Albie Alden," Seamie said quietly, his heart filling with dread. Seamie knew that Albie believed that Willa was dead. Is that why he was here? To tell them to call off the search? To let them know he'd found her body?

It's probably nothing to do with Willa. It's something to do with the march on Damascus, Seamie told himself, willing it to be so.

Albie and the pilot, who'd immediately been surrounded by gun-toting men, were quickly marched to Lawrence's tent. Lawrence greeted the two men as they approached him, but Albie, dusty from the plane ride and breathless from the march, cut him off.

"She made it out of Damascus alive," he said. "And she's trying to get to your camp, Tom. You've got to find her. Immediately. She's got maps on her showing the size and location of Turkish troops stationed between here and Damascus. They've set a trap for you. You've got to go after her. Now. The Turks are hot on her trail. They've put a price on her head. Anyone who finds her is under orders to recover the maps and bring her back to Damascus."

"How do you know this?" Lawrence asked.

"A camel trader in Damascus swears he sold her a camel and supplies the night she escaped from the city. She was on the run, dressed as a man. She told him she was in the service of the great sheik Lawrence, and he told her where your camp was. After she'd got out of the city, he told the story to his brother, a spice merchant who works the backcountry between Damascus and Haifa. The merchant, who visits a whorehouse in Haifa, told the madam who runs it, and the madam told me. For a fee, of course. But I trust her information. My colleagues tell me she's never been wrong."

"How long ago did she leave Damascus?" Seamie asked

"I'm not sure. Four days, maybe," Albie said.

"Then she should be close by now," Tom said. "She's an excellent navigator. She wouldn't have got herself lost."

"That's the problem," Albie said. "The trader who sold her the camel told her where to find your camp, Tom, but since then, you've moved camp."

"Bloody hell. She's trying to ride to the old camp," Seamie said. "And there's nothing there." He turned to the pilot. "Can you fly out to the old campsite?" he asked.

"It's about a seventy miles west of here," Lawrence added. "Have you got enough petrol?"

"Petrol's not the problem," the pilot said. "I know that area. It's all dunes. I can't land. If I got down, I'd never get back up again."

"Fly a recon, then," Seamie said. "I'll go with you. If we can spot her, we can turn around, get back here, and get a party of armed riders out to her straightaway."

"Let's go," the pilot said, starting back toward his plane. Seamie was hot on his heels, but Albie called to him, stopping him.

"What is it?" Seamie said.

"There's more to the story. According to the camel trader, Willa killed a high-ranking German officer—one Max von Brandt."

"*What?* The same Max we knew in London? The bloke who came to my wedding?"

"Yes. I think he's the spymaster, Seamie. The one I've been hunting. I think he worked for the German government while he was in London, that he established a link with an informant in the Admiralty while he was there, and that that link is still active. Still feeding information to the Germans on the whereabouts of our ships."

Seamie couldn't believe what he was hearing. "Do you have proof of this?"

"Not yet. Just a strong hunch. Von Brandt was in London as the information was beginning to flow to Berlin. Now he's here. Or rather, he was. It's too much of a coincidence. He was very valuable to the Germans, and they can't be happy about what happened to him." Albie paused for a few seconds. He swallowed hard, then said, "The camel trader said that when the Turks get her back to Damascus, they're going to shoot her. Find her, Seamie. Please. Before they do."

CHAPTER EIGHTY-FOUR

"HERE THEY COME," Willa said, stiffening in her saddle.

"Remember please that you are mute," Hussein said.

"I'll remember. And you remember that if you pull this off . . . if they let us through . . . that the pistol is yours," Willa said.

The boy Hussein grinned. His eyes sparkled. He was only fifteen or so. This was an adventure to him, a game. If he played it well, he would win a prize. For Willa, it was life or death.

Hussein spurred his camel on. Willa followed close behind on Attayeh, who had been fed and watered and was tractable once more. Which was a good thing, for Willa had to keep him closely reined in to make sure he didn't step on or kick one of the two hundred goats walking ahead of them. Attayeh, it turned out, didn't care much for goats.

Willa had arrived in Hussein's village early that morning. It was situated near a small oasis and had provided plenty of water for herself and her camel. Luckily it had not been home to raiders, or a Turkish outpost, and she was able to trade Max's money for food and water for Attayeh and a bottle of some horrible bitter liquid that was supposed to help with stomach ailments. She still could keep nothing inside her. The illness, whatever it was, was taking a toll on her.

The village was inhabited by goatherds mainly, many of whom pastured their animals at a nearby spring. Willa planned to stay there for a day, resting and recovering her strength. She and Attayeh had napped a bit under the shade of some date trees in the center of the village. Afterward, she'd asked a village elder if he knew where the sheik Lawrence camped. The man had shaken his head no, smiling regretfully.

"The other visitors wish to know the same thing," he told her.

The hairs on Willa's neck prickled. "What other visitors?" she asked, warily.

"The soldiers who come through. Most every day now. The Turks."

Willa had jumped to her feet. "Which way do they ride?" she asked the man.

"All ways," the man told her, making a back-and-forth motion with his hand. "They are looking for Lawrence. They stop here for water."

Willa panicked. An entire Turkish patrol could be here any minute. And from any direction. She quickly gathered her things, refilled her skin with water, and saddled Attayeh. She was looking all about as she did, nervously scanning the horizon for rising dust. As she rode out of the village, she saw two boys saddling up their camels—one about her height, one smaller. A herd of goats was milling about them.

Looking at them, she got an idea. She rode up to them and quickly told them that she needed to get past the Turkish patrol.

"Trade clothes with me," she said to the taller boy, "and stay here in your house while I pretend to be you and ride out with your brother. If I get past the patrol, there will a reward for you both. If I do not, I will say I kidnapped your younger brother while you were still in your house and forced him to ride out with me."

"The soldiers will know you are not one of us the minute you speak," the boy said.

"Then your brother must tell them I cannot speak. He will tell them I am deaf, too. And not right in my mind."

"You must not show your eyes. They are green, not brown like ours."

"I will look at the ground."

The older boy snorted. "You are a fool. It will never work. You must go with me instead," he said matter-of-factly. "You must wear a veil. I will say you are my sister and a mute and that I am bringing you to marry a man in the village south of the spring and that fifty of the goats are your dowry."

Willa blinked at him. "That's a brilliant plan," she said. "Simply brilliant!"

"Yes, it is. But I have not yet said I will do it. What is the reward?" he asked.

"One of these," Willa said, showing him one of the jeweled pistols she had stolen. His eyes widened. Willa knew the pistol was worth more money than he would make in a lifetime.

The boys talked among themselves, then the older one, Hussein, sent his younger brother home for women's robes. When the boy came back, Willa was pleased to see that the robes included a full head covering, with only a small cloth mesh for her eyes. Hussein was a genius. If she ever found Lawrence, she would tell him about the young man. He would be an asset to anyone's army. Willa quickly put the robes on. She hated the head covering, hated how it impeded her vision and her mobility, but she was glad of it also. Under it, she was a village woman, and as such, invisible to all but her family.

She and Hussein set off. They had ridden for half an hour before they saw a patrol on the horizon.

"Stay behind me," Hussein said now. "Bow your head. Like a village girl would."

Willa did as she was told. The Turkish soldiers stopped them and spoke rudely to Hussein.

"You there!" their captain shouted. "Where do you come from and where are you going?"

He told them, adding that he was taking his sister to her new husband's village.

"What is your name, girl?" the captain shouted at Willa.

"She cannot answer you, she is mute," Hussein said. "That is why I have so many goats. Because she is mute, my father must give fifty goats instead of twenty-five to marry her off."

"Is that so? And you are paying the husband extra? For a wife who cannot speak? That is a rare and wonderful thing. I wish my wife could not speak," the captain said, laughing. "My boy, the man should pay *you* extra!"

The captain circled around Hussein and Willa, fording his way through the bleating goats, never taking his eyes off Willa. She could see him through the mesh of her head covering. Her heart was pounding. Why did he not let them pass? Hussein's story was perfectly credible.

A split second later, Willa found out. The captain raised his riding crop and brought it down hard on her leg. Willa, expecting such a rotten trick, was ready for him. She doubled over in her saddle, noiselessly cowering, and grabbed her leg, rocking back and forth as if it hurt her terribly, when actually it didn't hurt a bit, as the captain had lashed her false leg.

Satisfied, the captain said, "Forgive me, my boy. I had to make sure of your story. There is another woman at large in the desert, and she is not mute. She is an Englishwoman, one of Lawrence's, and very dangerous. If you should see such a woman, please report her to me, or to any member of the Turkish Army, immediately."

"I will, sir," Hussein said. He told Willa to stop sniveling and follow him, then whipped his camel into a trot. Willa did the same with Attayeh. Half an hour later, when they were well out of sight of the patrol, she shouted at Hussein to stop. She tore her robes off and tossed them to him. Then she dug in her saddlebag for the pistol she'd promised him and tossed that to him, too.

"Thank you, Hussein. I owe you my life, and many others' besides," she said, wrapping a scarf around her head.

Hussein smiled, told her to go with God, then spurred his camel west. Willa turned Attayeh south. She would reach Salkhad soon, where Max thought Lawrence was. It was about a day's ride. If he was not there, she would press on, riding farther south. She was weary and ill and in pain; the horizon swam sickeningly before her eyes, but she did not stop, she did not even falter.

"One more day, Attayeh, old boy," she said aloud, trying to ignore the pain in her gut. "All we have to do is keep going for one more day."

CHAPTER EIGHTY-FIVE

"WHERE IS IT?" Willa mumbled, through cracked, blistered lips. "Where the hell is it?"

She turned in her saddle, looking all around, but could see no camp.

"Where is it?" she shouted hoarsely. Her voice, floating over the dunes that surrounded her, echoed back at her mockingly.

She had looked for Lawrence's camp at Salkhad, questioned some local boys, but had heard nothing of Lawrence, and had found nothing of him. Then she'd continued south, to where the camel trader had said he was—north of Azraq and east of Minifer. And again, she'd found nothing. Perhaps both Max and the trader were wrong. Or perhaps she'd simply missed the encampment, or missed signs like tracks or camel scat, that could have led her to it. It was hard to hold her head up now, to even see straight. It was hard to think. It hurt to even try. She had so little strength left.

Attayeh stumbled suddenly, and Willa lurched dangerously in her saddle. "Keep your seat, old girl," she told herself, her voice little more than a croak now. Her throat was as dry as dust. She'd drunk the last of her water yesterday. She couldn't remember exactly when. She had not stopped for the last forty-eight hours, but had driven Attayeh mercilessly. She had no choice. She was dying, she knew she was, and she had to get to Lawrence before the sickness in her gut finished her off.

It was certainly cholera. People sometimes recovered from it. If they had the proper medicines, and rest. She had neither. She desperately wanted to climb down. To stop. To rest. But she knew that if she did that, she would not get up again. She would die where she lay, for she would not have the strength to pull herself back up into the saddle.

Attayeh, exhausted and confused, stumbled again and wept. Willa knew that camels cried tears when they became dehydrated, and Attayeh had been ridden too hard and too long without rest, food, or water. Willa wanted to speak to the animal, to comfort him and encourage him, but she no longer had the strength to do so. She hoped she might be near a village, or a Bedouin camp, and that Attayeh, sensing the nearness of other camels, and water, might be able to get there on his own. She hoped so. She had to, for hope, fragile and fading, was all she had left.

Willa rode on for another half hour, her head lolling as Attayeh plodded along. The camel bellowed suddenly. He stopped short, then started walking again, at a brisker pace. Willa picked her head up; she squinted into the distance, hoping that by some miracle the camel had spotted an oasis, a small settlement, something. Instead, she saw dust on the horizon. She wondered for a moment if she was seeing things. She knew that people who were suffering from dehydration started to hallucinate. She squinted again. There *was* dust on the horizon, she was sure of it. She shaded her eyes and saw riders—three of them. One was in the lead, streaking ahead of the others, though they were all coming on fast.

Please, she prayed, don't let them be Turkish soldiers. Or raiders. Please. I've brought the maps this far, let these be good men. Willa knew she would never see Lawrence again, but she hoped these riders, whoever they were, would take the maps the rest of the way.

After what seemed like an eternity, the lead rider drew up to her. Willa saw that he was wearing plain white robes, dirtied by dust and sweat. He unwound his head scarf, and Willa knew then that her death was very close.

He was a real man, she was quite sure of that, because he was shouting at her, but his face . . . his face was a hallucination, a vision. For one last time, her fevered mind was showing her the one she most wanted to see—Seamie Finnegan.

"Willa, my God," he said. "It's all right. You'll be all right now,

Willa. We're here. We'll get you back to camp." There was fear in his voice as he spoke, and in his eyes.

His voice . . . it even sounds like Seamie's, she thought. And he knows my name. He must be one of Lawrence's. Oh, thank God!

Willa tried to speak to him, she tried to answer him, but she couldn't. Her throat worked, but no sound came out. Her voice was gone. She motioned for water. The man gave her some. She drank, then gasped as her gut was gripped hard by a fresh wave of cramps.

When the pain subsided, when she could breathe again, Willa rasped out her final words. She was swaying in her saddle now. There was nothing left inside her, no strength, no will. She was played out, but it was all right. She could let go now. This man would help her.

"Please . . . I have maps . . . documents . . . give them to Lawrence . . . tell him Jabal ad Duruz is a trap . . . tell my mother I'm sorry . . . tell Seamus Finnegan I love him . . ."

CHAPTER EIGHTY-SIX

"HE'S DEAD, I know he is," India said, dully. "That's the only explanation. He wouldn't not come home for days for the sheer hell of it. Something's happened to him. Something terrible."

It was a Sunday morning. Fiona was sitting with India and Jennie in the Brambles kitchen. She'd just cooked everyone breakfast and had sent the children outside to play. Charlotte and Rose had Wish, Elizabeth, and little James with them, as well as Fiona's younger children. Fiona and Jennie had brought their children with them expressly to keep India's children occupied, and to keep their minds off their missing father. India kept telling them that their dad had business in London, and that's why he wasn't home, but it had been a week since he'd left for London, and she couldn't go on saying that forever.

Fiona reached across the table and took India's hand. She'd been doing her best over the last few days to keep India's spirits up, and her own, but it was getting harder by the minute. India was right, of course, Sid would never simply take off on a jaunt, or a drinking binge, or some sort of mad spree. He would never have worried India that way. Fiona was frightened, though she refused to let on, that something terrible had indeed happened to him. And someone from his past was involved. She felt it in her bones.

"Joe will be here any minute now," she said. "He'll tell us what he's found out. He hired one of the best private investigators in London. The man's bound to have turned up something."

India picked her head up and looked at Fiona. "Yes, but what?" she said, her eyes filling with tears. "I'm sure he'll have found out something, but I'm not sure I'll want to hear what it is."

A few minutes later, there was a knock at the front door. Fiona ran to answer it. It was Joe, assisted in his wheelchair by Mr. Foster.

"Hello, love," Fiona said, kissing her husband. She greeted Mr. Foster. "What news?" she asked them.

Joe shook his head. "It's not good, Fee."

Fiona's heart sank. Not Sid, she thought. Please. "Come inside. Into the kitchen," she said in a hollow voice. "That's were India and Jennie are. It'll save you telling it twice."

Joe greeted both women. As Jennie poured tea for Joe and Mr. Foster, Joe asked India how she was holding up.

"Not very well, I'm afraid," she said.

The fear in her eyes was so great that it hurt Fiona to look at her. Sid was Fiona's brother, and she loved him, but he was India's whole life. They'd been through so much already. It wasn't fair that he should be taken from her now.

"What's happened to him, Joe? What did the investigator find out?" Fiona asked.

"We don't know what's happened," Joe said. "The investigator—

Kevin McDowell's his name—managed to find out that Sid was last seen going into Teddy Ko's offices in Limehouse last Sunday. Ko's an importer. Does his trade with China."

India remembered the little Buddha she'd found in Sid's pocket. "Teddy Ko . . . ," she said slowly. "I know that name. He's also an opium peddler. I once tried to get his place shut down."

"He still is an opium peddler. The biggest in London," Joe said.

"Why was Sid there?" India asked. "What on earth could he have wanted with Teddy Ko?"

"I don't know. All I know is that he was seen going into Ko's, but was not seen coming out," Joe said. He hesitated before continuing. It was the briefest of pauses, but Fiona felt it and so did India.

"What, Joe?" India said, in an anguished voice. "What are you not telling me?"

Joe took a deep breath, then said, "Billy Madden and two of his heavies were also seen going into Ko's. About five minutes after Sid went in."

India shook her head. She knew that name, too. They all did. "Why, Joe? Why did he go there?" she said, her voice breaking. She started to weep.

Jennie went to her side. She put her arms around her.

Fiona looked at Joe. "Billy Madden?" she said, tears starting in her own eyes. "What was Sid doing mixing with the likes of Billy Madden? Years ago, yes. But why now? He must've been mad, Joe. I don't understand it. I don't—"

Her voice was cut off by the sound of a door slamming. "Peter, is that you?" she sharply called to her son. "Go back outside, will you? And don't slam the door! I've told you a thousand times not to!"

"Sorry," a voice said.

It wasn't Peter.

"Bloody hell!" Joe said as Sid walked into the kitchen. "Look at your face! What happened to you?"

India's head snapped up. She leapt out of her chair, ran to Sid, and threw her arms around his neck. "I thought you were dead!" she sobbed. "I thought I'd never see you again!" She let go of his neck, grabbed fistfuls of his jacket, and shook him. "Why did you go to see Teddy Ko? And Billy Madden? Why did you do it?" she shrilled at him. "They could've killed you. It looks like they almost did!"

"India, how do you know all this?" Sid asked, looking stunned.

"We hired an investigator," Joe said.

"Mummy!" Charlotte said loudly. She was suddenly in the kitchen with Wish and the other children. "Was that Daddy who just came in?" Her excited smile fell when her father turned to her. "Daddy? What happened to you?" she asked, ashen-faced. Little Wish burst into tears. Sid's face was still a swollen mess of cuts and bruises.

"Excuse me, ma'am," Mr. Foster quietly said to Fiona. "But could you tell me where the brandy is kept?"

"In the cabinet above the sink, Mr. Foster," Fiona said, taking a semi-hysterical India by the arm and leading her to a chair.

While Sid comforted his children—telling him he'd been in a bit of an accident, that's all, and that's why he looked so terrible and hadn't come home to them right away, but now he was here, home again, and Mummy would take care of his hurts—Jennie herded James and the other children back outside into the garden. Foster poured brandy for the adults, then made some hot chocolate. He poured it into mugs, put some biscuits on a plate, and asked Charlotte, who was still in the kitchen, if she could help him carry the treats out into the garden.

"Thank you very much, Mr. Foster," Charlotte said politely. "But I do not require cocoa and biscuits. I require a proper explanation."

"It's all right, Mr. Foster," Sid said. "She's old enough to know what's going on now. She can stay." To his daughter, he said, "You were going to have to find out the truth about me and my past sometime. Might as well be now."

By the time Mr. Foster had gone outside, India had emptied her brandy glass and stopped sobbing. Fiona, Joe, and Jennie had drunk theirs, too. Sid sat down at the table and emptied his in one swallow.

"You can usually be counted on to turn up," Joe said. "Even when all the odds are against you. This time, though, you had even me worried. What the devil happened to you?"

Sid picked up the bottle and refilled everyone's glass.

"I'll tell you everything," he said. "Every last thing. But get that down yourselves first. Otherwise, you're never going to believe me."

CHAPTER EIGHTY-SEVEN

"DO YOU REMEMBER it, Willa? Mombasa? Do you remember the turquoise sea? And the pink fort? And the white houses? Do you remember the hotel where we spent our first night? They didn't have two rooms for us. We had to share a bed. I don't think I slept at all. I stayed up all night, just listening to you breathe. You didn't. Stay up, I mean. You fell asleep and snored."

Seamie was talking fast.

I sound like a madman, he thought. No, a salesman, rather.

For that's what he was doing—trying to sell Willa on the idea of staying. Here. In this world. He was trying to sell her on the idea of life. Her life. He talked to her of their childhood. Of sails with her, Albie, and her parents. Of climbs on Snowdon and Ben Nevis. Of rambles in the Lake District. He talked to her of Kilimanjaro and their time together in Africa. He reminded her of the animals moving across the veldt, the sunrises, the impossibly vast sky. He told her how much he loved her photographs of Everest. And how he dreamed, still, of going there with her one day. He tried to bring back her best memories, tried to create images for her fevered mind of the things she loved most in this world. He tried to make her hold on, to stay with him.

She was sick. God, she was so horribly sick. He'd given her aconite and opium. He'd tried quinine. Nothing worked. Nothing broke her fever, nothing stopped the spasms that racked her body. No food stayed in her. No water, either. It was as if her body, battered and broken from the years of punishment she'd meted out to it, was trying to expel the fierce and terrible spark that animated her—her will, her drive, her very soul.

He told her of the search for the South Pole, and how the howling of the Antarctic wind and the ceaseless groaning of the sea ice could drive a man mad. He told her about existing in a world devoid of all color, a world of white, and of the infinite ocean of stars at night.

He ran out of adventures to talk about, and so he told her about the rest of his life. About James, the son he loved beyond all reason. He told her about the small cottage in Binsey, where the boy was born. He told her about the mistakes he'd made, the things he regretted, and the things he refused to regret. He told her about Haifa and the ship that waited for him there, and that he had to go, but didn't want to leave her.

And then he stopped talking suddenly and rested his head in his hands. For two whole days he'd nursed her, watching over her, bathing her blazing skin, holding her as she shivered and retched and arched against the pain inside her. He had barely slept since he'd first arrived at Lawrence's camp, and was so exhausted now, he was nearly delirious himself. He had searched for her by plane but hadn't been able to spot her from the air, so he had ridden out from Lawrence's camp and during his second day of riding, had found her.

"Please don't die, Willa. Don't go," he said. "Don't leave me here in this world without you. Just knowing you're somewhere on this planet, doing something brave and amazing, makes me happy. I love you, Willa. I've never stopped loving you. I never will."

He raised his head and looked at her, at the ruined wraith of a woman lying on the ground in a tent in the middle of this godforsaken desert, in the middle of this godforsaken war. Yes, he loved her, and she loved him, and their love had brought them only grief. Was it love at all? he wondered now. Or was it merely madness?

"I love you, too, Seamie," Willa said, her eyes suddenly open.

"Willa!" Seamie said, reaching for her hand and squeezing it. "You're awake!

She swallowed, grimacing, then motioned for water. Seamie got her some, and sat her up to drink it. When she finished, he gently eased her back down on her pillow. Sweat had broken out across her brow, and her breathing was shallow and labored. He could see the effort it had cost her merely to drink.

"Lawrence?" she said, her voice raspy.

"On his way to Damascus with Auda and an army. They're heading well west of Jabad al Duruz, and the traps set for them there. Because of you."

Willa smiled. She gazed at him for a while, gathering her strength, then said, "You have to go now."

"How, Willa? I can't leave you here . . . you'll die . . . I can't . . ."

"I'm finished, Seamie," she said. "I'm so tired . . . so ill . . . I'm played out."

"No, Willa, don't say that," Seamie said, his voice breaking.

"I . . . I heard you . . . talking," she said. "About us. James. Your ship. Go, or you'll be court-martialed and shot." She swallowed again. Her eyes were filled with pain. "Is that what you want for your son?" she finished softly.

"No, but—"

She cut him off. "We have to let go, Seamie. Once and for all. We've hurt each other long enough. Hurt too many others." There were tears in her eyes now. "Go to Haifa," she said. "Stay alive. Please. Survive this damn war and go home again. Jennie . . . and James . . . they need you—"

Willa abruptly stopped talking. She leaned over and vomited into the brass urn at the side of her bed. Seamie held her head, then wiped her face. As he settled her down on her pillow once more, he felt her body go limp in his hands.

"No!" he shouted, terrified that he'd lost her. "Willa, no!"

He quickly checked her breathing and her pulse. She was still alive, but unconscious again. Her skin was horribly hot to the touch. Grabbing a rag, he dipped it into a bowl of water, and sponged her face and body.

"Don't go, Willa," he whispered. "Please don't go."

As he sat in the tent, in the stench and heat of Willa's sickness, trying desperately to cool her, he suddenly heard bells in the desert and the sound of camels bawling. He wondered who was coming. The camp was nearly deserted. Lawrence, Auda, and Khalaf, together with four thousand troops, had left this morning. They were going to ride east, not north, turn west again to meet Faisal at Sheik Saad and then march to Damascus, avoiding certain slaughter at Jabal ad Duruz. Because of Willa. If it hadn't been for her, for her courage, her luck, her refusal to quit, they would have ridden into a trap, one they could not possibly have fought their way out of.

Only a few men remained behind to guard Seamie and Willa. Seamie stood up now, stepped outside of the tent, and shaded his eyes against the sun. What now? he wondered, too spent to be afraid. What the hell is happening now?

He quickly saw that it was not the Turks. That's something, he thought. It was a group of Bedouin, some fifty strong. Men were in the lead, followed by a litter. More men brought up the rear. When they got close to him, the lead man, tall and angry-looking, dismounted from his camel, walked up to Seamie, and bowed.

"I bring Fatima, first wife of Khalaf al Mor, and her women. She has heard that the woman Willa Alden is here and in need of help. You will take her to see Willa Alden. You will do this now."

Fatima and her women, all heavily veiled, came forth. When she saw Seamie, Fatima removed the veil from her eyes.

"You found her, Seamus Finnegan," she said.

Seamie bowed. "I did. With your help."

"Not with my help. With Allah's help," she said. "Take me to her."

"She is very sick, Fatima," he said brokenly. "I've tried everything. For two days, I've tried everything I can think of."

"I have remedies. Desert herbs. They may help," Fatima said. "And I have her necklace. The one I gave her to keep evil spirits away. She will need it now."

Seamie led Fatima to Willa's tent. He went inside with her. Fatima tried to hide her shock at the sight of Willa's emaciated body, but failed.

"She's very bad, isn't she?" Seamie said.

"You will go to another tent now and sleep or I will be nursing two sick people, not one," she said sternly, fastening the necklace around Willa's neck.

"I can't. I have to leave. I have to get to Haifa."

"You will sleep first. If only for a few hours, or you will never make it to Haifa," Fatima said.

Seamie was too tired to argue. "Thank you for coming," he said. "Please save her."

"I will do all that I can for her, but it is in Allah's hands, Seamus Finnegan, not mine."

Seamie nodded. "Talk to Him, Fatima. He listens to you. Tell Him if He wants a life, He can have mine. A life for a life. Mine, not hers. Tell Him, Fatima. Tell Him to please let Willa Alden live."

CHAPTER EIGHTY-EIGHT

". . . AND JENNIE'S GATHERING the statistics on the number of single London women under thirty who own property, which we'll need for the letter-writing campaign to the Commons," Katie Finnegan was saying.

But Jennie didn't hear her. She was sitting in Fiona and Joe's drawing room, attending her Tuesday-night suffrage meeting, but she was a million miles away. Katie was talking about the group's latest campaign—a push to lower the voting age for women—but Jennie was back at the Brambles, two nights ago, listening to Sid's dreadful story. She was feeling her blood run cold as he told them why he had gone to Teddy Ko's, what had happened to him, and what he had learned—about Maud, and about Max von Brandt. She was remembering how she had sat there, barely moving, barely breathing, as Sid told them that Max was in all likelihood a German spy, and a murderer, too—Maud's murderer. She remembered India's terrible shock at the news—and her grief. And she remembered Joe's fury.

"We have to tell the PM about this. Immediately," he'd said. "Von Brandt left London, but it sounds like his man Flynn's still moving information. He has to be caught. And stopped. Now. Before any more British lives are lost."

"Hold on, Joe," Sid had said. "John Harris—the man who saved my life—is all mixed up in this. He never wanted to be, but he had no choice. Madden threatened him. I promised I would help him, that I would get him and his family out of London. We can't make a move on Flynn until we figure out a way to do it that won't land John in prison."

"But we can't allow Flynn to remain at large," Joe said. "He could do a runner at any second."

"We have a few days," Sid said. "Today's Sunday. John told me that the next rendezvous would be this Friday. That's when we have to move. We have to catch Flynn with the goods on him or we've got nothing—just an innocent man, wrongfully accused."

Nobody had noticed Jennie as they talked. Nobody noticed how pale she'd suddenly gone, or that her whole body had begun to tremble. And ever since then, she'd been veering wildly between belief and denial, between terror and despair, and it was tearing her in two.

One minute she would tell herself that Sid had made a mistake—Max was on the side of peace, just as he'd told her. The next minute, she would believe that he was all the things Sid said he was. After all, what reason did John Harris have to lie? No honorable man engaged in a good endeavor would have anything to do with the likes of Billy Madden. No honorable man would buy morphine from a drug lord, and no honorable man's paramour would turn up dead from an overdose only days after he'd bought it. Max von Brandt was a German spy. He'd been hurting the Allies, not aiding them. He'd been sending thousands upon thousands of British fighting men to their deaths. And she, Jennie herself, had helped him. She had blood on her hands as surely as he did.

The truth of this was so unbearable that Jennie could not accept it. So she didn't. She told herself, again, that Sid was wrong. And John Harris, too. And that it would all come out when they found the man they were searching for—Flynn. He would tell them who Max really was and what he was doing. He would set them all straight.

"Do you think you could have those figures ready by early next month, Auntie Jennie? Auntie Jennie?"

It was Katie.

"Oh! I'm so sorry, Katie. I don't know where my head is tonight," Jennie said.

"You look a little peaky. Are you all right?"

Jennie, smiling, waved her concern away. "I'm fine. Just a little tired."

Katie asked her question again, and Jennie said she would indeed have the figures ready for her next month. Katie thanked her, smiling sympathetically. Jennie knew that Katie would attribute her fatigue to the scare the whole family had been through with Sid, but in reality it was the dreadful doubts she'd been entertaining about Max that made her feel ill. She had a headache all the time now, and often felt attacks of nausea, or shivered with a sudden chill.

With difficulty, she forced herself to listen and participate in the rest of the meeting, but she was glad when it was over and she could return to Wapping—to James and her father. As usual, she walked to the bus stop with Gladys Bigelow. They rode the same bus east, though Jennie got off it earlier than Gladys did. When the bus had stopped for them, and they'd climbed aboard and seated themselves, Gladys wordlessly handed Jennie an envelope, as she had been doing for more than three years now.

Jennie was just about to put the envelope in her carpetbag, when instead she took hold of Gladys's hand.

"What is it?" Gladys asked her, in that flat, dead voice of hers. "What's wrong?"

"Gladys, I have to ask you something," Jennie said.

Gladys's eyes grew wide. She shook her head. "No, you don't," she said.

"I do. I have to know about Max."

Gladys yanked her hand free of Jennie's grip.

"I have to know, Gladys," Jennie said. "I have to know that he's who he says he is. He told me he was a double agent. That he's helping sabotage Germany's war efforts. I have to know what's in this envelope."

Gladys shook her head. She started laughing, but her laughter quickly turned to tears. She turned away from Jennie and would not speak. Watching her, Jennie realized with a sickening certainty that Sid was right—Max was a German spy.

"Gladys," she said. "We have to tell someone. We have to stop him."

Gladys turned around. She grabbed Jennie's arm and squeezed it hard. "You shut your mouth," she hissed. "You don't tell anybody anything! Do you hear me? You don't know him. You don't know what he's capable of. But trust me, you don't what to find out."

"Gladys, you're hurting me! Let go!" Jennie said.

But Gladys didn't. She tightened her grip. "You keep delivering that envelope. Just like you're supposed to. The war will end one day, and then we can put it all behind us and never talk about it, never even think about it, again."

And then she stood up, took a seat away from Jennie, and stared out of the window into the darkness. She was still sitting like that when Jennie reached her stop.

As Jennie walked home from the bus stop, she felt anguished. She didn't want to believe the worst of Max, but it was getting harder and harder not to. If he was indeed working for Germany, she had to tell someone. It was the right thing to do. The only thing to do.

But then something that Gladys had said came back to her: *You don't know what he's capable of. But trust me, you don't want to find out.*

Jennie thought back to the time that Max had come to visit her in the rectory. She remembered how he'd told her of his mission and had asked her to help him. He'd been courtly and kind, as he always was, but when she wavered, when she tried to say no to him, his eyes had hardened and he'd threatened to tell Seamie about Binsey.

The memory was like a knife to her heart now. She'd just sent Josie Meadows a letter, with a picture of James. In it, she'd told her old friend what a beautiful child James was, that he was growing strong and healthy, and that he was loved. So dearly.

She'd addressed it to Josephine Lavallier—Josie's new stage name. She felt frightened now to think that Max knew about Josie, about their letters, about James. She could not bear for Seamie to know the truth about what she'd done, could not bear for James to one day know that she and Seamie were not his real parents.

Jennie arrived at her father's house. A light was on in the hallway, but the rest of the house was dark. Her father and her son were already asleep. She did not take off her coat and jacket, but hurried directly into the kitchen.

There, she put the kettle on, but not for tea. She was going to steam the envelope open.

It was time to find out once and for all just who Max von Brandt really was.

CHAPTER EIGHTY-NINE

JENNIE SAT AT the kitchen table, in the light of a small, single lamp, and stared at the large manila envelope in front of her. The house was quiet except for the ticking of the clock atop the mantel. She was supposed to take the envelope to the church basement and put it in its usual hiding place. Instead, she had steamed it open. She had not yet pulled its contents out and read them, though. She was too afraid.

There would be no going back once she read whatever was inside the envelope. She would find out who Max von Brandt really was. And she would find out what she really was. She would learn if she'd helped him save innocent German lives, or helped him destroy British ones.

"You should have done this years ago," she whispered to herself. But it had been easier not to. Easier not to know the truth, to believe she was doing good. Easier to accept Max's help with Willa, than to earn his enmity and have him reveal the truth of James's parentage.

As Jennie reached for the envelope, a sudden wave of nausea gripped her. She ran to the sink and was sick. When the heaving had stopped, she rinsed her mouth out, wiped her face, and sat down again. She had felt horribly unwell ever since Sid arrived at the Brambles with his news. Her headaches and sour stomach had got worse over the last few days, and she felt feverish now, too. She was certain it was all a reaction to the shock of Sid's allegations against Max.

"It has to stop," she said. "Now."

She pulled out the envelope's contents, praying hard that all would be as Max had said. What she saw told her instantly that it would not.

The envelope contained carbons of letters from Sir George Burgess to Winston Churchill, First Sea Lord, and to various other high-ranking naval officers, cabinet ministers, and the prime minister himself. In them was information on the movement of British ships, the size of their crews, the number and sizes of their guns, the objects of their missions.

Jennie saw the names of ships: *Bellerophon*, *Monarch*, *Conqueror*, *Colossus*, and *Exeter*. Some were in the Atlantic Ocean. Some in the Mediterranean. There was information on Britain's oil fields in the Mideast, their production capabilities, and their security.

There were no identity papers of any nature. There were no names of safe houses in Germany and France. No contact information for the people in Britain who were supposed to be providing homes and employment for the dissenters smuggled out of Germany.

It was all a lie.

Jennie stuffed the carbons back into the envelope then put the envelope back into her carpetbag. She couldn't bear to look at it. She covered her face with her hands and moaned with the horror that confronted her. What had she done? How much information had she helped feed to Berlin? How many men had she helped Max kill?

She was filled with guilt, sick with remorse. She knew she should immediately take the envelope to her brother-in-law, Joe. He would know what to do with it. But she was also frightened. If she took the envelope to Joe, the authorities to whom he showed it would want to know how he'd got it. He would have no choice but to tell them. Would they arrest her? What about her father? It was his church that she'd used to move the documents. Would they arrest him, too? If they did, what would become of James?

Her stomach squeezed again. She tried to quell the nausea roiling inside her. As she did, a fresh, and terrible, realization hit her—those ships, the ones mentioned in Burgess's letters—some of them were in the Atlantic, others in the Mediterranean.

The Mediterranean.

"That's where Seamie is," she said aloud.

Jennie didn't know the name of his new ship. Seamie was not allowed to mention it in his letters to her, but she knew he would soon be on it, as soon as the injuries he'd received when the *Hawk* was sunk had healed. Maybe he was already on it, patrolling off the coast of Arabia again. And, thanks to Max's efforts over the last few years—and her own—maybe German submarines were waiting for him.

"Oh, God," she cried. "Oh, Seamie, no."

She saw, with a sudden, wrenching clarity, what she had done: She had helped Max von Brandt because she hadn't wanted him to tell Seamie the truth about her, and about James, but by trying so desperately to hold on to the man she loved, she had likely doomed him.

She bent down to pick up her carpetbag; she knew what she had to do. She would take the envelope to Joe. Now. Immediately. Word had to be got to Burgess and the Admiralty that the Germans knew everything, and that British ships were in greater danger than anyone could imagine.

As Jennie put her coat back on, the nausea overwhelmed her and she was sick again, violently so. When she finished, she stood over the sink for a few minutes, shaking and gasping. As soon as she caught her breath, she opened her eyes and that's when she saw it—blood in the sink.

Jennie touched her fingers to her lips, but they came away clean. She realized that the blood was coming from her nose. She reached into her pocket to get a handkerchief to stanch it, but the blood was coming faster now. As she pressed the cloth to her face, the room swam suddenly, then came back into focus.

"Mummy?" a little voice said.

Jennie turned around.

"I heard a noise," James said. "Mummy, your nose is bleeding."

"James," Jennie said. Her son looked blurry and far away.

"What is it, Mummy? What's wrong?"

"James," Jennie said, right before her legs gave way. "Run and get Granddad. . . ."

CHAPTER NINETY

"WHERE AM I?" Jennie Finnegan said, looking around herself. She was lying in a bed that was not her own, in some sort of nightgown that was not her own, in a room she didn't recognize, next to people she had never seen before.

Frightened, she sat up. She swung her feet over the side of the bed and tried to get up but was gripped by a fit of coughing so severe, it left her weak and breathless.

"Mrs. Finnegan!" a voice said. "Please lie still! You mustn't bring the coughing on."

Jennie looked up and saw a young woman—a nurse—hovering over her. She wore a white cotton mask over her face.

"Where am I? What's happened?" Jennie asked, panic-stricken.

"You're in hospital, Mrs. Finnegan. On the quarantine ward. You're very ill, ma'am. It's the flu. The Spanish flu," the nurse said, easing Jennie back into bed.

"The flu? My God," Jennie said, slumping back against her pillow.

She remembered now. She remembered standing in her father's kitchen, devastated by what she had learned about Max von Brandt. She remembered being sick, and dizzy, and the blood . . . she remembered the blood.

"What day is it? How did I get here?" she asked. And then a terrifying new thought occurred to her. "Where's my son? Where's James?"

"Please calm down, ma'am. Everything is all right," the nurse said. "It's Wednesday. Your father brought you here last night. He wanted to stay with you, but of course we couldn't allow it. He told me that if you woke, I was to tell you he had a neighbor woman, a Mrs. Barnes, come to stay with James last night. And that he would be taking the boy to your sister-in-law's—a Mrs. Bristow's—later today."

Jennie felt so relieved. James was in good hands; he would be well cared for.

"I'm Sister Connors, by the way," the nurse said. "I'm one of the nurses who'll be looking after you."

Jennie nodded. "Are my things here?" she asked her. "My carpetbag?"

"No. Your father didn't bring anything with him. Is there something you need? Something I can get for you?"

"Listen to me, please," Jennie said urgently. She had remembered something else—her determination to stop Max, to stop the flow of military secrets to Berlin. "You must get my brother-in-law here. Joseph Bristow. He's an MP. Something terrible is going on and he must know about it immediately."

"I'm afraid he won't be allowed on the quarantine ward, either," Sister Connors said gently.

"I must get word to him. Can I write him?"

"I'm afraid not. We can't pass along anything handled by the infected."

"What am I going to do, then?" Jennie said, agitatedly.

"I can't just go summoning MPs, Mrs. Finnegan. If you could just tell me what it's about," Sister Connors said kindly.

Jennie didn't want to, but it seemed she had no choice. "There is a spy ring at work in London. They're passing secrets to Berlin through a network of tunnels under the river. I know about it because I helped them," she said. "Now, can you please get Mr. Bristow? He has a telephone at his home and also at the House of Commons. Do you have a telephone on the ward? Perhaps I could get word to him that way."

"One moment, please, Mrs. Finnegan," Sister Connors said.

Jennie watched as she walked to the center of the room, where the ward sister was standing with a clipboard, writing something down. Sister Connors tried to keep her voice down, but Jennie heard every word that she said.

"The new patient—Mrs. Finnegan—she's talking about spies, Sister Matthews, and says she's helping them. I believe she's delirious."

The ward sister nodded. She came over to Jennie's bed. Her eyes were troubled. "Hello, dear. I'm Sister Matthews. Sister Connors tells me that you're rather upset. You must calm yourself," she said through her mask. "You are very ill and you need to rest."

"I know you think I'm off my head," Jennie said. "I promise you I'm not. My husband, and many others in the Mediterranean, are in great danger. I must speak with my brother-in-law."

Sister Matthews nodded. "Get Dr. Howell, please," she said to Sister Connors.

Thank God, Jennie thought. The doctor would listen to her. He would ring up Joe and tell him she needed to see him.

A few minutes later, a brisk, bearded man appeared. He looked weary and careworn. A stethoscope hung from his neck. The front of his white coat was flecked with spots of dried blood. He was holding a cup.

He introduced himself, and then before Jennie could speak, he said, "Now, now, Mrs. Finnegan. What's all this I'm hearing about spies? You mustn't worry yourself about such things. Your husband is quite safe, I'm sure. We have spies of our own, you know, working very hard to catch the baddies. That's their job. Yours is to get better. Now, drink this, please."

Jennie eyed the cup suspiciously. "What is it?" she asked.

"Medicine," the doctor replied.

Jennie shook her head. "It's a sedative, isn't it? You think I'm raving, but I'm not. You have to believe me, Dr. Howell. You have to—"

"Mrs. Finnegan," Dr. Howell said, interrupting her, "if you will not drink the medicine willingly, I shall have to resort to other means."

"No! I can't. I must speak with Joseph Bristow! Please!" Jennie said, her voice rising. Her agitation set off another round of coughing. It was so harsh and racking that blood dripped from her nose again.

Dr. Howell wiped the blood with a cloth and showed it to her. "You have a young son, do you not? And a husband," he said. "What would they say to you if they knew you were not doing all in your power to recover and return to them? What would they say to me for allowing it?"

Jennie realized that Dr. Howell did not believe her and that he would not be sending for Joe. She realized, too, what he was trying to say—that she was gravely ill and that there was a very real possibility that she might not return to her husband and son . . . ever.

With tears in her eyes, Jennie took the cup from Dr. Howell's hand and downed the bitter liquid inside it. It took only seconds to work. Almost before she knew it, her eyes were closing, and she felt herself being pulled under, into a deep and heavy sleep.

The last thing she felt was Sister Connors's gentle hands smoothing her hair back from her face. The last thing she heard was the nurse's voice saying, "Poor woman. I'm sure the barmy things she's saying are all coming from her worries about her husband, from him being in the war and all."

And Sister Matthews replying, "She should worry about herself. She has a fight ahead of her as bad as any of our boys on the front are facing. And about as much chance of winning it."

CHAPTER NINETY-ONE

"HELLO, MUM! YOU all right?" Gladys Bigelow said loudly, poking her head into their small sitting room. Her mum was a bit hard of hearing. Gladys had just put her umbrella in the hallway stand and her bag of marketing on the floor and was now unbuttoning her dripping raincoat.

Mrs. Bigelow, in her usual seat by the window, smiled tiredly and said, "Right as rain, love. How was your day?"

"Beastly. I'm glad it's over."

"And I'm glad you're home. It's a filthy night. Awfully wet for September."

"You don't have to tell me. I'm half-drowned. I bought us some nice gammon steaks for our tea. And a tin of pineapple rings to put on them. And peas. I think I'll make some mash, too. I know you're partial to gammon steaks with mash."

"Oh, Gladys. You shouldn't have to do it."

"Do what, Mum?" Gladys said, shrugging out of her raincoat.

"Work so hard all day, then come home and cook for me. It's too much for one person," Mrs. Bigelow said, fretting at the kerchief in her hands.

Gladys frowned at that. She put her raincoat on a peg near the door, sat down next to her mother, and took hold of her shaking hands. "What's the matter, Mum? Are you feeling low again today? What's happened?"

Mrs. Bigelow turned her head away.

"Come on now. Out with it. Tell me."

"Well, Mrs. Karcher came over today. She brought me some biscuits she'd made. . . ."

"That sounds very nice," Gladys said.

"Oh, it was. She's a lovely woman is Mrs. Karcher. She told me that her middle girl—Emily, her name is—is engaged to be married. Her fiancé's fighting in France, but he wrote her a letter and asked her would she marry him and said he's sorry he couldn't put a ring in the envelope, but he'll buy her one as soon as he gets home."

"Why would that make you sad, Mum?" Gladys asked. "That's a lovely story."

"It *is* a lovely story, Gladys, that's why it makes me sad. You should be telling stories like that. You should have lads asking you to marry them. But you don't. Because you can't. Because you're saddled with me."

"Oh, Mum, you silly thing. Is that what has you all teary?"

"I'm not silly, Gladys. It's not natural, a young girl like you stuck looking after her mother. You should have a lad of your own. And a place of your own. And children one day."

"I will, Mum. One day I will," Gladys said.

"Whatever happened to that one you were seeing . . . that Peter lad? A sailor, he was."

"I've told you, Mum. He was killed in the war. Early on."

"That's right, you did. What a shame, that. He sounded like such a nice lad, too. And none since? In all this time?"

"Well, they're a bit thin on the ground just now, aren't they?" Gladys said. "I mean, with a war on and all."

"I suppose they are," Mrs. Bigelow said.

"Just wait until the war's over and they all come back home. They'll be so tired of living in the trenches, with only other blokes for company, that they'll all be mad to find a girl. Then all of us unmarried girls, we'll just be able to pick and choose, won't we?" Gladys said, smiling, trying to jolly her mother into a better mood.

"I hope so," Mrs. Bigelow said.

"And I know so. No more of this silly talk from you. You're no trouble at all. I love to come home and tell you all about my day. What would I do if I didn't have you to talk to? Have to get a budgie, wouldn't I? And I can't stand the bloody things."

"Gladys!" Mrs. Bigelow said. "You shouldn't use such language. It's not ladylike."

But Gladys could see she was trying not to laugh. She kissed her mother's cheek and said she would have to start their tea, or they wouldn't be eating until midnight.

"Did the postman come today, Mum?" she asked on her way out of the sitting room.

"Yes, he brought a letter or two. Mrs. Karcher put them on the kitchen table."

Gladys picked up her marketing and walked down the short hallway into the kitchen. She put her groceries away in the icebox, then grabbed her pinafore from its hook on the back door and tied it around herself. She was worried about her mother. Her spirits were often poor, but lately the bouts of tears and anxiety had grown more frequent. She had talked to Dr. Morse about it just yesterday, and he said low spirits were common in the housebound. She'd asked, too, if there was any hope that the palsy that afflicted her mother so badly—Parkinson's disease, the doctor called it—would ever improve.

"I'm afraid it will not, Miss Bigelow," he'd said. "Parkinson's is a progressive disease. It will continue to cause degeneration in the central nervous system. Your mother's motor functions, and her speech, will only grow worse. You must be prepared for that."

Gladys did not know what she would do when her mother got worse. It was hard enough to care for her now. She wished she could be at home with her all day, but that was impossible. She had to work. They needed the money that she earned. The neighbors were wonderful, of course, and looked in on her during the day, but what would happen when she could no longer walk at all? Or talk? Or eat?

Gladys sighed. She wouldn't think of that now. Not tonight. She would get the tea, that's what she would do. Then she would wash the dishes and get her mother to bed. And then scrub the floor or wash a few things. Anything to keep herself busy. Gladys needed to be busy. Being busy kept her from thinking too much.

She set a pot of water to boil on the stove and smiled as she turned the knob on her new cooker. She'd just bought it last week. The old one had finally given out, and the man at Ginn's Appliances said it would be better to buy a new one than to keep repairing the old one. So she had. She'd splurged on a deluxe model. It was the best one in the shop Mr. Ginn had said—all cream enamel with bits of green here and there, four burners, a grill, and a roomy oven. It was a gas oven and ever so much nicer than the old one, which had been coal-fired. There was just one thing to be careful about, Mr. Ginn had said, and that was to make sure the knobs were turned off completely when she was finished using it.

"Otherwise, you'll gas yourself to death, Gladys," he said, "and we certainly don't want that. You're one of me best customers!"

She was, too. Just last year, she'd bought the icebox from him.

When Gladys had the potatoes boiling and the peas opened and on the stove, she set the table. Then she turned her attention to the day's post. There was a bill from the gas company and something from the savings and loan about buying war bonds. There was another envelope, too—a small buff-colored one with her name and address on it and nothing else, no return address. The postmark was from Camden Town. It had been mailed yesterday. Puzzled, Gladys opened it. She gave a small cry when she saw what was inside.

"Gladys? Was that you?" her mother called from the sitting room. "Are you all right?"

Gladys swallowed hard. "I'm fine, Mum!" she called back. "Just burned myself on the pot handle, that's all."

"Be careful, love."

"I will."

Gladys stared at the ugly photograph in her hand. It was of her. Max von Brandt had taken it nearly four years ago. In a boarding-house in Wapping. Feeling sick to her stomach, she turned it over. There was nothing written on the back of it. There was nothing else in the envelope. There was no message at all, but there didn't have to be. It was a warning. Something had gone wrong. And the person who'd sent the photograph was telling her she'd better put it right.

But what could have gone wrong? Whatever it was, Gladys was certain it involved Jennie Finnegan. She immediately thought back to last night, and the conversation she'd had with her on the bus on their way home from the suffrage meeting; she'd been able to think of nothing else the entire day.

Jennie had wanted to know about Max. She'd wanted to know what was in the envelope Gladys had given her. She'd even talked about going to the authorities. Had she actually done so? Could she have been that foolish? Gladys had warned her. She'd told Jennie to not open the envelope, to deliver it just as she'd always done, or she'd find out exactly what Max von Brandt was capable of. Surely Jennie had listened to her.

But if Jennie *had* listened, then why had this picture been sent?

Maybe, a small voice inside her said, someone else had been listening, too. There had been other people on the bus—a handful of men. Was it possible one of them was working for Max, had been told to watch his couriers, and had overheard them? Yes, Gladys realized with a cold dread, it was. Anything was possible where Max von Brandt was concerned.

The photograph was a warning, all right—a warning to her to keep Jennie Finnegan in line.

"My God, what am I going to do?" Gladys whispered, numb with fear.

If Jennie decided to open the envelope, and discovered what was really in it, she would certainly go to the authorities. And when she did, government men would come for her—Gladys. She would be arrested, tried, and found guilty of treason. If she wasn't executed, she would spend her life in jail.

To prevent this, she would have to frighten Jennie. She'd have to intimidate her into continuing to deliver Max's envelopes. But how? She believed that Jennie honestly hadn't known she was helping German spies smuggle British military secrets to Berlin. Jennie was an innocent; Max had told her he was on Britain's side and she believed him. But for some reason, she now no longer believed him. And what was she, Gladys, supposed to do about that? Force an innocent woman to betray her own country? Even if she had an idea how to go about such a thing, she had no stomach for it. She would not do to someone else the dreadful thing Max von Brandt had done to her.

Just as she had the first time Max had shown her the pictures, Gladys once again thought of killing herself. But now, as then, she could not bring herself to do it, because she did not want her mother to be taken to a home where no one would look after her properly.

"What am I going to do?" she whispered again, in despair.

Moving woodenly, she tore the picture into bits and put the pieces into the rubbish bin. She opened the tin of pineapple rings, took the gammon steaks out of the icebox, put them in a bowl, and poured the juice from the tin over them. While they sat in their marinade, she mashed the potatoes, drained the peas, then added butter and salt to both. Next, she put the kettle on for a pot of tea, struck a match, and lit the grill. As the gas hissed, then whooshed into bright orange flames, she found her answer.

When she finished grilling the steaks, she put them on two plates and decorated them with the pineapple rings. Then she put the mash and peas on the table, followed by tea made in the best teapot. The meal looked very inviting. She thought her mother would like it very much.

"Tea's ready, Mum!" she shouted as she went down the hall to get her mother. "It looks good, if I do say so myself. I hope you've an appetite tonight."

Gladys helped her mother down the hallway to the kitchen and eased her into her chair.

"Sit down now, Gladys," Mrs. Bigelow said. "You must get off your feet for a bit."

"I will do, Mum. It's drafty in here. I'm just going to close the window so we don't get a chill."

She did so, and then kicked a floor rug up against the bottom of the back door. Just before she sat down, she turned the gas on for all four burners, the grill, and the oven, pretending, as she did, that she was turning them off. She knew that her mother, with her bad ears, would never hear the hissing.

"This is lovely, Gladys!" Mrs. Bigelow said, as she struggled to cut her steak with her trembling hands. "It's just the thing to take the gloom off a miserable, rainy night."

"Thank you, Mum. I'm glad you like it," Gladys said.

Mrs. Bigelow must've heard the sad, strange note in Gladys's voice, for she suddenly looked up. "You all right, Gladys?" she said.

Gladys nodded. She smiled.

She had wiped away her tears before her mother could see them.

CHAPTER NINETY-TWO

"SHALL WE TRY again, gentlemen?" Joe said, wheeling himself into Sir George Burgess's office. Sid Malone came in behind him. "Can hostilities cease for the duration of this meeting?"

Sid nodded. Burgess, standing behind his desk, did the same. "Please sit down," he said, gesturing to the two chairs on the opposite side of his desk.

Sid pulled one of the chairs out of the way of Joe's wheelchair, then sat down in the other. Burgess poured tea for both of them from a big silver teapot. He splashed some on Joe's saucer as he did.

"Forgive me. I usually have a girl to do this—you know her, Joe—Gladys Bigelow—but she hasn't come to work today. Most unlike her. I hope it's not the Spanish flu. Just sent my man, Haines, around to her flat to see what's going on. I hear your sister-in-law's laid up with it."

"She is, indeed," Joe said. "She's in hospital."

"I'm very sorry to hear it."

"Thank you, Sir George," Joe said. He paused, then said, "All right, then. Let's get down to business. We've a spymaster, von Brandt, whom, it seems, we can't touch, and we've a courier, Flynn, whom we can catch. We know where to find him, and when. What we don't have is our inside man. The person inside the Admiralty who's getting the information to the courier. Are we agreed on that much?"

Both Sid and Burgess said that they were.

"Good," Joe said, relieved. "That's a start."

He had brought Sid to Burgess's office at the Admiralty two days ago so that Sid could tell Burgess everything he'd told Joe about Max von Brandt and the man called Flynn. Without naming him, Sid had also told Burgess about his friend John, who'd been ferrying Flynn to the North Sea, and who'd saved Sid's life.

Burgess, alarmed, had wanted to immediately take John in for questioning and to nab Flynn, too. Sid had told him they could not immediately nab Flynn, for he only came to John's boatyard every fortnight. He'd also informed him that he would not allow John to be taken in or questioned, because to do so might endanger his life. He explained Billy Madden's role in the proceedings and told Burgess that Madden had threatened John and his family.

Burgess, however, made it clear he didn't care about Billy Madden or his threats; he wanted John, and he wanted him now. Sid refused to give John up, and the meeting had devolved into a shouting match.

"God only knows how much havoc this network has wreaked, how many deaths it's caused!" Burgess had yelled, banging his fist on the table. "I must have the name of your contact, Sid. I demand that you give it me."

"You what?" Sid said, leaning forward in his chair. "You *demand* it?"

"I do indeed."

Sid laughed. "I'm giving you nothing. No names, dates, or places," he said.

"I could have you arrested. It's certainly within my power."

"Go ahead. I'll deny everything I've told you. You'll look even more of a git than you already do."

"Now, see here!"

"No, *you* see here. You've no understanding—none at all—for the hardship that drove my friend to do what he's done," Sid said. "I'll not have him sacrificed."

"What about all the other men who are being sacrificed? Right this very minute. Because of a spy ring that is operating in London. What about them?" Burgess had asked.

Sid, glowering, said, "Well, we'd better sit down and hash out a plan then, hadn't we?"

And they'd tried, but they'd failed. Neither man would give an inch. Sid would do nothing to endanger John and his family. Burgess would give no guarantees that he would spare them. Sid had finally stormed out, disgusted. He and Joe had left Burgess's office no closer to capturing von Brandt's spy than they had been when they walked in.

"We got nothing done, Joe," Sid had furiously said afterward. "Bloody nothing!"

"Welcome to the wonderful world of politics, old son," Joe replied.

Now, two days later, they'd decided to meet again in Burgess's office, to see if they could work together to fashion a plan. Joe knew, as did they all, that they could not afford to leave the premises today without one. Too much was at stake.

"So, chaps," Burgess began now, "the question remains: How do we take Flynn without implicating Mr. Malone's friend?"

Sid, apparently, was ready for the question. "We don't," he said. "At least not right now."

Burgess raised an eyebrow.

"Hear me out," Sid said. "You don't want Flynn by himself. Flynn's low-hanging fruit. Take him and you break the pipeline from London to Berlin, sure . . . but for how long? Von Brandt, wherever he is, just puts another courier into play. There are probably a dozen of them in London right now, just waiting for the nod. If you want to stop the flow of secrets to Germany, you have to find out who the inside man is—the man in the Admiralty—and get him at the same time that you get Flynn."

"Go on," Burgess said, intrigued.

But before Sid could, there was a knock on the door.

"Come in!" Burgess barked.

A young man hurried into the room and closed the door behind him.

"My assistant, William Haines," Burgess said. "What is it, Haines?"

"Sir George," the young man said breathlessly, "there's been a rather important development in the matter we were discussing earlier, and I—"

"What matter would that be? We discussed several."

"Well, sir, it's one of rather sensitive dimensions. . . ." Haines paused, glancing at Joe and Sid.

"Speak freely, old chap," Burgess said.

"Thank you, sir, I shall. We have just received a communication from Haifa indicating that a person of particular interest—a Mr. Max von Brandt—is thought to have been killed in Damascus. By a person close to Lawrence. A chap by the name of Alden Williams."

"Well, that's good news. One less spymaster to worry about, but unfortunately, his protégés are still at large in London. Thank you, Haines," Burgess said, waving the man away.

"There is one other thing, Sir George . . . ," Haines said.

"Yes? What is it?"

"The matter of Miss Bigelow's whereabouts. I'm sorry to tell you that Gladys has been found dead in her home."

"What?" Burgess said, shocked. "Gladys is *dead*?"

"Yes, sir. We were all rather upset about it, I might add. It was gas inhalation. Given where she works—worked—the police notified us immediately. The press was already sniffing about. At our request, the police have put it about that she accidentally left the gas turned on. She'd just bought a new oven, you see. But they—and we—actually suspect she committed suicide."

"Good God, man. Why do you think that?" Burgess asked.

"Because sir, all four stove burners were turned on. One doesn't leave all four on accidentally. And the grill. And the oven. The kitchen window was shut tight, and there was a rug pushed up against the bottom of the door."

"I see," Burgess said.

"Miss Bigelow's mother was with her in the kitchen. She, too, died from gas inhalation. Miss Bigelow left no note, but the two officers who found her also found this in the rubbish bin. They pieced it back together and gave it to us," Haines said, handing Burgess a glued-together black-and-white photograph.

"Bloody hell," he said. "Thank you, Haines, that will be all for now," he added, pushing the photograph across the desk to Joe and Sid.

"Somebody was blackmailing her," Joe said, as Haines closed the door behind him. "She looks drugged in this photograph. Or drunk. Somebody slipped her something, took this picture, then used it to make her do what he wanted—which was to smuggle secrets out of your office. Bet you a hundred quid it's von Brandt. Or rather, it *was* von Brandt."

"Looks like we've got our inside man," Sid said. "Sooner than we thought we would. Only she's a woman. And she's dead."

Burgess was silent for a bit, then he shook his head and said, "No, it's not possible. There is simply no way that Gladys Bigelow took those documents to Flynn."

"How can you be sure?" Joe asked.

"Because we had her watched and followed. On numerous occasions."

"You suspected her?" Sid asked.

"Not at all. In fact, if there was one person I trusted above all, it was Gladys," Burgess said sadly, "but when war was declared, we watched everyone. As a matter of course. To be absolutely certain of them. I am quite sure that I myself am regularly followed. At least I hope I am."

Burgess paused to pour more tea, then continued. "I read the surveillance reports on Gladys myself. Her movements were as regular as the rain. She had her knitting club and her suffrage meetings. She did her marketing at Hansen's. Bought her clothes at Guilford's. On Sundays she took her mother to the park. There were no men in her life, not one. I can tell you with utmost confidence that Gladys Bigelow was not meeting German spies in smoky pubs or on the riverfront in the dead of night or anywhere else. So how the devil did the documents get from her hands to Flynn's?"

"You think there was yet another person involved?" Sid asked. "Someone who took the documents from Gladys and got them to Flynn?"

"There had to be," Burgess said.

"So we're only slightly better off than we were ten minutes ago. We've got the inside man accounted for, but now there's another courier to find. And we've no idea who he is," Joe said.

"I'm afraid so," Burgess said. "I'm also afraid that we cannot wait to find out who he is. When we first spoke, Sid, you told me your friend is scheduled to depart on his North Sea run on Friday—tomorrow. Flynn undoubtedly reads the papers, just like the rest of us. He'll find out that Gladys Bigelow is dead. Without her, he can't get his information and has no reason to stay in London. He'll go underground or leave England altogether. We'll lose him, and more importantly, we'll lose any information we could've squeezed out of him." Burgess looked at Sid. "We have to make a move. There is simply no other choice. I am asking for your help. Not demanding, asking."

Sid nodded. "Give me a few hours. I'll come up with something," he said. "Give me until tomorrow morning."

Burgess nodded. "Until tomorrow morning," he said.

There was another knock on the door. "I'm sorry to interrupt again, Sir George," Haines said, "but we've just had an urgent message for Mr. Bristow, from his wife."

"What is it?" Joe asked, alarmed.

Haines read from the piece of paper in his hand. "Mrs. Bristow asks that you meet her at the Whitechapel Hospital immediately. She says that your sister-in-law is in a very critical state and not expected to live much longer." Haines looked up at Joe. "I'm so terribly sorry, sir," he said.

CHAPTER NINETY-THREE

"HOW IS SHE?" Joe asked Fiona, as Sid wheeled him into the lobby of the Whitechapel Hospital.

Fiona, her eyes red with tears, shook her head.

"It won't be much longer," India said. She'd also been crying. She'd loosened the mask she'd been wearing on the quarantine ward; it was hanging around her neck. "She's been in and out of consciousness for the last few hours. She's been asking for you, Joe."

"Me?" Joe said, puzzled. "Why?"

India took a deep breath, then said, "She says she needs to tell you something—something that concerns Max von Brandt . . . and the Admiralty."

"*What?*" Joe said, stunned. "What does Jennie know about von Brandt and the Admiralty?"

"We're not sure. At first the nurses and the ward doctor—Dr. Howell—thought she was delirious," India said. "But she's persisted in her claims, and earlier this afternoon, when I came to visit her, she made me fetch her carpetbag from home. She wouldn't settle until I'd done it. There was an envelope in there. It contains carbons. She says they're from letters sent by Sir George Burgess at the Admiralty."

"My God. How did Jennie get those?" Joe asked.

"I don't know. She didn't tell me. The whole thing sounds mad, but after the other night—after all the things that Sid told us about Max von Brandt—I couldn't dismiss it. I had to bring you here."

"I'm glad you did, India. Can I go in to her?"

"Normally the hospital won't allow anyone but medical staff in a quarantine ward, but I've explained to Dr. Howell that Jennie has critical information that needs to be shared with a member of government and he's agreed to let you on the ward for ten minutes. The Reverend Wilcott's with her, too. He's her minister as well as her father, and clergymen have special privileges. You'll have to wear this," she said, handing a mask to Joe. "And I must tell you that you are taking a great risk. The Spanish flu, if contracted by an adult, is often fatal."

"Let's go," Joe said, without hesitating.

"Sid, Fiona . . . we'll be back shortly," India said.

"Please give her our love. Tell her James is fine. That his cousins are taking good care of him . . . ," Fiona said, her voice breaking with grief.

Sid went to her and put his arm around her. "Go," he said quietly to India and Joe. "Hurry."

After a brief elevator ride, India and Joe were at the doors to the quarantine ward, on the hospital's second floor. India tied Joe's mask around his nose and mouth, and then he followed her through the ward's large double-door entry.

He stopped short a few feet into the ward, momentarily stunned by the sheer number of people there, and by their suffering. He saw one woman coughing up blood, another struggling grievously for air. A man, skeletally thin, was moaning deliriously.

"Where is she?" he asked.

"She's down this way," India said. "Are you all right?"

"I will be," he said.

He and India continued down the walkway. "Dad?" he heard a small, weak voice say, as they neared a bed in the center of the ward. "Dad, is that Joe? I thought I heard him. Will you get him for me?"

India stopped. Joe did, too. He looked at Jennie, but barely recognized her. She was horribly thin and her skin had a frightening blue tinge. Her breathing was labored. Her eyes were open. They were wild and glassy. He looked at the Reverend Wilcott, and the grief he saw in the older man's eyes was devastating.

"Dad!" she said again, louder this time.

"I'm right here, Jennie," the Reverend Wilcott said, rushing to take her hand.

"I need my bag," she said. Her voice was thin and agitated.

"It's right here, Jennie. Please calm down. You mustn't worry yourself over—"

"Please, Dad!"

"All right . . . yes, yes . . . it's here, right here," the Reverend Wilcott said, pulling a carpetbag out from under the bed. "What do you need from it?" he asked.

"There's an envelope inside it," she said. "Get Joe, Dad. Promise me you will. Get him and give him the envelope and tell him to read what's inside of it. Tell him—"

"Jennie, darling, Joe's here. He came. He's right here," the reverend said.

Jennie tried to sit up, but could not. Her father caught her in his arms and helped her.

"Jennie, what is it?" Joe said gently, wheeling himself over to her and taking her hand.

Jennie coughed hard; blood dripped from her nose. As her father wiped it away, Joe could see the effort it cost her to talk, to merely breathe, and he knew that she was fighting—not for her life, which was lost, but for a few extra minutes.

"I have to . . . I have to tell you something. In 1914, Max von Brandt came to me. . . ."

So it's true, Joe thought. No. God, no. Not you, Jennie.

". . . He told me he was a double agent and that he needed help smuggling forged papers to Germany, in order to get German dissidents out of the country. He told me I would receive an envelope—"

"From Gladys Bigelow," Joe said.

Jennie nodded. "How do you know?" she asked him.

"Gladys killed herself. We think she was being blackmailed," Joe said. "Jennie, we think Max is dead, too," he added, hoping it would give her some comfort.

Jennie closed her eyes. Tears slipped down her cheeks. A few seconds passed before she could continue. When she started speaking again, she sounded even weaker.

"He told me to put the envelope in the basement of the church, inside the statue of St. Nicholas, and that a man would come for it. He told me I'd be helping him save innocent people. And so I did it. But he lied. I opened the envelope last week. I should have done it years ago." She pushed her bag toward Joe. "It's in there. Take it. He's a spy and I've been helping him. All these years. They know, Joe. About Seamie. About all the ships. The Germans know. Please help him . . . help Seamie. . . ." She stopped talking, closed her eyes, and collapsed back against her father.

Joe opened the envelope. His blood froze in his veins as he saw the carbons from Burgess's office. He held one after another up to the light and read information on ships—their names, captains' names, the size of their crews, their whereabouts.

"Jennie . . . ," he started to say.

"Don't," the Reverend Wilcott said, crying. "She hasn't the strength. Can't you see that?"

But Jennie opened her eyes again. She looked at Joe.

"When were you supposed to put the envelope in the basement? What day exactly?"

"Wednesdays," Jennie said. "The day I always clean the sacristy."

"Does the courier—Max's man—pick them up on Wednesdays?"

"I don't know. I never checked. Every time I went down with a new one, the old one was gone," Jennie said.

"Thank you, love," Joe said. He squeezed her hand tightly. "We'll fix it, Jennie. I promise you. We'll set it to rights."

Jennie gave Joe a tearful smile. "Take care of James," she said. "Promise me you will. Tell him that I loved him . . . that he was always my beautiful boy, no matter what happens. Will you tell him that? Will you?" she said, suddenly agitated again. "Please tell him that. . . ."

"Shh, Jennie. Of course I will. James is fine. He's with his cousins and they're taking good care of him. He sends his love to you. Fiona and Sid, too."

Jennie closed her eyes. "Tell Seamie I love him, too . . . and tell him I'm sorry," she murmured.

"Oh, my darling girl, you've nothing to be sorry for. Nothing at all. Do you hear me, Jennie? Do you?" the Reverend Wilcott said.

But it was too late. Jennie was gone. The reverend leaned his head against hers and wept. India went to him. She put a soft hand on his back. Joe, still holding the envelope, quietly left them. A nurse stopped him outside the ward, took his mask off, and had him wash his hands. Then he went to find Fiona and Sid again.

"She's gone," Joe said, when he saw them.

Fiona shook her head. "James is home with Mr. Foster and the children. How will I tell him his mother is gone? How will I tell Seamie?" she asked. She wiped her eyes.

"Fiona, love," he said. "I'm sorry, but I have to go now. I'll be back and I'll do my grieving later, but if I don't get to Sir George right away, we might all be grieving another family member soon—Seamie."

"What Jennie told you . . . the things you asked her . . . they all have to do with what Sid told us the other night, don't they? With John Harris and Madden and Max von Brandt?"

"Yes, they do," Joe said. "Seamie's in great danger. Many men are."

"Go," Fiona said tearfully. "And for God's sake, stop that man Flynn."

Fiona went to wait for India, and Joe took Sid aside. He quickly explained to him exactly what he'd learned from Jennie.

"I'm going to the Admiralty," he told him. "I've got to tell Burgess what I just found out. Are you coming?"

"You go," Sid said. "Tell Burgess what you know, but give me the envelope."

"Why?"

"It's our only chance of catching Flynn. You said Jennie doesn't know what day he picks up the envelope. Maybe it's Wednesday. But maybe we'll catch a bit of luck and it's today—Thursday. If it is, we've got to make sure it's there—just like it always is—or he'll spook. If we're really lucky, he hasn't read about Gladys. And he can't know about Jennie—why would he? Hopefully, he'll come today, take the envelope, go on his merry way, and show up at the boatyard tomorrow night, right on time. Only difference is, I'll be there waiting for him. And you'll be waiting for me. Upriver. With a carriage."

Joe smiled.

"I'll meet you at your house," Sid said. "Tomorrow night. At five o'clock. Tell Burgess he's to be there, too. Waiting upriver with you."

"I'll have the carriage ready. Anything else I can do?" Joe asked, handing Sid the envelope.

"Yes, one other thing," Sid said.

"What?"

"Hope like hell we're not too late."

CHAPTER NINETY-FOUR

"HE'S NOT COMING," Sid said.

"He is. He's never here on the dot. Sometimes it's ten. Eleven. Midnight. It's always different," John Harris said.

"Something spooked him."

"The rain slowed him. It's pissing it down, in case you haven't noticed."

"He's twigged. I know he has. He's a wily one, our boy. He's managed to not get himself captured all these years. He's cagey and cautious and he can likely smell trouble from ten miles away. He'll not come tonight. I know it."

John threw the hand he was playing down on the table. "You're a right old woman, you know that, Sid?"

It was Friday night, nearly eleven o'clock. Sid and John were sitting playing spoil-five in the hold of John's lighter, which was moored at Billy Madden's boatyard. Sid's mind wasn't on his cards, though. He was too tense. John was as well, though he was doing a better job of not showing it.

They were waiting for Flynn. Sid had taken the envelope Jennie had given Joe and hidden it in the basement of St. Nick's, inside the broken statue of the saint. He'd done it immediately after he'd left the hospital, but had he been early enough?

He had no idea when Flynn came through the tunnels to pick up the envelope. What if he'd come earlier in the week? What if he'd heard about Gladys Bigelow? Burgess's office had told the newspapers to hold their stories for a day, but they couldn't keep Gladys Bigelow's neighbors and friends from talking. Or her landlord. The man who'd sold her a pound of apples the day before. Or the newsagent at the corner.

So much depended on timing tonight. On sheer bloody luck. Burgess needed Flynn. He needed to find out from him just how much Berlin knew. Sid needed him, too. He needed to find out how much trouble his brother Seamie was in. And John needed him. He needed Flynn to show up and get on the fucking boat. Now. He needed to look as if he was headed to the North Sea, as usual, so he could get a good three days' head start before Madden figured out he was gone for good.

"Go above and see if he's—" Sid started to say. And then they both heard it—the sound of footsteps on the dock. Sid rose from the table wordlessly and positioned himself so that he was close to the ladder, but so that Flynn would not see him as he came down it. John had told him that Flynn always climbed down facing the rungs.

Sid saw a pair of booted feet, then strong, slim legs, a satchel hanging down from a shoulder strap, and then the rest of what was a good-sized man. Looking at him, Sid was glad he'd taken Joe up on the offer of a pistol earlier in the evening.

As Flynn climbed down the last rung of the ladder, Sid stepped forward noiselessly and pressed the barrel of the gun to the back of his head. He cocked the trigger. The sound it made was unmistakable. Flynn froze.

"That's far enough, old son," Sid said. "Hands up now, where I can see them."

Flynn did as he was told. And then, just as Sid was going to snap a handcuff around one of his wrists, Flynn suddenly ducked, whirled around, and drove his fist into Sid's gut, knocking the wind out of him.

Sid staggered away from the ladder, his hands clutching his gut, trying to breathe, and Flynn scrambled up it.

No! Sid shouted silently, stumbling toward the ladder. But John was ahead of him. He shot up the ladder in a blur of speed, wrapped one arm around Flynn's neck, grabbed a fistful of his hair, and drove the man's head into a ladder rung.

Flynn screamed in pain. His hands came off the ladder. He lost his balance and fell, with John still hanging on to him. Both men crashed to the floor. John gave Flynn no time to recover. He was nowhere near as big as Flynn, but he was quick. He straddled the man and started throwing vicious jabs to his face. Flynn swung wildly at him, trying to knock him off. John ducked some blows and took others, but they didn't stop him. They didn't even slow him. He was fighting for his life—his and his family's.

Sid, in the meantime, had caught his breath. He found the handcuffs he'd dropped and snatched them off the floor. Flynn, already bleeding and bruised, was no match for two men. In a matter of minutes, Sid and John were able to cuff his hands behind his back, gag him, and bind his ankles.

"Well done," Sid said to John when they'd finished with him. Sid was breathing heavily. John was bleeding. But they'd both be fine.

"For a minute there, I thought we'd lost him," John said.

"Me, too. I—"

"John!" a voice bellowed from above. "John Harris!"

Sid and John froze. They knew that voice. It was Billy Madden.

"John! You down there?"

"Go up!" Sid hissed at him. "Act like you're waiting for Flynn."

"Right here, Billy!" John shouted.

Flynn's eyes followed him. Sid picked up a long, thin, horribly sharp knife that John used for cutting lines. He quietly bent over Flynn.

"One sound from you and I go up and shoot Madden. Then I come back down here. I won't shoot you, though. I'll cut your throat," he said. "Ear to ear and very slowly."

Flynn's eyes widened. He nodded.

"Where's Flynn?" Billy barked when John was abovedecks.

"He hasn't shown yet," John said.

Billy swore. "Bastard owes me money. Or rather his master does. I was getting an envelope every month, nice and regular. This month I've got nothing. You tell him—"

"Billy! Come on, darlin'!" a voice called. A woman's voice. It sounded farther away. "You said we wuz going to the Casbah, not a manky old boatyard!"

"Shut your mouth, you silly bitch!" Billy shouted. "Or I'll throw you off the dock!"

"Billeeee!" the woman whined.

"She doesn't watch herself, I'll have another body for you to dump off Margate," Billy said darkly. "Anyways, when Flynn shows up, you tell him I want to see him. The minute he sets foot back on land. I'm running a business here, not a charity."

"Aye, Billy, I'll tell him."

"When are you back?"

"Three or four days, as usual. Should be fair on the way out. Might get some weather on the way back. If we do, it'll slow us."

"Come see me when you're done. I've got another job for you. Paintings this time. Got 'em out of a big manor house in Essex. They need to go south."

"Will do."

Sid heard footsteps on the dock. He waited for John to come back belowdecks, but it was a good, and nerve-racking, ten minutes, before he did.

"Christ, lad, where were you? I'm nearly shitting meself here!"

"Making sure Billy was gone."

"Is he?" Sid asked.

"Aye. I watched him. Waited till he and his tart got back in his carriage."

"Let's go," Sid said.

John didn't need telling twice. He'd already untied the lines. Minutes later, he had the boat's engine going and they were off. They needed to make Millwall by one o'clock, and it looked like they would. About half an hour later, John and Sid were bringing the boat alongside a small dock behind the Wellington, a riverside pub. To both men's great relief, Maggie Harris and her children were on the dock waiting for them.

"Come on! Hurry!" John hissed at them, not even bothering to tie up. One by one, he got his family on board, looking fearfully about the whole time.

Earlier that day, Sid had gone to John and Maggie's rooms. He'd given Maggie five hundred pounds, an enormous sum of money that she'd been terrified to take, and a piece of paper with two addresses on it—one in Inverness, one in Point Reyes.

"You'll go to Inverness first," he had told her. "To Smythson's Estate Agents. A man there—Alastair Brown—will look after you. There's a little house waiting for you there. Rent's all taken care of. When the war ends and you can travel across the Atlantic again, you can sell your boat, get yourselves to New York, and then to California. I'll be waiting there for you. Hope you like cattle. I've got four hundred head."

Maggie had burst into tears then, and Sid had had to wait until she'd calmed down to explain the rest of the plan to her. He had to make sure she was listening, that she understood what he was telling her. There was no room for error.

When she'd dried her eyes, he told her that just before teatime, she and the children must leave their rooms with nothing but the clothes on their backs, and that they must get to Millwall, to the Wellington, check into the room he'd booked under a fake name, and stay there.

"You lot," he'd said to three of the older children, "you leave home one by one. As if you're going out to see a friend, or do an errand. Maggie, you take the others, and your basket, as if you're going to the market. No suitcases, you understand? You mustn't look as if you're leaving. Madden's got eyes and ears all over East London."

Maggie said she understood. The children all nodded.

"Good. Get yourselves to the Wellington and stay in the room. Just before one o'clock in the morning, get downstairs to the dock in back of the pub and wait there. Do it as quietly as you can. John and I will come for you then. Don't say a word about any of this to anyone."

As soon as the last of John's brood was belowdecks, with a caution to leave the man lying on the floor there alone, Sid pushed off, John gunned the engine, and they were under way again. It took only a quarter of an hour to get to their second destination, a Millwall wharf. BRISTOW was painted on the old brick building, in tall white letters. Two men were waiting for them on the dock there—one was in a wheelchair, the other was pacing and smoking a cigar.

Burgess stopped pacing when he saw the boat, and went to the edge of the dock to catch the line Sid threw him. When the boat was tied, Sid went belowdecks, cut the ropes that bound Flynn's legs, and told him to climb the ladder. Sid helped him from below, since his hands were still cuffed, and John from above. Together they got him off the boat and onto the dock.

"George, Joe," Sid said, "I'd like you to meet Jack Flynn."

Sir George shook his head in amazement. "I'll be damned," he said. "You did it."

"Keep hold of him," Sid cautioned, making Flynn sit down on the dock. "He's slippery as an eel."

Sid turned back to John. "Go now," he said quietly. "Get out of London. Get out of the life."

John nodded. "Sid, I . . . I don't know how to thank you."

"Because of you, I get to watch me kids grow up. That's all the thanks I need," Sid said. "Go. The more distance you can put between yourself and Billy Madden, the better."

"I'll see you again, Sid," John said. "One day."

Sid smiled. "You will, John."

Sid untied the line and threw it to John. He waved as the boat pulled away from the dock. He hoped he would see John again. He truly did. He wanted things to go well for John and his family, but there were no guarantees. It took a long time to outrun your old life. He knew that well enough.

Sid gave one last wave, then he turned around. "That's one problem solved. Now, let's get Mr. Flynn up and out of here," he said.

He and Sir George hoisted Flynn to his feet. They half marched, half carried him down the dock, to the warehouse. Joe came behind them in his chair.

"Were you able to get the telegram sent off?" Sid asked Burgess.

Ever since he'd seen the contents of the envelope Jennie had given Joe, with all of its information on British ships in the Mediterranean, Sid had been worried sick about Seamie. As they left the hospital where Jennie had been quarantined, Joe had promised him he'd get Sir George to telegraph warnings to naval command in the Mideast and to the ships themselves.

"We were," Burgess said now, "but it's a long and arduous chain of telegraphing to get a message from London to the Mideast. We cabled our offices in Haifa and we cabled the *Exeter* herself, but we're still awaiting confirmations. We hope to have them in another day or two."

"Thank God," Sid said. "That's a relief. A huge, bloody relief."

Sid, Burgess, Joe, and their prisoner were just about to enter the warehouse when they were hailed from the dock by a boat that had just pulled up to it.

"Jack Flynn!" shouted a male voice. "This is Chief Superintendent Stevens, of Scotland Yard. You are under arrest. Give yourself up immediately!"

"What the—" Joe started to say.

"Bloody hell!" Sid bellowed, as a beam from a bull's-eye lantern was shined in his face, blinding him.

"Stop! All of you!" It was the voice again. "Grab them!"

Sid heard footsteps—many of them—on the dock. Within seconds, he, Joe, and Sir George were surrounded by police officers.

"Who are you? What are doing? What is the meaning of this?" Burgess spluttered.

"I'm Chief Superintendent Stevens," a tall man in uniform said. "I'm here to arrest Jack Flynn on suspicion of receiving stolen property. I'll be taking you in for questioning as well."

"You'll be doing nothing of the sort!" he said, blocking Stevens's access to Flynn.

Stevens gently, but firmly, pushed Burgess aside. "Your name, sir?" he said to Burgess, as he took Flynn's arm and pulled the man toward him.

"Do you not *know* who I am, you damned ninny? I am Sir George Burgess, Second Sea Lord! Put your hands on me again, and I'll personally see to it that you're demoted to constable. Walking the beat in a one-horse village in Cheshire! Unhand that man! He's a German spy."

Stevens gave a quick nod to one of his men. In a twinkling, the officer had slapped handcuffs on Burgess, Joe, and Sid.

"You're making a mistake, Chief Superintendent," Joe said.

Stevens turned to him. "Am I now? And who might you be?"

"Joe Bristow, MP for Hackney. Sir George is right about Flynn—he's a German operative. I can prove it. He has an envelope on him. It contains carbons of letters written by Sir George and stolen from his office. The letters detail secret information on the whereabouts of British ships—information that Flynn's been passing to Berlin via ships in the North Sea. Open it. You'll see."

Stevens weighed Joe's words. Looking skeptical, he walked over to Flynn and opened the man's jacket. He found a large yellow envelope, folded over, inside the breast pocket and pulled it out.

Sid, who'd been holding his breath, quietly let it out, relieved. That was the same envelope Joe had received from Jennie. He recognized it. Now Stevens would see that they were right. He'd release them and allow them to take Flynn with them, to be held and questioned by Burgess and the Secret Service.

Stevens opened the envelope. He looked inside and smiled, then he tilted it and poured its contents—an assortment of diamonds, rubies, and emeralds—into his hand. Some of his officers moved in for a closer look.

"You're looking at about fifty thousand pounds' worth of stones, lads," he said. "Stolen from a jewelers' in Brighton and bound for Amsterdam." He threw a dark look in Joe's direction. "I don't know who those three are, or what they're doing here on a wharf in the middle of the night with Jack Flynn, but I mean to take them in and find out. What I do know is that Flynn is a notorious fence. We've been following him for some time, but we've never been able to catch him with the goods on him. Not until tonight, eh, Jack?" Stevens said, winking at Flynn. He carefully poured the jewels back into the envelope. "I only wish we'd been able to catch the boatman, too. The one who's been helping Flynn get his swag to Holland. He was moving too fast, though. It was either follow him or nab Flynn. Take them aboard, lads. All of them."

The three men were seated together on the deck of the boat. Joe's chair was secured so that it could not roll about the deck as the boat turned and maneuvered back upriver. Flynn was taken belowdecks. Sid looked at him as he was walked past them, and he could've sworn that he saw the ghost of a smile on his face.

"This is preposterous. A complete and utter farce!" Burgess spat, when they were under way. "It was the same envelope that came from Jennie Finnegan. The very same. I'm positive of it," he added. "There was even a carbon smudge on the flap. I distinctly remember it. What the devil happened?"

"Someone got to Flynn," Sid said. "Told him he was about to get nicked. Someone who didn't want him sent down as a spy. They got to the envelope, too. They took out the carbons and put in the jewels. Told him to go through with the run as usual. That's all worrying . . . but what's really worrying is that the someone is powerful enough to get the Yard to play along with it all."

They all fell silent as Sid's words sank in, then Burgess said, "But why? Why not just tell him to bolt? To get out of London? Go underground? Why go through the whole elaborate charade of arresting him as a fence? And taking us in, too? I'm sure they'll hold us for all of ten minutes, then release us with full apologies."

"Because that same someone wanted to prove us wrong. To discredit us. To put paid to our theories about von Brandt, Flynn, and Gladys Bigelow. Make it all look like utter nonsense," Sid said.

"But who would want to do that? Who else knew?" Burgess said. "Whom did you tell?"

"No one," Joe said.

"Likewise," Sid replied. "No one knew except the three of us. Unless *you* told someone, Sir George."

"I told Churchill. He told Asquith," Burgess said. "It can only mean one thing . . ."

"That Churchill's working for the kaiser," Sid said drily. "And Asquith, too."

Joe laughed, but his eyes turned hard and his voice grim as he said, "It means that Max von Brandt is still alive. He has to be. Because someone, someone quite high up, is working very bloody hard to protect him."

CHAPTER NINETY-FIVE

WILLA HEARD A woman singing, soft and low. She had heard the song before, but she couldn't remember where. Gentle hands sponged her brow, her cheeks, her neck. Her body felt cool. The terrible burning had stopped. She felt peaceful and light, as light as a desert breeze. She felt as if she were floating in a clear oasis lake, and that Seamie was nearby. She wanted to stay this way forever. In this beautiful place. With Seamie. And yet she could not, for something was not right. There was something she was supposed to remember, something she was supposed to do.

She sat up with a gasp and opened her eyes. "Lawrence," she said hoarsely. "The maps . . . I have to get to Lawrence. . . ." Her head started spinning from the sudden motion. She groaned.

"Shh, Willa Alden. Lie down," a woman's voice said. "Lie down now."

Willa looked behind herself, in the direction the voice had come from. A Bedouin woman stood there, wringing out a cloth over a basin. She turned around and smiled. Willa knew her face.

"Fatima?" she said. "Is that you?"

"It is."

"Fatima, I have to get to Lawrence. I have to tell him about the maps. I have to go."

Fatima hurried to the bedside and eased Willa back against her pillow. "Everything is fine. Just fine. Now, lie down."

"But there's a trap. The Turks are waiting for Lawrence!"

"Lawrence is safe. Faisal, Auda, Khalaf al Mor—all of them are safe. Do you not remember?"

"No. I . . . I can't remember anything. Everything's so hazy. Where are they?"

"In Damascus, of course."

Willa blinked. "You mean . . . ," she started to say.

Fatima smiled. "They have taken the city, Willa. Damascus is in the hands of the British, and Arabia, at long last, is once again in the hands of the Arabs. Allah be praised!"

Willa closed her eyes. She whooped for joy, then laughed out loud, then started to cough.

"Quiet yourself, please," Fatima scolded. "You have been very ill. It was cholera. We despaired of your life. More than once. You are not out of danger yet and must spend many days recovering."

"Tell me what happened, Fatima. My mind is so foggy. I remember being at a village with some goatherds, and nothing after that," Willa said.

"You rode almost all the way into Lawrence's camp," Fatima said, "but it was his old camp. Lawrence's riders found you, though you were half-dead when they did, so I am not surprised you remember nothing. You talked of maps. Lawrence searched your saddlebags after you were brought into camp. He found all that you had brought him. He saw how the Turks had positioned themselves, how they had set a trap for him."

"What did he do?"

"He avoided it, of course! He and his troops rode east of the Turks. Beni Sakhr, Howeitat, Rwala—all rode as one. They skirted the danger. The English sheik Allenby met them at Damascus, and together they took the city."

"They did it, Fatima," Willa whispered.

"Indeed they did," Fatima said. "Because of you, Willa Alden. Had you not arrived with the maps when you did, they would have ridden directly towards the Turkish soldiers and would have been attacked."

"How do you know all this?" Willa asked.

"We have had a messenger from Damascus. A man whom Khalaf sent. Here, drink this. You must have water now."

Fatima helped her sit up a little and held the glass while Willa drank from it.

"Thank you," Willa said when she had finished.

"It is nothing," Fatima said. "Only a little water."

"I mean thank you for saving me, Fatima. More people die from cholera than survive it. I owe you my life now."

"Oh, no. Not me," Fatima said. "I did very little. The credit belongs to another."

"Really?" Willa said. "Who?"

"Captain Seamus Finnegan."

Willa thought she might be hallucinating again. "What did you say?" she whispered.

"Seamus Finnegan. He was in Haifa when he heard what had happened to you. Apparently, your brother, too, is in Haifa, and word got to him that an airplane you were riding in crashed in the desert." Fatima explained how Seamie had hunted for her and how he'd finally found her. "He brought you back here," she said, "and somehow, only Allah knows how, he kept you from dying. I only arrived when the worst was already over."

Seamie, here with her. In the desert. Willa couldn't believe it. It was so unreal that it made her head spin all over again. Her heart filled with love and gratitude and sadness for this man whom she loved so much, whom fate brought back to her again and again, and yet never allowed her to have.

"I *thought* he was here, Fatima," she said. "The whole time I was sick, I thought he was here. I remember him talking . . . talking to God, I think. No, talking to you. Asking you to bargain with God. Asking Him to take Seamie's life and spare mine. But when I woke up, I was sure I'd only dreamt it."

"You did not. He was truly here."

"Where is he now? Could you ask him to come, Fatima?" Willa asked. "I want to see him."

Fatima looked at her sadly. "I cannot. He left camp. He's gone."

"But why? Why would he do such a thing? Why would he leave without even saying good-bye?" Willa asked, stricken.

"He had to get to Haifa. To take command of a ship," Fatima said.

"Yes, I remember now. He told me he had to go," Willa said tiredly. "Things are coming back to me, but in bits and pieces."

"He left a letter for you," Fatima said. She went to the small table where the basin of water stood and picked up a piece of paper, folded in two, that was next to the basin. Willa opened the letter with trembling hands and read it.

My darling Willa,

I am sorry to leave you before you are awake, but I know that you are out of the woods now and will only get better under Fatima's care.

I hope you will understand that I had no choice but to leave. I am due to take command of the ship Exeter, *and must get back to Haifa quickly.*

Perhaps someday I will see you again and you can tell me exactly how you came to be riding alone through the desert, so sick and so weary, with maps from the German high command in your possession. I'm sure it will be a hell of a story. Most everything that you do is.

Take care of yourself, Willa. Please. You have no idea how close you came this time. Closer, I think, than you came when you fell at Kili. Stop punishing yourself. For my sake, if not your own. We've made our mistakes. We're paying for them. But I don't know how I'd go on if something happened to you. I don't know what I'd do if you weren't there in my head, and my heart, every time I look up at the night sky or smell the sea or climb to the top of something—a mountain, an ice wall, or a bloody great sand dune—just to see what's beyond it.

I love you, Willa. Whether it's bad or good, I love you. I always have and I always will. Don't you ever take that away from me.

Yours, Seamie

Willa folded the letter closed. She wished she could cry. Crying would help. But she couldn't. The pain she felt was too deep for tears.

Fatima took the letter and put it back on the table. "The letter has caused you grief. I can see it. I would not have given it to you if I had known it would. You must ask Allah for help. He listens. He hears. He answers our prayers. He has answered mine. He will answer yours. And Seamus Finnegan's, too."

Willa smiled tiredly. She was quite sure God listened to Fatima, but He did not listen to her. And she doubted He listened to Seamie, either.

She thought again of how Seamie had asked Fatima to ask God to spare Willa's life. He'd said he'd give his own, if only God would spare hers.

A sudden chill gripped her at the memory. Why had he said that? she wondered. He shouldn't have.

She fervently hoped that Fatima was wrong and that she was right. She hoped that God did not listen to Seamus Finnegan.

CHAPTER NINETY-SIX

"REPORT, MR. WALKER?" Seamie asked his lieutenant.

"All clear, sir. We've sighted nothing all morning. Not even a fishing boat."

"Strange," Seamie said. "Captain Giddings was certain he'd seen something. Right about where we are now. He was certain it was a German gunboat. Said he pursued her, but she eluded him."

"She must've realized she'd been spotted. Probably cleared off," Walker said.

Seamie, squinting out over the brilliant blue sea, nodded. "Could well be. Keep me informed, Mr. Walker."

"Of course, sir."

"Set a course for north-northeast, Mr. Ellis," Seamie said. "Tell the gunners to take their positions. I'd like to take a look around the northern coast of the island."

"Aye, aye, sir," the quartermaster said.

Seamie and the crew of the *Exeter* were patrolling off the coast of Cyprus. Shortly before they'd left port—about twenty-four hours ago—Peter Giddings, the captain of a ship that had just returned to Haifa to refuel—had come aboard to tell Seamie that he'd seen a German gunboat at the top of Famagusta Bay. He'd followed it, but the gunboat had disappeared around the island's northeastern tip. His fuel was low, Giddings said, or he would've given chase. He cautioned Seamie to keep his eyes open for the boat.

"I'm worried that Gerry may be using it as a decoy," Giddings said. "He may be hoping to draw us around the point, where other gunboats are lying in wait."

Seamie thanked him for the information, and shortly afterward the *Exeter* had left port. It almost didn't leave at all. At least, not with Seamie at the helm.

He'd only made it back to port by the skin of his teeth. He was due to assume command of the *Exeter* at 0800 hours today. He got back into town just before six A.M., on a camel. He rode the animal to Albie's house and banged furiously on his door. When Albie opened it, rumpled and bleary-eyed, Seamie handed him the camel's reins and rushed past him, saying he needed to bathe and shave. Luckily, he'd thought to leave his uniform with Albie. He was washed and dressed by seven. He ran back downstairs, told Albie that his sister was alive, if not exactly well. He explained what had happened, and where he could find her, and told him to take his camel to go fetch her. Then he slurped down a cup of tea, crammed a slice of toast into his mouth, and ran out the door. He made it onto the ship at exactly twelve minutes to eight.

It had been an uneventful few hours since he'd left port, but now, as the *Exeter* headed north-northeast, Seamie felt uneasy. He wondered if the gunboat had truly cleared off, or if Giddings was right and it was trying to lure them into a trap. They would have to proceed cautiously.

As he was about to leave the bridge to inspect his guns, the radio suddenly crackled and popped. He turned around. They were too far away from port to be receiving any messages from naval command in Haifa. This had to be a ship-to-ship communication, which told Seamie there was some urgency to it. Ensign Liddell, the radio operator, dove for his headphones. He started twiddling knobs and pressing buttons, and then suddenly he was scribbling furiously. He stopped writing once or twice to ask for clarification, and two minutes later, he signed off. He pulled his headphones off and stood up. Seamie saw that his usually ruddy cheeks had gone white.

"Captain, sir," he said, "we've just received a message from the captain of the *Harrier,* which is currently southeast of us, approximately halfway between us and Haifa. Since naval command cannot reach us, they've asked the *Harrier* to relay the following message from London, from Sir George Burgess himself."

"Read it," Seamie said tersely.

"We are ordered to abandon our position immediately and return to port."

"*What?*" Seamie said. "We just bloody got here!"

"The SSB has confirmed intelligence reports that a German fleet has moved into the southeast Mediterranean and is massing off the eastern coast of Cyprus, a fleet of—"

"Fleet? What fleet? There isn't one bloody boat here!" Seamie said. "Not one! This is madness! We can't turn around now!"

"Begging your pardon, Captain Finnegan," Ensign Liddell said. "Allow me to clarify. Not a fleet of war ships . . . a fleet of U-boats."

The bridge went completely silent.

"Mr. Ellis," Seamie said, "Bring her about. Now. Set a course for—"

He never got to finish his sentence. The first torpedo clipped the *Exeter*'s starboard bow. The second one broadsided her. She burst into flames, and ten minutes later she sank to the bottom of the placid blue sea.

PART THREE

DECEMBER 1918

LONDON

CHAPTER NINETY-SEVEN

"OI! MISSUS! IF I was yer husband, I'd poison yer tea!" a drunken heckler shouted.

"And if I was your wife, I'd drink it!" Katie Bristow shouted back, laughing cheekily.

The heckler scowled; the crowd in the packed market hall erupted into laughter. She'd just proved to every man and woman present that she was one of them—tough, scrappy, able to take a jab.

Joe, whose mouth had been set in a hard, angry line, whose hands had been clenched into fists, laughed, too. He'd wanted to wallop the bollocks who'd just shouted at her, but he knew that Katie would be angry with him if he so much as traded words with the man. She'd warned him about interfering at her speeches, no matter how unruly it got.

"Listen, Dad, you can't come if you're going to get shirty every time some silly bugger opens his gob," she'd said to him. "How will it look? Like I need my father to fight my battles for me, that's how. That won't go over well—not for Sam's campaign, and not for my own one day. So if you do come, you've got to keep quiet."

Joe had promised her he would. He didn't want to be banished. He didn't want to miss a single word his daughter said. She was a dazzling speaker—quick on her feet and inspiring. But it was so hard for him to keep quiet. He had many campaigns under his belt—for himself and for other Labour candidates he'd come out to support—and he well knew the ugliness of which crowds were capable. But nothing he'd ever encountered in his entire career as a politician matched the vulgarities thrown at Katie.

A general election had been called for December 10, and Katie, a popular figure in East London with her pro-Labour newspaper and pro-union activities, was spending her Christmas holiday stumping for Samuel Wilson, Labour candidate for the Tower Hamlets seat, which included Limehouse, where they were now. As soon as she'd started campaigning for Wilson, the newspapers had jumped on her—calling her unladylike and unnatural. Some of the people she'd hoped to pull to Wilson's side called her far worse. Grown men catcalled and heckled and said things better suited to a barnyard than a public hall, things that would have made most women—and even some men—blush and falter and run from the podium.

Not his Katie. She simply clasped her hands in front of her, waited for her antagonist to finish, then gave it back to him twice as hard.

"Oh, Katie," Fiona had fretted, after she'd attended her daughter's first speech. "Those men were truly horrible. Doesn't it upset you?"

"I don't let it, Mum," Katie said. "I can't. One day I'll be campaigning for myself, and that will be even tougher. I've got a chance to learn how to deal with crowds now, during Sam's campaign. It's a good way to gain experience. I've got to be able to take what people throw at me and throw it right back at them."

Now, as Joe continued to listen to Katie, one bright spark pointed out that she was a woman and that a woman's place was in the house.

"Oh, I couldn't agree more," Katie said, smiling her impish smile. "That's partly why I'm here, you see. Because I very much want to be in the house one day—the House of Commons."

There was a great deal of laughter, and she joined in, but then she turned serious.

"Yes, I'm a woman," she said, suddenly steely-voiced. "And very proud of it. The war is over now. Armistice Day has come and gone. But let us never forget that it was women who held their homes together while their men were away. It was women who worked in the munitions factories and then came home and scraped meals together out of rations, night after night. It was women who kept families of this country going single-handedly for four long years. So yes, I am proud, but proud as I am, I do not stand here before you today and ask you to vote for my candidate because I'm a woman, I ask you to vote for Sam Wilson because I'm a member of the Labour Party and he is, too."

Cheers went up—the first of the evening.

"You women out there—your country called upon you in her time of need, and you answered that call," Katie said, hotly. "You worked and sacrificed and went without, never knowing if you would see your sons, brothers, and husbands again. Some of you got telegrams telling you that you never will. Who will be there for you now? During *your* time of need?"

A group of women seated near the front of the hall burst into applause.

"You men—you did not ask for this wretched war, but you got it," Katie continued. "You endured a living hell on the banks of the Somme and the Marne. In the Atlantic Ocean. The Mediterranean Sea. Hundreds of thousands . . . no, *millions* of your comrades died, leaving behind grieving mothers and fathers, wives, children. Many of you have returned to us injured, unable to work, sometimes too damaged to ever rejoin society at all. You fought for us—now who will fight for you?"

A new cry went up—no catcalls, no insults, just one word, loud and strong: "Labour! Labour! Labour!" Katie did not hush the voices, but let them chant their battle cry until the rafters of the market hall shook with the noise.

When the crowd had quieted again, she said, "Ladies and gentlemen, we are not the same people we were four years ago. We live in a changed world now, one of war's making, and we cannot accept tired, old-world policies. Give Sam Wilson a chance, give Labour a chance, to represent you in this new world. You fought, you gave, you endured . . . now it's Labour's turn. Let Sam fight. Let him fight for better jobs for the men who've come back, for better pensions for the families of those who didn't. Let him fight for more hospitals for the injured, for more schools for the children of our courageous soldiers and sailors. Ladies and gentlemen of Limehouse, let Sam Wilson fight for *you*."

A roar went up. Hats went up in the air. Voices, some five hundred strong, chanted, "Wilson! Wilson! Wilson!"

As Joe looked at his daughter—her cheeks flushed, her blue eyes shining, her head held high—he thought he would burst with pride. He didn't know many twenty-year-old girls who were pulling down excellent grades in their final year of university, publishing their own newspapers, and campaigning on behalf of a would-be MP during their school holidays.

"Looks like the acorn doesn't fall far from the tree," a man beside him said.

Joe turned toward him. He knew his voice very well. "Why, if it isn't Jimmy Devlin," he said.

James Devlin was the editor and publisher of the *Clarion*, an East London newspaper. Katie printed her paper, the *Battle Cry*, on the *Clarion*'s presses.

"She's a brave one, Joe. I have to give her that. I've seen men—seasoned politicians—turn tail and run when confronted by crowds like this."

"She's the bravest woman I've ever known. Besides her mother, of course," Joe said.

"She's read this crowd right," Devlin said admiringly. "Telling them how the war's changed things. It certainly has. And not for the better. But not every candidate's coming out and saying that. Armistice Day was a month ago, but a lot of them are still beating the drum, talking about honor and glory and all of that. Not a lot of glory in death. Is there?"

Joe shook his head. Devlin was right. The war was over, and the world, weary and heartbroken, was grateful for it, but it had changed things forever. Nothing was the same. No family was untouched. His had certainly suffered its share of losses. Poor, damaged Charlie was still battling shell shock. His progress was painfully slow. Jennie was dead. And Maud. Seamie, too. His ship had gone down in the Mediterranean and his body had never been found. They'd had nothing to bring home, nothing to bury. His little son, James, nearly four years old, was now an orphan. Joe and Fiona had taken him in immediately, loving him every bit as much as if he'd been one of their own. He had no one else. Jennie's father, the Reverend Wilcott, had succumbed to the Spanish flu shortly after his daughter. The man behind Maud's death, and Jennie's tortured conscience, and likely Seamie's death, too—Max von Brandt—was thought to be dead. But Joe didn't believe it—no one had been able to confirm or disprove the reports from Damascus—and he doubted that anyone ever would.

India and Sid had returned to California. The Harrises, who'd ridden out the war in Inverness, had followed them. The hospital India and Sid had started at Wickersham Hall continued to take in war veterans and rehabilitate them. India had handpicked her successor, Dr. Allison Reade, a young woman whom Harriet Hatcher had recommended. India and Sid, together with Joe and Fiona, continued to fund the hospital.

"You finding time to campaign for your own seat?" Devlin asked.

"Just barely," Joe said. He'd been appointed leader of his party and, as such, was busy traveling the country, supporting candidates for seats in constituencies far away from London.

"Well, see that you don't lose it," Devlin cautioned. "This time out, Labour really does stand to make gains. I've seen the proof of it. At rallies all across London."

"I think the best we can hope for is that Labour gains and the Liberals win," Joe said. "It will still be some years before we see one of our own in Number 10. Very likely it won't happen in my time, but I'm hoping it will happen in Katie's. Perhaps I'll still be alive to see it."

"You're going to stay in the fray for some years, then?" Devlin asked. "No nice, peaceful retirement for you?"

"Chance would be a fine thing, Jimmy," Joe said.

"Why not? The war's over. Haven't you heard?" Jimmy joked.

"I have, but I wonder sometimes if the war—the one we're fighting, the same one we've always fought—will ever be over. It's hard, Dev. It tires a body after a while."

"Yes, it does," Devlin said. "Especially old bodies. Like ours."

Joe laughed. He was now fifty-three years old, and though there were days—many of them—when he felt his age and longed to linger in his bed with a pot of tea and the morning papers, there were many more days when he felt every bit as passionately committed to the cause of social reform as he ever had. In fact, even more than he ever had. In addition to becoming head of his party, he'd also taken on the leadership of several government committees, on veterans' affairs, education, and unemployment. Fiona had had mixed emotions about his taking on all this extra work at his age. She'd asked him if he could maybe just take up stamp collecting and had wondered, as Devlin had, if he would ever live a peaceful life. But Joe knew that he wouldn't, because there was no peace to be had.

The pain of what had happened to Charlie made sure that there never would be. Not for him. Peace and contentment went out the bloody window every time he saw his damaged son, and the other poor ruined young men who still lived at Wickersham Hall and probably always would, because there was no other place for them. Peace and contentment went out the window every time he rode through the slums of East London, and the slums in Liverpool, Leeds, Glasgow, and Manchester, and saw that the war that had changed everything had changed nothing—not in those places.

"How about you, Dev?" Joe asked. "You're hardly a spring chicken. Are you going to give it up anytime soon? Leave your typewriter and take up fishing?"

Devlin snorted. "And leave London's news in the hands of Fleet Street? Certainly not. Somebody's got to put the truth out there."

Joe smiled. James Devlin had, in his own way, been fighting the good fight, too. He liked his blood and thunder—the murders and robberies, all the blood and gore that sold newspapers—but he'd run countless stories about dangerous working conditions at the docks and the sweatshops, and threats to the public health from unsanitary and crowded living conditions in the slums. In his own way, Devlin had done as much as Joe had to bring the public's attention to the appalling privations suffered by the poor of East London, and Joe knew that a strong sense of social justice was what got James Devlin up in the morning.

"Tell you what," Joe said, offering Devlin his hand, "when we've won our war—that one that's still raging—then we'll worry about the peace. Not before. Do we have a deal?"

Devlin smiled. "We do indeed," he said, taking Joe's hand and shaking it.

Another huge roar went up from the front of the market hall. Both Joe and Devlin turned in time to see several members of the crowd surge up to the podium and lift Sam Wilson, who'd just finished his own speech, onto their shoulders. When they'd got him, they reached for Katie and lifted her up, too. Then they marched through the hall and out the door into the streets, where even more people were cheering.

"Should be quite a contest," Devlin said, watching Sam and Katie disappear down the street. He shifted his weight from one foot to the other, groaning a bit. "Arthritis," he said, shaking his head. "Plays up a lot more now than it ever did before. Glad it's the young ones fighting it, I must say." He pushed his hat back on his head. "Wouldn't miss it, though."

Joe smiled. "Nor I, Dev," he said. "Not for all the world."

CHAPTER NINETY-EIGHT

"HOLD STILL, OSCAR," Willa said. "Just a few more and I'll let you get up. I promise. The light's so amazing right now and it won't last much longer. The days are far too short in December. Look out the window, will you?"

Oscar Carlyle, a musician, crossed his hands over his trumpet, turned, and gazed out of the window.

"That's it . . . perfect!" Willa said.

His eyes widened, just as Willa knew they would. A smile played upon his lips. The light from the sunset, streaming in through the giant windows of Willa's west-facing atelier, did that to people. It captivated them. Enchanted them. It softened them, made them drop their guard, opened them up for a few seconds, just long enough for her to capture the breathless surprise, the sense of wonder, on their faces. Just long enough for her to snatch a tiny bit of their souls and affix it to film forever.

"The sun going down over Paris. What an incredible sight," Oscar said, in his hard Brooklyn voice. "How do you get any work done here? I'd be staring out of the windows all day."

"No talking!" Willa scolded. "You'll ruin the picture."

She took shot after shot, working as rapidly as she could in the last few minutes of light left to her. She wanted something magical out of this sitting, something extraordinary.

The sitting had been commissioned by *Life* magazine; they were doing a piece on Oscar, a young, avant-garde composer, and they wanted an equally avant-garde photographer to shoot him.

The war had ended a month ago, and the world was beginning to pick itself up and dust itself off. Already people were starting to clamor for news of something other than death, disease, and destruction. Some of Willa's recent assignments had included portraits of the Irish writer James Joyce and of the fiery Spanish painter Pablo Picasso.

When *Life*'s editors heard that Oscar was traveling from his home in Rome to Paris to perform there, they immediately wrote Willa to schedule the sitting. She'd only been in Paris about two months—since early November—and already she'd made a name for herself.

After another thirty-odd frames, the sun dipped beneath the city's rooftops; its last golden rays disappeared, and Willa put her camera down.

"That's it," she said. "We're done."

"Thank God," Oscar said, standing up to stretch.

"I think I got some good shots. You have an amazing face. Sensitive and intense. It's a photographer's dream."

Oscar smiled. "Well, let's hope my pretty face can sell out a few music halls," he said. "God knows my agent isn't."

"Have a seat on the divan," Willa said. "Make yourself comfortable. I won't be a moment."

"The very last thing I want to do is sit down again," Oscar said, walking over to a wall where various black-and-whites were tacked up. "I'd much rather look at your work. I've been wanting to nose around ever since I arrived."

Willa lived and worked in what used to be a milliner's atelier in Montparnasse, on Paris's Left Bank. She'd just moved in a fortnight ago from the flat she'd had near the river. The atelier was at the top of a dingy, rundown building, but the space was much larger than her old flat, filled with light, and quite cheap.

"Suit yourself," she said.

She carried her camera to her darkroom—a small alcove she'd made by hanging blankets around the atelier's lone, cold-water sink—and carefully set it down on the counter. She would develop the film later, when she was alone. Next to the sink was a syringe, a length of rubber tubing she used as a tourniquet, and a vial of morphine. She would attend to those later, too. When Oscar was gone. When the film was developed. When she'd got back from haunting the late-night cafes with her friend Josie. When there was nothing else to do and nowhere to go and she was all alone with her ghosts and her grief.

A doctor had given her the morphine when she'd first arrived in Paris. She told him she needed it to control the pain in her damaged leg. It was true, sort of. The leg didn't pain her so much anymore, but other things did. It was peacetime now, but there was no peace, not for her, and there never would be.

Willa took a half-empty wine bottle down off a shelf, tugged the cork out of it, and filled two glasses. "Cheers," she said, as she re-emerged from the darkroom. "Thank you for being such a wonderful subject."

Oscar seemed not to hear her. He was walking around her flat, peering at the photographs on the wall. She walked up to him and handed him one of the glasses. "I came to your concert, by the way. The one you gave two nights ago at the Opera. I loved it," she said. "What are you working on now?"

"A new symphony. A new musical language for a new world," he said absently.

"Is that all?" Willa joked, sipping from her glass.

Oscar laughed. "I sound like a jerk, don't I?" he said, turning to her. "Sorry, I was distracted. How could I not be? This is incredible," he said, pointing at a silvery black-and-white nude.

Willa glanced at the shot. It was a self-portrait. She'd taken it about two weeks ago and had exhibited it, along with a few other photographs, at a local gallery. It had caused quite a stir. Titled *Odalisque,* it showed her sitting on her bed, without her artificial leg, completely bare, her body taut and scarred. She had not modestly turned her gaze away from the camera, but instead had stared into it nakedly and challengingly. It had been called "shockingly brazen" and "subversive" by the mainstream press, but other, more forward-thinking critics had called it "brilliantly symbolic," "wrenching," and "a modern, war-torn Odalisque for our modern, war-torn world."

"Weren't you afraid? To be so naked? So vulnerable?" Oscar asked her.

"No, I wasn't," Willa said. "What's left to be afraid of? I'm scarred. Damaged. I'm missing pieces of myself. After the last four years, aren't we all?"

Oscar smiled sadly. "Yes," he said. "Yes, we are."

He kept walking from one shot to the next. Some were framed. Some were simply pinned to the wall. More were fastened with clothespegs to a length of rope stretched from one end of the room to the other.

"I've never seen anything like these," he said quietly.

"No," Willa said. "Most people haven't. Which is the whole point, I suppose."

The shots Willa had taken were not pretty images of children and parks and bourgeois Parisians out for a Sunday stroll. They were photographs of prostitutes and pimps. Shots of armless and legless soldiers, begging on the streets. A drunk man lying in the gutter. A skinny, dirty girl singing for pennies outside of a restaurant. They were ugly, many of them, harsh, raw, and utterly compelling.

They showed the souls of a war-weary people, and they showed her own soul, for Willa poured everything inside her—her emotion, her passion, and her sorrow—into them. Her art was the only solace she had, the only thing that allowed her to express the inexpressible—the sadness and anger she felt at having survived the great war and its horrors, only to wish she hadn't.

"There are so many," Oscar said quietly. "You must never sleep."

"No, not if I can help it," Willa said. "I'm sitting down, even if you're not. I'm knackered," she added, flopping down on a cracked and torn leather divan.

Oscar sat down in a battered old armchair across from her, and Willa refilled their glasses.

"What happened to you? During the war, I mean," he asked, giving her a searching look.

"I rode with Lawrence, in the desert. I photographed him and his men."

"It sounds exciting."

"It was."

"What else happened? Something must have. These pictures . . ." His voice trailed off as his eyes lit on even more prints, stacked haphazardly on the table between them. "You must have experienced a very great sorrow to be able to so easily recognize it in others."

Willa smiled sadly. She looked into her wineglass. "I lost the person I loved most in the whole world," she said. "He was a naval captain. His boat was sunk in the Mediterranean."

"I'm so sorry," Oscar said, visibly moved.

Willa nodded. "So am I," she said.

She remembered that day now, the day she'd learned Seamie was dead. She'd been in Lawrence's camp, recovering from cholera. She'd been lying in her bed, eating some soup, when Fatima suddenly came into her tent, talking excitedly.

"Willa, you have a guest," she said. "He's tall and handsome and says that he knows you."

Willa put her soup bowl down. Was it Seamie? she wondered. Could he have come back? Her heart began to race.

The flap to her tent opened again and her brother came inside. His face was tanned. He was wearing a uniform. He took off his hat and held it in his hands.

"Hello, Willa," he said. "I've come to see you. And to bring you back to Haifa. To stay with me there. In a house. A rather nice one. If you'd like to come."

"Albie?" Willa said. "My goodness, this is a surprise! I thought . . . I thought that—"

"You thought that I was Seamie," he said, then quickly looked down at his hat.

"Yes, I did," she said awkwardly. "But I'm very glad to see you, Albie. I really am. Sit down."

Albie sat on the cushion next to her bed. He leaned over and kissed her cheek. "It's good to see you, Wills. It's been yonks, hasn't it. I've heard all about your exploits," he said. "How are you?"

"Much better. Getting stronger every day, in fact. My food and drink stay in me now. It doesn't sound like much, but believe me, it's a huge achievement."

Albie laughed, but his eyes were sad. Willa knew her brother well. They hadn't been on the best terms, hadn't even seen each other for years now, but it didn't matter—she knew him. And she knew when something was wrong.

"Albie, what is it?" she said.

"Oh, Willa," he said. "I'm afraid I've got some very bad news."

Willa grabbed his hand. "Is it Mother? It is, isn't it? Albie, what's happened to her?"

"It's not Mother. I received a letter from her just last week. She's fine." Albie stopped speaking. Willa saw that his throat was working. "It's Seamie," he finally said.

Willa shook her head. "No. No, Albie. Please."

"I'm sorry," he said.

"When? How?" Willa asked.

"A few days ago. Off the coast of Cyprus. His ship was broadsided by a German U-boat. It burned and then sank. No survivors were found."

Willa let out a long, trailing moan. She felt as if her heart was being ripped from her. He was gone. Seamie was gone. Forever. The pain of it was beyond bearing.

As she wept, she remembered what Seamie had said while he nursed her. She remembered how he'd asked Fatima to pray for Willa. She'd heard his voice in her fevered dreams then, and she heard it still—in her nightmares.

Talk to Him, Fatima. He listens to you. Tell Him if He wants a life, He can have mine. A life for a life. Mine, not hers. Tell Him, Fatima. Tell Him to let Willa live.

God had listened. And God had taken him.

"And you came here after the desert? Right to Paris?" Oscar said now, breaking in upon her sad memories.

"No," Willa said, shaking her head. "I stayed with my brother for a few days. He was stationed in Haifa. Then I went home to England. I stayed with my mother in London, but London was gray and sad and full of ghosts. Everywhere I looked, someone was missing. That, too, only lasted a few days and then I came to Paris, where the ghosts all belong to other people, not me."

She didn't tell Oscar how unhappy her mother was that she'd gone to Paris, or that she'd sent Albie to fetch her after he'd arrived home from Haifa. He'd come to her flat, taken one look at her, and said, "Still trying to kill yourself, eh? Only this time it's with a needle." He'd returned to London without her.

Oscar picked up a print of an actress painting her face. Willa had shot it as the woman was looking into her dressing room mirror. Her hair was twisted up in pin curls. Her enormous breasts were nearly popping out of her black corset. Her expression, as she rubbed white greasepaint onto her skin, was searching and intense, as if she'd hoped the mirror might tell her who she was.

"Josephine Lavallier, *l'Ange de l'Amour*," Oscar said.

"You know her?" Willa asked.

"I think all of Paris does. Thanks to that photograph of her at Bobino's, standing onstage in a pair of feathery wings and very little else. I saw it a few nights ago, hanging on the wall at La Rotonde. Did you take that one, too?"

Willa nodded. "That shot was published in one of the daily papers here. The editor was outraged such an act is permitted on a Paris stage. Ever since he ran it, Josie's show has been sold out," she said, laughing. "The show's very cheeky. Have you seen it?"

Oscar said he had not, and Willa said he must. "We'll go this very evening," Willa said. "I'll take you. Are you free?"

Oscar said he was, and Willa said it was a date, then. They'd get a bite at La Rotonde first.

"I thought you said the show's been sold out. Will we be able to get tickets?"

"Josie will get us in," Willa said. "We've struck up quite a friendship, Josie and I. We get along quite well. In fact, we've made a pact—neither one of us is allowed to talk about the past. There *is* no past when we're together, only the present. We don't talk about the war, or what we've lost. We talk about paintings and the theater and what we had for dinner, and whom we saw, and what we wore. And that's all. She's originally an English girl. Did you know that?"

"No, I thought she was as French as onion soup."

Willa laughed. "She lets me come backstage and photograph her and her fellow actresses. I get shots of everyone and everything. The stage manager. The back-door johnnies. The girls in their costumes. The romances and the rows. In return, I give her prints of anything I take of her."

Willa looked at the shot Oscar was holding and smiled. She was quite proud of it. "Josie's a fascinating entertainer," she said. "Even though she's English, she embodies Paris, a place that's been battered but not broken. A place that's still beautiful, still defiant."

Willa gazed at the photograph for a bit, then said they should get going. Coats and hats were gathered. As they walked toward the door, another photograph, one hanging over another divan—that Willa used as a bed—caught Oscar's eye. It showed a young man standing on top of a mountain peak, with what looked like the whole world spread out behind him.

"Where was that taken?" he asked.

"On Kilimanjaro. On top of the Mawenzi peak," Willa said.

"That's him, isn't it? The naval captain?"

"Yes, it is. It was taken just after we'd summitted. And just before I fell. And shattered my leg."

Willa told him the story.

"My God," he said, when she finished. "Can you still climb?"

"Only foothills," she said, touching the photograph gently. "I loved climbing more than I loved anything or anyone, except for Seamie. We had such plans, he and I. We were going to climb every mountain in the world. We used to talk about what made a good climber. We decided it was longing—the overwhelming desire to be the first, to lay eyes on a view no human being had ever seen before." She smiled ruefully, then added, "That was many years ago. Before I lost my leg. And Seamie lost his life. But I still think about it—Kilimanjaro, Everest, all of them. And in my dreams, I climb them. With him."

The aching note of sadness in her voice was not lost on Oscar. "It's an awful thing, isn't it?" he said quietly, as Willa opened the door for him.

"What is?" she asked, fishing her key out of her pocket.

"That which drives us," Oscar said, starting down the stairs. "The quest. We are prisoners, both of us. One of music. One of mountains. And neither will ever be free."

"Perhaps freedom is overrated," Willa said, locking the door. "What would either of us be without our quests? Me without my mountains. You without your music."

Oscar stopped midway down the flight of stairs. He looked up at her.

"Happy," he said. Then he turned and kept on walking.

Willa, laughing ruefully, followed.

CHAPTER NINETY-NINE

HE WAS GOING to die. He knew that now. He hadn't eaten for three days. Hadn't drunk for two. There was no more food, no more water, and no hope of getting either of those things.

The guards were gone. Two weeks after Armistice Day, they'd heard the war was over, and they'd left. News traveled slowly in the desert. They'd taken the camels, the goats, all the weapons, and plenty of food and water, and they'd buggered off, leaving their charges—seventy-two British prisoners of war, survivors of U-boat attacks in the Mediterranean—to fend for themselves. In the middle of the desert.

They'd unlocked the doors to the cells. That was something. It had enabled the men to get out—those who could walk, at least—and reconnoiter the prisoner-of-war camp to take stock of supplies.

It had been a very quick exploration. The prison, such as it was, was merely a series of stone huts—the remains of a small village, the men guessed—that had been fashioned into cells by bolting strips of sheet metal over the windows and adding padlocks to the doors. There were no toilets, no sinks, no cots. Just some rags on the ground upon which to sleep. For meals they had got whatever half-rotted mess their jailers saw fit to feed them. Temperatures usually reached 110 degrees during the day and often sank into the fifties at night.

Out of the seven who'd survived the U-boat attack with him, three had died of their injuries during the first week. Walker had starved to death three days ago. Liddell, last night. Benjamin was hanging on, but only barely. He'd likely be gone by nightfall.

And Ellis, well . . . he didn't know if Ellis was alive or dead.

Ellis had walked out with two other men nine days ago, vowing to make it to Damascus, but there were more than one hundred and fifty miles of heat and sand between this godforsaken place and that city, and he and his comrades had been sick, weak, and malnourished. Most likely, they'd dropped down dead one by one in the desert.

Which would mean that no one on their side knew now that he, Benjamin, and the other prisoners were even here.

The Germans had pulled him from the sea three months ago. He'd been clinging to a piece of wood. His clothes had been in shreds. Blood had been seeping from his nose and mouth. He'd had a deep gash across the back of his head. His right side was burned down the length of it—arm, torso, and leg.

"You were nearly dead by the time they pulled you out," Ellis, his quartermaster, had told him. "You were raving. Out of your mind. You didn't even know your own name."

Bir Güzel, the Turkish guards had called him—"beautiful one." It was their little joke, for with his bruised and swollen face, he'd been anything but beautiful.

When he was better, when he could open his eyes and talk, Ellis told him that he'd been unconscious for days. They'd tended to him—Ellis and the others—they'd kept him alive.

He couldn't remember a thing when he'd first come to. Little by little, though, the memories returned. The ship-to-ship message. The German U-boat. The torpedoes. The horrible way the rest of his crew had died. The noise and the fire and the screaming. And then the awful silence as the ship went under.

The guards told them little. They'd had no idea the Allies had won until the day the guards let them out of their cells and informed them that the war was over and they were free to go. They pointed south and told them Damascus was that way, and that it was in the hands of the British now, and that it would take them five days to reach it. On a camel. If they could find one. And then they'd ridden off. One had looked back and tossed Ellis a compass.

They'd talked among themselves that night, all the men, after they'd seen how little food and water they had, and decided to send a party south to the city. The three strongest would go. Hopefully they'd be able to get to Damascus and bring help back before it was too late for the ones left behind.

His burned legs had not healed and he could not walk. He could barely sit up. There was no question of him walking to Damascus. He had lain in his cell for most of the past eleven days, drinking and eating what little the others brought him. Until, finally, there was no more to bring.

They were good men, his fellow prisoners, and he hoped they survived. It was too late for him, but he hoped desperately that help would come for them.

He closed his eyes and fell into a deep sleep, hoping he would not wake again to the horrifying thirst and the gnawing pain in his guts. He dreamed of his young son. And of the boy's mother. He dreamed of a dark-haired woman with green eyes. She was standing at the foot of a mountain, smiling at him. She was so beautiful. She was a rose, his wild rose. He would let go now—let go of the pain and the sorrow and the suffering, let go of everything. But he would find her again one day. He knew he would. Not in this life, but in the next.

He was ready to die, death held no terror for him, but the sound of men's voices, loud and urgent, pulled him back from it.

"Holy Christ! There's a dead body in here! And another one there!"

He heard someone kicking at his door—closed most of the way against the fierce heat.

"This one's gone, too, Sergeant," a second voice said, a voice that was very close by. "Wait a minute! He's not . . . he's breathing! He's still alive!"

He opened his eyes and saw a soldier standing over him, a British soldier. He saw him kneel down, then he felt water on his lips and in his mouth, and he drank it greedily, clutching at the canteen with shaking hands.

"There you are, that's enough. Slow down or you'll be sick. There's plenty more where that came from. What's your name, sir?"

"Finnegan," he said, blinking into the bright desert light flooding into his cell. "Captain Seamus Finnegan."

CHAPTER ONE HUNDRED

"HERE, JAMES, LOVE, give one of these to Charlie and one to Stephen," Fiona said, handing her nephew two ornaments she'd taken from a huge box. It was Christmas Eve, and she, Joe, their children, and little James, were spending it with the men at the Wickersham Hall Veterans' Hospital.

James carefully took the ornaments from her, then walked over to a young man who was standing by the tree. "Here, Stephen," he said, handing him a snowman. "Put it high up. No, not there. Higher. Where we haven't got anything yet."

James then walked over to Charlie, who was sitting on a settee, staring ahead of himself. He placed the second ornament in Charlie's hand, but Charlie made no move to get up and hang it on the tree. James, too little to know what shell shock was, or to feel the tragedy of it in a seventeen-year-old boy, simply got impatient with him. "Come *on*, Charlie!" he said. "You've got to do your share, you know. That's what Granddad always said. He said we've all got to do our share and no shirking." When Charlie still didn't move, James took hold of his free hand and tugged on it until he did. "Go put yours by Stephen's," he said.

"A right little general, isn't he?" Joe said fondly.

Fiona, watching the two cousins, one tall and one so small, nodded and smiled. It was the simplest of actions—putting a Christmas ornament on a tree—and yet seeing Charlie do it made Fiona so happy. He was making progress—slowly, but steadily.

In the months since he'd come back from the front, his shaking had lessened, he'd learned to feed himself again, and he could now help with simple chores. He still had difficulty sleeping, though, and almost never spoke.

They had tried taking him home, Fiona and Joe, back in October, hoping that the sight of his old house might help to bring him out of himself. It had been hard going, though. The younger children had been devastated by the sight of him and day-to-day life with him was arduous. He had difficulty eating and sleeping. He had nightmares. It was hard for him to go up and down stairs. Reluctantly, she and Joe had decided to bring him back to Wickersham Hall, for he did better there. It was quieter and things were done on a schedule. Routine seemed to comfort him.

Fiona and Joe sent to Europe for specialists and brought them to the hospital, one after the other. None of them had helped Charlie at all. During one terrible visit, the doctor, a man from Prague, had decreed that Charlie was hopelessly insane, and said that he could only benefit from something called convulsive therapy—a new treatment he'd invented. A high does of a stimulant drug—the name of which Fiona couldn't even pronounce—would be administered to Charlie. It would induce a grand mal seizure.

"That's a generalized seizure," the doctor said, "one which affects the entire brain. It is my hope that by inducing the seizure, I will re-order the damaged pathways in his brain. Have no fear, Mrs. Bristow. He will be properly restrained. Leather straps and shackles work quite well, with little bruising or chafing to the patient." He'd smiled cheerily, then added, "And even less to the doctor!"

Furious, Fiona had told him to get himself back to Prague and out of her sight. She'd grabbed her unhappy child's hand and dragged him out of the room and off to the hospital's orchard. She sat him down in the grass so he could not hurt himself, then went to pick some pears for the cook. She'd only taken her secateurs with her, not a basket, so she gave the fruit—she'd cut off a lot—to Charlie to hold, forgetting in her anger and sadness that he shook so, he could hold nothing. When she turned around again, he had stopped shaking. Not entirely, but mostly. He was holding one of the pears and looking at it. He lifted it to his nose and inhaled its scent. And then he looked at her, really looked at her, for the first time since he'd come home, and smiled. "Thanks, Mum," he said, quite clearly.

Fiona had nearly shouted with joy. She'd hugged him and kissed him. He'd dropped his head again, looked away, as he always did when people came too close. But he'd made gains since then, talking every now and again, making eye contact. It was a slow awakening, a slow returning to them. But Fiona was convinced that she would have her son back one day.

The very next day, back in London, she turned over the running of her tea businesses to her second in command, Stuart Bryce. She made him chairman, and gave him absolute authority, letting go, in a matter of mere hours, the business she'd taken a lifetime to build.

"Are you sure, Fee?" Joe had asked her, when she told him of her decision.

"I am," she said, without a doubt, without a tear, without a second's hesitation. Her tea empire was important to her; she loved it, but she loved nothing else in the world as much as she loved her children. Her son Charlie needed her desperately, and now so did her little nephew James.

She spent as much time as she could at Wickersham Hall, always taking James with her, and sometimes the twins, too, and staying at the Brambles. Together, she, Charlie, and the children did the work that Wickersham Hall's gardener couldn't manage. They dug and planted and clipped and pruned, preparing the plants and trees for the winter. They planted two hundred crocus bulbs. Three hundred tulips. Five hundred daffodils.

Autumn had come, and with it, a gathering sense that the war would be over soon. The Americans had come into it, fighting on the side of the Allies. Their numbers tipped the balance. The kaiser couldn't hope to hold out much longer. Day by day, Fiona's hopes grew—hopes for a quick end to the fighting, and for the safe and speedy return of her brother, Seamie.

And then came the awful day Joe had arrived at the Brambles

unexpectedly and Fiona knew immediately what had happened. She didn't need to read the telegram he was holding; she could see it in his eyes.

"I'm sorry, Fiona," he said. "I'm so sorry."

Charlie had been the first one to go to her. The first one to put his arms around her. "There, there, Mum," he'd said to her as she sank down in a chair, keening with grief. For herself. And for James, who in the space of mere weeks had lost both of his parents. "There, there," Charlie had crooned to her, just as she had to him when he couldn't eat and couldn't sleep. When the memories were too much for him.

Sid had grieved, too. Deeply. The loss of his brother had hastened his decision to return to America. To a place that contained no memories of Seamie. India had hired another doctor—one who could take over her responsibilities: Dr. Reade. She'd left the hospital in her care, and then she, Sid, and the children had left for Southampton and America. They'd made it safely to New York, and then across the country to California and Point Reyes, the place they loved so much. Fiona missed them terribly, but she understood their wanting to leave.

Seamie's personal effects had arrived from Haifa a few weeks later. She had nothing of him to bury—there were no remains—so she simply put a headstone next to Jennie's, in the Finnegan family plot in a churchyard in Whitechapel, and then she and Charlie planted a yellow rose between the two graves. Yellow for remembrance. She would never forget the brother whom she loved so much. She knew he was with their parents now, and with their baby sister, Eileen, and with his wife, Jennie.

Whenever she went to visit her family's graves, Fiona asked her parents to hug Seamie for her, the poor, restless soul. Happiness wasn't his gift. Once, years ago, it had seemed that he'd found at least some happiness, when he'd found Jennie and they married. But even then, there was still something sad and restless about him. Fiona knew that he'd seen Willa Alden again, at her father's funeral, and she suspected that Seamie had married Jennie even though he'd never got over losing Willa. She understood the pain that came from that. She had very nearly done the same thing herself. A long time ago in New York, when she thought that Joe was lost to her forever, she'd nearly married another man whom she thought she loved—William McClane. Had she done so, she would have lost the chance for true love forever. She could hardly bear to imagine that, to imagine her life without Joe in it, and her heart hurt anew for her brother as she thought how he had missed out on a life with Willa, his own true love.

Fiona glanced at the Christmas tree now. James had at least eight men gathered around it, and Joe, too, and was still handing out ornaments. It seemed to do them good, the patients—having a tree in their midst, records on the gramophone, and cups of mulled cider and hot chocolate to drink. It was the first real Christmas most of them had had in the last four years.

Fiona was glad of the cheer the holiday brought, for the veterans' sakes—and for her family's. Earlier in the month, Joe had won a grueling campaign to retain his Hackney seat. The prime minister had been ousted, but Joe had been returned. In fact, he'd been appointed Labour secretary by David Lloyd George, the new prime minister. Sam Wilson—whom Katie had campaigned so hard for—had won his seat, and Labour as a whole had made many gains. It had been a hard contest, and Joe and Katie were exhausted. It would do them good to rest for a few days.

"Come, James, you take this one and put it on," Fiona said now, lifting another ornament out of the box and handing it to him. "You've got all the lads hanging ornaments, haven't you? It's time you put some on yourself."

"It's an angel, Auntie Fee," James said, admiring the pretty porcelain ornament as he took it from her.

"Yes, it is," Fiona said.

"My mummy's an angel," the little boy said. "My daddy, too. They're in heaven now."

Fiona had to steady her voice before she could reply. "Yes, my darling," she said, "they are."

Fiona watched as James put his angel on the tree. She was thinking that Seamie had been the same age as James when he lost both of his parents. She had raised him. Now she would raise his son.

When James had hung the ornament, he turned to her and said, "I'm hungry, Auntie Fee. Stephen ate all the mince pies." He left the common room, where they'd been working, and took off down the hallway, toward the kitchen.

"James? Come back, will you? Where are you off to now, you little monkey?" Fiona called after him. "To pester Mrs. Culver for another mince pie, no doubt," she said, sighing as she climbed down from the stepladder she was standing on. "Charlie, love, you can put some more ornaments on the tree, if you like. I've got to go after James." Charlie nodded.

Always exploring and roaming, our James, Fiona thought as she hurried down the hall after him. Just like Seamie when he was little. She doubted very much that her brother was in heaven, despite what James had said. Heaven couldn't hold him. He was at the South Pole, or the North Pole, or on top of Everest. She hoped that wherever Seamie was, he was finally at peace.

"There you are!" Fiona said, when she caught up with her nephew. He was sitting at the cook's worktable, next to his cousin Katie, who was laying out next week's edition of the *Battle Cry* and drinking a cup of tea. He was watching the cook roll out pastry for the meat pies she was baking. "I hope you're not bothering Mrs. Culver," Fiona said to him.

"Oh, he's no bother at all," Mrs. Culver said. "He's right good company, aren't you, laddie?"

James nodded. His mouth was full of mince pie. Mrs. Culver had readied two more platters of them for the common room.

"Leave him here, Mrs. Bristow. I don't mind a bit. He can help me roll out the dough."

"Are you sure, Mrs. Culver?"

"Quite."

"All right, then," Fiona said. "I'd very much like to finish with that tree." She touseled James's hair, picked up a platter of mince pies, and turned to leave the kitchen. As she was walking past the windows toward the hallway, she glanced outside and saw an older man, a hard-looking man, walking with one of the patients.

"Who is that? I don't think I've ever seen him here before."

Katie looked up from her paper. She followed Fiona's gaze. "That's Billy Madden," she said. "*The* Billy Madden."

Fiona stared, stunned. "How do you know that, Katie?"

"I spend a lot of time in Limehouse. So does he," Katie said wryly.

"Billy Madden . . . *here?*" Fiona said. "Why?"

She remembered, very well, how Billy Madden had tried to kill her brother Sid.

"He's here to visit his son. His youngest. The lad just arrived last week," Mrs. Culver said.

"Peter Madden," Fiona said. She'd seen his name on the roster of incoming patients last week, but she'd never imagined he was Billy's son.

"Aye, that's him. Billy's two older boys were killed on the Somme, I heard. The one here with us was shot in the head. He has brain damage. Dr. Barnes says there's no hope for him. He'll never be right," Mrs. Culver said.

"I know Peter," James said. "He's new. He's very quiet."

Watching the man, stoop-shouldered and broken-looking, walking past with his silent, shuffling son, Fiona almost felt sorry for him. Almost.

"I've heard such dreadful things about him," Mrs. Culver said, looking out of the window, "but they're hard to credit. I mean, look at him . . . he hardly looks like a fearsome villain, does he? He looks like he's been gutted."

"Who's gutted? Who's a villain?" James asked, looking out of the window, too.

Fiona, her eyes still on Madden, felt a shiver go up her spine.

"Auntie Fee? Who's a villain?" James asked again. "That man out there? Is he Peter's daddy? He doesn't look like a villain. He just looks sad."

"No one's a villain, James," Fiona said. "Eat your mince pie, love," she said, still gazing at Madden.

Madden, who had his son's arm, pointed at something, smiling. Fiona followed the direction of his finger. It was a huge hawk, circling a field.

Mrs. Culver thought Madden a broken man, a changed man, but Fiona wasn't so sure. Men like Madden never really changed. She knew that well enough. The violence never left them. It stayed inside, coiled like a viper.

Fiona suddenly heard a door open and bang shut again, and the next she thing saw was James running across the lawn. Running to Billy Madden. He had something in his hands.

"James!" she shouted, banging the platter of mince pies down and running after him. "James, come back!" she shouted again, once she was outside.

But James was already at Billy Madden's side. He tugged on Madden's jacket. Madden turned around and James handed him something. As Fiona drew closer, she saw it was a mince pie. He gave one to Peter, too.

"Merry Christmas," he said.

Madden, still holding his pie, knelt down to the boy. His face had gone white. As if he'd just seen a ghost. As Fiona watched, he reached out and took hold of James's hand.

"William?" he said. "Son, is it you?"

His voice sounded tortured. His eyes, huge in his pale face, were boring into James. He was scaring him.

"Let go of me," Fiona heard James say, as he tried to break free of his grasp.

Fiona, panting, finally reached them. "Let go of him," she said, her voice low and hard. "Now."

As if suddenly remembering himself, Madden released the boy.

He looked up at Fiona. "I'm . . . I'm sorry, ma'am," he said, sounding confused. "I didn't mean to frighten the lad. Or you. It's just . . . it's just that he gave me a bit of a shock. You see, he looks exactly like my oldest son William did when he was a boy. Spitting image. It's . . . it's downright uncanny." He swallowed hard, then said, "William was killed in France, ma'am. Last year."

"I'm very sorry," Fiona said. "I see you're walking with Peter. We won't disturb you. Come along, James."

James took Fiona's hand and together they walked back to the kitchen. Fiona could feel Madden's eyes on them as they did.

"What was that about, Mum?" Katie asked, as Fiona stepped back inside, shepherding James before her.

"Run along into the common room and check on your cousin for me, will you, love?" Fiona said to James.

"I'm not sure what that was about," Fiona said to Katie when he'd gone. "But I don't want James near that man again. You'll keep him inside, Mrs. Culver? If he comes in here again?" she asked, for suddenly, and quite inexplicably, she was afraid for the boy.

"I will, Mrs. Bristow. But you've nothing to fear from Billy Madden. He's been here three times already, and he's always the perfect gentleman."

Fiona nodded. She picked up the platter of mince pies again. You're being silly, she told herself. And yet, for some reason she could not explain, before she left for the common room she locked the kitchen door.

CHAPTER ONE HUNDRED ONE

"ARE YOU TRYING to be funny, Mr. Simmonds?" Admiral Harris bellowed, from within the confines of his office. The door was open, and Seamie, who was sitting on a bench outside the admiral's office, could hear everything. "Because I'm trying to relocate four warships, three gunboats, eight submarines, and two hundred sailors from the Mediterranean to the Atlantic at the moment and I haven't the time for pranks."

"I assure you sir, I am most definitely not being funny," Mr. Simmonds, the admiral's secretary, said.

Seamie, dressed in an army uniform loaned to him by the men of the unit who'd saved him and his fellow prisoners of war, had approached Mr. Simmonds only moments ago in his office at the Royal Navy's headquarters in Haifa and told him his story.

He listened now as the admiral said, "What I would like to know, Mr. Simmonds, is *how*. How, exactly, did this happen?"

"I don't know, sir. I gather the army had something to do with it. A unit stationed just west of Hama. Though I rather thought it might be best to allow Captain Finnegan to explain the details to you himself."

"Where is he now?"

"Right outside, sir."

"For God's sake, man, bring him in!"

Mr. Simmonds popped his head out of the doorway and motioned for Seamie to join them. Seamie walked into Admiral Harris's office, slowly and stiffly, and snapped him a sharp salute. The admiral stared, then blinked, then returned the salute.

"I'll be damned," he said softly. And then, much louder, "Sit down, lad! Where the devil have you been?"

"It's rather a long story, sir. Before I tell it, I should like you to know that Quartermaster Ellis and Midshipman Benjamin are also alive, if not exactly well, and will be traveling from Hama to Damascus as soon as they are able. Might I ask you, sir, if you have word of any other survivors from the *Exeter*?"

"I'm afraid not. You, and now Ellis and Benjamin, are the only ones I know of."

Seamie nodded sadly. He had hoped, foolishly, that more men had somehow survived. That they'd been missed by the Germans and taken by a British rescue boat, or that they'd washed up on the shores of Cyprus. Something. Anything.

"The *Brighton* received your distress call," the admiral said. "She arrived at Famagusta about an hour after the *Exeter* went down. She searched as best she could. A storm had blown in and the seas had become rough. They could find no survivors and did not know that a German ship had picked any up." The admiral paused, then said, "I imagine you are blaming yourself for what happened. You must not. You had no way of knowing about the U-boat."

"And yet I do blame myself," Seamie said.

The admiral sat back in his chair. "Of course you do, lad. Never had a captain under my command who didn't. The pain of it lessens, though. In time."

Seamie nodded. He didn't believe that. He doubted the admiral believed it himself.

"Deserted the navy for the army have you?" the admiral said, nodding at Seamie's uniform and trying to lighten the mood.

Seamie smiled. As Mr. Simmonds bustled in with a teapot and some biscuits, he told Admiral Harris what had happened aboard the *Exeter*, the injuries he'd sustained, and how he and the other survivors had been picked up by a German ship and handed off to the Turks, who'd thrown them into a terrible prison camp in the desert. He told the admiral how Ellis and the two other men had started out for Damascus, but had mistakenly veered east and ended up at Hama instead. It was an incredible piece of luck that they had, for they'd barely survived the trek to Hama and never would have made Damascus. They'd stumbled to the army barracks there and told the CO about the prison camp. He'd promptly dispatched twenty men on camels, each laden with food, water, and medicine, to the camp. They'd been too late to save some men, but they'd saved many of them.

"Incredible," the admiral said. "Absolutely astonishing. And the burns . . . they're healing?"

"They've begun to. I received good care at Hama, but I still can't move as well as I'd like," Seamie said.

"We'll have a doctor here take a look at them. At the rest of you, too. We'll wire your family to let them know the wonderful news." He paused for a few seconds, then said, "Captain Finnegan . . . Seamus . . . before I do that, I'm afraid I've got some rather bad news for you."

Seamie steeled himself. He'd heard about the terrible influenza epidemic and the havoc it had wreaked back home.

"Not my son," he said. "Please."

The admiral shook his head. "No, it's not your son. I'm afraid it's your wife. Mrs. Finnegan was stricken by the Spanish flu. She passed away last autumn."

Seamie grabbed the front of the admiral's desk to steady himself. He was reeling. He couldn't believe that Jennie had been taken ill, that she was gone. For a few seconds, he panicked, wondering where James was. Then he reminded himself that his family was in London. James would be with Fiona and Joe. He was certain of it. The knowledge helped to calm the panic, but did nothing for the grief he felt. Or the guilt. He'd wanted to be a better husband to her. He'd promised himself that when he got back home, if he got back home, he *would* be better. He'd be the man she truly deserved. But it was too late now. He would never have the chance.

"I'm so sorry, Captain Finnegan. I'm sure you would appreciate a bit of privacy just now. Another officer just left for England two days ago. His rooms have been cleaned and readied for their next occupant. I will have Mr. Simmonds escort you to them. And I will do everything in my power to get you back to London as quickly as possible."

"Thank you, sir," Seamie said softly. "I almost don't want to go. A part of me wishes I could stay here. If it wasn't for my son, I would."

"I think you'd have a good deal of company," the admiral said. "Most every man in this building would like to stay here. Myself included. It's easier, in many ways, than returning home to the graves and the grief. And yet we must do what we must do. Your son has lost his mother. He needs his father now as never before."

The admiral stood. Seamie did, too. "It's time we got you to your rooms now. You've had a terrible shock. You should rest. I'll have proper clothing sent over to you, some food, and a good bottle of wine."

"I appreciate it, sir. Very much," Seamie said.

The admiral put a kind hand on Seamie's shoulder. "It's hard to lose those whom we love, lad. Especially a beloved wife. It's the hardest bloody thing in the world."

Seamie nodded. The admiral's words, so well intentioned, caused him more pain than the man would ever know.

If only I *had* loved her, he thought. If only I had.

CHAPTER ONE HUNDRED TWO

"COME ON, WILLS, let's go," Josie Meadows said, pulling her fox stole around her shoulders. "I'm freezing my arse off. It's bloody cold in here!"

"We can't leave. We just got here," Willa said, opening the back of her camera and pulling out a spent roll of film. "I'm getting good shots."

"And I'm getting nervous," Josie said, looking around herself unhappily.

"They won't hurt you. If anything, they're afraid you're going to hurt them. Have another glass of wine, Jo. Relax," Willa said, holding her camera closer to the candle on top of the tiny table in the corner of the tattered, garish tent in which they were sitting.

It was a gypsy tent. It had been set up in a wild and remote corner of Paris's Bois de Boulogne. Willa had discovered it, and the people to whom it belonged, two weeks ago, as she was walking through the park, photographing prostitutes, vagrants, and other night people.

Willa had fallen for the gypsies instantly. Their hard beauty captivated her. Everything about them begged a photograph—the dark, haunted eyes of an old woman; the glint of an earring against black hair; the flash of a smile, sudden and unexpected and gone so quickly; the way a young man held a battered trumpet in his arms so tenderly, as if he were holding an infant; the wonder in the children's faces when a stranger appeared, the fear in the faces of their elders.

Willa had tried to photograph them right away, but they were shy, superstitious, and wary—always wary—and they would not let her. They were afraid of the police. Afraid of soldiers. Afraid of ordinary people who did not like them and wanted them to move on, and sometimes came armed with clubs in the middle of the night to make sure they did.

Determined to win them over, Willa had visited them every day, bringing small gifts—loaves of bread, a basket of apples, coffee, warm jumpers for the children. She tried to make them see that she meant them no harm, that she would not tell the police about them, not rile up a band of citizens against them. And little by little, they had warmed to her. A few of the men talked with her. One of the women made her a strong cup of coffee. A few of the children asked to see her camera.

And then finally, they had invited her to their tent. It was separate from their caravans—farther into the woods. It was where they sang and danced. One could go there, if one was known to them. One could buy a bottle of wine, a bit of cheese and bread, and listen as they poured out their stories in music and song.

She had told Josie about them, told her that she was going to their tent tonight in the hopes of photographing them. Josie thought it sounded like a grand adventure and had begged to come along.

Now, though, she was jittery. "They scare me," she said.

"I've already told you they won't hurt you," Willa replied impatiently, putting a new roll of film into her camera. It was hard going tonight. The gypsies had allowed her to photograph them, but they were still difficult, still shy about the camera. The light in the tent—from lanterns and candles—was horribly low. Now she had Josie's nerves to contend with, too. "What do you think they're going to do? Kidnap you? Sell you to their king?" she asked her.

"They've got magic. That one over there? With all the knives? He's got the eye."

"What on earth are you talking about?"

"He can see things. He can see right inside a person. I know it. I can always tell when someone has the eye. My mam had the eye. It's nothing to trifle with. Let's go."

"I didn't think *l'Ange de l'Amour,* the woman who shows *le tout Paris* almost everything God gave her every night but Monday, would be afraid of anything, never mind a few gypsies," Willa teased.

"Yes, well, *l'Ange de l'Amour* translates to 'the Angel of Love.' Not 'the Angel of Bloody Stupid Stunts That Will Surely Get Everyone Killed.' "

Willa took a small bottle from the pocket of her trousers. She shook out two white pills and washed them down with a slug of wine.

Josie saw her take the pills. "What are those?" she asked.

"Painkillers."

"Do they work?"

"No."

"Your leg still hurts?" Josie said, concerned.

"My leg's fine," Willa said.

Josie gave her a long look. "The dose you gave yourself in your darkroom, right before we left, that wasn't enough? Oh, don't look so surprised. I know what you do in there. Making pictures is only half of it."

"All the morphine in the world's not enough, Jo," Willa said.

"Bloody right about that," Josie said with a sigh. "Nor all the wine, men, money, jewels, and dresses. Go on, then, Wills. Go take your snaps. What's the death of a chorus girl in the service of great art?"

Willa laughed. She kissed Josie's cheek. Josie was the only one who understood. Even Oscar Carlyle, who'd recently become her lover, didn't.

Morphine didn't stop the pain, it only dulled it. For Willa, there was only one thing that stopped it—taking pictures. When she was behind a camera lens, concentrating on a shot, she forgot everything. Forgot she even existed.

As she advanced the film in her camera, the two musicians—a violinist and a singer—whom she'd been shooting left the small stage they'd been standing on. A girl, young, voluptuous, and scantily clad, took their place. She stood against the stage's wooden backdrop, placed her hands on her hips and her legs wide apart in a V.

As Willa and Josie watched, the man—the one who Josie said had the eye—stepped forward. He had half a dozen daggers in his hand. A boy dropped a basket at his feet that contained even more. Another man, short and sprightly, jumped up on stage and announced that the Amazing Antoine, knife-thrower extraordinaire, would now take the stage. He jokingly advised any in the audience with an aversion to blood to leave now. Then he quickly jumped down.

Willa quickly reached into her pocket. She pulled out a few francs, walked up to Antoine, and offered them to him, hoping the money might persuade him to allow her to photograph him. Antoine looked at the money and then at her. He shook his head, and Willa's heart sank, but then he pointed to her, and the stage.

Willa didn't understand at first, but then, looking into his dark eyes, the eyes that Josie was sure could see inside someone, she did. "All right, then. Yes," she said.

"What?" Josie said loudly. "What's going on? What did he say? Willa . . . you're not . . . you can't be serious. Have you lost your bloody mind?"

Willa held a finger to her lips.

"Don't, Willa! Please!" Josie said. "He's been drinking! I saw him!"

But Willa was already on the stage.

"I'm not watching this," Josie said. "I can't." She covered her face with her hands, then peeked through her fingers.

The man barked at the girl onstage and she quickly left it. Willa took her place. She positioned herself against the back drop, legs in a V, just as the girl had done, but instead of putting her hands on her hips, she raised her camera—a little Kodak Vest Pocket. She'd brought it with her tonight because it was small and unobtrusive, and had a quick shutter speed.

Willa steadied herself now, then gave the man a quick nod. Low, urgent murmurs rippled through the crowd. Willa ignored them. Every fiber of her being was focused on Antoine, waiting for the look or the movement that would signal the first throw. A drumroll was heard. Antoine paced. He spat on the ground. Then he took a deep breath and threw the first knife. It landed with a sharp *thuk* only inches from Willa's right ankle. There was applause, and a few gasps. Willa didn't even hear them. She'd got off a shot, but had she caught the throw? She wound her film forward and readied herself for the next one.

The man started throwing in earnest now. To Willa's left. To her right. Josie was shouting, but Willa couldn't make out her words. People were clapping, yelling, gasping. And the man kept throwing. Faster now. One knife pinned her trousers to the board. Josie screamed. Willa never moved. She never so much as flinched. She just kept clicking and winding as fast as she could, trying to capture the man's face as he took aim, the knife as it came speeding toward her, and the crowd in the background, their faces lit by candlelight and hidden by shadow. She never stopped, never lowered the camera, never lost her nerve. The knives kept coming, traveling up her legs. To her torso. Her shoulders. Her neck. And finally, her head.

"Stop it! Stop it, you'll kill her!" Josie shouted.

The gypsy threw the last of his knives rapid-fire. They made a halo around Willa's head. He paused, then threw his very last one. It landed an inch away from her left ear. He bowed then, to wild applause and ringing bravos, then swept his arm toward Willa. She, too, took a bow, to even louder cheers.

Her cheeks were flushed, her heart was pounding. She was certain she'd got something on film. Maybe even something amazing. Everyone was excited and happy. Everyone, that is, except Josie, who was flushed and furious.

Josie stood up, now that it was over, walked to the knife-thrower, and gave him what for.

Her harangue lasted a good two minutes and made both the knife-thrower and the audience laugh. Willa tried to get down and go to her friend but found she was pinned in more than one place. The knife-thrower's girl assistant came to her aid, pulling two knives out of the cloth of her trousers.

Willa jumped down off the stage. She trotted over to Josie just in time to see her poke a dainty, gloved finger into the knife-thrower's chest and angrily say, "That was a very stupid thing to do! You could've killed her!"

And just in time to see the gypsy smile and say, "No. Never. How can I kill what is already dead?"

CHAPTER ONE HUNDRED THREE

"CAPTAIN FINNEGAN! CAPTAIN Finnegan, over here, please!" the photographer shouted.

Seamie, walking to the door of his sister and brother-in-law's house, turned around. A dozen flashes went off, nearly blinding him.

"Captain Finnegan! How does it feel to be home?"

"Wonderful, thank you," Seamie said, dazed. "I'm very happy to be back in London."

Seamie had not expected this. He had expected an uneventful ride to Mayfair and a quiet arrival, but reporters and photographers had swarmed him the second he'd stepped out of the carriage. He'd quickly forded his way through them and made his way up the steps. He was about to knock on the door when it suddenly opened.

Joe was there, in his wheelchair. "Come inside, lad. Hurry. Before the piranhas eat you alive."

Seamie did as he was told, grateful to be out of the scrum of shouting, jostling men. Questions, shouted loudly, followed him.

"Captain Finnegan! Tell us about the attack on your ship!"

"Captain Finnegan! When did you find out your wife died?"

"Captain Finnegan! Is it true you married an Arabian girl?"

"That's all for today, lads," Joe shouted. "Captain Finnegan's very weary from his long voyage."

"Mr. Bristow! When did you learn that your brother-in-law was alive?"

"Has Captain Finnegan seen his son yet?"

"What was Mrs. Bristow's reaction?"

"Diabolical, that lot," Joe said as he wheeled himself back inside the house and slammed the door behind him.

In the foyer, Fiona, weeping, had already thrown her arms around her brother.

"We thought you were dead, Seamie. I can't believe you've come back to us," she said through her tears.

"It's all right, Fee. It's all right . . . ," Seamie said, holding her tightly. Admiral Harris had telegraphed Fiona and Joe back in January. It was nearly the end of March now. The doctors in Damascus hadn't wanted him to travel until his burns had healed further. That had taken a month. And then the boat had taken another six weeks to get to England. The separation had been hard on them all.

When Fiona could bear to let go of him, Peter hugged him. Then Katie, and the twins. Everyone was there to greet him but Rose and James.

"How is James?" Seamie asked, when they finally released him.

"He's a little nervous," Fiona said.

"I would think so," Seamie said.

James was bound to be nervous, if not downright frightened. He had recently lost his mother. And his father—or so he'd been told. But now his father—a man he didn't even know very well—was coming back into his life. Seamie had only seen James a handful of times, when he was just a baby. He doubted very much that James, who was four now, remembered any of them. He knew he would be a stranger to the boy.

"Does he want to see me?" Seamie asked.

"Yes, he does. He's upstairs with Rose right now. I thought it might be better to bring him down after we'd all calmed ourselves a bit. Me especially. We've told him all about you. He's quite impressed. He wants to hear all about the *Exeter*. And how you survived the attack. Shall I get him?"

"Yes," Seamie said.

Fiona sent a maid upstairs to fetch Rose, then suggested everyone follow her into the parlor. When they'd all sat down, Rose came in, holding hands with a little boy.

Seamie's heart melted at the sight of his son. Seamie had teased Jennie that he was the milkman's son, for he had nothing of the

Finnegans in him. He was fair-haired, with hazel eyes, like his mother. And, like her, he was beautiful.

James left Rose and went to stand by Fiona.

"Is he really my daddy, Auntie Fee?" Seamie heard him whisper.

"He really is, James," Fiona said. "Would you like to say hello?"

James nodded. He approached Seamie shyly and manfully offered him his hand. Seamie could see James was being very brave, and his son's courage touched him. He took the small hand in his and shook it.

"Hello, James," he said.

"Hello, sir," James said. He looked Seamie over uncertainly, then added, "My uncle Joe is a member of Parliament."

"Is he now? Then I shall have to be very careful how I tread around here," Seamie said.

"Are you a bloody Tory?" James asked cautiously. "The bloody Tories make him very angry."

Fiona gave Joe a look. "I told you not to bellow so! I told you the children could hear you!" she whispered scoldingly. Joe looked at the ceiling.

"I see," Seamie said, biting back his laughter. "Well, I'm a Labour man myself, so I don't think I'll have any trouble there."

"Have you come to take me away?" James asked suddenly, plaintively.

Seamie could see the worry in his eyes. The poor little blighter, he thought. He's been through so much.

"No, James," he said gently. "In fact, I was wondering if you would let me stay here for a bit. With you and your aunt Fiona and your uncle Joe. I'd like very much to stay. But only if you want me to."

James's little face brightened. He turned to Fiona. "Can he, Auntie Fee? Can he stay with us?"

"He certainly can," Fiona said. "We'll make up a bed for him."

James smiled. "I got a train set for Christmas," he said to Seamie. "Would you like to see it?"

"I would like that very much," Seamie said.

"Come on, then," James said, offering Seamie his hand.

Seamie took it. He followed James. For the first time in months, ever since the *Exeter* had gone down, he felt glad.

Glad he'd survived.

Glad to be home.

Glad for the one thing he'd managed to do right in his life. Glad for little James.

CHAPTER ONE HUNDRED FOUR

WILLA STRETCHED LANGUIDLY in her bed, then sat up. It was three A.M. She would get up soon. Make some prints. She was wide awake and full of energy. Making love had always had that effect on her.

She looked over at Oscar Carlyle, her handsome American lover. He was lying sprawled out on his back in a tangle of sheets, eyes closed.

Lover, she thought now, as she turned away from him and gazed at the night sky out of her huge windows. What a strange word for what he is to me.

Willa didn't love Oscar, or any of the men she'd been with since she came to Paris. She wished she did. She wished she could.

"I love you, Willa."

She'd only ever loved one man, and she knew, deep inside, that she would give her body now and again, but she would never, ever give her heart. She could not. It was gone. She had given it to Seamie, and Seamie was dead.

"I love you, Willa."

Grief filled her—thick, black, and choking. She couldn't bear that he was gone. She didn't know how to go on in a world that didn't have him in it. In her head and in her heart, she still talked to him. Still marveled at sunsets with him. Told him about her work. Shared her wishes to return to Everest one day. And in her head and her heart, she heard him answer her. How could he be gone?

Willa felt a hand on her back. She jumped, startled. "Where are you, Willa? Where'd you go?" Oscar said.

Willa turned to him and smiled. "Nowhere. I'm right here."

"I said I love you. Fifteen times."

Willa leaned over. She kissed his mouth. And said nothing in return.

"I'm starving," Oscar said. "You have any food in this joint?"

"Some chocolate, I think. And oranges," Willa said.

Oscar got out of bed. He was young—only twenty-seven. He had a glorious body, all bronzed, rippling muscle. They'd gone out on the town, more than three months ago, after she'd photographed him for *Life*, and had had a good time. That same night, they'd ended up in bed. He was kind and smart and funny. He was something warm to reach for in the middle of the night. He would have to return to his home in Rome in a fortnight. She would miss him when he left.

He grabbed a silk kimono of hers now and shrugged into it.

"You look very fetching, Madame Butterfly," she said.

He picked up a magazine and held it in front of his face, like a fan, then walked daintily across the room like a geisha, to fetch the bowl of oranges, which made her laugh.

He put the oranges on the bed. He found half a bar of chocolate, wrapped in silver foil, and another bottle of wine—they'd already emptied one—and brought them to her, too.

"It's cold in here!" he said, belting the kimono around himself. He padded over to the small iron stove, on the far side of the room near the windows, opened its door, and tossed in a few lumps of coal. As he was making his way back to the bed, he stopped suddenly, to look at a row of prints spread out on a long worktable.

He was silent for a few minutes as he looked at them. Picking some up. Shaking his head. Saying, "Damn, Willa."

Willa knew what he was looking at it—it was a series she'd taken two days ago, at a brothel. The photographs portrayed the prostitutes during the day, when they were off-duty. It showed them washing their sheets, their underthings. It showed them cooking, eating, and laughing. Taking care of their children. It showed them as human beings.

"These are astonishing," Oscar said quietly. "Totally amazing. The critics are going to go nuts."

"Good nuts or bad nuts?" Willa asked, smiling at his Brooklyn voice.

"Both," he said, getting back in bed. "You're fearless, Willa. But it's not because you're brave. It's because you don't give a damn what happens to you. You don't care if the tarts beat you up, or the gypsies, or the cops, or the critics." He looked at the oranges and frowned, then took a big bite of the chocolate. "You got anything else to eat here?"

"I don't think so."

"No wonder you're so thin," he said, breaking off a piece of chocolate and popping it into her mouth. "Come to my place tonight. I'll make you steak frites."

"That sounds delicious. I think I will," she said.

As Oscar poured them both more wine, Willa reached over to her night table, for the bottle of pills that was there. She tried to take two, discreetly, to help her cope with the sorrow she was still feeling over her memories of Seamie. Oscar saw her, though, and said, "More pills? Again?"

"I need them. For the pain," she said.

"What pain? Where?" he asked her.

"My leg," she said.

Oscar shook his head. "No," he said. "The pain's not there." He slid his hand under her breast, pressing his palm against her heart. "It's here," he said.

Willa looked away. She didn't want to talk about it.

Gently, tenderly, Oscar took her chin in his hand and turned her face to his. "Look at me, Willa. Why are you so sad, huh? Always so sad? Thin and sad." He took her arm, stretched it out, kissed the inner bend of her elbow. "Why do your arms look like pincushions? Why do you gobble all those pills?"

"Oscar, don't . . . ," Willa said.

"Because you lost someone? In the war? Yeah, I know. I've seen the picture you took of him. The one on your wall. But hey, here's some news: Everybody lost someone." He went quiet for a bit, then he said, "But you found me and I found you, and that should count for something. It could, too, if you would let it."

Oscar popped the last piece of chocolate into his mouth, then he took the silver foil that had covered it and twisted it into the shape of a ring, complete with a knobby diamond. He took Willa's hand in his, slipped the ring onto her finger, and said, "Marry me, Willa."

"Stop it, you fool."

"I'm dead serious. Never been more serious. Marry me."

Willa shook her head.

"Come on, Willa. Be my wife. I'll get you out of this dump. Take you back to Rome with me. Get you a nice house somewhere pretty. One with radiators. You can have a garden. And a kitchen. I'll buy you an apron. And a set of china . . ."

Willa burst out laughing.

". . . and a vacuum cleaner, too." Oscar's voice dropped. "I'm serious. We can have kids. And toast in the morning. And dinners at night. Real ones. Just like normal people."

"That sounds nice, Oscar. It really does," Willa says softly. The thought that he cared enough to want these things for her, these good and real things, touched her deeply.

"It *is* nice. It will be. Do it. Leave your ghost in the graveyard where he belongs and do it, Willa."

Willa knew he was a good man. A talented musician. And as handsome as a god. Most women would have killed to have a man like that propose to them.

"Come on, Willa. Marry me," he said, pulling her close. "I love you like mad. Whaddya say? I'm throwing you a lifeline here. Don't be a jerk. Take it."

Maybe he was right and she was wrong. Maybe there was a

chance for her. For them. Nothing she'd done had ever been able to make her forget Seamie, but then again, she'd never done anything this mad or this foolish. Maybe she could be happy married. In a house. With a vacuum cleaner. Maybe she could. At the very least, she owed him for that. For caring enough to try.

"All right, then, Oscar," she said. "Why not? Yes. I'll marry you."

CHAPTER ONE HUNDRED FIVE

"EXCUSE ME, PRIME MINISTER," said Amanda Downes, David Lloyd George's secretary, "but you and the cabinet are due downstairs now for photographs with the German trade commission."

Lloyd George, who'd replaced Asquith in the general election, and who was in the midst of haranguing his chancellor of the exchequer, Andrew Bonar Law, over the government's proposed budget, paused. "Thank you, Amanda," he said. He turned to his minister of trade, Archibald Graham. "Remind me, Archie, why we are going along to this dog and pony show. This was your idea, wasn't it? What's it all about?"

"Reestablishing trade with Germany. Lifting embargoes. Making loans. Abolishing tariffs," Graham said.

"Business as usual," Joe Bristow said, with a note of bitterness in his voice.

"Precisely. They want our tea. We want their motorcycles," Graham said.

"But none of it can happen until we put that slight incident behind us," Joe said.

Graham raised an eyebrow. "Slight incident?" he said.

"The war."

"I wouldn't have put it exactly like that," Graham said, "but yes, that is correct."

Lloyd George sighed. He stood up and picked his cravat up off his desk, where he'd tossed it earlier. "I suppose there will be press?" he asked, tying the cravat around his neck.

"Quite a bit from what I understand," Graham said. He, and the ten other men seated around the large mahogany table in Lloyd George's office, also rose. All but Joe, who pushed his wheelchair away from the table.

"The kaiser starts a war, kills millions, then he wants to sell us motorcycles," he said, disgustedly. "I want no part of this."

"What we want to do and what we must do are two separate things," Graham said patronizingly. "In politics we must sometimes make deals and compromises. You've been in the House a long time. You know that well enough. This particular compromise is for the greater good."

Joe cocked an eyebrow. "Is it?" he said.

"It will create trade. And trade creates jobs. Which the men who have fought for this country, and have returned home to it, desperately need. We treat with the enemy to secure our advantage."

Lloyd George sighed deeply. "You're right, of course, Archie."

"I usually am, sir," Graham said. "Now, gentlemen, if we can please present a united front to the press on this issue. Smiles and warm words would be helpful."

Joe, who had wheeled himself to the doorway, now turned his chair around, blocking everyone else's way out. "A united front?" he said, shaking his head regretfully. "I don't know, Archie. I have to tell you that this is going to be a very hard sell in East London," he said.

"Ah. Now we come to the heart of the matter. I'm surprised it took you so long," Graham said archly.

"I'm going to need something I can take to my constituents."

"Have you any ideas on what that something might be?"

"As a matter of fact, I do."

"I somehow thought you would."

"I'll want three new factories. One in my constituency, Hackney.

One in Whitechapel and one in Limehouse. If Gerry wants to sell us motorcycles, he can bloody well build them in East London." He paused, then said, "In politics, Archie, we must sometimes make deals and compromises. You've been in the House a long time. You know that well enough."

Graham crossed his arms over his chest. "Two factories," he said at length. "Put them wherever the hell you like."

"Done," Joe said, flashing the man a wide smile.

"If you gentlemen are finished?" the prime minister said.

"We are," Joe replied, wheeling himself out of the way so that Lloyd George could pass him.

The prime minister led the way from his office, down a series of corridors, to the foyer of Number 10 Downing Street, his ministers following in his wake. There, Lloyd George stiffly shook hands with the head of the German trade commission—Wilhelm von Berg—as his ministers mingled with the delegates. The conversation was cool. Both sides were coming together because they had to, not because they wished to.

Joe made small talk with a coal baron from the Ruhr Valley, an economist from Berlin, and a manufacturer of farm equipment. The atmosphere was stiff and uncomfortable, and Joe found himself actually wishing to be outside, in the bear garden of journalists and photographers that awaited.

"Congratulations on your reelection, Mr. Bristow," a voice behind him said, in impeccable, polished English. Joe turned. A tall, blond man stood nearby. As Joe looked at him, he realized he knew him. His hair was shorter than the last time Joe had seen him, and there was a vicious scar running down the left side of his face, but even so, he had not changed greatly over the last four years.

"Max von Brandt," the man said. "We met before the war. At Holloway prison. You invited me to your home. For your brother-in-law's wedding."

"Yes," Joe said coldly. "Yes, I did."

"I'm pleased to see you again," Max added, "this time in my role as delegate to the trade commission."

A terrible anger rose inside Joe at the sight of von Brandt. With great effort, he forced himself to contain it. He was conducting the people of Britain's business here, not his own. He had words for von Brandt, but they would have to wait. He forced himself to listen, politely and attentively, while Max, and two more men who'd joined him, greeted him and congratulated him.

"Gentlemen, this way if you will . . . ," Joe heard Archie Graham say.

They were all shepherded outside, in front of the prime minister's residence. Hordes of reporters, jostling behind a cordon, started peppering them with questions.

"Rather reminds one of standing in front of a firing squad," Graham, who was standing next to Joe, said.

"I think the firing squad would go easy on us compared to this lot," Joe replied.

It was announced that the prime minister, his cabinet, and their German guests would stand for pictures first and then take questions. Joe looked out over the sea of press and saw his daughter in the scrum. She had her notebook out and was scribbling in it furiously. She had a photographer with her. Joe frowned at her. She was no longer on her term holidays. She should have been up at university and must have skipped classes to come to London. Fiona would certainly be unhappy if she knew, and there would be a row. Joe was proud of Katie for her devotion to journalism, but that paper of hers could sometimes cause a good deal of trouble, too.

After three or four minutes of picture-taking, the questions started. Reporters were shouting, interrupting, demanding answers. An irate Fleet Street wanted to know why the government was holding trade talks with Britain's erstwhile enemy.

Graham spoke first, telling them how renewed trade ties would help strengthen Britain's economy. The prime minister followed, urging for magnanimity in victory, and then it was the Germans' turn. Max von Brandt, their spokesman, stepped forward. He carefully and cogently outlined his commission's plans, detailing benefits for both Britain and Germany. He talked for about ten minutes, then finished by saying, "We will, of course, explain our plans more fully during our meetings with our British counterparts here in London over the next few weeks, but we appreciate being able to outline our ideas for you here. Fleet Street has been ill-disposed toward us, and understandably so, but I wish to assure you that it is my sincere hope, and the hope of the German people—now that the hostilities between us have ended—that we can work together for peace and prosperity, and for the benefit of both our nations. Good day, gentlemen."

Throughout Max's speech, Joe sat in his chair smiling woodenly and all the while raging inside. Von Brandt's presence was a cruel taunt to him. It was unbelievable that this man who had caused so much damage to his family, and to countless others, could stand here, smiling and talking about better days to come, as if nothing had ever happened. Joe's rage boiled up inside him and he could not contain it.

After a few more minutes of questions, the prime minister gave the members of the press a wave good-bye and headed back inside Number 10.

"Mr. von Brandt," Joe said, as German and British statesmen followed him. "Might I have a moment?"

Max stopped. He turned around, a questioning expression on his face.

"In here, please," Joe said, gesturing toward a receiving room off the foyer.

Max followed Joe. Once they were both inside the room, Joe closed the door. "Berlin should have sent someone else. Anyone but you," he said.

"I'm sorry to hear you feel that way, Mr. Bristow. I hope my work has not been lacking in some way?"

"I know who you are. And what you are. Maud Selwyn Jones died at your hands, didn't she? Why? Because she saw something she shouldn't have? Gladys Bigelow killed herself because you were blackmailing her. Jennie Finnegan went to her grave tortured over the fact that she'd helped you, a German spy. Her husband was very nearly killed by the information your network passed to Berlin. But I guess all's fair in love and war, isn't it?" Joe said.

Max shook his head. He gave Joe a puzzled smile. "I'm afraid I have no idea what you're talking about, Mr. Bristow," he said. "But before you destroy a man's reputation by accusing him of espionage and murder, you'd better have proof. A good deal of it. British libel laws, from what I understand, are highly punitive."

Max was right, of course. Joe had nothing concrete with which to hang him. He believed Jennie Finnegan's and John Harris's stories, but others would not. And he remembered, too, what had happened with Jack Flynn when they'd tried to bring him in for spying.

"You heartless bastard," Joe said. "I'd nail your head to the floor if I could only get out of this chair."

"How lucky for me, then, that you cannot," Max said. The smile was gone. His blue eyes were cold and hard. "A bit of advice, if I may: Things are not always what they seem, Mr. Bristow, especially when it comes to politics. The war is over. The entire world has accepted that. I urge you to do the same. Good day."

Max smiled icily, then left the room, slamming the door behind him. Joe stared after him, knowing he couldn't touch Max. Knowing he had only theories and hearsay, no proof. Knowing a treacherous and deadly man once again walked the streets of London and that he had no way to stop him. If only he did. If only there was some way, some one, some thing, *anything*, that could show the world what Max von Brandt was.

"Damn you," Joe said aloud. He picked up a glass paperweight and hurled it at the door. It shattered into a million useless pieces.

CHAPTER ONE HUNDRED SIX

WILLA LAY SPRAWLED out on her bed, tangled in her sheets, dreaming. She had fallen into a deep, narcotic sleep. A length of rubber tubing lay on the floor next to the bed, along with a syringe. A thin trickle of blood dripped from the inside of her right elbow.

She dreamed that she was standing on a platform at a train station, all alone. It was late and dark. A cold wind howled. It was a dangerous place. She knew she had to get out of there, but she didn't know how. There were no exit signs, no doors or stairs, no way out.

She couldn't quite remember how she'd got here. The pain had been very bad tonight—she remembered that. She'd been walking by the Seine earlier in the evening. She'd gone to buy wine, bread, and cheese. She'd seen a man walking toward her. He was handsome and tall and had red hair, and for the merest of seconds, her heart had leapt and she though it was him: Seamie. But of course it wasn't. Seamie was dead.

She'd felt so heartbroken afterward, so crushingly alone. The pain of knowing that she'd never see his face again had been agonizing. She'd rushed back to her flat, thrown her food down on the table, tied the tourniquet around her arm, and shot herself full of morphine. Nothing could save her. Not her work. Not Oscar. He was a good man, but she didn't love him. Couldn't love him. Something in her had died when Seamie died—her heart. She wanted the rest of her to die now, too.

The train pulled in, billowing steam. She was so glad. The wind had grown colder, the darkness more menacing. She desperately wanted to get on board. Faces, gray and expressionless, looked at her from the windows, but she wasn't scared of them. Seamie will be on this train, she thought. I know he will. More than anything, she wanted to see his face again, to hear his voice, to touch him. She climbed the steps from the platform to the train, turned into the car itself, and started to walk down the aisle, looking around expectantly for Seamie, but she could not find him. She walked into the next car, and the next. "Where is he?" she said aloud. "Where?" She was running now. Calling his name. But he was not there.

"Willa!"

She stopped and turned around. Was that him? It must be. But where was he?

"Seamie!" she called out. "Seamie, where are you?"

"Willa. Come on, Willa, sit up. . . ."

She felt pain, sudden and sharp. Someone was slapping her face. Hurting her. Again and again.

"Stop it!" she cried. "Let me go!"

"You're conscious. Oh, thank God. Willa, open your eyes."

She tried. But it was so hard.

Hands pulled her into a sitting position. A glass was pressed to her lips. The voice urged her to drink. Willa did so, then forced her eyes open. Josie was leaning over her. She looked terrified. And well dressed.

"You look so nice. Going out?" Willa mumbled.

"That was the idea," Josie said tightly. "We were going to meet you for dinner. Oscar and me. Remember? How much did you take?"

"Not enough, apparently," Willa said.

"Come on. Get up," Josie barked. "You're going to drink some coffee and walk this off."

As Josie tried to get her out of bed, another voice was heard—a man's. It was coming from the doorway. "Damn it, Willa," he said. It was Oscar. He looked heartsick.

"I'm sorry," Willa whispered.

"How could you do it?" he asked her.

"Oh, Oscar," she said brokenly. "How could I not?"

CHAPTER ONE HUNDRED SEVEN

BILLY MADDEN PICKED up his glass of whiskey—his fifth in the last hour—and downed it. On the table in front of him—next to the bottle—was a photograph of his three sons. It had been taken right before they'd shipped off to France. All three were in uniform.

"I still can't believe it, Bennie," he said. "William and Tommy dead. And Peter in hospital and a right fucking mess. He can't talk. He can barely walk. All he can do is shake—so fucking hard that he can't hold a spoon, or a pen, or his own fucking cock. The nurses have to do everything for him."

Bennie Deen, one of Billy's heavies, was sitting across from him at a table in the Bark. He was reading a newspaper. It was four o'clock. The pub was quiet. Only a few other men were in it. Bennie lowered his paper now and said, "You've got him in a good place, guv. The best place. He'll get better there. Didn't that doctor—Barnes, was it?—say that they're making strides with some of the worst of the lot?"

"Better? What's better? Maybe one day he'll be able to walk by himself. Or eat by himself. But he's never getting out of there. He'll die in that place. He'll never have a life, a woman, kids, nothing. He might as well be dead, too."

Billy poured himself another whiskey. "It's hardest on me wife," he said. "She don't do nothing anymore. She won't talk. Won't eat. She just sits in the kitchen, looking out the window. Like she was waiting for them all to come home."

"Can't she have no more?"

"No more what?"

"Kids."

"No, you stupid git, she can't. She's old. Forty, forty-one . . . I don't know. And even if she could, kids aren't hats, you know. You lose one, you can't just fucking replace him. For Christ's sake, go back to reading the funny pages, will you?"

At that moment, the door to the Barkentine opened and a young, well-dressed woman came inside. She was carrying a stack of newspapers.

"Is Mr. Madden about?" she asked the bartender. The man was just saying no, when she spotted Billy seated in his usual spot by the windows. "Ah! There he is. Thank you so much!" she said to the barman.

"Mr. Madden, might I join you for a moment?" she asked, as she approached his table. "My name is Katie Bristow. I'm the editor and publisher of the *Battle Cry,* and I work for Sam Wilson, your local member of Parliament."

"I don't care who you are, lass, you're not welcome here," Billy said. "This ain't a pub for ladies."

"Mr. Madden, Sam Wilson has a matter of great importance that he wishes to discuss with you," Katie said.

"Then why doesn't he come here himself?" Madden growled.

Katie frowned. She looked down at the floor, then back up at Billy. "Just between us, Mr. Madden . . . I think he's afraid," she said. "It's not everyone who'll come down to this part of Limehouse."

"Oh, aye? And why aren't you afraid, you cheeky little snip?"

"Because I've seen you with your son Peter. At Wickersham Hall. At Christmastime. You ate mince pies and didn't seem terribly fearsome."

Billy sat back in his chair, dumbfounded that this girl knew about Peter and, moreover, that she had the stones to talk to him so plainly.

"My brother Charlie is a resident of Wickersham Hall, you see," Katie explained. "He came back from France with severe shell shock. Members of my family founded the hospital. My parents contribute to its upkeep. I go there as much as I can. It's difficult though, what with my classes, and the paper, and my work for Mr. Wilson. I was there in December, though, and I saw you both—you and Peter."

"What do want?" Madden said gruffly. He didn't like talking about his son with strangers.

"The government is in talks with the Germans about siting two motorcycle factories in London. One possible site is in Limehouse, but there is competition. Other MPs are against us. They want the factories situated in their own constituencies. Sam Wilson is going to hold a rally next Saturday in support of the factory. He wants you to come."

Bennie burst into laughter. "Maybe you can carry the banner, Boss. Hand out badges."

Madden laughed, too. "You must be joking. You want *me* to come to a rally . . . for the Gerries? The same people who started the war that killed two of my sons and damaged the third one?"

"It is not a rally for the Gerries," Katie said. "It is a rally calling on government to site a German factory here in Limehouse instead of somewhere else. Because the people of Limehouse desperately need work, Mr. Madden. It is one of the poorest areas of London, of the entire United Kingdom. Life expectancy rates here are among the lowest in the country, and everything else—infant mortality, unemployment, crime, malnutrition—are extremely high. You are a powerful figure in Limehouse, Mr. Madden . . ."

"Too right!" Bennie chimed in.

". . . and if people see you come out for it, they will come out for it, and we need numbers if we are to convince government to put the factory here."

Madden was getting tired of this girl and her tedious speeches. "You've got the wrong man," he said. "Rallies ain't in my line of work."

But Katie was not to be deterred. "I know what your line of work is. Must it always be? I saw you with your son, Mr. Madden," she said quietly. "You were kind and concerned. You were—"

Billy Madden had had enough. Talk of his son made him feel helpless, and feeling helpless made him furious.

"My son is none of your bloody business. Get out. Now," he said, his voice rising.

Katie blinked, but did not falter. "Can I leave a copy of my newspaper with you? It has a story on the factory. Maybe you could take a look at it sometime."

Billy was barely keeping his temper under control now. "If I say yes, will you fuck off out of here?" he asked.

"Right away," Katie replied.

"Yes, then. Leave your bloody paper. If nothing else, the pictures will keep Bennie here amused."

"Good-bye, Mr. Madden, and thank you," Katie said, as she placed a copy of the *Battle Cry* on top of his table.

Madden, staring out at the river, made no reply.

"The fucking cheek," he said when she was gone. "Wilson can take his bloody factory and stuff it up his arse. I'll never have anything to do with it or with the bloody Gerries." He pointed at Katie's paper. "Take that rag and burn it," he said to Bennie. Then he poured himself another drink and continued to stare at the river, remembering Peter as he once was.

Bennie reached for the *Battle Cry*. As he lumbered over to the fireplace with it, he read the cover article. There were photographs to go along with the story, photos of the prime minister and his cabinet and the German trade commission. He stopped short, staring at one of the pictures.

"Oi, guv," he said, walking over to Madden. "Take a look at this. . . . Isn't this the bloke who used to come here? The one who hired a boat from you to take his man out to the North Sea? Name's different, but I could swear it's him."

"What are you on about now?" Madden said.

Bennie put the paper on the table in front of him. "There," he said, pointing at a picture. 'Maximilian von Brandt, Spokesman for the German Trade Delegation,' it says. See him? Second from the left."

Billy squinted at the photograph. The whiskey had made his mind foggy. "You're right. It is him. Without a doubt," he said at length. "Peter Stiles he called himself. Says here his name is von Brandt, though. Well, whatever it is, the son of a bitch cost me a good boatman.

John Harris disappeared right after the busies took his man Flynn. If I ever see Harris again, I'll gut him for walking out on me."

Billy kept reading and as he did, the whiskey fog lifted. "Bennie, listen to this. It says here that von Brandt was an officer in the German Army during the war and was pals with the kaiser, and that he's now a high-ranking government man and that the new guv'nor, Friedrich Ebert, handpicked him to come over to London and make nice."

"Yeah? So?"

"So? *So?*" Billy said angrily. "So he lied to us! He came here to the Bark sounding as English as me grandmother. Made out like he was one of us. But that wasn't true. He was *German,* Bennie. An officer in Gerry's army. Pals with the kaiser . . . it says so right here!"

"So?"

"So, I'll bet you my right ball that it wasn't jewelry his man was taking to the North Sea!"

"You . . . you don't think he was a spy, guv?" Bennie said slowly.

"No, you daft bastard, I *know* he was a spy!" Billy said. He shook his head in disbelief. "All that time, Bennie . . . all that time I thought he was a villain moving some swag. But he wasn't. And me, Bennie? What was I doing? I was helping Max von bloody Brandt feed secrets to the Gerries. I was helping a dirty spy. Fuck me! No . . . fuck *him*!"

Billy stood up, grabbed the whiskey bottle, and threw it across the room. It nearly hit the barman and it shattered the mirror behind him.

"Easy, guv," Bennie said.

But it was too late. The table Billy had been sitting at went over. Then every table in the room did. Pictures were smashed. Windows, too. Chairs were thrown against the wall. Billy was screaming and cursing, out of his mind. He only stopped his mad rampage when there was nothing left to break.

"I bet it was him who did for my boys," he said then, wild-eyed and panting. "I bet it was him who gave the Gerries all the information they needed. It's his fault, Bennie. It's Max von Brandt's fault William and Tommy are dead and Peter's off his nut."

"You've got to calm down, guv. This is no good."

"Oh, I'll calm down all right, Bennie. Just long enough to find von Brandt."

"Billy, be reasonable," Bennie said. "Von Brandt's a government man. He spends his days with the likes of the prime minister. We couldn't even get close to him."

"Oh, but I am being reasonable," Billy said, his eyes blazing with rage. "In fact, I've reasoned it all out very nicely. I'm going to make his father grieve the way I'm grieving. I'm going to make the man know what it feels like to lose a son."

"You don't mean that. We can't just—"

"We can, Bennie," Billy said. "And we will. There's got to be a way. Whatever it is, I'll find it, and when I do, Max von Brandt is a dead man."

CHAPTER ONE HUNDRED EIGHT

MAX VON BRANDT poured himself a cup of strong coffee and sat down at the desk in his hotel suite. It was only half past three, but he was already exhausted. The day, full of meetings at Westminster and interviews with the London dailies, had been a grueling one.

He was due at the chancellor's house for supper tonight—an event which would likely go quite late, and before that, he had a dozen telephone calls to make and a thick stack of reports to read through. He was just reaching for the telephone when he heard a knock on his hotel room door.

"Telegram for Mr. von Brandt," a man's voice called.

"One moment, please," Max called back.

He rose, quickly crossed the room, and opened the door. Before he could even shout, the two men were on him. The first man, a broad-shouldered giant, drove his fist into Max's face, knocking him to the floor.

The second man quickly closed the door and locked it. "Get him in the chair, Bennie," the first man said. "Over there. Tie him."

Max, dazed from the blow and bleeding from the gash it had left on his jaw, felt himself being lifted up and dragged backward. He tried to reach into his pocket, to get hold of the knife that was there, but before he could, he was dumped into a chair and a length of rope was wound around him, pinning his arms tightly against his body.

"Well done, lad," the second man said. "He won't be going anywhere soon. Will you, Mr. Stiles?"

Max, who'd been straining against his bonds, looked up just in time to see Billy's fist come flying toward him. The blow opened up another gash—this one across his cheekbone. His head snapped back. Blood sprayed across the wall behind him in an arc.

When the pain had subsided a bit, when he could see properly, and speak, he said, "Hello, Billy. What a pleasure it is to see you again."

"Shut your mouth, you bastard. You cunt. You filthy spy."

"Billy, I don't—"

"Shut your mouth!" Billy screamed.

He pulled a pistol out of his coat pocket and pointed it at Max.

"You killed them," he said. "You killed my boys William and Tommy. You put Peter in hospital for the rest of his life."

Max realized he was in very great danger. Billy Madden had never been entirely right; now he seemed to have gone completely insane. His eyes were dark and mad and full of rage. Flecks of spit flew from his lips as he spoke. He was sweating and shaking.

"Billy, let me talk, listen to me. . . . I did not hurt your sons. I swear it."

"Listen to him, will you, Bennie? Listen to his lies. You *did* kill them," Madden shouted. "I saw you, von Brandt. I saw your picture in the paper. The German guv'nor himself sent you here to make nice with the prime minister. How stupid do you think I am? You're not Peter Stiles. You're not English. And that wasn't swag you were sending to the North Sea. You and that murdering bastard of a kaiser were thick as thieves. You stole information here, you and your men, and you gave it to Germany. You told the kaiser where my boys would be and he dropped his shells on them. You killed them sure as I'm standing here, and now I'm going to kill you."

Madden raised the gun again, and Max knew he had seconds, only seconds, to save his own life.

"It would be a terrible mistake to kill me, Billy," he said.

"I don't think so," Madden replied. He walked over to Max and pressed the pistol's barrel against his head.

"You have another son."

"The fuck I do," Madden said, cocking the trigger.

"Josie Meadows," Max said. "She was pregnant when she gave you the slip, wasn't she? Pregnant with your child. Put the gun down, Billy, and I'll tell you where she is."

CHAPTER ONE HUNDRED NINE

"DADDY?" JAMES SAID.

Seamie smiled. He loved the sound of that word on his son's lips. If he lived to be a hundred, he would never tire of hearing it.

"Yes, James?"

"Tell me about Lawrence again. And Auda and Faisal. Tell me about the desert."

Seamie, sitting on an old, squashy settee by the fireplace in the Binsey cottage, said, "Isn't it past your bedtime, lad?"

"Just one more story. Please, Daddy?"

Seamie smiled. He would happily have told him twenty stories.

"Did you wash your face?"

"Yes."

"Clean your teeth?"

"Yes."

"Come on then, come sit by me," Seamie said, patting the cushion next to him.

James, in his pajamas and clutching Wellie, his teddy bear, bounded onto the settee.

They'd come up to Jennie's old cottage, which belonged to Seamie now, to spend a week together, just the two of them. They'd got to know each other at Fiona and Joe's house over the last few weeks. James had been reticent at first, but had gradually warmed to Seamie and had even started to call him Daddy on his own. When Seamie asked him if he might like to visit the cottage in Binsey and do a little winter rambling around the Cotswolds, James had immediately said, "Would I! Let's go!"

Seamie had taken James into an outfitters on Jermyn Street and made a big production of getting him kitted out with a pair of hiking boots, gaiters, a small walking stick, a waterproof, mittens, and a good warm hat. They'd arrived at the cottage three days ago and had been having a wonderful time cooking for themselves, walking, having pub lunches, talking, and sitting by the fire. Seamie hoped to eventually be able to go on proper treks and climbs with James, but his injuries were still not fully healed.

"If you could have seen Lawrence in the desert just one time," Seamie began now, "you would want that one time to be right as he set off to take Damascus."

"Why, Daddy?"

"Listen and I'll tell you," Seamie said. "Lawrence was about to wage the biggest campaign of his life, a campaign that would affect the fate of nations, and of all the people living in them. He was going to try to take a desert city heavily fortified by Turkish forces. If he succeeded, he would deal a lethal blow to England's enemies, and he would accomplish nothing less than the liberation of all of Arabia. . . ."

Seamie went on to describe for a wide-eyed, spellbound James the scene in Lawrence's camp right before the march to Damascus. He told him about the yelling and bawling camels, the thousands of fearsome Bedouin fighters. He told him about Lawrence, riding at the head of the Arab irregulars with Faisal and Auda. He painted a picture for the boy of the sight the three men made in their robes, rifles slung over their backs—the regal Faisal; the warrior Auda, with his sharp features and piercing hawk's eyes; and Lawrence in his white robes, at once so English, with his blue eyes and easy smile, and yet a son of Arabia, too, belonging, at that moment, entirely to the desert and its people.

Seamie told James how it had taken hours and hours for all the soldiers to leave. How the dust clouds had risen in their wake, how they looked as if a sea of men was marching to Damascus.

And then James said, "But, Daddy, what were you doing there?"

"Where? At the camp?"

"In the desert. You're a sea captain, aren't you? There are no oceans in the desert."

"Right you are, James. Well observed."

James smiled proudly.

"I had been hunting for a friend in the desert. This friend had fought very hard on behalf of Major Lawrence, had been captured by the Turkish Army, but had escaped."

"Did you find him?"

"Her, actually. Yes, I did. And I took her back to Lawrence's camp."

"Her?" James said, wrinkling his nose. "You had a girl for a friend?"

Seamie laughed. "I did."

His voice was wistful now, his expression sad. He wondered what had become of Willa. He had not seen or heard from her since he'd left her with Fatima at Lawrence's camp. His ship had been attacked only days after he'd said good-bye to her. Albie, who was back in Cambridge, and whom he'd written to, said she was in Paris. He had no current address for her, though. He'd tried to fetch her home once, but it hadn't gone well, and they hadn't corresponded since.

He gave Seamie the last address he had for her, but she must've moved because his letter to her had been returned to him unopened. He wondered if she'd heard he was dead, wherever she was, and if she'd now heard the opposite. He would go to Paris soon. As soon as he and James were a little more settled. Not just yet, though. He'd just come back into the boy's life and felt he must not leave him again so soon.

"She must've been a very good friend for you to hunt for her all over the desert."

"She was a good friend. Even though she was a girl," Seamie said conspiratorially.

"Mummy was a girl," James said. "Did you love your friend like Mummy?"

Seamie faltered for a second, as all the old pain flooded back. He thought about the mistakes he'd made and the betrayals. He thought about the sorrow, the regret, the guilt, and the loss. How in the world could he ever explain that to anyone, never mind a small boy?

"You know what, lad?" he finally said. "That's a story for another day. Off you go now. It's late. Time for bed."

"All right," James said. He kissed Seamie's cheek. "I love you, Daddy."

Seamie was stunned. It was the first time James had said that. He leaned his head against his son's and quietly said, "I love you, too, James."

They sat close beside each other, father and son, staring at the fire. Seamie forgot all about bedtime. He forgot the painful thoughts he'd just been thinking, the painful emotions he'd just felt.

For the first time in a long time, he didn't think of the past. And of all the things he'd lost. He thought only of the present, and what he had. And how it was so much more than he deserved. And he prayed then that he would never, ever lose it.

CHAPTER ONE HUNDRED TEN

"IT'S A LIE," Billy Madden said. "You're making the whole thing up to save your hide."

"It's no lie. Untie me and I'll tell you more," Max said, hoping to convince Billy of the truth. Hoping to save his life.

"Maybe I'll just beat the shite out of you instead. That's another way of getting you to tell me more."

"I hope you're feeling strong. Or, rather, that your gorilla here is. I can take a beating, Billy. In my line of work, it's an essential skill. Go too far with the fists, though, and you might kill me. That would be unfortunate. Because I'm one of only two people who knows that you have a son. Josie also knows where the boy is. But you have no idea where she is, do you? Kill me, and you'll never find out."

Madden stared at Max thoughtfully, then said, "Untie him, Bennie."

As soon as the ropes had been removed, Max stood. "He leaves, first," he said, pointing at Bennie, "and then you unload the pistol and give me the bullets."

Madden did as Max asked.

When Bennie was on his way to the hotel's lobby, and the bullets were safely in Max's pocket, Max looked at Madden and said, "Listen carefully, I'm only going to say this once. And then you're going to leave."

Madden nodded.

"She's in Paris. I've kept tabs on her. She's an actress. She goes by the name of Josephine Lavallier. She performs at Bobino's in Montparnasse. She hid from you back in 1914, had the child—a boy—and gave him away. Then she left England for the continent."

"Gave him away? To who? Is he here in London? Is he at an orphanage?"

"She gave him to a woman. The woman died. The boy is still well. He lives with the woman's husband—a man whom he knows as his father."

"What woman? Stop playing silly buggers and tell me the husband's name!"

"Sorry, Billy, but I'm afraid that's not possible. That bit of information buys me a bit of time. It's my insurance policy against another afternoon like this one. As long as I know where your son is, you can't kill me."

"I'll still kill you, von Brandt. I'll just wait until I find that bitch of a Josie and get the name of the ones she gave my boy to. Then I'll nip right back and do for you. Nab you some night when you least expect it."

"I don't think so. By the time you get to Paris and find Josie and then get back to London again, I'll be back in Berlin. I'd advise you not to come after me there. I have many friends in that city."

Without another word, Billy Madden left, slamming the door behind him. Max locked it after him. He walked back to the sitting area, picked the rope up off the floor, and put it in his briefcase. He would dispose of it later. He got a facecloth from the bathroom, wetted it, and rubbed his blood off the wall.

Next he went into the bathroom and attended to his face. He would tell Lloyd George, Bonar Law, and the others at the dinner tonight that he'd got into a scuffle on the street with a man who'd lost his son in France and wanted to take it out on a German, any German. It wasn't so far from the truth.

After he'd cleaned himself up, Max poured himself a whiskey to steady his nerves. He'd very nearly had a bullet put through his head. As he downed the contents of the glass, he thought it would be a good idea to kill Billy Madden. Right away. Tonight. But he knew that was impossible. Madden always had at least one of his men around him, if not more. Max was too visible now to move around London freely, and even if he could put together some sort of disguise, how would he get the time to go after Madden? His evenings were full of parties and dinners. He was supposed to be acting the part of the civilized diplomat now, not making shadowy visits to East London, as he used to do.

He would have to let it go. There was no other choice. He felt a momentary ripple of unease over having told Madden about Josie, and about possibly endangering both Josie and her son. In his current state, Madden was probably insane enough to actually go to Paris.

What would Madden do if he found Josie there? Max wondered. He'd probably question her about the child. Probably rough her up a bit. She might tell him where the boy was and she might not, but even if she did, was Billy Madden crazy enough to try to take a child from the likes of Seamus Finnegan? The man was a war hero. He'd survived the best efforts of the German Navy. He'd kill anyone who tried to take his son, and even if Billy did get hold of the boy, once the story made the newspapers, the entire country would be looking for him.

No, Max decided, Billy Madden was currently unhinged because of grief over his sons. Once he calmed down a bit, he would see the lunacy of the whole thing and let it go. Of course he would.

Max finished his drink and tried to put the whole incident out of his mind. He had things other than some East End madman to worry about. He'd managed to accomplish none of the things he ought to have done. No telephone calls had been made, no reports had been read. And he now would need to bathe and dress if he had any hope of getting to his dinner on time.

And after his dinner, he had one more meeting to attend. A very private meeting. Back here, in his rooms. Quite late.

Max von Brandt had been put in charge of the trade and finance delegation for a reason, and it wasn't because he was all gemütlich with the German president, no matter what the papers might say. It was because he had other business in London, for which the delegation was merely a convenient cover. He had something far more important to achieve than selling motorcycles.

He had a chain to mend.

CHAPTER ONE HUNDRED ELEVEN

"*BONJOUR*, WILLA!" THE baker's wife called out, as Willa entered her shop.

"*Bonjour*, Adelaide. *Ça va?*" Willa called back.

"*Oui, ça va! Et toi?*"

"*Je suis bien, merci, mais j'ai faim. Un croissant, s'il vous plaît, à aussi une baguette.*"

As the baker's wife assembled Willa's order, she told Willa that she was too thin and would never get a man because what man wanted to embrace a woman who looked like a garden rake? She said she was going to give Willa two croissants, not one, and that she must promise to eat them both.

Willa forced a smile and said she would. She paid for her purchases and slowly walked back to her flat. There was no reason to hurry. No one was waiting for her there. When she got to her rooms, she put her croissants and the milk she'd bought on her table, then heated a pot of water for coffee. She hung up her coat and then, still cold, shrugged into the woolly cardigan that Oscar had left hanging on a hook by the door. It was soft and warm, and of a good quality. I should really give it back to him, she thought. I will. If I ever see him again.

Oscar had decided that a nice house with a set of china and a vacuum cleaner in it was not the answer to Willa's problems—and neither was he. They had parted company a few days after her overdose and he'd returned to Rome. Willa didn't blame him. She wasn't angry with him. She didn't want to live with herself. Why should he?

The water boiled. Willa ground some coffee beans, put them in her press, and poured the water over them. She poured some creamy milk into a bowl, added some coffee, then carried the bowl to the table. Morning sunshine was streaming in the windows. She turned her chair so its heat warmed her back. Then put her head in her hands and wept.

It was like this every day now. Sadness had overwhelmed her; it had nearly immobilized her. She could barely eat or sleep and didn't work at all anymore. She wished that Josie and Oscar hadn't found her. She wished she had died the night she'd overdosed. She would have been with Seamie, then, instead of always being without him.

She pushed her breakfast aside and grabbed the bottle of pills on her table. She'd run out of injectable morphine. The pills weren't as strong, but they were all she had left.

As she swallowed three, she heard a knock on her door. "Who is it?" she called out.

"It's your aunt Edwina! Let me in!"

"Aunt Eddie?" Willa said, in disbelief. She hurried to the door and opened it. Her aunt stood there in a traveling coat and hat, a valise in her hand.

"Oh, dear," she said in a dismayed voice, her eyes traveling over Willa. "That man was right. You do look a wreck. May I come in?"

"Of course, Aunt Eddie," Willa said, taking her aunt's valise. "What man? What did he say? Why are you here?"

"What a lovely greeting," Eddie sniffed. "And after I've come all this way."

"I'm sorry, Eddie," Willa said, hugging her aunt. "I'm glad you've come, of course I am. I'm just confused, that's all. About this man you mentioned."

"Some man wrote to Albie," Eddie explained, as she took her coat off and laid it over a chair. "Said he got Albie's address from a stack of old letters he found in your flat. He said you were in an awfully bad way and that he—Albie—should come and collect you. Since Albie already tried that once—with no luck—I decided to come. I'm here to bring you home, Willa."

"Wait a minute, Aunt Eddie . . . what's the man's name?" Willa asked, still puzzled.

"Oscar Something-or-Other. I can't remember. He said he knew you and cared for you but couldn't seem to do anything for you. He didn't think you should be alone. Is that coffee I smell?"

"Yes, it is," Willa said. "Let me get you some." So Oscar was behind this. He'd written to her family out of concern for her. That he would do that, after what she'd done, touched her so deeply she felt like crying again.

"Willa, I came because of Oscar's letter, because I was worried about you, but there's also another reason for my visit," Eddie said.

Willa, who'd been stirring milk into her aunt's coffee, turned around, alarmed.

"Don't look so worried. Your mother and brother are both fine. I have some news for you. It's good news, but rather shocking. I think you should sit down. Come," she said, patting the empty space next to her on the settee.

Willa sat. She handed her aunt a hot cup of coffee. "I must say that this is all very strange, Aunt Eddie. What news? What is it? Couldn't you have just written instead of making the trip all the way from Cambridge to Paris?" she asked her.

Eddie didn't reply. She leaned over to her valise, drew a newspaper out of it, and handed it to Willa. Willa saw that it was a copy of the London *Times* and that it was several weeks out of date.

"Read it," Eddie said.

The headlines talked of the transfer of Alsace from Germany to France, of reconstruction projects in the Marne area, and of the Belgian king's visit to Paris. Willa quickly scanned the articles, sipping her coffee as she did. "What is it I'm supposed to be looking for?" she asked.

Then she saw the photograph at the bottom right of the page, and the coffee bowl slipped out of her hand, bounced off the table, and smashed on the floor. Willa didn't hear it smash. She didn't see the mess on the floor. All she saw was Seamie's face.

"My God, Eddie . . . it can't be," she whispered. But it was.

BRITISH SEA CAPTAIN RETURNS FROM THE DEAD, the headline said. "Seamus Finnegan, captain of the *Exeter*," the caption read.

Willa touched the image with trembling fingers. She started to read the article and learned what had really happened to Seamie after his ship had been attacked. She started to laugh, then burst into tears, and then laughed again. She kept reading and learned that he'd arrived in London a month ago and planned to stay with his sister and her husband. At their home, he would be reunited with his young son, James, who'd been staying with his relatives. Willa was stricken to find out that the reason the boy was not with his mother was because he had lost her to influenza. Captain Finnegan had told the press that he would eventually be relocating with his son to a family cottage in the Cotswolds.

"I can't believe it. I simply cannot believe it," Willa said. "He's alive, Eddie."

"I know. Wonderful, isn't it? I wanted you to hear it from me. I hoped I would reach Paris before any of the London papers did. Oscar said you were in such a fragile state, I wasn't sure how you'd react."

Willa stood up, elated. She was crying again, but this time her tears were tears of joy. Seamie was alive. He was in this world still, not the next.

"Do you know where Seamie is in the Cotswolds?" Eddie asked.

"The paper said he was moving to a family cottage. I think it's in Binsey. He mentioned a cottage in Binsey once. It belonged to his wife. Perhaps you can go see him there. After we return home," Eddie said.

The smile on Willa's face faded. She shook her head. "No, Aunt Eddie, I can't," she said.

"Why not?"

Willa was silent for a moment, then she said, "Because back in the desert, after Seamie found me and brought me back to Lawrence's camp, I told him we had to let go of one another. To stop hurting ourselves and the people around us. It's not good, what we had. Or what we did. Before the war." She looked down at her hands. "Perhaps you don't know about that. Or perhaps you do."

Eddie nodded. "I didn't. I do now."

"Yes, well," Willa continued, "it's a hard, destructive thing to love someone you shouldn't, and it's caused nothing but grief."

"His wife's passed away, Willa," Eddie said gently. "He's a widower now."

"So what should I do, Aunt Eddie?" Willa said bitterly. "Run to him like some she-vulture? I won't. Too many mistakes were made, too many sins committed. Jennie deserved better. Albie did. Seamie himself did. No, I'm staying here. We ended it for a reason, and that reason remains—we're no good for each other. We weren't in Africa. We weren't in London back in 1914. And we wouldn't be now, either. I know that." Eddie let out a long, heavy sigh. Willa took her aunt's hands in hers and said, "I appreciate you coming here. I know you did it out of concern for me and I love you for it, Aunt Eddie, but I can't go back. I can't. It's far too painful."

Eddie nodded. "I understand, Willa. God knows what I'll tell your mother, but I do understand."

Willa kissed her. "Thank you. You won't go back right away, will you? Stay with me for a bit."

"Yes, I think I shall stay," Eddie said. "I quite fancy a bit of a holiday and some good French food." She frowned, then said, "Your hands are trembling, Willa, I can feel them. You were already in a state when I arrived and I fear I've made things worse."

Willa shook her head. "You've done no such thing. I'm happy, so deeply happy, to know he's alive," she said. "He is my heart, and my soul, and to know that he didn't die, that he . . ." Her voice trailed off as tears threatened to overtake her again. She struggled to gain control over her emotions, and when she had, she said, "I believe I'm in need of some air, a walk, something."

"That sounds like a good idea. A walk will clear your head. I'll help myself to more coffee while you're gone, and when you get back, perhaps you can show me around Montparnasse," Eddie said.

Willa kissed her aunt again then she grabbed her coat and got down the stairs from her flat to the street as fast as she could, forgetting her scarf, forgetting her hat, forgetting everything but the amazing, impossible news that Seamus Finnegan was alive.

CHAPTER ONE HUNDRED TWELVE

"JOSIE!" WILLA SHOUTED, knocking on the door to her friend's flat. "Jo, it's me, Willa! Open up, will you?"

She'd been knocking for a whole minute already, but Josie had not answered. Willa knew she was there. There was no way she would have left the flat this early. Not Josie. She usually slept until noon.

Willa wanted to see her. Josie was her closest friend and she wanted to tell her about Seamie. She wanted to have a good long talk. And a good long cry, too.

"Come on, Josie, you lazy wench! Wake up and open the door!" Willa shouted, banging on the door again.

But still there was no answer. "That's odd," Willa said. She tried the doorknob; it turned in her hand. That was odd, too. She pushed the door open. "Jo?" she called again, uncertainly.

It was dark inside the foyer. Willa's eyes took a few minutes to adjust. As soon as they did, and as soon as Willa walked into the flat proper, she saw that something was terribly wrong. The place looked as if it had been upended. Pictures were off the wall. Vases and statues lay on the floor in pieces. The draperies had been shredded. Cushions had been torn apart. The fine silk upholstery on Josie's furniture had been cut open. Stuffing spilled out of chairs and settees.

"Josie?" she called out, suddenly afraid. She heard a sound, like a moan, coming from the bedroom and hurried toward it.

The sight that greeted her as she entered the room made her scream.

Josie lay on her bed. Her face had been battered so badly that she was nearly unrecognizable. Blood had dripped down the front of her dress and all over her bedding.

"Josie . . . my God . . . ," Willa cried, running to her friend.

Josie reached for her. "I didn't tell, Willa," she sobbed. "I didn't tell him."

"Tell who? Who did this to you?" Willa said, taking her bloodied hand. She knelt down on the floor. "No, don't speak. Don't move. Don't do anything. I'm going to run for help."

"No!" Josie moaned.

"You need a doctor!" Willa said.

"There's no time. Listen, Willa, please. . . . I have a son," Josie said, with effort.

"What?"

"A little boy. Back in England. James. I used to go round with a villain . . . Billy Madden. He put me up the spout, then wanted me to get rid of it. I couldn't. I had the baby. Gave it to my friend Jennie. She used to be my teacher. She'd lost her baby. Her husband didn't love her and she thought he would, if she could give him a child, but she couldn't. She'd had an accident. I left London and hid in her cottage. In the Cotwolds. . . ." Josie stopped speaking for a minute. She closed her eyes, breathing heavily.

Willa felt her whole body go cold. Seamie's late wife's name was Jennie. She'd had a cottage in the Cotswolds. Their son's name was James. James was four years old. No, she thought, it can't be. It's a coincidence, that's all.

Josie opened her blackened, swollen eyes again. Willa could see the pain in them.

"Josie, don't talk," she said. "Save your strength. Let me go for a doctor. *Please.*"

"There's no time," Josie said. She gave a small groan, stiffening against something that hurt her terribly. "I told the doctor who delivered my baby that I was Jennie, so the right names would be on the birth certificate," she said. "I gave James to Jennie the day after he was born and then I left for Paris. Jennie lied to her husband . . . she pretended to be pregnant, then told him she'd had the baby herself. I asked her would she write me now and again . . . send me a picture . . . oh, God . . ." Josie's words became a whimper of pain.

"Josie, please . . . you must let me go for help."

Josie shook her head. "Somebody told Billy about the child, and now Billy wants him. He's gone mad, Willa. I thought he would kill me. He said he lost his sons in the war and now he's going to take James. He tried to get Jennie's name from me, and her husband's, but I wouldn't give them to him . . . I wouldn't . . . so he did this to me. He's going back to England. He's going to find James somehow and take him," Josie sobbed. Tears leaked out of her eyes. "Don't let him, Willa. Don't let him take James. . . ."

"Shh, Josie, shh . . ."

"I hid the letters," she said, hysterical now. "The ones Jennie sent me. Billy pulled the place apart, but he didn't find them. They're in my jewelry box. Take them. They have Jennie's address on them. Tell her what happened. There's money in there, too. Take it, Willa. Go to her. Warn her. Hurry."

"Where, Josie? Where's the jewelry box?" Willa said. She would find it. That would calm Josie down.

"In the sitting room."

Willa ran into the other room and searched through the wreckage for Josie's jewelry box. She found it near the window, but it was empty. The jewels it had contained had been dumped onto the floor. There were no letters inside it, no money, nothing.

"Damn it!" Willa hissed. "Where are they?" She knelt down again and start ripping the box apart. She ripped out the lining, tore out the drawers and shelves, but still she found nothing. She raised the box over her head and slammed it against the floor. Once, twice. On the third time the bottom splintered. Willa pulled the pieces apart, and there they were—a stack of letters, neatly tied with a ribbon, and a small leather pouch containing franc notes and pound notes, rolled up together.

Willa pulled a letter out of the stack and turned it over, dreading what she might find. "Oh, no. Oh, God," she said. The return address was in London. Willa recognized it. It used to be Seamie's. She recognized the name above it, too: Finnegan. J. Finnegan. Jennie had died, and Josie hadn't known it. And Jennie had been married to Seamie. And her son . . . James . . . he was the boy Billy Madden was after. And Seamie had no idea about any of this.

"Did you find them?" Josie asked weakly when Willa returned to her bedroom.

"I did," Willa said, putting the letters and the money on Josie's night table.

"You've got to tell her. Promise me!" Josie said fiercely.

Willa couldn't bear to tell Josie that her friend was dead. "I promise you, Jo. I swear. I'll do something . . . ring her . . . or . . . or send a telegram. Soon. Very soon. But right now, I'm going to see to you."

There was a lot of blood on Josie's clothing, and in the bed. Too much blood.

"What am I going to do? What the hell am I going to do?" Willa whispered to herself. An image flashed in her mind—of her pill bottle. She'd taken three morphine pills. No wonder she couldn't think straight. "Come on, Willa, shake it off," she told herself. "You've got to think!"

Two seconds later, she was out on the landing, battering on the neighbor's door. A man answered it. She quickly told him that her friend had been attacked and that she was badly injured and needed a doctor. The man said a doctor lived on the top floor of the building and then ran upstairs to fetch him. A few minutes later, the doctor was at Josie's side. Her attacker had split a vein in her chin, he told Willa, that's where most of the blood was coming from. He said he would cauterize it and then stitch up the worst of the wounds on Josie's face.

"She's going to be all right," he told Willa. "She might've bled to death if I hadn't got here when I did, though."

As the doctor set to work on Josie, Willa raced back into Josie's sitting room. The telephone was on the floor. Willa prayed that it still worked. She set the base upright and put the receiver in its cradle. After waiting for a few seconds, she picked the receiver up again and dialed for the operator. Almost instantly, she heard a woman's voice. She asked to be put through to the address on the envelope. No luck. Service to that address had been terminated, the operator informed her. She asked to be connected to the home of Miss Edwina Alden, at Highgate House, Carlton Way, Cambridge.

After a few minutes, a male voice, crackly and faraway-sounding, said, "Highgate House. Hello?"

"Albie?" Willa shouted. "Oh, thank God!"

There was a pause, then "Willa? Is that you?"

"Yes, it's me. Albie, I need your help. You've got to get hold of Seamie. His son, James, is in terrible danger. He's not really his son. The boy was given to Jennie by another woman—Josie Meadows. His real father is Billy Madden, a villain. From London. He's coming after the boy, Albie. He's just been here in Paris and he's beaten Josie very badly—"

"Willa," Albie said, cutting her off.

"Albie, don't talk. Just listen to me."

"No, I'm not listening. Not anymore. You're obviously off your head, Willa. And we both know why."

"Albie, I'm *not* off my head. This is real. You've got to call Seamie and tell him. Now!"

"Aunt Eddie's supposed to be there with you. Is she? Put her on the phone."

"I can't. She's at my flat. I'm at my friend's flat. Albie, you've got to listen to me." Willa's voice was shaking badly. She tried to keep it steady, but she couldn't.

"This is pathetic," Albie said. "I can't bear to listen to you. Don't ring me again, Willa. Not in this state. Not until you've quit the drugs."

"Albie, no! Wait! Don't hang up!"

"Just answer me this: Did you take anything today?"

She did not want to answer him. "Yes, but Albie, I—" she finally said.

"I thought so." There was a loud click and then a dull, dead tone.

"He thinks I'm a raving lunatic. Because of the morphine," Willa said out loud.

Of course he did. When he'd come to Paris to fetch her home, he'd been able to tell just by looking at her that she was addicted. And now she'd called him out of the blue with this outlandish story.

She started to panic. If she couldn't get hold of Seamie, and if Albie wouldn't help her, who would?

"Think, Willa, think," she told herself. She got an operator again and asked to be connected to Westminster, hoping to talk with Joe Bristow. This time it was the operator who hung up on her.

Willa was frantic, then she remembered the cottage—at Binsey. In the newspaper article, Seamie had said he was going to relocate to a family cottage in the Cotswolds. It had to be the Binsey place. It just had to be. A few seconds later, she was on the line again, asking the operator to see if she could connect her with a Seamus Finnegan in Binsey, but again she had no luck. The woman said she had no such listing.

"Is there *anything* in Binsey with a telephone in it?" Willa asked. "A church, a shop, a pub, anything?"

The operator said there was an inn and then put her through.

"The King's Head. May I help you?" a woman's voice said.

"Hello. Yes," Willa said. "I was wondering if you know of a Captain Seamus Finnegan?"

There was a slight pause, then "Is this another reporter? I've told you lot time and again—leave that poor man alone!" the woman said angrily.

"I'm not a reporter. I'm a friend of Captain Finnegan's," Willa said.

"Pull the other one. It's got bells on," the woman said. And then she, too, hung up.

Willa stood in the silence of Josie's flat, the phone in her hand. She didn't know who else to ring for help. She didn't know how to get hold of Seamie, to warn him. All she knew was that Billy Madden was on his way back to England. On his way to find James Finnegan.

And he would stop at nothing to get him. The battered woman in the other room was proof of that.

And suddenly, Willa knew exactly what to do.

She ran into Josie's bedroom and knelt down by the bed. "I'm sorry, Jo. I'm so sorry for what happened to you. And I'm sorry to leave you like this, but I have to go now. Back to England. I'm going to find Seamie—James's father—and tell him what's happened. I'm going to make sure Billy Madden is stopped. I promise you."

"Take the money, Willa. Get on a ferry. Hurry."

"I will, Josie. And I won't leave you alone. My aunt Eddie just arrived. She was supposed to fetch me home with her. I'm going to send her over. She'll take care of you."

Willa leaned over her poor friend and kissed her forehead. Then she stood up, grabbed the bundle of letters and the wad of bills from the night table where she'd put them, and shoved them into her trouser pocket.

"Good-bye, Jo," she said, then she left Josie's flat, let herself out of the building, and broke into a shambling run.

CHAPTER ONE HUNDRED THIRTEEN

"I CAN'T BELIEVE this," Willa said. "I can't bloody believe this!"

She had traveled all the way from Paris to Calais, and then Calais to Dover in just under twenty-four hours. She'd taken a hackney from the ferry terminal to the train station, yelling at the man to driver faster the whole way, only to discover that she'd missed the Dover to London train by six minutes. Six bloody minutes! And the next one was not for another five hours.

She didn't have five hours to waste twiddling her thumbs here.

Seamie and James didn't have five hours. God only knew where Billy Madden was. Fear chattered at her, telling her he could be back in London by now, looking for them. She clamped down on it, reminding herself—as she'd done ever since she'd left Josie's flat—that Josie had *not* given Madden Jennie's name. Or Seamie's. Without those names, he couldn't track James down. Without those names, there was still time. But then she remembered that someone had told Madden that Josie had a son—did that someone also know where the boy was now?

There had to be another way to get to London, and to Paddington Station, where she could get a train to the Cotswolds. Perhaps there was a bus going there, perhaps she could hire another hackney to at least take her partway. As she walked out of the train station, looking around, trying to figure out what that other way might be, she spotted a delivery boy on a motorbike with a wooden crate strapped to the back. He'd just dropped off a bundle of papers at a newsagents and was about to motor off again.

"Wait!" she shouted. "Don't go!"

The boy turned. She started running toward him, waving. He gave her a quizzical look and pointed at himself.

"Yes, you!" she shouted. "How much for the motorbike?" she asked breathlessly, when she reached him.

"Depends where you want me to go. For local deliveries, I charge by the mile. For trips to Canterbury, or any of the outlying towns, I charge a flat rate."

"I don't want to hire the bike. I want to buy it. How much?"

"It's not for sale, miss. It's me livelihood, that bike."

"I'll give you twenty pounds," Willa said, digging in her satchel for her wallet.

The boy's eyes narrowed. "You're not a fugitive, are you?"

"No. I have a very great emergency, though." Willa found her wallet, opened it, and pulled out a twenty-pound note. "Will you sell me the bike or not?"

The boy nodded. "Have you driven one of these before?" he asked her.

Willa told him that she had. She'd done so in Cairo countless times.

"Tank's half-full," the boy said, taking off his goggles and handing them to her. "You should buy petrol at Broughton's—it's on the west edge of town. You'll pass it on the way out. There's a petrol station another twenty-five miles down the road, but it's closed as often as it's open.

"Thank you," Willa said.

She put her satchel in the crate, started the engine, and put the bike into gear. She found the petrol station a few minutes later and asked the proprietor to fill the tank. As she waited, she walked around in the brisk air and stamped her feet, trying to wake herself up. Trying to shake off the nausea and headache that were plaguing her. She'd had no morphine for more than twenty-four hours and was feeling the symptoms of withdrawal. She'd tried to sleep on the ferry, hoping that would help to take the edge off, but it hadn't. If anything, it made things worse. Every time she closed her eyes, she saw Josie's battered face.

Willa had run straight home from Josie's flat. She'd told her aunt Eddie what had happened. Not much could shock her aunt, but that did. When Willa asked her if she would take care of Josie, Eddie jumped off the settee, put her coat on, and asked for the address. She was just heading out the door when Willa grabbed her arm.

"Aunt Eddie, after you see to Josie, will you please ring up Albie and tell him what's happened?" she asked her. "There's a telephone in Josie's flat. I rang him. I tried to tell him, but he wouldn't listen to me. He's thinks I'm mad. He'll listen to you."

"I'll ring him as soon as I get your friend seen to. Hurry, Willa. Go," she said.

Willa had quickly put a warm jumper on, a sturdy pair of boots, and a thick coat. Then she'd put Josie's money and letters into her satchel. She'd closed the door to her flat, run down the stairs, and headed for the train station, where she'd managed to get a ticket on a 4:30 P.M. train to Calais. When she arrived, she found that the next boat to Dover was full, so she'd booked a passage on the night ferry. It was early morning now, about eight o'clock.

When she'd first got back to her own flat, she'd thought about going to the police and telling them what had happened to Josie, and that the same man who'd beaten her was now trying to kidnap a child. But then she thought, What if they don't believe me? Worse yet, what if they do? They'll insist I come into the station with them. They'll ask me a thousand questions. Their first job will be to investigate what happened to Josie, not to protect a child in England. I'll be sitting in the station house, reconstructing the crime scene for them, and Madden'll be halfway across the channel.

Going to the Paris police would have done no one any good—not James and not Josie. What she needed to do was to warn Seamie that Billy Madden wanted his son. Since she had failed to get Albie to do that, or Joe Bristow, or the publican at Binsey, she would have to do it herself.

"You're all set, miss," the petrol man said. "You'll have to fill her up again just as you're nearing London."

He gave her the name of a town with a good petrol station and a good pub, in case she fancied a break from the road and a nice hot meal. Willa thanked him. She pulled her goggles down over her eyes, kick-started the bike's engine, and flew out of Dover.

As the town fell away behind her, she decided she would try Albie again when she stopped—if the pub the petrol man mentioned had a telephone. Maybe Eddie would've gotten through to him by then. And maybe this time she—Willa—could convince him to drive down to Oxford, find Seamie and James, and get them out of harm's way.

Just in case she was wrong. Just in case Billy Madden was a lot closer to Binsey than she thought.

CHAPTER ONE HUNDRED FOURTEEN

ALBIE ALDEN HEARD the telephone ringing all the way from the garage. He lifted his marketing out of the car and made a run for it. The weather was filthy; he got soaked through running the few yards between the garage and the back door.

"Yes? Yes? Speak up, please, I'm hard of hearing!" he heard as he entered the kitchen. It was Mrs. Lapham, a cleaning woman his aunt Eddie insisted they have in twice a week. "Will? Will who?" she yelled.

Albie winced. It was Willa. It had to be. He set his basket down on the table and walked over to where the telephone stood on a small round table.

"I'll take it now, Mrs. Lapham. Thank you!" he bellowed.

Mrs. Lapham jumped. "Oh, Albie, dear! Gave me a right good startle, you did! There's someone on the blower," she said.

"Yes, I gathered," Albie shouted.

Mrs. Lapham handed him the telephone and went back to her cleaning. Albie held the receiver to his chest, waiting until she was out of earshot, then remembered that the poor woman was always out of earshot.

"I thought I told you not to call until you'd stopped using morphine," he said into the mouthpiece.

"I *have* stopped. I've had nothing for well over twenty-four hours, and it's killing me. I feel like my head's going to explode," Willa replied.

Albie heard wind blowing and what sounded like rain sheeting down. The line crackled, went out for a few second, then came back again. "Where are you?" he said.

"At a petrol station just west of London."

"*What?* What the devil are you doing there?"

"Did Aunt Eddie call you?"

Albie looked around for a note. "No. I don't think so. But I've been out a good deal of the day," he said. "Why?"

Albie heard Willa groan. "I'm trying to get to Binsey. To Seamie."

"Willa, you must tell me where you are. Right now. I'll send someone to get you," Albie said sternly.

"Someone with a big net? Holding a jacket with buckles down the back?" Willa shot back, her voice breaking. "Albie, I've just seen my best friend beaten to within an inch of her life. I'm trying to save another friend from something far worse. I've been traveling for hours and hours—far too many of them in the soaking rain on a sputtering bastard of a motorbike. I'm not under the influence of anything now, and I'm not mad, either. Madness can only take you so far. It can't take you from Paris to Oxford in twenty-four hours. You have to be sane to pull that off. Which is what I am. I swear it. Terrified, yes. In shock, yes. But sane." She paused for breath, then said, "This is life or death, Albie. Seamie's and his son's. Ring the inn at Binsey. The King's Head. Ask them if they can get Seamie to the telephone. Maybe they can send a lad to his cottage for him, and he can walk to the pub and ring you back. If he does, tell him what I told you yesterday. Please, Albie. Do this for me and I'll never ask you for anything again. I'm on my way there, but I've still a ways to go. Please, please, please do this."

"Yes, all right. I'll ring the pub," Albie said, very worried now. "Just calm down, Willa."

There was more crackling and then the line went dead. Albie put the receiver back into its cradle and set the tall, candlestick telephone down on the hallway table. He took a deep breath, then blew it out again, trying to decide what to do.

Even without the influence of morphine, Willa had always been rash and unpredictable, heading up mountain peaks as a young girl that daunted many men. And later, heading off to Africa on a whim, then to Tibet, Arabia, Paris. She'd been heedless, thoughtless, even, at times, ruthless. Ruthless in her pursuit of what she wanted, ruthless to others if that's what it took to get it. Ruthless, most of all, in the way she drove herself. In one thing, however, she had always been constant, always steady, no matter how dearly it cost her: her feelings for Seamus Finnegan. It was those feelings, Albie thought now, and not the morphine, that had finally done her in. Being told he was dead, and then finding out he wasn't—it must have been a shock for her. Too great of a shock.

A few seconds later, he picked up the phone again. "Binsey, near Oxford, please," he told the operator. "The King's Head."

It took a few minutes to get the call through. "Trouble with the lines," the operator told him. Finally, he heard a man's voice say, "Good afternoon. The King's Head. Mr. Peters speaking."

"Hello, my name is Albert Alden. I'm a friend of Captain Finnegan's. I need to speak with him."

"Ah! You're in luck! They're here just now—Captain Finnegan and his son. Having their dinner. I'll fetch him for you."

Seamie got on the line. He was surprised, but pleased, to hear Albie's voice. Albie told him it was nice to hear his voice, too, and that he was sorry to disturb his supper, but he had something rather troubling to discuss with him.

As he finished talking to Seamie, he said he hoped he would come up to Cambridge one day soon, with James, for a visit. Seamie said Albie could count on it.

Albie said good-bye and hung up. Seamie and his son were just fine. No one had been beaten or murdered or kidnapped. Quite to the contrary. They'd just enjoyed a nice meal at a Cotswold pub and would soon be enjoying a leisurely walk back to their cottage.

"I should have known," Albie said to himself. "This is all utter nonsense. Just more of Willa's lunacy. Why do I even listen to her? If anyone's mad, it's me for taking her telephone calls."

He looked out of the window. The rain was still lashing down. It was cold, and getting dark as well. It was hardly a good time for a drive, and yet what choice did he have? His insane sister was about to descend on his best friend. Seamie couldn't be expected to deal with her. No one could. He would collect her and bring her back here, and then he would see about a doctor for her. It was time somebody did.

"Albie dear, are you off the blower yet?" Mrs. Lapham shouted from the sink.

"Yes, I am!" Albie shouted back, walking over to her.

"Oh, good! Before I forget, your aunt Edwina rang up . . ."

Albie groaned. Eddie was supposed to have brought Willa home with her, not allowed her to make a dash for it. He could only imagine what she wanted to tell him and he didn't want to hear it. Not now. He had one loonie to deal with this evening; he didn't need two.

". . . and she wants you to ring her back. Here's the number," Mrs. Lapham said, pulling a piece of paper from her pinafore pocket and handing it to him.

"Thank you," Albie said.

Mrs. Lapham smiled and went back to her work.

Albie stuffed the paper into his trousers pocket, then loudly said, "Mrs. Lapham, I'm going out for a bit. In the automobile. I won't be back before you finish. Please lock the door when you leave."

"Of course," Mrs. Lapham said, not looking up from her polishing. "Where are you going, Albie dear?"

"On a wild-goose chase."

"Mongoose Place?" Mrs. Lapham said. "What a strange name. Never heard of it. Sounds lovely, though! Have a good time, Albie. And don't forget your wellies."

CHAPTER ONE HUNDRED FIFTEEN

WILLA GUIDED HER motorbike down the long, trailing drive that led to Seamie's cottage. At least, she hoped it did. If the directions Mr. Peters at the pub had given her were any good, it would.

It was dark now, and the drive was rutted and muddy from the rain. It took all the strength Willa had left to keep the bike from skidding and going over. She was soaked, cold, and exhausted. Most of all she was frightened—frightened that she was too late, that Billy Madden had somehow got here before her.

"He can't have," she told herself yet again. "He doesn't know Jennie's name. He doesn't have the address of her cottage."

After a few minutes, a small stone house came into view. Willa rode up to it and cut the engine. As she was getting off the bike, the door to the cottage opened. Seamie came out. He held a lantern in one hand. He held his other hand over his eyes, as a block against the rain. He squinted into the darkness, unable to see her yet.

Willa's heart clenched at the sight of him—with love, so much love. Still. Always. She took her goggles off, wiped as much mud off her face as she could.

"Hello, Willa," he shouted into the rain. "Come inside."

Willa, who'd been walking toward the cottage, stopped short.

"Seamie . . . how . . . how did you know it was me?"

"Albie rang me."

Relief flooded through her. "Oh, thank God!" she said, walking up to him. "Then you know—"

"I do. He told me everything," Seamie said.

He pulled her to him and held her tightly, pressing his lips to her cheek. She melted into his embrace, craving the feel of him, his warmth and his scent, this man whom she'd loved her whole life, who'd come back from the dead.

"I thought you were gone," she said, fighting back tears. "I thought I'd never see you again." She pulled his face to hers and kissed him deeply. She wanted to stay like this, folded in his arms. She wanted it so much, but she knew she couldn't, not when Billy Madden could be close.

"Seamie, we have to—" she started to say.

"I know. We will. Come inside now," he said, "before you catch your death."

Was it her imagination or did his voice sound sad? Alarmed is what he should be right now, she thought. Not sad.

"I don't need to come inside. Is James with you?" Willa asked. "Is he all right?"

"What? Yes. Yes, he's fine. He just went to bed."

"He went to *bed*? Seamie, you have to get him up. You have to leave. Right now," Willa said. "Albie told you some of what's happened, but there's more to tell you. I'll explain everything later, when we're on our way, but right now, you have to pack a few things and go to Cambridge. To my aunt Eddie's house. You'll be safe there and—"

"Willa, come inside. You can get out of those wet clothes. I'll get you a glass of brandy."

Willa shook her head. Something wasn't right. This wasn't how Seamie should be acting. She wondered, for a second, if there was something wrong with him. Did he not understand the danger he and James were in?

"There's no time for brandy, Seamie," she said tersely. "Have you got a car?"

"Yes, but—"

"Where is it? I'll start it up."

Seamie stared at her. His eyes traveled from her gaunt, mud-splattered face, to her thin body, to her hands, blue with cold. His eyes, already filled with sorrow, suddenly filled with tears.

"Oh, Willa, what's happened to you?" he asked her. "Come inside. Please. You need to rest."

"Seamie, for God's sake! You and James are in danger. Very great danger."

"Willa . . . I know," Seamie said.

"You do?"

"I know about the morphine and your addiction," Seamie said. "Albie rang up the pub earlier tonight while James and I were having our supper. He told me about you, and Paris. About Oscar Carlyle and how you almost killed yourself one night. He told me everything."

Willa realized why Seamie looked so sad. Why James was asleep. Why no bags were packed. She realized what her brother had done. He'd told Seamie nothing about Madden, even though she'd begged him to. Instead he'd told Seamie that she was a morphine addict, out of her mind and raving about imaginary villains.

"Albie told you everything, did he?" she said now, angrily. "What did he tell you? That I'm a drug fiend? Well, sod him. And sod you, too! I survived Mawenzi, and Everest, and Damascus. I survived losing you. Over and over again. But now, apparently, I'm such a fragile thing that a bit of morphine's addled my brain and I'm making up stories about villains and switched children and I'm traveling from Paris to Binsey in the rain, in record time, for the sheer bloody hell of it."

"What? Willa, what are you saying? What villains? What children? Albie didn't mention anything like that."

Willa opened the crate on the back of her motorbike and grabbed her satchel. She walked past Seamie into the cottage. It was small inside. There was no foyer. They were standing in an open room that served as both sitting room and kitchen.

"I wanted this to be kinder, Seamie, I really did," she said. "I wanted you to hear it from Albie or from me. But since I'm totally bloody crackers, you'll have to find it out for yourself now."

She dug the letters out of the satchel and handed them to him. "Read fast," she said. "As soon as you finish, we're leaving."

Then she pulled a chair out from the kitchen table. "Take a seat," she added. "You're going to need it."

CHAPTER ONE HUNDRED SIXTEEN

SEAMIE WAS DIMLY aware that Willa had found the brandy he'd mentioned. She opened it, poured two glasses, and placed them on the table. Then she sat down and waited for him to finish reading.

About twenty minutes later, he looked up at her uncertainly. "Willa, I don't understand," he said. "Who is Josie Meadows? How did Jennie know her? How do you?"

"I met Josie in Paris a few months ago. We became friends. She was raised in East London. She told me that she went to Jennie's school. That's how they knew each other. When Josie got older, she performed in the East End music halls. That's how she met Billy Madden."

"But what do these letters mean?" Seamie asked, though deep inside himself he knew.

Willa took a slug of her brandy. "They mean that James is not your son," she said.

"But how . . . Jennie had a baby . . . at Binsey . . . she—" he said, feeling as if someone had taken his legs out from under him.

"Jennie lost the baby. Early on in the pregnancy. She couldn't have children, Josie told me. There was some reason. An—"

"An accident," Seamie said dully. "She was hit by a carriage when she was a child. She was badly injured."

It was all making sickening sense to him now. All of it—Jennie's unwillingness to sleep with him while she was pregnant, to even let him touch her. Her constant trips to Binsey. The telegram from her saying that she'd had the baby there and not to be alarmed, she was fine. They were both fine. God, how could he have been so blind? So stupid?

"Josie said that Jennie only pretended she was still pregnant. Josie, who really was pregnant, had the child—had James—in Binsey. She told the doctor she was Jennie, so the right names would be on the birth certificate. Then she gave James to Jennie. He wasn't Jennie's and your son." She shook her head. "No, I don't mean to say that. He *is* your son. But not your flesh and blood. He was Josie Meadows's—Josie's and Billy Madden's."

Seamie recognized that name. He knew Billy Madden was a villain and that he'd tried to kill Sid. "Did Madden know about James?" he asked Willa.

"He didn't know James had been born. Josie said he wanted her to get rid of the baby, and she didn't want to, so she fled London. She went to Binsey and stayed here in the cottage until she'd had the baby. Then she left for Paris."

"But he knows now," Seamie said.

"Yes, he does. Somehow he's found out that he fathered James. And he wants him back. Josie said that he's gone mad. That he told her he lost his sons in the war and now he wants his other son—James."

Willa paused here. In a weary, broken voice she said, "He beat her almost to death, Seamie. I saw what he'd done. He beat her to get information on James, but she wouldn't give it to him."

"So he doesn't know who Josie gave James to. He doesn't know about Binsey, doesn't know that I have him now."

"I don't know what Madden knows. Someone told him about James. I don't know who. Josie didn't know either. I'm worried that the same someone who told Madden about James knows about Jennie and Binsey and you as well. I'm worried that Madden went back to this person and got more information out of her. Or him. I'm worried—no, actually I'm scared to death—that he'll find out where you both are. That's why I want you both to leave the cottage. Right now."

"Willa, James is asleep. It's late. I can't just pile him into the car and show up on Eddie and Albie's doorstep. Surely, Madden couldn't find out any more information so fast. And even if he did, he wouldn't come out here and just snatch James—"

Willa stood up so quickly, so violently, that the chair she'd been sitting in went over. "For God's sake, Seamie, that's *exactly* what he would do! You didn't see Josie. I did! I saw what he'd done to her. She'll never be the same. She'll never be on stage again," she shouted. "*That's* why I traveled all the way here from Paris. Not because I'm mad. Not because I'm drug-addled. Because I've seen what Billy Madden is capable of. You have to leave. I don't care if it's late. You have to go to Cambridge and you have to go now. Until Madden is found and stopped, you have to hide James."

"All right, Willa, I—" Seamie started to say. He was interrupted by a little voice.

"Daddy? Daddy, are you all right? I heard voices."

A sleepy-eyed, pajama-clad James stumbled into the kitchen.

"Hello, lad," Seamie said. "I'm sorry we woke you. I'm fine. Everything's fine. I was just having a chat with my friend. James, I would like you meet Miss Alden. Willa, this is my son, James."

"Pleased to meet you, Miss Alden," James said. "Are you my father's friend from the desert? The one who rode with Major Lawrence?"

"I am, James. And I'm very pleased to meet you, too. Please pardon my appearance. I've been riding on a motorbike in the rain. Got myself rather soaked," Willa said, smiling.

Seamie looked at Willa as she spoke. She looked so haggard, so tired. She was soaking wet and trembling, from fear, or exhaustion, or the cold—he didn't know. She was scared and sorrowing for her friend and in shock, and yet she had raced here. She had got herself to Calais and Dover and had somehow got hold of a motorbike and ridden for hours through the rain and the mud to get here. For him and for James. Now she looked like she was going to collapse any second, and yet she was smiling, speaking in a gentle voice, trying her best not to upset a small child.

"James," he suddenly said, "we're going to take a ride together. You and I and Miss Alden. Can you be a good lad, go back into your room, and put some warm clothes on?"

"Isn't it a bit late to go motoring?" James asked.

"It is, but I'll make you a nice bed on the backseat and we'll pack some biscuits and make an adventure out of it. Would you like that?"

James nodded. He padded back to his bedroom.

"Make sure you put a jumper on!" Seamie shouted after him.

"He's the spitting image of her, of Josie," Willa said softly, as soon as the boy was out of earshot.

"He's my son, Willa. I don't give a damn who fathered him, who carried him, who gave him up to whom. He's *my* son."

"I know he is, Seamie. I know. That's why I came," Willa said, turning to him. "We need to go. Do you want to pack some things?"

"Yes," Seamie said. "I will." He turned and walked stiffly down the hall.

"What happened?" Willa asked, following him.

"Burns. All down my right side. I got them when my ship was torpedoed."

"We make quite a pair, don't we? Stitch us together and there might be enough working parts to make one good human being," she said wryly.

As Seamie packed his things, Willa went into James's room, found a suitcase, and put clothes into it for him. When she was finished, she carried the suitcase to the front door.

James and Seamie were already there. James was holding his stuffed bear. "Can Wellie come?" he asked.

"Of course, he can," Seamie said. "I wouldn't dream of leaving Wellie behind."

"Don't forget the biscuits."

"I won't. We'll take the whole tin."

"And tea? Can we have tea in a flask, Daddy? With lots of milk?"

"We haven't time to make it, James, but we'll take some—"

Seamie's words were cut off by a small, scraping sound. They all heard it at the same time and they all turned toward its source—the front door. As Seamie watched, he saw the doorknob turn—first to the right, then to the left. Then whoever was standing on the other side, rattled it. He knew the door would not open; he had locked it after he and Willa came inside. He knew, too, that the door was old, and the hinges rusty, and that he probably had only seconds.

Seamie grabbed James's hand and pulled him down the short hallway into his bedroom. He quickly opened his window. "Listen to me, James, and do exactly as I say. Lock your door, crawl out the window, and run to the village. To the King's Head. Tell Mr. Peters that your father needs help. That he's to send the constable."

"But Daddy . . ."

"Pretend I'm Major Lawrence. And you're Auda and that you're going to get help from Khalaf al Mor. The Turks are all around the fort. Don't let them see you."

James's little face brightened. He saluted.

Seamie saluted back. "Hurry, James. Lock the door behind me!" he said. "Go now!"

He closed the door, then listened as James shot the bolt. There was an old saber over the fireplace, if he could just get it down in time. He ran back to the sitting room and saw Willa desperately trying to lug the settee to the door, to block it. He lunged at the mantel and pulled the saber down off the wall. He was just raising it, his fingers tightening on the handle, when the door was kicked in.

CHAPTER ONE HUNDRED SEVENTEEN

"DROP IT. NOW. Or I'll shoot her," Billy Madden said.

He was quicker than any of them. He'd got into the house and across the room in seconds. Willa had had no time to run. He'd grabbed her hair with one hand and pressed the barrel of his pistol into her head with the other.

Seamie lowered the saber, but he did not put it down.

"Fucking drop it!" Madden yelled, yanking Willa's head back cruelly. She cried out in pain. Seamie did as he was told. "Make one move, and she's dead," Madden said to Seamie. He turned to the man with him. "Bennie, get the boy," he said.

"No!" Seamie shouted.

Willa couldn't see what was happening, but she could hear scuffling. She heard the horrible crack of bone against bone, heard someone fall heavily to the floor, then heard Seamie groaning. Next, she heard Bennie's footsteps going down the hallway. He tried the door, then kicked it open.

"Stop this," she said, in a strangled voice. "Please . . ."

"Shut yer gob," Madden growled, tightening his grip. He'd pulled Willa's head so far back, it had become hard for her to breathe.

Bennie came back into the room. "The boy's not there, guv," he said.

"What?" Madden said.

"He's not there. He's gone. The window's open. He must've climbed out."

"Where is he?" Madden shouted at Willa. He let go of her hair and slammed her against the wall, pinning her there by her neck, squeezing so hard, Willa thought he would crush her windpipe. "Bennie, go after him!" he yelled, when Willa would not answer.

Bennie lumbered out of the door, and Willa saw that he was also carrying a pistol. Madden turned back to her. "I'll do for you, I swear I will. And then I'll do for him," he said, pointing his gun at Seamie. "Where's the boy?" He was squeezing her throat so hard now that she was gasping for air. She scrabbled at his hand. Kicked at him. "Where's the boy?" he said again, when she finally stopped struggling. He waited for what seemed like an eternity, slowly choking the life out of her. The minutes dragged by, but Willa would not answer him. "I'm going to ask you one more time," he said. And then he raised his pistol again, pressed the barrel into her cheek, and cocked the trigger.

"Easy, Billy, there's no need for that," a voice said—a voice from Willa's nightmares. "We talked about this. There's to be no blood. Not in the cottage and not outside of it, either. We can't have the police suspecting foul play. It will ruin everything."

No, it isn't him, Willa thought. It can't be. It's the DTs. Or a lack of oxygen. Or maybe Albie's right. Maybe I am mad. Maybe my mind's finally come apart.

Madden relaxed his grip somewhat and Willa was able to breathe again. She looked to her left, toward the doorway, and saw him—a tall, blond man. He had a scar on the side of his face. She herself had put it there.

"*Namaste*, Willa Alden," Max von Brandt said, bowing slightly. "Once again."

CHAPTER ONE HUNDRED EIGHTEEN

"I KILLED YOU," Willa said, stunned, unable to believe what her eyes were telling her. "In Damascus."

"Almost," Max said. "But not quite. I'd tell you to be more thorough next time, but I'm afraid there won't be a next time."

Madden, still holding Willa by her throat, swung his pistol toward Max. "What are you doing out of the car? Don't you move! Don't move a fucking muscle, von Brandt, or I'll shoot you where you stand!"

"Easy, Billy," Max said again, as if he was trying to calm a wild animal. "You and Bennie are the ones with the guns, not me, right?" He slowly raised his hands, palms out, to show Madden he was carrying nothing.

"Where's Bennie?"

"Bennie's outside. He told me to come in after you. He's got the boy. He's got him tied up and in the car. He's ready to go."

"No," Seamie said groggily, trying to get off the floor. "You leave him alone. . . ." Blood dripped from a gash in his lip. Willa could see the terror in his eyes. She struggled against Madden. He banged her back into the wall.

"Max, you bastard!" she screamed at him. "How can you do this? James is a child! An innocent child. And you're delivering him to a criminal. A murderer!"

Madden hit her across the face with the butt of his pistol. To Max he said, "You know her?"

"Very well," Max replied. He was carrying two lengths of rope.

"I say we do them both right here. Right now. And be done," Madden said.

"No," Max said.

As Seamie, still dazed, tried again to get up, Max put a foot in the center of his back, grabbed his hands and tied them. He then tied Willa's.

"I've told you before, Billy," he said when he'd finished, "it has to be clean and neat or else you'll have every police officer in the country looking for the boy. Remember, Billy? Remember what I told you?"

Billy nodded. Willa chanced a glance at him. His eyes were dark and empty. This is what madness looks like, she thought. He would have killed them both, without a second's thought or remorse, if Max had not stopped him. But why had he stopped him? she wondered. She soon found out.

"A coat on the riverbank—Captain Finnegan's," Max said to Billy. "A walking stick. Field glasses. Broken ice. It will look like Captain Finnegan and his son went for a winter ramble. James walked out too far on the ice. He fell through. His father tried to save him, but he could not; his injuries had left him too weak. They both drowned—"

"No!" Willa shouted, cutting Max off. "It won't work. My brother . . . my aunt . . . they know—"

A vicious backhand from Max silenced her. Billy's eyes flickered uncertainly between Willa and Max, but Max, unconcerned by what Willa had said, continued to talk, his voice calm and measured.

"Pay no attention to her, Billy. She's the cleverest little liar I've ever met, and I've met quite a few. It *will* work. It will look so tragic, Billy, especially given all that Captain Finnegan has been through. His body will be found downriver. In the spring. Poor little James's never will. It'll be said that he was swept away by the currents, but really, he'll be living life with his new father. His real father. And I'll be happily back in Berlin, because I held up my end of the bargain—I helped you get him." Max paused. His eyes sought Billy's. "That's the plan, right, Billy? And we must stick to it. That's how we make sure you not only get James, but you get to keep him."

Max moved around the cottage as he spoke. He shoved the settee back in place, righted a small end table that had gone over, and cleaned up some splintered wood that had fallen on the floor near the front door.

"Right. That's right. All clean and neat-like. No messes and no clues," Billy said.

"Good," Max said. "Let's get Finnegan outside. A bash to the head and then into the water."

"You can't do this. Please, Max," Willa begged.

"What about her?" Billy said, ramming the pistol's barrel into Willa's head again.

Max smiled. "Don't worry about her. She's my problem and I'll take care of her. In fact, this is one problem I'll take great pleasure in resolving. Come on now, Billy, let's go."

He grabbed Seamie's jacket and walking stick. After getting Seamie up off the floor, he half marched, half dragged him outside. Madden followed with Willa, closing the cottage's door behind them.

"Let's be quick," Max said. "I want to get back on the road. We've been here too long as is," he said.

Outside, Willa saw Madden's car. He'd parked it up the driveway a fair bit. Probably to keep herself and Seamie from hearing it as the three of them drove in. Looking at it now, Willa knew that any ride she took in that car would be the very last ride of her life. She tried desperately to think of a way to save James, to save all of them—but there was none. Max and Madden were walking them toward the river. She and Seamie were bound. They were outnumbered. Madden had a gun and Bennie did, too. There was nothing she could do.

"I'll take this one to the car," Madden said. "You do for Finnegan."

"No, Billy," Max said. "Bring her to the water. I want her to see it. She nearly killed me. I spent a month in a hospital bed because of her. I want her to see him go in."

Madden, squinting in the darkness at the car and frowning, hesitated. "Where's that fucking Ben—" he started to say.

"You owe me that much, Billy," Max said tersely. "I got you the boy. Without me, you'd never even have known about him."

"All right, then," Billy said. "But be quick about it. Like you said, we've been here too long already."

It was over. Willa knew that now.

She had tried her best to save James, but she had failed. And now she would pay for her failure, she and Seamie both. With their lives.

CHAPTER ONE HUNDRED NINETEEN

"WALK, DAMN YOU!" Madden shouted, shoving Willa ahead of him toward the river. "Where's that bloody Bennie?"

"I told you, he's in the car with the boy," Max said. His grip on Seamie tightened. "Don't do anything foolish," he told him.

Seamie made no reply. He was looking ahead of himself, past Willa and Madden. He was looking at the river, trying to see a way out of this. The blow he'd taken had dazed him, but his head had cleared now. He could take von Brandt, if only he could get his hands untied. But even if he got Max, Madden had a gun on Willa. And Bennie, who also had a gun, was inside the car with James.

They got closer to the water. They were only about ten yards away now. Seamie strained against his bonds.

"Please," he said. "Don't do this. Not to her. Not to my son."

Max said nothing. His eyes were fixed on Willa, who had started to struggle with Madden. Max's grip on Seamie was steel-like.

"Stay still," he said quietly. "Don't move or I'll shoot her."

Willa kicked at Madden. She connected with his leg, causing him to stumble. He righted himself and hit her savagely. She staggered backward from the blow and fell to the ground.

"You bitch!" Billy shouted. "I'll fucking kill you!" He raised his gun and pointed it at Willa.

"No!" Seamie shouted.

They all heard the shot.

Billy's head snapped up. Seamie spun around. They both looked at Max at the same time, both saw the shiny glint in his hand, both realized that he was holding a smoking, silver pistol.

CHAPTER ONE HUNDRED TWENTY

WILLA FELT BLOOD, hot and wet, on her face and neck. Its thick, coppery smell was heavy in the damp night air.

Max had shot her. Not Madden, Max. She'd seen him raise the pistol and fire. There was no pain, though. She had been close to death before and the pain had been terrible. Now she felt nothing at all. Is this what it's actually like to die? she wondered. She looked down at her chest for a bullet hole. There was blood spattered across her jacket, but she could see nothing else. Had he hit her in the neck? The head?

"It's all right, Willa," Max said. "You're all right."

Willa, still on the ground, realized that Madden was no longer standing over her, screaming at her. Where was he? She sat up and saw that he was lying on the ground next to her. His eyes were lifeless. There was a dark, wet hole in his forehead.

She turned and looked up at Max. He untied her hands, then he took Madden's gun from the dead man's hands and shoved it into the waistband of his trousers.

"Where's James?" Seamie was shouting. "Where's my son?"

"I don't know, Mr. Finnegan," Max said.

"You said he was in the car!"

"I lied. Turn around. Let me untie your hands."

As soon as Seamie's hands were free, he raced off to Madden's car, shouting for James. Willa struggled to her feet and raced off after him.

She found him opening all the car doors. "He's not here," he yelled. "Oh, God . . . where is he?"

"Look in the boot," Willa said.

Seamie wrenched the boot's lid up and Willa screamed. Bennie, a livid gash across his throat, was lying inside it.

"James!" Seamie shouted, spinning in circles. "James, where are you?"

Willa was about to slam the boot lid down again when Max, suddenly close by, asked her not to. She turned and saw that he had his arms around Madden's chest. He had dragged him all the way from the river to the car.

"I . . . I don't understand," Willa said. Nothing made sense to her. Nothing at all. She felt as if she was in some horrible nightmare, one from which she could not wake.

As she stood there, trying to figure out what was happening, Max tumbled Madden's body into the boot, then slammed it shut.

"James!" Seamie called out again. His agonized cry echoed through the woods.

"We must help Captain Finnegan find his son," Max said to her.

"His son's fine," said a new voice. Slowly, a man emerged from the darkness. He was holding a shotgun and it was trained on Max. "I know where he is and he's safe."

It was a very disheveled Albie.

CHAPTER ONE HUNDRED TWENTY-ONE

"JAMES IS NEARBY, Seamie. He's in good hands," Albie said, still holding the shotgun on Max.

"Albie, what are you doing here? How did you get here?" Willa asked.

"By car. After you called, I thought I should come to Binsey, meet you here and take you back to Cambridge," Albie said. "I took Eddie's automobile, but it ran out of gas a few miles outside of the village. I left it at the side of the road and walked the rest of the way. When I got to the drive, I ran into James—literally. He was very frightened, but he managed to tell me what was happening. I took him to a neighbor's house, the Wallaces'. Mr. Wallace and James went to the village to get the police. They'll be here shortly."

"Did you borrow that gun from the neighbor, too?" Max asked, looking at the shotgun.

"Mr. von Brandt," Albie said, "I've been after you for a very long time, but never in a million years did I expect to find you in Binsey. I'd like to know what you're doing here."

"It's a long story, Mr. Alden," Max said.

"That's all right. You're not going anywhere."

Max told them all about Billy Madden's first visit to him at his hotel, and how he'd had to tell Billy about James in order to save his own life.

"I never expected Madden to actually track Josie Meadows down," he said. "I thought he was in a bad way due to his grief over his sons and that it would wear off in a day or two. I was wrong. He paid me a second visit this evening, as I was getting out of a carriage in front of my hotel. He was waiting by the door for me with a gun. He forced me into his car and told me he'd been to Paris and had found Josie and that she wouldn't tell him the boy's name or where he was. Then he threatened to kill me if I didn't take him to the boy. So I did, figuring the ride would give me time to think, time to figure out a way to kill him, for I saw then that he would never stop. Not until he had James, and I did not want that to happen. I did not want an innocent child's abduction on my conscience. I knew I could take Bennie if I could just get them apart. Sending James out of the window was a great help. Bennie went after him. I saw him go. And then I went after Bennie. I was able to get his gun off him, kill him quietly with a clasp knife Billy foolishly left in my trouser pocket, and get him into the car boot."

"But Max, how did you know Billy Madden in the first place? And Josie Meadows? And Binsey?" Willa asked.

"Mr. von Brandt knows a lot of things, Willa," Albie said. "Too many things. He was a spymaster in London before the war even started. That's how he knows Madden. He used one of Madden's boats to get naval secrets to the North Sea. He's going to tell us what he knows. Every last thing. Raise your hands, Mr. von Brandt. You're under arrest."

"No, actually, I'm not."

"I have a gun. I'm not afraid to use it," Albie said menacingly.

"You won't shoot me, Mr. Alden," Max said, a note of weariness in his voice. "You can't. That shotgun's ancient. The trigger's rusted. And you're holding it incorrectly. It's probably not even loaded, is it? And even if it is, I have two pistols and I'm a much better shot. I'll get you first."

Albie still refused to lower the shotgun.

"Mr. Alden, two prime ministers will be most unhappy with you if you shoot me. Mr. Asquith, who protected me for the duration of the war. And Mr. Lloyd George who continues to protect me. You are right, Mr. Alden . . . I am a spy. But I'm not working for Germany. I never was."

"My God. That . . . that means," Albie said, as the full weight of Max's words hit him.

"That you're a double agent," Seamie said. "Fucking hell."

Max smiled ruefully. "Yes, Captain Finnegan, that's it exactly—a total fucking hell."

CHAPTER ONE HUNDRED TWENTY-TWO

"WHEN, MAX?" WILLA asked. "When did you turn? When did you become a double agent?"

"I never turned. I was a double agent all along," Max replied. "I'm a high-ranking member of the British Secret Service and have been for quite some time. I long ago saw the writing on the wall. I saw that the kaiser was a madman who would find any pretext for going to war. Had it not been Sarajevo, it would have been something else. I wanted to do what I could to stop him, to stop the war."

Willa shook her head in disbelief. "But how? How did you pull it off?" she said. "It seemed very clear to me in Damascus which side you were on. And it wasn't the Allies'. I would never have even suspected you for a double agent."

"It was difficult," Max said, "but I had a part to play, and I played it. I first had to convince Berlin that I was a loyal to the kaiser. That was easy enough. I'd had a sterling record of military service, after which I became a member of the German Secret Service. They found out I had family in London and wished to exploit that. So they had me stage a fight with my uncle—an industrialist and the head of our family's firm, and a big supporter of the kaiser's. We had a public falling out—or what looked like one—in a restaurant over my dissatisfaction with the kaiser's policies. A few days later, banished by my uncle, I arrived in London. Because of my family connections there, and because I had been publicly critical of the kaiser, I was welcomed everywhere."

"You were above suspicion, which made it easy to run a spy ring and which is exactly what Berlin wanted," Albie said.

"Yes, of course. I assembled the ring as soon as I got to London. I had to feed Berlin information. Good information. Constantly. If I hadn't done so, they would've suspected me—hence the documents in the packets that Gladys and Jennie couriered. But I gave London far more than I ever gave Berlin. No one knew about me except Asquith. Not you. Not Burgess. Not even Churchill. They couldn't know; it would have been too dangerous for me. Asquith played along quite well, I must say. He even invited me to his country home at the same time as he invited other spies—German agents who he knew were in constant contact with Berlin—people who would report back that I was doing my job. In fact, Asquith himself told me, just two nights ago, that I'm the reason the Allies won the war. Though I have to share credit with the Spanish flu, I suppose. It carried off more German and Austrian soldiers than it did Allied ones."

"People died because of your activities in London," Seamie said angrily.

Max's eyes turned hard. "Yes, they did," he said. "Once I was here, it was very important to look like a German spy to other German spies. That involved cruel, even brutal actions. I regret Maud Selwyn Jones's death. And Gladys Bigelow's. I regret any suffering I caused Jennie Finnegan. But that is the cost of what I do, and it is a very high one."

"Jennie Finnegan was my wife. *My wife,*" Seamie said. "You had no business . . . you had no right . . ."

"Yes, she was your wife. And all those German sailors you sent to the bottom of the Mediterranean, Captain Finnegan, who were they? I shall tell you. Each of them was some mother's son. And probably some woman's husband, some child's father. Jennie suffered, yes. Maud and Gladys are dead—all at my hands. But how many more were saved because of what I did? How many were spared because I, and others like me, helped to shorten the war? Hundreds of thousands? Millions? Do we sacrifice the many for the one? Or the one for the many? It's a question that I'll never answer, Captain Finnegan, and one that will always haunt me."

In the distance, lights were suddenly seen shining through the trees.

"The constable, no doubt. With Mr. Wallace and James. It looks as if they're still a fair ways off, but even so, I must be going," Max said. "When they arrive, please tell them that Madden and his man were trying to break into the cottage to rob it. You, Captain Finnegan, shot at them with a pistol you keep in the cottage." He pulled Madden's gun from his waistband and handed it to Seamie. "Now is your chance, Captain Finnegan," he said quietly. "Take it, if you must."

Seamie shook his head. "The war's over," he said.

"Good-bye, Captain Finnegan," Max said. He offered Seamie his hand, but Seamie would not take it.

"Good-bye, Mr. von Brandt," he said. "Thank you for saving my son." He turned away and started walking toward the cottage. Albie followed him.

Willa stood where she was, too stunned and tired to move.

Max turned to her. "I am very sorry that I hit you. Back in the cottage," he said. "Forgive me, I had no choice. I had to quiet you. If you had kept talking about your brother and aunt, and what they knew, you would have spooked Billy, and he might've killed both you and Captain Finnegan right there."

"Oh, no worries, Max," Willa said bitterly. "I've no hard feelings toward you. Not for that, or anything else. None at all."

Max looked at the ground. "What will you do after tonight?" he asked.

"I don't know. Get out of these clothes. Sleep. Then go back to Paris, I suppose," she said wearily.

"Why? So you can finish the job?" he asked, looking up at her again.

"What job?"

"The job of killing yourself. You were always trying to. On Everest. In the desert. And now, apparently, with a needle. Oh, you needn't look so surprised. I know an addict when I see one. You must stop, Willa."

"Strange sentiments coming from you, Max. I should think you would want me dead. You were going to kill me yourself in Damascus. I saw the order. From Berlin. It was in with the maps I stole from your desk."

Max shook his head. "I follow most of my orders, but not all of them. I never would have killed you. Not you. I would have stalled Berlin. Told them you still had valuable information. I might have locked you up for a bit, but I never would have had you shot. I couldn't have. It would have been like killing myself." He paused, then ruefully added, "The best part of myself, that is."

It was Willa's turn to look away.

"Stop it, Willa. Once and for all. You're here. Seamie is here. You have always wanted to be together. You should stay with him now."

Willa laughed. "After everything that's happened? What I did to his wife?"

"What you did, eh?" Max said. "What did Seamie do, meeting you all those times at the Coburg? What did Jennie do, lying to him about their son? What have I done, Willa? To you in Damascus . . . to Jennie . . . to dozens more." He fell silent for a bit, then said, "Think about the boy. James would likely not be with his father right now if it wasn't for you. Seamie would not be alive. I doubt very much that things would have turned out the way they have without you. Think on that, and perhaps, in the days to come, it might help to balance the scales a little."

Willa looked at him. Her eyes filled with tears.

"Don't be stupid, Willa. Take what love you can find in this wretched world. There's little enough. Grab it with both hands. For yourself. For Seamie. For the boy."

Max gathered her in his arms then and held her tightly. He kissed her lips, then released her. It was time to go.

"Good-bye, Willa," he said.

"Good-bye, Max," she said.

She turned away and started walking toward the cottage. He opened the driver's side door of the car. As he was about to get in, he glanced up at the sky, hoping to get his bearings, to get an idea of which way he should head in order to get back to the main road. He saw something there that made him smile.

"Willa!" he called out, remembering her and how she looked at Rongbuk. So long ago. Sitting on a rock, staring up at the sky.

Willa turned. "What?" she said brokenly.

"Look," he said, pointing up.

She followed his gaze, and Max saw the tears on her cheeks, silvery bright. High above them the Great Hunter drew his bow. In the vast and infinite night, Orion sparkled.

EPILOGUE

Kenya, September 1919

WILLA WATCHED THEM, Seamie and James, as they ran through the grass, trying to get aloft a kite that they'd made out of newspaper.

She was sitting on the porch of a bungalow. The house was about twenty years old and had lovely, mature gardens. There were roses planted around the porch, and they were in full bloom now.

"Wild roses," said Arthur Wayland, the man who'd sold it to them. "Clipped from a hedgerow and brought all the way from England. They were my wife's favorites and she couldn't bear to leave them behind. They've done marvelously well here."

They'd just bought the bungalow, and two hundred acres of land that went with it, last week. Mr. Wayland was returning home to England after forty years in Africa. His wife had died. His two sons were in London. It was time to go back.

Willa had fallen in love with the house immediately. It faced west, giving them the most spectacular view of Kilimanjaro. They had been happy to move in and finally put their bags down. They'd spent months in ships, trains, hotels, and tents.

As she watched Seamie and James, Willa noticed that Seamie was moving slowly. The scars from his burns still troubled him sometimes. They ached. Willa's leg still hurt, too. In fact, it was why she was sitting down now instead of joining in the kite-flying. She was still getting used to the new prosthesis she'd bought right before they'd left England. The lightness and range of motion was better than anything she'd had before, but she'd had to adjust her gait, and she'd had to put up with soreness and chafing. Prosthesis manufacturers had made vast improvements to the artificial legs and arms they made. They'd had to. Thousands of men had come home from the front missing limbs. They needed to be able to work. To walk. To hold their children.

We're all scarred, all three of us. We're all damaged, Willa thought as she massaged her knee. Some of the wounds were on the outside. Some of them went a lot deeper. There were days when James still wept for his mother. And there were nights when he still woke up screaming that bad men were coming to get him.

Seamie, too, had his dark days. The aftermath of Billy Madden's visit to Binsey had been very hard on him. He'd had to come to terms with Jennie's lies, and why she'd told them. He was angry at times, he said, but mostly he felt deeply sad—sad that he'd failed Jennie. Sad that she'd been so desperate to hold on to his love that she'd deceived him, passing another woman's child off as her own. Sad that Josie Meadows had suffered for that deception at the hands of Billy Madden.

Willa had her doubts and fears, too—some of them were so strong, they sometimes made her want to reach for a syringe again, but she didn't. She had doubted that they could ever make a go of it—she and Seamie. She was afraid that too much had happened, that they would always be haunted by the mistakes of the past, that their love would always be a destructive one.

After Max had driven away, she had gone inside the cottage and collapsed in a chair. The constable arrived a few minutes later with Mr. Wallace and James. Seamie had explained to them what had happened, using the story Max cooked up. After he'd thanked both men and said good-bye to them, he put James to bed. Albie stoked the fire, made a platter of cheeses, pickles, ham, and bread, and got out the bottle of brandy.

They'd drunk the brandy, eaten the meal, talked for hours, and then they'd all fallen asleep—Albie in an armchair, Willa in another one, and Seamie on the settee. They had not been together like that for years, since they were teenagers. In the morning they'd decided they would tell Joe and Fiona what had happened, and Sid and India, but no one else. Telling anyone else, including the police, would only hurt James. Seamie would tell his son the truth. One day. When he was much older.

The next morning, Albie offered to take Willa back to Cambridge with him.

Seamie answered for her. "No," he said. "Stay, Willa. Please."

"Are you sure?" she'd asked him. He'd been through so much—he and James both—she thought they would want time to themselves. She loved him and she wanted to be with him, but she had no idea if he felt the same way—not with all that had happened.

"Please," he'd said again. And so she'd stayed.

They had talked—not of their feelings for each other, not of Jennie or Max or things long past, but of their more recent lives. Seamie told her about the prisoner-of-war camp, and how a part of him had very much wanted not to come back to England after the war. He told her he didn't know what his next step would be. What he would do with himself. Or how he would raise James. Willa told him of her life in Paris, and her photographs, and said she would have to go back eventually, for she found it impossible to be in London.

They were weary and shaken by what had happened, and what had almost happened. They lived quietly—just going for walks with James, or to the village market. Going for rides into the countryside or for lunch at the King's Head. Cooking breakfast. Reading. Playing games with James.

Seamie did not touch her or kiss her, and she understood. He was grieving. He was angry. He was tortured by guilt. She did not touch him, either, for fear of being turned away.

A week passed, and a month, and Willa realized she did not know what to do. She didn't know whether to stay or go. She wanted to know Seamie's feelings, but was afraid to ask. For once in her life, she was afraid. It was better not to know, to live in hope, than to know for sure that he no longer felt for her what she felt for him. That he no longer loved her.

And then, one night, he suddenly answered her questions.

"I don't want this," he said abruptly, while they were sitting by the fire.

Willa's heart sank. She thought he meant her. Them. She had hoped they might have a chance, but then again, how could they? There was so much hurt between them. So much sorrow. She was not surprised, but she was devastated.

She was also wrong.

"I don't want to be here in Binsey anymore," he said. "I can't bear it. I've tried to like it. For James's sake. Because he likes the country. And for yours, because you don't like London. But I don't. In fact, I hate it here. I hate this cottage. There are too many ghosts in it. I don't want to be in England anymore. I want to go back to where it all went wrong and put it right. I want to make a new start. With you and James. In Africa."

Willa was speechless.

"You think it's a bad idea," Seamie said, his disappointment evident on his face.

"No, I don't. In fact, I think it's a wonderful idea. How soon can we go?"

"As soon as you marry me."

"Seamie, I—"

"Say yes, Willa. Say yes right now or go back to Paris," he said, with an ache in his voice. "If you're going to walk away again, do it now. Before James loves you as much as I do. I can take the blow. He can't. He's been through too much."

"Yes," Willa said.

Seamie looked at her long and hard. Then he grabbed her hand, pulled her out of her chair, and led her to his bedroom. They made love there, in the darkness, fell asleep, and woke up together in the soft light of morning.

Seamie drove to Oxford the next morning. He put Willa on a train there so that she could return to Paris, for just a few days, to pack her belongings and have them sent to her mother's house. Then he went to a jeweler's and bought two gold rings. They were married in London at Willa's childhood home three weeks later. Albie gave her away. Mrs. Alden arranged a lovely breakfast for them. Fiona and Joe came. Charlie, who was talking again now, and Katie, who'd just graduated from Oxford and was preparing to stand as the Labour candidate for Southwark, and all the rest of their children were there, too.

The day after their wedding, Seamie and Willa walked up the gangplank of a steamer bound for East Africa, with James between them. They hired porters in Mombasa, as they had years ago, and took a long, leisurely trip from there, introducing James to Africa. They'd decided to settle here, in Kenya, near Kilimanjaro.

Willa finished rubbing her knee now. The pain had diminished. She knew that it would go away completely as time went by, as her body adjusted fully to the new leg. She stood now, shading her eyes, smiling at her husband, and at James. He was not her son, not yet. Perhaps one day. If he wanted to be. For now, he called her Willa and she called him James, and both of them were happy with that.

Willa put her full weight on her leg, stepped down off the porch, and walked toward Seamie and James. Her stride was easier and smoother than it had been since she'd lost her real leg. It was good, the new leg—so good that she thought that one day she might even be able to climb again. Not the Mawenzi peak, not this time—the Uhuru peak. She might be able to manage that one. It was a bit of a doddle, that climb. But that was all right.

Once, long ago, she had wanted to be bold. To be daring and brave. To be the first.

Now she just wanted to be.

She wanted to be still at night, to look up and admire the stars without asking them which way to go. She wanted to walk slowly over the veldt and through the jungle, not hurrying to make camp, but stopping to rest, to gaze at a herd of antelope, to call back to the beautiful birds who called to her. She wanted to watch, delighted, as little James marveled at an African sunset, watched a cheetah run, or made friends with a Masai boy just his age.

She wanted to sit by the fire at night with Seamie. Talking sometimes, and sometimes just listening silently and with wonder to the wild African night.

They had torn themselves apart, she and Seamie. Years ago. Here in Africa. And then in 1914, the world had torn itself apart. Now they, and the world, would put themselves back together. Slowly, with pain, regret, and with hope, they would find the way forward.

She didn't know how, exactly. She had no map. No answers. No guarantees.

All she had was this day.

This impossible mountain rising before her.

This sun and this sky.

This man and this child.

This terrible, wonderful love.

ACKNOWLEDGMENTS

I am indebted to the following works: *Everest: The Moutaineering History* by Walt Unsworth, *Lawrence of Arabia* by B. H. Liddell Hart, *Setting the Desert on Fire* by James Barr, and *Seven Pillars of Wisdom: A Triumph* by T. E. Lawrence—and to the following websites: www.firstworldwar.com; Wikipedia; www.parliament.net; www.bbc.co.uk/history; virus.stanford.edu/uda; www.cliffordawright.com; www.jordanjubilee.com; and the digital library at Cornell University, where I viewed online volumes of *Littel's Living Age*, a general interest magazine published from 1844 to 1900.

I would like to thank the late Sheri Nystrom for graciously sharing her knowledge and experience of limb amputation and its aftereffects with me. And I would like to thank Clay Nystrom, her husband, for sharing Sheri.

Thank you, as always, to my wonderful family for seeing me through.

Thank you, too, to my agents, Simon Lipksar and Maja Nikolic, and to my editors, Leslie Wells and Thomas Tebbe.

And last, but very far from least, thank you to the wonderful readers, booksellers, bloggers, and reviewers who've embraced the Rose books so warmly. I appreciate your enthusiasm, emails, and kind words more than I could ever say.

BIBLIOGRAPHY

The Rose stories never would have been written had I not, many years ago, stumbled across a four-volume survey of working-class Victorian London by Henry Mayhew titled *London Labour and the London Poor*. Mayhew interviewed everyone—costermongers, thieves, prostitutes, mudlarks, even people who made a living by picking up cigarette butts. He gave detailed descriptions of their work and how they carried it out, and best of all, he let them tell their own stories, in their own words. These books are pure magic. If you ever get the chance to read them, grab it.

Many other books helped me re-create the London and New York of my novels, various other locales, and the people in them. A bibliography for the entire Rose series follows.

Abbot, Willis John. *The Nations at War: A Current History*. New York and London: Syndicate Publishing Company, 1915.

Balson, Consuelo Vanderbilt. *The Glitter and the Gold*. New York: Harper & Brothers, 1952.

Barltrop, Robert, and Jim Wolveridge. *The Muvver Tongue*. London: Journeyman Press, 1980.

Barr, James. *Setting the Desert on Fire: T. E. Lawrence and Britain's Secret War in Arabia, 1916–1918*. New York & London: W. W. Norton & Company, 2008.

Beckett, Stephen. *In Living Memory: Photographs of Tower Hamlets*. London: Tower Hamlets Local History Library & Archives, 1989.

Berridge, Virginia, and Griffith Edwards. *Opium and the People: Opiate Use in Nineteenth-Century England*. New Haven and London: Yale University Press, 1987.

Black, Mary. *Old New York in Early Photographs 1853–1901*. Second revised edition. New York: Dover Publications, Inc., 1976.

Blair, Richard, and Kathleen Goodwin. *Point Reyes Visions*. Inverness, Calif.: Color & Light Editions, 2002.

Bonner, Thomas Neville. *To the Ends of the Earth: Women's Search for Education in Medicine*. Cambridge, Mass.: Harvard University Press, 1995.

Booth, Martin. *Opium: A History*. London: Pocket Books, 1997.

Boyles, Denis. *African Lives*. New York: Ballantine Books, 1988.

Breashears, David, and Audrey Salkeld, with a foreword by John Mallory. *Last Climb: The Legendary Everest Expeditions of George Mallory*. Washington, D.C.: National Geographic Society, 1999.

Burnett, John. *Plenty & Want: A Social History of Food in England from 1815 to the Present Day*. Third edition. London: Routledge, 1989.

Burrows, Edwin G., and Mike Wallace. *Gotham: A History of New York City to 1898*. New York and Oxford: Oxford University Press, 1999.

Byron, Joseph. Text by Clay Lancaster. *Photographs of New York Interiors from the Turn of the Century*. New York: Dover Publications, Inc., 1976.

Cannadine, David. *The Decline and Fall of the British Aristocracy*. New York: Vintage Books, 1999.

Chauncey, George. *Gay New York: Gender, Urban Culture, and the Making of the Gay Male World 1890–1940*. New York: Basic Books, 1994.

Chesney, Kellow. *The Victorian Underworld*. London: Penguin Books, 1989.

Churchill, Winston Spencer. *My African Journey*. London: Hamlyn Publishing Group, 1972.

Coleman, Elizabeth Ann. *The Opulent Era: Fashions of Worth, Doucet and Pingat*. Brooklyn, N.Y.: Brooklyn Museum, 1989.

Cooper, Diana. *The Rainbow Comes and Goes*. London: Rupert Hart-Davis, 1958.

Cox, Steven M., and Kris Fulsaas. *Moutaineering: The Freedom of the Hills*. Seattle, Wash.: The Moutaineers Books, 2003.

Darby, Madge. *Waeppa's People: A History of Wapping*. Colchester: Connor & Butler on behalf of The History of Wapping Trust, 1988.

Davies, Jennifer. *The Victorian Kitchen*. London: BBC Books, 1991.

Dickens, Charles. *The Uncommercial Traveller*. New York and Boston: Books, Inc., 1860.

Digby, Anne. *The Evolution of British General Practice 1850–1948*. Oxford: Oxford University Press, 1999.

Dudgeon, Piers. *Dickens' London*. London: Headline Book Publishing PLC, 1989.

Ellmers, Chris, and Alex Werner. *London's Lost Riverscape: A Photographic Panorama*. London: Viking, 1988.

Fido, Martin. *The Crimes, Detection & Death of Jack the Ripper*. London: Weidenfeld and Nicolson, 1987.

———. *Murder Guide to London*. Chicago: Academy Chicago Publishers, 1986.

Fishman, William J. *East End 1888*. Philadelphia: Temple University Press, 1988.

Flanders, Judith. *Inside the Victorian Home: A Portrait of Domestic Life in Victorian England*. New York and London: W. W. Norton & Company, 2004.

Foote, Edward B., M.D. *Plain Home Talk Embracing Medical Common Sense*. Chicago: Thompson and Thomas, 1870.

Foreman, Freddie, with John Lisner. *Respect*. London: Arrow Books, 1997.

Fraser, Frankie, as told to James Morton. *Mad Frank: Memoirs of a Life in Crime*. New York: Warner Books, 2000.

Fraser, Frankie, with James Morton. *Mad Frank's London*. London: Virgin Books Ltd., 2002.

Fried, Albert, and Richard M. Elman, editors. *Charles Booth's London: A Portrait of the Poor at the Turn of the Century, Drawn from his "Life and Labour of the People in London."* New York: Pantheon Books, 1968.

Gann, L. H., and Peter Duignan. *The Rulers of British Africa 1870–1914*. Stanford, Calif.: Stanford University Press, 1978.

Geniesse, Jane Fletcher. *Passionate Nomad: The Life of Freya Stark*. New York: The Modern Library, 1999.

Gernsheim, Alison. *Victorian and Edwardian Fashion: A Photographic Survey*. New York: Dover Publications, 1981.

Gilmour, David. *Curzon: Imperial Statesman*. New York: Farrar, Straus and Giroux, 2003.

Grimble, Frances, editor. *The Edwardian Modiste*. San Francisco: Lavolta Press, 1997.

Hart, B. H. Liddell. *Lawrence of Arabia*. A Da Capo Press reprint of *Colonel Lawrence: The Man Behind the Legend*. New York: 1935.

Heussler, Robert. *Yesterday's Rulers: The Making of the British Colonial Service*. Syracuse, N.Y.: Syracuse University Press, 1963.

Hood, Clifton. *722 Miles: The Building of the Subways and How They Transformed New York*. Baltimore and London: Johns Hopkins University Press, 1993.

Hughes, Kristine. *The Writer's Guide to Everyday Life in Regency and Victorian England*. Cincinnati, Ohio: Writer's Digest Books, 1998.

Hughes, M. V. *A London Girl of the 1880s*. Oxford and New York: Oxford University Press, 1988.

Huxley, Elspeth. *The Flame Trees of Thika: Memories of an African Childhood*. New York: Weidenfeld & Nicolson, 1987.

Huxley, Elspeth, and Arnold Curtis, editors. *Pioneers' Scrapbook*. London: Evans Brothers Limited, 1980.

Jackson, Kenneth T., editor. *The Encyclopedia of New York*. New Haven and London: Yale University Press, 1995.

Jalland, Pat, editor. *Octavia Wilberforce: The Autobiography of a Pioneer Woman Doctor*. London: Cassell, 1989.

Jasper, A. S. *A Hoxton Childhood*. London: Readers Union, 1971.

Johnson, Boris. *Friends, Voters, Countrymen: Jottings on the Stump*. London: HarperCollins Publishers, 2001.

Johnstone, R. W., C.B.E. *William Smellie: The Master of British Midwifery*. Edinburgh and London: E. & S. Livingstone Ltd., 1952.

Kisselloff, Jeff. *You Must Remember This: An Oral History of Manhattan from the 1890s to World War II*. San Diego: Harcourt, Brace, Jovanovich, 1989.

Knight, Stephen. *Jack the Ripper: The Final Solution*. London: Granada, 1983.

Lambert, Angela. *Unquiet Souls: The Indian Summer of the British Aristocracy*. London: Macmillan, 1984.

Lawrence, Lady (Rosamond Napier). *Indian Embers*. Palo Alto: Trackless Sands Press, 1991.

Lawrence, T. E. *Seven Pillars of Wisdom: A Triumph*. New York: Anchor Books, 1991.

Llewelyn Davies, Margaret, editor. *Maternity: Letters from Working Women*. London: Virago, 1989.

———. *Life as We Have Known by Co-operative Working Women*. New York: W. W. Norton & Company, Inc., 1975.

London, Jack. *The People of the Abyss*. Chicago: Lawrence Hill Books, 1995.

MacColl, Gail, and Carol McD. Wallace. *To Marry an English Lord or, How Anglomania Really Got Started*. New York: Workman Publishing, 1989.

Manton, Jo. *Elizabeth Garrett Anderson*. New York: E. P. Dutton & Co., Inc., 1965.

Maxon, Robert M. *East Africa: An Introductory History*. Second revised edition. Morgantown: West Virginia University Press, 1994.

Mayhew, Henry. *London Labour and the London Poor*, Vol. 1–Vol. 4. London: George Woodfall and Son, 1851.

McCormick, J. H., M.D., editor. *Century Book of Health*. Springfield, Mass.: The King-Richardson Company, 1907.

McGrath, Melanie. *Silvertown: An East End Family Memoir*. London: Fourth Estate, 2003.

McGregor, Deborah Kuhn. *From Midwives to Medicine: The Birth of American Gynecology*. New Brunswick, N.J.: Rutgers University Press, 1998.

Morton, James. *East End Gangland*. New York: Warner Books, 2000.

Naib, S. K., al-, editor, with R.J.M. Carr. *Dockland: An Illustrated Historical Survey of Life and Work in East London*. London: North East London Polytechnic, 1988.

National Cloak & Suit Co. *Women's Fashions of the Early 1900s: An Unabridged Republication of New York Fashions, 1909*. New York: Dover Publications, Inc.

Nevill, Lady Dorothy. *The Reminiscences of Lady Dorothy Nevill*. Sixth edition. London: Edward Arnold, 1902.

———. *Under Five Reigns*. New York: The John Lane Company, 1910.

Newsome, David. *The Victorian World Picture*. London: John Murray, 1997.

Nicolson, Juliet. *The Perfect Summer: England 1911, Just Before the Storm*. New York: Grove Press, 2006.

Nicolson, Louise. *Fodor's London Companion: The Guide for the Experienced Traveler*. New York and London: Fodor's Travel Publications, 1987.

Novak, Emil, A.B., M.D., D.Sc., F.A.C.S., F.R.C.O.G. *Gynecologic and Obstetric Pathology with Clinical and Endocrine Relations*. Third edition. Philadelphia and London: W. B. Saunders Company, 1952.

O'Neill, Gilda. *My East End: Memories of a Life in Cockney London*. London: Penguin, 2000.

Pratt, James Norwood. *The Tea Lover's Treasury*. San Ramon, Calif.: 101 Productions, 1982.

Peterson, Jeanne M. *The Medical Profession in Mid-Victorian London*. Berkeley: University of California Press, 1978.

Pullen, Bob. *London Street People: Past and Present*. Oxford: Lennard Publishing, 1989.

Reeves, Maud Pember. *Round About a Pound a Week*. London: Virago, 1988.

Rey, H. A. *The Stars: A New Way to See Them*. Boston: Houghton Mifflin Company, 1980.

Roberts, Bob. *Last of the Sailormen*. London: Seafarer Books, 1986.

Roberts, Robert. *A Ragged Schooling: Growing up in the Classic Slum*. Manchester, UK: Manchester University Press, 1987.

———. *The Classic Slum: Salford Life in the First Quarter of the Century*. London: Penguin Books, 1971.

Ruffer, Jonathan Garnier. *The Big Shots: Edwardian Shooting Parties*. Debrett-Viking Press, 1978.

Rumbelow, Donald. *Jack the Ripper: The Complete Casebook*. Chicago: Contemporary Books, 1988.

Scannell, Dorothy. *Mother Knew Best: Memoir of a London Girlhood*. New York: Pantheon Books, 1974.

Shonfield, Zuzanna. *The Precariously Privileged: A Professional Family in Victorian London*. Oxford and New York: Oxford University Press, 1987.

Speert, Harold, M.D. *Obstetrics and Gynecology: A History and Iconography*. Revised third edition of *Iconographia Gyniatrica*. New York: Parthenon Publishing, 2004.

———. *Obstetrics and Gynecology in America: A History*. Chicago: The American College of Obstetricians and Gynecologists, 1980.

Traxel, David. *1989: The Birth of the American Century*. New York: Alfred A. Knopf, 1998.

Trzebinski, Errol. *The Kenya Pioneers*. New York and London: W. W. Norton & Company, 1986.

Tuchman, Barbara W. *The Guns of August*. New York: Ballantine Books, 1962.

———. *The Proud Tower: A Portrait of the World Before the War 1890-1914*. New York: Bantam Books, 1989.

Unsworth, Walt. *Everest: The Mountaineering History*. Third Edition. Macclesfield: Bâton Wicks, 2000.

———. *Hold the Heights: The Foundations of Moutaineering*. Seattle: The Moutaineers, 1994.

Wallach, Janet. *Desert Queen: The Extraordinary Life of Gertrude Bell: Adventurer, Adviser to Kings, Ally of Lawrence of Arabia*. New York: Anchor Books, 1999.

Weightman, Gavin. *London Past*. Collins & Brown Limited, 1991.

White, Jerry. *Rothschild Buildings: Life in an East End Tenement Block 1887-1920*. London: Routledge & Kegan Paul, 1980.

Wohl, Anthony S. *Endangered Lives: Public Health in Victorian Britain*. Cambridge, Mass.: Harvard University Press, 1983.

Wolveridge, Jim. *'Ain't it Grand?' or 'This was Stepney.'* London: The Journeyman Press, 1976.

Woodward, Kathleen. *Jipping Street*. London: Virago Press, 1983.

Youngson, A. J. *The Scientific Revolution in Victorian Medicine*. New York: Holmes & Meier Publishers, Inc., 1979.